The Daily Telegraph

THE GOOD GARDENS GUIDE 2004

GW00371334

The Daily Telegraph

THE GOOD GARDENS GUIDE 2004

EDITED BY PETER KING
& KATHERINE LAMBERT

FRANCES LINCOLN

Text copyright © Peter King 2004

This paperback edition published 2004

Peter King has asserted his right to be identified as the author
of this work under the Copyright, Designs and Patents Act 1988

Botanical Editor: Ruth Stungo
Disk Editor and Administrator: Anita Owen
Maps: Neil Hyslop
Index: Angie Hipkin

Frances Lincoln Ltd,
4 Torriano Mews, Torriano Avenue, London NW5 7RZ

A CIP catalogue record is
available from the British Library

ISBN 0 7112 2262 2

10 9 8 7 6 5 4 3 2 1

Typeset by Hewer Text Ltd, Edinburgh
Printed in Great Britain

Contents

THE GARDENS

Acknowledgements

This is the fifteenth annual edition of the *Guide*. All of the gardens described are open to the public, and there is an emphasis on those open frequently or by appointment over several months of the year. Certain gardens only open once or twice are included on merit. Our thanks to everyone who has helped with the preparation of the *Guide* – to owners, custodians, professional gardening staff, and many others. In particular, we thank our inspectors and those who advised them. Some of those who have given advice do not wish to be listed and, although anonymous, they have been every bit as valuable. We are also obliged to staff of The National Trust, The National Trust for Scotland and English Heritage for their co-operation.

The following include inspectors and some past inspectors and advisors: Barbara Abbs, Jane Allsopp, Gillian Archer, Diana Atkins, Rosie Atkins, Diane and Peter Baistow, David Baldwin, Jenny Baldwin, Susan Barnes, Mr and Mrs Basten, Kenneth and Gillian Beckett, June Beveridge, Margie Bleeker, Lavender Borden, Kathryn Bradley-Hole, Hilary Bristow, Cecil Brown, Jennifer Brown, Christina Campbell, Adam Caplin, Shirley Cargill, Dr Joan Carmichael, Brian and Gillian Cassidy, Lady Cave, Liz Challen, Anne Chamberlain, Sir Jeremy and Lady Chance, Annabelle Chisholm, Timothy Clark, Sarah Coles, Anne Collins, E. Anne Colville, David Conway, Beatrice Cowan, Simon Cramp, Jo, Penelope, Rosie and Trixie Currie, Wendy Dare, Margreet Diepeveen-Bruins Slot, Marilyn Dodd, Rosemary Dodgson, Daphne Dormer, Lady Edmonstone, Matthew Fattorini, Daphne Fisher, Kate Garton, Leslie Geddes-Brown, Lucy Gent, Alison Gregory, Gwynne Griffiths, Fenja Gunn, Elizabeth Hamilton, Stuart Harding, Anne Harrison, Sunniva Harte, Charles Hawes, Tara Heinemann, Jane Henson, Steve Hipkin, Judith Hitchings, Hilary Hodgson, Christopher Holliday, Mariana Hollis, Caroline Holmes, Jackie Hone, Sophie Hughes, Pam Hummer, Jill Husselby, David Jacques, Judith Jenkins, Valerie Jinks, Vanessa Johnston, Rosemarie Johnstone, Belinda Jupp, Mary Keen, Jo Kenaghan, Margaret Knight, Jean Laughton, Virginia Lawlor, Andrew Lawson, Dr Elizabeth Lazenby, Anne E. Liverman, Malcolm Lyell, Charles Lyte, Rhian de Mattos, Pat McCrostie, Anna McKane, Christopher McLaren, Deirdre McSharry, Bettine Muir, Dr Charles Nelson, Hugh Palmer, Lucinda Parry, Victoria Petrie-Hay, Lady Pigot, Stephen Player, Jocelyn Poole, Heather Prescott, Lorna Ramsay, Terence Reeves Smith, Finola Reid, Anne Richards, Tim Rock, Christopher Rogers, Sue Roscoe Watts, Dorothy Rose, Jane Russell, Alison Rutherford, Sarah Rutherford, Peter de Sausmarez, Kathy Sayer, George and Jane Scott, Barbara Segall, Marjorie Sime, Gillian Sladen, Dr Gordon Smith, Michael Smith, Lady Smith-Ryland, Elaine Snazell, Margaret Soole, Camilla Swift, Marlene Storah, Vera Taggart, Sally Tamplin, Caroline Todhunter, Michael Tooley, Annetta Troth, Marie-Françoise Valery, Jackie Ward, Ian Warden, Jenifer Wates, Myra Wheeldon, Susan Whittington, Cynthia Wickham, Nigel Wilkins, John Wilks. The editors also express their appreciation of the dedicated assistance of Angie Hipkin, Pam Rainbow and Ruth Stungo, and especially of the *Guide*'s invaluable disk editor, Anita Owen.

Britain's Modern Gardens

Pioneers and modern practitioners

The Good Gardens Guide for 2004 has chosen to focus on modern gardens in Britain. We start by looking at the legacy inherited from the twentieth-century pioneers who over the century changed entrenched Victorian attitudes and pointed horticultural practices in a different direction. A reaction against the folly and the sheer extravagance of large-scale Victorian gardening had gradually been gathering momentum towards the end of the nineteenth century. Change was in the air, and not just a few trifling changes here and there – a positive sea-change.

The first major battle was between two redoubtable and stubborn protagonists – Reginald Blomfield and William Robinson. Blomfield was an architect and a formalist. Robinson (the elder of the two) was above all a gardener and a plantsman – the foremost advocate of natural gardening. The titles of their respective books say it all. Robinson's *The Wild Garden* (1870) and *The English Flower Garden* (1883) targeted the Victorian parterre and architects as garden designers, while Blomfield's *The Formal Garden* (1892) set out the case for a return to formality – he had in mind the formality of the seventeenth century, when Gloucestershire for instance had been able to boast of 33 Baroque formal gardens, all of which would have been listed Grade I if they had survived until the twentieth century.

To an extent both men achieved their objectives after a titanic struggle lasting for a decade. Edwardian country houses did become more classical, more 'Wrenaissance', and their gardens more natural. It was Robinson's legacy, however, that was the more important, and natural gardening remains to this day a cardinal principle of modern garden design. Gertrude Jekyll deserves the final say: 'Both are right, and both are wrong. The formal army are architects to a man . . . they do not suggest who is to play the very needful part of artist-gardener . . . those whose views are wider cannot accept their somewhat narrow gospel.'

Gertrude Jekyll's own partnership with Edwin Lutyens – twenty years her junior – began when they worked together to create Orchards, near Godalming in Surrey. She was in no doubt about what was needed to make it work. 'The truth appears to be that for the best building and planting the architect and the gardener must have *some* knowledge of each other's business, and each must regard with feelings of kindly reverence the unknown domains of the other's higher knowledge.' Christopher Hussey, ever percipient, wrote of Lutyens: 'It was a strange and rather tragic circumstance that the architect of so many entrancing gardens never had one of his own. But he was neither a garden lounger nor a garden grower by temperament. For him a garden was an occasion for a work of art that, once designed, he had no wish to see again until its components had reached maturity.' The partnership was blessed by a receptive press. It was not long before Avray Tipping was writing in *Country Life* of Hestercombe's gardens that 'they prove that an architect can be in unison with nature, that a formal garden can form part of a landscape'.

Country Life's campaigning contribution to the cause of the country house – as champion of its architecture and of its gardens – cannot be overstated in this crucially creative period. From the moment the magazine was founded in 1897, its owner Edward Hudson employed the best writers – Avray Tipping, Lawrence Weaver, Christopher Hussey, Gertrude Jekyll, William Robinson – and the best photographers – A.E. Henson and Charles Latham – to record houses and gardens that publishing has ever enjoyed. Hudson became a lifelong friend and major client of Lutyens.

Two years before the First World War overshadowed the Edwardian heyday of garden-making, Lutyens was commissioned to extend Folly Farm in Berkshire. It was to be the last joint venture of the partnership. The entire Jekyll-Lutyens syntax was set out – compartments, vistas, changes of level, steps, patterned paving, water, bold planting and, not least, a herbaceous border. Yet something was not quite right. His formality was no longer restrained; her informality struggled to compete.

The First World War brought country-house building to a total standstill, and the appalling slaughter meant that labour was simply not available to maintain the gardens of yesteryear. At the armistice all the major architects were employed to design cemeteries for the War Graves Commission, and the familiar classical vocabulary was rolled out to express the nation's grief. Added to the pall and gloom of economic depression was the legacy of the late-nineteenth-century fall in agricultural and land prices. Landowners' problems had been aggravated by new taxation and their spending power had passed to the *nouveaux riches*. Country estates came onto the market almost daily. Most of the major gardens of the twentieth century were those commissioned by people who had been in a position to buy land during the 1885–1925 decline of land prices.

In the vacuum that followed, one option for those who had survived the war and 'who were not especially rich yet enjoyed independent means' was to restore tumble-down manor houses rather than to build new country houses. Avray Tipping, the leading historian of Britain's country houses and gardens, created three successive gardens for himself in Wales. Then there was the 'ex-Foreign Office circle' – a group of relatively young men who did up the houses they managed to acquire with impeccable taste and created gardens to match, compartmented, formal and topiaried, but enriched by exuberant planting. John Cornforth in *The Inspiration of the Past* was the first to identify and write about such characters as Sir Louis Mallet (of Wardes, near Otham, Kent), Sir Walter Jenner (Lytes Carey, Wiltshire) and his brother Colonel Jenner (Avebury Manor, Wiltshire), E.G. Lester (Westwood Manor, Wiltshire). A number of these properties – Ightham Moat in Kent, Lytes Carey and Great Chalfield in Wiltshire – came eventually to the National Trust.

Colonel Reggie Cooper epitomised the restlessness and the talent of this ex-Foreign Office circle. His gardens were part and parcel of his love of manor houses, which he restored with great style and panache, and for which he created equally vibrant gardens. His first was Cold Ashton in Gloucestershire, which he left after two years for a new challenge, Cothay in Somerset – which even now is being nurtured within his original formal framework by two great plantsmen-gardeners of the twenty-first century, Alastair and Mary-Anne Robb. After twelve years Cooper moved to Julians in Hertfordshire; having restored the largely eighteenth-century house and garden with bravura, he moved to his last challenge, a fourteenth-century manor house called Knightstone in deepest Devon.

The inter-war years also saw brave attempts to introduce truly modern architecture and to a lesser extent truly modern gardens to Britain. Many of the giants of modernism in Europe took refuge in Britain, where they were politely called émigrés – a noble word compared with the blunt 'asylum-seeker' epithet of twenty-first-century Britain. They were briefly billeted in Hampstead before settling in Britain or departing to America. The architectural fraternity made them welcome and struggled manfully to find them work here. The Elmhirsts of Dartington toyed with the idea of an English Bauhaus to be headed by Walter Gropius.

By and large, however, the gardening establishment eschewed bold modernity, opting for a timid nod in its direction combined with backward-looking romanticism. Two exceptions were Geoffrey Jellicoe and Oliver Hill, who both joined the Institute of Landscape Architects (set up in 1929) at this time. Hill's huge talent enabled him to be up there with the modernists and just as likely down there with the romanticists. His drawings for Joldwynds in Surrey are models of modernism. This interlude lasted through the 1930s, when he retired to his beloved Daneway and took up the gentler mantle of Arts and Crafts.

Two houses by the émigrés stand out as proof of their commitment to the post-war world – Mendelsohn and Chermayeff's Shrubswood at Chalfont St Giles, and Chermayeff's own house, Bentley, at Halland in East Sussex. The garden there was designed by Christopher Tunnard – who had almost done himself out of a job by questioning whether a modern house should have a garden at all. He had gone on record as saying that if a Jekyll garden could be considered the 'perfect adjunct' to a Lutyens house, it was 'a very good reason for its being unsuitable for a modern house'. Tunnard's garden was modern, however. It did characteristically frame the landscape beyond and it seeped out into wild garden and woodland. Of British practitioners the most talented modern architects were Connell Ward and Lucas, who built High and Over for Bernard Ashmole at Amersham, Raymond McGrath for his St Ann's Hill at Chertsey and Land's End at Gaulby in Leicestershire and Christopher (Kit) Nicholson's Kit's Close at Henley-on-Thames. Geoffrey Jellicoe's time was yet to come.

As war again engulfed Europe and Japan, building ceased and gardens were dug for Victory. Post-Second War gloom was just as strong as the First World War pall. It was not until the Festival of Britain in 1951 that the British began to come out of their shells, to smile again, and to be reminded that gardening could be a tonic, not just an aid to survival. The modern garden was given a significant role to play at the Festival, especially in Peter Shepheard's inspirational moat garden with its water, rocks and exuberant planting. Gardens also featured in the Homes & Gardens pavilion and Frank Clark's brilliant, evocative Picassoesque island lying below the Regatta restaurant.

The Festival of Britain made people think about their own, long neglected gardens. Although its impact was immediate, it could not work a miracle, because post-war reconstruction took priority. Talk (and action) was all of public housing, public parks and public spaces. Sylvia Crowe and Brenda Colvin, Britain's two best-known landscape architects, spent most of their time on new towns, nuclear power stations and the routing of high-voltage power lines. Both women made a plea for a radical reappraisal of planting and landscaping. Colvin was acutely aware that something was wrong. She regretted that 'our experiments in the free groupings of an enormously increased range of plants within the framework of widely different gardening styles have often been more successful from a horticultural point of view than for their aesthetic value'.

Two key practitioners of the post-war era were Russell Page and Lanning Roper. The former, an associate initially of Jellicoe, was at once a modernist and a traditionalist, and his gardens were structural and structured. Page was an Englishman working latterly abroad, Roper a highly sensitive American working largely in England. His genius was as a plantsman, and his finest work was for Christopher Hussey at Scotney Castle and within Jellicoe's formal garden at RHS Wisley. As gardening correspondent for *The Sunday Times* (during a period when Vita Sackville-West was at *The Observer*), Lanning Roper's influence on the general gardening public was enormous.

The first major new post-war work was Arne Jacobsen's St Catherine's College, Oxford. It was commissioned by Alan Bullock, its founding Master, who was determined to create architecturally a college of its time. Jacobsen was a designer of the first order and a landscape architect of vision. Everything in his buildings – from light fittings to cutlery to furniture – was designed by him, and the grounds were all his creation. Building and landscape were a totality, unified by a long cool canal along a longitudinal hall of residence, flanked by an equally long lawn. His materials were restrained: tawny yellow brick walls, blocks of hedges and winding paths alongside brick walls. The site – Holywell Meadow – was superbly hidden, for many people an unknown backwater of the River Cherwell. Towards the end of his life he admitted that it was his favourite work.

At about the same time, John Brookes created a courtyard garden for Penguin Books at Harmondsworth, London. Based on a Mondrian abstract painting, it was a sensational landscape statement mirroring modern art. Not long after, Darborne and Darke built a new headquarters for Wiggins Teape in Basingstoke and with great imagination created a roof garden for the benefit of its staff. The flat, terraced roofs sprouted lush vegetation visible to the traffic gyrating on public roads at the foot of the offices, which stood on a landscaped dais. Sadly other flat-roofed offices in Basingstoke did not seek to emulate Gateway House.

In 1980 there began the work of creating what Jane Owen has described as 'the most interesting garden made in the twentieth century' in Britain. Having long been a hesitant modernist, Geoffrey Jellicoe at the age of eighty designed a garden at Sutton Place of unquestionable modernity. He chose the well-tried formula of a large garden divided into many small ones, but this did not prevent him from playing the scale game with huge success. Into one of the smaller compartments, known as the Magritte Avenue, he placed enormous classical urns acquired at the Mentmore sale, and in a relatively humble lily-pond garden he positioned a Carrara marble realisation of one of Ben Nicholson's 'White Reliefs' to provide a gigantic cool climax for the lily pond and for the garden as a whole. This is Jellicoe at his most majestic, yet most subtle.

Two more claims can be lodged for the most interesting modern gardens in twentieth-century Britain: Ian Hamilton Finlay's Little Sparta in Lanarkshire and Charles Jencks' Portrack in Dumfriesshire. Both creators use the same word to propose their own highly personal form of garden-making. Finlay's is 'Land Art' and Jencks' is 'Land Form'. Little Sparta is a natural landscape of 1.5 hectares with carefully positioned fragments of poems carved on stone tablets to be found in grass, on plinths, as plaques in trees, in walls or by the wayside. The beautifully carved lettering adds up to a celebration of Finlay's literary heroes, combined with a bellicose litany against the bureaucrats who in his view tried to close the garden down. Portrack is a skilful manipulation of land into curves and mounts, shaped by Jencks and his wife Maggie Keswick. To Jencks they represent a 'language of landscape' freely formed from the forces of nature. His wife died before the garden was finished, but he has gone on to design a second Landform in the grounds of the Scottish National Gallery of Modern Art in Edinburgh.

One of Britain's outstanding landscape architects, Arabella Lennox-Boyd's gardens always have scale and invariably bold imaginative planting. Her roof-top garden for the Coq d'Or restaurant at Number One Poultry is an invaluable green oasis of majestic scale in the heart of the City of London, surrounded on all sides by soaring buildings. Janet Jack's roof garden at Cannon Street Station is another green lung for office workers which has the added dimension of the Thames in full view.

Tom Stuart-Smith's huge new walled garden for a private client near Banbury in Oxfordshire, with its dramatic sloping site, rills and pools and the sheer panache of his planting, is a modern garden of outstanding quality by one of the younger practitioners. It exhibits a firm grasp of the historical development of British gardening and unhesitatingly uses many of the plants that Gertrude Jekyll would have been overjoyed to see in a modern garden. What makes this garden so vital is Stuart-Smith's ability to borrow the existing landscape, to exploit its fall and its rise and to settle his creation so firmly into a fold of Oxfordshire countryside.

Natural gardening – Robinson with a difference – has been gathering support from amateurs and young professionals alike. Pam Lewis at Sticky Wicket was the first to tackle the professionals head-on – her Dorset garden is featured on the cover of this year's Guide. Julie Toll followed her mould-breaking wild garden at the 1993 Chelsea Flower Show, which won the coveted Best of Show award, by creating at Jenningsbury in Hertfordshire a meadow garden well able to challenge the hitherto-unchallenged Dutch style of naturalism.

Now a new generation is beginning to show its mettle: James Fraser with his wacky and wilful tropical planting in a small London garden, Declan Buckley with his deft transformation of a back garden into a tropical water garden, Jinny Blom with her low-maintenance garden in Stockwell for two families. Among the present-day émigré visitors to Britain, Piet Oudolf and Henk Gerritsen are almost household names. But others less familiar are at work here too. The Italian Luciano Giubbilei has designed a minimalist garden in the Little Boltons, the American Katherine Gustafson a ring of bright water in Hyde Park, the New Zealander Ross Palmer a tropical jungle in Maida Vale.

At the start of the new millennium, gardening in Britain is changing direction with intelligence and energy, just as it did as it did a century ago.

Modern gardens in the *Guide*

What is a 'modern garden'? That is the first nettle to grasp when compiling such a list. Perhaps it is best summed up as one that could not be the product of any period other than our own. That, plus a certain edge or twist that means that the garden is not only imaginatively designed and well planted (there are plenty of those), but also has a *je ne sais quoi* that makes it somehow unexpected. Other gardens mentioned in these editorial pages are, for one reason or another, not in the *Guide*, but if our readers were to visit all those listed below, we believe they would get a fair idea of the best of modern gardening in Britain today. Some are the work of well-known designers – Arabella Lennox-Boyd, Rupert Golby, Xa Tollemache, Christopher Bradley-Hole – but many more have been created by individual garden owners. All are worth seeing.

Bedfordshire *The Manor House*
Berkshire *Waltham Place*
Buckinghamshire *Ascott (work by Arabella Lennox-Boyd), The Manor House (water and sculpture features), Turn End*
Cambridgeshire *Florence House, 21 Lode Road*
Cheshire *Eaton Hall (work by Arabella Lennox-Boyd)*
Cornwall *The Barbara Hepworth Museum, Bonython Manor, Bosvigo*
Devon *Castle Hill (walled garden by Xa Tollemache), Dartington Hall, The Garden House*
Dorset *Knoll Gardens, Millmead, Stanbridge Mill, Sticky Wicket*
Essex *The Beth Chatto Gardens, RHS Hyde Hall*
Gloucestershire *Bourton House, Brackenbury, Daylesford House, Hill Farm Barn, Kiftsgate (the pool garden), Mill Dene, Ozleworth Park, Rockcliffe*
Hampshire *Apple Court, Bury Court, Farleigh House, West Green*
Herefordshire *Bryans Ground, Hampton Court, The Lance Hattatt Design Garden, Lower Hope, Lower Hopton Farm*
Hertfordshire *Jenningsbury, Vineyard Manor*
Kent *Great Comp, Groombridge Place (work by Ivan Hicks and Myles Challis), Old Place Farm, Walmer Castle (the Queen Mother's Garden by Penelope Hobhouse)*
Lancashire *Gresgarth Hall, Mill Barn*
Leicestershire *Orchards*
Lincolnshire *Garden House, Lincoln Contemporary Heritage Garden, 32 Main Street*
London *7 The Butts, 66A East Dulwich Road, 70 Gloucester Crescent, 8 Grafton Park Road, 239A Hook Road, 1A Hungerford Road, Hyde Park (Kathryn Gustafson's water feature), Kensington Gardens (children's playground), London Wetland Centre, Mile End Park, Noel-Baker Peace Garden, Pembridge Cottage, 167 Rosendale Road, Thames Barrier Park*
Manchester *17 Poplar Grove*
Norfolk *East Ruston Old Vicarage, The Exotic Garden, How Hill Farm (river valley garden), Kettle Hill, Pensthorpe*
Northamptonshire *The Menagerie*
Northumberland *Alnwick Castle*
Nottinghamshire *'Pure Land'*
Oxfordshire *Cotswold Wildlife Park, Gothic House, Old Church House, St Catherine's College, Westwell Manor*
Shropshire *Brownhill House, Lower Hall, Swallow Hayes*
Somerset *Gants Mill, Hadspen, Lady Farm, 2 Old Tarnwell*

Suffolk *Bucklesham Hall, Wyken Hall*
Surrey *Great Fosters (Kim Wilkie's work), The Green House, RHS Wisley (gardens by Penelope Hobhouse, Piet Oudolf, Tom Stuart-Smith et al)*
Sussex *Burpham Place, Cobblers, Denmans, Great Dixter, Ketleys, Perch Hill Farm, Yew Tree Cottage*
Warwickshire *Avon Cottage, Compton Scorpion Farm, Woodpeckers*
Wiltshire *Abbey House, Bolehyde Manor, The Fovant Hut, The Old Mill*
Worcestershire *24 Alexander Avenue, Little Malvern Court, Witley Court (Jerwood Foundation Sculpture Park)*
Yorkshire *30 Latchmere Road, Eastgrove Cottage, Little Malvern Court, 21 Swinton Lane*
Ireland *Ballymaloe, Butterstream, The Dillon Garden*
Scotland *Dun Ard, Landform Ueda, Little Sparta, Mount Stuart (kitchen garden by James Alexander-Sinclair), Portmore (walled garden by Chrissy Reid)*
Wales *National Botanic Garden, Ridler's Garden, Veddw House*

Case study: A modern garden for Dyrham Park

At the beginning of the eighteenth century, Dyrham had a sensational modern garden – a Baroque extravaganza created between 1697 and 1704. By 1800 it had been swept away. Today, only the giant statue of Neptune is a reminder that he once commanded a lofty cascade plunging into a canal and that magnificent Baroque formal gardens extended in front and behind the Talman house. In 1801 Repton was set to work to create a new garden and replant the park. Jane Austen recorded that he charged £5 a day, which suggests that he worked at Dyrham for fifteen days.

The weakest part of the landscape and garden has long been the west garden behind the house, even though the terracing set against the hill on the northern side, with the church perched on top, has always been a memorable landscape feature. Now, to the surprise of many, the disquiet of several and the outrage of a few, the National Trust has decided to create a twenty-first-century garden here to reflect more closely the formality and symmetry of the 1700s' scheme, to address the recent loss of old trees and to encourage visitors to spend time in the garden rather than in the very fragile house. Arne Maynard was chosen for the task, and his design has tried valiantly to resolve the problems resulting from successive planting schemes which combined to rob the garden of any unity or calmness.

The major elements of his plan are big-boned and architectural. A double line of pleached *Parrotia persica* will be planted in front of the restaurant, so as to conceal the view across the present lawn towards the formal sunken Baroque water garden. Through the parrotia screen, access to the sunken garden will be reopened down the lines of the original steps and cloud-pruned beech hedges planted at the point where the land swoops downwards. Over centuries the formal water garden was gradually reduced to rhomboidal ponds, and clever plantings of reeds will realign the edges to a semblance of formality. A grass amphitheatre on the bank to one side will focus the line of sight across the water garden rather than up and down (west and east). The northern half of the sunken garden will have four low box-edged beds enclosing billowing meadow plantings as a reminder of the historical position of a parterre shown in Kip's magnificent bird's-eye view of 1710.

It is a brave venture. Planning permission has been applied for and a decision is awaited towards the end of 2004. The cost is expected to be of the order of £350,000. Head gardener Dale Dennehy has tremendous drive and enthusiasm for the scheme, and it is also backed by English Heritage which has recently completed six modern gardens of its own. It will be surprising if the Trust does not succeed eventually in getting planning permission through. Dyrham's gardens have seen massive changes over the centuries. Why not a sympathetic modern insertion within an historical framework?

Contemporary uses for sculpture and water

Sculpture, water and lighting may all be employed to introduce an immediately modern element into the garden. In a small urban plot, they can be overwhelmingly theatrical, but at their most effective they enhance and work with nature and act as a positive force for changing the character of the gardens we create today.

Sophisticated, sensitive and sensual exterior lighting schemes for the garden still trail behind those for the house. Their use is beyond our remit here for the simple reason that garden owners have by and large closed their gates to visitors before the time has come to flick the switch on their gardens. There are exceptions: for a fortnight in late October/early November a route through the garden at Abbotsbury in Dorset is traced with floodlights and candles, while Westonbirt Arboretum in Gloucestershire illuminates some of its trees with twinkling lights in the run-up to Christmas. At Great Fosters in Surrey, the opening of Kim Wilkie's new grass amphitheatre was heralded by a string quartet playing in the well, with the rising tiers lit by thousands of flickering candles; Alnwick also has plans to illuminate the new Wirtz garden.

Monet's garden at Giverny may be a universal symbol for water in the garden, Bomarzo perhaps for sculpture, but there are some notable examples in Britain too. Clearbeck Hall, for example, manages to combine the two to stunning effect. Most of those mentioned below are in the *Guide*, and they reveal how many people are now experimenting with ways of enlivening their gardens.

The earliest sculptures in the landscape seem to have had a religious meaning – standing stones, Celtic crosses, Easter Island statues and the figures lining the Spirit Road in China. Later they acquired a civic role, as bronze representations of local worthies or national heroes were put on plinths in public parks and market squares. The great equestrian statues commanding the skyline at Blenheim and Windsor were the three-dimensional equivalents of the swagger portraits inside the houses they surveyed. They had a political agenda, while the nymphs, gladiators and busts of Roman emperors dotted around in glades and *allées* had a social one, proclaiming membership of that exclusive club – the Grand Tour. It is only during the last decade or so that sculpture has become commonplace in our smaller domestic gardens.

In 1977, the first sculpture park was established in Yorkshire as an independent charitable trust, and modern art moved into the open air for the enjoyment of the masses. It took some considerable time for outlets such as garden centres to capitalise on the trend, and it was not until the 1990s that individual dealers started basing their contemporary sculpture ventures out of doors, more often than not in their own gardens. Lady Bessborough transferred her London gallery to the grounds of Roche Court in Wiltshire, while at the Hannah Peschar Gallery in Surrey the eponymous owner worked closely with her husband, the landscape architect Anthony Paul, to create a setting for the works on display. Their secluded valley has a completely different atmosphere from Roche, which is set on a hill with spacious views; different again is Sculpture at Goodwood, where the contemporary pieces stand in woodland looking outward to the Sussex landscape and the borrowed sculpture of Chichester Cathedral spire. The Garden Gallery in Hampshire is closer in feel to a traditional country garden, while Ramster in Surrey has acquired a new millennium garden to show off the annual exhibitions set up by the owners' daughter.

It is obviously helpful for anyone contemplating investing in a high-quality work to see a variety of pieces in a variety of settings, and to talk to the knowledgeable and committed owners. But 'investing' is the right word – many prices reach well into five figures. Another consideration is that of theft. Massively heavy (and costly) pieces may be less at risk than more lightweight ones. At Newnham Paddox in Worcestershire Lady Denbigh started an Art Park (part of the ArtParks International group, of which Sausmarez Manor in Guernsey is also a member) in 2003, partly as a means of replanting the 'Capability' Brown park. She is happy to advise clients about anti-theft devices – whether it be attaching mercury pods underneath, fitting bronzes with a homing chip during the casting process, locking the sculpture to a concrete base, or installing a radio sensor to cover each piece. But although effective security does not have to cost the earth, it helps to push many pieces out of reach of would-be purchasers. Even the entry price to these sculpture gardens is high – the Hannah Peschar Gallery charges £8, Sculpture at Goodwood £10.

By contrast, the Yorkshire Sculpture Park is free, as are other places where the sculptures on show are personal to the owners. The garden at the Barbara Hepworth Museum in Cornwall was designed largely by her as a showcase for her work, and Little Sparta in Scotland (the garden and all its works) is Ian Hamilton Finlay's unique inspiration, perceptively described by the art critic Richard Cork as a place where 'sculpture, landscape, poetry and philosophy are brought together in superbly orchestrated unity'.

At Lismore Castle in Ireland, the recent installation of sculpture on an impressive scale is an affair of the heart for the Marquess of Hartington – and there the entrance charge is a reasonable €4. Another modestly priced garden enriched by sculpture is Gants Mill in Somerset, where Brian and Alison Shingler have 'borrowed' works by local sculptors (members of a co-operative venture called Sculpture in the South), which are then sold on to visitors. They do not charge the artists a commission; unsurprisingly, this does not find favour with commercial gallery owners.

It must be said that the contemporary works on show and on offer from these various sources are by and large of a much higher quality than off-the-peg items at retail outlets. They come in sizes ranging from the miniscule to the massive, in materials ranging from bronze to wood to plastic, steel and glass, and in styles ranging from figurative to abstract to frankly incomprehensible.

The traditional human and animal representations still have a following, but there are many abstract works of great interest and imagination. Young buyers don't have a monopoly on these – Rachel Bebb of The Garden Gallery says that her most radical client is 82 years old.

In the right hands – such as Arabella Lennox-Boyd's at Gresgarth Hall – sculpture in the garden is a wonderful thing. This is what we say about the imaginatively designed and immaculately planted one-acre garden at Shepherd House in Scotland: 'The garden is full of sculptural surprises. Some – bird baths, sundials and tulip-filled urns – are elegant, while others – lead pigeons in the undergrowth, a large copper rose stuck in a bush and eye-stopping giant topiary creatures – are delightfully quirky.' Sculpture, as at Shepherd House, may be an important appendage to the planting, or it may have a decisive influence on it. The addition of a living-willow cabin or a pair of wire geese may be the closest that some owners get to engaging with a Christopher Bradley-Hole garden; for others the installation of a stainless steel pyramid or a giant glass globe will be the catalyst for creating a revolutionary new look.

In the Baroque gardens of the seventeenth century, water on a grand scale was an instrument of wealth and power. At Chatsworth in Derbyshire the Dukes of Devonshire used it to dazzlingly theatrical effect with the installation of Grillet's great cascade, adding an intricate joke in the form of a copper 'willow tree' spouting water from its branches. In the landscape gardens of the eighteenth century, particularly at Stourhead in Witshire, owners like Henry Hoare II made their point by commissioning a clutch of temples and follies to overlook the lake at all its focal points. Finest of all was John Aislabie's gigantic formal water garden at Studley Royal in Yorkshire – in his case almost a hobby after the ruin and disgrace brought by his involvement in the South Sea Bubble fiasco. Described by the late Christopher Hussey as 'one of the most spectacularly scenic compositions in England', in Aislabie's lifetime it was 'Look'd upon as the Wonder of the North'. A modern wonder of the North is presently taking shape at Alnwick, where the ambitious and expensive water scheme devised by the Wirtz family for the Duchess of Northumberland has been greeted by both praise and derision.

At the other end of the social scale are the mills that once threaded the landscape along the maze of Britain's waterways. Many, like Docton Mill in Spekes Valley, Devon, are ancient in origin. Some of the most appealing and imaginative modern gardens have been created around the priceless asset of a romantic old building in a watery landscape – think of Pin Mill at Bodnant in Wales. Three of these are new to the *Guide* this year: the 1290 working Gant's Mill in Somerset, and in Wiltshire Goulters Mill (mentioned in the Domesday book) and The Old Mill in Ramsbury. The garden at Goulters Mill is the more traditional of the three; the other two have a distinctively modern feeling in their plantings, proof that a profusion of pools, streams and waterfalls need not restrict the style to that of a cottage garden.

The introduction of water into the garden is, however, no longer confined to the lucky few who have it as a gift. Water features, in the shape of naturalistic ponds, formal pools, rills and fountains, are within most owners' budgets, and retail outlets such as Stapeley Water Gardens in Cheshire are in on the act, selling 60 different kinds of pump alone, and aquatic plants galore –

400 varieties of water lily, for example. North of the border, Teviot Water Garden is another showcase for aquatic plants and equipment.

One water garden to attract universal praise is the minimalist rectangular pool at Kiftsgate Court in Gloucestershire. Jane Owen of *The Times* described it like this: 'The inky darkness of the water is maintained by the black-painted pool. In contrast symmetrical white stone steps seem to float across it to a rectangle of mown turf in the centre. Beyond, water trickles from 24 cast-bronze and gold-leaf philodendron leaves on steel stems that sway in the breeze, created by the sculptor Simon Allison.'

The pool garden at Kiftsgate is enclosed by tall yew hedges, making it a place for solitude and contemplation. Antony Young's twin rectangular pools at Ozleworth Park in Gloucestershire are, by contrast, more open in character, surrounded by hedges kept deliberately low. The designer writes: 'The lily ponds at Ozleworth lie adjacent to the large rose garden, and the two are united by the scent wafting in the calm of a summer's evening over the dark mirror of the pools. Water is a fundamental element of life, and in its reflections can be seen the landscape beyond the garden and the changing moods of the sky. It acts quite differently, yet with equal effect, when its surface is rippled by a gusty wind, or in winter when turned to ice. Water has many different qualities but above all its presence in the garden reminds us that all life is utterly dependent on it.'

These two water gardens are self-contained, detached from the rest of the garden. A water feature within the garden itself, if it is to succeed, must relate to its surroundings. Although the traditional kidney-shaped pond fringed with irises, rushes and marsh marigolds is still very much in evidence, and lion's head masks remain the decoration of choice on many fountains, some elegant and satisfying water features are beginning to appear in British gardens.

In 2003 Jane Mooney designed a cool and sophisticated garden for Mercedes at the Hampton Court Flower Show, in which decking and white-painted 'furniture' emphasised the feeling of an outdoor living room. The water feature took the form of a 'coffee table' where a perspex shelf across part of its top supported champagne flutes while revealing the water pouring out from the centre into a geometrical lower pool. Elegant and eye-catching. Similarly, much interest was aroused by the Escher-like installation at the Dyson garden at Chelsea the same year, in which the water appeared to be flowing uphill.

It is, however, William Pye who is acknowledged by his peers as the water wizard of the present generation. At once sculptor, designer and master-plumber, his harmonious and beautifully crafted work features in gardens up and down the country, in show gardens designed by Arabella Lennox-Boyd and others, and in countless books and magazines (an article written by Sir Roy Strong appeared in *Country Life* in March 2003). By setting impossible standards for others, he has helped to raise them generally, and the use of water in the garden seems set to develop in challenging new directions. But the moderns don't scoop all the prizes – the deep, clear and bubbling pool made by the monks of Mottisfont in Hampshire remains the sublimely simple blueprint.

Global warming and the British garden
by Barry McWilliam

Global climate change is an established fact. Twenty thousand years ago much of northern Britain was covered by an icecap comparable with those in Antarctica today, while southern England must have been comparable with the periglacial ice-free fringes of Greenland. Even after this ice had been dispersed by a period of rapid warming, between 11,000 and 10,000 years ago another thousand years of cold caused small glaciers and icecaps to re-form in the higher parts of the Scottish mountains, the Lake District and north Wales. The current warm period is merely an interglacial, and until as recently as the 1960s the major cause for climatic concern was the imminent return of colder conditions beyond our control.

It is ironic therefore that our current preoccupation is entirely with the prospect, not of another ice age, but of global warming. Since the Industrial Revolution, the proportion of carbon dioxide in the atmosphere has been rising, the result of our increasing combustion of stored carbon and carbon compounds in the form of coal, petroleum and natural gas. Atmospheric carbon dioxide is not malign – without it the earth would be uninhabitably cold. Carbon dioxide acts like the glass in our windows and greenhouses, allowing the solar light energy in and acting as a barrier, preventing heat energy from escaping from the warmed surface into cold space. The resulting 'greenhouse effect' is intensifying: we may already have double-glazed the earth and be heading towards triple-glaze.

The prospect of major and progressive environmental change, with effects both predictable and unpredictable, has so agitated scientists and governments that huge amounts of time and money have been expended in attempts to predict the future. An international organisation, the Intergovernmental Panel on Climate Change, has been created to confer on theoretical and practical global warming; countless scientific papers have been produced. The current consensus is that in the next 50 years global temperature will rise by a few degrees and UK sea levels by between 10cm and 80cm, that warming will be greatest in high latitudes and that storm activity will increase. This could mean that events like the 'hurricane' of 1987 occur with greater frequency, or that the average number of gales per annum doubles. The fact that, worldwide, three of the warmest years ever recorded have occurred in the last decade is suggestion (but not proof) that the rise in global temperature has already begun.

It is important here to distinguish between climate and weather. Weather is what actually happens, and what affects our gardens. As we know only too well, it is the extremes of temperature, high as well as low, which damage our plants. Even occasional heavy wet snow can break branches irreparably, whereas a snow blanket may give protection from the severest frost. Heavy prolonged rain saturates the soil and subsoil, depriving roots of essential air and allowing the spread of fungus spores, while prolonged drought causes potentially fatal cell collapse. Strong winds may strip leaves, break branches and stems and ultimately uproot trees, and when combined with high temperatures and drought may be a major factor in summer plant losses.

Climate is often described as average weather. It is in fact a purely statistical construct useful for comparisons between places and times, and by definition is retrospective. The Met Office uses totals and averages over periods of thirty years as a way of ironing out the inherent variability of our weather both on a day-to-day and a year-to-year basis. These climatic figures are then used in weather reports and forecasts for specific locations.

Situated as we are in Britain on the western edge of Europe between 50° and 60° North latitude, our weather results from conflict between air masses coming from the Arctic, the continental interior, the Sahara and the Atlantic. Global warming may raise the temperature of all of these air masses by a degree or two, but there is no suggestion, as yet, that it will prevent their visits. So although most of us were taught in school of the equable nature of the British climate (the result of the moderating effect of our island position), when contrasted with the extreme climate of the continental interior, our weather is anything but equable, varying substantially from day to day. These weather fluctuations inevitably lead to periodic record-breaking at one or other of the hundreds of recording stations, leading the non-mathematical among us to imagine that these represent evidence of climate change.

So what is actually happening to our climate (and weather)? Since the 'Little Ice Age' of the late Middle Ages, when crop failures and famines in Europe were commonplace, the average annual temperature may have risen by just 1°C – a trifling amount compared with higher predictions of global warming. Most of this change took place before the last century and affected winters. Springs warmed up from 1900 to 1940, fell back to 1900 levels by 1970, but since then have warmed by about 1°C. Summers have remained remarkably unchanged for the last century or more. The valuable phenological records kept by dedicated recorders (once regarded as harmless cranks), often over a lifetime, confirm our earlier, warmer springs. Precipitation changes over the last century are consistent, with little change to annual totals, but greater concentration in the cooler months – ie. drier summers.

Such climatic changes reflect changes in the balance of weather, but they do not preclude horticultural catastrophes. It is not impossible for a rise in average spring temperatures to occur at a time when individual frosty nights are more severe than previously. For temperature-responsive species it might be argued that these earlier springs triggering soft growth or flowering could make them more susceptible to damage by a single night of Arctic or polar air. Having said that, in lowland north-east England it is several years since new rose shoots shrivelled and fell, and even the dwarf, early-flowering rhododendrons, usually a magnet for late frost, have succeeded for three years, and plums are fruiting for a third successive year. But sequences of warmer, drier, cooler or wetter seasons have occurred before. They did not persist, nor will our frostless springs.

One man-made weather change is, however, more reliable and may have helped to exaggerate the 'global warming' scare: the warming of our towns. The provision of car thermometers has made the 'heat islands' represented by our towns and cities very apparent to any observer. The heat escaping from buildings, pumped out by refrigeration systems and generated by vehicles, has the effect of warming city centres frequently by as much as 3°C above the surrounding countryside, and sometimes by as much as 5°C; its effect is most intense in summer and at night. This has immediate implications for the ability of urban gardeners, especially in our major cities, to succeed with tender species impossible in country areas. Increasingly, with the expansion of air conditioning, these 'heat islands' will extend to summer with as yet unknown consequences.

At first sight it might seem that otherwise nothing has, or will, change. This is not the case. There will be subtle changes. Oranges and bananas will not be widely grown outdoors in Britain, but vines may become more commercial, half-hardy and tender plants may be safely put out earlier, and some woody species, which fail now because of a too-short growing season to ripen wood, might succeed in future. The unchanging average summer temperature over a long period hides the fact that there have been short heatwaves in most recent summers, especially in south-east England. Combined with drier summers and hosepipe bans, this might militate against that long-established feature of the British garden – the lawn. In the south-east too the current vogue for succulents and Mediterranean drought-resisters might well develop, while the number of species which do better in Scotland and Ireland might greatly increase.

Global warming has become a convenient scapegoat for many horticultural mishaps, largely without evidence, much of it either fanciful or apocalyptic. Everything from algal blooms in ponds to the spread of box disease, the spread of lily beetle and the death of fruit and sorbus species from phytophthora infection, has been laid at the door of this – as yet scarcely perceptible – climate change. In no case that has been thoroughly investigated has climate been implicated. Usually the culprit is some change in garden or adjacent land management, or the introduction of a new pest or new strain of disease. The international trade in plants and the smuggling of plant material by returning holidaymakers are both instrumental in introducing new pests and new diseases, or new strains of disease, which are far more damaging than climate change. The only way in which weather can be implicated is that our summers have not warmed or dried enough to induce travellers to stay at home.

The case of the yews at Westbury Court Garden in Gloucestershire is instructive. As the entry in the *Guide* relates, the hedges flanking the long canal underwent serious decline in 2000 – 2001 due to an outbreak of phytophthora. A large proportion of the yews died and global warming was initially suggested as the cause. However, a detailed investigation on behalf of the National Trust concluded that a management change, the raising of the canal water level by 38cm for visual reasons, combined with soil compaction by the feet of an ever-increasing number of visitors, was actually responsible. It is doubtful whether that conclusion received the same prominent publicity as the original global warming theory: much less sexy.

Barry McWilliam, a retired teacher of geography, is a long-time student of Pleistocene and Holocene environments.

Garden History MA, University of Bristol

In 2004 fifteen students of all ages and scholastic backgrounds will enrol for the MA course in garden history at Bristol University, now in its fifth year. The core syllabus includes a practical introduction to interpreting archaeological, physical and visual evidence, and to conservation and management issues. The overall aim is to encourage scholarly investigation by walking the landscapes and undertaking research into documents and literary texts: the dusty archives and green wellies approach. The MA can be taken full-time over one year, or by part-time study over two years; the cost for either is £3300. It is also possible to take the full-time course on its own for a postgraduate diploma in garden history. Teaching consists of lectures and seminars as well as study visits to gardens and landscapes, and students then research and write a dissertation on a garden history topic of their choice. The emphasis is on British garden history from 1620 to 1820, but there are many optional units on offer which cover subjects as wide-ranging as Persian, Islamic, Italian Renaissance and Baroque gardens. Of particular interest to this edition of the *Guide* is the challenging option devoted to contemporary landscape and garden design.

Dr Tim Mowl, Reader in Garden History at Bristol and author of the new series of county guides to historic gardens published by Tempus, outlines this increasingly popular course. He writes:

'*From Jekyll to Jencks* traces the modernist aesthetic in twentieth-century British landscape design. After charting incipient modernist sympathies in several Edwardian gardens, the unit explores classic modernism in public housing and private estates of the 1920s and 1930s. This legacy was taken up by professional landscape architects – Jellicoe, Colvin and Gibberd – in various post-war reconstruction projects, while the return to classic principles is marked in such 1960s landscapes as Arne Jacobsen's St Catherine's College in Oxford, John Brookes' café for Penguin workers at Harmondsworth, and Sylvia Crowe's Commonwealth Institute in Kensington. Seminars on these designers are accompanied by visits to many of the gardens – St Catherine's, Colvin's Sutton Courtenay, and Jellicoe's Sutton Place and Shute House, for example. The end-of-the-millennium post-modern approach is examined through such diverse gardens as Charles Jencks' Dumfriesshire estate at Portrack and Derek Jarman's seaside plot at Dungeness. In addition to seminars, there are lectures delivered by the department's Professor of History of Art, Stephen Bann, who is the acknowledged expert on Bernard Lassus and Ian Hamilton Finlay. One MA graduate, Trish Gibson, is now writing the definitive biography of Brenda Colvin; another, Katie Campbell, is studying for a PhD on twentieth-century British design.

'On a 2003 visit to Paris, organised by Professor Bann, the students explored some fascinating recent landscapes. French rationality finds a distinctly modern expression in the celebrated 14-acre Parc André Citroën. More controversial is Bernard Tschumi's Parc de la Villette; rejecting traditional notions of the park as a natural oasis, he has created a futuristic urban space in which bicycle paths, *avant-garde* sculpture and provocative gardens are linked by iconic red follies. More intimate is the Parc Atlantique, suspended over Montparnasse Railway Station – a charming horticultural evocation of the Atlantic holiday coast, brimming with seaside metaphors.'

With the continued success of the MA course, the annual series of lively conferences on a wide variety of topics and the ambition of creating an international centre for garden history studies at the University, Bristol seems set to remain at the forefront of developments.

Twentieth-Century Gardeners

Christopher Bradley-Hole (b. 1955) Qualifying as an architect at the age of 21, he worked first on a range of building projects before moving over to landscapes and gardens. He can claim to be among the first of British minimalists to practise the art of garden design. He was awarded his first medal at Chelsea in 1994, but it was with an elegant and spare design in 1997 that his career took off. Winner of 'Best in Show', this was a garden of spaces, contained within concrete, steel and glass. His 2000 and 2003 Chelsea gardens also won gold. His garden for Portland Castle (Dorset) was one of six modern schemes commissioned by English Heritage, and he was shortlisted for the new V&A garden.

John Brookes (b. 1933) Designer of over 700 gardens here and abroad, he is in Jane Brown's estimation 'the most talented Modernist who has worked in Britain since the war.' His Mondrianesque garden for Penguin Books in Harmondsworth is his most elegant modern garden, Denmans his best-known.

Percy Cane (1881 – 1976) A visit to Harold Peto's garden at Easton Lodge inspired Cane to become a garden designer, much sought after in his day. He owned *My Garden Illustrated* from 1918 to 1920 and *Garden Design* from 1930 to 1939. A lapsed modernist, he nonetheless made a distinguished contribution at Dartington, creating a green staircase and opening up several important vistas.

Brenda Colvin (1897 – 1981) A highly influential landscape architect who worked at both ends of the scale on large projects such as land reclamation schemes and new towns, and small gardens for private clients. She helped to found the Landscape Institute, serving as its President from 1951 to 1953, and her magisterial *Land and Landscape* became a prime reference book for the profession. Three of her gardens remain as testimony to her planting skills – Clipsham in Rutland, The Manor House at Sutton Courtenay and Steeple Manor in Dorset.

Dame Sylvia Crowe (1901 – 98) She was responsible for many large-scale projects for a crop of new towns – Warrington and Washington, Harlow and Basildon – and became an acknowledged expert on the sympathetic integration of development schemes, such as the construction of power stations, with the surrounding landscape. She designed the roof garden for the Scottish Widows Fund in Edinburgh and a park in Canberra, Australia. President of the Landscape Institute from 1957 to 1959, examples of her work are to be found at Blenheim, Cottesbrooke and Lexham Hall.

Henk Gerritsen (b. 1948) One of the famous trio of Dutch garden designers (Piet Oudolf and Ton ter Linden being the other two), he has been involved in turning the 40-acre garden at Waltham Place into a wholly organic garden, combining native and cultivated plants in naturalistic flower beds.

Rupert Golby (b. 1961) A Kew- and Wisley-trained designer with a gift for decorative planting, he is especially skilled at fashioning new designs for old-established gardens. He spent a year working for Rosemary Verey at Barnsley House, and his skill in laying out and planting *potagers* is second to none, as his ornamental kitchen gardens at The Old Rectory in Sudborough, Daylesford and Osborne House attest. Winner of two gold medals at Chelsea for *Country Life*, he has written two books, *The Well-Planned Garden* and *The Container Garden*.

Isabelle van Groeningen (b. 1965) She arrived in the UK in 1983 from Belgium to train at Wisley and Kew. After working for the National's Trust's gardens advisers and acquiring a doctorate, she formed the Land Art practice in 1992 with the German landscape architect Gabriella Pape. Together they have tackled an exciting range of projects both here and in France and Germany – historic gardens, new private gardens, public parks and commercial sites. These include the re-design of the South Moat Garden at Eltham Palace for English Heritage, the replanting of Jellicoe's Secret Garden at Cliveden, two new display gardens at Ryton Organic and a sustainable garden at the London Wetland Centre.

Kathryn Gustafson (b. 1951) Unusually for a landscape architect, she started her professional career as a fashion designer. To her it was nothing more than moving on to another medium – instead of producing sketches for a workshop, she now turns to clay to model her landscapes. Influenced by painters and sculptors, her textures are typically twenty-first-century: concrete, steel, glass. Her most famous work to date is the new public park at Terrasson-La-Villedieu in the Dordogne, where her scheme opened up spectacular views of the town and the serpentine River Vezere. Currently her circular rill in Hyde Park as a memorial to Diana, Princess of Wales is under construction, and her design submitted for the new garden at the V&A is on display.

Ian Hamilton Finlay (b. 1925) A calligrapher and sculptor of the highest order, he is best known for his home in Lanarkshire, Little Sparta, which has been described by Sir Roy Strong as 'the most original contemporary garden in the country'. This is modernism at its most elegant and refined, and a showcase for a lifetime of his own work. Stockwood Park and the Serpentine Gallery in London also display his calligraphic inscriptions.

Penelope Hobhouse (b. 1929) One of the most admired gardening writers, her grasp of the history of gardening has been matched by her skill as a designer. Her practice is international – she has worked for clients in Britain, France, Italy, Australia and the United States. She revived the garden at Hadspen, then after her marriage to John Malins moved to Tintinhull, and with him restored the Arts and Crafts garden there. After his death she moved to Dorset and created a new garden at Bettiscombe which is both modern and Islamic-inspired.

Preben Jakobsen (b. 1934) Danish by birth, much of his working life as a landscape architect has been spent in Britain. After studying at Kew, he returned to his native country to study landscape design at the Danish Royal Academy of Fine Arts, where he learnt to admire the works of Alvar Aalto, Le Corbusier, Frank Lloyd Wright and especially Carl Theodor Sorensen. Returning to England, he worked at Dartington for the Elmhirsts and on several low-rise housing projects with Eric Lyons for Span, and devised a much-admired landscape scheme for a private client in Stanmore.

Gertrude Jekyll (1843 – 1932) Both by her writing and her planting (much of it accomplished in partnership with the architect Sir Edwin Lutyens), she has probably had as much influence on the appearance of British gardens as any other designer. As someone trained initially as a painter and an embroiderer, her great strength was in carefully considered and subtle use of plant colour. Finding inspiration in the informality of cottage gardens, she created large interwoven swathes of plants rather than confining them to precise 'spotty' patterns, and in so doing changed our attitude towards the way in which borders should be planted. One of the best examples of her work with Lutyens is Hestercombe Gardens. Others are at Barrington Court, Castle Drogo, Folly Farm, Goddards, Hatchlands, Knebworth, the Manor House at Upton Grey, Munstead Wood, Tylney Hall, Vann and Yalding.

Sir Geoffrey Jellicoe (1900 – 96) Shortly after becoming an architect, he made an extensive study of Italian gardens with J.C. Shepherd, which led to their producing in 1925 what has become a classic book, *Italian Gardens of the Renaissance*. The publication of *Gardens and Design* in 1927 helped to bring him interesting commissions, such as the design of a large formal garden at Ditchley Park in Oxfordshire, giving scope for the strongly architectural quality of his work. After World War II he was given much public work, including the large water garden in Hemel Hempstead town centre, the Cathedral Close in Exeter, the Kennedy Memorial at Runnymede and a vast theme park in Galveston, Texas. Among his work for private clients, the gardens at Sutton Place and Shute House are notable. His work may also be seen at Cottesbrooke, Mottisfont and Sandringham.

Charles Jencks (b. 1939) An American academic long resident in the UK, he is best known for his re-landscaping of the garden at Portrack in the Scottish Borders with his wife Maggie Keswick. The principal landscape elements, monumental earthworks, echo the Land Art movement of the 1960s, and stem from his conviction that 'nature is basically curved, warped, undulating, jagged, zigzagged and sometimes beautifully crinkly'. Since his wife's death, he has created the Garden of Cosmic Speculation (a scientific theme park) at Portrack, and the new Landform Ueda for the Scottish National Gallery of Modern Art in Edinburgh.

Lawrence Johnston (1871 – 1948) One of the most outstandingly stylish twentieth-century gardeners, he was an American who spent much of his youth in Paris and built two great gardens in Europe which influenced the design of a great many others, including Sissinghurst. In 1905 he began to make the garden at Hidcote, pioneering the creation of a series of sheltered and interconnected garden rooms, each of which surprised by its different content and treatment.

Mary Keen (b. 1940) A great plantswoman, her work is vigorous and aristocratic. Her design for the garden at Glyndebourne acts as a powerful backcloth to Sir Michael Hopkins' formidable new opera house, and for another member of the Christie family she restored and replanted the splendid terracing by Belcher at Tapeley Park. She has also transformed the grand terrace at Bowood in front of the Robert Adam orangery. Her own garden at Duntisbourne Rouse, created over the past 10 years, is full of colour – a remarkably contemplative place at peace with itself. As a gardening writer, she is noted for the forcefulness of her views: her trenchant assessment of the new garden at Alnwick Castle in *The Daily Telegraph* will long be remembered by its readers.

Arabella Lennox-Boyd (b. 1938) Italian by birth and upbringing, her childhood was spent in the Sabine Hills near some of the finest Renaissance gardens. She has designed some 300 – in Europe, Barbados, Canada, the United States and Mexico. Her best-known work in Britain is at Ascott and Eaton Hall, but her own garden at Gresgarth Hall is a good example of the clarity, vitality and elegance of her style. She has won five gold medals at Chelsea, including a 'Best in Show' award in 1998. For many years a Trustee of Kew Gardens, she is also a member of the Historic Gardens Panel of English Heritage.

Christopher Lloyd (b. 1921) The doyen of garden-makers and one of the most stimulating of garden writers, he has just celebrated 40 years as columnist for *Country Life*. He is the son of Nathaniel Lloyd, the architectural writer, who commissioned Edwin Lutyens to extend his house at Great Dixter and to design the garden. Christopher Lloyd has brought to it his great skill as a plantsman and an almost iconoclastic approach to Lutyens' planting. His replacement of the Edwardian rose garden with a vibrant tropical scheme initiated a trend in gardens countrywide.

Sir Edwin Lutyens (1869 – 1944) A gifted architect who between 1893 and 1912 created approximately 70 gardens in partnership with Gertrude Jekyll. Her subtle planting always softened and complemented the strong architectural nature of his garden designs, and they in their turn splendidly integrated the house with the garden and its site. A fine example of the work of the partnership is at Hestercombe, where his genius for using classical masonry forms in a highly imaginative and individual way is wonderfully displayed. Other examples are Abbotswood, Ammerdown, Castle Drogo, Folly Farm, Goddards, Heywood, Irish National War Memorial Park, Knebworth, Misarden, Munstead Wood and Parc Floral des Moutiers.

Hal Moggridge (b. 1936) The most experienced landscape architect in Britain, he trained as an architect before working for Geoffrey Jellicoe. A designer of restraint and subtlety, his range of commissions is astonishingly varied. He started his own practice in 1967 after advising the GLC on suitable sites for new towns, then two years later joined Brenda Colvin in practice as Colvin and Moggridge. As a firm they have designed industrial landscapes, public gardens and private parks, landscaped the National Botanic Garden of Wales and planted William Morris's diminutive garden at Kelmscott. They devised a strategy for the Royal Parks and a plan for the military town of Aldershot. Retired but still a working consultant, his advice is eagerly sought and generously given.

Piet Oudolf (b. 1944) One of the best-known proponents of naturalistic planting with perennials and grasses, he is a nurseryman as well as a garden designer. His own garden at Humelo near Arnhem receives visitors from all over the world. He has made a number of gardens in Britain – twin borders for the RHS at Wisley, a garden at Bury Court, and a remarkable millennium garden at Pensthorpe. With Arne Maynard, he won the 'Best in Show' award at Chelsea 2000 for *Gardens Illustrated*.

Russell Page (1906 – 85) Trained as a painter, he quickly became absorbed by garden design and between 1935 and 1939 worked in association with Sir Geoffrey Jellicoe. After the war he gained a reputation in Europe and America, designing the garden at the Frick Gallery in New York and the Battersea Festival Gardens in London. He encapsulated his ideas about garden design in *The Education of a Gardener*, first published in 1962. Examples of his work are at Longleat and Port Lympne.

Dan Pearson (b. 1964) While studying at Wisley and Kew, scholarships to Spain, the Himalayas and Israel introduced him to native plant communities growing in the wild which have inspired his work. He began his professional career in 1987, and has completed a wide range of private and public sector commissions: a romantic garden in the grounds of a ruined mediaeval village in Italy, a contemporary landform design for the walled garden at Broughton Hall in Yorkshire, a walled sculpture garden for the Scottish National Gallery of Modern Art and 14 roof gardens for a new development in Tokyo. He was responsible for re-landscaping the grounds of Althorp House and for the landscape design surrounding the Millennium Dome. He is a columnist for the *The Sunday Times*, joint author with Sir Terence Conran of *The Essential Garden Book* and presenter of series for BBC2, Channel 4 and Channel 5.

Harold Peto (1854 – 1933) A talented architect working for the partnership which later employed the young Edwin Lutyens, who undoubtedly influenced his style. A lover of Italianate formal gardens, one of Peto's best-known works was his own garden at Iford Manor, but his canal garden at Buscot Park and the Casita garden at Ilnacullin are his most notable achievements. Other examples are at Easton Lodge, Greathed Manor in Surrey, Heale House, Wayford Manor and West Dean.

Tim Rees (b. 1952) and Brita Schoenaich (b. 1958) Graduates of Kew and founders in 1991 of the Schoenaich Rees landscape design firm, their concentration on private commissions in the UK, Europe and the USA has broadened into the commercial arena. Their style is at once naturalistic and cosmopolitan, consulting the topography of the site as well as the specific demands of individual gardens. A good example of their style of introducing assured and sympathetic modern planting within an historical setting is at Buscot Park.

William Robinson (1838 – 1935) An Irishman who settled in England and became one of the most prolific writers and influential designers of his epoch. By his teaching and example he liberated gardeners from the prim rigidity which had begun to dominate garden design in the mid-nineteenth century, advocating a free and natural attitude towards the creation of herbaceous and mixed beds. It was Robinson's planting philosophy which early inspired Gertrude Jekyll. He founded a weekly journal, *The Garden* (later absorbed into *Homes and Gardens*), and wrote *The English Flower Garden*, which ran to 15 editions during his life alone. Examples of his work are at Gravetye Manor, High Beeches, Killerton, Leckhampton College in Cambridge and Shrubland Park.

Lanning Roper (1912 – 83) A Harvard graduate from New Jersey who adopted Britain as his home and became one of the most popular landscapers in the 30 years after World War II. His best schemes, such as that at Glenveagh Castle, involved a subtle handling of plants combined with interesting formal features. One of his most controversial designs was the ornamental canal in the RHS garden at Wisley. Other examples of his work are at Anglesey Abbey, Broughton Castle, Fairfield House, Lower Hall, The Old Rectory in Orford, Trinity College in Dublin, and Trinity Hospice.

Vita Sackville-West (1892 – 1962) With her husband, Harold Nicolson, she made two notable gardens in Kent. The first, at Long Barn, Sevenoaks, was based on a Nicolson design which she planted during and after World War I. The second and most famous, at Sissinghurst Castle, was begun in 1932 and developed during the rest of her life. The couple were friendly with Lawrence Johnston, and their attitude to gardening was influenced by the ideas which he exploited at Hidcote. Another example of her work may be seen at Alderley Grange. Although she was the inspired plantswoman, arguably her husband's conception of structure made a greater contribution to twentieth-century garden design.

Tom Stuart-Smith (b. 1960) A superb plantsman and a perfectionist, he has won gold at Chelsea four times, and in 2003 won the 'Best in Show' award. He aims to create 'informal and wild' gardens, and indeed his gardens are becoming increasingly naturalistic. He has created a garden at Rosemoor for the RHS and the Queen's Golden Jubilee garden at Windsor Castle, but most of his work is for private clients.

Xa Tollemache (b. 1949) Born and bred in Staffordshire, on marriage she moved to Helmingham Hall in Suffolk. There she developed her sense of scale in design and her skill with colour combinations and plant associations, as she made and remade the historic garden and created new gardens within it. In 1995 she started to design for other people and now her commissions are countrywide from Castle Hill in Devon to Dunbeath Castle in Scotland, from town house gardens in London and Oxford to country gardens in Northumbria and France. She was a medal-winner at Chelsea in 1997, 2001 and 2003.

Christopher Tunnard (1910 – 79) The only figure of substance in the world of modernist garden-makers in the 1930s. He spent his early years at Wisley and worked briefly as assistant to Percy Cane. His book *Gardens in the Modern Landscape* was a pioneering manifesto putting the case for landscape being accepted as an art in its own right, independent of academic traditions. He was responsible with Frank Clark for the first major landscape exhibition at the RIBA in 1939. Disillusioned with British attitudes towards modernism, he escaped to America, teaching at Harvard and Yale. He too became disillusioned with modernism and died largely unfulfilled.

Rosemary Verey (1918 – 2001) A renowned plantswoman, whose reinterpretation of the traditional English style has been hugely influential, both here and in America. She created a famous garden at Barnsley House and designed schemes for many others, including Highgrove and Nether Lypiatt in Gloucestershire and at Elton John's garden in Berkshire. Other examples of her work are at Holdenby House and The Old Rectory in Sudborough. She was also an inspiring lecturer and one of England's foremost gardening writers, author of 17 books including *The Englishwoman's Garden*, *Classic Garden Design*, *The Garden in Winter* and one about her own garden.

Kim Wilkie (b. 1955) A landscape architect of vision, he is also an urban designer and an environmental planner, and expert at introducing modern designs seamlessly into historic landscapes. Responsible for the Thames Landscape Strategy, he threaded together the eighteenth-century waterside villas and landscape and made the administrative authorities along the Thames look anew at their heritage. He has helped to revive the cut of earth sculpting with his grass terraces at Great Fosters and Heveningham Hall. His design for the new garden at the V&A is restrained, practical and elegant.

Glossary of Garden Terms

Arbour Any sheltered covered area open to one side which usually contains a seat. Often surrounded by masonry, hedging or trelliswork covered with climbing plants.

Allée or alley A path either cut through a thick shrubbery or woodland or closely flanked by a hedge or wall.

Auricula theatre A shelter rising in tiers housing a collection of auriculas – an early-nineteenth-century collectors' craze.

Bath house A rectangular sunken pool for cold-water bathing, with seating approached by steps.

Bosquet or bosket A block of closely planted trees with *allées* between.

Canal An ornamental water basin made in the form of an elongated rectangle. It can either be excavated into the ground or confined above ground within masonry walls.

Clair-voie or **clair-voyée** A gap in a wall or hedge which extends the view by allowing a glimpse of the surrounding countryside; also an openwork gate, fence or grille at the end of an *allée*.

Cottage orné A deliberately picturesque rustic dwelling designed to ornament a park.

Crinkle-crankle wall A serpentine wall sheltering fruit trees within its walls.

Exedra An area of turf within a semi-circular hedge which is commonly used to display ornaments or to locate a semi-circular seat; or the seat itself.

Eye-catcher A building such as a tower, temple, obelisk, etc., or sometimes merely a bench, large urn or outstanding long-lived plant designed to beckon the eye towards a particularly rewarding view.

Finial An ornament such as an urn or a pointed sculptural form used to cap features like gateposts, the tops of spires, the top corners of buildings, etc.

Folly A decorative building with no serious function except perhaps to lure attention along a vista or to improve the composition of the garden 'picture'.

Gazebo Dog latin for 'I will gaze', used to describe a building usually sited on a high terrace from which the surrounding countryside can be enjoyed.

Grotto/Nymphaeum An artificial garden feature made to simulate an underground cavern and usually dimly lit from a single small natural light source such as the cave mouth or an oval occulus pierced through the roof or wall. When rather dank and simply lined with natural rock, it can be a good example of art echoing nature. But when formally shaped and lined with statuary and a sophisticated encrustation of shellwork, a grotto can become a nymphaeum and an example of art inspired by, and improving upon, nature. Occasionally (as at Woburn Abbey) it can be made as an extension to the house, so offering a cool area in hot weather. Other functions are to shock and surprise visitors, play upon their perception of the garden or provoke a fruitful melancholy.

Ha-ha A deep ditch separating the garden from the landscape beyond. It allows the unscreened view to be enjoyed from the house but is profiled in such a way that livestock cannot enter the garden.

Hermitage A rustic building popularised in the eighteenth century, supposedly as a hermit's retreat.

Knot garden Geometric patterns of low-growing hedge plants such as box or shrubby germander which are made to appear as though they intertwine like knotted cord. The areas between the hedges are filled with plants or decorative gravel.

Moon door or gate A circular opening in a door or wall.

Mount An artificial hill usually surmounted by an arbour from which landscapes both inside and beyond the garden can be enjoyed from a different perspective. A feature specially of Tudor gardens.

Obelisk A tall, thin vertical column diminishing in width as it rises, and frequently tapered to a pyramid. Large-scale examples have been built to commemorate great events or notable people and often to act as eye-catchers in great landscape schemes. Smaller *treillage* versions have been used to beckon for attention in smaller gardens or to act as vertical frames for climbing plants.

Pagoda A feature in a few great landscape gardens based on Buddhist multi-storey towers of spiritual significance. In Britain they were first introduced during the eighteenth-century craze for things Chinese.

Palladian bridge A bridge with a classical superstructure, usually open-sided with columns supporting a roof.

Parterre An intricately patterned formal garden which usually includes other features such as statuary, water basins and fountains; much larger than a knot garden.

Patte d'oie Literally 'goose foot'; a series of usually three formal paths or grand avenues leading fan-wise from a single point through densely planted trees.

Pergola A framework of columns supporting beams, usually clad with climbing plants such as roses, clematis or wisteria. If the parallel rows of columns are joined by cross-beams and covered with summer foliage, pergolas can become tunnels.

Pleaching Training the branches of a line of trees horizontally by pruning and attaching them to wires, so that the remainder can be intertwined as they grow to form a screen of foliage.

Pulhamite Composition stone invented by James Pulham.

Quincunx A pattern (sometimes a repeat-pattern) of four trees at the corners of a square and one at the centre.

Red Book Bound books of proposals including 'flap' overlays, drawn by Humphry Repton for his clients.

Ribbon bed A very narrow band of bedding plants, which the Victorians were fond of using to border their lawns.

Rotunda Strictly, circle of classical columns on a raised circular plinth supporting a domed roof. Instead of a solid dome it may be topped with an open ironwork dome. Sometimes loosely called a kiosk.

Rustic work Garden features, such as garden houses, fences or seats, made from rough tree branches, and frequently embellished with such decoration as patterns made from sectioned pine cones.

Souterrain An underground chamber, usually in a grotto.

Stumpery Roots and stumps of trees arranged upside down and covered with trailing plants.

Stilt hedge Clipped trees, such as limes, which have all their branches removed for several feet above the ground to reveal a line of bare trunks like stilts.

Théâtre de verdure Similar to but usually more spacious than an exedra, a turf 'stage' with a backcloth of trimmed hedge and sometimes other hedges disposed like the wings of a theatre.

Treillage Architectural features such as arbours, obelisks or ambitious screens made out of trellis.

Trompe-l'oeil A feature designed to deceive the eye, such as a path which narrows as it recedes from a viewpoint to exaggerate the perspective and make the garden seem larger.

Wilderness Bosquet, grove or wood traversed by paths.

How to Use *The Guide*

The Guide is **arranged by counties**. Within each of these the gardens are listed alphabetically by the normal name of the garden/house. The index at the end of the book can also be used to find a garden whose name only is known to the reader.

Readers who do not have a specific garden in mind may like to take the following **procedure to discover gardens** in their particular area which are available for viewing:

1. Choose the county or neighbouring counties which will be your target area.
2. Search out (in these counties) the gardens which are open all year round, i.e. those marked with ○.
3. Having listed these gardens, pay particular attention to ★★ and then ★ gardens on the list.

Alternatively, readers can concentrate on the starred gardens, checking which of these are open on the days available to the visitor.

Symbols: These are intended to convey some useful information at a glance.

[NEW] entries new for 2004 edition; ○ open all year; ◑ open most of year; ◐ open for main season; ● open on a certain number of days and/or by appointment; ☕ teas/light refreshments; ✗ meals; ▦ picnics permitted; WC toilet facilities; <u>WC</u> toilet facilities, inc. disabled; ♿ garden partly wheelchair-accessible; 🐕 dogs permitted on lead; 🌱 plants for sale; 🛍 shop; 🎪 events held; ☺ children-friendly; B&B bed and breakfast.

This list is repeated in various places throughout the book and further explanation of symbols is given under **Detailed use of *The Guide*** (below).

Detailed use of *The Guide*
(information listed in order used in entry)

Garden name The name of the garden, or the building with which it is associated.

Stars To help give the reader the opinion which inspectors and editors have formed about the status of certain gardens, over 100 properties have been marked with ★★ to indicate that in our opinion these are amongst the finest gardens in the world in terms of design and content. Many are of historic importance, but some are of recent origin. Readers will appreciate that direct comparisons cannot be made between a vast estate like Chatsworth with its staff of professional gardeners and a tiny plantsman's garden behind a terraced house, although both may be excellent of their kind. Those gardens which are of high quality, though not perhaps as outstanding as the ★★ ones, are given a single ★. The latter will be worth travelling a considerable distance to see, and sometimes the general ambience of the property as a whole will make the visit especially rewarding. The bulk of the gardens in *The Guide* are not given a mark of distinction, but all have considerable merit and will be well worth visiting when in the region. Some of them will have distinctive features of design or plant content, noted in the description, which will justify making a special journey. To give readers an idea of scale, we estimate that some 5000 properties in the UK are open to the public on announced dates in the year, plus public parks and green spaces. We list well over 1000, of which over 100 have ★★ status, that is about ten per cent of the total listed by us, but two and a half per cent of the total open. On the maps at the end of *The Guide*, those gardens given ★★ status are distinguished from the others by being boxed in bold.

Address This is the address supplied by the owner or some other reputable source. In the index, gardens with street numbers are listed at the beginning rather than under the initial letter of the street name.

Telephone numbers Except where owners have specifically requested them to be excluded, telephone numbers to which enquiries may be directed are given for each property. To maintain the support and co-operation of private owners, it is suggested that the telephone be used with discretion. Where group visits are proposed, owners should be advised in advance and arrangements preferably confirmed in writing. Telephone code numbers are given in brackets. Visitors calling the Republic of Ireland from Britain should phone 00353 followed by the code (Dublin is 1) followed by the subscriber's 6-figure number. Northern Ireland and the Channel Islands follow the mainland system. France has 9-figure numbers prefixed by 0033, Belgium by 0032 and Netherlands by 0031.

Website Many gardens in *The Guide* now have their own websites, and we include these in a separate list on pages 619–22.

Owners' names given are those available at the time of going to press. In the case of The National Trust, some properties may be the homes of tenants of the Trust. Some other gardens are owned or managed by other trusts.

Location, travel and parking This information has been supplied by inspectors and is intended to be the best available to those travelling by car. No specific details are given where to park because it is assumed that most owners make some convenient arrangement for visitors' cars. However, if special circumstances apply (i.e. if parking is a long walk away) this is usually mentioned under Other Information. The unreliability of train and bus services makes it unrewarding to include many details, particularly as most garden visits are made on Sundays. However, a number of properties can be reached by public transport.

Opening dates and times (see also symbols as opening indicators, below). Dates and times given of access to house (if open) and to garden are usually the best available at the moment of going to press, but some may have been changed subsequently. Some owners unavoidably cannot give their opening information before we go to press. The details given are the most helpful we can present. The dates and times given for all entries are inclusive – that is, an entry such as May to Sept means that the garden is open from 1st May to 30th Sept inclusive, and 2 – 5pm also means that visits will be effective during that period, although some gardens may close to visitors beforehand, and it is wise to arrive half an hour before closing time. Please note that many owners will open their gardens to visitors by appointment. They will often arrange to give a personally conducted tour on these occasions.

Gardens in Great Britain which are open by courtesy of the owners for one of many charities are included where the gardens are of special interest even if, as on some occasions, they are open in this way on only one day in the year. Many owners will, however, also open by appointment on other days. However, many such gardens are also open at other specific times, such as for local charities or church restoration funds, and it is not generally possible to give dates for all these locally publicised openings. Readers should note that other nearby gardens, not listed in this guide for one reason or another, may well be open at similar times to those of listed gardens.

Entrance fees As far as is known, these are correct at time of going to press, but changes may be made without notice. Where there are variations, these will be upwards, but the amount of increase is usually small. Family tickets may be available with children charged at a lower rate. Numbers of children included in the family ticket may vary. Charges for parties are often at special rates. National Trust charges are explained in their literature with special concessions for members. The Trust is tightening its admissions policy: members who arrive without their membership card will have to pay the full entrance charges. Accompanied children are normally admitted by the Trust at half price and this is why no specific charge for children is usually listed for Trust properties. Figures for the Republic of Ireland are given in Euros. The Royal Horticultural Society, in addition to its own properties, has a 'free access' scheme to a wide range of other British gardens. RHS members will find details in the *Handbook*; otherwise consult the website (www.rhs.org.uk).

Other information This section gives helpful information notified to us which we pass on to the reader. It includes: extra attractions in or near the garden (eg a museum or nursery); facilities outside the garden but nearby (eg toilet facilities); facilities which are limited either by availability (eg teas on charity open days only), or by location (eg picnics in park only); warnings (eg no coaches), and helpful hints (eg possible for wheelchairs but some gravel paths).

Disclaimer

The information given is believed to be correct at the time of going to press but changes do occur, properties sold or ownership varied. There may also be closures of over-visited properties, or limitations imposed on opening times. Prices of entry may be changed without notice.

It has not been possible for *Guide* inspectors to visit every garden which was open to the public at some time in the year, and certain gardens in *The Guide* may not have been visited for over twelve months. In general, inspections have been made on an anonymous basis to ensure objectivity.

Symbols

NEW New garden this year.

○, ◑, ◐, ◕ **Opening times** These symbols indicate gardens are open as follows: ○ throughout the year; ◑ most of the year; ◐ more or less throughout the season from Easter to October for several days (i.e. more than two or three) each week; and ◕ on a certain number of days and/or by appointment.

☕, ✕, 🍱 **Refreshments**: a guide only. Where ☕ is given, this means that the owners have arranged to serve a simple tea or light refreshments on the property, or near at hand, at reasonable prices during opening hours. ✕ indicates that meals are served. 🍱 means that picnics are permitted, although probably in certain areas only.

WC, <u>WC</u> **Toilet facilities** WC indicates that access to a toilet or toilets is provided, while <u>WC</u> means that the toilet facilities are also suitable for disabled visitors. Where neither symbol is given, no specific toilets are available and enquiries will have to be directed to staff or owners.

& **Wheelchair suitability** Inspectors have told us where they believe a garden is partly or wholly negotiable by someone in a wheelchair. This symbol refers to the garden only and if a house or other building is also open, it may or may not be suitable for wheelchairs.

🐕 **Dogs** They are allowed in the property on leads (very often in restricted areas only).

🌿 **Plants for sale** Often these are grown on the property, but some owners now buy in plants from a commercial source for re-sale.

🏪 **Shop** refers to a sales outlet on the premises, such as National Trust shops, those selling souvenirs, etc.

🎪 **Events** These may be held during, or as well as, normal garden opening times. Those wishing to participate in (or to avoid) events should check before travelling.

🎈 **Children-friendly** Some owners pay particular attention to expanding the attractions for the whole family, while other gardens are by their design and content intriguing to children.

B&B **Bed and Breakfast** An increasing number of owners offer accommodation – a fine way for visitors to become acquainted with a garden.

No symbol means either that a certain facility is not available at a garden or that we have not been notified of it. However, it is worth checking under Other Information for details of partial availability.

BEDFORDSHIRE

The Manor House ★

Church Road, Stevington, Bedford MK43 7QB. Tel: (01234) 822064

Kathy Brown • 5m NW of Bedford off A428, through Bromham. In Stevington, turn right at crossroads; garden is on left after ¼ m • Open 16th May, 13th June, 2 – 6pm, 30th June, 6 – 9pm, 1st Aug, 2 – 6pm, and for parties by appt • Entrance: £3, children £1 ● ⬤ WC ♿ 🌷 🏵 ⚲

This is a garden of exuberant imagination and reworked classic gardening themes: for example, a fine French-style, formal garden with clipped hedges and patterns in box punctuated by two fountains, one a splendid modern one. The manor house itself is set off by a mound-strewn lawn and some old trees, but everything else has been created in the last ten years. Rectangular areas are subdivided into patterns of succulents and grasses, against gravels of different colours. Old-fashioned roses and *viticella* clematis vie for space on the pergolas and obelisks, and the wildflower meadow is a tapestry of colour and shape in June and July. The owner is known for her skilful assemblies of plants grown in containers, so there are confections of bulbs, herbs, roses, diascias, succulents, etc. in a most unusual collection of pots and baskets.

Seal Point ★

7 Wendover Way, Luton LU2 7LS. Tel: (01582) 611567

Mrs Danae Johnston • In NE of Luton. Turn N off Stockingstone Road into Felstead Way and take second turning on left • Open for individuals and parties by appt • Entrance: £2.50 ● ⬤ 🏵 WC 🌷

This small, sloping town garden with a Japanese theme goes from good to better, with interesting plant combinations (for example *Aeonium* 'Schwarz-kopf' associated with *Clematis florida* 'Sieboldii'), and gorgeous colour schemes. A hardy standard fuchsia is now over three metres high, and 20 or more different grasses are integrated into the borders. There is something unusual at every turn: a wildlife copse, a tiny bonsai garden, three pools (one with a waterfall), yin and yang beds, amusing topiary, original ornaments, and much more. The garden is almost entirely organic and the accent everywhere is on nurturing wildlife.

Stockwood Park

Stockwood Craft Museum, Farley Hill, Luton LU1 4BH. Tel: (01582) 738714

Borough of Luton • Leave M1 at junction 10 for Luton. Take Farley Hill (Chapel Street) turn off A505 Dunstable road out of Luton. Signposted from A1081 • Open April to Oct, daily except Mon (but open Bank Holiday Mons), 10am – 5pm (Sun and Bank Holiday Mons closes 6pm); Nov to March, Sat and Sun, 10am – 4pm. Guided tours available by appt • Entrance: free • Other information: Craft museum in stable block ◐ ⬤ WC ♿ 🏵 🍼 ⚲

Within the walled gardens of the old house, a series of period gardens – medieval, seventeenth-century knot, cottage and Victorian – has been designed by Robert Burgoyne, ably assisted by Peter Ansell, the head gardener. In the park is a landscape garden with sculpture by Ian Hamilton Finlay, whose work gives a convincing continuity to the landscape tradition by its location alongside the original ha-ha. Another of his sculptures is a curved inscribed wall, and his modern fragments of 'antique' buildings, partly buried, suggest the eighteenth-century ideal of a harmonious blend of parkland, planting, architecture and sculpture.

The Swiss Garden [Historic Garden Grade II*]

Old Warden Park, Biggleswade SG18 9ER. Tel: (01767) 627666

Bedfordshire County Council • 6m SE of Bedford. Take A1 to Biggleswade and follow signposts from roundabout. Also signposted on A600 Shefford – Bedford road. Entrance via Shuttleworth Collection • Open March to Sept, daily, 1 – 5pm (Sun and Bank Holiday Mons opens 10am); Jan, Feb and Oct, Sun only, 10am – 4pm (but open 1st Jan). Guided tours available • Entrance: £3, concessions £2, family ticket £8, season ticket £12, concessions £8. Special rates for parties • Other information: Restaurant in grounds of Shuttleworth Collection. Disabled parking. Two wheelchairs available for loan ◐ ☕ ✕ WC ♿ ✿ ♨*

This romantic 10-acre landscape garden with its unpeeled-bark rustic 'Swiss Cottage' is said to have been created in the early nineteenth century by the 3rd Lord Ongley for his Swiss mistress. The architect John Papworth lived nearby, and may have given advice; it is reminiscent of his work at White Knights (see entry in Berkshire). Neglected for 40 years from 1939, an ongoing programme of restoration has been underway since the late 1970s. Beautiful rustic iron bridges cross over miniature ponds and beside the little Swiss cottage sheets of spring bulbs flower beneath azaleas, rhododendrons and spring-flowering shrubs. The gloom of the grotto and the dazzling light of the fernery provide a dramatic contrast.

Toddington Manor ★

Toddington LU5 6HJ. Tel: (01525) 872576

Sir Neville and Lady Bowman-Shaw • 8m NW of Luton, 1m NW of Toddington, 1m W of M1 junction 12. Signposted from village • Open 31st May, 11am – 5pm, and for parties by appt • Entrance: charge • Other information: Rare breeds of goats and pigs. Vintage tractor collection ◑ ☕ ♿ ⬦ ✿ ✂

The garden is maintained to the highest standards, but shrubs and plants are allowed to grow and flower and seed in abundance. Each area is themed individually. The pleached lime walk – a most successful *allée* – is paved and surrounded by large herbaceous borders displaying an exuberance of hostas with many variations of leaf, blue delphiniums, white astilbes and *Helleborus argutifolius*, euphorbias and angelicas. Inside the walled garden are borders with dramatic sweeps of delphiniums, peonies, clematis and grasses, backed by shrubs. In the rose garden the air is scented by yellow and white floribunda roses and philadelphus with wonderful eremurus growing through; under the roses violas have spread in sheets. A stream flows through and feeds the larger ponds and the fountain. There is a good herb garden and greenhouse, and beyond the walls a wildflower meadow, orchards and 20 acres of woodland contributing to a fine display of natural beauty.

Woburn Abbey [Historic Park Grade I]

Woburn MK17 9WA. Tel: (01525) 290666

The Duke of Bedford and Trustees of Bedford Estates • 11m NW of Luton between A5 and M1 (follow signs from junction 13) • Open Jan to March, Sat and Sun only, 10.30am – 4pm; end March to Sept, daily, 10am – 4.30pm; Oct, Sat and Sun, 10.30am – 4pm • Entrance: £6 per car. Abbey and park £8, OAPs £7, children (12–16) £3.50, under 12 free (2003 prices) • Other information: Pottery and antiques centre ◐ ⬤ ✕ ▦ WC ⅙ ⇗ 🎪 ⚑

Early in the seventeenth century, Woburn was established as the principal seat of the 4th Earl of Bedford, who extended the abbey buildings and commissioned Isaac de Caus to build a grotto in the new north wing. By the time of the Restoration, a series of enclosed gardens had been laid out to the west of the house and woodland planted with rides cut through. By 1714, the park had been extended and George London's Bason Pond created as an integral part of his grand Baroque west approach. By 1738 Charles Bridgeman had largely removed all the formal gardens around the house. In 1760, Sir William Chambers was commissioned to design a bridge across a stream, known as the Basin Bridge; twenty years later Holland designed a greenhouse (later a sculpture gallery) and the Chinese dairy overlooking a small lake with a covered walk. At the same time informal gardens were created and enclosed to the east and south. The 6th Duke then employed Humphry Repton to draw up a landscape scheme for the park as a whole. By 1805 the result was Repton's finest Red Book. His proposals were a triumph, and he was able to claim that 'The improvements I have had the honour to suggest have nowhere been so fully realised as at Woburn Abbey.' These comprised the creation of a group of linked yet separate areas of garden: an American and a Chinese garden, a rosery, a menagerie and an aviary. He also reshaped the lakes westwards from the Abbey and rerouted the southern approach drive. In the 1930s the gardens were again developed by Percy Cane, and the 42 acres of gardens today are those made in the twentieth century. The park is still a deer park, largely pasture, and still surrounds the gardens and pleasure grounds of the past. The private gardens, which are open to the public at stated times, contain a large hornbeam maze, formal gardens, good herbaceous borders, and a most successful rose garden by Anita Pereire.

Wrest Park [Historic Park Grade I]

Silsoe, Bedford MK45 4HS. Tel: (01525) 860152

English Heritage • 10m S of Bedford, ³⁄₄ m E of Silsoe off A6 • Open April to Sept, Sat, Sun and Bank Holiday Mons, 10am – 6pm; Oct, Sat and Sun only, 10am –

5pm (last admission 1 hour before closing) • *Entrance: £4, OAPs £3, children (5–15) £2, family £10 (2003 prices)* ◑ ☕ 🖼 WC ♿ 🛍 ⛪ 🏮 ⚲

One of the few places in England where it is possible to see a Baroque formal garden of the early-eighteenth century. The Long Water – a canal – dominates the 'Great Garden', made for the 1st Duke of Kent. It provides the main axis of the grounds, and cuts through thick blocks of woodland. At its head stands the beautiful Thomas Archer pavilion – the Banqueting House – with strong echoes of a similar pavilion designed by Daniel Marot, only recently discovered. 'Capability' Brown worked here later, creating a naturalistic river to surround the grounds at their perimeter. The woods on either side of the Long Water are intersected by avenues and dotted with 'incidents of delight' and giant urns set in grassy glades by Thomas Acres. The later Bath House was built as a romantic classical ruin. Water catches the eye in every direction. The nineteenth-century house (not open) was built in the French style, fronted by terraces and parterres. The large orangery was designed by Cléphane.

FEEDBACK

Readers are invited to advise the *Guide* of any gardens which in their opinion should be listed in future editions, and where possible arrangements will be made to review such suggestions. Readers who would like to add information about gardens listed are warmly invited to write to the *Guide* with their comments, which may be used in future editions without attribution. Please send letters to the publishers, Frances Lincoln Ltd, 4 Torriano Mews, Torriano Avenue, London NW5 2RZ. All letters are acknowledged by the editors.

RESEARCHING GARDEN HISTORY

The Register of Parks and Gardens of Special Historic Interest is the official record of the nation's historic landscapes produced by English Heritage. It has been substantially revised and upgraded, parks and gardens added, and threatened landscapes 'spot-registered'. At the beginning of August 2003, the total number of entries was 1590. Each site is documented in a description of its historical evolution, accompanied by specially drawn paper maps delineating the historical boundaries of the park or garden and chronicling its development.

The *Register* is available for public consultation at English Heritage's National Monuments Record Centre in Swindon (open Tues – Fri, 9.30am – 5pm). Copies of individual entries or complete county registers can also be purchased and sent by post. For more information contact NMR Enquiry & Research Services (Tel: (01793) 414600; Fax (01793) 414606; Email: nmrinfo@english-heritage.org.uk). Additionally, each local planning authority will have a copy of the relevant descriptions and maps within their jurisdictions. Be sure to telephone in advance of a visit.

BERKSHIRE

Some gardens have postal addresses in one county and are physically situated in another. If in doubt, a check in the index will direct the reader to the page on which the garden appears.

Two-starred gardens are marked on the map with a black square.

Ashdown House

(see Oxfordshire)

Blencathra

Finchampstead, Wokingham RG40 3SS. Tel: (0118) 973 4563

Dr and Mrs F.W. Gifford • 8m SE of Reading, 3m S of Wokingham. 1m W of A321 near Crowthorne Station, at NW end of Finchampstead Ridges (B3348). Entrance 300 metres down joint private drive • Open for charity and by appt for individuals and parties • Entrance: £3, accompanied children free ● ▭ WC & ◁

The owners started their 11-acre garden in 1964, when they purchased an unmanaged woodland site and built themselves a house. Their enthusiasm for fresh ideas is inspiring, and the low-maintenance garden has evolved with minimal budget and help – none professional. Established shrubs, lawns and specimen trees surround the house, whose design blends well with the plantings. Features include woodland areas on either side of the drive and an extensive water garden, with three small lakes, a stream and small 'bog' areas. Spring bulbs, especially bluebells, rhododendrons and many conifers ensure colour and interest in all seasons. White Knights (see entry) is nearby.

Chieveley Manor

Chieveley, Newbury RG20 8UT. Tel: (01635) 248208

Mr and Mrs C.J. Spence • 4m N of Newbury, ½ m from M4 junction 13 via A34. In Manor Lane by church • Open 27th June, 2 – 6pm • Entrance: £3, children free ● ▭ WC & ▦

This well-presented garden provides a pleasing setting for the old brick manor house. Generous lawns, with some fine trees, merge into the immaculate paddocks of the adjacent stud farm. Brick steps edged with roses lead up from the lawn to the gravelled drive and the house, where borders of mixed planting soften the walls. The grassed walled garden at the back of the house has attractive trees – these include a variegated maple and a tulip tree – and soft pink roses planted against the mellow brick walls. Herbaceous borders flank the entrance from a sunken stone terrace: here the colour scheme has been carefully conceived with deep colours counterbalanced by pinks and white. The choice of perennials in bold groups is relatively traditional but the variety of clematis in the walled garden and elsewhere catches the eye. Four beds surrounding a circular stone sink are filled with purple sage interspersed with *Geranium sanguineun* 'Album', which together create the rich but muted colour effect of an old carpet. A swimming pool garden with a Mediterranean atmosphere leads off the main walled enclosure.

Englefield House ★ [Historic Garden Grade II]

Englefield, Theale, Reading RG7 5EN. Tel: (0118) 930 2221

Sir William and Lady Benyon • 5m W of Reading. Entrance on A340, near Theale • Open all year, Mon; also April to Sept, Tues – Thurs; all 10am – 6pm • Entrance: £3, children free ◑ 🍴 ⑤ ⚲

There has been a garden here since the seventeenth century. Today its seven acres have achieved a rare and successful balance between the formal and informal. Spacious areas of stone balustraded terracing close to the house provide an appropriately grand setting for the historic building and are also the best place to view the deer park with its lake. On the terraces box-edged borders set against stone walls are planted with a varied mixture of shrubs and perennials. An informal touch is added by swathes of meadow grass, where cowslips and camassias have established themselves under trees within an area of formal lawn. The ground rises steeply behind the terraces into tree-covered slopes – the glory of this garden. Underplanted with thickets of shrubs, azaleas and rhododendrons, mature trees give character with their varied outlines, foliage and colour. Within the woodland area a stream edged with candelabra primulas, ferns and bog plants winds below a slope covered with azaleas and richly coloured maples. There are well-placed seats in pleasant intimate corners: under a domed ivy-house, surrounding a sundial, round the new pebble garden and beside an arrangement of attractively planted pots. Although this is a garden on a grand scale, a place has still been found for whimsical details like the carved wooden bear rising out of bluebells and the child's garden with its water tricks.

Folly Farm [Historic Garden Grade II*]

Sulhamstead, Reading RG7 4DF. Tel: (Contact: Janet Findon) (01635) 841541

7m SW of Reading, 2m W of M4 junction 12. Turn onto A4 and left at road signed to Sulhamstead at Spring Inn 1m after Theale roundabout; entrance ¾ m on right • Open all year for parties of 10 – 25 by appt • Entrance £6, incl. coffee and biscuits ◕ 🍴 WC ⑤

The gardens surrounding the old Georgian house, with its distinctive Dutch-style extension added in 1906 and later extension of 1912, remain in essence an outstanding example of the Lutyens and Jekyll partnership. The garden and house were designed to blend together in a series of walled courts connected by brick-arched doorways and herringbone brick paths. The tank cloister and canal (now planted with pastel-coloured water lilies) and the octagonal pool in the rose garden are sublime examples of Lutyens' design with water. Although the planting of the gardens is no longer maintained according to Jekyll's plans, nothing has been done to obscure or detract from the quality of Lutyens' garden architecture. In some cases grass has replaced borders for ease of maintenance, so that the hard landscaping is seen without the intended softening of plants, but this only serves to expose the strong bones of his design and his insistence on meticulous craftsmanship. Contemporary plantings of grasses have supplanted the iris border, and a mixture of disease-resistant modern roses has replaced the original scheme in the dramatic circular sunken rose garden, with its intriguing changes of level and tall yew hedges. Organic vegetables are now grown in the once-neglected kitchen garden and the original greenhouses provide a home for a remarkable collection of tropical rainforest plants which is the life's work of Barry Findon.

Frogmore Gardens [Historic Garden Grade I]

Windsor SL4 2JG.

H.M. The Queen • At Windsor Castle. Entrance via signed car park on B3021 between Datchet and Old Windsor. Pedestrian access only from Long Walk • House open as garden in Aug • Garden usually open several days in late May and Aug – telephone (020) 7766 7305 for information • Entrance: house, gardens and mausoleum £5.20, OAPs £4.20, children £3.20 (children under 8 not admitted) ●

Set amid the extensive Home Park of Windsor Castle, 30 acres of landscaped and picturesque gardens surround the house, which dates from the 1680s and was purchased in 1792 for Queen Charlotte, consort of George III. It then passed through a succession of royal owners, becoming a favoured retreat of Queen Victoria and later of King George V and Queen Mary; its sense of peace drew Prince Albert and Queen Victoria to break with royal tradition and choose a corner of the garden to build a mausoleum for themselves. Other architectural features include a charming wisteria-covered Gothick ruin by Wyatt, Queen Victoria's tea house and an Indian kiosk brought from Lucknow after the Mutiny. Fine and unusual trees include a remarkable incense cedar planted in 1857. (Unfortunately, the limited opening means that the public will not see what must be one of the garden's chief glories, the 200,000 spring bulbs planted in Queen Mary's time.) During August and September there is extended access to allow visitors to view the East Terrace. It has a somewhat municipal air, quite different from the private garden for the royal family behind its walls, or the gardens in the Great Park, begun after 1931, or, for that matter, Frogmore itself.

The Living Rainforest

Hampstead Norreys, Nr Newbury RG18 0TN. Tel: (01635) 202444

The Living Rainforest • 7m NE of Newbury. Follow signs from M4 junction 13 • Open all year, daily except 25th, 26th Dec, 10am – 5.15pm (last admission ¾ hour before closing) • Entrance: £4.95, concessions £4.25, children (5 – 14) £3.25, children (3 – 4) £1.95 (2003 prices) ○ 🍺 🛍 WC ⛄ 🐾 ♿ 🔦 ⚬

A remarkable 1860-square-metre glasshouse with a fine collection of exotic plants, splendidly grown, which educates visitors in the beauty and diversity of the rainforest. The plants are displayed in an imaginative way, with paths at various levels allowing them to be enjoyed from above. There are two distinct environments – an area known as Lowland which mimics conditions of lowland rainforest, and an area called Amazonica which emphasises life in the forest canopy. In each is a representative collection of the animals to be found there, chosen to illustrate the symbiotic relationship between animals and plants in their natural environment.

Meadow House

Ashford Hill, Thatcham RG19 8BN. Tel: (0118) 981 6005

Antony and Harriet Jones • 8m SE of Newbury. From B3051 take turning at SW end of village to Wolverton Common. After 350 metres turn right down track to house • Open by appt. Parties of up to 40 welcome • Entrance: £3, children free • Other information: Park cars in meadow and coaches at top of lane. Plants for sale in nursery ● ● & ●

Essentially a plantsman's creation – a modest country house garden of just under two acres with a lawn sweeping down to a small lake supporting ducks and waterside planting. The nursery and greenhouse are screened by a tall trellis smothered with wisteria, clematis, rambler roses and honeysuckle. Woodland is underplanted with hostas, primulas, camellias and 'Annabelle' hydrangeas. The borders contain mixed shrubs, unusual herbaceous perennials and shrub roses.

Odney Club

Odney Lane, Cookham, Maidenhead SL6 9SR. Tel: (01628) 530011

John Lewis Partnership • 4m N of Maidenhead off A4094, in Cookham near bridge • Open 25th April, 2 – 6pm • Entrance: £2.50, children free ● ● ●
WC & ● ●

This huge 120-acre site along the Thames, well cared for and continuously developing, takes a full afternoon's visit. It was a favourite with Stanley Spencer, who often visited to paint the magnolia which featured in his work. There is a magnificent wisteria walk, and also specimen trees, herbaceous borders, small side gardens, and terraces with spring bedding plants.

The Savill Garden

(see Surrey)

Scotlands ★

Cockpole Green, Wargrave, Reading RG10 8QP. Tel: (01628) 822648

Mr Michael Payne • 4m E of Henley-on-Thames, off A4 at Knowl Hill, halfway between Warren Row and Cockpole Green • Open for various charities, and by appt • Entrance: £3, children free • Other information: Picnics permitted on Cockpole Green ● ● WC & ● ●

The attractive chalk-and-flint house, formerly a seventeenth-century barn, is surrounded by a series of courtyards, one with a lily pool. To the west is an oval swimming pool, guarded by yew hedges and the lead statue of a drummer boy. A gazebo overlooks the herb garden with patterned paving and box, roses, lavender and choice vegetables such as artichokes. To the east, a lawn sweeps down to woodland and pond gardens, with the Repton-style summer-house signalling the merging of the landscaped water garden with natural woodland. Mown grass paths lead to a waterfall with large rocks. Fine speci-men catalpa, cedars, Spanish chestnut and copper beech mark the boundary of the four-acre site.

Waltham Place ★

White Waltham, Maidenhead SL6 3JH. Tel: (01628) 825517

Mr and Mrs N.F. Oppenheimer • $3\frac{1}{2}$ m S of Maidenhead. From M4 junction 8/9 take A404M and follow signs to White Waltham. Turn left to Windsor and Paley Street. Parking signposted at top of hill • Open April to Sept – telephone for details or consult website – and for parties by appt all year • Entrance: £3.50, children £1 (2003 prices) • Other information: Organic meals available for groups by prior arrangement • ◑ 🍵 🖼 WC ♿ ◁▷ 🌱

Forty acres of ornamental gardens, including a kitchen garden and orchards, integrated within a 170-acre organic farm. There are several walled gardens, long borders, a butterfly garden, a *potager*, Japanese and knot gardens, a lake, and woodland underplanted with rhododendrons, camellias and bluebells. Henk Gerritsen, owner of the renowned Priona Gardens (see entry in The Netherlands), has brought about some exciting changes, combining native and cultivated plants in naturalistic beds within the existing structure of hedges and seventeenth-century walls.

White Knights

The Ridges, Finchampstead, Wokingham RG40 3SY. Tel: (0118) 973 3274

Mrs Heather Bradly • 9m SE of Reading between A327 and A321, midway along Finchampstead Ridges on B3348. Turn in through white gateposts on right between Crowthorne station and war memorial • Open by appt only • Entrance £2.50 • Other information: Refreshments available. Guide dogs only ● 🍵 ♿ 🌱 ☕

The large garden has been designed to look interesting throughout the year with minimum upkeep. The beds around the house are mainly planted with dwarf conifers of all hues and many varieties of heathers. A noble wisteria covers the south-facing wall. A Japanese garden complete with flowing water and tea house in the Zen tradition, a Mediterranean area with cacti, both hardy and overwintered in the greenhouse, and a Chinese courtyard alongside the swimming pool graced by a fountain, combine to give the garden an international flavour. Indoors, a model of a Tudor village will appeal to all ages.

BIRMINGHAM AREA

Ashover

25 Burnett Road, Streetly B74 3EL. Tel: (0121) 353 0547

Mr and Mrs Martin Harvey • 8m N of Birmingham. Take A452 towards Streetly, then B4138 alongside Sutton Park. Turn left at shops into Burnett Road • Open for NGS 16th May, 11th July, 8th Aug, 1.30 – 5.30pm, and by appt • Entrance: £2.50, children 50p • Other information: Teas and plants on NGS open days only ● ☕ WC ⚘

This is a garden for all who love colour – a third of an acre cleverly planted for year-round interest, from bulbs and azaleas in the spring through roses, clematis, lilies and herbaceous plants, both traditional and unusual, in summer and autumn. Colour-themed beds and an attractive water feature catch the eye and close planting constantly challenges the interest of the discerning visitor. Surprises round every turn make the garden appear larger than it actually is, and a luxuriant atmosphere is generated by the sheer variety, quality and quantity of plants amassed here.

The Birmingham Botanical Gardens and Glasshouses ★ [Historic Garden Grade II*]

Westbourne Road, Edgbaston B15 3TR. Tel: (0121) 454 1860

2m SW of city centre. Approach from Hagley Road or Calthorpe Road, following tourist signs • Open all year, daily, 9am – 7pm, or dusk if earlier (opens 10am on Sun) • Entrance: £5.50 (£6 on summer Suns and Bank Holiday Mons), OAPs, disabled, students and children £3, family £15 (£16 on summer Suns and Bank Holiday Mons) Parties of 10 or more £4.50 per person, concessions £2.70 (2003 prices) • Other information: Manual and electric wheelchairs available free of charge ○ ☕ ✕ 🍽 WC ♿ ⚘ ♨ ♀ ⚲

This 15-acre ornamental garden will appeal both to the keen plantsperson and to the everyday gardener. In addition to the unusual plants in the tropical and Mediterranean houses, there is a sub-tropical house and an arid house, a small display of carnivorous plants, aviaries with parrots and macaws, peacocks and a waterfowl enclosure. Less rarified gardeners will enjoy the beautiful old trees, the border devoted to E.H. Wilson plants, the raised alpine bed and the sunken rose garden beside the Lawn Aviary. The rock garden contains a wide variety of alpine plants, primulas, astilbes and azaleas. There are also herbaceous borders, a quaint cottage-style garden, a herb garden and model domestic-theme gardens, including an organic garden, plus a plantsman's area and a sculpture trail, where many of the exhibits are for sale. An attractive courtyard houses the National Collection of bonsai. The recently developed alpine yard has examples of the many ways to grow plants in a variety of raised beds and containers. An imaginative children's Discovery Garden, a playground and adventure trail make this a pleasant place for a family outing. Bands play on summer Sundays and Bank Holidays.

Castle Bromwich Hall Gardens ★ [Historic Garden Grade II*]

Chester Road, Castle Bromwich B36 9BT. Tel: (0121) 749 4100

Castle Bromwich Hall Gardens Trust • 4m E of city centre. 1m from junction 5 of M6 northbound; southbound leave M6 at junction 6 and follow A38 and A452. Signposted • Open April to Oct, Tues – Thurs, 1.30 – 4.30pm, Sat, Sun and Bank Holiday Mons, 2 – 6pm. Guided tours daily • Entrance: £3.50, OAPs £2.50, children £1.50 ◑ ☕ WC �𝄐 ⇪ 🌱 ⛲ 🕯 ⚲

The hall (not open), was built at the end of the sixteenth century and sold to Sir John Bridgeman in 1657. His wife, with expert help from John Evelyn, Captain William Winde, George London and Henry Wise, created a garden famous in its time. It fell into decay, but now has a series of formal connecting gardens – 10 acres in all contained within a west-facing slope which have been restored by a dedicated team of volunteers to give them the appearance and content of a garden of 1680–1740. They contain a large collection of rare period plants and a nineteenth-century holly maze. An elegant greenhouse and summerhouse stand at each end of a broad holly walk. In the formal parterre, re-created to a 1728 design and bordered by culinary and medicinal herbs, several heritage vegetables are grown, such as skirrets, scorzonera, orache, cardoons and salsify. Fruit trees have been planted in orchards and along paths.

City Centre Gardens

Cambridge Street B1 2NP.

Birmingham City Council • Off Cambridge Street, to rear of theatre and Symphony Hall on Broad Street • Open all year, daily during daylight hours • Entrance: free ○ 🍴 丟 ⇪

Half an acre of rough ground remaining after building demolition and subsequently used as a car park has been converted into a garden for all seasons. The layout is formal, the planting skilful and exuberant, with a great variety of bulbs, shrubs, perennials, roses and some annuals, many of them less usual and all blending harmoniously. Climbers cover the walls and fences.

15 St Johns Road

Pleck, Walsall WS2 9TJ. Tel: (01922) 441027

Mr and Mrs Allen • 10m NW of Birmingham. From M6 junction 10, head towards Walsall on A454 Wolverhampton road, and turn right into Pleck Road (A4148). St Johns Road is fourth right • Open one Sun for NGS, and for individuals and parties of up to 30 by appt • Entrance: £2, children free ◐ ☕ 🌱

This comparatively small garden is skilfully landscaped so as to appear larger. It contains a wide range of delights, from a tropical area near the house, past a pool and a varied collection of trees, shrubs, climbers (33 different clematis) and flowers, to a Japanese feature at the far end, where a stream runs under a little bridge leading to a tea house. The smaller trees include acers, and there are shrubs, grasses, ferns, hostas, perennials and clematis blooming through the season, with annuals adding splashes of colour.

University Botanic Garden ★

Winterbourne, 58 Edgbaston Park Road, Edgbaston B16 3TT.
Tel: (0121) 414 4944

University of Birmingham • 2m SW of city centre, off A38 Bristol road. On university campus • Open all year, Mon – Fri (but closed Bank Holiday Mons and some university holidays), 11am – 4pm • Entrance: £2 • Other information: Events at weekends ◐ 🍴 <u>WC</u> ⅏

The six acres of garden, belonging to a Grade-II-listed Arts and Crafts house, owe much to the landscape style developed by Edwin Lutyens and Gertrude Jekyll. Its wide range of plants and different features make it of interest to the ordinary gardener as well as the botanist. Geographical beds show typical trees and shrubs from Europe, Australasia, the Americas, China and Japan. The pergola is covered with clematis and roses and there are extensive herbaceous borders backed by brick walls covered with climbers. A miniature arboretum contains interesting specimens, including acers, conifers and a *Ginkgo biloba*, together with hedges of yew and copper beech. In the Commemorative Garden is a black mulberry planted to mark the centenary of Birmingham's status as a city. The range of plants continues with the sandstone rock garden, troughs, rhododendrons, heathers and alpines. Unusual features include a nut walk containing several varieties of *Corylus avellana* trained over an iron frame-work, and a crinkle-crankle wall. A special feature is the walled garden laid out with beds showing the history of the European rose. There are also water gardens, rock and scree gardens, a meadow, a bog garden and a Japanese tea house.

Wightwick Manor [Historic Garden Grade II]

Wightwick Bank, Wolverhampton WV6 8EE. Tel: (01902) 761400

The National Trust • 3m W of Wolverhampton off A454. Turn by Mermaid Inn up Wightwick Bank • House open Thurs, Sat, 1.30 – 5pm (last entry 4.30pm). Timed tickets • Garden open March to Dec, Wed, Thurs, Sat, Bank Holiday Suns and Mons, 11am – 6pm, and other weekdays by appt. Pre-booked parties accepted Wed and Thurs; family days in Aug • Entrance: £2.60, children free (house and garden £5.70, concessions £2.85) • Other information: Possible for wheelchairs but sloping site. Braille guide available ◐ 🅿 🍴 WC ⅏ ⟷ ⬛ 🕯 ⚲

This 17-acre garden, designed by Alfred Parsons and Thomas Mawson for Theodore Mander, the paint and varnish manufacturer, surrounds an 1887 neo-Tudor house strongly influenced in its design by William Morris and his Movement. Large trees form a delightful framework, the main feature of which is the magnificent octagonal arbour in the centre of the rose garden, hung with climbing roses and clematis. Through an old orchard is a less formal area with pools surrounded by shrubs and rhododendrons. There are herbaceous borders, two rows of barrel-shaped yews and beds containing plants from gardens of famous men. The peach house and the rose garden have been restored and the Mathematical Bridge, giving access to the Bridge Garden filled with spring bulbs, is now reconstructed.

BRISTOL AREA

Algars Manor

Iron Acton, Bristol BS37 9TB. Tel: (01454) 228372

Dr and Mrs John Naish • 9m N of Bristol between M5 and A432. Turn S from Acton bypass (B4059) and pass village green; garden is 180 metres beyond level crossing • Open for NGS, and by appt • Entrance: £2 [NEW] ● 🍴 WC �& ⬧

The seventeenth-century manor house stands on the edge of a rocky bank bordering the River Frome. The dendrologically minded visitor can learn a great deal about magnolias and camellias interplanted with a wide range of rare and specimen trees after an enlightening tour of the woodland garden with the owners, who like to share its fifty-year history under their devoted care. The natural surroundings of quarry, river and mill stream contribute to the garden's very special atmosphere.

Ashton Court Estate [Historic Garden Grade II*]

Long Ashton BS41 9JN. Tel: (0117) 963 9174

Bristol City Council • SW of city off A369 • Open all year, daily, 8am – dusk • Entrance: free ○ 🍴 🍴 WC �& ⬧ 💡 ✄

The Ashton estate is an astonishing survival to find in the urban heart of a conurbation. It has two deer parks, and its 850 acres include many ancient oaks. The house itself is fifteenth-century with a handsome seventeenth-century wing. The park was first landscaped in the 1600s; two hundred years later Humphry Repton was commissioned to redesign it. The year 2004 will – with luck – see the start of a major plan of restoration with help from the Heritage Lottery Fund.

Blaise Castle House ★ [Historic Garden Grade II*]

Henbury BS10 7QS. Tel: (0117) 903 9818 (Museum);
(0117) 950 3732 (Estate Office)

Bristol City Museum • 4m N of city, W of Henbury, N of B4057 • Museum open April to Oct, Sat – Wed, 10am – 5pm • Entrance: free pedestrian access to green • Other information: Visitors requested not to picnic or invade privacy of cottage owners ○ 🍴 WC �& ⬧ 💡 ✄

Blaise Hamlet is a picturesque village owned by The National Trust in the form of a green surrounded by nine cottages with private gardens, designed by John Nash with George and John Repton in 1809 for the pensioners of John Harford's estate. The village pump and sundial of 1812 remain. Jasmines, ivies and honeysuckles were planted around the cottages to reflect their picturesque names ('Jessamine', 'Rose Briar'), with ornamental shrubs added to the woodland setting. A spectacular drive can be taken from Henbury Hill to the entrance lodge of Blaise Castle House – another charming *cottage orné* is halfway. The driveway into the gorge and up to the house passes a Robber's Cave and Lovers' Leap. The view is exceptional. Near the house are the ornamental dairy and elegant orangery, both by Nash.

Bristol Zoo Gardens

Clifton BS8 3HA. Tel: (0117) 973 8951

Bristol Zoo Gardens • Signposted from M5 junctions 17 and 18 and from city centre • Open all year, daily except 25th Dec, 9am – 5.30pm (4.30pm in winter) • Entrance: £8.90, concessions £7.90, children (3 – 14) £5.20. Special rates for parties of 15 or more ○ 💷 ✕ 🍽 **WC** ♿ 🎁 🍵 ♀

Set up in 1835 as a garden as well as a zoo, the gardens will satisfy those with Victorian tastes for splashes of colour. Displays range from formal to informal, and botanically interesting plants are highlighted. The vibrantly colourful terrace bedding is complemented by herbaceous borders, a lake, rose and rock gardens, indoor displays and numerous interesting trees and shrubs. All is well contrived and maintained with evident love and care. Two National Collections, of hedychiums and caryopteris, are held here.

Emmaus House

Retreat and Conference Centre, Clifton Hill, Clifton BS8 4PD.
Tel: (0117) 907 9950

Sisters of La Retraite • From city centre take A4018 W to Clifton, then A4176 past Zoo, and turn left into Clifton Down Road. Follow through to Regent Street; house is at bottom of drive on right • Open five times a year and on weekdays by prior appt • Entrance: £2.50, children free ● 💷 ✕ **WC** ♿ 🌿 🍵 **B&B**

Covering one and a half acres, the gardens lie hidden from the road behind two imposing eighteenth-century merchants' houses. Walking down from the front entrance and around the side of the property, the visitor enters a succession of separate gardens set on different levels, all carefully linked and with extensive views towards the harbour and beyond. They have been considerably altered in recent years, but the Victorian kitchen garden is substantially intact, supplying fruit and vegetables to the house. The old greenhouse is still in use, containing apricots and a 150-year-old Black Hamburg vine. A formal herb garden framed by clipped box pyramids surrounds an ornamental fishpond. This leads down to a Zen Garden, where large stones and running water are imaginatively used to represent the Zen concepts of life and rebirth. At a lower level, the visitor enters the Secret Garden containing many old apple trees and underplanted with spring bulbs. Then, continuing round the beech lawn, the courtyard garden is enclosed by high walls with macleayas, robinias and vigorous euphorbias; an old pump provides the soothing noise of running water.

Goldney Hall [Historic Garden Grade II*]

Lower Clifton Hill, Clifton BS8 1BH. Tel: (0117) 903 4873

University of Bristol • In city centre at top of Constitution Hill, Clifton • Open 25th April, 2 – 5pm, and three other days for charity – telephone for details • Entrance: £1, guided tours £2 ● 💷 **WC** ♿

The eighteenth-century garden (or what remains) is a thrilling discovery in the middle of the city. Perched on a hillside, it is full of surprises, not least the small formal canal with an orangery at its head. From the largely nineteenth-century house the visitor is led through the shadows of an *allée* of yews to a dark grotto entrance whose façade is a striking example of early but sophisticated Gothick. The grotto itself is astonishingly elaborate: water really gushes through it and the walls are liberally encrusted with shells and minerals. Passing through the grotto and out by narrow labyrinthine passages, suddenly there is a terrace, a broad airy grass walk with magnificent views over the old docks. At the far end of the terrace is a Gothick gazebo, and towering above the other end a castellated tower. Although a new student hall has been allowed to encroach upon this historic setting, it is alleviated by Michael Balston's stylish planting and landscaping, which includes a circular pool and a brick amphitheatre as a crossing point for paths. Goldney also has follies, a parterre and a herb garden packed into its nine acres.

The Red Lodge

Park Row BS1 5LJ. Tel: (0117) 921 1360

Bristol City Council • In city centre • House open • Garden open June, July, Sat – Wed, 10am – 5pm. Opening hours vary – telephone (0117) 922 3571 for details • Entrance: free ●

This is a good reconstruction of the early-seventeenth-century garden of a merchant's town house, with old varieties of roses, shrubs and other plants, trelliswork re-created from a seventeenth-century design, and a knot garden based on a plasterwork pattern in the house. A list of plant names is available for a small charge. Georgian *Queen Square* in the city has also undergone major restoration with lottery funding. If you drive 6m south of Bristol on the A37 you reach *Blackmore and Langdon's Nursery*, open daily, a pleasure at any time, but particularly when the delphiniums are blooming (Tel: (01275) 525455).

9 Sion Hill

Clifton, Bristol BS8 4BA. Tel: (0117) 973 2761

Mr and Mrs R.C. Begg • In city, 100 metres from Clifton Suspension Bridge • Open by appt • Entrance: £2 ● ⌖ ⚲

This is not a typical town garden. On the contrary, twenty-five years of profuse planting have produced an overall impression of peace and plenty on a scale which belies the garden's true size. Entering through a working conservatory, a small grassed area is dominated by a vigorous black mulberry tree (planted by the owners and for once not in King James's time) and surrounded by densely planted borders. This leads to a central path the axis of which is established by the 'temple', an ivy-clad terracotta architectural finial from which paths radiate to various points. Looking back from the house, the garden is terminated by a seven-metre-high wall which acts as a backdrop. The timber pergola, unusual in spanning the entire width of the garden, is smothered in roses and clematis. The play of light and shade ensures a constantly changing effect. A town garden full of interesting ideas – the subtle placing of pots of various kinds is particularly successful.

University Botanic Garden [Historic Garden Grade II]

Bracken Hill, North Road, Leigh Woods BS8 3PF. Tel: (0117) 973 3682

University of Bristol • W of city centre. Cross Suspension Bridge from Clifton, turn first right (North Road) and go $\frac{1}{4}$ m up on left • Open all year, Mon – Fri, except public holidays, 9am – 5pm. Parties welcome at other times by appt – contact Superintendent for details • Entrance: free, but guided tours for parties £3.50 per person • Other information: Friends of UBG (subscription £20) have out-of-hours access and educational benefits ○ WC &

The Botanic Garden, relocated to this site in 1959, is an interesting place for the keen plantsman. Large collections of New Zealand and South African flora as well as comprehensive collections of aeoniums, cistus, hebes, peonies, pelargoniums, salvias and sempervivums are all cultivated in the attractive five-acre garden. There are also collections of native trees and shrubs and plants peculiar to the Avon Gorge, plus conservation collections of rare native south-west species. Glasshouses contain ferns, orchids, bromeliads, cacti and succulents, insectivorous plants and tender bulbs. Plants and borders are well labelled and arranged with various themes, such as poisonous, dye, economic, medicinal, sand dune and woodland. A garden of Chinese medicinal herbs has recently been planted.

GARDEN AND FLOWER SHOWS 2004
- 7th to 9th May: Spring Gardening Show, Malvern
  (Three Counties Showground, Malvern, Worcs)
  Ticket hotline: (01684) 584900; www.threecounties.co.uk
- 25th to 28th May: Chelsea Flower Show
  (Royal Hospital, Chelsea, London SW3)
- Early June to early Sept, International Festival of Gardens, Westonbirt
  (Westonbirt, Tetbury, Glos)
  Tel: (01666) 880220; www.festivalofgardens.co.uk
- 16th to 20th June: BBC *Gardeners' World* Live
  (National Exhibition Centre, Birmingham)
  Ticket hotline: (0870) 909 4133; www.necgroup.co.uk
- 6th to 11th July: Hampton Court Flower Show
  (Hampton Court Palace, East Molesey, Surrey)
- 21st to 25th July: RHS Flower Show, Tatton Park
  (Tatton Park, near Knutsford, Cheshire)
- 22nd to 24th June, 17th to 19th Aug: Wisley Shows
  (RHS Garden, Wisley, Woking, Surrey)
- 25th and 26th Sept: Autumn Garden & Country Show, Malvern (see
  above for details)

Unless otherwise given, for details of all these shows telephone the Royal Horticultural Society on (020) 7834 4333 or consult www.rhs.org.uk.

BUCKINGHAMSHIRE

Two-starred gardens are marked on the map with a black square.

Ascott ★★ [Historic Garden Grade II*]

Wing, Leighton Buzzard, Bedfordshire LU7 0PS. Tel: (01296) 688242

The National Trust • 7m NE of Aylesbury, ½ m E of Wing, S of A418 • House and gardens open April, Aug, Sept. Telephone for details. Parties must pre-book • Entrance: £4, children £2 (house and garden £5.60, children £2.80) (2003 prices) • Other information: Parking 220 metres from house ◑ **WC** ♿

Thirty acres of Victorian gardening at its very best, laid out with the aid of Sir Harry Veitch and overlaid with more recent designs and planting, principally by Arabella Lennox-Boyd. It is notable for its formidable collection of mature trees of all shapes and colours, set in rolling lawns. Fascinating topiary includes an evergreen sundial with a yew gnomon and the inscription 'Light and shade by turn but love always' in golden yew. Wide lawns slope away to magnificent views across the Vale of Aylesbury, glimpsed between towering cedars. Formal gardens include the Madeira Walk with sheltered flower borders, and the bedded-out Dutch garden. More topiary has been added, and there are new plantings of magnolias by Lady Lennox-Boyd. The Long Walk leading to the lily pond has been imaginatively reconstructed by her as a serpentine walk with new beech hedging, and a wild garden planted in Coronation Grove. Two stately fountains were created by Thomas Waldo Story – one a large group in bronze, the other a slender composition in marble. Interesting all year, spring gardens feature massed carpets of bulbs.

Blossoms

Cobblers Hill, Great Missenden HP16 9PW. Tel: (01494) 863140

Dr and Mrs Frank Hytten • 8m NE of High Wycombe. From Great Missenden follow Rignall Road towards Butlers Cross. After about 1m turn right into Kings Lane and up to top of Cobblers Hill. At T-junction turn right at yellow stone marker in hedgerow, and after 50 metres right again • Open by appt only • Entrance: £2 ◑ ☕ 🅿 📷 ♿ ✂

The five-acre garden has a good variety of trees: an acre of beech woodland, underplanted with bluebells and other spring-flowering bulbs, an old apple orchard, collections of eucalyptus, acers and salix, and other specimen trees such as *Tetradium daniellii* and a magnificent ivy-leaved beech. Interesting features include rock and cutting gardens, a small lake with an island, and sculpture by the owner and friends; two other water gardens and a paved well garden with sundial are linked by woodland paths.

Campden Cottage ★

51 Clifton Road, Chesham Bois, Amersham HP6 5PN. Tel: (01494) 726818

Mrs P. Liechti • 1m N of Amersham on A416. Turn into Clifton Road by Catholic church (opposite primary school). Close to traffic lights at pedestrian crossing • Open 29th Feb, 21st March, 18th April, 16th May, 13th June, 18th July, 15th Aug, 12th Sept, 10th Oct, 2 – 6pm, and by appt for parties (no coaches) • Entrance: £1.50, accompanied children free • Other information: School car park available for parking on open days by arrangement ◐ ⚘

The masterful design takes advantage of a magnificent weeping ash, and displays both the owner's fine collection of rare and unusual plants and her skill in putting together interesting associations of colour, shape and foliage. The sunny York-stone terrace, with its large and ever-increasing collection of terracotta pots planted for seasonal colour, contrasts pleasingly with the more formal area of yew hedge, walled border and extended lawns. The busiest open day is in March for the well-known collection of hellebore species and hybrids, but the garden is worth visiting month by month to keep in touch with all the developments.

Chenies Manor House ★

Chenies, Rickmansworth, Hertfordshire WD3 6ER. Tel: (01494) 762888

Mrs MacLeod Matthews • 3m E of Amersham off A404. If approaching via M25, exit at junction 18 • House open (extra charge) • Garden open April to Oct, Wed, Thurs and Bank Holiday Mons, 2 – 5pm • Entrance: £3, children £1.25 (2003 prices) ◑ ▆ ▩ WC ♿ ⚘ ▦ ⚲ ✂

The owners have created several extremely fine linked gardens in keeping with the fifteenth- and sixteenth-century brick manor house. The gardens are highly decorative and maintained to the highest standards. Planted for a long season of colour and using many old-fashioned roses and cottage plants, there is always something to enjoy here: formal topiary in the white garden, collections of medicinal and poisonous plants in a 'physic' garden, a parterre, an historic turf maze, an intricate yew maze area over two metres high, and a highly productive kitchen garden. On her visits here, Queen Elizabeth I had a favourite tree and the 'Royal Oak' survives.

Cliveden ★★ [Historic Garden Grade I]

Taplow, Maidenhead, Berkshire SL6 0JA. Tel: (01628) 605069

The National Trust • 6m NW of Slough, 2m N of Taplow off A4094 • House open April to Oct, Thurs, Sun, 3 – 6pm • Woodlands open all year, daily except 24th Dec to 3rd Jan, 11am – 6pm (closes 4pm Nov to 15th March). Estate and gardens open 15th March to Oct, daily, 11am – 6pm; Nov to 23rd Dec, daily, 11am – 4pm. Closed Jan and Feb • Entrance: £6, family £15 (house £1 extra, entry by timed ticket) • Other information: Refreshments in Conservatory Restaurant, 15th March to Oct, daily. Dogs allowed in specified woodlands only ◑ ▆ ✕ ▩ WC ♿ ⬦ ▦ ⚲ ✂

The setting of Cliveden is one of the most beautiful for any house in Britain. The flamboyant Duke of Buckingham found it and William Winde exploited it. He took the raw material – 'a cliffy ground as hanging over the *Tamise* and sum Busshis groinge on it' and created, by excavation and earth-moving, a platform for the house and a terrace for access. John Evelyn's verdict was that 'the house stands somewhat like *Frascati* on the platform . . . a circular view of the uttmost verge of the Horison, which with the serpenting of the *Thames* is admirably surprising . . . The *Cloisters*, Descents, Gardens, & avenue through the wood august and stately.' The present house (now an hotel), designed by Sir Charles Barry, incorporates a terrace with a balustrade brought by the 1st Viscount Astor from the Villa Borghese in Rome in the 1890s. The attractive water garden, the secret garden and herbaceous borders, the formal gardens below the house, and the Long Garden, fountains, temples and statuary contribute to this fine garden. Among famous designers who have worked on the grounds are Bridgeman (walks and amphitheatre), Leoni (Octagon Temple) and John Fleming (parterre). The Trust has restored Jellicoe's secret garden of 1959, the Long Garden and the parterre. An inner avenue of limes has been planted north of the house, and the Yew Walk steps have been restored.

Gracefield

Main Road, Lacey Green, Princes Risborough HP27 0QU. Tel: (01844) 345560

Mr and Mrs B.C. Wicks • 5m N of High Wycombe off A4010. In Bradenham turn right by Red Lion towards Walters Ash then turn left at T-junction to Lacey Green. Brick and flint house is beyond church facing Kiln Lane • Open May to Aug for parties by written appt • Entrance: £2, children free • Other information: Park at village hall ● ● & ⬦ ⬩

A steeply terraced water garden is a fine feature in this one-and-a-half-acre garden. Plants for the flower arranger; new designs for paved terraces and trough gardens; collections of clematis and shrub roses. Specimen trees include a special malus, M. 'Marshal Oyama', giving fantastic crab apple jelly. The owners are self-confessed plantaholics and have thoughtfully labelled many specimens in their unusual collection.

Hughenden Manor [Historic Garden Grade II]

High Wycombe HP14 4LA. Tel: (01494) 755573

The National Trust • 1½ m N of High Wycombe on A4128 • House open as garden, but 1 – 5pm • Park and woodland open all year. Garden open March, Sat and Sun only; April to Oct, Wed – Sun and Bank Holiday Mons; all 12 noon – 5pm. Parties not admitted on Sat, Sun or Bank Holiday Mons, and must pre-book at other times • Entrance: £1.60, children 80p (house and garden £4.50, children £2.75, family £11.50. Party rates on application) (2003 prices) ◑ ● ✕ <u>WC</u> & ⬦ ⬜ ⬩

A High-Victorian garden created by Mrs Disraeli in the 1860s and recently restored. Particularly pleasing is the human scale of house and gardens. The five acres include lawns, a terraced garden with a sub-tropical planting scheme, formal brightly coloured annual bedding (Mrs Disraeli's guests commented at the time on the blinding colour schemes she chose), woodland walks, and an orchard with old varieties of apples and pears. The unusual chimaera shrub *Laburnocytisus* 'Adamii' combines yellow flowers of *Laburnum anagyroides*, mauve sprays of *Cytisus purpureus* and some intermediate in late spring/early summer. The additional Victorian flower beds, usually at their best in July, have been restored.

The Manor House ★★

Bledlow, Princes Risborough HP27 9PB.

Lord and Lady Carrington • 8m NW of High Wycombe, ½ m E of B4009 in middle of Bledlow • Manor House Garden open 2nd May, 20th June, 2 – 6pm, and May to Sept for groups by written appt. Lyde Garden open all year, daily • Entrance: Manor House Garden £4.50, children free. Lyde Garden free • Manor House Garden: ◐ ☕ WC ♿ ✂ ✂ *Lyde Garden:* ○

With the help of landscape architect Robert Adams, Lord and Lady Carrington have created an elegant English garden of an exceptionally high standard. The highly productive and colourful walled vegetable garden has York-stone paths and a central gazebo. Formal gardens are enclosed by tall yew and beech hedges; in the centre of one is a water feature by William Pye. Mixed flower and shrub borders feature many roses and herbaceous plants around immaculately manicured lawns. Another garden approached through a yew and brick parterre was planned around existing mature trees on a contoured and upward-sloping site with open views. It is now thoroughly established, with its trees and lawns fulfilling the original landscaping design, and incorporates several modern sculptures (displayed with a wit typical of their owners). *The Lyde Garden*, across the lane, is a magnificent wild water garden of great beauty and tranquillity, supporting a variety of plants. A note of caution: although the manor house garden is children-friendly, in the Lyde Garden they need watching on the difficult slopes.

Nether Winchendon House

Nether Winchendon, Aylesbury HP18 ODY. Tel: (01844) 290101

Mr and Mrs R. Spencer Bernard • 7m SW of Aylesbury, 5m NE of Thame. Near church in Nether Winchendon • Open 2 days for NGS, and at other times by appt • Entrance: £2, children under 15 free (2003 prices) ◐ ☕ WC ♿ ✂

The gardens surround a romantic brick and stone Tudor manor which is approached by an unusual line of dawn redwoods (*Metasequoia glyptostroboides*) planted in 1973, continuing a centuries-old tree planting tradition by the Spencer Bernard family. Small orchards on either side of the house combine with fine specimen trees, including mature acers, catalpas, cedars, paulownias, liquidambars and, dominating the lawns at the back of the house, an eighteenth-century variegated sycamore and a late-1950s' oriental plane of almost equal height. There are also well-kept lawns, shrub and flower borders, and walled gardens, including a productive kitchen garden.

Spindrift

Jordans, Beaconsfield HP9 2TE. Tel: (01494) 873172

Norma Desmond-Mawby • 1m NE of Beaconsfield, N of A40 in Jordans village. At far side of green turn right into cul-de-sac next to school • Open by appt • Entrance: £3, children (under 12) 20p ◑ ☕ ✗ 🖼 WC ⅙ ⟲ B&B

A series of linked 'secret gardens' on different levels, with fine trees and hedges, sets off a wide range of unusual plants and shrubs and a fine display of spring bulbs. A miniature version of Monet's flower garden features irises, poppies, peonies and arches with climbing nasturtiums. A model fruit and vegetable garden is terraced on a hillside, and there are three greenhouses with vines. Large collections of hostas and hardy geraniums.

Stowe Landscape Gardens ★★ [Historic Garden Grade I]

Buckingham MK18 5EH. Tel: (01280) 822850

The National Trust • 3m NW of Buckingham via Stowe Avenue off A422 Buckingham – Brackley road • House (Stowe School) may be open in holidays. Check before visiting • Garden open March to 19th Dec, Wed – Sun, but open Bank Holiday Mons, 10am – 5pm (last admission 4pm, but 3pm in Dec). Closed 29th May • Entrance: £5, family £12.50 (house £2). All parties must pre-book • Other information: Refreshments for parties must be pre-booked through Group Bookings Co-ordinator. Picnics permitted in Grecian Valley only. Self-drive powered 2-seater batricars available, must be pre-booked (telephone (01280) 818825) ◑ ☕ ✗ 🖼 WC ⟲ 🏛 ♿ ⚲

This is garden restoration on a heroic scale. Stowe has had enormous influence on garden design from the mid-seventeenth century onwards under a succession of distinguished designers, including the owner, Viscount Cobham: Vanbrugh, Bridgeman, Kent, 'Capability' Brown, and then the new owner Lord Temple, who thinned out Brown's plantings after 1750. What remains today is a *locus classicus* of eighteenth-century landscaping – with a nineteenth-century overlay diversifying the landscape into distinct 'scenes', each with its own character. The aim over the last twenty years has been to reinstate them. The concept of the restoration was brilliantly planned, using the Trust's considerable management and computer resources to reinstate lost plantings and remove recent irrelevant additions. There are two ways of visiting. One is just to wander through the gardens enjoying the wonderful views, the water, the splendid trees and the historic buildings – Stowe has more than twice as many listed garden buildings as any in England – and its statuary. The other approach is to step back in time and try to understand what was meant by the political and philosophical programme that fashioned the landscape movement. Stowe exemplifies this intellectual platform, on which the design was based. It was immensely influential, not only in Britain but in Europe and beyond. The past decade has seen a wondrous change of a quite different order. Land has been bought back – 320 acres including the home farm and deer park, which included the Wolfe obelisk, the Gothic umbrello and a superb set of 1790s' farm buildings. The Chinese house has been returned from Ireland as a memorial to

Gervase Jackson-Stops and six of the seven Saxon deities have reappeared. What is staggering is that the Trust has to date restored 70 per cent of the listed buildings at Stowe and Cobham is back on his column. Heroic indeed.

Turn End ★

Townside, Haddenham, Aylesbury HP17 8BG. Tel: (01844) 291383

Mr and Mrs P. Aldington • 7m SW of Aylesbury. From A418 turn to Haddenham. From Thame Road turn at Rising Sun pub into Townside; garden is 250 metres on left • Open several days during summer – telephone for details. Parties by appt at other times • Entrance: £2.50, children (under 14) £1. • Other information: No parking at garden. Teas on charity days only ● WC ᯽ ⟨ᐳ ⬚

Peter Aldington's RIBA-award-winning development of three linked houses (now listed) is surrounded by a series of garden rooms evolved over the last thirty years. A sequence of spaces, each of individual character, provides focal points at every turn. There is a fishpond courtyard, a shady court, a formal box court, an alpine garden, hot and dry raised beds and climbing roses. A wide range of plants is displayed to good effect against a framework of mature trees.

Waddesdon Manor ★★ [Historic Garden Grade I]

Waddesdon, Aylesbury HP18 0JH. Tel: (01296) 653211; advance house bookings with charge, garden tours and events (01296) 653226

The National Trust • 6m NW of Aylesbury, 11m SE of Bicester on A41. Entrance in Waddesdon village • House (inc. wine cellars) open 31st March to 31st Oct, Wed – Sun and Bank Holiday Mons, 11am – 4pm (timed-ticket system in operation from 10am; recommended last admission 2.30pm) • Grounds (inc. gardens, aviary, restaurant and shops) open 3rd March to 23rd Dec, Wed – Sun and Bank Holiday Mons, 10am – 5pm. Telephone for details of after Christmas opening dates • Entrance: £4, children £2 (house and grounds £11, children £8) • Other information: Parking for disabled. Guide dogs only. Many special events – brochure on request ◑ ▣ ✕ ▧ WC ᯽ ♿ ⬚ ⚲

Baron Ferdinand de Rothschild's grandiloquent château (built 1874–1889) is set in appropriately grand grounds with fountains, vistas, terraces and walks laid out by Elie Lainé, his landscape designer and contain an extensive collection of Italian, French and Dutch statuary. The extensive parterre and fountains to the south require over 100,000 plants in the main summer display alone. John Sales describes the parterre as 'the central jewel of a rich Victorian scheme'. One of the original head gardeners used to quote an aphorism describing how the rich established their wealth by the size of their bedding-out plant list: 10,000 for a squire, 20,000 for a baronet, 30,000 for an earl and 50,000 for a duke. Waddesdon is truly regal. Parterres used to require a large staff but Lord Rothschild has called on experts who bed plants by computer. To the west of the parterre, an ornate, semi-circular aviary of eighteenth-century French Rococo style, erected in 1889, provides a distinguished home for many exotic birds. It also acts as an *exedra*, focusing on the pleasure grounds and the expansive views of the landscape beyond. The area in front of it has recently been replaced by a restoration of the original bedding-planted garden. The gardens undergo changes almost annually, with old features being restored and new ones added. Wildflower Valley has thousands of daffodils in spring, and in summer wild flowers, including cowslips, ox-eye daisies and a range of orchids, which are encouraged to seed. Close by, over 20,000 camassias, colchicums, lilies-of-the-valley and wild garlic have been naturalised in grassland and in the woodland garden.

West Wycombe Park ★★ [Historic Garden Grade I]

West Wycombe HP14 3AJ. Tel: (01494) 513569

The National Trust • 2m W of High Wycombe, at W end of West Wycombe, S of A40 Oxford road • House open June to Aug, Sun – Thurs, 2 – 6pm (weekday entry by guided tour, last admission 5.15pm) • Grounds open April to Sept, Sun – Thurs and Bank Holiday Mons, all 2 5.30pm (last admission 5.15pm) • Entrance: £2.60, children £1.30 (house and grounds £5, children £2.50, family £12.60) (2003 prices) ◑ WC ఉ ♀ ℀

The park was largely created by the second Sir Francis Dashwood and was influenced by his experiences on the Grand Tour, which included visits to Asia Minor and Russia. The first phase involved the creation of the lake with meandering walks, completed by 1739. Numerous classical temples and statues were added subsequently, as well as the delightful little flint and wooden bridges which span the streams. Later still, in the 1770s, the park was enlarged; Nicholas Revett was employed to design yet more temples and follies, including a particularly fine music temple on one of the three islands. Thomas Cook, a pupil of 'Capability' Brown, was entrusted with the planting of trees and alterations to the landscape. There are splendid vistas, especially towards the lake which is in the shape of a swan.

Wotton House [Historic Garden Grade II*]

Wotton Underwood, Aylesbury HP18 0SB.

Mrs April Gladstone • 8m W of Aylesbury off A41 • Open April to Sept, Wed, 2 – 5pm, and for parties by appt in writing • Entrance: charge ● ఉ ⇗

This remarkable landscape garden (250 acres) with over a dozen follies and other attractions shares a history with Stowe (see entry). Derelict after World War II, it has, under two generations of the Brunner family in the latter half of the twentieth century, been painstakingly restored. Much, however, remains to be done. George London's early-eighteenth-century design is still evident, with the remains of his two double avenues east and west of the house. The third avenue, to the south-west, was the work of 'Capability' Brown. South of the house is London's walled garden with a terrace, an orangery below it, a double staircase with a shell niche between its wings, and a pavilion, formerly the coach house. The unchanged wider view remains splendid, and was shaped by Brown between 1750 and 1767. His main work was to remodel the contours and create a large lake, connecting it to a smaller, existing lake by a serpentine canal. Note the bridges and the two Tuscan pavilions overlooking the water. The island grotto, the strikingly handsome Turkey Building and the rotunda are contemporary, but not Brown's handiwork.

CAMBRIDGESHIRE

Two-starred gardens are marked on the map with a black square. A few gardens with Peterborough postcodes are to be found in the Northampton-shire section.

Abbots Ripton Hall ★ [Historic Garden Grade II]

Abbots Ripton, Huntingdon PE28 2PQ. Tel: (01487) 773555

Lord and Lady De Ramsey • 2m N of Huntingdon, approached from B1090 • Open 22nd May, 20th June, 4th, 18th July, 1st Aug for charities, 2 – 5pm, and for individuals and parties by appt • Entrance: £3 on charity days; £8 (including plant guide) for parties of 12 or more ● ☕ WC ♿ ✿

This superb garden was designed in the 1950s by Humphrey Waterfield with contributions by Lanning Roper and Tony Venison. The circular rose garden consists of a ring of historic roses backed by grey foliage of sea buckthorn with a circular lawn at its centre. The spectacular herbaceous borders stretching from the eighteenth-century house are backed by columns of yew and philadelphus and punctuated by a circle of Gothick trellising. There is also a grey-leaved border planted with alpines and sun-loving perennials. The two follies are by Peter Foster, who also designed some of the timber bridges; other architectural features of note are the modern but rustic octagonal summerhouse, the Doric loggia and a fishing hut like a Chinese pavilion beside the fine lake.

Anglesey Abbey Gardens and Lode Mill ★★ [Historic Garden Grade II*]

Lode, Cambridge CB5 9EJ. Tel: (01223) 810080

The National Trust • 6m NE of Cambridge off A14, on B1102 • House open 2nd April to 2nd Nov, Wed – Sun and Bank Holiday Mons (but closed 18th April), 1 – 5pm • Garden open 2nd April to 2nd Nov, Wed – Sun and Bank Holiday Mons, and daily 1st July to 1st Sept (but closed 18th April), 10.30am – 5.30pm (last admission 4.30pm). Winter Walk open 1st Jan to March, 5th Nov to 21st Dec, Wed – Sun, 10.30am – 4pm • Entrance: £4, winter £3.25 (house, garden and Lode Mill: £6.40). Charge made for tours with Head Gardener • Other information: Five single and one double electric buggies available. Lode Mill machinery working first and third Sat of month ☾ ☕ ✕ WC ♿ ✿ ⏚ ♨ ✎

The Abbey's setting is one of England's finest twentieth-century gardens for high maintenance, superb plantsmanship and statuary of exceptional quality. It was the visionary creation of one man, the 1st Lord Fairhaven, started in the 1930s. You will need a whole day – many whole days – to absorb this place, its separate gardens, the parade of sculptures, trees and open spaces, and the changeful seasons. Avenues of mature trees lead the wanderer to intimate gardens enclosed by meticulous hedges; smooth lawns give way to meadows awash with cowslips, lady's bedstraw and ox-eye daisies; visitors will unexpectedly come upon dramatic vistas lined by superb trees, or glimpse the peaceful Bottisham Lode and Lode Mill. A semi-circular garden with a deep encircling herbaceous border is a highlight for the summer; the bold, imaginative planting of perennials is splendid, plumes of seakale and spires of delphinium mingling with mysterious sages. In another garden, 4500 hyacinths bloom in spring while dark-foliaged dwarf dahlias take their place in late summer. Narcissus gazes at his reflection surrounded by scented white- and yellow-blossomed shrubs. A curved border of randomly planted late-summer dahlias may not be to everyone's taste, but what garden is ever entirely perfect? This place is almost so. It is vast, too – 100 acres. The mile-long Winter Walk, underplanted with thousands of early small bulbs, features a serpentine walk and other paths, including a recently rediscovered Victorian one. A grove of giant redwoods marks the start of the walk, a forest of white-stemmed birches underplanted with the black-stemmed *Cornus alba* 'Kesselringii' its conclusion.

Cambridge College Gardens

Most colleges are helpful about access to their gardens, although the Masters' or Fellows' Gardens are often strictly private or rarely open. Specific viewing times are difficult to rely on because some colleges prefer not to have visitors in term time or on days when a function is taking place. The best course is to ask at the porter's lodge or to telephone in advance. However, some college gardens will always be open to the visitor, by arrangement with porters. Several now charge for entry.

Amongst college gardens of particular interest are the following: *Christ's* (see entry). *Clare* (see entry). *Downing College*: Spacious neo-classical domus (founded 1800), covering 16 acres, with lawns and many fine trees, including a cedar of Lebanon in the East Lodge Garden [Open most days by application to the porter's lodge]. *Emmanuel* [Historic Garden Grade II*]: large gardens with herb garden designed by John Codrington. Also memorable for its fine trees, including a Caucasian wing nut, swamp cypress, dawn redwood and the splendid plane tree, cloaked to the ground, in the Fellows' Garden. Informal shrubberies and herbaceous borders skirt the lawns, and there is a pond with a restrained piece of modern sculpture nearby [Open daily, 9am – 5pm; College Gardens and Fellows' Garden open one day in summer]. *Jesus*: a must for those interested in sculpture; there are a number of interesting pieces throughout the grounds including the Flanagan Venetian horse in First Court and 'The Head' in the cloisters. An award-winning nature trail follows the bank of Jesus Ditch. Elsewhere the St Radegund's garden has planting derived from the sixth-century garden in Poitiers, France [Open daily, but closed during Easter term – May to mid-June]. *King's* [Historic Garden Grade II*]: one of the greatest British architectural experiences, set off by fine lawns. Spring bulbs [College and Chapel open daily until 6.30pm, but grounds closed mid-April to mid-June, 9.30am – 4.30pm, and closed over Christmas period Entrance: £4, children and concessions £3 ㅎ]. Fellows' Garden with magnificent old specimen trees [Open one day in summer for NGS, 2 – 6pm]. *Leckhampton* (part of *Corpus Christi*) at 37 Grange Road: laid out by William Robinson, originally seven acres with two acres added [Open one day for charity 👤 WC]. *Magdalene*: Fellows' Garden [Open daily, 1 – 6pm. Closed May and June &]. *Pembroke*: extensive and varied garden, including orchard and winter bed, with notable range of unusual plants, most of which benefit from shelter provided by various walls, and a good selection of herbaceous perennials. Recent landscaping projects by Marina and Robert Adams [Open daily during daylight hours. Closed May and June &]. *Peterhouse*: varied, smallish gardens and interesting octagonal court with hot and cool sides. Extensive naturalised daffodils in spring [Open Mon – Fri, 1 – 5pm. Closed mid-May to early June &]. *Robinson*: Warden and Fellows' Garden, Grange Road [Open daily, 10am – 6pm]. This modern college was built around the edge of a 10-acre site so as to preserve the character of the Edwardian gardens in the centre. The older individual gardens now interconnect and merge around a wide lawn and small lake. Memorable old trees are preserved and the original flower borders have been renewed. Wild areas benefit local wildlife. *St John's* [Historic Garden Grade II*]: huge park-like garden with eight acres of grass, fine trees and good display of bulbs in spring. Wilderness (nearly three acres) introduced by 'Capability' Brown has spring bulbs including, from June to July, the spectacular Turk's cap lily (martagon lily). In the Master's Lodge Garden are quantities of *Arabis turrita*, probably the only specimens in the country. Rose garden. [Open Mon – Fri, 10am – 5pm, Sat and Sun, 9.30am – 5pm.] *Trinity* [Historic Garden Grade II]: a garden and grounds of 45 acres with good trees [Grounds open daily although restricted access with charge for entry, March to Sept; opening times from porter's lodge. Fellows' Garden open one day, 2 – 6pm]. Nearby is *Little St Mary's Church*: wild and natural garden developed since 1925 [Open all year].

Childerley Hall [Historic Garden Grade II*]

Dry Drayton, Cambridge CB3 8BB. Tel: (01954) 210271

Mr and Mrs John Jenkins • 6m W of Cambridge on A428 opposite Caldecote turn • Open mid-May to mid-July by appt • Entrance: £2.50 ◗ ▓

The hall lies between the sites of the two vanished villages of Great and Little Childerley, and the drive leading to the house, chapel and four-acre garden is nearly a mile and a half through flat open country, making it seem particularly still and remote. To one side is an ornamental Tudor moat and a yew hedge crowned by topiary birds. The south front of the house is on a raised terrace. From here the main garden, sunken and surrounded by raised grass walks, can be viewed; the corners of these walks were originally Tudor mounts. The backbone of the garden is a collection of over 350 different shrub and species roses flourishing in mixed borders – secret corners accessed by paths winding through trees and shrubs.

Christ's College ★★ [Historic Garden Grade II]

St Andrew's Street, Cambridge CB2 3BU. Tel: (01223) 334900

In city centre • Open mid-June to Sept, Mon – Fri, 9.30am – 12 noon; Oct to April, Mon – Fri, 9.30am – 12 noon and 2 – 4pm. Closed Bank Holidays, Easter Week, exam period (May and early June) and 23rd Dec to 2nd Jan ◗ & ✆

First impressions are telling, and the court beyond the porter's lodge is a spectacle that proclaims excellence. The summer display of fuchsias and petunias in window boxes and tubs is refined and peaceful, and tubs of hydrangeas welcome visitors into the immaculate gardens beyond. The well-planned herbaceous borders with considerable panache are augmented by bedded-out plants. On a mound in the far corner the venerable mulberry, contemporary with Milton, sheds its fruit onto the exemplary lawn. There are many other lovely trees, including Indian bean trees (*Catalpa bignonioides*) in full bloom in midsummer, and the cypress grown from seed from the tree on Shelley's grave in Rome. Charles Darwin's garden with its canal intrigues the visitor by the use of false perspective. To commemorate the college's 500th anniversary in 2005, one of the borders in the Fellows' Garden was planted in the autumn of 2003 with plants known to have been cultivated in Britain before 1505. Many of the varieties will also have symbolic links with the personalities involved in the foundation of the college: Henry VI and Lady Margaret Beaufort, mother of Henry VII.

Clare College Fellows' Gardens [Historic Garden Grade II]

Trinity Lane, Cambridge CB2 1TL. Tel: (01223) 333200

In city centre. Entry from Queens Road and Trinity Lane • Open April to Sept, daily inc. Bank Holidays, 10am – 4.30pm. Closed on graduation, May Ball and special events days • Entrance: College and garden £2 ◐

Reached by crossing the oldest bridge over the Cam from the college itself, or from Queens Road by walking along the avenue laid out in 1690, there are two gardens between the college buildings and the bridge. To the north the private Master's Garden and to the south the Scholars' Garden, where the planting relies on silver, blue, purple and white. Professor E.N. Willmer designed the present, well-regarded planting scheme for the Fellows' Garden; the fine trees are mainly the legacy of his predecessors. At the garden's heart, concealed by hedges, is a formal pool. The double herbaceous borders have a yellow and blue theme, while along the northern boundary is a ribbon of silver with a mass of white flowers, including some that show up well against walls and hedges. Summer bedding is used to insert oranges and reds in island beds by the river. Elizabeth Banks Associates has prepared a master plan for development over the next ten years.

Crossing House Garden ★

78 Meldreth Road, Shepreth, Royston, Hertfordshire SG8 6PS. Tel: (01763) 261071

Mr and Mrs Douglas Fuller • 8m SW of Cambridge, ½ m W of A10 • Open all year, daily, dawn – dusk • Entrance: by collecting box ○ **WC** ♿ ⟐

Highly recommended, a delightful, eccentric place which proves that plantsmanship is alive and well in Cambridgeshire. A small garden, started by the present owners over 30 years ago, it is crammed full of plants and is an eye-opener about what can be achieved in a small space. There are little pools, excellent dwarf box edging, an arbour in clipped yew, rockeries and a lawn, and three tiny glasshouses full of orchids and alpines. In all there are estimated to be about 5000 different plants here, so a visit at any time of year will be rewarding. Docwra's Manor (see below) is about 250 metres away.

Docwra's Manor

2 Meldreth Road, Shepreth, Royston, Hertfordshire SG8 6PS.
Tel: (01763) 261473/261557/260235

Mrs John Raven • 8m SW of Cambridge, ½ m W of A10. Opposite war memorial • Open all year, Wed, Fri, 10am – 4pm, first Suns of April to Oct, 2 – 5pm, and at other times by appt. Parties welcome • Entrance: £3, accompanied children under 16 free. Extra charge for guided and out-of-hours parties • Other information: Park in village hall car park ☾ WC ⅗ ⚬

'Simply a garden as reasonably varied as could be' – that was John and Faith Raven's original intention when they bought a manor house with one and a half acres of land in 1954, and this they have achieved. It is a garden with the romantic feel of *temps perdu*, now expanded by a further acre, divided into unexpected compartments by buildings, walls and hedges, and containing many choice plants. Seedlings are left where they appear, so the effect is wild in parts; other areas are more formal, with hosts of roses, spurges, clematis, eryngiums and philadelphus. John Raven (1914–80), a lecturer in classics and an eminent field botanist, wrote about the plants he and his wife grew here in *A Botanist's Garden* (1971; re-issued). The Crossing House garden (see above) is within easy walking distance.

Elgood's Brewery

North Brink, Wisbech PE13 1LN. Tel: (01945) 583160

Elgood's Brewery • In Wisbech, at W end of North Brink • Brewery open for tours, Tues – Thurs, 2pm. £6 inc. tasting • Garden open 27th April to Sept, Tues – Thurs, 11.30am – 4.30pm • Entrance: £2.50, OAPs and children £2 • Other information: Guide dogs only ◖ 🍽 WC ⅗ 🐾 🛍 🌱

Wisbech is an elegant market town and among its delights are several splendid Georgian terraces. North Brink, along the River Nene, is arguably the most spectacular. Peckover House (see entry) is near the eastern end of the Brink, while the brewery dominates the western end. Behind it is a large enclosed garden, now restored, with some superlative trees. The *Ginkgo biloba* near the public entrance catches the eye first. A few paces away stands a tulip tree (*Liriodendron tulipifera*) the like of which you will rarely see; in June every shoot bears a flower, a cup of orange and jade. Other dignitaries are a mulberry, a variegated sycamore, a weeping willow, a tree of heaven (*Ailanthus altissima*) and an oak. The deep pool has become home to a colony of great crested newts. Paths have been reinstated, and colourful herbaceous borders, a rose garden, a herb garden, a maze and a rockery planted. Onto this new planting the trees look down with grace and dignity.

Elton Hall [Historic Garden Grade II*]

Peterborough PE8 6SH. Tel: (01832) 280468 (during office hours)

*Sir William and Lady Proby • 8m W of Peterborough in Elton, just off A605 •
Hall open as garden • Garden open 30th, 31st May; June, Wed; July, Aug,
Wed, Thurs, Sun and Bank Holiday Mon; all 2 – 5pm. Hall and garden open
for tours by appt April to Sept • Entrance: £4 (hall and garden £6, accompanied
children under 16 free)* ● ● ✕ WC & ✈ ⚑ ♜

Steps cloaked in aubretia and lavender, guarded by two sphinxes, ascend to the
low castellated mansion, parts of which date from 1475. Beside the steps is a
knot parterre in box, elegantly wrought, and in front a smooth lawn that rises
to meet the surrounding pasture. A sunken pool, enveloped in a billow of
whites and blues with some purple, is the first feature visitors see as they enter
the main garden through an archway. Take the gravel path that encircles the
lawn, which has an ornamental well-head offset in the middle, and wander past
the immaculately clipped low yew hedges and tumps of golden yew and the
short ha-ha, to the restored rose garden, full of old-fashioned roses – summer
scents and colours. The distant sound of water will eventually beckon you on,
across a hornbeam-lined avenue punctuated with pyramids of box, into an
informal silvery shrubbery, under a fine *Paulownia tomentosa*, to discover a new
Gothick orangery set in an ornamental garden.

Florence House

Back Road, Fridaybridge, Wisbech PE14 0HU. Tel: (01945) 860268

*Mr and Mrs A. Stevenson • 3½ m S of Wisbech on B1101. In Fridaybridge turn
right at Chequers pub • Open for NGS 10th March, 7th April, 7th July, 4th
Aug, 10am – 4pm, also 9th May, 13th June, 5th Sept, 12 noon – 4pm, and by
appt • Entrance: £2, children 50p • Other information: Refreshments Suns only.
Unusual plants for sale* [NEW] ● ● & ✈

Although 25 years have gone into its making, this is essentially a garden in the
contemporary style, filled with an array of choice plants. One-and-a-half acres
of lawns, borders, trees and shrubs benefit from some of the most fertile soil in
the country. The paddock borders, planted in 2000, are big-boned and colour-
themed, starting with grasses and boldly architectural and exotic plants –
cannas, phormiums, heleniums, phlomis, euphorbias and eryngiums. The
mood changes as the colours shade into greens and creams, then finishes with
a flourish of mauves, reds and blues. Mrs Stevenson likes to experiment with
colours and combinations, and the borders change from year to year. Beyond,
the woodland area is underplanted with ferns, hellebores and bulbs.

Hardwicke House

High Ditch Road, Fen Ditton, Cambridge CB5 8TF. Tel: (01223) 292246

*Mr J. Drake • 3½ m E of Cambridge off A14, ½ m from centre of Fen Ditton.
From A1303 Newmarket road turn N by borough cemetery • Open one day in
late May for NGS, and by appt • Entrance: £3, children free* ● & ✈ ♜ ✿

Fenland gardens need shelter, and shelter is provided here by tall hedges, some of beech, some of conifers, with elderly pruned apple trees in between. The compartments within the garden are all different. Closely mown paths radiate through rougher grass providing vistas; the main one is lined by birch trees alternating with yellow-blossomed *Rosa* 'Cantabrigiensis'. In late spring and early summer the place is awash with columbines and cranesbills and filled with the fragrance of old roses; in autumn there are colchicums in abundance, while hellebores and daffodils provide spring colour. Unusual plants are scattered around, and a National Collection of aquilegias is here.

Island Hall

Post Street, Godmanchester PE29 2BA. Tel: (01480) 459676

Mr C. and Lady Linda Vane Percy • 2m S of Huntingdon, in centre of Godmanchester • Open 30th May for NGS, and for parties by appt, May to July and Sept • Entrance: £2 ● ● & ●

The garden is in two parts, separated by a mill-race yet linked by a Chinese-style wooden bridge erected in 1988. The Island was the pleasure garden in Victorian times – today it has tall trees, mainly horse-chestnuts, underneath which cow-parsley and other wild flowers are being encouraged. There are lovely views across the River Ouse to Portholme Meadow. Returning via the bridge, another vista embraces two fine cedars of Lebanon, one standing in front of the eighteenth-century house. On the terrace is a formal parterre with clipped variegated box hedges, box spirals and yew pyramids; the Mill Garden has a sundial ensconced in another parterre spilling over with white shrubby cinquefoil, white Scotch roses and columbines.

21 Lode Road ★

Lode, Cambridge CB5 9ER.

Richard Ayres • 6m NE of Cambridge. From A14 take B1102 to Lode • Open for charity 19th, 20th, 27th, 28th June, 11am – 5pm, and by appt • Entrance: £2 • Other information: Parking facilities at village hall. Possible for wheelchairs but narrow paths ● ● &

The owner's use of foliage in variety – glittering, golden, ferny, fulsome, silvery – and his placing of shrubs and trees to their best advantage are magisterial. The yellows and blues of the flowers, with occasional flashes of scarlet and crimson, and the subtle whites, form a brilliant tapestry through which the paths weave and wind, opening new views at every turn. Everything is compact – there is no sense of boundaries – and everything immaculate.

The Manor

Hemingford Grey, Huntingdon PE28 9BN. Tel: (01480) 463134

Diana Boston • 4m SE of Huntingdon off A14. Access off river tow path • House open by appt; tours daily in May, 11am and 2pm – booking advisable • Garden open all year, daily, 11am – 5pm (closes dusk in winter) • Entrance:

£2, children 50p. (House £4, OAPs £3.50, children £1.50) • Other information: Park in High Street ○ & ⬦ 🌱 🖐 ☕

A storybook garden for children of any age – but there is much more than a garden here, for the wonderful moated Norman manor (c. 1130) is perhaps the oldest continuously inhabited house in England. It was the home of Lucy Boston from 1939 and the setting for her *Green Knowe* children's books. She designed the garden, intermixing old-fashioned roses with herbaceous perennials, creating parallel herbaceous borders, a formal rose garden and topiary in the form of chess pieces. Trees in the lawns are underplanted with autumn crocuses. At the Norman front are ancient yews and a superb copper beech that has layered itself. Parts of the garden are left wild deliberately.

Netherhall Manor

Tanner's Lane, Soham, Ely CB7 5AB. Tel: (01353) 720269

Timothy Clark • 6m SE of Ely on A142; pass church and war memorial and take second road on left. From Newmarket turn right in Soham at second road after cemetery • Open 29th March, 2nd May, 1st, 8th Aug for NGS, 2 – 5pm, and for parties of 10 or more by appt • Entrance: £1 ● ☕

An elegant garden, touched with antiquity, and full of old-fashioned plants. In spring it blazes with Victorian hyacinths, crown imperials and old primroses, followed by the only display of florists' tulips and florists' ranunculus in the country. In high summer Elizabethan daisies, the rare double-flowered white Turk's cap lily originated here, and collections of nineteenth-century variegated pelargoniums command the borders. Entering through a courtyard with box-edged beds and a handsome fountain, visitors first glimpse the formal aconite garden (later filled with old fuchsias); behind is the organic vegetable garden. To the right runs a colonnade of lichen-encrusted columns linked by a balustrade on which pots of seasonal flowers are displayed; summer is represented by gold and silver tricolour pelargoniums, yellow and golden-brown calceolarias, heliotropes and double lobelias. Notable too are the old apples, specimen trees, vast clumps of violets and hepatica and, most remarkably, the double-flowered ornamental blackberry (*Rubus ulmifolius* 'Bellidiflorus') trained against the gable wall.

Nuns Manor

65 Frog End, Shepreth, Royston SG8 6RF Tel: (01763) 260313

Mr and Mrs J.R.L. Brashaw • 8m SW of Cambridge off A10, 270 metres from Melbourn – Shepreth crossroads • Open for NGS 16th May, 20th June, 2 – 5.30pm, and by appt (parties only in May and June) • Entrance: £2.50
NEW ● ☕

This excellent two-acre garden, surrounding a sixteenth-century farmhouse, was designed by the owners' son, a landscape architect, and is maintained with style and energy. Stretching away from the house are deep twin herbaceous borders designed to flower from May until autumn. Eremurus seed prolifically in the light chalky soil and make a spectacular start to the five-month flowering period. They are followed by oriental poppies: 'Goliath', 'Mrs Perry' and 'Patty's Plum'. Campanulas and epilobiums continue the display, together with self-sown *Verbascum blattaria* and many penstemons. A main vista from the house looks to the pond, a central feature surrounded by a thickly planted white, green and purple ruff of salix, verbenas, hostas and irises, and a circular lawn with a tall central birdbath has a warmer colour scheme of blues, reds and purples. The overall effect is vibrantly colourful – a combination of plantsmanship and sheer nerve.

Peckover House [Historic Garden Grade II]

North Brink, Wisbech PE13 1JR. Tel: (01945) 583463

The National Trust • In centre of Wisbech on N bank of River Nene • House open as garden, but Wed, Sat and Sun only, plus Thurs, May to Aug, Good Friday and Bank Holiday Mons, 1.30 – 4.30pm • Garden open 29th March to Oct, Sat – Thurs and Bank Holiday Mons, 12.30 – 5pm • Entrance: £2.50 (house and garden £4) • Other information: electric wheelchair available by prior application. Facilities available only when house open ○ 🍵 ✕ WC ♿ ⚘ ⛪ 🔦 ⚒

The red-brick town house was built in 1722, whereas the elongated, two-acre garden has a distinctly late-Victorian ambience. Stepping from the house onto the croquet lawn, the visitor is surrounded by greenery, mature trees and evergreen shrubs. In summer, bedding plants add colour and the scent of a host of roses is an invitation to bear westwards, passing a (reconstruction) formal pool, into compartments variously planted with flowering shrubs, perennials and those perfumed roses. Topiary peacocks overlook a second pool and summerhouse. Lilies, peonies, hydrangeas and 'Mrs Sinkins' pinks provide a succession of blooms in the walled garden, at the end of which is the orangery, full to bursting with flowering pot plants and three mature, fruiting orange trees. Further on, a new border, dominated by dark red, is maturing, backed by espalier pear trees. Vegetables and cut flowers are grown for the tea room and house. Everything is neat and tidy, bearing out the claim that this garden is 'the product of prudent tidiness, a period piece'. Elgood's Brewery (see entry) is close by.

South Farm

Shingay, Royston, Hertfordshire SG8 0HR. Tel: (01223) 207581

Mr P. Paxman • 11m SW of Cambridge, 6m NW of Royston off A1198, via Wendy • Open two days in June for NGS, and May to July for individuals and parties by appt. Gardening clubs especially welcome • Entrance: £2.50 (joint entrance with other properties) on charity days ● 🍵 🍽 WC ♿ ⚘

The main flower garden is enclosed and protected by a tall cypress hedge, pierced frequently by gates that allow you to glimpse the long fields of wheat. The hedge even has a *trompe-l'oeil* cut into it – not a bad use for the loathsome 'Leylandii'. A lily pond in one corner is awash with sedges and monkey flowers and around it an informal garden with such beauties as *Rosa chinensis* 'Mutabilis'. Familiar flowers abound: Jacob's-ladders, daylilies, plume poppies, loosestrife.

On the other side of the farmhouse is a pool terrace and an exotic conservatory, and a 1000-metre-square vegetable garden enclosed by espalier fruit trees and totally netted. Each rotation plot is subdivided by gravel paths, parterre-style, into some 15 beds holding over 150 varieties of vegetables and fruit. Beyond is a small wildflower meadow, and more wheat. A happy, not-too-tidy garden – the lucky ducks and their companion 'rare breeds' have some well-trained humans to keep it for them. Nearby is a private nature reserve with a three-acre lake, which is open to the public. *Brook Cottage* (Mr and Mrs Charvil), four minutes' walk away, is a much smaller garden with a crystal-clear stream – a real cottage garden with vegetables and poultry as well as honeysuckles and horsetails.

Thorpe Hall [Historic Garden Grade II*]

Longthorpe, Peterborough PE3 6LW. Tel: (01733) 330060

Sue Ryder Care • In Longthorpe, on W edge of Peterborough between A47 and A605 • Ground floor of house open for some events • Garden open all year, daily except 25th, 26th Dec and 1st Jan, 10am – 5pm (closed on event days) • Entrance: by donation ○ WC ⅋ ⅏ ⅏

A wooden door lets the visitor out of the courtyard into the L-shaped garden comprising a series of parterres and borders. Two elegant Georgian pavilions, far apart, are linked by a long vista which is interrupted as it pierces a third pavilion. A boldly planted herbaceous border and a restrained, lavender-hedged rose garden around an oval pond occupy parts of a longer axis. On the shorter axis is an architectural Victorian parterre planted with a strange mixture of perennials, including ornamental grasses, clipped bay laurel, box and yew, and bedded-out plants. The south court is planted with Cromwellian plants, the east border with 1850s' plants, while the west end has rose gardens typical of the 1920s and '30s. What has been achieved so far is pleasing and worthwhile, providing a diverting small garden with echoes of former grandeur, especially in its Grade-II-listed pavilions, ancient yews and spreading cedar trees.

University Botanic Garden ★★ [Historic Garden Grade II*]

Cambridge CB2 1JF. Tel: (01223) 336265

University of Cambridge • In S of city, on E side of A1309 (Trumpington Road). Entrance off Bateman Street • Open all year except 25th Dec to 1st Jan inclusive: summer 10am – 6pm, winter 10am – 4pm • Entrance: March to Oct, Mon – Fri, and weekends and Bank Holidays all year £2.50; Nov to Feb, Mon – Fri, free ○ ⅏ ⅏ WC ⅋ ⅏ ⅏ ⅋

This diverse and impressive garden covers 40 acres, and admirably fulfils its three purposes – research, education and amenity. A visit at any time is worthwhile, even during the coldest months when the winter garden, especially on a sunny day, is dramatic. The various dogwoods with red, black, green and yellow-ochre stems contrast with *Rubus biflorus*, while the pale pink trunk of the birch *Betula albo-sinensis* var. *septentrionalis* is stunning. The garden has the best collection of trees in the east of England, with limes, chestnuts, willows and conifers featuring prominently. Exotic trees include pawpaw (*Asimina triloba*), and good specimens of madrona (*Arbutus andrachne*), black walnut *Juglans nigra* and dawn redwood (*Metasequoia glyptostroboides*). The historic systematic beds display the hardy representatives of over 90 families of flowering plants, and there are both limestone and sandstone rock gardens. The glasshouse range is always fascinating, and in winter the tropical section can be a welcome retreat. It contains a green-flowered jade vine (*Strongylodon macrobotrys*), cycads, tropical economic plants and much more. In the alpine house, plants are changed regularly as they come into flower. A recent addition is the Dry Garden, which investigates how design and plant selection can reduce the need for watering in a typical city garden. The Limestone Mound has an illuminating display of British wild plants, including some rare and endangered species. Nearby is another novelty, a linear bed showing arable weed flora changes in UK agricultural history. The Genetic Garden is a new display which illustrates how the amazing diversity of flowering plants results from genetic variation due to mutation.

Wicken Fen

Lode Lane, Wicken, Ely CB7 5XP. Tel: (01353) 720274

The National Trust • 9m SE of Ely, 3m SW of Soham, S of A1123, signed to Wicken Fen Nature Reserve • Fen Cottage open April to Sept, Sun and Bank Holiday Mons, 2 – 5pm (also open Wed in Aug) • Entrance Fen Cottage and Nature Reserve £3.80 • Other information: Light refreshments, toilet facilities and shop in Reserve visitor centre opposite, open Tues Sun, 10am – 5pm (closed occasionally in winter) ● � WC ♿ ❂ ✆

A simple, effective garden with jumbles of foxgloves, hollyhocks, Shasta daisies, clary and golden yarrow in midsummer, a few roses, some butcher's broom, a patch of fruit and vegetables and lots of nettles – unpretentious, in keeping with the rural cottage. You can just peep over the garden hedge on your way to Wicken Fen National Nature Reserve, which is one of the wild treasures of Cambridgeshire.

Wimpole Hall [Historic Garden Grade I]

Arrington, Royston SG8 0BW. Tel: (01223) 207257

The National Trust • 7m SW of Cambridge, signed off A603 at New Wimpole • Hall open 22nd March to 2nd Nov as garden, but 1 – 5pm (Bank Holiday Mons opens 11am) • Garden open 22nd March to 2nd Nov, Tues – Thurs, Sat, Sun and Bank Holiday Mons, 10.30am – 5pm (Tues – Sun in July and Aug); Nov to March, Sat, Sun, 11am – 4pm. Pre-booked guided tours for parties with head gardener. Park walks open all year • Entrance: £2.60 (hall and garden £6.40, children £3.10) • Other information: Pre-booked self-drive vehicles available for disabled visitors ◑ ✕ ▨ WC ♿ ⬦ ✿ ❂ ✆

The colossal landscaped park mirrors almost every fashion in landscaping during the eighteenth and nineteenth centuries; Charles Bridgeman (1720s),

Lancelot 'Capability' Brown (1760s) and many others worked here. Today, their handiwork is in part immaculate, in part preserved, but elsewhere decrepit and in the process of restoration. Restoration of the walled garden is progressing well and the glasshouses have been rebuilt. The parterre before the north front of the house is planted in Victorian style. In the park vast avenues lead to the cardinal points of the compass, past lakes, bridges, a splendid 1770 folly which can be seen in the distance from the parterre, trees at all stages from ancient to newly planted, and rare breeds of cattle and sheep everywhere. To reach the folly an hour is needed; other marked walks take longer. A walks leaflet is available.

Wytchwood

Owl End, Great Stukeley, Huntingdon PE28 4AQ.

Mrs David Cox • 2m N of Huntingdon off B1043. In Great Stukeley, turn at village hall into Owl End • Open for NGS one day in July, 1.30 – 5.30pm, and at other times by appt in writing • Entrance: £2, children 50p • Other information: Parking at village hall ● ● & ⚘

Cascades of petunias and an ornamental wheelbarrow filled with annuals are striking preludes to the garden proper. The brightly planted borders have manicured, matching golden cypress columns as backdrops. Even the magnolia has been clipped. A small pool, and a blue spruce in a heather bed frame the patio. A few steps further on and the garden becomes altogether different. There is one and half acres of mown grass with large uncut islands full of wild grasses and native plants softly waving in the breeze, especially attractive to amphibians, butterflies and dragonflies. After the cliché of the front garden, which some will dislike but most will thoroughly enjoy, the restraint of the meadow islands, filled with lady's bedstraw and poppies, set with rowans and birches, is inspired. A spinney has recently been planted with native trees, ferns, hostas, foxgloves and spring bulbs.

GUIDANCE ON SYMBOLS
Wheelchair users: the symbol &, denoting suitability for wheelchairs, refers to the garden only – if there is a house open, it may or may not be suitable. Additionally, some areas of the garden may not be accessible by wheelchair, or may require assistance.
Dogs: ⚘ indicates that there is somewhere on the premises where dogs may be walked, preferably on a lead. The garden itself is often taboo – parkland, or even the car park, are frequently indicated for the purpose.
Picnics: ● means that picnics are allowed, but usually in certain restricted areas only. It does not give visitors the all-clear to feast where they please!
Children-friendly: the bat-and-ball symbol ⚘ suggests that there are activities specifically designed for children, such as an adventure playground or a discovery trail, or that the garden itself is likely to appeal to them.

CHESHIRE

We have included some gardens with Cheshire postal addresses in the Manchester Area for convenience. So before planning a day out in Cheshire it is worthwhile consulting pages 270–75.

Two-starred gardens are marked on the map with a black square.

Adlington Hall [Historic Garden Grade II*]

Adlington, Macclesfield SK10 4LF. Tel: (01625) 820875

Mrs C.J.C. Legh • 5m N of Macclesfield off A523. Signed in Adlington • Hall and garden open June to Aug, Wed, 2 – 5pm, and to parties all year by appt • Entrance: hall and garden £5, children £2, parties of 20 or more £4 per person ● ● WC & ✿ ♀

An attractive woodland park, mostly landscaped in the eighteenth century in the style of 'Capability' Brown. To the porticoed Georgian south front of the house a gravelled carriage-sweep encircles an oval lawn with a sundial at its centre, then leads through a pair of iron gates to a short avenue of limes dating from 1688; a path then bears eastwards to the shell house, a small brick building of 1794 embellished with shells in the mid-nineteenth century. The wood to the west of the house offers pleasant walks, especially one along the small river bank. In the centre, close to the bridge, is a temple to Diana, and various follies in the eighteenth-century wilderness have been restored. Formal gardens created in front of the early Elizabethan north front of the house include a maze and rose garden and a herbaceous border. East of the house across a cobbled area is a water garden dedicated to Father Tiber and a new penstemon garden.

Arley Hall and Gardens ★ [Historic Garden Grade II*]

Arley, Great Budworth, Northwich CW9 6NA. Tel: (01565) 777353/777284

The Viscount Ashbrook • 5m W of Knutsford off A50, 7m SE of Warrington off A559. Signed from M6 junctions 19 and 20 and M56 junctions 9 and 10 • Hall open (times vary) • Garden open 9th April to 26th Sept, Tues – Sun and Bank Holiday Mons; Oct, Sat and Sun; all 11am – 5pm • Entrance: £4.50, OAPs £3.90, children £2 (hall extra) • Other information: Spring Plant Fair 4th April, 10am – 4pm, Garden Festival 27th and 28th June, 10am – 5pm, Autumn Plant Hunters' Fair 5th Sept, 10am – 4pm ◑ ● ✕ ▓ WC & ◁▷ ✿ ▥ ♀ ✎

These gardens consist of many distinct areas, each with its own character and charm – the 'garden room' concept may have been adopted here from Elvaston (see entry in Derbyshire) – but it is for its superb herbaceous border that Arley is most famed. Dating from before 1846, this is one of the earliest of its kind in England. A watercolour by George Elgood of 1889 shows it looking much as it does today, with a broad grass walk and clipped yew buttresses. At one end a classical pavilion provides a focal point framed by chess-piece topiary, and a little to one side is a fine wrought-iron gate. The large range of perennials grown includes some varieties that were used here a century ago. Designed to give colour from June to September, the season begins with soft yellows, blues and silvers, before the spires of delphiniums and aconitums make their impact along with the softer forms of gypsophila and achillea; towards the end of the year the hotter colours of sedum, helianthus and crocosmia come to the fore. There is plenty of interest in other areas too: the walled garden has perennials and shrubs grown in attractive combinations, and in the kitchen garden is a vinery containing a good collection of tender plants and a fine border with shrub roses, irises and peonies. Some areas, such as the flag garden and herb garden, are intimate in scale, while others have large open vistas. Topiary, mellow brickwork and stone ornaments contribute to the structure and character throughout. Away from the more formal areas a woodland garden has been created since the early 1980s, where a large selection of trees and shrubs grow in a delightfully tranquil setting. Attached to the gardens is a nursery owned and run by Viscount Ashbrook's sister, with some unusual plants, especially perennials.

Bluebell Cottage Gardens (Lodge Lane Nursery)

Lodge Lane, Dutton, Nr Warrington WA4 4HP. Tel: (01928) 713718

Rod and Diane Casey • 4m SE of Runcorn, 6m NW of Northwich, S of M56 and A533. Signposted • Gardens, meadow and woodland open May to Aug, Fri, Sat, Sun and Bank Holiday Mons, 10am – 5pm. Parties by appt • Nursery open mid-March to mid-Sept, Wed – Sun and Bank Holiday Mons, 10am – 5pm. Entrance: gardens, meadow and woodland £2, children free ◐ 🍵 WC & ﾟ

Set around an old cottage, the gardens include three acres of woodland, three acres of wildflower meadow and a large well-run nursery. Clustered around the cottage are several small gardens divided by hedges and trellises covered in climbers. Each is devoted to a different theme: herb garden, yellow garden, raised vegetable garden, the mandatory area of grasses and a patio with a large collection of pelargoniums and other tender perennials grown in pots. In a larger open area sloping up to the canal a scree bed runs down to a pool; cut into the lawn is a series of large herbaceous borders giving an impressive display from May through August. In a garden with little natural shade, a corner next to the canal bridge has been developed as a woodland haven.

Bramall Hall

(see Manchester)

Bridgemere Garden World ★

Bridgemere, Nantwich CW5 7QB. Tel: (01270) 521100

On A51 7m SE of Nantwich. Signed from M6 junctions 15 and 16 • Open all year, daily except 25th, 26th Dec, 9am – 7pm (winter closes 6pm) • Entrance: free ○ 🍽 ✕ WC & ﾟ 🏧 ▯ ✆

This 25-acre garden centre is one of the largest in Europe. There are some 5000 different plants for sale including several rare and unusual varieties. It also has six acres of display gardens designed to show off many of the plants on offer growing in their favoured conditions. There are many distinct areas, all well designed, some modern in feel and some more traditional. The gardens change with the seasons and are constantly being altered; some beds are devoted to the very latest introductions. Bridgemere's Gold Medal Garden re-created from an earlier Tatton Show has a Mediterranean feel with an area of terracotta, a fine stout pergola and many plants with striking foliage. The castle garden has mock ruins overlooking a moat and an area devoted to damp lovers. A rockery and a pool (filled with water lilies and surrounded by varieties of iris and astilbe) are backed by a collection of pines. Close by is a bed of euphorbias that reminds us just how many fine varieties of this plant there are. The displays of tulips are particularly impressive and a good selection of azaleas and rhododendrons grow around the mound, from where the visitor gets a fine view across the whole garden. Statuary, trellises, grottoes and garden ornaments are used to good effect throughout.

Capesthorne Hall and Gardens ★

Macclesfield SK11 9JY. Tel: (01625) 861221

Mr W.A. Bromley Davenport • 7m S of Wilmslow, 1m S of Monks Heath on A34 • House open as gardens but 1.30 – 3.30pm only • Gardens open April to Oct, Wed, Sun and Bank Holidays, 12 noon – 5pm • Entrance: gardens and chapel £6.50, OAPs £5.50, children (5–18) £3 (hall extra charge) • Other information: Lunches, teas and suppers by arrangement. Dogs and picnics in park only ◑ ☕ <u>WC</u> ও 🌱

Set within a large estate, the gardens, although unspectacular, have something of a quiet majesty about them and include fine architectural features. The surrounding parkland was laid out in the seventeenth and eighteenth centuries with a string of lakes forming the southern perimeter. Vernon Russell-Smith designed the formal lakeside garden in the 1960s to replace the large kitchen gardens. It is mainly laid to lawn, but also has herbaceous borders containing a good variety of plants and a wonderful set of Rococo Milanese gates. There is a serene view from here across the lake and its attractive brick bridge. The mellow brickwork of the elegant eighteenth-century chapel (be sure to look inside) sets off the glossy foliage of the *Magnolia grandiflora*, camellias and cherry in the small garden which surrounds it. An arboretum has two enormous sweet chestnuts and some giant redwoods. The surrounding park and woodland offer excellent walks – the small guidebook describing a number of routes is good value for money.

Cherry Hill

Malpas SY14 7EP.

Mr and Mrs Miles Clarke • 6m NW of Whitchurch, 2m W of Malpas off A41. From B5069 turn N at Cuddington Heath towards Chorlton and continue for 1m; garden is on left • Open one day in June for NGS, 2 – 6pm, and by appt • Entrance: £3.50, children under 16 £1 ● ☕ <u>WC</u> ও ⟁ ♀

A pleasant mix of the formal and informal. The formal is to be found within an old walled garden divided into different areas, all with a strong geometric design. A path through the centre leads under a rose-covered pergola, through a double border of peonies, under another rose pergola and finally to a double herbaceous border, where soft blues and pinks are picked out against a purple prunus hedge. On one side of the walk is a rectangle of lawn bisected by a rill surrounded by lavender, shrub roses and weeping pear, with a rose-covered arbour looking over a knot garden. On the other side of the walk is a neatly kept *potager*, a fine restored Victorian greenhouse and a collection of shrub roses. Outside the formal area a long sweep of lawn drops away from the house with its magnificent backdrop of the Welsh hills to a trout pool with specimen ducks and black swans. A woodland walk leads to the pavilion and cricket ground.

Cheshire Herbs

Fourfields, Forest Road, Tarporley CW6 9ES. Tel: (01829) 760578

Ted Riddell • 9m E of Chester, on A49 close to junction with A54 • Open daily except 24th Dec to 3rd Jan, 10am – 5pm • Entrance: free ○ **WC** & ⬦ ⌇ ⑂

This is principally a nursery stocking some 400 varieties of herbs, but there is also a small garden in a lawned area enclosed by a yew hedge. It is a circular knot garden small enough to be emulated by most gardeners; the raised bank around it reminds us that such gardens are best seen from a higher level. Beyond is a larger area of beds, again circular in pattern, containing many herbs and planted in an informal manner. There is also a polytunnel full of large tubs of plants. The aroma here and in other parts of the nursery makes a visit more than worthwhile.

Cholmondeley Castle Gardens ★ [Historic Garden Grade II]

Cholmondeley Castle, Malpas SY14 8AH. Tel: (01829) 720383

The Marquess of Cholmondeley • 7m W of Nantwich, 6m N of Whitchurch on A49 • Open April to Sept, Wed, Thurs, Sun and Bank Holiday Mons, 11.30am – 5pm, and on other days by prior appt for parties of 20 or more • Entrance: £3.50, children £1.50 (2003 prices) ◑ ⬛ ✕ ▩ **WC** ⬦ ⌇ ⑂ ♨

Of Lord Cholmondeley's great formal gardens, laid out by George London in the 1690s, no trace remains. His canal and fruit garden are gone, as is his vast kitchen garden (138 x 246 metres with some 40 compartments), which was almost on the scale of Louis XIV's *potager* at Versailles. Instead, set in idyllic parkland and blessed with a most extensive range of mainly acid-loving trees and shrubs, the gardens are designed to take advantage of spectacular views. The nineteenth-century castle is perched majestically on a hill overlooking the estate, which includes two lakes and a superbly sited cricket pitch. The lawns which slope up to the castle are covered with bulbs in spring. The area of gardens that lies to the west of the castle has some of the most interesting plants. In the glade, sheltered by large trees, are varieties of magnolia and cornus, an *Abutilon vitifolium*, a *Davidia involucrata*, many rhododendrons and a large liquidambar. On a lower level are primulas, narcissi and cyclamens. The rose garden contains a mixture of old and new varieties – Lady Cholmondeley is constantly experimenting to find varieties that will thrive on sandy soil. This is one of the few formal areas, a pleasant layout of beds divided by stone-flagged paths; a fine *Magnolia sieboldii* stands at the entrance. The most impressive area of all is the temple garden, where the landscaping and architecture give a classical feel – a Claude painting contrived by a horticulturist. Around a pool with its two grassed islands are some attractive combinations of shrubs and trees, good use being made of purple, gold and blue foliage. Tower Hill is a wilder area, where mature woodland of beech, oak and sweet chestnut is underplanted with camellias, more magnolias, cornus and rhododendrons.

Dorfold Hall [Historic Garden Grade II]

Chester Road, Acton, Nantwich CW5 8LD. Tel: (01270) 625245

Mr R. Roundell • 1m W of Nantwich, S of A534 • Hall open • Garden open April to Oct, Tues and Bank Holiday Mons, 2 – 5pm • Entrance: House and garden £5, children £3 ◑ WC ও ⬧

A woodland garden of spring-flowering shrubs and bulbs is the chief horticultural attraction here. The formal gardens around the house, once laid out in ornate Elizabethan style, are now fairly austere, confined to large areas of lawn edged by narrow herbaceous borders. A statue of Shakespeare stands to one side of the house and a fine Jacobean gate to the other. A new garden against the old walled garden, enclosed by a yew hedge and a wrought-iron gate, shows promise, with borders of peonies, hostas, tulips and shrub roses backed by wall climbers. The woodland garden itself, set within a dell, has clipped grass paths running among areas of long grass planted with spring bulbs and clumps of azaleas giving off a heady scent. The valley then slopes steeply down towards a small stream fringed by primulas and arums, beneath a dense canopy of oak and sycamore. The landscaping has been well designed, with gravel paths winding among large boulders and revealing views across the garden.

Dunge Valley Hidden Gardens

**Windgather Rocks, Kettleshulme, Whaley Bridge, High Peak SK23 7RF.
Tel: (01663) 733787**

David and Elizabeth Ketley • 6m NE of Macclesfield, 12m SE of Stockport in Kettleshulme. Signed from B5470 Macclesfield – Whaley Bridge road • Open April to Aug, Thurs – Sun and Bank Holiday Mons; March, Sat and Sun (plant sales only); all 10.30am – 5pm • Entrance: £3, children £1, season ticket £5 • Other information: Mini-buses up to 12 seats only. Telephone for appt at other times to buy plants at Hardy Plant Nursery ◑ ☕ ✕ WC ⅌

A superbly sited garden nestling in a small valley high in the Pennines; the location is so remote that often only the song of the lark or the cry of the curlew can be heard. Walks wind across and around the rocky valley, disclosing wonderful views over the garden and into the rugged landscape beyond. It is a superb natural setting for many rhododendrons, camellias, acers and magnolias; shrub and species roses provide interest later in the season.

When the garden was begun in 1983 pine, larch and hemlock were planted as shelter belts and now, even at an altitude of 1000 feet, some surprisingly tender specimens – embothriums, *Eremurus robustus* and *Desfontainia spinosa* – survive. Rodgersias, rheums, primulas and other moisture-lovers cluster around the stream that runs through the valley, and close to the stone farmhouse are cultivated pockets of choice plants, including collections of meconopsis and peonies. The expanding nursery stocks such things as American magnolias, plus sorbus and meconopsis grown from seed collected by the owners in Nepal.

Dunham Massey

(see Manchester)

Eaton Hall ★ [Historic Garden Grade II*]

Eccleston, Chester CH4 9ET. Tel: (01244) 684400

The Duke of Westminster • 4m S of Chester off A483 Chester – Wrexham road • Open 11th April, 30th May, 30th Aug, 1.30 – 5.30pm • Entrance: £2.50, children £1 • Other information: Chapel open ● ▣ WC & ⬥

The gardens and parkland surrounding the modern hall are vast. There are several fine features: well-kept herbaceous beds and many stone statues and urns. A long, narrow greenhouse contains camellias, and a deep bed backing against the walled garden is planted for dramatic effect with hot-coloured perennials and shrubs such as cotinus and dark-flowering buddleia. There is also a large lake and a small Gothic-style cottage with stone and brick paths set within its own small herb garden. Close to the house is the imposing Italian garden surrounded by a high yew hedge; a large dragon fountain stands at the centre of a pool, and there are beds of annuals and more statues. Arabella Lennox-Boyd has been working on the garden for several years.

Gawsworth Hall [Historic Garden Grade II*]

Macclesfield SK11 9RN. Tel: (01260) 223456

Mr and Mrs T. Richards • 3m S of Macclesfield off A536. Signposted • Hall open • Garden open Easter to mid-June, Sun – Wed and Bank Holiday Mons; mid-June to Aug, daily; Sept to early Oct, Sun – Wed; all 2 – 5pm • Entrance: hall, park and garden £4.50, children under 16 £2.25, parties of 20 or more £3.50 per person • Other information: Open-air theatre in garden mid-June to mid-Aug ◗ ▣ ▥ WC & ⚲

The hall is approached by a drive leading between two lakes to the north end, where there is a large yew tree and lawns sloping down to one of the rhododendron-fringed lakes. A formal garden on the west side has beds of modern roses edged with bright annuals and many stone ornaments, including a sundial and a circular pool with a fountain; stone steps lead to a sunken lawn and mixed beds. To the south is another lawned garden surrounded by a high yew hedge and herbaceous borders. A grassed area containing mature trees lies to the west of these formal areas, from where there is a view of the groundwork for a Williamite garden begun but not completed by the Earl of Macclesfield, who died in 1694.

Hare Hill Gardens

Hare Hill, Over Alderley, Macclesfield SK10 4QB. Tel: (01625) 584412

The National Trust • 5m NW of Macclesfield, N of B5087 between Alderley Edge and Prestbury at Greyhound Road • Open 29th March to Oct, Wed, Thurs, Sat, Sun and Bank Holiday Mons, 10am – 5.30pm. Special opening for rhododendrons and azaleas 10th – 31st May, daily, 10am – 5.30pm. Parties by written appt • Entrance: £2.70, children £1.25. £1.50 per car refundable on entry to garden • Other information: Picnics at lakeside only ◑ 🥪 WC ⚬

Hybrid and species rhododendrons, some of enormous size, are the main attraction here. Other acid-lovers – azaleas, magnolias, acers and tree-like pieris – thrive in the damp, lush setting and sheltering canopy of beech and oak. A pool at the heart of the wood gives a break in the trees, and the colours of the rhododendrons are reflected in its waters; rustic timber bridges cross to a central island. Hare Hill also has a walled garden, once used for growing vegetables, but now rather sparsely planted – laid mainly to lawn with beds of roses and some good climbers. Along the drive to the south, majestic conifers and pines tower above rhododendrons and azaleas in an impressive group. Although at its peak in spring and early summer, the rolling countryside surrounding the garden and the views of the Pennines to the east make it a good centre for walks at any time of the year.

Henbury Hall ★

Macclesfield SK11 9PJ.

Mr S.Z. de Ferranti • 2m W of Macclesfield on A537 • Open one day for NGS • Entrance: £4, children £1 ◑ 🍵 WC ⚲

The hall, built in 1986, was based on Palladio's Villa Rotunda, and the French limestone goes well with its parkland setting. To the east the land slopes down to two lakes with ornamental bridges at one end. The 12 acres are well landscaped and planted with many mature trees, azaleas and rhododendrons. Further north the land rises again, and beyond more banks of trees and shrubs is a walled garden with a double herbaceous border and a laburnum arch. Close by is a unique design of tennis court and a large modern conservatory housing a swimming pool, a fernery and a grotto. At the other side of the walled garden a cottage has recently been renovated in the Gothic style.

Jodrell Bank Arboretum

Jodrell Bank Visitor Centre and Arboretum, Macclesfield SK11 9DL.
Tel: (01477) 571339

Manchester University • 11m W of Macclesfield, on A535 between Holmes Chapel and Chelford, 5m NE of M6 junction 18. Signposted • Open mid-March to Oct, daily, 10.30am – 5.30pm; Nov to mid-March, Mon – Fri, 10.30am – 3pm, Sat,

Sun, 11am – 4pm. Closed several days over Christmas and New Year – telephone to check • Entrance: free (charge for 3D-theatre and parking) ☾ 💬 🏷 **WC** ⅙ 🏛

The arboretum, begun in 1972 largely at the instigation of Professor Sir Bernard Lovell, is set in a flat landscape with all views to the west dominated by the massive radiotelescope. The large collection of trees covers 35 acres and includes National Collections of malus and sorbus. There is also a collection of hornbeams and shrubs such as berberis, fine specimens of *Ulmus minor* (syn. *U. elegantissima*) 'Jacqueline Hillier' and the cut-leaved form of the common walnut (*Juglans regia* 'Laciniata'). Broad grass walkways lead among the trees, and small natural ponds are dotted around the garden. There are also beds of shrub roses and azaleas. A new apple orchard is based on varieties that originated in Cheshire. A day out for the family and good value when all the attractions are considered.

Little Moreton Hall

Congleton CW12 4SD. Tel: (01260) 272018

The National Trust • 4m SE of Congleton on E side of A34 between Congleton and Newcastle-under-Lyme • Open 27th March to Oct, Wed – Sun and Bank Holiday Mons, 11.30am – 5pm; 6th Nov to 19th Dec, Sat and Sun, 11.30am – 4pm • Entrance: £4.75, children £2.35, family £11.50, party rates, £4 per person (hall and gardens) (2003 prices) • Other information: Wheelchair for loan. Guide dogs and hearing dogs only ◑ 💬 ✕ 🏷 **WC** ⅙ 🐾 🏛 ☕

The hall is one of the best-known and most astonishing timber-framed buildings in the country, and its gardens are pleasant in their own quiet way. Largely the creation of the Trust and a fitting complement to the house, they cover about an acre set within a moat. The hall has a central cobbled courtyard and is surrounded by herbaceous borders; a gravel walk follows the inside perimeter of the moat. To the west is a large lawn with fruit trees and an old grassed mound, to the north a yew tunnel and a knot garden laid out under the guidance of Graham Stuart Thomas following a seventeenth-century model – a simple design of gravel and lawn separated by a low box hedge. Behind the knot garden, four beds have been planted with medieval and culinary herbs and a selection of seventeenth-century vegetables.

Lodge Lane Nursery

(see BLUEBELL COTTAGE)

Lyme Park

(see Manchester)

Mellors Gardens [Historic Garden Grade II]

Hough Hole House, Sugar Lane, Rainow, Macclesfield SK10 5UW.
Tel: (01625) 573251

Mr and Mrs A. Rigby • From Macclesfield take B5470 Whaley Bridge road. In Rainow turn off to N opposite church into Round Meadow, then turn first left

*into Sugar Lane and follow road down to garden • Open 24th May, 23rd Aug
for charity, 2 – 5pm, and by appt for parties of 10 or more • Entrance: £1.50,
children free* ◖

Where can you pass through the Valley of the Shadow of Death, climb Jacob's
Ladder, see the Mouth of Hell and visit the Celestial City, all within the space of
ten minutes? Here, in a valley in a rugged but attractive part of the Peak District,
in the second half of the nineteenth century, James Mellor, much influenced by
Swedenborg, designed a unique allegorical garden which attempts to re-create
the journey of Christian in Bunyan's *Pilgrim's Progress*. There are many small stone
houses and other ornaments to represent features of the journey. Most areas are
grassed, with stone paths running throughout; at one end a large pond is
overlooked by an octagonal summerhouse. Excellent guide book.

The Mount

Andertons Lane, Whirley, Henbury, Macclesfield SK11 9PB.

*Mr and Mrs Nicholas Payne • 2m W of Macclesfield off A537. Turn into
Pepper Street opposite Blacksmith's Arms, and left into Church Lane which
becomes Andertons Lane. Garden is 200 metres further on. Signposted • Open
one day a year for NGS, and by written appt at other times for parties of 10 or
more • Entrance: £3, children 50p • Other information: Plants for sale on NGS
day only* ◖ ☕ 🖼 WC ♿

The two-acre garden, originally planted in the 1920s but enlarged, improved
and replanted by the present owners, is a fine setting for the Regency house.
Each distinct area has its own individual style. The terrace garden has an Italian
feel, with a swimming pool, many architectural features and brightly planted
terracotta pots. The shade garden is more informal, with rhododendrons,
azaleas and camellias underplanted with hostas and other shade-lovers. A
lawned area has two herbaceous borders; opposite is another small border
planted entirely with astilbes, and a conservatory containing a climbing
pelargonium. In one corner of the garden an area of grass has been cut to
different heights, forming patterns and paths leading to an obelisk looking
across the Cheshire plain towards Wales.

Ness Botanic Gardens ★★ [Historic Garden Grade II]

Neston Road, Ness, Wirral CH64 4AY. Tel: (0151) 353 0123

*University of Liverpool • 10m NW of Chester, 2m off A540 between Ness and
Burton • Open daily except 25th Dec: March to Oct, 9.30am – 5pm; Nov to
Feb, 9.30am – 4pm • Entrance: charge • Other information: Guide dogs only*
○ ☕ ✕ 🖼 WC ♿ 🐾 🏛 ♀ ⚲

Mr A. Bulley began gardening on this site in 1898, using seeds from plants
collected for him by George Forrest, the noted plant hunter. His daughter, Lois
Bulley, who gave the gardens to the University in 1948, was described in her
Times obituary as 'an exceptional human being, born into wealth, which she
rejected, a member of the Labour Party, Communist Party and Cheshire County
Council, a Quaker, a fighter against racism and for social justice and equality,

especially for women, a philanthropist with a shrewd business brain, a national benefactor of applied plant biotechnology and horticultural research'. Ness Gardens extend to over 60 acres, and those who have experience of the north-west winds blowing off the Irish Sea will marvel at the variety and exotic nature of the plant life. The secret is in trees planted as shelter belts. The aim has been to provide interest from spring onwards, through the herbaceous and rose gardens of summer, to the heather and sorbus collections of autumn. There are in addition areas of specialist interest, such as the native plant garden, which houses plants raised from seed or cuttings from wild plants and is used for propagation or the re-stocking of natural habitats. With the creation of an academic chair at the gardens in 1991 there has been a positive move to increase on-site research. Specialisms include sorbus, betulas, salix, rhododendrons and primulas. Maps, coloured guides and interest trails are available.

Norton Priory Museum and Gardens ★

Tudor Road, Manor Park, Runcorn WA7 1SX. Tel: (01928) 569895

The Norton Priory Museum Trust • 2m E of Runcorn. From M56 junction 11 turn for Warrington and follow signs to Norton Priory. From all other directions follow signs to Runcorn, then Norton Priory • Open all year, daily, 12 noon – 5pm (closes 6pm Sat, Sun and Bank Holiday Mons; 4pm Nov to March). Walled garden open April to Oct, daily, 1.30 – 4.30pm • Entrance: £3.95, OAPs and children £2.75, family £10 • Other information: Museum open. Teas and snacks in Museum ○ ⬛ 🧺 WC ⬥ ⬿ 🌣 ⬛ 🌼 ⚲

This is a garden of distinct halves. The woodland garden, covering 30 acres and containing many fine mature trees, surrounds the remains of the twelfth-century Augustinian priory. The stream glade is the most attractive area, planted with azaleas, candelabra primulas and astilbes; a water-lily tank has a statue of Coventina (goddess of wells and streams) at its centre. There are many modern sculptures dotted around both parts of the garden. At some distance to the north of the woodland garden is the clearly signposted walled garden, built in the mid-eighteenth century as a vegetable garden and rede-signed on more ornamental lines. A rose walk runs down the centre – two broad borders contain many different shrub roses, an orchard has many varieties of pear, plum, greengage and quince (the National Collection of *Cydonia oblonga*, tree quince, is held here). There is also a vegetable garden and a distinctive herb garden. Along the south-facing wall a series of brick arches, covered with vines and honeysuckles and sheltering two large figs, is fronted by beds of perennials, strongly planted with kniphofias, euphorbias, salvias and geums. Indeed the walled garden is a good illustration of the twin strengths of the garden as a whole – a bold, coherent design and a great variety of plants.

Peover Hall [Historic Garden Grade II]

Over Peover, Knutsford WA16 9MW.
Tel: (01565) 632358 (Tour Guide, I. Shepherd)

Mr R. Brooks • 4m S of Knutsford off A50 at Whipping Stocks Inn, down Stocks Lane, signposted • Hall open April to Oct, Mon only (but closed Bank

Holiday Mons), 2 – 5pm • Gardens open April to Oct, Mon and Thurs, 2 – 5pm • Entrance: £3, children £2 (hall, stables and garden £4.50, children £3) • Other information: Possible for wheelchairs but many grass paths. Dogs in park only, on lead. Teas on Mons only ◐ **WC** &

Peover Hall (pronounced Peever) and its 15-acre gardens are surrounded by a large expanse of flat parkland laid out in the early eighteenth century, but the gardens themselves are mainly Edwardian. On the north side of the Eliza-bethan house a broad grass walk leads from the forecourt through an avenue of pleached limes to a summerhouse overlooking a small circular lawn; both are enclosed by a high yew hedge. On the west side of the gardens is a wooded area containing many rhododendrons and an attractive grassy dell. Clustered around the south and west of the hall are small formal gardens – rose, herb, white and pink – separated by brick walls and yew hedges, some containing yew topiary. The lily-pool garden has a summerhouse with a tiled roof supported by Doric columns. Fine Caroline stables and a church to visit.

Queen's Park, Crewe [Historic Park Grade II]

Victoria Avenue, Wistaston Road, Crewe CW2 7SE. Tel: (01270) 537882

Crewe and Nantwich Borough Council • 2m W of town centre, S of A530 • Open all year, daily, 9am – sunset • Entrance: free • Other information: Parking off Queen's Park Drive ○ ▬ ▦ **WC** & ⟨⟩ ▯ ℺

The well-landscaped Victorian park, created in 1878, is oval in shape and covers 48 acres, with large grassed areas and a wide variety of mature trees. From the ornate entrance with two Gothick lodges and a clock tower, the drive carries on through an avenue of birches to the centre of the park, where a café overlooks the large boating lake surrounded by banks of trees and shrubs. From the west of the park a stream runs through a lightly wooded valley to join the lake. A path linking the entrance to this valley leads past some raised beds of heathers and under a laburnum tunnel. There is also a scented garden for the disabled. It merits a high grade for the quality of landscaping, the trees and the Victorian buildings, but in essence it is a large municipal park where the fight against vandalism and litter is fought hard.

The Quinta ★

Swettenham, Congleton CW12 2LD.

Sir Bernard Lovell, Cheshire Wildlife Trust and Tatton Garden Society • 5m NW of Congleton, E of A535 Holmes Chapel – Alderley Edge road, near Twemlow Green in Swettenham, next to church • Open all year, daily, 9am – dusk, twice for NGS and for parties on weekdays by appt • Entrance: £2 • Other information: Teas on NGS Sun openings only ◕ ⟨⟩ ℺

Sir Bernard Lovell began planting this garden in 1948 to satisfy his love of trees. It now contains a large variety of trees and shrubs. There are good collections of pines and birches, five of the six varieties of wingnut and an Oriental plane directly descended from the Hippocratic tree on the island of Cos. Most areas are informally planted and interspersed with grassed glades;

several avenues pass up and down the garden, including one of limes planted in 1958 to celebrate Sir Bernard's Reith lectures. Across the more recently planted areas to the west of the garden a walk taking in some marvellous views across the Dane Valley (SSSI) leads to the 39 steps that descend into the wooded valley of a small brook (one mile from the car park and back).

Reaseheath College

Reaseheath, Nantwich CW5 6DF. Tel (01270) 625131

Reaseheath College • 1½ m N of Nantwich on A51 • Open for College Open Day 16th May, and 19th, 26th May, 2nd June for NGS, 1 – 5pm • Entrance: by donation. Guided tours available. Prices on application ● ● 🐾 WC ⚘ 🛒 ♿

The attractive gardens must provide the College's students with constant inspiration. From the old brick hall a large lawn sweeps southwards to a lake, flanked on one side by a heather garden and on the other by a rockery. The lake is spanned by a wooden bridge and stocked with a variety of water lilies and marginals. On the south side is a woodland garden with many fine trees, including a large cut-leaf beech, underplanted by primulas, hostas, azaleas and other shade-loving plants. To the west of the lake another lawned area has island beds with a variety of small trees, shrubs and perennials. Other areas of interest include a new garden with water features, a herb garden, a model fruit garden, a range of glasshouses and a nursery.

Rode Hall [Historic Garden Grade II]

Church Lane, Scholar Green ST7 3QP. Tel: (01270) 882961

Sir Richard and Lady Baker Wilbraham • 5m SW of Congleton between A34 and A50 • House open as garden from 1st April, Wed and Bank Holidays only, and for parties by appt at other times • Garden open 7th to 22nd Feb (for snowdrops), 12 noon – 4pm; April to Sept, Tues – Thurs and Bank Holiday Mons, 2 – 5pm; plus 9th May for NGS, 1.30 – 5pm. Also for parties by appt at other times • Entrance: £3, OAPs £2 (house and garden £5, OAPs £3.50. Special parties at other times £8, including tea) ◐ ● WC ⚘ 🚗 ♿

A long drive leads through parkland to an attractive red-brick house with fine stable buildings. The gardens lie to the north and east, with many areas remaining as planned by Repton in 1790. The rose garden and formal areas were designed by Nesfield in 1860; these are mainly lawn, with gravel paths and clipped yews, and good views from here of the surrounding countryside and Repton's lake. In a dell to the west is a woodland garden with hellebores and flowering shrubs, rhododendrons, azaleas and some fine climbing roses. Old stone steps ascend the opposite side of the dell to a grotto and early-nineteenth-century terraced rock garden. A small stream is dammed at the open end of the dell with the resulting pond surrounded by marginals; a path leads from here to the lake. The two-acre Georgian walled kitchen garden is at its best in June, July and August. The ice-house in the park is also worth a visit.

Stapeley Water Gardens

London Road, Stapeley, Nantwich CW5 7LH. Tel: (01270) 623868

*Mr R.G.A. Davies • 1m SE of Nantwich on A51. Signed from M6 junction 16 •
Open all year, daily except 11th April, 25th Dec. Opening and closing times
vary from 9am – 10am and 4pm – 8pm • Entrance: Display gardens free. The
Palms Tropical Oasis £4.35, OAPs £3.90, children £2.50, parties of 15 or more
£3.85 per person, OAPs £3.45, children £2.25. Season tickets available • Other
information: Wheelchairs available* ○ 🍵 ✗ WC ♿ 🌿 ♿ 🔦 🪝*

Two acres of garden shopping under cover form the world's largest water-
garden centre. Within it a few areas are attractive gardens in their own right.
At the back are many pools containing the National Collection of water lilies;
the land around is landscaped with lawns and shrub borders. Another area has
small demonstration gardens. Across the car park is The Palms Tropical Oasis.
This huge greenhouse has none of the architectural merit of a Victorian palm
house, but the main hall is impressive, with a long rectangular pool flanked by
huge palm trees, a display from the Manchester Museum of the World of Frogs,
and other exhibits. Those with an interest in water gardens might comment
that this is a bleak description – think of the giant *Victoria amazonica* water lily
from Brazil, the rare breeding sting-rays, the *Nymphaea gigantea* from Australia.
Ooh-aah! And an angling centre for the non-horticultural.

Tatton Park ★★ [Historic Garden Grade II*]

Knutsford WA16 6QN. Tel: (01625) 534400

*Cheshire County Council/The National Trust • 3m N of Knutsford, signed from
M6 and M56 • House open April to Oct, daily except Mon, 12 noon – 4pm •
Gardens open April to Sept, daily except Mon, 10am – 6pm; Oct to March,
daily except Mon and 25th Dec, 11am – 4pm • Entrance: gardens £3, children
£2, family £8, park £3.90 per car, Discovery Saver Ticket (to any two attractions
excluding park entry) £4.60, children £2.60 (2003 prices) • Other information:
RHS Flower Show 21st to 25th July* ○ 🍵 ✗ 🍽 WC ♿ 🌿 ♿ 🔦

Tatton Park was, throughout four centuries, the home of the Egertons, an
immensely rich family who could indulge their every whim on their vast
estate. The 50 acres of gardens here are among the finest in England and
contain some unique features created by the best designers in the country.
Repton made a 'Red Book' for Tatton in 1791 and much of his work is still
visible in the wonderful rolling parkland that surrounds the gardens. When
Lewis Wyatt completed his work on the house in 1815 he was asked to
design the kidney-shaped flower garden and the elegant orangery. From
1859 Paxton was at work, and his fernery was built to take the collection of
plants made by Lord Egerton's brother; it now houses New Zealand tree
ferns. Also by Paxton is the Italian garden, the grandest and most formal
part of the gardens: an arrangement of terraces spaciously laid out with an
ornate design of clipped hedges and beds. They are overlooked by the south-
facing portico of the house and fine views stretch out across the parkland
from here. The Japanese garden constructed in 1910 by Japanese workmen

and recently restored has a wholly different feel. Set in a small valley, the contrasting textures of mounds of moss, delicate acer leaves, large stones and a gently flowing stream give this garden its particular charm, while large conifers provide a backdrop and give it intimacy. Tatton has much more besides: pools and lakes, huge numbers of rhododendrons and azaleas, a rose garden that has something of the feel of Lutyens about it, a maze and an arboretum with especially fine pines. The Trust is now embarking on a huge project to restore the walled gardens to their former working glory, with areas of fruit and vegetables and large greenhouses, including a pinery for forcing pineapples. One problem — these marvellous gardens attract huge numbers of visitors at peak times.

Walton Hall Gardens

Walton Lea Road, Higher Walton, Warrington WA4 6SN. Tel: (01925) 601617

Warrington Borough Council • 2m SW of Warrington on S side of A56 in Walton • Open all year, daily, 8am – dusk • Entrance: free • Other information: Pay-and-display car park. Heritage centre, children's zoo and play area, pitch and putt, crazy golf, bowls ○ 🍲 🍴 WC & 🐕 ⚗ 🕯 ⚘

The gardens are dominated by the dark brick Victorian mansion with its distinctive clock tower. To one side of the building a large pool containing carp is backed by an impressive rockery well planted with azaleas, rhododendrons, birches and other small shrubs and trees. Water cascades down the rocks to a pool furnished with water lilies and marginals, including a clump of gunneras. Behind the hall is a series of formal gardens separated by yew hedges and low stone walls and containing beds of bright tulips and annuals. Beyond some large beech trees, modern roses are set out in formal beds. The walk back down the west side of the garden passes through light woodland with a collection of camellias and some fine acers and magnolias. The council keeps these gardens in good condition; a Ranger Service organises public events.

85 Warmingham Road

Coppenhall, Crewe CW1 4PS. Tel: (01270) 582030

Mr and Mrs A. Mann • 3m N of Crewe off A530 between Warmingham and Leighton Hospital near White Lion Inn • Open mid-Feb to Sept by appt for parties of up to 40 • Entrance: £2, children free ● 🍲 WC & 🎗

Two-thirds of an acre with a small woodland, a large herbaceous border and a good display of hellebores and snowdrops. Many and various alpines are to be found here. In the first section of the garden, paths run among lushly planted beds lightly shaded by trees; there are perennials and small shrubs as well as a collection of lilies, and a small pond in the centre is planted with marginals such as golden sedge. Beyond this area is a lighter, more open section containing gravel screes, a rock garden and a peat bed. Diascias, violas and geraniums abound. There are also two greenhouses, one with a good collection of cacti and succulents.

The Well House

Tilston, Malpas SY14 7DP. Tel: (01829) 250332

Mrs S.H. French-Greenslade • *3m NW of Malpas, 12m SW of Chester off A41. Turn right after Broxton roundabout, then continue on Malpas road through Tilston. Garden is at antique shop* • *Open one day for NGS, 2 – 5.30pm, and March to July by appt* • *Entrance: £2, children 25p* • *Other information: Plants sometimes for sale* ● ☕ WC ⛾ ⚲

A one-acre garden set around a small natural stream, well worth visiting both for the range of plants grown and the natural landscaping of the site. Close to the house is a geometric layout of beds containing perennials such as campanulas and alstroemerias, backed by a rose-covered pergola and with a sundial at the centre. There is also an area devoted to rock plants and a patio on which a large number of plants are grown in containers – an inspiration for those with small gardens. Another area has plants chosen for foliage colour, including yellow robinia, purple berberis and silver pyrus. Moisture-lovers, including many ferns, line the stream that divides the garden, and a bridge leads across to a small hexagonal summerhouse. In the upper garden is a new triple waterfall feature. The land rises steeply from the stream, giving views back over the garden, and another fine view can be had from the balcony, where tea may be taken.

CORNWALL

Two-starred gardens are marked on the map with a black square.

Antony ★ [Historic Garden Grade II*]

Torpoint PL11 2QA. Tel: (01752) 812364

The National Trust and Trustees of Carew Pole Garden Trust • 2m W of Torpoint on A374, 16m SE of Liskeard. From Plymouth use Torpoint car ferry • House open as formal gardens • Formal gardens open April to Oct, Tues – Thurs and Bank Holiday Mons; also June to Aug, Sun, all 1.30 – 5.30pm (last admission 4.45pm). Woodland gardens open March to Oct, Tues – Thurs, Sat, Sun and Bank Holiday Mons, 11am – 5.30pm • Entrance: £3.50; combined gardens only £3.90 (house and formal gardens £4.60, children £2.20, pre-booked parties £3.80 per person, family £11.50) • Other information: Separate car parks for formal and woodland gardens ◐ ☕ ✕ 🧺 WC ♿ ⬆ ✀

Antony is a little off the beaten track, but it is well worth the effort to visit one of the country's finest early-eighteenth-century houses, in a magnificent natural setting. The house and adjacent formal gardens now belong to the National Trust, while the woodland gardens, which lie between the parkland and the River Lynher and are also open, belong to the family trust. The formal gardens, with a terrace round the house, wide lawns, extensive vistas, yew hedges and old walls, are of the highest quality. A water feature by William Pye on the west lawn mirrors the yew topiary nearby. Eighteenth-century statues, modern sculpture and topiary are features of the yew walk and of the formal compartments of the summer garden; the latter includes a pleached lime hedge, mixed shrub and herbaceous borders with roses, and a knot garden. The woodland gardens, also known as the wilderness – the central section – include Jupiter Hill and a late-Georgian bath house and are planted with superb camellias, magnolias and rhododendrons, with scented rhododendrons outstanding in May. A standing stone of Cornish granite has been erected on top of Jupiter Hill in memory of the present owner's parents, who created the woodland gardens. In the neighbouring woodland walk is a ruined fifteenth-century dovecote and Richard Carew's sixteenth-century Fishful Pond, and there are fine walks along the river banks. Two National Collections are held here: hemerocallis (610 cultivars) and *Camellia japonica* (300 cultivars).

Barbara Hepworth Museum and Sculpture Garden [Historic Garden Grade II]

Barnoon Hill, St Ives TR26 1AD. Tel: (01736) 796226

Administered by The Tate Gallery • In centre of St Ives. Signposted • Open March to Oct, daily, 10am – 5.30pm; Nov to Feb, Tues – Sun, 10am – 4.30pm • Entrance: museum and sculpture garden £3.75, OAPs £2 ○ WC ♿ ⬆ 🛍 ✀

The wonderful collection of Hepworth's own sculptures combines superbly with the architectural planting of her garden as a permanent testimonial to her importance. The house and half-acre sloping garden are kept as they were in her lifetime. The strong vertical and other architectural statements and the soft underplanting occlude views outside and provide a soft contrasting background for the sculptures. Trees shade the upper part of the garden and give transient light effects in the sun. They include *Cordyline australis*, bamboos and a metasequoia on the back wall, and below them *Magnolia grandiflora*, a ginkgo, and a row of *Prunus* 'Amanogawa' providing cover for a small but important pond and separating the upper garden from the small open lawn which forms the lower part. Below are herbaceous beds and a silver-grey path. In 2001 the garden was listed by English Heritage as being of special historic interest. It is within walking distance of the Tate St Ives; the small but attractive *Trewyn Garden*, well planted and with an immaculate lawn, adjoins.

Boconnoc [Historic Garden Grade II*]

The Stewardry, Boconnoc, Lostwithiel PL22 0RG. Tel: (01208) 872546

Mr and Mrs J.D.G. Fortescue • Between Lostwithiel and Liskeard, S of A390. Well signed on open days between Lostwithiel and Middle Taphouse • Open 18th, 25th April, 2nd, 9th, 16th to 21st, 23rd and 30th May, 2 – 5pm, and for parties of 10 or more by appt • Entrance: £2.50, children free • Other information: Guided tours of house, garden and estate by prior arrangement. Refreshments and holiday accommodation available ● 💮 WC ⅙ ⟁ 🌿 🍵 ⚲

The extensive grounds, with great landscape effects, were first laid out by Thomas Pitt, Lord Camelford, in the eighteenth century, and an extensive restoration programme is underway. The magnificent woodland garden, covering some 20 acres, contains fine flowering shrubs and many large and unusual trees. It is best seen by taking a walk along the well-kept paths. Not far away in Lostwithiel is the *Duchy of Cornwall Nursery*, reputed to be the best garden centre in the county (Tel: (01208) 872668).

Bonython Manor Gardens

Cury Cross Lanes, Helston TR12 7BA. Tel: (01326) 240234

Mr and Mrs R. Nathan • 5m S of Helston on A3083. Turn left at Cury Cross Lanes (Wheel Inn), and take second entrance on right signposted 'Bonython Estate' • Open May to 5th Sept, Tues – Thurs, 10am – 4pm • Entrance: £3, children £1.50, parties of 10 or more £2.50 per person ● 💮 WC ⅙ ⟁ 🌿 ⚲

A major new and exciting garden still in the process of development. The owners started in 1999 with an old walled garden, a few ornamental trees and shrubs, background trees, and essential shelter belts (now extended). The long drive lined with hydrangeas leads under copper beeches to a lawn surrounded by rhododendrons and azaleas. The Georgian house has been given a new courtyard garden with herbs and ornamental bamboos, a rill and a water feature. The walled garden contains herbaceous and shrub borders for summer show and some eucryphias, with a parterre planted with flowers and vegetables in a lower section. The areas below the walled garden are more sheltered: an orchard slopes down to Lake Joy against a background of specimen trees and shrubs. The sunny bank which dams it has a bold display of South African and Mediterranean plants. Below lies Lake Sue, surrounded by an outstanding collection of ornamental grasses, and from here a stream leads through the woodland garden and dell, filled with wild flowers, new rhododendrons and ferns, to the quarry lake with vertical cliffs beyond.

Bosahan ★

Manaccan, Helston TR12 6JL. Tel: (01326) 231351

Mr and Mrs R.J. Graham-Vivian • 10m SE of Helston, 1m NE of Manaccan • Open by appt for parties of 6 or more • Entrance: £4 per person • Other information: Coach companies must confirm in advance ● WC ⚭

The valley garden is some 100 years old and, together with the rest of the estate, is being restored. The main garden, which has fine views from the top and where golden pheasants wander, runs from the house down to an attractive stream and pond in the valley. It covers about four acres and contains mature conifers and rhododendrons as well as camellias and other trees and shrubs; there are also azaleas near the house and more recent plantings. Beyond the main garden a wood where mature tree ferns and pittosporums grow follows the stream down to the Helford River. The adventurous can follow its bank to the left and return up the remains of the overgrown path of the old fern glen, where ancient rhododendrons fight to survive.

Bosvigo ★

Bosvigo Lane, Truro TR1 3NH. Tel: (01872) 275774

Mr Michael and Mrs Wendy Perry • ¾ m W of Truro. From A390, turn into Dobbs Lane adjacent to Sainsbury foodstore roundabout. Entrance is 500 metres down lane on left, just after sharp left bend • Open March to Sept, Thurs, Fri, 11am – 6pm • Entrance: £3, children £1 • Other information: Rare and unusual plants for sale in nursery ◑ WC ♿ ♚

An immaculately maintained garden of great artistry and imagination. The three acres surrounding the Georgian house consist of several delightful enclosed and walled areas. The hot garden displays red, yellow and orange flowers, the Vean Garden white and yellow, and the walled garden many rare plants. Flowers and foliage are grouped with boldness or subtlety to enchanting effect. Not a typical Cornish garden (rhododendrons and camellias do not play a major part), it is at its best in summer when the mainly herbaceous plants start their display.

Burncoose Gardens

Gwennap, Redruth TR16 6BJ. Tel: (01209) 860316

Burncoose Nurseries • On A393 Redruth – Falmouth road between Lanner and Ponsanooth. Signposted • Open daily except 25th Dec, 8.30am – 5pm (Sun opens 11am) • Entrance: £2, children free ○ ☕ WC ♿ ⬧ ♚ ♨

This woodland garden, belonging to the Williams family of Caerhays Castle (see entry), was laid out originally at the turn of the twentieth century; it is now allied to the Burncoose Nurseries. It contains many fine camellias, magnolias, rhododendrons, acers and other spring-flowering shrubs and ornamental trees. Though the woodland extends to more than 30 acres, accessible by a network of paths, the main planted areas lie either side of the main drive and beside the pond.

Caerhays Castle Garden ★★ [Historic Garden Grade II*]

Caerhays, Gorran, St Austell PL26 6LY. Tel: (01872) 501310

Mr F.J. Williams • 10m S of St Austell. On coast by Porthluney Cove between Dodman Point and Nare Head • House open 15th March to May, Mon – Fri, 1 – 4pm • Garden open 16th Feb to May, daily, 10am – 5.30pm • Entrance: £5.50, children under 16 £2.50 (under 5 free) (house and garden £9.50, children under 16 £3.50. Party rates for 15 or more • Other information: Car park by beach; short walk to garden entrance ● 🍽 <u>WC</u> & 🐕 🌿 🍴

Unsurpassed in spring and one of the greatest of all Cornish and British gardens, this has an international reputation which is well deserved. Principally a woodland garden, it stretches up and around the extensive hillside above the romantic early-nineteenth-century castle. It can lay claim to a superlative collection of camellias and rhododendrons and an unrivalled collection of magnolias. All of these, as well as many other fine shrubs and trees, are not only huge themselves, but bear flowers of a remarkable size and depth of colour. Many of the plants were raised from material brought back by famous plant hunters or sent recently from China; it was at Caerhays that the famous 'Williamsii' camellias were originally propagated, and the National Collection of magnolias is held here. Half a day is required to do justice to the garden at its peak.

Carwinion

Mawnan Smith, Falmouth TR11 5JA. Tel: (01326) 250258

Mr and Mrs H.A.E. Rogers • 5m SW of Falmouth. From Mawnan Smith take left road by Red Lion. 500 metres up hill on right is white gate marked 'Carwinion' • Open all year, daily, 10am – 5.30pm • Entrance: £3, children free ○ 🍽 WC & 🐕 🌿 🏛 🍴 ९ B&B

Twelve acres of wild woodland garden leading down to the Helford River, containing the most comprehensive collection of bamboos in the country, plus large gunneras and rhododendrons. There are some impressive camellias in the attached *Towan Camellia Nursery*. The most interesting part of the lower woodland area is on the right bank of the stream.

Chyverton ★★ [Historic Garden Grade II]

Zelah, Truro TR4 9HD. Tel: (01872) 540324

Mr N. Holman • 8m NE of Redruth, 1m W of Zelah on A30. At end of bypass, turn N at Marazanvose; entrance is ½ m on right • Open by appt only by

personally conducted tour • Entrance: £6, parties of 20 or more £5 per person • Other information: Lunch or tea by arrangement for parties ● ▩ WC ◁▷

Chyverton is one of the greatest of Cornish and of woodland gardens. It covers perhaps 140 acres, depending on the distinction between garden and woods, and is maintained virtually single-handedly by the owner without the use of chemical sprays. It has benefited from 70 years of unbroken planting, hence the outstanding collection of magnolias in particular, but also of rhododendrons, camellias, ferns and many other plants of the greatest interest. All these thrive in an unspoilt setting which is certainly not over-manicured, aptly described by the owner as a 'magic jungle', and a photographer's paradise; such are the growing conditions that collectors and great botanical institutions send their rare plants and collections here. The garden surrounds the 1730s' house, which has a contemporary copper beech and a recently planted herbaceous border nearby, and stretches under mature trees along the bottom of the adjacent valley. It is being divided into 29 separate 'rooms', some of them given added interest by a new collection of statues.

Cotehele ★ [Historic Garden Grade II*]

St Dominick, Saltash PL12 6TA. Tel: (01579) 351346

The National Trust • 12m NE of Liskeard, 8m SW of Tavistock. Turn S off A390 at St Anne's Chapel • House open 15th March to Oct, daily except Fri (but open Good Friday), 11am – 5pm • Garden open daily, 10.30am – dusk • Mill open daily except Fri (but open Good Friday), 1pm – 5.30pm; July, Aug, daily, 1pm – 6pm; Oct, daily except Fri, 1 – 4.30pm • Entrance: garden and mill £3.60 (house, garden and mill £6.40, pre-booked parties £5.40 per person) • Other information: Holiday cottages available ○ ▯ ✕ ▩ WC ♿ ◁▷ ✿ 🏛 ☕ ✎

There are two separate parts to this 19-acre garden. The upper gardens around the beautiful sixteenth-century house are largely formal, with courts, herbaceous borders, walls, yew hedges, fine lawns, a pool and a formally planted terrace falling away from the east front of the house. There is a daffodil meadow, a grove of acers and an orchard. This area is probably at its peak in the late spring and early summer. The woodland valley garden lies in the view below the formal terrace. Here beneath large conifers and hardwoods are many colourful flowers, shrubs and ornamental trees; rhododendrons and azaleas are especially striking in spring. The valley tumbles down towards the River Tamar, and from a hilltop behind the house a tower offers fine views.

Creed House

Creed, Grampound TR2 4SL. Tel: (01872) 530372

Mr and Mrs W.R. Croggon • Mid-way between St Austell and Truro. Take A390 to Grampound, then road in main street signed to Creed. After 1m, opposite Creed church, turn left; entrance to house and garden is on left • Open all year, daily, 10am – 5.30pm, and 9th May for NGS and 6th June for charity, 2 – 5.30pm • Entrance: £2.50, children free • Other information: Teas, toilet facilities and plant sales on charity open days only ○ ✿ **B&B**

This seven-acre garden, devotedly restored and developed over the last three decades by the present owners, surrounds a handsome Georgian rectory and has views of the countryside through mature trees; below the lawn a delightful fishpond is a focal point. The fine trees and shrubs include azaras, camellias, magnolias and rhododendrons. A walled garden behind the house gives additional interest in summer. For maximum enjoyment use the garden guide to be found beside the front door, and view the historical photographic montage in the stable-block garage.

Eden Project

Bodelva, St Austell PL24 2SG. Tel: (01726) 811911

1½ m off A391 NE of St Austell, or by Luxulyan Road, St Blazey Gate on A390 E of St Austell, or from A30 (all signposted). Open all year, daily, 10am – 6pm (last admission 4.30pm); Nov to March closes 4.30pm (last admission 3pm). Closed 24th and 25th December • Entrance: £10, OAPs £7.50, students £5, children (5–16) £4, under 5 free, family £25 • Other information: Students must have ID ○ ⬤ ✗ <u>WC</u> ♿ ⌀ ⬛ 🍴 ⚲

This mammoth project was created in 2001 from a vast disused china clay pit. It contains two huge, transparent geodesic lean-to conservatories and a landscaped area with a large waterfall and flowing river planted with species from Amazonia, West Africa, Malaysia and Oceania. But Eden can no longer call itself a project. It is a resounding success, not a garden but a spectacular educational theme park of botany and ecology. Almost too successful, it is now having to extend itself by adding to its existing biomes a third one – the Dry Tropics biome, plus a new educational building, covered walkways, a field centre, accommodation for more horticultural staff, facilities for student training and increased exhibition space. £75 million is the figure named, 2006 the target completion date. The truth is that it has developed into a tremendously powerful tourist magnet far beyond initial forecasts. Two million people pass through every year, nearly double the figure originally projected. They have already made Eden the third most-visited tourist attraction in Britain and a real earner for the Cornish economy. The problem will be that of keeping the show going while capacity is being enlarged.

Fox Rosehill Gardens

Melville Road, Falmouth TR11 4DB. Tel: (01326) 319377

Carrick District Council • From A39 follow signs to beaches and hotels • Open all year, daily, 8am – dusk • Entrance: free • Other information: Plant sale in early June ○ ⬛ ♿ ⬅ 🍴

Established by the Fox family, owners of the Falmouth Packet Line, with specimens brought back by ships' captains, this is a truly remarkable small park of two acres. It is famous for its many exotic trees and shrubs, including an *Embothrium coccineum* (Chilean firebush) and a *Syragus romanzoffiana* (queen palm). There are also collections of myrtus and bamboo, all set amongst paths and two lawns. A delight for the ordinary visitor and of great interest to the plantsman.

Glendurgan Garden ★ [Historic Garden Grade II]

Mawnan Smith, Falmouth TR11 5JZ. Tel: (01326) 250906

The National Trust • 4m SW of Falmouth, ½ m SW of Mawnan Smith on road to Helford Passage • Open 14th Feb to Oct, Tues – Sat and Bank Holiday Mons, 10.30am – 5.30pm (last admission 4.30pm). Closed 9th April • Entrance: £4, family £10, booked parties £3.40 (2003 prices) ◖ ⬗ ✕ ▨ WC ♿ ♨ ⊞ ⚲

Set, like Trebah (see entry), in a ravine with a fine view of the Helford River, and adjacent and similar in size to it, Glendurgan is predominantly a spring-time and sub-tropical garden. It contains many fine mature trees and shrubs, including rhododendrons, camellias, a vast 150-year-old liriodendron and a large michelia. An attractive pond graces the lower valley, together with tree ferns, gunneras, hydrangeas and bamboos. There is also an 1833 maze of cherry laurel, and a Giant Stride for children. Its upkeep is immaculate, although some consider the effect rather sanitising.

Headland

Battery Lane, Polruan-by-Fowey PL23 1PW. Tel: (01726) 870243

Jean Hill • 8m E of St Austell off A3082. Take passenger ferry from Fowey and 7-minute walk up hill, or take car ferry from Fowey to Bodinnick and follow signs for Polruan (3m). Ignore first car park, turn left for second car park overlooking harbour, then turn left (on foot) down St Saviour's Hill • Open for charity 6th May to 9th Sept, Thurs, 2 – 6pm • Entrance: £2, children £1 • Other information: Beach for swimming ◑ ⬗ WC

This unique garden, set on a steep cliff face with fine sea views, has been developed with great determination and ingenuity by the present owners. The narrow interlocking paths and archways reveal hidden areas and intimate seats on many different levels which maximise the feeling of space. Despite the salt spray and gales, a fine collection of temperate, alpine, antipodean and sub-tropical plants with a sheltered aspect gives a colourful display, especially in summer. A path lined with trees and a steep flight of steps lead to a small sandy beach. This is a garden of tremendous character, but definitely not for the disabled, and small children should be supervised.

Heligan ★★ [Historic Garden Grade II]

Pentewan, St Austell PL26 6EN. Tel (01726) 845100

The Lost Gardens of Heligan • 5½ m S of St Austell off A390. Take B3273 signed to Mevagissey past Pentewan • Open all year, daily except 24th, 25th Dec, 10am – 6pm (last admission 4.30pm in summer, 3.30pm in winter). Guided tours by arrangement • Entrance: £7.50, OAPs £7, children (5–18) £4, family £20 ○ ⬗ ✕ ▨ WC ♿ ♨ ⊞ ⚱ ⚲

Started in the late eighteenth century but neglected since 1914, the renaissance of this large garden is, rightly, a well-known story. The restored productive gardens to the north of the house, a superb demonstration of horticultural archaeology (the pineapple pits are particularly fascinating), are surrounded by Victorian pleasure grounds laid out as a series of secluded enclosures with fountains and a sundial. Massive, mainly red rhododendrons enclose the large lawn; some were collected by Sir Joseph Hooker and show signs of their age. The Jungle, some ten minutes walk away, is a wild, beautiful valley, now largely cleared, where rhododendrons, bamboos, tree ferns and Chusan palms flourish. Further on, magical woodland walks can be taken in the Lost Valley. The Steward's House has a well-planted young garden with magnolias, and beyond that a pioneering wildlife conservation project is being developed.

Ince Castle

Saltash PL12 4QZ. Tel: (01752) 842672

The Viscount and Viscountess Boyd of Merton • 3m SW of Saltash off A38 at Stoketon Cross. Turn at sign for Trematon and then for Elmgate • Open 14th March, 18th April, 16th May, all 2 – 5pm, and for parties by appt • Entrance: £2.50, children under 14 free • Other information: Due to very narrow lanes, no large coaches. Picnics in car park only ● ● WC & ⇪ ℃

Five acres of formal and informal gardens are knit together here by strong design and the personalities of its two generations of creators. The formal areas and lawns, enhanced by statues and planted with summer flowers, are set round the castle, with dramatic views over the Lynher River and a background of mature trees. Daffodils and other bulbs create colour early in the year, while the woodland areas, with paths and an elliptical open space, contain camellias, rhododendrons, azaleas and other fine shrubs. The summerhouse is decorated internally with shells collected during the 1960s. The castle itself is romantic and stands at the end of a very long lane.

Ken Caro

Bicton, Liskeard PL14 5RF. Tel: (01579) 362446

Mr and Mrs K.R. Willcock • 5m NE of Liskeard. Turn off A390 at Butcher's Arms, St Ive, take Pensilva road to next crossroads, then road signed to Bicton • Open 28th March to Sept, daily except Sat, 10am – 6pm • Entrance: £3, children £1 ● WC & ℘

These four acres are planted in two sections. One consists of a series of small enclosed areas interconnected by well-kept paths, and contains shrubs, conifers, rhododendrons and flowers, all labelled. Some rare shrub specimens include *Eucryphia* x *nymansensis* and *Lomatia ferruginea*. In contrast to the enclosed area, the second part is open to pleasing views of the surrounding landscape. Beds with a fine collection of hemerocallis are well kept, and there is a large fish pond; a further large lily pond is flanked by island beds. A good visit for plantsmen and gardeners alike.

Ladock House

Ladock, Nr Truro TR2 4PL. Tel: (01726) 882274

Mr G.J. and Lady Mary Holborow • 7m E of Truro on B3275. Entrance by church • Open 16th April, 1st May, 2 – 5pm, and for parties by appt • Entrance: £2.50, children free 🍵 ⬛ **WC** 👤 ⬦ ℃

The Georgian rectory is set in six and a half acres of garden and woodland, all reclaimed and planted during the past quarter century. Spacious lawns are embellished with shrubs and flower beds, and a spring garden has clearings in wooded areas planted with rhododendrons, azaleas and camellias. On the other side of a park-like field are drifts of bluebells and another shrub garden.

Lamorran House ★

Upper Castle Road, St Mawes TR2 5BZ. Tel: (01326) 270800

Mr and Mrs R. Dudley-Cooke • Above St Mawes turn right at garage. Signposted at castle. Continue for $\frac{1}{2}$ m, and house is on left set behind line of pine trees • Open April to Sept, Wed, Fri and first Sat of each month, 10.30am – 5pm, and at other times by appt • Entrance: £4, children free • Other information: Coaches by prior appt only ◑ **WC** 👤

This four-acre garden on a south-facing slope above the sea enjoys a most favoured microclimate that supports wonderful collections of plants from the southern hemisphere, sub-tropical plants flourishing in the lower sections of the garden, temperate plants higher up. The latter include rhododendrons, evergreen azaleas and camellias. The garden has a fine collection of palms (over 30 varieties) and tree ferns, including varieties of cyathea. Paths in an intricate pattern zigzag down the steep hillside between enclosed compartments, some designed in Japanese or Italian style, and all with fine views over the sea to St Anthony's Head. There are many imaginative neo-classical statues and columns, and streams and pools permeate the whole slope. The planting is so dense and comprehensive that the paths, though there is often little space between them, are well screened from each other and so appear to magnify the total area. The immaculate upkeep of the garden enhances the overall effect. Nearby, in the grounds of *St Mawes Castle*, is another sub-tropical garden, with good views.

Lanhydrock ★ [Historic Garden Grade II*]

Bodmin PL30 5AD. Tel: (01208) 265950

The National Trust • $2\frac{1}{2}$ m SE of Bodmin off A38 and A30, or off B3268 • House open 27th March to Oct, Tues – Sun and Bank Holiday Mons, 11am – 5.30pm (closes 5pm Oct) • Garden open daily, 10am – 6pm (5pm in Oct) • Entrance: garden and grounds £3.90, children £1.95; (house, garden and grounds £7.20, children £3.60, family £18, pre-booked parties of 15 or more £6.10 per adult, £3.05 per child) (2003 prices) • Other information: Parking 600 metres from garden but disabled may park adjacent to garden ○ 🍵 ✕ ⬛ **WC** 👤 ⬦ 🛍 🍴 ℃

Although the collection of trees was started as early as 1634, the bones of this superb 30-acre garden, in a dramatic woodland and parkland setting, were put in place in 1857 by the first Baron Robartes. The architect of his choice was George Gilbert Scott, who had been brought in to restore and extend the seventeenth-century house, and to redesign the garden. The formal gardens remain largely as he conceived them. Behind the original seventeenth-century gatehouse is a formal lawn with 29 topiary yews in the shape of truncated cones and with rose beds in between, and, beside the house, a Victorian parterre flanked by six similar yews has spring and summer bedding plants. The herbaceous circle is planted for both spring and autumn. A shady stream fringed by water-loving plants runs off the hill behind the house. The Higher Garden is planted with large groups of 'Cornish Red' and other rhododendrons, many camellias, azaleas, magnolias and *Viburnum plicatum*. The hillside woods have fine walks beneath mature trees underplanted with large-leaved rhododendrons and bluebells, although for some visitors the heavily gravelled paths introduce a some-what artificial note.

Marsh Villa Gardens

Marsh Villa, St Andrew's Road, Par PL24 2LU. Tel: (01726) 815920

Mrs Judith Stephens •5m E of St Austell. Leave A390 at St Blazey traffic lights, then take first left; garden is 700 metres on left • Open April to Oct, Sun – Wed, 11am – 6pm • Entrance: £2.50, children free ◑ 🍵 🍴 WC ♿ ⚜ ⚘

This magical garden has been created in only fifteen years from a poorly drained meadow. Though it is worth visiting at any time, the herbaceous plantings ensure that it is at its best in summer. A long sinuous lawn, sometimes divided in the centre by flower and shrub beds into a number of paths, leads to a wild garden beyond, which is part of the unreclaimed marsh; here native iris thrive beneath willow and alder. A stream lies on one side, and a series of compartments, each one revealing the next, on the other. The semi-formal lawn is bordered by a cypress hedge and tall shrubs; on its far side are more beds, partially surrounding an enclosed pond. Beyond is a transverse avenue, and finally a rectangular herbaceous garden enclosed by escallonia hedges.

Morrab Subtropical Garden [Historic Garden Grade II]

Penzance. Tel: (01736) 336621 (Environmental Services Manager)

Penwith District Council • In centre of Penzance. Entrances in St Mary's Terrace, Morrab Road and Coulson's Place • Open all year, daily, dawn – dusk • Entrance: free ○ 🍴 ♿ ⚜ ⚘

This garden, though only of three acres and in the centre of Penzance, is genuinely sub-tropical and successfully creates its own atmosphere. It is beautifully maintained and planted with, *inter alia*, tree ferns, cabbage palms, myrtles, drimys, camellias and magnolias. It contains a fine bandstand, two ponds and a fountain.

Mount Edgcumbe House and
Country Park ★ [Historic Garden Grade I]

Cremyll, Torpoint PL10 1HZ. Tel: (01752) 822236

Cornwall County Council and Plymouth City Council • Access from Plymouth by Cremyll ferry (pedestrian) to park entrance or Torpoint ferry (vehicle) via A374 and B3247. Access from Cornwall via A38 to Trerulefoot roundabout then A374 and B3247 • House open as Earl's Garden • Park and formal gardens open all year, daily, 8am – dusk. Earl's Garden open April to Sept, Sun – Thurs, 11am – 4.30pm • Entrance: Park and formal gardens free. Earl's Garden and house £4.50, concessions £3.50, children £2.25, family £10, season ticket £7.50, groups £3.50 per person • Other information: Coaches must pre-book. World War II exhibition in house ○ 🍽 ✕ 🗑 **WC** ♿ ⬥ 🌳 🏛 ♨ ⚓

The gardens and Grade-I landscaped park created by the Edgecumbe family in the eighteenth century were praised by William Kent and Humphry Repton. There are three main areas of interest. Surrounding the house is the Victorian Earl's Garden, with a fine formal east lawn containing flower beds, statues and urns, and with superb views down the wide hardwood avenue to the formal gardens below. In the landscaped woodland above and beside the house a National Collection of camellias, currently semi-mature, is developing attractively. The entrance to the formal gardens, best reached from below, has a fine view of the house. With a background of holm oaks and other mature trees, they include a formal Italian garden with orange trees, less formal English and French gardens, and two commemorating the Edgecumbe family's connection with America and New Zealand. In the centre of these is the 2002 Jubilee Garden. Rhododendrons and azaleas make late spring an attractive time to visit, and a rose garden gives summer interest.

The Old Mill Herbary

Helland Bridge, Bodmin PL30 4QR. Tel: (01208) 841206

Brenda and Robert Whurr • 1m N of Bodmin between A30 and B3266 • Open May to Oct, Thurs – Tues, and 29th Aug for NGS, 2 – 5pm • Entrance: £3.50, Children £1.75 • Other information: Coaches by arrangement ○ 🗑 **WC** 🌳

The five-acre garden on the banks of the gently flowing River Camel, with its fourteenth-century bridge, is an oasis of tranquillity and has intriguing and original features. An open meadow between the river and an old mill-race is planted with individual and interesting specimen trees, while three sizeable islands support mature woodland trees, some 500 years old. The semi-wild garden on the slope above the mill-leat consists of horizontal paths and borders with many rare herbs and other plants. Here and around the buildings, the statuary, based on an unabashed Mediterranean fertility theme, is another unusual feature. A camomile lawn gives off an impressive scent.

Pencarrow ★ [Historic Garden Grade II*]

Washaway, Bodmin PL30 3AG. Tel: (01208) 841369

*The Molesworth-St Aubyn family • 4m NW of Bodmin. Signed from A389
Bodmin – Wadebridge road and B3266 at Washaway • House open 28th March
to 28th Oct, Sun – Thurs, 11am – 4pm • Garden open March to Oct, daily,
9am – 6pm • Entrance: £3.50, children free (house and garden £7, children
£3.50, parties of 20 – 30 £6 per person, parties of 31 and over £5 per person) •
Other information: Craft gallery* ◐ 👜 ✕ 🍽 <u>WC</u> ♿ ⬦ 🌿 ♨ 🌸 ☞

The magnificent Palladian mansion lies at the end of an impressive one-mile
drive, planted with flowering shrubs, conifers and hardwoods. The setting is
superb, with formal gardens on two sides, a rock garden above, and wide and
beautiful lawns in front of mature trees; these include an open beech grove.
The trees are underplanted with shrubs, including azaleas and huge mounds of
'Cornish Red' and other rhododendrons. There is a fine view over the formal
garden with its circular lawn from the main façade of the house. The park and
woodland, which extends to 50 acres, contain many rhododendrons and
camellias, and a woodland walk leads to a lake covered with water lilies.

Penjerrick [Historic Garden Grade II]

Budock, Falmouth TR11 5ED. Tel: (01872) 870105

*Mrs R. Morin • 3m SW of Falmouth between Budock and Mawnan Smith.
Entrance opposite Penmorvah Manor Hotel • Open March to Sept, Wed, Fri and
Sun, 1.30 – 4.30pm • Entrance: £2.50, children £1 • Other information:
Parking for one coach only, at gate. Plants for sale on charity days only* ◐ ⬦

Set in parkland created by the Fox family in the late eighteenth century, the
principal interest lies in the 10-acre garden situated above the road, where
large sloping lawns are planted with camellias, tree ferns, bamboos, rare trees
and, above all, rhododendrons. Although famous as the home of the rhododendron hybrids 'Penjerrick' and 'Barclayi', the Loderi cultivars are also
outstanding, as are *R. falconeri* and *R. augustinii* and several fragrant species. In
the valley, a wooden bridge leads to ponds and a waterfall. At the height of the
season, it is a magical place. Wellies are advised.

Penwarne

Mawnan Smith, Falmouth TR11 5PH. Tel: (01326) 250585/250325

*Mr and Mrs H. Beister • 3¼ m SW of Falmouth and 1¼ m N of Mawnan
Smith off Falmouth – Mawnan Smith road • Open one or two days for charity,
and by appt – write or telephone for details • Entrance: £1.50, children 50p •
Other information: Coaches by prior arrangement only* ◕ <u>WC</u> ♿ ⬦ ☞

The 12-acre garden, at its best in spring, has been restored since 1982 by the
present owners, who have skilfully interwoven mature plantings and younger,
or exciting new, schemes. Plantations of azaleas mark the approach to the fine
1726 house, and around it and below the lawn are large mounds of 'Cornish
Red' and other rhododendrons. The lawn and the adjacent dell – which boasts

a deep pond and a walled garden – have some fine old hardwoods, including a copper beech, mature rhododendrons (an enormous R. *luteum*), camellias and tree ferns, together with more recently planted shrubs. Beside and above the main gardens are other younger shrub plantings.

Pine Lodge Garden and Nursery ★

Cuddra, Holmbush, St Austell PL25 3RQ. Tel: (01726) 73500

Mr and Mrs R. Clemo • Just E of St Austell off A390 between Holmbush and turning for Tregrehan. Signposted • Open March to Oct, 10am – 6pm. Guided tours for parties of 20 or more by appt all year • Entrance: £4.50, children £2.50 ◑ 💺 ✕ WC 🔲 ❤ 🐾 ♿

Assembled in this immaculately maintained 30-acre garden is a wide-ranging collection of over 6000 different plants, all of them labelled. In the formal gardens, many less familiar shrubs from around the world complement the magnolias, camellias, rhododendrons and azaleas surrounding the perfect lawns, adding to the year-round interest. There are statues, too, and several ponds, including separate ones for koi carp, newts and frogs. Beyond is a tightly planted arboretum with tidily mown grass, flanked on one side by a four-acre pinetum with its collection of 80 different conifers and on the other by parkland leading down to the lake, where an island is home to black swans and many waterfowl. A Japanese garden has recently been added and a bell tower sited in a wildflower meadow. The National Collection of grevilleas is held here, and plants for sale in the nursery include some raised from seed collected on annual plant-hunting expeditions.

Polgwynne

Feock, Truro TR3 6SG. Tel: (01872) 862612

Mrs P. Davey • 5m S of Truro. Take A39, then B3289 to first crossroads. Continue on past garage on right following signs to Feock. At T-junction turn left down steep hill; garden is at bottom on right • Open 25th April, 30th May, 27th June, 2 – 5pm, and by appt all year • Entrance: £2.50 for charity, children free • Other information: Refreshments and plants for sale on open days only ◑ 💺 WC ❤ 🐦 🐾 ☕

Though comparatively small, this garden is superb in every respect: the layout, the rare and interesting plants growing in benign conditions, and the immaculate but not over-tidy upkeep, the whole pervaded by the personalities of the owner and her late husband, who created it over the last 40 years. The principal garden, four acres in extent, slopes sharply down towards the sea and is protected by an 2.5-metre wall. Within is a croquet lawn and less formal lawns featuring a stream and ponds, all surrounded by shady walks and borders. The upper part of the protective wall and some of the plants, including what may be the oldest female gingko in the country and a superb wisteria, predate the present ownership. Beside the walled garden is a similar area consisting of a formal garden and, below, a Victorian stepped wall and kitchen garden, surrounded by a grass bank with primroses.

Porthpean House

Porthpean, St Austell PL26 6AX. Tel: (01726) 72888

Mr and Mrs C. Petherick • 1½ m S of St Austell. Take A390 and then road signed to Porthpean. Pass Mount Edgcumbe Hospice and turn left down Porthpean Beach Road; house is white building at bottom of hill just before car park • Open by appt only, 2 – 5pm (coach parties welcome) • Entrance: £2, children free • Other information: Teas for parties only ● 🍴 WC ⅙ ⊲⊳ ⌿ ⌀

The three-acre garden was first developed by Maurice Petherick some forty years ago. It contains a special collection of camellias, also many azaleas and rhododendrons. The grounds have access to the beach and from the main lawn there is a magnificent view of St Austell Bay; on spring days cherry blossoms stand out sharply against the blue of the sea. There is also a nursery garden with Victorian greenhouses.

St Martin's Manor

St Martin-by-Looe, Looe PL13 1NX. Tel: 01503 262825

Dr Kenneth Olson • 1m NW of Looe off B3253 Plymouth road. Go down small lane almost opposite Looe Garden Centre to St Martin's Church; garden is adjacent • Open by appt only • Entrance: £2.50, children (over 6) £1 ● WC ⅙ ⊲⊳ ⌿

The garden is that rarity, a plantsman's delight that is also beautifully designed and planted, reflecting the creativity of its owner. Its four acres are on a hillside and surround a Georgian rectory. Much of the lower garden, including the pond, is visually enclosed, while the upper part has views of the country-side. The borders are closely planted with rare shrubs and perennials, and ferns and many tender plants are concentrated round the pound. Attractive all through the year, the garden is at its peak from mid-June to August.

St Michael's Mount ★ [Historic Garden Grade II]

Marazion, Penzance TR17 0EF. Tel: (01736) 710507

The National Trust • ½ m from shore at Marazion, ½ m S of A394. Access by ferry or across causeway • Castle open April to Oct, Mon – Fri, 10.30am – 5.30pm (last admission 4.45pm), and most weekends from June to Sept for charity, when NT members are asked to pay for admission. Nov to March, essential to telephone for opening arrangements in advance • Garden open April and May, plus weekends as above • Entrance: April and May gardens only £2.50, castle £4.80, family £13, pre-booked parties of 20 or more £4.40 per person) • Other information: Parking in Marazion ◑ 🍽 ✕ WC ⌿ 🏛

It is the private eighteenth-century walled garden belonging to the St Aubyn family that is important here. Rising in terraces from just above sea level at the south-eastern corner of the castle to the foot of its southern wall, such is the microclimate that, despite constant exposure to salt spray and gales, many tender and exotic sub-tropical plans thrive. Escallonia hedges provide some shelter, and much of the planting is amongst granite boulders. The private garden, laid out on several terraces near the top, is approached along an informal avenue of kniphofia across rough grass. Both here and above are groups of striking plants: *Agave americanum*, aeoniums, succulents, *Euphorbia mellifera* and yuccas. The view down from the higher terraces and the castle walls is outstanding, but the climb is steep and rough; sensible shoes are advised.

Trebah ★★ [Historic Garden Grade II]

Mawnan Smith, Falmouth TR11 5JZ. Tel: (01326) 250448

Major and Mrs J.A. Hibbert (Trebah Garden Trust) • 4m SW of Falmouth. Signed from A39/A394 junction at Treliever Cross roundabout, 500 metres W of Glendurgan Garden • Open all year, daily, 10.30am – 5pm • Entrance: £5, OAPs £4.50, disabled and children (5–15) £3, RHS members and children under 5 free, NT members free Nov to Feb (reduced rates Nov to Feb) • Possible for wheelchairs but paths steep in places • Other information: New visitor centre. Powered wheelchairs available ○ 💷 ✕ <u>WC</u> & ⏩ ⁂ 🏠 ⚲ ℀

The most remarkable feature of Trebah is the spectacular view over the massive clumps of rhododendrons, tree ferns and bamboos and into the ravine, which runs between tall trees down to the Helford River. The garden is about 25 acres in all and contains many interesting and beautiful mature trees and shrubs. An extensive collection of colourful sub-tropical Mediterranean plants, a stream and some carp ponds occupy the upper reaches, while in the lower parts is a lake, a vast plantation of gunnera, and acres of blue and white hydrangeas giving summer colour. Superbly maintained throughout, but in no way over-manicured.

Tregrehan ★ [Historic Garden Grade II*]

Par PL24 2SJ. Tel: (01726) 814389

The Carlyon Estate/Mr T. Hudson • 2m E of St Austell, on A390 Lostwithiel – St Austell road. Entrance opposite Britannia Inn 1m W of St Blazey • Open mid-March to mid-June, Wed – Sun and Bank Holiday Mons, 10.30am – 5pm (closed 11th April); mid-June to Aug, Wed, 2 – 5pm • Entrance: £3.50, children free. Guided tours for groups by prior arrangement ◐ 💷 <u>WC</u> & ⁂

Woodlands occupy most of the 20 acres here, planted with interesting conifers, hardwoods and many fine rhododendrons and camellias, and underplanted with a variety of shade-lovers; the bluebell walk is beautiful in spring. There are lovely views of the valley with its young plantings from South America and New Zealand. The nineteenth-century walled garden is the central focus, with a magnificent Victorian glasshouse range, an arch of *Acer palmatum* and a variety of flourishing climbers, many of them summer-flowering.

Trelissick ★ [Historic Garden Grade II*]

Feock, Truro TR3 6QL. Tel: (01872) 862090

The National Trust • 4m S of Truro on B3289 above west end of King Harry Ferry • Open 14th Feb to Oct, daily, 10.30am – 5.30pm (or dusk if earlier); telephone for winter opening times • Entrance: £4.60, children £2.30, family £11.50, pre-booked parties £3.90 per person. Parking charge £2 (refundable) • Other information: Wheelchairs and batricar available. Theatrical events during season plus autumn and winter events programme ◑ ♨ ✕ 🏕 **WC** ♿ ⟁ 🐾 ♨ 🍴

Trelissick ranks among the most beautiful of Cornish spring gardens, and also has many summer-flowering shrubs. It covers 27 acres, set in the middle of 500 acres of park and farm land, and offers panoramic views down Carrick Roads to the open sea. It is young compared to many similar gardens, and the plantings and layout date only from 1937. It has fine open lawns, particularly in the area known as the Carcaddon, and is known both for its collection of camellias, magnolias and rhododendrons in the spring, and for its large collection of hydrangeas and other tender and exotic plants. The woodland walks, surrounded by shrubs, have attractive views across the water below.

Trengwainton Garden ★ [Historic Garden Grade II*]

Penzance TR20 8RZ. Tel: (01637) 875404

The National Trust • 2m NW of Penzance on B3312, ½ m N of A3071 • Open 16th Feb to 2nd Nov, Sun – Thurs (but open Good Friday), 10am – 5.30pm (closes 5pm Feb, March, Oct) • Entrance: £3.90, family £9.75, pre-booked parties £3.20 per person • Other information: Teas at Trengwainton Farm, weather permitting ◑ 🏕 **WC** 🐾 ♨ 🛒

Trengwainton, the 'House of the Spring', was acquired by the Bolitho family in 1867. It will appeal to both the plantsman and the ordinary gardener for its magnificent collections of magnolias, rhododendrons and camellias and its series of walled gardens containing many tender and exotic shrubs and plants that would not survive in less mild areas of England. The stream garden alongside the drive, backed by a beech wood, provides masses of colour from candelabra primulas, lilies, lysichitums and other bog plants. Many of the rhododendrons were raised from seed collected by Kingdon Ward's expedition to north-eastern Assam and the Mishmi Hills of Burma. New Zealand tree ferns, pittosporums from China, Japanese maples, embothriums, olearias, acacias, eucryphias, and Chatham Island forget-me-nots are just a few of the beautiful plants to be seen during the spring and summer. The woodland walk also now features an ornamental pond. There are magnificent views of the hills leading down to the sea and St Michael's Mount.

Tresco Abbey ★★ [Historic Garden Grade I]

Tresco, Isles of Scilly TR24 0QQ.
Tel: (01720) 424105 (Garden Curator: Mike Nelhams)

Mr R.A. Dorrien-Smith • On island of Tresco. Travel by helicopter from Penzance heliport to Tresco heliport (reservations (01736) 363871 and (01720) 422970) or from St Mary's by launch • Open all year, daily, 10am – 4pm • Entrance: £8.50, children free, weekly tickets (7 days) £15 • Other information: Possible for wheelchairs but some paths very steep. Wheelchairs available at gate ○ ♨ 🏕 **WC** 🐾 ♨ 🛒 🍴 ✂

Tresco, located in the Scilly Isles 28 miles off Land's End and in the full Gulf Stream, is a unique sub-tropical garden of the very highest quality. A formal framework of paths, steps, the ruined walls of the old Abbey and high hedges is filled with a lush profusion of flourishing exotic plants that soften the outlines and provide striking colour and contrasting shapes and textures. Set on a south-sloping hillside with horizontal walks, the gardens are visually quite self-contained. From the top terrace views slant downwards to the sea, revealing the wonderful plantings below, especially those in the more open areas such as the pond, where four Mediterranean cypresses form strong verticals. Myrtles, and notably various metrosideros, are set amongst the background trees. Aeoniums, cacti, puyas, huge agaves (some with leaves 18 inches wide) and proteas stand out, and callistemons, banksias, agapanthus and *Geranium maderenese* play a major part. Just five gardeners plus some student help maintain the 17 acres. The gardens are probably at their peak from March to the autumn, and at their most colourful from late April to the end of June.

Trevarno Estate and Gardens and The National Museum of Gardening ★

Trevarno Manor, Helston TR13 0RU. Tel: (01326) 574274

Mr M. Sagin and Mr N. Helsby • 3m NW of Helston off A394 or B3302 • Open all year, daily except 25th, 26th Dec, 10.30am – 5pm • Entrance: £3.75, concessions £3.25, children 5 – 14 £1.50, under 5 free (house and garden £4.75, concessions £4.20, children (5 – 14) £1.75, under 5 free) (2003 prices)
○ ☕ ✕ 🍴 WC & ⚐ 🌿 🏪 🕯 ⚒

Great and continuing restoration has taken place on the estate and in the gardens, which combine formal and less formal elements. The lawn, with a splendid avenue of Japanese cherries to one side, leads to the formal Italian garden; from here a woodland walk descends to the lake, which sports a Victorian boathouse and a cascade at its top end and a fine rhododendron rockery beyond. Above this is the pinetum underplanted with shrubs, and the Georgian walled gardens and glasshouses. With rhododendrons, Japanese cherries, camellias and bluebells in the woodlands, it is probably at its best in the spring. The National Museum of Gardening is located near the entrance, and there are interesting craft workshops nearby.

Trewidden ★

Chyandour, Penzance TR18 3LW. Tel: (01736) 363021

Bolitho Estates • 2m E of Penzance on A30 • Open 18th Feb to 6th June, Wed – Sun, 10.30am – 4.30pm • Entrance: £3.50, under 16 free NEW ● ☕ 🍴 WC & ⚐ 🌿

Until 2002 this wonderful sub-tropical spring garden, created by the Bolitho family in the nineteenth century, was only rarely open to the public; now, after recent restoration after storm damage and pruning of over-mature camellias, it is essential visiting for serious gardeners. It covers 12 acres, including the separate South Garden, and consists mostly of informal woodland paths, some leading to an attractive pond with a Japanese lantern and a whale-tail sculpture. Although chiefly renowned for its camellias, of which there are over 300 varieties from India, China and other parts of the Far East, equally fine are the early-flowering magnolias, which shine forth above the other shrubs throughout. These include huge specimens of *M.* x *veitchii* 'Peter Veitch' and *M. hypoleuca (obovata)*, as well as outstanding examples of *M.* 'Trewidden Belle', *M. sargentiana* and varieties of *M. campbellii*. There is also a magnificent stand of tree ferns set in the remains of an early opencast tin mine.

Trewithen ★★ [Historic Garden Grade II*]

Grampound Road, Truro TR2 4DD. Tel: (01726) 883647

Mr and Mrs A.M.J. Galsworthy • On A390 between Truro and St Austell • House open April to July, Mon, Tues, 2 – 4pm • Gardens open March to Sept, Mon – Sat, 10am – 4.30pm (also Suns in April and May) • Entrance: £4.25, OAPs £4, children under 15 free, parties of 20 or more £4 per person (house and garden £6) ◑ 🐷 🖼 WC ♿ ⟨⟩ ℘ B&B

Trewithen is one of the greatest of all Cornish and British gardens. It covers 30 acres, mainly of woodland, and is known internationally for its great collections of magnolias, camellias and rhododendrons, and for many other rare trees and shrubs. The most magnificent feature is the long lawn in front of the 1730s' house, flanked by sinuous borders of mature rhododendrons, magnolias, acers and other shrubs and ornamental trees, and backed by mature hardwoods. To the west the shrub beds and paths are sheltered by beeches and other woodland trees. A deep sunken garden contains acers, camellias and tree ferns. The walled garden, contemporary with the house, is laid out as a herb and rose garden with herbaceous borders; it has a fish pond, an old summerhouse and a fine wisteria-clad pergola. Many hybrid rhododendrons and camellias originated here, some of them named by George Johnstone, the garden's creator, for members of his family, and the inspiration for Tom Leaper's new Magnolia Fountain derived from the great specimens to be found here.

Trewoofe House

Lamorna, Penzance TR19 6PA. Tel: (01736) 810269

Mr and Mrs H.M. Pigott • 6m SW of Penzance. Take B3315 from Penzance via Newlyn towards Lamorna. At top of hill take sharp right turn signed to Trewoofe • Open May, Wed, 2 – 5pm; June, Wed, Sun, 2 – 5pm, and May to Sept by appt; • Entrance: £2, children under 16 free • Coaches and groups by appt ◕ WC ♿ ℘

This two-acre garden, situated at the head of the Lamorna valley, is planted informally with shrub and herbaceous beds that give colour all year round. An ancient mill leat runs through it, enabling a bog garden to be developed with a wide range of moisture-loving plants, including many iris species and varieties. The garden is on two levels, linked by two bridges over the leat and using local granite. There is a small fruit garden with cordon- and espalier-trained trees, and a conservatory with semi-tender climbers.

CUMBRIA &
THE ISLE OF MAN

Two-starred gardens are marked on the map with a black square.

Acorn Bank Garden and Watermill

Temple Sowerby, Penrith CA10 1SP. Tel: (01768) 361893

The National Trust • *6m E of Penrith off A66 N of Temple Sowerby* • *Open March to Oct, daily except Tues, 10am – 5pm* • *Entrance: £3, children £1.30, family £6.80, pre-booked parties £2 per person* ◑ ☕ ✕ 🖼 <u>WC</u> ♿ ⬦ 🐕 🏛 ❦

The 'acorn bank' is the ancient oakwood sloping down to the Crowdundle Beck behind the house. In spring it is a carpet of daffodils and narcissi in many varieties planted profusely in the 1930s, and there are some 60,000 Lenten lilies. The walled gardens are then also a mass of blossom from the old varieties of apple, medlar, pear and quince, carpeted with wild tulips, anemones and narcissi. The orchard trees include later-blossoming apple varieties. Along the three sheltering walls are herbaceous and shrub borders, backed by good clematis and other climbers. A bed of species roses flanks the steps to a picturesque sunken garden, with a pond and alpine terraces. Through a gateway lies a splendid walled herb garden – a well-tended collection of some 250 medicinal and culinary herbs, now being redesigned and replanted. For those interested in alpines, it is worth taking the A686 over the spectacular Hartside fell to *Hartside Nursery Garden* about 14m away near Alston. [Open March to Oct, daily, 9.30am – 4.30pm (12.30 – 4pm weekends and Bank Holiday Mondays) and otherwise by appointment – telephone (01434) 381372.]

Ballalheannagh ★

Glen Roy, Lonan, Isle of Man IM4 7QB. Tel: (01624) 861875

Mrs Maureen Dadd • *On E of island in Glen Roy, 2m inland from Laxey* • *Open mid-March to mid-Oct, Sat, Sun, 10am – 4.30pm, Mon, Tues, Thurs, 1 – 5pm, Fri, 2 – 5pm (advisable to check in advance), and at other times by appt* • *Entrance: £2.50, children free* ○ ❦

Take a steep-sided valley, a ladder, some seedlings of exotic rhododendrons and forget all about digging pits to accommodate the roots. Just stick them into crevices among the mosses and ferns and wait a few years, never giving up. Outcome – paradise for plant-lovers. You expect to find a garden like Ballalheannagh in Cornwall or Kerry – but this is the middle of the Isle of Man. No visitor with an interest in gardening who is marooned on the island need fear boredom, for this is a botanical garden, not in name, but surely in content. Steep winding paths cling to the valley sides, and crystal water cascades below, carrying the bells of pieris to the Irish Sea. The lower portion contains lofty rhododendrons, while the upper parts of the valley have newer plantings that will certainly delight in years to come. Here are eucalyptus, drimys, epacris, epigaea, megacarpaea and betula (species with evocative names like *Betula tatewakiana*), and a host of others too, and the native mosses and ferns are a wonderful sight. The garden has been extended to more than 20 acres, with four miles of gravel walks and new oriental features, plus a millennium window.

Brantwood

Coniston LA21 8AD. Tel: (01539) 441396

Brantwood Trust • On E side of Coniston Water off B5285, signposted. Coniston Launch provides hourly service to Brantwood and other points around lake. Steam yacht 'Gondola' sails regularly from Coniston Pier • House open • Garden open 15th March to 11th Nov, daily, 11am – 5.30pm; winter season Wed – Sun, 11am – 4.30pm, but closed 25th and 26th Dec • Entrance: £3 (house and garden £4.75, students £3.50, children under 16 £1) (2003 prices) ◐ ☕ ✕ ▓ WC ⬠ ⚘ ♿ ⚱ ☂ ⚲

A superb site with wonderful views, atmosphere and history. The rocky hillside behind the house is threaded with a wandering network of paths created by John Ruskin to delight the eye and please the mind. A succession of eight small, individual gardens threads the landscape, exploring the many themes that fascinated the artist and visionary social reformer. This 'living laboratory' of ideas is being revived by Sally Beamish and her small team. Ruskin's own Professor's Garden, the woodland pond and harbour walk are maturing beautifully. An extensive collection of British native ferns surrounds an ice-house and several waterfalls. There is a British herb garden, and the allegorical Zig-zaggy depicting the levels of Purgatory found in Dante's *Divine Comedy* is now complete. The High Walk, actually a Victorian viewing platform, encourages contemplation of the magnificent Lakeland scenery beyond the garden.

Brockhole ★ [Historic Garden Grade II]

Lake District Visitor Centre, Windermere LA23 1LJ. Tel: (01539) 446601

Lake District National Park Authority • 1½ m N of Windermere on A591 • Grounds and gardens open all year, daily, 10am – dusk • Entrance: parking fee only; minibuses and coaches free if pre-booked • Other information: Centre open April to Nov, with slide theatre and exhibition. Cruises from jetty ○ ☕ ✕ ▓ WC ♿ ⬠ ⚘ ♿ ⚱ ⚲

A garden blessed with the Lakeland combination of western aspect and water to the hills beyond, in this case notably the Langdale Pikes. To frame this view Thomas Mawson worked closely (c.1900) with his architect colleague Dan Gibson. The ornamental terraces drop through old-fashioned rose beds, herbaceous borders and shrubbery to a wildflower meadow flanked by mature woodland. The original kitchen and herb garden has been restored; other special features are herbaceous plants, tender shrubs and rarities and the constantly changing colour from spring rhododendrons and azaleas through to late Chilean hollies, maples and eucryphias. In Troutbeck, between Windermere and Ambleside, is *High Cross Lodge*, a small fellside garden planted with rhododendrons, foliage and tender plants. Open several times for NGS and by appointment – write to Mr and Mrs Sydney Orchant, High Cross Lodge, Bridge Lane, Troutbeck LA23 1AA.

Copt Howe

Chapel Stile, Great Langdale, Ambleside LA22 9JR.
Tel: (01539) 437685 (Infoline)

Professor R.N. Haszeldine • 3m W of Ambleside on B5343 • Open 9th to 12th, 22nd to 24th April, 1st to 3rd, 29th to 31st May, 10th to 12th June, 11am – 5pm, for NGS and other charities; also many days mid-April to Sept (telephone for recorded weekly information). Private visits and parties by appt • Entrance: £2.50, children free ◐ 🐌 **WC** & ⬧ 🌿 ☭

This plantsman's fellside woodland two-acre garden, with magnificent views of the Langdale Pikes and interesting geological features, has an exceptionally wide range of rare acid-loving plants from many mountainous countries, including expedition plants from the Himalayas, China, Tibet, Japan, Bhutan, Tasmania, New Zealand and North and South America. The extensive collections includes acers, camellias, azaleas, quercus, fagus, large and dwarf conifers, pieris, kalmias, tilias, bamboos, cercis and cercidiphyllums; among herbaceous plants are many bulbous species with orchids and species lilies, *Tropaeolum tuberosum, T. tricolor* and *T. speciosum*. The varied plantings extend to alpine troughs, streams and woodland with mountain primulas, nomocharis, trilliums, hepaticas, hellebores, cardiocrinums, *Myosotidium hortensia* and many species of meconopsis, including *M. punicea*. Dramatic spring, early summer and autumn colours.

Dalemain Historic House and Gardens ★ [Historic Garden Grade II*]

Dalemain Estate Office, Dacre, Penrith CA11 0HB. Tel: (01768) 486450

Mr and Mrs R.B. Hasell-McCosh • On A592 3m W of Penrith on Ullswater road • House open 11am – 4pm • Garden open 28th March to 14th Oct, Sun – Thurs, 10.30am – 5pm • Entrance: £3.50, children free (house and garden £5.50, children (6–16) £3.50, family £14.50. Special prices for pre-booked parties) • Other information: Wheelchair and electric scooter available by prior arrangement. Dogs outside garden only, on lead ◐ 🍽 ✕ 🐌 <u>WC</u> & 🌿 🎁 ♿

Dalemain has evolved in the most natural way from a twelfth-century pele tower with its kitchen garden and herbs. The Tudor-walled knot garden is there, as are the Stuart terrace (1680s) and the walled orchard where apple trees like 'Nonsuch' and 'Keswick Codling', planted in 1728, still bear fruit. The gardens were re-established by the late Mrs Sylvia McCosh during the 1960s and '70s with shrubs, a collection of over 100 old-fashioned roses, and other rarities, together with richly planted herbaceous borders along the terraces and around the orchard; maintained and developed by her daughter-in-law, Mrs Jane Hasell-McCosh, they continue to improve. The wild garden on the lower ground features an outstanding display of Himalayan blue poppies in early summer and a walk past the Tudor gazebo into woods overlooking the Dacre Beck. Some thoughtful planting in the woodland augurs well for the future. A plantsman's garden with an artist's appreciation of form, texture and colour.

Graythwaite Hall ★

Ulverston, Graythwaite LA12 8BA. Tel: (01539) 531248

Graythwaite Estate • 4m N of Newby Bridge on W side of Lake Windermere • Open April to June, daily, 10am – 6pm • Entrance: £2, children free ◑ **WC** ◁◎

Essentially a spring garden landscaped by the late Victorian Thomas Mawson in partnership with Dan Gibson in a beautiful parkland and woodland setting. Azaleas and rhododendrons yield to cultivars of late spring-flowering shrubs, and there is a formal terraced rose garden. The finely wrought sundials and gate by Gibson, the Dutch garden and the stream and pond all add charm to this serene garden. For topiary admirers, Mawson employed interesting effects to contrast with his more billowy plantings. Notable are the battlemented yew hedge and some yew globes with golden yew in the top half and green in the bottom. While in Hawkshead, those interested in sculpture in nature should visit the *Grizedale Sculpture Trail*, organised by the Forestry Commission (Tel: (01229) 860373). The first piece was placed there over 20 years ago and there are now 80 sculptures.

Halecat

Witherslack, Grange-over-Sands LA11 6RU.
Tel: (01539) 552536 (Contact: Mrs K. Willard)

Mrs M. Stanley • 14m SW of Kendal, off A590. Signposted • Garden open all year, daily, 9am – 4.30pm (Sun opens 12.30pm) • Entrance: free • Other information: Plants, especially hydrangeas, for sale in adjoining nursery ○ ▧
WC ⅙ ◁◎ ⅌ ☖ ⅏

These two acres are the front garden of the mid-nineteenth-century house which stands at the head of a small valley with distant views of Arnside Knott and the Forest of Bowland. Mrs Stanley has created this pleasing, personal garden over the past fifty years as a series of terraces and squares, and the limestone quarried from the borders has been used to build the retaining walls and the perimeter wall separating the garden from the surrounding woodland. An azalea bed has been made on the bottom terrace by removing rock and filling the beds with peat from a nearby bog. The mixed borders are well maintained and filled with many shrubs, clematis, herbaceous plants, and shrub and climbing roses. There is also a wildflower meadow and a damson orchard. Look out for unusual wooden animals, especially the bear. The gazebo with stained glass quarries was designed by the architect Francis Johnson.

High Cleabarrow

Windermere LA23 3ND. Tel: (01539) 442808

Mr and Mrs R.T. Brown • 3m SE of Windermere off B5284 (opposite Windermere Golf Course) • Open for groups by appt only, April to Oct •

Entrance: £2.50, children under 12 free • *Other information: Teas by prior arrangement* ● 🍵 WC ♿ 🐾

A plantsperson's garden of approximately two acres, created by the owners and continually evolving. Set in a shallow bowl sloping gently down to a pond with waterside planting, it is sheltered at the rim by woodland; terraces and herbaceous borders have been created on the slope. The combination of shrubs, mixed borders, a rose garden, alpines, hostas and hellebores make it a garden for all seasons; azaleas, rhododendrons and hydrangeas create a magnificent display among the trees on the rocky outcrop. There are paths for exploring the terraces and borders and viewing the many interesting and unusual plants.

Holehird ★

Patterdale Road, Windermere LA23 1NP. Tel: (01539) 446008

Lakeland Horticultural Society • *1m N of Windermere on A592 Patterdale road* • *Open all year, daily, sunrise – sunset. Garden guides available April to Oct, 11am – 5pm* • *Entrance: by donation (minimum £2 appreciated)* • *Other information: Annual plant sale 1st May in local school* ○ WC ♿

Run by members of a society dedicated to promoting 'knowledge on the cultivation of plants, shrubs and trees, especially those suited to Lakeland conditions', this garden is maintained to an exceptionally high standard. It lies on a splendid hillside alongside the house with a natural water course and rock banks looking over Windermere to the Langdale Pikes. The Society has 10 acres of attractive gardens and trial areas. Much of the earlier planting has been preserved, including many fine specimen trees. Highlights are the summer-autumn heathers, winter-flowering shrubs, alpines and National Collections of astilbes, hydrangeas and polystichum ferns. The walled garden, now accessible for wheelchairs, has fine herbaceous borders, herbs and climbers. The site has expanded to encompass the lower Victorian terrace of the estate and includes original Victorian features. The views of the fells from the terrace are breathtaking, and there are many mature shrubs in this sheltered area. A new alpine house contains outstanding displays, and the Victorian greenhouses have been restored.

Holker Hall ★★ [Historic Garden Grade II]

Cark-in-Cartmel, Grange-over-Sands LA11 7PL. Tel: (01539) 558328

Lord and Lady Cavendish • *4½ m W of Grange-over-Sands, 4m S of Haverthwaite on B5278* • *Hall open* • *Garden open April to Oct, daily except Sat, 10am – 6pm (last admission 4.30pm)* • *Entrance: wide variety of entrance prices depending on visitor requirements – telephone or contact website for details.* • *Other information: Dogs on leads in grounds only. Holker Garden Festival 4th to 6th June* ◑ 🍵 ✕ 🍽 WC ♿ 🐾 ♨ 🌷 ✎

Set in 125 acres of parkland, the award-winning 25 acres of woodland walks and formal gardens at Holker (pronounced Hooker) have been constantly developed by the family ever since Lord George Cavendish established his 'con-

trived natural landscape' over 200 years ago. The woods now contain many
rare and beautiful specimens, most of them tagged and chronicled in the
excellent guide to the garden walks. The National Collection of styracaceae is
maintained here. Other features are the impressive cascade, evocative of the
Villa d'Este, and a beautifully contrived transformation of the croquet lawn
into summer gardens. This combination of formal beds and inventive planting
makes a wonderful Italianate-cum-English garden that typifies the spirit of the
place. There is also a sunken garden, which was formerly the rose garden and
contains many sub-tropical plants. Of particular note are the Elliptical Garden,
the rhododendron and azalea walk and the new labyrinth in the wildflower
meadow. Designed in part to link the formal gardens with the parkland and
wider landscape, it is based on a Hindu temple motif allied to a contemporary
version of a Cumbrian stone circle.

Holme Cragg

**Blea Cragg Bridge, Witherslack, Grange-over-Sands LA11 6RZ.
Tel: (01539) 552366**

*Mr J. Watson • 14m SW of Kendal, 3m N of Grange-over-Sands, off A590.
From A590, follow signs to Witherslack. Past telephone kiosk in Witherslack,
turn first left, first left again and follow signs to Newton (past Halecat) for
1¼ m over small bridge to third gate on left • Open all year, daily • Entrance: by
donation • Other information: Coaches must pre-book* ○ 🍴 **WC** ⚡ ↔ ↗ ♀

This is an amateur's and a plantsman's garden which has made magnificent use
of natural features of the site. Every rocky outcrop is clothed in alpines,
sedums, sempervivums and saxifrages. Azaleas and rhododendrons are an
important feature, as are the irises and candelabra primulas around the pond.
The shaded areas are filled with the blue of the Himalayan meconopsis, a grass
bank is covered with double and single Welsh poppies in colours ranging from
deep orange to pale yellow, and there is an interesting natural wildflower area.
Rhododendrons are followed by shrub roses; later the foliage of acers provides
colour interest.

Hutton-in-the-Forest [Historic Garden Grade II]

Penrith CA11 9TH. Tel: (01768) 484449

*Lord and Lady Inglewood • 6m NW of Penrith on B5305 (M6 junction 41) •
House open 9th to 18th April, then 2nd May to 3rd Oct, Thurs, Fri, Sun and
Bank Holiday Mons, 12.30 – 4pm • Garden open March to Oct, daily except
Sat, 11am – 5pm. Private parties by arrangement from April • Entrance: £2.50,
children free (house and garden £4.50, children (7–16) £2.50, family ticket
£12) • Other information: Electric scooter available for disabled (donation
requested). Light lunches and teas when house open, other meals on request*
◑ 🍵 🍴 **WC** ⚡ ↔ 🚻 ☘

This garden, a compelling setting for the appealing house, which ranges across
the centuries from a thirteenth-century pele tower to Salvin's handsome
addition, is itself a mixture of features from the seventeenth to the twentieth

centuries. It has great visual appeal, with a magnificent view from the seventeenth-century terraces now embellished with Victorian topiary. The beautiful walled garden, dating from the 1730s, is divided into compartments and has excellent herbaceous borders, trained fruit trees and roses. The backdrop of the house, the surrounding yew hedges and compartments and well-filled herbaceous borders combine to make a dramatic composition. Some of the mature woodland trees were planted in the early eighteenth century. Other features include a seventeenth-century dovecot and an eighteenth-century lake.

Levens Hall ★★ [Historic Garden Grade I]

Kendal LA8 0PD. Tel: (01539) 560321

Mr C.H. Bagot • 5m S of Kendal on A6 (M6 junction 36) • House open as garden, but 12 noon – 5pm • Garden open April to mid-Oct, Sun – Thurs, 10am – 5pm • Entrance: £5.50, children £2.50 (house and garden £7, children, £3.50). Party rates available (2003 prices) ◑ 💺 🗑 WC ⑆ 🌿 🎪 ℺

James II's gardener, Guillaume Beaumont, designed this famous topiary garden in 1694; it is one of very few to retain its original trees and design. The impeccably clipped yews and box hedges are set off by colourful spring and summer bedding and borders, and the primroses may be the start of a permanent collection. To celebrate the tercentenary of the garden in 1994 a new area, the Fountain Garden, was created with lime avenues meeting at the pool. Indeed there is much to see in addition to the topiary. Massive walls of beech hedge open to vistas over parkland. One avenue leads to the earliest English ha-ha. There is a picturesque herb garden behind the house. The record of only 10 head gardeners in 300 years, and the affectionate care by the Bagot family, account for the rare harmony of this exceptional garden, which clearly still has a stylish hand at the helm. Further developments include the installation of two pairs of clematis gates, a green-oak ticket booth disguised as a garden pavilion, and a pair of gates with hearts as handles – celebrating the old legend that a gambler acquired the property in the seventeenth century by turning over the ace of hearts.

Muncaster Castle ★ [Historic Garden Grade II*]

Ravenglass CA18 1RQ. Tel: (01229) 717614

Mr and Mrs Gordon-Duff-Pennington • 15m S of Whitehaven on A595 • Castle open 9th March to 2nd Nov, Sun – Fri, 12 noon – 5pm, or dusk if earlier • Gardens, owl centre and meadow vole maze open all year, daily, 10.30am – 6pm • Entrance: £5.70, children (5-16) £3.70 (under 5s free), family £17, parties of 12 or more £5, children £2.50 per person. Inclusive price for all attractions £7.80, children £5, family £21, parties of 12 or more £6.80, children £3.50 per person • Other information: Wheelchairs available for pre-booking ○ 💺 ✕ 🗑 WC ⑆ ⟜ 🎪 ℺ B&B

The castle is set against the splendid backdrop of Scafell and the hills, with a remarkable panoramic view from the terrace. The acid soil and the Gulf

Stream warmth provide ideal conditions for one of the finest collections of species rhododendrons in Europe, substantially from plant-hunting expeditions to Nepal in the 1920s (Kingdon Ward, Ludlow and Sheriff). There are excellent azaleas, camellias, magnolias, hydrangeas and maples, plus many unusual trees. The gardens are at their best in May and June but intensive new planting is ensuring constant pleasure for visitors in all seasons; extensive clearing and replanting continues and will take time to mature. The Sino-Himalayan Walk is now complete and maturing at an encouraging rate, and a new wild walk has been created, opening up the estate for visitors. The walk, which takes two and half hours and ends appropriately enough at the tea rooms, embraces a wide spectrum of sea, estuary and coastline views, revealing Ruskin's famous 'Gateway to Paradise', with glorious sights of the Fells.

Rydal Mount [Historic Garden Grade II]

Ambleside LA22 9LU. Tel: (01539) 433002

Rydal Mount Trust • 1m N of Ambleside on A591 • House open • Gardens open March to Oct, daily, 9.30am – 5pm; Nov to Feb, daily except Tues, 10am – 4pm • Entrance: £1.75 (house and garden £4, OAPs £3.25, students £3, children (5–15) £1.50, parties of 10 or more pre-booked £2.75 per person, non-booked £3.25 per person. Reciprocal discounts with Dove Cottage and Wordsworth's House) • Other information: Limited parking with awkward entry/exit ○ 🍴 WC ♿ ⤵ ⛪ ℀

The carefully maintained grounds of Wordsworth's house still follow the lines of his own plan, and it is easy to imagine the poet wandering along the upper terrace walk ('the sloping terrace') and down through winding, shaded paths to the lawns, or across a terrace to the ancient mound with its distant glimpse of Windermere. Apart from its poetic association the garden is also a visual delight, with good herbaceous borders, shrubs and unusual trees (e.g. the fern-leaf beech). Dora's Terrace, named after the poet's daughter, is now open. An addition to the spring display is the bank of dancing daffodils in nearby Dora's Field. Wordsworth's other house at Cockermouth has a pleasant town garden, but it is only worth it if the house, too, is to be visited.

Sizergh Castle ★ [Historic Garden Grade II]

Kendal LA8 8AE. Tel: (01539) 560070

The National Trust • 3½ m S of Kendal on A590 (M6 junction 36) • Castle and garden open April to Oct, 12.30 – 5.30pm (castle open 1.30pm) • Entrance: £3, children £1.50 (castle and garden £5.50, children £2.70, family £13.70, parties of 15 or more £4.50 per person) • Other information: Manual wheelchair and powered buggies available. Guided walks available ◑ ☕ WC ♿ ✿ ⛪

An exceptionally varied garden with colour from early spring daffodils to summer borders and climbers, culminating in glorious autumn tints (the Japanese maples all fiery red are a memorable spectacle). Other features encountered along shady paths are the herbaceous border and the terrace wall, with half-hardy shrubs and climbers not expected this far north. The kitchen garden is a new area with themed beds of vegetables, herbs and cut flowers. In the large limestone rock garden hardy ferns and dwarf conifers are of special interest. The restored Dutch garden, with its avenue of spring-flowering 'Shirotae' cherries, is part of the 16-acre garden round the tower. There are also wildflower banks with native limestone flora, including species orchids, an orchard and a lake.

Stagshaw

Ambleside LA22 0HE. Tel: (01539) 446027

The National Trust • ½ m S of Ambleside on A591 • Open April to June, daily, 10am – 6.30pm, July to Oct by appt (s.a.e. to NT Property Office, St Catherine's, Patterdale Road, Windermere LA23 1NH) • Entrance: £1.50 (2003 price) • Other information: Limited parking ●

A carefully blended area of azaleas and rhododendrons among camellias, magnolias and other fine shrubs with unusual underplanting on a west-facing hillside of oaks looking over the head of Lake Windermere. There is a large area of pink erythroniums. Rather difficult of access, with the volume of traffic on A591 making the exit especially dangerous, but worth the effort.

Yewbarrow House

Hampsfell Road, Grange–over–Sands LA11 6BE. Tel: (01539) 532469

Jonathan Denby • 15m SW of Kendal off A590. Take B5277 to Grange-over-Sands, continue up main street past railway station to mini roundabout and turn right. At crossroads turn right, then left up Hampsfell Road. Road narrows and goes into woodland; pass cottage on left, take left fork at footpath signed to Yewbarrow Wood, then left again up narrow unmade road to entrance gates • Open for NGS, and by appt. Parties of up to 25 people welcome • Entrance: £2 • Other information: Parking very limited. Unsuitable for coaches NEW ● WC ♿

This interesting two-acre fellside garden with a breathtaking view over Morecambe Bay is being redesigned by the owner with help from Christopher Halliday. It is on the site of a Victorian garden which had mostly, except for the kitchen garden, reverted to woodland; the mild west-coast climate, shelter from the prevailing wind by boundary trees, good well-drained soil and an almost frost-free microclimate enable exotica from all over the world to flower and survive. There are several individual gardens, divided by attractive limestone walls: Mediterranean and gravel gardens, ferns in woodland, a Japanese garden with a swimming pool disguised as a hot spring pool and a tea house, flower terraces and a rhododendron area. There are olive trees bearing flowers and some ripe fruit, phormiums, palms, yuccas, *Magnolia grandiflora*, *Paulownia tomentosa*, cannas and much more. The owner's aim is to have something in flower throughout the year alongside evergreen plants providing colour and structure. This is surely a Lakeland garden with a difference.

DERBYSHIRE

Two-starred gardens are marked on the map with a black square.

Calke Abbey [Historic Garden Grade II*]

Ticknall DE73 1LE. Tel: (01332) 863822 (office)

The National Trust • 10m S of Derby, off A514 at Ticknall • House open probably 1 – 5.30pm • Park open all year, daily. Garden and church open April to Oct, except 16th Aug, Sat – Wed and Bank Holiday Mons, 11am – 5.30pm (but telephone first to check) • Entrance: £3.20, children £1.60 (house and garden £5.60, children £2.80, family £14). £2.70 vehicle charge for entry to park (2003 prices) ◑ ☕ ✕ <u>WC</u> ♿ 🍴 ♿

Previously owned by the Harpur Crewe family, Calke has a long history and with a sympathetic approach could be another Trust jewel. The vinery in the physic garden has been restored, as have the tomato house, frames, pits, and the only early-nineteenth-century auricula theatre left in England. The gardeners are growing flowers, fruit and old varieties of vegetables in the two walled compartments formerly kept for flowers and physic herbs. The third and biggest compartment is the old kitchen garden, now disused, overlooked by an orangery and housing a head gardener's office of 1777. An orchard of old local apple varieties is of particular interest.

Chatsworth ★★ [Historic Garden Grade I]

Bakewell DE45 1PP. Tel: (01246) 582204

The Duke and Duchess of Devonshire • 4m E of Bakewell, 10m W of Chesterfield on B6012, off A619 and A6 • House open • Garden open 2nd April to 21st Dec, daily, 11am – 6pm • Entrance: £5, OAPs and students £3.50, children £2, family £12 (house and garden £10, OAPs and students £8, children £3.50, family £22) (2003 prices). Parking charge for cars only £1 ◑ ☕ ✕ 🍴 <u>WC</u> ♿ ⬥ 🌿 🍴 ⚲

The 105 acres of garden at Chatsworth have developed over 400 years and many areas still reflect the fashions of each century. The seventeenth-century gardens of London and Wise remain only as the cascade, the canal pond to the south and the copper 'willow tree' with water pouring from its branches. During the eighteenth century 'Capability' Brown destroyed much of the formal gardens to create a landscaped woodland park. Notable is the vista he created from the Salisbury Lawn to the horizon, which remains unchanged, as does the lawn itself since no liming or fertilisers are used, allowing many varieties of wild flowers, grasses, moss and sedges to thrive. Paxton's work still gives pleasure, including some rare conifers and the magnificent 84-metre water jet from the Emperor Fountain. Although his Great Conservatory was a casualty of the 1914–18 war and metre-wide stone walls in the old conservatory garden are all that remain to give an idea of its size, as part of the celebration of the bicentenary of Paxton's birth in 1803, damaged areas of his giant rockeries were rebuilt. From the twentieth century come the orange borders and blue and white borders, the terrace, display greenhouse, rose garden and old conservatory garden, which has lupin, dahlia and Michaelmas daisy beds, and a yew maze planted in 1963. In the arboretum and pinetum the suffocating rhododendrons, laurels and sycamores have been removed and many new trees planted. The double rows of pleached red-twigged limes added in 1952 and the 1953 serpentine beech hedge are both now rewarding features. The epitome of a cottage garden has been created near another recent addition, up the yew stairs to a 'bedroom' where the four-poster is of ivy and the dressing-table of privet. The kitchen garden has been resited and redesigned – it has been called 'indelibly British'. The first major piece of garden statuary to be placed in the garden for 150 years, 'War Horse' by Dame Elisabeth Frink, is sited at the south end of the canal, while Angela Connor's water sculpture 'Revelation' has been described by *Country Life* as 'terrific'.

Dam Farm House ★

Yeldersley Lane, Ednaston, Ashbourne DE6 3BA. Tel: (01335) 360291

Mrs Jean Player • 8m NW of Derby, 5m SE of Ashbourne on A52. Opposite Ednaston village turn, gate is 500 metres on right • Open some Suns for NGS, and April to Oct by appt only • Entrance: £3, children free • Other information: Teas on charity open Suns only. Groups and coach parties welcome ● 🍴 WC & ⚘ ℺

This wonderful garden, created from a field, owes its existence to the inspiration of the owner, whose knowledgeable eye for good plants of all kinds – trees, perennials, shrubs and roses – is evident throughout. It is this planting that gives the garden, including the vegetable garden, its special character. Garden rooms span outwards from the house, most enclosed by high beech and yew hedges and an evergreen tapestry hedge dividing the arboretum from the main garden. The scree is filled with choice alpines. Climbers are used abundantly for clothing walls, pergolas, even spilling down over high retaining walls. The farmyard has several stone troughs, now used for plants. One of the best gardens in Derbyshire, maturing after 22 years of collecting and intermittent planting.

Derby Arboretum [Historic Garden Grade II*]

Arboretum Square, Derby DE23 8FN. Tel: (01332) 716644

Derby City Council • Between Reginald Street and Arboretum Square with entrances on either side of Royal Crown Derby Factory • Open all year, daily • Entrance: free ○ 🍴 WC & ⬦

The first specifically designed urban arboretum in Britain, this was commissioned in 1839 from John Claudius Loudon, whose original plans involved the planting of 1000 trees. A useful leaflet now lists 40 varieties, many from around the world, all individually numbered, and also describes other parks in Derby, including the well-known *Markeaton Park*. While in the city, try to visit the refurbished market place, where there is a splendid water sculpture by William Pye, of free-falling water over a bronze cascade – it will give you the sensation of walking behind a waterfall.

Dove Cottage

Clifton, Ashbourne DE6 2JQ. Tel: (01335) 343545

Mr and Mrs S.G. Liverman • 1½ m SW of Ashbourne off A515. In Clifton turn right at crossroads then first left down lane (signed 'Mayfield Yarns'). House is 200 metres on left by River Dove • Open by appt for party bookings of 10 or more, and certain Suns May to Aug for charity, 1 – 5pm • Entrance: Parties £3.50 per person for guided tour, (£2.50 on charity open days), children free • Other information: Teas on charity days only ● ▣ WC ☜

It is only to be expected that this richly stocked cottage garden is above the average, for it has had the benefit of being developed and nurtured by an owner who is a qualified horticulturist. There are several hardy plant collections, including alliums, campanulas, euphorbias, geraniums and variegated plants; hardy perennials are being nurtured in a dry woodland area. A pleasant walk leads between a flower bed and the River Dove, where kingfishers may sometimes be spotted.

Elvaston Castle Country Park ★ [Historic Garden Grade II*]

Borrowash Road, Elvaston DE72 3EP. Tel: (01332) 571342

Derbyshire County Council • 2m SE of Derby on B5010 between Borrowash (A6005) and Thulston (A6). Signed from A6 and A52 • Open all year, daily, 9am – 5pm • Entrance: free. Parking charge ● ▣ ✕ 🏛 WC ☧ ☜ 🏭 ☕

The gardens were designed by William Barron in the early nineteenth century for the 4th Earl of Harrington and include Italian, parterre and Old English gardens, all enclosed within 11 miles of hedges. It is probable that these were the first 'garden rooms', which influenced others when, twenty years after their establishment, they were opened to the public. Discover the extensive topiary, tree-lined avenues and large ornamental lake, search out the golden gates, boat house and Moorish temple, and wonder at the distinctive cedars of Lebanon – Barron transplanted mature trees as high as 13 metres from as early as 1831, using his unique transplanting machines, one of which is housed at the Royal Botanic Gardens, Kew.

Fanshawe Gate Hall

Holmesfield S18 7WA. Tel: (0114) 289 0391

Mr and Mrs John Ramsden • 6m NW of Chesterfield, 6m SW of Sheffield, 1m E of Holmesfield. Follow B6054 and turn first right after Robin Hood pub • Open for charity 27th June, 4th, 11th, 18th July, 11am – 5pm, and for parties by appt June and July • Entrance: £2 ● ▣ WC ☧ ☜ ☕

Topiary, mixed borders, a variegated border, an Elizabethan garden and a sixteenth-century dovecot are features of this two-acre garden. The upper walled garden displays herbaceous plants, shrubs, ferns, water features and roses, while the lower courtyard has a knot garden and a herb border. The owners, who moved here over 40 years ago, have sought to use plants appropriate to the setting of the 700-year-old hall. The orchard has been redesigned and replanted with old varieties of English fruit trees, and a wildlife pond created. A *potager* is planned for the vegetable garden.

Fir Croft

Froggatt Road, Calver, Hope Valley S32 3ZD.

Dr S.B. Furness • 4m N of Bakewell, between Power filling station and A625/ B6001 junction • Open 25th April, 9th, 23rd May, 13th June, 2 – 5pm • Entrance: by donation • Other information: Plants for sale at adjoining nursery ● & ❧

The owner is a botanist and botanical photographer who has put his expertise into an extensive alpine garden. Started from scratch in 1985 and considerably extended in 2002, it has been planted with many new varieties and now contains one of the largest and most eclectic collections of alpines in the UK. A 'must' for those interested in alpine and scree gardens.

Gamesley Fold Cottage

10 Gamesley Fold, Glossop SK13 9JJ. Tel: (014578) 67856

Mrs G. Carr • 2m SW of Glossop off A626 – Marple road near Charlesworth. Turn down lane opposite St Margaret's School • Open for NGS, and May to Oct for parties by appt • Entrance: £2, children free • Other information: Wildflower nursery open all year, but telephone to check opening times ● ❧ WC & ❧ ℺

Although all gardeners will find much of interest here, those who like native or 'wild' flowers will be particularly impressed. The loosely planted beds are crammed with primulas, violets, campions and poppies, many of them self-seeded. Mixed in is a good variety of perennials, notably campanulas, euphorbias, geraniums, verbascums, meconopsis and others that go well with their wild neighbours. There is also a vegetable garden, an orchard and woodland. Wildlife abounds within the garden, especially butterflies lured here by the flowers, trees and shrubs; looking outward are extensive views of the surrounding countryside and hills.

Haddon Hall ★ [Historic Garden Grade I]

Bakewell DE45 1LA. Tel: (01629) 812855

Lord Edward Manners • 2m SE of Bakewell, 6½ m N of Matlock on A6 • House open • Garden open April to Sept, daily, 10.30am – 5pm, Oct, Thurs – Sun, 10.30am – 4.30pm • Entrance: hall and gardens £6.75, OAPs £5.75, children £3.50, family £18, parties £5.75 per person, school parties £3.25 per child (no garden-only ticket) (2003 prices). Parking charge for cars, coaches free ◑ ❧ ✕ WC ♿

The hall, perched high on a rocky outcrop, looks down to the River Wye over mature woodland. In origin a medieval house, it has gradually grown over the centuries into every semblance of a castle. Rex Whistler painted a delightful watercolour conversation piece of the 9th Duke with his young son and heir on the hillside above the hall – lords of all they surveyed. The gardens retain a seventeenth-century atmosphere. The south garden is terraced with views of the river below, flowing in a series of loops across the valley landscape. It is above all a haven for roses – an immense collection built up by the 9th Duchess, set against the massive house walls and buttresses – and in June and July they create a spectacular floral display.

Hardwick Hall ★ [Historic Garden Grade I]

Doe Lea, Chesterfield S44 5QJ. Tel: (01246) 850430

The National Trust • 9½ m SE of Chesterfield, 6½ m NW of Mansfield. Approach from M1 junction 29 then A6175 • House open 27th March to Oct, Wed, Thurs, Sat, Sun, Bank Holiday Mons and Good Friday, 12 noon – 4.30pm • Garden open 27th March to Oct, Wed – Sun, 11am – 5.30pm. Country park open all year, daily, 8am 6pm • Entrance: £3.40, children £1.70 (house and garden £6.40, children £3.20) (2003 prices) • Other information: Refreshments on days hall is open. Limited access for wheelchairs ◑ ☕ ✕ <u>WC</u> ⴹ ⌨

This famous Elizabethan mansion was built by Bess of Hardwick and designed by Robert Smythson in the late sixteenth century. Mature yew hedges and stone walls provide necessary protection in an otherwise exposed escarpment site. The borders of the south court have shrubs and herbaceous planting to give structure and extend the flowering period, while the west court's herbaceous borders are planted in strong, hot colours graduating to soft hues and are mainly late-summer- and autumn-flowering. The herb garden is outstanding: the south-east quarter is an orchard, with varieties of apples, pears, plums, gages and damsons, and the north-east orchard has been progressively replanted with old varieties such as crab apples, with the grass left long for naturalised daffodils and wild flowers.

The Herb Garden

Hall View Cottage, Hardstoft, Pilsley, Chesterfield S45 8AH.
Tel: (01246) 854268

Mrs Raynor • 6m SE of Chesterfield on B6039 Holmewood – Tibshelf road. 3m SW of M1 junction 29 • Open 15th March to 15th Sept, Wed – Sun, and 12th, 13th April, 3rd, 4th, 31st May, 1st June, 30th, 31st Aug; all 10am – 5pm • Entrance: £2, children free ◑ ☕ WC ⴹ ⌨ ⌨

A rich herb garden in a rural setting with a now-established parterre. Three speciality gardens have been added: physic, scented pot-pourri and lavender. The large range of herbs for sale includes some rare and unusual species.

Kedleston Hall ★ [Historic Garden Grade I]

Kedleston, Derby DE22 5JH. Tel: (01332) 842191

The National Trust • 4½ m NW of Derby on Derby – Hulland road between A6 and A52. Signposted • Hall open 22nd March to 2nd Nov, Sat – Wed, 12 noon –

4.30pm • Park open 22nd March to 2nd Nov, daily, 10am – 6pm; 3rd Nov to 21st March, daily, 10am – 4pm. Garden open 22nd March to 2nd Nov, daily, 10am – 6pm • Entrance: park £2.70 per vehicle; park and garden £2.60, children £1.30, family £6.50 (hall, park and garden £5.80, children £2.80, family £14.40) • Other information: Coaches must pre-book by writing to Property Manager. Electric stairclimber and batricar available ◑ 💺 ✕ WC ⎌ ⛵ 🔦 ⚲

The extensive gardens do not compete with this neo-classical Robert Adam palace – the ancient home of the Curzon family – but are of mature parkland where the eye is always drawn to the house. The rhododendrons when in flower are worth seeing in their own right, otherwise visit the gardens as a pleasurable way to view not only Adam's magnificent south front but also the hexagonal-domed summerhouse, the orangery, the Venetian-windowed fishing house, the bridge across the lake, the aviary and slaughterhouse (now a loggia) and the main gateway. The formal gardens have a sunken rose garden. The Sulphur Bath House, one of the earliest eighteenth-century landscape park features, where a small spa used to operate, has been restored but is not accessible to the public.

Lea Gardens

Long Lane, Lea, Matlock DE4 5GH. Tel: (01629) 534380

Mr and Mrs Tye • 5m SE of Matlock E off A6 • Open 20th March to 30th June, daily, 10am – 5pm, and at other times by appt • Entrance: £3.50, children 50p (season ticket £6) • Other information: Coaches by appt ◑ 💺 WC ⎌ ⚘ 🔦 ⛵

This garden has a comprehensive collection of rhododendrons, azaleas, alpines and conifers, all brought together in a beautiful woodland setting. John Marsden Smedley started his rhododendron garden in 1935, inspired by his visits to Bodnant and Exbury. Under the Tye family the collection now comprises some 550 varieties of rhododendrons and azaleas in a much-increased area.

Melbourne Hall Gardens ★ [Historic Garden Grade I]

Melbourne DE73 1EN. Tel: (01332) 862502

Lord Ralph Kerr • 8m S of Derby between A514 and A453, off B587 in Melbourne • House open, Aug, daily except 2nd, 9th, 16th, 2 – 5pm (last admission 4.15pm) • Open April to Sept, Wed, Sat, Sun and Bank Holiday Mons, 1.30 – 5.30pm • Entrance: £3, OAPs and children £2 (hall and gardens £5, OAPs £4, children £3) ◑ 💺 ✕ WC ⎌ ⛵

There has been little alteration to the Rt Hon. Thomas Coke's formal plan, so this is a visual record of a complete late seventeenth-/early eighteenth-century design laid out by London and Wise in the style of Le Nôtre. It is in immaculate condition with avenues culminating in exquisite statuary and fountains, including a lead urn of The Four Seasons by van Nost, whose other lead statuary stands in niches of yew. A series of terraces runs down to a lake, the Great Basin. A grotto has an inscription thought to be that of

Byron's troublesome mistress Caroline Lamb. Unique in English gardens is the Bird-cage iron arbour of 1706, which can be seen from the house along a long walk hedged with yews. Also in Melbourne, on the site of the four-teenth-century castle, is *Castle Farm*, a garden of interesting plants, open for private visits and groups by appointment; telephone Mr and Mrs John Blunt on (01332) 864421.

Pavilion Gardens

St John's Road, Buxton SK17 6XN. Tel: (01298) 23114

High Peak Borough Council • Near town centre • Open all year, daily • Entrance: free • Other information: Refreshments in complex ○ 🍽 ✕ 🏚 **WC** ♿ ⬦ ♞

Twenty-three acres of landscaped municipal park, woodland and two orna-mental lakes, this updated pleasure garden of 1871 has the distinction of having been laid out by Edward Milner, Paxton's chief assistant at Crystal Palace. The gardens are well maintained and the pleasing 1875 octagon (now used for many events) is a graceful backdrop. The conservatory is well stocked but many find the colour schemes of the bedding plants harsh; there are, however, band concerts to soothe shattered nerves. In the nearby Crescent, examples of the arcane art of well-dressing may be seen during summer. A Heritage grant has aided a refurbishment programme costing £4m over five years.

Renishaw Hall [Historic Garden Grade II*]

Renishaw, Sheffield S21 3WB. Tel: (01246) 432310

Sir Reresby and Lady Sitwell • 6m SE of Sheffield, 5m NE of Chesterfield on A6135. From M1 at junction 30, take A616 towards Sheffield for 3m through Renishaw • Open 2nd April to Sept, Thurs – Sun and Bank Holiday Mons, 10.30am – 4pm • Entrance: £3.50, OAPs £2.50 • Other information: Sitwell museum, costume museum, art gallery, performing arts gallery ◑ 🍽 ✕ **WC** ♿ ⬦ ♨ 👍 ♟ ♞

For nearly twenty years Renishaw had 'the most northerly vineyard in western Europe'. Also astonishing to see at this northerly latitude and on top of a hill are enormous specimens of rare and slightly tender shrubs. Sir George Sitwell spent much of his life in Italy and this is the style he re-created at Renishaw a century ago. Within a formal framework of vistas, walks and topiary, plants riot in ordered confusion in the sheltered gardens to the south of the house. Statues, terraces and the sound of splashing water enhance the Italianate atmosphere, and the present incumbents have added a stupendous water jet to increase the effect. They have also increased the number of different gardens (10 in all), divided and protected by yew hedges and columns, enlarged the borders, introduced innovative planting, and linked the garden to the wood with new planting and paths. At the end of the lime avenue on the top lawn stands Sir Hamo Thornycroft's statue of the Angel of Fame, recently regilded by Lady Sitwell. Beyond the brick wall is a greenhouse that contains the National Collection of yuccas, and below that winds a spinney that badgers now share with a statue walk. A nature trail leads into an avenue of camellias and on to the classic temple, Gothick lodge, old sawmill, cave and lakes.

DEVON

Two-starred gardens are marked on the map with a black square.

Andrew's Corner

Belstone, Okehampton EX20 1RD. Tel: (01837) 840332

Mr and Mrs R.J. Hill • 3m E of Okehampton off A30, signed to Belstone then Skaigh • Open 18th April, 2nd, 23rd, 30th May, 6th, 13th June, 2.30 – 5.30pm, 23rd, 24th July, 7 – 10pm, and by appt at other times • Entrance: £2, children free (evening openings £3 incl. wine and refreshments) • Other information: Teas on open days only ● ☕ ♿ ✿

High above sea level on north Dartmoor, facing the Taw valley and the high moor, in only one and a half acres (amazing that it is not larger) grows a wide variety of plants of all sorts not normally seen at such an altitude. The sense of space is achieved by the division of the garden into different levels by rhododendrons and trees, each area having its own microclimate, and all with glimpses through to other areas and to the wider landscape. Colour in spring comes from bulbs and meconopsis, in summer from herbaceous plants and lilies, in autumn from maples (many grown from seed) and gentians. There are drystone walls (a speciality of the area), a paved area and ponds with water plants; in stone and paving cracks lewisias and other alpines flourish.

Arlington Court [Historic Garden Grade II*]

Arlington, Barnstaple EX31 4LP. Tel: (01271) 850296

The National Trust • 7m NE of Barnstaple on A39 • House and carriage collection open as garden, but 11am – 5pm. Carriage driving school open March to Nov by appt • Garden open 27th March to Oct, daily except Tues, 10.30am – 5pm • Entrance: garden and carriage collection £4, children £2 (house, carriage collection and garden £6, children £4, family £15, parties of 15 or more £5.10 per person, children £2.40) ◗ ☕ ✕ 🧺 <u>WC</u> ♿ ⟁ ✿ 🛍 🍴 ❀

The Georgian house is set in a largely informal garden extending to 30 acres. The mild, damp climate, combined with acid soil, provides a perfect home for a wide range of plants, particularly rhododendrons, with many species of tree-like proportions; hydrangeas also thrive here. In spring, drifts of bulbs carpet the grass, followed by wild flowers. The wilderness pond is surrounded by rhododendrons, contrasting with the formal and symmetrical terraced Victorian garden with its annual bedding. There is also a double herbaceous border, a rockery and a conservatory. The one-acre walled kitchen garden is being restored, and the Victorian lean-to greenhouse has been rebuilt to the original design. A few miles SE of Barnstaple on the A377, in Pixie Lane, Umberleigh, *Glebe Cottage Plants* (the nursery owned by Chelsea gold-medal winner Carol Klein) stocks a mouth-watering range of rare and newly introduced perennials. [Open all year, Wed – Fri. Tel: (01769) 540554.]

✓ Bickham House

Kenn, Exeter EX6 7XL. Tel: (01392) 832671

Mr and Mrs John Tremlett • 6m S of Exeter on A38 before junction with A380. Leave dual carriageway at Kennford Services and follow signs to Kenn, then take first right and follow lane for ¾ m to end of no-through road • Open 18th, 20th, 21st April, 9th, 11th, 12th May, 13th, 15th, 16th June, 11th, 13th, 14th July, 8th, 10th, 11th Aug, 5th, 7th, 8th Sept, 2 – 5pm, and at other times by appt • Entrance: £2.50, children 50p ● 🍵 🎩 **WC** க் ⬠ ⌀

Six acres of garden in a peaceful wooded valley, overlooking a small lake. The house has been in the family since it was built in 1682, but the garden has been extensively remodelled over the last few years, and new features are being added all the time. There are lawns and fine trees, spring-flowering shrubs and many naturalised bulbs, and a box-hedged parterre around a lily pond. In the mixed borders great attention is paid to colour co-ordination. The one-acre walled garden, divided into rose beds, a formal herb garden and a highly productive flower and vegetable section, is full of colour and interest throughout the year; an avenue of palm trees leads to a new summerhouse. Colourful too is the small water garden. There is also a conservatory, leading into an enclosed cobbled area with raised beds and a wall fountain.

✓ Bicton College

East Budleigh, Budleigh Salterton EX9 7BY. Tel: (01395) 562353

2m N of Budleigh Salterton on A376 • Open all year, daily except 25th Dec to 1st Jan, 10.30am – 4.30pm • Entrance: £2, children free (2003 price) • Other information: Parking beyond student car park, short walk to garden ○ 🍵 ⬠ ⌀

The gardens of this Georgian house, set in parkland with a lake, form the horticultural department of Bicton College, and as such contain a large number of plants laid out for both study and general interest – truly a plantsman's paradise. As well as fine herbaceous borders there is an arboretum worth visiting at any time of the year and an old walled garden, all approached by an avenue of araucarias (monkey puzzle trees). Amongst the plants which provide both information and effect are National Collections of agapanthus and pittosporums. Ten miles to the north is *Escot Place*, Ottery St Mary, where the latest project of the designer Ivan Hicks is evolving in 220 acres of traditional woodland garden. Telephone (01404) 822188 for more information, or visit the website at www.escot-devon.co.uk.

✓ Bicton Park Botanical Gardens ★ [Historic Garden Grade I]

East Budleigh, Budleigh Salterton EX9 7BJ. Tel: (01395) 568465

Bicton Park • 2m N of Budleigh Salterton on B3178 • Open daily except 25th Dec, 10am – 6pm (closes 5pm in winter) • Entrance: £4.95, children (3–15) £3.95, concessions £3.95, family £14.95 ○ 🍵 ✕ 🎩 **WC** க் ⬠ ⌀ 🛍 🍴 ⌀

There is much to see in the 60 acres. The formal and informal gardens date from c.1735, largely landscaped in the style of Le Nôtre. There is a stream garden with a 150-year-old mulberry, azaleas, camellias and flowering cherries, herbaceous borders against magnolia-clad walls, an American garden established in the 1830s, and a hermitage garden with a lake and water garden. The pinetum, first planted in 1839 and extended in 1910 to take the collection of the famous botanist and explorer 'Chinese' Wilson, has some rare conifers, including the tallest Grecian fir ever recorded (41 metres). Perhaps Bicton's greatest glory is the palm house, built between 1825 and 1830, one of the oldest in the country; inside, endangered species such as bottle, loulu, triangle, cotton and kentia palms, and outside a Chinese tea plant. There are also arid and temperate houses, and a tropical house for bananas, bromeliads, figs and bougainvilleas. The Countryside Museum, one of the largest in the West Country, houses a collection of farm machinery, gardening tools and craft exhibits, reflecting changes in rural life since the 1700s. There is a new display of cacti and other succulents in a naturalistic desert-like landscape in the arid house, and one of Britain's earliest Victorian ferneries has been re-established by the planting of a large collection of ferns, including dicksonias, among the rocks around the shell house.

Blackpool Garden

Blackpool Sands, Blackpool, Dartmouth TQ6 ORG. Tel: (01803) 770606

Sir Geoffrey Newman, Bt • 3m S of Dartmouth on A379. Entrance through Blackpool Sands car park • Open April to Oct, daily (subject to weather), 10am – 4pm, and to private and school parties by appt • Entrance: £2.50, children free • Other information: Refreshments and toilets available at Blackpool Sands
NEW ◐ ☕ 🗑 ⚲

This engrossing secret garden is entered through a small green-painted door, overhung by a cascade of *Fuchsia magellanica* and set into a wall of beautifully laid Devon stone. Facing south and rising steeply, it overlooks the perfect crescent of Blackpool Sands. This chunk of Devon's Heritage Coast has been in the same family since the late-eighteenth century, but the landscaping of the three-acre woodland garden was begun by Robert Lydston Newman, Deputy Governor of the Bank of England, in 1896. He carved out four wide parallel paths the length of the garden, joining them by further paths and steps so that they climb upwards in a gentle zig-zag. The hillside between is filled with a wide variety of sub-tropical, temperate and antipodean trees and shrubs, some of great age, others introduced more recently, and all testimony to the fact that succeeding generations of Newmans have been keen collectors and plantsmen. An 1848 Monterey pine and an 1896 avenue of cork oaks with venerably pitted bark survive from the earliest period. The award of a European grant in 2000 enabled the present owner to regenerate the landscaping and rejuvenate the plantings. A new water garden is planned, centred on an existing pond garden above the terraces, so that water may in time cascade back down towards the stunning views, far below, of beach, craggy headlands and a shoreline fading away to distant Start Point. Then it's time to make your way back through the secret door, enjoy a swim, hire a kayak, and return to the real holiday world.

Buckland Abbey

Yelverton PL20 6EY. Tel: (01822) 853607

The National Trust and Plymouth City Council • 6m S of Tavistock, 11m N of Plymouth. Turn off A386 ¼ m S of Yelverton • House open as garden • Garden open 27th March to Oct, daily, 10.30am – 5.30pm; 21st Feb to 26th March, 6th Nov to 21st Dec, Sat, Sun, 12.30 – 5pm. Closed 22nd Dec to 21st Feb • Entrance: £5, children £2.50 (abbey and grounds £5, family £12.50) • Other information: Possible for wheelchairs but steep site. Motorised buggy usually available ◔ ☕ ✕ <u>WC</u> ♿ ✿ 🎋 ☤ ⚲

The garden is largely a twentieth-century creation. There is a box hedge parterre between the 30-metre-long medieval barn and the abbey, its pockets filled with over 50 different herbs, reputedly inspired by Vita Sackville-West. *Magnolia delavayi* and *M. grandiflora* grow against the abbey walls. A line of ailing yews on the north border of the lawn has been replaced by an Elizabethan garden, and a thyme area has recently been created. Delightful estate walks and glorious views of Devon and Cornwall.

Burrow Farm Gardens ★

Dalwood, Axminster EX13 7ET. Tel: (01404) 831285

Mr and Mrs John Benger • 4m W of Axminster off A35 Honiton road. After 3½ m turn N near Shute garage onto Stockland road. Garden is ½ m on right • Open April to Sept, daily, 10am – 7pm • Entrance: £3.50, children 50p, parties (discount rate) by appt ◑ ☕ 🍴 <u>WC</u> ♿ ⬥ ✿

These lovely 10-acre gardens, created from pasture land, are the inspiration of Mary Benger and her family. Foliage effect has been admirably achieved with a colourful array of azaleas and rhododendrons. A former Roman clay pit is graded from top to bottom through mature trees and shrubs to an extensive bog garden with a marvellous show of candelabra primulas and native wild flowers during the early part of the season. In summer the pergola walk, with its old-fashioned roses and herbaceous borders, is a picture. A courtyard garden and a terraced garden feature late-flowering herbaceous plants. The rill garden has ponds, a classical summerhouse and a ha-ha laid out in a formal design, luxuriantly and informally planted. The setting and sense of grandeur are more typical of gardens of greater repute. Magnificent views.

Castle Drogo ★★ [Historic Garden Grade II*]

Drewsteignton EX6 6PB. Tel: (01647) 433306

The National Trust • Between Okehampton and Exeter, 5m S of A30 or 4m NW of Moretonhampstead on A382; follow signs from Sandy Park • Castle open 29th March to 2nd Nov, Sat – Thurs, 11am – 5.30pm • Garden open all year, daily, 10.30am – 5.30pm • Entrance: £3 (reduced rate Nov to Feb, but castle extra). Reduced rate for parties by appt (2003 prices) • Other information: Coaches by appt only. Disabled parking. Access for wheelchairs by arrangement at reception. Croquet equipment for hire ◑ ☕ ✕ 🍴 <u>WC</u> ♿ ✿ 🎋 ☤ ⚲

The last castle to be built in England (begun 1910) was designed by Sir Edwin Lutyens. The plans for the planting of the garden were by George Dillistone of Tunbridge Wells. Evergreen oaks survey the magnificent views over the Teign Gorge, and a valley planted with rhododendrons, magnolias, camellias, cornus and maples. Nearer the house are formal terraces and borders with walls of granite, sharp-edged yew hedges with rose beds and arbours of *Parrotia persica*. The paths and parrotia arbours echo Lutyens' circle and square theme. Herbaceous borders are full of old varieties of crocosmias, lychnis, campanulas, irises and red-hot pokers. Under the granite walls perennials – euphorbias, hellebores, alchemillas and rodgersias – mingle with spring bulbs. Steps lead to a second terrace with yuccas and wisterias and a fragrant garden; then on up to shrub borders of enkianthus, azaleas, magnolias and lilies; and finally comes a splendid circular lawn surrounded by a tall yew hedge at the top, a huge green circle and a perfect stage set for croquet. Near Chagford, off A30 via Whiddon Down, are *Stone Lane Gardens*, Kenneth and June Ashbourner's informally landscaped five-acre arboretum. An annual sculpture exhibition is held from May to September. [Open mid-May to mid-Sept, daily, 2 – 6pm; at other times ring (01647) 231311 to check, or consult website on www.mythicgarden.com.]

Castle Hill [Historic Garden Grade I]

Filleigh, Barnstaple EX32 ORQ. Tel: (01598 760336, Ext.4)

The Earl and Countess of Arran • 7m SE of Barnstaple, 19m NW of Tiverton off A361. Leave at Little Chef roundabout, heading for Filleigh. Take second right, then after 2½ m turn right into drive at yellow lodge • Open 2nd April to 11th June, Mon, Fri, 11am – 5pm • Entrance: £4 NEW ● WC & ● B&B

The eighteenth-century landscape garden and park were created by the 1st Lord Fortescue in 1730 with temples, follies, ponds and across the valley a triumphal arch. At the top of the hill above the house is a castle (complete with cannons) from which Dartmoor, Exmoor and Lundy Island are visible on a clear day. The woodland garden shelters magnolias, camellias, rhododendrons, azaleas and thousands of bulbs, and there are also some spectacular trees in the arboretum. As if this were not enough, the millennium garden designed by Xa Tollemache has herbaceous borders planted with lilies, agapanthus, phlox and penstemon edged with box and lavender in gentle curves following the line of the hill. There is an avenue of formal clipped *Quercus ilex* underplanted with *Viburnum tinus* and a spectacular water sculpture by Giles Rayner. The walled kitchen garden has a pergola down the centre with herbaceous borders, greenhouses and a herb garden as well as an abundance of vegetables.

Cleave House

Sticklepath, Okehampton EX20 2NL. Tel: (01837) 840481

Ann and Roger Bowden • 3½ m E of Okehampton on old A30 towards Exeter. House is in Sticklepath on left just past small right turn for Skaigh • Open for NGS, and by appt at other times – parties and individuals welcome • Entrance: £1.50 ● WC & ✍

For the Bowdens hostas are not just a business, they are an abiding passion. Their one-acre garden, tucked away at the heart of a small Devon village, boasts some delightful mixed planting – both trees and shrubs – but hostas are the dominant feature. A few varieties, notably the brightly coloured, have been imported from the United States. This Mecca for the hosta enthusiast includes demonstration beds resplendent with over 600 different varieties, displaying fascinating variations in both colour and size. The collection has been designated an NCCPG reference (of modern hybrids).

Coleton Fishacre Garden ★ [Historic Garden Grade II*]

Brownstone Road, Kingswear, Dartmouth TQ6 0EQ. Tel: (01803) 752466

The National Trust • 3m E of Dartmouth, 3m S of Brixham off B3205. 2½ m from Kingswear, take Lower Ferry Road and turn off at toll house • House open from 2nd April as garden, 11am – 4.30pm • Garden open March, Sat, Sun, 11am – 5pm; 2nd April to 2nd Nov, Wed – Sun and Bank Holiday Mons, 10.30am – 5.30pm • Entrance: £3.90, children £1.95, pre-booked parties of 15 or more £3.30 per person (house and garden £5, children, £2.50, family £12.50, pre-booked parties £4.30) (2003 prices) ◑ ☕ ✕ 🍽 WC ⚒ 🌿 ⛪ 🔦 ⚲

Oswald Milne, a pupil of Edwin Lutyens, designed the house and the architectural features of this garden for Rupert and Lady D'Oyly Carte; the house was completed and the garden begun in 1926. The exceptionally mild setting is a Devon combe, sloping steeply to the cliff tops and the sea, and sheltered by belts of Monterey pines and holm oaks. The streams and ponds make a humid atmosphere for moisture-loving and sub-tropical plants. There is a collection of unusual trees like dawn redwood, swamp cypress and Chilean myrtle, and dominating all a tall tulip tree and tree of heaven (*Ailanthus altissima*) the same age as the house. The Paddock Woodland Walk runs from the Gazebo Walk near the house through woodland to a main viewing area. Formal walls and terraces create a framework round the house for a large number of sun-loving tender plants. There are various water features, notably a stone-edged rill and a circular pool in the herbaceous-bordered walled garden.

Dartington Hall ★ [Historic Garden Grade II*]

Dartington, Totnes TQ9 6EL. Tel: (01803) 862367

Dartington Hall Trust • 2m NW of Totnes, E of A384 • Open all year, daily, dawn – dusk. Parties by appt only • Entrance: by donation £2, guided tours by arrangement £4 • Other information: Coaches by appt ○ ☕ ✕ WC ⚒ B&B

In 1925, Leonard and Dorothy Elmhirst purchased the then-declining Dartington Hall estate in order to launch their great experiment in rural regeneration. At its heart is one of the most beautiful medieval manor houses in Devon; sitting snugly in its combe, it was shaped by many notable garden designers, including the American Beatrix Farrand, who was responsible for transforming the courtyard and opening up the woodland walkways. There are three walks, each using yew and holly as background plantings for the collections of camellias, magnolias and rhododendrons. Percy Cane introduced such features as the glade, the azalea dell and the impressive magnolia steps. More recently, Preben Jacobsen redesigned the herbaceous border and Philip Booth was commissioned to create the Japanese garden. The overall effect is strongly architectural, with the fourteenth-century tiltyard and its terraces at the heart.

Docton Mill ★

Lymebridge, Elmscott, Hartland EX39 6EA. Tel: (01237) 441369

Mr and Mrs J. Borrett • 14m W of Bideford, 12m N of Bude off A39. From north Devon travel via Hartland to Stoke or from north Cornwall to West Country Inn, then turn left signed Elmscott towards Lymebridge in Spekes Valley • Open March to Oct, daily, 10am – 6pm • Entrance: £3.50, OAPS £3, children £1 • Other information: coaches by appt ◐ ◲ ✕ 🍽 WC ◁◲ ✣ ◔ B&B

The garden, in its fine valley setting, and the water mill of Saxon origin were rescued from dereliction in the 1980s by the previous owners. This involved a large-scale clearance of the waterways – ponds, leats, footbridges over the river and many smaller streams. The whole purpose has been to make everything as natural as possible. In spring there are displays of narcissi, primulas, camellias and azaleas, with bluebells carpeting the woods; in summer the garden abounds in roses, including a bank of hybrid musk 'Felicia' and 'Pax'. A bog garden is planted with ligularias, primulas and ferns. The old donkey paddock has been transformed into a new magnolia garden with large herbaceous borders, and a woodland garden was planted in the spring of 2002.

Endsleigh House and Gardens [Historic Garden Grade I]

Milton Abbot, Tavistock PL19 0PQ. Tel: (01822) 870248

Endsleigh Charitable Trust • 4m NW of Tavistock on B3362 • Open April to Oct, daily, 11am – 5pm • Entrance: £3 (ticket machine) (2003 price) • Other information: Lunches and teas at hotel by arrangement ◉ ◲ ✕ WC ㉓ ◁◲ ✣

The house was built, starting in 1811, for the 6th Duke of Bedford from designs by architect Jeffry Wyatville and landscape gardener Humphry Repton. It is a good example of a *cottage orné* and was used as a fishing and hunting lodge by the Duke. It is now a quiet country house hotel. The house and the immediate garden have tight views overlooking the almost stream-like character of the upper Tamar, wooded on either bank. The garden has been restored to re-establish the nineteenth-century vision, and an uneasy truce established between the rich wilderness that has invaded Repton's landscape and the slow process of ongoing authentication. Rare tree species in the arboretum have largely survived the storms of the late 1980s. Buzzards and cormorants command the sky.

The Garden House ★

Buckland Monachorum, Yelverton PL20 7LQ. Tel: (01822) 854769

The Fortescue Garden Trust • 10m N of Plymouth, 2m W of Yelverton off A386 • Open March to Oct, daily, 10.30am – 5pm • Entrance: £4, OAPs £3.50, children £1 ◐ ◲ ✕ 🍽 WC ㉓ ✣

A garden in the 'new naturalism' style, providing colour and interest from spring through summer and into autumn. Largely north-facing and nearly 150 metres above sea level, it has to contend with up to 150 centimetres of rain *per annum*. Its origins are deep in the past, but in gardening terms its story began when Mr and Mrs Lionel Fortescue arrived in 1945 to breathe life into the derelict walled garden, which surrounded the ruins of a medieval vicarage and included a thatched barn and a tower. Through years of painstaking work, it has become one of the finest of its type in the country. In 1978 Keith and Ros Wiley came here and continued the work. Their modification and planting programme since the 1980s has been quite remarkable. Eight acres of pasture and paddock have been transformed by the planting of more than 3000 trees and shrubs, more than 1000 herbaceous plants and thousands of spring bulbs. A wisteria wood is now maturing, and the latest departure is a quarry garden with ponds and waterfalls and associated bog planting.

Gidleigh Park ★

Chagford TQ13 8HH. Tel: (01647) 432367

Kay and Paul Henderson • Off A382 11m SE of Okehampton. In Chagford Square turn right into Mill Street by Lloyds TSB. After 150 metres fork right (virtually straight across junction), and go to end of road – about 2m • Open all year, Mon – Fri (but closed Bank Holiday Mons) • Entrance: £6 (inc. coffee or tea with biscuits) • Other information: Lunches and teas served in hotel
○ ☕ ✕ WC

Gidleigh Park, the acclaimed hotel and restaurant, is set in 45 acres of magnificent and secluded grounds on the north bank of the River Teign, within Dartmoor National Park. The woodland garden and parkland were created between 1850 and 1930. Since 1980, under the direction of head gardener Keith Mansfield, the owners have undertaken an extensive programme of restoration. Among the many interesting features is a delightful water garden, rebuilt and planted in 1986 and extended significantly into the woodland in 1997. Visitors can take this in on their way round the Boundary Walk – a 45-minute stroll through natural mixed woodland, underplanted with azaleas and rhododendrons. The Teign is never far away, tumbling over granite boulders, past spring displays of rhododendrons. The mock-Tudor house gives way to a terrace resplendent with summer colour, while a parterre and a herb garden add a touch of formality. There is an interesting avenue of young pleached limes adjacent to the front lawn, and mention must be made of the croquet lawns, the very upmarket golf 'putting garden' and the pavilion – the final decadent flourishes.

Greenway

Greenway Road, Galmpton, Churston Ferrers, Brixham TQ5 0ES.
Tel: (01803) 842382

The National Trust • 4m W of Brixham. From A3022 Paignton – Brixham road, take road to Galmpton, then towards Greenway quay and ferry. Vehicles strictly limited. Parking spaces for cars and mini-coaches must be pre-booked (Tel:

(01803) 842382). No parking in lanes outside property. Please either take ferries from Dartmouth or Totnes (Tel: (01803) 833206); or bus from Paignton Esplanade or Goodrington station; or Greenway circular tour (Tel: (01803 862735) • Open 3rd March to 9th Oct, Wed – Sat, 10.30am – 5pm • Entrance: £3.70, children £1.75 (2003 prices) ◑ 💂 🐾 WC ⬧ 🌿 👜

The 30-acre ancient Devon garden is set high on the curving bank of the tree-lined Dart river which has beautiful woodland walks. The Trust's researches indicate that Repton may have worked here. There are so many indigenous trees over 150 years old – plus a giant tulip tree – that in high summer the river is completely hidden from the house, and even from Dittisham on the opposite bank the house is barely visible. Overall are many camellias, 30 varieties of magnolias, ceanothus, wisterias and abutilons. The banks of primroses and bluebells make it magical in spring. The natural glades are spangled with foxgloves, white irises, herb Roberts, pennyworts, ivies and hart's tongue and male ferns. The restoration of the camellia and fernery gardens and the redevelopment of the herbaceous border in the top garden are the latest projects. The house (Agatha Christie's holiday home for many years) and the area immediately around it are not open.

Hartland Abbey

Bideford EX39 6DT. Tel: (01237) 441264/234

Sir Hugh and Lady Stucley • 15m SW of Bideford off A39 Bideford – Bude road. Follow signs to Hartland; drive through village, take road to Hartland Quay. Signposted • House open April to 6th Oct, Wed, Thurs, Sun and Bank Holiday Mons, plus Tues, July, Aug; all 2 – 5.30pm • Garden and grounds open April to 6th Oct, daily except Sat, 2 – 5.30pm, and at other times by appt • Entrance: gardens and grounds £4, children 50p (house, gardens and grounds £6, OAPs £5, children £1.50) ◑ 💂 🐾 WC ⬧ ⬧ 🌿 👜 🍴 ✂

Once an Augustinian monastery, the abbey is set across a narrow sheltered valley. Because of the gales, gardens were not created around the house – although a row of 100-year-old bay trees survives – but were planted either side of the valley with azaleas, rhododendrons, camellias, hydrangeas, gunneras and many other shrubs and trees. Some of the paths in the bog garden were designed by Gertrude Jekyll, who used to be a guest at the abbey, and the Victorian fernery, also thought to be by her, has been replanted. The walk to the Atlantic, a mile away, is carpeted in spring with bluebells, primroses and violets. A series of eighteenth-century walled gardens, set in a south-facing, gently sloping valley five minutes' walk away, is filled with vegetables, herbaceous plants, roses and clematis.

Higher Knowle

Lustleigh, Newton Abbot TQ13 9SP. Tel: (01647) 277275

Mr and Mrs D.R.A. Quicke • 13m NW of Torquay, 8m NW of Newton Abbot, 3m NW of Bovey Tracey on A382 towards Moretonhampstead. After 2½ m, turn left at Kelly Cross for Lustleigh; after ¼ m left then right at Brookfield along

*Knowle Road; after ¼ m steep drive on left • Open 28th March to May, Sun
and Bank Holiday Mons, 2 – 6pm, for NGS, and by appt between these dates •
Entrance: £2.50, children free* ● 🏚 WC ⏦

The three-acre woodland garden surrounds a stone house built in 1914 with
many Lutyens-style features by his pupil Fred Harrild as architect. Situated on
a steep hillside with spectacular views to Dartmoor, the sheltered garden
usually avoids late frosts and is home to tender plants. The old oak wood is
carpeted with primroses and bluebells in spring, with mature Asiatic magnolias providing a fine display in late March, followed by camellias, new hybrid
magnolias, many rhododendrons and azaleas, and tall embothriums. Giant
Dartmoor granite boulders add natural sculpture to the woodland walks,
which include a water garden.

Hill House Nursery and Garden ★
Landscove, Ashburton, Newton Abbot TQ13 7LY. Tel: (01803) 762273

*Mr and Mrs Raymond Hubbard and Mr Matthew Hubbard • 3m S of
Ashburton. From Plymouth-bound A38, take second exit signed to Ashburton,
then left signed to Landscove, or from A384 Totnes – Buckfastleigh road follow
signs to Landscove. Signposted • Open all year, daily, except 19th Dec to 5th
Jan, 11am – 5pm. Booking required for parties • Entrance: free • Other
information: Tea room open March to Sept only* ○ ☕ ✗ WC ♿ 🐾 ♀

Hill House, once a Victorian vicarage next to its church – both by John
Loughborough Pearson – is known to enthusiasts for the garden created by
Edward Hyams and filled by him with rare, exotic and tender plants. Since the
1980s it has been restored by the present owners, plantsmen Raymond and
Matthew Hubbard, both as a private garden and a family-run nursery. Hyams'
eighteenth-century Grecian temple has also been restored. By the pond is a
pretty conservatory also designed by him and containing a grape vine, passion
flowers and a lemon tree. An integral feature of the garden is the commercial
nursery, which offers both everyday plants and tender, exotic and rare species.

Killerton ★ [Historic Garden Grade II*]
Broadclyst, Exeter EX5 3LE. Tel: (01392) 881345

*The National Trust • 7m NE of Exeter on W side of B3181 • House and
costume museum open 13th April to Oct, daily except Tues, 11am – 5.30pm •
Park and garden open all year, 10.30am – dusk • Entrance: £4.20 • Other
information: Tea room limited opening in winter. Motorised buggies with drivers
available for disabled. Dogs in park only* ○ ☕ ✗ 🏚 WC ⏦ 🐾 🎡 ♀ ✂

This large hillside garden surrounded by woods, park and farmland extends to
over 6000 acres. It was created by John Veitch in the late eighteenth century
and later involved the famous Victorian gardening writer William Robinson. The
actual garden area of 18 acres is a haven of delight. It will provide pleasure
and interest to all but particularly to the tree and shrub enthusiast. Many of
the plants for sale were propagated here. Besides the avenue of beeches, there
are Wellingtonias (the first plantings in England), Lawson cypresses, oaks,

maples and many other fine broadleaved trees. Trees and shrubs introduced by
Veitch are now reaching an imposing size. Terraced beds and extensive
herbaceous borders provide summer colour. Killerton has a rhododendron
collection with 95 different species, many brought back from China and Japan.
There is also an early-nineteenth-century summerhouse, the Bear's Hut, an
ice-house and rock garden. The handsome chapel has its own three-acre
grounds containing many other fine trees, notably an enormous tulip tree.

Knightshayes ★★ [Historic Garden Grade II*]

**Bolham, Tiverton EX16 7RQ. Tel: (01884) 254665 (Property Manager);
Tel: (01884) 253264 (Garden Office)**

*The National Trust • 16m N of Exeter, 2m N of Tiverton. Turn off A396 at
Bolham • House open 27th March to Oct, Sat – Thurs (open Good Friday),
11am – 5pm • Gardens open 27th March to Oct, daily, 11am – 5pm •
Entrance: £4.50, children £2.20 (house and gardens, £5.80, children £2.90) •
Other information: Dogs on lead in park and Impey Walk only* ◐ ♨ ✕ 🗑 WC
♿ ⬦ 🌿 🛍 🍴 ☕

The garden and landscaping was originally planned by Edward Kemp in the late
1870s when the house was being completed. It remained essentially unchanged
until Sir John and Lady Amory began replanting in the 1950s. The terraces are
planted with shrub roses, tree peonies and herbaceous plants in soft colours
and silvers. Yew encloses a paved garden in shades of pink, purple and grey
with two standard wisterias. Battlemented hedges frame the pool garden with
a backdrop of *Acer pseudoplatanus* 'Brilliantissimum'. Topiary hounds endlessly
chase a fox on a lower terrace. The Garden in the Wood shelters magnolias,
rhododendrons, cornus, hydrangeas and other rare and tender plants, some
grown in raised peat blocks. Drifts of pink erythroniums, white foxgloves and
cyclamen appear in their seasons. The Victorian walled kitchen garden has
recently been restored and opened; constructed in tiers with a central
ornamental pool, it provides organic vegetables, fruit and cut flowers.

Lee Ford

Budleigh Salterton EX9 7AJ. Tel: (01395) 445894

*Mr and Mrs N. Lindsay-Fynn • 3½ m E of Exmouth on B3178 Budleigh
Salterton – Knowle road • Open for charity for parties of 20 or more by appt •
Entrance: £4, children £2, (£5 with guided tour with head gardener, children
£3) • Other information: Refreshments by special arrangement* ◑ ♨ WC ♿

Inspired by the Savill Gardens (see entry in Surrey), the present owner's father
developed this woodland garden in the 1950s. Although at its peak in spring,
with acres of daffodils followed by rhododendrons, azaleas and magnolias,
there is now plenty to see later in the year. Following much recent landscaping, the formal garden round the house merges into the woodland rising
above it, with curving beds full of new planting that includes collections of
hydrangeas and fuchsias, together with many grasses and a bog garden. In the
woodland, with its fine tall trees and distant views of the sea, the mown glades

are surrounded by masses of azaleas, *ponticum* and other species rhododendrons, some rare; the large collection of camellias includes white varieties which are often in flower on Christmas Day. The nineteenth-century walled garden is still run as a traditional vegetable garden, with flowers for cutting and greenhouses. There is also a conservatory, an Adam pavilion and a little herb garden.

Lukesland

Harford, Ivybridge PL21 0JF. Tel: (01752) 893390

Mrs R. Howell • 1½ m N of Ivybridge off A38, on Harford road • Open 14th, 21st, 28th March, 4th April; then 11th April to 13th June, Wed, Sun and Bank Holiday Mons; all 2 – 6pm • Entrance: £3.20, children free (2003 prices) • Other information: Teas during main season only. Coaches by appt ● 💭 WC ♿ 🐕 ✎

More a botanical park than a garden – on entering the grounds you could be forgiven for believing you were in the foothills of the Himalayas. Lying on the hem of Dartmoor, Lukesland is Victorian in both origin and taste. The house was built in 1862 in the Victorian Gothic style by W.E. Matthews. The delightfully secluded valley of Addicombe Brook is the setting here for 15 acres of flowering shrubs, trees and carpets of wild flowers – a gem of its kind. Although recent planting has ensured a greater variety of all-year interest, it is in spring that the profusion of rhododendrons, camellias and azaleas show the garden at its resplendent best. The magnificent *Magnolia campbellii*, over 21 metres tall, is one of the many fine specimen trees. The pocket-handkerchief tree, planted in 1936, is thought to be one of the largest in the country. The brook, which tumbles and gurgles its way over ponds and waterfalls, is crisscrossed by a series of delightful bridges which enable the visitor to wander at leisure amid scenes of great tranquillity. James McAndrew undertook the first major landscaping of the garden in the 1880s. The late owner and his family have carried out further planting, including a fine pinetum, and the construction of more ponds and bridges, all in the spirit of the original, and this is continuing.

Marwood Hill ★★

Marwood, Barnstaple EX31 4EB. Tel: (01271) 342528

Dr J. Snowdon • 4m NW of Barnstaple off A361. Signposted • Open all year, daily except 25th Dec, dawn – dusk • Entrance: £3, accompanied children under 12 free • Other information: Teas on Sun and Bank Holidays and for parties by arrangement ○ 💭 WC 🐕 ✎

With its wonderful collection of plants and its delightful setting, this 20-acre garden is of special interest to the connoisseur but could not fail to give pleasure to any visitor. Five thousand different varieties of plants covering collections of willows, ferns, magnolias, eucryphias, rhododendrons and hebes, and a fine collection of camellias in a glasshouse. There is also a large planting of eucalyptus and betulas. Other features include a pergola draped with 12 varieties of wisteria, raised alpine scree beds, three small lakes with an extensive bog garden and National Collections of astilbes, clematis, *Iris ensata*, and tulbaghias.

The Moorings

Rocombe, Lyme Regis, Dorset DT7 3RR. Tel: (01297) 443295

Mrs E. Marriage • 2m NW of Lyme Regis. Take A3070 out of Lyme Regis, turn right to Rocombe and Rhode Hill. Over crossroads, after ½ m ignore left fork and park on left on verge near 'garden open' sign • Open 10th, 11th April, 2nd, 3rd May, 31st Oct for NGS, and by appt at other times • Entrance: £1.50, accompanied children free ● 🍵 WC ❀

Especially rewarding to visit in spring and autumn, the garden lies on a sheltered, steep, west-facing slope. Impressively, most of the arboretum trees have been grown from seed; there is a collection of eucalyptus, many unusual pines including umbrella and maritime pines (grown from seed gathered in the south of France) and nothofagus, including *N. obliqua* and *N. procera*, and the woodland is underplanted with snowdrops, daffodils and bluebells. *Hibiscus paramutabilis*, a hardy shrub with large flowers in August, is very rare in this country; there are camellias and a 10-metre-high magnolia, and a buddleia flowering rose-red in June. A point of interest is the collection of many different species of fern.

Overbecks Museum and Garden ★ [Historic Garden Grade II]

Sharpitor, Salcombe TQ8 8LW. Tel: (01548) 842893

The National Trust • 1½ m S of Salcombe, SW of South Sands • Museum open 30th March to Sept, daily except Sat, 11am – 5.30pm; Oct, Sun – Thurs, 11am – 5pm • Garden open all year, daily • Entrance: £3.20 (museum and garden £4.40) • Other information: No coaches ○ 🍵 🍽 WC ♿ 🌼 🏛 ♞

Palms stand in this exotic garden high above the Salcombe estuary, giving a strongly Mediterranean atmosphere. The mild maritime climate enables it to be filled with exotics such as myrtles, daturas, agaves and the rare example of a large camphor tree, *Cinnamomum camphora*. The Himalayan *Magnolia campbellii*, over 100 years old and 12 metres high and wide, is a sight to see in February and March. The steep terraces were built in 1901 and lead down through fuchsia trees, huge fruiting banana palms and myrtles to a wonderful *Cornus kousa*. In the centre of the garden are four large beds packed with herbaceous perennials, many of them rare and tender; they are spectacular from July through to September. The parterre of classical design is enlivened in season by orange and lemon trees. The range of unusual and exotic plants is being extended and some of the more hidden areas at the perimeters of the garden made more accessible.

Paignton Zoo Environmental Park

Totnes Road, Paignton TQ4 7EU. Tel: (01803) 697500

The Whitley Wildlife Conservation Trust • 1m W of centre of Paignton on Totnes Road • Open all year, daily except 25th Dec, from 10am (closing times vary according to season) • *Entrance: £8, OAPs £6.50, children £5.75 (2003 prices)* ○ 💬 ✕ 🍴 <u>WC</u> ♿ 🏛 🖈 ☕

Those with mixed views on zoos may be won over by Paignton; it is in the forefront of animal and plant conservation and one of the zoos worldwide involved in the breeding of endangered species. As well as the healthy and happy animals there are the plants. Over 80 acres in size, this was the first zoo in the country to combine animals and a botanic garden, laid out 80 years ago and added to over the years. There are five habitat areas: wetland, desert, savannah, forest and tropical forest. Plant selection is governed by many factors including toxicity and suitability for particular animals. Garden areas are themed geographically and botanically: hardy Chinese plants surround the baboon rock, while medicinal plants are used around the veterinary centre. One of the large glasshouses contains a desert exhibit with plants from arid areas. A tropical display area, complete with birds and reptiles, gives visitors the experience of this very different environment, and a garden of tender plants from around the world has been established outside the restaurant.

RHS Garden Rosemoor ★★

Great Torrington EX38 8PH. Tel: (01805) 624067

The Royal Horticultural Society • *7m SE of Bideford, 1m SE of Great Torrington on A3124* • *Open all year, daily except 25th Dec, 10am – 6pm (closes 5pm Oct to March)* • *Entrance: £5, children £1* ○ 💬 ✕ 🍴 <u>WC</u> ♿ 🌿 🏛 🖈 ☕

Lady Anne Berry created the original garden here and her eight acres contain over 3500 plants from all over the world, many of which she collected. Rosemoor was the Society's first regional garden, second in importance only to Wisley, with which it has a certain stylistic affinity. The 40 acres include a new formal garden with 2000 roses in 200 varieties, colour-themed gardens, a herb garden, a *potager*, cottage, foliage and winter gardens, an alpine terrace, three model gardens and extensive herbaceous borders. The new garden designed by Tom Stuart-Smith displays a wide range of plants grown mainly for their leaves, particularly grasses. The eighteenth-century gazebo from the grounds of Palmer House, Great Torrington has been reconstructed in the south arboretum, giving fine views across the garden and the valley. Elsewhere are stream and bog gardens and a large walled fruit and vegetable garden. National Collections of ilex (over 100 kinds) and cornus are planted throughout. Lectures, talks, garden walks and demonstrations are held all year; there are also many events (telephone for full programme). Free guide books for children.

Saltram House [Historic Garden Grade II*]

Plympton, Plymouth PL7 1UH. Tel: (01752) 333500

The National Trust • *3m E of Plymouth. From A379 turn N to Billacombe. After 1m turn left to Saltram* • *House open 27th March to Oct, daily except Fri (but open Good Friday)* • *Garden open all year, daily except Fri (but open Good Friday), 11am – 5pm (closes 4pm Feb, March)* • *Entrance: £3.50 (house and garden £6.90)* ◑ 💬 📖 🍴 <u>WC</u> ♿ 🌿 🏛 🖈 ☕

The original garden dates from the 1740s, with Victorian and twentieth-century overlays. There are three eighteenth-century buildings – a castle or folly, an orangery (home to orange and lemon trees during the winter months) and a classical garden house named Fanny's Bower after Fanny Burney, who came here in 1789 in the entourage of George III. A long lime avenue is underplanted with narcissi in spring and *Cyclamen hederifolium* in autumn, and a central glade has specimen trees like the stone pine and Himalayan spruce. Set against rolling lawns are several walks with magnolias, camellias, rhododendrons and Japanese maples which, with other trees, make for dramatic autumn colour. Tree walk guide available. The restored (2002) Graham Stuart Thomas border provides colour through the summer months, as do a wide variety of hydrangeas. Many areas of long grass abound with wild flowers throughout the spring and early summer.

Tapeley Park ★ [Historic Garden Grade II*]

Instow EX39 4NT. Tel: (01271) 342558

Mr H.T.C. Christie • 2m N of Bideford S off A39 Barnstaple – Bideford road • House open for pre-booked parties (additional £2.50 per person) • Gardens open 18th March to 1st Nov, daily except Sat, 10am – 5pm • Entrance: £4, OAPs £3.50, children £2.50. Special rates for parties of 5 or more ◐ 💺 ✕ 🍽 WC ⴵ 🐾 ♨ 🏛 ☕ ⚒

The mellow red-brick William and Mary house bestrides the narrow estuary of the River Torridge. It was the nobility of its elevated setting that inspired a much later hand – the architect John Belcher – to create a triple cascade of Italian terraces at the beginning of the twentieth century. These have now been restored to startling effect by Mary Keen, with planting of longitudinal bands of colour emphasising their length and formality. The way from the house to the lake winds down a beautiful woodland walk; the water is backed by magnificent *Thuja plicata*, said to be the oldest in the country. Within the gardens is a set of small buildings, which include a circular shell-lined grotto, a brick ice-house, a Georgian dairy, a handsome neo-Grecian lodge and a fine 1855 obelisk. The eighteenth-century walled kitchen garden is very much a working area, and there is a new organic garden producing fruit, vegetables, nuts and herbs. The wild garden houses farm animals and an adventure playground. For plantsmen there are fine specimens including exotics (*Abelia floribunda*, sophoras and accas from Brazil), and for those interested in landscape design there is ornamental water, yew hedges, an ilex tunnel, giant beeches and oaks. A garden for all tastes and all seasons, and a house owned by a family with a fascinating history – the Christies of Glyndebourne in Sussex. Mary Keen was also responsible for the new gardens around the rebuilt opera house at *Glyndebourne* itself, where Christopher Lloyd and head gardener Chris Hughes are also reinvigorating the existing planting schemes. Those interested in Victorian walled kitchen gardens should visit *Clovelly Court Garden* in Bideford, with its magnificent glasshouses [open March to Oct, daily, 10am – 4pm].

Tudor Rose Tea Rooms and Garden

36 New Street, The Barbican, Plymouth PL1 2NA.

Plymouth Corporation • *In old town centre* • *Open all year, Tues – Sun, 9.30am 5.30pm* • *Entrance: free* ○ ➍ ✕ WC ⅙ ⬳ ✎

An integral part of an area of Plymouth that is being refurbished, this is an interesting reconstruction of the type of Tudor garden that would have existed behind the houses in this ancient street. As far as possible only plants which grew in Elizabethan England have been established. Elsewhere in Plymouth the Corporation commemorates great Victorian seaside gardening with colourful carpet bedding, hanging baskets and tubs.

University of Exeter ★

Streatham Estate, Prince of Wales Road, Exeter EX4 4PX. Tel: (01392) 263059

University of Exeter • *On N outskirts of Exeter on A396, turn E onto B3183* • *Garden open all year, daily* • *Entrance: free* • *Other information: Coaches by appt only* ○ ⬳

There is much to see on a one-mile tour of these extensive gardens, which are based on those created in the 1860s by an East India merchant who inherited a fortune made by blockade-running in the Napoleonic Wars. The landscaping and tree planting was carried out by Veitch, whose plant collectors (E.H. 'Chinese' Wilson among them) went all over the world, and at that time many of the trees were unique in Europe. There is a series of lakes with wildfowl, dogwoods, birches, hazels and alders, callistemon shrubs (bottle brushes), wingnut trees (*Pterocarya stenoptera*) brought from China in 1860, and a maidenhair tree (*Gingko biloba*) sacred in Buddhist China. Rockeries have collections of alpines; there is a banana tree (*Musa basjoo*), a large *Gunnera tinctoria* and palm trees introduced by Robert Fortune in 1849. Formal gardens and bedding plants lead to a sunken scented garden. Exeter will house the National Collection of azaras, evergreens from Chile with scented yellow flowers. There are, of course, rhododendrons, magnolias, camellias in a woodland walk; also roses, eucalyptus and *Opuntia humifusa*, the prickly pear cactus flowering in summer.

POSTCODE PLANTS DATABASE

It is often difficult to find out which plants are local to an area. The Postcode Plants Database locates the names of flowers, trees, butterflies and birds for each of Britain's 26 million home addresses. The website is www.nhm.ac.uk/science/projects/fff; simply by typing in the first four characters of their postcode, householders, schools, garden centres and councils can obtain tailor-made lists of local plants which are both hospitable and garden-worthy. Also included are the names of butterflies and birds most likely to visit gardens in each area. The lists come from innovative software, developed by Royal Mail and *FLORA-for-FAUNA* in conjunction with the Natural History Museum, which searches through hundreds of distribution maps of fauna and flora in the British Isles.

DORSET

Two-starred gardens are marked on the map with a black square.

Abbotsbury Sub-Tropical Gardens ★★ [Historic Garden Grade I]

Abbotsbury, Weymouth DT3 4LA. Tel: (01305) 871387

Ilchester Estates • 9m NW of Weymouth, 9m SW of Dorchester off B3157 • Open March to Oct, daily, 10am – 6pm; Nov to Feb, daily except Christmas and New Year period (telephone to check), 10am – dusk • Entrance: £6, OAPs £5.70, children £3.80 ○ 💷 ✕ 🍴 wc ♿ 🐕 ♨ 🏠 🔦 ⚲

The walled garden of Abbotsbury Castle, established by the 1st Countess of Ilchester in 1765, remains the sole trace of the family's summer residence that burned down in 1913. It forms the nucleus of these famous gardens, which contain a rich selection of plants from the Mediterranean. Proximity to the sea and shelter from the north creates the microclimate that has turned the area into a botanical treasure trove. In 1899 the head gardener came from ten years spent at La Mortola in Italy, and it is possible that he introduced the first of the Mediterranean plantings. The same year a catalogue of 5000 plants was produced, while today there must be many more within the 20-acre site which has been extensively restored and replanted over the last two decades. Rare trees abound, such as the ancient wingnut (related to the walnut and one of the best specimens in the British Isles), 100-year-old Chusan palms over 20 metres tall, and the beautiful *Cornus* 'Bentham's Cornel', bright with sulphur yellow bracts in July. Bamboo groves, bog gardens, bananas from Ethiopia, masses of hydrangeas, azaleas, hostas – they are all here to be seen on the well-marked woodland walk, and much else besides. The nearby swannery on the eastern end of the village should not be missed.

Arnmore House

57 Lansdowne Road, Bournemouth BH1 1RN. Tel: (01202) 551440

Mr and Mrs David Hellewell • On B3064 just S of hospital • Open all year, by appt • Entrance: £2.50, children free ● ♿

This highly individual garden has been created over the past 25 years by its owner and reflects his interests as a composer who also has a strong feeling for Chinese art. Ease of maintenance has also been a priority as Mrs Hellewell is disabled. Shape, colour and texture are all-important, with many unusual specimen trees, topiary and box parterres. Trees and shrubs, many chosen for year-round colour and grown in pots, have been pruned and trained to give the desired effect. The formal parterre consists of neat diagonals of *Buxus sempervirens* complemented by clipped balls of *B.s.* 'Aureovariegata'.

Athelhampton House Gardens ★ [Historic Garden Grade I]

Athelhampton, Puddletown, Dorchester DT2 7LG. Tel: (01305) 848363

*Patrick Cooke • 5m NE of Dorchester, 1m E of Puddletown off A35 at
Northbrook junction • House and gardens open March to Oct, daily except Sat;
Dec to Feb, Sun; all 10.30am – 5pm or dusk if earlier • Entrance: £5.50,
children free (house and garden £7.50, OAPs £6.75, children free, parties of 12
or more £5.50 per person) • Other information: Picnics in riverside area only.
Self-catering accommodation available* ◐ 💶 ✕ WC ♿ 🎅 🛍 ♈

The four gardens and two pavilions of the Tudor manor house were
designed for Alfred Cart de La Fontaine in 1891 by F. Inigo Thomas, and
the late Robert Cooke extended the garden with great sensitivity. Courts
and walls follow the original plan with beautiful stone and brickwork arches.
Visitors will take away with them an abiding memory of some of the most
stylish architectural topiary in England, and of the River Piddle, girdling the
garden in its own right and busily harnessed within it to service pools,
fountains and a long canal studded with water lilies. Major features are a
fifteenth-century circular dovecot on the lawn facing the west wing of the
house, and the pleached lime circular grove behind the Pyramid Garden.
Here, twelve massive yews are fashioned to echo the obelisks on the raised
terrace walk, which has a matching pair of charming pavilions standing at
each end. The toll house to the south has been restored. The planting,
including tulips, rambling roses, clematis and jasmine, is big-boned, low-key
and sophisticated. A remarkable, unforgettably atmospheric interpretation
of the late-medieval ideal.

Cartref

Station Road, Stalbridge, Sturminster Newton DT10 2RG.
Tel: (01963) 363705

*Mrs Nesta Ann Smith • 10m SW of Shaftesbury. From A30 at Henstridge traffic
lights turn S for 1m to Stalbridge. Turn left opposite post office; house is 80
metres on right • Open two days for NGS, and April to Sept by appt • Entrance:
£2, children free* ◐ 💶 🛍 WC ♈

If one is to question what makes a good garden, a visit to this quarter acre
behind an unassuming semi-detached village house has the answer for inve-
terate collectors. In this comparatively small area, winding paths, lawn and
small woodland are crammed with clearly labelled rarities, each tree is a
framework for interesting climbers, and the microclimate encourages plants
such as *Cytisus battandieri, Poncirus trifoliata* and terrestrial orchids. The owner is
happy to talk about the plants from provenance to maintenance; her vast
knowledge is gleaned from experience gained by working in well-known
nurseries under such masters as Jim Archibald and the hosta expert, Eric
Smith. Many of the varieties are for sale.

Chettle House

Chettle, Blandford Forum DT11 8DB. Tel: (01258) 830858

Mr and Mrs Peter Bourke • 6m NE of Blandford on A354, turn left to Chettle •
House and garden open. Telephone for opening times. • Entrance: £3.50,
children free ◐ ◙ ▓ WC ♀ ♋

The tranquil site is approached through mature trees where a number of
different horse chestnut species may be seen. There is an elegant church in the
grounds. Beyond the wide lawns framing the impressive Queen Anne house
(designed by the Baroque architect Thomas Archer, of rounded style and
inverted scrolls fame), vistas appropriate to that period are preserved, with a
vineyard on the south slope. Lavish herbaceous borders contain many chalk-
loving plants (some rare), including no fewer than 20 varieties of honeysuckle,
a buddleia collection, and some fine clematis.

Chiffchaffs ★

Chaffeymoor, Bourton, Gillingham SP8 5BY. Tel: (01747) 840841

Mr and Mrs K.R. Potts • 7m NW of Shaftesbury, 3m E of Wincanton. Leave
A303 (Bourton bypass) signed to Bourton and continue to end of village • Open
April to Oct, Wed and Thurs; also 14th, 28th March, 11th, 25th April, 2nd,
16th, 30th May, 13th, 27th June, 29th Aug, 19th Sept; all 2 – 5pm. Also by
appt • Entrance: £2.50, children £1 • Other information: Refreshments and toilet
facilities for parties only ◐ ⚘

An impressive avenue of flowering cherries leads to the 400-year-old cottage
and its cottage garden, full of colour and interest, immaculately maintained,
with an invitation to more pleasures at each turn of the path. The terraces and
viewpoints afford glimpses of open country around, and the varied and
colourful beds and borders are delightful. There is a noteworthy collection
of dwarf bulbs, dwarf rhododendrons and old-fashioned roses, a wide range of
herbaceous plants, and interesting underplanting in the woodland area. 12
acres in all. The well-stocked nursery has a wide variety of healthy-looking
plants. Further along the lane is *Snape Cottage*, a half-acre, conservation-minded
garden with a selection of old-fashioned and unusual perennials. [Open
frequently for NGS, and for parties by appointment – telephone (01747)
840330, evenings only.]

Cranborne Manor Garden ★★ [Historic Garden Grade II*]

Cranborne, Wimborne Minster BH21 5PP. Tel: (01725) 517248

The Viscount and Viscountess Cranborne • 10m N of Wimborne on B3078.
Entrance via garden centre • Open probably March to Sept, Wed only, 9am –
5pm, and some weekends for charity – telephone to check dates • Entrance: £3,
OAPs £2.50 (2003 prices) • Other information: Garden centre open all year
◑ ◙ ✕ WC ♿ ⚘ ♨ ♀ ♋

Tradescant established the basic framework in the early seventeenth century,
but little is left of the original plan. Neglected for a long period, the garden has

been revived in the last three generations and now includes several smaller areas surrounded by tall clipped yew hedges, a walled white garden at its best in midsummer, wide lawns (again yew-lined) and extensive woodland and wild areas. Best of all is the high-walled entrance courtyard to the south, approached through an arch between the two Jacobean gatehouses, though sadly it is no longer grassed over and gravel has won the day. Here the plant selection along the lengthy borders is delightfully imaginative, providing the perfect introduction to what has been called 'the most magical house in Dorset' (not least for the garden which surrounds it). The excellent nursery garden specialises in traditional rose varieties, but also carries a wide selection of other plants, particularly clematis and herbaceous perennials. Another garden with an interesting historical pedigree, but an entirely different experience, is to be found at nearby *Ashley Park Farm*, Damerham. Created by a dedicated conservationist, there are unusual trees and shrubs in attractive woodland walks, ponds and a wildflower meadow, a farm and wild fowl and rare sheep. [Open for NGS and by appt. Tel: (01725) 518200.]

Dean's Court

Wimborne Minster BH21 1EE.

Sir Michael and Lady Hanham • In centre of Wimborne off B3073 • Open several days for NGS • Entrance: £2, OAPs £1.50, children 50p ● ● WC & ⚘ ℚ

A mellow, eighteenth-century brick house set in 13 acres of parkland containing a number of interesting and very large trees. A swamp cypress towers near the house, also a 28-metre tulip tree which flowers from June to July. The many fine specimens include Wellingtonias, Caucasian wing nut, Japanese pagoda tree, blue cedars and horse chestnuts. There are few formal beds, but a courtyard contains an unusually comprehensive herb garden. The walled kitchen garden, in which many of the old varieties of vegetable are grown by chemical-free methods, is extensive and obviously successful. A monastic stewpond where the medieval monks bred their carp can still be seen in this peaceful haven.

Edmondsham House

Edmondsham, Cranborne, Wimborne Minster BH21 5RE. Tel: (01725) 517207

Mrs J. Smith • 9m N of Wimbourne, 1m S of Cranborne. From A354 turn at Sixpenny Handley crossroads to Ringwood and Cranborne • House open 12th to 30th April, Wed and Bank Holiday Mon; Oct, Wed; all 2 – 5pm • Garden open April to Oct, Wed, Sun, 2 – 5pm, and by appt • Entrance: £1.50, children 50p (house and garden £3, children £1, under 5 free) • Other information: Refreshments April and Oct, Wed only ● ● WC & ⚘

The visitor should allow time for a tour of the interesting family house and dairy before venturing out into the large walled kitchen garden. No chemical fertilisers or pesticides are used here. Admire the beds of Russian comfrey, rhubarb, Jerusalem artichokes and asparagus, the herb gardens and the fruit cage before taking the path to the lean-to peach house. The Pit House is a sunken greenhouse, restored in 1990. The arch of the walled garden leads to the paddock and on to the drive and the dell. The pond has an island of *Sasa palmata* and a dawn redwood (*Metasequoia glyptostroboides*). An unusual circular grass hollow is said to have been a cockpit, one of only a very few 'naturalised' areas of the sort in the country. The massed spring bulbs together with the many spring-flowering shrubs make this the best season, but the peaceful, mellow atmosphere pervades the garden throughout the year. Allow time to visit the church to look for the clumps of mistletoe and two unusual trees, *Magnolia acuminata* (cucumber tree) and *Paulownia tomentosa* (foxglove tree).

Forde Abbey ★★ [Historic Garden Grade II*]

Chard, Somerset TA20 4LU. Tel: (01460) 221290

Mr M. Roper • 8m NW of Beaminster, 7m W of Crewkerne, 4m SE of Chard off A30 • House open April to Oct, Tues – Fri, Sun and Bank Holiday Mons, 12 noon – 4pm • Garden open all year, daily, 10am – 4.30pm • Entrance: £5.25, OAPs £4.75, children under 15 free (house and garden £7, OAPs £6.50, children under 15 free. Parties of 20 or more should telephone 01460 220231 for bookings (2003 prices) ○ 🍵 ✕ 🗔 WC ⌖ ⇗ ⚘ 🛒

This unique and fascinating former Cistercian abbey, inhabited as a private house since 1649, is set in a varied and pleasing garden. A canal at the end of the long set of buildings which comprises the stately abbey, and a large lake some distance away, are major features of the extensive garden. Old walls and colourful borders, wide sloping lawns, lush ponds and cascades, graceful statuary and huge mature trees combine to create an atmosphere of timeless elegance. There is something here for every gardener to appreciate: the bog garden displays a large collection of primulas and other Asiatic plants; the shrubbery contains a variety of magnolias, rhododendrons and other delightful specimens. The rock garden was revolutionised by the late Jack Drake, and a fine arboretum has been built up since 1947; at the back of the abbey is an extensive kitchen garden and a nursery selling rare and unusual plants which look in fine health. In nearby Bettiscombe Penelope Hobhouse's renowned garden at *The Coach House* is included among several open annually one weekend in summer. Watch the local press for details – not to be missed.

Frankham Farm

Ryme Intrinseca, Sherborne DT9 6JT. Tel: (01935) 872304

Mr and Mrs R.G. Earle • 6m SW of Sherborne off A37 Yeovil – Dorchester road. 3m S of Yeovil turn left; garden is ¼ m on left • Open 6 days for NGS, and by appt • Entrance: £2, children free ● 🍵 🗔 WC ⌖ ⚘

In spring and early summer, visitors to this charming garden can be assured of plenty of colour. Developed since the 1960s, the flat site of over two acres includes extensive plantings of roses and clematis. Well-stocked herbaceous borders frame a fine view of adjacent fields, with grass walks meandering through woodland and a wild garden planted with spring bulbs and shrubs making a pleasing contrast. A striking group of white foxgloves under eucalyptus leads from the neat kitchen garden into a small plantation of unusual trees, including the Chilean firebush (*Embothrium coccineum*) and *Aesculus pavia*, alongside rhododendrons, azaleas and camellias. Farm buildings form an attractive backdrop. This is a high-quality, very English garden in a tranquil setting.

Horn Park

Beaminster DT8 3HB. Tel: (01308) 862212

Mr and Mrs David Ashcroft • 1½ m N of Beaminster on A3066 on left before tunnel • Open April to Oct, Tues – Thurs, by appt • Entrance: £3.50 • Other information: Teas by prior arrangement ◑ WC ⅄ ⬗

Although the impressive house designed by Lawrence Dale, a pupil of Lutyens, dates from 1910, the garden is based partly on features discovered as the work progressed. A drive through parkland leads to the wide gravel sweep before the entrance porch, with terraced lawns to the front of the house and a panoramic view east and south towards Beaminster and the distant coast. Other features include rock areas, herbaceous and rose borders, unusual plants and shrubs, a water garden beneath a steep azalea bank, ponds, a woodland garden and walks among wild flowers, including orchids and blue-bells in spring. The natural wildflower meadow, with over 160 different flowers and grasses, is listed as a site of nature conservation interest.

Ivy Cottage ★

Aller Lane, Lower Ansty, Dorchester DT2 7PX. Tel: (01258) 880053

Anne and Alan Stevens • 12m NE of Dorchester, 10m W of Blandford in centre of triangle between A352, A354 and A3030. Take turning near Fox Inn, Ansty • Open May to Sept, Thurs, 10am – 5pm, and for parties by appt at other times • Entrance: £2.50 ◐ 🥬 WC ⚘

Mrs Stevens trained and worked as a professional gardener before coming to her cottage over 30 years ago. Although chalk underlies the surrounding land, this one-and-three-quarter-acre garden is actually on greensand; it has springs and a stream that keep it well watered and is therefore an ideal home for plants such as primulas, irises, gunneras, and in particular trollius and moisture-loving lobelias. Other delights are a thriving and ordered vegetable garden (which hardly ever needs a hose), large herbaceous borders giving colour all year round, drifts of bulbs and other spring plants surrounding specimen trees and shrubs, and three most interesting raised beds for alpines. Wildlife, especially birds, are actively encouraged.

Kingston Lacy ★ [Historic Garden Grade II]

Wimborne Minster BH21 4EA. Tel: (01202) 883402

The National Trust • 1½ m NW of Wimborne on B3082 • House open late March to early Nov, Sat – Wed, 11am – 5pm (last admission 4pm) • Park and garden open late March to early Nov, daily, 10.30am – 6pm; Nov to 22nd Dec, Fri, Sat, Sun, 10.30am – 4pm; Feb, March, Sat, Sun, 10.30am – 4pm. Additional opening for snowdrops – telephone for details • Entrance: garden and park: £3.60, children £1.75, family £9.50 (house, garden and park: £7.20, children £3.60, family £19, parties of 15 or more £5.80 per person, children £2.90) • *Other information: Volunteer-driven buggy on house-open days. Dogs in park only, on lead* ◑ ⬛ ✕ 🍴 WC ⬧ 🌿 ⬛ 🔫 ⚲

This 32-acre formal garden, with nine acres of lawn, also has a wonderful lime avenue planted in 1668, which leads to the Nursery Wood containing a fine collection of rhododendrons and azaleas. The terrace displays urns, vases and lions in bronze and marble, and there are interesting marble wellheads or tubs for bay trees; also an Egyptian obelisk and a sarcophagus. The parterre was laid out in 1899 for Mrs Henrietta Bankes in memory of her husband and is still planted in the seasonal schemes designed for her. During the spring they are filled with wallflowers and forget-me-nots, during the summer with salmon-pink *Begonia semperflorens* and *Heliotropum* 'Marine'. The Victorian fernery, planted with 25 different types of fern and the National Collection of *Anemone nemorosa*, leads to the once-fine cedar walk, where one of the trees was planted by the Duke of Wellington in 1827 and others by visiting royalty. Spectacular roses include 'Bonica', 'Cardinal Hume', 'Nozomi' and 'Amber Queen'. The garden also contains the National Collection of convallarias. There is a circular woodland walk, including children's play equipment. In spring, many areas are covered in snowdrops, daffodils and bluebells.

Kingston Maurward Gardens ★ [Historic Garden Grade II*]

Dorchester DT2 8PY. Tel: (01305) 215003

Kingston Maurward Gardens • *E of Dorchester off A35. Turn off at roundabout at end of bypass* • *Open 5th Jan to 19th Dec, daily, 10am – 5.30pm. Guided tours by appt* • *Entrance: £4, children £2.50, under 3 free. Family season tickets available (gardens and farm animal park)* ◑ ⬛ 🍴 WC ♿ 🌿 ⬛ 🔫 ⚲

Three distinct periods coexist harmoniously here. In 1720 the handsome house was built, dignified by a contemporary landscape park with 35 acres of fine trees, water and woodland. Then, between 1918 and 1920, the formal gardens to the west of the mansion were laid out by the Hanbury family, who also owned La Mortola in Italy. Within splendid stone terraces, balustrading, steps and yew hedges, they made a series of intimate enclosures, including water features, topiary, a yew maze, and other requisites of a grand Edwardian garden. Positioned on a steep hillside overlooking the 8-acre lake, the views are outstanding. The most recent phase in the gardens' history has been their determined restoration since 1990 by the present incumbents, the staff and students of the Dorset Agricultural College. Their utilitarian training facilities might occupy the perimeter, but the formal gardens are resplendent once more. National Collections of penstemons and salvias are held here, together with a large collection of herbaceous perennials; in spring drifts of bulbs occupy the sweeping lawns and the margins of the lake. Of particular interest is the statuary on long loan from the Palace of Westminster and the restored Grecian temple at the lake's edge. There is also a Japanese-style garden with Chusan palms, bamboos and maples, a tree trail with 65 different species to discover, and an animal park for children. Thomas Hardy's father helped with building work within the house itself, and *Hardy's Cottage*, now a National Trust property with a small colourful garden, is nearby.

Knoll Gardens and Nursery ★

Hampreston, Wimborne Minster BH21 7ND. Tel: (01202) 873931

Mr Neil Lucas • Between Wimborne and Ferndown, off Ham Lane (B3073). Leave A31 at Canford Bottom roundabout. Signed 1½ m • Open all year, Wed – Sun, 10am – 5pm (or dusk if earlier). Closed Christmas and New Year period • Entrance: £3.50, OAPs £3, students £2.50, children (5–15) £2, family £9.50. Reductions for parties of 15 or more ◐ 💷 **WC** & ☙

Twenty-five years ago this was a private botanic garden, but it is now laid out in an informal English setting with mature specimen trees and shrubs giving a relaxed and intimate atmosphere. Although only a little over four acres, the many different areas, winding pathways and constantly changing views give an impression of a much larger area. The owners continue to develop the garden and its plant collections, particularly with hardy perennials and grasses. The summer garden has a collection of exotic-looking tender perennials, the water garden has several waterfalls and the newly designed Dragon Garden boasts a fine collection of modern perennials and grasses around a central pool. There are areas planted for dry shade and for moisture and a newly extended gravel garden for drought-tolerant plants. National Collections of deciduous ceanothus, phygelius and pennisetums. Christopher Bradley-Hole's new amphitheatre garden at *Portland Castle* is 12 miles away.

Langebride House

Long Bredy, Dorchester DT2 9HU. Tel: (01308) 482257

Mrs Greener • 8m W of Dorchester off A35 Dorchester – Bridport road. Turn S to Long Bredy • Open two Suns for NGS, and at other times by appt • Entrance: £3 ◐ **WC** &

This garden has so many desirable features it is impossible to avoid making a list: 200-year-old copper beech rising from wide, lush lawns, underplanted with carpets of spring bulbs; a thriving enclosed vegetable garden of manageable size, backing onto a sloping grass area with colourful mixed borders along the tile-topped walls; a rising slope to the mixed wild woodland behind, where favourite trees have been planted in groups to allow for culling as they enlarge; a formal yew-lined lawn with pond, fountain and old stone features, from which steps descend through sloping shrubberies towards the front of the house. A miniature area of greensand allows a patch of acid-loving plants to provide contrast. A long line of pleached limes runs parallel with the bi-colour beech hedge along the road. There is also a sloping orchard, a tennis court with a tall rockery behind, planted with alpines, which acts as a viewing point and sun-trap, beds and borders, trellises for climbing plants and low stone walls for those that prefer to hang. All around, thousands of bulbs hide in waiting for the spring explosion which, in the owner's opinion, is the best season to visit.

Loscombe House

Bridport DT6 3TL. Tel: (01308) 488361

Mr and Mrs Andrewes • 3m N of Bridport, 2m SE of Beaminster, 1m E of A3066. In Melplash take Loscombe turn opposite Half Moon Inn and after ½ m turn right (signed to Loscombe). Continue 1m to bottom of lane • Open April to Sept, Sat – Tues, 11am – 6pm • Entrance: free (donations to Macmillan Cancer Relief welcome) ◐ 🐚 ♿

Once a 'lost combe', this is Dorset at its most rural. Set in a four-acre site, the garden has a background of hills which drop down close to the boundary. Hillside tree-planting undertaken in 1970 has now developed into woodland, improved from 1984 when the valley bog was drained. An attractive flowing stream is a focus, with grass paths winding among well-maintained and decorative shrubs and perennials, including roses, clematis and hostas, sustained by the microclimate within this sheltered site. A delightful, peaceful scene, far indeed from the madding crowd.

The Manor House

Sandford Orcas, Sherborne DT9 4SB. Tel: (01963) 220206

Sir Mervyn Medlycott, Bt • 2½ m N of Sherborne, turning off B3148, next to village church • House open • Garden open 12th April, 10am – 6pm, then May and July to Sept, Sun and Mon, 2 – 5pm. Also by appt for parties at other times • Entrance: £1.50 (house and garden £3, children £1.50). Reduced rates for pre-booked parties of 10 or more ◐ 🐚 WC ⟡ ℺

Looked at purely as a garden, this is not exceptional. It is the medieval house, ancient and redolent of its long history, which permeates the scene and dominates the garden. An old, flagged path slopes up between bordered lawns towards an open field. The stone walls at either side are attractive, and where they stop the eye travels on into the countryside beyond. There is a herb garden with a pleasant view across a lower lawn along the south side of the house. At the end of this lawn another viewpoint back towards the south front allows the attractive planting below the herb garden to show at its best. Roses and other climbing plants clinging to the honey-grey walls harmonise well with this gracious setting.

Mapperton ★★ [Historic Garden Grade II*]

Beaminster DT8 3NR. Tel: (01308) 862645

The Earl and Countess of Sandwich • 5m NE of Bridport, 2m SE of Beaminster between A356 and A3066 • House open 28th June to 6th Aug, Mon – Fri, 2 – 4pm, and by appt • Garden open March to Oct, daily, 2 – 6pm. House and garden tours available by prior appt (£2 extra) • Entrance: £4, children (5–18) £2.90, under 5 free ◐ 💌 ✕ 🐚 WC ♿ 🌿 🏛 ⚘

Dorset's combes are famously intriguing, and Mapperton offers one of the county's most atmospheric gardens set into a unique stepped valley. This is garden-as-opera-set, beginning on the first of three levels with the courtyard garden at the front of the charming sixteenth- and seventeenth-century manor house which introduces a cast of old roses and clematis. To the east, beyond the seventeenth-century house and below the main lawn, the drama quickens as land falls to the Fountain Court with its sculptured topiary and Italianate features. Pools of water, carved stone steps, a pergola and foaming Mediterranean borders, including *Artemisia* 'Powis Castle'. *Phlomis italica* and species salvias face the classical orangery, built by the current owner's father in 1968. A golden hamstone wall shows off a living wallpaper of pink *Erigeron karvinskianus* and a tree poppy, *Romneya coulteri*. The Baroque-inspired fountain, beautifully restored, is surrounded by box and yew to evoke the original 1920s' design (probably by Pike, a local architect) for the then owner, Mrs Labouchere. Below are deep fishponds reflecting 'walls' of yew and the tower house above. These yew walls repay attention, for their niches display evocative statuary. Down on the third level – the floor of the valley – is a small arboretum of species trees and shrubs, which opens into the 'wild' countryside beyond with cattle looming. Mapperton is a draw for garden lovers and for photographers and watercolourists in particular, because of the play of light across the planes of this extraordinary north-south valley.

Melbury House ★ [Historic Park and Garden Grade II*]

Melbury Sampford, Dorchester DT2 0LF. Tel: (01935) 83699 (Garden Office)

Mr James and The Hon. Mrs Townshend • 13m NW of Dorchester on A37 Yeovil – Dorchester road. Signposted • Open 13th, 27th May, 10th, 24th June, 8th, 29th July, 12th Aug, 2 – 5pm • Entrance: £3, OAPs and children £2 • Other information: Guided walks on normal open days at no charge at 2.30pm, and by arrangement for parties of up to 15 (£3.50 per person) ● ● WC ●

The outstanding eighteenth-century historic house (not open) is approached by a long drive through open parkland. Visitors are directed to the west side and enter through the large walled garden, a good part still maintained as a productive kitchen garden. A walk through the western part of the arboretum ends at the bottom of the south lawn with fine views of the house and across the lake to the deer park. The main part of the arboretum with its massed spring bulbs lies to the east in the Valley Garden, overlooked by the ancient family church (open). Herbaceous borders along the south of the house lead to a colourful walled flower garden. Recent seasons have seen much replanting so this garden will be a source of continuous interest.

Melplash Court

Melplash, Bridport DT6 3UH. Tel: (01308) 488418

Mr and Mrs T. Lewis • 5m N of Bridport on A3066 • Open 20th, 26th June, 2 – 6pm, and by appt • Entrance: £3 ● ● WC & ● ●

The elegant sixteenth-century house, set among the Dorset hills with the sea over the horizon, is approached through an avenue of mature trees. The owners have respected plans for the garden as laid out by the previous owner, Lady Diana Tiarks, but have extensively restored and extended the area so that new planting is a feature without disturbing the general concept. On the whole, muted colours are preferred and expressed in a wonderful variety of foliage, particularly on the banks above the stream garden. Each section, including the outstanding Japanese garden, is a surprise as the visitor progresses via walled areas into carefully planned bedding that dramatises the sloping contours. A walled kitchen garden features knots where again leaf shape, in the form of rhubarb, leek, cabbage, angelica, creates attractive patterns. Herbaceous borders have recently been planted on the croquet lawn stretching out from the house. Maintenance is first-class.

Millmead

Winterborne Stickland DT11 ONT. Tel: (01258) 880814

Michele Barker • 4m SW of Blandford. After The Crown pub, turn right down West Street, signed to Winterbourne Houghton, then first left after 30mph sign • Open two days for NGS, and by appt • Entrance: £2, children 50p ● ⇦ ⚘

This ⅓-acre site is a showcase for its owner, a talented garden designer. Situated in the picturesque Winterborne valley, it has been developed around a modern village house, with garden rooms that belie its sloping nature, each demonstrating good use of colour, architectural features and vistas through to each area. The modern trend for pebbles, pillars and coloured furniture is predominant, with clever use of screening and some arresting blue and purple planting. Any gardener wishing to renovate a small patch would benefit from a visit, learning from its good structure and strong contrasts.

Minterne [Historic Garden Grade II]

Minterne Magna, Dorchester DT2 7AU. Tel: (01300) 341370

Lord Digby • 9m N of Dorchester, 2m N of Cerne Abbas on A352 • Open March to 10th Nov, daily, 10am – 7pm • Entrance: £3, accompanied children free ◑ **WC** ⇦

Minterne is a grand house in a magnificent setting. There are many rare trees, and one and a half miles of walks with palm trees, cedars, beeches, etc giving spectacular spring and autumn colour. At the lower end of the valley the stream with its lakes and waterfalls is surrounded by splendid tall trees, among which the paths wind back towards the house. The lakes contain many water lilies, and ducks have been introduced to deal with the duckweed. The garden has an interesting collection of Himalayan rhododendrons and azaleas, spring bulbs, cherries and maples. A restful and attractive atmosphere – the informative and personally written labels will encourage visitors to linger.

Moreton Gardens

Moreton DT2 8RF. Tel: (01929) 405084

Richard and Liz Frampton-Hobbs • 7m E of Dorchester off B3390 • Open March to Sept, daily, 10am – 5pm. Groups and coaches welcome • Entrance: £2.50, accompanied children under 16 free • Other information: Moreton Tea Rooms open daily, 10am – 5pm, catering for parties and coaches by appt (Tel: (01929) 463647) ◖ 🍴 <u>WC</u> ⅛ ⚘ 🏛 ⚑ ⚲

This tranquil three-acre garden has been re-created in an old setting along the banks of a flowing stream in a picturesque village associated with Lawrence of Arabia – he is buried in the cemetery. The presence of water, the gentle undulations of the site, and the imaginative design and planting schemes result in a delightful scene in which the visitor is led from one pleasant vista to another. Although the new planting is well established, and the rose beds in particular make a great show, in future years the design will greatly benefit from fast-maturing trees; a pergola and eye-catching fountains provide a good structural framework. The extensive plant centre reflects the number of attractive specimens to be seen in the garden itself.

The Old Rectory

Litton Cheney, Dorchester DT2 9AH. Tel: (01308) 482383

Mr and Mrs Hugh Lindsay • 9m W of Dorchester, 1m S of A35 • Open for NGS probably 11th April, on other days for charity in May and June, 2 – 6pm, and by appt • Entrance: £2.50, children free ● 🍴 🍴 WC ⅛ ⚘ ⚲

The house rests comfortably below the church and is approached by a gravel drive which circles a small lawn; a thatched summerhouse stands to one side like a massive beehive. The small walled garden has outhouses and a large barn on two sides and borders around three, prolifically stocked with well-chosen and favourite plants in specific colour bands. A steep path leads down into the four acres of natural woodland, a surprisingly extensive area of mature trees with many springs, streams and ponds – never a water shortage here, even in the driest of summers. This area was reclaimed by the current owners, who are adding new young trees and shrubs as well as successfully encouraging many spring-flowering plant colonies, mostly native. Climbing back up to the house, the visitor arrives at the belvedere giving views over trees to farmland on the other side of the valley. Spring and autumn are the best times to see this garden, from which Reynolds Stone, the wood-engraver, drew inspiration.

The Old Rectory

Pulham, Dorchester DT2 7EA. Tel (01258) 817595

Mr and Mrs N. Elliott • 13m N of Dorchester, 8m SE of Sherborne on B3143. Turn E at Pulham crossroads and continue to church • Open for NGS, and for groups by appt • Entrance: £2.50, children free ● WC ⅛ ⚘ ⚲

A well-maintained three-acre garden with superb views, developed around a fine eighteenth-century house. Plants, sometimes rare and often for sale, are attractively placed within box parterres sheltered by yew hedging and mature trees. Beyond the formal areas lie a further four-and-a-half acres of recently planted woodland and shrubbery, with pleasant walks. There are also two ponds and a small arboretum.

The Old Rectory

Tarrant Gunville, Nr Blandford Forum, DT11 8JN. Tel: (01258) 830309

Mr and Mrs John Stoller • 7m NE of Blandford, off A354 at Tarrant Hinton •
Open for small groups by prior arrangement only. Please write or telephone •
Entrance: by donation to designated charity NEW ●

The entrance to the handsome eighteenth-century house is dominated by a
towering evergreen oak, indication of the climatic advantages of this tucked-
away village. The owners, originally gardeners in Minnesota, where they faced
extremes of seasonal temperature, have resurrected the one-acre garden from
near-dereliction in the last four years. They inherited high brick walls and a
backdrop of tall trees; within the garden their use of contrasting greens is
original, varying textures and tones against good pale stonework. Box sculpture and yew planting break up the grass area, and attractive divisions are
made by alternating juniper and laurel. Where borders do occur, their curving
edges trimmed to perfection, planting is immaculate and interesting. Roses
and clematis grace the walls. An altogether serene and sophisticated place.

The Priest's House Museum

23–27 High Street, Wimborne Minster BH21 1HR. Tel: (01202) 882533

The Priest's House Museum • In centre of Wimborne • Museum open • Garden open
April to Oct, Mon – Sat, 10am – 4.30pm; also July, Aug, Sun, 2 – 5pm. Advisable
to check before travelling • Entrance: £2.50, OAPs £1.90, children £1 (museum and
garden) • Other information: Refreshments in summer only ◑ 💻 WC ふ ⌗ 🏛 🔔 ℺

In the heart of this small town lies a walled garden, hidden from the busy
shopping thoroughfare by the frontage of the museum. Both are well worth a
visit. The 100-metre-long garden is laid out with some formal beds but mostly
lawn, herbaceous and herb borders. In late spring the wisteria on the back of
the house is particularly appealing. Sit on one of the seats dotted around and
enjoy the peaceful atmosphere of this well-cared-for garden staffed by volunteers who are only too pleased to answer questions about the plants.

Sherborne Castle ★ [Historic Park Grade II*]

Sherborne DT9 5NR. Tel: (01935) 813182

The Wingfield Digby family • Signed from Sherborne • Castle and garden open
April to Oct, Tues – Thurs, Sat, Sun and Bank Holiday Mons, 11am –
4.30pm (castle opens Sat 2.30pm) • Entrance: £3, children free (castle and
grounds £6, OAPs £5.50, children free, parties of 15 or more £5.25 per person)
• Other information: Private viewings for parties of 15 or more by arrangement
◑ 💻 ✕ 🍽 WC ふ ⌗ 🏛 🔔 ℺

As they are seen today, the castle grounds are based on landscaping undertaken in the late eighteenth century by 'Capability' Brown for the 6th Lord
Digby, when the lake was created out of the then-flowing River Yeo, and the
famous hanging gardens enjoyed by Sir Walter Raleigh and his wife Bess a
century earlier were lost forever. Sweeping acres of deer park surround the

impressive castle, and masonry salvaged from the crumbling ruin of the old castle, destroyed during the Civil War in 1645, gave rise to fine stable blocks, courtyards and nearby Castleton Church. A charming walled flower garden has been designed within one of the courtyards near the orangery, but the main attraction lies surely in the site's unique history, the colourful scene of water against graceful sloping lawns, and the ancient ruin visible across the lake. As Alexander Pope wrote with enthusiasm to a friend: 'This is so peculiar and its situation of so uncommon kind, that it merits a more particular description.' A visit to the delightful and comprehensive *Castle Gardens Plant Centre*, established in the original walled kitchen garden of the castle and accessible from the main road, is worth a detour.

Shute House ★

Donhead St Mary, Shaftesbury SP7 9DG. Tel: (01935) 814389

Mr and Mrs John Lewis • 5m NE of Shaftesbury, off A30. Near Donhead St Mary church • Open Mon – Fri by appt for parties of 20 to 40 • Entrance: £3.50 • Other information: Teas by arrangement ● ● ● WC & ●

The handsome early-eighteenth-century house (originally a fifteenth-century pilgrims' inn) standing at the edge of the estate close to the road is surrounded by a garden of many springs and ponds – the source of a river. The marvellous site faces south, overlooking a slope to farmland. Behind, mysterious shrubberies have a magical hold on the visitor, who is led by paths through groves of camellias and rhododendrons into knot gardens and borders and by placid pools and canals. The late Sir Geoffrey Jellicoe designed the musical cascade that tumbles down the slope over projecting copper Vs set in concrete – a 1972 flashback to his earlier involvement in the Modern Movement. This famous feature has been revived and replanted, while other structural features are being created by the present owners, who are respecting Jellicoe's overall design 'while introducing their own sense of fun'. Suzy Lewis is the renowned Esther Merton's daughter.

Springhead

Fontmell Magna, Shaftesbury SP7 0NU. Tel: (01747) 811853/811206

The Springhead Trust • 5m S of Shaftesbury, 6m N of Blandford Forum on A350 • Open 6th May (Woodland Day), and by appt. Check local press and website for other public open days • Entrance: £3, children free • Other information: Difficult for wheelchairs (many levels). Children must be supervised. Plant sales and teas on official open days only ● ● & ● ● ●

Although the *raison d'être* of Springhead is the promotion of ecology, education and the arts, its magical garden is also developing fast under the direction of the daughter of the original owners, Rolf and Mirabel Gardiner, who created here in the 1930s a centre for rural regeneration and planted over a million trees. Day and residential courses are held in the house, which is based on several cottages on the site of an old mill and overlooks a sweeping view of the lake. At the far end emerge the springs of absolutely clear water which give the place its name and its spirit – it is indeed a haven of peace and privacy, nestling in a small green valley below the Cranborne Chase. The upper garden surrounds the lake, informal planting (including a fine copper beech framing wild flowers and magnolias in the spring) giving way to a more formal area along the banks. Further down the stream, in the lower garden, Neal's Yard Remedies are growing herbs organically. Wildlife abounds. A walk leads up to the chalk down glorious with wild flowers and orchids in summer, and with spectacular views all year.

Stanbridge Mill ★

Gussage All Saints BH21 5EP. Tel: (01258) 841067

James Fairfax • 7m N of Wimborne on B3078 Cranborne road • Open 9th June, 10.30am – 6pm, for NGS, and for parties by written appt • Entrance: £3.50, children 50p ● ● ♿ ⚘

Designed in its initial stages by Arabella Lennox-Boyd with sensitive later additions by the present owner and head gardener, the 50-acre site greets the summer visitor with clouds of white ox-eye daisies either side of the drive. This wild theme is paramount throughout. Extensive water meadows, now tamed, harvest an abundance of wild flowers; grass drives meander alongside streams towards an elegant thatched summerhouse – an ideal point from which to view this pleasing profusion. The house itself, once a water mill, is surrounded by more formal areas, although the millstream remains a key part of the design. A particular feature is the Mound Garden, from where tiers of hedges – ranging from diminutive box through yew and beech to pleached lime – lead up to a higher level with a magnificent swimming pool and a pavilion. All is rectangular, with clever planting edged by neat box. A striking white-flowered *allée* lies beneath a series of iron archways; as one emerges into the wider landscape, crossing a wisteria walk alongside herbaceous borders stretching for some 60 metres. Everything is well maintained and shown off to perfection by paving and steps created in patterns by up-ended tiles, flints and bricks.

Stapehill Abbey, Crafts and Gardens

276 Wimborne Road West, Stapehill, Nr Wimborne BH21 2EB.
Tel: (01202) 861686

Mr and Mrs J. Pickard (Directors) • On old A31 Wimborne – Ferndown road, ½ m E of Canford Bottom roundabout • Abbey open • Garden open April to Sept, daily, 10am – 5pm; Oct to March, daily except Mon and Tues (but closed 21st Dec to 28th Jan), 10am – 4pm • Entrance: £7.50, OAPs and students £7, children (4–16) £4.50, family £18.50 • Other information: Guide dogs only. Craft workshops ○ ● ● WC ♿ ⚘ ● ●

Formerly home for 200 years to Cistercian nuns, this lovely old abbey has now been restored and the grounds transformed into award-winning gardens, including a Victorian cottage garden, a wisteria walk, a tropical house, a lake, a woodland walk and picnic area, a large rock garden with waterfall and pools, and a new Japanese garden. Craft shops in the abbey offer demonstrations of traditional crafts on most days. The restaurant is in the former refectory, off a lovely walled terrace so that one can eat out of doors in summer. The Country World museum has a good collection of tractors etc., and overlooks the farmyard. Nearby, between Wimborne and Sandown, is *Trehane Camellia Nursery*, with a vast range of camellias, magnolias and other acid-lovers. [Open all year, Mon – Fri, 9am – 4.30pm; spring weekends, 10am – 4pm.]

Sticky Wicket ★

Buckland Newton, Dorchester DT2 7BY. Tel: (01300) 345476

Peter and Pam Lewis • 11m from Dorchester and Sherborne, 2m E of A352, or take B3143 from Sturminster Newton. At T-junction midway between church and school • Open June to Sept, Thurs, 10.30am – 8pm, and for parties by appt (write for details) • Entrance: £3, children £1.50 ● ● WC & ⚘

The three-acre gardens and meadows are divided into four areas; each has an individual focus of wildlife interest with varied planting styles and harmonious colouring to complement and enhance the environment. Information boards guide visitors through gardens which are specially designed with features and planting to attract frogs, birds, bees and butterflies. Wildflower meadows are a particular attraction. This is very much the garden of conservation-minded plant lovers and is not suitable for most children; if the progress of recent years is maintained it is destined to become outstanding.

Weston House

Buckhorn Weston, Gillingham SP8 5HG. Tel: (01963) 371005

Mr and Mrs E.A.W. Bullock • 4m W of Gillingham, 4m SE of Wincanton. From A30 turn N to Kington Magna, continue towards Buckhorn Weston and after railway bridge take left towards Wincanton. House is second on left • Open by appt May to July for charity; parties welcome • Entrance: £2.50, children free • Other information: Teas by arrangement ● ● WC & ◁ ◊ ●

Since 1985 the owners have transformed a neglected rubble-strewn plot and paddock into a one-and-a-half acre garden vibrant with colour, designed around an exceptional collection of old-fashioned and English roses: currently 90 varieties are on display, all clearly labelled. Near the house stone walls enveloped in climbers create a colourful backdrop to mixed borders. An archway of white rambler roses frames a York-stone path edged with standard 'Polar Star' roses underplanted with blue and white. Hot colours in borders and a herb collection entice butterflies. Beyond the well-kept lawn, mown paths lead visitors to the meadow area with a pond and wild flowers as well as a fine view of the Blackmore Vale. The rough-cut grass is interspersed with some unusual trees; there is also a new plantation of old-fashioned roses. Throughout the summer this garden is full of interest and colour in a design which links the formal garden, trees, wild flowers and grasses to the country-side beyond.

DURHAM

Some gardens have postal addresses in one county and are physically situated in another. If in doubt, a check in the index will direct the reader to the page on which the garden appears.

Auckland Castle Deer Park [Historic Park Grade II*]

Auckland Castle, Bishop Auckland DL14 7NR.
Tel: (01325) 462966 (Smiths–Gore Chartered Surveyors)

The Church Comissioners for England (leased to Wear Valley District Council) •
*Leave A1(M) at junction 60 signed to Bishop Auckland. Follow A689 W
through Rushyford past Windlestone Hall and Coundon into Bishop Auckland* •
*Castle state rooms and St Peter's Chapel open 21st April to 29th Sept, Sun,
Mon, Thurs, 2 – 5pm* • *Park open all year, daily, 7.30am – dusk* • *Entrance:
Deer park free (state rooms, chapel and gardens within inner wall £3.50, OAPs
£2.50, children under 12 free)* • *Other information: Symbols relate to castle only
– no facilities in park* ○ 🌿 **WC** ♿ 🐶 ♨ ❡ ✆

A remarkable survival of an eighteenth-century deer house enclosed within part of the original park in the well-wooded valleys of the Coundon Burn and Gaunless River, a tributary of the River Wear. Visitors enter the park through the Gothick gateway crowned by a turreted clock and weather vane, designed by Sir Thomas Robinson with touches of Thomas Wright, and walk past the entrance to the castle, glimpsed through a *clairvoyée*. Suddenly, through Bishop Barrington's screen of 1796, designed by James Wyatt, they see the twelfth-century banqueting hall converted into a chapel by Bishop Cosin in the late seventeenth century. The inner and outer parks extend to 160 acres, with the remainder of the 800-acre deer park leased to local farmers and the golf club. Within them, the river traces a meandering course among precipitous bluffs and craggy outcrops. It has been canalised in places with a weir dating from the eighteenth century. There are avenues of Austrian pine and sweet chestnut and circular stands of trees, groves of ancient alders and clumps of holly trees amongst which dog roses climb. The gnarled and ancient hawthorns are also a feature. A listed ornamental building, a scheduled ancient monument under the guardianship of English Heritage, exists within the park: the deer house, designed in 1757 for Bishop Trevor by Thomas Wright, the Wizard of Durham, to provide shelter for the deer and wild cattle that roamed the park.

Bedburn Hall Gardens

Hamsterley, Bishop Auckland DL13 3NN. Tel: (01388) 4888231

Mr I. Bonas • *9m NW of Bishop Auckland. W of A68 at Witton-le-Wear. 3m
SE of Wolsingham off B6293* • *Open one day in summer for NGS, 2 – 6pm,
and at other times by appt* • *Entrance: £3, children 50p* • *Other information:
Teas and plants for sale on NGS open day only* ● 🍵 **WC** ♿ 🐶 ✿ ✆

A medium-sized terraced garden, largely developed by the present owner, beautifully situated by Hamsterley Forest. It is dominated by a lake with associated rhododendrons and bamboos. A 17-metre lavender bed and a fruit cage of similar size are recent additions, and a bog garden was planted along the mill race in 2003. A well-established conservatory contains passion flowers and other exotics. Lilies and fuchsias are a speciality.

The Bowes Museum Garden [Historic Garden Grade II]

Barnard Castle DL12 8NP. Tel: (01833) 690606

The Bowes Museum Charitable Trust • In Barnard Castle • Garden and park open all year, daily • Entrance: free (museum and garden £6, OAPs £5, children under 16 free) ○ 🍵 ✕ 🖼 WC ⴓ 🐕 🏧 🌼 ♿

In front of the museum to the south, beneath a stone balustrade, a traditional herbaceous border announces a formal parterre, laid out in 1981 to complement the style of the building designed in 1869 by Jules Pellechet for John Bowes. The raised beds of the parterre are edged with box, which if laid out would stretch for over one and a half miles. There are 23 acres of grounds, planted with 56 different tree species. A double avenue starts behind the east lodge and follows the park perimeter; the trees mark a carriageway which led from the main gate to the first site of the Bowes chapel. The low terrace wall and enclosed garden and tennis courts are on the site of this chapel, now a picnic area, and the yews survive from this scheme. The trees continue as a windbreak round the whole of the northern edge of the grounds, with exotics such as Wellingtonias planted in front of the native species. The mound behind the car park has been designed as a retreat, with arbours, shrubs and statues (removed from the Houses of Parliament during restoration work in the 1970s), and there is also a tree trail. The museum has an important collection of European art and hosts major exhibitions.

Crook Hall Gardens

Sidegate, Durham City DH1 5SZ. Tel: (0191) 384 8028

Mr and Mrs K. Bell • In centre of Durham, near Millburn Gate shopping centre and car park. Follow road next to river bank • House and gardens open 9th to 12th April, 3rd, 31st May, and Suns in May, Sept; then June, July, Aug, daily except Sat; all 1 – 5pm • Entrance: £4, concessions £3 ◑ 🍵 WC 🐕 🏧 🌼 ♿

The medieval manor house is surrounded by romantic themed gardens. These include secret walled gardens, a Shakespeare garden using Tudor plants, and the Cathedral Garden with magnificent views of the cathedral and castle. There is also a moat pool, a wildflower meadow and a recently planted maze. An attractive, peaceful place and a must for visitors to Durham.

East Durham and Houghall Community College

Houghall, Durham DH1 3SG. Tel: (0191) 386 1351

1m SE of Durham city S of A177 Durham – Stockton-on-Tees road. Or leave A1(M) at A177 signed to Peterlee and continue towards Durham • Open all year, daily, 1 – 4pm • Entrance: free ○ 🍵 WC ⴓ ♿

These campus grounds have been developed over the last 35 years as the county's main horticultural educational and training facility. They comprise some 24 acres of sports fields and ornamental features and contain one of the largest collections of hardy plants in north-east England. The gardens are in a frost pocket where some of the lowest temperatures in the country are recorded annually. Ornamental features include a water garden, woodland garden, alpine house, display greenhouses, rock garden, raised beds, troughs, narcissi naturalised under trees, heather garden and arboretum. Since this is a working college the visitor may see empty beds and much work in progress. The College is holder of National Collections of sorbus and meconopsis.

Eggleston Hall Gardens

Eggleston, Barnard Castle DL12 0AG. Tel/answerphone: (01833) 650115

Gordon Long and Malcolm Hockham • 5m NW of Barnard Castle on B6278 • House not open but available for private functions – telephone (01833) 450553 • Garden open daily except 25th Dec, 10am – 5pm • Entrance: £1, guided tours for parties £1 per person • Other information: Catering and guides for parties by arrangement ○ ▆ ✕ WC & ⟳ ⅌ ▬ ℃ B&B

The early-nineteenth-century house and its lodge were designed by Ignatius Bonomi, and the four acres of walled gardens include many plants of note – *Syringa emodi*, veratrums, epimediums, fritillaries, meconopsis and a host of rare perennials. The signature plant here is *Celmisia spectabilis* 'Eggleston Silver' from New Zealand. The winding paths within the main garden hold much excitement, rounding corners to reveal colourful vistas that change with the seasons. The old churchyard, with gravestones dating from the seventeenth century, has been lovingly restored and there are interesting plantings among the re-erected gravestones and within the sheltered, roofless area inside the church walls. Three Victorian greenhouses are still in working order and everyday use.

Raby Castle Gardens [Historic Garden Grade II*]

Staindrop, Darlington DL2 3AH. Tel: (01833) 660202

The Rt Hon. The Lord Barnard • 1m N of Staindrop on A688 Barnard Castle – Bishop Auckland road • House open as garden, 1 – 5pm • Garden open May, Sept, Wed, Sun; June to Aug, daily except Sat; plus 10th to 14th April, 1st to 5th May, 29th May to 2nd June, 28th Aug to 1st Sept; all 11am – 5.30pm • Entrance: £4, OAPs/students £3.50, children £2.50, season ticket (house extra charge) • Other information: Dogs in park only, on lead ◑ ▆ ✕ ▣ WC & ⅌ ▬ ℗ ℃

One of the country's most impressive medieval castles, once the seat of the Nevills and home to Lord Barnard's family for over 350 years, is set in a 200-acre deer park and has an interesting walled garden. This formal garden, dating from the mid-eighteenth century, was designed by Thomas Wright (the Wizard of Durham) for the 2nd Earl of Darlington and has a wide array of trees, shrubs and herbaceous plants. Thomas White advised on the landscaping along with Joseph Spence. The garden walls built from locally hand-made bricks have flues which used to enable sub-tropical fruits to be grown on the south terrace. The famous white Ischia fig tree, brought to Raby in 1786, still survives. Rose garden, shrub borders, original yew hedges, lakes and ornamental pond – all exceptionally well maintained.

University Botanic Garden

Hollingside Lane, Durham DH1 3TN. Tel: (0191) 374 7971

Durham University • 1m from city centre, E of A1050. Accessible from A1(M). From S leave A177 and drive NW through Bowburn and Shincliffe to Durham. From N leave at A690 and drive SW to Durham. Garden off Hollingside Lane • Open all year. Glasshouses open daily, 9am – 4pm. Visitor centre open March to Oct, daily, 10am – 5pm; Nov to Feb, daily except Christmas week and bad weather, 10am – 4pm • Entrance: £1.50, concessions 75p (2003 prices) • Other information: Wheelchair and map of wheelchair route available ○ 🍽 🖼 **WC** &. 🌿 🏛 ⚲

Established in 1970 as a centre for botanical study, this is now one of the few botanical gardens in the north of England. Of special interest are woodland walks with exotic trees from the Americas and the Himalayas. There is little in the way of herbaceous borders because throughout the garden trees and herbaceous plants are grown together as they would be found in the wild. There are, however, individual features devoted to heathers and conifers and to woodland plants, plus a North American arboretum, a Himalayan valley, a gazebo garden overshadowed by a huge monkey puzzle tree, and an alpine/ scree garden. The greenhouses contain tropical and Mediterranean plants and cacti, further details of which are available at the visitor centre. Near this centre is the Prince Bishop's Garden, comprising sculptures originally designed for the 1990 Gateshead Garden Festival; the figures of six of County Durham's famous sons were carved by Colin Wilburn from elm trees felled because of Dutch elm disease. While this has potential to be a very interesting botanical garden, some improvement in maintenance in specific areas will be required. Eighteen acres in all.

Westholme Hall

Winston, Darlington DL2 3QL. Tel: (01325) 730442

Mr and Mrs J.H. McBain • 5m E of Barnard Castle on B6274 between Staindrop and Winston • Telephone for opening dates and times • Entrance: £2, children 50p • Other information: Teas available on open days ● 🍽 **WC** &. ⬙ 🌿 ⚲

The Jacobean house and the garden (which was laid out in 1890) are reached by a short drive of limes with mature hollies on the north side. To the south is parkland. Immediately inside the garden enclosure (about five acres), there are lawns: on the right an old tree supports a 'Félicité et Perpétue' rose and a 'Comtesse de Bouchaud' clematis. From the front door in the south elevation an axial line leads to a stone-flagged bridge over a stream, the Westholme Beck – a tributary of the Alwent Beck – and thence to the River Tees. A stone retaining wall parallel to and south of the house forms the backing for a grass walk running east-west; then a grass slope descends to a wide croquet lawn with bold plantings of rhododendrons and thence to grass walks with cherries and specimen trees. Cross the stream that bisects the garden and there is a paddock and more walks through maturing woodland; one vista through what will one day become an avenue of beeches is closed by a massive stone plinth. Elsewhere the long grass terrace walk is terminated by a wall and an urn, and stone parapets salvaged from the Streatlam Park demolition sale of the 1930s now adorn the garden. There is a delightful shrub rose garden to the west of the house, partly sunken and overlooked by a summerhouse, with a good collection of Albas, Bourbons, etc. A newly planted woodland walk leads up the old Pennine Railway, making a 20-minute round trip from the garden to a lake. At Headlam Hall, about five miles east, excellent lunches and dinners are available.

RHS YEAR OF THE GARDEN

To celebrate its bicentenary, the Royal Horticultural Society has declared 2004 the Year of the Garden. It will be making its own presence felt more widely in all its areas of expertise, initiating plant-hunting lectures, science exchanges and debates, running an essay competition for horticultural college students and increasing the number of its specialist shows in Vincent Square. In addition, about 100 outside bodies – museums, galleries, the WI, boy scouts and girl guides groups etc. – have agreed to devise their own gardening-related celebrations. A bicentenary brochure appears in the January edition of *The Garden*.

RESEARCHING GARDEN HISTORY

The Register of Parks and Gardens of Special Historic Interest is the official record of the nation's historic landscapes produced by English Heritage. It has been substantially revised and upgraded, parks and gardens added, and threatened landscapes 'spot-registered'. At the beginning of August 2003, the total number of entries was 1590. Each site is documented in a description of its historical evolution, accompanied by specially drawn paper maps delineating the historical boundaries of the park or garden and chronicling its development.

The *Register* is available for public consultation at English Heritage's National Monuments Record Centre in Swindon (open Tues – Fri, 9.30am – 5pm). Copies of individual entries or complete county registers can also be purchased and sent by post. For more information contact NMR Enquiry & Research Services (Tel: (01793) 414600; Fax (01793) 414606; Email: nmrinfo@english-heritage.org.uk). Additionally, each local planning authority will have a copy of the relevant descriptions and maps within their jurisdictions. Be sure to telephone in advance of a visit.

ESSEX

Two-starred gardens are marked on the map with a black square.

Amberden Hall ★

Widdington, Saffron Walden CB11 3ST. Tel: (01799) 540402

Mr and Mrs D. Lloyd • 6m S of Saffron Walden, E of B1383 near Newport. Follow signs to Mole Hall Wildlife Park. Hall is ½ m past park on right • Open by appt only • Entrance: £2.50, children free ● WC ⅙

Lovely old walls covered in a variety of climbers, some of them rare, enclose this medium-sized garden set at one side of a fine house. The colour-themed borders are cleverly designed so that not all of the garden is visible at once. A *leylandii* hedge has been clipped and the sides corrugated. There is a good vegetable garden with raised beds to make it easier to cope with the heavy clay soil. The garden has been extended beyond the walls with an ivy *allée* – this has two viburnum hedges with poles rising out of them supporting different ivies. More recent additions are a secret garden inside a dismantled barn, a bog garden, a moss garden and a woodland walk.

Audley End [Historic Garden Grade I]

Saffron Walden CB11 4JF. Tel: (01799) 522399

English Heritage • 1m W of Saffron Walden on B1383 • House open as grounds but different opening and closing times • Garden open April to Sept, Wed – Sun and Bank Holiday Mons, 11am – 6pm; Oct, Sat and Sun, 11am – 5pm. Last admissions 1 hour before closing time • Entrance: £4, OAPs £3, children under 16 £2, family £10 (house and grounds £8.00, OAPs £6.00, children under 16 £4.00, family £20.00) (2003 prices) • Other information: Snowdrop walks in spring (Sat and Sun only) – telephone for details. Picnics in park only ◑ ☕ 🖼 WC ⅙ ⬟ 🏩 ⛲ ⚲

The house has long been a fascinating relic of an extraordinary Jacobean pile. Now visitors can enjoy an early version of the parterre garden, restored to the plans developed by the 3rd Lord Braybrooke and his wife *c.* 1830, advised by William Sawrey Gilpin. The design was inspired by classic seventeenth-century French parterres but with sheltering shrubberies to relate to the contemporary (1830) interiors. English Heritage has introduced the whole repertory of the flower garden of the period – irises, martagon lilies, roses, peonies and astrantias, violas, hypericums – all planted in some 170 beds. The herbaceous borders leading into the parterre have recently been planted out with a wide variety of perennials. The restoration has taken ten years and has been completed without interfering with the surrounding 'Capability' Brown landscape. His park buildings included a circular temple, a bridge, Lady Portsmouth's Column by Robert Adam, and a cascade constructed in the same year on the site of an ancient mill dam. There are fine planes, oaks and tulip trees, and a pond garden, laid out in 1868, containing many scented old roses and sub-tropical bedding, with a Pulhamite rock garden at one end. Everything is immaculately maintained. The walled kitchen garden, which includes a 52-metre-long vine house, a full set of service buildings, gardeners' bothy and orchard house, has been developed into a working organic kitchen garden laid out in the Victorian style, including fruit trees on the walls and a splendid variety of Victorian vegetables, which are also for sale in season. A Twenty-First-Century Garden is under development.

The Beth Chatto Gardens ★★

Elmstead Market, Colchester CO7 7DB. Tel: (01206) 822007

Mrs Beth Chatto • 3m E of Colchester, $\frac{1}{4}$ m E of Elmstead Market on A133 • Open March to Oct, Mon – Sat, 9am – 5pm; Nov to Feb, Mon – Fri, 9am – 4pm • Entrance: £3.50, accompanied children free • Other information: Parties by appt ○ 🍽 🏚 WC �& ⚘ 🛍

Beth Chatto designed these gardens in the 1960s from a neglected hollow which was either boggy and soggy or exceedingly dry. She, more than anyone else, has influenced gardeners by her choice of plants for any situation, and her ability to show them off to perfection. Her planting is a lesson to every gardener on how to use both leaf and flower to best advantage. The large gravel garden which she planted to replace the old car park is maturing well as a home for beautiful plants which can thrive in very dry conditions. In the last few years some of the earliest borders have been renewed, and part of the Mediterranean garden has been given over to scree beds – a setting for the smaller plants in the form of five irregular islands. The other major change has taken time to evolve: the creation of five large ponds, each slightly lower than the other, at the heart of the garden. On the perimeter of the garden, a patch of woodland garden nurtures shade-loving plants. The beautifully designed and photographed handbook (£3) includes a fully descriptive catalogue. Adjoining is the excellent *Unusual Plants* nursery. All compulsory visiting.

Bridge End Gardens [Historic Garden Grade II*]

Bridge Street, Saffron Walden CM6 1AN.
Tel: (01799) 510444 (Tourist Information Office)

In town centre. Entrance in Bridge Street and Castle Street • Gardens open all year, daily. Yew hedge maze open Mon – Fri (Sat and Sun obtain key from Tourist Information Office, No. 1 The Market Place) • Entrance: free but £10 refundable key deposit ○ 🏚 WC �& 🍴 ⚘

The early Victorian gardens were started by Atkinson Francis Gibson. The yew hedge maze, planted in 1840 in the Italian Renaissance style, has 610 metres of pathways, originally embellished with statues and columns and entered by richly ornamented iron gates. After some fifty years of neglect, restoration began in 1984; the maze was replanted with 1000 yews and officially re-opened in 1991. Other features include a rose garden and a Dutch garden with elaborate topiary and a viewing platform. On the common nearby is the ancient *Turf Maze of Saffron Walden* [Historic Garden Grade II], a circular labyrinth of medieval Christian design, 29 metres in diameter with only four outer bastions. It is probably the largest of its kind in the world and one of only eight in England. Not far away, at Ashdon, *Beeches Nurseries* sell a range of rare and exciting plants. [Open all year, daily except Christmas and New Year. Telephone (01799) 584362.]

Cameo Cottage

Chapel Lane, Purleigh, Chelmsford CM3 6PY. Tel: (01621) 828334

Mrs Joan Cook • 9m SE of Chelmsford, S of Maldon between B1010 and B1012. Locate hill that leads to church. Facing hill, turn right, take first left (Howe Green Road), then first right by black house (Chapel Lane). Cameo Cottage is first house on right • Open by appt for individuals and parties • Entrance: £1.50 ◐ 🍽 ♿

Set around a cottage, the early part of which dates from the seventeenth century, this one-acre cottage garden is immediately captivating. It is entirely filled with plants that tumble and spill gloriously around a maze of narrow paths and small courtyards, yet the apparent informality is restrained within particular colour schemes, forming the cameos that give the cottage its name. Additional depth and texture are provided by a variation in levels and numerous raised troughs made by the owner's late husband. A diverted field ditch has allowed the creation of a bog garden. This is an enthralling place for the plantsman as it contains many rare treasures among more familiar herbaceous varieties. It is also known as a garden for all seasons, providing interest from February onwards. American visitors will be interested to learn that George Washington's great-great-grandfather was rector of Purleigh from 1633 to 1643; the church itself dates back to the thirteenth century.

Cracknells ★

Great Yeldham CO9 4PT. Tel: (01787) 237370

Mr and Mrs T. Chamberlain • 10m N of Braintree, on A1017 between Halstead and Haverhill • Open by appt • Entrance: by donation to collecting box ◐

Mr Chamberlain started contouring this large plot even before he started building his house. The landscape rolls away down to the lake, also excavated at the start. This is not a garden in the accepted sense but 'a garden picture painted with trees', to use his own words. He has gathered together an impressive collection from all over the country. Here is the rare cut-leaf beech, *Fagus sylvatica* var. *heterophylla*, and its purple- and pink-leaved forms, 'Rohanii' and 'Purpurea Tricolor', as well as the variegated tulip tree, *Liriodendron tulipifera* 'Aureomarginatum'. There are also collections of birches, acers, sorbus and oaks. If you are a lover of trees, make your pilgrimage.

Easton Lodge, The Gardens [Historic Garden Grade II]

Easton Lodge, Little Easton, Great Dunmow CM6 2BB. Tel: (01371) 876979

Mr and Mrs B. Creasey • 11m W of Braintree, 1m N of Great Dunmow on B184. Signposted • Open Feb to Oct, Fri – Sun and Bank Holiday Mons (snowdrop season open daily), 12 noon – 6pm, and at other times by appt •

Entrance: £3.80, OAPs £3.50, children under 12 £1.50. Discount for parties.
(2003 prices) ☉ 🐛 🏞 <u>WC</u> ♿ 🐕 🌿 💡 ⚘

The old west wing survives of Warwick House where 'Darling Daisy' Countess of Warwick, the mistress of Edward VII, spent vast sums on making a wonderful garden and grounds and entertaining her royal lover. Harold Peto designed the garden for her in 1930. In 1950 the house was demolished and the garden abandoned, but in 1996 the pavilion was restored with a grant from Essex County Council, and latterly a vast amount of work has been done. The glade, originally dug by hand by 69 Salvation Army inebriates, has been cleared to reveal Peto's design of a gently sloping mown valley planted with mature trees and bulbs ending in a viewing platform overlooking a large lake. The ornamental pond with its stone balustrading has been revitalised by water lilies and massed penstemons and agapanthus, the fine vistas framed by yew hedges beckon once more. In the fine cobbled yard stone pots contain pine trees, and the raised terrace is massed with pink roses and charming bantams and peacocks. This is, alas, a requiem for a beautiful garden. Although maintenance continues, restoration has ceased as Stansted Airport is coming alarmingly close – an extension would bring a flight path directly overhead.

7A Ellesmere Gardens

Redbridge, Ilford IG4 5DA. Tel: (020) 8550 5464

Cecilia Gonzalez • Travelling E, off A12 Eastern Avenue between Redbridge roundabout (M11 interchange) and Gants Hill roundabout • Open by appt (garden only takes two at a time) • Entrance: £2.50 ☉

The charming split-level courtyard garden, only six metres square, is a treasure trove of unusual plants such as *Podranea ricasoliana, Cassia corymbosa, Grevillea rosmarinifolia, Impomoea indica* and *Solanum rantonnetii*, all thriving in the south-west-facing plot encased in greenery. The upper level is filled with imaginatively planted containers, the lower with dense tropical planting. Between May and mid-August it has a cottagey feel, with favourites old and newer – clematis, gauras, campanulas, *Verbena bonariensis, Knautia macedonica, Hesperis matronalis* – then from August onwards the tropical plants come into their own.

Feeringbury Manor

Coggeshall Road, Feering, Colchester CO5 9RB. Tel: (01376) 561946

Mr and Mrs Giles Coode-Adams • 6m E of Braintree between Coggeshall and Feering • Open April to July, 3rd Sept to 1st Oct, Thurs, Fri, 8am – 4pm, and by appt • Entrance: £2.50 ◑ 🏞 WC ♿ 🐕

This 10-acre garden is distinguished by detailed planting. A huge variety of plants is grown, ranging from damp-lovers by the well-planted ponds and stream to semi-tender specimens in sheltered places, and there is a small arboretum, with many trees grown from seed. The season is prolonged by interesting bulbs and climbers such as sweet peas and clematis, the latter a speciality. Notable, too, are the sculptured gates by Ben Coode-Adams.

Folly Faunts House

Goldhanger, Maldon CM9 8AP.
Tel: (01621) 788213 (Home), (01621) 788611 (Office)

*Mr and Mrs J.C. Jenkinson • On B1026 between Maldon and Colchester • Open
for charity several days in summer, 2 – 5pm, and at other times for parties of 6
or more by appt • Entrance: £2.50 • Other information: Teas and plants for sale
on charity open days only* ● 🍵 🏡 WC & 🐕 🌿 ✂

The 20-acre garden, created round an eighteenth-century manor house since
1963, is divided into compartments, each with a different theme, and has a
wide variety of unusual trees and shrubs. The plantings around the informal
and formal ponds are a special feature, and a small sunken garden has been
made recently with lawn, paving and special shrubs. The 16 acres of park and
woodland, divided by five double avenues, provide attractive walks.

The Gibberd Garden ★ [Historic Garden Grade II]

Marsh Lane, Gilden Way, Harlow CM17 0NA. Tel: (01279) 442112

*Gibberd Garden Trust • E of Harlow between A414 and B183. From M11
junction 7 take A414 to Harlow, follow signs to Old Harlow onto B183 (Gilden
Way) and continue for 1m. Marsh Lane is on left • Open April to Sept, Wed,
Sat, Sun and Bank Holiday Mons, 2 – 6pm • Entrance: £4, concessions £2.50,
children free* ● 🍵 WC & 🐕 🍴 🌸 ✂

This is the extremely individual creation of the architect and art collector Sir
Frederick Gibberd, an outstanding example of twentieth-century garden design. Hugh Johnson has stated that it 'must certainly be one of the most
important [gardens] in the history of the twentieth century'. The nine-acre
sloping site comprises a series of rooms designed to display his remarkable
collection of modern sculpture and architectural artefacts. The structure is not
restrictive; tranquillity as well as drama is provided by glades, groves and *allées*,
as they open up vistas or focus on statuary. A waterfall and quiet pools have been
incorporated into a small brook which borders the east of the property and
towards which run lushly planted channels of water. At one end of the brook
stands a moated castle. There are also natural ponds, a tree house and a gazebo.
The garden is now in the enthusiastic hands of the Gibberd Garden Trust, which
is aiming to realise his wish that it be kept open to the public in perpetuity.

Glen Chantry ★

Wickham Bishops, Witham CM8 3LG. Tel: (01621) 891342

*Mr and Mrs W.G. Staines • 9m NE of Chelmsford off A12, 2m SE of Witham.
Turn left off B1018 towards Wickham Bishops. Pass golf course, cross River
Blackwater bridge and turn left up Ishams Chase by Blue Mills • Open 2nd
April to 29th Sept, Fri and Sat, 10am – 4pm • Entrance: £2.50, children 50p •
Other information: D.I.Y. teas* ◑ 🍵 🏡 WC & 🌿

A large undulating garden, started in 1977. The huge, informally shaped beds
are filled with an imaginative mixture of bulbs, hostas, grasses, shrub roses and

a wide variety of unusual perennials. Some beds are raised at the centre, and this gives excellent shape to the planting. Other features include large rock gardens, a stream with waterfalls leading to ponds with rodgersias, iris and good foliage plants, and an attractive white garden. Overall, the plantings and colour schemes are spectacular.

Hill House

Chappel, Colchester CO6 2DX. Tel: (01787) 222428

Mr and Mrs R. Mason • 8m W of Colchester on A1124 between Colchester and Earls Colne • Open by appt • Entrance: by donation to charity ●

The large garden was designed by the owners on formal lines, using yew hedging and walls to create vistas, and with a lime avenue sited to lead the eye out into the country. A mixed planting of tough native trees like sorbus and hawthorn has been established as a windbreak. A small courtyard with a raised pool, reminiscent of a London plot, is planted with green-leaved plants and white flowers only. Another feature is a pond with two black swans. The bones of the garden are in place including urns, statues and seats, and all the colour and secondary planting has now been introduced. Further land has been acquired giving a fine view over the Colne Valley and Chappel Viaduct, and hedges and trees are being established here.

Ingatestone Hall

Ingatestone CM4 9NR. Tel: (01277) 353010

Lord Petre • 7m SW of Chelmsford on A12. From Ingatestone main street, take Station Lane at SW end. Signposted • House open • Garden open 10th April to 20th July, 4th to 30th Sept, Sat, Sun and Bank Holiday Mons; 21st July to 3rd Sept, Wed – Sun and Bank Holiday Mon; all 1 – 6pm • Entrance: £4, OAPs and students £3.50, children £2 ◑ 🍽 WC ⅋ 🌿 🏰 🌷

There have been buildings here since 950 AD, and the hall was built in the 1540s. A large stewpond, contemporary with the house, provided fish and fresh-water mussels; it is now bordered by huge gunneras and shady walks. The walled garden has magnificent standard roses and a lily pond. There is a nut walk and a grass walk, but the lime walk is haunted by Bishop Benjamin Petre's dog, which saved his life when he was set upon in 1740. His ghost still patrols. The extensive, immaculate lawns have specimen trees: mulberries, *Magnolia grandiflora* and weeping beeches. The house is well worth a visit.

Langthorns Plantery

High Cross Lane West, Little Canfield, Dunmow CM6 1TD. Tel: (01371) 872611

Mr and Mrs David Cannon and Edward Cannon • 3m W of Great Dunmow, 5m E of M11 junction 8, on A120 • Plantery open daily, 10am – 5pm • Garden open by appt (telephone or ask at Plantery) • Entrance: free ● 🍽 ⅋ ♿ 🌿 🏰

The owners, avid collectors of unusual plants, propagate in the nursery, which stocks one of the widest ranges of good-quality plants in the country, including trees, shrubs, conservatory plants, alpines and herbaceous perennials. There are also clematis and honeysuckles, and many unusual forms of tricyrtis, geraniums and salvias. The garden has now been revamped and is open to the public on a limited basis.

The Magnolias

18 St John's Avenue, Brentwood CM14 5DF. Tel: (01277) 220019

Mr and Mrs R.A. Hammond • From A1023 turn S to A128. After 300 metres turn right at traffic lights, over railway bridge. St John's Avenue is third on right • Open 21st, 28th March, 4th, 18th, 25th April, 2nd, 16th, 23rd, 30th May, 20th June, 18th July, 15th Aug, 19th Sept, 24th Oct, 10am – 5pm. Parties by appt • Entrance: £1.50, children 50p ● ❀

The garden may be a bit of a jungle, but it is a plantsman's delight, with 70 different magnolias, camellias, hostas, bamboos and epimediums. The front garden (7½ x 6 metres) has impressive trees and shrubs – *Carpenteria californica* with white-flowered *Solanum jasminoides* growing through it, *Cercis canadensis* 'Forest Pansy', *Sophora microphylla* and *Cytisus battandieri*. A dark path leads to a long narrow garden with seven ponds, and mature trees and plantings, including trilliums, *Embothrium coccineum* (Chilean firebush), a *Magnolia campbellii* which did its first reasonable flowering twenty-five years after planting, in time for the owners' silver wedding anniversary, and several flowering cornus including 'Norman Hadden'.

Olivers

Olivers Lane, Colchester CO2 0HJ. Tel: (01206) 330575

Mr and Mrs David Edwards • 3m SW of Colchester off B1022 Maldon road. Follow signs to Colchester Zoo. From zoo continue ¾ m towards Colchester and at round-about turn right. After ¼ m turn right again into Olivers Lane. From Colchester pass Shrub End church and Leather Bottle pub then turn left at second roundabout • Open 2nd, 3rd May, and by appt • Entrance: £2.50, children free ● 🍴 🛍 WC ᨕ ❀ ☕

The moment visitors arrive at the attractive Georgian-fronted house and step down onto the large York-stone terrace, beautifully planted in soft sympathetic colours, they are entranced. All around are 20 acres of garden and woodland. The view from the terrace is down over the lawn, fine borders, pools and woods to a natural meadow (cut only to encourage wild flowers and grasses) and to the trees bordering the river. A 'willow pattern' bridge crosses the first of a succession of pools dropping down to an ancient fish pond. *Taxodium distichum*, metasequoia and ginkgo flourish by the pools. There are yew hedges and a delightful woodland walk, where mature native trees shelter rhododendrons, azaleas and shrub roses in the rides.

RHS Garden Hyde Hall

Rettendon, Chelmsford CM3 8ET. Tel: (01245) 400256

The Royal Horticultural Society • 7m SE of Chelmsford, signed from A130 • Open all year, daily except 25th Dec, 10am – 6pm (closes dusk Oct to March)

(last admission one hour before closing) • *Entrance: £4, children (6–16) £1.*
Parties of 10 or more £3 per person • *Other information: Guide dogs only* ◑ ☕
✕ 🗑 <u>WC</u> � ✍ 🏭 ♿

The 20-acre hilltop garden is perched above the East Anglian wheatfields in a truly Tuscanesque manner. Notable are the beds of species roses with white peonies and naturalised *Eremurus robustus* growing through them. There is much else to see: a colour-themed herbaceous border; an informal pond; a spring garden of massed hellebores and many bulbs; a formal enclosed rose garden with pillars behind a broad planting of alliums and half-hardy salvias. This is on a double crossfall which poses a severe problem – but although it is against all classical garden design principles, it still produces a stunning display. The National Collection of viburnums is here. Three thousand young trees have been planted, the upper and lower ponds are being opened up and replanted, and the terrace (entered through a massive oak pergola adorned with clematis and wisteria) is being enlarged. Much new planting and several wildflower areas have been established in the Malus Field, and work is continuing on the winding, shallow riverbed, display and shrub beds and a shrub rose garden. The new dry garden is on fertile alkaline clay with huge glacial boulders from Scotland, and grows things like the self-seeding *Eremurus robustus*, *Erigeron karvinskianus*, a thousand bulbs and much more.

R. and R. Saggers ★

Waterloo House, High Street, Newport, Saffron Walden CB11 3PG.
Tel: (01799) 540858

R. and R. Saggers • *6m S of Saffron Walden on B1383 through Newport* •
Open all year, daily except Mon (but open Bank Holiday Mons), 10am – 5pm.
(Closed Sun, Jan, Feb, March, Aug) • *Entrance: free* • *Other information:*
Possible for wheelchairs but gravel paths ○ 🗑 <u>WC</u> Ġ ◁ ✍ 🏭

This small, immaculately kept nursery has a charming town garden running down to a stream between flint walls. The nursery stocks old-fashioned roses and rare and unusual plants, grown and propagated by Mr Saggers. Almost everything on sale is grown in the wide borders in front of the flint walls. As well as the many exciting shrubs and herbaceous plants, there is a good range of statuary, lead urns, Whichford pots and armillary sundials.

Saling Hall ★ [Historic Garden Grade II]

Great Saling, Braintree CM7 5DT.

Mr and Mrs Hugh Johnson • *6m NW of Braintree, halfway between Braintree and Dunmow on A120 turn N at Saling Oak* • *Open for NGS May to July, Wed, 2 – 5pm, and for parties by written appt, Mon – Fri* • *Entrance: £2.50, children free* ◑ <u>WC</u> Ġ

Hugh Johnson's wonderful garden is clearly the work of a tree lover – a rare example of a picturesque landscape created by a very wide-ranging dendrological collection. When the huge elms of Saling died, he turned the 12 acres of chalky boulder clay into an arboretum of genera that thrive on alkaline clay or gravel. A marvellous collection of pines, quercus, sorbus, aesculus, acers, prunus, tilias, fraxinus, fagus, salix and betulas leads the eye to a classical Temple of Pisces. There are many rarities like *Carpinus fangiana, Tilia oliveri, Toona sinensis, Staphylea colchica*, an unknown weeping juniper, incense cedars from Oregon seed and unusual pines on the east slope. The walled garden faces south-west. Apple trees are trimmed into mushroom shapes to contrast with a file of clipped cypress and a matching file of Irish junipers and pyramid box bushes. The borders are informal, with grey and blue plants of rather typical Mediterranean associations – agapanthus, euphorbias, etc. The disciplined planting in the various sections creates a distinct atmosphere in each. There is also a vegetable garden, a Japanese garden, a water garden, a secret garden and a strange menhir in its private glade. The old moat with its cascade boasts some substantial carp.

Stone Pine ★

Hyde Lane, Danbury, Chelmsford CM3 4LJ. Tel: (01245) 223232

Mr and Mrs David Barker • 4m E of Chelmsford from Runsell Green, 1m S of A414 leaving Danbury towards Maldon • Open by appt • Entrance: by donation to collecting box ● ▓ **WC**

This small garden, owned by a former Chairman of the Hardy Plant Society, is filled with choice and unusual varieties. The area of grass is minimal and paths wind around borders crammed with trees, acers being particularly popular, and shrubs. Surprising plants appear around each corner, like the rarely seen *Paris quadrifolia*. Mr Barker is also knowledgeable on lilies, hemerocallis, irises and grasses. National Collections of epimediums and Japanese anemones are here.

Tye Farm

Colchester Road, Elmstead Market, Colchester CO7 7AX. Tel: (01206) 822400

Mrs C. Gooch • 2m E of Colchester on A133, ½ m W of Elmstead Market • Open for parties by appt • Entrance: £2 ● **WC** ⅄ ⬧ ⅌

This one-acre garden is cleverly planted with hedges to make compartments to break the prevailing wind. The shrubs and perennials complement one another, and there are over 60 varieties of old and modern roses. Look for the gold area in the small walled garden. There is a formally planted, box-edged area in front of the conservatory, which contains many unusual plants.

Warwick House

(see EASTON LODGE, THE GARDENS)

GLOUCESTERSHIRE

Some gardens have postal addresses in one county and are physically situated in another. If in doubt, a check in the index will direct the reader to the page on which the garden appears.

Two-starred gardens are marked on the map with a black square.

Abbotswood ★ [Historic Garden Grade II*]

Stow–on–the–Wold GL54 1EN. Tel: (01451) 830173

Dikler Farming Co • 1m W of Stow on B4077 • Open one Sun each month April to Sept for NGS, 1.30 – 6pm • Entrance: £3, children free • Other information: Coaches must drop passengers at top gate and park in Stow ● ☕ 🍴 WC & ◈

The house is in one of the most beautiful Cotswold settings. From the car park it is approached via a descending stream and pools towards woodland carpeted in spring with flowers and bulbs, including one of the largest displays of fritillaries in season. The woods continue above and beyond the house and have been planted with rhododendrons, flowering shrubs and specimen trees. Near the house are terraces and formal gardens, including a box-edged rose garden and a water garden. Extensive heather plantings. The gardens round the house are by Lutyens – note especially his lily pool running up to the house, with a jet of water which, if the angle of the sun is right, shimmers spectacularly. Alas, other vertical features by Lutyens were removed by an earlier owner, though the planting remains faithful to his design.

Alderley Grange [Historic Garden Grade II]

Alderley GL12 7QT. Tel: (01453) 842161

Mr Guy and The Hon. Mrs Acloque • 6m N of Chipping Sodbury, 2m S of Wotton-under-Edge. Turn NW off A46 Bath – Stroud road at Dunkirk • Open during June by appt • Entrance: £3.50, children free ● WC &

A garden of character and charm in a tranquil walled setting, renowned for its collection of aromatic plants and scented flowers. Designed by the late Alvilde Lees-Milne, it is believed to be the last garden in which Vita Sackville-West had a hand. The fine house and a mulberry tree date from the seventeenth century; a pleached and arched lime walk leads to a series of enclosed gardens. There is a notable hexagonal herb garden with many delightful perspectives of clipped, trained or potted shrubs and trees, and abundant plantings of old roses, tender and unusual plants.

Barnsley House ★★

Barnsley, Nr Cirencester GL7 5EE. Tel: (01285) 740421

Rupert Pendered and Tim Haigh • 4m NE of Cirencester on B4425 • Open for NGS, and for small parties throughout the year, strictly by prior appt • Entrance:

£5 • Other information: Coaches on open days only by prior appt. Refreshments available at Village Pub opposite house ● WC &

This was a highly influential garden in its day, comprising many garden styles from the past, carefully blended by Rosemary and David Verey after they inherited the house from David's father in 1951. The 1697 Cotswold stone house (now a country-house hotel and restaurant) is set in the middle of the four-acre garden, surrounded on three sides by a 1770 stone wall. Borders create vistas and divide the garden into areas of distinct and individual character, and great attention is paid to colour and texture. The laburnum, allium and wisteria walk, best in mid-May to mid-June, and the *potager* with its numerous small beds, are especially renowned; the kitchen garden has been enlarged into the adjacent field to meet the demands made upon it by the hotel kitchen. It is impossible that Rosemary's unique planting style could be perpetuated indefinitely, and as some trees and shrubs age and bulk out and others die, the garden will inevitably move on. However, it will remain both her creation and her memorial.

Batsford Arboretum ★ [Historic Garden Grade I]

Batsford Park, Moreton–in–Marsh GL56 9QB. Tel: (01386) 701441

The Batsford Foundation • 1½ m NW of Moreton-in-Marsh on A44 to Evesham. Opposite entrance to Sezincote (see entry) • Arboretum open Feb to mid-Nov, daily; mid-Nov to mid-Feb, Sat, Sun and 26th Dec, 1st Jan, 10am – 5pm • Entrance: £5, OAPs £4, children £1 ○ ▭ ✕ 🦃 WC & ⬦ 🌳 👜 ♿

Over 1500 different species and varieties of trees, shrubs and bamboos in 55 acres of typical Cotswold countryside, plus an unusual collection of exotic shrubs and bronze statues from the Far East, originally collected for the garden by Lord Redesdale. It was expanded by the first Lord Dulverton in the 1960s, and includes fine collections of magnolias, the National Collection of Japanese cherries, plus spring bulbs and excellent autumn colour. A 'swampery' combines elements of a bog and a stumpery. Good views of the house (not open).

Bourton House ★

Bourton–on–the–Hill, Moreton–in–Marsh GL56 9AE. Tel: (01386) 700754

Mr and Mrs R. Paice • 2m W of Moreton-in-Marsh on A44 • Open 26th May to Aug, Wed – Fri; 2nd Sept to Oct, Thurs, Fri; also 30th, 31st May, 29th, 30th, Aug; all 10am – 5pm • Entrance: £4.50, children free • Other information: Parking across road ◑ ▭ 🦃 WC 🌳 👜

The exceptionally handsome eighteenth-century Baroque Cotswold house with fine views is enhanced by its medium-sized garden which is an inspiring alternative to traditional country-house acres. The diminutive geometrical *potager* is a particular delight. Well-kept lawns, quiet fountains, a knot garden and Cotswold stone walls are set off by a number of herbaceous borders in which the choice and arrangement of plants and shrubs make skilful use of current fashions in garden design. The colours and choice of plants are bold and sophisticated, mixing spiky, semi-tropical, traditional and unusual species in a versatile display. Each year there are new interests – the raised pond in the top garden, a topiary walk, and long terraces on the main lawn planted with low-growing shrubs, perennials and roses. The plantation in the field opposite is roaring along and a pleasure to roam, and a gallery of local arts, crafts and design has opened in the tithe barn. The cocoon-like shade-house is a flourishing environment for novel shade-loving plants. Many of the plants may be unfamiliar to visitors; labels would be welcome. Sezincote and Batsford, and Hidcote and Kiftsgate (see entries) are less than half an hour away.

Brackenbury

Coombe, Wotton–under–Edge GL12 7NF. Tel: (01453) 842238

Mr and Mrs Peter Heaton • 2m S of Dursley, 1m NE of Wotton-under-Edge off B4058. From Wotton church travel ½ m on B4058 Stroud road, then turn right (signed to Coombe). From Stroud, go 300 yards past Wotton sign, turn left (signed to Coombe) and garden is on right • Open for NGS 31st May, 27th June, 25th July, 30th Aug, 2 – 6pm • Entrance: £2.50, children free ● 🍵 WC 🍽 ✿

This small terraced garden with multi-layer planting is situated in a beautiful Cotswold valley, and is clearly designed by plantspeople with designer tastes. The garden has evolved over twenty years into an exuberant mix of plants growing in conditions that suit them best. A large bed has recently been created to accommodate more sun-loving plants, and foliage is a feature throughout. There are good mixed borders, a cottage garden, a pool, over 1000 different hardy plants and 200 different shrubs. The vegetable garden, laid out on the deep-bed system, includes a four-ton compost heap. It is worth a visit in June and July to see the National Collection of erigerons.

Cerney House Gardens

North Cerney, Cirencester GL7 7BX. Tel: (01285) 831300/831205

Sir Michael and Lady Angus • 3½ m N of Cirencester off A435 Cheltenham road. Turn left opposite Bathurst Arms, follow road up hill past church, signed to Bagendon, and turn in through gates on right • Open April to July, Tues, Wed, Fri, 10am – 5pm, and one Sun in May for charity. Open at other times for parties by appt • Entrance: £3, children £1 • Other information: Lunches and high teas by arrangement. Picnics in car park only ◑ 🍵 🍴 WC & ✿ 🏛

Around the house, remodelled by Decimus Burton in 1791, goats and sheep graze and wild flowers flourish in their meadow. The pleasantly unmanicured garden is not for those who like everything tickety-boo – the plants are happy and unrestrained, and dead-heading is not a priority. There are lawns, shrubs and trees around the house, and behind it a three-and-a-half-acre sloping walled garden restored since the mid-1980s with riotous herbaceous borders, vegetables, many old-fashioned roses, clematis and a delightful children's story-book pig (a Gloucester Old Spot, of course) beneath the apple trees nearby. A woodland walk is carpeted with snowdrops in February and bluebells in May. Behind the house is a colourful rockery with a waterfall. The herb garden, the geranium and thyme bank, and the pink border beside the swimming pool are well established, and there is a genera-garden leading down to the pond, and a tree trail. Garden labels are packed with information, particularly those in the new beds to the side of the house which tell the stories of plant-hunters and famous nurserymen. The locality is rich in Roman history, with Chedworth Roman Villa a few miles away. The nearby twelfth-century church is well worth a visit.

The Chipping Croft

26 The Chipping, Tetbury GL8 8EY. Tel: (01666) 503178

Dr and Mrs P. Taylor • In town centre proceed between The Snooty Fox and 'Ultima One' shop past parking in Chipping Square. Garden is at bottom on left behind wall with tall trees, entrance in driveway to courtyard • Open by appt • Entrance: £2.50 • Other information: Teas by arrangement ◕ ⴟ ⬠ ⚲

This is a most unusual town garden because of its size and secret character. Entering through a courtyard leading to a terrace, sunken patio and large lawn bordered by mature trees and a wooded walk, it extends to about two acres and is on three levels. At one time, the mostly late-seventeenth century house was used as a school, and since 1985 Dr Taylor has transformed a playground area into a courtyard with a small rectangular raised pool and a conservatory. He has replanted extensively, constructed a summerhouse/potting shed and added new steps connecting the various levels. Three formal terrace gardens contain a variety of perennials and cottage-garden flowers as well as unusual plants, fruit trees, vegetables and herbs, with the kitchen garden proper laid out as a *potager* on a higher level. Beneath the terraces is a wide walk with roses and perennials in borders either side and arches covered with roses, honeysuckle, wisteria and clematis leading back to the house.

Cotswold Farm

Duntisbourne Abbots, Cirencester GL7 7JS. Tel: (01285) 821857

Mark and Iona Birchall • 5m NW of Cirencester off A417. From Cirencester turn left signed to Duntisbourne Abbots, then at once right, right again after 270 metres, under the new dual carriageway, and house drive is opposite. From Gloucester 1m past Highwayman Inn, turn left signed 'Duntisbourne Abbots/ Services', turn right at once, and the drive is 270 metres on left • Open 8th, 9th Feb for snowdrops, 2nd May, 22nd Aug, and by appt at other times (good notice appreciated) • Entrance: £3 (2003 price) ◕ ⬛ WC ⌖

A mature garden planted in grand style and sustained with sensitive artistry surrounding a fine old house in a superb Cotswold setting. The terrace was designed by Norman Jewson in 1938. The formal walled gardens have a pool and are planted with shrub, bush and climbing roses, alpines, lavender and a collection of scented flowers. There are also established plantings of shrubs, herbaceous perennials and many small treasures overlooking an unspoilt wooded valley. A charmed garden redolent of another age in a remote and lovely situation.

Daylesford House ★ [Historic Garden Grade II*]

Daylesford, Moreton-in-Marsh GL56 0YH. Tel: (01608) 659888

Sir Anthony and Lady Bamford • Off A436 between Stow-on-the-Wold and Chipping Norton • Open one day for NGS, and for parties by appt, Mon – Fri • Entrance: £5 per person ◕ **WC** ♿

Warren Hastings, the first Governor-General of Bengal, bought the estate in 1785 and the house, like nearby Sezincote, was designed by Samuel Pepys Cockerell in the Anglo-Indian style. Hastings employed John Davenport to design the general layout, including the splendid Gothick orangery, walled garden and lakes. The present owners have undertaken a gradual restoration of this most inspiring estate. They have re-created the original combination of semi-natural parkland, with particular emphasis on the naturalised wildflower meadows and woodland, contrasting with the more formal areas. Every aspect is a delight: the lawns and lakes are magnificent; the orangery has a sensational display of blue *Salvia guaranitica* across the length of the large south-facing wall, as well as a collection of citrus and vine arches and exotics in huge clay pots. Behind the orangery is the secret garden, with a pavilion and a pool presided over by a seventeenth-century Neptune, *Rosa banksiae alba* tumbling down the balustrades and stunning blue and white planting schemes continuing into the spring border outside. Beyond the scented walk and stumpery is the two-acre walled garden. This displays the talents of Lady Bamford, Lady Mary Keen and more recently Rupert Golby: it contains peach and orchid houses and a series of yew-hedged areas leading to a raised rose garden and cutting border. There are also espaliered fruit trees and a large *potager* producing unusual organic vegetables. The top lake cascades into the dell and stream, a shady area with the accent on texture and foliage, behind which the wood is carpeted in spring with bluebells and colonies of wood anemones, mysosotis and spotted orchids.

Dyrham Park [Historic Garden Grade II*]

Chippenham SN14 8ER. Tel: (0117) 937 2501

The National Trust • 4m S of Chipping Sodbury, 8m N of Bath, 12m E of Bristol on A46. Take M4 junction 18 in direction of Bath • House (including Victorian domestic areas) open as garden but 12 noon – 5.30pm • Garden open 19th March to 7th Nov, daily except Wed and Thurs, 11am – 5pm (last admission 4.15pm) • Park open all year except 25th Dec, daily, 11am – 5pm or dusk if earlier • Entrance: park only £2, children £1; park and garden £3, children £1.50; house, garden and park £7.90, children £3.90, family £19 (2003 prices) • Other information: Possible for wheelchairs on terrace but park steep in places. All cars in car park at East Lodge, bus link to house and garden. Dogs in dog walking area only, on lead • Garden: ◑ ☕ ✕ 🞕 **WC** ♿ 🚻 ♨ ℺ *Park:* ○ 🞕 ℺

Only a tiny fragment of the extensive London and Wise Baroque garden shown in the view by Kip in 1710 survives. The terraces were all smoothed out in the late eighteenth century to form an 'English' landscape with fine mature beech, Spanish chestnut, Lucombe oak, red oak and black walnut. Avenues of elms survived until the mid-1970s when they were wiped out by Dutch elm disease;

they have since been replanted with limes. The cascade in the garden on the west side is still working and one can make out the form of the original garden and enjoy the terrace and Talman's orangery, all 30 metres now splendidly transformed and wonderfully scented. The views towards Bristol and the elegance of the 'natural' landscape, with the house and church tucked into the hillside, make this an outstanding example of English landscape gardening. In all, 263 acres of ancient parkland. The first stage of Arne Maynard's transformation of the garden behind the house is in place after years of debate and controversy. The great project begins (see page XIII) with the planting of a double row of *Parrotia persica* outside the stable block and will continue inexorably outwards over the next five years. One to watch.

Eastleach House ★

Eastleach Martin, Cirencester GL7 3NW.

Mrs David Richards • 6m SW of Burford off A361 Lechlade road or off A40 via Westwell and Eastleach Turville. House opposite church gates, up steep drive • Open June, July, Fri, 2 – 5pm, and for limited number of guided tours by owner for parties of 10 or more. Requests only in writing please • Entrance £5, accompanied children free • Other information: Limited parking and no access for coaches. Lunches and teas available in village at Victoria Inn ◗

In a hidden and unknown village on the Gloucestershire/Oxfordshire border is a beautiful and virtually unknown garden, twenty years in the making, which even the gardening *cognoscenti* have yet to discover. Stephanie Richards interweaves plants and combines colours and textures with skill and sensitivity, handles changes of level with panache, and creates interlocking spaces and outdoor rooms forming a coherent flow in so assured a manner that the visitor can only conclude that they were ever thus. The house, which is turn-of-the-twentieth-century, sits on the top of a hill and faces the four points of the compass. It has become the reference point, the fulcrum of the design; everything flows from it and every view is seen from it. It looks down the hill onto the rill, out to the countryside along a newly planted lime avenue, into the walled garden. Only one secret is kept from it – the sunken wildlife pond hidden beyond the walled garden. Roses wind through clematis and around fastigiate Irish yews; a meandering path through the miniature arboretum brings the visitor to the edge of the croquet lawn, surprisingly at eye level. Ascend the broad steps and opposite is an arbour and a terrace filled with flowers. Stand finally at the west end of the house, look down onto the rill and have your eye caught by the perfectly shaped balls of *Sorbus aria* 'Lutescens' beyond the borders of perennials embracing the entire colour spectrum. A garden of sheer delight. Sorry, don't miss the herb and kitchen garden.

The Ernest Wilson Memorial Garden

Leasbourne, High Street, Chipping Campden. Tel:(01386) 840884 (Dick Smith)

N of A44 between Evesham and Stow-on-the-Wold and S of Stratford-upon-Avon off A46 E of Broadway • Open all year, daily except 25th Dec, 9am – dusk • Entrance: free, but contributions welcome (donation box) ○ ♿

Because of its position near Hidcote, Kiftsgate and Charlecote, the town is a popular holiday stopping-off point, so it is fortuitous that it has a garden to appeal to horticulturally minded visitors. It was opened in 1984 in memory of 'Chinese' Wilson, who was born in Chipping Campden in 1876. The famous collector is estimated to have introduced 1200 species of trees and shrubs during his career, and the garden has several of his introductions, including *Acer griseum*, *Davidia involucrata*, and the plant for which he wished to be remembered, *Lilium regale*. It is a peaceful oasis, with seats and shade, backed by the beautiful church tower. Other gardens in Chipping Campden are open on certain days, and the charity Action Research arranges for some 20 gardens to open on the third weekend in June, 2 – 6pm.

Ewen Manor

Ewen, Cirencester GL7 6BX. Tel: (01285) 770206

Lady Gibbs • 4m S of Cirencester off A429. Turn at signpost for Ewen, 1m • Open 7th May to 9th July, Wed, Thurs, and probably two days for charity • Entrance: £2 • Other information: Teas on charity days only ● 🥤 **WC** ⅙ ⬦ ⚲

In the late 1940s this was a run-down manor garden which had in part been used as a Dig-for-Victory patch. The Georgian house had been moved here from across the Thames 200 years earlier. Backed by magnificent trees, it now contains a series of gardens with architectural features, and everywhere the planting is profuse. There are views across the pattern-mown lawn to the circular summerhouse with its conical Cotswold stone-tiled roof, and to the 200-year-old cedars of Lebanon in the woodland area all around. The main herbaceous border is backed by a high yew hedge, behind which is a large rectangular lily pool surrounded by masses of helianthemums, overlooked by the garden room (once the stables) with its plant-filled terrace and pots. Daffodils and spring bulbs abound. One of the most charming of traditional manor house gardens.

Frampton Court [Historic Garden Grade I]

Frampton-on-Severn GL2 7EU.
Tel: (01452) 740267 (Home); (01452) 740698 (Office)

Mr Rollo Clifford • SW of Gloucester, 2m from M5 junction 13, signposted. On left-hand side of village green through gates in long wall • House open all year by appt (by guided tours, £5) • Garden open all year by appt • Entrance: £2 • Other information: Refreshments in village hall on selected days ● 🥤 ⅙ ⬦ **B&B**

Home of the remarkable Clifford family of female artists, who created the *Frampton Flora* (1830-1860), the elegant 1730s' house stands on land owned by the family since the twelfth century. It was possibly designed by John Strahan in the style of Vanbrugh; the interior has exquisite woodwork and furnishings. The five-acre grounds are maintained with a minimum of labour and contain a lake, fine trees and a formal water garden of Dutch design, believed to have been made by the architects of the larger Westbury Court Garden (see entry) on the other side of the Severn. The Strawberry Hill Gothick orangery of 1750 (not always open but available for holiday letting), where the ladies are believed to have executed their work, stands reflected in the still water, planted with lilies and flanked by a mixed border. This garden is open in association with that of *Frampton Manor*, also occupied by Cliffords, where a boldly planted walled garden with many old roses is set off splendidly by a fine fifteenth-century timbered house.

Hidcote Manor Garden ★★ [Historic Garden Grade I]

Hidcote Bartrim, Chipping Campden GL55 6LR. Tel: (01386) 438333

The National Trust • 3m NE of Chipping Campden. Signposted • Open 27th March to 7th Nov, daily except Thurs and Fri (but open Good Friday), 10.30am – 5pm, but advisable to check before travelling. Parties by written appt only. On fine weekends and Bank Holidays garden less crowded after 3pm • Entrance: £5.90, children £2.90, family £14.50. No party concessions (2003 prices) • Other information: Coaches by prior arrangement only ◑ 🍴 ✕ <u>WC</u> ᕼ ✿ 🏛 ♿

One of the most famous gardens in Britain, impeccably kept throughout their 10 acres, particularly the miles of sculptured hedges. It is famous especially for its highly disciplined formal outdoor rooms, many of them filled with wonderfully dramatic plantings. It was created in the early years of the twentieth century by Lawrence Johnston, an American with a strong sense of design and great planting skills. He made many new introductions and rediscovered many forgotten plants, some of which he collected himself; several varieties now bear the Hidcote name. The Trust has, since its acquisition in 1948, done its utmost to retain the spirit of the Johnston original, but its researches and some new evidence suggests that his planting legacy may have been eroded over the years. The plan now is to make a gradual return to Johnston's own stated vision of 'a wild garden in a formal setting'. His plant house may be re-created and other features reinstated. As always, a garden to watch.

Hill Farm Barn (Special Plants Nursery)

Greenways Lane, Cold Ashton, Chippenham SN14 8LA. Tel: (01225) 891686

Derry Watkins • 7m N of Bath just S of junction A46 and A420. Turn into Greenways Lane (signed to nursery) • Open Aug, Wed, 11am – 5pm; also four Thurs, June to Sept for NGS, and for parties by appt • Entrance: £1.50 • Other information: Teas on NGS days only. Lectures and courses given by Derry Watkins in autumn and winter; telephone for details [NEW] ◑ 🍴 WC ✿

Set high on the Cotswold Way is the ¾-acre garden of Derry Watkins, owner of the adjacent Special Plants Nursery. Entirely created over the last six years, the structure and imaginative modern design are the work of her architect husband, Peter Clegg, while she has employed her discerning eye for colour and knowledge of a vast range of unusual perennials to produce a dramatic and brilliant display rising to a climax in late summer. The steepness of the south-facing site, mercifully sheltered by mature willows, ash and chestnut, enables many borderline tender plants and shrubs to flourish and grow to immense size in deep gravel terraces and richly planted borders. Bold shapes in gravel, water and grass echo the outlines of the magnificent surrounding scenery, and there are superb colour-associations, such as the deep crimson/almost black border and the shades of apricot edging the new gravel garden. The garden is still developing – the productive vegetable garden and a peaceful woodland walk are new features. The nursery itself is outstanding, selling a wide range of beautifully grown and well displayed perennials, both hardy and tender, and many new and well-tried introductions.

Hodges Barn ★

Shipton Moyne, Tetbury GL8 8PR. Tel: (01666) 880202

Mrs Charles Hornby • 3m S of Tetbury, 3m NW of Malmesbury, just outside Shipton Moyne on Malmesbury side • Open 18th, 19th April, 23rd, 24th May, 20th June, 6th, 7th, 9th July, 2 – 6pm, and at other times by appt; parties welcome • Entrance: £4. children free ● 🌳 WC & ⬤

In 1499 this was built as a dovecot or columbarium to a large house nearby which burnt down in 1556; it was converted to a home in 1938 and bought by the Hon. Mrs Arthur Strutt, the late Mr Hornby's grandmother, in 1946. She set about creating the basic structure of the garden with good stone walls and topiary, and had planted most of the trees before her death in 1973. Another influence was the once-famous Pusey House, near Faringdon, owned by Mr Hornby's parents, who supplied some of the fine plants at Hodges Barn. It is an extensive eight-acre garden, with plenty of interest for everyone – above all those who like roses (there are well over 100 different varieties). The spring garden, the water garden, the little wild woodland, the large cleared wood, the topiary and the splendid lawns are all enjoyable. The plantings reflect a preoccupation with colour, scent and variety, uninhibited by a desire to prevent one flower or shrub from growing into another. Note the planting in gravel along some of the many beds, and the tapestry hedges. This is a garden which reeks of enthusiasm – long may it continue.

Hullasey House

Tarlton, Cirencester GL7 6PA. Tel: (01285) 770132

Mr and Mrs Jonathan Taylor • 5m SW of Cirencester off A433. In Tarlton, follow lane marked 'Church'; drive is few 100 yds on right • Open 6th, 7th June, 2 – 5pm for NGS; and May and June by appt • Entrance: £2, children free ●

Mrs Taylor has achieved a mature, medium-sized traditional Cotswold garden here in little under ten years, overcoming the problem of a windy situation. With spectacular views, the front of the house is a formal area with a sweeping lawn and octagonal box-edged beds in purple, mauve, white and silver. The luxuriant herb garden is contained within a walled parterre, with fruit trees, yet more roses and a miniature camomile lawn. There is a splendid walled garden with an exuberant mixture of herbaceous plants and roses of every description, rambling around and beside the walls and over arches, intertwined with honeysuckle. Beyond is the spring garden, planted with wild daffodils and scillas, and the wild rose garden.

Hunts Court

North Nibley, Dursley GL11 6DZ. Tel: (01453) 547440

Mr and Mrs T.K. Marshall • 1½ m SW of Dursley, 2m NW of Wotton-under-Edge near North Nibley. Turn E off B4060 in Nibley at Black Horse Inn and fork left after ¼ m • Open all year except Aug, Tues – Sat, 9am – 5pm; also 12th April, 3rd, 31st May, and some Suns for NGS, 2 – 6pm. Closed 9th April and 25th Dec to 2nd Jan • Entrance: £2, children free • Other information: Teas on Suns only ⏰ 🖼 <u>WC</u> ♿ 🌿 ♋

A must for those with a love of old roses. June sees in excess of 400 varieties – species, climbing and shrub – filling the borders, cascading over rails, pergolas and trees and spilling out over the informal grass paths which weave a passage through rare shrubs and herbaceous perennials. Summer is inevitably dominated by roses, but this is not to deny interest in other seasons. A more formal sundial garden, the beds intersected with gravel paths, provides a home for hardy geraniums, penstemons and diascias. In another area mown paths draw the eye towards the Cotswold escarpment which commands the eastern landscape. In the adjoining nursery many of the plants growing in the garden are for sale, and the owner is on hand with advice. An arboretum has been added with acers and other more unusual trees and shrubs.

Kelmscott Manor

(see Oxfordshire)

Kiftsgate Court ★★ [Historic Garden Grade II*]

Chipping Campden GL55 6LW. Tel: (01386) 438777

Mr and Mrs J.G. Chambers • 3m NE of Chipping Campden and near Mickleton, very close to Hidcote, which is signposted • Open April, May, Aug and Sept, Wed, Thurs, Sun and Bank Holiday Mons, 2 – 6pm; June, July, daily except Fri, 12 noon – 6pm (Note: opening times not identical to Hidcote's) • Entrance: £4.50, children £1 (2003 prices) • Other information: Coaches by appt only ◗ 🍴 WC 🌿

The house was built in the late nineteenth century on a magnificent site surrounded by three steep banks, and the garden was largely created by the present owner's grandmother after World War I. Her work was carried on by her daughter, Diany Binny, who made a few alterations but followed the same colour schemes in the borders, and by her grand-daughter Anne Chambers, who continues to perfect her vision. In spring, the white sunken garden is covered with bulbs, and there is a fine show of daffodils along the drive. June and July are the peak months for colour and scent, but the magnificent old and species roses are the glory of this garden, home of *Rosa filipes* 'Kiftsgate'. Notable too are perennial geraniums, a mighty wisteria and many species of hydrangea, some very large. In autumn, Japanese maples glow in the bluebell wood. Unusual plants are sometimes amongst those available for sale. This garden should not be missed, not only because of its proximity to Hidcote, but because of its profusion of colour and apparent informality. This said, most visitors had thought of Kiftsgate as trapped in a time warp, when, lo and behold, the owners add a serenely simple flower-free water garden – flower-free that is, apart from Simon Allison's inspired foliage sculpture reflected in the black water of the pool.

Lydney Park Gardens

Lydney GL15 6BU. Tel: (01594) 845497

The Viscount Bledisloe • 20m SW of Gloucester. N of A48 between Lydney and Aylburton • Open late March to early June, Wed, Sun and Bank Holiday Mons, 11am – 6pm. Parties and guided tours by appt • Entrance: £3 (£2 on Weds), accompanied children 50p (2003 prices) • Other information: Picnics in deer park only. Iron Age fort, Roman temple site and New Zealand museum ● ➍ 🏵 WC ⬦ ✿ ⛪ ✆

The park dates from the seventeenth century, and although it has been in the hands of one family since 1723, a new house was built in 1875 and the old one demolished. An area near the house has an interesting collection of magnolias, and a picturesque sight is the bank of daffodils and cherries, splendid in season. From 1955 a woodland garden was developed in the wooded valley behind and below the house, with the aim of achieving bold colour at different times between March and June. Near the entrance to the main part of the gardens is a small pool surrounded by azaleas and a collection of acers. From here the route passes through carefully planted groups of rhododendrons and past a folly, brought from Venice, which overlooks a valley and bog garden. Criss-crossing the hillside are rare and fine rhododendrons and azaleas, including an area planted with unnamed seedlings. Enormous effort has gone into the plant design, colour combination and general landscaping, and those who are enthusiastic about rhododendrons, azaleas and all varieties of shrubs and trees will find enough to enjoy for a whole day. Nearby is the Roman camp and museum containing the famous bronze Lydney dog, while the park has a fine collection of trees and herds of white, roe and fallow deer.

Mill Dene

Blockley, Moreton-in-Marsh GL56 9HU. Tel: (01386) 700457

Mr and Mrs B.S. Dare • 3m W of Moreton-in-Marsh on A44. Follow brown tourist-signs from Bourton-on-the-Hill • Open April to Oct, Tues – Fri, 10am – 5pm (also Suns in May and June, 2 – 6pm), and for individuals and parties by appt • Entrance: £4, children £1. Special rates for parties • Refreshments summer only ◑ ➍ 🏵 WC ♿ ✿ ⛲ B&B

A most attractive and unusually situated 2½-acre garden, built around the mill pond and stream and climbing in steep terraces, each with its own character and colour scheme, to a *potager* and fruit garden with a summerhouse and little fountain at the top and a rose walk and cricket lawn on the way. Scented plants are a priority, and there are splendid views of the Cotswold hills and surrounding picturesque village. Quirky surprises include a grotto and *trompe-l'œil* effects. Rupert Golby helped design the North Shade garden, which has garden sheds with planted roofs and a disguised telegraph pole and is decorated with glass fossil sculptures. Up to a dozen other gardens in this popular hillside village are open on one day in June for the NGS and are well worth a visit. Nearby is *Peartrees*, a small cottage garden full of treasures, open by appointment (telephone (01386) 700464).

Misarden Park Gardens ★ [Historic Garden Grade II*]

Miserden, Stroud GL6 7JA. Tel: (01285) 821303

Major M.T.N.H. Wills • 3m NW of Cirencester, 3m off A417. Signposted •
Open April to Sept, Tues – Thurs, 10am – 5pm, and for parties by appt •
Entrance: £3.50 (inc. printed guide), children free. Reduction for parties of 20 or
more. Guided tour extra • Other information: Adjacent nursery open daily except
Mon ◑ 🍽 **WC** & ⬙ 🌿 ℃

This lovely, timeless English garden, which commands spectacular views over the Golden Valley, has most of the features one expects of a garden started in the seventeenth century. There are extensive yew hedges, a York-stone terrace, a Lutyens loggia overhung with wisteria, and a good specimen of *Magnolia* x *soulangeana*. The south lawn sports splendid grass steps. West of the house the ground ascends to the nursery in a series of grassed terraces. Two good herbaceous borders lead to a new parterre of tulips, alliums, hebes and lavender, and a rill and summerhouse have been added. There are many fine specimen trees, and the spring show of blossom and bulbs is notable. The seventeenth-century manor house is not open.

Moor Wood

Woodmancote, Cirencester GL7 7EB. Tel: (01285) 831397

Mr and Mrs Henry Robinson • 3½ m N of Cirencester off A435. At North
Cerney turn uphill signed to Woodmancote. In Woodmancote go through white
gates on left beside lodge. Parking at end of drive • Open for NGS probably 27th
and 30th June, 2 – 6pm, and by appt • Entrance: £3, children free • Other
information: Teas on open days only ◑

With its attractive valley setting, this is the perfect home for a National Collection of rambler roses – 140 in all, crawling over every wall surrounding the gardens of this Cotswold family house and its cottages and stables. Since 1984 the owners have been gradually building up the collection and restoring the gardens, a continuing process. There are two acres of cottage gardens, a formal lawn and borders, an orchard and a terraced garden. What was the old walled vegetable garden is now a mass of wild flowers, all contributing to a delightfully natural atmosphere in keeping with the surrounding farmland.

The National Arboretum, Westonbirt ★★ [Historic Arboretum Grade I]

Westonbirt, Tetbury GL8 8QS. Tel: (01666) 880220

The Forestry Commission • 3m SW of Tetbury on A433, 5m NE of A46 junction
• Open all year, 10am – 8pm (or dusk if earlier) • Entrance: Charges vary

seasonally – maximum for individuals £7.50, OAPs £6.50, children £1, family £15 (reduced rates for disabled, educational, and parties) (2003 prices) ○ ● ✕ 🐗 <u>WC</u> ﴾ ⬦ 🌿 ⬦ ﴿ ⚲

This is perhaps the finest arboretum in Britain – 600 acres in all. Started in 1829 by Robert Stayner Holford, it was expanded and improved by successive generations of the same family until it was taken over by the Forestry Commission in 1956. Numerous grass rides divide the trees into glades used for special plantings, such as the famous collection of Japanese maples. Westonbirt is noted for its vast range of stunning mature specimen trees and the Forestry Commission is continuing with new planting. Across the valley from the original arboretum is Silkwood, with collections of native, Asian and American species that in spring are carpeted with primroses, wood anemones and bluebells. There are in excess of 18,000 numbered trees and 17 miles of paths. Colour is best in May (rhododendrons, magnolias, etc.) and October (Japanese maples, fothergillas, etc.). From mid-November until Christmas the garden is illuminated at weekends with hundreds of twinkling lights after dark, and many champion trees are floodlit. Westonbirt also hosts the International Festival of Gardens with show gardens, inspired by Chaumont in France, open to visitors from mid-June to early September.

Newark Park [Historic Garden Grade II]

Ozleworth, Wotton–under–Edge GL12 7PZ. Tel: (01453) 842644

The National Trust (contact: Michael Claydon) • *1½ m E of Wotton-under-Edge. 1¼ m S of A4135 and B4058. Follow signs for Ozleworth* • *Open 31st Jan, 1st, 7th, 8th, 14th, 15th Feb for snowdrops; April, May, Wed, Thurs and Bank Holiday Mons; June to Oct, Wed, Thurs, Sat, Sun and Bank Holiday Mon; all 11am – 5pm* • *Entrance: House and garden £4, children £2* ◑ 🐗 WC ﴾ ⬦

The former deer park, set within 700 acres, leads to the Tudor hunting lodge, and beyond to a landscape of hills and wild woodland brought vividly to life by the drama of a vertical drop on the southern side. The sixteenth-century house, greatly enlarged and Gothicised by James Wyatt in the 1790s, has now been rehabilitated with great taste; much of the credit for this goes to Robert Parsons, who was tenant here from 1970 to 2000 and whose work is continued with the Trust's support by Michael Claydon. The house is set amongst woodland walks which end at the foot of the escarpment (the planting here is yet to be restored) with a carp pond partially enclosed by a crinkle-crankle wall, a summerhouse and an arbour. Wildflowers abound in their season – aconites, snowdrops, daffodils and spring- and autumn-flowering cyclamen. No lover of classic English landscape should miss a visit to Newark with its majestic panoramic views to the distant Mendip Hills.

The Old Barn

Upper Dowdeswell, Cheltenham GL54 4LT. Tel: (01242) 820858

Dawn and Jamie Adams • *5m E of Cheltenham off A40. Turn right after reservoir to Dowdeswell, then right at crossroads at top of hill past church and after 180 metres right again into Upper Dowdeswell. Park outside Manor on left and walk short distance to garden • Open all year by appt • Entrance: £3, children free* ● & ■ ⬦ ℘ ℺

Dawn Adams, a garden designer, has cleverly combined style and naturalism in this beautifully kept three-quarter-acre hillside garden, which perfectly complements its fine Cotswold setting with splendid views. Developed from a field over the past twenty years and following gently sloping contours, individual areas are bounded by immaculate beech and yew hedges and stone walls. Planted for year-round appeal with many unusual species, there are traditional colour-themed borders, a rose-and-clematis-covered pergola, a croquet lawn, a fruit garden and a white garden – something of interest in and around every corner. Snowdrops and bluebells, auriculas and hellebores flower in profusion in their seasons. A one-acre woodland walk on the other side of the road overlooks the Severn Vale and Malvern Hills. Sunsets here are spectacular.

The Old Rectory ★

Duntisbourne Rouse, Daglingworth, Cirencester GL7 7AP

Charles and Mary Keen • 3m NW of Cirencester off A417. From Daglingworth take narrow valley road for the Duntisbournes. After ½ m house is on right next to church • Open 16th Feb, 15th March, 26th April, 21st June, 19th Sept, 11am – 5pm (6pm in summer), and by written appt for parties of 10 or more • Entrance: £3.50, children free. Parties negotiable • Other information: Light refreshments available in winter. Wheelchair access difficult, but not impossible ● ☕ WC ⬦ ℺

Visitors should start their tour by taking themselves up to the former schoolroom and browsing through the latest collection of cuttings and comments about the garden, giving themselves time to take in the peaceful atmosphere. Since 1983 the garden writer and designer Mary Keen has created an intimate and inspiring 1½-acre garden full of colour, variety and interest at every season. House and garden nestle among softly wooded Cotswold hills beside a tiny, unspoilt Saxon church. The garden has been designed with its exceptional setting in mind, its views drawing the eye towards the surrounding countryside. It is divided into many different areas of changing levels and moods, separated by yew or box hedges. The initial calm expanse of lawn at the front of the house gives way to sunken areas of exuberant colour, an auricula house, a winter garden, and a dark reflective pool. A partially hidden pathway lined with snowdrops leads to a shrub dell carpeted by wood anemones and more snowdrops. Behind the house, steps lead up through seasonally changing borders past the recently restored schoolhouse, to a greenhouse filled with special treasures, a gooseberry garden, a wildflower orchard with a hazel walk and mown pathways, and on into the vegetable garden and borders facing the churchyard. A particular feature is the exceptional use of colour and shape, well-summed up by the designer herself when she says, 'I like to think of a garden as a place to be, rather than a thing to look at.'

The Old Rectory

Quenington, Nr. Fairford, Cirencester GL7 5BN. Tel: (01285) 750358

Mr and Mrs D. Abel Smith • 2m N of Fairford, 9m E of Cirencester on A417 • Open one day in April for charity, one day in June for NGS, and by appt • Entrance: £3 on charity days only • Other information: Biennial show of contemporary sculpture usually July (next show 2005) NEW

The owners have taken full advantage both of the River Coln meandering through their garden and the more formal mill race (constructed by the Knights Hospitallers) to display their growing collection of sculpture. Personally chosen works are to be found in the formal garden behind the house, and more can be discovered when walking among the trees towards the river and its bridge – a natural setting for the collection of permanent works in many materials (note the growing interest in glass). Some 200 works are displayed during the biennial show. Today sculpture 'parks' are far from a rarity, but few enjoy the benefit of the fine riverside setting which has the feeling of an amphitheatre.

Owlpen Manor [Historic Garden Grade II]

Uley, Dursley GL11 5BZ. Tel: (01453) 860261

Mr and Mrs N. Mander • 6m SW of Stroud, 3m E of Dursley off B4066, 1m E of Uley. Signposted • House open • Garden open April to Sept, Tues – Sun and Bank Holiday Mons, 2 – 5pm • Entrance: £2.80 (house and garden £4.80, children £2) ◑ ⚇ ✕ WC

Situated in a remote, beautiful and vertiginous Cotswold valley, this is an unusually complete survival of a small formal manorial garden of the seventeenth century. Laid out on seven hanging terraces with topiary yews, box parterres, old roses, and steps leading steeply down to the mill pond, the garden plays a major role in creating a romantic setting for the house and its church. Today, however, the topiary has lost some of its crispness, the infilling of the parterres its freshness, the espaliered trees their rhythm. An unsympathetic modern viewing platform gazes out across the stream to a slightly dispirited garden – but it is a magical place nonetheless.

Ozleworth Park ★

Ozleworth, Wotton–under–Edge GL12 7QA. Tel: (01453) 845591

Michael Stone • 5m S of Dursley off A4135 Tetbury – Dursley road. At junction with B4058, turn S on single-track lane signed to Ozleworth, and follow signs for 2m until reaching gates with eagles on gate posts • Open one day for NGS, and for a limited number of small groups by appt NEW

The garden surrounding the handsome house is quite simply magnificent: in the generosity of its spaces, the scale and sophistication of its plantings and the artistry of its design. The present owners commissioned a complete reconstruction from Antony Young; later work by Jane Fearnley-Whittingstall, Charles Hornby and the head gardener Colin Durber amended the initial plans to produce the garden as it looks today. The tone is set from the moment of arrival in the park behind the house, where three venerable cedars stand on a huge lawn sweeping to a quarter-mile-long ha-ha. The stable courtyard to the east is substantial too, and the octagonal-towered Norman church is drawn into the assembly of outbuildings. There is space here only to hint at a few of the multiple enclosures laid out within yew hedges or beautiful old walls: a stepped rill with slabs of stone and square ponds, rising up a steep hillside to a wild area at the top; an espaliered pear pergola underplanted with lavender reached by a green yew corridor; an 1806 bath house (the garden's only source of irrigation) encircled by a walkway; wide and deep borders planted with a subtle, exuberant range of shrubs and perennials; a rose garden that really is given over to roses; a little stream crossed by a wooden bridge and thickly planted with moisture-lovers. One of the most successful spaces is the water garden, tucked away at the perimeter, where two long rectangular pools studded with water lilies and separated by a bronze girl with a bow are flanked on the inner side by a plump lavender hedge on top of a low wall and on the outer by an equally low yew hedge. Plus greenhouses, and a cutting garden, and a vast vegetable garden. Ten acres in all, this is a twenty-first-century garden of truly Edwardian opulence and panache.

Painswick Rococo Garden ★ [Historic Garden Grade II*]

Painswick GL6 6TH. Tel: (01452) 813204

Painswick Rococo Gardens Trust • ½ m from Painswick on B4073. Signposted • Open 10th Jan to Oct, daily, 11am – 5pm • Entrance: £4, OAPs £3.50, children £2 • Other information: Coaches by appt ○ ☕ ✗ 🏛 WC ⬦ 🌿 🏪 ⚱

A great deal of time, money and effort is going into the continuing restoration (almost complete redevelopment) of this rare Rococo survival. Much of the work is now completed with new plantings becoming established. At present, the best features are the eighteenth-century garden buildings, the views into beautiful surrounding countryside, and the marvellous snowdrop wood spanning a stream that flows from a pond at the lower end. This must be one of the best displays of naturalised snowdrops in England. There are some splendid beech woods and older specimen trees. Wild flowers are allowed complete freedom. Rococo gardening was an eighteenth-century combination of formal geometric features with winding woodland paths, revealing sudden incidents and vistas – in essence, a softening of the formal French style, apparent from about 1715 onwards in all forms of art. The basis for Painswick's present restoration is a painting of 1748 by Thomas Robins (1716–78) for Benjamin Hyett, who created the garden in the grounds of the house built by his father in 1735. To celebrate the 250 years of its existence, Painswick's owners have planted a yew hedge maze, designed by Angela Newing, in adjoining farmland; something to look forward to as it matures. In total it is a large estate and visitors (who should be fit for some steep inclines) must allow three-quarters of an hour even for a brisk walk round its many beauties.

Rockcliffe ★

Lower Swell, Stow-on-the-Wold GL54 2JW

Mr and Mrs Simon Keswick • 3m W of Stow-on-the-Wold on B4068 • Open 10th, 16th, 23rd, 24th June, 10am – 5pm • Entrance: £3, children under 15 free ◕ **WC**

The house was built in the late nineteenth century for the dowagers of Eyford Park, the estate that marches with it, and looks due west towards a glorious stretch of unspoilt country enclosed by a curving shelter belt of mature park trees. Two elegant pavilions added by Nick Johnson to the house pull the whole composition together and create a generous forecourt. Here the garden starts. On the stone slabs is a series of geometric box patterns, intertwined and tubular, including a centrepiece in the form of a box-edged spoked wheel with a stone wellhead in the centre; the paving froths lime-green with *Alchemilla mollis*. From the forecourt the view is of beech obelisks stalking up the broad grass ride towards the new ha-ha and beyond to open country-side. Between the terrace and the tree-lined boundary to the north is a shady enclosure where a stone-edged pool is overhung by six elegant *Cornus controversa* 'Variegata'. This lower-level garden leads to another where two simple canals of reflective water are framed by York-stone paving. In this placid green space are parallel lines of pleached hornbeams; a deep herbaceous border in pastel shades is relegated to a supporting role. Then come three flower-filled *boîtes* – two yew-edged rooms, richly planted in shades of white and purple-blue, and a scented swimming-pool garden with four huge standard bay trees and a pool-house covered with *Rosa* 'Zéphirine Drouhin'. A garden on the grand scale using a limited palette and a discriminating range of plants. As you leave the garden, cast an eye at the kitchen and cutting garden, beyond which the garden is being extended upwards and outwards up a steep bank where yew topiary birds perch in pairs, to an octagonal stone dovecote.

Rodmarton Manor ★ [Historic Garden Grade II*]

Rodmarton, Cirencester GL7 6PF. Tel: (01285) 841253

Mr and Mrs Simon Biddulph • 6m SW of Cirencester, 4m NE of Tetbury off A433, halfway between Cirencester and Tetbury • House open as garden, and for pre-booked guided group visits at other times • Garden open for snowdrops 8th, 12th, 15th Feb, from 1.30pm; 3rd May to Aug, Wed, Sat and Bank Holiday Mons, plus Mons in June, July; and 29th Aug for NGS; all 2 – 5pm • Entrance: £4, accompanied children 5-15 £1 (house and garden: parties of 20 or more £7 per person, children £3.50) • Other information: Coaches use holly (west) drive. Tea and biscuits by prior arrangement ◐ 🍴 **WC** ♿

The manor and its garden, designed by Ernest Barnsley for the Biddulphs from 1909, is an excellent example of the English Arts and Crafts Movement at its best. The drive lies between impeccably clipped tapestry hedges, and the garden, which retains virtually all its original features, comprises a series of outdoor rooms, each with its own character, bordered by the fine hedges of yew, beech, holly and box for which it is famous. In front of the house is the terrace and topiary garden, the recently replanted trough garden, a sunken garden and white borders leading to the cherry orchard, which has a wide variety of snowdrops in early spring as well as shrubs and roses. There is a good rockery, a wild garden with a hornbeam avenue, and many attractive vistas. The large working kitchen garden features both culinary and ornamental plants, old apple arches, a collection of old-fashioned and scented roses, and a row of sinks. Several areas have been replanted since 1991 when the present owners moved into the manor, including parts of the leisure garden and the four large herbaceous borders, which are now quite magnificent. The shrubbery has also been renovated. Beautifully kept, this garden is full of romance and excitement. Helpful and interesting booklet available.

Sezincote ★★ [Historic Garden Grade I]

Moreton–in–Marsh GL56 9AW.

Mr and Mrs D. Peake • 1½ m W of Moreton-in-Marsh on A44 just before Bourton-on-the-Hill • House open May to July, Sept, Thurs, Fri, 2.30 – 6pm (no children in house) • Garden open Jan to Nov, Thurs, Fri and Bank Holiday Mons, 2 – 6pm (or dusk if earlier), and 7th July for charity • Entrance: £3.50, children £1, children under 5 free (house and garden £5) • Other information: Teas on charity open day only ☾ 🍽 **WC** ♿

The entrance to Sezincote is up a long dark avenue of holm oaks that opens into the most English of parks, with a distinct feeling of Repton influence – fine trees and distant views of Cotswold hills. Turning the last corner is the surprise, for there is that fascinating rarity, an English country house built in the Moghul architectural style by Samuel Pepys Cockerell. The form of the garden has not changed since Repton's time, but the more recent planting was carried out by Lady Kleinwort with help from the late Graham Stuart Thomas, and on her return from India in 1968 she laid out the Paradise Garden in the south garden with canals and Irish yews. Behind this is the curved orangery, home to many tender climbing plants. The house is sheltered by great copper beeches, cedars, yews and limes, which provide a fine backdrop for the exotic shrubs. Streams and pools are lined with great clumps of bog-loving plants, and the stream is crossed by an Indian bridge, adorned with Brahmin bulls. Planted for year-round interest, the garden is particularly strong on autumn colours. Graham Stuart Thomas's instructive guidebook is highly recommended.

Snowshill Manor ★ [Historic Garden Grade II]

Broadway WR12 7JU. Tel: (01386) 852410

The National Trust • 3m S of Broadway off A44 • House closed in 2004 for re-servicing • Garden open 27th March to Oct, Wed – Sun and Bank Holiday Mons; July, Aug, Mon, Wed – Sun, 11am – 5.30pm • Entrance: gardens £3.60, children £1.30 (house and gardens £6.40, children £3.20, family £16) (2003 prices) • Other information: Coaches and school parties by written appt only. No entry from Snowshill village. Car park 500 metres from manor with entry via footpath; motorised buggy available ◑ ☕ ✕ 🍽 **WC** ♨ 🏬 🔦 ⚲

From a design by M.H. Baillie-Scott, the owner Charles Wade transformed a 'wilderness of chaos' on a Cotswold hillside into an interconnecting series of outdoor rooms in Hidcote style from the 1920s onwards. Wade was a believer in the Arts and Crafts rustic ideal and the garden, like the house, expresses his eccentricities. Seats and woodwork are painted 'Wade blue', a powdery dark blue with touches of turquoise which goes well with the Cotswold stone walls. The simple cottage style conceals careful planting in shades of blue, mauve and purple. Organic gardening is employed here.

Stancombe Park ★ [Historic Garden Grade I]

Stancombe, Dursley GL11 6AU. Tel: (01453) 542815

Mrs Gerda Barlow • Between Wotton-under-Edge and Dursley on B4060 • Open for parties by appt • Entrance: £3, children 50p ◐ 🍴 ♿ WC

People still rush to view the most curious park and garden south of Biddulph Grange (see entry in Staffordshire), built in 1811. Set on the Cotswold escarpment, it has all the ingredients of a Gothick best-seller. A narrow path drops into a dark glen, roots from enormous oaks, copper beeches and chestnuts trip your feet, ferns brush your face, walls drip water, and ammonites and fossils loom in the gloom. Rocks erupt with moss, Egyptian tombs trap the unwary, tunnels turn into grottoes. Even plants live in wire cages. But it is not a place of gloom; indeed the secret garden can be light and friendly when it is not raining. There is another side to Stancombe – a pretty rose garden, twentieth-century follies around the house, patterned borders and extensive gardens created by the owner and by the designer Nada Jennett. A millennium folly with a peace motif placed at the head of a small pond has reused the façade of a small ruined chapel found in the woods; a bog garden has been planted behind.

Stanway House [Historic Garden Grade I]

Winchcombe, Cheltenham GL54 5PQ. Tel: (01386) 584469

Lord Neidpath • 1m E of B4632 Cheltenham – Broadway road, 4m NE of Winchcombe • House open • Garden open July and Aug, Tues and Thurs, 2 – 5pm. Tours for parties at other times by appt • Entrance: House and garden £4, OAPs £3, children £1 ◐ WC ♿

Stanway is a honey-coloured Cotswold village with a Jacobean 'great house' which has changed hands just once since AD 715. It was much frequented by Arthur Balfour and 'The Souls' in the latter years of the nineteenth century. The garden rises in a series of dramatic terraced lawns and a rare, picturesque 'grasswork' to the pyramid, which in the eighteenth century stood at the head of a 190-metre-long cascade descending to a formal canal on a terrace above the house. This was probably designed by Charles Bridgeman, and exceeded in length and height (36 metres) its famous rival at Chatsworth (see entry in Derbyshire). Inside the house is a fascinating painting recording the cascade as it looked in the eighteenth century. The canal, the upper pond behind the pyramid, a short section of the cascade, and the upper fall below the pyramid were restored in 1998, and a 20-metre-high single-jet fountain added in the middle of the canal. The medieval pond in the Lower Garden, recently restored, has enhanced the beauty of the fourteenth-century tithe barn. It is hoped soon to restore the pyramid itself, a banqueting house from which guests could watch the sluices being opened and the water falling down towards the house. A high walk along the hillside above the cascade reveals the splendid park trees and the good progress made with water features.

Stone House

Wyck Rissington GL54 2PN. Tel: (01451) 810337

Mr and Mrs Andrew Lukas • 1½ m S of Stow-on-the-Wold off A429 just NE of Bourton-on-the-Water. Last house in village, past church on opposite side of road • Open April to Oct for individuals and parties by appt • Entrance: £3 • Other information: Teas by prior arrangement. Plant fair 31st May ● ▓ WC &

This plantsman's garden is the perfect antidote to all those daffodil-lined Cotswold lanes, as it avoids horticultural clichés all year round. Note, for example, the bold use of euphorbias. Its two acres are filled with unusual bulbs, shrubs and herbaceous perennials, including an abundance of aquilegias and hostas. There is a crab-apple walk, rose borders and a herb garden, and fritillaries have started to naturalise in the meadow walk. A spring-fed stream flowing into the River Dikler bubbles throughout; the area of sloping, box-edged lawns leading down from a terrace via rounded Lutyensesque brick steps to the water's edge is especially charming. The overall design makes full and sensitive use of the sloping site and the views out across a ha-ha to unspoilt countryside; major elements such as a swimming pool and tennis court are cunningly concealed. The annual plant fair is prized for its wide range of good and unusual plants, with some of the stands manned by professional nursery-men fresh from Chelsea triumphs. The attractive village has an unusual church with a fine tower, where Gustav Holst was organist for a period at the princely annual stipend of £4.

Sudeley Castle ★ [Historic Garden Grade II*]

Winchcombe, Cheltenham GL54 5JD. Tel: (01242) 602308

Lord and Lady Ashcombe • 8m NE of Cheltenham off B4632 at Winchcombe • Castle open April to Oct, daily, 11am – 5pm • Gardens open March to Oct, daily, 10.30am – 5.30pm. Private guided tours in and out of season by arrangement • Entrance: castle and gardens £6.70, concessions £5.70, children £3.70; party rates and season tickets available ◑ 🍽 ✕ ▓ WC & ⬗ ✿ ♛ ♿ ⚲

There has been a house on this magnificent site, with views of the surrounding Cotswold hills at every turn, for over 1000 years, and today the emphasis is on tourism, with pleasant facilities and special exhibitions. The extensive grounds contain ten integrated but individual gardens, notably the Queen's Garden with its outstanding collection of old-fashioned roses, surrounded by immaculately clipped double yew hedges. These were laid out in the nineteenth century by an ancestor of the present owners on the site of the original Tudor parterre. In recent years Jane Fearnley-Whittingstall guided the restoration of this area, as well as designing the knot garden and a newly planted buddleia walk featuring 23 different varieties. The gardens surrounding the ruins of the banqueting hall and the tithe barn with its carp pond are exceptionally lovely, with old climbing roses and (should you be lucky enough to avoid the coachloads) a romantic atmosphere. There is a white garden, a secret garden recently replanted by Charles Chesshire, and a new tree peony garden under construction. The Victorian kitchen garden is managed in collaboration with the Henry Doubleday Research Association to produce seed for propagation.

Upton Wold

Northwick Estate, Moreton-in-Marsh GL56 9TR. Tel: (01386) 700667

Mr and Mrs I.R.S. Bond • 5m NW of Moreton-in-Marsh on A44. Pass Batsford, Sezincote and Bourton House (see entries), continue up Bourton hill, pass Troopers Lodge Garage at A424 junction, and drive is 1m further on right • Open two days for NGS, 2 – 6pm, and by appt May to July, 10am – 6pm • Entrance: NGS openings £4, children free; May to July openings £6 ● ● WC ⅀ ⌖

One would never know, travelling along the busy A44, that four fine gardens lie along this stretch of a few miles, the newest and best concealed of these being the garden set around a small seventeenth-century manor house hidden in a wold. The owners arrived here in the 1970s and have created, from scratch, what is now one of the most distinguished of typical Cotswold gardens. The view from the south-east façade of the house (not open) stretches out across a lawn and ha-ha to the valley. To the left is a long border, which leads to the pond and wild garden (fritillaries bursting through in season). The walk on the opposite side of the central lawn is bordered by a tunnel of yew. Beyond this the ground slopes up through the Hidden Garden and hedged croquet lawn to a long level area containing an ornamental fruit garden, a fine vegetable garden and greenhouses. Imaginative planting is evident everywhere (note the owners' passion for standards), with particular care taken to provide pleasing views from the house windows, such as the bank of old roses below the dovecot.

The Urn Cottage

19 Station Road, Charfield, Wotton-under-Edge GL12 8SY. Tel: (01453) 843156

Mr A.C. and Dr L.A. Rosser • 3m E of M5 junction 14. In Charfield turn off main road at the Railway Tavern; garden is 370 metres on left, a short walk from parking • Open by appt only • Entrance: £3, children £1 ● ● WC ⅀ ⌖

This splendidly varied garden around an old stone cottage has been entirely created by the owners since 1982. The trees they planted for shelter have now matured and frame beautiful views of the Cotswolds from its edge-of-village setting. Dr Rosser is a horticultural design consultant and lecturer, and her expertise is evident in the skilful design and planting of this attractive ¾-acre garden. Her preference for well-behaved plants results in a wide and remarkably healthy selection, all maintained to a high standard. Long-season interest is achieved throughout the garden, from the stylish schemes around the house to planting beside a shady stream and even on a patch of volcanic rock. A small vegetable garden is cleverly terraced with wooden railway sleepers, and interesting sculptures are imaginatively displayed.

Westbury Court Garden [Historic Garden Grade II*]

Westbury-on-Severn GL14 1PD. Tel: (01452) 760461

The National Trust • 9m SW of Gloucester on A48, close to church • Open March to June, Wed – Sun and Bank Holiday Mons; July to Aug, daily; Sept to 26th Oct, Wed – Sun; all 10am – 5pm. Individuals at other times by appt and parties of 15 or more by written appt • Entrance: £3, children £1.50 • Other information: Braille plan available ◑ 🐌 **WC** ♿ ⚒

The future of this remarkable Dutch water garden – restored by the Trust in the 1960s is still in jeopardy following an outbreak of phytophthora in 2002. Substantial sections of the formal yew hedging flanking the Tall Pavilion have died and therefore disfigure one fundamental component of the ensemble of *allée,* canal, *clairvoyée* and vista, and the Trust has been advised that the garden could be flooded with increasing frequency in the decades to come. Nevertheless, the replanting of the hedges is said to be under positive review. The other elements of this rare seventeenth-century survival remain in good shape and retain their interest for garden historians. Parallel to the long canal and its unhappy yews is a T-shaped canal with Neptune bestriding a dolphin in the centre of the arm. There is an elaborate seventeenth-century seat in the 'bowling green', a central area which has been returned, as in the Kip engraving, to growing period vegetables, fruit and herbs. To the north-east is a charming gazebo, one side of which overlooks a small walled enclosure where species of plants to be found growing in England prior to 1900 grow now in box-edged beds. Beyond is the parterre: beds of simple shape containing box topiary; this in turn is surrounded by the quincunx, a formal arrangement of small trees and clipped evergreens. Further to the north, on the Herefordshire border, is *Cinderdine Cottage,* where Daphne Chappell has over 100 varieties of snowdrops. [3m NE of Newent off B4215, south of Dymock; look for sign Ryton/Ketford; cottage is on right after ¾ m. Open frequently in February and March and at other times throughout the year, including every Tues. Telephone (01531) 890265 for details.]

Westonbirt Arboretum

(see THE NATIONAL ARBORETUM, WESTONBIRT)

Westonbirt School Gardens [Historic Garden Grade I]

Tetbury GL8 8QG. Tel: (01666) 880333

Westonbirt School • 3m SW of Tetbury on A433 opposite Westonbirt Arboretum • Open two days for NGS, 2 – 4.30pm, at certain times during school holidays (telephone for details), and at other times by appt • Entrance: £3.50, children £2 (2003 prices) • Other information: Teas when open during summer holidays only ● & ⬦ ▮

The house, modelled on Wollaton Hall, Nottinghamshire, was built by the eminent Victorian plant collector Robert Stayner Holford. A pioneer collector of trees, shrubs and flowers from around the world, he had already started to plant trees when he inherited the estate from his father in 1839, and the spectacular 40-acre gardens which we see today had started to take shape before the house was completed in 1872. After his death in 1892 his son George, who had also inherited his father's love of horticulture, becoming one of the most successful amateur gardeners of his time, continued the development of both arboretum and garden. He was particularly keen on orchids and exotics. The garden is designed to have leisurely walks and a few surprises. Sweeping lawns and terraces lead down to the fountain pool, with views across the ha-ha, which hides the road, to farmland beyond. The other axis leads from the church to the sunken garden, with its pond and statue of Mercury. An Italian garden with exuberant ogee-roofed pavilions and a pergola walk complete the formal eastern side of the house, while the other side is more informal, with irregular groups of trees and shrubs (many rare and exotic), a lake, grotto and rockery. Many of the trees are over 100 years old, and some are the largest of their kind in the country.

THE HERITAGE BULB CLUB

This is both a commercial venture and a conservation-minded horticultural service. It is based at Tullynally Castle (see entry in Wales), with none other than Helen Dillon as its President and Martyn Rix, formerly botanist at Wisley and author of *Growing Bulbs* as its botanical adviser. Membership of the so-called Heritage Collection secures an autumn and a spring delivery totalling some 128 bulbs in a dozen rare varieties, while the Plantsman Collection offers a smaller number in still rarer varieties. The fee structure is geared to different budgets, ranging from £45 to £110 p.a., with the opportunity of seeing a different variety in flower every month of the year. But it is also very much a club aimed at kindling interest and spreading knowledge, with visits to gardens here and abroad, expeditions to see wild species in flower, and the opportunity to buy normally unobtainable bulbs and exchange seeds. Enquiries to Heritage, Tullynally Castle, Castlepollard, Co. Westmeath, Ireland (Tel: (44) 62744 (Ireland), 0845 300 4257 (UK); or consult the website on www.heritagebulbs.com.

HAMPSHIRE &
THE ISLE OF WIGHT

Gardens on the Isle of Wight will be found at the end of the Hampshire section.

Two-starred gardens are marked on the map with a black square.

Abbey Cottage

Rectory Lane, Itchen Abbas, Winchester SO21 1BN. Tel: (01962) 779575

Col. Patrick Daniell • 2m W of New Alresford on B3047, 1m E of Itchen Abbas • Open 14th April, 9th, 16th June, 2 – 5pm; 2nd, 3rd May, 12 noon – 5pm • Entrance: £2.50 ◕ ▆ ▩ WC ⛄ ⚘ ⚲

A series of vistas linked by steps, slopes and hedge corridors leads the visitor into this one-and-half-acre organic garden with varied levels and enclosures. The framework of yew and other hedging makes a satisfying foil to shrubs and perennials, while an oval window cut through the hedge of one garden gives glimpses into the next, of a pond and an immaculate box bench with box cushions. Walls are covered with species clematis such as *C. x aromatica* and *C. fargesii* and the perennial climber *Malvastrum lateritium*; among many striking plants are *Magnolia x loebneri* 'Merrill', flowering against the yew hedge in spring, *Cornus alternifolia* 'Argentea' and ancient, well-groomed apple trees. One meadow is planted with spring bulbs and young specimen trees, another with late-summer wild flowers, and at the highest point in the garden there is a new plantation containing native trees.

Amport House [Historic Garden Grade II]

Armed Forces Chaplaincy Centre, Amport, Andover SP11 8BG.

4m W of Andover, S of A303 • Open by appt only in writing to the Principal • Entrance: £3 ◕

This little-known garden of the Lutyens/Jekyll partnership has a great water terrace on two levels, with rills, a central oval mirror pond and square lily pools, and is said to be the prototype for the water gardens at New Delhi. Since Lutyens found the Victorian house designed by Sir William Burn unattractive, he sought to distract the eye to his terraced gardens and waterways. Note his hallmark arrangement of millstone and diaper paving. Other features are herbaceous borders, a sunken rockery, pleached limes, a splendid Victorian parterre with the Winchester coat of arms, parkland and a ha-ha. A few miles E of Andover, on B3400 Whitchurch road, is Mr and Mrs Beeson's one-acre eco-friendly garden, *Forest Edge*, brimming with wild flowers, many native species and wildlife galore. [Open 25th April, 16th May, 27th June, and for B&B – telephone (01264) 364526 for details.]

Apple Court

Hordle Lane, Hordle, Lymington SO41 0HU. Tel: (01590) 642130

Charles and Angela Meads • 200 metres N of A337 between Lymington and New Milton along Hordle Lane opposite Royal Oak • Open March to Oct, Fri – Sun and Bank Holiday Mons, 10am – 5pm • Entrance: free • Other information: Plants for sale in adjoining nursery ☾ 🍽 WC ♿ ⚘

The garden is a showcase for a National Collection of hostas and is the only American Hemerocallis Society display garden in Europe. The daylily garden is at its peak in July and August, when the flowers, mostly American introductions, are mixed with agapanthus, crocosmias, kniphofias and phormiums, and has a frothy rectangle of ornamental grasses at its centre. The white garden has a different drama – a square of yew hedging contains an oval border of white flowers and silvery-leaved grasses viewed through an inner oval of pleached hornbeam which frames them like a series of lit pictures. The effect is architectural, like entering a square with a circular colonnade. Three rectangular ponds are connected by cascading rills, and there is also a fern path and herbaceous borders lined with rose-covered rope swags.

Bramdean House ★ [Historic Garden Grade II]

Bramdean, Alresford SO24 0JU. Tel: (01962) 771214

Mr and Mrs H. Wakefield • 9m E of Winchester, 5m SE of New Alresford on A272 in middle of Bramdean • Open 29th Feb, 11th April, 9th May, 13th June, 11th July, 8th Aug, 12th Sept, 2 – 5pm, for NGS, and by appt at other times • Entrance: NGS days £3, other days £4, children free ● 🍵 WC ♿ ⚘

The mellow brick eighteenth-century house is well protected from the main road by a huge undulating yew and box hedge. The six-and-a-half-acre garden on chalk slopes away from the house and is divided into three parts. One contains the famous mirror-image herbaceous borders, and surrounding beds have a large array of usual and unusual plants, shrubs and small trees. Fine wrought-iron gates lead through into the walled working kitchen garden, cultivated entirely by hand, containing fruit and vegetables grown for the house, old-fashioned sweet peas, perpetual carnations, a peony walk and a trial area for plants. Ornamental flower beds along a central path lead through a second wrought-iron gate into the orchard area, featuring fruit trees underplanted with massed daffodils and terminated by a blue-doored apple house and belfry. To the east are interesting shrubs and trees and castellations of yew. In spring there are carpets of aconites, snowdrops, crocuses and other early bulbs.

Brandy Mount House

Brandy Mount, Alresford SO24 9EG. Tel: (01962) 732189

Mr and Mrs M. Baron • In town centre. Take first right in East Street before Sun Lane • Open 4th, 7th, 8th Feb, 11am – 4pm; also Suns in early March, early April, early May (telephone to check) • Entrance: £2, children free • Other information: No vehicular access. Parking in station car park and Broad Street. Teas available except in Feb. Children must be supervised ● 🖪 ⅙ ⬥ 🍃

This informal one-acre garden of trees, shrubs, beds and grass is very much for the plantsman. Michael Baron is on hand to guide visitors through his National Collections of at least 220 named snowdrops in winter and spring, and over 130 varieties of daphne, and will discuss the problems of growing shrubs on chalk. There are woodland plants by the pond, and hellebores, ferns, trilliums, pulmonarias, epimediums, erythroniums. Unusual plants, such as *Paeonia* 'Smouthii', may be discovered all over the garden. The alpine house has a good display of dwarf narcissi and alpine primulas, where they are a delight on cold spring days. The *potager* is packed with vegetables.

48 Broad Street

New Alresford, Alresford SO24 9AN. Tel: (01962) 732441

Mr and Mrs David Ashdown • In town centre • Open by appt • Entrance: £2.50 ●

This town garden turns a long and narrow plot into a journey of light and dark through varied passages and rooms. Near the house are pots, paving, *Trachelospermum jasminoides* and the silver-leaved *Elaeagnus angustifolia* grown as a standard with *Clematis viticella* 'Etoile Violette' weaving through it. Next comes the lawn, sculpture and box-edged beds of lilies, perennials and roses. Then you reach miniature woodland and a geometric garden in shades of lavender with slate chippings. The transition to Hampshire countryside is completed by a nut walk leading to a view of fields and a glimpse of Alresford pond. Everywhere there is the sound of water bubbling from low fountains.

Bury Court

Bentley, Farnham, Surrey GU10 5LZ. Tel: (01420) 520351

John Coke • 6m NE of Alton, 5m SW of Farnham, 1½ m N of Bentley on road signed to Crondall • Open for NGS and for parties by appt • Entrance: £2 ◐ 🍽 ✕ <u>WC</u> ⅙

The walled garden is the work of the Dutch designer Piet Oudolf and displays both his naturalism and his characteristic use of grasses. Surrounded by walls of brick and stone, curved oast houses and other buildings with a glimpse of the countryside beyond, the asymmetrical beds are dominated by robust perennials and varied grasses, planted so as to evoke an idealised or dreamlike natural landscape. With lawns, cambered sett paths, a set-piece of planks emerging from water, sculptural clipped box, and a fine gravel bed with blue-flowered and grey-leaved plants, it is a good example of Oudolf's work. A new garden has been made with help from the minimalist designer Christopher Bradley-Hole, using raised beds edged with rusted steel and planted with drifts of grasses and wild-looking but non-weedy perennials.

Cadland Gardens ★ [Historic Garden Grade II*]

Fawley, Southampton SO45 1AA.

Mr and Mrs Maldwin Drummond • 16m SE of Southampton off A326/B3053 • Open May to July, Sept and Oct, by written appt for parties of 20 or more • Entrance: £4 • Other information: Teas by arrangement. House also open by arrangement ● 🍵 WC & ⬥

The landscape garden of eight acres, laid out for the banker Robert Drummond in 1775, is 'Capability' Brown's smallest surviving pleasure ground. It has been restored to the original plan, using plants available before 1780. A path with tiered shrubs (roses, brooms, *Viburnum tinus* 'Lucidum', *Bupleurum fruticosum*) and underplanted with wild flowers, winds from the modern house (encapsulating the original thatched *cottage orné* designed by Brown and Henry Holland), along the Solent shore and back through a lime walk and a Georgian flower border. Broad vistas alternate with carefully orchestrated views of the sea. There is a kitchen garden with fruit houses and a gravel garden. A second walled garden has a red border, a cool grey border and rare plants – *Astelia chathamica*, *Pileostegia viburnoides*, tender acacias and leptospermums.

Conholt Park ★

Chute, Nr Andover SP11 9HA

Prof. Caroline Tisdall • 5m NW of Andover off A342. Turn N at Weyhill church and continue 5m through Clanville and Tangley Bottom. Turn left for Conholt; house is 1/2 mile on right just off Chute causeway • Open 6th June, 4th July, 2 – 6pm • Entrance: £3, children free ● 🍵 🌿 WC ⬥

Surrounding the Regency house is an imaginative 10-acre garden created over the past few years. Spacious lawns, towering cedars and fine views are gracenotes providing a dignified setting for a variety of individual spaces, including rose, secret, winter and Shakespeare gardens, an Edwardian Ladies' Walk and a laurel millennium maze, in the shape of a foot and possibly the longest in the country. The walled kitchen garden has good glasshouses, a sunken pool and tunnels of runner beans, herbs and flowers. Future plans include a meadow rose garden with the roses allowed free growth through an existing meadow – something which has been done in France but rarely over here.

Exbury Gardens ★★ [Historic Garden Grade II*]

Exbury, Southampton SO45 1AZ. Tel: (023) 8089 1203

Mr E.L. de Rothschild • 15m S of Southampton. From M27 junction 2 take A326 then B3054. 2½ m SE of Beaulieu, after 1m turn right for Exbury. Signposted • Open March to Oct, daily; Nov, Dec, Sat and Sun only; all 10am – 5.30pm (or dusk if earlier) • Entrance: main-season £5.50, OAPs £5 (£4.50 on Tues, Wed and Thurs), children (10–15) £3.50, parties of 15 or more £5 per person. Seasonal discounts ◑ 🍵 ✕ 🌿 WC & ⬥ 🌱 🏪 🍴 ♿

Established between the wars by Lionel de Rothschild, these gardens of rhododendrons and azaleas are the most outstanding of their kind in the south. Winding paths meander over 200 acres and proceed under a light canopy of trees, mostly oak and pine, over a bridge and beside ponds to the Beaulieu River. Many rhododendrons and azaleas, such as *R. yakushimanum* and *R.* (Hawk Group) 'Crest', were introduced here and are to be found growing beside purple Japanese maples and candelabra primulas. At times the colour associations seem bold – harsh orange beside blush, metallic magenta beside pale blue – but a glade of towering white blooms, pink in bud, more than makes up for this. In March early rhododendrons, camellias and the daffodil meadow flower; in April the rock garden, miniature mountain scenery with screes and valleys, is at its peak with alpine rhododendrons among 'Skyrocket' junipers. May is the high season. In summer the modern rose garden is a mass of colour and the garden of herbaceous plants and grasses is full of interest. For autumn interest there is a superb collection of deciduous trees, shrubs, notably acers, which exhibit fiery hues next to the ponds. The most recent addition is the Summer Lane Garden, which opened in 2001 with the steam railway. Its contemporary design was inspired by Piet Oudolf, combining huge swathes of herbaceous plants, grasses, bulbs and wild flowers, and including an apple and pear orchard.

Fairfield House ★

East Street, Hambledon, Portsmouth PO7 4RY. Tel: (023) 9263 2431

Mrs Peter Wake • 10m SW of Petersfield in Hambledon • Open one day in April and June for NGS, and by appt. Suitable for parties • Entrance: £3, children 50p • Other information: Teas by arrangement only ● WC & ⬦ ⌀ ℚ

This magnificent collection of species and old roses, climbers and ramblers, together with some modern roses, was established by Peter Wake over thirty years ago with advice from Lanning Roper, and continues to flourish with replantings and additions by Marion Wake and her son Edward. The roses are planted informally on five acres, divided by yew hedges and brick walls which display to perfection larger ramblers like 'Cooper Burmese'. Elsewhere the lower stems of the shrub roses and species like 'Wolley-Dod' and *Rosa* x *alba* 'Maxima' are contained within stakes from which they rise and flower as if from giant urns. None of the roses are sprayed. On the spreading lawns are mature cedars, limes and copper beeches, as well as sorbus, malus, robinia, *Ptelea trifoliata* and fern beech, indicating the range of trees which can grow on a thin chalk soil. Among the herbaceous plants by the house, *Amsonia orientalis* flourishes in the dry chalk.

Farleigh House

Farleigh Wallop, Basingstoke RG25 2HT. Tel: (01256) 842684

The Earl and Countess of Portsmouth • 3m SW of Basingstoke off B3046. Leave M3 at junction 7 and follow signs from Dummer • Open for parties by appt • Entrance: £3 NEW & ⬦

An exemplary modern garden in the classic tradition, designed by Georgia Langton, immaculately maintained and complementing the knapped-flint house. The large kitchen garden has a herbaceous border running with blue clematis *C.*

durandii, and culminates in a conservatory (with a pond), scented with various brugmansis, rare passion flowers and other choice plants. The quadripartite fountain garden, of roses, lavender and alchemilla, is followed by an area of species roses with grey metallic seagulls wheeling overhead. A simple maze leads, via two topiary peacocks pecking at strawberries, to a rectangular waterlily garden; beyond, at the end of the Scots pine walk new wrought-iron gates open onto a 1½-acre lake. Note the details: a huge smooth granite apple in woodland is lit by a shaft of light . . . another pair of wrought-iron gates decorated with tools, flowers and abstract geometrical patterns . . . hedges dipping to give glimpses of gardens beyond . . . the little barrel seat above the ice-house. Good shrubs and trees, including a fine *Cornus controversa* 'Variegata'.

Furzey Gardens ★

Minstead, Lyndhurst SO43 7GL. Tel: (023) 8081 2464

Mrs M.M. Cole (Administrator) • 8m SW of Southampton, 1m S of A31, 2m W of Cadnam and end of M27, 3½ m NW of Lyndhurst • Open daily except 25th, 26th Dec, 10am – 5pm (earlier in winter) • Entrance: summer: £3.50, OAPs £2.80, children £1.50, families £9; winter: £1.50, OAPs £1, children 50p, families £3. Reductions for parties by arrangement • Other information: Art and craft galleries. Sixteenth-century cottage open daily March to Oct ○ ☕ ▦ WC ☇ ⚘ ♨ ✇

The eight acres of this well-maintained woodland garden were laid out by Hew Dalrymple in the early 1920s. In early March the acacia tree in full fragrant bloom, a group of *Corylopsis pauciflora* dripping with pale yellow flowers, species daffodils, *Magnolia stellata* and banks of heathers make a visit worthwhile. Among the plants which revel in the sandy acid soil of the New Forest are the ubiquitous rhododendrons and azaleas, the Chilean fire bush (*Embothrium coccineum*) flowering bright scarlet in May, and a host of shrubs and trees from Australasia. There is also a lake and a water garden with yellow skunk cabbage, ferns, etc., and a sensory garden. The children's play area has been extended with a tree house, log cabin and a living willow tunnel. Sir Arthur Conan Doyle is buried in the churchyard of the fine village church.

The Garden Gallery

Broughton, Nr Stockbridge SO20 8AZ. Tel:(01794) 301144

Mr and Mrs G. Bebb • 12m W of Winchester • Open May to Oct for parties of 10 or more by appt • Entrance: £3 • Other information: telephone for exhibition opening times ◑ ☇

Rachel Bebb's one-acre cottage garden, designed as a series of stylishly informal enclosures with varied plantings, displays a range of modern sculpture for sale. Some are set among flowers beside the small formal pond, others on gravel, in an orchard and a field, or showing up against a background of shrubs. Wind chimes, abstract shapes, urns, benches, tables, sundials and figures in stone, bronze, resin, ceramic, clay, wood and other materials – all are harmoniously sited, encouraging visitors to relate them to their own gardens.

Gilbert White's Garden

The Wakes, Selborne, Alton GU34 3JH. Tel: (01420) 511275

Oates Memorial Trust • 4½ m S of Alton, 8m N of Petersfield on B3006 • Open April to 24th Dec, 11am – 5pm • Entrance: £4.50, OAPs and students £4, children £1. Special rates for parties • Other information: Public car park behind Selborne Arms. Unusual plant fair 19th, 20th June and other non-horticultural events later (telephone to check dates) ☾ ☕ WC ᕗ ⚘ ♨ ☕

Here the naturalist Gilbert White wrote his classic *The Natural History of Selborne* (published 1788), and the garden is exceptionally well documented. The sundial and ha-ha beyond the lawn, with its splendid views of the beech-clad hanging wood, were there in his day. A copy of the amusing wooden cut-out of the Hesperian Hercules which he set up in the park in 1758 (12½ feet high, compared with the 30-foot versions at Vaux-Le-Vicomte and Caserta) has been created by sculptor David Swinton and re-installed in the garden. The quincunx, a square pattern of five cypresses on a mound, was also originally conceived by White. Borders and beds near the house contain many plants from his time, including hollyhocks ('hollyoaks'), sweet Williams, pinks, species foxgloves, santolinas, martagon lilies and old roses, Gallicas, Damasks, etc. Later additions include a laburnum tunnel, a herb garden, a fine tulip tree planted in 1910 and some yew topiary. The garden is being restored to its eighteenth-century form with historic varieties of fruit (including White's favourite melons), vegetables, herbaceous plants, annuals and wild flowers. Look out for the revolving wine barrel.

Heathlands ★

47 Locks Road, Locks Heath, Southampton SO31 6NS. Tel: (01489) 573598

Dr John Burwell • 5m W of Fareham. Leave M27 at junction 9. Locks Road runs due S from A27 at Park Gate • Open 7th March, 11th April, 9th May, 22nd Aug, 2 – 5.30pm • Entrance: £2, children free ● ☕ ⚘

A row of paulownias, grown from seed by the owner, is a memorable sight in May and raises the expectations of any visitor to this remarkable garden on the outskirts of Southampton. The lawn stretches through spring bulbs to a more wooded area. To the north a pond with a small herbaceous border is separated from the kitchen garden by a yew hedge sporting topiary balls and a peacock, its tail in low relief, its head and crown rising above the hedge line. The kitchen garden has four bay cones and Worcesterberries grown espalier-fashion. A huge holly drum is one of over 1000 different plants, including the architectural *Yucca gloriosa* and *Phormium tenax*, ferns, pieris, *Rhododendron sinogrande*, corylopsis, and a National Collection of Japanese anemones. There is also a part-yew walk focusing on an obelisk, a secret garden with a tiny pool, a new cutting garden and a conservatory.

Highclere Castle and Gardens [Historic Garden Grade I]

Highclere, Newbury, Berkshire RG20 9RN. Tel: (01635) 253204 (infoline)

The Earl and Countess of Carnarvon • 4½ m S of Newbury, W of A34 • House open as garden • Garden probably open July to early Sept (telephone for exact

*dates), daily, 11am – 5pm (Sat closes 3.30pm) (last admission 1 hour before
closing) • Entrance: £3.50, children £1 (castle and gardens £7, OAPs/students
£5.50, children (5–14) £3, family £17, season ticket £25, parties of 20 or more
£5.50 per person, children £3) (2003 prices)* ◑ 💭 ✕ 🖦 <u>WC</u> ♿ 🕯 🕯

At first glance it seems that the Houses of Parliament have flown and settled in
a parkland setting of lawns and cedars. Not surprising, since Highclere Castle
(1840) was designed by the same architect, Sir Charles Barry, who remodelled
a Georgian mansion to create a fine Victorian home for the 3rd Earl of
Carnarvon. Three follies, a rotunda beside the lake, a roofless temple called
Jackdaw's Castle, and Heaven's Gate on Sidown Hill opposite the castle are
remnants of the garden before 'Capability' Brown remodelled the grounds in
1774 to give a gloriously simple vista of valley and hills. Tucked out of sight is
the walled garden and the flower garden, designed by the late James Russell.

Hillier Gardens

(see THE SIR HAROLD HILLIER GARDENS AND ARBORETUM)

Hinton Ampner ★

Hinton Ampner, Bramdean, Alresford SO24 0LA. Tel: (01962) 771305

*The National Trust • 8m E of Winchester, 1m W of Bramdean on A272 •
House open • Garden open 21st, 28th March, then 3rd April to Sept, Sat –
Wed, 12 noon – 5pm. Parties of 15 or more by appt • Entrance: £5.80, children
(5–16) £2.90 • Other information: Coaches must use entrance through village.
Plants usually for sale* ◑ 💭 <u>WC</u> ♿

Approached through parkland, this quintessentially English garden has been
well restored in recent years. It was created by Ralph Dutton, later Lord
Sherborne, who inherited the estate in 1935. A dramatic series of terraces
with downland views descends to the south, and from the cross-axis of each
terrace you see – as if by happy chance – urns, a temple, an obelisk or a
silhouetted statue of Diana luring you to the garden's limits. The route leads
through a series of secret gardens. Huge, immaculately trimmed topiary
mushrooms give a surreal *Alice in Wonderland* effect. The features are interesting, the planting self-assured, ranging from an avenue of domed yews to a
waterlily pond, a garden of hexagons and a dell with philadelphus, lilies,
cotinus etc. In August, furnished with blue and white agapanthus, *viticella*
clematis, species salvias and *Romneya coulteri*, the garden stays resplendent.

Houghton Lodge [Historic Garden Grade II*]

Stockbridge SO20 6LQ. Tel: (01264) 810912

*Mr and Mrs Martin Busk • 1½ m S of Stockbridge. Signposted • Open March to
Sept, daily, except Wed, 2 – 5pm (opens 10am Sat, Sun and Bank Holiday
Mons) • Entrance: £5, children free* ◑ <u>WC</u> ♿ ⬦ ⚲

Superbly sited on an eminence, overlooking an open and gently curving
stretch of the River Test with its swans and water meadows, the early

eighteenth-century *cottage orné* (some cottage!) and its garden is the centre-piece of a miniature 30-acre estate. The lodge stands at the corner of a stable yard with 'stabling for fourteen and four carriages'. Beyond is the one-acre organic kitchen garden. Divided in two by a central path, it is contained by chalk 'cob' walls – once a feature of Hampshire, now more likely to be found surviving in Dorset and Wiltshire. Fine mature specimen trees, all of them proper parkland stock – planes, oaks and horse chestnuts – stand proudly on the ridge beyond the lawns. The garden abounds in topiary, including a peacock garden with a patterned box parterre, and in spring is a mass of snowdrops and daffodils. Dr David Jacques advised on the restoration. There is also a modern hydroponicum in which plants are cultivated without soil, and a new orchid collection.

53 Ladywood ★

Eastleigh SO50 4RW. Tel: (023) 806 15389

Mr and Mrs D. Ward • Leave A33/M3 at junction 12 on A335 signed to Eastleigh, turn right at roundabout into Woodside Avenue, second right into Bosville, fifth right into Ladywood • Open for NGS on three Suns, 11am – 5.30pm, and April to Sept, Tues pm by appt • Entrance: £2, children £1 • Other information: Parking in Bosville only ● ℘

This suburban garden, 14 metres square, containing 1800 different labelled plants, is subdivided into several more miniscule areas: a water garden with water hawthorn (*Aponogeton distachyos*) and water lilies, a scree garden, a shade garden with hostas and variegated plants and a tiny oval lawn. Among the healthy plants are alpines, erodiums, hardy geraniums galore, the white *Clematis* 'Henryi', *C. viticella* climbing through shrubs and trelliswork, roses, grasses, the miniature *Philadelphus* 'Manteau d'Hermine', and a good collection of *Phlox paniculata*. All are sensitively arranged with good colour associations and contrasts – for example, the black viola 'Molly Sanderson' and black grasses *Ophiopogon planiscapus* emerging from pale shingle.

Lake House

Northington, Alresford SO24 9TG.

Lord Ashburton • 3m NW of Alresford off B3046. Follow English Heritage signs for Northington and The Grange, and turn sharp left before entrance to Grange • Open probably two days for NGS • Entrance: £3, children free ● 🍽 🏵 **WC** ♿ 🐕 ℘ 🍂

The tall and handsome walls of the old kitchen gardens of the ruined Grange make a pleasing contrast with the low modern house nearby. The walled garden has herbaceous borders and box-edged plots filled with old roses and perennials, as well as a vegetable and cutting area with espalier apples, a rose and wisteria pergola and an avenue of Irish yews leading to a moon gate. The house – surrounded by a conservatory, a terrace, a formal pond and pots – looks across lawns to the lake with a scenic walk which includes views of the neo-classical shell of the old house, a nineteenth-century cascade, ancient cedars, a castle folly and an arched flint bridge. *The Grange* itself, designed by William Wilkins and formerly home of the Ashburton family, is now owned by English Heritage [Historic Park Grade II*] and may be visited at any time.

Longstock Park Water Garden ★★

Longstock, Stockbridge SO20 6EH. Tel: (01264) 810904

John Lewis Partnership (Leckford Estate Ltd) • 5m S of Andover, 2m N of Stockbridge. From A30 turn N on A3057. Signposted • Open April to Sept, first and third Sun of each month, 2 – 5pm, and by appt for parties • Entrance: £4, children £1 • Other information: Refreshments and plants for sale at nursery ● ♥ WC & ♨ 🏛

The seven acres of these superb water gardens, created by John Spedan Lewis in 1948, are fed from the River Test and surrounded by acid-loving trees and shrubs. They form an archipelago connected by narrow bridges and causeways. Gunneras, swamp cypresses (*Taxodium distichum*) surrounded by stilts, royal ferns and Japanese angelica trees (*Aralia elata*) are just some of the plants reflected in the clear waters moving with gold carp, and a walk along the paths gives a succession of views followed by more intimate spaces. Aquatics include 48 different water lilies. Do not miss a visit to *Longstock Park Nursery* nearby (also open daily), set in a walled garden with climbing plants, and the fine herbaceous border reached through a gate in its wall. This runs parallel to a pergola planted with roses and an exquisite and extensive collection of *viticella* clematis. A National Collection of buddleias, with over 100 varieties, may be seen by request.

Longthatch Gardens

Lippen Lane, Warnford, Southampton SO32 3LE. Tel: (01730) 829285

Mrs Vera Short • 14m SE of Winchester on A32 • Open 3rd March – 30th June, Wed; plus 14th, 21st, 28th March, 25th April, 30th, 31st May, 20th June for NGS; all 10am – 5pm • Entrance: £2.50 • Other information: Teas available on NGS days only NEW ●

The three-acre plantsman's garden descends to woodland paths winding across and beside the River Meon. The hellebores (part of a dispersed National Collection and including such delights as 'Old Ugly') make a fine show in spring. Huge kingcups are among the bog plants growing in spring-fed ponds beside the river, and trees shelter daffodils, pulmonarias, primulas, *Anemone nemorosa*, mounds of a mauve-flowered parasite living off willow roots, and many other rarities. In summer meconopsis, hostas, gunnera, ferns, digitalis and arum lilies merge with the wild and watery scene, and near the house are borders with cottage-garden favourites: geraniums, oriental and other poppies, Jacob's ladder, *Gladiolus byzantinus*, a huge sculptural giant fennel, and of course roses.

The Manor House ★ [Historic Garden Grade II*]

Upton Grey, Basingstoke RG25 2RD. Tel: (01256) 862827

Mr and Mrs J. Wallinger • 6m SE of Basingstoke in Upton Grey, on hill immediately above church • Open April to Oct, Mon – Fri (but closed Bank

Holidays), by appt only • Entrance: £4 (includes guide/leaflet) • Other information: Teas available by arrangement ● ☕ WC &

Over the past 18 years this garden has been meticulously restored by Mrs Ros Wallinger to the original 1908 Gertrude Jekyll planting plans, copies of which are on display, and the tender care invested makes it more than a unique museum piece. Here are formal beds with lilies, peonies and roses edged with lamb's ears, drystone walls clothed with plants, terraces, pergola and yew hedging, as well as Jekyll's only surviving restored wild garden with a pond, daffodils and rambling roses. A living example of many Jekyll theories, it is worth noting her use of colour, with hot reds moving through yellows to distant greys and blues, the proportions of the steps, and the relation of the garden to the house (designed in grand vernacular style with hung tiles, etc by Ernest Newton for Charles Holme, founder and owner of *The Studio* magazine). This is claimed to be the most authentic Jekyll garden reconstruction, supported by a useful booklet and plant list.

Marycourt

43 High Street, Odiham, Hook RG29 1LF. Tel: (01256) 702100

Mr and Mrs M.N. Conville • 7m E of Basingstoke, 7m W of Aldershot off A287 1½ m from M3 junction 5 • Open 27th June, 4th July, 2 – 6pm, 7th July, 9am – 6pm, for NGS, and by appt • Entrance: £2, children free ● 🍃 WC & 🐕

The large, long town garden is approached from the drive in the High Street. Splendid mixed borders (alpines, clematis, honeysuckles, roses, shrubs, bulbs, phormiums, perennials) along the walls open out to a riot of primary colours (ligularias, heleniums, bergamot, achilleas) beside the swimming pool. The detail and the variety of plants in the alkaline soil of this garden is remarkable; note particularly the half-hardy plants. Near the grass tennis court, with its copper beech and climbing roses, are over 20 varieties of ivy, grown as ground cover, in pots, as shrubs and, best of all, 'Paddy's Pride' draping a shed. Blue and white beds are planted with agapanthus, white roses and delphiniums and edged with lavender. Hostas grown with Solomon's seal and *Lilium regale* in a tunnel of overhanging apple trees are most effective.

Mottisfont Abbey Garden ★★ [Historic Garden Grade II]

Mottisfont, Romsey SO51 0LP. Tel: (01794) 340757

The National Trust • 15m NW of Southampton, 4¼ m NW of Romsey, ½ m W of A3057 • Open 1st to 16th March, Sat, Sun, 10am – 6pm; 22nd March to 2nd Nov dates vary – telephone to check. During rose season, 7th to 27th June, open daily, 11am – 8.30pm (last admission 1 hour before closing) (check recorded message on (01794) 341220, June only, for state of roses) • Entrance: £6.50, children £3, family £15. Party rates on application • Other information: Coaches must pre-book. Picnics in grounds only. Four-seater golf buggy available. No smoking in walled garden during rose season ◑ ☕ ✕ 🍃 WC & 🌿 🏛 🎔 ✎

This famous collection of historic roses, based on the design and selection by Graham Stuart Thomas, was established in 1972 in the original walled kitchen garden, quartered with paths and box hedging – a formal design given additional interest by herbaceous borders, a central pond and a fountain. Here are the Albas, Damasks and Gallicas of the Middle Ages, cabbage and moss roses, and the earliest Chinas, Bourbons, hybrid perpetuals, French nineteenth-century Gallicas and Albas as well as Rugosas, and ramblers up walls, arches and stands – in all, a National Collection of 300 old-fashioned roses (also a few species and New English roses), now being renovated. The best time to visit is on midsummer evenings, when the coaches have gone. Sweeping lawns around the house, cedars, the largest London plane tree (*Platanus* x *hispanica*) in the country, a magically deep and bubbling pool, and a spring running down to the River Test provide a tranquil contrast to the heady and scented delights of the roses. The simple but effective design of grass terraces, yew octagon and pollarded lime walk is the work of the late Sir Geoffrey Jellicoe, while Norah Lindsay contributed the small lavender- and box-edged parterre infilled with spring bulbs and summer annuals.

Moundsmere Manor [Historic Garden Grade II*]

Preston Candover, Basingstoke RG25 2HE. Tel: (01256) 389207

Mr and Mrs Andreae • 6m S of Basingstoke on B3046. Manor gates on left just after Preston Candover sign • Open one day for NGS, and for parties by appt • Entrance: £2, children 50p • ● WC &

The 'Wrenaissance' house was inspired by Hampton Court and designed in 1908 by Sir Reginald Blomfield (1856–1942). To its south lies Blomfield's formal garden, with herbaceous borders backed by yew hedges and buttresses at either side, then yew avenues, and at the centre a sunken garden edged with roses and a central pool in which the house is pleasingly reflected from the far end. There is also a pinetum and good hothouses with streptocarpus, abutilons, figs, etc. This is Edwardian gardening on a grand scale, characteristically architectural, and exemplifies Blomfield's theories in *The Formal Garden in England*, in which he attacks the informal style supported by William Robinson. Other examples of Blomfield's work can also be found at Athelhampton House (Dorset) and Godinton Park (Kent) (see entries).

Redenham Park ★

Redenham, Nr Andover SP11 9AQ. Tel: (01264) 772511

Lady Clark • 4m NW of Andover on A342 • Open for parties by appt • Entrance: £4.50 • Other information: Teas by arrangement ● 🐾 WC

The perfect setting for a Jane Austen novel, this classic five-acre garden embraces its early-nineteenth-century ashlar-faced house. Views of parkland with sheep and cedars are followed by an enclosed paved rose garden with a circular pond (home to zantedeschia and white iris) and a fountain, then by herbaceous borders leading to a pleached lime walk and a moon gate. There are also fine borders, sculptural clipped yews, a tapestry hedge of copper- and green-leaved beech bordering the croquet lawn, and a low pear and apple espalier in a walled garden, where walls and paths drip in June with scented roses. The walled kitchen garden is immaculate, and the mass of exotic fowls includes an ebony cock and hens.

Rotherfield Park [Historic Garden Grade II*]

East Tisted, Alton GU34 3QE. Tel: (01420) 588207

Sir James and Lady Scott • 4m S of Alton on A32 • Open for NGS, and for parties by appt in May and Sept • Entrance: £2.50, children free ◐ 🍴 🏞 WC

The Grade-I-listed house was built between 1815 and 1822 by the Scott family, with later additions in a medley of medieval and Tudor styles – note the laundry house chimney like Rapunzel's tower – and is an integral part of the Picturesque landscape, looking to the church which was rebuilt as a *point de vue* complete with little tower. The quadripartite walled garden is approached via splendid yew hedges supported by golden yew buttresses, and entered through magnificent wrought-iron gates. These open to herbaceous borders terminated by a Victorian summerhouse with enamelled tiles. There is a fruit section with espalier apples and pears along the walls, standard gooseberries and other fruits, a vegetable plot and flower and shrub sections. In May the 60-acre pleasure ground is a haze of bluebells. Elsewhere, a rose garden with old roses, an orchard and maze, and many fine trees and shrubs.

Selborne

(see GILBERT WHITE'S HOUSE AND GARDEN)

The Sir Harold
Hillier Gardens ★★ [Historic Garden and Arboretum Grade II]

Jermyns Lane, Ampfield, Romsey SO51 0QA. Tel: (01794) 368787

Hampshire County Council • 3m NE of Romsey, 9m SW of Winchester, $\frac{3}{4}$ m W of A3090 along Jermyns Lane. Signed from A3090 and A3057 • Open all year, daily, except 25th, 26th Dec, 10.30am – 6pm (or dusk if earlier) • Entrance: £5.25, concessions £4.75, children under 16 free, parties of 10 or more £4.25 per person • Other information: Plants for sale and shop in adjacent nursery ○ 🍴 ✕ 🏞 WC ♿ 🌷 ⚲

Administered by Hampshire County Council since 1977, this collection of hardy trees and shrubs, the largest in the world, was begun in 1953 by the late Sir Harold Hillier, using his house and garden as a starting point. It extends to 180 acres and includes approximately 12,000 different species and cultivars, with many rarities. Eleven National Collections are held here, more than any other garden, including quercus and hamamelis. Weekly lists of plants of current-season interest are produced, and lead the visitor to herbaceous, scree, heather and bog gardens. With a total of about 40,000 plants it is impossible at any time of year not to be impressed or learn something about what, where and how to plant. Notable among the trees are *Eucalpytus nitens* and *E. niphophila*, *Magnolia cylindrica*, *Zanthoxylum* spp. (the prickly ash or toothache tree) as well as acers and sorbus. Among the shrubs is a wide range of rhododendrons, azaleas, camellias and hydrangeas. The winter garden specialises in plants at their best from November to March, and includes gold- and black-stemmed bamboos and the white-stemmed *Rubus thibetanus*. Much more than an arboretum, this attractively laid-out garden can be enjoyed at many levels. The new entrance pavilion is approached by a curved walk of *Metasequoia glyptostroboides*, and the visitor now approaches the arboretum with a view of rare trees merging with the Hampshire countryside beyond. Nearby at *Broadlands* there is a 'Capability' Brown landscape [Historic Park Grade II*]. It is also worth the detour into Winchester to view *Queen Eleanor's Garden*, the recreation of a small medieval plot designed by Dr Sylvia Landsberg behind the Great Hall of Winchester Castle.

Spinners ★

School Lane, Boldre, Lymington SO41 5QE. Tel: (01590) 673347

Mr and Mrs P.G.G. Chappell • 1½ m N of Lymington. Follow county signs on A337 between Brockenhurst and Lymington • Open 15th April to 13th Sept, Tues – Sat, 10am – 5pm (Sun and Mon by appt); mid-Sept to March nursery and part of the garden open on same days – telephone for details • Entrance: £2 • Other information: Plants for sale in nursery ◑ 🗑 WC ⚜ ♿

This informal woodland garden on the acid soil of the New Forest, created by the Chappells and praised by Roy Lancaster and other plantsmen, is remarkable for its plant associations and the owners' careful choice of scale. Nothing is over-large or dwarfs the smaller pleasures. In spring the sun shines through the canopy of trees, lighting camellias and dwarf rhododendrons, exochordas, magnolias, *Cornus kousa* and the brilliant coral leaves of *Acer palmatum* 'Shishio Improved'. Admire at ground level the carpets of cyclamen, *Erythronium revolutum* like pale pink stars, and the white and strange maroon trilliums (a National Collection held here). Beside the spring near the house the yellow-greens of ferns and variegated iris synchronise with white and yellow skunk cabbage. Ferns, primulas and hostas thrive in the bog garden, and good autumn colouring comes from *Nyssa sinensis* and other trees.

Staunton Country Park [Historic Park Grade II*]

Middle Park Way, Havant PO9 5HB. Tel: (023) 9245 3405

Hampshire County Council and eight other public bodies • 2m N of Havant on B2149. Signposted • Open daily: summer 10am – 5pm; winter 10am – 4pm • Entrance: £4.30, OAPs £3.90, children £3.30, family £14.20 (2003 prices) ○ 🍽 ✕ 🗑 WC ⚐ ♿ ♿ ⚜ 🏛 ♿ ⚘

Formerly the Leigh estate, belonging to the nineteenth-century horticulturist and adventurer Sir George Staunton. The walled garden has a crinkle-crankle wall to the south, and within it lies a major restoration of Victorian greenhouses. Here are the passion flowers, pepper vines and exotics grown by him, including the giant *Victoria amazonica* lily in its original circular pool. The great house has gone and the park is split by a main road, but fine specimen trees remain, as well as the Gothick library and follies such as the shell house and the beacon, also the terrace and the lakes, the Chinese bridge, and the remains of the lake fort where Staunton used to fire guns and fly the imperial yellow flag of China. Don't miss the ornamental Regency farm, stocked, as in the 1800s, with peacocks, deer, pigs, sheep, goats and horses. The Golden Jubilee Maze, planted in yew, has hand-crafted arbours and gates and reflects the spirit of the formal gardens and rose displays that existed in Staunton's time.

The Tudor House Museum

Tudor House, Bugle Street, Southampton SO14 2AD. Tel: (023) 8033 2513

Southampton City Council • Near Docks in Bugle Street, off Town Quay Road • Museum open • Garden open all year, Tues – Fri, 10am – 12 noon, 1 – 5pm; Sat, 10am – 12 noon, 1 – 4pm; Sun, 2 – 5pm • Entrance: free ○ **WC** & ⚑ ℺

This delightful museum, with its dark polished floors and gallery, includes a garden designed by Dr Sylvia Landsberg. It incorporates many features from Tudor gardens, such as heraldic beasts on poles, a camomile seat, a knot garden with twisting lines of santolina, germander and box, a skep for bees, a fountain surrounded by camomile and hyssop, an arbour hung with vines, and many herbs, labelled with details of their associations and uses. With its old walls and buildings, this is a peaceful corner in the heart of the city.

Tylney Hall Hotel ★ [Historic Garden Grade II*]

Rotherwick, Hook RG27 9AZ. Tel: (01256) 764881

Access from M3 junction 5 (take A287 via Newnham) or from M4 junction 11 (take B3349 via Rotherwick) • Open 23rd May, 13th, 27th June for NGS, and for meals to non-residents • Entrance: £2, children free • Other information: On garden open days main hotel closed except to guests with reservations, but refreshments available to garden visitors. Plants for sale on June open day ● ➥ ✕ **WC** & ℘ ♔ B&B

An Edwardian period piece. The elaborate brick house with gardens stretching to 66 acres was built in 1900 by Seldon Wornum for Sir Lionel Phillips, a South African diamond merchant. Wornum and Robert Weir Schultz designed the gardens, with an Italian terrace and fountain overlooking the boathouse lake, a Dutch garden, a fine avenue with Wellingtonias and splendid vistas framed by trees to the north and south. Schultz obtained designs from Gertrude Jekyll for the wild water garden, where two rivulets fell from one lake to another. When the house became a school in 1946, hard tennis courts were built on the Italian terrace, the lakes became choked and balustrades and statuary were lost. It is now a hotel, and the gardens have been restored by estate manager Paul Tattersdill and five gardeners. A fountain plays again on the Italian terrace, the boathouse lake is cleared and its bridge rebuilt, the water gardens are restored with rivulets, lakes and bogside planting, the kitchen garden has regained its rose pergola, the orchards stock 20 varieties of apple, and the vistas with their mature trees now look better than in the photographs of earlier days. Fine specimen trees.

West Green House Garden ★★

West Green, Hartley Wintney, Hook RG27 8JB. Tel: (01252) 844611

Miss Marylyn Abbott • *10m NE of Basingstoke, 1m W of Hartley Wintney, 1m N of A30* • *Open 24th April to Aug, Thurs – Sun and Bank Holiday Mons; Sept, Sat and Sun; all 11am – 5pm* • *Entrance: £5* ◑ ☕ ✕ WC & ☙ ⏚ ♀

Nestling in a wooded corner of Hampshire is this ravishingly attractive 1720s' manor house, where busts of gods, emperors and dukes look down from the walls onto two major gardens. The inner gardens, enclosed by eighteenth-century walls, are all devoted to parterres. One is filled with water lilies, another is of classical design with box topiary, and a third enacts the whimsy of *Alice in Wonderland* with the story's characters in ivy and box topiary surrounded by roses of red and white. The main walled garden is planted in subtle hues of mauve, plum and blue, contained in beds that have been faithfully restored to their original outlines. A decorative *potager* is centred around berry-filled fruit cages where herbs, flowers and unusual vegetables are designed into colourful patterns. All this is surrounded by a second garden, a remarkable neo-classical park studded with follies, birdcages and monuments designed by Quinlan Terry, a partner of the late Raymond Erith, hidden beside a tree-fringed lake, especially attractive in spring. A grand water garden, the Nymphaeum, spills down rills and steps from a devil's mouth into serene ponds. Work continues with planting aimed at resolving the landscape lacuna between the lake and the Nymphaeum, leading to a woodland planting and a new white and grey garden. A green theatre, a picturesque orangery and long *allées* of green all add to a fine and dramatic restoration undertaken by the well-known Australian gardener Marylyn Abbott, who purchased a 99-year lease from the National Trust to remake this enchanted place after some years of neglect (and worse). Now drifts of fritillaries and early spring flowers are naturalised beside the lake and flamboyant groups of tulips echo the walled garden's imaginative colour schemes.

White Windows ★

Longparish, Andover SP11 6PB. Tel: (01264) 720222

Mrs Jane Sterndale-Bennett • *5m E of Andover. Turn off A303 to Longparish on B3048* • *Open four days for charity, 2 – 6pm, and by appt April to Sept, Wed, 2 – 6pm* • *Entrance: £2* ◑ WC & ☙

The owner is the former Chairman of the Hardy Plant Society and crams a wealth of hardy perennials into the undulating beds of her immaculate garden. Three mini-gardens stretch in sequence from the house, each giving informal but theatrical views to adjacent areas. The fragrant white columbine grows among a mass of glaucous foliage, including *Artemisia ludoviciana* 'Valerie Finnis', and grasses like *Calamagrostis brachytricha* and *Carex comans*. Gold, variegated and purple-leaved shrubs, as well as unusual trees like *Malus transitoria* with its hawthorn-like leaves, make this a garden of interest throughout the year.

ISLE OF WIGHT

Barton Manor

Whippingham, East Cowes PO32 6LB. Tel: (01983) 528989

Robert Stigwood • From East Cowes take A3021, 500 metres beyond Osborne House on left • Open for four themed charity days, 10am – 5pm • Entrance: £3, children £1 • Other information: Coaches welcome. Guide dogs only ● ☕ ▦ WC & ⬛

Prince Albert's original design included fine trees and the cork grove; the grand terraces were added by Edward VII. In 1968 Hillier's laid out an intriguing water garden on the far side of the lake, home to carp and water-fowl, on what was originally Queen Victoria's skating rink. There is also a secret garden planted with azaleas and roses and impressive herbaceous borders. The present owner (a keen conservationist) has spared no effort in restoring and maintaining the estate. National Collections of kniphofias and watsonias are here. The most recent addition is a rose hedge maze which is the largest such attraction on the island – it is now tall enough to get lost in. Another former royal residence, Osborne (see entry), is nearby.

Morton Manor

Brading, Sandown PO36 0EP. Tel: (01983) 406168

J.B., J. and J.A. Trzebski • 3m from Ryde on A3055. Turn right at Brading traffic lights, signposted 100 metres up hill • Manor open (guided tours) • Garden open April to Oct, daily except Sat, 10am – 5.30pm • Entrance: £4.50, OAPs £4, children (6–16) £2. Parties of 15 or more £3.50 per person (house and garden) (2003 prices) • Other information: Vineyard and winery ◐ ☕ ✗ ▦ WC & ⬠ ⌀ ⬤ ⚲

The history of Morton goes back to the thirteenth century. The Elizabethan sunken garden has old-fashioned roses and is shaded by a magnificent *Magnolia grandiflora*. The terraces are nineteenth-century with extensive herbaceous borders and a huge London plane. Masses of spring bulbs are followed by rhododendrons and traditional herbaceous displays. Among the wide range of fine trees is an Indian bean (*Catalpa bignonioides*) and a *Cornus kousa*; particularly lovely in early June is *Robinia hispida*. There are also 100 different varieties of Japanese maple, and several varieties of acer imported from New Zealand are now on sale. Another feature is a pagoda covered with the vine variety 'Baco'. Little remains of the old walled garden, but in the corner behind the herbs are the restored bee boles (an old telephone box has a beehive inside so that visitors can view in safety). Also a turf maze made for children and a vineyard.

North Court ★

Shorwell, Newport PO30 3JG. Tel: (01983) 740415

Mr and Mrs J. Harrison • 4m S of Newport on B3323. Entrance on right after rustic bridge, opposite thatched cottage • Open one Sun in May, 2 – 5.30pm for

NGS, and one evening in June, 6 – 8pm (pre-booked guided tour) – telephone for details. Special openings for pre-booked parties of 10 or more at other times • Entrance: approx. £2.50 (varies according to charity) ● ☕ WC ⚲ B&B

Fifteen acres of wooded grounds surround a Jacobean manor house, with varied gardens consisting of seventeenth-century landscaped terraces leading down to the stream and water gardens, herbaceous borders, woodland walks, a sunken rose garden and a walled kitchen garden. Terraces with a south-easterly aspect have been made into a maritime garden with far-reaching views of the sea. The garden specialises in more tender plants – abutilons, salvias, diascias and argyranthemums all thrive here, especially in the new Mediterranean garden. The 'secret walled garden' at the top has been cleared and planted in sub-tropical style. The cottage garden of *Little Northcourt* open at the same time as North Court, is full of hidden delights especially in May and June. Swinburne, the poet, stayed and wrote at the big house. 3m W on B3399, the National Trust's *Mottistone Manor* has good views of the Channel and a herb garden.

Nunwell House [Historic Garden Grade II]

Coach Lane, Brading PO36 0JQ. Tel: (01983) 407240

Col. and Mrs J.A. Aylmer • 3m S of Ryde, signed off A3055 in Brading into Coach Lane • House open, tours 1.30pm, 2.30pm, 3.30pm • Garden open 30th, 31st May, 5th July to 8th Sept, Mon – Wed, 1 – 5pm, and for parties by appt • Entrance: £3.50 (house and garden £4, OAPs and students £3.50, accompanied children under 10 £1) ◗ 🍴 WC ⚹ ⚱

Nunwell House stands in six acres of gardens with wonderful views across the park to Spithead. The rose garden (a bowling green in the seventeenth century) is set at the top of a slope in front of the walled garden, which is now replanted with a double herbaceous border. The Long Walk leads down past the side of the house to the front garden. Among the varied shrubs and plants in the borders are several pretty *Lavatera* 'Barnsley', a notable acanthus, an enormous *Elaeagnus* x *ebbingei* and a *Cotoneaster* x *watereri* 'Cornubia'. There is also a 45-metre run of *Rosa* 'Frensham' and a *Cornus kousa*, and on the front of the house are three large myrtles. A steep flight of steps bordered by lavender leads up to the woods. To the rear of the house is an arboretum laid out by Vernon Russell-Smith in 1963.

Osborne House [Historic Garden Grade II*]

East Cowes PO32 6JY. Tel: (01983) 200022

English Heritage • 1m SE of East Cowes off A3021 • House open as grounds, 10am – 5pm • Grounds open April to Sept, daily, 10am – 6pm; Oct, daily, 10am – 5pm. Telephone for winter opening times • Entrance: £4, OAPs £3, children £2 (house and grounds £7.50, OAPs 5.60, children £3.80, family £18.80) (2003 prices) ◗ ☕ ✕ 🍴 WC ⚹ ⚘ ⚱ ⚲

Built by Queen Victoria in 1845–51 as a family retreat, the royal apartments are open to the public. The gardens, designed jointly by Victoria and Albert in the formal Italianate style, are now being restored and replanted to the original designs. Old cultivars have been used for the 'Victorian' bedding on the terraces, and the borders have been replanted with plants of the period. The park and gardens are notable for their magnificent trees. The Swiss Cottage Garden, in what were the royal children's gardens, has nine plots, each with 14 beds, planted with old varieties of soft fruit, flowers and vegetables. The children's gardening tools, wildflower meadow and orchard, and Queen Victoria's bathing machine are on show here. The one-acre walled garden has been restored sympathetically by Rupert Golby using historic plants within a modern design to celebrate the lives of Queen Victoria and Prince Albert. The plantings in the walled garden fully exploit the island climate, enhanced by the protective walls of the garden. The usual wall-trained fruit of vines, figs, pears, plums and cherries are complemented by an olive, an orange and a lemon tree. Drifts of multiple plantings span the length and width of the garden, ensuring a continuous display of striking colour throughout the summer, and broad rows of herbaceous plants are offset by extensive plots of annually sown flowers, herbs and vegetables. The glasshouses commissioned by Prince Albert have been restored and house collections of plants from South Africa and plants introduced to Britain during the Victorian period. The frequent use of entwined V & A motifs in the furnishings of the house is also employed in the garden, on ironwork arches, garden benches and terracotta pots.

Pitt House

Love Lane, Bembridge PO35 5NF.

L.J. Martin • Near village centre and Maritime Museum • Open June to Aug, Thurs, 2 – 5pm • Entrance: by donation ● &

Four acres with lovely views of the Solent through the trees. On a lower level from the house is a delightfully shady dell with a waterfall, ponds and water plants. In the main part of the garden are pergolas hung with roses and honeysuckle, and a Victorian greenhouse with two magnificent yellow daturas. Interesting trees include a crinodendron and a paulownia.

Ventnor Botanic Garden ★ [Historic Garden Grade II]

Undercliff Drive, Ventnor PO38 1UL. Tel: (01983) 855397

Isle of Wight Council • 1m SW of Ventnor. Signed from A3055 • Garden open all year, daily, dawn – dusk. 'Green' House and visitor centre open March to Oct, Sat and Sun, 10am – 4pm • Entrance: Garden free; charge for 'Green' House and car parking • Guided tour for parties by appt, £3 per person • Other information: New visitor centre with exhibition area, gift shop and restaurant
○ ● ✕ ▨ <u>WC</u> & ⬠ ✿ ⊞ ⛺ ⚲

Twenty-two acres, sheltered from the south by *Quercus ilex* and escallonias, and from the north by an escarpment growing cistus, echiums and olearias, were originally planted by Sir Harold Hillier to house the tender trees and shrubs in his collection. Almost destroyed by the gales of 1987 and 1990, the collections have been restored, and *Acer sikkimensis*, *Citrus ichangensis* from China, the flowering tree

Lyonothamnus floribundus subsp. *asplenifolius* from California, *Cestrum elegans* from Mexico, banana plants from Japan, and olive trees from the Mediterranean are but a few of the exotics to flourish in the unique microclimate of the Undercliff. The National Collection of pseudopanax is held here, including *P. ferox* and *P. crassifolius*. The New Zealand garden holds the largest collection of native plants grown in this country, and in July the South African garden includes a beautiful array of agapanthus. On the sunny slopes an amazing colony of four-metre-tall *Echium pininana* has naturalised. In the Palm Garden stately foliage plants like yuccas, cordylines, phormiums and beschornerias are underplanted with watsonias, cannas and kniphofias. The only drawback to this attractive municipal garden is that the labelling of plants leaves much to be desired. The 'Green' House has been re-landscaped with a series of water features, and the adjoining plant sales area has a range of unusual varieties on offer, mostly raised from seed and surplus to the garden's requirements. *Deacon's Nursery*, Godshill [open Oct to March, Sat only] has a large variety of fruit trees and bushes together with hops and nut trees. Their catalogue contains over 200 varieties of apples. A few miles inland is the ruined shell of the eighteenth-century *Appuldurcombe House*, now owned by English Heritage, which stands in grounds landscaped by 'Capability' Brown. [Open April to Oct, 10am – 6pm.]

NATIONAL COUNCIL FOR THE CONSERVATION OF PLANTS AND GARDENS

The NCCPG publishes a *National Plant Collections Directory*. Those interested in particular families of plants who want to see some of the rarer species and garden varieties will find this an invaluable publication. The latest edition, which offers information on about 600 collections comprising more than 50,000 plants and contains articles by holders of the collections, is available from NCCPG, The Stable Courtyard, RHS Garden, Wisley, Woking GU23 6QP (Tel: (01483) 221465; Fax: (01483) 212404; Website: www.nccpg.com. The new edition will be published in February or March 2004.

POSTCODE PLANTS DATABASE

It is often difficult to find out which plants are local to an area. The Postcode Plants Database locates the names of flowers, trees, butterflies and birds for each of Britain's 26 million home addresses. The website is www.nhm.ac.uk/science/projects/fff; simply by typing in the first four characters of their postcode, householders, schools, garden centres and councils can obtain tailor-made lists of local plants which are both hospitable and garden-worthy. Also included are the names of butterflies and birds most likely to visit gardens in each area. The lists come from innovative software, developed by Royal Mail and *FLORA-for-FAUNA* in conjunction with the Natural History Museum, which searches through hundreds of distribution maps of fauna and flora in the British Isles.

HEREFORDSHIRE

Abbey Dore Gardens ★

Abbey Dore, Hereford HR2 0AD. Tel: (01981) 240419

Mrs C.L. Ward • 11m SW of Hereford off A465 • Open April to Sept, Tues, Thurs, Sat, Sun and Bank Holiday Mons, 11am – 5.30pm, and by appt • Entrance: £3, children 50p ◐ ☕ ✗ <u>WC</u> ♿ ✍

A most intolerant garden! Only first-rate plants are allowed to grow here: flower, colour or shape – everything is in some way exemplary. The six acres, two of them left wild, incorporate a large part of the original Abbey Dore Court garden (laid out in 1858 but developing its present character and plantings since the late 1960s), plus all of Huntsman's Cottage. A new area, designed around a delicate gazebo, is quickly becoming established. The purple, gold and silver borders, created some years ago at the suggestion of Graham Stuart Thomas, are eye-catching and retain year-round interest. They lead to a wild riverside walk, and across the River Dore a meadow is planted with rare trees and shrubs, intersected by mown paths. A walled Victorian garden with wide borders punctuated by white foxgloves and cimicifugas has been developed with a sure eye for colour and form. The fruit trees have now all gone and a wide path dissects the old orchard area. There is a wire seat at the end looking down to an original water feature. Extravagant plantings, laid out with flair and imagination, delight the eye on every side. Hellebores, peonies and astrantias are specialities.

Arrow Cottage

(see THE LANCE HATTATT DESIGN GARDEN)

Berrington Hall [Historic Garden Grade II*]

Leominster HR6 0DW. Tel: (01568) 615721

The National Trust • 4m N of Leominster, W of A49 • House and garden open 29th March to 2nd Nov, Sat – Wed (but open Good Fri), house 1 – 5pm, garden 12 noon – 5pm (closes 4.30pm Oct, Nov). Park walk open July to 2nd Nov, 1 – 5pm. Parties of 15 or more by written appt • Entrance: £3.40 (house and grounds £4.60, children £2.30, family £11.50) • Other information: Two wheelchairs and batricar available for pre-booking. Telephone for wheelchair access to restaurant. Picnics in car park and play area in walled garden ◐ ☕ ✗ 🧺 <u>WC</u> ♿ 🎁 🍼 ✎

Spherical golden yews line the path to the formal eighteenth-century house designed by Henry Holland. The grounds, landscaped by 'Capability' Brown, are an excellent example of naturalistic parkland, containing many specimen trees. The walled garden houses a small orchard of pre-1900 apple varieties and handsome mixed borders which include lupins and red-hot pokers. A children's play area nearby sports a living willow tunnel.

Bryan's Ground ★

Letchmoor Lane, Stapleton, Nr Presteigne LD8 2LP. Tel: (01544) 260001

David Wheeler and Simon Dorrell • 2m E of Presteigne between Stapleton and Kinsham • Open 28th March to 30th Aug, Sun, Mon, 2 – 5pm, and at other times by appt for parties of 10 or more • Entrance: £3.50, children £1 ◐ ☕ 🏠 WC ♿ ✿ 🏛

Home of *Hortus*, the widely acclaimed quarterly magazine, this eight-and-half-acre garden is a feast of horticultural delights. The entrance sets the tone: the orchard plats flanking the main drive are thickly planted with squares of blue *Iris sibirica*, stunning against the ochre-yellow walls of the Edwardian house. Colour, both strong and subtle, is used everywhere to great effect. The Sulking House (hung with tattered velvet, adorned with dried teasels) looks out onto a double border where dark red, mauve and purple predominate, backed by copper beeches. At every turn, strong architectural lines of clipped yew or box hedging are softened by exuberant clumps of aquilegia, cranesbill, astrantia; the sweet smell of *Elaeagnus* 'Quicksilver' fills the air. The square pool in one quarter of the walled kitchen garden is as peaceful as a chapel, enclosed by its hornbeam cloister; water materialises also as a 19-metre canal in the Dutch Garden, and a 'cold bath' with a water spout in the old kitchen garden. Other delights include a crinkle-crankle beech hedge, a three-storey timber-framed dovecot, a restored Edwardian greenhouse and a large collection of hellebores in a wild woodland area. The arboretum has been extended to the river bank, and there is a new vegetable garden.

Croft Castle [Historic Garden Grade II*]

Leominster HR6 9PW. Tel: (01568) 780246

The National Trust • 5m NW of Leominster off B4362 • Garden open 6th to 28th March, Sat and Sun; April to Sept, Wed – Sun and Bank Holiday Mons; 2nd to 31st Oct, Sat and Sun; all 12 noon – 5pm. Parties of 15 or more by written appt. Parkland open all year • Entrance: £3.10. Car parking charge £2 per car (refundable on entry), £10 per coach • Other information: Picnics in car park only. Braille guides available. Dogs in parkland only, on leads ◐ ☕ WC ♿ 🚲 ✿ 🏛 💡 ⚲

The Welsh Marches castle dates from the fourteenth century and commands a spectacular landscape of open countryside. The walled garden has a collection of interesting and unusual plants, while the park is notable for its fine avenue of Spanish chestnuts, possibly 350 years old, and for its venerable pollarded oaks. There are charming walks in the Fishpool valley. Berrington Hall (see entry) is nearby.

Darkley Gardens

Norton Canon, Nr Weobley HR4 7BT. Tel: (01544) 318121

Jill and Malcolm Ainslie • 10m NW of Hereford off A480. Follow signs to Norton Wood and Hurstley. Gardens 1m on left-hand side • Open mid-May to

mid-Sept, Thurs, Sun, 1 – 5pm, and by appt • Entrance: £3, children free
● ▊ WC ⅃ ✿ ☙ B&B

This peaceful traditional garden is tucked away down a quiet lane, with views across
to the Black Mountains. The many herbaceous borders are carefully colour-
themed: a yellow bed with hemerocallis and euphorbias, a pink bed of roses
and geraniums under a silver pear tree, a striking purple bed of heucheras and
deep-coloured penstemons. An arch of golden hops leads through to a well-kept
potager, while the walled garden adjoining provides a tranquil retreat with bubbling
water and scented thyme paths. The garden is host to 150 varieties of clematis,
many of them in the clematis and rose walk which leads to a wilder pond area, the
domain of a charming family of call ducks. A friendly and very English garden.

Hampton Court Gardens ★

Nr. Hope under Dinmore, Leominster HR6 0PN. Tel: (01568) 797777

*Hampton Court Gardens (Herefordshire) Ltd • 5m S of Leominster, on A417 near
junction with A49 between Leominster and Hereford • Open all year, Tues – Sun
and Bank Holiday Mons, 11am – 5pm (closed Christmas week) • Entrance: £5,
OAPs £4.75, children £3, family £14. Prices may vary on event days; reduced
rates in winter – telephone for details* ● ▊ ✕ ▦ WC ⅃ ⌂ ✿ ⌨ ☕ ☙

This magnificent garden has only been in creation since 1996. Surrounding a
fifteenth-century Grade-I-listed building (already fully restored by the American owners), the grounds have been designed on a suitably grand scale by
Simon Dorrell. A *potager*-style kitchen garden is now established, producing
organic fruit and vegetables. The water garden is a large, geometrically laid-
out walled enclosure, with a pair of octagonal pavilions surrounded by canals
and ornamental water steps; the borders, lushly planted with lilies, lavenders,
macleayas and cardoons, create an effective contrast to their crisp formality. It
is worth puzzling your way through the intricate yew maze (based on the
owners' initials) to reach the tower, from where a bird's eye view of the walled
garden – like a medieval pleasaunce with the crenellated house beyond – is
especially beguiling. From the tower a dark, subterranean tunnel leads to a
thatched hermitage beside a cascade and sunken pool. These contrasts – light
and dark, high and low viewpoints, formal and wild planting schemes – all add
to the sense of playfulness and enjoyment. A nineteenth-century wisteria arch
is magically sweet-smelling in flower, and leads to the calm tranquillity of a
Dutch-inspired water garden. Wide lawns surround the house; the ha-ha
allows an interrupted view of cattle grazing under some magnificent trees in
the park beyond. The quality of workmanship from gardeners, carpenters,
stonemasons, bricklayers and blacksmith involved in this huge project is very
high, and the garden repays repeated visits to watch the grand scheme unfold.

Hergest Croft Gardens ★ [Historic Garden Grade II*]

Kington HR5 3EG. Tel: (01544) 230160

*W.L. Banks • 14m W of Leominster, ½ m W of Kington off A44 • Open April
to Oct, daily, 12.30 – 5.30pm; May and June, 12 noon – 6pm • Entrance: £4,*

children under 16 free, season ticket £15, parties of 20 or more £3.50 per person
◑ ⬛ ✕ ▥ <u>WC</u> ♿ ⬧ ⌾ ♨ ⬥ ☕

A large, varied garden, created over 100 years by three generations of the Banks family. Over 50 acres, the design was much influenced by the writings of William Robinson, and is laid out in four sections: the plantings around the house itself, the kitchen garden, the azalea garden, and Park Wood. The lawns and borders that surround the Edwardian house are filled with a large collection of herbaceous plants and shrubs, backed by some outstanding specimen trees, including a huge sycamore planted c. 1800. The croquet lawn is like a restful, empty room amid all this fascinating variety, featuring only its clipped yew hedges and large urns filled with lilies. The kitchen garden is traditional, with an avenue of ancient apple trees and double borders of spring flowers, with many coloured tulips and forget-me-nots under the blossoming trees – an ordinary enough combination, but somehow particularly pretty here. The exotically coloured azalea garden is outstanding, shaded by many of the magnificent birches and maples that form part of the National Collections held here. A grove of maples has been planted recently by Elizabeth Banks, many of them new or re-introduced species from China. The outer reaches of Park Wood are retained as natural beech and oak woodland, carpeted with anemones and bluebells in spring, but at its heart lies a secret valley of giant rhododendrons, a positively Himalayan scene.

Kingstone Cottages

Weston under Penyard, Nr Ross–on–Wye HR9 7PH. Tel: 01989 565267

Michael and Sophie Hughes • 2m E of Ross-on-Wye off A40. Turn left at Weston Cross public house signed to Bromsash, then left signed to Rudhall. Garden is ³/₄ m down this lane, on left • Open 3rd May to 10th July, daily except Sat, 10am – 5pm, and by appt • Entrance: £2, children free • Other information: Refreshments by arrangement for pre-booked parties NEW ◑ ⬛ ▥
WC ♿ ⌾ ⚲

The garden has only been in existence since 1976, but thanks to the owners' skilful use of reclaimed brick and stone it has the mellow atmosphere of a much older one. The planting is subtle and varied, well balanced between flowering plants and foliage. A pond, full of bulrushes and water lilies, is overhung by a cleverly constructed summerhouse, creating a magically secret spot. Other plantings frame fine views out to the Black Mountains. A grotto, a honeysuckle and clematis tunnel and a small formal water garden are other attractions, with a 'scrap-iron' garden adding a more surreal note. A special feature is the National Collection of old dianthus, with 140 varieties on show. Dianthus and other unusual plants for sale.

The Lance Hattatt Design Garden ★

Ledgemoor, Weobley HR4 8RN. Tel: (01544) 318468

Mr and Mrs L. Hattatt • 10m NW of Hereford between A4110 and A480, 1½ m E of Weobley • Open April to Sept, Wed, 10am – 5pm • Entrance: £3.75 • Other information: Unsuitable for children ◑ WC ⌾ ☕

The clever layout of this garden makes it seem much larger than its two-acre site. A series of well-defined areas, each named (Zion, for instance, is planted with 10 apple trees, *Malus* 'Ten Commandments') offers the visitor a cornucopia of contrasting shapes, colours and moods. A long, peaceful rill of water, punctuated by pots of agapanthus, terminates in a simple and elegant fountain, whose gentle splashing sound permeates the garden. Elsewhere, old shrub roses flower in informal profusion. A designer's garden, it is in a constant state of evolution, and offers many ideas to take home. Its versatility will only be fully appreciated after several visits.

Lower Hope

Ullingswick HR1 3JF. Tel: (01432) 820557

Mr and Mrs Clive Richards • 7m NE of Hereford. At roundabout on A465 near Burley Gate take A417 towards Leominster. After 2m turn right, signed to Pencombe and Lower Hope; garden is ½ m on left. Signposted • Open for NGS 28th March, 30th May, 11th July, 8th Aug, 3rd Oct, 2 – 6pm • Entrance: £3, children £1 • Other information: Guide dogs only ● ▆ WC & ⚘

This eight-acre garden is dazzlingly colourful and immaculately maintained. Bog gardens boast impressive gunneras and swathes of candelabra primulas, while the swimming-pool garden, with its palm trees and air of quiet seclusion, feels positively Mediterranean. A laburnum walk is magnificent in early summer. The many large island beds are sheets of bright flowers and coloured foliage, and interesting sculptures are artfully placed within the grounds. Melons, palms, orchids and other exotic plants flourish in a fine glasshouse. A tree-fern stumpery has been added, and a recently established lime tree walk leads onto a new lake surrounded by wild flowers and marginal bog plantings, the haunt of a great variety of water birds, dragonflies and other wildlife.

Lower Hopton Farm

Stoke Lacy, Bromyard HR7 4HX. Tel: (01885) 490294

Mr and Mrs Giles Cross • 10m NE of Hereford off A465 Bromyard – Hereford road • Open for individuals and parties of 20 or more only, by personal introduction, to be confirmed in writing • Entrance: By donation – guideline individuals £10 per person, parties of 45-50 £6 per person ● ▆

This five-acre garden, created from a field since 1992, is a testament to the skill and vision of Mrs Cross (the garden designer Veronica Adams), who tends it single-handedly. Rare plants abound. There are over a hundred named cultivars of snowdrops, unusual coloured roses – grey, green, buff – and splendid, towering cardiocrinums. The moated island holds rare shrubs and ferns and unusual varieties of peony, hellebore and magnolia among many other treasures. The prize in this collection is the ethereal, mauve-white giant bell-flower (*Ostrowskia magnifica*), flowering happily in a sunny border. These wonderful rarities are seamlessly woven into an imaginative design, with subtle colour schemes and light, humorous touches: two clipped yew giraffes are growing well, and a topiary fox peers out from a border. An elegant gazebo gives a view upstream to a series of small waterfalls, with climbing roses cascading from overhanging trees, and 'Paul's Himalayan Musk' towering overall. A new area, planted with white Judas trees, arching white wisteria and 'Debutante' roses, leads to a small fountain. A tunnel of airy robinias heralds a garden of old shrub roses, and a lacquer-red Chinese bridge adds an exotic note, leading to an area of pink and lime-green plants – a refreshing colour combination. The cleverly created 'ruin' provides a sheltered spot for tender perennials. Overall a triumph of creativity and much hard work.

Monnington Court

Monnington-on-Wye HR4 7NL. Tel: (01981) 500264

John and Angela Bulmer • 9m W of Hereford, off A438. Turn left opposite Portway pub, follow lane to end • Open 28th to 30th Aug, 10am – 5pm, and for parties by appt • Entrance: £4 (2003 price) • Other information: Special Morgan Horse displays 3.30pm each open day ● ☕ WC ໖

The 20 acres around this historic house are full of surprises and delights: black swans swim on the large, man-made lake, peacocks show off their fine plumage and all around are many interesting sculptures, both abstract and figurative, including most recently a bronze of the late Queen Mother by Mrs Bulmer – she is the well-known sculptress Angela Conner. Monnington Walk, a mile-long avenue of pine and yew trees, leads to the house. This is also the Foundation Farm of the Morgan Horse in Britain, a beautiful, old-fashioned-looking breed which originated in the United States.

Stockton Bury Gardens

Kimbolton, Leominster HR6 0HB. Tel: (01568) 613432

Mr G. Fenn and Mr R. Treasure • 1m NE of Leominster. From A49, turn right onto A4112 Kimbolton road. Garden is 300 metres on right. Signposted • Open April to mid-Oct, Wed – Sun and Bank Holiday Mons, 12 noon – 5pm • Entrance: £3.50 • Other information: Unsuitable for children ◑ ☕ ✕ WC ໖ ⌖

A true plantsman's garden, thoughtfully laid out and beautifully cared for, containing a wealth of unusual clematis, shrubs, climbers and herbaceous plants. The four-acre site is divided into different areas by brick and stone walls and yew hedges; The Dingle, created from an old quarry, is the most recently cultivated and beginning to look well established, with clumps of marginal plants fringing the water's edge. Cultivars are grown, especially of peonies, pulmonarias, viburnums and lilacs; rare and beautiful plants greet the visitor round every corner. The enchanting little double wood anemone, (*Anemone nemorosa* 'Vestal') makes a delightful underplanting. Many of the more unusual plants are for sale, all of them of good size, well labelled and reasonably priced – typical of the owners' meticulous attention to detail.

The Weir Garden

Swainshill, Hereford HR4 8BS. Tel: (01981) 590509 (Infoline)/(01684) 855372

The National Trust • 5m W of Hereford on A438 • Open 17th to 31st Jan, Sat and Sun, 11am – 4pm; Feb, Wed – Sun, 11am – 5pm; March, daily, 11am –

6pm; April to Sept, Wed – Sun, 11am – 6pm, Oct, Sat and Sun, 11am – 6pm
• *Entrance: £3, children £1.50, family £7.50 (2003 prices)* • *Other information:*
No coaches ◐ 🗑

The woodland garden which runs along the northern banks of the River Wye is at its best in spring when daffodils, bluebells, chionodoxas, camassias and naturalised tulips carpet the ground. The rockery (made with stone from Cheddar Gorge) contains a selection of colourful Japanese maples, conifers and ferns. A newly created willow arbour frames a seat giving a delightful view over the river to the weeping willows on the opposite bank, peaceful meadows beyond, and the Black Mountains in the distance. A collection of tightly clipped yew balls sits rather oddly in this otherwise 'wild' garden – have the aliens landed? Some of the paths are steep, and muddy in wet weather; sensible shoes are a good idea.

Whitfield House [Historic Garden Grade II]

Wormbridge HR2 9BA. Tel: (01981) 570202

Mr and Mrs Edward Clive • *8m SW of Hereford on A465 Abergavenny road* •
Open by appt • *Entrance: £2.50, children free* ● 🗑 **WC** ⅖ ⟁

A splendid 15-acre garden surrounds the house, plus extensive woodland walks. The estate boasts some magnificent trees, including a stand of giant redwood planted in the mid-nineteenth century and reputed to be the largest in Europe. The gardens adjacent to the house have been redesigned by Arabella Lennox-Boyd, and are currently under construction; cubes of yew and pleached limes will add a crisp formality. A string of lakes leads away from the façade, where golden orfe fry turn the water in the Fountain Pool positively gold in early summer. Castle Pool has a folly island, created by the late owner, a rare creation in the twentieth century. A fernery, punctuated with martagon lilies, flourishes in the shade of a large copper beech, and there are some fine magnolias. An extensive walled garden is reached through the camellia house, with a classical portico; a vinery and a gingko tree with the greatest girth in the country are amongst the delights therein. The epitome of the English country house garden, on a grand scale, Whitfield is a tribute to the knowledge of the late owner, George Clive (a dendrologist of renown), the enthusiasm of the present owners and the energy of their gardener. An obviously much-loved place, with lots of atmosphere.

SYMBOLS
[NEW] entries new for 2004; ○ open all year; ◑ open most of year; ◐ open during main season; ● open rarely and/or by appt; 🍵 teas/light refreshments; ✕ meals; 🗑 picnics permitted; WC toilet facilities; <u>WC</u> toilet facilities, inc. disabled; ⅖ partly wheelchair-accessible; ⟁ dogs on lead; 🌱 plants for sale; 🏠 shop; 🍷 events held; ℀ children-friendly; B&B bed and breakfast available.

HERTFORDSHIRE

Two-starred gardens are marked on the map with a black square.

The Abbot's House

10 High Street, Abbots Langley WD5 0AR. Tel: (01923) 264946

Peter and Sue Tomson • 5m N of Watford, in Abbots Langley. Approach via M25 junction 19 (from W) and 21A (from E) or M1 junction 6 • Open 2nd May, 4th July, 29th Aug, 2 – 5pm. Parties welcome by appt • Entrance: £2, children free • Other information: Plants for sale in nursery ● ❤ WC ♿ ⚘

This plantsman's garden is full of delights: *Crinodendron hookerianum*, *Itea ilicifolia*, *Hoheria sexstylosa* 'Stardust' and *Halesia carolina*, and many outstanding shrub and tree specimens, some of which must be tender. The sunken garden has plants thriving between the brickwork. There is also a Mediterranean semi-formal garden, a shrub border with contrasting foliage, borders of differing colour schemes, an annual and wildflower meadow and a conservatory.

Ashridge Management College [Historic Garden Grade II*]

Berkhamsted HP4 1NS. Tel: (01442) 843491

Ashridge (Bonar Law Memorial) Trust • 3½ m N of Berkhamsted (A41), 1m S of Little Gaddesden off A4146 • Open 9th April to Sept, Sat, Sun and Bank Holiday Mons, 2 – 6pm • Entrance: £3, OAPs and children £1.50 ● 📖 ♿ ⚘

A total of 150 acres, comprising 90 acres of garden with the rest woodland. The nineteenth-century design was influenced by Humphry Repton; following his death the gardens were laid out by Sir Jeffry Wyatville, retaining many of Repton's suggested small gardens. An orangery with an Italian garden and fountain leads round to the south terrace, which is dominated by clipped yews approximately 100 years old, and spring and summer bedding. The main lawn in front of the terrace links many small gardens and has within it a group of ancient yews and a large oak planted by Princess (later Queen) Victoria. The circular Rosarie is sited virtually where Repton intended. The Monk's Garden and Holy Well comprises box laid out to represent an armorial garden depicting the four families closely associated with the property. The conservatory dates from 1864 and was used as a fernery. The grotto is constructed of Hertfordshire pudding-stone, and the *souterrain* leading from it of flints hung on an iron framework; this follows the original boundary between Hertfordshire and Buckinghamshire. Crossing the main lawn brings visitors to a sunken garden formerly used as a skating pond. Beyond a disused moat is an avenue of Wellingtonias planted in 1858 and underplanted with rhododendrons, leading to the arboretum with many specimen trees and a Bible garden featuring a circle of incense cedars.

The Beale Arboretum

**West Lodge Park Hotel, Cockfosters Road, Hadley Wood EN4 0PY.
Tel: (020) 8216 3900**

*Beales Hotels • Leave M25 at junction 24 and take road S towards Cockfosters
(A111). West Lodge Park is 1m further on left • Open all year, daily, 2 – 5pm;
also 16th May, 2 – 5pm, and 17th Oct, 1 – 4pm, for NGS. Organised parties
of 10 or more, including tour and luncheon or tea, by appt all year • Entrance:
£2, children free • Other information: Possible for wheelchairs but undulating
gravel paths* ● ▉ ✕ WC & ◁❐ ⏻ B&B

The late Edward Beale bought West Lodge Park Hotel in 1945 with the intention
of enriching its fine eighteenth-century park with many more trees. Today,
there are 10 acres of arboretum with some fine rare trees. These, together with
the three acres of more formal garden, the lake, the many azaleas and rhododendrons, and the impressive four-star hotel, make a visit to this little-known
gem, only 12 miles from central London, memorable. Certainly if he were to visit
the property today, as he did in 1675, the diarist John Evelyn would still be able to
say that it was 'a very pretty place – the garden handsome', although he would
probably fail to recognise the strawberry tree which was believed to be there at
the time of his visit and which has become one of the largest in England.

Benington Lordship ★★ [Historic Garden Grade II]

Benington, Stevenage SG2 7BS. Tel: (01438) 869668

*Mr and Mrs C.H.A. Bott • 5m E of Stevenage • Open Feb/March for snowdrops
(telephone end of Jan for recorded message on opening dates); spring and
summer Bank Holidays (Suns 2 – 5pm, Mons 12 noon – 5pm); and 26th June
to 4th July, daily, 2 – 5pm. Also open by appt all year • Entrance: £3.50,
children free* ● ▉ ▨ WC ℘ ℀

Surrounding the manor house, Norman gatehouse and Victorian folly is a
romantic hill-top garden of timeless charm, with fine views over the lake and
open countryside. The massive and well-filled herbaceous double borders are
designed with a glorious feeling for texture and colour, backed on one side by
the kitchen garden wall and a sloping bank planted with an informal mixture of
foliage and flowering plants. The formal, lavender-edged rose garden, set in a
square in the centre of the old bowling green, has repeat-flowering roses in
shades of cream, pale yellow and apricot infilled with perennials. There is also a
shrub rose border, flowering in May. The kitchen garden is ornamental as well
as functional, with borders of gold and silver and another filled with penstemons. The garden has an outstanding display of snowdrops. Sheets of
flowers cover the moat and the surrounding grounds, followed by scillas.

Bromley Hall

Standon, Ware SG11 1NY. Tel: (01279) 842422

*Mr and Mrs A.J. Robarts • 6m W of Bishop's Stortford near A120 and A10
on Standon – Much Hadham road • Open 6th, 19th, 20th June, 2 –*

5.30pm, and for parties by appt • Entrance: £3.50, children free ● 🅿 **WC**
♿ 🐾

Mrs Robarts has created this four-acre garden over the last thirty years. It is both an architectural and a plantsman's garden with an immaculate kitchen garden tended by Mr Robarts. On a very windy site, good use has been made of walls and hedges, including one of copper beech, to shelter borders filled with a pleasing mixture of shrubs, foliage plants and unusual and elegant perennials. Vistas reveal mown paths and rough grass, mature trees and the countryside beyond the garden.

Cheslyn House

54 Nascot Wood Road, Watford WD17 4SL.
Tel: (01923) 235946 (Watford Council)

Managed by Watford Council • In north Watford off A411 Hemel Hempstead road or Langley Road, near M25 junction 19 • Open daily except 25th, 26th Dec, 1st Jan, 9am – dusk. Pre-booked tours with resident gardener available for parties • Entrance: free ○ 🍴 **WC** ♿ 🐕 🔌 ♀

This three-and-a-half-acre garden has woodland, lawns, a bog garden and pond, herbaceous borders, a rock garden and an aviary and an inheritance of fine trees. Among these are *Sequoiadendron giganteum*, *Catalpa bignonioides*, a particularly good *Diospyros kaki* and a large *Eucryphia* x *nymansensis* 'Nymansay', spectacular in late-summer bloom. The woodland, a haven for wildlife, is well planted with mature rhododendrons, azaleas, camellias and pieris, and there are drifts of spring and autumn bulbs among the trees. The herbaceous borders have been redesigned and replanted and feature a collection of hemerocallis.

Great Munden House

Dane End, Ware SG11 1HU. Tel: (01920) 438244

Mr and Mrs D. Wentworth-Stanley • 7m N of Ware off A10. Turn off W of Puckeridge bypass • Open April to July for small parties by appt only, with refreshments • Entrance: £3 ● 🅿

The charming three-and-a-half-acre garden, beautifully planned, immaculately kept and containing a great variety of plants, is situated down the side of a valley with a backdrop of wheat fields and trees. Beech hedges surrounding lawns act as necessary windbreaks against the wind funnelling down the valley. The mixed borders are imaginatively planted with shrubs, shrub roses, phlox and excellent foliage plants. Spring colour and interest come from bulbs and blossom. The main border in May is blue, mauve and pink with early irises, pale and dark alliums, aquilegias and perennial geraniums. A paved pond area is surrounded by silver plants and roses, with a *Juniperus virginiana* 'Skyrocket' in each corner. Many climbing roses ramble through old apple trees, and there is an additional damp area with shade-loving plants. Primulas and hostas surround a small statue, and the herb garden is protected by a clipped *Lonicera nitida* hedge.

Hanbury Manor Hotel

Ware SG12 0SD. Tel: (01920) 487722

Hanbury Manor Hotel • 2m N of Ware on A10 • Open all year • Entrance: free (charge on charity days) • Other information: Refreshments, toilet facilities and shop in hotel ○ ♿ ⬧

Edmund Hanbury inherited the property in 1884 and replaced the old house with a Jacobean-style mansion designed by Sir Ernest George. The Hanbury family were gifted horticulturists and the original gardens, now part of the hotel complex, were widely acclaimed both for their species trees and for their orchid houses. Today, a colourful pre-Victorian walled garden with a listed moon gate has extensive herbaceous borders, a herb garden and fruit houses. The original pinetum with its centuries-old sequoias still stands, and major restoration work has seen the revival of the period rose gardens and bulb-planted orchard. A more recent secret garden in a woodland setting is well worth a visit. On the outskirts of Ware, on A1170, is *Van Hage's Nursery*, superbly run with top-class plants and a wide range of garden furniture and accessories. [Open daily except Easter Sun, Christmas Day and Boxing Day, Mon – Sat, 10am – 6pm, Sun, 10.30am – 4.30pm.]

Hatfield House ★★ [Historic Garden Grade I]

Hatfield AL9 5NQ. Tel: (01707) 287010

The Marquess of Salisbury • 2m from A1(M) junction 4 off A414 and A1000, opposite Hatfield railway station • House open as garden, but 12 noon – 4pm (guided tours weekdays only) • Park, West Gardens, restaurant and shops open 11th April to Sept, daily, 11am – 5.30pm. East Gardens open Fri only • Entrance: Park and gardens £4.50, children £3.50. Park only £2, children £1 (house, park and gardens £7.50, children £4; Fri, house, park and gardens £10.50, park and gardens £6.50) • Other information: Dogs in park only ◑ ☕ ✕ 🍴 WC ♿ ⌾ 🎁 🅿 ⚲

Laid out originally in the early seventeenth century by Robert Cecil and planted by John Tradescant the Elder, the garden underwent various changes in the following centuries, particularly in the Victorian era, but during the past three decades it has enjoyed a splendid transformation at the hands of the Dowager Marchioness of Salisbury. She began the work of restoration with an imaginative and bold stroke – a new garden as the setting for the Old Palace. From there she went from strength to strength. Not all her re-created gardens are open (the maze, for example, is a protected space) but all, including the splendid East Gardens, can be viewed on Fridays (Connoisseurs' Day). The Dowager Marchioness is well known for her creative work on other private gardens, but here at Hatfield are many splendours, such as the south-front inner courtyard. The plantings are her particular skill – see the mop-headed *Quercus ilex* imported especially for the garden, and the wild garden around the New Pond (formed in 1607), landscaped and planted since the devastation by two hurricanes. Amongst the many features are the varied knot gardens and a charming herb garden in the scented garden, all planted following her own designs, and sited, like those in Tudor times, to be viewed from above; they are filled with plants used from the fifteenth to seventeenth centuries. Those interested in so-called wild gardens should spend time in the Wilderness and note that its splendours have not been achieved by throwing flower seeds about but by planting up to 20,000 bulbs a year.

Hopleys ★

Much Hadham SG10 6BU. Tel: (01279) 842509

Mr A. Barker • 5m W of Bishop's Stortford off A120. 50 metres N of Bull pub in Much Hadham • Open March to Dec, Mon, Wed – Sat, 9am – 5pm, Sun, 2 – 5pm, and also on special days for charities • Entrance: free (donations welcomed) • Other information: Self-service refreshments ○ 🍴 **WC** ♿ ⚘

The owner and his parents have been working on this four-acre plantsman's garden for many years, and it has been expanding annually. The pool and bog area are now well established, there are numerous borders filled with shrubs and hardy plants, most of which are for sale in the nursery, and the conifer bed is a graphic illustration of the different sizes and shapes of mature specimens. Much Hadham has two other properties of interest to gardeners. In Bourne Lane (Tel: (01279) 842685) is the headquarters of *Andrew Crace*, who designs and sells a wide range of fine garden furniture and bronze and stone ornaments; and *Dane Tree House* is the home of the *Henry Moore Foundation*. Moore lived here for forty years and his collection, studios and workshops remain very much as they were in his lifetime, standing in parkland with many native trees and particularly fine ancient hedgerows. Larger works are placed in the surrounding fields with sheep grazing round them – as he intended. [Open April to Sept, Tues – Thurs, mornings only by appointment or 2.30pm for tour. Tel: (01279) 843333.]

Jenningsbury Farm House

Haileybury, Hertford Heath SG13 7NS. Tel: (01992) 583978

Mr and Mrs Barry Fox • 3m SE of Hertford between A414 and A10. Take B1197 to Hertford Heath and Haileybury College; garden is ½ m on right • Open for NGS early June, and by appt • Entrance: £3 [NEW] ○ **WC** ♿ ⚘

The seventeenth-century farmhouse stands in eight acres of ground encompassed by two-thirds of a thousand-year-old moat haunted by the Mayor of Hertford who drowned in it, and includes three acres of wonderfully atmospheric flower meadow. Cut-grass paths wander through a profusion of camassias, tradescantias, ox-eye daisies, orchids and much else. The path leads past a large pond, a bog garden with *Geum rivale*, primulas, handsome grasses and a fernery. Round the pond is a mixed planting of wild and cultivated species; a wide border, hiding the farm buildings, contains purple-leaved hazel, yew, golden comfrey and huge, massed *rugosa* roses. It is teeming with wildlife, home to kingfishers, herons, owls, coots and moorhens, tench, carp, golden orfe and grass snakes. By contrast, the garden round the house, dominated by a huge cedar, is immaculate: a formal pond with water lilies and a gunnera, and a white wisteria on the pagoda. Then out into the field by the car park where Daisy Roots' exciting nursery has many rare plants.

Knebworth House ★ [Historic Garden Grade II*]

Knebworth, Nr Stevenage SG3 6PY. Tel: (01438) 812661

The Hon. Henry Lytton Cobbold • 2m S of Stevenage off B656. Access from A1(M) junction 7 • House open as garden, 12 noon – 5pm • Garden open 27th, 28th March, 24th April to 23rd May, 12th to 27th June, 4th Sept to 26th Sept, daily; 3rd to 18th April, 29th May to 6th June, 3rd July to 31st Aug, Sat, Sun and Bank Holiday Mons only; all 11am – 5.30pm. • Entrance: £7.50, OAPs and children £7 • Other information: Guided tours available. Dogs in park only, on lead ◑ ● ✕ ▤ WC ◁ ▥ ℗ ℺

As the historic home of the Lytton family, the garden evolved from a simple Tudor green and orchard to Sir Edward Bulwer Lytton's elaborate Victorian design of the mid-1800s. Edwin Lutyens redesigned the garden at the beginning of the twentieth century with twin avenues of pollarded lime trees leading to the rose garden, lily ponds and herbaceous borders with tall yew hedges behind. Beyond lie the Green Garden, the Gold Garden, the Brick Garden with a blue and silver theme, and a pergola. To one side is a pets' cemetery, to the other a crab apple walk. Other features are the maze (replanted in 1995), the ponds, and the Gertrude Jekyll herb garden, designed in 1907 but not laid out until 1982. The Wilderness with its woodland walk is a carpet of daffodils in spring followed by blue alkanet, foxgloves and other wild flowers. The redeveloped walled garden has a collection of culinary herbs and vegetables. In all there are 25 acres of garden to explore. A few miles north at Hitchin are the rose gardens of R. Harkness & Co [open all year, Mon – Sat, 10am – 5.30pm, Sun and Bank Holiday Mons, 10am – 4.30pm].

Pelham House

Brent Pelham, Buntingford SG9 0HH. Tel: (01279) 777473

David and Celia Haselgrove • 7m NW of Bishop's Stortford, E of Brent Pelham on B1038 Buntingford – Newport Road • Open 28th March, 18th April, 9th May, 12 noon – 5pm, and by appt at other times • Entrance: £2.50 ◑ ● WC ⅊ ◁ ℘

The garden is the creation of the present owner, a plantsman, avid plant hunter and keen member of the Alpine Garden Society. He has won his battle with an extremely unprepossessing site – a cold and windswept clay field – and achieved a most interesting and ambitious garden. Raised beds are a feature, and among the noteworthy plants are hellebores, erythroniums, trilliums, a host of orchids, euphorbias, *Daphne cneorum*, *Cornus kousa*, excellent magnolias and a collection of betulas. Where the land has been drained, masses of bee orchids have sprung to life.

St Paul's Walden Bury ★ [Historic Garden Grade I]

Whitwell, Hitchin SG4 8BP. Tel: (01438) 871218

Mr and Mrs Simon Bowes Lyon • 5m S of Hitchin, ½ m N of Whitwell on B651 • Open probably four Suns in April, May or June, 2 – 7pm, and to parties at other times by appt • Entrance: £3, children 50p, parties £5 per person
● ● ● & ⬩

The formal landscape garden was laid out in 1730 and is one of the few to survive. It covers an area of 40 acres. The long mown rides or *allées* are lined with clipped beech hedges and fan out from the eighteenth-century house – the heart of the layout – through *bosquets* to temples, statues, ponds and a medieval church. In one of the *bosquets* is an elegant green theatre. The Bowes Lyon family have lived at St Paul's for more than 250 years, and it was here that the late Queen Mother spent her childhood. Interesting plants are grouped in small gardens of differing character, woodland is underplanted with shrubs, and spring bulbs abound. The lake, with its beautiful temple and wonderful vistas, is well worth walking to.

Vineyard Manor

Much Hadham SG10 6BS Tel: (01279) 843761

Mr and Mrs H. Tee • 5m W of Bishop's Stortford off A120 • Open May to Aug by appt • Entrance: £3 • Other information: Teas by arrangement ● ● &

A garden of vivid imagination created by the present owners since 1995. Visitors enter up a slope planted with ferns, exciting hostas and other shade-loving plants under mature trees, past an amusing man's head with two clutching hands by Mark Hall. Behind the house a terrace with a wide border let into the hillside is planted in shades of gold, silver and bronze with good colour contrasts. This leads to a swimming pool surrounded by, and lined with, grey Chinese slate – a most ingenious solution. An old dew pond restored by Anthony Paul has been taken into the garden and planted in generous blocks of colour, with a mass of dark sedums, vast drifts of ligularias, *Gunnera manicata* and drifts of tall grasses in variety. This is a garden humming with ideas.

OPENING DATES AND TIMES

Times of access given are the best available at the moment of going to press, but some may have been changed subsequently. In the entries, the times given are inclusive – that is, an entry such as May to Sept means that the garden is open from 1st May to 30th Sept inclusive, and 2 – 5 pm means that entry will be effective during that period. Please note that many owners will open their gardens to visitors by appointment, and they will often arrange to give a personally conducted tour on these occasions. Unavoidably some owners cannot give their opening details before we go to press, and in such cases we attempt to give the best guidance we can. If in doubt, it is wise to telephone before making a long journey.

KENT

We have included some gardens with Kent postal addresses in the London section for convenience. So before planning a day out in Kent it is worthwhile consulting pages 234–69.

Two-starred gardens are marked on the map with a black square.

Abbotsmerry Barn

Salmans Lane, Penshurst TN11 8DJ. Tel: (01892) 870900

Mr and Mrs K. Wallis • 5m SW of Tonbridge off B2176 towards Leigh. Turn left 180 metres N of Penshurst; house is 1m down lane • Open for NGS and for parties by appt • Entrance: £3, children free ● ▆ WC ⑁

The five-acre, south-facing garden is tucked away down a long narrow road, with distant views towards Penshurst Place (see entry). With steeply sloping lawns running down towards the River Eden and a series of well-planned dells, it is laid out in a series of different areas. There are hollows filled with herbaceous plants, a vertical quarry garden colonised by ferns, places for moisture- and shade-loving plants, groupings of alder and birch, an orchard in a wildflower meadow and, on the eastern boundary, a careful planting of old-fashioned, highly perfumed roses. A large circular paved area near the house has rock plants growing in the cracks. Seats provide resting places to absorb the atmosphere of each part of this magical garden in turn.

Bedgebury National Pinetum and
Forest Gardens ★ [Historic Arboretum Grade II*]

Goudhurst, Cranbrook TN17 2SL. Tel: (01580) 211781

Forestry Commission • 10m SE of Tunbridge Wells off A21, on B2079 Goudhurst – Flimwell road • Arboretum open all year, daily, 10am – 5pm (4pm in winter) • Entrance: £3, OAPs £2.50, children £1.20, family £7 (2003 prices) ○ ▆ ▆ WC ⇪ ⌂ ♨ ⚲

The modern pinetum was founded in 1924, but some of the larger specimen trees dating from 1850 are still flourishing. The conifer collection has been listed as the best in the world by the International Dendrological Research Institute based in America and Hungary. As well as conifers, it has many deciduous trees, including rare oaks and maples, and a wide range of rhododendrons flowers from January to August. The pinetum has five National Collections: Lawson and Leyland cypresses, junipers, yews and red cedars.

Beech Court

Challock, Ashford TN25 4DJ. Tel: (01233) 740735

Mr and Mrs Vyvyan Harmsworth • 5m N of Ashford, W of A251/A252 crossroads, off The Lees • Open 22nd March to 2nd Nov, Mon – Thurs,

10.30am – 5.30pm, Sat and Sun, 12 noon – 6pm, and at other times by appt •
Entrance: £3.75, OAPs £3.30, students and wheelchairs £2, children 5 and over
£1, parties of 12 or more £2.50 per person ◑ 🍵 🎒 ♿ 🐕 🧺 ⚲ ℀

One hundred and fifty metres above sea level in a pocket of acidic clay on the
edge of the North Downs, this 10-acre woodland garden was designed with
Inverewe in mind (see entry in Scotland) and has many acres of rhododendrons, azaleas, hydrangeas and viburnums. Spring colour from the rhododendrons, azaleas and acers is augmented by bulbs, summer interest is provided by
roses, philadelphus and hydrangeas, and the many specimen trees give good
autumn colour. Mature acers and various oaks, a rose walk and buddleia and
viburnum avenues encourage a natural feeling of tranquillity in this garden of
meandering paths and surprising vistas. A small sunken pond has well-planted
margins and is set in a lawn edged with herbaceous plants.

Belmont ★ [Historic Garden Grade II]

Belmont Park, Throwley, Faversham ME13 0HH. Tel: (01795) 890202

Harris (Belmont) Charity • 4m SW of Faversham, 1½ m W of A251 Faversham
– Ashford road. From A2 or M2 junction 6, take A251 S towards Ashford.
Signed at Badlesmere • House open • Garden open April to Sept, daily except Fri,
10am – 6pm • Entrance: £2.75, children £1 (house, clock museum and gardens
£5.25, children £2.50) • Other information: Teashop open from 3pm Sat, Sun
and Bank Holiday Mon only ◑ 🍵 🎒 **WC** ♿ 🚐 🐕 🧺 ⚲

The eighteenth-century house by Samuel Wyatt has been the seat of the Harris
family since 1801 and, though somewhat off the beaten track down winding
lanes, it is well worth a visit. It was built at a time when beautiful country-
house architecture was required to blend in with equally beautiful and well-
planned surroundings, exemplified here by 40 acres of formal and informal
gardens merging into 150 acres of parkland to give marvellous vistas of aged
and noble trees. There is also a yew walk and a pinetum. The walled garden
includes borders, a pool and a rockery; note also the shell grotto and folly. The
two-acre kitchen garden has been restored and replanted, and the surrounding area was transformed with grasses, wild flowers and nut trees; it contains a
formal garden based on a Hindu design, thus perpetuating the Harris family's
long connection with India.

Broadview Gardens

Hadlow, Tonbridge TN11 0AL. Tel: (01732) 850551

Hadlow College • 8m SW of Maidstone, 3m NE of Tonbridge, on A26 • Open
all year, daily, 10am – 5pm (closes 4pm Suns) • Entrance: £2 ◑ 🍵 🎒 **WC** ♿
🐕 🧺 ℀

The gardens in the grounds of Hadlow College – 10 acres and growing – offer
an inspiring range of old and new designs in a series of well-planted areas. The
sub-tropical garden with four different varieties of musa, canna lilies, stooled
paulownia and golden catalpa, leads to a 100-metre-long herbaceous border.
The cottage garden has dwarf trained fruit trees, herbs and flowers, and in the

Sensory Garden a water rill at waist height falls over cobbles and raised beds. The contrast between the Heaven and Hell gardens is achieved by planting the former with scented herbs and subtly varied foliage colour, the latter with hot colours in both flowers and foliage. A half-acre Japanese garden has all the appropriate oriental elements and appropriate planting. There is also a low-maintenance gravel garden, an Italian garden and a one-acre lake edged with bog plants. National Collections of hellebores and Japanese anemones are held here.

Chart's Edge

Westerham TN16 1PL.

Mr and Mrs Bigwood • S of M25 and A25, ½ m S of Westerham on B2026 towards Chartwell • Open 21st April, 9th, 23rd May, 23rd June, 4th July, 2 – 5pm • Entrance: £2.50, children free ● ☕ WC & ⬦ ✿

The removal of some mature trees during storms over the last 10 years has opened up areas of this seven-acre garden to provide sweeping lawns, space for some interesting trees and the reclamation of some of the original Victorian features. Whilst a large part of the planting, especially many trees and rhododendrons, dates from the 1960s, new and unusual plants have been introduced since then. A 90-metre-long raised herbaceous border leads down to the atmospheric dell garden with acers, ferns, hostas and other bog plants, and a series of stone terraces has been created for exotic plants and a cascade. An interesting feature here, built into the hillside, is a Victorian grotto lined with flint; adjoining is a brick-lined room with steps leading down to what was probably a bath with a lead pipe. Around the house are borders with roses, a large and well-planted rockery, a terrace with views over the North Downs framed by two *Acer palmatum* var. *dissectum*, and an old mulberry.

Chartwell [Historic Garden Grade II*]

Mapleton Road, Westerham TN16 1PS. Tel: (01732) 866368 (Infoline)

The National Trust • S of M25 between junctions 5 and 6, 2m S of Westerham off B2026 • House open • Garden open late March to early Nov, Wed – Sun and Bank Holiday Mons; also Tues in July and Aug; all 11am – 5pm (last admission 4.15pm) • Entrance: £3.25, children £1.60 (house and garden £6.50, children £3.25, family £16.25) ◑ ☕ ✕ WC & ⬦ 🏛 🍴 ✦

Within this garden on a hill, with vast views over the Weald of Kent, the first feature to greet the visitor is the water garden with fish pools and the swimming pool constructed by Sir Winston Churchill. Well-established trees along a path lead the way to a walled rose garden, its perimeter planted with herbaceous plants such as hostas, peonies and penstemons. A cloud of shrub roses perfumes the terrace, and ceanothus, white potentillas and dark red double *rugosa* roses invite the visitor on towards the house, one wing of which is covered by a huge *Hydrangea petiolaris*. The south wall has a large *Magnolia grandiflora*. A vine-covered pergola leads to a gazebo and viewpoint. There is also a series of smaller terraces, one planted with silver-foliage plants, and a Golden Rose walk bordered by clipped beech hedges. Maintenance and labelling are excellent, but remember that Churchill bought Chartwell above all for its magnificent view.

Church Hill Cottage Gardens ★

Charing Heath, Ashford TN27 0BU. Tel: (01233) 712522

Mr and Mrs M. Metianu • From M20 junction 8 (from Maidstone) or junction 9 (from Folkestone) join A20; ½ m W of Charing, turn S from A20 dual-carriageway section to Charing Heath and Egerton. Fork right after 1m at Red Lion pub, take next right, and gardens are 250 metres on right • Open 22nd March to Sept, daily except Mon (but open Bank Holiday Mons), 10am – 5pm. Coaches by appt • Entrance: £2, children free • Other information: Nursery open Feb to Oct ◗ 🏦 WC ⅃ ⬠ ⅌ ℺

In these tranquil one and a half acres surrounding a sixteenth-century cottage there is a strong sense of design in the curves of borders and island beds, but they are so well matched by the fine and well-developed planting that the whole seems natural. Established birches form a central point. Beds are varied, some with colour themes, others with shrubs underplanted with a wide range of unusual hardy plants and bulbs in season. Of particular interest to the plantsman are the large collections of dianthus and violas, which include between 30 and 40 varieties of old forms dating from the sixteenth to the eighteenth century. The woodland area has been improved by the addition of two fine fern and hosta beds.

Copton Ash Gardens

105 Ashford Road, Faversham ME13 8XW. Tel: (01795) 535919

Drs Tim and Gillian Ingram • 1m S of Faversham. Just N of M2 junction 6 on A251 Faversham – Ashford road • Nursery and garden open Feb to Oct, Tues – Sun, 2 – 6pm, but check before travelling. Gardening parties welcome by appt • Entrance: £2 (but free for nursery visitors), accompanied children free ◗ 🏦 ⅃ ℺

Despite its position close to the M2 there is a pleasant atmosphere in this plantsman's garden created since 1978 on the site of an old cherry orchard. About one and a half acres in extent, it accommodates over 3000 species in herbaceous borders and island beds with specimen plantings. There is a collection of fruit varieties, alpines are grown in raised beds, and experiments are underway to examine the hardiness of species from Australia, New Zealand and South America. From the garden, Tim Ingram has developed a specialist nursery with an emphasis on plants for dry situations, including cistus, peonies and umbellifers. Some significant new plantings have been and are being made, including many novel and rarely seen species from wild-collected seed. A collection of over 100 different snowdrops and early bulbs, along with hellebores and other woodland plants, make visits early in the year particularly rewarding. So is *Brogdale Horticultural Trust*, which holds the National Collection of fruit – over 4000 varieties. Seek them out in Brogdale Road, Faversham – open Easter to Dec, 9.30am – 5pm.

Doddington Place Gardens [Historic Garden Grade II]

Doddington, Sittingbourne ME9 0BB. Tel: (01795) 886101

Richard and Amicia Oldfield • 6m S of Sittingbourne. From A20 turn N at Lenham, from A2 turn S at Teynham. Signposted • Open April to July, Suns, plus 1st, 29th Aug, 19th Sept, all 2 – 6pm, and at other times for parties by appt • Entrance: £3.50, children over 5 75p, groups £3 per person • Other information: Picnics in park only ◑ 💭 WC ᕕ ⇗ 🦋 🏛 💡

The theatrical quality of the gardens where, appropriately, open-air opera is performed each year, is significantly heightened by newer features. The scale is intrinsically grand – smooth lawns are punctuated by towering specimen trees and enclosed by extraordinary yew hedges pruned into amorphous, cloud-like shapes, and a Wellingtonia avenue planted in the mid-nineteenth century is contemporary with the house. A young *allée* of upright *Sorbus aucuparia* 'Beissneri' accentuates the geometry of the Pond Walk, and a mirror-glass obelisk is the striking focus of the flower-filled grasses of the Spring Walk. A new brick-and-flint Gothick folly marks the transition between the formality of the Folly Walk and the wildness of the three-acre woodland garden beyond, where camellias, rhododendrons, acers and bulbs are spectacular in May and June. The formal rose and sunken gardens have imaginatively modern planting schemes, and a pool has been added to the Edwardian rock garden, which is undergoing gradual restoration.

Dolly's Garden

(see London)

Down House

(see London)

Edenbridge House

Main Road, Edenbridge TN8 6SJ. Tel: (01732) 862122

Mrs M.T. Lloyd • 1½ m N of Edenbridge on B2026 • Open April to Sept, Tues and Thurs, 2 – 5pm, and for parties by appt • Entrance: £2.50 (2003 price) • Other information: Refreshments on charity open days only ◑ 🍽 WC ᕕ ⇗ 🦋

This five-acre garden, originally made in the 1920s, is set on a south-facing slope. The part-sixteenth-century house is surrounded on three sides by a wide terrace on which a large variety of tender plants – datura, *Punica granatum*, *Streptosolen jamesonii* and *Cestrum elegans* – flourishes in pots. A walled courtyard to one side of the house contains a parterre filled with displays of annuals. Roses, *Itea ilicifolia*, *Clerodendrum bungei*, wisteria, jasmine and a *Magnolia grandiflora* drape the walls. Garden rooms are linked to the house by a lawn containing a fountain pool guarded by elegant drum-shaped golden yews. A small stream, crossed by two wisteria-clad bridges, meanders down to a small lower pool. The banks of the stream are edged with rocks and planted with moisture-loving plants. There is a large kitchen garden, a soft-fruit cage and an apple and cherry orchard. Part of the kitchen garden has been turned into an arboretum and planted with a selection of trees and shrubs to give a wide range of colour: *Amelanchier canadensis*, liquidambar, *Ginkgo biloba*, *Acer platanoides* 'Crimson King' and *Gleditsia triacanthos* 'Sunburst'. A 21-metre-long peach house now contains plumbago, passiflora and a large *Cobaea scandens* f. *alba*. This is a plantsman's garden, with year-round interest provided by displays of early spring bulbs, colourful summer herbaceous borders and the foliage colours of autumn. A gravel garden, which is hot and sheltered with the added benefit of a boggy area, has hostas, bamboos, various grasses, ferns (including a tree fern), spiky agaves and palms.

Emmetts Garden ★ [Historic Garden Grade II]

Ide Hill, Sevenoaks TN14 6AY. Tel: (01732) 868381

The National Trust • 1½ m S of A25 and M25 junction 5, 1½ m N of Ide Hill off B2042 Edenbridge – Sundridge road • Open 20th March to June, Wed – Sun and Bank Holiday Mons; 3rd July to Oct, Sat, Sun, Wed and Bank Holiday Mon; all 11am – 5pm (last admission 4.15pm) • Entrance: £4, children £2, family £9 • Other information: Buggy available from car park to entrance ◑ 💷 🖼 WC ⅋ ⬧ 🏧 🕯 ⚲

Set on the top of Ide Hill, the garden gives a superb view over the Weald of Kent and provides an impressive setting for this plantsman's collection of trees and shrubs. It is a garden to visit at any time of the year, but is particularly fine in spring, with its bluebell woods and flowering shrubs. First planted by Frederick Lubbock, the owner from about 1890 until his death in 1926, it is noted especially for its rhododendrons and azaleas. It follows the late-nineteenth-century style of combining exotics with conifers to provide a 'wild' garden; the plants are all listed in the guidebook. A rose garden, a rock garden and a collection of acers planted for autumn colour extend the interest throughout the year. The enforced clearance of some trees and shrubs after the gales of 1987 has enabled new planting to keep the traditions of the garden and also to expand it – the rock garden in particular is becoming established. A splendid site and a fascinating garden.

Godinton House [Historic Garden Grade I]

Ashford TN23 3BP. Tel: (01233) 620773

The Godinton House Preservation Trust • Off M20 junction 9, 1½ m NW of Ashford in Godinton Lane at Potter's Corner (opposite Hare and Hounds pub) • House open 18th April to 5th Oct, Fri – Sun • Garden open 15th March to 5th Oct, Thurs – Mon, 2 – 5.30pm • Entrance: £3, children free (house and garden £5, children free) • Other information: Coaches by appt only. Garden tours available by prior arrangement. Refreshments available when house is open and for pre-booked parties ◑ 💷 🖼 WC ℘

The outstanding feature of the garden is the great boundary hedge planted to Blomfield's original design, one of the largest in the country; it has been cut back to encourage new growth and will re-establish itself within a few years.

This hedge encloses Blomfield's first formal garden with its lawns, pond, terraces, topiary and the box-hedged Pan Garden. The wild garden is famous for its show of daffodils, and the fine trees here include a huge tulip tree and two of the largest 'Tai Haku' cherries in Britain. In the walled garden, delphinium borders have been established in partnership with the Delphinium Society, and 25 varieties of *Clematis montana* have been planted amongst the wall-trained fruit trees. The new greenhouse has vegetables as well as an extensive range of cut flowers. The rose garden has been redesigned and replanted, as has the architectural Italian garden adjoining the walled garden, where restored statuary is on display. The parkland is also being restored: 400 trees will be planted over the next eight years, and the perimeter fence surrounding the garden has been replaced with traditional park railings.

Goodnestone Park ★★ [Historic Garden Grade II*]

Goodnestone, Nr Wingham, Canterbury CT3 1PL. Tel: (01304) 840107

Lady FitzWalter • 5m E of Canterbury. A2 to Dover, turn left at junction B2046 for Wingham/Aylesham, then E after 1m • House open by appt for pre-booked parties • Garden open 31st March to 3rd Oct, Mon, Wed – Fri, 11am – 5pm, Sun, 12 noon – 6pm. Pre-booked parties daily • Entrance: £3.50, OAPs £3, students £1.50, children (under 12) 50p, family £5.60 (guided tours £4.50 per person) • Other information: Teas available April to Sept only ◑ 🍽 🏪 WC & ⌖ ♿ ☕

Goodnestone (pronounced Gunston) Park is a 14-acre garden in a rural setting. Built in 1700 by Brook Bridges, the Palladian-style house was rebuilt and enlarged by his great-grandson, Sir Brook Bridges, 3rd Baronet, whose daughter Elizabeth married Jane Austen's brother Edward. In her letters Jane makes frequent reference to Goodnestone and her Bridges cousins. There are pleasant vistas within the garden and good views out to open countryside. The garden ranges in time from the walled area behind the house, which dates from the sixteenth and seventeenth centuries to mid-eighteenth-century parkland with fine trees and cedars. The garden tour leads along a broad terrace in front of the house, planted with a parterre for the millennium, to a lime avenue. Next comes a new venture – a gravel garden inspired in part by Beth Chatto. The small woodland garden, laid out in the 1920s, gives pleasant walks among rhododendrons, camellias, magnolias, hydrangeas and many cornus. A cedar walk leads, between spring borders on the left and a red and grey border on the right, to a walled garden overlooked by the church tower. Old roses mingle with mixed underplanting, and walls bear clematis, jasmine and climbing roses.

Great Comp ★

Comp Lane, Platt, Borough Green, Sevenoaks TN15 8QS. Tel: (01732) 882669/886154

Great Comp Charitable Trust • From M20 junction 2, take A20 towards Maidstone. At Wrotham Heath take B2016. Signposted • Open April to Oct, daily, 11am – 6pm • Entrance: £4, children £1. Annual ticket £10, OAPs £7 ◑ 🍽 🏪 WC & ⌖ ☕ ♿

A half-day is likely to be required to do justice to this imaginatively planned seven-acre garden, which offers all-year interest. Although the setting for an early-seventeenth-century house, it was only created since 1957 by Mr Roderick Cameron and the late Mrs Joyce Cameron out of the neglected earlier garden, rough woodland and paddock. Long grass walks intersect the beds and borders, providing ever-changing views to tempt visitors to stray from their intended route. Focal points and interest are given by statuary, a temple and ruins built from the tons of ironstone dug up over the years. There are woodland areas, herbaceous borders, a heather garden, a rose garden, formal lawns and a new Italianate garden, designed to set off a collection of Mediterranean plants. Hellebores, especially *H. orientalis*, are a feature. The *Taxus baccata* at the front of the house was planted in 1840. Other specimen trees include a young dawn redwood (*Metasequoia glyptostroboides*) and a Californian redwood (*Sequoia sempervirens* 'Cantab'). A music festival is held here each year, with recitals in the former stables.

Groombridge Place ★ [Historic Garden Grade II*]

Groombridge, Tunbridge Wells TN3 9QG. Tel: (01892) 863999

4m SW of Tunbridge Wells. Take A264 towards East Grinstead, then after 2m B2110 to Groombridge • Open April to Oct, daily, 9am – 6pm • Entrance: £8, OAPs £7, children £6.50, family £25 (2003 prices) • Other information: Canal boat rides, birds of prey ◐ 🖤 🐌 WC & 🌿 🛍 🍴 ♿ ✎

This mid-seventeenth-century moated house (not open to the public) is set at the bottom of a valley with enclosed formal gardens sloping up to the north: the Drunken Garden with topiary of drum yews and junipers leaning at angles; the Oriental Garden containing some very old gnarled cut-leaf acers; the Draughtsman's Garden (the eponymous film was filmed here) and the White Rose Garden. These areas are subdivided by topiaried yews, a nut walk and a 'bowling alley'. There are many magnificent trees, such as the four nineteenth-century Wellingtonias to the west of the house. Beside the moat is a parterre knot from which a door in the wall leads into the Secret Garden – a small shady area planted with candelabra primulas alongside a stream flowing among mossy rocks. Dotted around are information boards giving details of the garden's historical and literary associations. Peacocks wander freely. A walk up through the vineyard gives access to the Enchanted Forest, through the Chime Walk and on up to the wooded hillside with magnificent views across the Weald. Several theme gardens designed by Ivan Hicks, plus an imaginative Spring of Life by Myles Challis, are to be found along this walk, which then leads back beside the canal to the formal gardens and the Golden Key Maze.

115 Hadlow Road

Tonbridge TN9 1QE. Tel: (01732) 353738

Mr and Mrs Richard Esdale • 1m N of Tonbridge. From High Street take A26 signed to Maidstone. House is 1m on left in service road • Open 11th July, 1st, 29th Aug, 2 – 6pm, and by appt • Entrance: £2 ◐ 🖤

A third-of-an-acre terraced suburban garden with many interesting specimen trees such as *Catalpa bignonioides* 'Aurea', *Acer negundo* 'Flamingo', *A. japonicum*

'Aureum', golden elm and *Sorbus cashmiriana*. A herbaceous border and an array of clematis, hardy fuchsias, ferns, grasses (*Stipa gigantea*), alpines, roses, shrubs and summer bedding provide additional colour, and a small pool with a fountain contains water-loving plants. There is also a small, well-stocked fruit and vegetable garden.

Hall Place

(see London)

Hever Castle and Gardens ★★ [Historic Garden Grade I]

Hever, Edenbridge TN8 7NG. Tel: (01732) 865224

Broadlands Properties Ltd • 3m SE of Edenbridge off B2026, between Sevenoaks and East Grinstead • Castle opens 12 noon • Gardens open March to Nov, daily, 11am – 6pm (closes 4pm March and Nov). Pre-booked guided tours available for both castle and gardens for parties • Entrance: £6.50, OAPs £5.60, children (5–14) £4.30, family £17.30; castle and gardens £8.40, OAPs £7.10, children (5–14) £4.60, family £21.40. Rates for parties of 15 or more available (2003 prices) ① ▆ ✕ ▆ WC & ⬠ ⬡ ⬢ ⬣ ⬤

The gardens were laid out between 1904 and 1908 to William Waldorf Astor's designs. One thousand men were employed, 800 of whom dug out the 35-acre lake; steam engines shifted rock and soil to create apparently natural new features, and teams of horses moved mature trees from Ashdown Forest. Today the gardens have reached their maturity and are teeming with colour and interest throughout the year. Among the many superb features is an outstanding four-acre Italian garden, the setting for a large collection of classical statuary. Opposite is a magnificent pergola, supporting camellias, wisteria, crab apple, Virginia creeper and roses. It fuses into the hillside beyond, which has shaded grottos of cool damp-loving species such as hostas, astilbes and polygonums. Less formal areas include the rhododendron walk, Anne Boleyn's orchard and her walk, which extends along the full length of the grounds and is particularly attractive in autumn; in keeping with the Anne Boleyn connection a so-called Tudor herb garden has been added, and the Sunday Walk nearby runs beside a stream past newly created borders in mature woodland. The 110-metre herbaceous border has been re-created and the water maze on Sixteen-Acre Island, planted with a range of aquatic plants, offers peaceful walks down to the millennium fountain.

Hole Park

Rolvenden, Cranbrook TN17 4JA. Tel: (01580) 241251

Mr D.G.W. Barham • 4m W of Tenterden, on B2086 between Rolvenden and Benenden • Open April to June, Oct, Mon, Wed; plus ten Suns for NGS; all 2 – 6pm, and by appt • Entrance: £3.50, children (under 12) 50p • Other information: Refreshments by prior arrangement. Plants for sale on NGS Suns only ● WC &

Situated midway between Sissinghurst and Great Dixter, Hole Park affords the visitor an opportunity to enjoy a peaceful garden of great beauty far away from the crowds and very different from its popular neighbours. The 14-acre gardens were designed and created by the owner's grandfather in the early 1920s, when extensive yew hedges were planted. These, together with fine trees, broad lawns and old walls, provide the background for herbaceous and mixed plantings as well as pools, statuary and pleasant places in which to wander at will. A feature is the millennium water garden. There are splendid views over the beautiful parkland to Rolvenden's famous seventeenth-century postmill and towards the Weald of Kent. In the wild garden to the north of the house, daffodils in great variety are followed by flowering shrubs, rhododendrons and azaleas, and the dell is cool and inviting. In May bluebells fill the woodland walk, and autumn colours are a speciality, making the garden a sight for all seasons. Nearby is *Great Maytham Hall* (Country Houses Association), said to have inspired *The Secret Garden* [open May to Sept, Wed and Thurs, 2 – 5pm].

Ightham Mote

Ivy Hatch, Sevenoaks TN15 0NT. Tel: (01732) 810378

The National Trust • 6m E of Sevenoaks off A25, $2\frac{1}{2}$ m S of Ightham off A227 • House open • Garden open 23rd March to 9th Nov, daily except Tues and Sat, 10.30am – 5.30pm • Entrance: £6, children £3, family £15, pre-booked parties of 15 or more £5 per person (2003 prices) • Other information: Disabled parking ◑ 💺 ✕ 🍴 WC 🚾 ⛪ 🔥 ✎ ℺

Situated in a wooded cleft of the Kentish Weald, this medieval and Tudor manor house lies in the valley of Dinas Dene, where a stream has been dammed to form small lakes and the moat which surrounds the house. The design of the gardens has evolved over several centuries – the present lawn replaces the medieval stew pond, which was used for breeding fish for the table; further domestic needs were satisfied with vegetables and herbs for culinary and medicinal purposes, and flowers for decorating and scenting the house. During the nineteenth century the garden emerged as an excellent example of the ideal 'old English' garden, and the Trust is gradually restoring this with extensive replanting. Six acres of woodland walks with fine rhododendrons are re-established and the long border has returned to its former glory.

Ladham House ★

Goudhurst TN17 1DB

8m E of Tunbridge Wells, NE of Goudhurst off A262 • Open two days for NGS, 2 – 5.30pm, and by written appt for individuals and parties • Entrance: £3.50, children 50p, £4.50 for private visits • Other information: Teas must be pre-booked ● 💺 WC 🚾 ⟁

The house, Georgian with additional French features, is surrounded by 37 acres of garden and parkland. It is interesting to see the bog garden replacing a leaking pond, and the arboretum replacing the old kitchen garden. The mixed shrub borders are attractive; notable are the magnolias – two *M.* x *wieseneri* over 10 metres tall and a deep-red-flowering 'Betty Jessel', a seedling from Darjeeling. Amongst the other rarer trees and shrubs are *Cornus kousa*, embothriums, American oaks, *Aesculus parviflora, Carpenteria californica* and *Azara serrata*. The arboretum is maturing and has some unusual and interesting trees. Developments continue: the Fountain Garden has been completely reconstructed, the rock garden restored with a waterfall incorporated, a 200-metre-long Kentish ragstone ha-ha built to the north of the house, and a woodland walk down the side of the park opened up. A new garden close to the swimming pool uses tropical and hot-coloured plants.

Leeds Castle ★ [Historic Garden Grade II*]

Maidstone ME17 1PL. Tel: (01622) 765400

Leeds Castle Foundation • 7m E of Maidstone on B2163 near M20 junction 8 • Castle opens 11am (10.15am in winter) • Park and gardens open all year, daily, 10am – 5pm (closes 3pm Nov to Feb). Closed 28th June, 5th July, 8th Nov, 25th Dec • Entrance: castle, park and gardens £11, OAPs and students £9.50, children (4–15) £7.50, family £32; (Nov to Feb, £9.50, OAPs and students £8, children (4-15) £6, family £27) (2003 prices) ○ 🍽 ✕ 🍴 **WC** ♿ 🌿 ♨ 🚻 🐕

Visit the castle and grounds for its romantic, wooded setting, covering some 500 acres. The woodland garden, with its old and new plantings of shrubs, is especially beautiful in daffodil time. The atmosphere is also much enhanced by wildfowl. The Culpeper Garden, in a secluded area beyond the castle, provides the main interest for the keen gardener. This is not a herb garden as often thought, though a small area does include some herbs, but is named after a seventeenth-century owner, distantly related to the herbalist. Started in 1980 by Russell Page on a slope overlooking the River Len, and surrounded by high brick walls of stabling and old cottages, the garden already has an established feeling of old-world charm. A simple pattern of paths lined with box contains areas of old roses, riotously underplanted with herbaceous perennials. Old greenhouses have been replanted with peach trees, and there is an excellent fuchsia display in the summer months. National Collections of monardas are situated in one corner of the Culpeper Garden. The spectacular grotto built in 1987 beneath the maze has been much publicised. The garden is complemented by some rare and attractive birds in the duckery and aviary, which are well placed amid numerous shrubs and small trees. The terraced Italian-style Lady Baillie Garden overlooking the Great Water has stunning sub-tropical plants.

Longacre

Perry Wood, Selling, Faversham ME13 9SE. Tel: (01227) 752254

Dr and Mrs G. Thomas • 5m SE of Faversham. From A2 (M2) take A251 S signed to Selling. Pass White Lion on left, second right, then left, continue for $\frac{1}{4}$ m. From A252 at Chilham, take road to Selling at Badgers Hill Fruit Farm, turn left at second crossroads, first right, next left, then right • Open for NGS 11th, 12th, 25th April, 2nd, 3rd, 16th, 30th, 31st May, 8th, 29th, 30th Aug, and at other times by appt • Entrance: £2, accompanied children free • Other information: Teas and plants for sale on NGS open days only ◑ 🍽 **WC** ♿ 🌿

This is a jewel of a small garden in a tranquil country setting next to Perry Woods into which the borders of the garden melt. Created entirely by the present owners, it offers all-year interest of colour and form, replicating in miniature woodland, damp and dry areas. There are mixed borders, a small pond with running water and a large gravel garden. Trellis around the area supports sun-loving climbers, and vegetables in raised beds are cropping well. A new conservatory displays a wide range of tender plants.

Marle Place Gardens and Gallery ★

Brenchley, Tonbridge TN12 7HS. Tel: (01892) 722304

Mr and Mrs G. Williams • 5m E of Tunbridge Wells, 1m SW of Horsmonden, W of B2162. Signposted • Open 18th April to 1st Oct, daily, 10am – 5.30pm (but telephone in advance to confirm garden is open), and by appt • Entrance: £4, OAPs and children (4-12 years) £3.50 • Other information: Art exhibitions in gallery throughout season ◐ ☕ 🥾 WC ☕ 🌱 ♿ ⚘

This 10-acre garden surrounding a seventeenth-century house hidden away in the byways contains a wide range of garden features. Close to the house is a small shady fern garden and a border of several varieties of cistus (at their best in early June), set off by an old wall furnished with interesting climbers. A double herbaceous border leads to an area of alliums and ornamental grasses, also at its peak in June. Near the house is an old ornamental pool garden with a wildflower bank and aromatic plants, a croquet lawn and several interesting specimen trees, such as an old *Acer pseudoplatanus* 'Brilliantissimum' and a weeping form of *Ginkgo biloba*. The use of different-coloured foliage hedges as a background to many of the borders illustrates the artistic flair of the owner (her studio is open to garden visitors). Other features include a Victorian gazebo, an Edwardian rockery and two lakes approached by a woodland walk; a red Chinese bridge leads over a boggy area planted with bamboos. A mosaic terrace has been laid within the blue and yellow border. Areas of wild flowers, both within the garden and in the 10-acre wood of native trees, and several large iron skeletal sculptures of horses and other work by varied artists, plus carved wooden furniture made by the owners' daughter, add to the eclectic charm. Along the woodland walk visitors come upon a two-acre 'gallery wood', where they are invited to participate in creating artworks made from the natural objects surrounding them. A recently planted five-acre arboretum is carpeted with scented clover and a *potager* includes several varieties of special vegetables.

Mount Ephraim [Historic Garden Grade II]

Hernhill, Faversham ME13 9TX. Tel: (01227) 751496

Mrs Mary Dawes and Mr and Mrs E.S. Dawes • 6m W of Canterbury, 3m E of Faversham off A299. At Duke of Kent pub turn to Hernhill; garden is through village on left, signposted • Open 20th April to Sept, Wed, Thurs, Sat, Sun and Bank Holiday Mons, 1 – 6pm (Bank Holiday weekends 11am – 6pm) • Entrance: £3.50, children £1, parties £3 per person (2003 prices) • Other information: Craft shop Suns only ◐ ☕ 🥾 WC ☕ 🍴 ♿ ⚘

The fine ten-acre gardens surrounding the house mirror two centuries of changing horticultural fashions. From its eminent position, with far-flung views over fruit orchards to the Thames estuary, the house overlooks sweeping lawns, huge borders and magnificent specimen trees, including a sweet chestnut planted to commemorate the Battle of Waterloo. The steeply sloping site retains the original formal plan in the rose terrace, with flights of steps hedged in venerable yew, leading to the tranquil lake and a newly developed water garden. The arboretum was planted to celebrate three centuries of ownership by the Dawes family and the eightieth birthday of the indefatigable Mary Dawes. In 1950 she and her husband began the restoration work, which continues today with the creation of an elegant garden filled with fragrant new and old-fashioned roses. A long herbaceous border, skilfully planted and sheltered by old stable walls, lines the topiary garden with its idiosyncratic collection of birds, animals and First World War memorabilia in clipped yew. The restored Japanese and rock gardens are a turn-of-the-century feature, but the cricket pitch and pavilion are new. Nigel Lee Evans was responsible for the layout of the new rose garden, Sarah Morgan for the planting.

Nettlestead Place ★

Nettlestead, Maidstone ME18 5HA. Tel: (01622) 812205

Mr and Mrs R.C. Tucker • 6m SW of Maidstone off B2015. Next to church • Open for NGS 11th June, 6 – 8.30pm, 9th May, 26th Sept, 2 – 5.30pm, and at other times by appt • Entrance: £4 ● & ⟨ᴅ 🌣

From the early-fourteenth-century gatehouse an avenue of Irish yews leads down to the thirteenth-century manor house set in seven acres on the banks of a tranquil stretch of the River Medway. A long gravel garden planted with rock plants and dwarf bulbs lies along the eastern side of the house, which is clothed with akebia, sophora, fremontodendron and *Rosa* 'Frances Lester'. A large sunken pond bounded by a ragstone wall provides a sheltered environment for tender plants, and a natural spring flowing down the hill in the glen garden is edged with hostas, primulas, dwarf pines, astilbes and other damp- and shade-lovers. The astounding plantsman's collection continues throughout the garden – shrubs, hybrid tea and floribunda roses in the large rose garden, and specialised trees and shrubs in a series of island beds, a comprehensive range of plants in the herbaceous garden, and a small, recently planted China rose garden. An arboretum containing over 30 different acers delights in spring with its interesting bark variations and in autumn with its vibrant foliage colours. A wonderful experience for the enthusiast.

Old Buckhurst

Markbeech, Nr Edenbridge TN8 5PH. Tel: (01342) 850825

Jane and John Gladstone • 4m SE of Edenbridge via B2026. At Queen's Arms turn E to Markbeech; after 1½ m garden is first on right after leaving village • Open May to July, Wed, 11am – 5.30pm, and for NGS • Entrance: £2.50 ● 🦐 WC & 🌣

The fifteenth-century farmhouse, draped in wisteria, roses, a fig and summer jasmine, sits on top of a wide, flat ridge. It is surrounded by an acre of garden containing an exuberance of cottage-garden plants, old-fashioned roses and clematis. The planting becomes wilder towards the perimeter, the better to blend into the countryside, but in the heart of the garden native species give way to more sophisticated effects. A courtyard enclosed by low walls has a silver pear tree and a series of box globes for structure and winter interest. A short pergola leads to the kitchen garden; a small pond surrounded by damp-loving plants and a gravel garden provide contrasts. The wide variety of plants propagated from the garden for sale in the little nursery is an added bonus. The owners' daughter, Claire Gladstone, is a garden designer who keeps a watching brief on this charming place.

Old Place Farm

High Halden, Ashford TN26 3JG. Tel: (01233) 850202

Mr and Mrs J. Eker • 10m SW of Ashford. From A28, opposite Chequers pub in High Halden, take Woodchurch road and follow for ½ m • Open by appt only • Entrance: £3 ● 🕷 WC ⅻ

A four-acre garden surrounding a period house and farm buildings, created since 1968, mainly designed by Anthony du Gard Pasley. The lake of two-thirds of an acre provides a near focus from the house, and an elegant gazebo is an idyllic setting for contemplation. The borders behind have an apricot, gold and cream colour theme offset by blues, purples, silvers and greys. An avenue of *Crataegus prunifolia*, underplanted with white-flowering bulbs from February to May, leads to a fine sheep statue. There is a nut plat, a philadelphus walk and, to provide summer shelter from the sun, two large *Catalpa bignonioides*. A parterre herb garden is linked to a circular brick feature with a sundial by an avenue of *Malus* 'Golden Hornet'. A pergola draped with the rose 'New Dawn', white wisteria and purple vines divides the cutting garden from a small *potager*. Two new bridges over the stream connect the garden to the wood and fields beyond.

Owl House Gardens

Lamberhurst TN3 8LY. Tel: (01892) 891290

Estate of the late Maureen, Marchioness of Dufferin and Ava • 6m SE of Tunbridge Wells, S of Lamberhurst off A21. Signposted • Open all year, daily except 25th Dec and 1st Jan, 11am – 6pm • Entrance: £4, children £1 • Other information: Coaches by appt. Tea room shut Sept to April ○ 🍽 🕷 WC ⅻ ⬥ 🐾

In 1952 Lady Dufferin fell in love with a cottage which had the crookedest chimney in Kent and was the county's oldest building. In 1522 its tenants paid a yearly rental of one white cockerel to the monks at Bayham Abbey. During the sixteenth century it was a hiding place for wool smugglers who, at the approach of the law, hooted their warning, hence its name. Within its 16½ acres a beautiful year-round garden was created over the years by Lady Dufferin. Swathes of daffodils and bluebells start the season, followed by camellias, azaleas and rhododendrons. Summer interest is ensured by large numbers of old roses, *R. longicuspis*, 'Bobbie James' and 'Rambling Rector', climbing into the many fine trees; philadelphus and clematis also abound.

Statues of owls are dotted about the garden, with seats placed to overlook viewpoints. There is a wisteria temple, a grove of *Parrotia persica*, and four walks: of iris, apple blossom, laburnum and blue hydrangeas. Three water gardens provide a peaceful setting for contemplation.

Penshurst Place and Gardens ★ [Historic Garden Grade I]

Penshurst, Tonbridge TN11 8DG. Tel: (01892) 870307

Lord De L'Isle • 5m SW of Tonbridge on B2176, 7m N of Tunbridge Wells off A26 • House open as garden, but 12.30 – 5.30pm • Gardens open weekends from 6th March, then daily from 27th March to Oct, 10.30am – 6pm. Garden tours available for parties of 20 or more • Entrance: £5, children £4.50, family £17 (house and gardens £7, OAPs and students £6.50, children £4.50, family £18). Parties of 20 or more £6 per person • Other information: Garden history exhibition. Guide dogs only ◑ 🍽 🧺 WC ♿ 🐾 🎁 💡 ⚲

The 600-year-old gardens, contemporary with the house, reflect their creation under the Tudor owner, Sir Henry Sidney, and the restoration by the present owner, his father and his grandfather. An example is the 640-metre double line of oaks, their planting completed in 1995 as part of a 15-year programme to re-create the historic parkland structure. The many separate enclosures, surrounded by trim and tall yew hedges, offer a wide variety of interesting planting, with continuous displays from spring to early autumn. Just inside the entrance is a garden for the blind, with raised beds of aromatic plants, a small wooden gazebo and the constant music of water splashing on pebbles. The Italian garden with its oval fountain and century-old ginkgo dominates the south front of the magnificent house. Herbaceous borders are teeming with colour. Note also the borders designed by Lanning Roper in the late 1960s and the blue and yellow border. Contrast is made by the nut trees and over a dozen different crab apples underplanted with daffodils, myosotis, tulips, bluebells, Lenten lilies, and a magnificent bed of peonies bordering the orchard. Even in late summer the rose garden is colourful with 'Anisley Dickson' and 'Anna Olivier', and their perfumes mingle with those of mature lavender bushes. A lake and woodland trail have been developed so that the style of design so much enjoyed here by Gertrude Jekyll and Beatrix Farrand is fully recaptured. Two medieval fish ponds have been reclaimed and stocked with fish. There is an imaginative play area for children.

The Pines Garden

Beach Road, St Margaret's Bay CT15 6DZ. Tel: (01304) 852764

St Margaret's Bay Trust • 3m NE of Dover off A258, through St Margaret's at Cliffe, just before beach • Open all year, daily, 10am – 5pm • Entrance: £3.50, concessions £3, children 50p, family £5 • Other information: Teas and gift shop in St Margaret's Museum opposite, open Easter and May Bank Holidays, end-May to early Sept, Wed – Sun, 2 – 5pm ○ 🍽 🧺 WC ♿ ⬦ 🎁 ⚲

It is hard to believe that this well-stocked and organically maintained garden was scrubland until 1970. Fred Cleary, founder of the St Margaret's Bay Trust, transformed the original six-acre site, known as the Barrack Field, once the home and training ground for soldiers in the Napoleonic Wars. Now the garden is established, with a good variety of trees, gently undulating lawns, flowering shrubs, bulbs and herbaceous plants. The lake with its cascade of waterfalls provides further interest. A bronze statue of Sir Winston Churchill by Oscar Nemon looks across the garden to the famous white cliffs of Dover. A Romany wedding caravan (as used by gypsies of Romney Marsh) stands in the garden, and at the other end there is a seventeenth-century façade from a London Cheapside property. To celebrate the millennium, Pauline Gould (Fred Cleary's daughter) created a large new bed near the entrance to the garden with perennial plants that have been introduced into Kent over the past few hundred years. A new water feature has been built at the entrance, with a lily pool and two terraced gardens leading up to the visitor centre which houses creative displays of the Trust's work.

Port Lympne [Historic Garden Grade II*]

Lympne, Hythe CT21 4PD. Tel: (01303) 264647

Aspinall family • 3m W of Hythe, 18m S of Canterbury on B2067 • House open • Garden open all year, daily, 10am – 6pm (last admission 4.30pm, 3pm in winter) • Entrance: £11.95, OAPs and children £8.95 (house, garden and wild animal park) (2003 prices) ○ 🍵 ✕ 🛍 WC ♿ ♨ 💡 🌳 ♀

This is one of those gardens which is hugely enjoyed by some people and leaves others cold. It stands in a 300-acre wild animal park with views across the Channel. The interior of the Lutyens-style house is noted for the murals by Rex Whistler and Spencer Roberts. After a period of distinction in the 1920s and '30s it fell into decay until it was rescued in the 1970s by the late John Aspinall, who wanted the surrounding land for his private wild animal park. He reconstructed the 15-acre garden to something like its original design with advice from experts, including the late Russell Page. Visitors enter down a great stone stairway of 125 steps, flanked by clipped yews, to the paved west court and lily pool. Beyond is the lime tree walk and a series of terraces planted with standard fig trees and vines. Everywhere there is fine stone paving and walls with appropriately placed urns, statues from Stowe, etc. Bedding and bedding-out are used extensively. The late Arthur Hellyer admitted that 'for years it has been fashionable to denigrate Port Lympne' but he admired it; he also waxed lyrical about the beautiful wrought-ironwork by Bainbridge Reynolds.

Priory Gardens

(see London)

Riverhill House Gardens [Historic Garden Grade II]

Sevenoaks TN15 0RR. Tel: (01732) 458802/452557

Rogers family (correspondence to Mrs John Rogers) • 2m S of Sevenoaks on A225 • House open to bona fide booked parties only. No children inside house •

Garden open April to 13th June, Wed, Sun, 12 noon – 6pm • Entrance: £3, children 50p (house and garden for parties of 20 or more £4 per person) • Other information: Coaches by appt ● 💭 🍴 WC ♨ 👍 ✄

This was originally one of the great smaller country-house gardens, housing a plantsman's collection of trees and species shrubs as introduced by John Rogers, a keen horticulturist, in the mid-1800s. Massive rhododendrons, many of them species, are topped by a cedar of Lebanon planted in 1815, and azaleas and outstanding underplanting of bulbs make a fine show in spring and early summer. Other features include a woodland garden, a rose walk, an orchard with a Wellingtonia planted in 1860, magnolias and much more.

Rock Farm ★

Nettlestead, Gibbs Hill, Maidstone ME18 5HT. Tel: (01622) 812244

Mrs P.A. Corfe • 6m SW of Maidstone. From A26 turn S onto B2015, then turn right 1m S of Wateringbury • Open 15th, 18th May, 12th, 15th, 19th, 22nd, 26th, 29th June, 3rd, 7th, 10th, 13th July, 11am – 5pm, for private visits by appt • Entrance: £3 ◐ 🍴 WC B&B

This Kentish farmhouse, set on an east-facing slope, is surrounded by a two-acre plantsman's garden. Natural springs supply water for two ponds at different levels and for a small stream whose banks are planted with primulas and other bog plants. The soil is alkaline and there are excellent specimens of ceanothus, a huge *Solanum crispum*, a *Fremontodendron californicum* and a *Magnolia grandiflora*. The best season is May to July when the large herbaceous border is at its peak. An iris border provides a colourful entry to the garden. Of special interest is the *Chionanthus virginicus* or fringe tree. The two ponds are bordered with cupressus of various foliage colours. A *Catalpa bignonioides* 'Aurea' is cut annually to give huge golden leaves, and a *Sequoia sempervirens* is also pruned drastically, resulting in rarely seen new foliage of this coniferous forest tree.

Scotney Castle Garden and Estate ★ [Historic Garden Grade I]

Lamberhurst, Tunbridge Wells TN3 8JN. Tel: (01892) 891081

The National Trust • 8m SE of Tunbridge Wells, 1m S of Lamberhurst on E side of A21 • Old Castle open as garden • Garden open May to mid-Sept – telephone (0870) 458 4000 for details • Entrance: £4.40, children £2.20, family £11. Pre-booked parties (weekdays only) £3.80 per person (2003 prices) • Other information: Possible for wheelchairs but hilly approach ◐ 💭 🍴 WC ♿ ⟨⟩ 👍 🍷

This is an unusual garden designed in the romantic manner by the Hussey family, following the tradition established by William Kent and using the services of William Gilpin, the artist and landscape gardener, who also advised on the site of the new house, completed in 1843. Of the fourteenth-century castle only one of the four towers remains, plus some of the sixteenth- and seventeenth-century additions. The landscape garden includes smaller garden layouts in the overall area. A formal garden overlooks a quarry garden and the grounds of the Old Castle enclose a herbaceous border backed by roses and clematis; there is also a herb garden. The lakeside planting adds an air of informality. Evergreens and deciduous trees provide the mature planting, linking shrubs and plants to give something in flower at every season. Daffodils, magnolias, rhododendrons and azaleas are the most spectacular; also notable are the kalmias and hydrangeas. In a good autumn, the colours are amazing. In some ways the planting seems occasional and haphazard, 'Picturesque' in the true sense, but visit this garden for its setting on a slope that gives fine views of open countryside, and for the romantic eighteenth- to nineteenth-century theme uniting it. A great pity there are no refreshments as there is plenty of space.

Sissinghurst Castle Garden ★★ [Historic Garden Grade I]

Sissinghurst, Cranbrook TN17 2AB. Tel: (01580) 710700 (infoline)

The National Trust • 13m S of Maidstone, 2m NE of Cranbrook, 1m E of Sissinghurst on A262 • Open 20th March to Oct, Mon, Tues, Fri, 11am – 6.30pm, Sat, Sun and Bank Holiday Mons, 10am – 6.30pm (last admission 5.30pm or dusk if earlier). Parties of 11 or more by appt. Garden much quieter after 3.30pm • Entrance: £6.50, children £3, family £16 (2003 prices) • Other information: Coaches by appt. Picnics beyond car park and in front of castle only. Wheelchairs restricted to two chairs at one time because of narrow, uneven paths; pushchairs not admitted ◑ ▆ ✕ 🍴 WC ⚅ ♨ ♨ B&B

'Profusion, even extravagance and exuberance within the confines of the utmost linear severity', was Vita Sackville-West's description of her design when creating Sissinghurst with her husband Harold Nicolson. It is a romantic garden within a formal framework, with seasonal features throughout the year. Certain colour schemes have been followed, as in the purple border, the orange and yellow cottage garden, and the white garden, which is probably the most beautiful garden at Sissinghurst, itself one of the outstanding gardens in the world. The Nicolsons added little to, but saved much of, the Elizabethan mansion. The site was first occupied in the twelfth century, when a moated manor was built where the orchard now stands. The long library and Elizabethan tower are open and the latter is well worth climbing in order to see the perspective of the whole garden and surrounding area. All is kept in immaculate condition, well labelled, with changing vistas at every turn of the winding paths or more formal walks. The rose garden contains many old-fashioned roses as well as flowering shrubs such as *Ceanothus impressus* and *Hydrangea villosa*, which together with iris, clematis and pansies fill the area. There is a thyme lawn leading to the herb garden filled with fragrance and charm. It is a truly magnificent example of Englishness and has had immense influence on garden design because of its structure of separate outdoor rooms within the garden. *Knole* [Historic Park Grade I] will also interest Vita's fans [park open daily, Lord Sackville's garden on first Wed in every month, May to Sept].

Southover

Grove Lane, Hunton, Maidstone ME15 0SE. Tel: (01622) 820876

Mr and Mrs David Way • 6m S of Maidstone between A229 and B2010. From Yalding take Vicarage Road to Hunton. Almost opposite school turn left into

Grove Lane; house is about 180 metres on right. From Coxheath turn down Hunton Hill to Hunton; Grove Lane is immediately past school • Open for NGS, and by appt; parties welcome • Entrance: £3, accompanied children free • Other information: Wheelchair users must be accompanied ● &

The typical fifteenth-century timber-framed house in the centre of a south-sloping site is surrounded by a garden designed to complement it. Work started in 1980. The foundations of a much larger house were uncovered and planted with hedges to enclose a true garden room. Two ponds, filled in over the centuries, have been redeveloped – one re-excavated, the other planted as a damp garden. Higher up, a bank flows with ground-cover plants. Beyond is a woodland walk and wildflower meadow. The spring garden is complemented by an autumn border. Nearer the house are two 'secret' gardens: one, adjoining the house, is a cottage garden planted with roses and scented flowers, the other, similar in size but quite different in atmosphere, is known as the Meditation Garden, a study in greens. A third garden room has been developed as a *potager*. Impressive herbaceous borders to the south of the house contain many unusual plants. Penstemons are a speciality and one border displays over 40 varieties. Other features are a sunken walk in green and white, a fern area, a brown garden featuring sedges and grasses, and new beds for winter- and spring-flowering bulbs.

Squerryes Court [Historic Garden Grade II]

Westerham TN16 1SJ. Tel: (01959) 562345/563118

Mr and Mrs John Warde • ½ m W of Westerham on A25, near M25 junctions 5 and 6 • House open as garden, 1.30 – 5.30pm • Garden open April to Sept, Wed, Sat, Sun and Bank Holiday Mons, 12 noon – 5.30pm. Parties of 20 or more by appt • Entrance: £3, OAPs £2.50, children under 14 £1.50, family £7; (house and garden £4.60, OAPs £4.10, children £2.50, family £12). Reduced rates for pre-booked parties (2003 prices) ◑ 🍽 🍴 <u>WC</u> & ⬠ 🏺 ♟

The 20 acres of gardens, laid out around 1700 in the formal Anglo-Dutch style, were landscaped again in the eighteenth century. The view over the large lake leads to a gazebo, built around 1740, from where a former member of the family used to watch his racehorses in training; nearby is a fine old dovecot. The main feature is the restored formal area to the rear of the house; a 1719 print has been used as an outline on which to base the changes. These reflect the mellow brickwork of the handsome house; beds, edged with box, contain lavender, purple sage and santolina. Two long Edwardian borders have been planted with roses and herbaceous perennials. All are framed by well-kept yew hedges. There are several other mixed borders and a Victorian rockery with fine examples of topiary. The woodland garden, currently being restored, contains rhodo-dendron and azalea shrubberies, which, together with a broad variety of spring bulbs, makes this a garden for all seasons. Many fine magnolias around the house and a cenotaph in memory of General Wolfe (a family friend) complete a most attractive garden. The house is worth a visit, too, for its collection of paintings; particularly interesting is the portrait of the proud squire and his family in front of the handsome house he had acquired. Those with a historical bent will wish to visit nearby Chartwell (see entry), although this, horticulturally speaking, has a less interesting garden.

Stoneacre

Otham, Maidstone ME15 8RS. Tel: (01622) 862871

The National Trust • 3m SE of Maidstone, 1m S of A20 from Bearsted, at N end of Otham • House open • Garden open mid-March to mid-Oct, Wed, Sat and Bank Holiday Mons, 2 – 6pm (last admission 5pm), and at other times by appt • Entrance: house and garden £2.60, children £1.30 • Other information: Disabled parking at gate. Picnics in car park ◑ ⅙ ⌀

The Kentish hall house was restored and embellished in the 1920s by Aymer Vallance, Oxford aesthete, writer and friend of William Morris. Within the framework of yew hedges and ragstone walls, the current tenants have considerably reworked the charming garden of borders and lawns along more sculptural and textured lines. The lawns and hedges have been reshaped to reflect the surrounding landscape, and the old *potager* has been transformed into a secluded rose garden planted with many varieties of scented old roses in shades of red. The gardens at the front of the house contain borders with unusual colour schemes, including one with many interesting black and dark plants. At the rear of the house is a wild garden – particularly beautiful when the cow parsley is in bloom – with apple orchards and three ponds.

Walmer Castle [Historic Garden Grade II]

Kingsdown Road, Walmer, Deal CT14 7LJ. Tel: (01304) 364288

English Heritage • On coast 2m S of Walmer on A258, off M20 at junction 13 or from M2 to Deal • Castle open • Garden open April to Sept, daily, 10am – 6pm; Oct, daily, 10am – 5pm; Nov, Dec and March, Wed – Sun, 10am – 4pm; Jan, Feb, Sat, Sun, 10am – 4pm. Closed 24th to 26th Dec and when Lord Warden in residence. Telephone in advance of visit to check, particularly in Oct and winter months • Entrance: castle and garden £5.50, concessions £4.10, children (5–16) £2.80, family £13.80. Discount for parties of 11 or more (2003 prices) • Other information: Guided garden tours. Wheelchair available. Guide dogs only ◐ 🍵 ✕ 🖼 WC ⅙ ⌀ 🏛 🔦 ⚲

English Heritage is restoring the gardens of this, the official residence of the Warden of the Cinque Ports, to their former status in the early twentieth century. The castle overlooks the sea and the 10-acre gardens are surrounded by shelter belts and meadows. The formal core of the garden consists of three areas. The first is the double herbaceous border which is backed by large crinkle-crankle yew hedges ending in terraces with a croquet lawn. Then comes the traditional kitchen garden with a cut-flower area producing decoration for the castle, and a vegetable area with espaliered apple and pear trees, cold frames and glasshouses. Finally the Queen Mother's Garden, situated in the old walled garden, was redesigned by Penelope Hobhouse to commemorate her late Majesty's 95th birthday. It includes a 30-metre-long formal pond, yew pyramids, box topiary and a mount topped by yew hedges clipped in the shape of a castle. A dry moat is planted with roses and shrubs. An informal woodland walk encircles a wildflower meadow, and there are picnic tables and deck chairs on the oval lawn from which to relax and enjoy it all. The restored glasshouse displays a range of conservatory plants, providing an added attraction in winter and early spring.

Waystrode Manor ★

Spode Lane, Cowden, Edenbridge TN8 7HW. Tel: (01342) 850695

Mrs Jill Wright • 8m W of Tunbridge Wells, 4½ m S of Edenbridge, off B2026 Edenbridge – Hartfield road • Open some Weds and Suns from May to July for NGS • Entrance: £3, children 50p ● ☕ WC ₺ ⌀ ⑂

This eight-acre garden on Wealden clay has been developed over the last thirty years and surrounds a beautiful half-timbered sixteenth-century house. An avenue of red-candled horse chestnut trees leads to the house, which is flanked on one side by an old barn supporting wisteria, clematis, actinidia and schizophragma. A stone-flagged area at the rear has herbs growing out of it and, as a central feature, an old mill grinding-wheel planted with low-growing plants. From the house the eye is led via the serpent fountain garden to a small yew-enclosed white garden. A large and decorative wooden building contains tender and tropical plants. There are several pergolas of wisteria, laburnum and roses. Two small pools connected by a waterfall are crossed by a charming arched bridge. Borders of irises, old roses and geraniums are dotted around, and the whole is complemented by some excellent and unusual specimen trees, such as *Ulmus minor* 'Dampieri Aurea', *Abies koreana*, *Betula utilis* var. *jacquemontii* and *Cedrus deodara* 'Pendula', and a collection of unusual oaks.

Weeks Farm

Bedlam Lane, Egerton Forstal, Ashford TN27 9DA. Tel: (01233) 756252

Robin and Monica De Garston • 2½ m E of Headcorn. From Headcorn, take Smarden road, then third turning on left. House is 1½ m on right • Open for NGS and by appt (please telephone evenings) • Entrance: £2 ● WC ₺ ⑂

The two-acre garden is informally laid out round a typical Kent farmhouse. The prime asset here is a glorious annual display of naturalised spring bulbs, started thirty years ago by the previous owner on a badly drained site, and topped up annually with more bulbs – hyacinths, daffodils and tulips. A new pond, linked to an older one, is generously stocked with fish. The overall effect is much more than a cottage garden, with subtle oriental elements such as bamboos repeated throughout, and for good measure there are two deep mixed borders lining the sweeping drive.

Yalding Organic Gardens

Benover Road, Yalding, Maidstone ME18 6EX. Tel: (01622) 814650

HDRA – the organic organisation • 6m SW of Maidstone, $\frac{1}{2}$ m S of Yalding on B2162 • Open May to Sept, Wed – Sun; April and Oct, Sat, Sun and Bank Holiday Mons; all 10am – 5pm • Entrance: £3, accompanied children free, parties of 14 or more £2.50 (£1 extra for garden tour) ◐ ⬛ ✕ 🧺 WC ♿ ⌖ ⛟ ⓟ ⚲

The pergola of hop poles at the heart of Yalding links it closely to the surrounding oasts and hop gardens of Kent. The gardens offer a tour of garden style through history, beginning with the natural woodland that once dotted our hills and valleys. Visitors pass through a thirteenth-century apothecary's garden, an Elizabethan Paradise Garden and Tudor knot, an early-nineteenth-century cottager's plot, a Victorian artisan's garden with an original nineteenth-century glasshouse, sweeping Edwardian borders and a utilitarian 1950s' allotment before being shown an organic vision of the future. A children's garden completes the tour. Impressive, well-kept and an experience for the whole family.

GARDENING FOR THE DISABLED

- The Gardening for the Disabled Trust (Charity No. 255066) collects donations to assist people with improvements to their gardens, or to supply equipment which will enable them to continue to garden. Information from Mrs Angela Parish, Frittenden House, Nr Cranbrook TN17 2DG (Fax: (01580) 852120; Email: apparish@hotmail.com.
- Thrive is a national charity promoting the use of gardens and horticulture as a therapy for restricted or disabled gardeners (Tel: (0118) 988 5688; Email: info@thrive.org.uk; Website: www.thrive.org.uk or www.carryongardening.org.uk
- For information on the Disabled and Older Gardeners' Association (including workshops etc.), write to Growing Point, Holme Lacy College, Hereford or telephone Sue Eaton on (01432) 268876.
- Demonstration gardens to assist the disabled are on view at a number of properties open to the public and are also featured in the *Guide*. They include two in Battersea Park (for an appointment with the Horticultural Therapy Unit telephone (020) 7720 2212), Capel Manor and Broadview Garden.
- Open days for the disabled are also held from time to time at other gardens described in the *Guide*, such as Dolly's Garden.

LANCASHIRE

Two-starred gardens are marked on the map with a black square.

Ashton Memorial [Historic Garden Grade II]

Williamson Park, Quernmore Road, Lancaster LA1 1UX. Tel: (01524) 33318

E of Lancaster town centre. Signposted • Open daily except 25th, 26th Dec and 1st Jan: April to Sept, 10am – 5pm; Oct to March, 10am – 4pm • Entrance: park and ground floor of memorial with exhibition free; memorial viewing gallery 50p; butterfly house, mini-beast house, conservation garden and free-flying bird enclosure £3.50, OAPs £3, children £2 ○ ⬥ ⊕ ⚲

Ashton Memorial, described by Pevsner as 'the grandest monument in England', stands at the highest point of Williamson Park looking down on the town of Lancaster. There are many views of the surrounding country from various points in the superbly landscaped park. Broad paths run through the grounds, much of which is woodland with an underplanting of rhododendrons and other shrubs. A small lake is spanned by a stone bridge, and nearby a large stairway leads to the huge domed monument. Not far away is the butterfly house and pavilion. Both monument and butterfly house were designed in 1906 by John Belcher in Baroque Revival style. A three-year restoration programme for the park and woodland is due to be completed in 2007.

Catforth Gardens ★

Cherry Tree Lodge, Roots Lane, Catforth, Preston PR4 0JB. Tel: (01772) 690561

Mr and Mrs T.A. Bradshaw • 5m NW of Preston. Turn S off B5269 to Catforth. Roots Lane is S of village – telephone for further directions • Open May to July by appt • Entrance: £2, children 50p ● ▦ WC ⚲ ⬥ ⌀

The one-acre garden is informally laid out with grass paths running among well-planted beds. Some unusual trees and shrubs, interspersed with climbing roses and clematis, provide height; a good selection of ferns and grasses gives variety to the planting, but it is perennials that will impress most. This is the home of a National Collection of hardy geraniums (over 400 varieties), and the charm and versatility of the genus is well demonstrated. In woodland areas they mingle with dicentras, pulmonarias, anemones and many other shade-lovers; in sunnier areas they combine with large collections of euphorbias, poppies, campanulas and delphiniums followed by lythrums, sidalceas, phlox, eryngiums and many others. A pond is surrounded by banks of alpines, and a waterfall, stream and bog gardens are planted with candelabra primulas, irises, ligularias, astilbes and other water-loving plants. The smaller front garden is designed as a summer flower and rose garden.

Clearbeck House

Higher Tatham, Lancaster LA2 8PJ. Tel: (01524) 261029

Peter and Bronwen Osborne • 10m E of Lancaster. From M6 junction 34 take A683 towards Kirkby Lonsdale, turn right on B6480 and follow signposts from Wray village • Open for NGS 27th June, 4th July, 11.30am – 5.30pm, and for parties by appt • Entrance: £2, children free ● ■ ☕ ᇰ ⬦ ⬧ ☕

Art and water are the two key features of this garden, but there is plenty more in the way of plants, follies and landscaping. The old stone house has a large balcony where tea can be taken overlooking the garden; beneath is a terrace planted with shrubs and perennials – hebes, geraniums and heathers – and with an unusual glass sculpture. Below the terrace a large irregular lawn has grass paths radiating outwards. One path follows a series of ponds planted with water lilies down to a large wildlife lake with lush margins (75 bird species were noted last year), which has been extended to give an illusion of flowing under a bridge into the distance. There are two boathouses, one in the form of a cavern, its access down 'Ratty'-like steps from an alder avenue. Behind the larger pond is a Tuscan-order Temple of the Tall Trees, which is backed by a mount with a viewing point on top. A brick tower with a lancet window is open-fronted to give a view up to a further folly in the form of a monastic pillar. Another path leads to a pyramid, then on to a small secret garden with its own pool. Beyond a second, raised terrace are fine views over the garden and lake. There is a bog garden surrounding a small natural stream and throughout the garden many shrub roses, grasses and bamboos. But it is the sculpture that fits so well with the natural look of this distinctive garden.

Gawthorpe Hall [Historic Garden Grade II]

Padiham, Burnley BB12 8UA. Tel: (01282) 771004

Lancashire County Council (on lease from National Trust) • 2½ m NW of Burnley, N of A671 just E of Padiham town centre • Hall open April to Oct, daily except Mon and Fri (but open Good Friday and Bank Holiday Mons), 1 – 5pm • Gardens open all year, 10am – 6pm • Entrance: free (hall £3, concessions £1.50, children free) • Other information: Refreshments when hall open only
○ ■ ▒ **WC** ᇰ ⬦ ⬧ ▯ ☕

This garden, though botanically not particularly special, sets off the Elizabethan hall. To the front is a formal layout of lawns and gravel paths, and to the rear a parterre by Sir Charles Barry in the form of a sunburst overlooks the River Calder. The woodlands that surround the formal garden are planted with rhododendrons and azaleas and traversed by many walks, with views back to the house and across the valley.

Gresgarth Hall ★★

Caton LA2 9NB. Tel: (01524) 770313

Sir Mark and Lady Lennox-Boyd • 4m NE of Lancaster. From M6 junction 34 take A683 towards Kirkby Lonsdale, then turn right in Caton village, signed

'Quernmore' • Open 11th April, 9th May, 13th June, 11th July, 8th Aug, 12th Sept, 11am – 5pm • Entrance: £4 ◐ ☕ WC ♿ ✿

You expect something special from the garden of such a renowned designer as Arabella Lennox-Boyd, and you will not be disappointed. Over this large area she has experimented with different styles of gardening and produced some superb results – all the more surprising since the weather in this part of northern Lancashire can be harsh. At the front of the house are formal areas – herbaceous borders, protected by yew hedges, to the south a pool and bog garden with a large selection of moisture-lovers, including many ferns. An arboretum contains a large sequoiadendron, acers, lilacs and many other fine specimens, while the walled garden has a happy mix of vegetables, fruit and flowering plants. To the east an attractive terrace and belvedere overlook a rocky beck that rushes through this part of the garden. A Chinese bridge leads to a woodland garden where azaleas, cornus, magnolias and many unusual plants flourish in the light shade. Sculpture, classical and modern, is used creatively throughout. There are woodland walks, a huge variety of plants and so much else that this description can only serve as the briefest of introductions to a fine garden.

Hoghton Tower [Historic Garden Grade II]

Hoghton, Preston PR5 0SH. Tel: (01254) 852986

Hoghton Tower Preservation Trust • 5m SE of Preston, mid-way between Preston and Blackburn, on old A675 • House open for guided tours (£5, OAPs and students £4, children £4, family £12) • Garden open Bank Holiday Suns and Mons (except Christmas and New Year); also July to Sept, Mon – Thurs, 11am – 4pm, Sun, 1 – 5pm. Private tours by arrangement • Entrance: £2 ◑ ☕ ✕ WC ♿

Hoghton Tower, a sixteenth-century fortified manor house built of local stone, occupies a hilltop position with good views to all sides and outwards to the surrounding countryside. The house and outbuildings are constructed around two courtyards which, although not qualifying as gardens, are fine spaces. Surrounding the house are three walled gardens. The first, the Wilderness, contains a large lawn and herbaceous borders. The second, the rose garden, has a rectangular lawn flanked on two sides by clipped yews; in the centre is a raised square pond with an elaborate stone fountain. The third is mainly lawn with access to the tops of two crenellated towers. Around the walled gardens runs the Long Walk, which passes under large beech trees and holly trees (especially weeping hollies) and is planted with shrubs, mainly rhododendrons and azaleas. There is a tradition that Shakespeare lived here during a formative period, and James I knighted a piece of beef 'Sirloin' on 17th August 1617.

Leighton Hall

Carnforth LA5 9ST. Tel: (01524) 734474

Mr R.G. Reynolds • 8m N of Lancaster, 1m W of Yealand Conyers, signed from M6 junction 35 • Hall open • Gardens open May to Sept, Tues – Fri, Sun, 2 –

5pm (opens Aug 12.30 – 5pm) • Entrance: house and garden £5, OAPs £4.50, children £3.50, parties of 25 or more £4 per person, schools £3 per child (2003 prices) • Other information: Dogs in park only, on lead ◑ 🍵 🏠 WC ⅃ ⌘ 🏛 ⚑ ⚲

Very striking when first seen from the entrance gates, the white stone façade (c. 1822) shines out in its parkland setting with the hills of the Lake District visible beyond. The most interesting area of the gardens, which lie to the west of the house, is the walled garden with its unusual labyrinth in the form of a gravel path running under an old cherry orchard. Opposite is a vegetable garden made in a geometric design with grass paths. There are also herbaceous borders and an aromatic herb garden containing a wide variety of perennials, with climbing roses on the wall behind.

Lindeth Dene

38 Lindeth Road, Silverdale LA5 0TX. Tel: (01524) 701314

Mrs B.M. Kershaw • 12m N of Lancaster. From M6 junction 35, turn right at Carnforth traffic lights and follow signs to Silverdale; ¼ m after level crossing turn left into Hollins Lane. At T-junction turn right into Lindeth Road and continue to fourth gateway on left • Open by appt • Entrance: £1.50, accompanied children free ● ⅃ ⌾ ⚑

A garden of one and a quarter acres set in an area of beautiful countryside with fine views over Morecambe Bay. Informal in layout, much of the garden consists of a large limestone rock garden planted with a wide range of perennials and alpines; there are many saxifrages and geraniums, and in the shadier parts (some large mature trees at this end of the garden) hostas, epimediums and varieties of ferns. Close to the house away from the trees are beds containing dwarf conifers and other small shrubs, also a heather garden, stone troughs and an organic kitchen garden. There is much of interest for the plantsman and for anyone looking for planting ideas for a small garden. Be sure to visit the excellent nursery next door, which stocks a large range of plants, including ferns.

Mill Barn ★

Goose Foot Close, Samlesbury Bottoms, Preston PR5 0SS. Tel: (01254) 853300

Dr C.J. Mortimer • 6m E of Preston on A677 Blackburn road, turn S into Nabs Head Lane, then Goose Foot Lane • Open 13th, 14th, 20th, 21st June, 11am – 5pm, and for parties by appt • Entrance: £1.50, children free • Other information: 'Art and Garden' exhibition 13th, 14th June. Refreshments and plants for sale on open days ● 🍵 WC ⅃ ⌾ ⚑ ⚲ B&B

On the site of an old mill by the River Darwen, this garden has been designed to make the most of its superb setting. A path leads along a high stone embankment overlooking the fast-flowing river. It passes through a series of features: a unique temple to alchemy created from an old sluice gate, a rose-clad pergola, a picturesque ruin constructed to hide a septic tank. Near here a fine 'Paul's Himalayan Musk' rose climbs high up into a tree. Finally there is a rectangular pool set into the wall containing a good variety of water plants and marginals, with a stretch of lawn and an heptagonal summerhouse beyond. A long herbaceous border runs back to the house, containing plants chosen for their contrasting foliage and architectural effects. A bridge crosses the river giving access to a belvedere looking back over the garden. The quarry is becoming a secret garden in a modern style.

Pendle Heritage Centre

Park Hill, Barrowford, Nelson BB9 6JQ. Tel: (01282) 661701

The Heritage Trust for the North West • N of Nelson, near M65 junctions 13 and 14. In Barrowford at A682/B6247 junction • Open all year, daily except 25th Dec, 10am – 5pm. Parties welcome by appt • Entrance: Walled garden, barn and woodland £1.20, concessions 80p. Museum £1, concessions 80p

○ ☕ ✕ WC ♿ ⚘ ♨ 🔧 ♀ ❧

In the centre of Barrowford among a group of fine old stone buildings (eight Grade-II-listed) is a walled garden dating from the 1780s. This has been restored and replanted under the guidance of the NCCPG, using only plants that were available in the eighteenth century. There are culinary and medicinal herbs and plants that were used in the production of dyes, as well as traditional varieties of fruit and vegetables. All plants are organically grown in beds divided by gravel paths and edged in clipped box. A woodland walk takes the visitor up a steep wooded bank planted with native wild flowers to a viewing point that looks back over the garden and surrounding countryside to a cruck-frame barn saved and re-erected on the site.

The Ridges

Limbrick, Chorley PR6 9EB. Tel: (01257) 279981

Mr and Mrs J. M. Barlow • From M61 junction 8 follow signs for Chorley on A6, then for Cowling and Rivington • Open June and July, Wed and Bank Holiday Suns and Mons, 11am – 5pm (closed Easter); and by appt at other times • Entrance: £2.50, children free ● ☕ WC ♿ ◁▷ ♨ ❧ B&B

In the first area of the garden an herbaceous border contains hemerocallis and geraniums, shaded by fruit trees. The seventeenth-century house has French windows leading onto a small lawn – part of the old walled garden – where a small pool in one corner is set within paving, and two new arches over seating have been thoughtfully planted with jasmines, fragrant climbing roses and herbs. A path leads beneath a laburnum arch and between two large thujas into a large rectangular-lawned space surrounded by woodland, with beds of perennials, shrubs and trees. There is also a large Victorian glasshouse, a mock ornamental pond with a central urn, a water feature with ponds, and a stream fringed with wild flowers and moisture-loving plants.

Rivington Terraced Gardens

(see Manchester)

Rufford Old Hall

Rufford, Ormskirk L40 1SG. Tel: (01704) 821254

The National Trust • 7m NE of Ormskirk, N of Rufford, E of A59 • Hall and garden open 3rd April to 29th Oct, Sat – Wed, 11am – 5.30pm (hall opens 1pm, last admission 4.30pm) (telephone for winter opening times) • Entrance: £2, children £1 (house and garden £4.30, children £2) (2003 prices) ◑ ☕ ✕ 🍴 WC ⌐ 🅿 🔦 🐾

The gardens complement the exceptional sixteenth-century timber-framed house, having been laid out by the Trust in the style of the Victorian/ Edwardian period. On the south are lawns and gravel paths designed in a formal manner. The many island beds are formal in layout, too, but the shrubs, small trees and herbaceous plants they contain are planted in a more relaxed way. In the centre a path leads from two large topiary squirrels to a beech avenue that extends beyond the garden towards Rufford. There are many mature trees and rhododendrons in this area dating back to the 1820s. To the east of the house by the stables is an attractive cobbled space with climbing plants on the surrounding walls. Look out for the cottage garden to the north side of the house, in which grow many old-fashioned plants enclosed by a rustic wooden fence.

Swiss Cottage

8 Hammond Drive, Read, Burnley BB12 7RE. Tel: (01282) 774853

Mrs Doreen Bowker • 5m NW of Burnley on A671. In Read turn by Pollards Garage into George Lane, then at T-junction left into Hammond Drive • Open for parties by appt • Entrance: £2 per person ● ⌐ 🅿 🐾

A modern garden of one and a half acres set on a steeply sloping south-facing site. The west side is backed by mature woodland and planted to enhance the woodland feel. Small trees such as sorbus, salix, acers and birch are here as well as a *Cornus nuttallii*, a particular favourite of the owners. Beneath the trees are rhododendrons, azaleas, camellias and skimmias, while hostas, tiarellas, helle-bores and other shade-lovers fill the remaining space. Close to the centre of the garden a small stream rises and is taken through a series of rock pools bordered by beds of astilbes, irises and calthas; there is also a bed of grasses. The east side of the garden close to the house has irregularly shaped beds meandering down the slope, which is much steeper here. They are mulched with gravel as the owners find that this breaks up the Lancashire clay better than bark or other mulches. Dwarf conifers, alpines and sun-loving perennials like the conditions. The planting is well considered; there is good variety and inspiration here.

Towneley Park [Historic Park Grade II]

Todmorden Road, Burnley BB11 3RQ. Tel: (01282) 424213

Burnley Borough Council • 1½ m SE of Burnley on A671 • Hall open Mon – Thurs, 10am – 5pm, Sat, Sun, 12 noon – 5pm. Closed Christmas week • Park open all year, daily during daylight hours • Entrance: free • Other information: Shop in hall ○ 💽 🏵 <u>WC</u> � ⬦ 🎁 💡 ℃

The hall dates from 1500, but its exterior is largely the work of 1816 to 1820. The frontage looks out over a pond and beyond a ha-ha to open parkland laid out in the late eighteenth century. There are some formal beds to the east of the house planted with bright annuals. Herbaceous plants and shrubs have been chosen for the area around the hall, and the Small Lime Walk has been opened up by removing old rhododendrons, replacing them with a better selection of choice shrubs and ground cover. Further to the east, as well as to the south and west, are extensive woodlands containing many large rhododendrons, and long walks. There is also a museum of local crafts and industries, a nature centre and an aquarium.

Weeping Ash

Glazebury, Leigh, Manchester WA3 5NT.
Tel: (01942) 266303 (Bent's Garden Centre)

John Bent • 14m W of Manchester. Turn S off A580 at Greyhound Hotel roundabout onto A574 to Culcheth. Garden is $\frac{1}{4}$ m further on left • Open Feb to Nov, 3rd Sun in each month, 11am – 5.30pm • Entrance: £2, children free • Other information: Parking, teas, toilet facilities, plants for sale and shop at adjacent award-winning garden centre ● 💽 ✕ <u>WC</u> ⅆ 🎁 ℃

This garden has been created by a retired nurseryman, so it is only to be expected that a great variety of plants is found here. John Bent has a good collection of small trees, particularly sorbus, and many shrubs, especially roses. The herbaceous border is 90 metres long. There is a large range of perennials, including over 50 hellebores and many bulbs; one large bed is devoted to lilies. But it is his ideas on design that bring so much to the garden. Broad grass paths snake around the mixed beds and small offshoot paths give interesting views back into the main areas. There are views over the whole garden from a ruined Doric temple on a mound – a feature inspired during a visit to Cyprus. Many structures have been created as hosts to climbing plants, the best being a rustic gazebo built entirely from scrapwood, which is now covered by a passion flower and a golden hop.

Woodside

Princes Park, Shevington, Wigan, Manchester WN6 8HY. Tel: (01257) 255255

Barbara and Bill Seddon • 3m NW of Wigan. From M6 junction 26 or 27 follow signs for Shevington • Open by appt • Entrance: £1.50, children free ● 💽 🌿

This is a suburban garden of two thirds of an acre on an attractively undulating site, surrounded by mature trees. Broad grass paths designed to accentuate the landscaping lead round beds of mainly acid-loving plants – azaleas, small rhododendrons, camellias, magnolias, acers and conifers. Of particular note are collections of hostas, peonies and hellebores. An attractive water feature stands at the centre of the garden – a large stone trough with water bubbling up through stones guarded by a pair of ornamental geese. The well-established herbaceous border is delightful from mid-June until September, and in August dozens of hydrangeas and three mature *Eucryphia x nymansensis* are in flower. There is also a stone-banked dell excavated at one end of the garden and a waterfall. Everything is exeptionally well kept, and there is a surprising amount to see in what is not a vast garden. A recent addition is a well-planted gravel bed with driftwood features.

Worden Park [Historic Garden Grade II]

Leyland PR25 2DJ. Tel: (01772) 422316

Borough of South Ribble • 4m S of Preston. Take B5253 S from Leyland. Signposted • Open all year, daily, 8am – dusk • Entrance: free • Other information: Refreshments at craft centre ○ 💻 ✕ 🍽 WC ♿ ⏀ 🔦 🐾

The gardens are set around part of an old house and a stable block that now contains craft and theatre workshops (the rest of the house was burnt down in the 1940s). The maze is unusual, being made of hornbeam hedges in a circular pattern. A little distance away is a large conservatory with a rockery to one side and a herbaceous border to the other. They face a formal sunken lawned area enclosed by a low balustrade and some fine ironwork gates. Large areas of open parkland surround the gardens, which contain a children's adventure play area, mini golf, a model railway, an ice-house and an arboretum. Areas in the parkland are being developed to attract wildlife. Full events programme (some without charge) – telephone for details.

2005 GUIDE

The 2005 *Guide* will be published before Christmas 2004. Reports on gardens for consideration are welcome at all times of the year, but particularly by early summer (May 2004) so that they can be inspected that year.

GARDENING WEBSITES

Many gardens now have their own websites, and we list these at the back of the Guide. Others useful for garden visitors are:

Dept of Environment (Ireland): www.heritageireland.ie
English Heritage: www.english-heritage.org.uk
Historic Houses Association: www.hha.org.uk
Historic Royal Palaces: www.hrp.org.uk
Historic Scotland: www.historic-scotland.gov.uk
Landmark Trust: www.landmarktrust.org.uk
National Gardens Scheme: www.ngs.org.uk
National Trust: www.nationaltrust.org.uk
National Trust for Scotland: www.nts.org.uk
Royal Horticultural Society: www.rhs.org.uk
Welsh Historic Monuments: www.cadw.wales.gov.uk

LEICESTERSHIRE

For gardens in Rutland, see pages 334–5.

Beeby Manor ★

Beeby LE7 3BL. Tel: (01162) 595238

Mr and Mrs Philip Bland • 5m E of Leicester. Turn off A47 in Thurnby and follow signs through Scraptoft • Open by appt • Entrance: £2 ● 🍵 🍽 WC ♿

Three acres of mature gardens in the form of a series of romantic rooms enclosed by lofty yew hedges, with roses everywhere in soft colours on frames and mellow walls or tumbling through arbours. A parterre leads to formal lily ponds and exuberant herbaceous borders which are overblown and carefully untidy. An arboretum is under development. This is a charming Old English garden in the grandest cottage style, evoking a bygone age. The attractively designed *Kaye's Garden and Nursery*, on the A607 at 1700 Melton Road, Rearsby, has a collection of interesting and unusual plants for sale [open March to Oct, daily, 10am – 5pm, and Sun, 10am – 12 noon].

Belvoir Castle [Historic Garden Grade II]

Belvoir, Grantham, Lincolnshire NG32 1PD. Tel: (01476) 871002

The Duke of Rutland • 10m NE of Melton Mowbray off A607 by Belvoir. Signposted • Castle open • Garden open April, May, June, Sept, daily except Mon and Fri; July, Aug, daily; all 11am – 5pm (last admission 4pm). Spring garden open all year for pre-booked parties • Entrance: castle and garden £7, OAPs £6.50, children £4.50, family £19. Spring garden £5, OAPs £4.50 per person for pre-booked parties of 20 to 40 persons (2003 prices) ● 🍵 ✕ 🍽 WC ♿ 🏛 🍴 ⚲

The castle, straddling an isolated hill at the edge of the Vale of Belvoir, is the third to occupy this dramatic natural belvedere. The first was eleventh-century Norman, the second a mid-seventeenth-century house by John Webb with a remarkable sloping formal garden. All were swept away at the beginning of the nineteenth century, and James Wyatt's mock Gothic castle for the 5th Duke stands in their stead. On her return from the Grand Tour in 1819 the Duchess redesigned the garden in the Renaissance manner. By the mid-nineteenth century terraced gardens had been created, divided into smaller enclosures by the discreet use of topiary and hedging. During the 1870s spring bedding was introduced; now various areas are devoted to roses, peonies and daylilies, and elsewhere snowdrops and daylilies are naturalised. In the early twentieth century the rose garden was laid out and yew hedges were planted around two sides of the garden. To the north-east runs a curving terrace path, probably the broadwalk depicted in Badeslade's view of 1731; some of the Caius Cibber statues which lined it are now in the Statue Garden. The present Duchess is moving the restoration and upkeep of these historic gardens forward with great care and taste. Her private woodland garden, known as the Spring Garden, was laid out in 1810; it is set in a natural amphitheatre and contains statuary and a recently restored hexagonal root house dating from 1841.

Goadby Hall

Goadby Marwood, Melton Mowbray LE14 4LN. Tel: (01664 464202

Mr and The Hon. Mrs Westropp • 4m NE of Melton Mowbray between A606 and A607 • Open by appt only • Entrance: £3 • Other information: Teas by arrangement NEW 🦽 WC ᕗ ⟁ ☕ B&B

The approach to this exciting and romantic garden is at the head of a string of ornamental lakes extending to over a mile. These have been meticulously restored to the beauty the Duke of Buckingham must have imagined when he created them in the eighteenth century. Surrounding the handsome 1760s' manor house is a variety of separate gardens: a children's garden leads to the croquet lawn, then past the church to the secret rose and west walled gardens. There is also a *potager* and a recently restored stable garden, and a small orchard. All have been brought back to life over the past three years with the love, imagination and hard work of the knowledgeable owner, who worked for some time with Rosemary Verey.

Long Close ★

**Main Street, Woodhouse Eaves, Loughborough LE12 8RZ.
Tel: (01509) 890616 (business hours)**

Mr J.T. Oakland and Miss P. Johnson • 5m S of Loughborough between A6 and M1 junctions 22 and 23 • Open March to July, Sept to Oct, Mon – Sat, 9.30am – 1pm, 2 – 5.30pm, and two Suns for NGS. Parties by appt • Entrance: £3, children 50p • Other information: Tickets for daily visits to be purchased from Pene Crafts gift shop opposite the garden. Park in adjacent public car park. Teas on NGS open days, and for parties by arrangement only ◐ WC ᕗ ⟁ ⌷ 🏛

When Mr and Mrs George Johnson bought Long Close in 1949, they began to restore the five-acre garden, based on the framework and potential left by their predecessor, Colonel Gerald Heygate. Taking advantage of the lime-free loam, they nurtured a large collection of rhododendrons, azaleas and magnolias, which are now in magnificent maturity, adding many camellias and other shrubs and trees. Formal terraces lead to more informal gardens, with winding paths between specimen trees and finally to a natural dappled pool. In spring there are drifts of snowdrops, daffodils and bluebells and in summer prolifically planted herbaceous borders. The present owners have extended the plantings and created a *potager* and penstemon collection in the old walled kitchen garden. A courtyard plays its sheltered part with magnificent wall-covering plants. This is sometimes described as a Cornish garden in Leicestershire due to the many quite tender trees and plants rarely to be found elsewhere so far north. Truly a plantsman's garden. For contrast, stroll along the ancient pasture wildflower meadow walk.

Orchards ★

Hall Lane, Walton, Lutterworth LE17 5RP. Tel: (01455) 556958

Mr and Mrs G. Cousins • 10m S of Leicester, 4m E of Lutterworth. Leave M1 at junction 20 signed to Lutterworth, then follow signs to Walton • Open 22nd, 23rd, 30th, 31st May, 26th, 27th June, 24th, 25th July, 21st, 22nd Aug, 2 – 5pm, and at other times by appt • Entrance: £2, children free ● ⬤ WC & ⚘

Tucked away behind a modern bungalow, this garden is a success story. There are ideas here that relate to almost any medium-sized plot in town or country – a round pool surrounded by a circle of trees, old brick paths, views through sculpted walks, vistas terminating in unusual artistic arrangements. Most notable is the series of colour-themed gardens full of rare and unusual plants, with views of the countryside beyond.

Stoke Albany House

Stoke Albany, Market Harborough LE16 8PT. Tel: (01858) 535227

Mr and Mrs Alfred Vinton • 4m E of Market Harborough. Turn S off A427 onto B669. Garden ½ m on left • Open 4th April, (Daffodil Sunday), 12th, 19th, 26th May, 2nd, 9th, 16th, 23rd, 30th June, 7th, 14th July, all 2 – 4.30pm, and for parties by appt • Entrance: £2.50, children free • Other information: Teas on Daffodil Sun only ● & ⚘ ☕

A country-house garden set in four acres with picturesque landscape sweeping beyond. There are fine trees and wide herbaceous borders, striped lawns, good displays of bulbs in spring and roses in June. The walled grey garden shows splashes of white, and the clever avenue of *Nepeta* 'Six Hills Giant' has 'Mme Alfred Carrière' roses skilfully trained over arches. A rose-filled box parterre, a *potager*, topiary, a beautifully maintained greenhouse, a new water feature and a Mediterranean garden – tradition brought up to date in a perfect English setting.

Wartnaby Gardens ★

Wartnaby, Melton Mowbray LE14 3HY. Tel: (01664) 822296

Lord and Lady King • 4m NW of Melton Mowbray. From A606 turn W in Ab Kettleby for Wartnaby • Open April to July, Tues, 9.30am – 12.30pm, and by appt • Entrance: £2.50, children free • Other information: Plant sale 27th April, plant fair and picture exhibition 20th June ● ⬤ 🗋 WC & ⬥ ⚘

The garden has delightful little gardens within it, including a white garden, a rose garden, a purple border of shrubs and roses, good herbaceous borders, climbers and old-fashioned roses. Two large pools with primulas, ferns, astilbes and several varieties of willow extend to further pools and woodland walks. There is an arboretum with a good collection of trees and shrubs. A long drive leads to the house, with an avenue of lime trees underplanted with beech hedging in a crenellated pattern. To round it all off is a well-furnished kitchen garden and orchard with arches and a collection of climbing roses and clematis.

LINCOLNSHIRE

Aubourn Hall ★

Aubourn, Lincoln LN5 9DZ. Tel: (01522) 788270

Lady Nevile • 7m SW of Lincoln between A46 and A607 • Open for charity 18th April, 16th May, 13th June, 5th Sept, 2 – 5pm, and for parties by appt (telephone (0781) 6202 353) • Entrance: £3 • Other information: plants sometimes for sale ◑ 🍽 WC ⅋ ♨

First impressions of the 10 acres of gardens at this lovely red-brick hall (c. 1600) are of spacious simplicity. Glorious undulating lawns and borders sweep through rose arches or along grassy swathes to further lawns and gardens beyond. The enviably deep and diverse borders are carefully planted to give maximum effects of colour, shape and texture. There are also secluded areas in which to linger: the formal rose garden with its fine central tiered copper planter, the Golden Triangle edged with yew and planted with ornamental crab apple trees and spring bulbs, the ponds, the woodland dell and walks, and the swimming pool surrounded by a rose- and clematis-covered pergola. The nearby church, one of the smallest in Lincolnshire, is also open to visitors on garden open days.

Ayscoughfee Hall [Historic Garden Grade II]

Churchgate, Spalding PE11 2RA. Tel: (01775) 725468

South Holland District Council • In centre of Spalding • Hall open March to Oct, daily, 9am – 5pm (Sat opens 10am, Sun 11am), Nov to Feb, Mon – Fri, 9am – 5pm. Closed 25th Dec, 1st Jan • Gardens open all year, daily, 8am – dusk. Closed 25th Dec, 1st Jan • Entrance: free • Other information: Refreshments in main season ○ 🍵 🛍 WC ⅋ 🛬 ⛲ ♨

The gardens of this late-medieval wool merchant's house are in a beautiful setting next to the River Welland. Entirely enclosed by lovely old walls, they are worth visiting for the bizarrely shaped clipped yew walks, the old rectangular fish pond with fountains, and the fascinating late-medieval red-brick hall, now housing the Museum of South Holland Life, with displays on the history of bulb growing in the Fens. In addition there are good bedding displays, particularly in the 1995 Garden of Peace, an ice-house, a garden for the visually impaired, lawns, a pergola and wall shrubs, including a fruiting vine. Nearby is the *Pinchbeck Engine and Land Drainage Museum* – a reminder of how the Fens achieved and maintained their prosperity.

Belton House ★ [Historic Garden Grade I]

Belton, Grantham NG32 2LS. Tel: (01476) 566116

The National Trust • 3m N of Grantham off A607 • House open 12.30 – 5pm • Gardens open 31st March to Oct, Wed – Sun and Bank Holiday Mons, 11am – 5.30pm. Free access to park on foot from Lion Lodge gates all year (closed for

special events), but this does not give admittance to house, garden or adventure playground • *Entrance: house and gardens £6.50, children £3, family £15*
◑ ☕ ✕ 🍴 <u>WC</u> ♿ ⛪ 🔦 ⚲

The park and gardens are, like the house, composed with perfect harmony and proportion. Serenity, order, and strong architectural conviction are the keynotes. The house itself is superb in its own right, but there are also good views from first-floor windows of the formal gardens and of the East Avenue rising imperiously to the distant Bellmount Tower. The extensive woodland has two lakes, a small canal and noble cedars, and a maze re-created from the 1890 original. The radiating avenues are an impressive reminder of the late seventeenth- and early eighteenth-century predilection for introducing drama into the landscape. However, it is the formal area to the north of the house that makes a visit memorable. The 1870s' Dutch garden is a satisfying composition with pillars of green yew and cushions of golden yew, pale gravel, formal beds cleverly planted and edged with lavender, and generously filled urns. The earlier sunken Italian garden is more reliant on Wyatville's architectural features: a large central pond with a fountain, a lion-headed exedra and, the high point, the superbly restored and replanted orangery. Behind the orangery a little church is glimpsed; it is filled with memorials to generations of Custs, who built the house, and Brownlows, who created the garden.

Belvoir Castle

(see Leicestershire)

Burghley House [Historic Park and Garden Grade II*]

Stamford PE9 3JY. Tel: (01780) 752451

Burghley House Preservation Trust. Custodian: Lady Victoria Leatham (née Cecil) • ½ m E of Stamford on Barnack road, close to A1. Signposted • House open, daily, April to Oct, 11am – 4.30pm • Sculpture garden and parkland open daily, 10am – 5pm (closes 4pm in winter); South Garden open April • Entrance: free except weekends in June, July, Aug, then £2, children free (house £7.50, OAPs £6.80, children £3.70) (2003 prices) • Other information: Limited access for wheelchairs. Dogs in park only, on lead ◑ ☕ ✕ 🍴 <u>WC</u> ♿ ⟳ ⛪ 🔦 ⚲

The main attraction at Burghley is the magnificent Elizabethan house with its immense collection of art treasures, built by William Cecil, created Lord Burghley by his Queen. The parkland, landscaped by 'Capability' Brown, is delightful and extensive, even though in the process he swept away the George London Baroque garden of 1700 which had 'canals, rising flights of terraces, ornamental fish-pools, a maze, a vineyard and other conceits'. In addition to creating a large serpentine lake, Brown built a new stable block and an orangery. The finest surviving small building is his recently restored lakeside 'temple', which can be seen while the South Garden is open for its spectacular display of spring flowers in April. Twelve acres of garden have been reclaimed from woodland in recent years and extensively planted with specimen trees and shrubs. This area has an annually changing display of contemporary sculpture alongside a number of permanent site-specific sculptures, one of the most dramatic being a group emerging Excalibur-like from the surface of the lake.

21 Chapel Street

Hacconby, Bourne PE10 0UL. Tel: (01778) 570314

Mr and Mrs C. Curtis • 3m N of Bourne off A15, turn E at crossroads to Hacconby • Open 21st, 22nd Feb, 11am – 4pm (snowdrop and hellebore weekend), 4th March, 2 – 6pm, 12th April, 11am – 5pm, 3rd June, 5 – 9pm, 5th Aug, 2nd Sept, 2 – 6pm, 3rd Oct, 11am – 5pm; and at other times by appt • Entrance: £1, children (under 16) free (2003 prices) ◑ ◙ WC ✿

The gay and cottagey impression of this village garden has been achieved by minimising lawn area and replacing it with planting space. The circuitous path passes rockeries and scree beds, small trees and shrub roses, rustic arches, troughs and a pond, all exuberantly planted and underplanted to ensure year-round colour, from snowdrops in February to red, yellow and gold herbaceous plants in late summer and asters extending the season into October. There are hundreds of varieties of bulbs, alpines and herbaceous plants here to satisfy both the casual gardener and the seeker of the rare.

Croft House

Pitmoor Lane, Ulceby, Brigg DN39 6SW. Tel: (01469) 588330

Mr and Mrs P. Sandberg • 9m NW of Grimsby, 7m SE of Barton-upon-Humber on A1077 • Open for NGS, and by appt • Entrance: £2, children under 12 free • Other information: Refreshments by arrangement and plants for sale on open days ◑ ◙ & ✿

Although set within a formal design of high walls, clipped *Lonicera nitida* hedges, a pergola walk and gravel paths, this two-acre garden could not seem less formal. The eclectic planting of old favourites among sought-after varieties gives a refreshingly cottagey air, intensified by flowers allowed to seed freely in the gravel. In fact the owners have a rare affection for garden 'thugs', using them to advantage throughout the garden. There is a tiny, paved secret garden with an unusual thyme table, and many other features and areas of interest, including mixed, herbaceous and woodland borders, a meadow, a gravel bed, a loggia and a Victorian vinery.

Doddington Hall [Historic Garden Grade II*]

Doddington, Lincoln LN6 4RU. Tel: (01522) 694308

Mr and Mrs A.G. Jarvis • 5m W of Lincoln on B1190 • House open May to Sept • Garden open 15th Feb to April, Sun only; May to Sept, Wed, Sun and Bank Holiday Mons; all 2 – 6pm. Parties at other times by appt • Entrance: £3.60, children £1.80 (house and garden £5.20, children £2.60, family £14.50), special rates for disabled in wheelchairs and parties of 20 or more ◑ ◙ WC & ♨ ✦ ✾

The romantic gardens of the Elizabethan house are a successful combination of many different styles and moods. The simplicity of the gravel, box and lawned courtyard – with its paired yews and topiary unicorns from the Jarvis family crest – and of the croquet lawn, pleached hornbeams and gravel walk along the kitchen garden wall contrast with the walled west garden, restored in Elizabethan style in 1900. Here are elaborate parterres of roses and irises edged with box, and good herbaceous borders. The lower terrace has two octagonal ponds and beds of flag irises; from here fine eighteenth-century Italian gates open onto an enclosed lawn and a formal yew *allée*, with an avenue of limes beyond. The yews make a fine transition to the wild garden, where meandering walks take in a turf maze, a stream, ancient specimens of sweet chestnut, cedar, yew and holly, and a Temple of the Winds designed and built by the present owner. The explosion of spring bulbs starts in time for the February openings, when rhododendrons are in flower along with the snow-drops.

The Garden House

42 Wragby Road, Bardney LN3 5XL. Tel: (01526) 397307

Lee and Peter Heykoop • 10m E of Lincoln on B1202 • Open 6th, 27th June, 11th July, 30th Aug, and by appt • Entrance: £2, children free NEW 🅿 WC ⅋ ℗

Conventional design rules have been consciously ignored in this relatively small garden and nursery. There are no obvious focal points, defined edges, traditionally grouped and stepped plantings or secret areas; instead the deep borders, planted with a mainstay of grasses and unusual herbaceous perennials, are designed to create sensuous waves of light, colour and movement. Like a series of veils, the grasses diffuse the often hot colours and tempt the eye through and beyond, giving an illusion of boundless natural landscape. Plants with similar demands are grown together, and by establishing a damp area next to a surprisingly formal pond and by exploiting different aspects and shady spots, the range has been greatly extended.

Goltho House

Lincoln Road, Goltho LN8 5NF. Tel: (01673) 857768

Mr and Mrs S. Hollingworth • 10m E of Lincoln on A158, 1m on left before reaching Wragby • Open for NGS, and by appt • Entrance: £2 • Other information: Teas on open days and by arrangement ● ⅋ ℗

This 4½-acre garden was only started in 1998, but already looks established and holds out much promise for the future. A long grass walk flanked by abundantly planted mixed borders forms a focal point; paths and walkways span out to other features – a nut walk, planted mostly for spring interest, an experimental prairie border, a small woodland area (still in its infancy, but maturing) and a stunning wildflower meadow. Nearer the house and its range of interesting old farm buildings lies a large pond area, still undergoing development, a peony and iris garden and a delightful rose garden. In contrast to the large-scale effect of the garden as a whole, the *potager*, with its brick and stone paths and geometric planting, offers an intimate experience of a wide variety of herbs and vegetables. The garden is laid out with a strong feeling for colour, form and texture in flowers and foliage, and reflects the owners' interest in a wide range of plants, many of them rare. Future plans include the development of a winter walk and a dry garden.

Grimsthorpe Castle [Historic Garden Grade I]

Grimsthorpe, Nr Bourne PE10 0LY. Tel: (01778) 591205

Grimsthorpe and Drummond Castle Trust Ltd • 4m NW of Bourne on A151 Colsterworth – Bourne road • Castle open 1pm, last admission 4.30pm • Garden open April to July, Sept, Thurs, Sun; Aug, Sun – Thurs; all 11am – 6pm • Entrance: Park and garden £3.50, OAPs £3, children £2 (additional £3.50 for castle, OAPs £3) ◑ 🖳 ✕ 🖼 WC ⅄ ⬳ 🏚 ⬣ ⚲

The impressive house, part-medieval, part-Tudor and part-eighteenth-century, with a dramatic forecourt and north front by Vanbrugh, is surrounded on three sides by good pleasure gardens in which 'Capability' Brown had a hand. The Victorian knot garden to the east of the house has beds of lavender, roses and catmint with edges of clipped box. To the south are two yew-hedged gardens with topiary, a yew broad walk and a retreat. Leading to the west terrace is a double yew walk with classic herbaceous borders; beyond is a shrub rose border and a row of 70-year-old cedars. The yew hedging throughout the garden is superbly maintained and differs in design from one area to another. Beyond the pleasure gardens is an arboretum, a wild garden, an unusual geometrically designed kitchen garden with clipped box and bean pergola, and extensive parkland. Views of the old oak and chestnut avenues and of the parkland with its lake and Vanbrugh summerhouse are provided by cleverly positioned vistas and terraces.

Gunby Hall ★ [Historic Park and Garden Grade II]

Gunby, Spilsby PE23 5SS. Tel: (01909) 486411

The National Trust • 7m NW of Skegness, $2\frac{1}{2}$ m NW of Burgh-le-Marsh on S of A158 • Hall and garden open, Wed, 2 – 6pm • Garden open 31st March to Sept, Wed, Thurs, 2 – 6pm, and Tues, Fri by written appt to Mr and Mrs J.D. Wrisdale. Coaches and parties pre-book in writing • Entrance: £2.70, children £1.30, family £6.70 (hall and garden £3.80, children £1.90, family £9.50) • Other information: Possible for wheelchairs but some gravel paths; no wheelchair access to hall ◑ 🖼 WC ⅄ ⬳ 🍃 ⬣ ⚲

The charming William and Mary house, its walls smothered in fine plants, sits in parkland with avenues of lime and horse chestnut. The shrub borders, wild garden, lawns with old cedars and restrained formal front garden of catmint and lavender beds backed by clipped yew provide a startling contrast to the main attraction of Gunby – its walled gardens. The dazzling pergola garden with its apple-tree walkway has a maze of paths leading to beds of old roses, a herb garden and brimming herbaceous and annual borders. The second walled area houses an impressive kitchen garden reached after passing more borders of perfectly arranged herbaceous plants and hybrid musk roses. Backing onto its wall is another wonderfully classic herbaceous border and, beyond that an early-nineteenth-century long fish pond, a focal point for walks on either side. This is a gorgeous garden. It is fitting that it was the subject of Tennyson's *Haunt of Ancient Peace*.

Hall Farm and Nursery ★

Harpswell, Gainsborough DN21 5UU. Tel: (01427) 668412

Mr and Mrs M. Tatam • 7m E of Gainsborough on A631 • Open all year, daily (for winter weekend opening please telephone to check), plus 5th Sept for NGS (with free seed collection), 10am – 5.30pm. Also by appt • Entrance: donation to charity • Other information: Coaches by appt. Teas on charity open day only ○ WC & ✿ ♔

This garden combines the formal and the informal in a most imaginative way. The owners' sheer delight in plants, satisfied by their adjoining nursery, is evident everywhere; there are hundreds of varieties of unusual herbaceous plants, roses and shrubs. A rose pergola leads from a decorative paved terrace to the main area behind the farmhouse. Subdivided into six separate areas, each with at least two entry points, the whole becomes a fascinating maze of garden rooms linked by border-edged paths and pergolas; they include a walled top terrace, a formal double border walk, a sunken garden with seasonal planting and an informal area with a wildlife pond. A newly planted orchard includes a giant chessboard and set of chessmen. A short walk away is an interesting medieval moat.

Harrington Hall [Historic Garden Grade II]

Harrington, Spilsby PE23 4NH. Tel: (01790) 754570 (Gardener)

Mr and Mrs D.W.J. Price • 5m E of Horncastle, 2m N of A158 • Open 6th, 27th June, 18th July, 8th Aug, 2 – 5pm • Entrance: £2, children free ◑ ☕ WC ◁▷ ✿

Given an idyllic setting in the Wolds, the mellow red-brick walls of the Tudor and seventeenth-century hall provide the perfect backdrop for a great variety of superb wall shrubs, climbers and deep herbaceous borders. No visitor would guess that the hall itself was practically destroyed by fire during the tenure of the present owners. Referred to in Tennyson's *Maud*, it is hard to imagine that these romantic gardens, walks and terraces have ever changed, although they were in fact replanted during the 1950s after a spell of wartime vegetable cultivation. Ironically, the one-acre kitchen garden immediately east of the house is a much more recent restoration. Formal in design and subdivided by a variety of hedges and paths, it is a happy combination of the functional and the purely decorative, with excellent trained fruit trees, borders and a raised sitting area with a pond. With the recent opening of two new areas, these gardens rank again amongst the best in Lincolnshire.

25 High Street

Rippingale, Bourne PE10 0SR. Tel: (01778) 440693

Mr and Mrs Beddington • 6m N of Bourne off A15 • Open 14th, 15th Feb in conjunction with Manor Farm, Keisby (see entry)(hellebore and snowdrop Sat and Sun), 11am – 4pm, and at other times by appt • Entrance: £1.50, children free • Other information: Refreshments and plants for sale on open days only
● ➤ WC & ↻

What at first seems a small informal garden of lawn, borders and island beds in fact provides half an acre of many delightful surprises. There are shady paths and secret corners, a bog garden, ponds, pergola and paved areas, and through a small gate an inspirational vegetable garden complete with a fruit cage and rhubarb pots. The assiduous care of the knowledgeable owners ensures a display of unusual herbaceous plants, shrubs and bulbs throughout the year. With its almost exclusively pastel palette, gentle curves and emphasis on wildlife habitats, the garden invites the visitor to linger and absorb its tranquillity.

The Lawn

**Sir Joseph Banks Conservatory, Union Road, Lincoln LN1 3BL.
Tel: (01522) 873629.**

Lincoln City Council • Off Burton Road beside Lincoln Castle • Open all year, Thurs – Sun, 10am – 5pm (closes earlier Fri and in winter) • Entrance: free, but parking charge ○ ➤ ▤ WC & ↻

When Lincoln City Council bought this disused Georgian mental hospital in 1985 they aimed to establish a botanic collection to represent Lincoln's partnership with cities and countries around the world. Central to this is the Sir Joseph Banks conservatory. Here, an excellent use of water, and arrangements of plants in areas corresponding with parts of the world visited by Banks on his three-year voyage with Captain Cook, have made this small area both exotic and interesting. The nearby walled *John Dawber Garden* continues this international theme, with mini-gardens representing England, Germany, China and Australia.

Lincoln Contemporary Heritage Garden

Medieval Bishops Palace, Minster Yard, Lincoln LN2 1PU. Tel: (01522) 527468

English Heritage • On S side of Lincoln Cathedral • Open April to Sept, daily, 10am – 6pm (closes 5pm in Oct); Nov to March, Wed – Sun, 10am – 4pm. Closed 24th, 25th, 26th Dec, 1st Jan • Entrance: £3.20, children £1.60, OAPs £2.40 (2003 prices) NEW ○ ➤ ▤ ↻ ▥ ♨ ↻

Mark Anthony Walker's heritage garden is a landscaper's answer to the New York loft conversion. In this case an antique terrace, first recorded as a garden site in 1320, has been given a pure and uncluttered design which must surely convert the anti-modernist. Deceptively simple, it makes clever allusion to the garden's history, linking it perfectly to the surrounding ruins and nearby cathedral. Brick paths create a lattice pattern across a lawn, and fastigiate hornbeams have been planted within steel discs at the intersections. Like the ribs and bosses of the cathedral's vaulted ceilings which inspired the design, the lattice succeeds in resolving the problem of asymmetry created by the irregular quadrilateral site. Clipped lavender and the red 'Guinée' rose give localised colour. The garden may be enjoyed from two seats set in yew niches, but the best views are from the East Hall terrace above, where the full impact of what is in effect a contemporary knot garden can be appreciated. The entry charge includes access to the palace ruins and the superb vineyard on a lower terrace.

32 Main Street

Dyke, Bourne PE10 0AF. Tel: (01778) 422241

Mr and Mrs D. Sellars • 1m N of Bourne, off A15 • Open by appt; parties especially welcome • Entrance: £1, children 25p ◐ ⚘

This small area (30 x 15 metres) is subdivided into tiny compartments allowing an astonishing number of planting schemes. Every available space is crammed with a choice plant, ornament, trough or architectural feature. The majority of plants are grown in concealed pots, allowing schemes to be changed throughout the growing season. An interesting and unusual garden which reflects the owners' involvement with display gardens at Chelsea.

Manor Farm

Keisby, Lenton, Bourne PE10 0RZ. Tel: (01476) 585607

Mr and Mrs C.A. Richardson • 9m NW of Bourne, N of A151 between Lenton and Hawthorpe • Open 14th, 15th Feb (snowdrop and hellebore weekend), 11am – 4pm, and 27th June, 2 – 5pm, for charity • Entrance: £2 ◐ ⚑ WC ⟨♿⟩ ⚘

Artistically planned and planted in harmonious colours, this pretty, informal garden is a delight. The tiny paths to the pergola, the stream and the one formal area of herbaceous beds and clipped yews meander through the garden, allowing close inspection of the many choice plants, including perennials, shrub roses, ramblers and clematis. A walk along the stream bank leads to a new half-acre garden made in a former farmyard. In complete contrast to the cottagey style of the original, this open, south-facing area of lawns, gravel and beds is hot and continental in feeling. Here the emphasis is on outdoor living, with sitting areas and a gazebo from which to enjoy the variety of grasses and sun-loving plants. There is also a large collection of hellebores and snowdrops, plus other rarities for the plantsperson.

Normanby Hall

Normanby Hall Country Park, Normanby, Scunthorpe DN15 9HU. Tel: (01724) 720588

North Lincolnshire Council • 4m N of Scunthorpe on B1430 • Hall and Farm Museum open April to Oct, daily, 1 – 5pm • Park open all year, daily, 9am – 5pm (closes 9pm in summer). Victorian walled garden open daily except 25th

Dec, 1st Jan, 10.30am – 5pm (4pm in winter) • Entrance: hall, gardens and farm museum £4, concessions £3, family £11. Season tickets available (2003 prices) ○ ⬛ ✕ 🖼 **WC** ♿ ⬤ ⌖ ♨ 🍴 💡 ℺

The Regency hall designed by Sir Robert Smirke is set in 300 acres of parkland boasting some fine mature trees, including a grand old holm oak looking like a surreal climbing frame and good avenues of copper beech and Wellingtonia. There are also woodland and stream walks, a bog garden and an accessible deer park. Elsewhere great improvements have been made to restore the pleasure gardens to their former beauty and to give year-round interest. The formal garden south of the hall includes a 'boar's head' parterre and a sunken garden with a rectangular pond surrounded by pastel borders. Further away are two gardens enclosed by tall old walls and holly and conifer hedges. The first secret garden has good wall shrubs and climbers; double herbaceous borders planted Gertrude-Jekyll-fashion move from hot to cool colours. The second is a lavish restoration of the original Victorian kitchen garden, complete with potting shed, bothy, vinery, fern house and display house. Fruit trees are trained against the walls – those in the south-facing peach cases are under glass. There are decorative borders and four box-edged plots filled with fruit and vegetables which are sold in season. All varieties here are true to the period, organic, and as far as possible grown using Victorian techniques.

The Old Rectory

Church Lane, East Keal, Spilsby PE23 4AT. Tel: (01790) 752477

Mrs R.F. Ward • 12m W of Skegness, 2m SW of Spilsby on A16 • Open 4th April, 6th May, 6th June, 29th Aug, 2 – 5pm, and by appt • Entrance: £2, children free ◑ ⬛ **WC**

Nestled on a hillside in the beautiful Wolds, this gorgeous three-quarter-acre garden boasts possibly the best views of all those listed in Lincolnshire. It has been planted by the owners to complement the many old walls, paved areas and yew hedges. There are paths everywhere – grass, brick, stone and granite-sett – all meandering from one delight to another. Essentially the garden is cottagey, with lawn kept to a minimum and masses of flowers tumbling over rockeries, ponds, borders and retaining walls. The one formal border, edged with box, sings out with hot bedding – exotic tulips when visited in spring. Great efforts are made not to repeat planting in the different areas, which results in a wide variety of plants for the enthusiast to appreciate. There is also an extensive vegetable garden, an orchard, a rhododendron walk and a swimming pool area converted into an enclosed pool garden with a bog surround.

Pinefields

Main Street, Bigby, Barnetby DN38 6ER. Tel: (01652) 628327

Mr and Mrs R. Hill • 10m SE of Scunthorpe, 4m E of Brigg off A1084 • Open 23rd June to 4th July, Wed – Sun, 1.30 – 5.30pm, and for parties by appt • Entrance: £2 • Other information: Plants on sale from specialist delphinium nursery on open days ◑ ⬛ 🖼 **WC** ♨

The rear of this simple-fronted village garden comes as a refreshing surprise. By capitalising on its length and cross-slope to give two levels, a potentially awkward ¾-acre site has been transformed into a garden full of interest. From a paved terrace, sloped gravel beds lead to lawn paths and mixed borders crammed with covetable specimens. An informal pond acts as a pivot, opening up to a formal area of clipped box and gravel paths, a pergola, a wild garden and a delphinium bed where at least 30 different colours are displayed. Lacking the advantage of old walls for the many climbers grown here, support is provided by pillars with swagged ropes, trellises and obelisks.

4 Ringwood Close

Birchwood, Lincoln LN6 OLN. Tel: (01522) 683960

Margaret and John Brown • 2m SW of Lincoln. From A46 Lincoln by-pass take Skellingthorpe Road, signed to Birchwood. Turn right at traffic lights, then first right and first right again • Open 27th June, 25th July, and May to Sept for individuals and parties of 10 or more by appt • Entrance: £2 NEW ● ☕ 🌵

For many, gardening on the edge of a wood could be dispiriting, but here the owners have used their sylvan backdrop to enhance the colour and composition of their young planting. From a paved driveway with planters and conifers, the ⅓-acre back garden sweeps away into the distance, encompassing very different growing conditions. A damp shaded courtyard allows hostas, ferns and acers to flourish, while the dry wide borders flanking the meandering lawn paths contain an exciting mix of desirable herbaceous plants, roses, shrubs and grasses. The recently planted Blue Garden, a final project for a design course, provides a perfect spot in which to sit and contemplate the different areas.

Springtyme

Station Road, Sibsey, Nr Boston PE22 0SA. Tel: (01205) 750438

Mr and Mrs J. Lynn • 6m N of Boston on B1184 • Open by appt • Entrance: £1.50, children free ● ♿ 🌵

Walking through the gate from the small front garden, one is certainly hit by the 'wow' factor: the long, curvy, quarter-acre garden, bursting with luxuriant growth and blossom, stretches away to a gazebo and open fields beyond. Small paved areas are filled with troughs and containers displaying unusual alpines or more tender beauties. Elsewhere height is achieved by raised, stone-edged beds and borders and carefully positioned small trees and shrubs, most of them draped with one of the 100-plus clematis grown here. These are not the only plants of interest, however. There is an alpine house, cyclamens and sempervivums in variety, choice herbaceous perennials and grasses – all clearly labelled for the enthusiast.

LIVERPOOL & WIRRAL

Birkenhead Park ★ [Historic Park Grade I]

Birkenhead, Wirral CH62 8BP.
Tel: (0151) 637 6218 or (0151) 652 5197 (Ranger)

Metropolitan Borough of Wirral • 1m from centre of Birkenhead, S of A553 • Open all year, daily, during daylight hours • Entrance: free ○ 🐌 **WC** ♿ ⟨⟩ ⚲ ℘

Historically Birkenhead Park is a milestone in garden history. Opened in 1847, it was the world's first urban park to be built at public expense. Designed by Joseph Paxton, it was also highly influential in the creation of New York's Central Park. Paxton's master-stroke at Birkenhead was to separate 'through' from peripheral traffic; he also banked up the edges of the lakes to keep them hidden, and made them sinuous in shape to provide walkers with a constantly changing view. No subsequent public park has succeeded in fashioning such a subtle yet masterly landscape. The banks on the eastern side of the lake are planted with trees and shrubs; a Swiss-style bridge links two islands, and a fine stone boathouse has recently been restored. The western lake has weeping willows and rhododendrons planted around its edge. The park has been continuously under restoration since receiving multiple grants totalling nearly £11 million. Work began at the end of 2003 and will be phased over five years.

Croxteth Hall [Historic Garden Grade II]

Croxteth Hall Lane, Liverpool L12 0HB. Tel: (0151) 228 5311

Liverpool City Council, Leisure Services • Turn N off A5058 Liverpool ring road into Muirhead Avenue on NE side of city. Signposted • Hall and Victorian farm also open • Garden open 9th April to Sept, daily, 10.30am – 5pm (winter times on request) • Entrance: grounds free; walled garden £1.20, OAPs and children 70p; all facilities £4, OAPs and children £2, family £9.90 • Other information: Dogs in outer park only. Shop in hall ◑ 🍽 ✕ **WC** ♿ ⟨⟩ ℘ 🏪 ⚲ ℘

The hall, formerly the ancestral home of the Barons Sefton, stands in 500 acres of its original parkland, with large areas of woodland and many rhododendrons. For gardeners the centre of interest is the large walled garden to the north of the house. Interpreted as a working Victorian kitchen garden and divided up by gravel paths, this contains a great variety of fruit, vegetables and decorative plants, organically cultivated; espalier fruits are grown against the walls and trained on wire fences, and the south-facing wall has a broad herbaceous border containing a good variety of perennials and ornamental grasses. Several greenhouses and a mushroom house are also open, and there is a small herb garden.

Liverpool Botanic Gardens ★

Calderstone Park, Liverpool L18 3JD. Tel: (0151) 233 3000

Liverpool City Council, Environmental Services • 4m SE of city centre, S of A562 • Park open all year, daily. Old English garden and Japanese garden open all year, daily except 25th Dec, 8am – 6pm (Oct to March closes 4pm) • Entrance: free • Other information: Dogs in park only ○ 🍵 🏛 <u>WC</u> ♿ 🐕 🌳 ☕

These botanic gardens are a credit to the city council and will amply repay a visit to enjoy a wide variety of plants in a most attractive setting. Essentially Calderstone is a large, well-landscaped park with mature trees, a lake and a rhododendron walk. At its heart, close to the house, is an area of gardens set around the old walled garden. To the front a long herbaceous border, six metres deep, has a range of strong-growing perennials; beyond, the flower garden features large clumps of grasses and daylilies and beds of annuals. Overlooking it is a greenhouse containing a sample of the National Collections of codiaeums, dracaenas and aechmeas, many fine orchids, an impressive collection of cacti, and much else besides. To the rear of the greenhouse the Old English flower garden has beds of perennials, bulbs and shrubs set within a formal layout of paths, with a circular lily pool and pergolas bearing clematis, vines, golden hops and honeysuckle at its centre. In the Japanese garden a chain of rocky streams and pools is fringed by acers, pines and clumps of bamboo. Altogether one of the best 'free' gardens in the country.

Ness Botanic Gardens

(see Cheshire)

Reynolds Park Walled Garden

Church Road, Woolton, Liverpool L24 0TR. Tel: (0151) 724 2371

Liverpool City Council (controlled by Environmental Services, Calderstone Park) • 4½ m SE of Liverpool city centre. Turn left off A562 up Beaconsfield Road to end and right into Church Road; park is on left • Open 18th April to Sept, Mon – Fri, 10am – 5.30pm • Entrance: free ○

The walled garden is planted with herbaceous borders, large dahlia beds and excellent wall climbers. Other features include a large grass area with mature trees, an unusual clipped yew garden and a small rose garden – all in very good condition, litter-free and maintained by only two staff. East of the city centre in Knowsley, within the 35-acre Victorian Court Hey Park, *The National Wildflower Centre* has demonstration areas of different plantings, including a garden of medicinal plants and herbs, plus a sculpture garden, workshops and activities for children. [Open April to Sept, Wed – Sun and Bank Holiday Mons, Oct to March Wed only, 11am – 4pm.]

Sefton Park [Historic Park Grade II*]

Liverpool. Tel: (0151) 225 4868; (0151) 726 9304 (Palm House enquiries)

Liverpool City Council • 3m SE of Liverpool city centre, N of A561 • Open all year, daily • Entrance: free • Other information: Palm House used for functions, so not always open ○ 🍵 🏛 <u>WC</u> ♿ 🐕 🌳 ☕

One of the country's most impressive Victorian parks, endowed by the Sefton family, conceived on a vast scale, and close in size to Hyde Park. It was planned as one of a series of parks ringing Liverpool to serve as an amenity for the growing population of the city. The competition for its design was won by Edouard André and Lewis Hornblower. Its layout of huge ellipses and circles owes much to Parisian gardens – André had worked with Haussmann in his grand bid to transform the French capital. For this English park he devised many views towards the interior, cleverly using planting to enhance perspective, with large-leaved trees around the perimeter and finer-leaved varieties in the centre. Hornblower, who had worked under Paxton at Birkenhead, was responsible for the many fine lodges, gates and kiosks dotted around the park. The most magnificent building of all is not, however, his. The palm house was built in 1896 thanks to the generosity of a local millionaire; octagonal in plan, it is 39 metres across with a vast glass dome built in three tiers, and contains tropical and exotic plants from Africa, Asia and Australasia. Each continent has an excellent guidebook. Its recent restoration is greatly to be welcomed, although it is unfortunate that much of the floor has been concreted over to serve the needs of functions. Sefton in the past has suffered badly from vandalism – let's hope its current good fortune continues.

Speke Hall

The Walk, Liverpool L24 1XD.
Tel: (0845) 585702 (Infoline) or (0151) 427 7231

The National Trust • 8m SE of city centre, S of A561. Signposted • Hall open – telephone for details • Garden open all year, daily except Mon (but open Bank Holiday Mons), 11.30am – 5.30pm (closes earlier in winter). Closed 24th to 26th and 31st Dec, 1st Jan • Entrance: £2, children £1, family £5 (2003 prices) • Other information: Picnics in orchard only. Self-drive wheelchair available for grounds; accessible path around Stocktons Wood ○ 🅿 🖼 WC ♿ 🏛 💡 ⚒

The remarkable gardens at Speke are neither as old nor as impressive as the Elizabethan hall. They are extraordinary, however, for although they are situated in one of the most heavily industrialised areas of south Liverpool and close to the airport, they seem to be set in the heart of the countryside. In front of the house is a large lawn with shrub borders to the sides containing mainly rhododendrons and hollies. On the side opposite the house a ha-ha allows views to the fields and woodland. A stone bridge leads over a drained moat to the ornate stone entrance of the hall. The moat continues to the west where there is a herbaceous border with a variety of perennials; a large holm oak stands opposite. To the south are new Victorian borders, and a formal rose garden contains fragrant varieties of old-fashioned roses. In the centre of the house is a large cobbled courtyard in which grow two enormous yews. The Trust is continuing to develop many areas of the gardens, and a mid-Victorian-style stream garden has been planted with rhododendrons, azaleas, camellias, ferns and other plants. New beds have been planted on the south lawn. A minibus service from Speke Hall will take visitors to the tiny garden at *20 Forthlin Road*, former home of Sir Paul McCartney, where the Beatles composed and rehearsed in their earliest days.

LONDON AREA

At the end of this section we include some of London's most attractive open spaces: City parks and gardens, squares and other retreats. The famous parks justify an entry of their own, but we have listed others of merit with a brief description under 'London's Open Spaces'.

Two-starred gardens are marked on the map with a black square.

33 Balmuir Gardens

Putney, London SW15. Tel: (020) 878 80931

Mrs Gay Wilson • Nearest station Putney mainline (5 mins). Buses 14, 74, 377, along Upper Richmond Road • Open for NGS, and by appt • Entrance: £3 NEW ◑

Pleasure in Putney: a small garden with romantic mixed planting for sun and shade. A paved path patterned with slate and pebble mosaics meanders between a small lawn and under an apple tree to a dipping pool and wall pond. The artistic owner intersperses the densely planted borders of shrubs, ferns and hostas with a soft colour palette of annual plantings, and the many climbers – roses, wisteria and the like – are discreetly nipped and tucked to give an abundant backdrop to this delightful garden.

Barbican Conservatory

The Barbican, Silk Street, London EC2Y 8DS. Tel: (020) 7638 4141

City of London • In Barbican Centre, on 3rd floor • Open Sun and Bank Holiday Mons only, 12 noon – 5.30pm. Telephone to confirm opening times as conservatory is sometimes used for conferences • Entrance: free ◑ WC ♿

The lift to the third floor of the Barbican propels you from the streets of the City to a lush jungle of temperate and semi-tropical plants. Planted in the autumn of 1980–81 using 1600 cubic metres of soil, the imaginative conservatory was opened in 1984 and is arguably the best single piece of architecture of the whole of the Barbican. Twin *Dicksonia antarctica* grace the main entrance, while a vast banyan tree (*Ficus bengalensis*) in the eastern section threatens to burst through the roof. Many familiar houseplants like *Ficus benjamina* have reached gigantic proportions, and a colossal Swiss cheese plant (*Monstera deliciosa*) produces edible fruits after flowering. The arid house on the second level, added in 1986, contains epiphyllums and cacti. There are finches in the aviary and the ponds are alive with fish. Another interesting contemporary garden is at the *Broadgate Arena* at the far end of Liverpool Street Station concourse.

Battersea Park [Historic Park Grade II*]

Battersea, London SW11 4NJ. Tel: (020) 8871 7530/8800

Wandsworth Borough Council • On S side of River Thames, from Chelsea Bridge to Albert Bridge • Open all year, daily, 7am – dusk • Entrance: free, but parking charge ○ ☕ ✕ 🗑 WC ♿ 🚻 🌷 ⚲

LONDON AREA • 235

There is something for everyone in this 200-acre Victorian park. The attractive Pump House, now a contemporary art gallery, is always a joy to visit. You can hire a tandem or a penny-farthing to pedal sedately round to the Peace Pagoda, watch cricket on the green, and admire sculpture by Barbara Hepworth and Henry Moore. The Thames Broad Walk – giving arguably the finest unspoilt view of the Thames – the Lakeside café, the 15-acre boating lake, with its ring of Pulhamite rocks recently restored, and Lanning Roper's Festival of Britain garden are worth seeing. Locals may bemoan the loss of the children's zoo and the neglect of the Thrive Garden by Albert Bridge Road Gate, but the Old English Garden within its walled enclosure, although also in need of attention, still has its fans.

Buckingham Palace [Historic Garden Grade II*]

Westminster, London SW1A 1AA. Tel: (020) 7766 7300

Crown Estate Commissioners • On N end of Buckingham Palace Road, on N side beyond Royal Mews and Royal Gallery. Entrance through courtyard to S of palace • Open Aug to Sept (but opening and closing dates may vary), daily, 9.30am – 4.30pm by timed ticket • Entrance combined with admission to State Rooms: £12, over 60s £10, children under 17 £6, children under 5 free, family £30, group rate (minimum 15 persons) £11 per person (2003 prices) • Other information: Advance tickets available via website or by telephone on (020) 7321 2233. Ticket office in Green Park Aug to Sept. Coaches must contact visitor officer (Tel: (020) 7839 1377) well in advance ◐

Visitors to the Palace end their tour of the State Rooms along a 450-metre guided route on the south side of the garden, and halfway along the three-acre lake are then directed out into Grosvenor Place. Although they may not roam freely they will be able to marvel at a 39-acre walled garden in central London – part parade ground, part ecological and dendrological oasis and part wildlife habitat. The magnificent trees were planted by William Aiton – head of Kew in the nineteenth century – and latterly by the Royal Family in acts of commemoration. The romantic and naturalistic lake is host to more than 30 types of bird. The visitors' view of Nash's handsome garden front of the palace is a privilege in itself.

15A Buckland Crescent ★

London NW3 5DH. Tel: (020) 7586 2464

Lady Barbirolli • Near Fitzjohn's Avenue at Swiss Cottage end. 5-min walk from Swiss Cottage tube station and various buses • Open 30th May, 2.30 – 6pm. Private visits welcome for parties of 25 or more, by appt • Entrance: £2, children free ◐ ♿ 🌿

The strong sense of space and line that musicians often possess is expressed in this dignified third-of-an-acre town garden, in which the ground plan combines flowing unfussy lines and ingenious geometry. Planting is everywhere discriminating, ranging from a functional but decorative vegetable patch to some unusual plants such as citrus and other interesting shrubs, including a small bamboo 'grove'. A generous terrace is enhanced by boldly planted urns.

5 Burbage Road

Herne Hill, London SE24 9HJ. Tel: (020) 7274 5610

Crawford and Rosemary Lindsay • Close to Half Moon Lane. Nearest station: Herne Hill • Open on special open days for NGS (telephone for information); otherwise by appt only • Entrance: £2 ◐ ⚘

An attractive garden in a tranquil and sheltered setting, with well-kept lawns, a quietly splashing fountain and herb beds. There is year-round interest and a continual introduction of unusual plants; borders are filled with choice arrangements of herbaceous perennials and shrubs, and good use is made of a variety of pots holding climbers, ferns and alpines.

Bushy Park [Historic Park Grade I]

Hampton, Surrey. Tel: (020) 8979 1586

Royal Parks • N of A308 Hampton Court road, between Kingston Bridge and Hampton Court Bridge. Access from Hampton Court or Twickenham. Entrance to Waterhouse Plantation via gate on Hampton Court road • Open all year, daily, 9am – dusk • Entrance: free ○ 🖐 WC ⬦

Once a royal hunting ground, the park adjoins Hampton Court (see entry) to the north. The vast avenue of four rows of limes and one of chestnuts planted by Wise for William III created a grand approach to the palace. It was punctuated by a formal basin in which Queen Anne resited the Arethusa fountain (long called the Diana fountain) from the Old Privy Garden. In the *Waterhouse Plantation* paths wind round mass shrub plantings and open onto small lakes and the Longford River with many bridges.

7 The Butts

Brentford TW8 8BJ. Tel: (020) 8232 8597

Mrs Susan Sharkey • Off Manor Road and Half Acre (A3002), a short walk from Brentford High Street. Buses 235 and 267. Nearest mainline station Brentford • Open for NGS, and by appt • Entrance: £2 ◐ ♿

A garden designer's garden (27 x 14 metres) cleverly planted with an abundance of foliage plants. It is separated into three sections. Next to the house a terrace has raised beds and strong use of colour. Leading from a plant-festooned pergola to a well-kept lawn framed by cloud-pruned box-edged beds, the garden opens up and gives a feeling of space, before revealing the final secret area with an original water feature and unusual planting for year-round interest.

Camley Street Nature Park

12 Camley Street, London NW1 0PW. Tel: (020) 7833 2311

London Borough of Camden; managed by London Wildlife Trust • Off Goods Way, near King's Cross railway station • Open all year, daily except Fri, 9am – 5pm (opens 11am Sat and Sun; winter, 10am – 4pm or dusk if earlier) • Entrance: free, but donations welcome ○ 🖐 WC ♿ 🛈 ⚘

An innovative project created in the early 1980s and now a designated local nature reserve, this is an example of a successful and thriving urban wildlife park and garden created against all the odds. Just over two acres between the Regent's Canal and the railway have been landscaped with a large pond and include a visitors' centre with an environmental education classroom. This tranquil space has a fine sighting record of birds and other wildlife. Views of the canal and passing narrow boats are offset somewhat romantically by relics of Victorian industry. The park will remain open throughout the Channel Tunnel rail link works in the area.

Cannizaro Park [Historic Park Grade II*]

West Side Common, Wimbledon, London SW19 4UE. Tel: (020) 8946 7349

London Borough of Merton • West Side Common, Wimbledon • Open all year, daily, 8am – sunset (opens 9am Sat, Sun and Bank Holidays) • Entrance: free • Other information: Teas on summer Suns only. Top garden possible for wheelchairs ○ 🍴 **WC** ⟨⟩ 🌱

Formerly the grounds of Cannizaro House, the park is entered through imposing gates up a formal drive, lined with beautifully kept seasonal bedding. The trees are the principal attraction here: cork oaks, mulberries and sassafras, enormous and beautiful beeches and mature red Japanese maples are among the many attractions. At the southern wooded end of the park, Lady Jane's Wood, the main feature is the magnificent and vibrantly colourful azalea dell. In the midst of the trees a secluded picnic area, set with tables, contains – somewhat unexpectedly – a bust of the Emperor Haile Selassie of Ethiopia, who sought refuge in Wimbledon. There is a small aviary, a pretty walled rose garden, an azalea and a rhododendron collection. The old garden, a formal garden and a pool are found down a steep slope directly in front of the house, with a wild garden in the same location. A sculpture exhibition is held in the park in June and an open-air theatre season in July and August.

Capel Manor College

Bullsmoor Lane, Enfield EN1 4RQ. Tel: (020) 8366 4442

Capel Manor Charitable Corporation • From M25 junction with A10, via Turkey Street/Bullsmoor Lane (signposted), or walk from railway station • Open March to Oct, daily, 10am – 6pm (last admission 4.30pm), Nov to Feb, Mon – Fri (times vary, so telephone before travelling) • Entrance: £5, OAPs £4, children £2. Special prices for show weekends • Other information: Plants for sale at special events ○ 🍴 ✕ 🍴 **WC** ♿ ⟨⟩ 🌱 🏪 🌱 ✎

These busy gardens of the well-known horticultural college have several functions. They show the history of gardening from the sixteenth century to the present, and also serve as a design centre for the garden industry and as an instructional venue, with a wide variety of plants, combination plantings and features such as water, paving and buildings. Although inevitably any sense of unity (such as at nearby Myddelton House – see entry) is lacking, pleasure can be found in individual features. Sponsors are secured each year for the many small show gardens. A large area has been established by *Gardening Which?* which includes demonstration plots, an A-Z of shrubs, a theme garden and a low-allergen garden designed for the National Asthma Campaign by Lucy Huntingdon. Suitable for a family outing, enhanced by a maze and rare breeds of farm livestock including Kune-Kune pigs and Clydesdale horses.

Chelsea Physic Garden ★ [Historic Garden Grade I]

66 Royal Hospital Road, Chelsea, London SW3 4HS. Tel: (020) 7352 5646

Chelsea Physic Garden Company • Entrance in Swan Walk, off Chelsea Embankment and, for wheelchair users only, in Royal Hospital Road • Open April to Oct, Wed, 12 noon – 5pm, Sun, 2 – 6pm; also during Chelsea Flower Show and Chelsea Festival Week, 12 noon – 5pm. There are some Sun openings and sales in winter (telephone for details) • Entrance: £4, students, children and unemployed £2 (2003 prices) ● ➤ WC ♿ ✿ ⯃ ▯

Founded in the seventeenth century to train London's apothecary apprentices in herbal medicine, the garden is still actively involved in displays of herbal medicine, as well as playing an important botanical role. Its three and a half acres are well worth visiting, not only for the fascinating range of medicinal plants, but also for the rare and interesting ones, including trees like the magnificent olive tree (*Olea europaea*). The garden also houses what is believed to be one of the earliest rock gardens in Europe, created with basaltic lava brought back by Sir Joseph Banks from Iceland in 1772 and restored in 2001. The main part of the garden is devoted to systematically ordered beds of plants, but there are also displays associated with the plant hunters and botanists who have played their part in the development of the garden, including Banks, Philip Miller, William Hudson and Robert Fortune, as well as an attractive woodland garden, glasshouses and a Garden of World Medicine showing the use of medicinal plants by tribal peoples. A Pharmaceutical Garden showing plants linked to modern pharmaceutical drugs was opened for the millennium. A National Collection of cistus is held here.

Chiswick House ★★ [Historic Park and Garden Grade I]

Burlington Lane, Chiswick, London W4 2RP. Tel: (020) 8995 0508

London Borough of Hounslow and English Heritage • 5m W of central London; entrance on A4 • House open April to Oct, daily, 10am – 6pm (closes 5pm in Oct). Private tours by arrangement Nov to March; telephone for details • Gardens open all year, daily, 8.30am – dusk • Entrance: garden free (house £3.50, concessions £3, children £2) • Other information: Dogs outside Italian garden only ○ ➤ ▤ WC ♿ ⬟ ⯃

The handsome eighteenth-century gardens, stretching over many acres, with a lake, statues, monuments, bridges and magnificent trees, were created from 1726 and extended by William Kent to complement the Palladian villa built by Lord Burlington in 1729. They are full of splendid vistas, avenues and changes of contour. Drawings of the time show the degree of perfection the English landscape had reached even in the early eighteenth century. The large canal-shaped lake has at its southern end a cascade designed by Kent in 1738 to mimic an underground river flowing from a rocky hill. He failed to make the cascade work but English Heritage – using information from archaeological excavation and from the archives at Chatsworth – has succeeded. After Kent's day, the Victorian garden with parterres was created and is now filled with vividly coloured bedding plants in front of a handsome conservatory. In co-operation with the London Borough of Hounslow, English Heritage plan to complete the restoration of the Victorian gardens; a first bid is in for a major lottery grant. West of the lake, the oriental plane walk has been restored with holly hedges, re-creating the walk in the manner of the mid-nineteenth century. William Kent's carriage drive and the raised walk that flanked the drive have also been re-created. Although this is not yet open to the public, visitors can walk the length of the *allée* leading from the Burlington Gate to the classical bridge. There is an outstanding camellia collection with early-nineteenth-century specimens; a new outdoor camellia garden is envisaged to the south of the Italian garden. Further work is planned in Burlington's Orange Tree Amphitheatre and in the northern and western wildernesses. From about Easter there are two return trips a day by boat from Westminster (telephone (020) 7930 4721) – but note these are lengthy.

College Garden and Little Cloister

Westminster Abbey, London SW1P 3PA. Tel: (020) 7222 5152

Dean and Chapter of Westminster • Entrance via Broad Sanctuary (west end of Abbey) then Dean's Yard, Great Cloister and Fountain Court (signposted) • Open all year, Tues to Thurs, 10am – 6pm (Oct to March closes 4pm), and for NGS • Entrance: free but donations welcome • Other information: Band concerts (free) July and Aug, Thurs, 12.30 – 2pm as advertised ○ 💷 ⠪ 🐾 ☕

The eleventh-century College Garden (a little over one acre) has been under cultivation for more than 900 years, and therefore qualifies as one of the oldest in England. It was originally the source for herbs used in the monastic infirmary of the Benedictine Abbey, and this theme is continued by the growing of herbs in the knot garden. Landscaping by John Brookes encourages visitors to move towards the south and east, from where some of the best architecture of the abbey may be viewed. In the south-west corner is a shaded area with a crucifixion group in bronze. Some interesting small gardens with topiary and intensive planting adjoin the buildings to the north of the area. The Little Cloister Garden is a miniature study in green and white, with a fountain and fish pond in the centre. There are fine trees throughout, and for flowers the best time to visit is February to May.

156 Dalling Road

Hammersmith, London W6 0EU. Tel: (020) 8741 2994

Kim Whatmore • Off King Street, Hammersmith. Buses 27, 190, 266; underground station Hammersmith (10 mins) • Open for NGS, and by appt • Entrance: £1.50 ☕ 💷

Key plants – large tree ferns, camellias, cordylines and box – are repeated throughout the small and tranquil garden to give cohesion. Trellis covered with *Clematis* 'Nelly Moser' and purple wisteria make secret partitions; York-stone paving liberally interspersed with pebbles and planting leads to an arbour painted pale green. This is a garden where every inch of space counts.

Dolly's Garden

43 Layhams Road, West Wickham, Kent BR4 9HD. Tel: (020) 8462 4196

Mrs Dolly and Miss Mary Robertson • Off A232 and A2022. Semi-detached house opposite Wickham Court Farm • Open all year by appt only • Entrance: by donation to collecting box ● WC & ⬡

An organic garden designed for a disabled owner now in her 80s, who maintains this much-loved 8 x 23 metres with her daughter. In raised beds excellent fruit and vegetables are fed by organic mulches and protected by slug guards. Perennials, combined with shrubs and climbers, are surrounded by native trees, holly, bay and bamboo, with a purpose-built greenhouse tucked among the raspberry canes.

Down House [Historic Garden Grade II]

Luxted Road, Downe, Kent BR6 7JT. Tel: (01689) 859119

English Heritage • 2m NE of Biggin Hill off A21 • Open 5th Feb to 23rd Dec, Wed – Sun and Bank Holiday Mons, 10am – 6pm (closes 4pm in winter) • Entrance: £6, OAPs £4.50, children £3 ○ ☕ ✕ WC & ⬡ ⬡ ⬡

Charles Darwin and his family lived in the house for forty years from 1842, and his daughter wrote: 'Many gardens are more beautiful and varied but few could have greater charm or repose.' The great scientist used the garden, woodland and meadows as his open-air laboratory while he for-mulated the theories which culminated in his ground-breaking work, *On the Origin of Species*. This garden is historic rather than horticultural. For visitors one of the most famous features of the garden is his 'Sand-walk' or 'thinking path'. The greenhouse where he studied plant growth and pollination has been restored and now houses orchids, carnivorous and climbing plants. The nearby ¼-acre kitchen garden, which provided fruit, vegetables and flowers from the vegetable plots as well as material for his experiments, has been re-created. The flower garden outside the drawing room, now restored to its appearance during the late 1870s, was used by the family as an extra room. Outside, on the lawn, is a 'wormstone' laid out here by Darwin's son Horace in an experiment to measure soil displacement. The estate is home to over 200 species of fungi, including rare grassland species such as wax-caps.

66A East Dulwich Road

East Dulwich, London SE22 9AT. Tel: (020) 8693 3458

Kevin Wilson • Behind Goose Green, opposite Dulwich swimming baths. Buses 37, 175, 176; underground station East Dulwich (20 mins) • Open by appt; parties of 10 or more welcome • Entrance: £2.50 ● &

The 30-metre-long garden is distinguished by lush planting, ponds, a willow tree and climbing plants used to great advantage. The owner is an artist and a garden designer, and his unique method of festooning may-poles with climbers, head-height seating areas and plant-filled antique hip baths defy all the rules. Large plantings of slug-free hostas and hanging baskets of ferns line the gravel path leading to a decking area, and pots of helxines march up wooden steps. Before reaching the large workroom, a pole with a mirrored top reflects the abundant planting. A viewing platform made from decking, with a double swing underneath, a seating area and a plunge pool near the summerhouse/studio entice you to the end of this unusual garden.

The Elms

**13 Wolverton Avenue, Kingston upon Thames, Surrey KT2 7QF.
Tel: (020) 8546 7624**

Professor and Mrs R. Rawlings • 1m E of Kingston on A308, 100 metres from Norbiton station. Entrance opposite flats in Manorgate Road • Open 13th, 14th March, 17th, 18th April, 15th, 16th May, 2 – 5pm, and for parties of 10 or more by appt • Entrance: £1.50 ● ☕ ☙

This is a true collector's garden with some rare and unusual plants, featuring rhododendrons, magnolias, camellias, conifers and a wide range of evergreen and deciduous shrubs. In a very small area (just $16\frac{1}{2}$ x $7\frac{1}{2}$ metres) are small trees, herbaceous ground cover, and a two-level pool with a geyser and well-planted margins; room is even found for plums, pears and soft fruit. The roof garden (open to private visitors only) is an object lesson in the possibilities of such high-level spaces.

Eltham Palace Gardens [Historic Garden Grade II*]

Court Road, Eltham, London SE9 9QE. Tel: (020) 8294 2548

English Heritage • Near Eltham High Street, $\frac{1}{2}$ m from Eltham railway station (then Bus 161) or $\frac{3}{4}$ m from Mottingham railway station (then Bus 126 or 131) • Palace open as garden • Garden open Feb to Sept, Wed – Fri, Sun and Bank Holiday Mons, 10am – 6pm (closes 5pm Oct, 4pm Nov to March). Closed 22nd Dec to Jan • Entrance: £4, OAPs £3, children £2 (house and garden £6.50, OAPs £5, children £3.50, family £16.50) ● ☕ ▨ WC ♿ ♨ ♀

The palace has one of the oustanding Art Deco interiors in London, though little now remains of the medieval building except the hall. The gardens were laid out in 1936 for Stephen and Virginia Courtauld, and a major programme of garden repair and restoration is in progress. The rose garden has been replanted using early hybrid tea and hybrid musk varieties, a permanent planting scheme created in the Triangle Garden, and the cascade rock garden is under reconstruction. Wide paths have been mown in the wild meadows and framed views of the palace opened up on the route from the new car park. Contemporary planting in the spirit of the 1930s' garden has been achieved in the 120-yard-long South Moat border and White Wood by designer Isabelle van Groeningen. Within the series of enclosures created by unusual evergreen shrubs and trees, including *Ligustrum lucidum* and *Ilex pernyi*, are spring-and-summer flowering shrubs underplanted with a variety of perennials and bulbs. There is also a developing collection of viburnums. The wildflower lawns in spring, the autumn colour of the extensive collection of trees and shrubs, and the attractive setting with long views to the City of London and countryside combine to ensure interest at all times of year.

Fenton House

Hampstead Grove, London NW3 6RT. Tel: (020) 7435 3471

The National Trust • In centre of Hampstead in Hampstead Grove behind Heath Street • House open • Garden open 6th to 28th March, Sat and Sun, 2 – 5pm; 3rd April to Oct, Sat, Sun and Bank Holiday Mons, 11am – 5pm, Wed – Fri, 2 – 5pm. Parties at other times by appt • Entrance: house and garden £4.60, family £11.50 • Other information: Toilet facilities if house is also visited ◑ WC ও ⚲ ⚱

The entrance to the handsome seventeenth-century house – described by *Country Life* as 'London's most enchanting country house' – and the garden is through the grand iron gate into an avenue of robinias or by a side gate near the yew bower, from which the south garden is visible. The one-and-a-half acre walled garden is formal, with gravel walks and herbaceous borders planted to give summer-long interest, edged by neatly clipped box. Standard hollies are a feature, and the walls are particularly well planted; note the collection of *Clematis viticella* varieties. The ground drops on several levels to a sunken rose garden and a late-summer/autumn border surrounded by tall yew hedges dividing the formal lawn area from the rose garden. Steps then lead down to an ancient orchard delightful in spring with narcissi, fritillaries and bluebells. At one end is the reinstated glasshouse with a herb border alongside (note the two olive trees in pots), at the other the vegetable garden and cutting borders. In collaboration with the HDRA, the garden was chosen to be part of a pilot project aimed at providing the Trust with an organic gardening blueprint for the future.

The Ferry House

Old Isleworth TW7 6BD. Tel: (020) 8560 6769

Lady Caroline Gilmour • 2m W of Kew Bridge, adjacent to Syon Park gates. Bus 267 from Hammersmith, Bus 37 from Richmond; signed from A315/310 at Bush Corner • Open for parties of 10 or more by appt • Entrance: £4 per person for charity • Other information: Plants sometimes for sale ◑ ☕ WC ও ⚲

A three-acre garden of exceptional charm on the bend of the Thames opposite Richmond Old Deer Park, with Kew to the south-east. A terrace commands a view of a completely unspoilt stretch of the river, framed in spring by white cherry blossom. The terrace itself, flanked by pleached lime trees, is planted mainly in white, with a profusion of plants in urns and tubs and splendid mature climbers on the old brick walls around the house. The borders are full of old-fashioned roses and other scented flowers, aromatic herbs and variegated and golden shrubs. On one side of the house is a large walled area, to which the fine old trees of nearby Syon Park provide a backdrop. Here there are avenues of whitebeam, groups of well-chosen trees and shrubs, winding paths with shaded seats, wildflower areas and, in spring, carpets of bulbs. Fine gazebo, attractive vegetable and fruit cage.

Fulham Palace [Historic Garden Grade II*]

Bishop's Avenue, London SW6 6EA. Tel: (020) 7736 3233

London Borough of Hammersmith and Fulham • Off Fulham Palace Road down Bishop's Avenue • Museum open March to Oct, Wed – Sun, 2 – 5pm; Nov to Feb 2005, Thurs – Sun, 1 – 4pm • Garden open all year, daily except 25th Dec, 1st Jan, 8am – dusk. Tours of Palace and garden 2nd and 4th Sun of each month, 2pm; other tours by appt • Entrance: free (museum tours £3 per person) • Other information: Plants for sale in nearby nursery. Annual plant sale end April/early May, 11am – 4pm. Garden walks once a season ○ 🐦 ♿ 🛒 🍴 ☕

The palace, surrounded in its prime by a moat, was the former home of the Bishops of London; in the seventeenth century Bishop Compton used his missionaries to help him establish here a collection of shrubs and trees sent back from America. The museum tells the story of the site and its garden. The east front of the house looks over lawns with enormous cedars and other trees, including an ancient evergreen oak. The holm oak, estimated over 500 years old, has been nominated a Great Tree of London. The romantic old walled garden contains a very long (if ruined) vinery built along a curved wall, and an elliptical box-edged herb garden enclosed by a magnificent old wisteria pergola. Another part has order beds and an orchard, recently replanted using historic varieties. The small courtyard at the front of the house (part Henry VII, part Victorian) has euphorbias, some climbers and other plants and a fountain.

Geffrye Museum Herb Garden

Kingsland Road, London E2 8EA.
Tel: (020) 7739 9893/(020) 7739 8543 (Infoline)

Geffrye Museum Trust • 200 metres N of Shoreditch Church. Take underground to Liverpool St. (Bishopsgate exit) then buses 149 or 242. Buses 243, 242, 67. Front garden open all year, daily except 1st Jan, 9th April, 24th to 26th Dec; herb garden open April to Oct, daily except Mon (but open Bank Holiday Mons); all 10am – 5pm (opens 12 noon Suns and Bank Holiday Mons) • Entrance: free • Other information: Guide dogs only ○ 🍽 ✕ 🐦 WC ♿

The enjoyable museum and gardens are on the site of eighteenth-century almshouses formerly belonging to the Ironmongers' Company; the walled herb garden entrance is tucked away by the side of the museum. This mature garden has 170 different herbs, including sweet woodruff (*Galium odoratum*), sweet cicely (*Myrrhis odorata*) and buckler-leaf sorrel (*Rumex scutatus*). Flower beds contain informal, labelled groupings of herbs showing those for aromatic, culinary, cosmetic, dye, household and medicinal uses, and a special bed is designed to attract bees. Secluded arbours with roses and climbing plants surround a delightful fountain. Period gardens lead from the herb garden and are arranged chronologically to reflect the museum's main displays of period rooms. These include a seventeenth-century garden of raised beds for herbs and vegetables, a Georgian garden with box edging, York-stone paths and clipped yew; a Victorian garden with seasonal, massed bedding; and an Edwardian garden with a pergola, a circular pool and informal planting of cottage-garden favourites.

70 Gloucester Crescent

London NW1 7EG. Tel: (020) 7485 6906

Lucy Gent and Malcolm Turner • Near junction of Gloucester Crescent and Oval Road 350 yards SW of Camden Town underground • Open by appt; visitors most welcome • Entrance: £2 ●

Mrs Charles Dickens once lived in this end-of-crescent house, and the garden, with its idiosyncratic shape, is strong on character. The three areas – a square at the front, a triangle at the side and a wedge at the back – show how a difficult town site may successfully be exploited. The owner, a garden designer and author, has created a place of strong geometry and infinite interest. The contrast with the bustle of nearby Camden Lock is quite something.

8 Grafton Park Road

Worcester Park, Surrey KT4 7HS. Tel: (020) 8337 1110

Robin Green and Ralph Cade • S of A3. From A240 Kingston-Epsom road take slip road signed to Worcester Park, turn right at Hogsmill Inn, left at next junction (Grafton Road). Grafton Park Road is first left • Open by appt only • Entrance: £3 in June, £2 in July, children 50p • Other information: Unsuitable for people unsteady on their feet ●

A steeply sloping, north-facing back garden 50 metres square with a lawn that was difficult to mow has been terraced and developed into an imaginative, witty Mediterranean oasis. Steps lead up past palms and bananas to a sun deck with a beach hut. A weeping tree shades a throne. Herbs grow among tender plants, with *objets trouvés* displayed among them. There is even a long, narrow, intensively planted vegetable patch. A camomile seat faces fountains supporting metal balls and there are pots everywhere – some 400 in all.

4 The Grove ★

Highgate Village, London N6 6JU.

Mr Cob Stenham • In Highgate Village, off Hampstead Lane • Open 6th June, 2 – 5pm, and May and June by appt only • Entrance: £2, OAPs/children £1 ● ⚘

The seventeenth-century house sits behind a dignified front courtyard, beautifully paved with brick and surrounded by lush plantings of evergreens such as skimmias and ivy grown along the railings, with spring-flowering magnolias in the borders. A side passage brings the visitor through to an outstanding vista: the terrace, with a formal pool surrounded by dramatic planting, is the foreground to an immaculate lawn with well-planted mixed borders. Beyond this is an extensive backdrop to the wooded slopes of Hampstead Heath. An arbour of silver pears overlooks this stunning view, and a ceanothus arch leads down, through a tunnel of *Vitis coignetiae*, to the lower garden. This comprises an orchard with an old mulberry tree and some good statuary. One yew hedge conceals the well-ordered compost/bonfire area, and another balances this to enclose a secret garden dominated by a *Cladrastis kentukea*. *Rosa* 'Cooperi' flourishes on the south wall of the house, and the whole garden, which is beautifully designed and maintained, has exceptional charm. No. 7 The Grove (see below) is usually also open on the same day in June.

7 The Grove ★

Highgate Village, London N6 6JU. Tel: (020) 8340 7205

Thomas G. Lyttelton • In Highgate Village, off Hampstead Lane • Open 28th March, 6th June, 26th Sept, 2 – 5.30pm • Entrance: £2, OAPs and children £1 • Other information: Teas available on open days ● ● & ℁

A half-acre London walled town garden behind a handsome Victorian house of c.1830, splendidly designed by the owner for low maintenance, but with a variety of good planting schemes and ideas. Tunnels, arbours and screens abound, providing inspiration for busy garden-owners who would still like to have an interest outside the house. A series of nineteenth-century brick-built arches across the width of the garden separates it into two compartments. The area near the house is formal with a lawn, the area beyond the screen much less so, with fine compartments and features. Secret paths and unexpected views make this a magical place for children. Much use is made of evergreens and there are some exquisite shrubs, including a row of camellias down one wall and a massive *Hydrangea petiolaris*. There are many species and varieties of a particular genus – five varieties of box and even more of ivies, for example. The owner describes it as a green and yellow garden, with glimpses of white and red here and there. The canal feature was restructured and enhanced into a water garden in autumn 1996. No. 4 The Grove (see above) is also open on the charity day in June.

Hall Place [Historic Garden Grade II]

Bourne Road, Bexley, Kent DA5 1PQ. Tel: (01322) 526574

Bexley Heritage Trust • Just N of A2 near A2/A223 junction • House open April to Oct, Mon – Sat, 10am – 5pm, Sun, 11am – 5pm; Nov to March, Tues – Sat, 10am – 4.15pm • Garden open all year, daily, 9am – dusk. Model allotment, parts of nursery and glasshouses open all year, except 25th Dec, Mon – Fri, 9am – 5pm (4pm in winter) • Entrance: free ○ ● ✕ WC & ℀ ⊞ ♟ ℁

Surrounding a splendid Tudor mansion, this is arguably the most interesting and best-kept public garden in south-east London. Although there is a strong emphasis on municipal annual bedding plants like geraniums, lobelias and marigolds to provide summer colour, they are used with restraint and good taste, as are the roses in the large classical rose garden and the herbaceous plants in two splendid borders separated by a turf *allée* and backed by a characterful old brick wall on one side and a tightly clipped yew hedge on the other. Features include a raised walk overlooking one of Britain's finest topiary gardens, several rich shrubberies, a large and beautifully designed patterned herb garden, a wildlife-friendly garden, a rock garden, meandering stretches of the River Cray, a heather garden and acres of lawn studded with evergreen and deciduous trees to provide vistas. The working nursery has a wide range of tropical floral displays, including model gardens and an orchard, carpet bedding and an environmental education garden with pond-dipping, a wildflower meadow and a time garden reflecting the origins of the house.

Ham House ★ [Historic Garden Grade II*]

Ham Street, Richmond, Surrey TW10 7RS. Tel: (020) 8940 1950

The National Trust • On S bank of Thames, W of A307 at Petersham • House open 22nd March to 2nd Nov, Sat – Wed, 1 – 5pm • Garden open all year, Sat – Wed, 11am – 6pm (or dusk if earlier). Closed 25th, 26th Dec, 1st Jan • Entrance: House and garden £6, children £3, family £15 • Other information: Parking 400 metres by river, disabled on terrace. Refreshments main-season only except Sat and Sun ○ ♥ ✕ 🍽 WC ♿ 🐾 🏛 🔦 ⚲

The approach to the impressive house is along a tree-lined walk running past meadows bordering the River Thames, giving no hint of the architectural framework of the seventeenth-century gardens beyond. Clipped balls of santolina and lavender set amongst parterres of box and hedged with yew lead to the raised south terrace, where historic pots and planting are backed by healthy pomegranate trees. Beyond lie the grass plats. The Trust is at the last stage of returning the gardens to their appearance c. 1670–80. The restoration of the wilderness as it lies on the main axis of the house re-creates one of the highlights of the original garden. Replicas of seventeenth-century wooden garden seats mark its entrance, and hornbeam hedges provide a setting for spring bulbs and summer wild flowers. The replacement of the statues will mark the culmination of this project. The walled kitchen garden, planted with period herbs, fruit and vegetables, is the perfect adjunct to the earliest surviving orangery in the country. Then cross the river by ferry to Marble Hill (see entry), or visit the *Palm Centre* at Ham Central Nursery. [Open Mon – Fri, 10am – 6pm. Tel: (020) 8255 6191.]

116 Hamilton Terrace

St Johns Wood, London NW8. Tel: (020) 7625 6909

Mr and Mrs I.B. Kathuria • Nearest underground station Maida Vale (5 mins), St John's Wood (10 mins). Buses 16, 98 from Marble Arch to Cricklewood. Parking in Hamilton Terrace • Open for NGS, and by appt • Entrance: £2 NEW ◗

Spot the house duck on the small front-garden pool in this prize-winning garden. The considerable visual appeal of the neighbouring church and surrounding trees gives a peaceful quality to the large and interesting back garden. Prize hostas flourish at different levels and the walls are covered with a variety of clematis, roses and other climbers. The garden reflects the owners' interest in a wide range of plants. Exuberance is balanced by restraint in many effective planting combinations, as the changes are rung in open areas, damp and shady sites, and containers, all beautifully maintained.

Hampton Court Palace ★★ [Historic Park and Garden Grade I]

East Molesey, Surrey KT8 9AU. Tel: (0870) 752 7777

Historic Royal Palaces Trust • On A308 at junction of A309 on N side of Hampton Court Bridge over Thames • Palace open • Gardens open all year, daily, dawn – dusk • Entrance: Rose, Wilderness and East Front Gardens free; Maze £3, children £2; Privy Garden, Sunken Garden and Great Vine £3, children £2 (free to palace ticket-holders). Afternoon garden history tours, including entrance to Privy Garden, weekends only from May to Sept, £3 (free to palace ticket-holders, limited places); special pre-booked morning tours by arrangement. Admission fee for gardens may change at short notice ○ ⬤ ✕ ▨ WC ♿ ⬧ ⬛ ⬤ ⬲

The gardens, which provide the setting for the palace, are an exciting and eclectic mixture of styles and tastes, with many different areas of character and interest. They are traditionally famous for the Great Vine, planted in 1768 – probably the oldest in the world and still producing hundreds of 'Black Hamburg' grapes each year (for sale to the public when harvested in August) – and the 1702 maze, the oldest hedge-planted maze in Britain. The Pond Gardens offer a magnificent display of bedding plants, and there is a 1924 knot garden with interlocking bands of dwarf box, thyme, lavender and cotton lavender infilled with bedding plants. On a truly grand scale, the great Fountain Garden, an immense semi-circle of grass and flower beds with a central fountain, is probably the most impressive element, but the Wilderness Garden in spring, with its mass of daffodils and spring-flowering trees, has the most charm. The laburnum walk – a tunnel of trained trees with butter-coloured rivulets of flowers in May – off the Wilderness Garden is another great attraction. The former kitchen garden now houses a rose garden. The restored Privy Garden of William III is a spectacular and unique example of the Baroque, with parterres, cutwork, clipped yews and spring and summer displays of seventeenth-century plants. It now forms a magnificent setting for Sir Christopher Wren's south front of the palace and the elaborate gilded ironwork railings by Jean Tijou. An area of the gardens sometimes missed by visitors is the secluded twentieth-century garden, an area developed originally for the training of apprentices, but now also open to all. It is located just over the canal next to the Fountain Garden (signposted) and is open daily. Too much to see in one day – plan at least two trips; one in spring and one in summer to walk in only part of the 66 acres of gardens and the informal deer park ten times that size. By-the-by, try making the journey by boat from Westminster pier down to Hampton Court – the most charming approach to the garden – although be aware that it can take four hours. The park is also the venue for the annual Hampton Court Palace International Flower Show in July. Bushy Park (see entry) lies across Hampton Court Road.

37 Heath Drive

London NW3 7SD. Tel: (020) 7435 2419

Mr C. Caplin • Off Finchley Road • Open 13th June, 18th July, 2.30 – 6pm, and for parties by appt • Entrance: £2, children 50p ● ♨ WC & ♨ ♋

A square garden of about one-fifth of an acre with a vast number of unusual and interesting plants packed into it – abutilons, tree peonies, tree ferns, rhododendrons, palms, brooms, black and other bamboos, a tamarisk tree, a handkerchief tree, figs and a mulberry tree. Features include an attractive pergola walk, pools and rockeries, a fruit tree pergola, raised beds and a greenhouse and conservatory for exotics. The garden has an effective compost heap hidden behind a hedge of delightful cut-leaved alder. In the front garden is a highly scented stauntonia flowering in spring, and a very large *Rhododendron davidsonianum*.

Highwood Ash

Highwood Hill, Mill Hill, London NW7 4EX. Tel: (020) 8959 1183

Mr and Mrs Roy Gluckstein • From central London via A41 (Watford Way) to Mill Hill Circus, turn right up Lawrence Street, bear left at top up Highwood Hill. House is at top on right • Open 15th, 16th, May, 2 – 6pm, for NGS, and May to Sept for groups by appt • Entrance: £2, children 50p • Other information: Refreshments and plants for sale on NGS open days only ● & ♨

This is a surprising country-sized garden in north London – some three and a half acres in all. The house (not open) dates from the sixteenth to the eighteenth centuries, during which time it was home to, among others, the noted traveller Celia Fiennes (d. 1741). A spacious lawn takes the eye to boundaries of mature trees with a brick wall on one side fronted by a broad mixed border. On the opposite side are headlands of juniper planned by the late Percy Cane, who helped with the design in its early phases. His main feature was a formal rose garden. Another noted designer, John Brookes, assisted with the late 1980s' water features in the lower garden. Two large pools have imaginative planting at their edges, with an old mulberry over one bank and ornamental trees elsewhere. Behind a copper beech are white-barked birches, *Betula utilis* var. *jacquemontii*, partially shielding the Secret Garden with its spring bulbs. Other surprises include a terrace with a raised herb bed and a covered arbour leading to the swimming pool. Rhododendrons and azaleas are a spring feature.

The Hill Garden [Historic Garden Grade II*]

Inverforth Close, North End Way, London NW3 7EX. Tel: (020) 8455 5183

Corporation of London • From Hampstead pass Jack Straw's Castle on road to Golders Green, on left hand side. Inverforth Close is off North End Way (A502) • Open all year, daily, 9am – dusk • Entrance: free ○ ♨ ✕ WC &

Overgrown in parts, the chief charm here lies in the secluded setting. The pergola, now restored, was built between 1906 and 1925 to a design by Thomas H. Mawson to screen Lord Leverhulme's house, The Hill (now known as Inverforth House), from its kitchen gardens and to shield it from people walking on the Heath. It is one of the best examples of its type, with all its columns and timber features intact. The pergola walk and the former kitchen garden have both been replanted. Other features include a large formal lily pond, herbaceous borders, undulating lawns and many shrubs and trees. There are wonderful views across the Heath.

Holland Park [Historic Park Grade II]

Kensington, London W8/W11. Tel: (020) 7471 9813

Royal Borough of Kensington and Chelsea • Between Kensington High Street and Holland Park Avenue, with several entrances • Parking (pay and display) from Abbotsbury Road entrance • Open all year, daily, 7.30am – dusk • Entrance: free ○ ☕ ✕ 🍽 <u>WC</u> ♿ ⬧ 🍴 🐾

Most of the famous Holland House was destroyed by bombs in World War II, but the formal gardens, created in 1812 by Lord Holland, have been maintained. The 53-acre park contains some rare trees such as Pyrenean oak, Chinese sweet gum, Himalayan birch, violet willow and the snowdrop tree, which flowers in May. The rose walk has now been replanted with a variety of azaleas. There is a small iris garden round a fountain. Peacocks strut the lawns and drape the walls with their tail feathers, and in the woodland section birds and squirrels find sanctuary from London's noise and traffic. There are excellent children's play areas. In 1991 the charming and beautifully maintained one-acre Kyoto Garden was opened as a permanent souvenir of the Japanese Festival. This is one of the most pleasant small London parks, although paths and grass can look worn and tired after the busy summer period, and not everyone will admire the bedding plants. Don't miss William Pye's fountain in the garden behind the orangery.

The Holme

Inner Circle, Regent's Park, London NW1 4NT.

Crown Estate Commissioners • In Regent's Park, just W of Inner Circle • Open several days for NGS • Entrance: £2.50, children £1 • Other information: Parking in Outer Circle. Refreshments and toilet facilities in café opposite ◖ ♿

The garden was designed to enhance the setting of one of the best-positioned houses (by Decimus Burton) in central London, overlooking Heron Island in Regent's Park Lake. Wisely, waterfowl are excluded. A gravel path leads down through a shrubbery towards sweeping lawns and herbaceous beds at the back of the house. A spectacular rock garden with stream, pond and waterfall is not to be missed, nor is the formal garden with its pool, fountain and arbours. Find time to sit at some of the many vantage points to admire the mature trees, good planting schemes and views.

239A Hook Road

Chessington, Kingston–upon–Thames, Surrey KT9 1EQ. Tel: (020) 8397 3761

Derek and Dawn St Romaine • On Hook road (A243) close to Hook underpass and A3. Opposite recreation ground • Open 13th June, 2 – 6pm, 16th June, 6 –

9pm, and by appt • Entrance: £2 • Other information: Parking in recreation ground opposite ● ₺ **B&B**

Created since 1985, this garden of many visual delights reflects the artistic skill of the garden-photographer owner and his wife. An attractive patio leads out onto a gravel garden and dining area planted with grasses and drought-tolerant plants. Around the circular lawn are standard hollies and box balls act as edging to the wide and effective borders. A circular pond and an L-shaped rose tunnel lead into the *potager*, where thriving vegetables are given designer willow supports and fruit trees are underplanted with patterns of herbs, vegetables and low hedges. Look out for the picturesque garden shed with its cobwebby windows, which puts in an appearance in many garden photographs.

Horniman Gardens [Historic Public Park Grade II]

Horniman Drive, London SE23 3BT. Tel: (020) 8699 8924

Horniman Museum • On South Circular at 100 London Road, SE23 • Open all year, daily except 25th Dec, 7.15am – sunset (Sun opens 8am) • Entrance: free ○ ☕ ✕ 🖼 **WC** ₺ ⬦ 🏛 ♟ ℀

This charming, rather old-fashioned park has a fine setting, with extensive views over the North Downs, St Paul's and west London, and its attractions include formal bedding, a rose pergola, a bandstand – with a band on summer Sunday afternoons and children's entertainment in August. The herbaceous and mixed borders have been replanted, and the area round the main entrance to the museum has been relandscaped by Elizabeth Banks Associates. The large and impressive Victorian conservatory was rebuilt recently behind the museum; it does not contain any plants in winter but is used for functions and for the concert series held in spring and autumn. There is a nature trail along a stretch of disused railway line with a pond and wildflower meadow and also an animal enclosure.

1A Hungerford Road

London N7 9LA. Tel: (020) 7607 0072

David Matzdorf • Short walk from Caledonian Road tube station. Buses 29, 253 to Hillmarton stop in Camden Road, 17, 91, 259 to last stop in Hillmarton Road, 10 to York Way and 274 to junction of Market Road and Caledonian Road • Open two days for NGS, 1 – 6pm, and by appt • Entrance: £1.50, children 50p NEW ● **WC**

The small walled garden in front of the eco-house co-designed by the owner and architect Jon Broome is planted as an exotic sub-tropical space with acacias, palms, brugmansias in plunge pots, bananas, cannas and ginger lilies – in essence a conservatory without a roof. The 'green roof' of the house (accessible at visitors' own risk) is fashioned with a densely packed array of alpines, sedums, grasses and aromatic herbs. An unusual house and garden, and a good example of creativity in a small space.

Hyde Park [Historic Park Grade I]

Rangers Lodge, London W2 2UH. Tel: (020) 7298 2100

Royal Parks • Open all year, daily, dawn – midnight • Entrance: free • Other information: Dogs not permitted in rose garden ○ ♨ ✕ WC ♿ ⬦ 🏛 ⛲ ⚲

A popular retreat from the surrounding streets is the rose garden. This enclosed area has matured well, with plenty of seats from which to admire the colour-coordinated planting in many flower beds. The heavy metal pergola has in part been covered by 'Sander's White Rambler' roses. The plan is to match the growth and flowering times of a range of rambling roses and to plant them, together with varieties of clematis, to complement the adjoining flower beds. The meadow area around the police station has a wide variety of native grasses; it is mown in late summer. The dell is a charming enclosed area, with a waterfall, stream, ducks and even a few rabbits. The Holocaust Memorial stone stands close by among a small grove of trees. The seven-mile-long walk in memory of Diana, Princess of Wales, through Kensington Gardens, Hyde Park, Green Park and St James' Park, was opened in 2000. A circular rill in her memory, designed by Kathryn Gustafson, will occupy in 2004 the site of the car park next to Serpentine Bridge at the west end of the park.

Isabella Plantation ★

Richmond Park, Richmond, Surrey TW10 5HS. Tel: (020) 8948 3209

Royal Parks • Richmond Park, Broomfield Hill • Open all year, daily, dawn – dusk • Entrance: free • Other information: Parking in Broomfield Hill car park, Pembroke Lodge, Roehampton Gate, disabled at north entrance by way of Ham Gate. Refreshments at Pembroke Lodge. Toilet facilities in summer only. Motorised wheelchair available weekdays. Telephone to book by 12 noon previous day ○ WC ♿ ⬦

The remarkably rich wooded plantation features many fine indigenous forest trees – oaks, beeches and birches – as well as more exotic specimens like magnolias, camellias, witch hazels and styrax trees. The principal glory is the collection of rhododendrons and azaleas, the earliest rhododendron, 'Christmas Cheer', blossoming in the New Year, but the garden is at its best from April until June, when the dwarf azaleas and the waterside primulas around the several ponds, streams and a bog garden, are also in flower. The garden is a notable bird sanctuary – nuthatches, tree-creepers, kingfishers, woodpeckers and owls have all been spotted, and herons fish regularly in the ponds. The Waterhouse Plantation in neighbouring Bushy Park (see entry) is also fine.

Kensington Gardens [Historic Park and Garden Grade I]

London W2 2UH. Tel: (020) 7298 2100

Royal Parks • Entrances off Bayswater Road, Kensington Gore and West Carriage Drive, Hyde Park • Palace State Apartments open all year, daily, 10am – 5pm (closes Sun 6pm, Nov to Feb 4pm). Orangery open daily; for information telephone (020) 7937 9561 • Gardens open all year, daily, from 6am (closing time displayed at gate) • Entrance: free (State Apartments £10, OAPs/students £7.50, children £6.50, family £30) ○ 🍵 🥤 **WC** ♿ 🚲 ♨ 🔦 ⚲

The 274 acres of finest park adjoining Hyde Park have their own pleasures, including sculpture by G.F. Watts. Children and older enthusiasts will relish on the northside of the park at the western corner the Peter Pan statue and a whole new imaginative Peter Pan world – a playground in memory of Diana, Princess of Wales, which features a pirate ship, wigwams, a tree house and a splendidly realistic crocodile among its many attractions. The Albert Memorial is a glittering treat, and the elegant Baroque orangery by Hawksmoor and Vanbrugh, with decoration by Grinling Gibbons, is well worth a visit. So, too, is the sunken water garden surrounded by beds of bright seasonal flowers, which can be viewed from 'windows' in a lime walk. From the Broad Walk south to the Albert Memorial, semi-circular flower beds are kept planted against a background of flowering shrubs. *The Serpentine Gallery*, host to some of London's most exciting and talked-about modern exhibitions, is situated at the convergence of two of Bridgeman's avenues. It is distinguished by a crescent of slate benches and a stone circle by Ian Hamilton Finlay inscribed with the Latin names of all the trees in the park, and other outdoor sculpture is also sometimes on display.

Kenwood [Historic Park Grade II*]

Hampstead Lane, London NW3 7JR. Tel: (020) 8348 1286

English Heritage • On N side of Hampstead Heath, on Highgate – Hampstead road • House open April to Oct, 10am – 5.30pm (closes 5pm Oct, 4pm Nov to March). Closed 24th to 26th Dec, 1st Jan • Park open all year, daily, 8am – 8.30pm (closes winter 4.30pm) • Entrance: free • Other information: Parking at West Lodge car park, Hampstead Lane ○ 🥤 ✕ 🍵 **WC** ♿ 🚲 ♨ 🔦 ⚲

The picturesque landscape was laid out by Humphry Repton at the end of the eighteenth century. Vistas, sweeping lawns from the terrace of Kenwood House and views over Hampstead Heath (and London) predominate, and the magnificent mature trees include oak and beech. There are large-scale shrubberies dominated by rhododendrons, and a kitchen garden with walls once heated. Walks follow Repton's original plan. The pasture ground slopes down towards two large lakes, and woods to the south of the lakes fringe the heath side of the pasture ground, with several gates onto the heath itself. It is a good place to walk at any season, but particularly when the trees are turning in autumn, to recall that the lime walk was a favourite of that great gardener of the eighteenth century, Alexander Pope. Look out for the ivy arch which opens out on to the lakes (one of Repton's famous 'surprises') and the sham bridge on the Thousand Pound Pond, which has been faithfully rebuilt with its single upside-down baluster. There is also some worthwhile modern sculpture, including a Henry Moore and a 1953 Barbara Hepworth. On the western side are haymeadows which change colour from May to July; natural regeneration of the ancient woodlands (SSSI) is being encouraged.

Kew Gardens

(see ROYAL BOTANIC GARDENS)

38 Killieser Avenue

Streatham Hill, London SW2 4NT. Tel: (020) 8671 4196

Mrs Winkle Haworth • Off Streatham Hill, near Streatham Hill station. From Sternhold Avenue take second turning right • Open to parties of 5 or more by appt • Entrance: £3 ● 💭 ♨ B&B

This much-visited South London garden is lovingly tended and full of carefully chosen plants and shrubs evoking a romantic atmosphere. Lush and skilful planting divides the garden into two distinct areas where perennials and annuals blend harmoniously – creamy nasturtiums surround box balls, old-fashioned roses, clematis and violas. An obelisk, a rose arch and a water cascade give architectural interest, while box cones beside a delightful rose-clad Gothick arbour introduce visitors to a second level, with a parterre and wall fountain providing an element of formality.

London Wetland Centre

Queen Elizabeth's Walk, Barnes, London SW13 9WT. Tel: (020) 8409 4400

The Wildfowl and Wetlands Trust • From M4 junction 1 take A4 to Hammersmith, then follow signs to Barnes (A306), crossing Hammersmith Bridge. Travel ³⁄₄ m along Castelnau to traffic lights; at Red Lion pub turn left into Queen Elizabeth Walk. Nearest underground station Hammersmith; Buses 33, 72, 209, 283 from Hammersmith Bus Depot (alight at Red Lion pub). • Open all year, daily, except 25th Dec, 9.30am – 6pm (5pm in winter) (last admission 1 hour before closing) • Entrance: £6.75, OAPs £5.50, children £4, family £17.50 ○ 💭 ✕ 🍽 WC ♿ 🚻 ♨ ♞

Within 105 acres of the wetlands in an area close to the visitors' centre, three high-profile young garden designers have focused on the theme of sustainability and created gardens to motivate and encourage conservation gardening. The first, designed by Land Arts, has a loosely laid spiralling path of slate curving from the outer edge of the garden to finish in a tight central oval resembling a butterfly's proboscis. Block planting of perennials rich in pollen and scent has been chosen to give interest for the partially sighted and to attract insects. By contrast, Arne Maynard's garden consists of structured formal planting with turf-topped walls formed from split oak logs, radiating across the site in undulating curves; the planting is meadow-like. The third garden is a tongue-in-cheek Bouncing Bomb/Barnes Wallis/Barnes Wetlands by Cleve West and Johnny Woodford. It is surrounded by cobalt-blue spikes, with a seat resembling sharp teeth. The eye is led to the central pond with the 'bouncing bomb' skimming the surface; reed beds surround the pond and planting is simplified to increase the sculptural impact. Find time to include the Wildfowl and Wetland Trust areas, and look out for the hides with their roofs of succulents.

London Zoo

Regent's Park, London NW1 4RY. Tel: (020) 7722 3333

London Zoo • In Regent's Park to N of Outer Circle. Take Bus 274 from Camden/Baker Street to Prince Albert Road and walk across bridge to main gate; tube to Camden Town/Baker Street; waterbus from Camden Lock or Little Venice • Open all year, daily except 25th Dec, 10am – 5.30pm (4pm in winter) • Entrance: £12, OAPs and students £10.20, children under 15 £9, under 3 free, family £38 • Other information: Car park at zoo or metered parking in Outer Circle. Wheelchairs and buggies available from information kiosk at main gate
○ 🍵 ✕ 🐾 WC ⅖ ♿ ♨ ⚘

Listen to the dramatic cries of the macaws in the distance as you enter the main gate and observe the mixed carex planted in front of their enclosure. All the enclosures are designed to provide the conditions the animals need. The keepers choose the most appropriate materials, all grown on site for each species: sand or earth for burrowing animals, hard surfaces for hoofed animals, branches and perches for arboreal species. Note the tree of heaven (1870) with the listed penguin pool built around it, and the old black mulberry (wrongly labelled 'white' a century ago). Find time to walk over the timber bridge below the 'stream' of blue slate in the Water-wise Garden. As part of the 'Bugs' exhibition, housed within the Millennium conservation centre, a native wildlife garden has been created. This includes habitats such as meadows, woodland and hedgerow, along with ideas for a domestic garden including a rockery and a herb garden, and reveals ways that birds, butterflies and animals can be attracted to a city garden.

4 Macaulay Road

Clapham, London SW4 0QX. Tel: (020) 7627 1137

Mrs Diana Ross • Off Clapham Common Northside • Open by appt only • Entrance: £5 per person (10 people min.) inclusive of guided tour ◗

A walled garden (24 x 15 metres) set out on strong, clear lines with formality heightened by box hedges, topiary and lots of pots. A circular lawn is surrounded by dense mixed planting, arches and a pergola. There is a grotto with a fernery around it and many exotic shrubs and herbaceous plants chosen for their handsome foliage. The garden has been designed to look as good in winter as in summer.

Marble Hill [Historic Park Grade II*]

Richmond Road, Twickenham TW1 2NL. Tel: (020) 8892 5115

English Heritage • S of Richmond Bridge off Richmond Road. Additional access by river launch • House open April to Oct, daily, 10am – 6pm (closes 5pm Oct). Nov to March, parties by appt only • Park open all year, daily, 7.30am – dusk • Entrance: £3.50, concessions £3, children £2 ○ 🍵 🐾 WC ⅖ ♿ ♨ ⚘

The gardens, originally laid out in the 1740s for the Countess of Suffolk, are still being restored by English Heritage and awaiting the result of a Heritage

Lottery bid based on the Thames Landscape Strategy – a conservation plan for the whole of this historic area. Alexander Pope, a neighbour of the Countess, took an interest in the layout, and excavation revealed one of the two grottos known to have been constructed. There is an ice-house and a young Sweet Walk. The gardens (if they can be called that, as now they are largely sports pitches and a venue for summer music concerts) lay claim to one of the largest and oldest black walnuts in the country and also some of the tallest bay willow and Italian alder trees. Then take the ferry to Ham House (see entry) over the river. You can also visit *Strawberry Hill* (eponymous station nearby) where Horace Walpole's 'little Gothick castle' and Grade-II* garden can be seen from Easter to Oct on Sunday afternoons for parties by appointment. Telephone (020) 8892 0051.

Mile End Park

Mile End Road, London E3. Tel: (020) 7364 5000

London Borough of Tower Hamlets • Access from Burdett Road (A1205), St Paul's Way, Mile End Road (A1), Grove Road (A1205). Nearest underground station: Mile End • Open all year, daily • Entrance: free ○ 🌿 **WC** & ⬥ ▯ ℀

This great green lung in the heart of Tower Hamlets has been welcomed by schools, youth clubs and community groups; all have been invited to take part in planting trees – rowans, pines and hornbeams – shrubs and bulbs. Already the green bridge and terraced gardens have established creatively wild planting, and swathes of grasses, euphorbias, sisyrinchium, *Viburnum* x *bodnantense* and galegas are covering the ground to give a mature feeling. Exciting mounds have appeared, one with wide grass steps and a winding path topped by standing stones. Then there are designer ponds and views of the canal with sections set aside for wildlife. The recently completed ecology park and arts park, each with its own earth-sheltered building, host various activities throughout the year.

Museum of Garden History

Lambeth Palace Road, London SE1 7LB. Tel: (020) 740 8865

In Lambeth Palace Road, parallel to River Thames on S bank, hard by Lambeth Bridge • Open early Feb to mid-Dec, daily, 10.30am – 5pm • Entrance: Voluntary admission charge £3, concessions £2.50 • Other information: Historic collection of garden tools and artefacts. Courses, exhibitions, lectures, plant fairs and concerts ◑ 🍽 WC & ⬥ 🛍 ▯

The garden in the churchyard was created in 1981. It commemorates the two John Tradescants (father and son), gardeners to Charles I and II, who are buried in a fine tomb in the replica seventeenth-century garden, which contains plants grown at that time. Lady Salisbury's knot garden design incorporates some of the Tradescants' own introductions. Well-labelled herbs abound amongst pretty perennials, making a delightful backcloth for the table tombs, whilst the walls are clothed in Virginia creeper, ivy, roses and clematis.

Museum of London Nursery Garden

London Wall, London EC2Y 5HN. Tel: (020) 7600 3699

Museum of London • Take underground to St Paul's or Barbican, then follow signs • Open 9th April to Oct, daily, 10am – 5.30pm (opens Sun 12 noon) • Entrance: free • Other information: Possible for wheelchairs but shallow steps make assistance necessary ◐ ☕ ✕ WC ও ⛪ ⚲ ⚭

Garden designers Colson and Stone totally revamped the internal courtyard in 1990 to coincide with the exhibition of London's gardens, and have transformed an almost lifeless area into a living history of plantsmanship in the City from medieval times to the present day. Legendary names like Henry Russell, who sold striped roses in Westminster, and James Veitch, who sold exotica like the monkey-puzzle tree from his nursery in Chelsea, are represented. This tiny roof garden is flanked on four sides by high buildings, yet the designers have still managed to incorporate a tumbling rill and a rock garden.

Myddelton House Gardens ★ [Historic Garden Grade II]

Bulls Cross, Enfield EN2 9HG. Tel: (01992) 702200

Lee Valley Regional Park Authority • S of M25 on A10 (junction 25), turn first right into Bullsmoor Lane, left into Bulls Cross; house is on right at junction with Turkey Street • Open all year, Mon – Fri, 10am – 4.30pm; plus Suns and Bank Holiday Mons, 11th April to Oct, 12 noon – 4pm; and for NGS. Closed Christmas week and Bank Holidays • Entrance: £2.10, concessions £1.50 • Other information: Teas on NGS Suns and charity days only ○ 🍴 WC ও ⚲

A magnificent, diverse plant collection set in four acres was built up by the famous E.A. Bowles and is now restored. Splendid spring bulbs, followed by an award-winning iris collection, then by autumn crocus and impressive varieties of autumn-remontant iris, make this garden a joy all year round. Sternbergia and nerines are but a few of the autumn bulbs, and there is a fine *Crinum moorei* near the old conservatory. This is by no means a municipal garden, and the impressive plant collection is displayed attractively in a well-designed area surrounding the Regency house. The garden is still unified by Bowles's plants and vision and it is worth reading details of his plan, which included a Lunatic Asylum planted with botanical misfits. Other attractions include the carp lake, a magnificent wisteria and part of the old London Bridge.

17A Navarino Road

Hackney, London E8 1AD. Tel: (020) 7254 5622

John Tordoff • Off London Fields, near Hackney Central station. Buses 30, 38 • Open by appt for parties of 10 or more • Entrance: £2 per person (2003 price) ◑ ⚭

An imaginative explosion of design occupies just 25 x 8 metres, yet this garden visit must not be hurried, starting with the Italianate courtyard with its fountain guarded by white pottery doves – the doves, archways, Mount Fuji, tea house and mirrored alcove are recycled or made by the owner. Clipped yews lead to a new perspective – a Japanese garden. Do not miss the seating area on the right which shares the pool with neighbours. Miniature conifers and well-placed rocks bring the eye down to the small scale of the design, and the whole is kept together by the rich green carpet of *Soleirolia soleirolii* (baby's tears). The clear stream is a haven for many birds. Memorable.

Noel-Baker Peace Garden

Elthorne Park, Hazelville Road, London N19.

London Borough of Islington • Entrances to Elthorne Park in Beaumont Road and Sunnyside Road • Open all year, daily, 8am – dusk (Sat opens 9am, Sun 10am) • Entrance: free • Other information: Toilet facilities in adjacent playground ○ &

This is a small, well-designed formal garden within a London park, created in 1984 in memory of Philip Noel-Baker, winner of the Nobel Peace Prize in 1959. It is an interesting example of late-twentieth-century garden design and planting, centering on a water feature and a striking bronze figure (with a horizontal bronze reflection). Much use is made of brick and York-stone paving, and raised beds together with lawns; the overall effect is softened and enlivened by the excellent planting, with many unusual species (e.g. *Acca sellowiana, Clerodendrum bungei, C. trichotomum*). The emphasis is on green, grey and white, lifted here and there by splashes of colour and linked by the strong lines of the asymmetrical design. There are several secluded sitting areas. The garden receives extensive use and support from the local community, and although the results of limited maintenance are sometimes apparent, the overall impression is of well-loved amenity. In adjacent *Elthorne Park* is a good children's playground and a fitness trail.

Pembridge Cottage

10 Strawberry Hill Road, Twickenham TW1 4PT. Tel: (020) 8287 8993

Ian and Lydia Sidaway • 1m from Twickenham town centre, approached from Cross Deep or Waldegrave Road. Strawberry Hill station; buses 33, 110, 267, 281, 290, 490 • Open 13th, 20th June for NGS, and by appt • Entrance: £1.50 ● ■ WC

A carefully maintained artist's garden which is an excellent example of a green garden without the ubiquitous lawn. Interesting at all seasons, it is designed with recessed areas framed by structural shrubs – bay, elaeagnus, fig, olive, viburnums, box and photinia. Gravel paths are outlined by groups of large river stones. Bamboos, strong ferns and grasses have stylishly planted terracotta pots placed among them. The journey ends at the artist's studio. Ask to see the imaginative scrapbook showing the garden's progress over the past six years.

Priory Gardens [Historic Garden Grade II]

Orpington, Kent. Tel: (020) 8464 3333 ext. 4471

London Borough of Bromley • Off Orpington High Street • Open all year, daily, 7.30am – dusk (opens 9.30am Sat, Sun and Bank Holiday Mons) • Entrance: free • Other information: Separate area for dogs ○ ■ WC & ♀

Adjacent to an attractive medieval priory building (now Bromley Museum), this is one of the most tastefully gardened public spaces in outer London, documentation of which dates from 1634. Pre-1939 the gardens were extended in the formal Arts and Crafts style. It has an excellent example of patterned annual bedding, a recently replanted herbaceous garden, a rich rose garden, fine mature trees and shrubs and a refurbished lake.

Regent's Park ★ [Historic Park and Garden Grade I]

Inner Circle, Regent's Park, London NW1. Tel: (020) 7298 2000

Royal Parks • Off Marylebone Road. Many other entrances to park • Open all year, daily, dawn – dusk • Entrance: free • Other information: Dogs in park only ○ ☕ ✕ 🏭 **WC** ⧗ ⚑ ⚑ ⚑

Within the park, *Queen Mary's Rose Garden*, well-laid-out and beautifully manicured, is justly famous. Playing host to more than 60,000 roses – dominated by hybrid teas and floribundas, although also including old-fashioned, shrub and species roses – the sight and scent of the garden in high summer is a magnet for thousands of visitors. It must be said, however, that this style of rose garden is not to everyone's taste. The roses are grown with almost military discipline and are in perfect condition. Swagged and garlanded climbers surround the circular rose garden, but the herbaceous borders are also worth visiting, particularly in late July and August, as is the large ornamental lake with its central island. It attracts many varieties of waterfowl, including herons which nest on the island. The Broad Walk (five minutes away, between the Inner and Outer Circle towards Cambridge Gate) is another exquisitely maintained Victorian-style area of planting. Its side walks are lined with urns and fountains following Nesfield's originals. Cypress lookalikes line the paths. There are 32 ornamental urns and tazzas (shallow bowls) and eight fountains. Nesfield's planting precision has been described as performing the same function as a military band – it provides entertainment for park visitors. Do not miss the charming little St John's Lodge garden. Nearby, at 66 Portland Place, W1 (a short walk from Oxford Circus) is the *Royal Institute of British Architects* (RIBA). The delightful roof garden on the first floor adjoining the café which features gleaming steel containers with clipped box and other architectural foliage plants, and a William Pye fountain, is open to the public during office hours. Another stylish sculpture garden in the area, which also has a café, is to be found at *The Wallace Collection* in Manchester Square.

The Roof Garden [Historic Garden Grade II]

99 Kensington High Street, London W8 5ED. Tel: (020) 7937 7994

Virgin Group • In Derry Street off Kensington High Street by lift • Telephone to check gardens open before attempting to visit • Entrance: free ● ✕ ⚑

A fantasy one-and-a-half-acre garden 30 metres above the ground on the sixth floor of what was Derry and Toms 1938 department store. Now a private members' club with restaurant facilities, the gardens which surround the bar and dining room are also used for functions and conferences. Ralph Hancock designed them to give three distinct illusions – a formal Spanish garden with canal, an English woodland garden and a Tudor garden. The soil is nowhere thicker than a metre, so it is remarkable that more than 500 varieties of trees and shrubs, including palms, figs and vines, survive up here. Ducks swim about in their high-rise ponds, watched over by flamingos, and there is a delightful maze of small paths, bridges and walkways, with peepholes in the outer walls giving glimpses across the city skyline.

The Rookery [Historic Garden Grade II]

Streatham Common South, London SW16. Tel: (020) 8671 0994

Lambeth Council • Streatham High Road (A23), then Streatham Common South. No entrance by car from Streatham North Crown Lane • Open all year except 25th Dec, 9am – dusk • Entrance: free • Other information: Dogs on leads on top terrace only ○ 🥤 🧺 WC ♿ ℗

This surprising garden space up the hill from Streatham High Road was once part of a private garden. In over a quarter of a mile there is much to enjoy: an abundantly planted English garden with quiet seating areas, a rock garden and stream, a small yew-hedged pond area close by a wisteria-clad pergola. The white garden, at its peak in July, almost rivals Sissinghurst. Further down the hill through shrubbery-lined paths is a quiet orchard picnic ground. On the way back up the hill seek out the well – one of the three original wells of Streatham's spa waters, dating from 1659. A fenced and gated play area with large paddling pool, much used by local families, is next to the parking area.

167 Rosendale Road

West Dulwich, London SE21 8LW. Tel: (020) 8766 7846

Mr and Mrs A. Pizzoferro • Off South Circular Road at junction of Rosendale and Lovelace Roads. Nearest train stations Tulse Hill or West Dulwich • Open for NGS, and by appt • Entrance: £1.50 ● ℗

The warm colour theme of the front garden gives no hint of the charm to be found in the small woodland area, the natural winter stream and child-safe wildlife pond in the back garden. This is a place to visit for ideas: bamboo canes topped with holed flints; massed perennials and winding bark paths, one of which leads to an old wooden ladder leaning against a fruit tree; grasses massed in pots, houseleeks at home in bricks, hostas planted at eye level for inspection, agapanthus and bulbs in pots, are just a few of the visual delights.

Royal Botanic Gardens ★★ [Historic Park Grade I]

Kew, Richmond, Surrey TW9 3AB. Tel: (020) 8332 5655 (24-hour message)

Trustees • Kew Green, S of Kew Bridge • Kew Palace (maintained by Historic Royal Palaces) closed for refurbishment • Gardens open all year, daily, except 25th Dec and 1st Jan, 9.30am – 4pm/7.30pm depending on season; glasshouses close earlier. Guided tours daily from Victoria Gate visitor centre, 11am and 2pm • Entrance: £6.50 (last hour of admission £4.50), OAPs, students £4.50, children under 16, blind, partially sighted and essential carers free, season ticket (for Kew and Wakehurst Place) £24, season ticket for couples £43. Other season tickets and Friends of Kew Membership available • Other information: Parking in Kew Green/Brentford Gate car park in Ferry Lane. Coach parking in Kew Road. Wheelchairs may be reserved in advance free of charge. Guide dogs permitted ○ 🍽 ✕ 🎒 wc ♿ 🐾 ℘

Kew's delightful and varied gardens and grounds of 300 acres have something for everyone: in spring, the flowering cherries, crocuses, daffodils and the fine rock garden; in May and June, the bluebell wood, the lilacs (made famous by the song) and the water-lily house; in summer the Duke's Garden, the rose garden; in autumn bulbs and trees; in winter, the winter-flowering cherries and (indoors) the alpine house. The trees range from ash and birch collections through conifers, eucalyptus and mulberry to walnut. The lake, once a disused gravel pit, has an abundance of wildfowl. Year-round pleasures are Decimus Burton's Palm and Temperate Houses and the elegant modern Princess of Wales Conservatory (named after Princess Augusta, founder of the Botanic Gardens in 1759) with its computer-controlled microclimates. The huge glasshouses, some of which are kept at tropical temperatures, have their unique collections of exotic and unusual plants, ranging from banana trees to giant water lilies. There is an Evolution House, and Museum No. 1 (opposite the Palm House) exhibits the Economic Botany collection. The somewhat formal rose garden, the delightful rock garden and the grass and bamboo gardens should not be missed. The Japanese gateway has been completely restored and the area around landscaped. All these buildings and gardens are elements in 'working' Kew, which is primarily a botanic research institution, collecting, conserving and exchanging plants from all over the world. There is another Kew – historic and royal. The palace (still disgracefully empty and not restored internally) became in 1729 home to Frederick, Prince of Wales. It was he who commissioned the gardens here, his Lord of the Bedchamber, the 3rd Earl of Bute, who created them, and his consort, Princess Augusta, who after Frederick's death commissioned Sir William Chambers to design the splendid buildings which today give Kew its historical hinterland – the three temples dedicated to Aeolus, Arethusa and Bellona, the 1761 orangery, the ruined arch and the pagoda. A relic of an earlier age, the seventeenth-century Queen's Garden beside the palace, has been re-created in period style. The disabled will find most parts of Kew accessible; indeed there is a Secluded Garden, designed by Anthea Gibson, created with the partially sighted and disabled in mind. (Telephone (020) 8332 5622 for details.) Children will enjoy the imaginative mangrove swamps, Mohave Desert and carnivorous plants in the Princess of Wales Conservatory, and the Palm House with its bananas and Marine Display showing seaweeds and fish from around the world. In 2003 Kew was awarded World Heritage Site status as an international unique cultural landscape – a great fillip for the world's greatest botanic garden.

Royal Hospital, Chelsea (Ranelagh Gardens) [Historic Park Grade II]

Royal Hospital Road, London SW3 4SR. Tel: (020) 7881 5204

Royal Hospital Chelsea • Through Royal Hospital London Gate in Royal Hospital Road, and through next gate into South Grounds, then through small gate on left • Open all year, daily (except 1st Jan, 25th, 26th Dec, and mid-May and early June due to Chelsea Flower Show), 10am – 1pm, 2pm – sunset (Sun, 2pm – sunset only) • Entrance: free ○ **WC** ♿ 👍

The elegant and attractive gardens are sited to one side of the Royal Hospital, with over a mile of wide walkways through undulating park-like grass and handsome tree and shrub plantings, and a few perennial and shrub borders. Formerly the pleasure grounds of Ranelagh, complete with a large rotunda (now demolished) and laid out in formal style, they were redesigned by Gibson in the nineteenth century, turned into allotments for pensioners between the two world wars, and later reconstructed according to Gibson's plan. A summerhouse by Sir John Soane, near the entrance to the garden, houses several seats plus glass cases with a history and a map of the gardens indicating the major trees. These include many species of poplar, birch, beech, holly, cherry, chestnut, lime, oak and so on, with a couple of more exotic ones – the tree of heaven and the maidenhair tree. To one side of the park is the area used to house the Chelsea Flower Show. A long avenue of plane trees marks the western boundary of the gardens.

Southwood Lodge

33 Kingsley Place, Highgate, London N6 5EA. Tel: (020) 8348 2785

Mr and Mrs Christopher Whittington • Off Southwood Lane, Highgate • Open one day for NGS, 2 – 6pm, and April to July by appt • Entrance: £2, children 50p • Other information: Plants for sale on NGS Suns only ● ☕

An imaginatively designed garden created in 1963 from a much larger, older one, set at the highest part of London with a magnificent view to the east 'as far as the Urals'. In approximately a third of an acre on a fairly steep site, there is much variety of mood and planting. By the house, a densely planted paved area is enclosed on two sides by a high beech hedge, through which steps lead down to a grassy walk planted with shrubs, clematis and herbaceous plants. A wooded area in the lowest part of the garden, with many shade-loving plants, leads up past two pools to the soothing sound of trickling water, and suitable bog plants. Alpines grow in troughs on a low wall.

7 St George's Road ★

St Margaret's, Twickenham W1 1QS. Tel: (020) 8892 3713

Mr and Mrs R. Raworth • Off A316 between Twickenham Bridge and St Margaret's roundabout • Open 6th, 20th June, 2 – 6pm, 10th June, 6 – 8pm, and by appt • Entrance: £2.50, children 50p, evening opening £3 including wine • Other information: Home-made teas and plants for sale on open days only ● ☕ 🌿

A most successful result of garden design, inspired by Hidcote and Tintinhull on a miniature scale. This is one of the most interesting and well-maintained private gardens in the west London area and well worth going out of one's way to see. Among its many striking features are impressive hedges of privet, yew, box and hornbeam, which enclose various rooms and a new formal knot garden. Entering through a sunken Mediterranean garden and a sink garden full of interesting small plants, the visitor passes by a rose-covered pergola to an emerald grass carpet, flanked by flower borders backed by old trees in a private park. In one corner is a water feature, a pool with waterside planting and a bog garden surrounded by wooden decking and crossed by a charming bridge. The new parterre gives an air of formality amongst the rare shrubs and containerised plants; plant lovers will also be drawn to the large, elegant conservatory on the north-facing wall filled with old-fashioned Victorian plants.

St James's Park ★ [Historic Park Grade I]

London SW1A 2BJ. Tel: (020) 7298 2000

Royal Parks • Extends from Buckingham Palace on W to Horse Guards Parade on E, The Mall on N and Birdcage Walk on S • Open all year, daily, 5am – midnight • Entrance: free ○ ☕ ✕ 🍴 WC ♿ ⟡ 🔦 ✎

One of the smaller royal parks but one of the prettiest. It was Henry VIII who turned this swampy field into a pleasure ground and nursery for deer. After the Restoration in 1660, Charles II sought advice from the French garden designer Le Nôtre, who planned the gardens at Versailles, to refashion the park into a garden. Le Nôtre gave advice, via his nephew, Claude Desgots, on a formal canal and included a pitch for King Charles to play the old French game of *paille maille*, a crude form of croquet, which gave its name to neighbouring Pall Mall. Nash remodelled the lake and gardens in 1827–29. The islands are still home to a wide variety of birds. Don't miss the picturesque skyline view from the bridge across the lake looking east. Bands play on summer weekend afternoons near Marlborough Gate. There is a small playground for younger children at the eastern end of the park.

Syon Park ★ [Historic Park Grade I]

Brentford TW8 8JF. Tel: (020) 8560 0882

The Duke of Northumberland • 2m W of Kew Bridge, marked from A315/310 at Bush Corner • Telephone for house opening dates, times and entrance charges • Garden open all year, daily except 25th, 26th Dec, 10am – 5.30pm (or dusk if earlier) • Entrance: £3, concessions/children £2.50, family £7 ○ ☕ 🍴 WC ♿

The Tudor house, with interiors redesigned by Robert Adam c.1760, is the London seat of the Percy family. The park shows British gardening on a grand scale and is one of the oldest landscapes in the country. A few statistics: 3200 trees here, one in four of which are over 100 years old and about one in seven over 200 years old. There are wonderfully mature oaks and swamp cypresses among over 200 different species in this park landscaped by 'Capability' Brown, but the most glorious asset is the great curving conservatory designed by Charles Fowler, which is said to have inspired Paxton when he was working at Chatsworth. One wing is full of scented flowers, leading to a collection of succulent plants, the other is planted with vines, leading to a fern-covered waterfall; the central part with its renovated dome is used for receptions and contains palms in timber planters. The formal garden in front of it has been simplified and now has an austere Italianate feel. The brashly commercial architecture of the garden centre and the crude, unshielded parking area in front of the house have done great damage to the setting, yet the house remains serene and the direct view to the river from it is remarkably untouched. The surrounding park and lakeside walk are of great interest, and a new path was opened in 1999 to allow visitors to walk the complete circuit of the lake. Wildflower areas are being developed, including a spectacular display along the entrance drive in midsummer. The rose garden has been redesigned and replanted with old varieties. One of the glories of Syon has always been the view from the ha-ha across water meadows towards the Thames; here new vistas and the famous axis to the Palm House at Kew are being opened up, and soon it will be possible to see across to the observatory and the pagoda. Much work still needs to be done, but there is a continuing programme for improvement and conservation, including work in the woodland garden and a new gravel garden planted with grasses and perennials. The future is bright indeed. Nearby *Osterley Park* [Historic Park Grade II*] – 650 acres surrounding the neo-classical villa by Robert Adam – has a farm, ornamental lakes, classical buildings and fine old hills, and is a delightful place for a walk, especially in May when the paddocks and chestnut trees are in flower. [Open all year, daily, 9am – 7.30pm or sunset.]

Thames Barrier Park

Barrier Point Road, Off North Woolwich Road, London E16 2HP.

London Borough of Newham • Nearest underground station Canning Town, mainline station Silvertown/London City Airport • Open all year, daily, 7am – dusk • Entrance: free ○ 🅿 📧 WC ♿ ⬦ 🚻 ☕

After Lee Valley Regional Park, Thames Barrier Park is the first significant modern park in London and only new riverside public park to be created since the war. The distinguished French landscape designer Alain Provost of Groupe Signes teamed up with the English architects Patel Taylor and engineers Ove Arup and won the competition to transform a contaminated brownfield site into a 23-acre park on the north bank of the Thames adjoining the river's most significant modern work of engineering, the Thames Flood Prevention Barrier. It is simultaneously a brave act of regeneration and a landscape *tour de force*. Its river promenade gives a setting to the Barrier, and a raised walkway opens up views along and over the river. The high-level plateau is planted with a variety of trees and wild flowers to create meadows suitable for recreation and events. The plateau is cut through to replicate the scale and depth of the giant dock structures and to create a microclimate for the Green Dock. Bridges reveal extensive views at the same level and a water plaza forms a dramatic entrance (as well as a dampening experience on windy days). It has already attracted private investment of £50 million to the area.

Trinity Hospice ★

30 Clapham Common North Side, London SW4 0RN. Tel: (020) 7787 1000

Trustees of the Hospice • Off N side of Common • Open for charity 17th, 18th April, 12th, 13th, June, 4th, 5th Sept, 2 – 5pm, and by appt at other times • Entrance: £1, children free � 🅿 WC ♿ 🌿

The gardens at Trinity Hospice were created primarily for the benefit of patients, their families and the staff. Stretching over nearly two acres, they are set out on slightly rolling park-like terrain and were designed by John Medhurst and David Foreman of London Landscape Consortium on the principles laid down by Lanning Roper. The latter had originally been asked by the Sainsbury Family Charity Trust to design these gardens on a dilapidated site, but his illness caught up with him before he could do much. The gardens were finished thanks to donations made by his friends and called the Lanning Roper Memorial Garden. Perennials and shrubs predominate, but there is also a wild garden at one end, a large pool with a mobile sculpture by George Rickey and a smaller one with a water feature by William Pye.

Victoria and Albert Museum (The Pirelli Garden)

Cromwell Road, London SW7 2RL.

In Cromwell Road, close to South Kensington tube station • Open all year, daily except 24th to 26th Dec, 10am – 5.45pm • Entrance: free • Other information: Refreshments during summer only. Music, wine and food lectures, etc. available on Wed evening openings (seasonal) – telephone (020) 7942 2209 for details
○ WC ♿ ♨ ☕

The Pirelli Garden of 1987 is to be replaced. Six short-listed landscape designers have already produced proposals, and their plans were on show in 2003 to enable visitors to comment on the idea before the final judgement is made. They were: Christopher Bradley-Hole and Kim Wilkie (UK), Adriaan Geuze of West 8 (Netherlands), Kathryn Gustafson, Olin Partnership and Martha Schwartz (all USA). The brief was to create a garden that could alternate as a large open space. Olin and Schwartz both have mobile gardens. Bradley-Hole proposes a version of I.M. Pei's Washington sunken restaurant with a glass roof. Gustafson suggests a central lozenge-shaped pool capable of being drained and refilled at will. Wilkie has a central lawn with a swimming-pool-cover-in-reverse that can be flooded on special occasions. And West 8 relies on fastigiate cypresses – on stilts. A description of the winning garden next year. On the corner of Cromwell Road and Exhibition Road is *The Natural History Museum Wildlife Garden*, an evolving garden which is a pleasant surprise among the many museums in this area of London. Pursuing a rigorous programme of conservation and ecology, 1000 trees and 20,000 wild flowers have been planted in a 1-acre site landscaped to re-create British nature sites. [Open April to October for tours and special-interest parties (telephone (020) 7938 9461) and on weekdays for school parties (telephone (020) 7938 9090).]

London's Open Spaces

OTHER LONDON PARKS

W10: *Emslie Horniman Pleasance Park* in Kensal Road has bespoke timber benches and sculptures set among colourful perennials and shrubs.

NW3: *Golders Hill Park*, North End Way, a 36-acre park with a vibrant two-acre flower garden, a water garden and a menagerie.

N19: *Waterlow Park*, Dartmouth Park Hill [Historic Park Grade II], has three ponds, tree-lined walkways, mature shrub beds and a terraced garden surrounding historic Lauderdale House, all set on undulating hillside with panoramic views.

E7: *West Ham Park*, Forest Gate, originally a late-eighteenth-century garden rivalling Kew, now a well-maintained 77-acre park with fine trees, Victorian bedding schemes, a rose garden and entertainments for children and adults.

E10: *Lee Valley Regional Park* totals 10,000 acres. Telephone information centre at Waltham Abbey Gardens (01992) 702210.

SE9: *Avery Hill Park*, Eltham, is notable for its rose gardens, three giant conservatories and aviary.

SE10: *Greenwich Park*, Greenwich [Historic Park Grade I], the oldest enclosed royal park, covering 183 acres, has sensational views especially from the observatory and historic buildings. Deer park, flower garden, rose and herb gardens, playground and children's entertainments.

SE20: *Crystal Palace Park*, Crystal Palace Park Road [Historic Park Grade II*], 200 acres surrounding Paxton's resited Crystal Palace created for the Great Exhibition of 1851 (alas burnt down in 1936). Terraces and features remain, and there is plenty of family interest.

SE24: *Brockwell Park*, Tulse Hill [Historic Park Grade II], a peaceful refuge with a walled garden, shrubs, trees, formal bedding and three ponds.

Morden: Just over the border in Surrey is *Morden Hall Park* [Historic Park Grade II], a former deer park with ancient haymeadows, waterways and collection of stables, mills and cottages. Nearby is a garden centre, a city farm (closed Mons except Bank Holidays) and craft workshops (closed Tues).

CITY OF LONDON PARKS AND GARDENS

Although there is inevitably a certain similarity in the design and planning of any group of gardens administered by a public body, those within the City of London (numbering around 150), being principally located on bomb sites, churchyards and former churchyards, have more variety than might be expected. For tourists and workers these gardens provide a welcome respite from the City traffic, and almost all are provided with lots of benches. *They are open 8am – 7pm or dusk, 7 days a week unless otherwise stated.*

EC1: *Christchurch – Greyfriars Rose Garden*, Newgate Street. A collection of hybrid teas and climbing roses trained up wooden pillars with linking ropes. *Postman's Park*, Aldersgate Street (close to St Paul's Cathedral). Formal bedding in the centre with mature trees and shrubs, a small pool with fountain and goldfish, together with tombs and headstones – the area is still a churchyard. An arcade protects the Watts Memorial, a tiled wall commemorating the deeds of those who died in their efforts to save others.

EC2: *Finsbury Circus* [Historic Garden Grade II]. [Closed Oct to March at weekends.] The largest public open green space in the City and London's first public park (1606). Apart from the ubiquitous London plane trees, it also boasts the only bowling green in the City, surrounded by low box hedges, bedding plants, shrubs, a drinking fountain and a small bandstand. *St Anne and St Agnes Churchyard*, Gresham Street. [Permanently open.] Here the church still stands, alongside the remains of part of London Wall and those of a Roman fort, surrounded by trees and shrubs. *St Botolph-without-Bishopsgate Churchyard*,

Bishopsgate. [Permanently open.] Apart from the usual planting, there is also a tennis court and a netball court and a former school house, restored in 1952 by the Worshipful Company of Fan Makers to serve as a church hall. *St Mary Aldermanbury*, Love Lane. [Permanently open.] Made within the low ruined walls of a Wren church destroyed in the Blitz, the stumps of remaining pillars mark different levels of the garden. A shrubbery encloses a monument to Shakespeare's pals, John Heminge and Henry Condell. There is also a small knot garden. *St Mary Staining*, Oat Lane. [Permanently open.] Another patch of grass surrounded by shrubs, roses and benches. A rare opportunity to see a design by the late David Hicks is available at *Salter's Garden*, Fore Street. Hicks before his death ensured that there were benches for office workers and visitors. Paved areas alternate with grass alleys dividing rectangular box-edged beds. Formally placed obelisks in the beds have been planted with climbing roses and some of the *allées* run below honeysuckle-clad tunnels. Three fountains. *St Alphage Highwalk Garden*, London Wall is nearby. [Permanently open.] This roof garden beside London Wall can be reached via the escalator at Moorgate station and consists of a series of raised beds and extensive trellis work. The planting is a mixture of shrubs, climbers and herbaceous plants with an interesting collection of grasses as a centrepiece.

EC3: *Pepys Garden*, Seething Lane. [Open weekdays only, 9am – 5.30pm.] A splinter of garden on the site of the Navy Office, where Samuel Pepys lived and worked. A surprising number of trees in a tiny area. *St Dunstan-in-the-East Church Garden*, St Dunstans Hill. The most romantic garden in the City, it has been created within the walls of a Victorian Gothick church which was bombed during World War II. Only the Wren tower survived and was restored. The remaining walls, containing arched windows and doorways, are covered with creepers and climbing plants and the spaces between planted with small trees and shrubs. There is a small fountain surrounded by benches and large tubs with standard fuchsias and bedding plants.

EC4: *Bow Churchyard*, just off Cheapside, will interest US visitors as in its small garden is the statue of Captain John Smith, 'citizen and cord-wainer', who was leader of the first settlers in Virginia.

E1: *Portsoken Street Garden*, between Portsoken Street and Goodman's Yard. A tiny oasis with a bubbling fountain, brick walls, small trees and shrubs.

LONDON SQUARES

When this *Guide* first appeared over a generation ago, the squares of London were mostly municipal in appearance, even though the majority of them were in fact private, and their gates firmly locked to visitors except residents or those with a key. Now the story is different. The gardens in the squares get much more attention from professionals as well as amateurs, and for several years now many are open to the public on the second Sunday in June. Some have events such as Punch and Judy shows as well as the opportunity for visitors to buy plants. London has about 400 squares, of which only about 15 per cent are currently open on this one day in the year designated London Garden Squares Day, though a few of the others welcome the public more frequently, some on a daily basis.

The squares were mostly built in the eighteenth and nineteenth centuries to provide an outlook for the fashionable houses which surrounded them and in not-so-fashionable areas like Pimlico so that the lesser classes could imitate the behaviour of their betters. A few squares still remain the joint property of the owners of houses (and today, flats) round them, the grandest being Belgrave Square built by Basevi in 1825, Cadogan Square and Eaton Square. Other private squares, hardly less grand, include Brompton, Carlyle, Edwardes, Lowndes, Montpelier, Onslow, Pembroke and others to the west of Hyde Park Corner.

Many of London's squares are listed on the English Heritage *Register*. Historic Gardens Grade II* are Gray's Inn, Lincoln's Inn and Victoria Embankment, while the Inner and Middle Temple are Grade II. Historic Squares Grade II* are Bedford and Bloomsbury; Grade II are Belgrave, Eaton, Eccleston, Russell, Brunswick, Mecklenburgh, Tavistock, Woburn, Edwardes, Berkeley, Grosvenor, St James's and Cadogan.

One enthusiast, Roger Phillips of Eccleston Square, says that in order to keep the squares going for the benefit of residents and the visual pleasure of passers-by, it is necessary to wage a horrendous battle against potential developers. By contrast, Michael Heseltine once said that 'someone, somewhere, should get a grip' on London squares. There should be tree-planting schemes, seats for the elderly, statues or water features – possibly provided by sponsors.

Amongst gardens which have recently joined the 'open day' scheme are Eaton Square, the Inner and Middle Temple Gardens, Little Venice along the canal, and Portman Square in the West End. For information about the scheme, tickets and descriptive booklets are available from May by writing with a s.a.e. to London Gardens Squares Day, c/o London Historic Parks and Gardens Trust, Duck Island Cottage, St James Park, London SW1A 2BJ. Further information may be available from English Heritage Customer Services from May (020) 7973 3434. Of the many other squares and 'gardens' open to the public outside the one-day scheme, the following may be worth a visit.

Northern area: Despite its name probably the least romantic was the home of the Bloomsberries, *Bloomsbury Square*. *Russell Square* has been imaginatively restored, thanks to a £1.4m lottery grant, to Repton's original design, with elegant railings, a new fountain, a hornbeam hedge and an ornamental shrubbery around the perimeter. Then come *Queen Square*, with its statue of Queen Charlotte, after whom it is named; *Brunswick Square*, beyond which is the walled garden, usually a haven of peace; *Coram's Fields* [Historic Garden Grade II], a children's play area, open 10am-5pm with *Mecklenburgh Square* adjoining; *Tavistock Square* (quietest in the area); *Woburn Square*; *Gordon Square* (closed weekends); and *Fitzroy Square*, the work of Sir Geoffrey Jellicoe (not open but viewable). Further north is *Edward Square*, Copenhagen Street/Caledonian Road, with a small orchard, nature and picnicking areas. Nearby is *Gibson Square*, with plenty of seats, much grass, fine trees and too many municipal roses.

Central area: *Berkeley Square*; *Cavendish Square*; *Grosvenor Square*. *Phoenix Gardens,* a community-run site with a 20-year lease which shows what can be done by London residents, and which, unlike many others, is open 24 hours a day; and *St James's Square*, the earliest London square, begun 1665, and the quietest. *Mount Street Gardens* is a well-hidden leafy retreat much loved by locals while the throng of the city seems to pass it by. Tasteful planting and lofty trees make it the perfect spot to take your ease after shopping. Versailles tubs planted with palms, beds of sugar-pink and white geraniums or other interesting and varied schemes can be enjoyed from dozens of wooden benches donated by those who have enjoyed this garden's charm. [Open spring and summer, weekdays, 8am – up to 9.30pm; autumn and winter, 8am – 4.30pm; Sun and Bank Holidays, open from 9am.] Also within walking distance are *Covent Garden* and *Soho Square* and *St Paul's Churchyard*, a visual treat and a much-needed restful space under the shadow of St Paul's, with well-designed, densely planted beds, an oval lawn and many seats.

Eastern area: *Embankment Gardens*, if rather municipal, are leafy and tranquil. At *Gray's Inn* Field Court is open to the public during weekday lunchtimes in the summer. *Inner and Middle Temple Gardens* stretch up from the Embankment (no entrance here) to Fleet Street. Their fourteenth-century origins are reflected in the names of some of the individual squares. The Inner Temple's Great Gardens, with majestic trees, were extended in the early eighteenth century and again in the nineteenth. The smaller Middle Temple has fine borders and a small rose garden. Alas, the future of these beautiful, historic and unique gardens is in jeopardy because of a plan to build a bridge, with twin towers as high as the dome of St Paul's, on their very doorstep. At *Lincoln's Inn* one of the 'squares', New Hall, is open Mon – Fri, 12 noon – 1.30pm only. The newest square in London is surrounded by offices, not houses. This is *Arundel Great Court*, which may be viewed from The Strand, south of Aldwych and entered from Arundel and Norfolk Streets. To the south is the luxurious courtyard garden of the *Norfolk Hotel*.

Southern area: *Cadogan Place* (above the car park halfway down Sloane Square (to its E) and *Cadogan Square* (to the W) are sometimes open for two or three days in early June for the Chelsea Festival.

OTHER LONDON 'PUBLIC' SPACES

N1: *New River*, a narrow man-made stream and park off Canonbury Road. *St Mary's Churchyard Gardens*, Upper Street, opposite the King's Head Theatre.

EC1: *Angel/Upper Street.* Three charming courtyard gardens have been built below the new office block, Regent's House, in Upper Street, just a few metres from the Angel tube exit. Nowhere to sit, but a pleasant strolling space. *Bunhill Fields Burial Ground*, between Bunhill Row and City Road. [Open Mon – Fri, 7.30am – 7pm (4pm Oct to March), weekends 9.30am – 4pm.] A burial ground, unused since 1853, containing many fine tombs and memorials, including those of William Blake and John Bunyan. Most of the tombs are behind railings, but part of the grounds which were bomb-damaged has been planted with grass, trees and shrubs. Fine planes and a mulberry. *Fortune Street Garden*, NW of the Barbican between Beech Street and Old Street. *Myddleton Square*, St John Street, which houses St Mark's Church.

EC3: *Trinity Square*, Tower Hill, home to Wyatt's Trinity House.

SE1: The gardens of *Southwark Cathedral* are newly reconfigured, making this the only historic green space remaining under continuous development in Bankside. The new *Globe Theatre* may have an Elizabethan knot garden on its one-acre site. For further details contact Shakespeare Globe Trust (Tel: (020) 7902 1400). At *Tate Modern* Bankside, close block planting of young birch trees and wide grass verges flank the main entrance path, while in the South Garden a green amphitheatre of crab apples and quinces creates a quiet, open space.

The London Eye has been given a narrow public space between County Hall and Jubilee Gardens with seating areas, yew hedging and an avenue of *Prunus avium* to encourage orderly queues.

SE15: *Centre for Wildlife Gardening*, 28 Marsden Road, near East Dulwich railway station, gives information and sells plants for gardeners who want to attract wildlife. [Open Tues – Thurs and Sun, 11am – 4pm, but telephone first (020) 7252 9186 🐾 ♿ 🌿 🍴 🍷]

SE23: *Sydenham Hill Woods*, near Forest Hill railway station. Over 180 species of trees and plants.

SW1: *Whitehall Court*. Parallel to N bank of River Thames, between Horseguards Avenue, Whitehall Place and Victoria Embankment. A Grade-II-listed garden, owned by Westminster City Council, re-created in 1994. The excellent planting plan takes into account the proximity of heavy traffic along Victoria Embankment and gives occasional views of the River Thames. Cross over Northumberland Place and visit the rest of *Victoria Embankment Gardens*, especially Bryant's small lily pond and Sullivan's Victorian memorial, which are well supported by planting. Maintenance is to a high standard. *Tate Britain* in Millbank is a pleasant place to stroll after visiting the museum – an exercise in restraint and a garden for all seasons.

WC2: *Somerset House*, The Strand. The Great Courtyard and River Terrace open up a walk from Covent Garden to the South Bank.

W9: *Clifton Nurseries* is a commercial establishment for the sale of plants and garden paraphernalia, but for all that it has the charm of a small enclosed London green space, worth visiting at all times of year (nearest tube station: Warwick Avenue) WC ♿ 🌿 🍴. Nearby is *Rembrandt Gardens*, a small municipal triangle by the side of the canal where, if the weather is suitable, the newspaper can be read in pleasant surroundings.

W10: Some London cemeteries have a gardenesque style, or have acquired one over the centuries. *Highgate* [Historic Cemetery Grade II*] in N6 is one of the best known. The longest-surviving cemetery still in private ownership is the 77-acre *Kensal Green* [Historic Cemetery Grade II*] in Harrow Road. (Tube to Kensal Green on Bakerloo line or bus No 18. Parking access via West Gate WC ♿ ♿.) It also has more free-standing mausoleums than any other in England – the majority were constructed to the owners' approved designs before being put to use. Several are Grade-II-listed. There are fine trees here as well as grand graves. The company which established Kensal Green in 1832 aimed to create a spacious park that would complement the fine monuments. They succeeded, and their work is now assisted by subscription-paying 'Friends'. [Open April to Sept, 9am – 5.30pm, Oct to March, 9am – 4pm (opens 10am Suns and Bank Holidays). Guided tours 2pm on Suns throughout the year.]

MANCHESTER AREA

We have included some gardens with Manchester postal addresses in Cheshire and Lancashire for convenience, so it is also worthwhile consulting pages 36–50 and pages 210–17.

Bramall Hall

Bramall Park, Bramhall, Stockport, Cheshire SK7 3NX Tel: (0161) 485 3708

Stockport Metropolitan Borough Council • 3m S of Stockport on A5102 between Bramhall and Stockport. Signposted • Hall open April to Sept, daily, 1 – 5pm; Oct to Dec, daily except Mon and 25th, 26th Dec, 1 – 4pm; Jan to March, Sat and Sun • Grounds open all year, daily • Entrance: free (hall £2.95, OAPs and children £2) ○ 🍵 WC ✦ ⬤ ⬛

The gardens round the magnificent black-and-white timber-framed house are of mixed interest, the best parts being those at a little distance from the front of the house where, in a narrow strip of land, formal beds contain bright annuals and a herbaceous border is enclosed by a hedge. The parkland is another matter. In the valley of a small river broad areas of grassland encircle a number of small lakes. Woods, which contain some very large beech trees, surround the park and hide all sign of the suburbs of Stockport. The riverside walk has banks covered in wild flowers.

Dunham Massey ★ [Historic Garden Grade II*]

Altrincham, Cheshire WA14 4SJ. Tel: (0161) 941 1025

The National Trust • 3m SW of Altrincham off A56 • House open April to 1st Nov, Sat – Wed, 12 noon – 5pm • Garden open April to Oct, daily, 11am – 5.30pm (closes 4.30pm in Oct). Park open all year, daily • Entrance: car park £3, garden £3.80, house and garden £5.80 (2003 prices) • Other information: Manual wheelchairs and batricar available. Dogs in park only, on lead ◑ 🍵 ✕ 🍴 WC ✦ ⬤ ⬛ 🅿 🌳 ⬤ ✎

Between the conurbations of Liverpool and Manchester sits the 3000-acre estate of Dunham Massey, where fallow deer still roam free in a 300-acre park. A miraculous survival, medieval in origin, the avenues predate the English Landscape School of the eighteenth century. The broad stretch of water curling round the north and west sides of the house is an Elizabethan moat, and the semi-circular promontory jutting out into the moat was the site of the Elizabethan mount. The house, described as of 'beautifully proportioned austerity', is an eighteenth-century replacement of the Elizabethan mansion. Enough of the formal seventeenth-century Baroque lay-out of the park to the west and the south remained for the Trust to repair and replant the six long avenues which radiate out from a *patte d'oie* in front of a triple row of lime trees each side of the southern forecourt. In the garden proper, becoming known as one of the finest plantsman's gardens in the North-West, other historical layers remain, including an Edwardian parterre planted in purple and gold by the north front of the house, an eighteenth-century orangery and an old well-house. The acid conditions and varied site permit a wide range of shade- and moisture-loving plants, all set among lawns, mixed borders and woodland. Visitors to the house will find an attractive courtyard in the centre with four beds of shrubs and herbaceous plants.

Fletcher Moss Botanical and Parsonage Gardens ★

Mill Gate Lane, Didsbury M20 2SW. Tel: (0161) 445 4241

Manchester City Council Leisure Department • 5m S of city centre on Mill Gate Lane, S of A5145, close to centre of Didsbury • Open all year, daily, 9am – dusk • Entrance: free ○ 🍴 📷 WC ᕫ 🏛

Here, close to a busy part of south Manchester, is a tranquil green oasis with a large range of plants, an historic rockery, and a water garden. What's more, it's free. It was in 1889 that Robert and Emily Williamson began to create this garden, focusing on its most important feature, the large rockery (in effect a mountainside in miniature) on which to grow their collection of alpines. It is still impressive. Large stones embedded in the steep south-facing slope form a series of terraces with pockets of soil for the plants and paths for the visitor, and in them are massed alpines, bulbs and small shrubs, plus many conifers and the odd well-placed small tree. Japanese maples cast their light shade in places; there is a large tulip tree and sheltered at one end of the garden a collection of Chusan palms. A small stream cascades down the rocky terraces to the rich foliage of the water garden. A restful walled terrace gives views across the garden to the meadows and trees of the Mersey Valley. Emily Wiliamson had another interest beside plants: she founded the RSPB here in 1889. Close by are the public *Parsonage Gardens*, entered through an old stone arch in Didsbury's busy High Street. Rhododendrons, camellias, magnolias, hellebores and ferns grow beneath the canopy of trees, and in a brighter area a deep L-shaped herbaceous border is backed by a wisteria-covered wall.

Haigh Hall Gardens

Haigh Country Park, Haigh, Wigan WN2 1PE. Tel: (01942) 832895

Metropolitan Borough of Wigan (Department of Leisure) • 2m NE of Wigan, N of B5238. Signposted • Open all year, daily, during daylight hours • Entrance: free, but parking charge during summer • Other information: Wheelchairs available from information centre. Craft gallery. Children's rides, model village and railway ○ 🍴 WC ᕫ 🏛 🚂 ⚲

The hall is set in the midst of mature parkland, and a short distance to the east are formal gardens, probably of Victorian and Edwardian origin. In an open area of lawn rose beds and specimen shrubs surround an oval pool. Three walled gardens adjoin. The middle one contains a good herbaceous border and a well-stocked shrub border. The second, to the south, has shrubs around the walls and young specimen trees planted in a lawn in the centre, and the low wall to the south gives a view across a wild garden with a pond. The third, at the northern end, can only be entered at peak times, and here against the south-facing wall is a cactus house; on the west side a landscaped area has heathers and conifers. The rest of the layout is formal, with roses, yew hedges and lawns and, against the east wall, a border of shrub roses. The arboretum, featuring acers set in woodland, is developing well.

Heaton Hall [Historic Park Grade II]

Heaton Park, Prestwich M25 2SW.
Tel: (0161) 236 5244 (Hall enquiries); (0161) 773 1085 (Park enquiries)

Manchester City Council • 4m N of Manchester city centre on A576 just S of junction with M66 • House open summer months only • Garden open all year, daily, during daylight hours • Entrance: free, but parking charge on Sun and Bank Holiday Mons • Other information: Some areas possible for wheelchairs but telephone first ○ 💭 WC ♿ 👍 ℀

The hall, designed in 1772 by James Wyatt, was described by Pevsner as 'the finest house of its period in Lancashire'. The 650-acre park, landscaped between 1770 and 1830, contains a number of other neo-classical buildings. To the front of the hall are formal, brightly planted Edwardian gardens. The stables to the west have a small heather garden in front and a large formal rose garden behind. A path leads through a tunnel to an attractive dell of mature trees and many rhododendrons, then follows a stream through a series of pools and waterfalls to a large boating lake. On the Prestwich side of the park small demonstration gardens are enclosed within old walls.

73 Hill Top Avenue

Cheadle Hulme, Cheshire SK8 7HZ. Tel: (0161) 486 0055

Mr and Mrs Martin Land • 2m S of Cheadle. From A34 follow B5094 to Cheadle Hulme. Take 2nd left turn into Gillbent Road, go to end and turn right at roundabout into Church Road, then 2nd left into Hill Top Avenue • Open two days for NGS, and by appt • Entrance: £2.50, children free 💭 ℘

Perennials are the mainstay of this small suburban garden, and the variety is huge. A lawn snakes through the length of the garden. To one side is a border in full sun, its soil lightened over the years; it contains delphiniums, campanulas, penstemons, hemerocallis, achilleas and other sun-lovers. Shade-lovers, including ferns, are grown in the opposite border in heavier soil. Providing colour later in the year are phlox in variety, dahlias, asters and crocosmias. A selection of small shrubs has been chosen for foliage colour: *Cercis canadensis* 'Forest Pansy', berberis, golden elm (*Ulmus minor* 'Dampieri Aurea'), *Salix exigua* and silver elaeagnus. A small pool has a selection of moisture-lovers, and there are shrub roses and clematis. Don't get the impression, however, that this is just an impressive plant collection, for the planting has been planned for its aesthetic effect and the result is a most attractive garden.

Lyme Park ★ [Historic Garden Grade II*]

Disley, Stockport, Cheshire SK12 2NX. Tel: (01663) 762023/766492

The National Trust • 6m SE of Stockport just W of Disley on A6 • House open as garden, 1 – 5pm • Garden open 28th March to 28th Oct, Fri – Tues, 11am – 5pm,

Wed and Thurs, 1 – 5pm; Nov to 21st Dec, Sat and Sun, 12 noon – 3pm. Guided tours by arrangement • Entrance: Garden £2.70. Park: pedestrians free, car and occupants £3.80 (house and garden £5.80) 🕐 🅿 ✕ 🖼 WC ♿ ♨ 🏵

The hall, a Palladian-style mansion, is set in spectacular parkland in the foothills of the Pennines with panoramic views of the Cheshire Plains. The 17-acre gardens are of great historic importance, retaining many original features from Tudor and Jacobean times. It is regarded as one of the foremost National Trust gardens for its high-Victorian-style bedding in magnificent formal beds, using many rare and old-fashioned plants such as *Penstemon* 'Rubicundus' (bred at Lyme in 1906). Important features include a well-planted orangery (by Lewis Wyatt, 1814) containing two venerable 150-year-old camellias; a spectacular Dutch garden with a rare example of a *parterre de broderie* using Irish ivy; a fine Gertrude Jekyll-style herbaceous border designed by Graham Stuart Thomas; a wooded ravine garden with a stream and fine collections of rhododendrons, azaleas, ferns and other shade-loving plants; a collection of rare trees and plants associated with that eminent plantsman, the Hon. Vicary Gibbs; a large lake; a 300-year-old lime avenue; extensive lawns and a recently restored Edwardian rose garden. A rare garden designed by Lewis Wyatt (1817) has been re-created and the Sundial Terrace restored.

17 Poplar Grove ★

Sale M33 3AX. Tel: (0161) 969 9816

Gordon Cooke • SW of city centre off M60 junction 6. From A6144 at Brooklands Station turn into Hope Road; Poplar Grove is 3rd turning on right • Open two days for NGS, and by appt in June • Entrance: £2.50, children 50p • Other information: Teas on NGS open days only 🅿 WC 🌀

That the owner is a landscape gardener and potter is soon evident, for in a suburban setting and a fairly small area he has created a very distinctive garden. A masterstroke was to set the paths at diagonals to the main axis and this, together with the changes in level and varied use of building materials, creates interest throughout. Many of the plants are chosen for their foliage shape and colour: phormiums, thistles, alliums, euphorbias, cordylines, grasses and ferns all contribute to the variety. At one side is an unusual grotto sunk into the ground with plants growing over the top, which overlooks a long rectangular pool surrounded by pieces of modern sculpture. Other water features and fine ceramics are spread around the garden.

Rivington Terraced Gardens [Historic Garden Grade II]

Rivington Lane, Horwich, Bolton, Lancashire BL6 7SB.
Tel: (01204) 691549 (Great House Information Centre, Rivington)

United Utilities • 1m NW of Horwich. Follow signs to Rivington from A673 in Horwich or Grimeford. Gardens are 10-min. walk from Rivington Hall and Hall Barn • Open all year, daily • Entrance: free • Other information: Parking, refreshments, toilet facilities at Hall Barn and refreshments, toilet facilities and information at Great House Barn 🔵 🖼 ⬧ ☕

These are not gardens as such but the remains of gardens built by Lord Leverhulme and designed by Thomas Mawson in the early part of the twentieth century. Set mainly in woodland on a steep west-facing hillside, they have fine views across Rivington reservoirs. Particularly impressive is a rocky ravine, the remains of a Japanese garden and the restored pigeon tower. The number and variety of mature trees and rhododendrons indicate that this must once have been a very grand estate. Take care on the steep, sometimes slippery paths.

Weeping Ash

(see Lancashire)

Woodside

(see Lancashire)

Wythenshawe Horticultural Centre

[within Wythenshawe Park – Historic Park Grade II]

Wythenshawe Park, Wythenshawe Road M23 0AB. Tel: (0161) 998 2117

Manchester City Council • 7m S of Manchester city centre, $\frac{1}{4}$ m S of M63 junction 9, $\frac{1}{2}$ m SE of M56 junction 3, S of B5167 • Open all year, daily except 25th Dec, 10am – 4pm • Entrance: free ○ 🍵 🥪 WC ♿ 🐾 🪑 🌳

Once this nursery grew bedding stock for the city's parks; now it is a demonstration garden where a large number of different plants can be seen growing. To the right of the entrance a large lawned area runs along a chain of pools planted in large effective clumps with many moisture-lovers, including irises and astilbes. The developing area, backed by mature woodland, already looks attractive. The Safari Walk through a long array of greenhouses leads past a series of plant collections – cacti, tropical plants, carnivorous plants, a fernery – and some unusual displays, including one on rice-growing. Behind the greenhouses is an area of demonstration gardens – a heather garden, a pool and rockery, a collection of shrubs and small trees, a well-labelled herbaceous border and a section of dwarf conifers. Another area is devoted to fruit, with many of the bushes and trees grown as cordons.

13 Yew Tree Cottages

Compstall, Beacomfold, Nr Stockport SK6 5JU Tel: (0161) 427 7142

Mr and Mrs M. Murphy • Off B6104 Marple Bridge – Romiley road. Turn into Compstall village signed to Etherow Country Park, and take second left after Andrews Arms pub • Open for NGS, and by appt • Entrance: £2.50, children £1, (parties £5) ● 🍵 🐾 🪴

A small garden that is a delight to visit, not just for its horticultural merits but also its superb location high on a hillside overlooking the Etherow Country Park and the historic mill town of Compstall. You can start your visit by drinking tea on the grass terrace, surrounded by beds of small shrubs and perennials, and from here a number of small stone paths lead up through winding routes into the steeply rising garden, which is dotted with pools, streams and water features and has areas devoted to moisture-lovers. Pergolas and trellises giving height and structure accommodate many climbers, and shrubs and small trees are used to create distinct and intimate areas. Shrub roses and geraniums are well represented, but there are many other perennials, including a bed of delphiniums. The other, more formal section of the garden lies across a small track, on a site that is less sloping and more sheltered. Scented and climbing roses and clematis climb up pergolas and other structures in an attractive, mainly gravelled area. There is also a vegetable garden with views across the valley, and a shaded area where hostas and ferns grow beneath small trees. On one of the open days gardens close by at Edith Terrace are also on show, and these combine with the enjoyable walks in the local countryside to make a good day out.

2005 GUIDE

The 2005 *Guide* will be published before Christmas 2004. Reports on gardens for consideration are welcome at all times of the year, but particularly by early summer (May 2004) so that they can be inspected that year.

GARDEN AND FLOWER SHOWS 2004

- 7th to 9th May: Spring Gardening Show, Malvern
  (Three Counties Showground, Malvern, Worcs)
  Ticket hotline: (01684) 584900; www.threecounties.co.uk
- 25th to 28th May: Chelsea Flower Show
  (Royal Hospital, Chelsea, London SW3)
- Early June to early Sept, International Festival of Gardens, Westonbirt
  (Westonbirt, Tetbury, Glos)
  Tel: (01666) 880220; www.festivalofgardens.co.uk
- 16th to 20th June: BBC *Gardeners' World* Live
  (National Exhibition Centre, Birmingham)
  Ticket hotline: (0870) 909 4133; www.necgroup.co.uk
- 6th to 11th July: Hampton Court Flower Show
  (Hampton Court Palace, East Molesey, Surrey)
- 21st to 25th July: RHS Flower Show, Tatton Park
  (Tatton Park, near Knutsford, Cheshire)
- 22nd to 24th June, 17th to 19th Aug: Wisley Shows
  (RHS Garden, Wisley, Woking, Surrey)
- 25th and 26th Sept: Autumn Garden & Country Show, Malvern (see above for details)

Unless otherwise given, for details of all these shows telephone the Royal Horticultural Society on (020) 7834 4333 or consult www.rhs.org.uk.

NEWCASTLE UPON TYNE AREA

Bede's World Herb Garden

Church Bank, Jarrow, South Tyneside NE32 3DY. Tel: (0191) 489 2106

Bede's World • 8m NE of Gateshead off A185, or S entrance to Tyne Tunnel off A19 • Museum open all year except Good Friday • Garden open all year, daily except Good Friday, 10am – 5.30pm (Sun opens 12 noon, Nov to March closes 4.30pm). Telephone for details of Christmas openings • Entrance: free (museum, Anglo-Saxon farm and garden £4.50, concessions £2.50, family £9) (2003 prices) ○ ⬤ ✕ 🌂 <u>WC</u> & ⬤ 🍴 🔦 ⚲

A small garden of interest to the herbalist, with a wide range of herbs in four sections: culinary, Anglo-Saxon medicinal, aromatic and medicinal. There are also narrow beds in a second part of the garden based on the plans of a medicinal herb garden found at St Gall (*c.* AD 816), and a bricked area at the top of the garden with seating, planted around with rosemary, lavender and with two banks of herbs below it leading down to the St Gall area. An 'Anglo-Saxon' farm has been developed on adjacent land – an 11-acre site with fields, crops, animals and timber buildings. Some herbs and early vegetable strains are grown here, together with pond and stream plants and trees of species available at the time of the Venerable Bede (AD 673–735). The adjacent museum building has a courtyard with four raised beds planted in the style of a late-medieval formal garden. The herb garden is maintained by a team of volunteers.

Gibside [Historic Garden Grade I]

Burnopfield, Gateshead NE16 6BG. Tel: (01207) 542255

The National Trust • 6m SW of Gateshead, 20m NW of Durham from B6314, off A694 at Rowlands Gill. Signed from A1(M) • Open all year, daily, except Mon (but open Bank Holiday Mons), 10am – 4.30pm. Closed 25th, 26th Dec • Entrance: £3.50, children £2 (2003 prices) • Other information: Chapel open, service first Sun each month ○ ⬤ ✕ 🌂 <u>WC</u> & ⬤ 🍴 🔦 ⚲

Gibside was once one of the finest designed landscapes in England of the eighteenth century, created by a Whig MP, George Bowes of the Bowes Lyon family, another of whom fashioned St Paul's Walden Bury (see entry in Hertfordshire). In 1729, amongst wooded slopes cut through with radiating avenues, he commissioned and positioned a series of buildings – an early, more formal version of Stowe (see entry in Buckinghamshire). Each building was admirably sited, and all were constituents of a harmonious plan. Employing various architects, he built a Gothick banqueting house, an orangery and stables. The landscape *pièce de résistance* was a grand terrace flanked by an avenue of Turkey oaks with a statue to British Liberty – on a column taller than Nelson's in London – at one end, the architectural masterpiece – James Paine's stately Palladian chapel – at the other.

The Trust, assisted by the National Heritage Memorial Fund, has acquired 354 acres to secure the future of this great landscape garden and to protect its chapel setting. Wel-marked walks have been opened up with views to the ruined hall, orangery and other estate buildings in the grounds. Restoration of the ruined buildings and removal of the Forestry Commission's intrusive tree planting is a rolling programme which, although started in the 1970s, is still nowhere near completion. Bowes also made a walled garden, which is now the car park – an open space waiting to be filled.

Jesmond Dene [Historic Park Grade II]

Jesmond NE7 7BQ. Tel: (0191) 281 0973

Newcastle City Council • 1m E of city centre along Jesmond Road • Open all year, daily • Entrance: free • Other information: Parking in Benton Bank. Visitor Centre open at weekends. Café open daily ○ ☕ 🍴 WC ☕ ⬠ 🏤 🍴 ☕

Presented to the city in 1883 by Lord Armstrong, the famous engineer, and only a mile from the city centre, this steep-sided, thickly wooded dene provides extensive walks in an entirely natural setting, complete with a waterfall, a ruined mill and some fine old buildings. There is a well-run pets' corner, and from Freeman Road the upper park has a children's play area and a pond. For a city park, its condition is quite exceptional. Cragside (see entry in Northumberland) was also the creation of Lord Armstrong.

Mowbray Park and Winter Gardens [Historic Park Grade II]

Burdon Road, Sunderland SR1 1PP. Tel: (0191) 553 2323

Sunderland Museum and Winter Gardens • In city centre • Open all year, daily • Entrance: free ○ ☕ ✕ WC ☕ ⬠ 🍴 ☕

Restored to its former Victorian splendour, Mowbray Park is awash with colour – in rose arbours, in colourful shrub borders and in formal bedding displays. Winding paths lead to a quarry garden and a limestone crag at the more naturalistic southern end. Not to be missed within the park are the Winter Gardens, which are attached to the museum. Here is a new and amazing glass and steel structure housing a variety of exotic plants. Tree ferns, banana plants, citrus trees and scented flowering shrubs create a lush canopy, which can be viewed from a tree-top walk. A specially commissioned water sculpture by William Pye cascades in torrents, adding to the exotic atmosphere.

HOW TO FIND THE GARDENS

Directions to each garden are included in the entry. This information has been supplied by the owners and garden inspectors. It is aimed to be the best available to those travelling by car, and has been compiled to be used in conjunction with a road atlas. Some gardens may be reached by train or bus, but the unreliability of these makes it unrewarding to include details, particularly as many garden visits are made on Sundays.

NORFOLK

Two-starred gardens are marked on the map with a black square.

Besthorpe Hall ★

Besthorpe, Attleborough N17 2LJ. Tel: (01953) 450300

Mr J.A. Alston • 14m SW of Norwich, 1m E of Attleborough on Bunwell Road. Entrance on right, past church • Open by appt only ◐ **WC** &

A pool and fountain occupy the centre of the entrance forecourt. Beyond the house, more pools and fountains are set among lawns skirted by high clematis-hung walls of Tudor brick which form a backdrop to long herbaceous borders. The largest lawn, believed to have been a tilt yard once, has developing topiary, while on another is an enormous and shapely Wellingtonia. Among the many fine trees are paulownias and a variety of birches, acers and magnolias, including a sumptuous *M. delavayi*. There is also a walled kitchen garden, a nuttery and a herb garden. A small lake is home to wildfowl, and on another pool lives a pair of black swans. Bearded irises are the June feature. *Peter Beales Roses*, London Road, Attleborough is not far away [open daily, 9am – 5pm (4pm on Sun)].

Blickling Hall ★ [Historic Garden Grade II*]

Aylsham, Norwich NR11 6NF. Tel: (01263) 738030

The National Trust • 15m N of Norwich, 1½ m NW of Aylsham on N side of B1354 • House open end March to early Nov, Wed – Sun, 1 – 4.30pm • Garden open end-March to early Nov, Wed – Sun and Bank Holiday Mons, plus Tues in Aug, 10.15am – 5.15pm; late Nov and Dec, Thurs – Sun, 11am – 4pm; Jan to March, Sat and Sun, 11am – 4pm • Entrance: £3.90 (house and gardens £6.90) (2003 prices) • Other information: Picnics in walled garden only. Dogs in park only, on lead ◑ **♨** ✕ **▦ WC** & ⟁ ✿ ⏏ ⛾ ℀

Although the gardens seem a perfect setting for the handsome Jacobean house, they incorporate features from the seventeenth to the twentieth centuries. From the earliest period come the massive yew hedges flanking the southern approach. To the east is the parterre originally planned by Nesfield and Wyatt in 1870. Its complicated flower beds were replaced in 1938 by Norah Lindsay's four large corner beds of herbaceous plants in selected colours surrounded by borders of roses edged with catmint. The central pool has a seventeenth-century fountain. In the centre of the eastern side flights of steps mount to the highest terrace where a central vista cut through blocks of woodland leads to the Doric temple of 1730 high in the parkland beyond. The two blocks are intersected by *allées* in seventeenth-century style planted in 1861–64 and now replanted using Turkey oak, lime and beech. On the southern side the orangery of 1782 by Samuel Wyatt houses half-hardy plants and a 1640s' statue of Hercules by Nicholas Stone. In the corner of the northern block is the Secret Garden, a remnant of a larger eighteenth-century garden for which

Repton made recommendations, consisting now of a lawn with a central sundial surrounded by high beech hedges. The shrub border through which it is approached and the dry moat around the house are also by Norah Lindsay. North of the parterre is a raised grassy area, possibly a remnant of the Jacobean mount, topped by an enormous, sprawling Oriental plane. To the north-west is landscaped parkland where woods descend to the curving lake formed before 1729 and later extended. West of the house stands a cedar of Lebanon and a collection of magnolias around a nineteenth-century fountain. Elsewhere in the park is the Gothick tower of 1773 and the mausoleum of 1796 – a pyramid nearly 14 metres square by Joseph Bonomi. The Trust has now restored the park to its 1840 limits and replanted 30 acres of the Great Wood. Truly a garden for all seasons.

Bradenham Hall ★

Bradenham, Thetford IP25 7QP. Tel: (01362) 687243/687279

Mr and Mrs Christian Allhusen • 8m E of Swaffham, 5m W of East Dereham S off A47 • Open April to Sept, 2nd and 4th Suns in month, 2 – 5.30pm, and for NGS 25th April, 25th July, 26th Sept. Coach parties on open days or at other times by written appt (with meals if requested) • Entrance: £3, children under 12 free • Other information: Plant sale 22nd Aug ● ☕ WC & ⚘

The gardens sit near the top of one of Norfolk's highest hills and give a fine view to the south over rolling farmland. The gardens and arboretum comprise about 27 acres and surround a fine early-Georgian brick house (not open). Since the site is windy, the gardens are divided by many yew hedges screening 90 yards of herbaceous borders, backing onto shrubs and the Philosophers' Walk. There is a paved garden and a large old-fashioned rose garden. The other borders contain a plantsman's collection of shrubs, flowers and trees. The house and garden walls are covered with a wide range of shrubs, climbers and fruit. The walled kitchen garden has vegetables, cut flowers and a mixed border backed by laburnums, and there are two glasshouses, an attractive old barn and a millennium aviary. The arboretum, of about 800 varieties (all labelled), is underplanted for spring with fritillaries and large drifts of naturalised daffodils (some 90 cultivars). Noted gardeners have described Bradenham as 'exceptional' and 'a must' for visitors.

Bressingham Gardens ★

Bressingham, Diss IP22 2AB. Tel: (01379) 686900

Mr Alan Bloom and Mr and Mrs Adrian Bloom • 2½ m W of Diss on A1066 • Open early April to end Oct, daily: Dell Garden, 10.30am – 4.30pm (closes 4pm Oct), Foggy Bottom, 12.30 – 4.30pm • Entrance: £7.50, OAPs £6.50, children £5 (includes entry to Steam Experience) (2003 prices) ◑ ☕ ✗ 🍴 WC & ⚘ 🏛 ♿ ☕ B&B

Over 14 acres of beautiful gardens still under creation by the Bloom family with over 8000 species and varieties of plants on display in five gardens. Alan Bloom created the six-acre *Dell Garden* with its famous island beds set in park-like meadow between 1955 and 1962. Planted with perennials to give colour and interest from spring to autumn, the wide and varied collection includes many Bressingham-raised varieties. The *Summer Garden* is at the entrance, and here the National Collection of miscanthus mingles with early- to late-summer-flowering plants like crocosmia, agapanthus, helenium and phlox. The new *Winter Garden* opens in autumn 2004. *Foggy Bottom* is a different style of garden, designed and created by Adrian Bloom over 30 years ago. It sparkles with colour, principally from the excellent collection of blue and gold conifers, shrubs and ornamental trees, which provide a backdrop for seasonal plantings of perennials, grasses and bulbs. The 'River of Blood', a snaking broad drift of massed plantings of the Japanese blood grass *Imperata cylindrica* 'Rubra', is a stunning sight from midsummer onwards. Linking the Dell Garden and Foggy Bottom, a new pathway goes through the *Shrub Garden*, planted with mature ornamental species, and *Adrian's Wood*, which contains a collection of North American native plants. Then visit the national Dad's Army Collection and the steam museum where engines and trains chug away and whistle — but these nostalgic sounds do not detract from the overall peace of the garden.

Castle Acre Priory

Castle Acre, King's Lynn PE32 2AF. Tel: (01760) 755394

English Heritage • 5m N of Swaffham, ¼ m W of Castle Acre, off A1065 • Open April to Oct, daily, 10am – 6pm (closes 5pm in Oct); Nov to March, Wed – Sun, 10am – 4pm. Closed 24th to 26th Dec and 1st Jan • Entrance: £4, OAPs £3, children £2, family £9.30 (2003 prices) ○ 🍽 🛍 WC ♿ ⟨♿⟩ 🛍 🌳 ⚲

This is a walled herb garden divided into four sections containing medicinal, decorative, culinary and strewing herbs. Lavenders line the walls, where there are also three apple trees dating from the sixteenth century; a central circular bed contains a bay tree. Two small beds on the outside of the boundary wall are planted with medieval-period flowers. The Old Rectory, South Acre (see entry) is nearby, and *West Acre Gardens*, a commercial nursery for rare plants set in a two-acre walled kitchen garden, about four miles away.

Congham Hall Hotel

Lynn Road, Grimston, King's Lynn PE32 1AH. Tel: (01485) 600250

Julie Woodhouse, General Manager • 7m NE of King's Lynn. From A149/A148 interchange, follow A148 signed 'Sandringham/Fakenham/Cromer' for 100 metres. Turn right for Grimston. Hotel is 2½ m on left • Open April to Sept, daily except Sat. Small parties by appt at other times • Entrance: free • Other information: No coaches ◑ 🍽 ✕ WC ♿ 🌿 ⚲

The hotel, set in 40 acres of parkland with a neat parterre full of bright bedding at the entrance, is listed in the *Good Food Guide*. It merits an entry in this *Guide* for its formal herb garden with about 650 varieties of both culinary and medicinal herbs, each labelled in an eccentric manner, although it also has some herbaceous plantings and pergolas with roses. The herb garden was started some 13 years ago to supply the hotel kitchen, and is thus a working garden. A 'woodery' accommodates the increasing collection of herbs, using timber salvaged from fallen trees instead of rocks.

Corpusty Mill Garden ★

Corpusty, Norwich NR11 6QB Tel: (01263) 587223

Roger Last • 6m S of Holt. Turn off B1149 at Corpusty; mill is in centre of village • Open for parties only by appt • Entrance: £5 ◗

This four-acre garden is as unexpected as it is intriguing, gradually revealing itself as a complex series of interlinked spaces, each with a mood and character of its own. The planting is varied and lush with a rich collection of trees, shrubs, herbaceous and water-loving plants. Water is everywhere, in fountains, ponds, a stream, a small lake and a river. Buildings and follies are discovered as the garden unfolds: a long high flint wall inset with heads of Roman emperors, a Gothic arch with knapped flints, and a pitch-dark and mysterious four-chambered grotto, built of moss-covered ginger sandstone. Elsewhere, a Gothick ruin with a spiral staircase, a flint humpback bridge and a classical pavilion in the kitchen garden, with ornamental compost containers. A separate area, rich in trees, has been developed as a landscaped meadow. Here a small lake with a raised bank and walkway on one side is dominated by a gunnera and a tall, slender stainless steel cone. A water-filled cave reveals a figure drowning or rising up from the mud. To the north, the River Bure forms a tranquil natural boundary. By the house a contemporary formal garden, with a stainless steel water column and a central rill and pool, completes a highly eclectic but well-judged sequence of different styles and moods.

Courtyard Farm ★

Ringstead, Kings Lynn PE36 5LQ.

Lord Melchett • 16m NE of King's Lynn, 3½ m E of Hunstanton, 2m E of Ringstead, on road crossing Ringstead Common to Chosely and Burnham Market • Open all year, daily • Entrance: free ○ 🐾 ⬦

The primeval gardener was a stone-age farmer who enjoyed the wild flowers that spattered his little fields of ripening grain, and Courtyard Farm harks back to those prehistoric days of marigolds and corncockles. The best time to visit is in July. Take a circular walk through fields of ripening grain and acres of wild flowers – 93 plant species have been identified in the grassland areas, 29 in the cornfields. This is not gardening on a small scale, but it is a most praiseworthy effort to retain our natural heritage of wild and cultivated plants. On many farms the cornflowers have been exterminated as weeds – there are no weeds here! Most heartening.

East Ruston Old Vicarage ★★

East Ruston, Norwich NR12 9HN. Tel: (01692) 650432 (daytime)

Graham Robeson and Alan Gray • 15m NE of Norwich, 4m E of North Walsham. Turn off A149 signed to Walcot and Bacton, then left at T-junction. After 2m, the house is next to the church • Open 28th March to 30th Oct, Sat,

Sun, Wed, Fri and Bank Holiday Mons, 2 – 5.30pm, and by appt for coach parties • Entrance: £4, children £1, season ticket £12.50 ◑ 🍵 **WC** ♿ 🌿 🔦

This garden has as much to offer in style as in substance, for its twin strengths are the architectural framework of walls and hedges and an astonishing profusion of plants. Two Norfolk churches and a lighthouse are visible from the garden, and play a fundamental role as focal points at the end of skilfully crafted vistas. Within the garden the value of theatre is not forgotten. Tall dark hedges with openings beckon the visitor on to yet more discoveries: a box parterre and sunken garden, superb herbaceous borders, a Mediterranean garden and, one of the most striking elements, a tropical border recently trebled in size and relocated. How rare to find bananas growing one and a half miles from the North Sea, their leaves intact, surrounded by equally luxurious foliage of cannas and many other exotics. Rare plants are everywhere, set in gravel or in borders; because of the garden's coastal setting, many are semi-hardy and shrubs from the southern hemisphere are well represented. On the perimeter, a cornfield achieves an astonishing density and brilliance of summer colour, and the garden continues to be developed with apparently limitless energy on the part of the owners. A Desert Wash has mature palms, agaves, dasylirions, colourful lampranthus, delospermas, cacti and self-sown annuals, all left out for winter.

Elsing Hall ★

Elsing, East Dereham NR20 3DX. Tel: (01362) 637224

Mr and Mrs D.H. Cargill • 5m NE of East Dereham. Signed off A47 • Open June to Sept, Sun, 2 – 6pm, and by appt • Entrance: £3, children free ◑ 🍵 🧺 **WC** ♿ ◁▷ 🌿

The romantic appearance of the garden is in complete harmony with the moated half-timbered and flint house which it surrounds. It is rich, lush and unrestrained, and in midsummer is filled with the scent of the old roses which cover the walls and fill the borders. The lawn between the house and the moat has been abandoned to wild orchids; wildfowl nest among the reeds. Both the moat and a nearby stewpond are encircled by moist borders supporting luxuriant growth. On the walls of the kitchen garden grow more old roses, many of which seem unique to this place, and more are continually being added. A large variety of trees has been planted, a formal garden developed, and an avenue of ginkgos established.

The Exotic Garden

6 Cotman Road, Thorpe, Norwich NR1 4AF. Tel: (01603) 623167

Mr W.R.S. Giles • In E Norwich off A47 Thorpe road, ¼ m from Norwich station. From Yarmouth follow one-way system towards city centre, turn right at traffic lights opposite DEFRA building. New entrance and car park via side entrance of Alan Boswell Insurance, 126 Thorpe Road, next to DEFRA building • Open 27th June to 10th Oct, Sun, 1.30 – 5.30 pm, and for parties of 10 or more by appt • Entrance: £3.50, children free, parties £5 per person incl. refreshments ◑ 🍵 🧺 **WC** 🌿 ⚲

An exotic garden of half an acre on a south-facing hillside, with tall trees and hedges creating a sheltered microclimate. The unusual collection of plants includes gingers, bananas, aroids and succulents. The garden reaches its peak in high to late summer, when such exotics as cannas and brugmansias are in full bloom. It is also renowned for its use of house plants as bedding plants. Tillandsias may be spotted in the branches of trees which are underplanted with codiaeums, guzmanias and tradescantias. Philodendrons and *Monstera deliciosa* are also used in this way, flourishing in the summer months. There are many flint walls and two raised pools. A feeling of fantasy pervades the whole place, especially in the evening when the various scents are at their headiest. A new half-acre garden has been added for hardy exotics that need far less maintenance and tolerate winter cold.

Fairhaven Woodland and Water Garden ★

School Road, South Walsham, Norwich NR13 6DZ. Tel: (01603) 270449

The Fairhaven Garden Trust • 9m NE of Norwich. At South Walsham, follow brown tourist-signs on A47 at junction with B1140 • Open all year, daily except 25th Dec, 10am – 5pm; May to Aug, Wed, Thurs, 10am – 9pm. Guided walks for parties • Entrance: £3.50, OAPs £3, children £1.25, under 5 free. Annual membership £12.50, family membership £30, wildlife sanctuary £1. Discounts for parties • Other information: Boat trips available May to Aug ○ ⬤ ✕ 🖌 WC 🚾 ♿ ⬱ ⚘ 🏕 🔦 ⚒

A garden created in natural woods of oak and alder extending to about 180 acres and surrounding the unspoiled (private) South Walsham Inner Broad. Paths wind among banks of azaleas and large-leaved rhododendrons and lead to the edge of the broad itself. Much of the area is wet and supports a rich variety of primulas, especially candelabras, with lysichitums, hostas, astilbes, ligularias and gunneras of exceptional size merging into the natural vegetation, among which are many royal ferns and some majestic oaks. Although particularly colourful during the flowering of the azaleas and rhododendrons in the spring, the garden gives pleasure at all times of the year if natural beauty is preferred to man-made sophistication. Three miles of woodland walks with fine views.

Felbrigg Hall ★ [Historic Garden Grade II*]

Felbrigg, Norwich NR11 8PR. Tel: (01263) 837444

The National Trust • 2m SW of Cromer off A148. Entrance on B1436 • Hall open as garden, 1 – 5pm • Garden and walled garden open 20th March to Oct, Sat – Wed, 11am – 5pm; garden also open 22nd July to 3rd Sept, daily, 1 – 5pm. Park and woodland walks open all year, daily, dawn – dusk • Entrance: £2.50, children £1 (house and gardens £6, children £3, parties £5.10 per person) • Other information: Self-drive scooter available • Garden: ◑ ⬤ ✕ 🖌 WC ♿ ⚘ 🏕 🔦 ⚒ *Park:* ○ ⬱ ⚒

The Jacobean house faces south across the park, which is notable for its fine woods and lakeside walk. William Windham III, the great-grandson of the builder of the hall, was Humphry Repton's landlord. A ha-ha separates the park from the lawns of the house, where there is an orangery planted with camellias. To the north the ground rises and there are specimen trees and shrubs, including many of North American origin. At some distance to the east a large walled kitchen garden is now richly planted with a combination of fruit, vegetables and flowers in a formal design behind clipped hedges; it contains a vine house and a great brick dovecot with a flock of doves. In early autumn there is a display of many varieties of colchicums: the National Collection is kept here. The gardens are in immaculate order, and restoration, renewal and replacement continue at a brisk pace. Sheringham Park, also by Repton (see entry), is nearby.

Fritton Lake Countryworld

Fritton, Great Yarmouth NR31 9HA. Tel: (01493) 488208

Lord and Lady Somerleyton • 5m SW of Great Yarmouth off A143 • Open April to Sept, daily, 10am – 5.30pm • Entrance: £5.80, OAPs £5, children £4. Discounts for parties • Other information: Falconry, heavy horses, golf, putting, boats, children's farm, pony rides, miniature tractors, miniature railway, cycle trail, self-catering accommodation ◑ ☕ ✕ 🏬 WC ⑇ 🏛 ⛲ ⚲

The large lake remains almost unspoilt and separate from the tea rooms and other commercial attractions of this country park. An unusual feature is a Victorian garden of about half an acre in the gardenesque style with irregular beds surrounded by clipped box hedges and filled with shrubs and herbaceous perennials. In addition to the formal lakeside gardens there are woodland walks and gardens, including the Lost Gardens of Fritton Hall – the Victorian hall burned down in 1957 and the gardens were left to go wild – which contain a large collection of rhododendrons and azaleas intersected by paths.

The Garden in an Orchard

Mill Road, Bergh Apton, Norwich NR15 1BQ. Tel: (01508) 480322

Mr and Mrs R.W. Boardman • 6m SE of Norwich off A146 at Hellington Corner • Open Bank Holiday weekends and several others May to Sept, 11am – 6pm (but check before visiting) • Entrance: £1.50 • Other information: Refreshments on Suns only ◑ ☕ 🏬 WC ⑇ ⚘ ⛲

The garden started as a three-and-a-half-acre commercial orchard and over the years has been planted up bit by bit with rare and unusual plants and trees. Narrow paths meander through dense plantings of species roses, giving eye-to-eye contact with their flowers, then open up to similar plantings of herbaceous walks. Mr Boardman is a professional plantsman and among his rare trees are *Phellodendron amurense*, *Prunus padus* 'Colorata', *Paulownia tomentosa* and nine species of eucalyptus. *Lonicera ledebourii* catches the eye, along with *Malva sylvestris* subsp. *mauritanica* and many special clematis scrambling through trees. A half-acre wildflower meadow, with a wide range of British flora, is maturing.

Hales Hall

Hales, Loddon NR14 6QW. Tel: (01508) 548395

Mr and Mrs Terence Read • 12m SE of Norwich, off A146. Signposted • Open all year, Mon – Sat, 10am – 4pm, Sun and Bank Holiday Mons, 11am – 4pm. Closed 9th April. Guided parties by arrangement • Entrance: £2 (Great Barn and gardens) • Other information: Fifteenth-century thatched Great Barn ○ WC ⅃ ⚘

A moat surrounds the remaining wing of a vast house of the late fifteenth century and a central lawn with well-planted borders and topiary of box and yew backed by high brick walls. Work is continuing on the restoration of the garden after centuries of neglect. A fruit garden has been planted, and there is a pot-grown orchard. The owners specialise in rare and unusual perennial plants, and look after National Collections of citrus, figs and greenhouse grapes. The associated century-old nurseries offer an extensive range of conservatory plants, vines, figs, mulberries, and many peach, apricot, nectarine and greengage varieties.

Holkham Hall ★ [Historic Garden Grade I]

Wells-next-the-Sea NR23 1AB.
Tel: (01328) 710806 or (01328) 711636 (Holkham Nursery Gardens)

The Earl of Leicester • 23m W of Cromer, 2m W of Wells on A149 • Hall and Terrace Garden probably open end May to Sept – telephone to check. Nursery gardens open daily except 25th, 26th Dec, March to Oct, 10am – 5pm, Nov to Feb, 11am – dusk • Entrance: Terrace and nursery gardens free (hall and bygones museum £10, children £5, family £25). Discount for parties of 20 or more • Terrace gardens: ◑ ♨ ✕ 🗃 WC ⅃ 🛖 ♀ ✊ *Nursery gardens:* ○ ⚘

The vast park, famous for its holm oaks, was laid out originally by William Kent but altered by 'Coke of Norfolk' and the 2nd Earl. On the west side of the house, lawns sweep down to the great lake. The terrace which fronts the south façade was added in 1854, but the scale of the house and park is so great that, from a distance at least, this does not seriously disrupt the vision of the two. The formal beds designed by W.A. Nesfield flank a great fountain representing St George and the Dragon, said to be designed by R. Smith. The nursery gardens in the original eighteenth-century walled kitchen garden in the grounds extend to over six acres, subdivided into six areas with perennial borders and the original greenhouses. Alpines, shrubs, perennials, herbs, roses, bedding and house plants are for sale. About five miles away, at South Creake, is another nursery worth visiting, the *Creake Plant Centre*.

Houghton Hall ★ [Historic Garden Grade I]

King's Lynn PE31 6UE. Tel: (01485) 528569

The Marquess of Cholmondeley • 13m NE of King's Lynn off A148 • Hall open as garden • Park and gardens open 20th April to 28th Sept, Thurs, Sun and Bank Holiday Mons; plus June to Sept, Wed; all 2 – 5.30pm • Entrance: £3.50,

children £2 (hall, park and gardens £6, children £3) (2003 prices) ◐ ☕ 🥄
WC ♿ 🐾 🏛

One of the most magnificent houses in Britain curiously never seems to have
had a formal garden in the eighteenth century: it was not until the 1890s
that it acquired a garden on the west front. Since 1991 the five-acre walled
kitchen garden has been completely renovated by the present Marquess
with a double herbaceous border as its centrepiece. The remainder of the
space is divided by yew hedges into 20 individually themed garden rooms,
including a box-edged rose parterre. A wide outer border has some of the
older rose varieties and a mixture of foxgloves, pinks and delphiniums. In
the kitchen garden proper are trained fruit trees, a huge rustic fruit cage
and vegetable beds filled with unusual varieties; elsewhere, pleached limes
surround a grassy area planted with 200 plum trees and spring and summer
bulbs. The cherry walk is underplanted with irises, and a wisteria pergola
runs along the western edge of the garden. Behind, a border is given over to
peonies and lilies, while an autumn border of asters, Japanese anemones and
sunflowers provides a blaze of colour from August onwards. The rebuilt
glasshouses contain an expanding orchid collection, an unusual water feature
by Julian Bannerman. A rustic temple, a Kent seat, Italian statues, a sunken
pool and a modern obelisk add architectural flourishes.

Hoveton Hall Gardens

Wroxham, Norwich NR12 8RJ. Tel: (01603) 782798

*Mr and Mrs Andrew Buxton • 9m NE of Norwich, 1m N of Wroxham on
A1151 • Open 11th April to Sept, Wed, Fri, Sun and Bank Holiday Mons, plus
Thurs in May, all 11am – 5.30pm. Coach parties and tours by arrangement •
Entrance: £3.75, wheelchairs £2, children (5–14) £1, season tickets £9.50,
family £20* ◐ ☕ 🥄 WC ♿ 🐾 ☕

Set in the Norfolk Broads area, the gardens are amply supplied with water and
streams. For mid-May and early June the rhododendrons and azaleas, many
rare varieties, are spectacular, dominating and scenting the woodland walks.
The formal walled garden, planted and enclosed in 1936, with herbaceous
borders of that period, is being renewed; a delightful gardener's cottage is set
picturesquely in one corner, covered in roses. The adjoining walled kitchen
garden is a good example of traditional vegetable planting. The entrance to the
two walled gardens has an intriguing iron gate in the shape of a spider, hence
the formal garden is called the Spider Garden. A water garden, leading to the
lake, has good water plants, vast *Gunnera manicata*, peltiphyllums, hostas and
fine stands of bamboos. The whole area is laced with streams and interesting
bridges, and birds, both migratory and native, abound.

How Hill Farm ★

Ludham, Gt. Yarmouth NR29 5PG. Tel: (01692) 678558

*Mr P.D.S. Boardman • 15m NE of Norwich, 1m W of Ludham off A1062.
Follow signs to How Hill. Farm Garden S of How Hill • Open probably 23rd*

May, 2 – 5pm, and to parties at other times by appt • Entrance: £2.50, children free ● ☕ 🐾 ← ⬭ ✎

The garden around the farm is comparatively conventional, with a new garden and pond in the old bullock yard and a large Chusan palm planted in a dog cage from which it threatens to escape. Here, too, is a collection of over 100 varieties of *Ilex aquifolium* as well as many other rare ilex species. Over the road in the river valley is a rich combination of exotics mingled with native vegetation. Around a series of pools, banks of azaleas merge into reed beds, rhododendron species rise over thickets of fern, wild grasses skirt groves of the giant *Arundo donax*, with birches, conifers and a collection of 50 different bamboos against a background of a recently created three-acre broad, thick with water lilies. The soil acidity ranges from pH 2.8 to pH 7.5, supporting a wide variety of trees and shrubs.

Kettle Hill ★

Blakeney NR25 7PN. Tel: (01263) 741147

Richard and Frances Winch • 11m W of Cromer, just outside Blakeney on B1156 Langham road • Parking • Open for parties by appt • Entrance: £5 (includes coffee), children free ● ☕ WC ← ⚹

With the help of Mark Rumary, the owners have transformed this garden into a luxurious and elegant delight. A box-edged rectangular parterre with heart-shaped beds, heightened with topiary spirals and mop heads, reflects their interest in the *Romantic Garden Nursery* at Swannington. A cleverly sited brick wall shelters a long mixed border packed with colour and unusual plants and leads to a circular secret garden. A large lawn, featuring a delightful Gothick summerhouse by George Carter, extends from the house to mature wood-land, to which many ornamental trees have been added and which is carpeted in spring with bluebells and naturalised lilies. A new rose garden has been planted adjoining the house to replace an old one in the wood which had passed its peak.

Lake House Water Gardens

Brundall, Norwich NR13 5LU. Tel: (01603) 712933

Mr and Mrs Garry Muter • 5m E of Norwich. From A47 roundabout take Brundall turn and turn right at T-junction into Postwick Lane • Open 11th, 12th April, 11am – 5pm; and for parties of 20 or more by appt • Entrance: £3, children free • Other information: Sale of unusual plants on open days ● ☕ 🐾 ⬭ ✎

Two acres of water gardens, once part of a 76-acre private estate and arboretum planted about 1880, are set in a steep cleft in the river escarpment. From the top of the hill the gardens fall away to a lily-covered lake at the bottom. New water features, a fountain and waterfall have recently been added. Plant associations throughout the garden reflect Mrs Muter's talent as a flower arranger. Surrounding the formal areas are drifts of primroses, blue-bells and daffodils in season; wild flowers abound. The formal planting has many rare and interesting species: *Zantedeschia aethiopica* 'Green Goddess' and 'Crowborough' in a large clump cool down a flamboyant *Hemerocallis* 'Frans Hals'. A wide variety of hardy geraniums blooms in succession and a good collection of hybrid helianthemums awaits those who visit by appointment in June.

Lawn Farm

Cley Road, Holt NR25 7DY. Tel: (01263) 713484

Mr and Mrs G.W. Deterding • From Holt take Cley Road opposite King's Head pub in High Street. After 1m, turning is signposted on right after Holt Hall School gates • Open April to July by appt • Entrance: £3, children free ◐ WC ♿

The six-and-a-half-acre garden was designed and laid out by the owners in 1987. There are five natural ponds with three water gardens, and a very damp wooded area with hydrangeas and azaleas. A completely different atmosphere is to be found in the two medieval flint-walled courtyards; here roses and many interesting and unusual shrubs and climbers flourish in the hot and sheltered microclimate. Mrs Deterding has a magpie's eye for the rare and difficult to find, including a good collection of unusual trees.

Lexham Hall [Historic Garden Grade II]

East Lexham, King's Lynn PE32 2QJ. Tel: (01328) 701288/701341

Mr and Mrs Neil Foster • 6m N of Swaffham, 2m W of Litcham off B1145 • Open two Suns in Feb for snowdrops – please telephone for details; 16th May, and May to July mid-week for parties of 20 or more by appt • Entrance: £3, parties £4 per person ◐ WC

The seventeenth- and eighteenth-century hall sits well amid beautiful parkland with sheep and interesting trees. The ground falls away to the river forming a lake and canals crossed by elegant bridges; the garden was the inspiration of the present owner's mother who, with the help of the late Dame Sylvia Crowe, laid out its bones. Massive yew hedges reveal intimate views of the park, taking the eye to the distance beyond. Wide terracing to the south of the house is well planted and colourful, and a long grass walk edged with herbaceous plants and shrubs progresses to woodland full of rhododendrons, azaleas, camellias, rare trees and spring bulbs. (In early spring, the parkland and adjoining churchyard are awash with snowdrops.) There is a colourful rose garden, and the kitchen garden has an early eighteenth-century crinkle-crankle wall covered with fruit, a cutting border, greenhouses with plants for the house and tender vegetables, the whole a picture of health. A wood to the south, known as the American Gardens, is reputedly planted from seeds collected in America.

Magpies

Green Lane, Mundford IP26 5HS. Tel: (01842) 878496

Patricia Cooper • 7m NW of Thetford, ½ m N of A134 Downham Market – Thetford road at Mundford roundabout, or off A1065 Swaffham road • Open

May to July, Tues – Sun; nursery open March to Sept, daily except Wed; all 11am – 5pm. Closed 24th, 25th Aug • Entrance: £1.50 per person for group visits (for charity) • Other information: Picnic facilities by arrangement only ◐ WC ✍

The garden in midsummer is a living display of vegetable fireworks, but for all that it is a tranquil, subtle place. Shimmering fountains of golden oats (*Stipa gigantea*) are its hallmark. Larches and birches provide a light canopy over irregular island beds boldly planted with perennials. Tall mulleins and evening primroses are mixed with chicories and plume poppies, while the fragrance of jasmine and honeysuckle hangs in the air. It is a real cottage garden of informal rooms, each one filled to the brim with interesting plants. There is a pond and shady nooks and crannies where you may even chance to see a wandering hedgehog snuffling about under the billowing cranesbills. Many of the excellent, modestly priced plants are for sale. Worth visiting, on the A1065 Swaffham road, is *Lynford Arboretum* and, to the south, Lynford Lakes and Zig-Zag Covert. Lynford Hall, a hotel specialising in organic food, is also nearby.

Mannington Hall ★ [Historic Garden Grade II]

Saxthorpe, Norwich NR11 7BB. Tel: (01263) 584175

Lord and Lady Walpole • 5m SE of Holt off B1149. Signposted • Open May to Sept, Sun, 12 noon – 5pm; also June to Aug, Wed – Fri, 11am – 5pm • Entrance: £3, OAPs and students £2.50, children free ◐ ☕ 🍽 WC ♿ ✍ 🏛 ♀

A romantic garden of 20 acres with a fifteenth-century house. Lawns run down to the moat, crossed by a drawbridge, to herbaceous borders backed by high walls of brick and flint. The moat also encloses a secret, scented garden in a design derived from one of the ceilings of the house. Outside the moat are borders of flowering shrubs flanking a Doric temple, and woodlands beyond contain the ruins of a Saxon church and nineteenth-century follies. Within the walls of the former kitchen garden, a series of rose gardens has been planted following the design of gardens from medieval to modern times and featuring roses popular at each period. A twentieth-century rose garden incorporates a planthouse, a vegetable plot and a children's garden. There are now more than 1500 varieties of roses here. In 2003 a sensory garden was created on the south lawn with a narrow channel of water and four large beds with plants chosen for scent, touch, sight, taste and hearing. A lake, woods and meadowland with extensive walks are other features.

Norfolk Lavender

Caley Mill, Heacham, King's Lynn PE31 7JE. Tel: (01485) 570384

Norfolk Lavender Ltd • 13m N of King's Lynn on A149 • Open all year, daily except 25th, 26th Dec, 1st Jan, 10am – 5pm (closes 4pm Nov to March) • Entrance: free ○ ☕ ✕ WC ♿ 🚲 ✍ 🏛 🍽 ♀ ✂

Fields of lavender, stretching into the distance like giant stripes of corduroy, are a splendid sight in July and August. There is a more intimate display of named lavender (designated as a National Collection) near the Victorian watermill that serves as the visitor centre for this major commercial enterprise. A small herb garden is well tended and labelled, and the beds in the rose garden are lavender-edged. The four-acre fragrant garden has helped to reduce the pressure of visitors, particularly in July and August.

Oxburgh Hall [Historic Garden Grade II]

Oxborough, King's Lynn PE33 9PS. Tel: (01366) 328258

The National Trust • 7m SW of Swaffham off A134 • House open 20th March to 7th Nov, Sat – Wed, 1 – 5pm (Bank Holiday Mons opens 11am) • Garden open 28th Feb to 14th March, Sat, Sun, 11am – 4pm; 22nd March to July, Sept to 2nd Nov, Sat – Wed; 31st July to Aug, daily; all 11am – 5.30pm • Entrance: £2.80, children £1.40 (hall and garden £5.50, children £2.80, family £14.50) (2003 prices) ◑ ☕ ✕ 🍽 WC ⅊ 🚻 ♿

The gatehouse is the glory of Oxburgh, and the mellow red-brick early-Tudor manor house seems to float in its rectangular moat above a haze of fringed water lilies. Both house and garden are concealed from view until you have walked past the orchard of quince, plum and greengage trees. Then you look down over the formal parterre, a Victorian copy of a Le Nôtre design consisting of a moderately restrained pattern of beds edged with clipped box hedges, punctuated by clipped tumps of yew. Yellow, red, violet and silver are the colours of the annual bedding – a vibrant carpet. Behind a long yew hedge is a narrow border edged with wispy catmint, with carefully repeated clumps of perennials: loosestrife, golden-rod, daisies and mallows. There are some fine trees, and circular walks lead into the park and woodland, full of snowdrops and winter aconites in early spring.

Pensthorpe

Pensthorpe, Fakenham NR21 OLN. Tel: (01328) 851465

Mr and Mrs B. Jordan • 1m E of Fakenham on A1067 Norwich – Fakenham road. Signposted • Open March to Dec, daily; Jan to March, Sat and Sun; all 10am – 5pm (Nov to Jan closes 4.30pm) • Entrance: £5.50, OAPs £5, children £3. Special rates for parties of 15 or more ○ ☕ ✕ 🍽 WC ⅊ 🐾 🚻 ♿ ⚲

The 200-acre park and nature reserve, already well-known for one of Europe's finest collections of endangered and exotic water birds, also has a feature of considerable interest to gardeners. In 1999 the well-known Dutch designer and plantsman Piet Oudolf was commissioned to create a millennium garden overlooking one of the lakes. Extending to nearly an acre, it is one of the largest project he has undertaken in the UK. The perennial planting style for which he has become famous is both spectacular and sensitive, blending well into the environment of the park where a traditional English garden would have looked out of place. There are large drifts and clumps of herbaceous plants, interspersed with grasses such as miscanthus and calamagrostis to contrast with other areas of deschampsia and lower-growing sesleria. The early flowering of *Nepeta subsessilis*, a spectacular planting of *Cimicifuga simplex*

'James Compton', various geraniums and monardas help ensure that this remains one of the finest plantings of perennials in the country. The garden is at its best in July, August and September, but should not be forgotten through the autumn, especially if your visit coincides with a hoar frost. The darker areas near the water provide excellent growing conditions for lobelias, drifts of Lythrum salicaria 'Stichflamme' and L. virgatum. Oudolf has also used substantial plantings of eupatoriums, thalictrums and echinaceas. The garden is a paradise for huge numbers of butterflies, bumble-bees and insects. A woodland garden was planted in 2002. There is also an adventure playground for children and walk-through aviaries for all ages.

The Plantation Garden [Historic Garden Grade II]

4 Earlham Road, Norwich NR2 3DB.
Tel: (01603) 621868 (Trust chairman: Mr B.M. Adam)

Plantation Garden Preservation Trust • Entrance off Earlham Road, next to Beeches Hotel • Open daily, 9am – 6pm, or dusk if earlier. Guided parties by arrangement • Entrance: £2 (honesty box), accompanied children free, guided parties by arrangement ● WC ⅊ ⚘ ☕

This unusual surviving example of a high-Victorian suburban garden, framed by mature trees, was created by Henry Trevor in a disused chalk quarry just outside the medieval walls of Norwich. The first feature in his garden, an idiosyncratic Gothick fountain over nine metres high, was built in 1857. There followed terraces with walls in the medieval style (random rubble), built using an extraordinary conglomeration of materials: industrial waste, locally made fancy bricks, flint and stone. Flights of steps with Italianate pedestals and balustrades, a rustic-style bridge and summerhouse, flower beds and woodland paths combine to make a garden simultaneously typical of its period and the personal vision of one individual. Conservation and restoration is an on-going process. It is also an area of ecological interest with birds and lime-loving wild flowers. The replica summerhouse on the upper terrace gives a view over the whole garden.

Raveningham Hall [Historic Garden Grade II*]

Raveningham, Norwich NR14 6NS. Tel: (01508) 548152

Sir Nicholas Bacon • 14m SE of Norwich off A146. Turn left at Hales on B1136, then first right • Open 11th, 12th April, 2nd, 3rd, 30th, 31st May, 27th, 28th June, 29th, 30th Aug, 2 – 5pm • Entrance: £2.50, children free ● ☕ WC ⅊ ⚘

Set in a fine landscaped park, the garden has a rich variety of trees, shrubs and herbaceous plants, and is notable in spring for a large collection of galanthus species and varieties. Its eighteenth-century and Victorian past are still in evidence: the herb garden incorporates physic plantings, and the walled kitchen garden and greenhouses are still in use. An arboretum with some unusual trees is being extended towards the lake. Sculpture is well placed all around this peaceful garden.

Sandringham House ★ [Historic Garden Grade II*]

Sandringham, King's Lynn PE35 6EN. Tel: (01553) 772675

H.M. The Queen • 9m NE of King's Lynn on B1440 near Sandringham Church • House open as garden • Garden and park open Easter to July, early Aug to Oct, daily, 11am – 4.45pm • Entrance: museum and grounds £5.50, OAPs £4.50, children £3.50, family £14.50 (house, museum and grounds £6.50, OAPs £5, children £4, family £17) ◑ ☕ ✕ WC 🚾 ↻ ⌂ ♿

The huge Victorian house stands among broad lawns with an outer belt of woodland through which a path runs past plantings of camellias, hydrangeas, cornus, magnolias and rhododendrons, with some fine specimen trees including *Davidia involucrata* and *Cercidiphyllum japonicum*. The path passes the magnificent cast- and wrought-iron Norwich Gates of 1862. In the open lawn are specimen oaks planted by Queen Victoria and other members of the Royal Family. To the south-west of the house the eastern side of the upper lake is built up into a massive rock garden using blocks of the local carrstone, and now largely planted with dwarf conifers. Below the rock garden, opening onto the lake, a cavernous grotto was intended as a boathouse; above is a small summerhouse built for Queen Alexandra. There are thick plantings of hostas, agapanthus and various moisture-loving plants around the margin of the lake. The path passes between the upper and lower lakes set in wooded surroundings. To the north of the house is a garden designed by the late Sir Geoffrey Jellicoe for King George VI.

Sheringham Park ★ [Historic Garden Grade II*]

Upper Sheringham NR26 8TB. Tel: (01263) 823778

The National Trust • 4m NE of Holt off A148 • Open all year, daily, dawn – dusk • Entrance: £2.80 per car inc. parking and all occupants. Coaches £8.40 • Other information: Coaches must pre-book with Warden during rhododendron season. Refreshments available April to Sept only ○ ☕ 🛍 WC 🚾 ↻

Located in a secluded valley at the edge of the Cromer/Holt ridge, close to the sea but protected from its winds by steep wooded hills, the house and park, both designed by Humphry Repton, are now the property of the Trust, although the house is in tenanted occupation. The park is remarkable not only for its beauty and spectacular views but also for an extensive collection of rhododendrons which thrive in the acid soil. Crowning an eminence is a modern classical temple based on a Repton design and erected to mark the 70th birthday of Mr Thomas Upcher, the last descendant of the original owner to live at Sheringham. This is the most-admired and best-preserved work of Repton.

Stow Hall ★

Stow Bardolph, King's Lynn PE34 3HU. Tel: (01366) 383194

Lady Rose Hare • 2m N of Downham Market, E of A10 • Open 28th March, 25th April, 30th May, 20th June, 3rd Oct for NGS, 2 – 6pm, and for parties by appt • Entrance: £3, children free • Other information: Possible for wheelchairs but some gravel paths ● ☕ 🛍 WC 🚾 ↻ ⌂ ♿

Majestic plane trees, beeches and cedars of Lebanon certainly two centuries old provide a changing backdrop for a garden that is in effect a long series of imaginative and interesting gardens linked by a straight path of red bricks and gravel. The high, warm walls of the old stableyard and the house are swathed in roses and wisteria – this is a paradise for anyone enthralled by old roses. Shrubs more usually seen in milder gardens also have congenial homes in the shelter of these walls – vanilla-scented *Azara microphylla*, white and blue abutilon, sun roses, Californian lilac, and many others. Amble along the path from the house to the nineteenth-century walled kitchen garden and you pass small elegant formal gardens, a mixed perennial garden including irises, a Dutch garden, cloisters with more roses, and a croquet lawn. Inside the kitchen garden you will find formal beds of fruit and vegetables tended by retired people living in the village, gnarled apple trees and pear trees, a venerable mulberry, and more roses. A collection of antique apple trees has recently been planted. The cottage garden next to a greenhouse is an exuberant mixture of scented plants, herbs and alpines. Everything is carefully maintained.

Thrigby Hall Wildlife Gardens

Filby, Great Yarmouth NR29 3DR. Tel: (01493) 369477

Mr K.J. Sims • 6m NW of Great Yarmouth on A1064. Signposted • Open all year, daily, 10am – 6pm (or dusk if earlier) • Entrance: £6.50, OAPs £5.50, children (4 – 14) £4.50 ○ 🍵 ▦ WC ♿ 🏺 ⚲

The chief attraction here is a collection of Chinese plants arranged to form the landscape of the willow-pattern plate, complete with pagodas and bridges across a small lake. Complementing the collection of Asiatic animals, the plants are those particularly associated with temple gardens and include *Ginkgo biloba*, *Pinus parviflora*, *Paeonia suffruticosa*, *Nandina domestica* and *Chimonobambusa quadrangularis*, set against a background of willows of many species.

Wretham Lodge

East Wretham, Thetford IP24 1RL. Tel: (01953) 498997.

Mr Gordon Alexander • 6m NE of Thetford off A1075. Turn left by village sign, right at crossroads, then bear left • Open 11th, 12th April, 11am – 5pm, 27th June 2 – 5pm, and for parties by appt • Entrance: £2.50, children free ● 🍵 WC ♿ 🌿

Extensive lawns surround the handsome flint-built former rectory set in its own walled park; there are wide mixed borders around the house and within the walled kitchen garden. Roses are massed in informal beds and cover the high flint walls, and plants worthy of note include espalier and fan-trained fruit trees, a large indoor fig and unusual vegetables. A wide grass walk runs around the park and through mature and recently established trees where daffodils are naturalised; a long walk among narcissi and bluebells leads to a grove of flowering trees. Spring sees the flowering of many bulbs, and in summer the wildflower meadows are a haze of colour. New developments include a double herbaceous border and a small area of woodland planting.

NORTHAMPTONSHIRE

Two-starred gardens are marked on the map with a black square.

Althorp House [Historic Garden Grade II*]

Althorp, Northampton NN7 4HQ. Tel: (01604) 770107 (House and Park Office)

*Earl Spencer • 6m NW of Northampton on A428 Northampton – Rugby road •
House and grounds open July to Sept, 10am – 5pm (closed 31st Aug) •
Entrance: house and gardens £10, OAPs £8.50, children (5–17) £5 (pre-booked
tickets) (2003 prices)* ◐ ☕ 🐾 WC ♿ ♨

The Caroline-fronted Elizabethan house was surrounded by formal gardens
with a vast walled garden to the east. John Evelyn remarked in 1675 on
Althorp's 'stately woods and groves in a Park and with a Canale' and 'Gardens
furnished with the choicest fruite in England and exquisitely kept'. They were
all swept away during the fashionable eighteenth-century improvements by
the architect Henry Holland, helped by Samuel Lapidge, 'Capability' Brown's
assistant. The present gardens were laid out in the 1860s by the architect W.M.
Teulon and enclosed by stone walls and balustrades. To the side and rear the
gardens are also laid to lawn, although the talented designer Dan Pearson has
recently planted beds with a subtle blend of bronze fennel, aconitum, potentillas and *Verbena bonariensis* outside the stable block, which now houses a
shop, and the same restricted palette is used in other borders, harmonising
wonderfully with the honey-coloured stone. This was the home of the late
Diana, Princess of Wales, and the Earl, her brother, engaged Pearson to
produce an unusual memorial – a two-mile walk in the grounds through
the park and house to the island where the Princess is buried, leading through
a green meadow of long grasses and wild flowers by the lake colonised by 1000
white water lilies and black swans.

Boughton House Park [Historic Park Grade I]

Kettering NN14 1BJ. Tel: (01536) 515731

*The Duke and Duchess of Buccleuch and Queensberry • 2m NE of Kettering off
A43, entry via Geddington. Signposted • House open as garden • Garden open
Aug, daily, 2 – 5pm. Park and plant centre open May to 1st Sept, daily except
Fri, 1 – 5pm. Specialist and educational parties welcome at other times by prior
arrangement • Entrance: £1 (house, gardens and park £6, OAPs and children
£5) • Other information: Tearoom open August and weekends only. Dogs in
park only, on lead* ◐ ☕ 🐾 WC ♿ ⟁ 🌿 ♨ 🎵

Although only limited formal gardens remain, Boughton will be attractive to
garden enthusiasts and the whole family. The large sixteenth- and seven-
teenth- century house, with monastic origins and a strong French influence,
contains an extensive collection of paintings and furniture. The magnificent
surrounding park, with its lakes and canalised river, and avenues of trees, was
laid out by the 1st Duke of Montagu before 1700 with the help of a Dutch

gardener, Van der Meulen, who had experience of reclamation work in the Fens. The 2nd Duke, known as John the Planter, added a lake and a colossal network of avenues of elms and limes in the 1730s to an ambitious plan of Bridgeman, though not even 'The Planter' was prepared to carry out the complete network and indeed in 1731 he sacked Bridgeman. Even so the avenues stretched to 23 miles with rides through woods extending another twenty or so. Today, the garden close to the house includes herbaceous borders and some fine planted vases. To the south of the house a small circular rose garden leads to the outstanding rectangular lily pond, beyond which the walled garden houses a long herbaceous border and well-stocked plant centre. Work is ongoing to restore some of the more important features, such as the Star Pond and its cascade. In the 350-acre park are walks and trails, including one for the disabled, and a woodland adventure play area for children (open subject to weather conditions).

Canons Ashby House [Historic Garden Grade II*]

Canons Ashby, Daventry NN11 3SD. Tel: (01327) 860044

The National Trust • 6m S of Daventry off A361 Daventry – Banbury road • House open • Garden open 22nd March to 29th Oct, Sat – Wed, 11am – 5.30pm, or dusk if earlier (closes 4.30pm in Oct); Nov to 21st Dec, Sat, Sun, 11am – 3pm • Entrance: £2 (house and garden £5.60, children £2.80, family £14. Reductions for pre-booked parties) • Other information: Parking 200 metres from house. Disabled telephone in advance and park near house. Wheelchairs available. Tape and braille guide available. Picnics in car park. Dogs in home paddock only, on lead ◖ 🍽 🏛 WC ᕙ ⬦ ℘ 🏚 ⛽ ℺

The brooding, romantic house where Spenser wrote part of *The Faerie Queene* was the first to be rescued by the National Heritage Memorial Fund. The historical framework of the garden has been painstakingly re-created over the past decade by the Trust. Formal, with axial arrangements of paths and grass terraces, high stone walls, lawns and gateways, the design dates almost entirely from the beginning of the eighteenth century; a cedar planted in 1781 survives from the original six. The garden is maturing well, with trees and shrubs beginning to give the required height and scale. Hexagonal beds, part of the later Inigo Trigg's plan of 1901, have been reinstated and feature seasonal bedding. Borders have majestic plants such as acanthus and cardoons, while the green court contains fine topiary. Old varieties of soft fruit bushes and fruit trees include espaliered pears grown from the original stock planted in 1710 by Edward Dryden, whose family owned the house. The wild gardens are in direct contrast to the formal, carefully maintained terraces at the highest level, from where the eye is irresistibly drawn down the principal vista to the Lion Gates and the fine Baroque gate piers.

Castle Ashby Gardens [Historic Garden Grade I]

Castle Ashby, Northampton NN7 1LQ. Tel: (01604) 696187

Earl Compton • 5m E of Northampton, between A45 Northampton – Wellingborough road and A428 Northampton – Bedford road • Open all year daily, 10am – 6pm (closes 4pm in winter), with occasional closures when house can be hired as corporate venue. Tours for parties by appt • Entrance: (tickets from machine when entrance unattended) £2.50, OAPs/children £1.50, season tickets £32 (2003 prices) • Other information: Teas available in garden if pre-booked for coach parties or large groups. Possible for wheelchairs but uneven paths. Farm shop and craft centre in village ○ &. ⟨⊅ ⌀ ℺

Originally Elizabethan, then a park landscaped by 'Capability' Brown, and later given a Matthew Digby Wyatt terrace, Italian garden and arboretum. The house is never open to the public, but there is access to most of the gardens (except the east terrace, although there are good views of it from near the church) which present a glorious combination of views. A nature walk past mature trees leads over a terracotta bridge and to the 'knucklebone arbour' (sometimes open) – a summerhouse with what are probably sheep or deer knuckles set in the floor. Among the wild and naturalised plants are carpets of aconites and snowdrops, winter heliotropes, butterburs, daffodils, bluebells, wood anemones, celandines, bush vetches, wood buttercups and a wide selection of lake and pondside plants. An orangery, archway greenhouses, topiary and well-planted large vases are to be found in other parts of the garden. Restoration is on a continuing basis.

Coton Manor Garden ★

Guilsborough, Northampton NN6 8RQ. Tel: (01604) 740219

Mr and Mrs Ian Pasley-Tyler • 10m NW of Northampton, 11m SE of Rugby near Ravensthorpe Reservoir, signed from A428 and A5199 • Open April to Sept, Tues – Sat and Bank Holiday Suns and Mons, plus Suns in April and May, 12 noon – 5.30pm • Entrance: £4, OAPs £3.50, children £2.50 ◑ ⛾ ✕ WC &. ⌀ ⛺ ♀

Dating from the 1920s, when the original seventeenth-century farmhouse was bought and added to by Mr Pasley-Tyler's grandparents, this is a beautifully maintained garden of exceptional charm, with unexpected vistas at every turn. There is something for everyone here: a most attractive assortment of pelar-goniums in pots on the terrace by the house leading to the rose garden, a contrastingly shady woodland garden, a water garden, lush lawns sloping down to a large pond complete with black swans and ornamental ducks, and magni-ficent mixed borders, particularly striking in July with campanulas and phila-delphus. There is a surprise around every corner (do not rub your eyes should you think you see a real crane or flamingo beside the neatly clipped yew hedge – no verdigris imitations here) and strategically placed seats from which to enjoy the views and effects of Mrs Pasley-Tyler's marvellous eye for colour. The garden has continued to develop since the present generation moved into the house in 1991. The Mediterranean bank, rose walk and herb garden are now well established, along with the replanted rose bank and the midsummer and late-summer borders. The bluebell wood is magical in May and the wildflower meadow a mass of colour during June and July. A water staircase has just been completed running down between old apple orchards. A helpful and interesting booklet and plant list is available; don't miss a visit to the extensive nursery.

Cottesbrooke Hall ★★ [Historic Garden Grade II]

Cottesbrooke, Northampton NN6 8PF. Tel: (01604) 505808

Mr and Mrs A. Macdonald-Buchanan • 10m N of Northampton between A5199 and A508 (A14, junction 1 – A1/M1 link road) • House open as garden • Garden open May to June, Wed and Thurs; July to Sept, Thurs only; plus 3rd, 31st May, 30th Aug; all 2 5.30pm. Parties by appt • Entrance: £4, children £2 (house and gardens £6, children £3) ◗ 💭 <u>WC</u> & ⚘

A beautifully maintained formal garden surrounding a fine Queen Anne house, set in a large park (also open) with lakes and a stream, vistas and avenues. Designs by Edward Schultz, Geoffrey Jellicoe, Dame Sylvia Crowe and the late Hon. Lady Macdonald-Buchanan are being continued by the present family – particularly the planting. The result is a series of delightful enclosed courtyards and gardens around the house with superb borders, urns and statues. Be sure to visit the intriguingly named Dilemma Garden and to wander through the Statue Walk. The spinney garden is at its best in spring with bulbs and azaleas. New trees, borders, yew hedges, gates and vistas have recently been added, and Philip Astley, formerly head gardener at Hardwick, is beginning to make his mark here. Beyond the thatched Wendy house, the wild garden surrounds a running stream and cascades, with azaleas, rhododendrons, acers, cherries, spring bulbs and wild flowers. The magnolia, cherry and acer collections and the ancient cedars are notable. The house contains fine furniture and paintings, including several distinguished Stubbs, and was possibly the model for Jane Austen's Mansfield Park.

Deene Park [Historic Garden Grade II]

Corby NN17 3EW. Tel: (01780) 450278/450223

Mr Edmund Brudenell • 6m N of Corby off A43 Kettering – Stamford road • House open • Gardens open 8th, 15th Feb, 11th, 12th April, 2nd, 3rd, 30th, 31st May; June to Aug, Sun, Bank Holiday Mon, all 2 – 5pm. Parties by appt • Entrance: £3, children (10-14) £1.50, accompanied children under 10 free (house and gardens £5.50, concessions, £5, children (10-14) £2.50, accompanied children under 10 free) (2003 prices) ● 💭 ✕ 🍴 <u>WC</u> & ⚘ 🍺 ♿

The house, created by generations of the Brudenell family, is an amalgam of architectural styles of all periods which co-exist without a quarrel. The glory of Deene is its trees. Fine mature specimens and groups fringe the formal areas and frame tranquil and enchanting views of the parkland and countryside. The main features of the garden are the long borders, the old-fashioned roses, the parterre and the huge winding lake, crossed by a commanding bridge. The parterre, designed by David Hicks, is a particularly fine feature, running along the whole south side of the house. Gardens, parkland, house and church together provide a delightful, interesting and relaxing afternoon for visitors in what was the home of the Earl of Cardigan who led the Charge of the Light Brigade in 1854.

Delapre Abbey

London Road, Northampton NN4 8AW. Tel: (01604) 761074

Northampton Borough Council Leisure Department • 1m S of Northampton on A508 • Walled gardens open April to Sept, Mon – Fri, 9am – 3pm (closes Fri 2.30pm). Park open all year, daily • Entrance: free ◑ WC ♿ ⬇ ♀

Largely rebuilt in the seventeenth century, the house, on the site of the former nunnery of St Mary of the Meadow, together with 500 acres of land, passed into public ownership in 1946. With improving standards of maintenance (although some associated buildings are in need of repair), it is still possible to glimpse the hey-day of a lovely garden. Beyond the walled former kitchen garden, well-tended lawns, perennial, annual and rose beds and an eighteenth-century thatched game larder are walks through the wilderness garden with fine trees, shrubberies and lily ponds. There are lakes and a golf course in the park, and at the roadside close to the entrance one of the Queen Eleanor Crosses commemorates the funeral procession in 1290 of Edward I's queen.

Holdenby House Gardens and Falconry Centre [Historic Garden Grade I]

Holdenby, Northampton NN6 8DJ. Tel: (01604) 770074

Mr and Mrs James Lowther • 7m NW of Northampton, signed from A5199 and A428 • House open 12th April, 3rd, 31st May, 30th Aug, and by appt • Garden and falconry centre open April to Sept, Sun and Bank Holiday Mons, 1 – 5pm, July and Aug, daily except Sat, 1 – 5pm • Entrance: £4.50, OAPs £4, children £3 (house and gardens £6, OAPs £5, children £4) • Other information: Meals by appt. Special events Easter, May Day, Whitsun and Aug Bank Hols, 11am – 6pm ◑ ☕ 🛍 WC WC ♿ ⬇ 🌿 🏛 ♀

Two grassed terraces, a fish pond and the palace forecourt with its original arches remain of the extensive Elizabethan garden which surrounded the vast mansion built by Elizabeth I's chancellor, Sir Christopher Hatton, in the late sixteenth century. The gardens still link the surviving remnant of the house (one-eighth of its former size) to its past, especially the delightful Elizabethan garden, designed in 1980 by the late Rosemary Verey as a miniature replica of Hatton's original centrepiece, using only plants available in the 1580s. Other garden features include the fragrant border (now replanted by Rupert Golby), part of the nineteenth-century garden, a silver border and a kitchen garden, the falconry centre, and an authentically reconstructed seventeenth-century farmstead. A children's garden is currently being planned by garden designer Roddy Llewellyn with bronze statuary, magic planting and hidden surprises.

Kelmarsh Hall ★

Kelmarsh, Northampton NN6 9LT Tel: (01604) 686543

The Kelmarsh Trust • 11m N of Northampton on A508 near A14 junction 2 • House open 11th April to 5th Sept, Sun and Bank Holiday Mons, plus Thurs

in Aug • Garden open 11th April to Sept, Sun – Thurs, 2.30 – 5pm •
Entrance: £3.50, OAPs £3, children £2 (house and garden £4.50, OAPs £4,
children £2) ◑ 🍴 WC ♿ ⟿ 🦮 🍽

The Palladian house, designed by James Gibbs and built in 1730, is set in an
eighteenth-century landscape and has twentieth-century gardens made by
Nancy Lancaster, who was advised by Norah Lindsay in planting the lavish
herbaceous borders. The deep terrace on the garden front of the house,
designed by Geoffrey Jellicoe, looks out across the lake and has rows of
pleached limes on either side. (Nancy Lancaster and Geoffrey Jellicoe had
already worked together at another Gibbs house – Ditchley Park in
Oxfordshire.) A sunken garden, surrounded by billowing box hedges, is
filled with sweetly scented plants in pale pastel colours. The fan-shaped rose
garden, filled with old-fashioned roses, looks across a meadow towards the
church; a herd of British White cattle grazes. Early in the year, the garden is
rich with spring flowers, from fritillaries naturalised down the drive to large
drifts of daffodils in the woodland walk. A great sense of peace pervades this
very private garden, and its well-articulated design and sure sense of style
are re-emerging as the major features are restored, including the renovation
of the walled garden glasshouse with the aid of a Heritage Lottery Fund
grant.

Kirby Hall [Historic Garden Grade II*]

Deene, Corby NN17 5EN. Tel: (01536) 203230

English Heritage • 4m NE of Corby off A43 on road W of Deene • Open April to
Sept, daily, 10am – 6pm; Oct, daily, 10am – 5pm; Nov to March, Sat and
Sun, 10am – 4pm. Closed 24th to 26th Dec, 1st Jan. Please telephone before
travelling • Entrance: £3.50, concessions £2.60, children £1.80, family £9
(2003 prices) ○ 🍵 🍴 WC ♿ ⟿ 🏛 🍽 ⚲

The gardens date from at least the period when Sir Christopher Hatton
owned the hall in Elizabethan times. However, it was in the late seventeenth
century that they achieved considerable fame through the work of the
fourth Sir Christopher Hatton, who devoted his energies to the gardens
until his death in 1705. In the 1930s the Great Garden was laid out following
the pre-war idea of how a Baroque formal garden would have appeared.
Since then, following extensive research of the period, the 1930s' garden is
being buried and the parterre re-created using a design based on Longleat
(see entry in Wiltshire), which will provide a more accurate view of how
this garden would have looked in 1686. Over 80 two-metre-high clipped
yew cones, holly mopheads and box balls, many placed in oak barrels similar
to those used in the Hampton Court restoration, surround the dramatic
geometric design of the *gazon coupé* parterre of wide gravel paths and cut-
through patterns of lawn. The north border was replanted in 1995 with
species following as closely as possible those mentioned by Hatton in his
notebooks. These include old varieties of fruit trees – apples, pears and
cherries – trained against the walls.

Lamport Hall and Gardens [Historic Garden Grade II]

Lamport, Northampton NN6 9HD. Tel: (01604) 686272

Lamport Hall Trust • 8m N of Northampton on A508 • Hall open • Garden open 11th April to 3rd Oct, Sun and Bank Holiday Mons, 2.15 – 5.15pm (last admission 4pm), also Aug, Mon – Fri, for one tour only at 2.30pm. Coach parties at any time by arrangement • Entrance: (Hall and gardens) £4.50, OAPs £4, children £2 (2003 prices) • Other information: Dogs in grounds only, on lead. Regular programme of events – telephone for details. Agricultural museum ● � WC & ▱ ♀*

The principal façade of the hall is one of the only surviving country houses by John Webb; it was extended by the Smiths of Warwick. The grounds, initially laid out by Gilbert Clarke in 1655, have been restored, and there are now considerable herbaceous and mixed borders and lawns, a box bower, a small Italianate garden with a shell and coral fountain and the Privy Garden, opened in 2002. Sir Charles Isham's local ironstone rockery, the home of the first garden gnome, stands over 5 metres tall.

Lyveden New Bield [Historic Garden Grade II*]

Oundle, Peterborough PE8 5AT. Tel: (01832) 205358

The National Trust • 4m SW of Oundle off A427, 3m E of Brigstock • House, Elizabethan water garden and visitor information room open 3rd April to 2nd Nov, Wed – Sun, 10.30am – 5pm; 3rd Nov to April, Sat, Sun, 10.30am – 4pm • Entrance: £2.50, children £1.20, family £6.20 • Other information: Access ½ m along farm track; parking at property for less able visitors. Teas for groups by prior arrangement ● � WC ▱ ♀ ♆*

This is not so much a garden, more the remains of an unfinished late-Elizabethan project. Its principal elements were water and sculpted landform, both of which remain largely intact. Part of the canal system survives, as do the remains of a banqueting house or lodge. The latter is a three-storey building in the shape of an equal-armed cross as a celebration of the Passion of Christ. Alas, there is no planting of the period, though the raised grass terrace with its broad walk is still in place, with turf pyramids at each end. The Trust is undertaking a project to reveal the extensive remains of an elaborate water garden, containing a series of truncated pyramids and circular mounds, surrounded by moats and terraces, and has begun the re-planting of the Elizabethan orchard containing over 300 fruit trees.

The Menagerie [Historic Park Grade II]

Horton, Northampton NN7 2BX.
Tel: (01604) 870957 (Leave message for Administrator)

Mr A. Myers • 6m SE of Northampton, on B526 turn left 1m S of Horton into field. Watch out for tiny notice on gate • Open April to Sept, Mon and Thurs, 2 – 5pm, also last Sun of these months, 2 – 6pm • Entrance: £3.50, children £1.50 (2003 prices) ● � WC ▱*

The informal approach through a farm gateway and across uncultivated fields gives no hint of the delights of the journey beyond. This is a garden where the past is still present – in the formal water gardens and wetlands surrounding the house, an eighteenth-century folly where Lord Halifax had his private zoo, and one of the most important surviving works of Thomas Wright of Durham. It is also a garden where the present was sadly consigned to the past with the untimely deaths of Gervase Jackson-Stops, who rescued the Menagerie, and Ian Kirby, who helped him create a new garden here in the 1980s. They planted a central lime avenue, drawing the eye to a mount with a spiral path leading to the obelisk on top and two hornbeam *allées* ending in eighteenth-century ponds with fountains. Two thatched arbours were built – one circular and classical, the other triangular and Gothick – with shrubberies screening them from the house. The charming rose garden enclosed by yew hedges was designed by Vernon Russell-Smith in 1989. Fortunately, the garden has fallen into sympathetic hands and continues to develop. Jackson-Stops' plan for a walled garden has been carried out (larger than the one he envisaged) beyond the rose garden, and a disused railway cutting is to be cleared and planted.

The Old Rectory ★

Sudborough, Kettering NN14 3BX. Tel: (01832) 733247

Mr and Mrs Anthony Huntington • 7m SE of Corby off A6116 Corby – Thrapston road, A14 junction 12 • Open April to June, Tues, Sat, July to Sept, Tues, all 10am – 4pm; and by appt. (parties welcome) • Entrance: £3.50 (£5 with tea and biscuits), children under 16 free • Other information: Evening parties by arrangement ● ☕ WC & ✿

A delightful three-acre rectory garden in a beautiful stone and thatch village. Much has been accomplished in recent times to develop plantings throughout the year, with a fine collection of hellebores in spring and many containers, especially in summer. Copious planting in the mixed borders, around the pond and many climbers. The *potager*, begun in 1985 by the late Rosemary Verey and completed by Rupert Golby, is charming, with small beds and brick paths leading to a central wrought-iron arbour; standard roses, gooseberries and tents of runner beans and marrows provide vertical features. A small wild garden with interesting trees and a woodland walk along the stream completes the picture.

The Prebendal Manor House

Nassington, Peterborough PE8 6QG. Tel: (01780) 782575

Mrs Jane Baile • 6m NE of Oundle off A1, in Nassington opposite church • Open 12th April, then 18th April to Sept, Sun, Wed, 1 – 5.30pm • Entrance: £4, children £1.50 ◑ ☕ ▦ WC & ✿ 🏮 ♋

From a window sill of the early thirteenth-century tawny stone house two carved heads gaze down, guardians of the secrets of this ancient place. Scattered around the six acres are reconstructions of various types of medieval garden. The herber has grass seats, a fig tree and scented plants, while the trellis garden's compartments overspill with poppies and mallows. Concealed by an ancient wall and protected by a fine withy fence is a vegetable patch with broad beans, herbs and wheat; nearby is a small vineyard, and a nut walk leads to two fishponds. Patches of wild flowers sit in the lawn; old willows, the other guardians of the manor's secrets, billow silvery in the breeze. The tithe barn contains an interpretative museum display with some look-alike farm tools. Rare-breed sheep and pigs are in fine fettle in June and early July.

Rockingham Castle Gardens [Historic Garden Grade II*]

Market Harborough LE16 8TH. Tel: (01536) 770240

James and Elizabeth Saunders Watson • 2m N of Corby on A6003. Signposted • Castle open as garden but from 1pm • Garden open April, May, June, Sept, Suns and Bank Holiday Mons; July, Aug, Tues, Thurs, Sun and Bank Holiday Mon; all 12 noon – 4.30pm • Entrance: £4 (castle and gardens £6, OAPs £5.50, children £4, parties of 20 or more £5.50 per person) (2003 prices) • Other information: Disabled park near entrance ◑ ☕ ✗ 🧺 WC ♿ 🐕 🛍 🎪 ✯

Rockingham sits on a hilltop fortress site with stunning views of three counties. It has remains from all periods of its 900-year history, with major features ranging from formal seventeenth-century terraces and yew hedges to the romantic wild garden of the nineteenth century. There is a circular rose garden surrounded by a yew hedge and also good herbaceous borders. The wild garden was replanted with advice from Kew Gardens in the late 1960s and includes over 200 species of trees and shrubs. The result is a delightful blend of form, colour, light and shade.

SYMBOLS
[NEW] entries new for 2004; ○ open all year; ◑ open most of year; ◐ open during main season; ☕ open rarely and/or by appt; ☕ teas/light refreshments; ✗ meals; 🧺 picnics permitted; WC toilet facilities; WC toilet facilities, inc. disabled; ♿ partly wheelchair-accessible; 🐕 dogs on lead; 🌱 plants for sale; 🛍 shop; 🎪 events held; ✯ children-friendly; B&B bed and breakfast available.

BED AND BREAKFAST FOR GARDEN LOVERS
The biennial paperback *Bed and Breakfast for Garden Lovers* contains some 200 B&Bs run by keen and knowledgeable gardeners. Some of the gardens are stylishly modern, the work of their landscape-designer owners. Several of these are described in the *Guide* – Gants Mill, Ridleys Cheer and The Garden Lodge, for example – but visitors with contemporary tastes will also enjoy a stay at Court Hall in Devon, Cerne River Cottage in Dorset, 80 Bromfelde Road in London, Heaseleigh in Surrey, Little Orchard House in Sussex, The Old Vicarage, Darley in Yorkshire and 11 Warriston Crescent in Edinburgh. Full details from *BBGL*, available in bookshops or direct from Alastair Sawday Publishing – telephone (01275) 464891 or consult www.specialplacestostay.com.

NORTHUMBERLAND

Two-starred gardens are marked on the map with a black square.

Alnwick Castle ★ [Historic Park and Garden Grade I]

Alnwick NE66 1NQ.
Tel: (01665) 510777 (Mon – Fri), (01655) 511100 (Infoline)

Duke and Duchess of Northumberland • 35m N of Newcastle upon Tyne. Take A1 and turn W at Alnwick. Signposted • Castle open Easter to Oct (extra charge) • Grounds open, daily, 11am – 5pm or dusk if earlier (last admission 4.15pm). Closed 25th Dec. The Alnwick Garden open all year, daily except 25th Dec, 10am – 8pm (or dusk if earlier) • Entrance: Grounds free. The Alnwick Garden £4, OAPs/students £3.50, accompanied children (16 or under) free; parties of 14 or more £3.50 per person. (2003 prices) ◐ 🍵 WC ♿ 🚫 ☕

Set in a 'Capability' Brown landscape, the castle (remodelled in the 1850s) and its grounds have long been open to the public. The landscape survives almost intact, but in 2001 the first stage of a remarkably ambitious and dramatic new garden – the Alnwick Garden – was completed. Within the 12-acre Victorian walled former kitchen garden, a Grand Cascade has been constructed which in effect will become the spine of the garden. It is enclosed by an arched hornbeam tunnel with clipped openings along its length. Designed by the Wirtz father and sons team from Belgium, the cascade sends water tumbling down a series of 27 weirs; the garden is on a slope, so the way to the rose garden is uphill. The path then leads through trees on the Water Tower Walk to a formal ornamental garden, reached through three interlinked stone arches. This walled enclosure contains the largest collection of European plants in Britain (16,500) – a must for any plant lover. Pergolas and arbours are covered in ramblers and vines, and rills lead to secret enclosed gardens with yew hedges.

Ashfield

Hebron, Morpeth NE61 3LA. Tel: (01670) 515616

Barry and Rona McWilliam • 3m N of Morpeth, 1m E of A1 on C130 S of Hebron • Open all year by impromptu appt • Entrance: £2, children free ◐ 🍵 🏡 WC ♿ 🚫

The original half-acre garden surrounding the house overlooks a terrace dense with bulbs in spring and a carpet of alpines, many tumbling over the supporting wall. The lawn slopes gently downwards, sheltered by beech and prunus hedges and punctuated by island beds filled with bulbs, shrubs and small trees, including many varieties of sorbus. Beyond this is a three-acre garden developed from a ploughed field over the past fifteen years. Here again is an expanse of lawn with colourful herbaceous borders, together with a small pinetum, beds of shrubs, a willow 'temple' and a crab-apple walk. In the one-and-a-half-acre wood the mature trees form a canopy for spring bulbs, hellebores, hostas, other shade-loving plants, and small trees – sorbus, betulas, acers. Many plants come from abroad and have been grown from seed, as in the scree bed planted with Sino-Himalayan alpines near the entrance. The owner is a keen plantsman and the five-acre garden reflects his knowledge and enthusiasm. Planting and development continue.

Belsay Hall, Castle and Gardens ★★ [Historic Garden Grade I]

Belsay, Newcastle-upon-Tyne NE20 0DX. Tel: (01661) 881636

English Heritage • 14m NW of Newcastle on A696 • Hall and castle open • Gardens open all year, daily, 10am – 6pm (closes 5pm Oct, 4pm Nov to March). Closed 24th to 26th Dec, 1st Jan • Entrance: £4.50, OAPs £3.40, children £2.30, family £11.30. Reductions for parties of 11 or more • Other information: Advance notice preferred for coaches. Refreshments Easter to Oct only. Wheelchairs available for loan. Annual NCCPG plant sale in June ◖ ☕ ✕ 🍴 WC ♿ ⟨💧⟩ 🌿 🏭 💡 ⚲

The 30-acre gardens are the creation of two men who between them owned Belsay in succession from 1795 to 1933. Sir Charles Monck built the severe neo-classical hall with formal terraces leading through woods to a 'garden' inside the quarry which provided the building with its stone. Sir Arthur, his grandson, took over in 1867, adding Victorian features. Both were discerning plantsmen. The result is an exceptionally well-cared-for collection of rare, mature and exotic specimens in a fascinating sequence. The terrace looks across to massed June rhododendrons. Other areas (flower garden, magnolia terrace, winter garden) lead to woods, a wild meadow and the quarry garden itself. This was carefully contrived and stocked to achieve a wild romantic effect, and the sheltered microclimate has resulted in the luxuriant growth of some remarkable and exotic trees and shrubs, dramatically beautiful in the light and shade of the sandstone gorge. Here, among the massive hewn slabs silvered by lichen are memorable corners: the well of a natural amphitheatre, cascading with ferns; stepped rock ledges carpeted with moss; a host of fritillaries naturalised in grass. The path from the eighteenth-century hall leads through formal gardens to the quarry garden and thence to the fourteenth-century castle, a distance of about half a mile, all on fairly level ground. The winter garden, with its heathers, also has a 28-metre-high Douglas fir planted in 1839 and rhododendrons. An unexpected pleasure is the croquet lawn, which is in regular use. The one-and-a-half-mile Crag Wood walk is a stepped, serpentine path which passes by the lake and through the hanging woods opposite the hall to the south.

Bide-a-Wee Cottage ★

Stanton, Netherwitton, Morpeth NE65 8PR. Tel: (01670) 772262

Mark Robson • 7m NW of Morpeth, 3m SW of Longhorsley, off A697 Morpeth – Coldstream road towards Stanton • Open 24th April to Aug, Sat and Wed, 1.30 – 5pm. Parties of more than 18 by appt • Entrance: £2.50 ◖ ♿ 🌿

One of the most enchanting and richly planted gardens in the North-East. Combining formal, informal and wild features, it occupies a long-abandoned stone quarry and some of the higher surrounding land. The varied topography, soil and climate allow for a diversity of plants to be grown, from marsh-loving to drought-tolerant species. The beauty of the natural rock faces has been exploited to the maximum and enriched by truly sympathetic planting. More quarry wall has been exposed with new planting and another seat from which to view the garden. As well as being a highly refined plantsman, the owner is also a splendid mason whose stonework has done much to embellish the garden, and a shady corner has a timber summerhouse with an adjacent planting of arisaemas. The National Collection of centaureas is held here. There is an excellent plant sales area with unusual species (catalogue available).

Chillingham Castle [Historic Park and Garden Grade II]

Chillingham NE66 5NJ. Tel: (01668) 215359/215390

Sir Humphry Wakefield, Bt • 12m NW of Alnwick between A1 (signposted), A697, B6346 and B6348 • House open • Gardens open May to Sept, Sun – Fri, 12 noon – 5pm, and by appt • Entrance: £5, OAPs £4.50, children over 16 £2, parties of 10 or more £4.30 per person. Guided tours £30 ◑ ☕ WC ♿ ✿

Since the 1200s this has been and continues to be the family home of the Earls Grey and their relations. Sir Humphry has restored the ancient castle and garden along with the grounds, landscaped in 1828 by Wyatville (of Windsor Castle and Royal Lodge fame). The Elizabethan-style walled garden has been virtually excavated to rediscover its intricate pattern of clipped box and yew (enlivened by scarlet tropaeolum), with rose beds, fountains, a central avenue and a spectacular herbaceous border running the whole length. Outside are lawns and a rock garden, delightful woodland and lakeside walks through drifts of snowdrops, spring displays of daffodils, bluebells and, later, rhododendrons. The medieval castle provides a spectacular backdrop to the gardens.

Chipchase Castle Garden

Wark NE48 3NT. Tel: (01434) 230203

Mrs P. Torday • 11m NW of Hexham on B6320 to Wark and Kielder. Turn right in centre of Wark following brown tourist-signs and right again on far side of bridge; Chipchase 1m • Castle open 1st to 28th June, daily, 2 – 5pm • Garden open April to July, Thurs – Sun and Bank Holiday Mons, 10am – 5pm • Entrance: £3, concessions £2.50 (house and garden £5, concessions £4)
NEW ◕ WC

The impressive castle was built in 1621 incorporating a fourteenth-century pele tower. The eighteenth-century walled garden with immaculate beds of vegetables and herbaceous borders has been redesigned by the present owners, who are also responsible for the fine herbaceous borders in the formal garden extending on two terraces to the castle walls, with superb views across the North Tyne valley. In the 1860s' pond garden a high canopy of fine old trees including a Wellingtonia and a Douglas fir shelters rhododendrons, magnolias and specimen trees planted for spring and autumn colour, and there is more colour beside the lake, where hostas, irises, candelabra primulas, ligularias, deutzias and much else bestow a succession of flowering interest. The one-and-a-half-acre nursery in an adjoining walled garden is under separate management and well worth a visit (Tel: (01434) 230083).

Cragside House [Historic Garden Grade II*]

Rothbury, Morpeth NE65 7PX. Tel: (01669) 620333

The National Trust • 13m SW of Alnwick off A697 between B6341 and B6344 • House open April to 28th Sept, 1 – 5.30pm (last admission 4.30pm), 30th Sept to 2nd Nov, 1 – 4.30pm • Gardens and estate open April to Oct, Tues – Sun and Bank Holiday Mons, 10.30am – 7pm (last admission 5pm); 3rd Nov to 19th Dec, Wed – Sun, 11am – 4pm • Entrance: Gardens and estate £4.80, children (5-17) £2.40, family £12, parties of 15 or more £4 per person (house, gardens and estate £7.20, children (5-17) £3.60, family £18, parties of 15 or more £6.10 per person) (2003 prices) • Other information: Main car parks either near to house (with ½ m walk to formal garden) or near formal garden, with further car parks along estate drive. Visitor centre (some distance from garden) with toilet facilities and shop ○ ☕ ✕ ▓ WC ౬ ♨ ♀ ⚲

Lord Armstrong, one of the greatest of Victorian engineers, clothed this hillside above the Coquet Valley with millions of trees and shrubs as the setting for a house designed by R. Norman Shaw (the first ever lit by hydro-electricity) that was then the wonder of the world. From the car park nearest to the house the path (signposted 'Garden') affords views of the rock gardens below the house. These are again planted with an impressive display of heathers, shrubs, alpines and dwarf rhododendrons, which are spectacular in spring. The path descends sharply into the Debdon gorge, crosses the river by a rustic bridge (magnificent views of the elegant iron bridge soaring above) and climbs through majestic conifers to the clock tower (1864) which over-looks the formal garden. This walled area, laid out in high-Victorian style, is set on three terraces and restoration is continuing. On the upper terrace are rock ferneries, grottos and a small canal. The middle terrace contains the imposing orchard house, with its rotating fruit pots of sixteen types of fruit, to one side of which is a bed planted with small foliage plants in formal patterns typical of the 1870s. Carpet bedding is taken literally at Cragside: two of the beds mirror the design of floor-coverings and fittings in the house. In the formal beds some 6000 tulips are planted in autumn for spring colour. Between the middle and lower terraces is the Dahlia Walk, planted annually with 650-700 mixed cultivars and at its best in September and October. On the lower Italian terrace is the loggia made of bold, pierced cast-iron, another unique remnant of the extensive range of glass structures once found on this terrace. The quatrefoil pool has been reinstated as the centrepiece of the whole terrace, giving a focal point to the overall design and an Italian feel to the area. The walk back through the gorge impresses on the visitor the contrasting forces of wild romanticism and industrial technology which influenced this estate in equal measure. Two hundred rare North American coniferous species, given to the Trust by the Royal Botanic Gardens in Edinburgh, have been planted on the estate. The climatic conditions and historic landscape of the property make it an ideal site for a collection of specimen conifers. Major engineering work is in progress (a five-year project) to restore and improve deteriorating water systems and to ensure the restoration and long-term preservation of the rock garden. It has to be said that the replanting and rerouting and all the infrastructure here subtract somewhat from the romance which must have characterised the original. Helpful leaflets.

The Garden Cottage

Bolam Hall, Bolam, Morpeth NE61 3UA. Tel: (01661) 881660

Heather and John Russell • 15m NW of Newcastle. Turn off A696 after turn to Belsay Hall, follow sign to Bolam – telephone in advance for directions • Open 8th, 29th June for NGS, and for parties by appt • Entrance: £2.50 • Other information: Possible for wheelchairs but gravel paths. Refreshments for parties by arrangement NEW ● ▓ WC ஃ ♨

Protected by a long south-facing wall, the owners – who have been gardening here for twenty years – have been able to overcome the problems of the cold and wet Northumbrian site and to create a one-acre garden of great artistry and imagination. The centrepiece is a large bed modelled on a dry gravelled river course and surrounded by a terrace with beds built up to suggest river banks, creating the impression of a sunken garden. Everywhere there is an exuberance of colours, both warm and cool, and an inspiring range of planting variations. Structural planting is well conceived – a beech arch, buttressed by a pair of cone-shaped yews, finds an echo in a single beech near the southern boundary – and winter interest is sustained by the coloured stems of cornus and willow. Abstract and animal sculptures enliven the main garden, where there are also secluded areas with seats for relaxation, a table for meals, well-filled tubs and a vegetable garden. North of the protective wall a large wild meadow is being developed.

The Garden Station

Langley, Hexham NE47 5LA. Tel: (01434) 684391

Mrs J. Torday • 9m W of Hexham off A69 Newcastle – Carlisle road. Turn onto A686 near Haydon Bridge. Continue past Langley Castle Hotel for 2m, then follow yellow signs • Open May to Aug, Tues – Sun and Bank Holiday Mons, 10am – 5pm, and for small parties Mon – Fri by appt • Entrance: free • Other information: Gardening and art courses 7th March to Nov – essential to book ● ▣ WC ஃ ⬦ ♨ ▦ ♟ ⚲

One of the most unusual and attractive gardens in Northumberland, surrounding a pretty, restored railway station and itself sheltered by mature woodland. The main garden is on three different levels. On one side is a heavily wooded bank, which drops down to the old platform, now the stage for a small gravel suntrap full of pots; along the foot of the station building are beds of scented plants arranged in the traditional English manner, while a deep row of plants for sale creates the illusion of a herbaceous border. The lowest level is the railway track, now laid to lawn; a richly planted woodland walk extends the garden along the route of the old railway line, passing under the arches of two magnificent Victorian railway bridges, which frame a long vista.

Herterton House ★

Hartington, Cambo, Morpeth NE61 4BN. Tel: (01670) 774278

*Frank and Marjorie Lawley • 11m W of Morpeth, 2m N of Cambo off B6342,
signed to Hartington • Open May to Sept, Mon, Wed, Fri – Sun, 1.30 –
5.30pm • Entrance: £2.40, children £1 (under 5 free)* ◐ **WC** ♨

The Lawleys took over this land and near-derelict Elizabethan building, with
commanding views over picturesque upland Northumberland, in 1976. With
vision and skill they have created four distinct areas. In front, a winter garden
with views over the Northumbrian countryside; alongside, a cloistered
'monastic' knot garden of mainly medicinal, occult and dye-producing herbs;
and to the rear, their most impressive achievement, a flower garden with
perceptively mingled hardy flowers chosen with an artist's eye. This part of
the garden contains some impressive topiary (spirals, columns and balls),
which is altogether appropriate to this formal setting in front of a period
house. Many unusual varieties of traditional plants (including many species
from the wild) flourish within the newly built sheltering walls. The fourth
area, the Fancy Garden, although still in its infancy, shows great promise. The
views from the gazebo contrast well; to the north over a large field of cattle
and to the south over this new garden and beyond to the formal garden with
its flowers and topiary.

Howick Hall ★ [Historic Garden Grade II]

Howick, Alnwick NE66 3LB. Tel: (01665) 577285

*Lord Howick of Glendale (Howick Trustees Ltd) • 6m NE of Alnwick, 2m N of
Longhoughton, off B1339 • Open early April to late Oct, daily, 1 – 6pm •
Entrance: £3, concessions £2, children under 16 free* ◐ 🍴 **WC** ♿

Acquired by the Grey family in 1319, the accident of woodland which
sheltered this site from the blasts of the North Sea enabled Lord and Lady
Grey to start building a fine collection of tender plants. Although the main
house is unoccupied, Stephen Anderton describes the ambience as 'a genial
lived-in garden of the best kind'. The lower terrace has a pond and excellent
borders and the lawns run down through shrubs to a stream. Winding paths
lead through shrubbery or parkland to Silverwood, under whose magnificent
trees the visitor passes among numerous fine shrubs and woodland flowers.
There are good varieties of rhododendrons, azaleas and camellias, and outstanding species hydrangeas (*H. villosa*) apart from other unusual varieties. In
the woodland garden are drifts of unusual perennials such as meconopsis,
erythroniums, candelabra primulas etc. The colour is memorable at every
level. A large pondside garden is maturing well, with a great variety of
moisture-loving plants making an impressive display. Although a catalogue
of plants would be advantageous, Lord Howick's five gardeners are most
helpful to visitors. This is a garden for plant lovers, but there are many delights
for the aesthete, such as the agapanthus of varying blues on the terrace. In
early April visitors will be impressed by the spectacular view of drifts of
daffodils in the parkland, followed in May by tulips of many colours scattered in

the meadow areas near the house. One of the signed walks is the Long Walk, a one-and-a-half-mile path to the sea.

Loughbrow House

Hexham NE46 1RS. Tel: (01434) 603351

Mrs Kenneth Clark • 20m E of Newcastle, 1m S of Hexham. Take B6306 off Whitley Chapel road and at fork is brick lodge and long drive to house • Open 20th June, 8th Aug, 2 – 5pm, and by appt at other times • Entrance: £2, children free ● ● WC & ⊲ ⌖ B&B

The garden here is expansive and a source of inspiration for both plant lovers and those who enjoy original design concepts. The lawns are generous, the planting of shrubs and roses bountiful. On the terrace is an interesting canal. The two deep herbaceous borders show the owner's colour concepts to great advantage, and beyond is a woodland garden, maturing well. There is also a kitchen garden. The small lake from which the house derives its name ('lake c ' the brow of the hill') has been re-created, the bog garden extended, and an arboretum developed around the lake.

Mindrum

Cornhill-on-Tweed TD12 4QN. Tel: (01890) 850246

The Hon. P.J. Fairfax • 14m SW of Berwick-upon-Tweed. From A697 turn onto B6351 at Akeld, join B6352 towards Kirk Yetholm and continue 3m to Mindrum • Open 20th June, 11th July for NGS, and by appt • Entrance: £2 • Other information: Teas and plants for sale on open days only ● ● WC ⊲ ⌖ ⚲

From the nineteenth-century house built on flat ground there are fine views co the valley of the Bowmont Water (you can actually see the Scottish Borders to the south), and the creators of the three-acre garden have taken good advantage of the different levels of the site. From the lawn at the side of the house – over 90 metres above sea level – a path leads down a gentle slope to a walled garden with many flowering shrubs and roses. Opposite this, and separated from it by a sage hedge, is a rose garden with yew hedges on the far sides. The path then descends steeply, winding down a rocky bank beside a small stream which flows into a pool at the foot and then joins a tributary of Bowmont Water. The bank is densely planted with a rich variety of colourful perennials and flowering shrubs at every level – old-fashioned roses, clematis, many varieties of acer, abutilons, golden yews, irises and candelabra primulas by the water, with spires of white foxgloves adding to the dramatic effect. The tributary is crossed by wooden bridges leading to the riverside walk. The far bank has rhododendrons, azaleas, acers, and planting still continues.

Northumberland College at Kirkley Hall

Ponteland NE20 0AQ. Tel: (01670) 841200

11m NW of Newcastle off A696; turn right at Ponteland on C151 for 2½ m. Signposted • Open April to Sept, daily, 10am – 3pm • Entrance: free ◗ ● WC & ⌖ ☗ ⚲

The 10-acre grounds with a three-acre Victorian walled garden have in the past been a showcase for all the gardening arts. The long border in front of the hall and the many colourfully planted containers make a brilliant show. The lawns and hedges are well maintained, and the succession of beds carefully planted with many mature trees, shrubs and perennials give variety of profile and continuity of colour. A National Collection of beeches is held here. The sunken garden is almost completely restored with cushions of alpines on the raised beds. The herbaceous borders in the three-acre walled garden are again filled with a great variety of colourful perennials. New projects include a small wildlife garden with a living willow arch. It is cheering to see progress being made after a period of neglect.

Nunwick ★ [Historic Garden Grade II]

Simonburn, Hexham NE48 3AF.

Mrs L. G. Allgood • 8m NW of Hexham on B6320 • Open 20th June, and for parties by appt in writing • Entrance: £2.50 • Other information: Teas and toilet facilities on open day only ◕

This is one of the most interesting gardens in a county full of remarkable ones. The house (not open) was described by Pevsner as perfect for its date (1760). It looks out over lawns and parkland, with fine trees which the owner has been meticulous in caring for and replacing when necessary. Walking down to the gardens, it is clear that the design combines a clever sense of colour and shape with an interest in unusual plants. The herbaceous borders are cut back from their sheltering wall to ease maintenance, and there are fine beech hedges and shrub roses to provide shelter on the orchard side. The large Victorian walled kitchen garden is excellently maintained. Mrs Allgood experiments with varieties of vegetables – there were about 12 named potato varieties when our inspector visited. Good flowers, too, along the walks. Behind one wall is a small and elegant orangery containing a camellia over 100 years old. The other fascinating feature is the woodland path to the bog garden (*en route* note the stone wellhead), where the visitor first becomes aware of a profusion of hostas. The latter become evident again after crossing the recently built stone bridge over the burn and reaching the eighteenth-century Gothick kennels. Its four rooms, now open to the sky, house a spectacular collection of hostas, and the walls are planted with purple erinus, ivies of many kinds, toadflax and ferns. Trees and plants are well labelled. Back beside the house is a large collection of stone farm troughs with alpines, and an attractive large fountain. It is difficult to do justice in words to the charm of this garden.

Seaton Delaval Hall [Historic Garden Grade II*]

Seaton Sluice, Whitley Bay NE26 4QR. Tel: (0191) 237 1493/0786

Lord Hastings • 10m NE of Newcastle, ½ m inland from Seaton Sluice on A190 • Parts of house open together with coach house, stables and ice-house • Garden open 3rd, 31st May; June to Sept, Wed, Sun and Bank Holiday Mon; all 2 – 6pm • Entrance: £4, OAPs £3, children £1 ◑ ♨ WC ⅔ ⬥ 🏭 ℀

The original grounds of this architectural masterpiece by Vanbrugh no doubt matched its magnificence, but little is known save for an early painting showing a swan lake. A notable weeping ash survives from that time, and there is a venerable and impressive rose garden, its beds outlined by box hedges 60 cm high and 30 cm wide. Since 1948 an excellent parterre has been laid out by Jim Russell, now embellished by a large Italianate pond and fountain. An attractive shrubbery (rhododendrons, azaleas, etc.), herbaceous borders and a laburnum walk have been established on the south side towards the fine Norman chapel. Replanting continues, including many ornamental trees, and the garden is clearly in good hands.

Wallington ★ [Historic Garden Grade II*]

Cambo, Morpeth NE61 4AR. Tel: (01670) 773600

The National Trust • 20m NW of Newcastle off A696 (signed on B6342) • House open • Walled garden open April to Oct, daily, 10am – 7pm (Oct closes 6pm) or dusk if earlier; Nov to March, daily, 10am – 4pm. Grounds open all year, daily, during daylight hours • Entrance: £5, children £2.50, family £12.50, parties of 15 or more £4.50 • Other information: Self-drive scooters and guided tours available ○ 🍵 ✕ 🛍 <u>WC</u> ♿ ⬥ 🌱 🏛 ♨

The handsome eighteenth-century house is set in a 100-acre landscape of lawns, terraces (fine views) and flower beds – serene, quiet and quintessentially English – but it is the walled garden, quite some distance away across the entry road via an attractive woodland walk, which has the most appeal. A rill runs from the pond to narrow lawns fringed with beds on two levels, and climbers cluster in prodigal numbers on the lovely old walls. (Alas, two of the elegant statues that graced the balustrade were stolen and the rest have been removed for safe-keeping.) The sloping site reveals the layout and invites exploration of the harmonious and generously filled herbaceous border. There is a garden house designed in Tuscan style by Daniel Garrett; the Victorian peach house is now restored, and the spectacular Edwardian conservatory is home to many treasures, with a rich tapestry of colour at every turn. Outside, the walks step down from a classical fountain past beds re-designed by Lady Trevelyan in the 1930s, including notable heathers and many herbaceous perennials. Trees planted by the Duke of Atholl in 1738 include a great larch, the survivor of three, by the China Pond.

NATIONAL COUNCIL FOR THE CONSERVATION OF PLANTS AND GARDENS
The NCCPG publishes a *National Plant Collections Directory*. Those interested in particular families of plants who want to see some of the rarer species and garden varieties will find this an invaluable publication. The latest edition, which offers information on about 600 collections comprising more than 50,000 plants and contains articles by holders of the collections, is available from NCCPG, The Stable Courtyard, RHS Garden, Wisley, Woking GU23 6QP (Tel: (01483) 221465; Fax: (01483) 212404; Website: www.nccpg.com. The new edition will be published in February or March 2004.

NOTTINGHAMSHIRE

Clumber Park [Historic Park and Garden Grade I]

Clumber Estate Office, Clumber Park, Worksop S80 3AZ. Tel: (01909) 476592

The National Trust • 4½ m SE of Worksop off A1 and A57, 11m from M1 junction 30 • Open all year, daily during daylight hours, except 10th July, 21st Aug, 25th and 26th Dec • Walled kitchen garden open 15th March to Oct, daily, 10am – 5.30pm • Entrance: £1. Vehicle charge for park: cars £3.80, caravans and mini-coaches £4.60 • Other information: Wheelchairs available for adults and children. Bicycles for hire. Chapel open (telephone for details) ○ ☕ ✕ 🍽 WC ⅃ ⬦ 🌱 🏛 🔦 🔍

The park of 3800 acres was enclosed from Sherwood Forest in the eighteenth century, and the Dukes of Newcastle had their seat here. The garden was largely the creation of the 9th Earl of Lincoln (subsequently the 2nd Duke of Newcastle) in the second half of the eighteenth century, when he landscaped the park and laid out the pleasure ground, serpentine walks and shrubberies, possibly with advice from his architect Stephen Wright and his friend and mentor Joseph Spence. Wright designed two temples and a bridge for the lake, which remain today. In 1824 William Sawrey Gilpin created the Italianate terrace to the south of the house, island beds and picturesque walks in the pleasure ground. The two-mile-long lime avenue of 1838 and the Lincoln Terrace of 1845 were completed by other hands. From the nineteenth century also are Charles Barry's stable block and clock tower and G.F. Bodley's ornate Gothic chapel built in the pleasure garden. Since the demolition of the great house in 1938 (Barry's being the last in the line), the chapel has become the focus of the garden. The Trust purchased Clumber in 1946 and has kept in good order the wide expanse of park, peaceful woods, open heath and rolling farmland with a superb serpentine lake at its heart. The vinery and palm house have been restocked and the extensive glasshouses (138 metres) are the best and longest in the Trust's properties. The walled kitchen garden contains an impressive herbaceous border as well as cut-flower, fruit and vegetable and herb borders, a collection of old varieties of apple trees and a working Victorian apiary. The Atlantic cedars and sweet chestnut trees in the cedar avenue are of breath-taking size.

Felley Priory ★

Underwood NG16 5FL. Tel: (01773) 810230

The Hon. Mrs Chaworth Musters • 10m NW of Nottingham, ½ m from M1 junction 27. Take A608 signed to Heanor and Derby. Garden is on left • Garden and nursery open all year, Tues, Wed, Fri, 9am – 12.30pm (March to Oct, second and fourth Weds in month, 9am – 4pm, third Sun in month, 11am – 4pm). Snowdrop Sun 8th Feb, 11am – 4pm. Also open for NGS 11th April, 11am – 4pm, and for parties by appt • Entrance: £2.50, children free. Other information: NCCPG Plant Fairs 6th June, 3rd Oct, 12 noon – 4pm ◑ ☕ WC ⅃ 🌱 🔦

Despite the M1 being only half a mile away, the first impression is of a garden with quiet English countryside as a backdrop. The owners have, with the use of hedging, created several gardens within the one, the original ancient walls unifying the parts as well as providing shelter and support for many unusual and slightly tender bulbs, perennials, shrubs and climbers. Snowdrops in variety abound. Over 90 different kinds of old-fashioned roses plus dozens of clematis scrambling up obelisks, make the rose garden a fantastic sight when in full bloom. Water lilies adorn the large natural pond, which is fringed by bamboos, irises, primulas and eucomis. Two pergolas are surrounded by parterres. Home-made cakes, excellent nursery and a welcoming owner.

Hodsock Priory ★

Blyth, Worksop S81 0TY. Tel: (01909) 591204

Sir Andrew and Lady Buchanan • 6m NE of Worksop, 2m W of A1 at Blyth off B6045 Blyth – Worksop road • Open 31st Jan to 7th March, daily, 10am – 4pm • Entrance: £3.50, children (6 16) 50p • Other information: Best displays depend on weather (telephone before travelling). Coaches must book. Dogs in park only ❶ ☕ 🍴 WC ♿ ⚘

Beyond the imposing red-brick Tudor gatehouse which is the entrance to Hodsock Priory stretches one of the most beautiful winter gardens in England. Snowdrops, magenta cyclamen and golden aconites are everywhere – spreading through the borders of the five-acre garden, in the grass and under the trees. Coloured stems of cornus and willow, and the brilliant white trunks of *Betula jacquemontii* reflect in the lake. There are two ferneries and banks of hellebores (almost 1000 plants in one), and the hedges of sarcococca and avenues of winter honeysuckle add fragrance to the whole. The working Victorian apiary is a great attraction to visitors. The Victorian Fan Garden was re-created in 2002 as a low-maintenance feature to be at its best in February and March. Among the many old and interesting trees are *Cornus mas*, *Catalpa bignonioides*, swamp cypress, tulip trees, acers and a pawlonia. An additional walk in the snowdrop wood has been opened up.

Holme Pierrepont Hall [Historic Garden Grade II]

Radcliffe-on-Trent NG12 2LF. Tel: (0115) 933 2371

Mr and Mrs R. Brackenbury • 5m SE of Nottingham off A52/A6011. Continue past National Water Sports Centre for 1½ m • House open as garden • Garden open June, Thurs; July, Wed, Thurs; Aug, Tues – Thurs and Bank Holiday Mon; all 2 – 5.30pm. Parties by appt all year, inc. evening visits • Entrance: £2 (house and garden £4, children £1) ❶ ☕ WC ♿ ⚘ 🍽

The hall is a medieval brick manor house, but the listed garden and box parterre of 1875 have been restored by the present owners. The parterre is the outstanding feature of the gardens, and the herbaceous borders next to the York-stone path (replacing old rose beds) enhance the courtyard garden further. (The Jacob sheep are friendly lawnmowers.) The owners work hard with improvements and new plantings in this peaceful house and garden and willingly provide information. Their innovations include a winter garden, an outer east garden and the planting of yews, shrubs, roses and fruit trees. Recent years have seen great improvements as those mature and increase.

Mill Hill House

Elston Lane, East Stoke, Newark NG23 5QJ. Tel: (01636) 525460

Mr and Mrs R.J. Gregory • 5m SW of Newark. Take A46, turn left into Elston Lane (signed to Elston); house is first on right • Open April to Oct, Bank Holiday Mons, 11am – 5pm, and for NGS; parties and individuals welcome by appt only • Entrance: £1.50, accompanied children free • Other information: Parking 100 metres past house in nursery ◗ 🍂 WC ⬠ ℘

A half-acre cottage garden generously filled with a wide variety of plants provides year-round interest and tranquillity. The garden is well screened from the road and visitors have often commented 'What a beautiful surprise' or 'One of the best kept secrets in Nottinghamshire'. Birds, bees and butterflies have no difficulty in finding it, however. This garden uplifts the spirit as it demonstrates how to overcome the problems of a formerly exposed site. The plants provide a wealth of propagating material for the nursery, and the garden holds a National Collection of berberis.

Newstead Abbey ★ [Historic Garden Grade II*]

Newstead Abbey Park, Nottingham NG15 8NA. Tel: (01623) 455900

Nottingham City Council • 11m N of Nottingham on A60 • House with Byron memorabilia open April to Sept, 12 noon – 5pm • Open all year, daily except 26th Nov and 25th Dec, 9am – dusk • Entrance: £5, children £2.50
○ 🍴 ✕ 🍂 WC ⅋ ⬠ 🏛 ♨ ✂

Water predominates in the estate which the poet Byron inherited, and where he lived from 1808 to 1814. In most of the extensive and immaculate gardens there is much of interest. The Japanese gardens are justly famous and the rock and fern gardens worth visiting. Indeed, the waterfalls, wildfowl, passageways, grottos and bridges provide plenty of fun for children, but in addition there is an excellent, imaginatively equipped play area with bark mulch for safety. The tropical garden and the monks' stewpond are visually uninteresting but they are of laudable age. It is a pity that the large walled kitchen garden is now a rose garden – rose gardens, however pretty, are commonplace, but large kitchen gardens to the great houses are now rare. The old rose and carnation garden, until recently the iris garden, has been replanted as a herb garden.

'Pure Land' Japanese Garden

North Clifton, Nr Newark NG23 7AT. Tel:(01777) 228567

Buddha Maitreya • 10m N of Newark on Trent on A1133. Signposted • Open April to Oct, Tues – Fri, 10.30am – 5.30pm, Sat, Sun and Bank Holiday Mons, 10am – 5.30pm • Entrance: £4.50, OAPs £3.50, children £2.50 (under 5 free), season ticket £25, OAPs £20 • Other information: Limited access for wheelchairs ◗ 🍴 WC ⅋ ✂

The garden of about one and a half acres, created since 1980, is laid out in the Japanese style to provide a calm and contemplative setting for the relaxation and meditation centre based here. Narrow paths, steps and stepping stones lead the visitor up and down to various features of the garden, including the pagoda, tea house, Zen gravel garden and koi-filled pond. Appropriate ornaments and sculpture combine with carefully pruned and shaped trees and shrubs to create an oriental atmosphere which never descends into cliché. The sound of running water is always present from the small waterfalls and streams that weave their way through the garden. The hardy herbaceous, essentially English planting is informal and relaxed, contrasting successfully with the cloud pruning of many familiar conifers. The singular theme has enabled the owners to achieve an exceptional ambience, and yet the garden remains full of inspiration for any visitors thinking of adding a Japanese element to their own gardens.

Rufford Country Park [Historic Park Grade II]

Ollerton, Newark NG22 9DF. Tel: (01623) 822944

Nottinghamshire County Council • 9m NE of Mansfield, 2m S of Ollerton on A614 • Rufford Abbey Cistercian area open • Park open all year, daily, 9am – 5pm • Entrance: free. Parking charge from April to Dec at weekends and Bank Holidays, and through school summer holidays • Other information: Four wheelchairs available for pre-booking ○ 🍽 ✕ 🛍 wc ♿ 🎣 🐾 🏛 💡 ✂

This contains almost everything that might be expected of an important country park: lake, lime avenue, mature cedars, etc. A visit to the eight themed gardens within the formal gardens is well worthwhile, and there is a rose garden in front of the abbey ruins. Large areas are managed with wildlife in mind, but ball games are allowed on the lawns beneath cut-leaved beeches and cedars. The Reg Hookway arboretum, established in 1983, has a good collection of oaks and birches, all well labelled.

Wollaton Park [Historic Park and Garden Grade II*]

Nottingham NG8 2AE. Tel: (0115) 915 3900

Nottingham City Council • W of city centre on A609. From M1 junction 25 take A52, turn left onto A614 and left onto A609 • Natural history museum in hall open all year, daily, 11am – 5pm. Closed 24th to 26th Dec, 1st Jan • Garden open April to Sept, 11am – 5pm, Oct to March, 11am – 4pm • Entrance: Mon – Fri free, charge at weekends and Bank Holidays ○ 🍽 wc ♿ 🎣 💡 ✂

This large park and garden – the setting for Robert Smythson's masterpiece – is surrounded by the city, but because of its size the visitor feels deep in the country, although near the periphery of the park the roar of traffic dispels that illusion. The polyanthus in spring are spectacular, as are the colourful summer bedding planting schemes. The formal gardens at the top of the hill afford views of huge cedars and holm oaks, lime avenues and the deer in the park.

OXFORDSHIRE

Two-starred gardens are marked on the map with a black square.

Ashdown House [Historic Park and Garden Grade II*]

Lambourn, Newbury, Berkshire RG16 7RE. Tel: (01488) 72584 (Estate Office)

The National Trust • 9m E of Swindon, 3½ m NW of Lambourn on W side of B4000 • House (hall, stairway and roof) open by guided tour only, Wed – Sat, 2.15pm, 3.15pm, 4.15pm • Garden open April to Oct, Wed, Sat, 2 – 5pm. Woodlands open all year, Sat – Thurs, dawn – dusk. Parties must pre-book in writing • Entrance: Woodlands free (house £2.10). No reduction for parties • Other information: Parking 250 metres from house. New visitor reception/ information area in South Lodge ● 🍴 ♿ ☕

Set in a hauntingly beautiful valley, the exquisite hunting lodge built by the 1st Lord Craven for Elizabeth of Bohemia appears at first to have a tall central section complete with cupola flanked by two lower wings. It is only when the visitor approaches the front entrance that it becomes obvious that the wings are quite separate from the central block. The remains of a large formal park are present in a western lime avenue, and a complementary lime avenue planted in 1970 to the north of the house is maturing well; the avenue west of the parterre has been replanted. A.H. Brookholding-Jones's appropriately intricate parterre was laid out in the 1950s; the avenue west of the parterre has been replanted. In spring thousands of snowdrops, naturalised in the avenue and woodland, are at their showiest.

Blenheim Palace ★★ [Historic Park and Garden Grade I]

Woodstock, Oxford OX20 1PX. Tel: (01993) 811325

The Duke of Marlborough • 8m NW of Oxford. At Woodstock on A44 • House open as garden • Park open all year, daily except 25th Dec, from 9am. Garden open mid-Feb to Oct, 10.30am – 5.30pm (last admission 4.45pm) • Entrance: Park only (inc. herb garden, maze, play area, butterfly house and train): pedestrians £2.50, children £1, cars inc. occupants £7.50. Gardens only £3.50 (house and gardens £10.50, OAPs £8, children £5) (2003 prices) • Park: ○ 🍴 ♿ ⬇ 🚽 🌡 ☕ *Gardens:* ◐ ☕ ✕ WC ♿ 🐾 🚽 🌡 ☕

Walking through Hawksmoor's Triumphal Arch into Blenheim Park, the visitor is greeted by one of the greatest contrived landscapes in Britain. The architect Vanbrugh employed Bridgeman and Henry Wise, Queen Anne's master gardener and the last of the British formalists. Wise constructed a bastion-walled 'military' garden, laid out kitchen gardens, planted immense elm avenues and linked Vanbrugh's bridge to the sides of the valley. The gardens were ready when the 1st Duke of Marlborough moved into the palace in 1719. Major alterations were made by the 4th, 5th and 9th Dukes, one of the earliest of which was the removal and grassing-over of Wise's formal gardens by 'Capability' Brown after 1764. Brown also landscaped the park, installing the lake and cascade, and removed Wise's military garden. The gardens today include formal areas designed by Achille Duchêne early this century to replace those destroyed by Brown. He made formal gardens to the east and west, the latter as two water terraces in the Versailles style. To the east of the palace is the elaborate Italian garden of patterned box and golden yew, interspersed with various seasonal plantings. To the south-west from the terraces are the rose garden and arboretum. From the vast south lawn 'one passes through a magnificent grove of cedars . . . part shrubberies of laurel and an exedra of box and yew, the whole exemplifying the Victorian pleasure grounds'. In 1991, as a contribution to the celebration of the 300th anniversary of the replanting of the maze at Hampton Court, the Duke planted in part of the kitchen garden a maze which is maturing well, providing visitors with a puzzling and pleasurable experience. The former garden centre has been redeveloped as a lavender and herb garden.

Brook Cottage ★

Well Lane, Alkerton, Banbury OX15 6NL. Tel: (01295) 670303/670590

Mrs D. Hodges • 6m NW of Banbury. From A422 Banbury – Stratford-upon-Avon road, turn W signed to Alkerton. With small war memorial on right, turn left into Well Lane and right at fork • Open 12th April to Oct, Mon – Fri, 9am – 6pm. Weekends, evenings and all group visits by appt only • Entrance: £3, OAPs £2, children free • Other information: Refreshments for parties must be pre-booked. Unusual plants for sale ◗ 🍵 🏠 WC ⅙ ⊲⊳ ⌀

A four-acre garden of great originality and variety, created since 1964 in a west-facing valley as a series of interconnecting and intensively planted areas. It is the work of the plantswoman owner and her late husband and shows what can be achieved by those who 'Consult the Genius of the Place in all'. Once past the terrace below the house, slivers of paths force visitors into single file, making their emergence onto open lawn above the stream and lower pond all the more exciting. Here, the planting is bold and confident, grouped tellingly in individual clumps or in beds with skilful combinations of colour. In the bog garden a splendidly broad band of foliage plants contrasts with feathery or piercing flower spikes. The hanging garden of shrub roses is the most famous feature in its season, but for those who wish to see a profusion of plants, many of them rare, disposed in a masterly way, Brook Cottage is a living workshop of ideas at any time.

Broughton Castle ★ [Historic Garden Grade II]

Broughton, Banbury OX15 5EB. Tel: (01295) 276070

Lord Saye and Sele • $2\frac{1}{2}$ m SW of Banbury on B4035 • Castle open • Garden open 11th, 12th April; May to 16th Sept, Wed, Sun and Bank Holiday Mons (plus Thurs, July and Aug); all 2 – 5pm. Also by appt for parties all year • Entrance: £2.50 (house and garden £5.50, OAPs and students £4.50, children £2.50, family £13.50). Party rates for private guided tours • Other information: Teas on open days only. Refreshments for parties by arrangement ◗ 🍵 🏠 WC ⅙ ⌀ 🏪 🍵

More of a house than a castle, with gardens that are unexpectedly domestic within the confines of the moat, Broughton sits in a beautiful flat-bottomed valley. In 1900 there were 14 gardeners, now there is one maintaining the overall splendour. The most important changes were made after 1969 following a visit from Lanning Roper, who suggested opening up the views across the park. There are now two magnificent borders, where great planting skill is evident in the serpentine flows of colour. The west-facing border, backed by the battlement wall, is based on blues and yellows, greys and whites, the other on reds, mauves and blues. On the south side is the walled 'ladies' garden' with box-edged, fleur-de-lys-shaped beds holding floribunda roses. Another wonderful border rises up to the house wall. Everywhere is a profusion of old-fashioned roses and original planting.

Buscot Park ★ [Historic Park and Garden Grade II*]

Faringdon SN7 8BU. Tel: (01367) 240786

Administered by Lord Faringdon on behalf of The National Trust • On A417 between Lechlade and Faringdon • House open as garden (but closed Mon and Tues) • Garden open April to Sept, daily, except weekends of 3rd, 4th, 17th, 18th April, 15th, 16th May, 5th, 6th, 19th, 20th June, 3rd, 4th, 17th, 18th, 31st July, 1st, 7th, 8th, 21st, 22nd Aug, 4th, 5th, 18th, 19th Sept, 2 – 6pm • Entrance: £4.50, children £2.25 (house and grounds £6.50, children £3.25) • Other information: Teas available when house open ◑ ◕ ▦ WC ⟨⟩

The huge walled estate is situated in the flatlands of the Thames, with a house built in 1780. Its garden, however, was only developed during the twentieth century. The water-garden-within-a-wood was created by Harold Peto in 1912; later, avenues linking lake to house were cut through, branching out from a goose-foot near the house, with fastigiate and weeping varieties of oak, beech and lime. The Egyptian avenue created by Lord Faringdon in 1969 is guarded by sphinxes and embellished with Coade-stone statues copied from an original from Hadrian's Villa. Two new gardens at *allée* intersections – the Swinging Garden and the Citrus Bowl – provide enclosed areas of great charm. The large walled kitchen garden was rearranged in the mid-1980s, and is now intersected by a pleached avenue of ostrya (hop hornbeam) and a Judas tree tunnel. Deep borders under the outside walls have unusual and skilled planting by Tim Rees, mixing old roses and climbing vegetables (gourds, marrows, beans, cucumbers) which lay themselves out over the rose bushes after their flowering is over. Walkways both outside and inside the kitchen garden are between wide borders which use the exterior and interior walls and trellises as screens. In the latter the planting by the late Peter Coats and imaginative development by Lord Faringdon is exceptionally effective. The small garden at the elegant seventeenth-century *Buscot Old Parsonage*, also a Trust property, has different opening times.

Chastleton House [Historic Garden Grade II*]

Chastleton GL56 0SU. Tel: (01608) 674355

The National Trust • 6m NE of Stow-on-the-Wold off A436 • Open 31st March to 2nd Oct, daily, 1 – 5pm (last admission 4pm), 6th to 30th Oct, 1 – 4pm (last admission 3pm). Ticket numbers restricted and prospective visitors strongly advised to telephone in advance. Pre-booked guided tours available (charge applies including NT members). Groups of 11 – 25 by prior appt only • Entrance: £5.80, children £2.90, family £14.50 • Other information: No large coaches. Parking 270 metres from house – telephone for details of parking for disabled. Braille guide available ◗ **WC** &

The beguiling, somewhat gawky early seventeenth-century house was in a state of pleasing decay when it was in private hands, but the Trust has sensitively retained the atmosphere. The garden, which was at its peak in the early twentieth century and survived more or less intact until the 1960s, has been treated in the same spirit. The impressive topiary, probably a Victorian re-creation of a seventeenth-century design, still makes an emphatic statement; the rest provides a pleasant setting for the enchanted house. The rules of modern croquet were first codified at Chastleton and one of the original croquet lawns has been restored. At *Chastleton Glebe* Prue Leith's garden is usually open one day a year for the NGS.

Clock House

Coleshill, Swindon, Wiltshire SN6 7PT. Tel: (01793) 762476

Denny Wickham and Peter Fox • 3$\frac{1}{2}$ m SW of Faringdon on B4019 • Open 16th May, 13th June, 12th Sept, 3rd Oct, 2 – 6pm; April to Oct, Thurs, 2 – 5pm (closes 8pm in June); also by appt • Entrance: £1.50, children free • Other information: Teas in courtyard in fine weather ● ☕ **WC** &

Situated on a hillside with inspiring views over the Vale of the White Horse, this exuberant, delightful garden was created by Denny Wickham in the last 40 years on the site of one of the most beautiful Caroline houses, Coleshill (tragically burned, then wilfully demolished in the 1950s). The ground-plan of the original house is planted out in box and lavender, to show the layout of walls and windows. The gravel 'rooms' are full of self-sown poppies in June and *Verbena bonariensis* in late July. There is a courtyard with a collection of plants in pots, and a sunny walled garden in the old laundry-yard with roses and mixed planting and a fine greenhouse. The lime avenue at the front of the house sweeps down to the views, and a pond and terrace are sheltered by tall shrubs. The mixed herbaceous borders are filled with interesting and unusual plants. This is an original garden, designed by an artist, with a large collection of plants in imaginative settings.

Cotswold Wildlife Park and Gardens ★

Burford OX18 4JW. Tel: (01993) 823006

John and Reggie Heyworth • Open all year, daily; March to Sept, 10am – 6pm (last admission 4.30pm), Oct to Feb, 10am – 4.30pm (last admission 3pm). Closed 25th Dec • Entrance: £8, children (3-16) £5.50, OAPs £5.50 (discount for parties of 20 or more) (2003 prices) ○ ☕ ✕ **WC** & ⟲ 🛒 ✇

Varied and extensive grounds – 160 acres in all – surround the listed Victorian Gothic manor house. Head gardener Tim Miles and his team have achieved wonders here in the past four years. The tropical house is outstandingly atmospheric with its spectacular plants and birds – the original Eden Project in miniature – and the exotic theme is carried through into the exuberant walled garden. Here are hot colours and the largest collection of tender perennials in the country, together with immaculate traditional bedding in an effective combination of pink and silver shades, fruiting bananas and avocados, and a range of containers and hanging baskets with original and flamboyant displays. The planting schemes throughout complement and enhance the settings of the various animals and birds: don't miss the meerkats in their landscaped desert with its flowering cacti and succulents. The terrace beside the house, which has a formal pond and parterre, is in cool contrast, featuring blues and mauves and masses of white roses. Areas of prairie planting with grasses and bamboos continue to develop, and the parkland, home to many endangered animals, has fine specimen trees: Wellingtonias, giant redwoods, cedars and an immense oak six hundred years old. There are delights here for all ages, whether in prams or invalid chairs.

Gothic House ★

Charlbury, Chipping Norton OX7 3PP, Tel: (01608) 810654

Mr and Mrs Andrew Lawson • In centre of Charlbury on B4022 Witney – Enstone road • Open one day for NGS, and for parties by appt • Entrance £2.50, children 50p ● WC &

A third-of-an-acre walled town garden, designed by one of the country's leading garden photographers and his sculptress wife. Artistic flair is evident everywhere, although it is sad to report that the dead tree painted electric-blue has succumbed, replaced now by a crab apple. There is a chess-board arrangement of squares set into gravel which included a charming box-edged reflective pool, a wigwam, two thyme squares, naturalistic planting in greys and purples, and an assemblage of pots. An imaginatively planted broad border leads through to the rear garden, which is dignified by espaliered fruit trees alongside a pleached lime walk and has many artful touches. *Objets trouvés* amid the foliage and the whole effect delightful. Briony Lawson's sculptures are everywhere, numbered and for sale. Regular visitors find inspiration here year on year.

Greys Court ★ [Historic Garden Grade II]

Rotherfield Greys, Henley-on-Thames RG9 4PG. Tel: (01491) 628529

The National Trust • W of Henley-on-Thames, E of B481. From town centre take A4130 towards Oxford, at Nettlebed mini-roundabout take B481. Signposted to left shortly after Highmoor • House open April to Sept, Wed – Fri and Bank Holiday Mons, 2 – 6pm • Gardens open March, Oct, Wed, 2 – 6pm; April to Sept, Tues – Sat and Bank Holiday Mons, 2 – 6pm • Entrance: £3.40, children £1.70, family £8.30 (house and garden £4.80, children £2.40, family £12) • Other information: Picnics in car park only ◑ ☕ WC & ⌂

The statue symbolising St Fiacre, the protector of gardeners and commemorating Charles Taylor, a former head gardener, stands modestly in this beautiful garden, or several gardens, set against the ruins of a fourteenth-century fortified house. The largest area, an orchard, is divided by hedges of *Rosa mundi*. An ancient wisteria forms a canopy over a walled area, approached on one side through a tunnel of wisterias and *Robinia hispida*. The impeccably kept peony bed and rose garden glow against the ancient walls. Beyond the kitchen garden – now an ornamental garden of unusual vegetables – across the nut avenue, is the grass Archbishop's Maze, interesting for its symbolism. Seek out also the donkey wheel and the restored ice-house. In collaboration with the HDRA, the garden was part of a pilot project aimed at providing the Trust with an organic gardening blueprint for the future.

The Harcourt Arboretum [Historic Arboretum Grade I]

Nuneham Courtenay, Oxford OX44 9PX. Tel: (01865) 343501

Oxford University Botanic Garden • 6m S of Oxford off A4074 • Open all year, daily except 9th to 12th April and 22nd Dec to 4th Jan: May to Oct, daily, 10am – 5pm; Nov to April, Mon – Fri, 10am – 4.30pm • Entrance: free, but £2 car parking charge • Other information: No coaches ○ ▩

The village and church of Nuneham were demolished in the 1670s to make way for a classical landscape to be seen from the house (not open); Oliver Goldsmith's poem *The Deserted Village*, written in 1770, may be based on that upheaval. Horace Walpole, in 1780, described the gardens, designed by 'Capability' Brown and William Mason (the poet-gardener), as the most beautiful in the world. The garden was then full of flowers, not only along the walks, but in carefully planted beds. This 85-acre site, one and a half miles from the house, and now owned by Oxford University Botanic Garden, dates from 1835 when the Harcourt family, who owned the Nuneham estate at the time, planted a pinetum with the help of William Sawrey Gilpin. Many of those plantings are now magnificent mature specimens underplanted with camellias, rhododendrons, bamboos, magnolias and a collection of acers. There is also a 10-acre bluebell wood and a 22-acre meadow.

Hill Court

Tackley. (Enquiries to Court Farm, Tackley, Kidlington OX5 3AQ. Tel: (01869) 331221)

Mr and Mrs Andrew C. Peake • 9m N of Oxford, off A4260. From Oxford turn opposite Sturdy's Castle; from S turn off at Tackley sign • Open 12th, 13th June, 2 – 6pm, and for parties by appt daytime only (fee payable) • Entrance: £2, children free ● ▣ WC ㅅ ⚘ ♋

A two-acre, sixteenth-century walled garden formerly attached to the house, which was demolished *c.* 1960. Remains of the manor house, also demolished, can be seen across the park, which dates from 1787. The garden, the design of which was influenced by Russell Page, is unusual because it is terraced uphill from the entrance. The rose beds were removed a decade ago and the sensitive and original planting which replaced them is the work of Rupert Golby.

Home Farm

Balscote, Banbury OX15 6JP. Tel: (01295) 738194

Mr and Mrs G.C. Royle • 5m W of Banbury, ½ m off A422 • Open 3rd, 31st May, 9am – 6pm, and March to Oct by appt • Entrance: £2 • Other information: Teas on open days only, otherwise light refreshments if pre-booked ● ➤ 🏠 WC 🚻 🐕 🌿

This sophisticated hilltop garden of half an acre has been created by the Royles since 1984 from a farmyard on a gently sloping site, with soft pastoral views of grazing sheep. There is nothing mimsy here. Mrs Royle has a firm way of using colour, and the garden is abundantly planted with unusual flowering shrubs, bulbs, herbaceous plants, alpines and roses – designed to give all-year interest, with a special love of coloured or contrasting foliage.

Kelmscott Manor [Historic Garden Grade II]

Kelmscott, Lechlade, Gloucestershire GL7 3HJ. Tel: (01367) 252486

The Society of Antiquaries • 4m NW of Faringdon, 2m E of Lechlade in Kelmscott • House open as garden • Garden open April to Sept, Wed, 11am – 1pm, 2 – 5pm; also first Sat July and Aug, and third Sat April to Sept, 2 – 5pm. Tours for parties by appt on Thurs and Fri • Entrance: £2, children free (house and garden £7, children/students £3.50) ● ➤ ✕ 🏠 WC 🚻 🍴

'A magical house in a remarkably unchanged village' was *Country Life's* verdict. Its strange atmosphere will be relished by those who are attracted by the Pre-Raphaelite Brotherhood in general, or William Morris in particular. The impression one forms of all Morris's gardens is that they had an unruly beauty where weeds might well have been encouraged if they were decorative. Above all the choice of flowers was essentially artistic and romantic because, for him, gardens were places of magic and mystery, fairytale worlds where lovers met under rose-covered arbours. The present garden, designed by Colvin and Moggridge, re-creates some of that romanticism – what Morris himself described as 'a heaven on earth . . . and such a garden! Close down on the river, a boat house and all things handy.'

Kingston Bagpuize House

Kingston Bagpuize, Abingdon OX13 5AX. Tel: (01865) 820259

Mrs Virginia Grant • 5½ m W of Abingdon at junction off A415 and A420. At entrance to village, park by large ornamental gates • Open 7th, 8th, 21st, 22nd, 29th Feb, 14th, 27th, 28th March, 11th, 12th, 25th April, 2nd, 3rd, 9th, 23rd, 30th, 31st May, 13th, 27th June, 11th, 24th, 25th July, 8th, 22nd, 29th, 30th Aug, 11th, 12th, 26th Sept, 10th Oct; all 2 – 5pm. Open to parties by appt all year. Guided tours available • Entrance: £2.50 (house and garden £4.50, OAPs £4, children (5–15) £2.50) • Other information: Home-made teas. Meals available for groups by arrangement ● ➤ WC 🚻 🌿 🍴 🍷

The beautiful mellow brick Baroque house, neither too small nor too large, set in its compact park, was owned by Miss Marlie Raphael, an enthusiastic and much-travelled plant collector, from 1939 until her death in 1976. With the help of Sir Harold Hillier and other friends, she created a 15-acre garden with its mind-boggling variety of rare and unusual trees, shrubs and plants. Since inheriting the house in 1995, the present owner, together with her late husband, Francis, successfully uncovered and restored much of Miss Raphael's original planting, adding to it with their own complementary and innovative ideas. Within the framework of mellow brick walls and hedges of yew, beech and laurel (and even of brachyglottis), there is an air of relaxed informality, the plants thriving in the fertile greensand soil. An enormous mixed border 10 metres deep is packed with tall perennials, many self-sown, covering a broad spectrum of harmonious colours. At every turn in the three-acre woodland garden are rare and interesting trees and shrubs, including several magnolias. Many of them are quite spectacular, and beneath the jungle canopy are carpets of snowdrops and other bulbs, followed by drifts of geraniums, astrantias, campanulas, vincas, hellebores, lilies and other shade-loving perennials. Along the edge of the Garden Park with its beech avenue, Wellingtonias and other specimen trees, the shrub border reveals yet more rarities. The terrace walk has a growing cistus collection and provides an excellent vantage point from which to enjoy a view of the house and different aspects of the garden, which is planned to give colour and interest throughout the year.

Lime Close ★

35 Henleys Lane, Drayton OX14 4HU.

Mme M.C. de Laubarede • 2m S of Abingdon off B4017; turn left into Henleys Lane, house 200 yds on left • Open for NGS 18th April, 6th June, 2 – 5.30pm, and at other times for parties of 10 or more by written appt • Entrance: £2.50, children 50p (under 4 free) ● ● ● ▤ ₺ ⬛ ⅏ ℅

The owner, a garden designer, has created an unexpected three-acre oasis here, following in the footsteps of her grandfather, Charles Christie-Miller, a tree, shrub and iris specialist, and her aunt, an alpine enthusiast, from whom she inherited the garden. Grassy walks and vistas, and mixed and shade borders distinguished by rare perennials, including *Clematis recta* 'Lime Close', and clever colour combinations, are all surrounded by mature trees and a wide variety of more recently planted rare trees and shrubs. Yew hedges and topiary are beautifully maintained and privet hedges enclose the flower-filled *potager* with its Italian-Renaissance-style pergola and increasing iris collection. Beside the Elizabethan house formal areas include a parterre, a charming little herb garden designed by Rosemary Verey, a lawn and herbaceous borders. Peonies, roses, honeysuckles and clematis put in an appearance everywhere. The planting throughout is relaxed and informal, the colour effects enviably subtle and delicate. Masses of bulbs from late February onwards, and spectacular autumn leaves. A new cottage garden is in the making.

The Mill House

Sutton Courtenay, Abingdon OX14 4NH. Tel: (01235) 848219

Mrs Jane Stevens • 1½ m S of Abingdon off B4016. Leaving town over river bridge, entrance gates in main street opposite Fish pub • Open by appt for parties of 10 or more • Entrance: £4 per person • Other information: Teas by prior arrangement ● WC &

Although the stone house behind high walls suggests promise, the romantic experience of the garden cannot be guessed at as the visitor approaches through the winding main street of the village. Of course, few gardeners have the gift of the Thames in their territory, but the present owner has made remarkable use of it. She had the benefit of a structure laid out by Colonel Peter Laycock, a colleague of Eric Savill, who planted rare and unusual trees and has added imaginative touches of her own – like the circles of comfrey. This eight-and-a-half-acre garden is to be walked in, sat in and savoured. The old mill in the middle of the garden, now a ruin, was used for printing banknotes up until the middle of the eighteenth century. There are formal areas near the early Georgian house, but once past these, the wanderer will be lost in a sylvan idyll amongst the water, trees and groves. There are three islands, planted with a mass of wild flowers, and seasonal interest comes from the fine bulbs in spring, old-fashioned roses in summer, and charming autumn colours. For those who like to conjure up dreams of previous owners, Herbert and Margot Asquith lived here before 1916 while he was Prime Minister and entertained all the great figures of the day for Friday-to-Monday weekends. The nearby *Manor House*, with a garden by Brenda Colvin (replacing Norah Lindsay's), is open once a year for the NGS.

Old Church House

2 Priory Road, Wantage OX12 9DD. Tel: (01235) 762785

Dr and Mrs Dick Squires • Near Wantage Market Square next to parish church and opposite Vale and Downland Museum • Open April to Oct, Tues – Sat, 10.30am – 4.30pm, Sun, 2 – 5pm, and by appt • Entrance: By donation to charity (tickets available at museum). Children welcome • Other information: Park in nearby public car park. Refreshments and toilet facilities at Museum ◖ ● & ⏦ ℆ B&B

An unusual and exciting town garden running down to Letcombe Brook. Dr and Mrs Squires have transformed his childhood garden into a series of rooms leading away from the existing lawns and mature trees. There is a sunken water garden, a Mediterranean garden, a pergola garden and a wild garden, all filled with unusual plants and shrubs, follies and highly imaginative building. It is an inspiration to see what can be achieved in less than three years. Some fascinating documentation shows the development of the planning and the work itself in before-and-after style.

The Old Rectory ★

Farnborough, Wantage OX12 8NX. Tel: (01488) 638298

Mr and Mrs Michael Todhunter • 4m SE of Wantage off B4494 • Open for NGS, 2 – 5.30pm, and by written appt • Entrance: £2.50, children free on open

days, and £5 by appt • Other information: Teas nearby on charity open days and for parties ● ☕ WC ♿ ✿

At nearly 250 metres, and despite being prey to winds from the Downs, this four-acre garden has been created over thirty years, based on a good original structure of large trees and hedges, with magnificent views. Its house is as pretty as any village old rectory could be, and sits at the heart of the garden looking out at the downs. Deep, parallel herbaceous borders are backed by yew hedges. The planting by the front of house is subtle and effective, and smaller areas have been laid out for sun- or shade-loving plants. Woodland contrasts with shrubs and lawns, and the fast-growing arboretum now contains over 150 trees. The swimming pool is surrounded by a large *Hydrangea sargentiana* and potted lilies, with mixed roses and clematis around the outside walls. There is a collection of old roses and small-flowered clematis, and wild flowers line the front lawn by the ha-ha. The tennis court has been turned into a *boule a drôme* – a place in the middle to play boule – with four large beds, pretty wrought-iron gates and a gazebo. Those who like John Betjeman's poetry will be interested to know that he lived here from 1945 to 1950 and can look for the ghost of Miss Joan Hunter Dunn in the shrubberies. A John Piper window in the church is in his memory.

Oxford Botanic Garden ★★ [Historic Garden Grade I]

Rose Lane, Oxford OX1 4AZ. Tel: (01865) 286690

University of Oxford • In city centre opposite Magdalen College near bridge • Open all year, daily: April to Sept, 9am – 5pm (closes 8pm, Thurs, June to Aug)(glasshouses 10am – 4.30pm); Oct to March, 9am – 4.30pm (glasshouses 10am – 4pm). Closed 9th April and 25th Dec • Entrance: April to Sept £2.50, children under 12 free; Oct to Feb by donation • Other information: Plants for sale April to Sept. Professional photography and music prohibited ○ WC ♿ ✿ ▥ ♒

This is the oldest botanic garden in Britain, founded in 1621 for physicians' herbal requirements, surrounded by a Grade-I-listed wall and entered through a splendid archway by Nicholas Stone. Nowhere else on earth, it is claimed, are there so many different plants in four and a half acres, 8000 species in all, and representatives of over 90 per cent of families of flowering plants. One yew survives from the 1650 plantings, and there is a series of family beds containing herbaceous and annual plants in systematic and labelled groups. The old walls back beds with tender plants, including roses and clematis. To the left is a collection of glasshouses, modern ones replacing those built in 1670. A rock garden has been renovated, as has the bog garden and late summer/autumn borders. A National Collection of euphorbias is held here. Recently, Nori and Sandra Pope, who have taken over Hadspen in Somerset (see entry), were commissioned to make some new autumn borders. They have planted dark and silver shrubs with spectacular autumn colour at the back of the border. The site amply justifies its original purpose 'to promote learning and glorify the works of God'. Outside the front entrance is a large rose garden donated to Magdalen College by Americans in memory of those university staff who developed penicillin. Six miles away at Nuneham Courtenay (south of the A4074) is the Harcourt Arboretum (see entry). Guided tours of both gardens are available – contact the Botanic Garden for details.

Oxford College Gardens

Most colleges are helpful about access to their gardens, although the more private ones, such as the Master's or Fellows', are rarely open. Specific viewing times are difficult to rely on because some colleges prefer not to have visitors in term time or on days when a function is taking place. The best course is to ask at the porter's lodge or to telephone ahead of visit. However, it is fair to say that some Oxford college gardens will always be open to the visitor, by arrangement with porters, even if others are closed on that particular day. Some colleges have a policy of allowing public entrance on official guided tours only and others now make a charge for entry.

There are eight college gardens that are on the English Heritage *Register*. Each one is identified in the text that follows. As well as these, amongst the college gardens of particular interest are the following: *Christ Church*: the War Memorial Gardens on St. Aldate's, with its attractive herbaceous borders, and, just beyond, the rose garden with its water feature, [open daily except 25th Dec, Mon–Sat, 9am – 5.30pm, Sun, 11.30am – 5.30pm]. So are the splendid Christ Church Meadows [Historic Park Grade I], with the herd of Old English Longhorns resident in summer and autumn months. Most of the other gardens – Master's, Cathedral and Pocock – are open once a year, usually mid-Aug, for the NGS, allowing a sight of the Oriental plane planted in 1636 and of the Cheshire Cat's horse chestnut tree – a reminder of the college's connection with Lewis Carroll. WC ♿ ♀ *Corpus Christi* [Historic Garden Grade II]: the smallest college, with an attractive small garden overlooking Christ Church Meadow [Normally open 1.30 – 4pm]. *Exeter*: Fellows' Garden [Open most days, 2 – 5pm] is walled on all sides with part of boundary formed by the old Bodleian Library and Divinity Schools. The mound at the end gives excellent views across Radcliffe Square with the Camera, Church of St Mary the Virgin and All Souls College all clearly visible. Visitors are requested to keep to the paths. Herbaceous borders, shrubs and mature trees. Also the Rector's private garden [Open for NGS in conjunction with New College Warden's Garden one Sun in late June/early July, 2 – 5pm]. *Green College*: alas this institution with its environmental name is only open to the public once a year. *Holywell Manor*, part of Balliol: a restful, well-maintained garden of one acre [Open 10.30am – 6.30pm]. *Kellogg College*: an unusual and pleasant inner courtyard with three separate walled gardens at the back situated in Rewley House, Wellington Square [Open all year – telephone (01865) 270383 WC ♿]. *Lady Margaret Hall*: eight formal and informal acres, mainly designed by the Edwardian architect Blomfield, who was also responsible for some of the buildings. Fine specimen trees and good borders [Open 2 – 6pm or dusk if earlier. All visitors are requested to call at the porter's lodge ♿]. *Magdalen College* [Historic Park Grade I]: 100 acres of meadows including a deer park adjacent to the college buildings and Fellows' Garden (open to the public). The water meadows bounded by the River Cherwell and circled by Addison's Walk, named after the eighteenth-century essayist and garden enthusiast, are famous for the display of fritillaries in April [College and gardens open nearly all year, 2 – 6pm. Refreshments sometimes available ☕ WC ♿]. *New College* [Historic Garden Grade I]: admirers of the writings of Robin Lane Fox will be able to see examples of his plantings, outstanding mixed borders against Oxford city wall, rose borders, cloister garden. The mound was completed in 1649. [Open Easter to Oct at New College Lane Gate, 11am – 5pm; winter at Holywell Gate, 2 – 4pm]. *Nuffield*: formal gardens in two quadrangles with water features and sculpture by Peter Randall-Page [Open Mon – Fri, 9am – 5pm, but closed Christmas, Easter and August Bank Holiday. No large parties]. *Queen's*: The gardens are a worthy modern setting to a college with a history stretching back to the fourteenth century. Wrapped around the buildings on several levels, they are planted with elegance, flair and a vital sense of colours that work well together [College, Fellows' and Provost's garden open 27th June for charity, but not to casual visitors during year except those on guided tours arranged through the Information Centre]. *Rhodes House*: not a college and not a pretty building but an unexpectedly pleasant garden behind [9am – 5pm weekdays only]. *St Catherine's* [Historic Garden Grade II]: in the midst of so much ancient charm in garden design it is pleasing to be able to recommend a modern garden (1960–4) created by the distinguished Danish architect Arne Jacobsen (1902–71). Noted for his concern for integrating building and landscape, this is a remarkable example. It has a fine water feature, and John Brookes says that, later in the season, when the water planting is at its best, the canal comes into its own – [Open except Easter, Aug and Christmas]. *St Hilda's*: five acres of lawns and beds extending along the banks of the River Cherwell; flood plain meadow with wild flowers including fritillaries. Jacqueline du Pré Music Building accessible for visits and concerts [Open during daylight hours but dogs not permitted]. *St Hugh's*: an interesting 10-acre garden largely created by Annie Rogers, a Fellow. [All visitors are requested to call at the porter's lodge ♿]. *St John's* [Historic Garden Grade II]: landscaped in the eighteenth century and still immaculately kept. Striking in spring when bulbs in flower. William Pye has designed a new water sculpture. See also the new Garden Quad, opened in 1993, designed by MacCormac Jamieson & Pritchard and described as 'one of the most important buildings of the 'nineties anywhere in Britain' [Open daily, 1 – 5pm or dusk if earlier. Better to go during the week, rather than at weekends, to avoid crowds ♿]. *Trinity* [Historic Garden Grade II]: broad sweeping lawns, magnificent herbaceous borders and informal woodland carpeted with bulbs in spring; interesting trees including 1737 catalpa and a splendid fraxinus. Remarkable stone Baroque gateway at the end of Trinity College's garden onto Parks Road, probably by Hawksmoor. [Open daily, 10.30am – 12 noon, 2 – 5pm WC ♿]. Trinity Fellows' and President's Gardens, recently developed with choice plants, statuary and fountain [Open for NGS, one Sun in late March or early April and Aug, 2 – 5pm ☕ ⚘]. *Wadham* [Historic Garden Grade II]: herbaceous borders, new 'fragrant' garden, rare and fine old trees [Open 1 – 4.30pm WC ♿]. *Wolfson*: nine acres designed around modern college buildings by Powell and Moya. Mature beds of perennials and shrubs, formal lawns and mature trees in a peaceful riverside setting. [Open daily, daylight hours **WC** ♿ ❐]. *Worcester* [Historic Garden Grade II*]: the only true landscaped garden in Oxford, including a lake, made from a swampy area in 1817. Brightly coloured beds in front quad [Open term time 2 – 6pm, vacation 9am – 12 noon and 2 – 6pm. Organised parties not admitted except by prior written arrangement]. The Provost's Garden, open on special occasions, has a charming rose garden stretching to wooded lakeside walks and orchards. *The University Parks* (a short walk from Rhodes House past the amazing museum): these were laid out in 1864 and are the perfect place for walking in all weathers and across the bridges to Mesopotamia or the Spalding Nature Reserve. The herbaceous border near South Lodge Gate is laid out in colour themes. The borders along the West and North Walks contain a broad collection of shrubs and groundcover plants chosen especially for their drought tolerance, grouped in strong associations to create a focus in the middle distance. The extended pond provides a habitat for moisture-loving plants, while Cox's Corner has an emphasis on winter colour. The Parks have a fine collection of mature trees mixed with newer plantings [Open daily, except 3rd Sept, 8am – dusk **WC** ♿].

Pettifers ★

Lower Wardington, Banbury OX17 1RU. Tel: (01295) 750232

Mr J. and The Hon. Mrs Price • 5m NE of Banbury on A361 Daventry Road from M40 junction 11. Opposite church • Open for NGS 8th July, 16th Sept, 3.30 – 7.30pm, and by appt • Entrance: £4 (£5 for private visits) ● 🍴 **WC** ♿

Created since 1988, the garden has now matured and totally changed in concept. It has an air of peace and romance which stems from the stunning view dominating the landscape. It is an all-year garden. Spring starts with tulips and a meadow spangled with fritillaries, anemones, narcissi, miniature daffodils and bluebells, while summer is characterised in the borders by exciting perennials interspersed with miscanthus and roses in variety. Late in the year an autumn border and a parterre filled with annuals, sweet peas and sunflowers of different colours come into their own. In winter the seed heads are allowed to remain in the herbaceous borders, and the crocus lawn flowers into life.

The Priory

Charlbury OX7 3PX. Tel: (01608) 810417

Dr D. El Kabir and others • On B4022 Witney – Enstone road. In Charlbury adjacent to church • Open 20th June, 2 – 6pm, and occasionally for individuals and parties by appt • Entrance: £2.50, children 50p ● 🍴 ⚘

In this formal terraced topiary garden with Italianate features, the owners have aimed to create a poetic and contemplative atmosphere through terraces, parterres, foliage colour schemes, statuary and water features. They have also tried to make it low-maintenance and accordingly have ruled out annuals. Over one acre is planted with many unusual specimen trees and shrubs, mainly in various 'rooms' and a young three-acre arboretum has about 200 different trees.

Rousham House ★★ [Historic Park and Garden Grade I]

Nr Steeple Aston, Bicester OX25 4QX. Tel: (01869) 347110

Charles Cottrell-Dormer • 11m N of Oxford, 2m S of Steeple Aston off A4260 and B4030 • House open April to Sept, Wed, Sun and Bank Holiday Mons, 2 – 4.30pm • Garden open all year, daily, 10am – 4.30pm • Entrance: £3 • Other information: children under 15 not admitted ○ 🏚 **WC** &

This is much admired because William Kent's design of 1738 is effectively frozen in time. Historical enlightenment can be combined with the enchantment of the setting and the use he made of it. In fact, before Kent it was already a famous garden, described by Alexander Pope as 'the prettiest place for water-falls, jetts, ponds, inclosed with beautiful scenes of green and hanging wood, that ever I saw'. Kent's design, influenced perhaps by stage scenery, created a series of effects. There are splendid small buildings and follies, fine sculpture, water and many seats and vantage points. The best way to view the garden is to follow these one by one, in the order Kent intended, and for this a guidebook is necessary. By taking the effects *seriatim*, a feeling for the whole will then gradually emerge. This was also one of the first places where the garden took in the whole estate, 'calling-in' the surrounding countryside, to use Pope's words. Walled gardens next to the house, which pre-date Kent, have been made into a major attraction with herbaceous borders, parterre, rose garden, dovecot and vegetable garden.

Shotover House [Historic Park and Garden Grade I]

Shotover Estate, Wheatley, Oxford OX33 1QS.

Lt Col Sir John Miller • 6m E of Oxford on A40 (S carriageway) • Open probably April and July for NGS, but check Oxford Times newspaper for dates • Entrance: £1.50, children free • Other information: Possible for wheelchairs but some unsurfaced paths ● 🍴 🏚 **WC** & ⬦ 🌳 🔱 ⚲

The landscaped park and garden were begun *c.* 1718, and William Kent was involved in the design in the 1730s, constructing a domed octagonal temple (now ringed by cherry trees) and, on another axis, an obelisk – he was working at nearby Rousham (see entry) from 1738. Rare cattle and sheep, including black varieties, greet visitors as they walk from the car park at the end of the drive round to the colonnaded back of the eighteenth-century house (not open). Much is being done to enliven the planting in the formal garden surrounding it and to revive the statuary. From the rear arcade the view is of a long canal ending in a Gothick folly, which can be reached by walking via the pet cemetery and interestingly decorated wooden chalet. From the west front of the house, visitors will enjoy strolling down the long avenues carved out of what was once part of the royal forest of Wychwood. There is also a small obelisk erected to commemorate visits by H.M. Queen Elizabeth II and the late Queen Mother, who was a regular visitor for more than a decade. Allow an hour to explore this pleasant park, but be warned that the noisome A40 is all too present.

The Skippet ★

Mount Skippet, Ramsden, Chipping Norton OX7 3AP. Tel: (01993) 868253

Dr M.A.T. Rogers • 4m N of Witney off B4022 Charlbury road. At crossroads signed to Finstock turn E and almost immediately right. After 500 metres turn left up no-through-way lane • Open March to Sept by appt • Entrance: £1 for charity ● WC ◁▷

Tucked away between the village pond, which he maintains was contructed by the Romans 1700 years ago, and ancient ridge-and-furrow farmland not far from Akeman Street, the owner, a retired research chemist now in his nineties, has developed over the last quarter-century a two-acre garden of exceptional interest. It is literally crammed with rare and fascinating plants of every description, in luxuriant herbaceous borders reminiscent of Monet, in rockeries, in greenhouses and in an enormous number of pots and containers of all shapes and sizes. There are exotic and unusual climbers both in the conservatory and all around the largely seventeenth-century house. A court-yard with a profusion of spring bulbs and annuals, mostly self-sown, leads to the prolific vegetable garden. Across the lawn, surrounded by a large variety of shrubs, are attractive vistas, and the alpine house contains many treasures. There is an interesting tufa collection, unusual shrubs and trees in the wild garden, a mass of bulbs in the orchard, and snowdrops beside the pond. Most of the plants are labelled, some rare specimens are for sale, and, if you are lucky, the owner will delight in giving you an enthusiastic and highly informative tour.

Stansfield ★

**49 High Street, Stanford–in–the–Vale, Faringdon SN7 8NQ.
Tel: (01367) 710340**

Mr and Mrs D. Keeble • 16m SW of Oxford, 3½ m SE of Faringdon. Turn off A417 opposite Vale Garage • Open 6th April, 4th May, 1st June, 6th July, 3rd Aug, 7th Sept, 10am – 4pm, and by appt; parties and evening visits welcome • Entrance: £1.50 ● ☕ 🖼 ♿ 🌿

A one-acre-plus plantsman's garden with many island beds and borders, and a large collection of plants for both damp and dry conditions. All-year round interest is provided by a wide use of foliage and seasonal flowers, starting with species spring bulbs – indeed, attention is focused on the number and variety of plants rather than the design and layout, which includes woodland, a grass border, a scree garden and a model vegetable garden. Alpines in sinks and troughs give interest on a smaller scale. Rabbit-proof fencing encloses perforce the entire property.

Stonor Park [Historic Park Grade II*]

Stonor, Henley-on-Thames RG9 6HF. Tel: (01491) 638587

Lord Camoys • 5m N of Henley-on-Thames on B480 • House open • Open April to Sept, Sun, Bank Holiday Mons; July to Aug, Wed, Sun; all 2 – 5.30pm.

Parties by arrangement Tues, Wed or Thurs (am and pm) • Entrance: £3.50 (house and gardens £6, children under 14 in family parties free). Party rates on application (2003 prices) • Other information: Lunches for parties by arrangement. Wheelchairs by arrangement ◑ ☕ 🌿 WC & 🏪 ☕

The long eastern façade of the house masks a complex E-shaped Tudor building with twelfth-century origins. It is set in a bowl on the east side of a hill facing west to open parkland and large trees. Behind and to the side of the house on higher land, sheltered against the hill, are flower and vegetable gardens. Lawns lead up to a terrace with pools, stone urns and planting along the steps. The orchard, with its cypresses and espaliered fruit trees, and the lavender hedges are attractive features.

Wardington Manor

Wardington, Banbury OX17 1SW. Tel: (01295) 750202/758481

Lord and Lady Wardington • 5m NE of Banbury off A361 from M40 junction 11 • Open by appt • Entrance: £4 ● WC & �—

Great lawns spread themselves in front of the Caroline manor house with its wisteria-covered walls. The topiary is impeccable too, and there are attractive borders. Away from the house, the owners have created a flowering shrub walk with interesting ground cover, which leads to a walled area planted with hostas. To the left is a rockery and a large pond with a peripheral walk. Nearby is The National Herb Centre (see entry under Upton House, Warwickshire).

Waterperry Gardens

Wheatley, Oxford OX33 1JZ. Tel: (01844) 339226

9m E of Oxford, 2½ m N of Wheatley off M40 junction 8 from London, or 8A from Birmingham. Signposted • Open daily, 9am – 5pm but closed Christmas and New Year holidays. 15th to 18th July open only to visitors to Art in Action (enquiries (020) 7381 3192) • Entrance: Nov to March, £1.60; April to Oct, £3.85, OAPs £3.35, children £2.35 (under 10 free), coach parties (of 20 or more) by appt only, £3 per person • Other information: Art and craft gallery. Teashop and museum closed 17th to 20th July ○ ☕ WC & �— 🐕 🌿 🏪 ☕

Waterperry has to be included in this *Guide* although its 20 acres are difficult to categorise. There is a strong educational atmosphere going back to the 1930s when Miss Beatrix Havergal opened up a small horticultural school. There is also a commercial garden centre which occupies large areas of the walled garden. The herbaceous nursery stock beds are in the ornamental gardens and form a living catalogue, with the plants grown in rows and labelled. Intermixed with this are major features of the old garden, lawns and a substantial herbaceous border – also new beds containing collections of alpines, dwarf conifers and other shrubs, a new rose garden and a water-lily canal. The clay bank is planted with shade-lovers. The owners describe the place as one where 'the ornamental and the utilitarian live side by side'. The greenhouses in the nursery are interesting too, containing a good stock of houseplants for sale, usually including orchids and tall ficus; another, in the old walled garden, has

an enormous citrus tree A few miles east down the M40 is *Le Manoir aux Quat'*
Saisons, in Church Road, Great Milton (off A329 Thame–Stadhampton road).
The 12-acre garden surrounding Raymond Blanc's renowned hotel includes an
impressive *potager*, a water garden, a Japanese garden, an orchard etc. It is open
one day for the NGS and can be viewed by patrons.

Westwell Manor ★★

Burford OX18 4JT.

Mr and Mrs T.H. Gibson • 10m W of Witney, 2m SW of Burford off A40 •
Open 6th June, 2 – 6.30pm, and by written appt for horticultural parties of 20
or more (£10 per person) • Entrance: £3, children 50p • Other information: Teas
available in village on open day ◐ WC ℘

It is worth braving the inevitable crowds on the one day a year on which this
seven-acre garden is open for the sheer variety and ingenuity which Mrs Gibson,
a garden designer, has achieved here since 1978. Expecting perhaps a traditional
Cotswold manor garden, the visitor will find that there is much, much more to
discover. The Tudor manor hides behind huge walls, and even through the gate,
the forecourt gives no hint of what lies beyond. Each of the 20 or so garden rooms
behind the house and barn leads to another, offering surprises and originality as
well as traditional features. A charming water garden and a *pièce d'eau* complete
with boat and containing black-dyed water reflect Mrs Gibson's fascination with
the element. Other features include two rills lined by a pleached lime *allée*, an
unusual lavender terrace, a sundial garden, a moonlight garden, an alder basket,
a knot garden and splendid deep herbaceous borders in muted pastels contrasting with areas of meadow and long grass. There is also a vegetable garden, a
nut walk and a Bunny Walk laid along a ley line. Mown paths lead to a mount
constructed from surplus earth moved during the making of a ha-ha. Mrs Gibson
claims no great master-plan, continuing to develop the garden with flair and
unrestrained enthusiasm: a miniature paddy-field with rice from the Camargue,
in all its varying shades of greeny-yellow, a grass amphitheatre in the old
orchard. She plans next a late-summer border with umbelliferous plants and
an orchard with carefully selected old fruit tree varieties.

Wilcote House ★

Wilcote, Finstock, Chipping Norton OX7 3DY. Tel: (01993) 868606

The Hon. and Mrs Charles Cecil • 4m N of Witney, 3m S of Charlbury E off
B4022 • Open by written appt • Entrance: £3, children free, parties negotiable •
Other information: Conducted tours for private parties on weekdays by
arrangement. Teas available by prior arrangement ◐ ☕ ▦ WC ♿ ⬧ ⚲

Surrounding and complementing a fine sixteenth- to nineteenth-century
Cotswold stone house, the large garden is itself a period piece, with extensive
beds of old-fashioned roses and mixed borders and a 40-metre laburnum walk
at its best at the end of May. An unusual feature is the large wild garden
intersected by grass paths, planted within the last two decades with an
increasing selection of trees now beginning to feature, particularly those with
autumn colour. Nearby is the former walled kitchen garden, now leased to

Bridewell Organic Gardens and transformed into a productive and decorative acre of fruit, vegetables and flowers. There is a smithy and most surprising of all, a five-acre vineyard on a sloping hillside with splendid views. The whole place is maintained to a high standard by a team of willing volunteers with a range of health problems, for whom it is a therapy. Full entry next year. [Open Day in Sept; also open for gardening and other interested parties evenings by appt. Telephone (01993) 868445 for details.]

Wroxton Abbey [Historic Park and Garden Grade II*]

Wroxton, Banbury OX15 6PX. Tel: (01295) 730551

Wroxton College of Fairleigh Dickinson University of New Jersey, USA • 3m W of Banbury off A422 • House open only by appt • Grounds open all year, daily, dawn – dusk, but closed for 3 weeks in Aug and late Dec to early Jan • Entrance: free • Other information: Parking in village; vehicles not permitted in grounds ○ &

The drive that leads up to the Jacobean house is lined with trees. Its gardens and parkland with its extensive lawns, specimen trees and woodlands, natural-looking waters and 'eye-catcher' buildings are of considerable historic interest, a good example of the early Picturesque style of gardening. The formal garden designed by Tilleman Bobart, pupil of Henry Wise, which was laid out between 1727 and 1732, was swept away. The grounds were remodelled and extended less than 10 years later by Sanderson Miller for the first Earl of Guilford. Well-kept lawns flow down the valley behind to the Great Pond and Great Cascade, the serpentine river, the Chinese bridge and the Little Cascade, with a viewing mount. Miller's various buildings include a Gothick dovecot, the Drayton Arch, an ice-house and a Doric temple above the formal rose garden and knot garden, with a vista to the obelisk – all restored from their derelict state by the American owners in the late 1970s. There are 56 acres in all, with pleasant lakeside and woodland walks.

THE FIELD FLORICULTURE RESEARCH STATION, LITHUANIA

When Lithuania gained its independence from Russia in 1990, unfettered communication with the West was possible for the first time. Dr Rita Razinlyte, head of a research station in Vilnius specialising in lilies, irises, sempervivums and hyacinths (some 3000 varieties), began a correspondence with the RHS and several UK flower growers, including Alan Shipp, holder of a National Collection of hyacinths in Waterbeach, Cambridgeshire. They exchanged bulbs – he acquired the 'Double Yellow' variety then extinct in the West, for example. Growers and buyers come from all over Lithuania to the biennial plant sale, and the research station exhibits also in Moscow. But it receives no public funding and Dr Razinlyte is concerned for the future of the collections. She also works for a charity, SOS Lithuania Children. If you are in a position to help either venture, please write to Dr Rita Razinlyte, Uab Lauko Gėlininkystės Bandymų Stotis (The Field Floriculture Research Station), V. Kojelavičiaus 1, 2048 Vilnius, Lietuva (Lithuania) (Tel: 00370 2) 67 17 18.

RUTLAND

For gardens in Leicestershire, see pages 218–20.

Ashwell House

Ashwell, Oakham LE15 7LW. Tel: (01572) 722833

Mr and Mrs S.D. Pettifer • 3m N of Oakham via B668 towards Cottesmore, turn left to Ashwell • Open by appt only • Entrance: £1 ● 💭 WC ⅗ 🌀

Next to the fourteenth-century church of St Mary's Ashwell the spacious vicarage garden has been designed by the present owners to provide all-year colour in the shrubs and borders. Fine trees on all sides, some distant, give the impression of a park-like setting. Architectural features by George Carter enliven some shaded areas, and a classical summerhouse offers a peaceful retreat. The colour schemes achieve a successful balance of light and dark: in the front garden *Cedrus atlantica* 'Glauca', eucalyptus and white roses act as a cool foil to the copper beech and red-leaved berberis on the other side. A striking group of silver birches fans out in two arcs, surrounded by purple cut-leaf alders and 'Ispahan' and 'Blanche Double de Coubert' roses. The old walled vegetable garden, although well stocked with fruit and vegetables, has in part been taken over by the pool and millennium gardens, with an abundance of roses: an avenue of standard 'Iceberg', a fan of 'Wedding Day', and columns draped with purple 'Raubritter'.

Barnsdale Gardens

The Avenue, Exton, Oakham LE15 8AH. Tel: (01572) 813200

Nick and Sue Hamilton • 3m NE of Oakham off A606 • Open March to Oct, daily, 9am – 5pm (closes 7pm June to Aug), Nov to Feb, daily, 10am – 4pm (last admission 2 hours before closing time). Parties by appt • Entrance: £5, children under 16 free, season ticket £12.50 each or £23.50 per couple • Other information: Pre-booked wheelchairs available on free loan ◑ 💭 ✕ WC ⅗ 🌀 🏺 🍵 ⚲

Here are the show gardens immortalised by the late Geoff Hamilton on *Gardeners' World*, and now run by his son and daughter-in-law. They are impressive in their range and variety. Themes include town and country paradises, modern estate, cottage gardens, allotment, ornamental kitchen garden, woodland, stream, bog and parterre – all excellent aids to planning or redesigning green spaces. The adjoining nursery sells a wide range of plants propagated from the gardens.

Lyddington Bede House

Blue Coat Lane, Lyddington LE15 9LZ. Tel: (01572) 822438

English Heritage • In Lyddington, 7m S of Oakham, 1m E of A6003 • Open April to Oct, daily, 10am – 6pm (closes 5pm in Oct) • Entrance: £3.20, OAPs

£2.40, children £1.60, family £8 (2003 prices) • *Other information: Parking off road 20 metres from entrance via cobbled alley* ◑ 🍴 ♿ ⬇ 🏛 ⚲ ✎

Originally a medieval palace of the Bishops of Lincoln, the house retains many of its original features; it was later converted into an almshouse. It is set in small gardens among picturesque golden stone cottages and beside the handsome parish church of St Andrew. Situated in a sunny corner at the entrance and backed by walls, the herb garden forms an L-shape and includes culinary and medicinal herbs of the period. Beds are edged with low box hedging.

The Old Hall

Market Overton, Oakham LE15 7PL. Tel: (01572) 767276

Mr and Mrs T. Hart • *6m NE of Oakham, 2m N of Cottesmore off B668* • *Open one day for NGS, 2 – 6pm, otherwise by appt only* • *Entrance: £2, children 50p* ◑ WC ♿

Five acres of softly agreeable grounds. Carefully coloured borders lead from a sunken lawn which falls away gently to distant vistas and a trickling stream; the formal enclosed swimming pool in the walled kitchen garden has views through ornamental gates and avenues of mature trees. Two large borders, designed by Neil Hewertson, have been planted on the old tennis court lawns against the stone walls. The long borders are divided by yew buttresses and have wide steps in the centre coming down from the croquet lawn terrace. There are many interesting focal points, including a raised pond with enchanting tiny frog sculptures that spout from lily leaves into the jaws of a lion mask. The pleached lime screen now coming into its own is elegant and well placed. The whole is at one with its beautiful surroundings of Rutland stone and rolling landscape.

The Old Rectory

Teigh, Oakham LE15 7RT. Tel: (01572) 787681

Mrs D.B. Owen • *5m N of Oakham between Wymondham and Ashwell* • *Open by appt in April, June and July. Parties welcome* • *Entrance: £1* • *Other information: Teas by arrangement* ◑ 🍴 WC ♿

A delightful, partially walled garden of three-quarters of an acre. First laid out in the 1950s, the existing garden has evolved from its original design over the last 25 years under the present owners, with much successful thought given to colour and juxtaposition of plants. There is a good show of spring bulbs and blossom, but perhaps the best month is July. Roses are used cleverly, connecting shapes and contrasts of foliage, and fine trees and climbing plants everywhere complement the mellow walls of the eighteenth-century stone rectory. The special Strawberry-Hill-Gothick church next door is a testament to the grandeur of an earlier incumbent.

SHROPSHIRE

Two-starred gardens are marked on the map with a black square.

Attingham Park [Historic Park Grade II*]

Attingham, Shrewsbury SY4 4TP. Tel: (01743) 708162

The National Trust • 4m SE of Shrewsbury. Turn off B4380 at Atcham • House open 19th March to 31st Oct, Mon, Tues, Fri, 1 – 5pm, Sat, Sun and Bank Holiday Mons, 11am – 5pm. Parties by arrangement • Deer park and grounds open all year except 25th Dec, 9am – 8pm (Nov to Feb closes 5pm) • Entrance: £2.60, children £1.30 (house and grounds £5.20, children £2.60, family £13). Party and out-of-hours rates available • Other information: Two self-drive electric scooters available by pre-booking ○ 🍽 ✕ 🛍 <u>WC</u> ♿ � ⌨ 🍴 🔌

This is a landscape mainly of large trees and shrubs, including a magnificent grove of Lebanon cedars, as the setting for a grand neo-classical pile. A mile-long ambulatory walk created by the River Tern in the eighteenth century is enlivened by daffodils in spring followed by azaleas and rhododendrons; autumn colour is provided by dogwoods and American thorns. A longer walk through the deer park affords fine views of the house and the restored Repton landscape. The Trust has bravely and rightly removed the formal 1920 garden in front of the house and returned it to Reptonian grass. The eighteenth-century orangery has also been restored.

Benthall Hall

Broseley TF12 5RX. Tel: (01952) 882159

The National Trust • 4½ m S of Telford, 1m SW of Broseley off B4375 • Part of house open same times as garden • Garden open April to June, Tues, Wed and Bank Holiday Suns and Mons; July to Sept, Sun, Tues, Wed and Bank Holiday Mon; all 1.30 – 5.30pm. Coaches and parties by arrangement only • Entrance: £2.50 (house and gardens £3.75) (2003 prices) • Other information: Parking 150 metres down road ◑ <u>WC</u> ♿

A small garden containing interesting plants and features, including topiary. George Maw and Robert Bateman both lived in the house and contributed to the garden design and plant collection. The rose garden has fine plants and a small pool and there is a delightful raised scree bed. A good collection of geraniums and ground-cover plants, together with a peony bed, and clematis and roses growing through trees and shrubs, create a pleasant place to stroll through. The old kitchen garden now contains a collection of crab apples, roses, wall plants, etc. In spring daffodils and the crocus introduced by George Maw provide interest, and the large specimens of Scots pine, beech and chestnut are stunning features. A monument to botanical history.

Brownhill House

Ruyton XI Towns, Shrewsbury SY4 1LR. Tel: (01939) 261121

Roger and Yoland Brown • 10m NW of Shrewsbury on B4397 • Open May to Aug by appt, and several times in summer for NGS, 1.30 – 5.30pm • Entrance: £2.50, children free • Other information: Parking at Bridge Inn 100 metres away ● ● WC ⌖ ⌖ B&B

Out of an impossible north-facing cliff a most unusual and distinctive garden of great variety has been created since 1972. The slope has been transformed from a scrap-covered wilderness into a series of terraces and small gardens connected by over 600 steps that wander up and down the hill through plantings of trees and shrubs, patches of wild flowers and open flower-filled spaces. At the bottom a riverside garden runs from an open lawn to a bog garden. A series of formal terraces includes a laburnum walk, and at the top there are paved areas with a pool, gazebo, parterre, a long walk with herbaceous border, flower beds and a large kitchen garden with glasshouses. Also incorporated into the design are a folly, Thai spirit house, grotto, summerhouse, large Arabic arch, cascade and a unique design of Menorah. Developments are continuing on the extensive terracing on which grow many of the collection of over 100 varieties of hedera, and a Japanese 'dry' garden has replaced the rockery. This is a garden that has to be seen to be believed, and fun for children, who can tax their brains with a challenging quiz. A few miles away, just west of the A5 at Kinnerley, is *Hall Farm Nursery*, which has an award-winning selection of herbaceous perennials.

Cruckfield House

Shoot Hill, Ford, Shrewsbury SY5 9NR. Tel: (01743) 850222

Mr and Mrs G.M. Cobley • 5m W of Shrewsbury off A458. Turn left signed to Shoot Hill • Open probably one Fri in May and one Sun in June and July, and for parties of 25 or more by appt • Entrance: £4, children £1 ● ● WC ⌖ ⌖

Sheltered and surrounded by mature trees, the romantic and tranquil four-acre garden, managed organically for many years, is designed in traditionally English formal style with an abundance of roses and peonies in their season as part of the attraction. There are exuberant plantings of shrubs and herbaceous plants, many of them rare or unusual. Specimen trees set in wildflower grassland and a pretty bog area surround a large pond. The ornamental kitchen garden is set off by attractive outbuildings and an adjoining courtyard garden.

David Austin Roses

Bowling Green Lane, Albrighton, Wolverhampton WV7 3HB.
Tel: (01902) 376300

Mr and Mrs David Austin • 6m SE of Telford between A41 and A464. Take junction 3 off M54 towards Albrighton, turn right at sign 'Roses and Shrubs', then second right • Open all year, Mon – Fri, 9am – 5pm, Sat, Sun and Bank

Holiday Mons, 10am – 6pm (closes dusk mid-Oct to mid-March). Closed 24th Dec to 1st Jan • Entrance: free ○ 💷 WC ♿ ⬦ 🐾

David Austin is one of the country's leading rose breeders, so this is an ideal place for inspecting them *en masse*. There are about 900 varieties, including shrub, climbing, species and old roses. Claire Austin presides over the hardy plants department, which stocks more than 1000 species and varieties of hardy perennials and grasses. The nursery also has comprehensive selections of irises and peonies, including tree peonies.

Dorothy Clive Garden

(see Staffordshire)

The Dower House

Morville Hall, Morville, Bridgnorth WV16 5NB. Tel: (01746) 714407

Dr Katherine Swift • 3m NW of Bridgnorth at A458/B4368 junction, within Morville Hall grounds • Open 4th April to 29th Sept, Wed, Sun and Bank Holiday Mons, 2 – 6pm; 13th June, 2 – 6pm, with other local gardens for NGS; and at other times, inc. evenings, by appt. Guided tours for parties • Entrance: £3, children (under 16) 50p • Other information: Parking in churchyard ◐ 💷 ♿ ⬦

Starting in 1989, the present owner, a well-known gardening writer, has transformed a one-and-a-half-acre site within the grounds of Morville Hall, with the aim of relating the history of English gardens in a sequence of separate features: a turf maze, a medieval cloister garden, a knot garden, a seventeenth-century plat and flower beds, a William and Mary canal garden with formal water feature and box-edged *plates-bandes*, an eighteenth-century flower garden, a Victorian rose border, a nineteenth-century wilderness and, finally, an ornamental fruit and vegetable garden. Particular attention is given to the use of authentic plants and construction techniques; old roses are a speciality.

Dudmaston [Historic Park and Garden Grade II]

Quatt, Bridgnorth WV15 6QN. Tel: (01746) 780866

The National Trust • 4m SE of Bridgnorth on A442 • House open • Garden open April to Sept, Sun – Wed, 12 noon – 6pm (last admission 5pm). Special openings for pre-booked parties only, Mons. Estate open free of charge for pedestrian access throughout the year • Entrance: £2.50 (house and garden £4.10, children £2, family £9.50, parties of 15 or more £3.50 per person) • Other information: Batricar available. Dogs in Dingle only, on lead ◐ 💷 🧺 WC ♿ ⬦ 🐾 ♨ 🍽 ☕

To garden historians, Dudmaston is a shrine. Its valley wilderness is the best surviving exemplar of William Shenstone's gardening philosophy of the Picturesque – 'pleasing the imagination by scenes of grandeur, beauty or variety'. The Dingle is a romantic creation of the late eighteenth century by one of Shenstone's former gardeners, working directly with the owners, the

Whitmores of Dudmaston. The William and Mary house sits on the other side of the park, in a landscape of woods, hills and water. The terraces which connect the hall to the Big Pool – actually the largest of a series of lakes – were made in 1816; they anticipated the creation of more formal gardens here. Today eight acres of garden in proximity to the house include a large pool and bog garden, island beds filled with shrubs, azaleas, rhododendrons, viburnums and fine old roses. Large specimen trees, old fruit trees and mature shrubs lend an established feel. The rock garden has been restored and the Big Pool is now framed by attractive plantings. There are two estate walks.

Gate Cottage

English Frankton, Ellesmere SY12 0JU. Tel: (01939) 270606

G.W. Nicholson and Kevin Gunnell • 10m N of Shrewsbury on A528. At Cockshutt take road to English Frankton; garden 1m on right • Open for NGS 16th May, 6th June, 1 – 5pm, and for parties by appt • Entrance: £2.50, children 50p • Other information: Teas on charity open days only ● ☕ ♿ ⚲

This garden is changing and developing all the time to accommodate a vast range of plants. Roses and clematis scramble through old fruit trees, and there are many other fine roses along the exterior fence and in the herbaceous borders. Aquatic interest comes from pools and a bog garden with primulas. In the extended area shrubs have been planted for colour effect. Large pebbles create attractive features, and there are unusual brown and black foliage plants and some interesting grasses. The rock and gravel plantings now include an area of hardy carnivorous plants.

Hawkstone Park [Historic Park Grade I]

Weston-under-Redcastle, Shrewsbury SY4 5UY. Tel: (01939) 200611

13m NE of Shrewsbury via A49, 6m SW of Market Drayton on A442 Telford – Whitchurch road. Entrance on road from Hodnet to Weston-under-Redcastle. Signed from Hodnet • Open April to June, Sept, Oct, Wed – Sun; July, Aug, daily; all 10.30am – 5pm (last admission 4pm); Jan to March, Sat and Sun, 10am – 2.30pm. Dates may vary, telephone to check • Entrance: £5.50, OAPs £4.50, children £3.50, family £15 (peak time 2003 prices). Reduced rates for pre-booked parties ◐ ☕ 🧺 WC ♿ 🏛 ♿ ⚲ B&B

In its day Hawkstone was as famous as Stowe and Stourhead, and the grounds have now been returned to their eighteenth-century grandeur and sublimity (the latter was supposed to induce awe if not fear). A series of monuments, now reconstructed, is linked by winding paths and tunnels. Ascending towards the White Tower, the visitor passes the thatched buildings, in one of which was a mechanical hermit famous for his artificial cough (now replaced by a hologram), then a grotto and the so-called Swiss bridge (a fallen tree across a gorge). Much remains to be done to the Red Castle, which is genuinely medieval. The whole thing is a triumph for all involved, including English Heritage. A walk through the park is approximately three and a half miles, but visitors should be warned that it involves climbing and descending many steps.

Hodnet Hall ★★ [Historic Park Grade II]

Hodnet, Market Drayton TF9 3NN. Tel: (01630) 685786

Mr A.E.H. and The Hon. Mrs Heber-Percy • 12m NE of Shrewsbury, 5½ m SW of Market Drayton, at A53/A442 junction • Open April to Sept, Tues – Sun and Bank Holiday Mons, 12 noon – 5pm • Entrance: £3.50, OAPs £3, children £1.50 ◑ WC ♿

The 60-acre parkland offers a constant succession of interest, although the greatest effect comes in autumn when the acers, sorbus and birches present their display. The grounds are grouped around a series of lakes and water gardens, home to black swans. This is essentially splendid large-scale parkland planting: magnolias, azaleas, rhododendrons in late spring are followed in summer by fuchsias, astilbes and gunneras, matched with water lilies on the lakes. For the herbaceous gardener there are shrub roses, tree peonies and the more traditional border plants. The working walled kitchen garden is well maintained, and there are also displays of flowers and pot plants grown especially for use in the hall, together with many varieties of fruit and vegetables.

Limeburners

Lincoln Hill, Ironbridge, Telford TF8 7NX. Tel: (01952) 433715

Mr and Mrs J.E. Derry • 4m SW of Telford. Turn off B4380 W of Ironbridge at traffic island. Take Church Hill for ½ m; garden on left below Beeches Hospital • Open April to Sept by appt • Entrance: £2.50, children free ◕ WC ♿

The garden was started in 1970 with the then not-so-fashionable vision of planting for wildlife. Now the mature garden continues to act as a haven for butterflies and birds with its collection of buddleias, nectar-rich flowers and native trees and shrubs of holly, broom, blackthorn, alder and dogwood. Shrub roses abound. The central pool (which looks natural but is man-made) features a waterfall with a stream splashing in.

Lower Hall ★

Worfield, Bridgnorth WV15 5LH. Tel: (01746) 716607

Mr and Mrs C.F. Dumbell • 4m NE of Bridgnorth. Take A454 Wolverhampton/ Bridgnorth road, turn right to Worfield and after village stores and pub turn right • Open for NGS 13th June, 2 – 6pm, 26th, 27th June for charity, 2 – 6pm. Also by appt for a limited number of horticultural groups • Entrance: £3, children under 12 free • Other information: Access for large coaches difficult. Garden room available for parties of 20 – 40 for pre-booked refreshments ◕ ✕ WC ♿

This modern four-acre plantsman's garden has been developed by the present owners since 1964, helped originally by the designer Lanning Roper. The courtyard and its fountain are featured in many design books. The walled garden has a magnificent display of roses, clematis and irises in season. Everywhere the use of colour combinations and plant associations is good –

a red border, another of white and green giving a cool effect. Roses abound. The water garden is separated from the woodland garden by the River Worfe with two bridges and two weirs. A deck built over the pool exploits the view across to the colourful primula island. The woodland garden includes rare magnolias, a collection of birches with bark interest, acers, cornus, magnolias and amelanchiers – all-year variety and colour.

Millichope Park [Historic Park Grade II*]

Munslow, Craven Arms SY7 9HA. Tel: (01584) 841234

Mr and Mrs L. Bury • 8m NE of Craven Arms, 11m N of Ludlow on B4368 • Open for NGS 3rd May and one Thurs each month during summer and autumn, 2 – 6pm, and for parties by appt • Entrance: £2.50 per person • Other information: Teas on Bank Holidays only. Picnics in woodland only ● 🏮 WC ♿ ⬧ ℺

The glory of Millichope is its magnificent landscaping, commissioned in the 1760s by a father seeking a fitting memorial to his four sons, all of whom had predeceased him. The main memorial was an elegant Ionic temple now dramatically sited away from the house across a lake. The present owners have commissioned a fine Chinese-style bridge across one of the gorges, and Mrs Bury has added a set of herbaceous borders disposed in elegant 'rooms' framed by yew hedges. Away from Georgian classicism, romantic wilderness plantings of roses and philadelphus combine to make this a most beautiful park and garden; below the lake the grass has been managed as a flower-rich hay meadow.

Oteley

Ellesmere SY12 0PB. Tel: (01691) 622514

Mr and Mrs R.K. Mainwaring • 8m NE of Oswestry, 1m E of Ellesmere near A528/495 junction. From N past the Mere turn left opposite convent • Open 3rd, 31st May, 2 – 6pm, and by appt • Entrance: £2, children 50p • Other information: Possible for wheelchairs if dry ● 🖤 WC ♿ ⬧ 🐾 ℺

The magnificent 10-acre garden, set in park and farmland with glimpses of the Mere beyond surrounding trees, has extensive lawns with architectural features, interesting and old handsome trees set about the lawns, a grey/ silver border, decorative island beds, rhododendrons, azaleas, roses and shrubs in a gracious setting, with a collection of peonies flowering simulta- neously. Herbaceous borders are backed by high walls covered with roses, clematis and other climbing plants, and a folly and a walled kitchen garden provide the finishing touches. All this plus a superlative plant stall.

The Patch

Acton Pigot, Acton Burnell, Shrewsbury SY5 7PH. Tel: (01743) 362139

Mrs Margaret Owen • 8m SE of Shrewsbury between A49 and A458. From Acton Burnell take Cressage Road. After ½ m turn left signed to Acton Pigott • Open 29th Feb, 11am – 3pm, 11th, 12th April, 2 – 5pm, 16th May, 6th June,

10th July, 10am – 5pm, 26th Sept, 2 – 5pm, and for parties by appt at other times • *Entrance: £2.50, children free* ● 🍽 WC ♿ ☕

Do not be deceived by this three-quarter-acre garden – allow time. It is filled with beauties, starting in spring with snowdrops, hellebores, erythroniums, dicentras, trilliums and violas. On into summer go *Paeonia mlokosewitschii* and *P. daurica*, roses and epimediums. National Collections of camassias, dictamnus and veratrums are held here, and other specialities include nerines and schizostylis. The garden is bordered by a broad grassy path, and at its centre lies a white garden. It is graced with tree rarities such as *Eucalyptus pauciflora* spp. *debeuzevillei*, *Styrax obassia*, *Toona sinensis* and *Sorbus aria* 'Chrysophylla'.

Preen Manor

Church Preen, Church Stretton SY6 7LQ. Tel: (01694) 771207

Mrs A. Trevor-Jones • *5m W of Much Wenlock on B4371. After 3m turn right for Church Preen and Hughley; after 1½ m turn left for Church Preen, over crossroads. Drive is ½ m on right* • *Open several dates in summer and autumn for NGS, and by arrangement for parties of 15 or more in June and July* • *Entrance: £3.50, children 50p* ● 🍽 WC ☕

The grounds are blessed with a beautiful south-east aspect facing Wenlock Edge. Despite the attractions of the more formal part of the gardens, it is the wooded landscaped walks beside the pools and natural stream which are the most outstanding feature. Rodgersias, *Primula japonica*, *Rhododendron ponticum* hybrids and magnificent yews and cedars create a noble setting on the banks which fall away from the former manor house. The formal gardens are akin to a pretty cottage garden, with roses, deutzias and violas planted to good effect. Other gardens, including a chess garden, pebble garden and gazebo complete with parrot and cat, demonstrate an esoteric style of gardening which may appeal to some. East of Preen are *Wenlock Abbey* [Historic Park Grade II] and the ruined *Wenlock Priory* with imaginative topiary.

Radnor Cottage

Clunton, Craven Arms SY7 0JA. Tel: (01588) 640451

Mr and Mrs David Pittwood • *12m W of Ludlow, 8m W of Craven Arms. 1m E of Clun on B4368 between Clun and Clunton* • *Open 6th, 20th April, 1st June, 2 – 6pm, and for parties by appt* • *Entrance: £2.50, children 50p* ● 🍽 ☕

Overlooking the Clun valley in A.E. Housman's Marcher countryside, the two-acre garden has been continually developing since it was taken on in the 1980s by its present enthusiastic owners. Set on a south-facing slope, it embraces the surrounding countryside by means of drystone walling, a wildflower meadow with snakeshead fritillaries and the old cottage-garden pheasant's eye narcissi. The wide range of garden habitats includes sunny terracing and paving, alpine troughs, and damp shade lightened by golden foliage. There is a pond, a stream, and a small arboretum with native sorbus; roses are of the old-fashioned variety such as *R. mundi*.

Ruthall Manor

Ruthall Road, Ditton Priors, Bridgnorth WV16 6TN. Tel: (01746) 712608

Mr and Mrs G.T. Clarke • 7m SW of Bridgnorth. Ruthall Road signed near garage; garden is ¾ m further on • Open by appt and for parties • Entrance: £2 ● & ⟐

Set below the heights of Abdon Burf, the one-acre garden, designed for ease of maintenance, is now coming to maturity. It offers a mixture of settings – from a delightful old pond planted to great natural effect to more formal plantings near the house, a woodland area and a vegetable garden – and a variety of well-sited trees and shrubs combined with climbers and perennials. A gravelled area beyond the lawn stretching out from the house will be given over to an increasing collection of modern sculptures.

Swallow Hayes ★

Rectory Road, Albrighton, Wolverhampton WV7 3EP. Tel: (01902) 372624

Mrs Michael Edwards • 9m SE of Telford, 7m NW of Wolverhampton. Turn off M54 at junction 3, then off A41 into Rectory Road after garden centre • Open 18th Jan (for National Collection of witch hazels), 11am – 4pm, and several days in spring by appt – telephone for details • Entrance: £3 (on open days), parties £3.50 per person (incl. tea and biscuits), children 10p • Other information: Teas on open days only ● ☕ ▦ WC & ⟐ ⅋ ℃

A delightful two-acre modern garden with many design features, colour and foliage contrasts, and a beautiful display of plants, shrubs and trees. Although easy maintenance is an object, it contains nearly 3000 different types of plants (most of which are labelled), and gives year-round interest. The Mediterranean wall has tender plants, and elsewhere small pools, ferns and a woodland area provide contrast. National Collections of witch hazels and lupins are here, plus an interesting area of small gardens to copy at home, vegetables and fruit trees, nursery stock beds and a hardy geranium trial of over 100 labelled hardy varieties.

Walcot Hall [Historic Park Grade II]

Lydbury North SY7 8AZ. Tel: (01588) 680570

Mr C.R.W. Parish • 7m NW of Craven Arms, 3m S of Bishop's Castle, off B4385. Turn left by Powis Arms in Lydbury North • House open for parties by appt • Garden open May to Oct, Fri – Mon, 12 noon – 4.30pm • Entrance: £3, children free ◑ ☕ ▦ WC & ⟐ ⅋

The handsome red-brick eighteenth-century house was remodelled by Sir William Chambers for the 1st Lord Clive of India. Don't miss the courtyard stabling. Its beautiful setting in the borderland hills enhances the arboretum planted by his son. Rhododendrons and azaleas sweep down to pools and are set amid many fine specimen trees. The lake and pools display the fine collection to advantage, enhanced by the lovely vision of Chambers' clock towers among the rolling hills. Although only open for a short period each year, the arboretum is well worth a visit if in the area to those who particularly enjoy landscape settings.

Weston Park ★ [Historic Park Grade II*]

Weston–under–Lizard, Shifnal TF11 8LE. Tel: (01952) 852100

Weston Park Enterprises • 6m E of Telford on A5, 7m W of M6 junction 12, 3m N of M54 junction 3 • House open as garden • Garden open April to Sept (enquire for days, times and events list) • Entrance: park and gardens £2.50, OAPs £2, children £1.50 (house, park and gardens £4, OAPs £3.50, children £2.50) ◐ 🍵 ✕ 🧺 WC ⬦ 👜 🔟 ⚲

A handsome seventeenth-century house with a distinctive 'Capability' Brown park as its setting. There are almost 1000 acres of delightful woodland planted with rhododendrons and azaleas, together with beautiful pools; magnificent trees form a handsome backcloth to the many shrubs. A rose walk leads to the deer park, and the rose garden by the house and the Italian parterre garden have been restored. The architectural features in the park – Temple of Diana, Roman bridge and orangery – were all designed by James Paine. Children will enjoy the adventure playground, the Weston Park Railway and the pets' corner. Gourmet dinners and open-air events are also on offer.

Wollerton Old Hall ★★

Wollerton, Hodnet, Market Drayton TF9 3NA. Tel: (01630) 685760 (Daytime)

John and Lesley Jenkins • 12m NE of Shrewsbury off A53. Brown-signed from Hodnet and Tern Hill A53/A41 junction • Open 9th April to Aug, Fri, Sun and Bank Holiday Mons, Sept, Fri, 12 noon – 5pm • Entrance: £3.80, children £1 (2003 prices) ◑ 🍵 ✕ WC ♿ 🌿 🔟

In design and layout this is a garden in the classic English mode. Within a little over three acres is a series of beautifully planted rooms, each distinct in character yet very much part of the whole. This effect is achieved through the careful positioning of a number of principal and secondary axes upon which the overall plan of the garden depends. The framework, seemingly a constant, has on occasion had to change. A wonderful new planting of yews replaced the former box-edged compartments (struck by the dreaded fungal disease), creating an all-embracing, deeply green atmosphere. Within the different garden rooms, contrasts are much in evidence. Fiery borders in the hot garden, stunning in August, are tempered with cool whites in a scented garden; openness, in the form of a broad expanse of lawn, contrasts with the intimacy of a pergola dripping with roses and clematis. But this garden is not just about plantsmanship and design. It is charged with atmosphere, enhanced by a number of most appealing structures; in recalling the Arts and Crafts Movement of the early years of the last century, it is redolent of many fashionable ones of the present.

SOMERSET

Two-starred gardens are marked on the map with a black square.

Ammerdown House [Historic Garden Grade II*]

Radstock, Bath BA3 5SH.

The Hon. Andrew Jolliffe • 10m S of Bath, ½ m off A362 Radstock – Frome road on B3139 • Open for charity 12th April, 3rd, 31st May, 30th Aug, 11am – 5pm • Entrance: £3, children free • Other information: Pre-booked catering for parties at Ammerdown Study Centre. Tel: (01761) 433709 ● ● WC ● ●

The Bath-stone house was designed by James Wyatt, with panoramic views on one side and a garden on the other; the garden was a brilliant conception by Lutyens, who wanted to link the house with the orangery. Walking through the Italianate 'rooms' of yew and sculpture and parterre, one is unaware of the tricks of space that are being played. Massive yew planting, now mature and nearly four metres high, creates enclosed formal areas which lead irresistibly one from another – the spaces between being almost entirely filled with hedging. The originality and grandeur remain, as do some particularly clever details such as the clipped Portugal laurels, honeysuckles trained over wire umbrellas, and ancient lemon verbenas in pots in the orangery and on terraces. Daffodils, narcissi and cowslips are spring features; fountains and statues add architectural interest at all seasons.

Barford Park ★

Spaxton, Bridgwater TA5 1AG. Tel: (01278) 671269

Mr and Mrs M. Stancomb • 5m W of Bridgwater. From Bridgwater – Spaxton road, turn to Enmore • House and garden open by appt, May to Sept • Entrance: £3, children free ● ● WC ● ●

This is a garden in the eighteenth-century style developed over the last 32 years, set in parkland and protected by a ha-ha on three sides. After watching the golden orfe darting around the lily pond, stroll down a sweep of lawn to a stand of tall trees. In spring the woodland glade is a carpet of many shades of primulas. The eighteenth-century walled garden unusually is sited in view of the house – a lawn with deep herbaceous borders on each side makes a colourful vista.

Barrington Court Garden ★ [Historic Garden Grade II*]

Barrington, Ilminster TA19 0NQ. Tel: (01460) 241938

The National Trust • 5m NE of Ilminster, on B3168 in Barrington • Open March, Thurs – Sun, 11am – 4.30pm; April to Sept, Thurs – Tues, 11am – 5.30pm; Oct, Thurs – Sun, 11am – 4.30pm • Entrance: £5.20, children £2.50, family £13, parties of 15 or more, £4.50 by arrangement with visitor services manager (2003 prices) • Other information: Self-drive buggy and wheelchairs available ● ● ✕ ● WC ● ● ● ●

In 1917, at the end of her career, Gertrude Jekyll planned the planting for the Lyle family, the Trust's first tenants at Barrington, and planting schemes today are based on her original ideas. Set in a park with avenues of mature chestnut trees, the gardens are in the Hidcote style of separate 'rooms'. The lily garden has a central pool with surrounding beds of annuals and perennials planted with a 'hot' theme of oranges, reds and yellows. The white-flowering and silver-leaved plants are seen in the White Garden *à la* Sissinghurst, though this is a Lyle, not a Jekyll, scheme. It is interesting that this was part of the farm before the Lyle lease, and the cattle troughs can still be seen in the beds. Beyond, a pergola (also not Jekyll) supports clematis, wisteria and honeysuckles in profusion. Note the cattle sheds, *c.* 1800, of considerable visual appeal. The vast walled kitchen garden produces a wide variety of fruit and vegetables, and further afield a cider orchard provides raw material for the liquid refreshments.

Bath City Gardens

The City of Bath has two interesting gardens which are well worth a visit. At the *William Herschel Museum* in New King Street, historical research has resulted in the re-creation of a charming town garden with a curious arbour and plants such as might have existed in the great astronomer's time. [Open 10th February to November, daily except Wednesdays, 2 – 5pm (11am – 5pm at weekends).] On Lansdown Hill the Grade-II burial ground adjacent to *Beckford's Tower* is planted with shrubs as used by the writer, collector and aesthete in his extensive garden. The Greek Revival building of 1827 was designed for him by Goodridge as a retreat. [Open Easter to Oct, Sat, Suns and Bank Holiday Mons, 10.30am – 5pm.]

Cannington College Gardens

Cannington, Bridgwater TA5 2LS. Tel: (01278) 655000

Cannington College • 3m NW of Bridgwater on A39 • Open April to Oct, daily, 9am – 5pm, and for parties by appt • Entrance: £2, OAPs and children (5–16) £1 (2003 prices) • Other information: Teas for parties by arrangement. Guide dogs only ◑ 🍽 🍴 WC ♿

The gardens, enclosed within a medieval priory wall surrounding the fifteenth-century Cannington Court, contain one of the largest collections of rare and unusual plants in the South-West, including National Collections of abutilons, argyranthemums, osteospermums and wisterias. The gardens are planted individually on various botanical themes, among them an Australasian Garden and the Bishop's Garden, featuring plants from the eastern Mediterranean. In total, the college gardens cover an area of approximately two-and-a-half acres.

City of Bath Botanical Gardens

Royal Victoria Park, Upper Bristol Road, Bath BA1 2NQ.

City of Bath • In Royal Victoria Park • Open all year, daily, 8.30am – dusk • Entrance: free • Other information: Toilet facilities in park ○ ♿ 🔄 🎈 ♋

Located in the city's Royal Victoria Park, the botanical gardens were formed in 1887 to house a collection of plants assembled over a lifetime by Mr C.E. Broome of Batheaston, an enthusiastic amateur botanist and plant collector. It has become one of the finest collections, certainly in the West Country, of plants on limestone. To mark the centenary in 1987, the gardens were extended to take in the adjacent Great Dell. The herbaceous border was replanted in 1990. Ongoing improvements to the plant collections and educational aspects received a grant from the Heritage Lottery Fund and developments are afoot in the park.

Claverton Manor [Historic Garden Grade II]

Claverton, Bath BA2 7BD. Tel: (01225) 460503

The American Museum • 2m SE of Bath off A36, signed 'American Museum' • Garden open late-March to Nov, daily except Mon, 1 – 5pm. Pre-booked private garden tours by arrangement • Entrance: grounds and galleries: £3.50, children £2. House, grounds and galleries: £6, OAPs £5.50, children £4. Garden tours £3 per person • Other information: Museum and new gallery ◐ ☕ 🛍 WC ♿ ⟡ ✿ ☕

The house, designed by Jeffry Wyatville, and garden are set on the side of the valley of the Avon in a stunning position with splendid views from the terrace. The rather stark high walls of the house and the terrace support honeysuckle, clematis and old climbing roses, and fastigiate yews make strong buttress shapes up the south-facing wall. The Colonial Herb Garden is modest in size but the little herbarium is popular for seeds, herbs, tussie-mussies and so on. The Mount Vernon Garden, a colonial interpretation of George Washington's famous garden, with rampant old-fashioned roses, trained pear trees and box and beech hedges, is surrounded by white palings. There is a replica of the octagonal garden house used as a school room for Washington's step-grandchildren. The seven-acre arboretum, which contains a fine collection of exclusively native American trees and shrubs, is believed to be the only one of its kind outside the USA. Labelling is extensive and a map listing trees and shrubs is available. An orchard contains American apple varieties, and there is also a fernery, a cascade and a waterfall.

Cothay Manor ★★

Greenham, Wellington TA21 0JR. Tel: (01823) 672283

Mr and Mrs Alastair Robb • 5m W of Wellington. From W (M5 junction 27) take signed A38 signed to Wellington, then after 3½ m turn left to Greenham. From N (junction 26) take Wellington exit; at roundabout take A38 signed to Exeter. After 3½ m turn right to Greenham (1½ m) and right again on left-hand corner at bottom of hill. House is 1m further, always keeping left • House open for parties by appt • Garden open May to Sept, Wed, Thurs, Sun and Bank Holiday Mons, 2 – 6pm • Entrance: £3.50 • Other information: Coaches by appt ● ☕ WC ♿ ✿

The house is reputed to be one of the finest small medieval manors in the country, and its outstanding garden appears integral to the house, each a natural extension of the other. In fact the gardens seen today were laid out only in the 1920s. They have been redesigned and replanted over the last few years, within the original yew-hedged compartments which were created to provide a serene seventeenth-century promenade complete with 'conversation arbours'. The 70-yard-long Walk of the Unicorn, an avenue of *Robinia pseudoacacia* 'Umbraculifera' underplanted with *Nepeta* 'Six Hills Giant', is a wonderful sight in May when a thousand white tulips in bloom appear through the nepeta. Surrounding meadows, planted with specimen trees, shrubs and spring bulbs, lead on to herbaceous borders, a cottage garden and a magical white garden. There is also a bog garden. Masterly planting is everywhere evident, exuberance balanced by restraint, as the owners are never afraid to repeat a theme within an enclosed space. Particularly unusual is the effective way in which complementary greys and mauves flow into the house walls. The newly created pond beyond the main garden and the bog garden alongside the fast-flowing river are beginning to make an impact. Plants propagated from the garden are for sale. If you are heading back to Taunton, 3m south-west is *Broadleigh Gardens Nursery* [open Mon – Fri only], where bulbs and herbaceous plants may be ordered after viewing them in flower in the garden.

Crowe Hall ★ [Historic Garden Grade II]

Widcombe Hill, Bath BA2 6AR. Tel: (01225) 310322

Mr John Barratt • Behind Bath Spa station off A36 within walking distance of station • Open for NGS 4th April, 6th June, also 9th May, 11th July, 2 – 6pm, and for parties by appt • Entrance: £2.50, children £1 ● ☕ WC & ⬈ ℺

These gardens, which extend to 11 acres on the hillside above Widcombe, are some of the most mysterious and beautiful in Bath. Through the gates is an intriguing view of a drive, portico and terrace, and once inside the grounds few gardens in the area offer so many surprises and delights. The owner describes it as an island of classical simplicity surrounded by romantic wilderness. Around the Regency-style house are Italianate terraces, a pond, grottos, tunnels, woods, glades, kitchen gardens and a long walkway with a stone statue facing a stunning view of Prior Park (see entry). Vistas and views are a feature of this steeply banked garden, where down one walk you suddenly come upon the roof of the fifteenth-century church of St Thomas à Becket. The loss of 20 trees in storms is regarded as an improvement by the owner because new vistas have opened up. Beyond the restored grotto is a meadow garden and an amusing garden dedicated to Hercules, with a theatrically ferocious hero. This garden has been redesigned, and Hercules now appears in a mosaic pool as well as on dry land. Magnificent trees include mulberries, beeches and limes. The charming little enclosed Sauce Garden, with its trelliswork and canal-like pool, was created in 1995, and the 1852 greenhouse has been restored to its former glory. The Teazle Garden (in memory of a much-loved dog) has a cascade, a fountain, a pergola and many climbing plants. For its stunning setting in the meadows above and facing away from Bath and for the romantic ambience Crowe Hall is an experience not to be missed.

Dunster Castle ★ [Historic Garden Grade I]

Dunster, Minehead TA24 6SL. Tel: (01643) 821314

The National Trust • 3m SE of Minehead on A39 • Castle open Sat – Wed •
Garden and park open daily, 10am – 5pm (Oct to Dec, 11am – 4pm). For
Christmas details telephone (01643) 823004 • Entrance: £3, children under 16
£1.50, family £7.50 (castle, garden and park £6.20, children under 16 £3.10,
family £15.50, pre-booked parties £5.20 per person) (2003 prices) • Other
information: Self-drive batricar and volunteer-driven multi-seater available ○
WC ⅙ ⊞ ⬙ ⅗

The Luttrell family, who had lived here since the fourteenth century, gave the
castle and gardens to the Trust in 1976. A fine border of rare shrubs surrounds
a lawn by the keep and is well worth the steep climb to view. On the formal
terraces below and along the river thrives a variety of sub-tropical plants,
camellias and azaleas. Thousands of bulbs have been planted, and after the
daffodils and snowdrops come fine displays of forsythias, camellias and early
rhododendrons. There is a National Collection of arbutus and a huge 18-metre
Magnolia campbellii. Views stretch across to Exmoor, the Quantocks and the
Bristol Channel. The park totals 28 acres in all.

East Lambrook Manor Gardens [Historic Garden Grade I]

South Petherton TA13 5HH. Tel: (01460) 240328

Robert and Marianne Williams • 3m SW of Martock off A303, 2m NE of South
Petherton • Open Feb to Oct, daily, 10am – 5pm • Entrance: £3.95, OAPs,
students, groups £3.50, children £1 (2003 prices) • Other information: Art
gallery and café open throughout summer ○ ⬙ ✕ WC ⅙ ⬨ ⊞ ⬙

In essence this is a cottage-style garden with mixed areas of planting, small
lawns and narrow paths, but it remains iconic as the creation of the great
plantswoman Margery Fish, who established the garden for endangered
species. It still houses a remarkable collection of plants many of which she
saved from extinction. Thanks to the previous owner, Andrew Norton, the
National Collection of geraniums (cranesbill) species and cultivars also remains
here. The present owners aim to improve historically important areas of the
Grade-I-listed garden, famous not only for its plants but also for its controlled
luxuriance of growth, colour and scent. This will include restoring the green
garden, replacing the pudding trees and clearing the top terraces and the
colosseum. The nursery has been relocated in its original site.

Gants Mill and Garden

Bruton BA10 ODB. Tel: (01749) 812393

Alison and Brian Shingler • ½ m SW of Bruton, signed off A359 • Open 15th
May to Sept, Sun, Thurs and Bank Holiday Mons, 2 – 5pm, and for parties by
appt • Entrance: £2 (mill and garden £4) NEW ◐ B&B

Approached down the greenest of lanes on the edge of historic Bruton are the
old buildings of Gants Mill. The mill itself (still working) is dated 1290, but

today's visitor can also revel in the half-acre English summer garden designed by Philip Brown and realised by Alison Shingler since 1995. The emphasis is on the masses of repeat-flowering climbing roses and clematis on pergolas, surrounded by swathes of perennials and summer bulbs in complementary shades. The vibrant scent and colour create an unforgettable effect from mid-May until late September, while the strong and intricate design holds all together. The backdrop of river and trees provides a calm setting, and the skilful use of water as a main feature contributes sound and movement overall. An annually changing exhibition of sculptures – some abstract, many figurative, and all for sale – benefits the garden as well as the artists. There can be few cottage gardens that look as good as this.

Greencombe ★★

Porlock TA24 8NU. Tel: (01643) 862363

Greencombe Garden Trust (Miss Joan Loraine) • *7½ m W of Minehead, ½ m W of Porlock off B3225* • *Open April to July, Sat – Wed, 2 – 6pm* • *Entrance: £4.50, children £1* • *Other information: Coaches by arrangement* ◐ 🍵 WC ও ⌀ ℺

Created in 1946 by Horace Stroud, this garden has been extended by the present owner over the last three decades. Overlooking the Bristol Channel, set on a hillside where the sun cannot penetrate for nearly two months in the winter, it glows with colour. The formal lawns and beds round the house are immaculate. Roses, lilies, hydrangeas, maples and camellias thrive. By contrast the woodland area, terraced on the hillside and traversed by a maze of narrow paths, provides a nature walk of great interest; here a wide variety of rhododendrons and azaleas flowers in the shelter of mature trees, and ferns and woodland plants also flourish. At the far end comes a surprise: a circular chapel of fine workmanship, open to the sea view, which houses a tender Madonna and child ('Our Lady of the Secrets'), sculpted from a Greencombe sweet chestnut by Tom Preator of Taunton. No sprays or chemicals are used in the cultivation of this completely organic garden, which contains National Collections of erythroniums, gaultherias, polystichums and vacciniums.

Hadspen Garden and Nursery ★★

Castle Cary BA7 7NG. Tel: (01749) 813707

N. and S. Pope • *3½ m NW of Wincanton, 2m SE of Castle Cary on A371* • *Open March to 1st Oct, Thurs – Sun and Bank Holiday Mons, 10am – 5pm* • *Entrance: £4, children 50p* • *Other information: Coaches by arrangement* ◐ 🍵 ✕ 🍽 WC ও ⌀ ℺

Set in parkland, this is a classic English walled garden, curved here to raise the temperature within. The basic plan was devised by Margaret Hobhouse in the Victorian gardening 'boom' days, to provide a setting for the eighteenth-century hamstone house. Over the years the garden became overgrown and formless until it was reclaimed in the mid 1980s by Canadians Nori and Sandra Pope, who retained the best of the original plan and have embellished it with a variety of new plantings. Their thing is colour – bold, innovative, thought-provoking colour. Indeed, you could say it is their trademark. The borders therefore have schemes ranging from silver and white through the spectrum to the deepest purple and black; flowers and foliage are combined in the most effective ways. Other features include a lily pond, shrub walks and a wild-flower meadow. Hostas are a speciality.

Hestercombe Gardens ★ [Historic Garden Grade I]

Cheddon Fitzpaine, Taunton TA2 8LG. Tel: (01823) 413923

HGP Ltd/Somerset County Council • 4m NE of Taunton off A361, just N of Cheddon Fitzpaine. Signposted • Open all year, daily, 10am – 6pm (last admission 5pm). Parties by written appt only • Entrance: £5, OAPs £4.70, children (5–15) £1.20, under 5 free (2003 prices) • Other information: Coaches by arrangement ○ 🍵 ✕ WC ⅙ ⟁ 🌿 🏧 💡 ✎

This is a superb product of the collaboration between Edwin Lutyens and Gertrude Jekyll, blending the formal art of architecture with the art of plants. The detailed design of steps, pools, walls, paving and seating is Lutyens at his most accomplished, and the rills, pergola and orangery are also fine examples of his work. To the north of the house is the Combe, laid out two centuries earlier than the main gardens and a unique example of eighteenth-century pleasure grounds unchanged until the timber was felled in the 1960s. Visitors are now able to see the eighteenth-century parkland designed between 1750 and 1786 by Coplestone Warre Bampfylde, and his (restored) Great Cascade; he also designed the cascade from the lake at Stourhead (see entry in Wiltshire). He described Hestercombe's as one 'that will rivet you to the spot with admiration'. This ambitious restoration of a Grade-I-listed landscape is likely to continue for a further five years, and will form a 35-acre landscape garden in its own right. The restoration of the Victorian terrace is now complete, and a programme is well advanced to recreate the shrubbery in the style of William Robinson, c. 1880. Be sure to see the Doric temple, the mausoleum, the rebuilt witch's hut and the Gothic alcove, which commands views of Taunton Vale. There is still a sense of nature enhanced rather than transformed, with the set pieces so well sited and spaced that they seem to relax into the natural setting. A major reassessment and renewal of Jekyll's planting is underway and the formal garden will be mostly replanted, as close as possible to her original plans, in time for the garden's centenary in 2004, when the heroic pergola will also be restored.

Jasmine Cottage

26 Channel Road, Clevedon BS21 7BY. Tel: (01275) 871850

Mr and Mrs Michael Redgrave • 12m W of Bristol. From M5 junction 20, take road to seafront, continue N on B3124 and turn right at St Mary's church • Open by appt May to Sept • Entrance: £1.50, children free • Other information: Plants for sale in nursery ● WC ⅙ 🌿

Something for everyone in this exuberant garden: old-fashioned roses, climbers, mixed shrubs, herbaceous borders, island beds, a pergola walk and a vegetable garden – all crammed into one-third of an acre. An inspiration for suburban enthusiasts, especially as it is only about 100 metres from the sea. The rectangular shape is cleverly disguised, with island beds in one area, and a secret garden enclosed by a hedge over three and a half metres high and cut annually. Through the hedge is the so-called cottage garden with unusual climbers, including *Rhodochiton atrosanguineus*, *Dregea sinensis* and *Dicentra macrocapnos*.

Lady Farm ★

Chelwood, Bristol BS39 4NN. Tel: (01761) 490770.

Malcolm and Judy Pearce • 9m S of Bristol on A368, ½ m E of Chelwood roundabout (A37/A368) • As we go to press, we learn that due to re-landscaping works the garden will be closed to visitors in 2004, reopening in 2005 ● ⚘ WC ⬧

Set on the side of a valley and covering approximately eight acres, this is an essential visit for anyone interested in the changing face of gardening. Here is the pioneering continental style set down in the English countryside. Water is an essential component. A spring-fed water course with marginal planting and waterfalls flows into a lake with adjacent rock features, then flows on down to join a further lake, made by damming a stream in the valley bottom, where lakeside and woodland walks are being developed. But the greatest excitement is reserved for the sunny slopes on the other side of the waterfall. One slope is planted as a steppe garden, peaking from May to July, with rhythmical clumps of foliage plants and splashes of colour from spring bulbs and strong-hued summer flowers. Another has a large area of perennial prairie planting, with substantial groups of heleniums, achilleas, rudbeckias, eupatoriums and the like, and many ornamental grasses; this is at its most colourful from July to December. Elsewhere are wildflower meadow areas, a meandering walk of birch species underplanted with hostas, hellebores, alliums and grasses. A formal garden has a thatched summerhouse and herbaceous perennials, in rich plum and purple shades, in a four-square design with a circle in the centre. From there a path leads through a formal topiary garden. This is a garden with a future, and one for all seasons.

✓ Lower Severalls

Crewkerne TA18 7NX. Tel: (01460) 73234

Mary Pring • 1½ m NE of Crewkerne off A30 • Open March to 15th Oct, Mon – Wed, Fri, Sat, 10am – 5pm (plus Suns in May and June, 2 – 5pm) • Entrance: £2.50 • Other information: Coaches by appt. Teas for pre-arranged parties only. Plants for sale in nursery ◑ ⚘ WC ♿ ✿ ☕

A typical cottage garden of some two and a half acres with herbaceous borders against the stone-walled house. The garden extends through stone pillars which make a frame for the view of the valley over lawn and varied shrubs and a bog garden. Additional features include arches made from recycled farm machinery, and a 'dogwood basket'. Water gardens, fed from a spring in adjacent farmland, have been created, together with a 'wadi' or dry garden built up to form a windbreak for a sheltered valley. A pavilion for contemplation – a green-roofed octagonal building covered in sedums and sempervivums – has replaced the old horse chestnut of 200 years' standing.

Lytes Cary Manor [Historic Garden Grade II]

Charlton Mackrell, Somerton TA11 7HU. Tel: (01458) 224471

The National Trust • 9m N of Yeovil, 2½ m NE of Ilchester, signed from A303 • Open April to Oct, Mon, Wed, Fri and Sun, 11am – 5pm (or dusk if earlier) • Entrance: £4.60, children £2 (2003 prices) • Other information: Building works to house roof may cause some disruption ◑ 🍴 **WC** &

Once the house of the medieval herbalist Henry Lyte (although nothing of his botanic garden remains), the main feature is a long, wide border which has been replanted in line with Graham Stuart Thomas's original design, with a mixture of roses, shrubs and herbaceous plants. There are also pleasing lawns with hedges in Elizabethan style and some topiary, a large orchard with naturalised bulbs and mown walks with a central sundial. A little over five miles to the west, at Langport, is the legendary nursery *Kelways*, a leading grower of peonies (Tel: (01458) 250521). [Open daily, weekdays 9am – 5pm, Sat 10am – 5pm, Sun 10am – 4pm.]

Manor Farm

Middle Chinnock, Crewkerne TA18 7PN. Tel: (01935) 881895

Simon and Antonia Johnson • 5m W of Yeovil off A30 • Open one day for NGS, and by appt • Entrance: £2, children free ● 🍴 **WC** & ⬥ ℺

Despite being the recent creation of the owner, designer Simon Johnson, the garden succeeds in making the visitor feel that it could always have been here, and that its scale and proportion are right for both the site and the family life that goes on in and around it. The hamstone farmhouse has architectural distinction without being grand, and this is reflected in the garden spaces. There is a traditional framework of stone walls and hedges – yew and hornbeam – allowing areas for plants and colours, for architectural austerity and lush wildness, for fruit- and vegetable-growing. Contrasts appear throughout, and everywhere are seats from which to take in the views of the landscape beyond the garden. Despite its air of timelessness and maturity, the garden is still evolving, with structures and new plantings appearing as time and funds allow, including a walled garden surrounding a renovated cottage, and a pond complete with an island.

Milton Lodge ★ [Historic Garden Grade II]

Wells BA5 3AQ. Tel: (01749) 672168

Mr D.C. Tudway Quilter • ½ m N of Wells. From A39 Wells – Bristol road turn N up Old Bristol Road • Open 11th April to Oct, Tues, Wed, Sun and Bank Holiday Mons, 2 – 5pm • Entrance: £2.50, children under 14 free • Other information: Parties and coaches by special arrangement. Teas on Sun and Bank Holiday Mons only ◑ 🍴 **WC** ℀ 🛍

The terraced garden, replanted by the present owner in the 1960s is cultivated down the side of a hill overlooking the Vale of Avalon, affording a magnificent view of Wells Cathedral. A wide variety of plants, all suitable for the alkaline soil, provides a succession of colours and interest from March to October. Many fine trees can be seen in the garden and in the seven-acre arboretum opposite the entrance to the car park.

Montacute House ★ [Historic Garden Grade I]

Montacute TA15 6XP. Tel: (01935) 823289

The National Trust • 4m W of Yeovil. Signposted from A3088 and A303 near Ilchester • House open 19th March to Oct, daily except Tues, 11am – 5pm • Park and garden open all year: Jan to 18th March, daily except Mon and Tues, 11am – 4pm; 19th March to Oct, daily except Tues, 11am – 6pm; 3rd Nov to 25th March 2005, daily except Mon and Tues, 11am – 4pm • Entrance: March to Nov, garden and park £3.70, children £1.70; Nov to March 2005, £2, children £1 (house, garden and park £6.80, children £3.20, family £17) • Other information: Picnics in designated areas only. Dogs in park only, on lead. Plants for sale April to Sept ○ 🍽 ✕ 🛍 WC �&. ⏀ 🚽 ⏀ ⚲

This Elizabethan garden of grass lawns surrounded by clipped yews set in terraces is a triumph of formality. The surrealism of the topiary, which some claim was inspired by a dramatic snowfall, adds immensely to the effect. A large water feature has replaced the original Elizabethan high circular mount, and there is a charming raised walk, two original pavilions and an arcaded garden house probably devised by Lord Curzon while he was a tenant. Colour is provided by herbaceous borders and from midsummer by twin scented rose borders. The gardens are surrounded by graceful parklands giving vistas and an impression of space. An avenue of 72 limes is now established.

2 Old Tarnwell

Upper Stanton Drew BS39 4EA. Tel: (01275) 333146

Mr and Mrs K. Payne • 6m S of Bristol, W of Pensford between A368 and B3130 • Open June and July for small groups by appt • Entrance: £2 ●

A tiny garden full of contrasts and interest. The front garden was remodelled in 2003 to reflect the owners' interest in steppe-style planting, proving that it can be effective on a miniature scale. Based on apricots, coral, yellows and brown, with a hint of purple, this random planting style of contrasting foliage effects is set against flint gravel. Slate monoliths add interest and structure, echoed by columnar box and *Ilex crenata*. The back garden retains its cottage style of cool colours encased by rampant clematis. Features include a misty pool, a wall covering of clipped ivy and auricula theatres, all enhanced by good planting.

Prior Park Landscape Garden ★ [Historic Garden Grade I]

Ralph Allen Drive, Bath BA2 5AH. Tel: (01225) 833422 (General Enquiries)

The National Trust • No parking at garden or nearby; catch Badgerline bus from city centre or walk up A3062 from Widcombe • Open Feb to Nov, Wed –

Mon, 11am – 5.30pm; Dec to Jan, Fri – Sun, 11am – dusk. Closed 25th, 26th Dec and 1st Jan • Entrance: £4.10, children £2 (£1 discount, on production of ticket, for those arriving by public transport or pre-booked coach) • Other information: Small area for disabled parking (must be pre-booked), but limited access for disabled ◔ 🍽 🏞 <u>WC</u> ♿ 🌿 ⚘

This remarkable restoration by the Trust, when completed, will have transformed Prior Park. The Palladian mansion, designed by the architect John Wood from 1735 for Bath's leading entrepreneur and philanthropist Ralph Allen, dominates the steeply sloping landscape and provides stunning views of the city. While the mansion is owned and used by Prior Park College and is not open to the public, the grounds below are well worth the circular walk (allow 1½ hours) from the entrance gate off Ralph Allen Drive. Allen landscaped and planted continuously over a period of 30 years from 1734 to 1764, helped by several gardeners, notably 'Capability' Brown, who eliminated areas of formality. Alexander Pope inspired the area known as the Wilderness, which includes a Rococo sham bridge and the ruins of Mrs Allen's grotto (full restoration of the Wilderness is ongoing). The walk continues from the mansion viewpoint down the east side of the valley (steep in places) to the lakes and the Palladian bridge of 1755, returning by the west side of the valley via the Rock Gate. Undoubtedly two-star are the views – sensitively created by the Trust – of the Palladian bridge, the mansion from the bridge and the city of Bath.

Sherborne Garden

Pear Tree House, Litton BA3 4PP. Tel: (01761) 241220

Mr and Mrs J. Southwell • 15m S of Bristol, 7½ m N of Wells on B3114, ¼ m beyond Litton and The Kings Arms • Open 7th June to 27th Sept, Mon and occasional Suns, 11am – 6pm, and other days by appt • Entrance: £2.50, children free ◑ 🏞 <u>WC</u> ♿ ⬥ 🌿 ⚘

A large, rather surreal garden that displays a very personal choice of specimen trees, grasses and water garden features in a four-and-a-half-acre site reclaimed from farmland. It is an excellent example of how natural pasture land may be tamed and surface water channelled into ponds. The owners are compulsive tree people who since 1963 have planted hundreds of native and exotic trees, expanding the original cottage garden and paddock into a mini-arboretum. The garden now boasts a one-acre spinney of native species, a pinetum, nut hedges, a collection of species roses, gravel beds with collections of giant and miniature grasses and about 150 varieties of hemerocallis, a Prickly Wood that offers 100 varieties of holly, and a collection of over 250 ferns. In such experienced and creative hands this garden never stands still, and the twin themes of trees and water – a 'wadi' was constructed as a millennium project – are continually being celebrated and extended.

Ston Easton Park ★ [Historic Garden Grade II]

Ston Easton, Bath BA3 4DF. Tel: (01761) 241631

Von Essen Hotels • 11m SW of Bath, 6m NE of Wells on A39 • Open all year, daily, 10am – 5pm (closes 6pm Sat and Sun) • Entrance: free • Other information: Teas and toilet facilities in hotel ● ● ✕ WC & ⇗ ⏚ ⏚ ♨ B&B

The magnificent Palladian house is set in a park replanned and replanted by Humphry Repton in 1792, reached by a suitably impressive drive winding past the old stables. The glory is the view from inside the great Saloon, or from the terrace immediately outside, over the River Norr with a bridge and cascades. Repton made a Red Book with his proposals for improvement, and Penelope Hobhouse worked with the previous owners on the restoration of the park to his plans. Beyond the terrace are wide lawns with fine specimen trees and extensive woodland with many glades and paths. At some distance from the house is a vast sheltered walled garden, partly ornamental and partly productive. Many new projects and plans are now under way in this area, and maintenance has greatly improved.

Tintinhull House Garden ★ [Historic Garden Grade II]

Farm Street, Tintinhull, Yeovil BA22 9PZ. Tel: (01935) 822545

The National Trust • 5m NW of Yeovil, ½ m S of A303. Signposted • Open April to Sept, Wed – Sun and Bank Holiday Mons, 12 noon – 6pm • Entrance: £4, children £2 (2003 prices) • Other information: Disabled parking by arrangement ◗ ● WC & ⏚

Developed from the 1930s by Phyllis Reiss, this relatively small modern garden, barely two acres, which achieves an impression of greater size with a series of vistas created under the influence of Hidcote. The Eagle Court near the house has fine borders and passes on to a small white garden; from here, an opening leads to the stylish kitchen garden with an orchard beyond. The pool garden is particularly splendid, with its 'hot' and 'cool' borders, although overall some visitors have queried the standard of maintenance. The Cedar Court has some old trees, including a yew said to be 400 years old. An inventory is available for interested visitors.

Wayford Manor ★ [Historic Garden Grade II]

Crewkerne TA18 8QG. Tel: (01460) 73253

Mr and Mrs R.L. Goffe • 3m SW of Crewkerne off B3165 at Clapton • Open 11th April, 2nd, 3rd, 23rd May, 13th June, 2 – 6pm, and for parties by appt • Entrance: £2, children 50p ● ● WC ⇗ ⏚

A well-maintained garden of flowering shrubs and trees complementing a fine manor house dating from the thirteenth century with Elizabethan and Victorian additions. This is a fine example of the work of Harold Peto, who redesigned the garden in 1902. The formal upper terrace with yew hedges and topiary fronting the house leads down to the next level, a walled garden with rose and herbaceous beds, lawns and gravel paths. It descends again to a rockery and a grass tennis court enclosed on three sides by a yew hedge. Below is an area of informal, partly wild garden with extensive plantings of mature trees and shrubs, including rare and colourful maples, cornus, magnolias, rhododendrons and spring bulbs. Water features throughout, from a spring-fed pond on the top terrace through streams and ponds at all levels. The millennium project was the replacement of a timber pergola by a stone-pillared one to complement the loggia designed by Peto.

Windmill Cottage

Hillside Road, Backwell BS48 3BL. Tel: (01275) 463492

Mr and Mrs Alan Harwood • 8m SW of Bristol on A370. Cottage is 10-min walk up Hillside Road, single-track lane. Park in Backwell and New Inn (telephone for special arrangements for disabled etc.) • Open May to Oct for parties by appt • Entrance: £2 ● ● & ⌖

A wooded background to a rocky hill site facing north is hardly the best plac ˙ for a garden, but the owners have accepted the challenge and over several years have achieved a remarkable result. Interspersed with a range of shrubs and grasses, beds of varying shape and content climb the hill. A pretty pool area, a dry stream and scree beds are reached by winding grass paths and lead on to an unfolding progression of unusual plants in strong but blended colours. A pergola is home to a variety of roses and honeysuckles, and a magnificent 'Etoile de Hollande' rose covers the cottage wall. A rare *Holboellia latifolia* survives the winters. Clematis abound, blue and white ones bedecking the ruined windmill overseen by the donkey in its orchid and wildflower patch.

Woodborough

Porlock Weir TA24 8NZ. Tel: (01643) 862406

Mr and Mrs R.D. Milne • 6m W of Minehead. From A39 at Porlock take B3225 towards Porlock Weir. At Porlock Vale House on right, take tarmac lane uphill immediately opposite. Garden first on right • Open by appt only • Entrance: £2.50, children under 10 free • Other information: No coaches ● ⟨⟩

This fascinating garden created on a steep (1 in 4) hillside has magnificent views over Porlock Bay. The wide variety of shrubs includes some of the lesser-known hybrid rhododendrons and a number of Ghent azaleas. The garden is at its most colourful in May but a bog garden and two pools designed by the owners' landscape architect son add interest over a longer season. The owners will happily share with visitors their hard-won experience in garden restoration and their battle with the dreaded honey fungus.

Yarlington House

Yarlington, Wincanton BA9 8DY. Tel: (01963) 440344

Count and Countess Charles de Salis • In village of Yarlington S of Castle Cary, signposted off A371 • Open one day for NGS, and for parties of 10 or more by appt • Entrance: £2.50, children free (2003 prices) NEW ● ● WC &

A large and varied formal garden blessed with an ideal mix of design and planting. The fine pleached lime square surrounding the rose garden and the romantic sunken Italian garden, complete with classical statuary and balustrades and awash with scent and soft colours, complement the scale and style of the distinguished 1780s' house. Created by the present owners over forty years, the garden is at a satisfying stage of maturity within the setting of the fine surrounding parkland. Within some two acres it achieves skilful mood changes, moving gradually from the more formal areas to an unusual circle of crab apples trained in the shape of a bandstand (J.C. Loudon's 'apple house') and down towards a dell replete with ferns and shade-loving specimens. Vegetables and fruit trees are grown within a magnificent walled garden approached through impressive gates. Early in the year the daffodils make their point before the laburnum walk comes into flower over a Gothic-arched pergola. The Emperor Napoleon is commemorated in the Italian garden, surrounded by roses – 'Empress Josephine' and 'Souvenir de la Malmaison' of course.

RHS YEAR OF THE GARDEN

To celebrate its bicentenary, the Royal Horticultural Society has declared 2004 the Year of the Garden. It will be making its own presence felt more widely in all its areas of expertise, initiating plant-hunting lectures, science exchanges and debates, running an essay competition for horticultural college students and increasing the number of its specialist shows in Vincent Square. In addition, about 100 outside bodies – museums, galleries, the WI, boy scouts and girl guides groups etc. – have agreed to devise their own gardening-related celebrations. A bicentenary brochure appears in the January edition of *The Garden*.

THE HERITAGE BULB CLUB

This is both a commercial venture and a conservation-minded horticultural service. It is based at Tullynally Castle (see entry in Wales), with none other than Helen Dillon as its President and Martyn Rix, formerly botanist at Wisley and author of *Growing Bulbs* as its botanical adviser. Membership of the so-called Heritage Collection secures an autumn and a spring delivery totalling some 128 bulbs in a dozen rare varieties, while the Plantsman Collection offers a smaller number in still rarer varieties. The fee structure is geared to different budgets, ranging from £45 to £110 p.a., with the opportunity of seeing a different variety in flower every month of the year. But it is also very much a club aimed at kindling interest and spreading knowledge, with visits to gardens here and abroad, expeditions to see wild species in flower, and the opportunity to buy normally unobtainable bulbs and exchange seeds. Enquiries to Heritage, Tullynally Castle, Castlepollard, Co. Westmeath, Ireland (Tel: (44) 62744 (Ireland), 0845 300 4257 (UK); or consult the website on www.heritagebulbs.com.

STAFFORDSHIRE

Two-starred gardens are marked on the map with a black square.

Alton Towers ★ [Historic Park Grade I]

Alton ST10 4DB. Tel: (08705) 204060

Alton Towers • From N take M6 junction 16 or M1 junction 28, from S take M6 junction 15 or M1 junction 23A. Signposted • Theme park, ruins and grounds open 5th April to 2nd Nov daily, 9.30am – 5pm, 6pm or 7pm (1 hour before rides open until 1 hour after they close). Telephone for winter opening times • Entrance: Charges vary seasonally – maximum for individuals £26, OAPs £16, children £21. Party rates available ○ 🍵 ✕ 🧺 WC & 🏛

This fantastic Elysium of ornamental garden buildings was created between 1814 and 1827 by the 15th Earl of Shrewsbury. It contains many beautiful and unusual features, including the three-storey cast-iron Chinese pagoda fountain – a copy of the To Ho pagoda in Canton. W.A. Nesfield was active here (one of his parterres is still *in situ* though in need of restoration). The enormous rock garden is planted with a range of conifers, acers and sedums. The fine domed conservatory houses geraniums etc. according to the season, and the terraces have rose and herbaceous borders. There is a Dutch garden, Her Ladyship's Garden featuring yew and rose beds, the Italian garden, a yew-arch walkway and woodland walks. Water adds further beauty and interest. And of course, there are all the attractions of the theme park.

Arbour Cottage

Napley, Market Drayton, Shropshire TF9 4AJ. Tel: (01630) 672852

Mr and Mrs D.K. Hewitt • 4m NE of Market Drayton. From A53 take B5415 signed to Woore. In 1¾ m turn left at telephone box • Open 9th April, 2 – 5.30pm, and for parties by appt • Entrance: £3, children 50p ● 🍵 WC & 🌿

The owners have established a two-acre garden of wide-ranging interest and year-round colour in a stretch of beautiful countryside with many species of trees. There are peonies, grasses, bamboos, tender specimens such as New Zealand flax, and a collection of shrub roses and alpines. Plenty here for the plantsman, including screes and rockeries, and a large greenhouse with tropical plants, some for sale.

Biddulph Grange Garden ★★ [Historic Garden Grade I]

Grange Road, Biddulph, Staffordshire Moorlands ST8 7SD. Tel: (01782) 517999 (Garden Office)

The National Trust • 3½ m SE of Congleton, 7m N of Stoke-on-Trent. Access from A527 Biddulph/Congleton road • Open April to Oct, Wed – Fri, 12 noon – 5.30pm, Sat, Sun and Bank Holiday Mons, 11am – 5.30pm (or dusk if earlier); Nov to 19th Dec, Sat and Sun, 11am – 3pm. Guided tours by appt only • *Entrance: £4.80, children £2.40, family £12, parties of 15 or more £4 per person; Nov and Dec free* ☾ ☕ WC ♨ 👐

This is one of the most remarkable and innovative gardens of the nineteenth century. There is an Egyptian garden with a pyramid and obelisks of clipped yew. The Chinese garden has a joss house, a golden water buffalo overlooking a dragon parterre, a watch tower and a temple reflected in a calm pool. In front of the house terraces descend to a lily pond. The Stumpery demonstrates an innovative Victorian way to display suitable plants. The verbena, araucaria and rose parterres and the Shelter House and Dahlia Walk (with over 600 dahlias) have now been restored just as they were in the middle of the nineteenth century, and the long Wellingtonia avenue, felled and replanted in 1995, is beginning to make its presence felt again. In all, one of the country's most unusual gardening rediscoveries and restorations – it should not be missed.

12 Darges Lane

Great Wyrley, Walsall WS6 6LE. Tel: (01922) 415064

Mrs A. Hackett • *2m SE of Cannock. From A5 (Churchbridge junction) take A34 towards Walsall. First turning on right over brow of hill. House on right on corner of Cherrington Drive* • *Open 25th April, 23rd May, 2am – 6pm, and by appt* • *Entrance: £2* • *Other information: Plants for sale on open days* ● ☕ ♨

A quarter-acre garden on two levels, attractively laid out, well stocked and of great interest to plantsmen. Fine trees and large variety of shrubs and foliage plants are the background to a comprehensive collection of flowering plants and small shrubs, some unusual, even rare. A National Collection of lamiums is here. There are borders and island beds, and a small water garden. Every inch is used to grow or set off the plants, and there is year-round appeal for flower arrangers. The overall effect is attractive as well as enticing to the plant lover. Plants for sale include some more unusual ones.

The Dorothy Clive Garden ★

Willoughbridge, Market Drayton, Shropshire TF9 4EU. Tel: (01630) 647237

Willoughbridge Garden Trust • *7m NE of Market Drayton, 1m E of Woore on A51 between Nantwich and Stone* • *Open 14th March to Oct, daily, 10am – 5.30pm* • *Entrance: £3.80, OAPs £3.30, children (11–16) £1, under 11 free* • *Other information: Disabled parking* ● ☕ ✕ 🛍 WC ♿ ◁

Created by the late Colonel Clive in memory of his wife, with the help of distinguished gardeners including the late John Codrington, this garden has wide appeal in terms both of design and inspired planting. The guidebook identifies the highlights season by season. These include the rhododendrons and azaleas in the quarry garden and the pool with the scree garden rising on the hillside above it. In spring there are unusual bulbs and primulas, in summer colourful shrubs, unusual perennials and many conifers; other trees provide autumn colour. The scree garden must give gardeners many good ideas. The garden has been extended, and new features include a laburnum arch with roses and other climbers, and a small pool with a bog garden.

The Garth

2 Broc Hill Way, Milford, Stafford ST17 0UB. Tel: (01785) 661182

Mr and Mrs David Wright • 4½ m SE of Stafford. On A513 Stafford – Rugeley road, at Barley Mow turn right, then left after ½ m • Open 6th, 27th June, 2 – 6pm, and by appt for parties • Entrance: £2, children free ● ● WC ⌁ ⌁ ℺

This half-acre garden surrounded by countryside contains specialist areas which should give inspiration and ideas to any gardener. The visitor moves down the different levels to discover old caves at the bottom of the slope. The range of plants includes six unusual beeches, 20 different ferns, 30 varieties of clematis, magnolias, rhododendrons, pulmonarias, hostas, azaleas, penstemons and astilbes, berberis, fothergillas, garryas, amelanchiers and *Holodiscus discolor*, all planted to provide foliage interest and colour combinations. Archways are covered with roses and loniceras, and in the herbaceous borders are heathers, campanulas and osteospermums. There is also a pool and a bog garden.

Little Onn Hall

Church Eaton, Stafford ST20 0AU. Tel: (01785) 840154

Mrs I.H. Kidson • 6m SW of Stafford, 2m S of Church Eaton, midway between A5 and A518 • Open by appt only • Entrance: £3, children 50p ● ● ▨ WC ♿ ⌁ ℺

The driveway to this six-acre garden is flanked by long herbaceous borders backed by yew hedges. The large rose garden contains standards, shrub and hybrid teas. An unusually shaped pool known as the Dog Bone is planted with water lilies; bog plants reside elsewhere in the medieval moat, a delightful feature. Since 1971 the present owner has been planting new trees and is trying to maintain Mawson's original scheme. Many rhododendrons, spring bulbs and large beeches and conifers ensure colour for a long season. Some eight miles north-west, at Offley Brook, Eccleshall, is *Heath House*, where the varied and interesting garden contains a wide selection of unusual plants. [Open for NGS and by appt – telephone (01785) 280318.]

Moseley Old Hall

**Moseley Old Hall Lane, Fordhouses, Wolverhampton WV10 7HY.
Tel: (01902) 782808**

The National Trust • 4m N of Wolverhampton, 5m SW of Cannock. From S take M6 then M54, exiting at junction 1 on A460 to Wolverhampton. From N on M6 exit at junction 11, then take A460. Coaches must use A460 • House open as garden but opens 1pm • Garden open 20th March to 7th Nov, Wed, Sat, Sun; also Bank Holiday Mons and Tues following, 12 noon – 5pm; Nov to 19th Dec, Sun only, 12 noon – 4pm • Entrance: £4.40, children £2.20, family £11; parties of 15 or more £3.70 per person (house and garden) (2003 prices) ◐ ● ✕ ▨ WC ♿ ⌁ ℘ ⛪ ● ℺

Around the Elizabethan house where Charles II hid after the Battle of Worcester is a garden mainly for the specialist interested in old species, as all are seventeenth century except for a few fruit trees. The knot garden is from a design of 1640 by The Rev. Walter Stonehouse. A wooden arbour is covered with clematis and *Vitis vinifera* 'Purpurea'. Fruit trees include quince, mulberry, medlar and a morello cherry. The walled garden has topiary and annual borders, and fritillaries grow in the nut walk. There is a small herb garden and boles for bees. It is interesting to see plants grown in times past to provide dyes and for cleansing and medicinal purposes.

Oulton House

Oulton, Stone ST15 8UR. Tel: (01785) 813556

Mr and Mrs W.A. Fairbairn • 8m N of Stafford, ½ m NE of Stone. From Stone take Oulton road and after Oulton village sign turn left. After houses turn right up long drive • Open February to July by appt • Entrance: £2, children 75p
● ⬤ WC ♨

This three-acre garden with fine views, surrounded by parkland, has been developed by the present owner over more than 25 years. A range of large trees provides shelter. The conservatory contains vines, camellias and roses. Herbaceous borders are distinguished by interesting colour combinations and a wide range of plants, including geraniums, delphiniums, euphorbias and astrantias. Old shrub roses abound, and a grey-and-silver border by the house has clematis and roses climbing its walls. A new border features yellow, blue and white perennials and the bank behind is covered with ivies, loniceras and roses. There is also a rhododendron walk, a large rockery, a patio area, a golden corner, a white area, and a large vegetable and fruit garden. Although not a weed-free garden, there is plenty to delight the eye; it is hoped it may be open more often as the borders contain a mass of snowdrops and tulips which must be a delight to see in spring and early summer.

Rode Hall

(see Cheshire)

Shugborough ★ [Historic Park Grade I]

Milford, Stafford ST17 0XB. Tel: (01889) 881388

Staffordshire County Council/The National Trust • 6m E of Stafford on A513 • House, museum and Park Farm open • Garden open 27th March to 26th Sept, daily except Mons (but open Bank Holiday Mons), 11am – 5pm; Oct, Suns only. Open for pre-booked parties all year from 10.30am • Entrance: £2 per vehicle to parkland, gardens, picnic area, walks and trails. Extra charge for house, museum and farm • Other information: Batricars available. Dogs in park only, on lead ◐ ⬤ ✕ ▦ WC & ⊞ ☘

Shugborough is of interest to garden historians because Thomas Wright of Durham worked here. Many of the buildings and monuments are ascribed to James 'Athenian' Stuart and were built for Thomas Anson from the 1740s onwards. These are some of the earliest examples of English neo-classicism, and there is also an early example of Chinoiserie based on a sketch made by one of the officers on Admiral Anson's voyage round the world. It has been suggested that the buildings were randomly scattered, but another view is that they were put in place as 'hidden architectural treasures' to surprise. As for the garden, the Victorian layout with terraces by Nesfield was revitalised for the Trust in the mid-1960s by Graham Stuart Thomas, who also worked on the Edwardian-style rose garden. Due to an outbreak of phytophora, all the roses except the ramblers are being replaced by herbaceous plantings, harmoniously grouped in small beds. Seasonal attractions include azaleas, rhododendrons and a fine herbaceous border. The first stage of a major tree-planting scheme has begun with over 1000 young oaks, the aim being to restore the landscape to its original eighteenth-century layout with more hedgerows and wooded areas. There is also a woodland walk, and guided tours of the garden are available.

Trentham Gardens [Historic Park Grade II*]

Stone Road, Trentham, Stoke-on-Trent ST4 8AX. Tel: (01782) 657341

Trentham Leisure Ltd • 2m S of Stoke-on-Trent on A34, 2m E of M6 junction 15 • Open early April to Sept, daily, 10am – 4pm (telephone to check dates) • Entrance: £1, concessions/children 50p (2003 prices) ◑ 🏠 **WC** ♿ ⟨⟩ ♀ ♞

The 750 acres of parkland were designed by 'Capability' Brown. Nesfield added a large Italian garden and Sir Charles Barry laid out formal gardens for the Duke of Sutherland. The gardens have been greatly simplified but still retain many features, such as Brown's large lake. There is a good selection of shrubs including hebes, potentillas and buddleias, and magnificent trees alongside the River Trent, which flows through the gardens, and in the woodland area by the lake. The long-neglected buildings and hundreds of acres of parkland have been given the go-ahead for a major refurbishment, which started with the restoration of the Italian gardens, formal gardens, woodland and lake in 2004, and will take three years.

GARDENING WEBSITES
Many gardens now have their own websites, and we list these at the back of the Guide. Others useful for garden visitors are:
Dept of Environment (Ireland): www.heritageireland.ie
English Heritage: www.english-heritage.org.uk
Historic Houses Association: www.hha.org.uk
Historic Royal Palaces: www.hrp.org.uk
Historic Scotland: www.historic-scotland.gov.uk
Landmark Trust: www.landmarktrust.org.uk
National Gardens Scheme: www.ngs.org.uk
National Trust: www.nationaltrust.org.uk
National Trust for Scotland: www.nts.org.uk
Royal Horticultural Society: www.rhs.org.uk
Welsh Historic Monuments: www.cadw.wales.gov.uk

SUFFOLK

Two-starred gardens are marked on the map with a black square.

Abbey Gardens [Historic Garden Grade II]

Bury St Edmunds.

Borough of St Edmundsbury • In town centre • Open all year, daily, 9am – dusk • Entrance: free • Other information: Refreshments and toilets available summer only ○ 🍵 ✕ 🖼 **WC** ♿ 🔁 🎪 🚻 ◔

This is a most surprising garden. In 945 the Benedictines founded the Abbey, which undoubtedly had gardens for herbs and vegetables. The abbey ruins (it was dissolved in 1539) form the bones of the present-day landscape; if for no other reason, visit the place to see the great walls, like some extraordinary geological feature, now dissolving into flinty stumps. Then think forward 900 years and bring to mind that one Nathaniel Hodson actually formed a botanic garden on this site in 1821. The present arrangement of formal beds on the site of the Great Court of the abbey mirrors his garden, of which perhaps only a few trees remain. The planting in the central area may be bright – lots of begonias and busy lizzies in summer and polyanthus and pansies in the winter and spring – but in its way it is the modern equivalent of Hodson's choice. A sensory garden for the visually impaired has been created and the water garden and wall shrub border have been refurbished.

Barham Hall ★

Church Lane, Barham, Ipswich IP6 0PT. Tel: (01473) 830055

Mr and Mrs Richard Burrows • 5m NW of Ipswich off A14 (A45). Take third turning to Claydon, ½ m up Church Lane • Open 27th June for charity, 2 – 6pm • Entrance: £3, children £1.50 ◑ 🍵 **WC** ♿ 🌿

The garden, seven acres in all, includes a water garden and a lake surrounded by bog plants, a woodland shrub garden, many herbaceous borders and a collection of Victorian roses. The whole impression is of immaculate care and attention to detail, achieved during the past ten years, with extensive remodelling over the past five. In 2000 a new border and a water canal were added. If the perfection of maintenance will not make you green with envy you must see this garden – if it does, go anyway to see the Henry Moore sculpture in the church.

Blakenham Woodland Garden

Little Blakenham, Ipswich. Tel: (07760) 342131

4m NW of Ipswich, 1m off B1113. Signed from The Beeches in Little Blakenham, 1m off old A1100 (now B1113) • Open March to June, 1 – 5pm. Parties welcome by appt • Entrance: £3 ◑

A Tory cabinet minister, who became Lord Blakenham, planted five acres on a hill above the village between 1950 and 1982. It was his rural retreat from urban political life where he could hear the birdsong and relax in its peace. He succeeded admirably. Though this woodland is clearly managed (and very well labelled), the birds still sing in the trees above a carpet of native primroses and bluebells in due season. Other planting is more exotic: rhododendrons, azaleas and magnolias flower blithely alongside bamboos and phormiums now interspersed with sculptures, belvederes and rustic huts from which to enjoy the serenity. Even the badgers have their own reserved dell. A delight on a spring or early-summer day.

Bucklesham Hall ★

Bucklesham, Ipswich IP10 0AY. Tel: (01473) 659263

Mr and Mrs D.R. Brightwell • 6m SE of Ipswich, ½ m E of Bucklesham. Entrance opposite and N of primary school • Open by appt • Entrance: £3 • Other information: Coaches by appt. Refreshments by arrangement ● ▬ ▦ & ⚥ ♿

The great interest of Bucklesham is how these seven acres of interlocking gardens, terraces and lakes have been created from scratch since 1973 by the previous owners and added to and further improved by the present owners since 1994. A Monet-type bridge was built in 1999 with a waterfall falling between two lakes. A 16-step water staircase has also been made so that the water flows from an island lake into the streams. Round the house are secret gardens so packed with flowers that no weed could survive; beds of old-fashioned roses overflow their borders, and a courtyard garden has been created with the use of every kind of container. Descending terraces of lawns, ponds and streams lead to the woodland and beyond; round each corner is a new vista. Skill, wide horticultural knowledge and imagination have resulted in a remarkable display of plants, shrubs and trees.

East Bergholt Place

East Bergholt CO7 6UP. Tel: (01206) 299224

Mr and Mrs Rupert Eley • 8m SW of Ipswich, 2m E of A12 on B1070 • Open March to Oct, daily, 10am – 5pm. Closed 11th April • Entrance: £2.50, children free ◗ ▦ WC & ⚥ ♿

The garden was originally laid out between 1900 and 1914 by Charles Eley, the present owner's great-grandfather, and many of the existing plants originate from the great plant collector George Forrest. The 15 acres are an interesting blend of the formal and informal, and are particularly lovely in spring. The yew topiary and terrace area are linked to undulating informal walks by water features, including a pool and a stream. The large collection of rare specimen trees and shrubs includes many camellias, magnolias and rhododendrons. There is an extensive plant centre in the attractive walled garden.

Euston Hall ★ [Historic Park Grade II*]

Thetford, Norfolk IP24 2QP. Tel: (01842) 766366

The Duke and Duchess of Grafton • 11m NE of Bury St Edmunds, 3m S of Thetford on A1088 • House open as garden • Garden open 17th June to 16th Sept, Thurs, plus 27th June, 18th July and 5th Sept; all 2.30 – 5pm • Entrance: £2 (house and garden £4, OAPs £3, children £2 (under 5 free), parties of 12 or more £3 per person) ◐ ⏚ 🖾 WC ♿ ⛲

The pleasure grounds, laid out in the seventeenth century by John Evelyn, have grown into a forest of yew, but straight rides trace out the original formal layout. Also from this period are the stone gate piers which, together with the remnants of a great avenue, mark the original approach to the house. Fronted by terraces, the mellow red-brick hall stands among extensive lawns and parkland along a winding river, the work of William Kent in the 1740s, as is the splendid domed temple isolated on an eminence to the east and the pretty garden house in the formal garden by the house. A small lake created by 'Capability' Brown reflects the house across the park, and there are many fine specimen trees and a wealth of shrub roses.

Garden House Farm ★

Rattlesden Road, Drinkstone, Bury St Edmunds IP30 9TN. Tel: (01449) 736434

Mr and Mrs Hans Seiffer • 8m E of Bury St Edmunds, 3m SW of Woolpit off A14; from Woolpit follow signs to Drinkstone Green • Open 24th April to Sept, Wed, 2 – 5pm, 20th June, 2 – 6pm, and at other times by appt • Entrance £3 ◐ ⏚ 🖾 🌣 B&B

Formerly the display gardens of Barcocks Nursery, there are now 11 acres of hedge-lined gardens. The summer garden, planted with many old-fashioned roses and exuberant herbaceous perennials, contrasts with a fiery-coloured foliage and flower garden. In the formal secret garden paths radiate from a central pond. There is also a winter garden, a lake, large woodland areas filled with rare and unusual plants and many fine trees.

Haughley Park ★

Stowmarket IP14 3JY. Tel: (01359) 240701

Mr R.J. Williams • 4m NW of Stowmarket, signed to Haughley Park (not to Haughley) on A14 • House open by appt • Garden open two Suns for bluebells (telephone for details), and May to Sept, Tues, 2 – 5.30pm • Entrance: £3, children under 16 free (2003 price) • Other information: Coaches by appt. Teas and plants for sale on bluebell Suns ◐ 🖾 WC ♿ ⏚ 🌣 🍶

A hundred acres of rolling parkland at the heart of 100 more acres of woodland surround the seventeenth-century Jacobean mansion. Unexpected secret gardens with clipped hedges or flint and brick walls hide immaculate flower beds, climbers and flowering shrubs; each garden has its own character. The main lawn is surrounded by herbaceous borders, with a splendid lime avenue at the end drawing the eye across many miles of open countryside. Rhododendrons, azaleas and camellias grow on soil which is, unexpectedly for Suffolk, lime-free. The trees include a 12-metre-wide magnolia and a flourishing oak over nine metres in girth, reputed to be a thousand years old. Beyond are the walled kitchen garden, the greenhouses and the shrubbery. In spring the broad rides and walks through the ancient woodland reveal not only the newly planted trees, specimen rhododendrons and other ornamental shrubs, but 10 acres of bluebells, two acres of lilies-of-the-valley and half a mile of mauve *ponticum* rhododendrons.

Helmingham Hall Gardens ★★ [Historic Garden Grade I]

Stowmarket IP14 6EF. Tel: (01473) 890363 (Contact Jane Tresidder)

Lord Tollemache • 9m N of Ipswich on B1077 • Open 2nd May to 12th Sept, Sun, 2 – 6pm; also Wed, 2 – 5pm, by appt • Entrance: £4, OAPs £3.75, children £2, parties of 30 or more £3.75 per person ● ◕ ▦ WC ⅃ ⟨⅃⟩ ⅟ ⅏ ⚘

Nineteen generations of Tollemaches have lived here, and though there have been many changes over the past five centuries the property retains a strong Elizabethan atmosphere. The double-moated Tudor mansion house of great splendour and charm, built of warm red brick, stands in a 400-acre deer park. A nineteenth-century parterre, edged with a magnificent spring border, leads to the Elizabethan kitchen garden which is surrounded by the Saxon moat with banks covered in daffodils. Within the walls the kitchen garden has been transformed into an enchanting *potager* most subtly planted; the meticulously maintained herbaceous borders and old-fashioned roses surround beds of vegetables separated by arched tunnels of sweet peas and dangling gourds. Large beds along the walls have been cleverly split up with iron dividers and planted with geometrically arranged herb and box beds. Outside is a lushly planted south-facing spring border which includes many irises and peonies. There are wildflower areas, fruit trees, a shady yew walk, knot and herb gardens. Lady Tollemache is an extremely clever plantswoman and garden designer, with Chelsea medals to her name, and this garden increasingly benefits from her skill.

Ickworth Park [Historic Garden Grade II*]

Horringer, Bury St Edmunds IP29 5QE. Tel: (01284) 735270

The National Trust • 3m SW of Bury St Edmunds; signposted • Park open daily (except 25th Dec), dawn to dusk. Garden open Jan to 21st March, 3rd Nov to 21st Dec, Mon – Fri, 10am – 4pm; 22nd March to 2nd Nov, daily, 10am – 5pm • Entrance: £2.80, children 80p (2003 prices) ○ ◕ ✕ ▦ WC ⅃ ⅟ ⅏ ⚘

The vast park, girdled by woodland, is in part the work of 'Capability' Brown and provides a formidable setting for the late-eighteenth-century house. At first the building is not obvious, but the huge rotunda soon looms large, and the great domed drum emerges with its vast curving wings, dominating the gardens which surround it. A formal garden, in the Italian style, lies to the south of the house. It features many Mediterranean species and provides an intriguing point of contrast to the thoroughly bucolic, English landscape of the grazed parkland beyond its boundary wall. Within the Italian garden, there is box everywhere (the property holds a National Collection). Bands of Jerusalem sage and catmint, and bedded-out scarlet pelargoniums, provide occasional colour. Hidden behind the clipped hedges you can discover a series of hidden gardens – spring, silver and gold – and the extraordinary stumpery complete with bits of the Giant's Causeway, signalling one of the other stupendous creations of Ickworth's builder, the fourth Earl of Bristol (also Bishop of Derry): his Mussenden Temple at Downhill on the north coast of Northern Ireland. The park and woods at Ickworth contain many other delights, including an ornamental canal and summerhouse which pre-date the house, a recently planted vineyard, miles of way-marked woodland walks, and a deer enclosure complete with hide.

Melford Hall [Historic Garden Grade II*]

Long Melford, Sudbury CO10 9AA. Tel: (01787) 880286

The National Trust • 14m S of Bury St Edmunds, 3m N of Sudbury, in village, W of A134 • Hall open with Beatrix Potter exhibition • Garden open April, Sat, Sun and Bank Holiday Mon; May to Sept, Wed – Sun and Bank Holiday Mons; all 2 – 5.30pm • Entrance: principal rooms and garden £4.50 • Other information: Disabled driven to hall. Wheelchairs provided ◑ 🐾 WC ♥

The magnificent sixteenth-century house of mellow red brick is set in a park and formal gardens. A plan by Samuel Pierse of 1613 shows that the park was separated from the hall by a walled enclosure, outside which was the moat; part of this is now the sunken garden. The avenue at the side of the house has been replanted with oaks grown from acorns taken from the existing trees. The octagonal brick banqueting house on the north side of the path, a rare and beautiful example of Tudor architecture, overlooks the village green and the herbaceous borders inside the garden, which are being restored to their original Victorian and Edwardian design and planting. Around the banqueting house clipped box hedges and a bowling-green terrace lead past dense shrubbery. The garden has many good specimen trees, including the rare *Xanthoceras sorbifolium*. Great domes of box punctuate the lawns, and an interesting detail is the arrangement of yew hedges to the north of the house. Outside the walls stand topiary figures. Round the pond and fountain are beds originally planted with herbs in 1937.

North Cove Hall ★

North Cove, Beccles NR34 7PH. Tel: (01502) 476631

Mr and Mrs B. Blower • 3½ m E of Beccles, 50 metres off A146 Lowestoft road • Open by appt only • Entrance: £2, children free ● 🐾 WC ＆ ⬦

Climbing roses adorn the sunny Georgian house set in lawns surrounded by mature park trees. The walled garden partly encloses the half-acre pond studded with water lilies and bordered by majestic *Gunnera manicata*, *Taxodium distichum* var. *imbricatum* 'Nutans', a group of *Betula jacquemontii* and *Alnus glutinosa* 'Imperialis'. A small stream with waterfalls has recently been constructed and planted. Inside the walls are herbaceous and shrub borders, pergolas and a kitchen garden, and there also is a small scree garden. Outside are woodland walks among mature trees and various younger conifers. About 10 miles south of Beccles is *Woottons* of Wenhaston, a small garden of one acre attached to a nursery run by Mr Loftus, well laid-out and labelled, and full of rare and unusual plants.

The Old Rectory

Orford, Woodbridge IP12 2NN. Tel: (01394) 450063

Mr and Mrs Tim Fargher • 10m E of Woodbridge. Take B1084 Woodbridge – Orford road; house is on left behind church • Open mid-June to mid-July, Mon – Fri, 10am – 4pm – please telephone in advance • Entrance: £4, OAPs and children £2 (2003 prices) • Other information: Parking for disabled only. No dogs. Visitors are asked to make themselves known to gardener, Mr Denny ◐

This extensive five-acre garden, tucked behind Orford church, is immaculate, secluded and unexpected. It was designed for the owners' parents by Lanning Roper, with additions by Mark Rumary, and its beautifully planned borders and vistas surround the house, which has a large conservatory.

Playford Hall

Playford, Ipswich IP6 9DX. Tel: (01473) 622509

Mr and Mrs Richard Innes • 3m NE of Ipswich, 1m N of A1214 between Ipswich and Woodbridge, on edge of Playford • Open by appt only • Entrance: £5 ◐ 🍽 ♿ ⇪

A beautiful moated Elizabethan house set in 10 acres of outstanding gardens. Trees, lawns and a lake surround the house, with yew hedges dividing herbaceous and shrub borders full of unusual plants. Roses cascade over the house and moat walls, and there is also a pergola rose garden underplanted with lavender and other old favourites. The orchard contains a small vegetable and herb garden.

The Priory ★

Stoke by Nayland CO6 4RL. Tel: (01206) 262216

Mr and Mrs Henry Engleheart • 8m SE of Sudbury on B1068 • Open 16th May, 20th June, 2 – 6pm, and by appt in writing • Entrance: £3, children free ◐ 🍽 🛍 WC ♿ ⇪ 🌿

An exceptional nine-acre garden, with fine views over Constable country. Around the house is a splendid selection of plants and roses in terraces and mixed borders. Lawns slope down to a series of six small lakes, planted with a mass of water plants and water lilies; spring-flowering rhododendrons and azaleas ring the water under large trees. A Chinese bridge links to a tea pavilion by one of the lakes. A garden of mixed planting in the walled garden leads into the greenhouse/conservatory, with its colourful collection of tender plants.

Shrubland Park ★ [Historic Park and Garden Grade I]

Coddenham, Ipswich IP6 9QQ. Tel: (01473) 830221

Lord de Saumarez • 4m N of Ipswich. Turn off A140/A14 interchange slip road towards Ipswich, then turn signed to Barham • Open April to Sept (telephone for dates and times). Guided tours for parties of 10 or more at other times by appt • Entrance: £3, OAPs and children £2 ◑ 🏚 WC ♿ ℘

The magnificence of the hall is reflected in the Victorian gardens, laid out by Sir Charles Barry and later modified by William Robinson. They are among the most important of their type remaining in England. From the upper terrace outside the house visitors descend by a stunning cascade of a hundred steps and terraces to a garden of formal beds, fountain and eye-catcher loggia. Beyond is the wild garden, which merges into the woods and is bordered by the park with its many fine trees, some reputed to be 800 years old. The gardens are punctuated by a series of enchanting follies, ranging from a Swiss chalet to an alpine rockery and magnificent conservatory. The box maze is now established and growing well, and the old dell garden undergoes slow restoration. The hot wall has been totally restored.

Somerleyton Hall and Gardens ★★ [Historic Garden Grade II*]

Somerleyton, Lowestoft NR32 5QQ.
Tel: (01502) 730224 (732950 during opening hours)

Lord and Lady Somerleyton • 5m NW of Lowestoft, 8m SW of Great Yarmouth on B1074. Signposted • House open 1 – 5pm • Gardens open 31st March to Oct, Thurs, Sun and Bank Holiday Mons; July and Aug, Tues, Wed, Thurs, Sun and Bank Holiday Mon, 12 noon – 5.30pm. Private tours of hall and gardens for parties by arrangement with Administrator • Entrance: £5.80, OAPs £5.50, children £2.90, family £16.40, parties of 20 or more rates on application (2003 prices). Check prices and opening details on website ◐ ☕ 🏚 WC ♿ ℘ ♨

The former Jacobean house was extensively rebuilt in the mid-nineteenth century by Sir Morton Peto as an Italianate palace, and the gardens splendidly reflect this magnificence with 12 acres of formal gardens, a beautiful walled garden, an aviary, a loggia and a winter garden surrounding a sunken garden displaying statues from the original nineteenth-century winter garden. Special are the 1846 William Nesfield yew hedge maze and the 90-metre-long iron pergola covered in wisteria, vines and roses. The extraordinary peach cases and ridge-and-furrow greenhouses designed by Sir Joseph Paxton now contain peaches, grapes and a rich variety of tender plants. Victorian kitchen garden and museum of bygone gardening equipment.

Sun House ★

Hall Street, Long Melford, Sudbury CO10 9HZ. Tel: (01787) 378252

Mrs J. Thompson • 3m N of Sudbury. In centre of Long Melford opposite Cock and Bell pub and next to Swags and Bows shop • Open by appt only • Entrance: £3 ◑ ℘ B&B

Into a third-of-an-acre under a noble false acacia have been shoehorned a tiny bluebell wood, a flinty 'ruin', a hot border, a shady border, and a flagged courtyard including a large pond with water lilies and around 100 clematis, mostly different varieties. Then there's the secret garden, walled with ancient bricks, which, unlike the main area, is formal, Italianate and so peaceful it seems leagues away from the busy main street of Long Melford. This is a garden for all seasons: snowdrops are succeeded by primulas, then tulips, before the herbaceous beds and clematis strike up along with the old-fashioned roses. The owner, a fine plantswoman with notable colour sense, can name virtually everything.

The Thumbit

Badwell Road, Walsham–le–Willows IP31 3BT. Tel: (01359) 259414

Mrs Ann James • 10m NE of Bury St Edmunds off A143. From crossroads by church, follow road signed to Badwell Ash to outskirts of village. Parking on roadside • Open for NGS 10th, 11th July, 2 – 6pm, and by appt • Entrance: £2, children free [NEW] ● 🍵 💷 🏵 WC �&ન ⬦

The gardens of this tiny thatched cottage are no bigger than a town garden, but the owner has designed the space so skilfully that they include a fish pond, fed by an ancient iron kettle, an ornamental herb garden with a frame of runner beans and plenty of places to sit out. Winding paths of the most immaculate grass edge circular and curvaceous beds, heavily planted with colourful perennials and given height by loggias, and trellises covered in clipped ivy. Even the cornfield beyond has been hijacked to give a long view over the Suffolk countryside. Mrs James will happily discuss her design theories with visitors.

Wyken Hall ★

Stanton, Bury St Edmunds IP31 2DW. Tel: (01359) 250287

Sir Kenneth and Lady Carlisle • 9m NE of Bury St Edmunds on A143. Leave A143 between Ixworth and Stanton. Signed to Wyken Vineyards • Open April to Oct, daily, except Sat, 2 – 6pm • Entrance: £3, OAPs £2.50, children under 12 free • Other information: Vineyard ◑ 🍵 ✕ WC �&ન ⬦ ⚘ 🏛 ℀

This outstanding garden covers four acres, most of them planted in the last twenty years. It is divided into a series of rooms, starting with the wild garden and winter garden, which leads into the south and woodland garden, and so into the dell. Mown paths meander between shrubs and into the newly planted copper beech maze next to the nuttery and gazebo, then on to the rose garden, enclosed on three sides by a hornbeam hedge and on the fourth by a rose-laden pergola. Beyond the wall are the knot and herb gardens, separated by yew hedges and designed by Arabella Lennox-Boyd. An 'edible garden' and a kitchen garden have been planted to the north of the house, and there is a new pond just beyond the garden. The whole place is remarkable for its colours and scents, particularly in high summer. An eccentric dog kennel, a chapel (with armchair), a contemplation garden, a giant stride and a curious veranda with rocking chairs are the personal touches of Lady Carlisle.

SURREY

We have included some gardens with Surrey postal addresses in the London section for convenience. So before planning a day out in Surrey it is worth consulting pages 234–69.

Two-starred gardens are marked on the map with a black square.

Albury Park Gardens ★ [Historic Park Grade I]

Albury, Guildford GU5 9BB. Tel: (01483) 202964

Trustees of the Albury Estate/Country Houses Association Ltd • 5m SE of Guildford. Turn off A25 onto A248 (signed to Albury). After $\frac{1}{4}$ m turn left; entrance immediately left • House open as grounds • Gardens around house open May to Sept, Wed and Thurs, 2 – 5pm. Pleasure grounds open two days only, for NGS • Entrance: £2.50 ● & ⇗

John Evelyn designed the 14 acres of pleasure grounds in the mid-seventeenth century. Two dramatic terraces, a quarter of a mile long, extend across the grounds. A tunnel entrance in the upper terrace leads through the hillside to a semi-circular pond which was originally fed by water from the Silent Pool; the bathhouse on the lower level is dated 1676. In the grounds are about 70 different species of trees, a lake and a small canal. The gardens around the house have impressive trees, a bank of azaleas and a formal rose garden. On one of his rural rides in 1882, Cobbett described the gardens as 'without exception the prettiest in England; that is to say, that I ever saw in England'.

Barnett Hill

Wonersh, Guildford GU5 0RF. Tel: (01483) 893361

Barnett Hill Conference Centre Ltd • 5m SE of Guildford off A281. After $1\frac{1}{2}$ m cross railway bridge and turn left at Shalford village green for Wonersh. Continue for $1\frac{1}{2}$ m and turn left signed 'Conference Centre'. Entrance at top of hill on right • Open 16th May, 2 – 5.30pm • Entrance: £3, children under 14 free ● ● ● WC & ⇗ ⌖ ●

In 1906 the grandson of Thomas Cook, the founder of the travel agency, built the Queen Anne-style house on a levelled hill top 360 feet above sea level, employing 14 gardeners to tend the 26 acres of grounds. Traces of that period remain – the architectural yew hedges, a formal garden with a lily pond, a summerhouse and a delightful Wendy house built for their only child. It is a garden of great diversity – a terrace with surprising, distant views, a long herbaceous border and paths leading through banks of azaleas, rhododendrons and camellias, plus a rockery, heathers and a $\frac{3}{4}$-mile woodland walk. More recent developments include alpine beds, an area of grasses and herbaceous drifts.

Brook Lodge Farm Cottage

Blackbrook, Dorking RH5 4DT. Tel: (01306) 888368

*Mrs Basil Kingham • 1m S of Dorking. From A24 turn left in Mill Road for
Leigh and Brockham, then left at T-junction. Garden is short distance on left •
Open monthly through summer for NGS, and by appt • Entrance: £2.50,
children free* ● ♨ WC ♿ ✿

The present owner created this immaculately kept plantsman's garden fifty
years ago, the emphasis being on plant associations and foliage. Now mature
trees shelter flowering shrubs, clematis, roses, herbaceous and tender plants,
and towering specimen conifers. The fruit and vegetable gardens lead to a heated
greenhouse full of tender flowering plants and the gardener's cottage garden.

Busbridge Lakes [Historic Park Grade II*]

Hambledon Road, Godalming GU8 4AY. Tel: (01483) 421955

*Mr and Mrs Douetil • $1\frac{1}{2}$ m S of Godalming off B2130 Hambledon road •
Open 9th to 18th April, 2nd, 3rd, 30th, 31st May, 22nd to 30th Aug, all
10.30am – 5.30pm; pre-booked parties any day April to Sept by appt • Entrance:
£4, OAPs and children £3, under 5 free • Other information: Refreshments at
weekends and on Bank Holidays only* ● ♨ ▨ WC ♿ ⚒ ℺

Parkland was created here in the 1650s and the grounds were landscaped in
1750 by Philip Webb MP. Beside the largest of the three lakes stands an early-
nineteenth-century Gothick boathouse, recently restored, with delicate blind
windows, a room with a fireplace and two verandahs. At the end of the lake,
what appears to be a bridge, multi-arched and built of rocks, proves to be an
illusion. Huge plane trees dominate the lakeside; the 30-metre chestnuts,
probably planted in 1660, may be the tallest in England. Tulip trees (*Liriodendron
tulipifera*) and a fine cedar of Lebanon stand near the orchard; a sequoia towers
above the house. Across the canal lake is a hermit's cave, excavated in 1756 as a
tomb for the then owner's wife and two of their children. Further up, a late-
eighteenth-century Doric temple with two porticos has recently been restored; below it a grotto contains the spring which feeds the lakes. There are
peacocks on the lawns, and the site abounds with attractive, rare and
endangered species of ducks, geese, swans and pheasants, all flourishing –
as are the gardens. 2m SW of Godalming on the A3100 is *Secretts Garden Centre*,
Portsmouth Road, Milford (Tel: (01483) 426633), where the plants for sale are
placed in imaginatively designed settings and a garden with a large pond
displays National Collections of cornus and kalmias.

Chilworth Manor

Chilworth, Guildford GU4 8NL. Tel: (01483) 561414

*Lady Heald • 3m SE of Guildford on A248. Turn off in Chilworth up
Blacksmiths Lane • House open Sat and Sun only • Garden open for NGS, and
by appt • Entrance: £2 (house £1.50), children free • Other information: Teas on
open days only* ● WC ♿ ⬫

A lovely old garden, particularly in spring and summer, but with something to see all the year round. The house stands on the site of a monastery. Laid out in the eighteenth century, a walled garden was carved in three tiers out of the side of the hill by Sarah, Duchess of Marlborough. The high walls, backed by wisteria, shelter many fine plants, a herbaceous border, lavender walk and shrubs. There is also a woodland area with magnolias, rhododendrons, azaleas, an oak tree reputed to be 400 years old and a Judas tree. Candelabra primulas flourish along the stream and golden carp swim in the monastic stewponds.

Clandon Park [Historic Park Grade II]

West Clandon, Guildford GU4 7RQ. Tel: (01483) 222482

The National Trust • 3m E of Guildford on A247 at West Clandon; or take A3 to Ripley then join A247 via B2215 • House open as garden • Garden open April to Oct, Tues – Thurs, Sun, Good Friday and Bank Holiday Mons, 11am – 5pm. Parties, Tues – Thurs only, must book • Entrance: House and garden £6, children £3, family £15, parties of 15 or more £5 per person, combined ticket with Hatchlands (see entry) £9 • Other information: Disabled parking near front of house. Dogs in picnic area only, on lead ○ ⚑ ✕ 🍴 WC ᕙ 🏛 ♀ ⚲

The house was built by the Venetian architect Giacomo Leoni in the early 1730s for the 2nd Lord Onslow, whose family still owns the park although the house and garden are owned by the National Trust. The seven-acre garden is on a hillside and gives a fine view of the lake. An interesting feature is the Maori meeting house, known as 'Hinemihi', brought from New Zealand over a century ago by the then Lord Onslow. Note also the grotto, parterre and herbaceous border, and the bedding and colours in the sunken Dutch garden.

Claremont Landscape Garden ★ [Historic Park Grade I]

Portsmouth Road, Esher KT10 9JG. Tel: (01372) 467806

The National Trust • E of A307, just S of Esher • House (not NT) and belvedere open – telephone for details • Garden open Jan to March, daily except Mon, 10am – 5pm; April to Oct, Mon – Fri, 10am – 6pm (closes 7pm Sat, Sun and Bank Holiday Mons); Nov to March, daily except Mons, 10am – 5pm or sunset if earlier (closed 25th Dec, 1st Jan). Coach parties must book • Entrance: £4, children £2, family £10, pre-booked parties £3.50 per person (2003 prices) • Other information: Dogs, Nov to March only, on lead ○ ⚑ ✕ 🍴 WC ᕙ 🏛 ♀ ⚲

One of the most important historic landscapes in England. Practically all the great landscape designers of the eighteenth century adapted it in turn for the new owner – the immensely wealthy man who became Duke of Newcastle – who bought the house from Sir John Vanbrugh. For him Vanbrugh designed the belvedere (the views from the top are amazing). The Duke then employed Bridgeman in 1716, followed by Kent in the 1730s; the latter adapted the garden to create picturesque settings, evoking various moods, and also enlarged the pond to make the lake, with a pavilion (recently restored). When the Duke died, Clive of India purchased the estate. He brought in 'Capability' Brown, who also designed the house and, in typical form, diverted the London-Portsmouth road to improve the viewpoints, the most striking of which is the grass amphitheatre. In the nineteenth century it was a favourite retreat of Queen Victoria and her younger son. The 50 acres restored by the Trust are only a part of the original estate, which was broken up in 1922 when the house became a school. A useful leaflet describes the various contributions to the park, which will appeal to everyone interested in its sensitive recon-struction of the eighteenth-century English style, even if it has little to please a plant lover, except perhaps the camellia terrace. A few miles east, in Leather-head Road, Chessington, *Chessington Nursery* (Tel: (01372) 744490) offers a wide range of plants for both house and garden, attractively displayed. [Open all year, daily, 9am – 6pm (10am – 4pm on Suns).]

Coverwood Lakes, Garden and Farm

Peaslake Road, Ewhurst, Cranleigh GU6 7NT. Tel: (01306) 731103

Mrs C.G. Metson and Mr and Mrs N. Metson • 7m SW of Dorking, 6m SE of Guildford, $\frac{1}{2}$ m S of Peaslake off A25 • Gardens and farm open for NGS 18th, 25th April, 2nd, 9th, 16th, 23rd, 30th May, 2 – 6pm; 24th Oct, 11am – 4.30pm. Also for parties by appt • Entrance: £3, children £1 • Other information: Home-made teas available on April and May open days, hot soup and sandwiches on Oct open day ● ➾ WC ♿ ✿ B&B

The original gardens were designed in 1910 by a rich Edwardian businessman. Now it is a woodland estate surrounding four lakes, the water for which comes from the natural springs in the bog garden. Each lake has a different character, from the towering rhododendrons reflected in the calm water of the highest to the largest alongside the arboretum. This was planted early in 1990 and contains 100 different trees, which are prospering in this natural setting. Bordering the paths are a great many varieties of hostas, trilliums and candelabra primulas, and lilies-of-the-valley form a carpet below a dazzling display of rhododendrons and azaleas. There is a marked farm trail with wonderful views.

Crosswater Farm

Millais Nurseries, Crosswater Lane, Churt, Farnham GU10 2JN. Tel: (01252) 792698

Mr and Mrs E.G. Millais • 6m SE of Farnham, 6m NW of Haslemere, $\frac{1}{2}$ m N of Churt off A287. Signed 'Millais Nurseries' • Open 19th April to 11th June, daily, 10am – 5pm • Entrance: £2.50, children free ● ➾ ▧ WC ♿ ✿ ⛪

These six acres of woodland gardens were begun in 1946 by the present owners, who specialise in azaleas and rhododendrons and have assembled an exceptional international collection. Among the mature and some more recent plantings are rare species collected in the Himalayas and hybrids raised by them, including *Rhododendron* 'High Summer'. The plants are labelled and most are available from the adjoining nursery, which grows more than 750 different varieties. There is also an excellent collection of sorbus trees. The surrounding garden features a stream, ponds and attractive companion plant-ings, including magnolias, Japanese maples and woodland perennials.

Dunsborough Park

Ripley, Woking GU23 6AL. Tel: (01483) 225366

Baron and Baroness Sweerts de Landas Wyborgh • 3m NE of Guildford. Take A247 or A3 to Ripley. Entrance across Ripley Green • Open four times a year for charity, and by appt (please telephone for dates) • Entrance: £2.50, children £1.25 ◐ 🍵 **WC** ♿ 🌿 💡 🐾

The 10-acre garden of the Georgian house has recently been restored as a showplace for the owners' extensive collection of statuary. Herbaceous borders lead to the extensive walled gardens, now redesigned as pleasure gardens; a row of ginkgo trees, grown originally for sale, became too big to move and now forms an unusual feature. A hidden garden encloses an ancient mulberry. At the end of the water garden the bridge, with its belvedere, is now accessible, and the fine Victorian glasshouses have been restored. RHS Wisley (see entry) is nearby.

Feathercombe

Feathercombe Lane, Hambledon, Godalming GU8 4DP. Tel: (01483) 860264

Campbell • 6m SW of Godalming between A283 and B2130. Feathercombe Lane is off Hambledon Road between Hydestile crossroads and Merry Harriers pub • Open for NGS one weekend in April and one in May, 2 – 6pm, and by appt during May only • Entrance: £2.50, children 50p (2003 prices) [NEW] ◐ ♿ 🌿

The romantic 12-acre garden was designed and created in 1910 by Surrey author and journalist Eric Parker and his wife Ruth, daughter of Ludwig Messel of Nymans (see entry in West Sussex); now it is maintained by their grandchildren. High banks of rhododendrons, azaleas, tree heathers and shrubs, including a huge exochorda, are sheltered by mature trees – in spring spectacular tall *Embothrium coccineum* (Chilean firebush) blaze out their scarlet flowers. A mature yew topiary garden surrounds a formal goldfish pool, and *Wisteria floribunda* cascades from a pergola. There are amazing views to the Surrey hills: Blackdown, Hindhead and the Hog's Back.

Gatton Park [Historic Park Grade II]

Reigate RH2 0TW. Tel: (01737) 649068 or (0794) 157 2434

The Royal Alexandra and Albert School • 3m NE of Reigate. From A23 or Gatton Bottom, turn into Rocky Lane • Open Feb to Oct, 1st Sun each month, 1 – 5 pm • Entrance: £3, children free ◐ 🍵 🧺 **WC** ♿ ♿ 🌿 💡 🐾

The Domesday Book records a manor and deer park at Gatton. In the fifteenth century it became a rotten borough: a diminutive town hall still stands opposite the impressive portico, which is all that remains of the Italianate mansion, burnt down in 1934 and rebuilt in plainer style in 1937. There are magnificent cedars and sequoias around the house, and ancient oaks below in the parkland. In the eighteenth century, 'Capability' Brown swept away earlier formal gardens and created the 28-acre lake and a chain of smaller ones; he also landscaped the parkland, woods and vistas, enhancing the spectacular setting on the North Downs. This was one of his larger commissions, for which he was paid £3000. In the late Victorian and Edwardian eras Jeremiah Colman, the mustard magnate, developed the gardens, building a dramatic rock and water garden on a slope with Pulhamite pools, massive rocks and curving steps. Most of this garden has been restored and is now shaded by yews and appropriately planted. Colman also created a Japanese garden with interlacing pools and paths and waterside plants; now restored, it is overlooked by a thatched tea house. Restoration work continues.

Goddards

Abinger Common, Dorking RH5 6JH.
Tel: (01306) 730871 (Ticket bookings during office hours)

The Landmark Trust • 10m SE of Guildford, 4m SW of Dorking off A25. At Wotton take right turn for Abinger Common. House on green opposite Victorian well • Open 23rd April to 29th Oct, Wed only, 2 – 6pm, strictly by appt • Entrance: £3 (2003 price) • Other information: Limited parking, must be booked ● WC &

Sir Edwin Lutyens designed the house originally in 1898 as a home of rest for ladies of small means. He planned it around a courtyard garden, facing slightly west of south and overlooked by all the principal rooms – in effect an outdoor room. Gertrude Jekyll collaborated on the structure of the garden, which remains intact. A dipping well in the centre, providing water for the plants, is surrounded by paved paths, low walls, curved beds and a raised sundial. There are flower borders under the windows and vines and wisteria grow against the house walls. Architectural yew hedges enclose the formal gardens around the house, and yew arches give vistas over lawns, a ha-ha and across a meadow to a curving backdrop of woods. The house, cared for by the Landmark Trust, may be rented for self-catering holidays. Strangely, Goddards is not on the English Heritage Register of Gardens.

8 Grafton Park Road

(see London)

Great Fosters [Historic Garden Grade II*]

Stroude Road, Egham TW20 9UR. Tel: (01784) 433822

Great Fosters (1931) Ltd • 1m SW of Staines off M25 junction 13, 1m S of Egham. From railway station follow Manorcroft Road into Stroude Road and continue 1m. Hotel on left • Open all year, daily, during daylight hours • Entrance: free • Other information: Refreshments and toilet facilities in hotel ○ ● ✕ WC & B&B

Built in the late sixteenth century, possibly as a Windsor Forest hunting lodge, the house has been a hotel since 1929. The garden, developed in 1918, has recently been restored, with Kim Wilkie as consultant. Behind the hotel, a long, paved terrace gives views of a wide semi-circular lawn and a lime avenue truncated at the far end by an amphitheatre designed by Wilkie; the new lake is also his creation. Steps lead down to four knot gardens with box edging, topiary and statues surrounding a sixteenth-century sundial, the whole outlined by a U-shaped Saxon moat. Wisteria drapes the Japanese bridge, which arches over the moat and leads to a pergola underplanted with lavender. A circular, sunken rose garden with an octet of steps down to a lily pool and fountain is bordered by rose arches and a paved path and surrounded by yew. Two square iris and peony gardens, also enclosed by yew hedges, are on a more intimate scale. At the side of the hotel a vista garden with serpentine yew hedges is developing. An orangery has been built at the southern end, and orange trees in containers stand on the terrace in summer.

The Green House

69 Station Road, Chertsey KT16 8BN. Tel: (01932) 567725

Steven Leon and Stephanie Grimshaw • Leave M25 junction 11 for A317. Turn left at roundabout, left at Eastworth Road, left at Highfield Road, then right into Station Road • Open by appt only • Entrance £1.50 (2003 price)
◐ ♿ ⚲

Only seven metres wide, the garden feels totally secluded – secret, shady and full of surprises. It is enclosed by hazel, ash and eucalyptus trees, unusual shrubs and arches swathed in climbers. On the sheltered terrace tender plants grow in pots – a bottlebrush, *Nicotiana langsdorffii* and, on the back of the house, *Clematis armandii*. A winding path of stepping-stones and gravel leads to a Japanese-style bridge and four pools, with a profusion of bulbs, flowering plants and those with architectural foliage. Raised beds have been given extra height by lowering the level of the path to make gardening easier for the disabled owner. Mirrors and holes in the fence create a *trompe-l'oeil* effect, adding width to the garden, and at the far end is a circular seating area and a folly.

Guildford Castle Gardens

Castle Street, Guildford GU1 3TU. Tel: (01483) 505050

Guildford Borough Council • From High Street walk through arches into Tunsgate. Castle opposite at far end • Open all year, daily, dawn – dusk • Entrance: free ○ ♿

This ruined keep built by William the Conqueror (close to the present city centre) once formed part of the garden of a private house bought by Guildford Corporation in 1885. Clever use has been made of the original moat. A path runs around the bottom, and shaped beds, retaining their interesting Victorian designs, are cut into the sloping turfed sides. They are bedded out for spectacular spring and summer displays with much the same plants as the Victorians would have used. There are plenty of seats. A tunnel, its damp, shady approach brightly planted, leads up to a bandstand and a bowling green with attractive borders and clipped hedges.

Hannah Peschar Sculpture Garden

Black and White Cottage, Standon Lane, Ockley RH5 5QR. Tel: (01306) 627269

Hannah Peschar • 6m S of Dorking, 1m SW of Ockley off A29. Follow signs for 'Golf and Country Club'. Entrance on right in Standon Lane 400 metres past low bridge over stream • Open May to Oct, Fri and Sat, 11am – 6pm, Sun and Bank Holiday Mons, 2 – 5pm; other days, except Mon, by appt only • Entrance: £8, OAPs £6, children under 16 £5 • Other information: Refreshments and meals for parties by arrangement only. Details of lecture tours, party and school visits on request ◑ 🧺 WC ⚿ ⬳ ▮ ⚲ B&B

In Victorian times the heart of the 20-acre valley garden was part of the Leith Vale Estate, and when Hannah Peschar and her husband, the landscape designer Anthony Paul, came here in 1977, the place had been neglected for many years. He kept the old trees, and under their canopy has encouraged some 400 native species to spread among his favourite, more restricted palette of architectural plants – dynamos such as gunneras, *Ligularia* 'The Rocket', a variety of grasses and stands of bamboo. It is another-worldly experience to wind along the narrow paths looking down on streams, lakes and precarious wooden bridges; and the Hansel-and-Gretel buildings at the heart of the garden enhance the effect. But the garden is only half the story. It has primarily been designed as a showcase for Hannah Peschar's own business – the sale of contemporary sculpture of the highest quality, unerringly placed among vegetation or against water to bring out the character and quality of each piece.

Hatchlands Park

East Clandon, Guildford GU4 7RT. Tel: (01483) 222482

The National Trust • 5m NE of Guildford, E of East Clandon, N of A246 • House and garden open April to Oct, Tues – Thurs, Sun and Bank Holiday Mons, also Fri in Aug, 2 – 5.30pm; park walks and grounds open April to Oct, daily, 11am – 6pm. Parties by appt Tues – Thurs only • Entrance: park walks £2.50 (house, garden and walks £6, family £15, parties of 15 or more £5 per person, combined ticket with Clandon (see entry) £9) ◑ ☕ ✕ 🧺 WC ⚿ 🧺 ⚲

The restoration of these gardens has been successfully completed and the Gertrude Jekyll garden re-created most effectively with herbaceous planting and roses. Beside the garden is a magnificent 200-year-old London plane tree, a temple and an ice-house. A wildflower meadow is left uncut until July. The Italianate garden at the front has been returned to its original Reptonian design of lawns and vistas, and the park has also been restored on Reptonian principles. There are three woodland walks to enjoy, including a bluebell wood. Surprisingly, not on the English Heritage Register of Gardens.

Hethersett [Historic Garden Grade II]

Littleworth Cross, Seale, Farnham GU10 1JL.

Lady Adam Gordon • 4m E of Farnham, S of Hog's Back (A31). 1½ m from Seale Church on Elstead road, or 1m N of B3001 on Seale Road • Open 16th

*May for NGS, 11am – 5pm, and for parties by appt during May • Entrance:
£3, children free (conducted tours for parties £5 per person)* ● ⬠ ⚘ ⚲

This magical 25-acre woodland garden, rarely open, was created at the end of
the nineteenth century by H.A. Mangles, an early hybridiser of rhododendrons. Under mature trees, many of his hybrids and species have grown as tall
as trees themselves, intermingling with shrubs and varieties of ground cover.
In clearings there are splashes of colourful azaleas, and a circular walk, with
intersecting paths and seats at intervals, guides the visitor through the wood.

Knightsmead

Rickman Hill Road, Chipstead CR5 3LB. Tel: (01737) 551694

*Mrs C. Jones and Miss C. Collins • 7m E of Epsom, 1m SW of Coulsdon, 3m SE of
Banstead, off B2032 • Open 10th June, 11am – 4pm, 13th June, 2 – 5.30pm,
and by appt • Entrance: £2, accompanied children 50p* ● ⬛ WC ⚹ ⚘

When the present owners came here over a decade ago, the half-acre garden was
overshadowed by vast Lawson cypresses. Now there are shrub roses and clematis,
with arcs of smaller trees underplanted with spring bulbs and woodland plants
such as erythroniums, trilliums and pure-colour-bred hellebores. A graceful 18-
metre deodar cedar dominates this well-designed plantsman's garden, and a lily
pond, roses climbing over an arch and beds of shrubs and perennials give year-
round interest. On heavy clay soil, a bog garden, peat bed and limestone scree
provide ideal conditions for choice plants. Walls support climbers and a conservatory extends the range. There is also a pergola and water features.

22 Knoll Road

Dorking RH4 3EP. Tel: (01306) 883280

*David and Anne Drummond • From one-way system turn left up Horsham Road
(A2003). Knoll Road is on right just after Bush Inn • Open 30th May, 2nd
June for NGS, and for individuals and parties by appt • Entrance: £2, children
free* NEW ● ⬛ WC ⚹ ⚘ ⚲

Approaching up a short steep drive cut through banks, the visitor is introduced first to the garden lying behind the house. The owners' love of plants is
evident everywhere: in the large collection of alpines in troughs and raised
beds, and in the interesting mixed borders surrounding the lawn, which has a
labyrinth of ancient design cut into it. A catalpa stands in a miniature meadow,
and room is also found for a pond, a peat bed, a fern *allée* and a conservatory.
Arranged around the garden are intriguing artefacts from many countries; a
list with their histories is available. The front garden, with its pebbles and
dramatic plants, comes as a complete surprise.

Langshott Manor

Langshott, Horley RH6 9LN. Tel: (01293) 786680

*Mr and Mrs Peter Hinchcliffe • 6m S of Redhill, 4m N of Crawley. From Horley
on A23 turn right at Chequers Hotel roundabout into Ladbroke Road and*

continue about 1m. Manor is on right • Open all year, daily • Entrance: free
○ 🍵 ✕ WC ᵫ ⊲ 🌡 ♿ B&B

This beautifully restored Grade-II Elizabethan manor house, draped in roses, clematis and a huge *Magnolia grandiflora*, is tucked away down a country lane; it is now a hotel. The peaceful setting is enhanced by a garden whose design complements the house. A sunken rose garden with borders edged in box contains an interesting star-shaped brick-and-tile feature with roses growing up a central pillar. The terrace of mellow stone and brick is edged with lavender. A pleached lime avenue curves around one side of the croquet lawn, and a hornbeam pergola leads from the entrance drive down towards it. A small orchard of old varieties of fruit on dwarf rooting stock contains a turf seat and a colourful mixed bed of herbs and salad plants. There is also a small lake with ducks and a rustic stone bridge separating the birds' domain from the ornamental part, planted with water lilies and moisture-loving plants.

Leith Hill Rhododendron Wood

Tanhurst Lane, Coldharbour. Tel: (01306) 712711/712153

The National Trust • 5m S of Dorking. Take Coldharbour Road and continue to Leith Hill. At next junction keep right, then fork left. Wood immediately on left • Tower open 9th April to Sept, Wed, 10 – 5pm, Sat, Sun and Bank Holiday Mons, 11am – 5pm; Oct to March, Sat, Sun, 11am – 3.30pm. Closed 25th Dec • Rhododendron wood open all year, daily, during daylight hours • Entrance: £1.50 per car for wood (2003 price) • Other information: Light refreshments when tower open ○ 🍴 ᵫ ⊲

The wood was originally part of the estate of Leith Hill Place, once the home of the composer Ralph Vaughan Williams. Beside the car park is an extensive picnic area, and below this the rhododendrons and azaleas are a blaze of colour in April and May. There has been some replanting and the paths have been improved. An immense tulip tree, *Liriodendron tulipifera*, can be seen in the field beyond, and there are spectacular views. Further on, the mature trees create a shady area for rhododendrons in soft colours.

Little Lodge

Watts Road, Thames Ditton KT7 0BX. Tel: (020) 8339 0931

Mr and Mrs Peter Hickman • 1m N of Esher. From London take A3. In Thames Ditton village follow High Street down Watts Road. Giggs Hill Green is ahead, house is opposite library • Open 6th June, 11.30am – 5.30pm, 9th June, 2.30 – 8.30pm, and by appt at other times • Entrance: £2.50 (£3.50 after 6pm), children free ● 🍵 WC ᵫ 🌿 ♿

The house rests comfortably in its own lush surround, and in the front garden a pond and wild planting with formal topiary beds give little hint of the large cottage garden behind the house. Against the densely covered house walls is a paved suntrap with a wide variety of containers and unusual plants. The main lawned area has herbaceous borders and island beds with secret spots defined by yew hedges. A vegetable garden with raised well-stocked beds edged in box adds to the charm of this much-visited garden.

Loseley Park ★

Compton, Guildford GU3 1HS. Tel: (01483) 304440

Mr and Mrs M.G. More-Molyneux • 3m SW of Guildford, W of A3, off B3000 • House open 2nd June to Aug, Wed – Sun and Bank Holiday Mons, 1pm – 5pm • Garden open 3rd May to Sept, Wed – Sun and Bank Holiday Mons, 11am – 5pm • Entrance: £3, OAPs/disabled £2.50, children £1.50 (house and garden £6, OAPs/disabled £5, children £3) ◑ ☕ ✕ WC & ✿ ⚭ ☗

The Elizabethan house is surrounded by parkland. Hidden away at the side of the house, the vast walled garden has been transformed: based on a Gertrude Jekyll design, six gardens have been created, each with their own theme and character. The old mulberry is still there and a medlar with a group of palms. An enchanting rose garden with low box hedges is filled with old-fashioned roses, carefully labelled; box balls and circles emphasise the design, while pillars of roses and hollies give height. Along one side is an arcade of vine and clematis. A herb garden displays culinary, medicinal and ornamental herbs in triangular beds and others used in cosmetics, lotions and dyes, all well labelled. Quartets of domed acacias stand at the intersections of the main paths, and golden malus (crab apple) form a square avenue in the fruit and flower garden, which is planted in bold fiery colours. In contrast, the fountain garden is planted with white and silver flowers and foliage to create a romantic atmosphere. A wide range of produce is grown in the attractive vegetable garden. Future plans include a wildflower meadow. The moat walk shelters a long border of sun-loving plants, including yuccas (don't step back while admiring them). Near the entrance to the garden is an ancient wisteria and a good herbaceous border.

Munstead Wood ★ [Historic Garden Grade I]

Heath Lane, Busbridge, Godalming GU7 1UN. Tel: (01483) 417867

Sir Robert and Lady Clark • From Godalming take B2130 to Busbridge. Heath Lane is on left opposite church • Open 18th April, 23rd May, 13th June, 2 – 6pm, and by appt • Entrance: £3, OAPs £1.50, children free ◐ ☕ WC & ✈ ✿

Gertrude Jekyll began to make her own garden here in 1883, when she was forty; the house, designed by Edwin Lutyens, was built thirteen years later. The garden, carefully restored to Jekyll's original plans over the past decade, reveals the extent of her genius for both planting and design. A river of daffodils flows onto the front lawn from a birch copse. A wide grass path through mature rhododendrons creates a vista to and from woodland and the house, and there are walks among scented azaleas in soft and vibrant colours. The wide west lawn leads past a sunken rock garden and shrubbery to the main border, 60 metres long, backed by a high wall of local Bargate stone. Jekyll grew hot red and orange flowers in the centre, shading out through yellows, blues and mauves to white at either end. The spring and summer gardens are reached through an arched doorway. Returning towards the house, past the rose-covered pergola and summerhouse, visitors discover the nut walk and the aster garden, white borders and lavender-fringed paths; a primula garden is hidden away to one side. At the back of the house is a cool courtyard with festoons of *Clematis montana*, paving and a pool. Jekyll had eight gardeners tending 15 acres: now 10 acres are maintained by just two.

Painshill Park ★★ [Historic Garden Grade I]

Portsmouth Road, Cobham KT11 1JE. Tel: (01932) 868113

Painshill Park Trust • 4m SW of Esher, W of Cobham. From M25 junction 10, take A3 and A245. Entrance 200 metres from A245/A307 roundabout • Open all year: March to Oct, Wed – Sun and Bank Holiday Mons, 10.30am – 6pm; Nov to Feb, Tues – Thurs, Sat, Sun and Bank Holiday Mons, 11am – 4pm or dusk if earlier. Closed 25th Dec. Parties of 10 or more (incl. school parties) by appt • Entrance: £6, concessions £5.25, children (5–16) £3.50 • Other information: Children under 16 must be accompanied. Wheelchairs and electric buggies available by prior booking ◑ ⬛ ✗ 🖼 WC ᪥ ♨ ◉ ✑

The Hon. Charles Hamilton created Painshill – contemporary with Stowe and Stourhead – between 1738 and 1773, when it was sold after he ran out of funds. The garden was well maintained until World War II, then in 1948 it was sold off in lots and all but lost. Between 1974 and 1980 Elmbridge Council bought up most of the land; the following year the Painshill Park Trust was formed and began the task of restoration. The landscaped park, which now covers 160 acres, was designed around a serpentine 14-acre lake fed from the River Mole by a spectacular waterwheel. The restored Chinese bridge, opened in 1988, leads to an island and a magical grotto, the main chamber of which is 12 metres across, hung with stalactites and lined with shards of glistening felspar. The mausoleum, near the river, was depicted on one of the plates of Catherine the Great's Wedgwood 'Frog Service'; a further reach of the lake reflects an abbey ruin. The focal point of the garden is the elegant Gothick temple on higher ground. It is approached across a grassed 'amphitheatre' encircled by formal eighteenth-century-style shrubberies. A dramatic blue and white Turkish tent with a gold coronet stands on a plateau among informal plantings. In the distance is the Gothick tower. The great cedar of Lebanon, 36½ metres high and with a girth of 10 metres, is reputedly the largest in Europe. The vineyard has been replanted on a southern slope as it was in Charles Hamilton's day. Much has been achieved, and the Trust has plans to complete the restoration of the grotto and rebuild more of the original features, including the 'missing' Temple of Bacchus. Painshill needs 80,000 visitors annually to meet running costs, and the capital costs of completing the project will be the subject of fund-raising appeals for some years to come.

Polesden Lacey ★ [Historic Garden Grade II*]

Dorking RH5 6BD. Tel: (01372) 452048/458203 (Infoline)

The National Trust • 5m NW of Dorking, 2m S of Great Bookham off A246 Leatherhead – Guildford road • House open 27th March to 7th Nov, Wed – Sun and Bank Holiday Mons, 11am – 5pm • Grounds open all year, daily,

11am – 6pm, or dusk if earlier (last admission 5pm) • Entrance: £4, children £2 (house and grounds £7, children £3.50, pre-booked parties of 15 or more £6 per person) • Other information: Parking 150 metres away. Disabled parking area. Batricar available on pre-booked basis. Braille guide available. Picnics and dogs permitted outside formal garden only. Open-air theatre and concerts last two weeks in June ○ ☕ ✕ 🍴 WC & ⬥ ✍ 🎁 ♿

This 30-acre garden has grown up over several centuries. Richard Brinsley Sheridan, the dramatist who owned the house for over twenty years, lengthened the Long Walk before he died here in 1816. The present house was built a few years later by Cubitt in the Greek classical manner for an owner who made extensive alterations and planted over 20,000 trees. In the Edwardian era the society hostess The Hon. Mrs Greville laid out the formal walled gardens; her tomb stands near the house in the centre of a lawn surrounded by yew hedges. The garden was further developed early in the twentieth century and given to the Trust in 1944. The walled rose garden is in four square compartments divided by paths and arched over by wooden pergolas, and the area is dominated by a water tower covered with an ancient Chinese wisteria. Small gardens of peonies, bearded irises and beds of different kinds of lavender lead to a winter garden overshadowed by ironwood trees (*Parrotia persica*), a long herbaceous border and a sunken garden. A fragrant evergreen *Clematis armandii*, flowering in April, grows on the wall of the house. A detailed garden guide is available. Stunning walks through the landscape of the North Downs have been constructed on the estate, including one suitable for wheelchairs.

Ramster

Chiddingfold, Godalming GU8 4SN. Tel: (01428) 654167

Mr and Mrs P. Gunn • NE of Haslemere, 1½ m S of Chiddingfold on A283 • Open 24th April to 27th June, daily, 11am – 5pm, and for parties by appt • Entrance: £4, children free • Other information: Teas daily in May, and on weekend open days. Sculpture exhibition 1st to 26th May, daily, 11am – 5pm. Possible for wheelchairs in dry weather only ○ ☕ 🍴 WC & ⬥ ✍ ♿

A local nursery originally laid out the garden in 1890 in the Japanese style fashionable at the time. Bamboos, stone lanterns and a splendid double row of *Acer palmatum* 'Dissectum Atropurpureum' remain from that time. In 1922 the property was bought by Sir Henry and Lady Norman, Mrs Gunn's grandparents. Lady Norman grew up at Bodnant and many of the plants at Ramster came from there. The 20 acres of natural woodland, stream and lakes provide an ideal setting for rhododendrons and azaleas, camellias, magnolias and unusual trees. A collection of over 200 old hardy hybrid azaleas is a more recent addition, and a bog garden was planted in 1998. The millennium garden on the old tennis court, by contrast, is paved, with two ponds connected by a rill, and four raised beds of three tiers each, built of concrete blocks. The planting follows the colour wheel, with an appropriate tree (*Acer palmatum* 'Senkaki' in the 'hot' section), underplanted with bulbs, herbaceous perennials and shrubs.

RHS Garden Wisley ★★ [Historic Garden Grade II*]

Wisley, Woking GU23 6QB. Tel: (01483) 224234

Royal Horticultural Society • 7m NE of Guildford, on A3. Signed from M25 junction 10 south. Trains to West Byfleet or Woking; taxi service usually available at stations, and bus service from Woking station early May to end-Sept (departs 11am, returns 4pm) • Open all year, daily, 10am – 6pm (opens 9am Sat and Sun, closes 4.30pm Nov to Feb) • Entrance: free to RHS members; otherwise £6, children (6–16) £2, under 6 free; companion for wheelchair-bound or blind visitors free (2003 prices) • Other information: Disabled and shaded parking ○ ⬤ ✕ 🐾 WC ♿ 🌿 🛒 🍽 ⚲

Wisley Garden was presented to the Royal Horticultural Society in 1903 by Sir Thomas Hanbury, who created the famous La Mortola garden in Italy. The Society's first major development was the rock garden, a fashionable feature at the time, sections of which were reconstructed in the 1980s. The broadwalk leads between double mixed borders, each over $120 \times 5\frac{1}{2}$ metres, to a country garden designed by Penelope Hobhouse, then to rose gardens and onwards to Battleston Hill and East Battleston, with azaleas, rhododendrons, hydrangeas and lilies. Over the crest of the hill, on the southern slope, is the Mediterranean garden, planted since the Great Storm of 1987 and, beyond it, the Portsmouth Field. Here the Society, as the leading international trials institution, holds trials of plants, flowers and vegetables, including, every year, delphiniums, sweet peas and dahlias. To the east is the winter garden; to the west the 32-acre Jubilee Arboretum encircles the fruit field, where growing trees can be compared. In 1980 displays of hedging and ground cover were planted between the arboretum and the glasshouses to compare rates of growth. The temperate house, the central section of the main glasshouse, has been completely redesigned: at one end is a curved area for subjects preferring arid conditions, at the other end a water feature with plants enjoying moisture, and in the centre a circular seasonal display area. The orchid house is naturalistic, with a stream and bridge. Nearby the popular model gardens include a collection of bonsai and prize-winning gardens transported from the Chelsea Flower Show; others display fruit and vegetables – 1000 varieties of top, bush and soft fruit are grown. Lucy Huntington's redesigned herb garden is now open. The peaceful pinetum, the riverside walk and the new heather garden in Howard's Field lie beyond the restaurant. The lakes nearby have been enlarged and made more naturalistic, with planting mainly for winter effect. Sir Geoffrey Jellicoe designed the canal and loggia in front of the laboratory. Martin Lane Fox and the garden staff have transformed the walled garden – a sun trap which now shelters Italian cypresses, Chusan palms, tree ferns and a host of tender plants. Beyond the rockery along the lower path through the trees are new, dramatic meadow-style borders, each 11 metres deep and 146 metres long, designed by the Dutch garden designer and plantsman Piet Oudolf. An avenue of *Cornus kousa* var. *chinensis* and shrubs backs herbaceous perennials and grasses planted in diagonal drifts to give a ribbon effect. At the top is the staff's own millennium project, a fruit mount with a spectacular view of the Surrey countryside; stepover apples grow round the base and the spiral path is bordered by blackberries and vines. Occasional displays of sculpture are among the most recent attractions. The laboratory, built in 1916 in Tudor style, is the hub of the Society's advisory service to members: identifying plants, answering queries on pests and diseases and gardening problems. Talks and demonstrations of gardening techniques are given, informative walks conducted, and a training programme run for students. The combination of learning and pleasure is the essence of Wisley, as well over half a million visitors discover each year as they explore the 240 acres. A reading room is near the restaurant, and the bookshop should be visited.

Savill Garden ★★ [Historic Park Grade I]

Wick Lane, Englefield Green TW20 0UU. Tel: (01753) 847518

Administered by the Crown Estate Commissioners • 4m W of Staines, 5m S of Windsor. From A30, turn into Wick Road and follow signs, or follow signs from Englefield Green • Open all year, daily, 10am – 6pm (closes 4pm Nov to Feb). Closed 25th, 26th Dec • Entrance: £3.25 – £5.50, OAPs/parties £2.75 – £5 (all seasonal), accompanied children under 16 free (2003 prices). Guided tours available ○ ☕ ✕ WC ⅙ ✿ 🏬 🍽

A particularly fine woodland garden covering some 35 acres, it contains a wide range of rhododendrons, camellias, magnolias, hydrangeas and a great variety of other trees and shrubs producing a wealth of colour throughout the seasons. A wonderful collection of hostas and ferns flourishes in the shadier areas. Meconopsis and primulas are splendid in June, while lilies are the highlight of high summer and the tweedy autumn colours are almost as satisfying in their mellowness as the jauntier spring hues. A more formal area is devoted to modern roses, herbaceous borders, a range of alpines and an interesting and attractive dry garden. The Golden Jubilee Garden, planted in cool colours, has a central vista lined by pink and blue lavender; at its heart is a water sculpture designed by Barry Mason. An imposing temperate house was opened in 1995 where tender subjects – tree ferns, mimosas, eucryphias and delicate shrubs – are arranged in tiered beds and underplanted with exotics. Metal obelisks support non-hardy climbers; *Lapageria rosea* is on the main wall. The minimum temperature maintained in the 36½ x 18-metre glasshouse is only 2°C (38°F), easily achieved in a conservatory.

Shulbrede Priory

(see West Sussex)

Street House

The Street, Thursley, Godalming GU8 6QE. Tel: (01252) 703216

Mr and Mrs B.M. Francis • 6m SW of Godalming, just W of A3 between Milford and Hindhead, near road junction in Thursley • Open several times April to July for charity (telephone for details). Private parties welcome by appt • Entrance: £2.50, children 50p • Other information: Parking on recreation ground behind house, off A3 ● ☕ WC ⅙ ◁▷ ✿

Sir Edwin Lutyens spent his early years at this listed Regency house, and it was said that he first met Gertrude Jekyll here. There are three separate gardens around the house. A walled garden is full of interesting plants, trees and shrubs, including an immense false acacia (*Robinia pseudoacacia*), a Japanese snowball tree (*Viburnum plicatum* 'Sterile') and *Rubus* 'Benenden'. The main lawn is surrounded by shrubs with a curving backdrop of fine limes, while the lower lawn is framed by dazzling rhododendrons and azaleas and has splendid views. There is an unusual astrological feature constructed with Bargate-stone unearthed from the garden and local ironstone.

Sutton Place ★★ [Historic Garden Grade II*]

Guildford GU4 7QV. Tel: (01483) 504455

Sutton Place Foundation • 3m N of Guildford off A3 • Open by appt for pre-booked parties, but property up for sale, so essential to check ◑ WC &

Henry VIII gave Sutton Place to Sir Richard Weston in the early sixteenth century and it remained in the family until this century. Paul Getty lived here in the 1960s and '70s; in 1980 Stanley Seeger, the oil magnate, arrived and commissioned Jellicoe to design a new garden on a grand scale. In 1986 Sutton Place was sold and Sutton Place Foundation established. Further restoration and development included a rose garden in soft colours with a central arbour, the beds divided like a cake and edged with box. The walls are clothed in climbers and the borders punctuated by conical yews. A long rose arch separates it from a *potager*. Beyond the wall a Jellicoe path with false perspective passes huge decorative urns bought from Mentmore. Thoughtfully surrounded by yew hedges is Ben Nicolson's magnificent and cool 'White Wall' sculpture. The Ellipse Garden is approached by curving paths through a shrubbery planned to give scent throughout the year; in the centre is a pool with a funereal fountain bordered by an ellipse of pleached hornbeams. As well as a camellia garden and an 18-acre woodland garden going down to the River Wey, there is an orchard of different varieties of apples, pears and plums, underplanted with daffodils. Across the south front of the house is a vast lawn with mature trees, including a magnificent Atlas cedar, its branches sweeping the ground; a dramatic Victorian fountain has been placed as the focal point of a yew bauble avenue leading from the mansion. Citrus trees grow in boxes in front of the house, with herbaceous borders on either side, one in hot and one in cool colours. High-arching pleached limes lead to Jellicoe's two-storey summerhouse, designed to balance a sixteenth-century one in the old walled garden. His Paradise Garden, now more prosaically renamed the East Walled Garden, is a delight of rose arbours around little fountain pools, curving brick paths, tall laburnum arches and mixed planting. A moat with water lilies divides it from the house. Jellicoe's secret moss garden has gone, and now the enormous, central plane tree, with its welcome circular seat, stands on a square lawn with borders planted in purples and blues. The pool garden has a silver and old gold scheme and a Gertrude Jekyll shelter. At the front of the house, beyond a double avenue of American oaks, is a vast lake designed by Jellicoe in the shape of a foetus, part of his allegorical theme.

Titsey Place [Historic Garden Grade II]

Titsey Hill, Oxted RH8 0SD. Tel: (01273) 407077/407056 (Information line)

Trustees of the Titsey Foundation • 1m E of Oxted, 9m W of Sevenoaks. Leave M25 at junction 6. From A25 E of Oxted, turn left into Limpsfield (signed to Warlingham). At end of High Street fork left into Blue House Lane and first right into Water Lane • House open • Garden open 12th April, 3rd May; 31st May to 30th Aug, daily; all 1 – 5pm • Entrance: £2, children £1 (house and garden £4.50, no concession for children) • Other information: Parking through park near walled garden, or by gate for woodland walks with long walk to garden ● WC ⬥*

The recently restored 18-acre gardens and grounds have been in the same family for 400 years. An unusual knot border stretches across the front of the house, and below it herbaceous borders curve round a fountain. An ancient yew guards old gravestones. Two modern rose gardens are attractively planned, but the colour schemes are unappealing. Magnificent mature trees dominate the lawns, which lead down to two lakes divided by a bridge and a cascade; the larger lake has an island, and a stream has been planted with marginals. The walls of the one-acre Victorian kitchen garden, damaged by a World War II bomb, are now rebuilt, supporting espaliered fruit behind deep borders of old-fashioned roses and annuals. It is divided classically at crossing points, two ironwork gazebos giving height in the centre. Box-edged beds are filled with vegetables, salad crops, herbs and 100 varieties of tomatoes, raised from seed collected all over the world. There are strawberries too, and flowers for cutting. Against the south wall greenhouses shelter collections of alstroemerias, pelargoniums and tender varieties of tomatoes and peaches. The central glasshouse displays exotic and more familiar plants in pots, and from here the central path leads out into the gardens. Two woodland walks are open, free, all the year.

Vale End

Albury, Guildford GU5 9BE. Tel: (01483) 202296

Mr and Mrs J. Foulsham • 4½ m SE of Guildford. From Albury take A248 W for ¼ m • Open for NGS, and by appt • Entrance: £2.50, children free ● 🖳 🧺 WC ⬥ 🌱

In an idyllic setting with views of a mill pond backed by woodland, this one-acre walled garden is arranged on different levels. In spring it has a mass of bulbs, especially tulips. The sloping lawn is bordered by old roses and old favourites as well as less familiar perennials. The terrace in front of the house is a sun trap, the border filled with subjects that thrive in hot, dry conditions. Beyond a yew hedge, a cool area is shaded by a spreading magnolia; above, edging a walk, stand clipped yew boxes and a catenary of posts and rope swags, festooned with roses, wisteria and vines. An attractive courtyard is hidden behind the house. Steps by a new pantiled cascade lead up to a fruit, vegetable and herb garden level with the roof.

The Valley Gardens (Windsor Great Park) ★★

Wick Road, Englefield Green TW20 0VU. Tel: (01753) 847518

Administered by the Crown Estate Commissioners • 4m W of Staines, 5m S of Windsor. From A30 turn into Wick Road and look for burgundy-coloured signs to car park entrance adjoining Valley Gardens, avoiding a 2m round walk • Open all year, daily, 8am – 7pm (or dusk if earlier). Possible closure if weather inclement • Entrance: car and occupants £4 (April, May £5.50) (10p, 20p, 50p and £1 coins only) (2003 price) • Other information: Refreshments and plants for sale at Savill Garden (see entry) ○ 🌱 **WC** ♿ ♿

One of Britain's most discriminating and experienced garden visitors, the late Arthur Hellyer, suggested that the Valley Gardens are among the best examples of the 'natural' gardening style in England. With hardly any artefacts or attempts to introduce architectural features, they are merely a tract of undulating grassland (on the north side of Virginia Water) divided by several shallow valleys, that has been enriched by the introduction of a fine collection of trees and shrubs. They were started by the royal gardener Sir Eric Savill, when he ran out of room in the Savill Garden. One of the valleys is filled with deciduous azaleas. In another, the Punchbowl, evergreen azaleas rise in tiers below a canopy of maples. Notable too are collections of flowering cherries, a garden of heathers which amply demonstrates their ability to provide colour during all seasons, and one of the world's most extensive collections of hollies. Lovers of formal gardening might be forgiven for suggesting that the Valley Gardens have something of that rather too open, amorphous, scrupulously kept feel found in America. *Virginia Water Lake* [Historic Park Grade I], off the A30, adjacent to the junction with the A329, was a grand eighteenth-century ornamental addition to Windsor Great Park created by the Duke of Cumberland, who became its Ranger in 1746. It had dams, rockwork and a cascade. There was a fake 'Mandarin yacht', a Chinese pavilion and a Gothick belvedere with a mighty single-arch bridge spanning the water. Alas, almost all have disappeared, but the woodland and the lovely one-and-a-half-mile lake, full of fish and wildfowl, survive, and there is still a colonnade of pillars from the Roman site of Leptis Magna in Libya.

Vann [Historic Garden Grade II]

Hambledon, Godalming GU8 4EF. Tel: (01428) 683413

Mrs M.B. Caroe • 11m S of Guildford, 6m S of Godalming. Take A283 to Wormley, turn left at Hambledon crossroads into Vann Lane and continue for 2m • Open several days for NGS mid-March to Sept, and by appt. Parties by written appt • Entrance: £3.50, children 50p • Other information: Refreshments for parties by prior arrangement and on some open days only. Limited toilet facilities. Limited access for wheelchairs ◖ **WC** ♿ ♿

The Grade-II-listed house (not open), standing in five acres of garden, dates from 1542 – the name derives from the word 'fen'. The oldest part of the garden is at the front, enclosed by clipped yew hedges, divided by paths and planted in cottage-garden style. Behind the house a stone pergola (W.D.

Caröe, 1907), underplanted with shade-lovers, strides out towards an old field pond. The woodland water garden was designed with the help of Gertrude Jekyll, who supplied the plants in 1911. It has a winding stream, crossed and recrossed by Bargate-stone paths and swathed in lush planting; above the pond a narrow, stone-walled stream is enclosed by a yew walk planted in 1909. A serpentine crinkle-crankle wall supports fruit trees, and there are double borders in the vegetable garden and island beds in the orchard.

The Walled Garden

Sunbury Park, Thames Street, Sunbury–on–Thames. Tel: (01784) 451499 (Community Services)

Spelthorne Borough Council • 3m E of Staines, in Sunbury-on-Thames via B375 Thames Street. Entrance through car park • Open all year, daily except 25th Dec, 8am – dusk • Entrance: free • Other information: Wheelchair available on request ○ **WC** &

The original house was built for a courtier of Elizabeth I, and the hearth return for 1664 shows it, with its 27 hearths, to have been the largest domestic building in Sunbury. A later house was pulled down in 1946 and the site bought by Surrey County Council; the local borough council began to develop the walled garden in 1985. A pergola leads to beds of roses of the Victorian era. Adding interest are knot gardens of lavender and box, parterres, modern roses and island beds of plants from all over the world. There are climbers against the walls and gates which lead through to Sunbury Park. During the summer, exhibitions of sculpture, paintings, etc. are on view and a band plays at published times.

Winkworth Arboretum

Hascombe Road, Godalming GU8 4AD. Tel: (01483) 208477

The National Trust • 2m SE of Godalming, E of B2130. Signposted • Open all year, daily, dawn – dusk (but may be closed in bad weather, especially high winds) • Entrance: £4, children (5–16) £2, family £10, cyclists and public transport users 50% discount, carers with the disabled free. Pre-booked guided tours available • Other information: Coaches must pre-book. Disabled parking. Possible for wheelchairs but some steps and steep paths. Shop and tearoom closed Mon and Tues but open Bank Holiday Mons ○ 🅿 🍴 **WC** & ♿ ♿ ♿ ♿

Winkworth is open 365 days of the year, so is a great place to take the family for a walk on Christmas Day or any other. A new brochure celebrates fifty years of Trust ownership. The 60 plant families and 150 genera grown here provide variety and interest throughout the year. In spring there are slopes carpeted in bluebells, then azaleas, rhododendrons, cherries, and in the autumn sorbus, liquidambars, acers and nyssas. The arboretum contains a National Collection of whitebeams. The hillside setting and two lakes give pleasing views from almost all of the site. The boathouse is a tranquil resting place with views over the water from the balcony.

SUSSEX, EAST

Two-starred gardens are marked on the map with a black square.

Bateman's [Historic Garden Grade II]

Burwash, Etchingham TN19 7DS. Tel: (01435) 882302

The National Trust • 14m E of Uckfield, 10m SE of Tunbridge Wells, ½ m S of Burwash off A265 • House and mill (which grinds flour most Sats in open season) open 3rd April to Oct, Wed – Sat, 11am – 5pm • Garden open 6th to 28th March, Sat, Sun, 11am – 4pm; 3rd April to Oct, Sat – Wed (but open Good Friday), 11am – 5pm • Entrance: £5.20, children £2.60, family £13, pre-booked parties of 15 or more £4.40 per person (house, mill and garden) • Other information: Picnics in area provided. Dog creche available ◑ ☕ ✕ 🍽 WC ⅗ ♿ ♀

Kipling may be more screened than read these days, but his home from 1902 to 1936 is much visited. The house was built in 1634 and the rooms and study remain as they were during the period when he wrote many of his best-known works. Much of the garden was his doing and contains formal lawns with yew hedges, a rose garden and pond, a wild garden, and, on the right as you descend from the car park, an exceptional herb garden. Not far away in Rottingdean is the *Grange Museum* [open weekdays, 10am – 4pm and Sun, 2 – 4pm], opposite which are two acres of garden, formerly part of the house the Kiplings rented on their return from India. These *Kipling Gardens* are open on weekdays.

Bates Green

Arlington, Polegate BN26 6SH. Tel: (01323) 482039

Mrs Carolyn McCutchan • 7m NW of Eastbourne, 2½ m SW of A22, 2m S of Michelham Priory (see entry) at Upper Dicker. Approach Arlington passing Old Oak Inn on right, continue for 350 metres, turn right along small lane. Signposted • Open for NGS, and by appt • Entrance: £2.50 ◑ ☕ 🍽 WC ⅗ ♀ **B&B**

Successful and original groupings of plants express the owner's flair for using colour and foliage to create atmosphere and effect. Overall this might be described as a 'plantsman's artistic garden'. A splendid mature oak isolated after the 1987 hurricane has been underplanted with foliage plants rejoicing in the dappled shade. Bark paths interweave between the planting and under the young trees. The warm and sheltered area of the former vegetable garden has colour-themed borders of sun-loving plants and foliage contrast. A serpentine path leads from the front of the old farmhouse to the pond where water-loving plants are skilfully grouped. Views from the pond are of the adjoining woodland where there are delightful walks in the bluebell season. A raised-bed vegetable area includes a glasshouse and frames and an adjacent monocot garden.

Brickwall [Historic Garden Grade II]

Northiam, Rye TN31 6NL. Tel: (01797) 253388

The Frewen Educational Trust • 9m N of Hastings on B2088 • Open July, Aug,
Wed, 2 – 5pm • Entrance: £3, children under 10 free • Other information:
Coaches by appt ● ㅎ ☜ ⚲

This is an interesting example of a Stuart garden, and care has been taken to
use the plants, such as daylilies, bergamots, *Lychnis chalcedonica*, Cheddar pinks
and columbines, chosen by Jane Frewen when she was making and planting it
between 1680 and 1720. There are two old mulberries, groups of clipped yew,
and a superb pleached beech walk. A striking modern addition is a garden with
green and golden yew chessmen in iron frames, set in squares of white and
black limestone chips. Great Dixter (see entry) is not far away.

Charleston

Firle, Lewes BN8 6LL. Tel: (01323) 811265/811626

The Charleston Trust • 6m E of Lewes on A27 between Firle and Selmeston •
House open (guided tours Wed – Sat) • Garden open April to Oct, Wed – Sun
and Bank Holiday Mons, 2 – 6pm (opens July and Aug, 11.30am, Mon – Sat,
2pm Suns and Bank Holiday Mon) • Entrance: £2.50, children £1 (farmhouse
and garden £6, children £4.50) ◐ ☕ ▦ WC ㅎ ⏥ ⚲

Created by artists of the Bloomsbury Group, this is a delightful example of a
garden fashioned during the 1920s by an idiosyncratic group of highly creative
people. The walled garden has been meticulously restored through painstaking research and from the memories of people who visited when Vanessa Bell
and Duncan Grant lived at the farmhouse and of those like Angelica Garnett
and Quentin Bell who spent their childhood there.

Clinton Lodge ★

Fletching, Uckfield TN22 3ST. Tel: (01825) 722952

Mr and Mrs Hugh Collum • 4m W of Uckfield off A272. Turn N at Piltdown
and continue 1½ m to Fletching. House is in main street surrounded by yew
hedge • Open for NGS probably 6th, 7th, 18th, 25th June, 2nd, 9th July, 20th
Aug, 2 – 5.30pm, and for private parties by appt • Entrance: £3.50 ● ☕ WC
ㅎ ⚲

The house was enlarged by the Earl of Sheffield for his daughter, who married
Sir Henry Clinton, one of the three generals of Waterloo. The eighteenth-
century façade is set in a tree-lined lawn, flanked by a newly created canal, and
overlooking parkland. The 1987 storm removed the old oaks but these have
been replanted in a Repton-style landscape leading to a tall stone pillar on the
hill. The garden itself is of about six acres of clay soil divided into areas by
period. The Elizabethan herb garden has camomile paths and turf seats, and
four knot gardens. The Victorian era is represented by a tall white, yellow and
blue herbaceous border; the Pre-Raphaelites by an *allée* of white roses,
clematis, purple vines and lilies; the twentieth century by an unusual swim-

ming pool garden encircled by an arcade of apples. A wildflower meadow is reached through an avenue lined with fastigiate hornbeams, and a pleached lime avenue leads to the medieval herb garden and a *potager*. An enclosed garden of old and English roses is trained at nose height to enjoy the scent.

Cobblers ★

Mount Pleasant, Tollwood Road, Jarvis Brook, Crowborough TN6 2ND. Tel: (01892) 655969

Martin and Barbara Furniss • On A26 at Crowborough Cross take B2100 towards Crowborough and Jarvis Brook station. At second crossroads take Tollwood Road • Open several days May to Sept for NGS, all 2 – 5pm • Entrance: £4 (inc. home-made tea), children £1 ◕ ☕ ✕ WC WC ♿

A lifetime's gardening creativity and enthusiasm by architect Martin Furniss has made this a superb example of a plantsman's garden. The sloping site, sheltered by fine trees and mature shrubs, has been most skilfully exploited, with magnificent mixed borders at the highest point and lawns sweeping down to the beautiful water garden fed by a plant-fringed stream, where lush architectural foliage is offset by flowering marginals. Throughout the two acres surrounding the early-seventeenth-century house, a perfect balance has been achieved between a seemingly artless informality and a strong visual sense of scale, contrast and form. Near the house, the controlled profusion of planting creates a tapestry of colour and texture to provide interest from spring to autumn; huge shrub roses enhance the summer spectacle. The weathered brick paths and unusual seats made by the owner add character to a fine garden.

Great Dixter ★★ [Historic Garden Grade I]

Dixter Road, Northiam, Rye TN31 6PH. Tel: (01797) 252878

Christopher Lloyd and Olivia Eller • 10m N of Hastings, ½ m N of Northiam. Turn off A28 at Northiam post office • House open • Garden open April to mid-Oct, daily except Mon (but open Bank Holiday Mons), 2 – 5pm • Entrance: £4.50, children £1 (house and garden £6, children £1.50) (2003 prices) ◑
WC ♿

One of the best-known gardens in Britain surrounds the fifteenth-century house bought in 1920 by Nathaniel Lloyd and restored by Lutyens. The sunken garden was designed and constructed by Mr Lloyd, and his son Christopher has continued his family's great gardening tradition, backed up by a strong team under head gardener Fergus Garrett. Within the series of gardens is to be found fine topiary, a magnificent mixed long border, and an exotic garden, spectacular in autumn; the latest development is a pebble mosaic of two reclining dachshunds. Throughout the complex of gardens are pockets of wild flowers, and spring at Great Dixter is famous for the huge drifts of naturalised bulbs. Another feature is the use of theme plants such as forget-me-nots and verbena, which have, as Christopher Lloyd has written, a unifying role and are threaded through the borders. This is truly a plantsman's garden, but also a joy for anyone who enjoys gardening in the finest tradition. Over the past decade, when many might have thought of him as an established pioneer of the British garden, Lloyd has made it clear that he regards his life's work as being to coax new and exciting effects out of plants of all kinds, employing his wizardry with colour, shape and texture to create idiosyncratic and unforgettable plantings. To see what this means, visit Dixter.

Hailsham Grange

Hailsham BN27 1BL. Tel: (01323) 844248

Mr Noel Thompson • 8m N of Eastbourne off A22. Turn off Hailsham High Street into Vicarage Road and park in public car park • Open 6th June, 4th July for NGS, 2 – 5.30pm, and for parties by appt • Entrance: £2, children free NEW ⬤ WC ♿ ⚘

The present owner has devised a horticultural stage set with the handsome early-eighteenth-century former vicarage centre-stage. Masterly use of stilted hornbeam and box hedging divides the garden into a series of formal rooms where the restraint of clipped foliage, gravel and brick contrasts with romantic, colour-themed planting. A central turf path leading to a rose-swagged gazebo reveals a *coup de théâtre* of hidden double borders filled with cream, yellow and apricot perennials, skilfully planted for texture and form and set against the backdrop of church and sheltering trees. Box parterres, a tiny white garden, a shady secret wilderness and a bulb-filled spinney combine with topiary and statuary to create a classical estate in miniature.

Herstmonceux Castle [Historic Garden Grade II*]

Hailsham BN27 1RN. Tel: (01323) 833816

Queen's University (Canada) • 14m N of Eastbourne, off A271 Hailsham – Bexhill road • Open 9th April to 24th Oct, daily, 10am – 6pm (last admission 5pm) • Entrance: £4.50, children (under 15) £3, children (under 5) free, concessions £3, family £11 ◗ ⬤ 🗑 WC ♿ ⬤ ⚘ 🍴 🍵

The approach to the impressive and beautiful red-brick fifteenth-century castle, set in parkland, is past the science centre housed in the erstwhile observatory buildings. The path continues alongside the moat (filled with water lilies) and under gnarled but stately 300-year-old sweet chestnuts. The gardens are contained within ancient walls and yew hedges, some castellated; they include a herb garden, a Shakespeare garden, rose gardens and herbaceous borders. An orchard has been planted with old varieties of fruit trees. A woodland area has an azalea walk and a lake, sculptures and a folly garden. In all, 550 acres of woodland and gardens, including a nature trail.

Ketleys

Rosemary Lane, Flimwell TN5 7PS. Tel: (01580) 879300

Helen Yemm • 12m SE of Tunbridge Wells on A21. At Flimwell traffic lights turn onto B2087 signed to Ticehurst. Rosemary Lane is ½ mile on right • Open two days in June for NGS, and for small parties of 10 – 20 by appt • Entrance: £3 • Other information: Very limited parking NEW ● ⬤

The two-and-a-half acres surrounding the weather-boarded farmhouse have been transformed in the last five years by garden writer Helen Yemm into distinctively contrasting areas. The tiny cottage front garden and sheltered gravel garden near the kitchen are filled with a profusion of herbs, low-growing grasses, euphorbias, alliums and annual poppies. Little wooden gates lead to the old orchard, filled with wild flowers, where roses scramble through the apple trees, and to a sophisticated lawned area with distant views of Bewl Water and a formal pool shaded by a huge willow. There is a tiny kitchen garden and beyond lies the wilderness, where a natural pond and a bog garden lush with gunnera and bamboo have been created. Mown paths lead through a spinney of larch and birch filled with bracken and foxgloves to a circular glade. The skilled planting demonstrates how to use plants for varying situations; to explore the garden in the company of its lively and knowledgeable creator brings the whole place alive.

King John's Lodge

Sheepstreet Lane, Etchingham TN19 7AZ. Tel: (01580) 819232

Mr and Mrs R.A. Cunningham • 10m NW of Hastings, 2m SW of A21/A265 junction. In Etchingham, turn into Church Lane leading to Sheepstreet Lane • Open April to Sept, daily, 11am – 6pm, and by appt • Entrance: £3, children free • Other information: Shop selling statuary ◑ 🍵 🍽 WC & ⬦ ⚘ ☕ B&B

This romantic four-acre garden has been developed since the present owners came here more than a decade ago. The 1980s' hurricane removed sixty per cent of the mature trees, leaving some rhododendrons, a small number of formal and informal water features and a wild garden incorporating bulbs in spring and roses in summer. Main borders include softly coloured old roses and herbaceous plantings. The Secret Garden leads to an attractive garden house, which then passes through a meadow to a barn covered in roses and honeysuckle. The historic Jacobean house forms a delightful backdrop. The garden has been increased to feature a large pond near the wild garden, with a bridge leading to a shaded garden and on through gates to the parkland with its many fine trees.

Lamb House

West Street, Rye TN31 7ES. Tel: (01892) 890651

The National Trust • In centre of Rye, in West Street, facing W end of church • House open • Garden open 2nd April to Oct, Wed, Sat, 2 – 6pm • Entrance: house and garden £2.60, children £1.30, family £6.50, groups £2.20 per person • Other information: No parking near house ◑

Although the author Henry James professed to have no horticultural knowledge, with help from Alfred Parsons he left a town garden of charm and interest. An oasis of calm in this crowded town, there are unusual trees and shrubs, vegetable and herb gardens and herbaceous plantings enclosed within the one-acre walled garden.

Merriment Gardens ★

Hawkhurst Road, Hurst Green TN19 7RA. Tel: (01580) 860666

Mr and Mrs Mark Buchele and Mr David Weeks • 7m N of Battle, on A229 (formerly A265) between Hawkhurst and Hurst Green • Open April to Sept, daily, 10am – 5pm • Entrance: £3.50, children £2 (2003 prices) ◑ ♨ ✕ <u>WC</u> ⬚ ⬚ ⬚ ⬚

Pools and pergolas surrounded by boldly curving beds of impressive colour-themed planting create a rich source of inspiration particularly relevant to modern gardens, Well-designed and labelled schemes show plant associations for every situation, from a shady bog garden filled with lush marginals to the sun-baked gravelled entrance garden where *Humulus lupulus* 'Aureus' scrambles over striking yellow arches. Between these extremes are imaginatively stocked borders in every colour combination, filled with herbaceous plants and shrubs underplanted with tulips, alliums and hostas. Fine specimen trees like *Gleditsia triacanthos* 'Sunburst' and *Catalpa bignonioides* 'Aurea' have been chosen for their decorative foliage. Benches, arbours and summerhouses afford good vantage points, and handsome containers and sculpture make effective focal points. The health and vigour of the plants, which include many excellent varieties of clematis, is remarkable. A welcoming tea room and a shady terrace combine with a superbly stocked nursery.

Michelham Priory ★

Upper Dicker, Hailsham BN27 3QS. Tel: (01323) 844224

Sussex Past • 10m N of Eastbourne off A22 and A27. Signposted • House, museum and gardens open March to Oct, Tues – Sun and Bank Holiday Mons, 10.30am – 5pm; Aug, daily, 10.30am – 5.30pm (closes 4pm March and Oct) • Entrance: £5, OAPs and students £4.30, children (5–15) £2.60, family £12.20. Rates available for pre-booked parties of 15 or more (2003 prices) • Other information: Working watermill and museum ◑ ♨ ✕ ⬚ <u>WC</u> ⬚ ⬚ ⬚ ⬚ ⬚

Initially, the main horticultural interest of this historic monastic site – more a Tudor manor than a monastery – was the physic garden, but every visit reveals new areas of interest within the moated site of the old priory. The stewponds have been re-excavated and fringed with exotic waterside plants, particularly those with dramatic foliage. The widely sweeping herbaceous border is planted in swathes of bold colour and form and leads into new areas of mixed planting alongside the moat and adjoining the buildings. A fine ornamental *potager* with vegetables, flowers and a central pergola lies behind the walls of a yew hedge. Young liquidambars and catalpas are gaining strength and enliven the foreground to the more natural moatside planting. A cloister garden in the well courtyard, inspired by illustrations of medieval Marian gardens, includes an arbour, turf seat and raised beds for medicinal plants.

Monk's House ★

Rodmell, Lewes BN7 3HF. Tel: (01892) 890651

The National Trust • 4m S of Lewes off old A275, now C7. In Rodmell follow signs to church and continue 400 metres to house • House and garden open 2nd April to Oct, Wed, Sat, 2 – 5.30pm • Entrance: £2.60, children £1.30, family £6.50 ◑ 🦽 WC ♿

This was the cottage home of Virginia and Leonard Woolf from 1919 until his death in 1969. There are three ponds, one in dewpond style. An orchard, underplanted with spring bulbs, contains a comprehensive collection of daffodils, and Leonard's vegetable area is still thriving. Flint stone walls and yew hedges frame the more formal herbaceous areas, leading to a typical Sussex flint church at the bottom of the garden. The one-and-three-quarter-acre garden is a mixture of chalk and clay, nurturing a wide variety of species. Among the interesting specimen trees are *Salix hastata* 'Wehrhahnii', *Magnolia liliiflora*, walnut and mulberry.

Pashley Manor ★

Ticehurst TN5 7HE. Tel: (01580) 200888

Mr and Mrs James A. Sellick • 16m N of Hastings, 10m SE of Tunbridge Wells on B2099 between Ticehurst and A21. Signposted • Open probably April to Sept, Tues – Thurs, Sat and Bank Holiday Mons, 11am – 5pm. Coach parties by appt only • Entrance: £6, OAPs £5.50 (2003 prices) ◑ 🍽 🦽 WC ♿ 🌿 🎁 🍵

The Grade-I-listed Tudor timber-framed ironmaster's house of 1550 with a George I rear elevation dated 1720 stands in some eight acres of formal garden, being completely renovated with advice from Anthony du Gard Pasley. The planting is subtle, with emphasis on colour and form, pale colours blending with carefully chosen foliage. From the terrace and over the magnificent fountain there is a view of the Mad Jack Fuller obelisk at Brightling Beacon several miles away. A series of enclosed gardens is surrounded by beautiful eighteenth-century walls. Grass paths, some concealing the original Victorian gravel beneath, lead through camellia and rhododendron shrubberies. A large fountain, and the natural springs which feed a series of ponds falling away from the house and medieval moat, ensure that the sound of falling water is heard over most of the garden. Access to a small island with a classical temple is by a decorative iron bridge. A golden garden has been created, and other projects include an extensive planting of tulips to complement the Tulip Festival held in May; an avenue of pleached pear trees underplanted with box so arranged as to give a view through to magnificent hydrangeas; and a garden of old-fashioned roses to complement the Summer Flower Festival held in June. In the 1½ -acre garden to the south-east of the old walled garden, ample herbaceous borders are planted with strong colours and sculptural plants for late-summer flowering.

Perch Hill Farm

Willingford Lane, Brightling, Robertsbridge TN32 5HP, Tel: (01424) 838899

Sarah Raven and Adam Nicholson • At Burwash Weald on A265, turn down Willingford Lane opposite Wheel Inn; garden 1 mile • Open 1st, 3rd May, 28th, 30th Aug, 12th Sept, 11am – 4pm, and for parties by appt • Entrance: £4, children free • Other information: Flower-arranging talks by Sarah Raven on open days, £25 (must pre-book). Wide range of courses available May to Dec
[NEW] ● 🍴 ✕ WC 🚻 ♿ ♨ 🏛 🌱 ✿

Set high on a windy hill, with stunning views across valleys to the distant Brightling Beacon, the Sussex farmhouse is surrounded by a series of character-ful garden spaces – 1½ acres in all. The Oast Garden, now sheltered by a loggia and handsome walls, is planted with bold architectural plants and washes of brilliant colour. The vegetable garden, divided by brick paths and chestnut hurdles, is filled with unusual vegetables on trial, and the herb garden is a decorative delight defined by box topiary. The hot colours of cosmos and cannas add late-season interest in the dahlia garden. A constant supply of favourite flowers for Sarah Raven's courses comes from the large cutting garden, where a hazel tunnel clothed in sweet peas is sensational in summer. Inspirational.

Royal Pavilion Gardens [Historic Garden Grade II]

Brighton BN1 1EE. Tel: (01273) 290900

Brighton & Hove City Council • In central Brighton • Royal Pavilion open April to Sept, daily, 9.30am – 5pm; Oct to March, daily except 25th, 26th Dec, 10am – 4.30pm • Garden open all year, daily • Entrance: gardens free (Royal Pavilion £5.80, concessions £4, children under 16 £3.40) (2003 prices) • Other information: New garden entrance to Brighton Museum and Art Gallery (open Tues – Sun) ○ WC ♿ 🏛 ✿

The gardens surrounding the Royal Pavilion have been restored to their original splendour, closely following John Nash's plans of the 1820s. Nash conceived the building and grounds as a unity, and his vision will be fully realised as the plants and shrubs continue to flourish and mature. The beds are of mixed shrubs and herbaceous plants, a combination first applied in the Regency period. Species and varieties have been selected to conform as closely as possible to the original lists of plants supplied to the Prince Regent (later King George IV). The gardens and grounds reflect the great revolution in landscape gardening that began in the 1730s, when straight lines and symme-trical shapes were banished, and in their place appeared curving paths and 'natural' groups of trees and shrubs undulating gracefully over the lawn. As visitors pass through the grounds, the magical Royal Pavilion is disclosed by a succession of varying views through the shrubs and thickets.

Sheffield Park Garden ★★ [Historic Park Grade I]

Sheffield Park TN22 3QX. Tel: (01825) 790231

The National Trust • 5m NW of Uckfield, midway between East Grinstead and Lewes E of A275 • Open 3rd Jan to Feb, Sat and Sun, 10.30am – 4pm; 2nd

March to Oct, Tues – Sun and Bank Holiday Mons, 10.30am – 6pm; 2nd Nov to 23rd Dec, Tues to Sun, 10.30am – 4pm, (last admission 1 hour before closing) • *Entrance: £5, children £2.50, family, £12.50, pre-booked parties £4.25 per person, children £2.50* • *Other information: Teas at Oak Hall. Wheelchairs and self-drive powered vehicles available* ◑ 🅿 **WC** & 🕭 ⚘ ℺

A 120-acre landscape garden and arboretum with two lakes (later extended to four, in an inverted-T formation below the house) created by 'Capability' Brown for the Earl of Sheffield in 1776. Repton worked here in 1789, and a waterfall and cascades were added later. Between 1909 and 1934 a collection of trees and shrubs notable for their autumn colour was planted, including many specimens of *Nyssa sylvatica*. These and other fine specimen trees, particularly North American varieties, provide all-year-round interest. The Trust aims to plant 9000 new trees and shrubs over the next five years to repair storm damage. Features include good water lilies in the lakes, the Queen's Walk and, in autumn, two borders of the Chinese *Gentiana sino-ornata* of amazing colour. Three new beds of brightly coloured azaleas include varieties recently rediscovered, expanding the National Collection of Ghent azaleas.

Warren House

Warren Road, Crowborough TN6 1TX. Tel: (01892) 663502

Mr and Mrs M.J. Hands • *7M NE of Uckfield off A26. From Crowborough Cross turn towards Uckfield, take 4th turning on right; garden is 1m down Warren Road. From south, take 2nd turning on left after Blue Anchor pub* • *Open for NGS, and by appt* • *Entrance: £2.50* ◑ 🅿 🍴 **WC** &

Situated in a commanding position overlooking Ashdown Forest, this is a splendid example of a garden made and tended by the owner alone – all nine acres of it. Extensive plantings of trees, shrubs, grasses and flowers skirt the sweeping lawns, and a series of different vistas display a wealth of rhododendrons and azaleas. There are wisteria and laburnum walks, and the woodland, with its ponds and tree-lined avenues, is a peaceful place in which to stroll. The original infrastructure of walls, paths and terraces has been restored, blending with the garden as a whole harmoniously into the surrounding forest.

Wellingham Herb Garden

Wellingham Lane, Nr Lewes BN7 5BSW. Tel: (01435) 883187

Grant Brickell • *2m N of Lewes off A26* • *Open Easter to Sept, Sat and Sun, 10.30am – 5.30pm* • *Entrance: free* ◑ & ℘

Enclosed within a walled garden is a delightful and aromatic herb garden, created since 1992. Herbs are displayed in four main box-edged beds. The walls are clothed with fruit, including medlars, and accompanied by old roses and perfumed shrubs.

SUSSEX, WEST

Two-starred gardens are marked on the map with a black square.

Berri Court

Yapton, Arundel BN18 0ED. Tel: (01243) 551663

Mr and Mrs J.C. Turner • 8m E of Chichester, 5m SW of Arundel on B2233, in Yapton between post office and Black Dog pub • Open several days during summer – check local press for details. Parties by arrangement • Entrance: £2, children free ● ▆ WC ⅋ ⌁ ℘

A series of sheltered gardens within a one-and-a-half-acre garden of great interest to plant enthusiasts. A mass of daffodils flowers in spring, together with azaleas and rhododendrons. The borders have an impressive display of herbaceous plants and many varieties of shrubs and climbing roses. Around the house are magnificent *Magnolia grandiflora*, *Drimys winteri* and *Clematis rehderiana*. Elsewhere, *Clematis* x *jackmanii* clambers through trees, and different varieties of eucalyptus are grown throughout the garden. The vigorous *Rosa glauca* (syn. *Rosa rubrifolia*) provides spectacular foliage colour contrast, and *Tropaeolum speciosum* create splashes of vermilion through the borders.

Borde Hill Garden ★ [Historic Garden Grade II*]

Balcombe Road, Haywards Heath RH16 1XP. Tel: (01444) 450326

Borde Hill Gardens Ltd • 1½ m N of Haywards Heath on Balcombe – Haywards Heath road • House open to groups by appt • Garden open all year, daily, 10am – 6pm (or dusk if earlier); guided tours by arrangement • Entrance: £6, children £3.50, season ticket £16.50, children £10 ○ ▆ ✕ ▆ WC ⅋ ⌁ ℘ ▦ ☕ ℘

This is one of Sussex's fine plant-hunter gardens. Created from 1893 with trees and shrubs collected from Asia, Tasmania, the Andes and Europe, it has award-winning collections of azaleas, rhododendrons, magnolias and camellias surrounded by 220 acres of parkland and bluebell woods. New classic rose and Italian gardens have been designed by Robin Williams, and Heritage Lottery funds have been used to restore the glasshouse area and create a new area in the old potting sheds – now a series of small rooms with herbs and tender species. The Long Dell has much new planting of Sino-Himalayan species surrounding Chusan palms, which survived the 1987 hurricane. The Round Dell is a lush hidden area with Chusan palms, bamboos and huge gunneras. A white garden was created in 2002, together with further planting in the Italian garden and restoration of the woods. Additional attractions include a pirates' adventure playground, coarse and children's fishing, extensive woodland walks and lakes.

Burpham Place

Burpham, Arundel BN18 9RH. Tel: (01903) 884833

Elizabeth Woodhouse • ½ m S of Arundel, turn off A27 Arundel – Worthing road and continue for 2m through Wepham to Burpham • Open by appt • Entrance: charge ◐ ☕ **B&B**

Most of the small garden was redesigned in 2002 by the garden designer/owner. New colour-themed herbaceous borders were introduced around two circles of grass with a succession of unusual and native plants from May to September. Special emphasis is on 'sad' colours – black, brown, peach, silver and grey plants and grasses flow through several beds. New varieties of verbascum, foxglove and iris star, and other beds feature mauve/lime and magenta/pink plantings. A Gothic arch leads to a path in the small wild garden full of cow parsley and mullein which meanders through silver birch trees down to a stream and folly. The whole is designed to blend with the Downs beyond.

Champs Hill

Coldwaltham, Pulborough RH20 1LY. Tel: (01798) 831868

Mr and Mrs D. Bowerman • 2m SW of Pulborough off A29. At Coldwaltham turn W towards Fittleworth. Garden is 300 metres on right • Open on many days for NGS, 11am – 4pm (Sun 2 – 5pm). Private parties welcome – please telephone • Entrance: £2.50, children free ◑ ☕ **WC** ಈ ℘

This fine and unusual heathland garden, with over 300 varieties of heather grown alongside dwarf conifers and other interesting plants, is complemented by spectacular views of the Arun Valley and South Downs. The heathers are best viewed in March and August, but a walk in May through the 27 acres of natural woodland interplanted with a wealth of rhododendron and azalea species is a real bonus, and sculptures and a trickling stream add to the appeal.

Chantry Green House

Church Street, Steyning BN44 3YB. Tel: (01903) 814824

Mr R.S. Forrow and Mrs J.B. McNeil • 8m N of Worthing, 10m NW of Brighton off A283. From Steyning High Street, opposite White Horse Inn, turn into Church Street. House is 150 metres on left • Open 12th, 13th June, 2 – 5pm • Entrance: £2, children 50p • Other information: Parking in Fletchers Croft car park opposite church ◐ ☕

A sheltered and well-maintained one-acre town garden with some interesting features – a water garden, a kitchen garden, an American garden and an arboretum with unusual trees, including *Liriodendron tulipifera* 'Aureomarginatum', *Lagerstroemia indica*, the crape myrtle, and *Eriobotrya japonica*, the Japanese loquat. In a corner, an old wall fountain is the focus of a shady area planted with ferns and hostas. Also of note are the many varieties of cistus.

Chidmere House

Chidham Lane, Chidham, Chichester PO18 8TD. Tel: (01243) 572287

*Jackie and David Russell • 6m W of Chichester, 4m E of Emsworth, S of A259.
Turn right at S end of Chidham • Open in 2004 by appt only • Entrance: £2,
children free* ● ● WC & ◁ ◁◁

The Tudor house (not open) is excitingly situated next to Chidmere Pond, so
much so that the well-filled greenhouse which borders the mere almost feels
like a houseboat. The garden was laid out in 1930–36 by the late Hugo
Baxendale, and is divided into separate compartments by tall hedges of
hornbeam and yew. Flowering cherries, sheets of daffodils and bluebells
ensure that it is spectacular in the spring. There are other fine flowering
trees, while the house supports a Banksia rose and two wisterias. Later, the
roses, a fine herbaceous border, a tulip tree and *Taxodium distichum* command
attention. The garden will be expanded by 12 acres and include a wildflower
meadow and orchards of fruit trees.

Coates Manor

Fittleworth, Pulborough RH20 1ES. Tel: (01798) 865356

*Mrs G.H. Thorp • 3m W of Pulborough, ½ m S of Fittleworth off B2138 • Open
by appt only • Entrance: £2, children 20p* ● ● WC

This one-acre garden has an abundance of trees and shrubs carefully chosen to
give long-term pleasure. There are ferns, grasses such as *Stipa gigantea* like
frozen waterfalls, *Phlomis italica* and *P. chrysophylla*, blue and white agapanthus,
and many specimen trees chosen for their foliage, berries or autumn colour. A
small paved walled garden has *Clerodendrum trichotomum*, clematis, phlox and
other scented flowers. The owner is particularly interested in colour contrasts
and light and shade, and goes to considerable lengths to find the best species
available. Look out for a variegated ivy contrasting well with *Cotinus coggygria*
'Notcutt's Variety' on a wall by the house; a mature copper beech tree stands
nearby. The delightful Elizabethan house is partly covered in variegated ivy
and euonymus, linking it with the surrounding countryside.

Denmans ★

Fontwell, Arundel BN18 0SU. Tel: (01243) 542808

*John Brookes • 5m E of Chichester. Turn S off A27, W of Fontwell racecourse •
Open March to Oct, daily, 9am – 5pm • Entrance: £2.95, OAPs £2.65,
children over 4 £1.75, parties of 15 or more £2.50 per person if pre-booked
(2003 prices)* ◑ ● ✕ ▦ WC & ◢ ⛪ ◁

John Brookes, one of Britain's most influential designers, moved here in 1980.
The whole site relies for its drama on foliage plants – even in spring, in spite of
the early flowering bulbs, visitors come away with minds full of euphorbias,
yuccas, phormiums and mounds of clipped box. The centre of the garden is a
river of pebbles and gravel against which the leaves of thistles and bamboo
show up dramatically. There are some choice tulips and other spring bulbs,

interesting primulas and spring-flowering shrubs, including a *Stachyurus praecox*. The walled garden contains many old roses as well as a herb garden and perennials and is at its finest in late June and July. Outside the house is the south garden; very tender species are planted in another gravel area near a circular pond. In late summer a large border of *Romneya coulteri*, the Californian tree poppy, is at its best, while autumn and winter interest are given by the stems of willow and cornus, and by the leaves of *Parrotia persica* and staphylea, the bladder nut.

Duckyls

Sharpthorne, East Grinstead RH19 4LP. Tel: (01342) 811038

Lady Taylor • 4m SW of East Grinstead, 6m E of Crawley. Take B2028 S at Turners Hill and fork left after 1m to W Hoathly. Turn left at sign to Gravetye Manor (see entry) on right • Open April, May, July, Tues, Thurs, 11am – 5pm, and for small parties by appt • Entrance: £3, children £1 ● ▄ ▓ WC ♿ ✿ B&B

These 14 acres of terraced and hilly garden, with breathtaking views of woods and Weir Wood Reservoir, are established with rhododendrons and azaleas among carpets of bluebells and daffodils. The secret garden is now a parterre garden with some beds underplanted with irises. There are ponds and a bog garden with gunnera and philadelphus, and some interesting new trees are maturing near the house. The woods are occupied by a small flock of Soay sheep. Only a portion of the garden is maintained to the same standard as that around the house, yet the place stays immensely attractive.

Frith Hill

Northchapel, Petworth GU28 9JE. Tel: (01428) 707531

Mr and Mrs P. Warne • 8m NE of Midhurst, 7m N of Petworth on A283. In Northchapel turn E into Pipers Lane by Deep Well Inn; after ³/₄ m turn left into bridleway past Peacocks Farm • Open three times a year for charity (send s.a.e. for further details) and for parties of 10 or more by appt • Entrance: £3, children free • Other information: Possible for wheelchairs but gravel paths ● ▄ WC ♿ ✿

This one-acre garden of variety and charm surrounds a brick-and-tile-hung house and relates effortlessly to the countryside beyond, with surprises in every corner. The first walled garden has a huge herbaceous border to the north and leads to another walled area with an arbour and old-fashioned roses enclosed by clipped box, then proceeds through a gate to a millennium pond facing splendid views of the rolling weald. Overlooking the view is a third garden with a paved area and beside the gazebo a shady white garden with massed *rugosa* roses ('Blanc Double de Coubert'), water bubbling over a millstone, and a herb garden with alliums, mallows and almost black opium poppies as well as culinary herbs. There are also massive white ramblers, lilies, good hydrangeas and interesting pots everywhere.

Goodwood House and Sculpture Park

(see SCULPTURE AT GOODWOOD)

Gravetye Manor [Historic Garden Grade II*]

Vowels Lane, East Grinstead RH19 4LJ. Tel: (01342) 810567

Mr P. Herbert • 4m S of East Grinstead between M23 and A22. By M23, take exit 10 onto A264 towards East Grinstead. After 2m, at roundabout, take 3rd exit on B2028. 1m after Turners Hill fork left and follow signs • Open all year to hotel and restaurant guests, perimeter footpath only for public, Tues and Fri • Entrance: free • Other information: Parking in drive in lay-by before gates. Toilet facilities for hotel and restaurant guests only ●

This historically important garden has been carefully restored in the style pioneered here by William Robinson. The area around the hotel (which can only be visited by guests or visitors having lunch or dinner) can be viewed from a public footpath which passes through wildflower meadows to the north and south. Several large shrubs and trees – parrotias, rhododendrons and pines – are part of the original planting. The path down the magnolia walk bordered by shrubbery and large camellias leads down through Smugglers Lane to a lake, continues along the lakeside and completes the circumnavigation back to the entrance. For those interested in the Robinsonian doctrine, it is well worth giving yourself a treat, either by spending a night at Gravetye or simply going for a meal, though do not plan a visit without asking about prices and availability beforehand. For a complete contrast, not far away is *Birch Farm Nursery* (formerly part of the original Robinson estate), open all year for the sale of Ingwersen's renowned alpines – 1800 different varieties.

Hammerwood House

Iping, Midhurst GU29 0PF. Tel: (01730) 813635

The Hon Mrs Lakin • 3m W of Midhurst, 1m N of A272 • Open 9th, 16th May, 2 – 5pm • Entrance: £2.50, children free ● 🍵 WC ♿ ⬧ 🌱 ℺

This is a peaceful country garden, formerly part of a Regency vicarage, planted with care and a fine eye for good plants. Although the rhododendrons and azaleas give it its most spectacular flowering season, there are some splendid camellias, magnolias, cornus and other specimen trees. Across a meadow from the main garden is the woodland walk by a stream. Wild flowers abound.

High Beeches Gardens ★ [Historic Garden Grade II*]

Handcross RH17 6HQ. Tel: (01444) 400589

High Beeches Gardens Conservation Trust • 5m S of Crawley, 1m E of Handcross, S of B2110 • Open March to June, Sept, Oct, Thurs – Tues, 1 – 5pm • Entrance: £5, accompanied children under 14 free. Guided parties of 10 or more by appt any day or time, £8 per person with refreshments by arrangement ◑ 🍵 ✕ 🍽 WC ℺

The delightful woodland and water garden of over 25 acres encourages its visitors to explore the different walks that meander, like the streams, through the collection of rare trees and unusual shrubs. Alongside the National Collection of stewartias are glades of rhododendrons, azaleas and magnolias. (In 2003 *Magnolia campbellii* 'Lanarth' flowered for the first time – after a wait of 50 years.) Originally designed by Colonel Loder in 1906, the garden is always extending its collection, which is well labelled. There are many benches and a summerhouse from which to enjoy the scents and colours. Starting with bluebells in spring, stunning cornus, a wildflower meadow, a glade of *Gentiana asclepiadea* (the only naturalised site of willow gentian in Britain) and *Eucryphia glutinosa* in late August, and a carpet of *Cyclamen hederifolium* at the base of the oak tree at Centre Pond adding to the wonderful autumn colours, this is a garden of many seasons.

Highdown [Historic Garden Grade II*]

Littlehampton Road, Goring-by-Sea BN12 6PE. Tel: (01903) 501054

Worthing Borough Council • 3m W of Worthing, N of A259 • Open April to Sept, daily, 10am – 6pm; Oct to March, Mon – Fri, 10am – 4.30pm (closes 4pm Dec, Jan) • Entrance: free – donation box • Other information: Refreshments at peak times only. Toilet facilities available to wheelchair users only with key ○ 🍴 **WC** ᕕ ᕐ

Gardeners everywhere, but particularly those who garden on chalk, must be grateful to Worthing Council for their continuing high standard of care for Sir Frederick Stern's chosen site in 1910 in and around a bare chalk pit donated to Worthing in 1968. The season starts with a mass of hellebores; narcissi and cowslips follow, and then peonies and iris. Brilliant scarlet anemones are naturalised in the grass; later come agapanthus, eremurus and autumn crocus. And these are just the flowers. There are also fine specimen trees – davidia, arbutus and cornus – and many shrubs, including roses, ceanothus, kolkwitzia and laburnum, with buddleia and paulownia to follow. Dramatic banks of pittosporum are a striking feature. Highdown is a plantsman's garden – it doesn't have a lot of shape – and unfortunately there are few labels. There is, however, an explanatory display at the entrance.

Leonardslee – Lakes and Gardens ★★ [Historic Garden Grade I]

Lower Beeding, Horsham RH13 6PP. Tel: (01403) 891212

The Loder family • 4m SW of Handcross and M23 on B2110/A281 • Open April to Oct, daily, 9.30am – 6pm • Entrance: April £6, May, Mon – Fri £7, Sat, Sun £8, June to Oct, £6, children £4. Season tickets £16 • Other information: Victorian motor car collection ◑ 🍽 ✕ 🍴 **WC** 🌿 ♿ 🏛

The garden was enlarged by Sir Edmund Loder, who raised the famous *Rhododendron* 'Loderi' hybrids with their huge scented flowers. This 240-acre valley with its seven lakes, its collection of rhododendrons (some are nearly two hundred years old), azaleas, camellias, acers, magnolias, snowdrop tree and other shrubs, and sweeps of bluebells, combines to form a beautiful landscape in a peaceful setting. Wallabies (used as mowing machines) have lived semi-wild in parts of the valley for over 100 years. The immense scale and the mature trees give the garden a special quality. In the morning light the colours of the rhododendrons and azaleas glow and their heady scent fills the air. The rock garden has ferns and Kurume azaleas in perfect small scale. Nor should visitors miss the excellent bonsai exhibition, the alpine house with 400 species of alpines, and the miniature landscape of the 'Behind the Doll's House' exhibition. Selehurst (see entry) is opposite.

Little Wantley

Fryern Road, Storrington RH20 4BJ. Tel: (01903) 740747

Hilary Barnes • 10m NW of Worthing, 1m N of Storrington on Fryern Road towards West Chiltington; entrance on right • Open for NGS and by appt for small parties • Entrance: £2.50 • Other information: Teas by arrangement
[NEW] ● WC

Before 1997 the garden was 1½ acres with a 2½ -acre field adjoining. The owners bought the field, wanted a lake and got one – all 1½ acres of it! By the top pond *Rosa* 'Grouse' creates an enchanting arch over the waterfall into the main lake, which has lush marginal planting. The surrounding area, including newly landscaped mounds, has been extensively planted. Among the willows, bamboos, birches and conifers is a pretty stand of cut-leaf alders and a trio of swamp cypresses. Once the trees are more mature the autumn colour will be stunning. There is also a rose walk (*R. pimpinellifolia*) and a nut walk. Roses are a passion and abound everywhere. There are walks from which you can look down on the lake and the views back to the house; the run-off from the lake has been planted up as a lush stream with a path beside it. An arch of golden hop leads into a *potager* with four stunning *Rosa* 'Helexa' (*R.* 'Super Excelsa') standing sentinel. Beyond the hedge is the front drive and lawn with a beautiful copper beech, a cedar and a dawn redwood. The long front border has magnificent hostas, and tucked away behind the rhododendrons is a fern gully. On the other side of the house an old wooden pergola heralds a small hidden garden, and a new metal pergola smothered in roses, wisteria and clematis invites the visitor round another border and back towards the lake.

Nymans ★★ [Historic Garden Grade II*]

Handcross, Haywards Heath RH17 6EB. Tel: (01444) 40032/0016/00157

The National Trust • 4m S of Crawley. At southern end of Handcross, off A23/ M23 and A279. Signposted • House open as garden, 11am – 4.30pm • Garden open April to Oct, Wed – Sun and Bank Holiday Mons, 11am – 6pm (or dusk if earlier); Nov to Feb, Sat and Sun, weather permitting (telephone for details) • Entrance: house and garden £6, children £3, family £15, parties of 15 or more £5 per person. Joint ticket available with Standen (see entry) Wed – Fri only, £9 (2003 prices) • Other information: Coaches must pre-book. Batricar, wheelchairs and braille/audio guide available on free loan. Map of wheelchair route available ● 🍽 ✕ 🍴 WC ♿ ♨ 🏛 ♿

An historic collection of fine trees, shrubs and plants in a beautifully structured setting, full of outstanding and almost theatrical effects: sheets of white narcissi under sorbus trees, a circle of camellias around a lawn with an urn in the centre, a vista down a lime avenue with a 'prospect' at the end and several borders of great splendour. Originally started by Ludwig Messel in 1890, it was continued by his son Leonard and daughter-in-law Maud, and then by his granddaughter, Anne, Countess of Rosse. Although the garden was given to the Trust in 1954, Lady Rosse continued to live there until her death in 1992. The library, drawing room and walled garden have been preserved and opened to the public. These rooms lead out to the forecourt and a knot garden. The picturesque ruins of the original building (built *c.* 1928 to resemble a medieval manor house and largely destroyed by fire in 1947) are planted with clipped yew and other topiary. The Messel creations include a pinetum, a sunken garden with a stone loggia, a laurel walk, a croquet lawn, a heather garden, roses in beds and over arbours, and magnificent herbaceous borders. Some of these areas can be viewed from on high from the mound. Bedding is always beautifully done and the whole is exceptionally well maintained. *Magnolia* x *loebneri* 'Leonard Messel' and *Eucryphia* x *nymansensis* were both raised at Nymans. An exhibition of garden history situated within the garden is a recent welcome addition. On the opposite side of the road is The Rough, a wild garden. The Trust also have in hand some 600 acres of park. This is one of the most outstanding gardens in an area of interesting ones.

Orchards

Off Wallage Lane, Rowfant, Nr. Crawley RH10 4NJ. Tel: (01342) 718280

Penelope S. Hellyer • 4m E of Crawley. From Turners Hill crossroads, turn N on B2028 for 1½ m, left into Wallage Lane, and after ¼ m right immediately after railway bridge, up farm track • Open March to Oct, Wed – Sat, 1 – 4pm; Mon, Tues by prior appt only • Entrance: £3, OAPs £2.50, accompanied children free • Other information: B&B available – send s.a.e. for details ◐ ☕ WC B&B

The late Arthur Hellyer acquired this 7½-acre plot of south-facing land in 1934. Full use has been made of the sloping terrain. Viewed from the house, an open area with magnificent conifers on either side leads down to a small pond with lush marginal plantings of *Gunnera manicata*. It is mainly a woodland garden with many striking mature specimen trees. Penelope Hellyer and her husband have added a herb and vegetable garden, a grass garden and lush herbaceous borders planted for a long season. Beneath an old apple tree is a meadow planted with wild flowers. The old swimming pool has been filled in and narrow borders around three sides planted with bearded irises; sandstone paving is laid on the fourth side with an eye-catching 'cartwheel' seat. Numerous camellias, a bluebell wood, apple orchards, a mass of bulbs, rhododendrons and late-autumn asters, conifers and a heather border make this a year-round garden.

Parham House and Gardens ★ [Historic House Grade II*]

Nr Pulborough RH20 4HS. Tel: (01903) 742021/744888

4m SE of Pulborough on A283, equidistant from A24 and A29 • House open as garden but 2 – 6pm (last admission 5pm) • Garden open 11th April to Sept, Wed, Thurs, Sun and Bank Holiday Mons, 12 noon – 6pm (last admission 5pm), also Tues, Fri in Aug. 10th, 11th July for garden weekend, and 4th, 5th Sept for flower-arranging weekend. Private parties and guided tours on other days • Entrance: £4, children £1, family £9, season ticket £16 (house and garden £6, OAPs £5.50, children £2, family £14, season ticket £24). Pre-booked parties per person: unguided of 20 or more £5; guided of 25 or more £7.50 (2003 prices) • Other information: Telephone for details of garden study and flower painting courses. Advance notice required for wheelchairs ◑ 🍴 🧺 WC 🛗 ⬳ 🖼 💡 📷*

Set in the heart of a medieval deer park on the slopes of the South Downs, the award-winning gardens of this Elizabethan house are approached through Fountain Court. A broad gravelled path leads down a gentle slope through a wrought-iron gate guarded by a pair of Istrian stone lions to a walled garden of about four acres, which retains the original quadrant layout divided by broad walks and includes an orchard and teak walk-through greenhouse. Over the last ten years the scope and character of the walled garden have been enhanced with new borders and plantings of Edwardian opulence, reaching their peak from July onwards. Recent additions are a *potager*, a rose garden and a green border, planted along the outer west wall, and a lavender garden. In one corner is an enchanting miniature house with its own garden, a delight for both children and adults. The pleasure grounds of about seven acres provide lawns and walks under stately trees to the lake, with views over the cricket ground to the South Downs. A brick and turf maze is a feature here. This is a garden for all seasons, and in spring it is dominated by the splendid 'sacred' grove of 'Mount Fuji' white-flowering cherry, over fifty years old.

Petworth House ★ [Historic Park Grade I]

Petworth GU28 0AE. Tel: (01798) 342207

The National Trust • 6½ m E of Midhurst on A272 in Petworth • House open 27th March to Oct, Sat – Wed, 11am – 5.30pm (but open Good Friday) • Pleasure ground open 13th, 14th, 20th, 21st March, 12 noon – 4pm, then 27th March to Oct, Sat – Wed, 11am – 6pm. Deer park open all year, daily, 8am – dusk • Entrance: pleasure ground £1.50, children free; deer park free (house and pleasure ground £7, children £4, family £18. Pre-booked parties of 15 or more £6.50 per person) • Other information: Parking ½ m N of Petworth on A283. Disabled visitors by arrangement, special parking available. Refreshments only on days house open • Pleasure Ground: ◑ 🍴 ✕ WC 🛗 ⬳ 💡 📷 *Deer park:* ○

Petworth is a stately palace, with one of the finest late-seventeenth-century interiors in England. The house sits in a magnificent park developed over centuries from a small enclosure for fruit and vegetables in the sixteenth century to its present size of 705 acres; it is enclosed by an impressive five-mile-long stone wall. George London worked here at the end of the seventeenth century. From 1751—63, for the 2nd Earl of Egremont, 'Capability' Brown was modifying the contours of the ground, planting cedars and many other trees and constructing the serpentine lake in front of the house. It was one of Brown's earliest designs, planned while he was still at Stowe (see entry in Buckinghamshire). Turner painted fine views of the park (as well as the interior of the house) and it is interesting to see these and have them in one's mind when strolling around the park, as Turner himself must have done many times while staying at Petworth. This is not a garden for the botanist, but it is a splendid experience all year round, and the individual trees and shrubs, including Japanese maples and rhododendrons, deserve close study. Majestic veteran trees now tower over wildflower meadows and ornamental shrubs, providing interest throughout the year. It is worth noting that at the turn of the century Petworth had over two dozen gardeners (they were always counted in dozens). Far fewer staff have, since the storms of 1987 and 1990, planted in the region of 40,000 trees.

Rymans

Apuldram, Dell Quay, Chichester PO20 7EG. Tel: (01243) 783147

Mrs Suzanna Gayford • 1m SW of Chichester. Turn off A259 (old A27) at sign to Dell Quay, Apuldram, garden on left • Open for NGS, and by appt • Entrance: £2.50, children 50p ● 🌸 WC ♿ ◁

Previously owned by Lady Anne Phillimore, a member of the Dorrien-Smith family of the famous Tresco Abbey Gardens, Isles of Scilly (see entry in Cornwall), the garden holds a number of plants with Tresco connections. Surrounding a fifteenth-century house with mellow Ventnor-stone exterior, the garden is being developed by the present owner. A walled garden filled with flowering shrubs and roses and furnished with a new pergola leads to a modern architectural water feature. The paddock opposite the old stables is now planted with a selection of trees, and two wildflower glades. Seen from within the walled garden an avenue of black poplars, *Populus nigra*, stretches beyond a magnificent wrought-iron gate to nearby twelfth-century Apuldram church. Planted with massed daffodils, the avenue is a picture in springtime. A spiral *potager* is maturing, and there is a new dahlia walk.

Sculpture at Goodwood ★

Goodwood, Chichester PO18 0QP. Tel: (01243) 538449

Mr and Mrs Wilfred Cass • 7m N of Chichester, 3m S of East Dean, between A286 and A285 (telephone (01243) 771114 for directions) • Open April to Nov, Thurs – Sat, 10.30am – 4.30pm • Entrance: £10, OAPs £8, students/children £7 (2003 prices) ◑ WC ♿ 🏛 🔦 ◁

Twenty acres of woodland have been shaped to provide a finer setting for British contemporary sculpture than any indoor gallery. The quality of the work is outstanding; the trees act as screens, giving each piece its own stage, and sometimes opening to give a backdrop of the Sussex countryside. Beautiful new gates by Wendy Ramshaw herald the entrance to the park, while at the end of one walk the spire of Chichester cathedral is borrowed sculpture of the most majestic kind. Pieces, mostly for sale, vary as works are commissioned to provide about twenty new works a year. It is worth following the directions of the printed guide on a tour of the wood – at present the visitor begins walking down to a gallery designed by architect Craig Downie. You could construct a novella with macabre undertones from the titles of some of the more recent pieces on show: Peter Burke's 'Register', Diane Maclean's 'Spine', Kenneth Armitage's 'Legs Walking', David Mach's 'Fire Breaker', Peter Randall-Page's 'Give and Take', Marc Quinn's 'The Overwhelming World of Desire' and Bill Woodrow's 'Regardless of History'.

Selehurst

Lower Beeding, Horsham RH13 6PR. Tel: (01403) 891501

Mr and Mrs M. Prideaux • 4½ m SE of Horsham on A281, opposite Leonardslee (see entry) • Open 16th May, 1 – 5pm, and for parties by appt • Entrance: £3 ● 🍽 🏷 WC ও 🌿 ♋

The 20-acre woodland garden is now emerging as a romantic landscape garden in the skilful hands of garden designer and novelist Sue Prideaux. Near the house a 30-metre rose and laburnum tunnel is underplanted with ferns, phormiums and hostas in a striking tapestry of foliage. The Italian border has purple old-fashioned roses and darkest delphiniums. A box-patterned herb knot is scented with lilies and moss roses. The walled garden shelters a huge white wisteria and herbaceous borders, the woodland a collection of tender scented rhododendrons and specimen trees, including the tallest eucalyptus in the kingdom, according to the late Alan Mitchell. A series of ponds linked by waterfalls leads ultimately to Pope's Vale, a green theatre with urns and a spring-fed tear-drop pond. A Gothick folly tower is being decorated with shells, while the Chinese pavilion on the water is planted with black bamboo and cloud-pruned myrtles; gold dragons fly through the red lacquer interior.

Shulbrede Priory

Linchmere, Haslemere, Surrey GU27 3NQ. Tel: (01428) 653049

Laura Ponsonby and Ian and Kate Russell • 2m SW of Haslemere off B2131 • Open 30th, 31st May, 29th, 30th Aug, 2 – 6pm, and by appt • Entrance: house and garden £3, children £1, parties (maximum 30) £4 per person (guided tour included) ● 🍽 🏷 WC ও 🚻

Originally an Augustinian priory, twelfth-century Shulbrede became the home of Lord Ponsonby, a writer and former pacifist MP early in the twentieth century. He and his wife Dorothea created a garden here which delighted Dorothea's father, Sir Hubert Parry, the composer and Director of the Royal College of Music, who often visited Shulbrede and composed the *Shulbrede Tunes* for piano. Their grand-daughter, Laura Ponsonby, continues to improve the garden. Cottage-style borders are seen and smelt from the house, a sunken garden gives an Italianate air, a waterside walk in the wild garden inspires a sense of mystery, and vast yew hedges enclose a series of individual gardens planted to great effect. A gem on the Sussex/Surrey borders.

Somerset Lodge

North Street, Petworth GU28 0DG. Tel: (01798) 343842

Mr and Mrs R. Harris • 6½ m E of Midhurst on A272 in Petworth, 100 metres N of church • Open some days in June, 12 noon – 6pm, and for parties by appt • Entrance: £2, children 50p ◗ 🍵 WC ⟊ 🌿 ℺

This seventeenth-century house near Petworth House (see entry), has a steeply sloping garden with splendid views towards the North Downs. In just over a decade the present owners, retired architects, have transformed an ancient orchard by creating different elements on several levels. There are small collections of classic old and species roses. Herbaceous borders, a wild garden leading to a *potager*, ponds and a gazebo contribute to the peaceful yet exuberant atmosphere. The superb woodwork has been designed and built by Mr Harris.

St Mary's House

Bramber BN44 3WE. Tel: (01903) 816205

Peter Thorogood • 8m NE of Worthing off A283 in Bramber, 1m E of Steyning • Open Easter to Sept, Thurs, Sun and Bank Holiday Mons, 2 – 6pm (last tour 5pm). Parties by appt daily, 9am – 6pm, except during public open times. Secret Garden open May to Sept, first Sun in month; tours 2.15pm, 3.15pm, 4.15pm • Entrance: formal gardens £3, children 50p; Secret Garden £2 extra, children free (house and formal gardens £5, concessions £4.50, children £2) (2003 prices) ◗ 🍵 ✕ WC ⅄ 🐾 ♖

From the small gravel garden with clipped box and yew, the path leads over a pretty stone balustraded bridge and up to the topiary garden (strange animals and birds) in front of the fifteenth-century timber-framed house. The yew tunnel beyond the gate leads to the Monk's Walk. The top lawn is enclosed by herbaceous beds, while the lower lawn has clipped yew hedges and roses; there is a beautiful *Ginkgo biloba* and lower down a small pond. The Victorian Secret Garden is now a rose garden, and a border has been planted in memory of the late Queen Mother, and the circular orchard is under restoration. A rural museum has been created in the Boulton and Paul potting shed, while the unusual 40-metre fruit wall has been cleared and will be replanted, and the pineapple pits with their original stove-house proclaim their purpose once again. Two herbaceous borders and new yew hedges are in their infancy, but will give structure to the planned knot and rose gardens. The woodland walk has been underplanted with bluebells and primroses but is mostly left to the native wildlife, with a huge fallen willow starting into growth again as an amazing living structure.

Standen

East Grinstead RH19 4NE. Tel: (01342) 323029

The National Trust • 2m S of East Grinstead, signed from A22 at Felbridge, and from B2110 • House open as garden, 11am – 5pm • Garden open 22nd

March to 9th Nov, Wed – Sun and Bank Holiday Mons, 11am – 6pm; 14th Nov to 21st Dec, Fri – Sun, 11am – 3pm • Entrance: £3, children £1.50 (house and garden £5.70, children £2.85, family £14.25); joint ticket available with Nymans (see entry) Wed – Fri only, £10, children £5 (2003 prices) • Other information: Picnics in picnic area only. Dogs in woodland walks only ◐ 💻 ✕ 🍴 WC ♿ 💝 🛍 🔦

The Philip Webb house and estate have close connections with Morris and Co., and the garden reflects much of the Arts and Crafts period of the latter part of the nineteenth century. It is made up of a succession of small, very English gardens, and the helpful leaflet lists twelve different areas or features, including bamboo and rose gardens. Perhaps the most outstanding is the little quarry (with its restored bridge), which has survived as a Victorian fernery. There are good views from this hillside garden across the Medway Valley. Two woodland walks are described in the leaflet, but these can be muddy.

Stansted Park Victorian Walled Garden

Rowlands Castle, Hampshire PO9 6DX. Tel: (023) 9241 3090

7m W of Chichester, 2m N of Westbourne, off B2149 • Garden centre and walled gardens open May to Oct, daily, 10am – 5pm (opens 10.30am Suns) • Entrance: free ◐ 💻 WC 💝 🛍

Now a garden centre, the Victorian glasshouses, conservatories and complex of walled gardens, and the circular well-head garden in the arboretum, have recently been restored. The upper walled garden holds a collection of sculptures from the 'Sculpture in the South' organisation; all of these are for sale. The site also includes a seven-acre arboretum, a falconry and a resident glass-blower on site. In the lower walled garden, Ivan Hicks' quirky and intriguing *Garden in Mind* has been replaced by a formal yew maze.

Town Place

Ketches Lane, Freshfield, Nr Scaynes Hill RH17 7NR. Tel: (01825) 790221

Mr and Mrs Anthony McGrath • 3m E of Haywards Heath. From A275 turn W at Sheffield Green into Ketches Lane (signed to Lindfield); garden is 1¼ m on left • Open 13th, 17th, 27th June, 4th, 11th, 15th July, and for parties of 20 or more by appt • Entrance: £3.50, children free ◐ 💻 WC ♿ 💝 ☕

A wonderful 3¼-acre garden created since 1990 by an ultra-keen husband-and-wife team – each year it gets a bit bigger. Wrought-iron gates open onto a lawn enclosed by low walls and old brick paths; the one to the left leads up steps to an apple tunnel and herb garden with wide downland views, then down past a big hollow oak to the dell with its attractive free-form raised pond and fountain. From here you look back across the main lawn to the 1650s' house (not open) and a 46-metre-long herbaceous border backed by a magnificent flame tapestry hedge. A rose pergola shields a small sunken rose garden, replanted in 1993 with over 100 Floribundas, and this in turn leads into the orchard and a new area by the pool with gravel paths and beds block-planted with box, screened by a line of *Rosa* 'Excelsa'. Amble through the orchard, carpeted in spring with daffodils, to the shrubbery, where you are surrounded by the astonishing circular, clipped, striped conifer hedge; beyond is the English rose garden, box-edged and planted with over 300 roses of 36 different cultivars. Tucked away in a corner are a spring garden and a hidden secret garden – follow the sound of water. There is more – copper beech hedges, a hornbeam walk, a *potager* and cutting garden and the New Territories, where a hornbeam *allée* has recently been planted. From here you can return to the main lawn to soak up a bit more of that sumptuous border.

Trotton Old Rectory

Trotton, Petersfield GU31 5EN. Tel: (01730) 813612

Captain and Mrs John Pilley • 3m W of Midhurst on A272 • Open for parties by appt • Entrance: £3 ◗

Set in the pretty Rother valley, the one-and-a-half-acre garden consists of several different areas of varying shapes and sizes, each with its own character. Many are lavishly planted, and they are separated from each other by hedges of yew, holly and beech as well as a trellis screen and walls. To the north of the house are newly planted pleached limes and box, to the south a terrace leads out into a formal rose garden. This is planted with attractive pink and white roses, contrasting with the old roses in the circular rosarium in the garden beyond, which is surrounded by mixed borders where lavender, delphiniums, campanulas and many other plants provide a riot of colour. A restful enclosure dominated by a venerable oak has gunneras, clipped yew and a lawn speckled with bulbs in spring to give variations of texture and shades of green; against the hedge are the graves of family pets. Another garden surrounds the croquet lawn. To the east of the house at a lower level is a large pond surrounded by clumps of handsome *Iris ensata*. Linking the different areas are walks lined with shrubs and hostas, hemerocallis and lilies.

Wakehurst Place Garden and
Millennium Seed Bank ★★ [Historic Garden Grade II*]

Ardingly, Haywards Heath RH17 6TN. Tel: (01444) 894066 (Infoline)

The Royal Botanic Gardens, Kew • 7m N of Haywards Heath on B2028. From London take A(M)23, A272, B2028 or A22, B2110 • Part of house open • Garden open all year, daily, except 25th Dec and 1st Jan: Nov to Jan, 10am – 4pm; Feb, 10am – 5pm; March, Oct, 10am – 6pm; April to Sept, 10am – 7pm. Guided walks available 11.30am and 2.30pm Sat, Sun and Bank Holiday Mons • Entrance: £6.50, OAPs, students and UB40 £4.50, children (under 16) free. Season tickets and Friends of Kew membership available (2003 prices)
○ ➍ ✕ 🖼 WC 🚹 ♨ 🏠 🔦 ⚲

Dating from Norman times, the estate was bought by Gerald W.E. Loder (Lord Wakehurst) in 1903. He spent thirty-three years developing the gardens, a work carried on by Sir Henry Price. The gardens have been managed by the Royal Botanic Gardens, Kew, since 1965. They have a fine collection of hardy plants arranged geographically and display four comprehensive National

Collections – betulas, hypericums, nothofagus and skimmias. Unique is the glade planted with species growing at over 3000 metres in the Himalayas. A plantation of Japanese irises is part of the extensive and fascinating water gardens. There are two walled gardens, one given over to colourful bedding schemes, the other to herbaceous borders, delightfully planted in subtle shades. Wakehurst is a place for the botanist, plantsman and garden lover, offering features of year-round interest, particularly the winter garden which bursts into colour about late November. The Wellcome Trust Millennium Building, home to an international seed bank and interactive public exhibition, opened in 2000 – futuristic and even slightly sinister in appearance, the design and presentation are masterly.

Weald and Downland Open Air Museum

Singleton, Chichester PO18 0EU. Tel: (01243) 811348

Weald & Downland Open Air Museum • 5m N of Chichester on A286 • Open March to Oct, daily, 10.30am – 6pm (last admission 5pm); Nov to Feb, Sat, Sun, 10.30am – 4pm • Entrance: £7, children £4, under 5 free, family £19, OAPs £6.50 (2003 prices) ○ 🍴 📷 ⬱ ℘ 👜 🔦 ⚲

Set in the heart of the South Downs, the main exhibits of this museum (founded in 1967) are over 45 traditional buildings, ranging from medieval to Victorian, rescued from certain destruction, restored and rebuilt on the museum's countryside site. Complementing the buildings, seven historic gardens have been researched and planted to demonstrate the changes and continuities in domestic gardens from the early 1400s to 1900. The earliest garden has only a few plants, including wild garlic and edible weeds such as fat hen. A complete medieval farmstead has been re-created around Bayleaf Farmhouse, and the replica fifteenth-century garden is planted to fulfil the gastronomic and medical needs of six adults, their children and servants from beds over four metres long and a metre wide. By the Victorian era, represented by a typical cottage garden of the period, the gardens were not only practical but showed the introduction of flowers for their beauty alone. A delightful, educational experience for those keen to enjoy period husbandry.

West Dean Gardens ★ [Historic Garden Grade II*]

West Dean, Chichester PO18 0QZ. Tel: (01243) 818210

Edward James Foundation • 6m N of Chichester on A286 • Open March to Oct, daily, 11am – 5pm (May to Sept opens 10.30am). Parties by appt • Entrance: £5, OAPs £4.50, children £2. Pre-booked parties of 20 or more £4 per person ◐ 🍴 ✕ 📷 WC ♿ ℘ 👜 🔦 ⚲

There have been gardens here since 1622; in 1836 a number of rare trees were mentioned by J.C. Loudon, and in 1891 William James bought the property and Harold Peto designed the magnificent 100-metre-long pergola. If you want to see fruit and vegetables growing, this is the garden to visit. The restored Victorian glasshouses are immaculate and the regimented rows of fruit and vegetables excellently labelled. In the orchard, backed by an old crinkle-crankle wall, are fruit trees trained in a variety of shapes and an unusual circular thatched apple store. The potting sheds now house garden-themed exhibitions. Outside the 3.5-acre walled garden you can explore the 35 acres of pleasure garden – designed around the house (now an Arts and Crafts College). Stroll the length of the pergola with its lush planting designed to flower from spring through to early autumn, then relax in the sunken garden, a mass of tulips in spring, before taking the woodland walk. The west end of the garden has been restored and replanted. The spring garden, with its enchanting summerhouse, laburnum tunnel and flintwork bridges over the River Lavant, is given an exotic jungle atmosphere by a planting of Chusan palms and bamboos; beyond is the wild garden, which has some unusual trees and is planted in more naturalistic style to blend into the surrounding parkland. From here there is an enjoyable walk through the park to *St Roche's Arboretum*, where Edward James is buried beneath the trees he loved so much.

Yew Tree Cottage ★

Turner's Hill Road, Crawley Down RH10 4EY. Tel: (01342) 714633

Mrs Hudson • 1m S of A264 between Crawley and East Grinstead. On Down Lane (B2028) opposite Grange Farm entrance, turn right and cottage is second of semi-detached on left • House open for small parties, 50p extra per person • Garden open by appt for small parties • Entrance: £1.50, children free ● 🏵 🌐

A plantsman's delight and an encouragement to all with small gardens; it is not surprising that this third-of-an-acre plot has been a prizewinner. Changes to reduce maintenance include the use of gravel and the introduction of drought-resistant plants. Inspired by the Dutch designer Piet Oudolf, several grasses have been added, such as the low-growing, feathery *Stipa tenacissima*, which has proved most successful. To the rear of the house a black marble sculpture, underplanted with hellebores, stands over a well, while the borders are bursting with colour and unusual plants. *Cornus kousa*, *Veronica virginica*, Miss Willmott's Ghost, the pink-flowered bronze elderflower, lysimachia, and a range of hellebores and astrantias are but a few of the interesting plants in this exceptional garden.

POSTCODE PLANTS DATABASE
It is often difficult to find out which plants are local to an area. The Postcode Plants Database locates the names of flowers, trees, butterflies and birds for each of Britain's 26 million home addresses. The website is www.nhm.ac.uk/science/projects/fff; simply by typing in the first four characters of their postcode, householders, schools, garden centres and councils can obtain tailor-made lists of local plants which are both hospitable and garden-worthy. Also included are the names of butterflies and birds most likely to visit gardens in each area. The lists come from innovative software, developed by Royal Mail and *FLORA-for-FAUNA* in conjunction with the Natural History Museum, which searches through hundreds of distribution maps of fauna and flora in the British Isles.

WARWICKSHIRE

Arbury Hall ★ [Historic Garden Grade II*]

Arbury, Nuneaton CV10 7PT. Tel: (024) 7638 2804

The Viscount and Viscountess Daventry • 10m N of Coventry, 3½ m SW of Nuneaton off B4102 Fillongley/Nuneaton road • House and garden open 11th, 12th April, 2nd, 3rd, 30th, 31st May, 29th, 30th Aug, 2 – 6pm (hall closes 5pm) • Entrance: £4.50, children £3 (hall and gardens £6.50, children £4, family £16, parties of 25 or more £5.50 per person) ● ▉ WC & ⬦ ⬛ ♔

A formal rose garden and climbing roses are features of this delightful, peaceful garden, distinguished also by the lakes with their wildfowl, the parkland, the drive and the bluebell woods. Especially memorable are the pollarded limes, the old walled garden and the beautiful old trees. Bulbs at the start of the season are followed by rhododendrons and azaleas, then roses in June and autumn colour from trees and shrubs. A canal system was installed years ago as a method of transport.

Avon Cottage

Ashow, Kenilworth CV8 2LE. Tel: (01926) 512850

Neil Collett • 5m NE of Warwick, 1½ m E of Kenilworth. From A452 Kenilworth – Leamington road turn onto B4115 (signed to Ashow and Stoneleigh), after ¼ m turn right into Ashow and right again. Continue to end of Ashow. Cottage is beside church • Open 5th, 6th June, and by appt • Entrance: £2, children 50p • Other information: Refreshments and toilet facilities available in village club on Suns ● ⬙

A peaceful one-and-a-half-acre garden surrounding a picturesque eighteenth-century listed cottage in a lovely riverside setting. The owner, a landscape architect, has worked organically to protect valuable wildlife habitats and there is plenty of interest in the sensitive use of reclaimed materials. Moving through archways covered with clematis, roses and honeysuckles there are surprises at every turn, and seats are strategically placed to enjoy the views, including a new one of camomile on slate. There are riotous mixed herbaceous borders, with vegetables and herbs growing among the flowers, an orchard area with domestic and water fowl, a rhododendron walkway, a collection of old-fashioned shrub roses and masses of daffodils in spring. Don't leave without crossing the footbridge to the twelfth-century church, or you will miss a sensational view of the garden.

Barton House

Barton-on-the-Heath, Moreton-in-Marsh, Gloucestershire GL56 0PJ. Tel: (01608) 674303

Mr and Mrs I.H.B. Cathie • 6m S of Shipston-on-Stour off A3400, 4m E of Moreton-in-Marsh off A44 • Open for NGS 30th May, 2 – 6pm, and for parties

of more than 25 by appt • Entrance: £3, children £1.50 • Other information:
Refreshments in coach house on open day ● 💭 WC & ♨ ℺

Borders of rhododendrons greet the visitor to the six-acre garden, set
around a manor house by Inigo Jones (not open), and throughout the
garden an excellent collection of American, species and hybrid types
provides a long flowering period. A secret garden has magnolias and
maples underplanted with camellias, pieris, embothriums, arbutus, crino-
dendrons, euphorbias and geraniums. Viewing points have been made to
enjoy the surrounding countryside, and there are some fine mature trees,
many rare plants plus National Collections of nothofagus and stewartias,
and masses of spring bulbs. Among the varied features and surprises are a
catalpa walk, a collection of moutan tree peonies (*Paeonia suffruticosa*), a
rose garden with beds of individual colours surrounding an oblong lily
pool, a Himalayan garden, a Japanese garden, herbaceous and shrub beds,
statues, archways and a copy of the portico of St Paul's, Covent Garden. A
paved roundel in the centre of the walled kitchen garden is being
developed as a Mediterranean garden with palm trees, olives and cypresses. The ornate cast-iron atrium from the Royal Exchange in Thread-
needle Street forms the roof of the orangery. The ha-ha has been lined
with clay, filled with water and furnished with an ornate iron bridge, a
Neptune platform and a garden house. Also well worth seeing is *Whichford*
Pottery off the other side of the A3400 [open all year, daily except Sun].
Although not strictly a garden, it is well worth visiting for its design ideas
as well as its stylish pots, and Jim Keeling's own garden, if you can get to
see it, is inspirational.

Charlecote Park [Historic Park Grade II*]

Charlecote, Wellesbourne, Warwick CV35 9ER. Tel: (01789) 470277

The National Trust • 5m E of Stratford-upon-Avon, 1m W of Wellesbourne •
House open as garden but 12 noon – 5pm • Garden and grounds open 6th
March to 7th Nov, Fri – Tues, 11am – 6pm (also Weds, July, Aug and Bank
Holiday weeks; closes 4.30pm, Oct, Nov). Parties by appt • Entrance: £3,
children £1.50 (house and garden £6.40, children £3.20, family £16) • Other
information: Braille guide available ◑ 💭 ✕ WC & 🏛 🌱 ℺

Home of the Lucy family since the thirteenth century, the pink brick gatehouse is the only remnant of the early Tudor house left untouched. A
courtyard garden has been designed in front of the house and a parterre
re-instated. The wild garden is interesting and the cascade will attract those
who like water features – these include a pond in the small wilderness garden,
full of wildlife. The Shakespeare border has now been made smaller and is
situated in front of the summerhouse. A new herbaceous border has been
created to give colour from early spring to the first frosts, and there is also a
new sensory garden. The park was laid out by 'Capability' Brown, who was
directed not to destroy the avenues of elms (later eliminated by Dutch elm
disease).

The Coach House

Bitham Hall, Avon Dassett CV47 2AH. Tel: (01295) 690255

Mr and Mrs G.J. Rice • 12m SE of Warwick, 7m N of Banbury off B4100. Leave M40 junction 12 at Gaydon, or from Leamington take A462 to join Banbury road. 3m after Gaydon turn left to Avon Dassett; entrance to garden is on hill. Parking on hill and in village • Open for NGS, and by appt • Entrance: £2, children free **WC** & ⬥

These two acres, set on sloping ground overlooking Edgehill, originally formed part of a Victorian garden, and are now planted for year-round interest, with many varieties of trees, shrubs, climbers and perennials. Walls give shelter to tender plants. Two areas are devoted to bush and cordon fruit trees and vegetables, and there is also a wet garden. The woodland has well-established trees and some 70 young native trees, underplanted with new shrubs, including camellias, rhododendrons and peonies. Flowering bulbs and primroses give spring interest.

Compton Scorpion Farm

Ilmington, Shipston-on-Stour CV36 4PJ. Tel: (01608) 682552

Mrs T.M. Karlsen • 8m S of Stratford-upon-Avon, 4m NW of Shipston-on-Stour off A3400. Take left fork uphill at Ilmington village hall. After 1½ m turn left down steep narrow lane and house is on left • Open all year, Mon, 2 – 5pm, and by appt • Entrance: £2, children free ● **WC** & ⬥

One of the most stunning views in the county unfolds as you drive along the ridge from Ilmington towards this farmhouse, which in 1989 was surrounded by a mere meadow, sloping steeply towards the house. The owner has worked wonders, from the small walled garden behind the house aiming at Jekyll-inspired single colour schemes, to the rose-encrusted slope beyond and the rabbit-proof vegetable garden around the old sheep shed. A spring-fed pond has been added in the orchard, and a wildflower meadow in the wild garden on the hillside is now well established. In countryside as beautiful as this you could say that she started with an advantage, but the stylish planting is all her own.

Coombe Country Park

Brinklow Road, Binley, Coventry CV3 2TL. Tel: (024) 7645 3720 (Ranger Service)

Just E of Coventry on B4027 • Open all year, daily, 7.30am – dusk • Entrance: free but parking charge ○ 🍽 ✕ 🏪 & ⬥ 🎁 🍵 🐾

Nearly 400 acres of beautiful parkland including woodland and lakeside walks, all-weather pathways, wildflower meadows and historic gardens by William Andrews Nesfield and William Miller. There are also the remains of a duck decoy and an arboretum: a SSSI includes the vast lake originally designed as part of the 'Capability' Brown landscape, which is home to wildlife, a bird hide and a heronry. Facilities include an information centre, a history video, a wildlife discovery centre and play areas.

Coughton Court ★

Alcester B49 5JA. Tel: (01789) 400777

Mrs C. Throckmorton • 8m NW of Stratford-upon-Avon, 2m N of Alcester on A435 • House open • Garden open April to June, Sept, Wed – Sun; July, Aug, Tues – Sun and Bank Holiday Mons; Oct, Sat, Sun; all 11am – 5.30pm. Parties by appt • Entrance: £5.10, children £2.50 (under 5 free), family £15, parties £4.10 (house and garden £7.45, children £3.95 (under 5 free), family £26.50) ◑ ♨ ✕ 🍴 **WC** 占 ⬥ ⚘ 🏛 ♨ ♋

The grounds complement the mid-sixteenth-century house and include a variety of gardens both formal and informal. The main garden, courtyard and walled garden were designed by Christina Williams. The redesigned orchard contains many old local varieties and there is also a chef's herb garden. The large lawn is bordered by cloistered lime walks, while a peaceful stroll beside the River Arrow reveals willows, wild garlic, ferns, hellebores and native trees and shrubs. In spring there is a bluebell wood and many bulbs to enjoy. A second lake has been drained to form a bog garden. One of the finest features is the large walled garden with 'hot' and 'cold' herbaceous borders dedicated to Professor d'Abreu – Mrs Throckmorton's father – containing a superb display of plants to give colour and interest through the seasons. The red and white gardens are surrounded by hornbeam hedges being trained to provide windows. In the rose labyrinth masses of roses and clematis grow over arches and pedestals, with herbaceous underplanting. In the early summer garden wisteria is trained over raised hoops with peonies beneath, and pale colours change to deeper shades of blue and red. The architectural features are also good. A pond and fountain is surrounded by benches and planted in green and white as a peaceful place for contemplation.

Elm Close

Binton Road, Welford–on-Avon CV37 8PT. Tel: (01789) 750793

Mr and Mrs E.W. Dyer • 5m SW of Stratford-upon-Avon on B439. Turn left after 4½ m to Welford • Open for NGS, and for parties by appt • Entrance: £2, children free ◕ **WC** 占 ⚘

A relatively small garden filled with fresh ideas and a wide range of plants. Clematis (over 300) are trained over pergolas and climb through trees and shrubs, and there are dwarf conifers, a rock garden, hellebores, a pool, alpine troughs, raised beds and an excellent variety of bulbs. Herbaceous plants and shrubs, including a wealth of peonies, cornus, hostas, daphnes and magnolias, provide interest and colour throughout the year.

Farnborough Hall [Historic Garden Grade I]

Farnborough, Banbury, Oxfordshire OX17 1DU. Tel: (01295) 690002

The National Trust/Mr and Mrs Holbech • 5m N of Banbury, ½ m W off A423 or 1½ m E off B4100 • House open as garden • Grounds open 7th April to 25th Sept, Wed, Sat, and 2nd, 3rd May; all 2 – 6pm. Closed Good Friday •

Entrance: garden and terrace walk £1.90, (house and grounds £3.80, children £1.90) ◗ **WC** ᕕ ⬳ ⚲

The house has been in the same family since 1684. It was reconstructed in the eighteenth century with fine Rococo plasterwork and the grounds were improved in the 1740s with the aid of Sanderson Miller, the architect, landscape gardener and dilettante who lived at nearby Radway. Climbing gently along the ridge looking towards Edgehill is the fine S-shaped terrace walk built by William Holbech in order to greet his brother on the adjoining property. *The Oxford Companion* describes it as a majestic concept marking the movement towards the great landscaped parks at the end of the eighteenth century. There are two temples and a game larder along the walk and an obelisk at the end. The trees are beeches, sycamores and limes. Beyond the cedar tree is part of the site of the former orangery, a rose garden, and a yew walk with steps at the end, where there is a seat with a fine view over the river, the cascade and the countryside towards Edgehill. The cascade fountain suppresses the otherwise-invasive hum of the M40. A uniquely interesting site.

The Hiller Garden

Dunnington Heath Farm, Alcester B49 5PD. Tel: (01789) 772771

Mr and Mrs R. Beach • 9m W of Stratford-upon-Avon, 3m S of Alcester at former A441/A435 junction, now B4088 • Open all year, daily, 10am – 5pm • Entrance: free ◯ ☕ ✗ **WC** ᕕ ⬳ ☘ ✋

An established two-acre garden with year-round interest. Large beds of herbaceous perennials with frequent new introductions enable visitors to the garden centre to see mature, well-labelled plants in good colour combinations and so judge their suitability for personal use. The garden also embraces an extensive rose garden, which includes more than 200 varieties and has a Victorian rose area as its centrepiece. The owners' adjacent private garden is also open for pre-booked visits by horticultural societies.

Jephson Gardens [Historic Public Park Grade II]

Leamington Spa CV32 4AD.
Tel: (01926) 450000 (Amenities Department, Warwick District Council)

Warwick District Council • In Leamington Spa, main entrance off Parade • Open all year, daily, 8am – dusk (opens 9am Sun and Bank Holiday Mons) • Entrance: free • Other information: Parking in Newbold Terrace ◯ ☕ **WC** ᕕ ⬳

The spa town has always made a great effort to provide floral displays in its streets, and this vibrancy can also be enjoyed at its peak in the intensive bedding-out of the principal formal public garden. Besides flowers, it contains a remarkable collection of trees. Leamington has a string of parks and gardens running along the River Leam right across the town – an almost unique piece of town planning of a century ago. It is possible to walk their length: Mill Gardens, Jephson Gardens, Pump Room Gardens, York Promenade and Victoria Park. There are some fine listed examples of Victorian iron bridges, as well as earlier stone ones. On the outskirts of nearby Kenilworth is the ruined *Kenilworth Castle*, whose reconstructed Tudor garden [Historic Garden Grade II*] is worth a visit in memory of what it once was.

The Master's Garden [Historic Garden Grade II]

Lord Leycester Hospital, Warwick CV34 4BH.
Tel: (01926) 491422 (Contact: Susan Rhodes)

Board of Governors of Lord Leycester Hospital • In High Street • Open end March to Sept, daily except Mon (but open Bank Holiday Mons), 10am – 4.30pm • Entrance: £1.50 (2003 price) ◑ 🍵

The restoration work of this garden is remarkable. Old cobbles from the summerhouse have been relaid in the new circular house with its thatched roof of Norfolk reeds, and archways dating from the 1850s have been copied to support roses, clematis and other climbers. A brick pathway through the centre of the garden repeats the feathered pattern. The 150-year old pleached lime avenue remains, and on the walls is a fig tree, along with gooseberries and redcurrants. An eighteenth-century dovecot has been converted into a gazebo, and a pineapple frame is to be restored. A circular herb garden has a sundial at its centre, and there is a vegetable and fruit area. Through the seasons the borders are filled with 4000 tulips and various perennials. A twelfth-century Norman arch frames a Nileometer – a finial from a stone column installed by the Romans on the Nile to record the rise and fall of the river – which was a gift from Lord Leycester in the eighteenth century. It leads into the other half of the garden, which includes a Victorian rock garden, shrubs, roses and perennials. Also in Warwick, at Hill Close, the *Victorian Pleasure Gardens* are an interesting example of nineteenth-century plots grown by local craftsmen, and tradesmen. They are now being restored, with their high hedges, summerhouses and old fruit trees.

Packwood House ★ [Historic Garden Grade II*]

Lapworth, Solihull, Birmingham B94 6AT. Tel: (01564) 782024

The National Trust • 11m SE of central Birmingham, 2m E of Hockley Heath on A3400 • House open 3rd March to Oct, Wed – Sun, Good Fri and Bank Holiday Mons, 12 noon – 4.30pm • Garden open 3rd March to Oct, Wed – Sun and Bank Holiday Mons, 11am – 4.30pm (closes 5.30pm May to Sept) • Park open all year, daily • Entrance: £2.80, children £1.40 (house and garden £5.60, children £2.80, family £14. Parties of 15 or more by written appt only • Other information: Picnic site opposite main gates. Combined entry ticket with Baddesley Clinton – see below ◑ 🍵 🍽 WC ♿ 🏛 🌷 ⚘

Hidden away in a rather suburban part of Warwickshire, this garden is notable for its intact layout, dating from the sixteenth and seventeenth centuries when the original house was built. There are courtyards, terraces and brick gazebos. Even more remarkable is the almost surreal yew garden, unique in design. Tradition claims that it represents the Sermon on the Mount, but in fact the 'Apostles' were planted in the 1850s as a four-square pattern round an orchard. Never mind, the result is now homogeneous. A spiral mount of yew and box is a delightful illusion; note also the clever use of brick. G. Baron Ash, who gave the property to the Trust, made a sunken garden in the 1930s and restored earlier design features. He also introduced colourful border plantings, and now the gardens are worth seeing at all seasons of the year. In spring drifts of daffodils follow the snowdrops and bluebells carpet the copse, while shrubs flower on red-brick walls. The herbaceous border, the sunken garden, the terrace beds and climbing roses and honeysuckles are a riot of colour in summer, and autumn brings changes in foliage. The head gardener, who moved here from Powis Castle in 2000, is clearing and replanting some beds and slowly restoring the walled kitchen garden after many years of neglect. It promises to be splendid. There is a combined entry ticket with nearby *Baddesley Clinton* [Historic Garden Grade II]. The medieval moated manor house has a walled garden containing herbaceous borders, climbers, herbs and greenhouses, and there are pleasant walks round the lake, a wilderness walk and a discovery trail quiz for the young.

Ragley Hall [Historic Park and Garden Grade II*]

Alcester B49 5NJ. Tel: (01789) 762090

Marquess and Marchioness of Hertford • 8m W of Stratford-upon-Avon, 1m S of Alcester off A435 • House, garden and park open April to 3rd Oct, Thurs – Sun and Bank Holiday Mons; daily during school holidays, 11am – 5pm • Entrance: £6, concessions £5, children £4.50 (house, park and garden, £7, concessions £6, children £5.50) • Other information: Dogs in park only, on lead

◑ 🍽 ✕ 🏢 WC & 🔈 🏛 🔦 ☗

The 27 acres of formal and informal gardens date from the 1870s and include some vast trees – blue cedar, picea, abies and Wellingtonia. Near the house (the scene of a great range of entertainments) is a border of unusual and tender perennials and, beyond, the rose garden with beds of individual varieties. There are also roses on the pillars of the house. There is a 'fumpery' with ferns, rhododendrons, hydrangeas and foxgloves. The Secret Garden has a central fountain and beds of herbaceous plants. A new bog garden is planted with gunneras, primulas and astilbes to encourage wild life, and a meadow contains wild flowers, orchids and fritillaries. There are lovely views of the surrounding parkland and pleasant walks through woodland and around the lake. Children will enjoy an adventure area. A yew walk is to become a topiary area, and overall there is steady development across this very large property.

Ryton Organic Gardens

Ryton-on-Dunsmore, Coventry CV8 3LG. Tel: (024) 7630 3517

HDRA – the organic organisation • 7m NE of Leamington Spa, 5m SE of Coventry. Turn off A45 onto Wolston road • Open all year, daily except Christmas period, 9am – 5pm • Entrance: £3, accompanied children free, parties of 14 or more £2.50 per person (50p extra for guided tour) (2003 prices) • Other information: Guide dogs only ○ 🍽 ✕ 🏢 WC & 🌿 🏛 🔦 ☗

Ryton was set up in 1985 to be a centre of excellence for organic horticulture. Since then the 10 acres have been steadily developed, in a beautifully landscaped setting, to provide a wide range of inspirational and educational displays of herbs, roses, unusual vegetables, fruit, wildlife gardening and plants for bees. The individual gardens include demonstrations of organic methods of looking after soil, and of pest and disease control. There are also gardens for the visually impaired and those with other special needs, and a children's play area with a growing willow structure that invites exploration. At the centre of the garden is a vibrant display of herbaceous perennials in an informal drift of form and colour. The most recent additions are a garden for the enthusiastic cook, a highly acclaimed Paradise Garden created in memory of the late Geoff Hamilton by award-winning designer Isabelle van Groeningen, a recycled garden and a children's trail. Events and courses are held throughout the year.

The Shakespeare Houses and Their Gardens

Stratford-upon-Avon. Tel: (01789) 204016

Shakespeare Birthplace Trust • Located in Stratford-upon-Avon and surrounding area • All properties open all year, daily, except 23rd to 26th Dec. Opening and closing times vary – times and prices on application • Other information: Parking on site at Anne Hathaway's Cottage and Mary Arden's House, otherwise in town car parks. Restaurant/tea shop at Hall's Croft and café and picnic area at Mary Arden's House ○ 🍽 ✕ 🧺 WC � ⅍ 🛍 ℺

Some claim that little is known about Shakespeare and less still about his gardens. The Trust has made them interesting adjuncts to the houses. They include: *The Birthplace Garden*, a small informal collection of over 100 trees, herbs, plants and flowers mentioned by the Bard. *Mary Arden's House*, the front a *mélange* of box, roses and flowers, the rear a stretch of lawn with a wild garden beyond. Country museum with tools, etc. *Anne Hathaway's Cottage* [Historic Garden Grade II]: a typical English cottage garden dating from the end of the nineteenth century, including a small garden with varieties of Victorian vegetables, and a nearby tree garden with examples of those mentioned in the *Works*, where a circular yew maze was planted in 2001 based on an Elizabethan model. Garden centre with plants and herbs for sale grown by the Trust's gardeners, and a small display of Victorian and Edwardian garden tools. *Nash's House and New Place*: the house Shakespeare bought for his retirement, demolished in the eighteenth century; the foundations are planted with a garden beyond which, it is suggested, his orchard and kitchen garden lay. Reconstructed Elizabethan knot garden with oak palisade and 'tunnel' or 'pleached bower' of that time. *Hall's Croft*: a walled garden, including a herbal bed, bearing little resemblance to its probable form in the period when it was owned by the Bard's son-in-law. All the above are Trust houses and fee-charged. Beyond the knot garden is the *Great Garden* with free access. Also free, but not part of the Trust, are *Bancroft Gardens* in front of the Theatre and the long stretch owned by the Royal Shakespeare Theatre, along the River Avon between the Swan Theatre and the church where Shakespeare is buried.

Stoneleigh Abbey [Historic Park and Garden Grade II*]

Kenilworth CV8 2LF. Tel: (01926) 858535

Stoneleigh Abbey Ltd (Charitable Trust) • 4m N of Leamington Spa, 5m NE of Warwick, 7m S of Coventry, off M40 junction. Turn off A46 onto B4115, then follow signs to Ashow; entrance on right between two lodges • House open as garden • Garden open 9th April to Oct, 10am – 5pm • Entrance: £2, children free (house £5, OAPs £3.50, children, one free, additional child £2.50) • Other information: Dogs allowed in park only, on lead ◑ 💭 🦽 WC ♿

Over the last few years, extensive restoration by the charitable trust in which ownership was vested in 1997 has included the Baroque west wing of the abbey and its grand state rooms, the fourteenth-century gatehouse, the conservatory overlooking the River Avon, and the early-nineteenth-century stables and riding school. From now on it will be the turn of the park and gardens, which will be made accessible as one of Humphry Repton's most imaginative and picturesque landscape plans is gradually reinstated. The estate was the focus in 1809 of one of his finest and largest Red Books. Not all Repton's proposals were executed, but under his aegis the Avon was widened, a stone bridge built, an inspirational reflective pool created to mirror the south façade, and next to it, as counterpoint, a weir built to churn the waters of the river. Work is concentrated on the development of the water features which played such a part in Repton's proposals. This takes in such eclectic features as the eel catchers' hut. Later hands responsible for shaping the landscape included a pupil of Wyatville, C.S. Smith, who in the 1810s and 1820s provided many of the buildings in the park, and Percy Cane who restored and replanted the western terrace. W.S. Nesfield's strident Italianate garden, created overnight for a visit by Queen Victoria in 1858, may be left as a footnote in gardening history, but two herbal parterres, still in their infancy, have been planted in the manner of Nesfield in front of the west wing.

University of Warwick

Gibbet Hill Road, Coventry CV4 7AL. Tel: (02476) 524189 (Estate Office)

Warwick University • Nearer to Coventry than Warwick, most direct access is off A46 signed 'University of Warwick/Stoneleigh' just S of Coventry • Open all year. Term dates: 5th Jan to 13th March, 19th April to 26th June, 29th Sept to 3rd Dec • Entrance: free ○ 💭 ✕ WC ♿

The university buildings have been the subject of early controversy but their impact has been mellowed by clever landscaping, including the creation of new sports fields south of Gibbet Hill Road, the planting of many trees and the use of bedding schemes. Interesting in a smaller space is a wisteria-covered pergola in the Social Studies quadrangle. Formal gardens are being created, and around the Warwick Arts Centre and at sites across the university is a sculpture trail which features work by Richard Deacon, Liliane Ljin, Keir Smith, Bettina Furne, William Pye *et al*. The university now has seven lakes with a wetlands environment and nature reserve. There are several walks through and around the extensive grounds.

Upton House ★ [Historic Garden Grade II*]

Banbury, Oxfordshire OX15 6HT. Tel: (01295) 670266

The National Trust • 12m SE of Stratford-upon-Avon, 7m NW of Banbury on A422 • House open (timed tickets at peak times) • Garden open 3rd April to Oct, Mon – Wed, 12 noon – 5pm, Sat, Sun and Bank Holiday Mons, 11 – 5pm; 6th Nov to 12th Dec, Sat and Sun, 12 noon – 4pm (but garden closed on inclement days). Parties of 15 or more by appt • Entrance: £3.20 (house £6.40, children £3.20). No reductions for parties • Other information: Coaches by arrangement with visitor services manager. Possible for wheelchairs in parts but very steep in places. Motorised buggy with driver available for access to and from lower garden ◐ 🍽 ✕ 🖿 WC ♿ 🛍 ♀*

The house, which dates from 1695, contains a fine collection of paintings including three superb Stubbs. More interesting to the garden visitor is that it stands on limestone, over 210 metres above sea level on Edgehill, near the site of the famous battle. Below a great lawn, the garden descends in a series of long terraces, along one end of which an impressive flight of stone steps leads down to the large lake. In the centre of the terraced area is a huge sloping vegetable garden, well labelled to indicate varieties. The grand scale of the plan is the main interest, but there are many unusual plants, particularly perennials and bog plants, and the National Collection of asters spp. *amellus, cordifolius* and *ericoides* is here. *The National Herb Centre*, with small display gardens, good herb nursery, research glasshouses, exhibition and herb bistro, is nearby on B4100 at Warmington [open all year, daily, 9am – 5.30pm. Tel: (01295) 690033].

Warwick Castle ★ [Historic Park Grade I]

Warwick CV34 4QU. Tel: (0870) 442 2000

The Tussauds Group • In Warwick • Castle open • Grounds open all year, daily except 25th Dec, 10am – 6pm (Oct to March closes 5pm) • Entrance: Charges vary seasonally – maximum for individuals £13.50, OAPs £9.75, students £10, children £8, family £36 (2003 prices) ○ 🍽 ✕ 🖿 WC ♿ 🛍 ♀ ⚲

The castle stands on the banks of the River Avon, surrounded by 60 acres of beautiful grounds landscaped by 'Capability' Brown. He had previously been in employment as gardener to Lord Cobham at Stowe, but after the latter's death in 1749 decided to take on commissions of his own. His work at Warwick Castle for the 1st Earl (Francis Greville) is thought to have been his first independent commission, for which he received much praise, encouragement and publicity. He removed the old formal garden outside the wall and shaped the grounds to frame a view using an array of magnificent trees, notably cedars of Lebanon. In 1753 he began to landscape the courtyard, removing steps, filling in parts of the yard and making a coachway to surround the large level lawn. He then worked on the creation of the park on the other side of the eleventh-century mound. In 1779, when Brown's remodelling was barely twenty years old, the 2nd Earl embarked on a grandiose scheme of expansion which involved demolishing several streets in the town. In 1786 he constructed the conservatory at the top of Pageant Field, which today houses a replica of the famous Warwick Vase. From here visitors can view the panorama before them – the Peacock Garden and the tree-lined lawn of Pageant Field which meanders down to the gently sloping banks of the River Avon. On the other side of the castle entrance is the Victorian rose garden re-created in 1986 from Robert Marnock's designs of 1868. Also in the town is The Master's Garden (see entry) at Lord Leycester Hospital. The castle itself is ★★.

Wheelwright House

Long Compton CV36 5LE. Tel: (01608) 684478

Richard and Suzanne Shacklock • 6m S of Shipston-on-Stour on A3400. At S end of Long Compton take road signed to Little Compton and continue for 300 metres; house is on left • Open by appt only • Entrance: £2, children free • Other information: Teas for parties by prior arrangement ● ● WC & ⬧ ⌖

The central feature of this attractive one-acre garden surrounding the early eighteenth-century Cotswold stone house is a natural stream, with little waterfalls, distinctive bridges and banks covered in moisture-loving plants. In eleven years the owners have created a garden with a variety of moods, aspects and colour themes, containing many interesting and unusual plants. There is a formal lily pond with a rose pergola adjoining, a woodland garden, shady areas with ferns, hostas and pulmonarias, a Mediterranean garden in a sheltered sunny spot, a collection of pots, and several mixed borders designed for year-round colour. Seats are strategically placed to enjoy the various vistas. The garden continues to develop: the latest project is a box wheel in the front garden accompanied by a topiary wheelwright. Barton House (see entry) is nearby.

Woodpeckers ★

The Bank, Marlcliff, Bidford–on–Avon B50 4NT. Tel: (01789) 773416

Dr and Mrs A.J. Cox • 7m SW of Stratford-upon-Avon off B4085 between Bidford and Cleeve Prior • Open by appt all year • Entrance: £3, children free • Other information: Wheelchair users must be accompanied ● ▦ WC & ⌖

This two-and-a-half-acre garden, planned for year-round interest, contains a wide range of design and planting ideas, and blends well with the surrounding countryside. A small arboretum with a wide selection of choice trees provide contrast in form and colour. Moving around the garden, there are many surprises – a collection of old roses, with clematis climbing through, an attractive small *potager*, colourful and unusual herbs and vegetables. A knot garden has been created from three varieties of box, and room has been found for topiary, an ivy arbour with statue, a fern border, a white and apricot bed, several island beds with splendid ranges of colour and plants, a Mediterranean garden, a cactus and succulent greenhouse and a round greenhouse for tender plants including mimosas, abutilons, salvias and clematis. The terrace has a range of troughs and alpine plants, and there is a delightful pool and bog garden. A belvedere of framed English oak affords fine views of the garden, including a wildflower area in spring. A two-storey oak building with a balcony overlooks the arboretum and rose garden.

WILTSHIRE

Two-starred gardens are marked on the map with a black square.

Abbey House Gardens ★

Malmesbury SN16 9AS. Tel: (01666) 822212 *RECORDED MESSAGES.*

Barbara and Ian Pollard • In town centre next to Abbey • Open 21st March to 21st Oct, daily, 11am – 6pm, and for parties by appt • Entrance: £5.50, OAPs/ students £5, children (5–15) £2 (2003 prices) • Other information: Car park close to garden ◐ ☕ 🏠 WC & ♨ ⚲

A remarkable five-acre garden, created in only eight years. The owners' passion and enthusiasm are reflected in the exuberant planting schemes. The setting around a late-Tudor house beside the abbey is unique, the effect overwhelming, with thousands of roses (the largest private collection in the country), an enormous arcade-encircled herb garden, a generously proportioned laburnum tunnel and many other triumphs. Also included are a Celtic cross knot garden echoing its historic surroundings, huge herbaceous borders in riotous colours, water features, a river and woodland walk (with kingfishers and water voles if you are lucky), rhododendrons, and a bog garden with an exceptional display of meconopsis in spring. The season starts with a dazzling display of thousands of tulips and continues right through to the autumn. As well as clematis and climbing roses, there is a large and interesting collection of cordon fruit trees around an arcade, with sweet peas for added colour, a foliage walk and a maple walk.

Avebury Manor

Marlborough SN8 1RF. Tel (01672) 539250

The National Trust • 6m W of Marlborough, 1m N of A4 Bath road on A4361. Manor on N side of High Street, behind church • House open Mon, Tues, Sun and Bank Holiday Mons, 2 – 4.40pm • Garden open April to Oct, daily except Mon and Thurs (but open Bank Holiday Mons), 11am – 5pm • Entrance £2.90, children £1.40 (house and garden £3.80, children £1.90) • Other information: Parking in outer village. Alexander Keiller Museum, Barn Gallery exhibition, refreshments and shop adjacent ◐ ☕ ✕ WC & ♿

The house and gardens were purchased by the Trust in 1991. The much-altered house has monastic origins with notable Queen Anne alterations. The rose garden in the shadow of the church tower is a fragrant delight, herbaceous borders are set neatly behind low box hedging, and there is a splendid lavender walk at the main entrance to the house, which on the south-west is framed by lawns and topiary. The orchard has been replanted with old apple varieties from Wiltshire. In the topiary garden the pond has been restored and the box hedges are in the design of overlapping diamonds, inspired by a plaster ceiling in the house.

Bolehyde Manor ★

Allington, Chippenham SN14 6LW. Tel: (01249) 652105

*Earl and Countess Cairns • 1½ m W of Chippenham on A420 Bristol road.
Turn N at Allington crossroads; garden is ½ m on right • Open 20th June, 2.30
– 6pm for NGS, and for parties by appt • Entrance: £2.50 • Other information:
Teas and plant sales on NGS open day only* ● &

A four-acre garden at once steeped in tradition and bursting with innovative
ideas. The characterful manor house dates from the fifteenth century. Owned
by the Abbot of Glastonbury until after the dissolution of the monasteries,
Bolehyde was sold in 1635 to the Case family, who lived there for the next 400
years. The house, outbuildings and gatehouses developed into a charming
huddle of beautifully weathered Cotswold stone buildings, and this is reflected
in the series of linked garden rooms disposed around the house. Within a semi-
formal framework are splendid contrasts, gracefully achieved: a pear walk,
some lovely wildflower meadow planting, a new and exciting *potager*. Sheltered and sunny formal areas are edged with colourful narrow beds, and
satisfyingly chunky topiary abounds. Planted for year-round interest, the
garden is nevertheless at its stunning best in midsummer, when masses of
roses bloom on the old walls and the half-hardy planting of the courtyard –
much of it in dark glowing jewel colours – is nearing the peak of a brilliant
display.

Bowood House ★ [Historic Park and Garden Grade I]

Bowood House, Derry Hill, Calne SN11 0LZ. Tel: (01249) 812102

*The Marquis and Marchioness of Lansdowne • 5m SE of Chippenham, 4½ m
W of Calne off A4, 8m S of M4 junction 17. Separate rhododendron walks off
A342 Chippenham – Devizes road midway between Derry Hill and Sandy Lane
• House open • Garden and pleasure grounds open April to 2nd Nov, daily,
11am – 6pm or dusk if earlier. Rhododendron walks open daily end-April to
early June (depending on flowering season) • Entrance: House and gardens
£6.25, OAPs £5.15, children (5-15) £4, (2-4) £3.15, rhododendron walks
£3.50 extra, children free* ◑ ☕ ✕ 🍴 WC & ♿ 🚻 ⚘

The house and its pleasure grounds cover over 100 acres and lie in the centre of
'Capability' Brown's enormous park. Other splendours include a tranquil lake,
arboretum and pinetum, Doric temple, cascade waterfall and hermit's cave.
Thousands of bulbs bloom in spring. The Robert Adam orangery (converted
into a gallery) is particularly fine, and in front of it are formal Bath-stone
terraces with rose beds, standard roses and fastigiate yews. *Fremontodendron
californicum* flourishes on the Italianate terrace. The upper terrace was laid out
in 1817 and the present fountains were added in 1839. In the twentieth
century, when elaborate bedding schemes became too time-consuming, the
parterre was planted with hybrid tea roses, thus blurring the edges. Mary
Keen advised replacing the grass paths with gravel and compensating for the
loss of green by putting box hedges around the beds. New planting has
ensured that the flowering season starts almost three months earlier than

it used to. In the nineteenth century it was the aim of every garden to be 'as clean as a drawing room', and Bowood is now in this class once again. The rhododendron walks are situated in a separate 50-acre area, which is only open when the rhododendrons are flowering. Robert Adam's mausoleum (a little gem well worth a visit) is in this area.

Broadleas Garden

Broadleas, Devizes SN10 5JQ. Tel: (01380) 722035

Lady Anne Cowdray/Broadleas Garden Charitable Trust • 1m S of Devizes on A360. Signed from Devizes town centre • Open April to Oct, Sun, Wed, Thurs, 2 – 6pm • Entrance: £4, children (under 12) £1. Parties of 10 or more £3.50 • Other information: Coaches must use Devizes town centre approach. Teas on Suns until end of Aug only ◑ ☕ WC & ⬧ ⌀

This garden was bought just after World War II and started from nothing by Lady Anne Cowdray in a combe below Devizes. Mature and semi-mature magnolias grow on each side of a steep dell. As good as any Cornish garden, it is stuffed with fine things that one would think too tender for these parts – large specimens of everything (much of it now over 40 years old),including *Paulownia fargesii, Parrotia persica*, all manner of magnolias, azaleas, hydrangeas, hostas, lilies and trilliums of rare and notable species. There has also been much planting in recent years, including many rhododendrons and camellias. It is a garden of tireless perfectionism, at its most stunning in spring when sheets of bulbs stretch out beneath the flowering trees. Rarely seen in such quantities for instance are the erythroniums or dog-tooth violets. Many of the more unusual plants, both shrubs and perennials, are grown for sale at Broadleas. There is also a woodland walk, a sunken rose garden and a silver border. This is serious plantsmanship and dendrology.

Conock Manor [Historic Garden Grade II]

Conock, Devizes SN10 3QQ.

Mrs Bonar Sykes • 5m SE of Devizes, off A342 near Chirton • Open 24th May, 2 – 6pm • Entrance: £2.50, children under 16 free • Other information: cream teas available ◑ & ⌀ ⌀

Set between distant views of Marlborough Downs and Salisbury Plain, the Georgian house looks out over lawns with specimen trees, ha-has and a recently planted arboretum, which includes unusual trees, such as *Aesculus* x *mutabilis* 'Induta' and *Catalpa fargesii* f. *duclouxii*. From a Reptonesque thatched dairy near the house, a long brick wall and a mixed shrub border lead to the stable block, in early Gothic-Revival style, with a copper-domed cupola. Beyond, yew and beech hedges and brick walls frame unusual trees and shrubs, a small kitchen garden and a 1930s' shrub walk. Beech forms attractive bays and box makes clipped balls. Notable are the pleached limes and a magnolia garden including malus, sorbus, prunus and eucalyptus.

Corsham Court [Historic Garden Grade II*]

Corsham SN13 0BZ. Tel: (01249) 701610

James Methuen-Campbell • 4m W of Chippenham on A4 • House open • Garden open Jan to 19th March, Sat and Sun, 2 – 4.30pm; 20th March to Sept, daily except Mon (but open Bank Holiday Mons), 2 – 5.30pm; Oct and Nov, Sat and Sun, 2 – 4.30pm. Closed Dec. Also open by appt for parties of 15 or more • Entrance: £2, OAPs £1.50, children £1, season tickets £10 (house and garden £5, OAPs £4.50, children £2.50, parties £4.50 per person) • Other information: Teas by prior arrangement for parties ☽ 🍱 WC ᕕ ⟨⟩ ℺

Approaching from Chippenham, look out for a glimpse of this house on your left, once framed by an avenue of elms now replaced by some lime trees. The house, which has a fine collection of pictures and furniture, is surrounded by a landscape of 'Capability' Brown's devising finished off by Humphry Repton (the lake and boat-house particularly). It is an example of this kind of gardening at its best. Rare and exotic trees look entirely at home: black walnuts, Californian redwoods, cedars, Wellingtonias, and the most astonishing layered Oriental plane tree, shading beeches, oaks, sycamores and Spanish chestnuts. There are 340 tree species. The Bath House designed by Brown leads out into a small enclosed garden with flowers and catalpas. Repton's roses trained over metal arches encircling a round pond are a rare surviving example of the elegance of early-nineteenth-century flower gardens. Here the borders contain the unusual *Clerodendrum trichotomum* and enormous iron supports for roses and *Clematis* x *jackmanii*. A box-edged garden, a hornbeam *allée*, urns, arbours and seats add further elegant touches.

The Courts Garden ★ [Historic Garden Grade II]

Holt, Trowbridge BA14 6RR. Tel: (01225) 782340

The National Trust • 3m SW of Melksham, 3m N of Trowbridge, 2½ m E of Bradford-on-Avon on B3107 • Open March to mid-Oct, daily except Wed, 11.30am – 5.30pm, and by appt at other times • Entrance: £4.20, children £2.10 (2003 prices) • Other information: Parking at village hall ◗ ᕕ 🎃 ℺

The distinguished eighteenth-century house is surrounded by lawns, topiary and hedging laid out originally in the 1920s, and these are now exploding into new and creative plantings. Passing through huge stands of cotinus and other red-leaved shrubs, the visitor reaches water gardens which include a rectangular lily pond bordered by hundreds of pale *Iris sibirica* with a luxuriant planted 'dye pond' beyond, dating from its old history as a mill. Borders are brilliantly conceived and maintained – the blue and yellow one is particularly fine – within traditional enclosures of yew, beech and holly. The head gardener came from Sissinghurst six years ago and throughout these 7 acres has achieved a dynamic mix of new planting in a well-defined framework, taking in the newly restored, colourful and productive vegetable garden and orchard and the arboretum beyond. Planted in 1952, this is now peaceful and beautiful all year round, with rare and splendid trees and masses of scillas and narcissus in spring.

Fonthill House

Tisbury, Salisbury SP3 5SA. Tel: (Estate Office) (01747) 820246

Lord and Lady Margadale • 12m W of Salisbury, E of Hindon on B3089. Entrance is S of Fonthill Bishop, on farm road over bridge and through deer park • Open usually three or four times a year during April, May, June, July for charity, 2 – 6pm. Telephone for details • Entrance: £2.50, children free ● ▬ WC & ⬧ ⬧ ⬧

The 1970s' neo-Georgian house, built on the site of a demolished Detmar Blow masterpiece on the estate, stands at the head of a combe with fine views and is backed by mature beech and oak trees. Throughout this woodland grow camellias and rhododendrons and, in spring, a carpet of bluebells. The charm and isolation of the place add to its magic, particularly in spring when the woodland is a mass of colour. Five acres in all. For children, there is a heated swimming pool open from mid-May.

The Fovant Hut

Fovant, Salisbury SP3 5LN. Tel: (01722) 714756

Christina and Nigel Oates • Off A30 between Salisbury and Shaftesbury. At W end of Fovant, take road signed to Broadchalke and Bowerchalke. Follow road up steep hill and just before crest turn right into unmade-up road; garden is few hundred yards on right • Open 12th April, 3rd, 31st May, 2 – 5pm. Special openings and guided tours for parties • Entrance: £4 ●

The 'hut' – in fact an old coaching inn – stands on an ancient byway in an area of outstanding natural beauty, and the most impressive feature of the garden is the successful blending of the more intimate areas with the vast and beautiful panorama of the surrounding downland. It is a 'modern' garden in the best sense – conceived and realised since 1992 by garden designer Christina Oates and her husband Nigel. Through design and planting they have succeeded in creating a brilliant one-acre garden on a north-facing sloping site with chalky soil and fierce winds. Skill and dedication have enabled them to achieve areas of shelter, generously planted with specimens that suit the conditions. An original and fresh use of many familiar ideas distinguishes the garden here – the 'hot' borders are narrow and run steeply downhill to the distant view; the imaginative use of decking and water leads to a most delightful garden room/conservatory; in the fruit garden masses of alliums flower under a fine lilac; and the area around a small wildflower patch has produced new ideas and experiments. Note, for instance, the 3-metre clipped *leylandii* drums used as a windbreak.

The Garden Lodge

Chittoe, Chippenham SN15 2EW. Tel: (01380) 850314

Mrs Juliet Wilmot • Off A342 Chippenham – Devizes road, signed to Chittoe; garden marked on right after 1m • Open by appt only • Entrance: £3 ● WC & B&B

In 1990 the present owner bought the house and its abandoned 2-acre Victorian walled garden in the peaceful hamlet of Chittoe. Since then, taking advantage of a sheltered, sloping site, she has created within the mellow surrounding walls a many-levelled formal garden of immaculate design. The upper level consists of a long curving sweep of lawn, backed by a deep raised border which leads to a fine mature oak tree. A large pond on a lower level is lavishly furnished with marginal and water plants, and a stone rill drops to an amphitheatre and a central area planted with 'Sander's White' rambler roses. Clematis and roses abound on walls, pillars and pergolas. Original features include a grass-and-brick maze and a brick sundial let into the grass, and a serpentine yew-edged path leads to an elegant pavilion complete with an ingenious snakes-and-ladders game. The seclusion in this appealing garden is accentuated by the borrowed landscape of mature trees on the encircling skyline.

Goulters Mill

Nettleton, Nr. Castle Combe, Chippenham SN14 7LL. Tel: (01249) 782555

Mr and Mrs Michael Harvey • 6m W of Chippenham on B4039 between Burton and The Gibb • Open 11th April to 26th Sept, 2 – 5pm, by appt • Entrance: £3.50 NEW ● ● WC & ⚘ B&B

The idyllic ¾-acre garden lies deep in seclusion and silence. Ancient tracks radiate from the mill, mentioned in the Domesday Book, and the present seventeenth-century house preserves an atmosphere of timelessness and peace. Looking out from the house a sea of colour and movement is achieved with beautifully chosen hardy perennials and self-sown annuals, framed by attractive paths and accented by topiary figures. The dense planting leads to a small lawn surrounded by ancient apple trees entwined with roses and overlooking a lily-fringed stream and pool, then on to a happily planted gravel area. Irises and sisyrinchium abound here, and poppies and eremurus are also a speciality. The river, tree house and vine planting may be glimpsed beyond a wild area currently under review. The spring invites walks to bluebell woods beyond, and in the summer there is a wash of wild flowers and rare butterflies in the meadow paths.

Great Chalfield Manor [Historic Garden Grade II]

Melksham SN2 8NJ. Tel: (01225) 782239

The National Trust • 3m SW of Melksham off A350 and B3107 via Broughton Gifford Common • Open April to Oct, Tues – Thurs, 12 noon – 5pm, and for parties by appt • Entrance: £4.20 ● WC & ⚘ B&B

The moated fifteenth-century house and its surroundings were restored by Robert Fuller in the early 1900s, and given to the National Trust forty years later. It remains the home of his grandson's family, and they now manage the property. Fuller employed Sir Harold Brakspear as his architect, and Alfred Parsons designed the gardens to complement the house; Brakspear also contributed a gazebo. The spacious lawns are broken up by vast jelly-mould yew shapes, and have substantial borders, recently replanted. There are some splendid old-fashioned and rambling roses. Good views open up from the moat walk and, nearby, a shrubbery is managed as a semi-natural area with woodland plants.

Hazelbury Manor [Historic Garden Grade II]

Box, Corsham SN13 8LB. Tel: (01225) 812088

5m SW of Chippenham. From Box take A365 towards Melksham, turn left onto B3109, next left, and right immediately into private drive • Open one weekend for NGS, and by appt • Entrance: £2.80, OAPs £2, children £1, under 6 free (2003 prices) ◑ WC ⓱ ⚘

The extensive formal gardens, surrounding a sprawling Elizabethan house, are undergoing restoration based on evidence from old photographs. The rock garden at the front of the house is impressive, although it could not be called in keeping with the house and makes as big a twentieth-century statement as the earlier Edwardian garden. The formal garden has a large lawn, with a chess set and other topiary sculpture, banked up on either side by high walks between clipped beeches. In spring the *allées* are carpeted with polyanthus, cowslips and wallflowers. Mammoth herbaceous borders blaze in summer. Other features include a beautiful arched laburnum walk, a lime walk and terraced alpine garden.

Heale Gardens ★ [Historic Garden Grade II*]

Middle Woodford, Salisbury SP4 6NT. Tel: (01722) 782504

Mr and Mrs Guy Rasch • 4m N of Salisbury between A360 and A345 • Open all year, Tues – Sun and Bank Holiday Mons, 10am – 5pm. Snowdrop Sundays 1st, 18th Feb • Entrance: £3.75, children (5–15) £1.50, under-5s free ○ ☕ 🧺 WC ⓱ ✿ 🏛

This is an idyllic garden with mature yew hedges, much of it designed by Harold Peto. A tributary of the Avon meanders through, providing the perfect boundary and obvious site for the sealing-wax red bridge and thatched tea-house which straddles the water. This was brought over from Japan and assembled in 1910 with the help of four Japanese gardeners and extends under the shade of *Magnolia* x *soulangeana* along the boggy banks planted with bog arums, *Rodgersia aesculifolia*, candelabra primulas and irises. There are two terraces to the west of the house. The topmost has beds containing two aged wisterias among tall herbaceous plants, backed by clipped yew. A central path of old York stone links both terraces and is rampant with alchemilla. The other has two stone lily ponds and two small borders given height by tall wooden pyramids bearing roses, clematis and honeysuckles. The Long Border contains many dark-leaved plants including *Cercis* 'Forest Pansy', *Physocarpus* 'Diabolo', and interesting herbaceous perennials; behind is a border of musk roses. The walled kitchen garden achieves a satisfying marriage between practicality and pleasure: the formal nature of rows of vegetables is made into a feature, and plots are divided by espaliered fruit trees forming apple and pear tunnels, and by a pergola and hedges. The wonderful flint-and-brick wall provides protection for many plants including *Cytisus battandieri* and an ancient fig tree. This is a walled garden where one is encouraged to linger on the seats and in the shaded arbours and enjoy and admire the extraordinary tranquillity of the place. Look out for the ancient mulberry, the very old *Cercidiphyllum japonicum* (the second tallest known in Europe), and the *Magnolia grandiflora*. The plant centre is comprehensive and the shop appeals to the discerning. Unique wrought-iron plant supports can be bought here.

Home Covert Gardens and Arboretum ★

Roundway, Devizes SN10 2JA. Tel: (01380) 723407

Mr and Mrs John Phillips • 1m N of Devizes. Turn off A361 on edge of built-up area NE of town, signed to Roundway. In Roundway turn left towards Rowde. House is ³/₄ m on left. Signposted • Open for NGS, and by appt. Guided parties (12–40 persons) welcome • Entrance: £3, children free • Other information: Teas and plants for sale on Sun charity open days only ● ċ ⬙

This garden, developed in the 1960s, has been created by the present owners out of amenity woodlands of the now-demolished Roundway House. In front of the house is a large lawn on a plateau edged with grasses, herbaceous plants and alpines producing colour throughout the year. Beyond this, grass pathways meander through a collection of trees and rare shrubs. A steep path drops from the plateau to a water garden, lake, waterfall and bog garden, rich with colour from bog primulas and other moisture-loving plants, and shaded by fine specimen trees. Excellent collections of magnolias, camellias, erythroniums and hydrangeas are scattered informally throughout, and roses and clematis scramble over walks and through trees. Described as 'a botanical madhouse', this garden offers wonderful contrasts.

Iford Manor ★★ [Historic Garden Grade I]

Bradford-on-Avon BA15 2BA. Tel: (01225) 863146

Mrs Cartwright-Hignett • 2m S of Bradford-on-Avon off B3109, 7m SE of Bath via A36. Signposted • Open April, Sun; May to Sept, Tues – Thurs, Sat, Sun and Bank Holiday Mons; Oct, Sun; all 2 – 5pm. Other times and parties by appt • Entrance: £4, OAPs, students and children over 10 £3.50. Children under 10 free, Tues – Thurs only • Other information: Teas May to Aug, Sat, Sun and Bank Holiday Mons only ◑ ➤ WC ċ ℘

Harold Peto found himself a near-ideal house in the steep valley through which the River Frome slides langorously towards Bath. The topography lends itself to the strong architectural framework favoured by Peto and the creation of areas of entirely differing moods. The overriding intention is Italianate with a preponderance of cypresses, junipers, box and yew, punctuated at every turn by sarcophagi, urns, terracotta, marble seats and statues, columns, fountains and loggias. In a different vein is a meadow of naturalised bulbs, most spectacularly martagon lilies. A path leads from here to the cloisters – an Italian-Romanesque building of Harold Peto's confection made with fragments collected from Italy. From here one can admire the whole, and the breathtaking valley and the walled kitchen garden on the other side. Perhaps somewhat incongruously, at the top of the garden, there is a Japanese area, pleasantly done but not apparently completed by Peto himself. Westwood Manor (see entry) is nearby.

Lacock Abbey [Historic Park Grade II]

Lacock, Chippenham SN15 2LG. Tel: (01249) 730227

The National Trust • 3m S of Chippenham off A350 • Abbey open 29th March to 2nd Nov, daily except Tues, 1 – 5.30pm • Grounds, cloisters and museum of photography open March to 2nd Nov, daily, 11am – 5.30pm. Closed 18th April • Entrance: grounds, cloisters and museum £4.20, children £2.50, family £11.80 (abbey, grounds, cloisters and museum £6.50, children £3.60, family £17.60, parties £6 per person, children £3) (2003 prices) • Other information: Refreshments and shop in village. Batricar available ◑ WC ᏸ 🏛 ⚲ ⚲

The thirteenth-century abbey, set in meadows beside the River Avon, was turned into a private house by Sir William Sharington after the Dissolution, and was gothicised by John Ivory Talbot in the eighteenth century. The romantic Victorian woodland garden is best viewed in spring when sheets of crocuses, daffodils and later, fritillaries, replace the large drifts of snowdrops and aconites. Lady Elisabeth's Rose Garden, originally created for the mother of William Henry Fox-Talbot, inventor of photography, has been re-created from the original photograph of 1840, which is probably the earliest known photograph of a garden. Fox-Talbot was also an eminent botanist, and planted many unusual trees which can still be seen today, including specimens of the American black walnut, the Judas tree and the swamp cypress. His walled 'Botanic Garden', once fallen into use as allotments, has reopened after restoration. An eighteenth-century grotto will also be restored.

Larmer Tree Gardens [Historic Garden Grade II*]

Rushmore Estate, Tollard Royal, Salisbury SP5 5PT. Tel: (01725) 516228

Mr W. Gronow Davis • 16m SW of Salisbury, 7m SE of Shaftesbury off B3081. Signposted • Open 11th April to Oct (but closed in July), Sun – Fri, 11am – 6pm • Entrance: £3.75, concessions and groups £3, children £2.50. Discount entry available with Chettle House (see entry in Dorset) (2003 prices) • Other information: Tea rooms and shop open April, Sun and Bank Holiday Mon; May, June, Aug, Sept, Wed – Fri, Sun. Closed July ◑ 🍴 ✕ 🏺 WC ᏸ ⚸ 🏛 ⚲ ⚲

These 12-acre pleasure grounds were laid out in 1880 by General Pitt-Rivers as a place of public enlightenment and entertainment. Today, they remain an exceptionally fine example of Victorian vision and extravagance. The gardens contain a unique collection of buildings, including a Roman temple, an open-air theatre and Nepalese rooms which the General introduced as points of interest for those with small knowledge of the outside world. The buildings surround the main lawn, off which radiate laurel-hedged rides forming small enclosed wooded arbours originally intended for picnickers. Restoration of the gardens began in the 1990s with the aim that they would continue to be a place of pleasure and entertainment. Regular concerts, theatrical events and festivals are held throughout the summer and local bands play on the stage most Sundays. The gardens provide stunning views north to the Cranborne Chase and south to the Solent.

Longleat [Historic Park and Garden Grade I]

Warminster BA12 7NW. Tel: (01985) 844400

The Marquess of Bath • 3m SW of Warminster, 4½ m SE of Frome on A362 •
House open • Garden open all year, daily except 25th Dec, 10am – 5.30pm
(closes 3pm Nov to March) • Entrance: £3, OAPs and children £2, coaches free
(house extra) (2003 prices) • Other information: Helicopter landing pad
available by prior request ○ 🍵 ✕ 🧺 WC ఈ ⟨⇔ 🏛 🕯 ℺

This garden has been rearranged and developed by most of the great names in
English landscape history. There is nothing left today of the two earliest
gardens here – one Elizabethan, the other, spectacularly elaborate, created by
London and Wise in the 1680s–90s. Sadly it was barely half a century before
'Capability' Brown ironed out the formality and landscaped a chain of lakes set
amongst clumps of trees and hanging woods, best admired today from
Heaven's Gate. The park was slightly altered by Repton in 1804 and added
to in the 1870s when it became fashionable to collect exotic trees and to make
groves of rhododendrons and azaleas. It remains both beautiful and rewarding
for all who delight in trees. In this century the fortunes of the garden came
under the guiding hand of Russell Page. The nineteenth-century formal garden
in front of the orangery to the north of the house was simplified and improved
upon by him to great effect, although, alas, most of his work has since been
swept away. The orangery itself is a dream of wisteria. A quarter of a mile to
the south there is a pleasure walk in a developing arboretum, with many
spring bulbs and wild flowers. To the immediate west of the house the small
private garden is not open to the public. Lord Bath says this was designed
around the two commas within the yin and yang symbols: bulbs and fruit trees
in the first and a lily pond in the second. There is a large dovecot in one corner
– inspired by the turrets on the roof of the house. The 6th Marquess planted
one of the world's longest hedge maze at Longleat in 1975, and new ones
planted by the persent Marquess are at various stages of growth, from the Sun
Maze and Lunar Labyrinth to the east of the house to the Love Labyrinth in
front of the orangery. Future examples of the genre will encompass a variety of
styles and materials. Elsewhere, the safari park and other attractions.

Mompesson House

The Close, Salisbury SP1 2EL. Tel: (01722) 335659

The National Trust • In city centre, N of Choristers' Green in Cathedral Close •
House open as garden • Garden open April to Oct, Sat – Wed (plus Fri, 9th
April), 11am – 5.30pm (last admission 4.30pm); • Entrance: 80p (house and
garden £3.90, children £1.95, parties £3.40 per person) (2003 prices) • Other
information: Parking in city centre. Teas when house open. NT shop nearby
◑ 🍵 WC ఈ 🕯

If visiting Salisbury, the Cathedral and the Close are a must. Take time also to
visit this small walled garden, which is in the Old English style. Its tranquil
atmosphere is very refreshing. Summer is best, with the old-fashioned roses in
bloom, but it is attractive throughout the open season.

Oare House ★ [Historic Garden Grade II]

Oare, Marlborough SN8 4JQ. Tel: (01672) 562613

*Mr Henry Keswick • 2m N of Pewsey on A345 • Open two days for NGS, 2 –
6pm • Entrance: £2, children 20p* ● ●

The 1740 house was extended by Clough Williams-Ellis in the 1920s and the
garden created from 1920 to 1960 by two successive owners, Sir Geoffrey Fry
and Henry Keswick. The house is seen as the backdrop to a cathedral-like nave
of limes, a worthy overture to many good things. The main garden is
approached through a wisteria-covered pergola enlivened by a lily pond
and tinkling fountain. Great yew hedges enclose the garden outside the
library, from which an elegant loggia can be spied along a formal axis of
pleached limes. Below is a long, corridor-like secret garden where good brick
walls have been used for interesting planting. In the impressive kitchen garden
fruit and vegetables are arranged around the edge in purposeful manner
behind their lavender hedges, espalier fruit trees and shrub roses. One of
the two axial paths is dominated entirely by white roses while in the other a
mossy gravel path threads its way through a tunnel of herbaceous plants with
yellow and white violas spilling out beneath clumps of richly coloured phlox
and heleniums. The lawns to the west of the house are very much in the grand
manner. Substantial borders on either side of the main lawn lead down to a
gate in the wall to a massive swimming pool flanked by herbaceous borders.
From this side of the house the eye is drawn up a broad and steep ride flanked
by an avenue of mature limes and twin bluebell woods, shimmering blue in
spring. I.M. Pei's two-storeyed glass pagoda may terminate the ride but it is
kept in its place by the grand encircling sweep of the Marlborough Downs.

The Old Mill

Ramsbury SN8 2PN. Tel: (01672) 520266

*James and Annabel Dallas • 5m NE of Marlborough. Go down High Street, turn
right at The Bell pub (signed to Hungerford); garden is 90 metres on right
behind yew hedge • Open 12th May, 20th June, 15th Sept for NGS, 2 – 6pm,
and by appt • Entrance: £3, children free* [NEW] ●

It would be hard to imagine a more idyllic setting for a garden than the
grounds of this ancient rambling mill house. The River Kennet runs through
and therefore divides the garden, so that from the formal areas near the house
on one side of the river there are lovely views of a wilder and more natural
landscape across the flow of water. The pool, mill stream, mill race and
numerous channels, all once part of the original working mill, dominate
and shape the five acres of cultivated land, giving the garden its special allure
and character. The design never intrudes on the natural beauty of the site –
this is due to Mrs Dallas' light touch with colour and choice of plants, many of
them grown from seed, which veers away from anything that looks too
contrived. The whole place is full of experiment and ideas which are constantly
being developed. Close to the house are ebullient borders of salvias, other
colour-themed borders and an attractive area combining an informal arrange-

ment of pots with planting in gravel. Wooden bridges cross streams to extend the garden into different areas: an enclosure of lawn and herbaceous borders leads into a green garden backed by an old brick wall, and thence to the bog garden and wilder parts at the periphery.

The Old Vicarage ★

Edington, Westbury BA13 4QF. Tel: (01380) 830512

J.N. d'Arcy • 4m NE of Westbury on B3098 to West Lavington. Signposted • Open once for charity in mid-June, and by appt • Entrance: £4, children free (includes other neighbouring gardens) • Other information: Parking in church car park ● &

Every year new discoveries mark the travels of this peripatetic gardener, who has created a varied, scented garden on a two-and-a-half-acre escarpment set high on the north side of Salisbury Plain. To be shown round by Mr d'Arcy is a treat as he mixes wit with erudition. Swags of clematis, cistus and mahonias enliven the plain façade of the former vicarage; a wide lawn – croquet of course – leads to a meadow artful with wild flowers beneath rare varieties of chestnut, sorbus and maple. The National Collection of evening primroses gives pleasure after dusk. Stunning views towards Edington Church lift the visitor's eyes through well-planted vistas. Dividing the garden is a dense yew hedge, only 17 years old, which is clipped so that the base gets the light. 'For a mature hedge it is agreeably slim,' he says. An *allée* of fastigiate hornbeams points the view towards Devizes. Newly built brick walls create rooms and shelter exotic plants and trees, and a base of natural greensand over clay and a mulch from elaborate bays of compost ensure vigorous plants. Waves of phlomis species mark the hot garden, while a sunken garden to the rear of the house is romantically planted in cool shades round a 15-metre well. Nepetas, a particular passion, run riot. Towards the end of the tour a gravel bed is a sea of agapanthus and eryngiums, and everywhere seedlings push through the gravel – phlomis, dieramas, *Acanthus discoridis* and *Oenothera caespitosa* 'Marginata', an unusual evening primrose with white flowers. The strong salvia, *S. darcyi*, is a souvenir of his Mexican tour – 400 species there.

Old Wardour Castle [Historic Garden Grade II*]

Tisbury, Salisbury SP3 6RR. Tel: (01747) 870487

English Heritage • 2m SW of Tisbury off A30 • Open April to Oct, daily, 10am – 6pm (closes 5pm in Oct); Nov to March, Wed – Sun, 10am – 1pm and 2 – 4pm. Closed 24th to 26th Dec, 1st Jan • Entrance: £2.50, concessions £1.90, children £1.30 (2003 prices) ○ ☕ 🏴 WC & ⬗ 👍 💡

In a picture-book setting, the ruins of this fourteenth-century castle stand overlooking a lake and surrounded by woodland. The small garden was laid out in the eighteenth century when the nearby New Wardour Castle was built, and remnants of this landscape can still be seen in some fine trees and shrubs. There is a pavilion in Gothic style and a picturesque grotto built of stone, brick and plaster by Josiah Lane, a noted creator of rockwork grottos in Wiltshire in the eighteenth century. Paths and tunnels twist between ancient-looking weathered rocks containing nooks and alcoves. Notable among the trees is a stand of yews around 400 years old, Atlas Mountain cedars of between 150 and 200 years old, and a mighty cedar of Lebanon.

Pound Hill Garden

West Kington, Chippenham SN14 7JG. Tel: (01249) 783880

Mr and Mrs Philip Stockitt • 8m W of Chippenham, 2m NE of Marshfield between A420 and M4 • Open Feb to Oct, daily, 2 – 5pm, and for parties by appt • Entrance: £3 • Other information: Plants for sale in adjacent plant centre open daily except Jan, 10am – 5pm ◐ ☕ ✕ WC ⅏ ✣ ⍟

A Cotswold garden in two acres around a sixteenth-century stone house. The viewer takes in the effect from the plant centre through to an 'old-fashioned rose garden' (planted and labelled David Austin roses) leading to a Victorian vegetable garden with espaliered fruit trees, then through a wisteria, rose and clematis tunnel, culminating in a statue. Beyond is an orchard, a Cotswold garden with topiary, herbaceous border and drystone walls showing off a parterre of clipped box, *Rosa* 'The Fairy', seasonal pots and rose-covered obelisks. A water garden, with many shade-loving as well as moisture-loving plants, is surrounded by yew hedging to create another small garden. A corridor lined by *Betula utilis* var. *jacquemontii*, underplanted with *Pulmonaria officinalis* 'Sissinghurst White' and 'Queen of the Night' tulips, leads on to a rose walk lined with clipped sweet chestnuts underplanted with old-fashioned roses. The courtyard has many interesting planters. The nursery sells progenies from 2000 varieties of rarer plants as well as roses, topiary and specimen plants.

The Priory

Kington St Michael, Chippenham SN14 6JG. Tel: (01249) 750360

Mme Anita Pereire • 3m N of Chippenham off A350 between Chippenham and M4 junction 17. Drive through village, then turn left down lane opposite stud farm on right at bottom of hill • Open by appt only • Entrance: £3 ◐ ☕ WC ⅏

Since 1994 the owner, a well-known writer and garden designer, has created a magical garden around the buildings of an ancient priory. A firm overall structure and lavish planting have combined to make this a most satisfying and elegant garden. Radiating from a central patchwork stone path lined with an avenue of weeping silver pears (Mme Pereire's signature tree) are well-defined and separate areas. These include a ha-ha-cum-rockery, a breathtaking 'French' garden of topiary and standard roses (the long-lasting 'The Fairy' and 'Ballerina'), an exquisite water garden, a ha-ha ablaze with rock plants, perennials and flowering shrubs, and a classic rose garden filled with colour and scent from masses of old-fashioned roses. Beyond the hedge-enclosed part of the garden lies a meadow with mown paths forming a maze among the long grasses. In the wild garden further mown grass paths, edged with wild roses, lead down to a gravel garden which blends seamlessly into the surrounding meadowland.

Ridleys Cheer

Mountain Bower, Chippenham SN14 7AJ. Tel: (01225) 891204

Mr and Mrs Antony Young • 8m W of Chippenham off A420. Turn N at The Shoe pub, take second left, then first right • Open 4th April, 16th May, 13th June, 2 – 6pm, and for parties by appt • Entrance: £2.50, children under 14 free, parties £3.50 per person • Other information: Picnics in meadow only, from 1pm ● ➤ 🍵 WC & 🌿 🔍 B&B

The garden, created over the past 20 years, covers some three acres, two of which hold a young and interesting arboretum, and there is also a three-acre wildflower meadow. The garden is on two levels, connected by a broad flight of steps and a grass walk, and contains many fine examples of rarer shrubs and trees. The shrub roses, including some 120 species and hybrids seldom encountered, are a major summer feature. There is a small *potager*, and a gravel garden planted with box and yew outside the conservatory. Autumn colour is given by a growing number of maples, beeches, tulip trees, oaks and zelkovas. In the main, this in an informal garden, full of appeal for plantsmen, who can derive much information from the knowledgeable owners. A small nursery sells trees, shrubs and perennials, many of them unusual.

Sharcott Manor

Pewsey SN9 5PA. Tel: (01672) 563485

Captain and Mrs David Armytage • 1m SW of Pewsey off A345 • Open April to Oct, first Wed in month, 11am – 5pm, two days for NGS, 2 – 6pm, and for parties by appt • Entrance: £2.50 • Other information: Teas on NGS open days and for groups on request ● WC & 🌿

A fine six-acre garden, mainly informal in character and largely created over the last twenty-five years. More formal areas with lawns and generous borders lead on to water and woodland plantings which include many rare and beautiful trees. The owner is an avowed plant collector and enthusiast, and the whole garden is densely planted with a rich choice of colourful subjects. The family atmosphere of the garden is much appreciated by visitors, and those more expert can revel in the fine effects and groupings that have been achieved. The widely varied plantings ensure a long season of interest, such as the thousands of bulbs blooming in the woodlands in spring and the climbing roses cascading through the trees in late June; an avenue of *Pyrus calleryana* 'Chanticleer', leading down the lower lawn towards the stream, gives scarlet autumn colour. The small collection of waterfowl is an unexpected delight.

Stourhead ★★ [Historic Garden Grade I]

Stourton, Warminster BA12 6QF. Tel: (01747) 841152

The National Trust • 3m NW of Mere (A303) at Stourton off B3092 • House open April to Oct, Fri – Tues, 11am – 5pm (or dusk if earlier) • Garden open all year, daily, 9am – 7pm (or dusk if earlier) • Entrance: House or garden, April to Oct:

£5.10, children (5–16) £2.90, family £12.70; garden only, Nov to Feb, £3.95, children £1.90, family £9.50; house and garden £8.90, children £4.30, family £21.20 (2003 prices) • Other information: Refreshments in restaurant or at Spread Eagle Inn at garden entrance. Wheelchairs available. Buggy service from car park in peak season. Dogs Nov to Feb only ○ ▇ ▇ WC ♿ ♨ ▇ ● ✎

An outstanding example of an English landscape garden, designed by Henry Hoare II between 1741 and 1780, a paragon in its day and almost the greatest surviving garden of its kind. The sequence of arcadian images is revealed gradually if one follows a route anti-clockwise around the lake, having come from the house along the top route, so seeing the lake from above. Each experience is doubly inspiring: visitors glimpse classical temples across the water, almost unattainable and mirage-like, and when they reach their goal some other vision always attracts the eye – the boat-house, Temple of Flora, turf bridge, Temple of Apollo, rock bridge, cascade (these two are tucked away and very surprising), Pantheon, Gothic rustic cottage and grotto. The view from the Temple of Apollo (1765) was described by Horace Walpole as 'one of the most picturesque scenes in the world', by which he meant that it was as fine as a painting. To gain a better idea of how these buildings would have looked had the surrounding planting remained as it was originally, take a walk by Turner's Paddock Lake below the cascade. Between 1791 and 1838 Hoare's grandson Richard Colt Hoare planted many new species, particularly from America, including tulip trees, swamp cypresses and Indian bean trees. He also introduced *Rhododendron ponticum*. From 1894 the 6th Baronet added to these with the latest kinds of hybrid rhododendrons and scented azaleas, and a large number of copper beeches and conifers, such as the Japanese white pine, Sitka spruce and Californian nutmeg, of which many are record-sized specimens. In the early nineteenth century Stourhead boasted one of the best collections of pelargoniums in the world, over 600 varieties. The latest effort to emulate Richard Colt Hoare's interests consists of over 100 varieties of pelargoniums in a 1910 lean-to greenhouse. Especially wonderful in winter when the garden is quiet, and more views are afforded through the bare trees. Adjacent to Stourhead, and sharing the same car park, is *Stourton House Flower Garden*, a colourful five-acre garden with a wide range of rare species and profusion of plants for drying (many for sale). [Open April to Nov, Wed, Thurs, Sun and Bank Holiday Mons, 11am – 6pm.]

Westwood Manor

Bradford–on–Avon BA15 2AF. Tel: (01225) 863374

The National Trust • 1½ m NW of Trowbridge, 1½ m SW of Bradford-on-Avon off B3109. In Westwood beside church • Open April to Sept, Sun, Tues, Wed, 2 – 5pm, and at other times for parties of up to 20 by written appt with s.a.e. • Entrance: £4.20 (2003 price) ◐

Turning from the Italianate glories of Iford Manor (see entry) one mile away, topiarists and others might like to contemplate the dense green geometry of the garden here. There are no flowers, other than the lilies in the pond set into the lawn and the swathes of wisteria on the wall leading to the entrance. A small garden links the ancient barns to the medieval manor house which the yew hedges enfold and enclose. This simple design looks centuries-old but dates from the early part of the twentieth century, when Mr Edgar Lister purchased and restored the house and created and designed the garden, both of which he later left to the Trust. The late James Lees-Milne wrote that the exquisite manor in its present form 'was his [Lister's] creation and should be his memorial'. It must be emphasised that the garden should be visited as an adjunct and a complement to the house, which is lived in and administered by the Trust's tenant.

Wilton House ★ [Historic Garden Grade I]

Wilton, Salisbury SP2 0BJ. Tel: (01722) 746729

The Earl of Pembroke • 3m W of Salisbury on A30 • House open • Grounds open 2nd April to Oct, daily, 10.30am – 5.30pm (last admission 4.30pm) • Entrance: £4.50, children £3.50, family £14 (house, grounds and exhibition areas £9.75, OAPs £7.50, children (5–15) £5.50, family £24, parties £7 per person) • Other information: Plants for sale in garden centre ◑ ☕ ✕ 🍴 WC & 🦽 🏛 🚻 ♿

The first garden the visitor used to see, in the north courtyard, was designed by David Vickery in 1971. It incorporated formal pleached limes in a rectangular layout, the geometry being further emphasised by a box parterre infilled with lavender and a central, torrential fountain which provides a cool haven in summer. It created a green space with immense style which manages to answer the architecture of the house. A wrought-iron gate adjoining the courtyard leads to the east front with wall-trained shrubs and extensive herbaceous borders. Looking to the south, the Palladian bridge built in 1737 spanning the River Nadder is a focal point. Beside this stands a fine golden oak, *Quercus robur* 'Concordia', raised and grafted in 1843 at a nursery in Ghent. Going east along the broad gravel walk among many specimen trees set in eighteenth-century landscaped parkland, the visitor reaches the walled rose garden containing a large collection of old-fashioned English roses. This adjoins a pergola clothed with climbing plants and a water garden containing roses, aquatic species and ornamental fish. Beyond is the Whispering Seat with its unusual acoustic properties and a loggia facing the statue from the Arundel collection, all enclosed by a short avenue of *Quercus ilex*, with the river a glistening vista in the distance. Within the central courtyard of the house, the current (17th) Earl commissioned Xa Tollemache to design the fourth new garden (visible but not visitable) where, echoing designs from the central, ninth-century Venetian wellhead, a border of cotton lavender encloses quadrants of clipped box hedge. For children there is fun and excitement in a large adventure playground; for historians, interest in searching out those parts of the garden which show the work of Isaac de Caus (*c.* 1632), the 8th Earl, the 9th 'Architect Earl', Sir William Chambers and James Wyatt (1801). Tree-trail leaflet available. Nearby is *Philipps House*, Dinton (Tel: (01985) 843600), a National Trust house by Wyatville *c.* 1816, open all year with 100-acre *Dinton Park*. The house (ground floor only) is open 4th April to Oct, Mon, 1 – 5pm and Sat, 9am – 1pm. Walks in the park and woodland start from the car park.

WORCESTERSHIRE

24 Alexander Avenue

Droitwich WR9 8NH. Tel: (01905) 774907

David and Malley Terry • Take M5 exit 5 or 6, then A38 • Open 25th April, 6th June, 11th July for NGS, and by appt • Entrance: £2 ● & ⚘

This small garden is a lesson in what can be done in a small space and a short time. The present owners moved here in the winter of 1995 and have turned a barren patch of grass into a paradise. High hedges obscure the views of neighbouring houses, and through them climb some of the 100 clematis the garden grows. The borders are stuffed with a dazzling array of interesting plants, many of them rare; most shrubs have climbers growing through them. There is a fine collection of ferns, and alpines grow in many old stone troughs or the gravel bed in front of the house. A garden of immaculate artistry.

Barnard's Green House

**10 Poolbrook Road, Barnard's Green, Great Malvern WR14 3NQ.
Tel: (01684) 574446**

Mr and Mrs Philip Nicholls • Just E of Great Malvern at B4211/B4208 junction • Open April to Sept, Thurs, 2 – 6pm, 4th April, 27th July for NGS, and at other times by appt • Entrance: £2.50, children free ● ▦ WC & ⚘ ⬤

This immaculately kept, quintessentially English garden, set behind a neat seventeenth-century house, has at its centre a tranquil lawn with a great cedar and a young cut-leaved beech. Beyond this, winding paths and gateways lead to areas of differing character, the highlight in summer being the splendid herbaceous borders. Mrs Nicholls is a plantswoman with an eye for colour, and here mauves, blues and pinks are lifted by touches of magenta and by gold and silver foliage. Pink roses cascade over a pergola behind. Entered through an arch cut into a venerable yew hedge, and set beneath mature limes and horse chestnuts, is a shady garden filled with euphorbias, ferns, hostas, geraniums, epimediums and hydrangeas. A vegetable, fruit and cutting garden lays out its offerings in a more formal hedged enclosure, intersected in a traditional way by herringbone brick paths and edged with box; the rows of peonies, roses and delphiniums are particularly impressive. Elsewhere is a small white border, a red border, and a well-planted shrub border containing fine hydrangeas and philadelphus, as well a rockery, a small pond and rose borders.

Burford House Gardens ★

Tenbury Wells WR15 8HQ. Tel: (01584) 810777

Burford Garden Company • 19m SW of Kidderminster, 1m W of Tenbury Wells on A456; 8m S of Ludlow via A49 and A456 • Open all year, daily, 9am – 6pm (or dusk if earlier). Closed 25th, 26th Dec • Entrance: £3.95, children £1.

Parties of 20 or more by prior arrangement £3 per person • Other information: Plants for sale, especially clematis, at Burford Garden Company opposite ○ ☕ ✗ <u>WC</u> ♿ ✿ ⌂

John Treasure's gardens, planned and planted over forty years from 1954, are now mature and a classic of their time. The approach to the gardens via the large garden centre has become rather impersonal, but once through the garden gate there has been little change. A huge variety of species is grown here in the broad sinuous mixed borders, which cross the smooth lawns, with much of the herbaceous planting devised for late summer colour. Elsewhere, streamside gardens look attractive in spring and early summer, while *Erigeron mucronatus* clothes the more formal terraces against the house, which is draped with a magnificent *Wisteria macrobotrys* 'Burford'. The gardens remain a showcase for clematis, in which the garden centre specialises. An exciting recent development across the brook which skirts the main garden is the meadow garden, the work of the designer Charles Chesshire, who also improved the run-down areas of the garden when he moved to Burford House in 1993. Mown grass paths curve through the meadows into circular enclosures of amelanchier or cherry, or dive into a maze of beech hedging which serves as a sculpture gallery in summer. A tiny track leads down through the wild flowers to the banks of the River Teme. The whole forms a perfect balance to the more contrived informality of the original gardens.

Conderton Manor ★

Conderton, Tewkesbury, Gloucestershire GL20 7PR. Tel: (01386) 725389;

Mr and Mrs William Carr • 8m SW of Evesham, 5½ m NE of Tewkesbury between A46 and B4079. Opposite Yew Tree Inn in Conderton • Open for NGS, and by appt • Entrance: £4 • Other information: Refreshments by prior arrangement and at Yew Tree Inn. Toilet facilities by arrangement ◗ ♿

The seven-acre garden of this fine seventeenth-century manor house has spectacular views. Completely restructured over the last ten years, it has an attractive parterre containing foliage plants on the terrace, an old vegetable garden transformed with rose arches and mixed borders, and a 135-metre-long border with unusual shrubs. The quarry garden and bog bank includes cornus and salix for winter stem colour with ferns and primulas for the summer. The vistas through the box walk, cider apple avenue and the fountain garden are quite magnificent. Unusual trees, the owner's special interest, are everywhere. A garden for all seasons.

Croome Park [Historic Park Grade I]

High Green, Severn Stoke WR8 9JS. Tel: (01905) 371006

The National Trust • 8m S of Worcester, E of A38 and M5 • Open 21st March to 2nd Nov, Fri – Mon, 11am – 5pm. Guided tours by appt in writing • Entrance: Gardens £4, children £1.70, family £8.50 • Other information: For disabled access, telephone in advance ◑ ▦ <u>WC</u> ◈

'Capability' Brown's career as an independent landscape designer and architect was effectively launched at Croome Court, of which today's park was once an integral part. The house (not open) was sold by the family who commissioned it and remains in private hands. In 1996 The National Trust purchased 670 acres of the parkland with generous help from the Heritage Lottery Fund and Royal & Sun Alliance. The ten-year restoration plan involves dredging all of Brown's considerable water-works, including the serpentine lake, and restoring the bridge across the lake, its small classical temple, and the rockwork tunnel under the main road, together with numerous other listed park buildings by Robert Adam and James Wyatt. Some 1400 trees have been planted as replacements for those lost from the original planting scheme.

Eastgrove Cottage Garden Nursery ★

Sankyns Green, Shrawley, Little Witley WR6 6LQ. Tel: (01299) 896389

Malcolm and Carol Skinner • 8m NW of Worcester on road between Shrawley (B4196) and Great Witley (A443) • Open 8th April to July, Thurs – Sun and Bank Holiday Mons; 2nd Sept to 16th Oct, Thurs – Sat, plus 26th Sept; all 2 – 5pm. Closed Aug • Entrance: £3, children free ◑ WC & ℗

This delightful cottage garden with a profusion of colour has been carefully designed to give each plant maximum impact, the interaction of variegated foliage and strongly coloured shrubs creating backdrops for a variety of perennials. A collection of flowers and foliage by the front door, looking stunningly casual, turns out to be all in pots. The brick paths lead through areas of clever colour combinations. The romantic Secret Garden, concentrating on pinks, mauves, silver and strong burgundy, leads into the Great Wall of China, a raised bed stuffed with sun-lovers and backed by old apple trees – a different atmosphere altogether. The arboretum, now extended, is artistically planted to give maximum effect to the variously coloured foliage. A wide range of well-grown, less usual plants is for sale, all propagated at the nursery.

Eastnor Castle [Historic Park Grade II*]

Eastnor, Ledbury HR8 1RL. Tel: (01531) 633160

Eastnor Estate • 8m SW of Great Malvern, 2m E of Ledbury on A438 • Castle open selected days for collections of armour, tapestries and fine art • Garden open 11th April to 3rd Oct, Sun and Bank Holiday Mons; July, Aug, daily except Sat; all 11am – 5pm • Entrance: £3.50, children £2.50 (house and garden £5.50, children £3.50) (2003 prices) • Other information: Refreshments on castle open days ◑ ☕ ▦ WC & ⬧ ♨ ⬛ ♿ ℗

The arboretum here contains some of the earliest plant-hunter collections of exotic trees in the country, especially of conifers. Roughly contemporary with the more famous arboretum at Westonbirt, the main collection was established between 1840 and 1860, with seed being brought from around the world throughout the nineteenth century. A tree trail leads to the most important and interesting specimens, and to far-flung areas of the extensive grounds. A lakeside walk gives fine views back to the fairytale Gothick castle. Restoration is ongoing: new groves of cercidiphyllums and acers, for example, will add to the variety of colour and texture for all seasons. Near to the castle, the terraces have not been restored to their nineteenth-century character; instead, a long border is planted for mid- to late-summer colour, while the upper terrace has an iris border, together with lavenders, santolina and other sun-loving shrubs. A cottage-style garden is being planted near the maturing yew maze. In Eastnor itself *The Long Barn*, Roger Oates' textile design studio, has a small, stylish garden reminiscent of a medieval *hortus conclusus* divided into square plots and enclosed by walls, hedges and trellis festooned with honeysuckle and roses. [Open for NGS, and to studio visitors.]

Hanbury Hall [Historic Garden Grade I]

School Road, Hanbury, Droitwich WR9 7EA. Tel: (01527) 821214

The National Trust • 4½ m E of Droitwich, off B4090 or B4091 • House open as garden, but Mon – Wed, 11am – 5pm, Sat and Sun, 1 – 5pm • Garden open March to Oct, Sat – Wed, 11am – 5.30pm • Entrance: £3.50, children £1.80, family £8.50 (house and garden £5.40, children £2.70, family £13, parties £4.60 per person) (2003 prices) • Other information: Batricar available
❶ 🍵 🏠 WC ⅙ ⬧ 🌢 🏛 💡 ⚲

The Trust has restored much of the early eighteenth-century garden design by George London, and the formal garden, typical of the period, comprises a sunken box-edged parterre, a fruit orchard and a wilderness. Structural additions include two summerhouses, two timber bowling-green pavilions and an obelisk. Lawns spread round to the orangery, which houses citrus trees. Further on a cedar walk leads to a fine ice-house. An almost three-metre pond has its fountains operated by solar panel. Near Droitwich is the 50-acre nursery *Webbs of Wychbold*, where Chelsea gold-medal winner Marigold Webb has created themed Riverside Gardens, including a new series of areas planted with naturalised perennials by Noel Kingsbury. [Open all year, daily except 25th, 26th Dec, 11th April, Mon – Sat, 9am – 6pm, Sun, 10.30am – 4.30pm.]

Lakeside

Gaines Road, Whitbourne, Worcester WR6 5RD. Tel: (01886) 821119

Mr D. Gueroult • 9m W of Worcester off A44. Turn left at county boundary sign, signed to Linley Green (ignore sign to Whitbourne) • Open by appt for parties of 10 or more • Entrance: £2.50, children free ❶ 🍵 WC

The first glimpse of this six-acre garden is a moment of sheer delight: a dramatic vista of the lake at the bottom of a steep grassy slope. The main part of the garden lies within the walls of what was the fruit garden of Gaines House nearby and consists of mixed beds and borders with many unusual plants, including bulbs and climbers. The main lake is the largest of three medieval stewponds. A small pinetum is maturing well, as is a large bog garden. A short woodland walk, bordered by ferns and different varieties of holly, leads to the attractive lakeside walk. Don't miss the view from the top of the heather garden.

Little Malvern Court

Little Malvern, Nr Malvern WR14 4JN. Tel: (01684) 892988

Mrs T.M. Berington • 4m S of Great Malvern on A4104 S of junction with A449 • Open 14th April to 15th July, Wed, Thurs, also 21st March, 3rd May for NGS, all 2 – 5pm. Private visits welcome weekdays only by appt NEW ● WC &

Tucked into the side of the Malvern Hills, and spread out beside an ancient gabled manor house and priory church, this is a garden of great romantic charm. The medieval fish ponds, bulging yew hedges clipped into fantastic shapes and a venerable lime tree remain from earlier gardens, but much dates from 1982 onwards, originally laid out by Arabella Lennox-Boyd and continued by Michael Balston. Close to the house, a classic English combination of clipped hedges and pergolas defining formal areas filled with soft planting creates satisfying contrasts. Moving from area to area, themes develop and vistas are opened up. Pale colours and soft textures are used to great effect, and the garden gains a modern edge by the elegant simplicity of some of the planting, such as a clipped box hedge set against a clipped yew hedge and a billowing choisya in the entrance forecourt, and elsewhere a simple horseshoe of pleached limes around a small lawn. Below the house a series of small lakes connected by weirs is embraced by mown grass paths, flanked by wildflowers and maturing trees. At the top of the first lake is a new rock garden and a watery gravel bed where primulas and irises are naturalising. This evolving, imaginative and immaculately presented garden repays several visits.

Luggers Hall

Springfield Lane, Broadway WR12 7BT. Tel: (01386) 852040

Mr and Mrs R. Haslam • In Broadway turn off High Street by Swan Hotel, bear left into Springfield Lane, garden is 270 metres on left • Open three days for NGS, and May to Sept for parties of 20 or more by appt • Entrance: £2, children free NEW ● ● WC & ⬦ ✿ B&B

The Victorian painter of gardens and landscapes Alfred Parsons built the house for himself in 1911 and designed the $2\frac{1}{2}$-acre garden in the style typical of the Arts and Crafts Movement centred around Broadway at that time. The present owners have been gradually restoring the garden since 1995, retaining its overall character and adding ideas of their own. The main lawn, with hedged compartments opening off it, has a splendid battlemented yew hedge to one side, and the rose garden remains unchanged with criss-cross paths of broken Cotswold stone. The parterre, reconstructed with the aid of an original black-and-white aerial photograph, has been replanted with white roses and blue perennials. Mrs Haslam's colour effects are superb: themed borders in the walled garden and elsewhere range from palest yellows through blues to intense shades of pink, with many unusual plants including a wide variety of salvias. A white garden is tucked away, and there is also a *potager* and a tranquil leafy corner where the former swimming pool has been transformed into a home for the koi carp. Gravel paths with strategically placed seats connect the different areas, and Broadway Tower may be glimpsed between the trees.

The Manor House

Birlingham, Pershore WR10 3AF. Tel: (01386) 750005

Mr and Mrs D. Williams-Thomas • 8m W of Evesham, 2m SW of Pershore, off A4104 in Birlingham • Open for NGS 12th, 13th June, 11.30am – 5.30pm, and May to June for individuals and parties of 20 or more by appt • Entrance: £3, children free • Other information: Rare plant fair 13th June, entrance £3.50

● ● ● WC ● ●

The charm here lies in the successful blend of spacious, informal areas, made up of sweeping lawns, wide, well-stocked borders and splendid views over open countryside, with more enclosed, formal gardens where a sense of secrecy and intimacy is maintained. Notable is a partly walled white garden where old brick paths weave amongst massed plantings of roses, hardy geraniums and campanulas complemented by grey-foliage plants. On the south side of the house an expanse of lawn carries the eye over a ha-ha and meadow to the river, a view echoed from the windows of a pretty little summerhouse retreat. Mature trees and hedges, climbing roses and free-flowering clematis give an air of tranquillity.

Overbury Court ★ [Historic Garden Grade II*]

Overbury, Tewkesbury, Gloucestershire GL20 7NP. Tel: (01386) 725528

Mr and Mrs Bruce Bossom • 9m SW of Evesham, 5m NE of Tewkesbury, 2½ m N of Teddington (A46/A435) roundabout • Open by appt only • Entrance: £2, children free (2003 price) ● ●

The superb garden, largely laid out in the late nineteenth and early twentieth centuries, provides the setting for a fine early-eighteenth-century house. It is bordered by lush parkland giving unspoiled views in all directions. Everywhere there is water. Behind the house, a brook issues into a tufa grotto. Rough steps wind between cascades and through naturalistic plantings of hostas, filipendulas, wild garlic and ferns, backed by mature box bushes. The brook, emerging along a broad rill bordered on one side by meadow and on the other by lawn, descends through gentle cascades and winds around a series of pools beyond a great lawn. Huge plane and lime trees contrast with the smoothness of grass and water. The simplicity is magical. Massive yew hedges separate this part of the garden from the more formal area to the south, where the centrepiece is an avenue of Irish yews flanked by a sunken bowling lawn and a formal pool. Again, the planting is simple yet stunning – to the east a glorious crinkle-crankle border of gold and silver foliage by Peter Coates, and to the west a sunken double mixed border displaying mainly old-fashioned and species roses, underplanted with geraniums and *Alchemilla mollis*. Near the house is a small terrace with silver and white borders, and well-trained shrubs and climbers clothe the house walls.

Pershore College

'Avonbank', Pershore WR10 3JP. Tel: (01386) 552443

7m SE of M5 junction 7, 1m E of Pershore on B4084 • Open 6th June for College Open Day, 10am – 5pm, and weekdays by appt for large parties • Entrance: £1, coaches by appt on open day ● 🐾 <u>WC</u> ♿ 🌿 🧺 🌡 🐕

The grounds are working areas designed with an educational bias, and include 'model gardens' created by students, and a variety of specialist gardens. There is also an arboretum, orchards, automated glasshouses and a hardy plant production nursery and plant centre. The RHS Pershore Centre is on the campus, and the Alpine Garden Society has its national HQ here; the college also holds National Collections of penstemons and philadelphus.

The Picton Garden

Old Court Nurseries, Colwall, Great Malvern WR13 6QE. Tel: (01684) 540416

Mr and Mrs P. Picton • 3m SW of Great Malvern on B4218 • Open Aug, Wed – Sun; Sept, 1st to 12th Oct, daily; all 11am – 5pm; and by appt May to July, 21st to 31st Oct • Old Court Nurseries open as garden • Entrance: £2.50, children under 15 free ◑ 🌿

A one-and-a-half-acre plantsman's garden on the site of Ernest Ballard's Old Court Nurseries. A large collection of herbaceous perennials ensures plenty of late summer interest, while shrubs and shade beds create year-round diversity. The National Collection of Michaelmas daisies is here, growing in every imaginable variety, notably as the dominant force in the former alpine and rose gardens. Another interesting garden close by is *Caves Folly Nursery* in Evandine Lane, off Colwall Green, B4218 between Malvern and Ledbury [open Thurs–Sat, 10am–5pm all year]. The garden is open twice for NGS and group visits are welcome at other times (Tel: (01684) 540631).

Shuttifield Cottage

Birchwood, Storridge, Malvern WR13 5HA. Tel: (01886) 884243

Angela and David Judge • 8m SW of Worcester off A4103. Turn right opposite Storridge church to Birchwood. After 1¼ m turn left down tarmac drive. Park on road and walk down this drive • Open 18th April, 1st, 22nd May, 10th July, 14th Aug, 25th Sept, 2 – 5pm, plus 19th June (Rose Day), 12 noon – 5pm, and at other times by appt • Entrance: £2.50, children free ● 🍵 🌿

Lawns lead down the sloping site in a succession of pleasure and interest, past borders and beds planted with shrubs and flowering plants – many of them unusual – to the rose garden. This has space for a large collection of old varieties to spread, sprawl, climb and bloom abundantly in what is almost a secret garden. Beyond is a 20-acre wood carpeted with wood anemones and bluebells. In other parts are colour-themed beds, splendid trees, herbaceous plants, a woodland walk, a vegetable garden, a deer park and ponds. The planning and planting are skilful, the effect is natural and unstudied.

Spetchley Park [Historic Park Grade II*]

Spetchley, Worcester WR5 1RS. Tel: (01905) 345224/213

*Trustees of Spetchley Gardens Charitable Trust • 3m E of Worcester on A44 •
Open April to Sept, Tues – Fri and Bank Holiday Mons, 11am – 5pm, Sun, 2
– 5pm (last entry 4pm) • Entrance: £4, children £2* ◗ 🍵 WC ঌ

The grand Victorian gardens, surrounded by seventeenth-century parkland,
were laid out and extended by successive generations of the Berkeley family.
Ellen Willmott, a relative, was a frequent visitor and helped to fashion the
planting, evidenced by *Eryngium* 'Miss Willmott's Ghost' still self-seeding in the
vast herbaceous borders. The current owner, a plant collector, is expanding
the area under cultivation, with a view to allowing the plants to do their own
thing, even in more formal parts within and around the old walled garden.
Everywhere gravel or daisy-strewn grass walks lead you on between yew
hedges or old shrubberies to discover further areas punctuated by statue and
fountain, and a visit in June is rewarded by spectacular expanses of naturalised
Martagon lilies, together with *Campanula pyramidalis*. In the extensive woodland
garden, the varied collection includes many dogwoods and acers, and extensive recent plantings supplement the many fine mature trees. The Park Lake is
fringed with water lilies and bulrushes, with views to the deer park beyond.

Stone House Cottage Gardens ★

Stone, Kidderminster DY10 4BG. Tel: (01562) 69902

*Mr and Mrs James Arbuthnott • 2m SE of Kidderminster via A448 • Open
March to Sept, Wed – Sat, 10am – 5.30pm, and Oct to March by appt •
Entrance: £2.50, children free* ◗ WC ঌ ⌖

The garden has been created since 1974, and looking round it now, it is difficult to
believe that the whole area was once flat and bare. The owners have skilfully built
towers and follies to create small intimate areas and at the same time provide
homes for many unusual climbers and shrubs. Yew hedges break up the area to
give a vista with a tower at the end, covered with wisteria, roses and clematis.
Hardly anywhere does a climber grow in isolation – something will be scrambling
up it, usually a small late-flowering clematis. Raised beds are full to overflowing,
shrubs and unusual herbaceous plants mingle happily. In a grassed area shrubs are
making good specimens. In June during two evenings of music the towers have a
secondary purpose as platforms for wind ensembles. You are invited to picnic in
the garden for a modest fee – the effect is akin to non-pretentious Glyndebourne
transplanted to San Gimignano. At other times you may ascend the towers to view
the garden as a whole for the price of a donation to the Mother Theresa charity.

21 Swinton Lane

Worcester WR2 4JP. Tel: (01905) 422265

*Mr A. Poulton • 1½ m W of city centre off Bransford road (B4485) from St
Johns to Rushwick. Turn left between Portobello pub and Worcester golf course •
Open by appt only • Entrance: £2* ◗ ⌖

Behind the 1930s' house, in a space no greater than one third of an acre, the owner has created a most imaginatively planned, splendidly planted, atmospheric garden. Clever use of divisions, hedges, trees, shrubs and trelliswork has resulted in distinct areas or enclosures, notably a beautifully conceived and executed silver and white garden, designed for all-year interest, a hot late-summer border and an area devoted to shade-loving plants. Throughout, herbaceous borders are supplemented with pot-grown, tender perennials, which are moved in and out of key positions according to flowering season.

Witley Court [Historic Garden Grade II*]

Worcester Road, Great Witley, Worcester WR6 6JT. Tel: (01299) 896636

English Heritage • 10m NW of Worcester on A433 • Open April to Oct, daily, 10am – 6pm (5pm in Oct); Nov to March 2005, Wed – Sun, 10am – 4pm. Closed 25th, 26th Dec, 1st Jan. Evening guided tours available by appt • Entrance: £3.80, OAPs £2.90, children £1.90, family ticket £9.50 (2003 prices) • Other information: Disabled parking available ◐ 🍽 🧺 WC �& ⟴ 🏺 ⚲

Witley Court is an early Jacobean manor house which in the nineteenth century was turned into a vast Italianate mansion, with porticos by John Nash. It is now a spectacular ruin. The elaborate gardens, William Nesfield's 'Monster Work', still contain immense stone fountains. Gravel walks lead around the lake and through woodland to the house and the skeleton of the formal Victorian gardens, which it is hoped will soon be restored. The Jerwood Foundation Sculpture Park is being created here in the North Park, with Elizabeth Frink's 'The Walking Man' as its first permanent installation. Other sculptures have followed, including three by Michael Ayrton and one each by Lynn Chadwick, Antony Gormley and Kenneth Armitage. The landscape architects Colvin and Moggridge are creating spaces within the restored nineteenth-century wilderness to house the sculpture; they are also involved in new plantings in the Governor's Garden.

GUIDANCE ON SYMBOLS

Wheelchair users: the symbol &, denoting suitability for wheelchairs, refers to the garden only – if there is a house open, it may or may not be suitable. Additionally, some areas of the garden may not be accessible by wheelchair, or may require assistance.

Dogs: ⟴ indicates that there is somewhere on the premises where dogs may be walked, preferably on a lead. The garden itself is often taboo – parkland, or even the car park, are frequently indicated for the purpose.

Picnics: 🧺 means that picnics are allowed, but usually in certain restricted areas only. It does not give visitors the all-clear to feast where they please!

Children-friendly: the bat-and-ball symbol ⚲ suggests that there are activities specifically designed for children, such as an adventure playground or a discovery trail, or that the garden itself is likely to appeal to them.

YORKSHIRE (N. & E. RIDING)

Two-starred gardens are marked on the map with a black square.

Aldby Park ★ [Historic Park and Garden Grade II*]

Buttercrambe, York YO41 1XU. Tel (01759) 371398

Mr and Mrs G.M.V. Winn • 7m NW of York off A166 Bridlington road. Turn left at sign to Buttercrambe and continue ½ m past Gate Helmsley • Open one Sun for charity, and by appt • Entrance: £2, children £1 • Other information: Teas and other refreshments on open days only. Plants for sale in adjacent nursery ● ♨ ▨ WC & ◁ ℘

The fine 1726 house stands on a wooded hillside site which includes the mound and dry moat of King Edwin's seventh-century castle. The original terraced garden was created by Thomas Knowlton in 1746. In 1964 Mr Winn, who had known and loved the pre-war garden as a child, took over the house, and with a single gardener began the huge task of restoring what was by then a jungle to the garden we see today. The result is a triumph – a truly romantic garden which lifts the heart as it reveals itself to you. A glimpse through ornamental trees leads to a grassy terrace around a mound, decked on the sunny side with day lilies, yuccas and agapanthus. Pale colours contrast with the dark yews and box and range from white and yellow to silver and pink. In shady areas electric-blue geraniums take over, and a band of hostas flourishes free of slugs, thanks to hungry hedgehogs. Golden elders, *Hypericum* 'Hidcote' and corkscrew hazels add interest. Now a steep drop to the river is revealed, and the path leads down to a grassy walk along the water's edge, where kingcups and primulas glow and dark ferns thrive. On the water are black swans, greylag geese and ducks. Back up towards the house, a 'Kiftsgate' rose has smothered a large yew tree, and fine shrub roses, selected for looks and fragrance, abound.

Arden Hall

Hawnby, York YO62 5LS. Tel: (01439) 798396

The Earl and Countess of Mexborough • 11m NE of Thirsk, 9m NW of Helmsley off B1257 • Open two or three times a year for charities, and possibly by prior appt to suitably interested parties • Entrance: £3 ● ♨ WC ℘

Formerly the site of a Benedictine convent, the house (not open) was built in the eighteenth century, and the gardens are a series of formal terraces, dominated by a massive yew hedge at least 250 years old. A natural spring supplies four gallons of water a minute, a bonus imaginatively developed under the direction of gardener Stephen Mead. A formal Italianate pond is fed through a series of rills in stone troughs which pass through the terraces. An 80-feet-long laburnum walk and splendid borders have been made by the old croquet lawn. A 1920s' swimming pool (too cold for use) has been converted into a wildlife-oriented pond which flows into a stream and a series of pools before disappearing down the valley, rich in wild plants, especially wood garlic. Mead's philosophy is to progress from the naturally informal environment – an 'Arden' indeed.

Beningbrough Hall [Historic Garden Grade II]

Shipton-by-Beningbrough, York YO30 1DD. Tel: (01904) 470666

The National Trust • 8m NW of York off A19 York – Thirsk road at Shipton • House open as garden, but 12 noon – 5pm, with National Portrait Gallery loan exhibition • Gardens open 27th March to Oct, Sat – Wed; also Good Friday and Fri in July and Aug; all 11am – 5.30pm (last admission 4.30pm) • Entrance: gardens and exhibitions £5, children £2.50, family £12.50 (house, gardens and exhibitions £6, children £3, family £14) • Other information: Picnics in walled garden only ◐ 🍽 ✕ WC ⛨ ✿ 🏧 🍷 ⚲

The main formal garden, comprising geometrically patterned parterres, was laid out at the time the house was built in 1716, but replaced during the late eighteenth century by sweeping lawns and specimen trees, part of an estate of 365 acres. This is essentially a pleasure garden with an historic framework, amongst which considerable recent planting has been integrated. The wilderness and two privy gardens have been restored to the original standards, and there is a nineteenth-century American garden and a Victorian conservatory. The main border has been planted as part of a three-stage redevelopment project. New planting has brought the walled garden back to life, including more than 5000 lavender plants, flowers for cutting, blocks of vegetables, and soft fruit, with vegetables surplus to the restaurant requirements sold in the shop. Don't miss seeing the superb interior of the Baroque house.

Bolton Percy Churchyard

Bolton Percy, York YO23 7BA.

7½ m SW of York, 5m E of Tadcaster. Open all year, daily • Entrance: donation welcome ○ ⛨ ✿

The enthusiasm of Roger Brook has brought a wilderness under control in the splendid one-acre village churchyard, and it is now in all respects a paradise of garden plants growing in the new perennial style of gardening, with limited maintenance required – a lesson for churchwardens the country over. Roger Brook, who still maintains the churchyard, is now converting *Worsborough Village Cemetery* on the same principles [located five minutes from M1 at A61, near St Mary's Church, Birdwell, Worsborough].

Burnby Hall Gardens and Museum ★

The Balk, Pocklington, East Riding YO42 2QF. Tel: (01759) 302068

Stewart's Burnby Hall Gardens and Museum Trust • 13m E of York off A1079 in Pocklington • Open April to Sept, daily, 10am – 6pm • Entrance: £2.50, OAPs £2, children (5–15) £1, under 5 free. Parties of 20 or more £1.50 per person (2003 prices) ◐ 🍽 🍴 WC ⛨ ✿ 🏧 🍷 ⚲

When the gardens were established on eight acres of open farmland in 1904 by Major Stewart, the original ponds, which covered two acres, were constructed for fishing, but in 1935 they were converted to water-lily cultivation. The large collection of hardy water lilies here forms part of the National Collection. They may be seen from June to mid-September in a normal year, and in July and August the two lakes are covered in blooms from 80 different varieties.

Burton Agnes Hall

Burton Agnes, Driffield, East Riding YO25 4NB. Tel: (01262) 490324

Mrs Susan Cunliffe-Lister/Burton Agnes Preservation Trust Ltd • 5m S of Bridlington, 5m NE of Great Driffield on A166 • House open • Garden open April to Oct, daily, 11am – 5pm • Entrance: £2.60 (hall and garden £5.20, OAPs £4.70) ◑ 🍽 ✕ 🖼 WC ⛩ 🐕 🖽 👜 ℘

The beautiful Elizabethan hall – designed by Robert Smythson, master mason to Elizabeth I and builder of Longleat and Hardwick – is approached through the gatehouse archway, up a wide gravel drive flanked by rows of fig-shaped yew hedges, with lawns beyond. Little evidence remains of the garden's history, any former flower planting in sight of the hall having succumbed to lawn on all sides. However, the walls of the former enormous kitchen garden conceal a riot of colour (including campanulas, thymes, clematis, hardy geraniums and old roses). The *potager* of vegetables and herbs supplies the needs of the household. There are two herbaceous borders, a scented garden, a jungle of bamboos and giant exotic species, and a maze. A series of large-scale games (including chess, draughts and snakes and ladders) is laid out on paving at the end of the walled garden. Behind the hall is a woodland garden and a one-mile arboretum walk. Adjoining is the English Heritage *Burton Agnes Manor House*, a rare example of a Norman house open 'any reasonable time'.

Burton Constable Hall [Historic Park Grade II*]

Burton Constable, Hull, East Riding HU11 4LN. Tel: (01964) 562400

Burton Constable Foundation • 7½ m NE of Hull off A165 • House open as grounds, but 1 – 5pm (last admission 4pm) • Grounds open 3rd April to Oct, daily except Fri, 12.30 – 5pm • Entrance: £1, children 50p (hall and grounds £5, OAPs £4.50, children £2, family £11, parties please telephone for details) ◑ 🍽 🖼 WC ⛩ 🐕 🖽 ℘

The fine Elizabethan house, once the seat of the Chichester-Constables, was rescued by the National Heritage Memorial Fund in 1992 with a £3.5m endowment, and 300 acres of parkland were vested in Burton Constable Foundation. In 1999 work started on a ten-year programme to restore the 1770s' 'Capability' Brown park, replant the avenues, repair the ha-ha and Brown's bridge-cum-dam between the lakes, and reinstate the Victorian park fencing. An additional £1m in grant aid has been spent on the repurchase of important furnishings sold from the house.

Castle Howard ★★ [Historic Park Grade I]

York YO60 7DA. Tel: (01653) 648333

Castle Howard Estates Ltd • 17m NE of York, 5m SW of Malton off A64 • House open • Garden open mid-Feb to early Nov, daily, 10am – 4.30pm. Special tours of woodland garden and rose gardens available for pre-booked parties • Entrance: £6, children (4–16) £4, (house, gardens and grounds £9, OAPs £8, children (4–16) £6) (2003 prices). Rates for garden tours on request • Other information: Dogs permitted, on lead ◑ 🍵 ✕ 🏪 WC & ⟳ ⌀ 🛍 🏵 ⚲

Described as one of the finest examples of the heroic age of English landscape architecture, the house and grounds were first designed by Sir John Vanbrugh, assisted by Nicholas Hawksmoor. This architectural framework still basically exists, although over time features have been added, for example the impressive fountains designed by Nesfield. Although known principally as a fine landscape with remarkable park and buildings, there is also much for the garden lover. It holds one of the largest collections of old-fashioned and species roses in Europe, with the soil of the two gardens having been completely replaced in recent years and 2000 new roses planted. The Ray Wood and the adjacent area accommodate fine collections of magnolias, rhododendrons, sorbus and vacciniums, an adjunct to the newly extended arboretum, which will soon be one of the largest and most important in the country. An association has been formed between the Royal Botanic Gardens, Kew and Castle Howard to manage the wood. Most of the plants are well labelled.

Constable Burton Hall [Historic Park Grade II]

Leyburn, North Yorkshire DL8 5LJ. Tel: (01677) 450428

Mr Charles Wyvill • 16m NW of Ripon, 3m E of Leyburn on A684 • Open 21st March to 12th Oct, daily, 9am – 6pm. 3-day Tulip Festival 1st – 3rd May • Entrance: £2.50, OAPs £2, children 50p (honesty box) ◑ 🍵 WC & ⟳ ⌀ 🏵

In a walled and wooded parkland setting is a perfect Palladian mansion designed by John Carr of York in 1768. Built in beautiful honey-coloured sandstone, it rises from the lawns shaded by fine mature cedars. The owners have made a great effort to replant and develop. A delightful terraced woodland garden of lilies, ferns, hardy shrubs, roses and wild flowers drops down to a lake enhanced by an eighteenth-century bridge (no access). Near to the entrance drive are a stream and rock garden, and a new lily pond has been added. This substantial garden is a pleasure to visit because, after placing their entry coins in the honesty box, visitors can follow the numbered directional arrows using the concise notes to pass from one area of the garden to another (a technique that many other gardens could use with advantage). Surprises abound, such as *Lilium monadelphum* (yellow Turk's cap) in profusion and many mad climbers and shade-loving ground-cover plants. A herbaceous garden and several grand borders (over 6000 tulips planted each year to spectacular effect in May) have replaced the old formal rose garden. A fine morning or afternoon outing at all times of year.

Duncombe Park [Historic Park Grade I]

Helmsley, North Yorkshire YO62 5EB.
Tel: (01439) 770213/771115 (during open hours)

Lord Feversham • 12m E of Thirsk, 1m SW of Helmsley off A170 • House and garden open probably Easter to Oct – telephone for details. Parkland Centre and National Nature Reserve also open • Entrance: gardens and park £3.50, concessions £3, children (10 – 16) £1.75, parties of 15 or more £2.75 per person; park £2, children (10 – 16) £1 (house, garden and park £6.50, concessions £5, children (10 – 16) £3, family £13.50, parties of 15 or more £4.750 per person). Discounts for pre-booked parties visiting house and grounds • Other information: Parking at Parkland Centre. Alternative entrance for wheelchair users ◑ 🍽 ✕ 🏪 <u>WC</u> ♿ ◁⏀ 🛒 ♀ ✎

Home of the Duncombes for 300 years, the mansion has recently been restored as a family home by Lord Feversham. Its 35-acre garden, set in 300 acres of dramatic parkland, dates from *c.* 1715 and was described by Sacheverell Sitwell as 'the supreme masterpiece of the art of the landscape gardener'. Impressive are the tree-lined terraces, classical temples, statues and vast expanses of lawn. The magnificent trees, mostly dating from the original eighteenth-century planting, include the tallest ash and lime trees, according to the *Guinness Book of Records*. The ha-ha is one of the earliest ever built, pre-dating Bridgeman's at Stowe (see entry in Buckinghamshire). There is also a yew walk and an orangery.

Fountains Abbey

(see STUDLEY ROYAL AND FOUNTAINS ABBEY)

Gilling Castle [Historic Park Grade II]

Gilling East, North Yorkshire YO62 4HP. Tel: (01439) 788238

The Right Reverend The Abbot of Ampleforth • 20m N of York on B1363 York – Helmsley road • Great chamber and entrance hall of castle open by appt during term only • Garden open by appt, daily, 10am – 4pm • Entrance: £1.50, children free ○

A lovely garden in outstanding scenery. The terraces have been constructed on the south-facing side, four of them tumbling down the slope from an expansive lawn at the top. Many old-fashioned flowers grow in the borders, with a backdrop of majestic trees.

Hackfall Wood [Historic Landscape Park Grade I]

Grewelthorpe, North Yorkshire.

Woodland Trust • 6m NW of Ripon off A6108, between Grewelthorpe and Masham • Open all year, daily • Entrance: free ○ ◁⏀

The site is a spectacular gorge cut out by the River Ure. Now battered by neglect, this romantic woodland garden, painted by Turner and praised by

Wordsworth, was laid out by William Aislabie between 1750 and 1765 as a counterpoint to the splendour of Studley Royal (see entry) created by his father. In the 112 acres of entirely overgrown semi-natural scenery, paths lead to a pool, a grotto and a number of small Arcadian ruins. The crumbling banqueting hall commands magnificent views over the gorge. Restoration of the paths, sometimes soggy, is underway. Spring sees masses of flowering wild garlic and bluebells, and tall ferns flourish in late summer amid beech, Turkey oak, elder and elm.

Harlow Carr Botanical Gardens

(see RHS GARDEN HARLOW CARR)

Millgate House ★

Richmond, North Yorkshire DL10 4JN. Tel: (01748) 823571

Austin Lynch and Tim Culkin • In Richmond, in corner of Market Square opposite Barclays Bank • Open mid-March to mid-Oct, daily, 10am – 5.30pm, and at other times by appt • Entrance: £2 ◐ 🖢 B&B

This small but outstanding award-winning town garden is walled on two sides, with the continuous sound of waterfalls on the River Swale in the background. Clematis, roses and jasmine jostle for place against the walls. Hostas and ferns are at the roots of the rose 'Boule de Neige', while 'Maigold' hangs in fragrant swags from the Regency balcony that runs across the first floor of the house. The lower garden houses over 28 varieties of roses, the clematis list is equally spectacular, and there is a specialist collection of hostas. A jewel providing plenty of ideas for the small garden.

Mount Grace Priory

Staddle Bridge, Northallerton, North Yorkshire DL6 3JG. Tel: (01609) 883494

English Heritage • 12m N of Thirsk, 7m NE of Northallerton on A19 • Open April to Sept, daily, 10am – 6pm; Oct, daily, 10am – 4pm; Nov to March, Wed – Sun, 10am – 4pm. Closed 24th to 26th Dec, 1st Jan • Entrance: £3.20, concessions £2.40, children £1.60 ◐ 🍽 🛍 WC 🐾 ♿ ⚲

The ruins of the priory guest house, incorporated into a seventeenth-century manor, were combined in 1900–1901 with a larger house which is an important example of the Arts and Crafts Movement. The monks' cells in the monastery were occupied from 1398 to its dissolution in 1539, and each cell had its own garden. Some have been replanted, with the latest crop of herbs illustrating varieties used for medicinal purposes. The design of the cell-garden is in the form of paths and raised beds. A low box hedge surrounds the central bed, which is filled with blocks of herbs; every second year these follow a different theme. The one-acre early-twentieth-century garden of stepped terraces falling away from the house is being re-created, with rock plants spilling over the edges. There are shrubberies and narrow borders and a garden with ponds, colourful maples, rhododendrons and azaleas.

Nawton Tower ★

Highfield Lane, Nawton, York YO62 7TU. Tel: (01439) 771218

Mrs Sylvia Ward • 14½ m E of Thirsk, 2½ m NE of Helmsley, off A170 Scarborough road. In Nawton and Beadlam, turn left up Highfield Lane for 2m • Open May, June, Sat and Sun, 2 – 6pm, and at other times by appt • Entrance: £1.50, children 75p ● ▧ ⬦ & ♨ ℃

This remarkable, atmospheric 12-acre garden on the edge of the North York Moors was created during the 1930s by the Earl of Feversham. It consists of a series of formal grassy walks between living tapestries woven from a masterly selection of trees, rhododendrons, azaleas and old shrub roses. Every junction from the central walk leads to a fresh surprise: a statue on a pedimented gazebo as the focal point of another pathway; a yew-hedged topiary garden; a quiet contemplative clearing with a silent stone fountain at its centre. A magical experience.

Newby Hall and Gardens ★★ [Historic Garden Grade II*]

Ripon, North Yorkshire HG4 5AE. Tel: (0845) 450 4068

R. Compton • 4m SE of Ripon on B6265, 3m W of A1 • Open April to Sept, Tues – Sun and Bank Holiday Mons, 11am – 5.30pm • Entrance: £5.70, OAPs £4.70, children £4.20 (house and gardens £7.20, OAPs £6.20, children £4.70) (2003 prices) • Other information: Wheelchairs available. Dogs in area adjacent to picnic area only ◑ ☕ ✕ ▧ <u>WC</u> & ♨ ♨ ♀ ℃

The much-loved home of the Compton family, who have restored this famous Adam house to its original beauty and have renovated and developed 25 acres of award-winning gardens. Some features remain from the nineteenth century, such as the east-to-west walk marked by Venetian statuary and backed by yew and purple plum. The south front has long wide green slopes down to the River Ure, with herbaceous borders on either side backed by clipped yew hedges and flowering shrubs. Cross-walks lead to smaller gardens full of interest. These include species roses and tropical, autumn, rock and stepped water gardens, as well as a fine woodland area attributed to Ellen Willmott. A National Collection of cornus is here. There is also a garden restaurant, a children's adventure garden and a miniature railway. Events such as craft and plant fairs are held in the summer, with special admission prices. The Newby plant stall is operated in conjunction with *Oland Plants*, a nursery and garden five miles west of Ripon on B6265.

Ormesby Hall

Ormesby, Middlesbrough, North Yorkshire TS7 9AS. Tel: (01642) 324188

The National Trust • 3m SE of Middlesbrough, W of A171 • Open 30th March to 2nd Nov, Tues – Fri, Sun and Bank Holiday Mons, 12.30 – 4.30pm (house opens 1.30pm) • Entrance: £2.50, children £1 (house, garden, railway and exhibitions £3.70, children £1.80). Party rates available (2003 prices) • Other information: Disabled parking near house. Braille guide available. Dogs on leads, in park only ◑ ☕ ▧ & ♨ ♀ ℃

There have been recent developments in the gardens, including the reintroduction of the original ironwork fencing and the planting of many new bulbs and shrubs. The main rose beds have been renewed, and further ground-cover planting is taking place in the Holly Walk. Seasonal mini garden guides are available. The hall itself is licensed for wedding ceremonies, and the stable block is used by the local mounted police.

Parcevall Hall Gardens ★ [Historic Garden Grade II]

Skyreholme, Skipton, North Yorkshire BD23 6DE. Tel: (01756) 720311

Walsingham College (Yorkshire Properties) Ltd • 10m NE of Skipton, 1m NE of Appletreewick off B6265 Pateley Bridge – Skipton road • Open April to Oct, daily, 10am – 6pm, in winter by appt, and for NGS • Entrance: £3.50, children 50p • Other information: Teas available – for opening times telephone (01756) 720630. Picnics in orchard only ◑ 🍵 🏠 WC ◈ 🌿 ♿

A garden of interest to the plantsperson all year round, many of Sir William Milner's treasures having survived years of neglect. Much of the garden has been renovated – and each year another area is restored, currently the old rose garden. There are red borders, an extended woodland walk, fish ponds and a rock garden. A fine range of rhododendrons, many originally collected in China, still thrive in the walk here. It is worth a visit just to enjoy the spectacular views of Simon's Seat and Wharfedale from the terrace.

Plumpton Rocks [Historic Park Grade II*]

Plumpton, Knaresborough HG5 8NA. Tel: (01423) 863950

Edward de Plumpton Hunter • Midway between Harrogate and Wetherby, 1m SE of A661 junction with Harrogate S bypass • Open March to Oct, Sat, Sun and Bank Holiday Mons, 11am – 6pm • Entrance: £2, concessions £1 • Other information: Guided tours by arrangement [NEW] ◑ ◈

This is not so much a garden as a dramatic natural feature enhanced by man – a place for those seeking peace, quiet and dramatic beauty. Owned by the Plumpton family since the 1080s, the present Lord of the Manor of Plumpton is Edward de Plumpton Hunter, who represents the 27th generation of the family. The estate was acquired around 1750 by Daniel Lascelles and it is he who was responsible for creating the wonderful pleasure grounds painted by Turner and surviving today. Two thousand mixed trees, costing just over £17, were planted in 'plumps' and 'acorns, beech mastes, chestnuts and fir seeds of all sortes were sown and left to take their chances'. In 1757 he gave instructions for a mix of flowering shrubs and evergreens – the cost was £13 so it seems likely that again about 2000 were planted. Today we are reaping the benefit. On Lascelles' death the estate passed to his cousin, the owner of Harewood, and it remained in the ownership of the Harewood family until 1950, when it passed back to the Plumptons. Plumpton Rocks covers over 30 acres, including a six-acre lake (originally a string of fishponds). Paths run over the massive reddish-purple rocks, under the rocks, alongside the lake and through woodlands. It is impossible to become tired of this imposing yet restful place: one could spend all day exploring and not see it all.

RHS Garden Harlow Carr ★

Crag Lane, Harrogate, North Yorkshire HG3 1QB. Tel: (01423) 565418

Royal Horticultural Society • 1½ m W of Harrogate on B6162 Otley road • Open all year, daily, 9.30am – 6pm (or dusk if earlier) • Entrance: £4.50, OAPs £4, accompanied children 11-16 £1, under 11 free. Parties of 20 or more £3.50 (2003 prices) • Other information: Manual and electric wheelchairs for loan. Guide dogs only ○ 🍽 ✕ 🛍 WC ⅌ ⅌ 🏧 🔦 ⚲

For over fifty years Harlow Carr has been a showcase garden assessing the suitability of plants for growing in a cold climate, and it has now become the Royal Horticultural Society's first garden in the north of England. In its 58 acres are flower and vegetable trial gardens, several National Collections, scented, herb and foliage gardens, and contemporary grass borders. Clustered along the banks of the stream is one of the best collections of moisture-loving plants in the North, and there is also woodland and an arboretum. An extensive range of gardening courses and workshops widens the educational scope and supplements the natural attractions.

Rievaulx Terrace ★ [Historic Park Grade I]

Rievaulx, Helmsley, North Yorkshire YO6 5LJ. Tel: (01439) 798340

The National Trust • 10m E of Thirsk, 2½ m NW of Helmsley on B1257 • Open 20th March to Oct, daily, 10am – 6pm (last admission 5pm), (closes 5pm Oct, last admission 4pm). Ionic temple closed 1 – 2pm • Entrance: £3.80, children £3, family £9.60, parties £3.20 per person • Other information: Coach park. Possible for wheelchairs but steps to temples. Electric runaround available for pre-booking; one manual wheelchair also available. Exhibition of landscape design in basement of Ionic temple ◑ 🛍 WC ⅌ ⟊ 🏧 🔦 ⚲

This is a unique example of the eighteenth-century passion for the romantic and the picturesque – that is, making landscape look like a picture. The work was done at the behest of the third Thomas Duncombe around 1754 and consists of a half-mile-long serpentine grass terrace high above Ryedale with fine views of the great ruins of one of the finest of all of Britain's Cistercian abbeys. At one end is a Palladian Ionic temple-cum-banqueting-house with furniture by William Kent and elaborate ceilings, at the other a Tuscan temple with a raised platform, from which are views to the Rye Valley. The concept is wonderfully achieved, its beauty is breath-taking. Those who want to see flowers will have to concentrate their attention on the grass bank below the terrace which is managed for wildflower content – fine displays of cowslips, primroses, orchids, violets, bird's foot trefoils, ladies' bedstraws, etc. There is also blossom throughout the spring season, such as cherry (bird and wild), blackthorn, rowan, whitebeam, elder and lilac.

Ripley Castle [Historic Park Grade II]

Ripley, Harrogate, North Yorkshire HG3 3AY. Tel: (01423) 770152

Sir Thomas Ingilby, Bt • 3½ m N of Harrogate off A61 Harrogate – Ripon road • Castle open Sept to May, Tues, Thurs, Sat, Sun; June to Aug, daily; all 10.30am – 3pm • Garden open all year, daily, 10am – 5pm • Entrance: £3, OAPs £2.50, children £1.50. Parties of 25 or more £2.50 per person • Other information: Guide dogs only ○ 🍴 ✕ WC ♿ 🌿 🚻 ◑ B&B

The mid-eighteenth-century 'Capability' Brown landscape with formal gardens has been developed by Peter Aram for a family that has lived here since the fourteenth century. The formal areas have been completely restored and the huge herbaceous borders – a total of 110 metres long – are amongst the most spectacular in the north of England. Other features include a lake with an attractive Victorian iron bridge, an eighteenth-century orangery and summerhouses. There are magnificent specimen trees. A woodland walk leads to a temple with fine views, and a lakeside walk takes the visitor through the deer park. Extensive plantings of a rich variety of spring-flowering bulbs have been made to complement a National Collection of hyacinths here, and the tropical plant collection formerly owned by Hull University at Cottingham Botanical Gardens is now at Ripley and is open to the public in the restored listed greenhouses. The vegetable garden has rare species adopted from the Henry Doubleday Research Association. Nearby, at the arts centre in Knaresborough, is a 'garden of the senses' designed for *Henshaw's College* for children with disabilities. Telephone (01423) 886451 for details.

Shandy Hall

Coxwold, York YO61 4AD. Tel: (01347) 868465

The Laurence Sterne Trust • 18m N of York, 7m SE of Thirsk. From York, take A19 towards Thirsk, turn off to Easingwold and follow signs to Coxwold. From crossroads go 150 metres past church • House open May to Sept, Wed, Sun, 2 – 4.30pm • Garden open May to Sept, daily except Sat, 11am – 4.30pm • Entrance: £2.50 (house and garden £4.50, children £1.50) • Other information: Refreshments in village nearby. Permanent Sterne exhibition. Art and pottery gallery ◑ 🍽 WC ♿ 🌿 🚻

A delightful small-scale, three-part garden, full of year-round interest, surrounds the pretty fifteenth-century cottage in which Laurence Sterne wrote *Tristram Shandy* during the 1760s. In the Barn Garden, borders of herbaceous plants and shrub roses enfold on three sides, with a view out to Byland Abbey and the North York Moors beyond. The Old Garden is approached through a small orchard where some of the gnarled trees are covered with climbing roses. A wide selection of old-fashioned roses in raised beds against drystone walls is interspersed with herbaceous planting in which careful thought is given to plant associations for colour and form. The foliage of a silver poplar provides a perfect backdrop for shrub roses such as 'Kassel', 'Fantin-Latour' and 'La Reine Victoria'. The third section is a surprise garden, created within a long-abandoned adjacent quarry and devoted mainly to a wonderful display of wild flowers underplanted with bulbs. Starting in the spring with narcissi and then bluebells, the tree-fringed quarry garden changes colour through the year, from yellow to blue to pink, then purple (in July) and on to a deep bosky green, punctuated by clematis and climbing roses, before moving into autumn colours. Four magnificent ash trees form a centrepiece, and grassy paths wind through its undulations, past rustic seats and bowers.

Sledmere House [Historic Park Grade I]

Sledmere, Great Driffield, East Riding YO25 3XG. Tel: (01377) 236637

Sir Tatton Sykes, Bt • 9m NW of Great Driffield off A166. Signposted • House open • Garden open 9th to 12th April for flower festival, then 2nd May to 19th Sept, Tues – Fri, Sun and Bank Holiday Mons, 11am – 4.30pm • Entrance: £3, children £1 (house, park and garden £5, OAPs £4.50, children £2) ◐ ✕ 🍴 WC & 🐾 ♿ ⚲ ⚲

Sledmere is among the best-preserved of 'Capability' Brown's landscape schemes. Dating from the 1770s, it clearly reveals his characteristic belting and clumping of trees and carefully controlled diagonal vistas to distant 'eye-catchers'. His use of a ha-ha allows the park to flow up to the windows of the house (whence it is best seen) across extensive tree-planted lawns. To the rear of the house is a well-stocked herbaceous border and parterre. The eighteenth-century walled gardens are planted mainly with roses, herbaceous plants and fruit trees, and there is an attractive iron pergola running the length of this area.

Sleightholme Dale Lodge

Fadmoor, Kirbymoorside, North Yorkshire YO62 7JG. Tel: (01751) 431942

Dr and Mrs O. James • 20m NE of Thirsk, 3m N of Kirbymoorside, 1m from Fadmoor off A170 Thirsk – Scarborough road • Open for NGS and NHS, and by appt in writing • Entrance: £2.50, children 50p ◑ WC ♿

This garden occupies a unique position on the side of a wooded valley opening onto the moors. In the spring it is a blaze of blossom, wild daffodils and azaleas, and through the summer the walled garden, which runs steeply up the hill to the north, is breathtaking in the colour and exuberance of the parallel borders. This is described as 'a gardeners' garden' and there are many rare plants to be seen, notably meconopsis. Descending terraces, built at the beginning of the century to the south of the house, have deep shrubberies. The lowest of them is a grass platform separated from the meadow beyond by a ha-ha. A fine series of steps runs down through the terraces.

Stillingfleet Lodge ★

Stillingfleet, York YO19 6HP. Tel: (01904) 728506

Mr and Mrs J. Cook • 6m S of York. From A19 York – Selby road take B1222 signed to Sherburn in Elmet. In Stillingfleet turn opposite church; garden is at end of lane • Open for Pulmonaria Day on 18th April, 1.30 – 4.30pm; May to

Sept, Wed, Fri, 1 – 4pm; plus 9th May, 20th June, 1.30 – 5.30pm for NGS •
Entrance: £2.50, children 50p • Other information: Parking and plants for sale
at nursery ● 🍵 WC ♿ 🌱

An eclectic and most attractive garden has been unfolding here since the
owners started developing their windswept plot sloping down to the River
Fleet in 1974. Vanessa Cook is a notable plantswoman with an instinctive
feeling for both naturalistic and formal planting styles. The wilder areas which
include a meadow, a grassy walk dominated by beehives and wild flowers, and a
large pool generously fringed with exotic and native species have no quarrel
with the magnificently ordered double herbaceous borders, furnished with
trees, shrubs and many bulbs for year-long colour interest. Many climbing
roses and clematis, and a good use of foliage plants in soft colours, give the
garden a romantic feel. A National Collection of pulmonarias is here. The
nursery, well stocked with unusual plants, is also well worth a visit. [Open
April to mid-Oct, Wed, Fri, 10am – 4pm.]

Studley Royal and Fountains Abbey ★★ [Historic Park Grade I]

Ripon, North Yorkshire HG4 3DY. Tel: (01765) 608888

The National Trust • 4m SW of Ripon, 9m N of Harrogate. Follow Fountains
Abbey sign off B6265 Ripon – Pateley Bridge road • Deer park open all year
during daylight hours. Abbey and garden open all year, daily except 24th, 25th
Dec and Fridays from Nov to Jan, 10am – 6pm (closes 4pm Oct to March, or
dusk if earlier). Free guided tours April to Oct, daily • Entrance: Studley park
free. Abbey, mill and garden £5, children £3, family £14. Special rates for pre-
booked coach parties (2003 prices) • Other information: Parking free at main
visitor centre car park but £2 at Studley park (pay-and-display, NT members
free). Self-drive powered runarounds available by prior booking ○ ☕ ✗ 🍵 WC
♿ 🐕 ♿

The gardens of Studley Royal were created by John Aislabie, who had been
Chancellor of the Exchequer but whose career was ended by his involvement
with the South Sea Bubble in 1720; he retreated to his estate in 1722 and
worked until his death in 1742 to make the finest water garden in the country.
The lakes, formal canals and water features, with buildings such as the Temple
of Piety, turned what is essentially a landscape with large trees and sweeping
lawns into one of the most beautiful green gardens in the world. The views
from Colen Campbell's Banqueting House are remarkable. Then there is its
intimate and dramatic relationship with Fountains Abbey – probably the
noblest monastic ruin in Christendom – visible at first only distantly from
the Surprise View, a door in a small building. Studley Royal Park is deservedly
a World Heritage Site. Restoration of Anne Boleyn's seat, a timber gazebo
with a fine view, is now complete. A further £10 million is being sought to
continue a major programme of restoration, including the repair of river
banks, fords and bridges, and an on-going programme of woodland management and tree planting.

Sutton Park ★

Sutton-in-the-Forest, York YO61 1DP. Tel: (01347) 810249/811239

Sir Reginald and Lady Sheffield • 8m N of York on B1363 • House open April to Sept, Sun and Wed, also Good Friday and Bank Holiday Mons, 1.30 – 5pm. Private parties by appt at other times • Gardens open April to Sept, daily, 11am – 5pm • Entrance: £3, concessions £2, children 50p (house and gardens £5.50, concessions £4.50, children £3, parties of 15 or more £5.50 per person) • Other information: Coaches by appt (£4 per person). Specialist plant fair 6th June
◑ ☕ ✕ WC ♿ 🏧 🍴 ✎

The distinguished English garden designer Percy Cane came in 1962 to this Georgian house and its terraced site with views over parkland said to have been moulded by 'Capability' Brown, and started the elegant planting which has been most carefully expanded by the present owners. There are several fine features on the terraces – a tall beech hedge curved to take a marble seat, ironwork gazebos, and everywhere soft stone. The woodland walk leads to a temple. A water feature has been created in the old walled garden, planted with 3000 wildflowers, and the herb garden and fernery are also recent additions.

Thorp Perrow Arboretum and Woodland Garden ★ [Historic Arboretum Grade II]

Bedale, North Yorkshire DL8 2PR. Tel: (01677) 425323

Sir John Ropner, Bt • 10m N of Ripon, 2m S of Bedale, signed off B6268 Masham road • Open all year, daily, dawn – dusk • Entrance: £5.75, OAPs and concessions £4.40, children (4–16) £2.95, family £16 and £19 • Other information: Electric wheelchair available. Tea room open mid-Feb to mid-Nov, thereafter weekends only ○ ☕ 🍴 ♿ ⟷ ✿ 🏧 🍴 ✎

The arboretum was established many years ago and has one of the finest collections of trees in the north of England, containing over 2000 species. Within the 85 acres is a Victorian pinetum, sixteenth-century woodland and National Collections of ash, limes, laburnums and walnuts. You can follow the tree trail, the nature trail or simply amble at your own leisure. Thousands of naturalised daffodils and bluebells in spring, glorious wild flowers in summer and stunning autumn colour. There are new plantings and continual improvements in the arboretum. Falconry demonstrations and children's trail. *Norton Conyers*, 4 miles north of Ripon, has a 2 ½-acre walled garden (listed Grade II) with an orangery and herbaceous borders. A pleasant place with an historic feel and a house with Charlotte Brontë associations. [Open regularly during main season – telephone (01765) 640333 to check.]

Valley Gardens ★ [Historic Public Park Grade II]

Valley Drive, Harrogate, North Yorkshire. Tel: (01423) 500600

Harrogate Borough Council • In centre of Harrogate; main entrance near Pump Room Museum and Mercer Art Gallery • Open all year, daily during daylight

hours • Entrance: free • Other information: Art exhibition 30th, 31st May, 29th, 30th Aug in Sun Pavilion (also available for events – telephone (01423) 522588)
○ � ▩ WC ᕫ ⇦ ▯ ℺

One of the best-known public gardens in the north of England, laid out earlier this century at the time Harrogate was fashionable as a spa. The Sun Pavilion has been restored. The standard of formal bedding remains high, and the dahlia border gives a fine display in late summer. Children will enjoy the range of activities on offer – paddling and boating pools, play area, tennis courts, pitch-and-putt course and crazy golf.

Wytherstone House

Pockley, York YO62 7TE. Tel: (01439) 770012

Lady Clarissa Collin • 15m E of Thirsk, $2\frac{1}{2}$ m NE of Helmsley off A170. In Pockley, past church • Open by appt • Entrance: £2.50 (2003 price) ◖ ▭ ▩ WC ᕫ ⌀

A large and expanding plantsman's garden created from a green-field site over thirty-five years, with a wide range of rare shrubs, perennials and roses. It consists of a series of interlinked compartments, each with its own character. The spring garden has a tapestry of azaleas and rhododendrons and peat terracing. Next to the spring garden is a rock garden with some rare alpines. A sunken garden of mixed shrubs and herbaceous plants, enclosed by tall beech hedges, leads through to other delights beyond, past an arboretum and pond to a woodland walk. Back in the conservatory garden, climbing roses smother trees, and fine herbaceous plants and old roses create borders full of interest and colour, along with plants not normally thought to be hardy in the North of England, such as *Melianthus major*, thriving and flowering year after year.

RESEARCHING GARDEN HISTORY

The Register of Parks and Gardens of Special Historic Interest is the official record of the nation's historic landscapes produced by English Heritage. It has been substantially revised and upgraded, parks and gardens added, and threatened landscapes 'spot-registered'. At the beginning of August 2003, the total number of entries was 1590. Each site is documented in a description of its historical evolution, accompanied by specially drawn paper maps delineating the historical boundaries of the park or garden and chronicling its development.

The *Register* is available for public consultation at English Heritage's National Monuments Record Centre in Swindon (open Tues – Fri, 9.30am – 5pm). Copies of individual entries or complete county registers can also be purchased and sent by post. For more information contact NMR Enquiry & Research Services (Tel: (01793) 414600; Fax (01793) 414606; Email: nmrinfo@english-heritage.org.uk). Additionally, each local planning authority will have a copy of the relevant descriptions and maps within their jurisdictions. Be sure to telephone in advance of a visit.

YORKSHIRE (S. & W. AREA)

Bramham Park ★ [Historic Park Grade I]

Wetherby LS23 6ND. Tel: (01937) 846000/846002

Mr G. Lane Fox • 10m NE of Leeds, 15m SW of York, 5m S of Wetherby just off northbound A1 • House open by written appt only • Garden open April to Sept, daily, 11am – 4.30pm (closed for horse trials, please telephone for dates) • Entrance: £4, OAPs/children £2, under 5s free. Reduced rates for parties of 20 or more ◑ ▦ WC ☷ ⬙ ⵎ

Created by Robert Benson after the style of Le Nôtre nearly 300 years ago, this is one of the most important formal landscape gardens in the French style to survive in this country. Although a great storm early in 1962 caused extensive damage to trees and avenues, the original concept has been maintained and the layout restored. Apart from their unique design, the gardens also have a substantial rose garden providing summer-long colour, and an interesting herbaceous border. However, it is the splendid architectural features (such as the Gothic pavilion) with trees and water, that are outstanding. Mary Keen calls it 'forest gardening' – a genre practised by generations of the owner's family. In 1991 the remains of a massive eighteenth-century cascade were found. Apparently the family of the day had a change of mind, so they carefully grassed it over without ever starting to build a pond at the bottom of the valley.

Brodsworth Hall [Historic Garden Grade II*]

Brodsworth, Doncaster DN5 7XJ. Tel: (01302) 722598

English Heritage • 5m NW of Doncaster. Access from A1(M) junction 37 off A635 • House open as garden, but from 1pm • Garden open April to Oct, Tues – Sun and Bank Holiday Mons, 12 noon – 6pm, and in winter, Sat and Sun, 11am – 4pm – telephone for details • Entrance: summer £3.50, concessions £2.60, children £1.80; winter £2, OAPs £1.50, children £1 (hall and gardens £6, OAPs £4.50, children £3) ◑ ☕ ✕ ▦ WC ☷ ⬗ ⵎ ⚲

The 15 acres were designed and planted when the Italianate house was being built in the mid-1860s on a site with many fine established trees. It also featured a long, deep quarry dating from the eighteenth century. Main features in the garden are tamed evergreen shrubberies and a border where trimmed shrubs are underplanted with Japanese anemones, daylilies, aconites, ferns and fuchsias. Beyond, around a marble fountain, an intricate bedding scheme uses the original shapes cut in the lawn filled with such delights as tulips and nineteenth-century pelargonium varieties. Trees overhanging the old quarry shade a maze of walkways and bridges in fine rockwork; these offer vistas into the recently restored fern dell. Cooled by an elegant cascade, it is planted with an historic collection of period ferns together with shrubs, bulbs, herbaceous perennials and dwarf conifers. This part of the garden, including the rose garden, is undergoing further restoration and planting. The lawns are rich in natural flora. A collection of the Portland group of roses has been planted here, along with other historic varieties, and a large herbaceous border provides a fine backdrop. New for 2004 is the restored woodland garden near the house.

East Riddlesden Hall

Bradford Road, Keighley, Bradford BD20 5EL. Tel: (01535) 607075

The National Trust • 1m NE of Keighley off B6265, 3m NW of Bingley • House open • Garden open end-March to 2nd Nov, Sat, 1 – 5pm; Sun, Tues and Wed, 12 noon – 5pm. Also open Good Friday, Bank Holiday Mons and Mons in July, Aug. Parties must pre-book • Entrance: £3.60, accompanied children £1.80, family £9 ◑ 🍵 🐌 **WC** ♿ 🐕 🌿 ♨ ⛱ ⚘

In spring, the garden designed by Graham Stuart Thomas is dotted with primroses, violas and 'Baby Moon' narcissi. A fragrant medicinal herb border based on Culpeper's *Herbal* leads into a small walled garden, which in summer is filled with honeysuckles, roses, lavenders, clematis, herbaceous perennials and mophead acacias. The Orchard Garden has been planted with Yorkshire apple trees; spring bulbs and wild flowers provide a changing carpet of colour from season to season.

Golden Acre Park ★

Otley Road, Leeds. Tel: (0113) 246 3504

Leeds City Council • NW of Leeds off A660 Leeds – Otley road at approach to Bramhope • Open all year, daily, during daylight hours • Entrance: free ○ 🍵 **WC** ♿ 🐕 ⛱ ⚘

Until 1945, when it was purchased by Leeds Corporation for £18,500, this was a privately owned pleasure park. Since then it has been developed as an important public park and minor botanic garden. It stands on a pleasant undulating site leading down to a lake, and has an extensive tree collection. Rhododendrons are a feature, together with alpine plants both in the rock garden and the alpine house. The park is noted for its fine collection of sempervivums and heathers. Demonstration plots are maintained where instruction is provided for home gardeners; the quality of planting and vegetables improves annually.

Harewood House ★ [Historic Park and Garden Grade I]

Harewood, Leeds LS17 9LQ. Tel: (0113) 218 1010

The Earl and Countess of Harewood • 7m N of Leeds on A61 • House open, 11am – 4.30pm • Grounds open 11th Feb to Oct, daily, Nov to mid-Dec, Sat and Sun, all 10am – 6pm (or dusk if earlier) • Entrance: Terrace Gallery, Bird Garden and grounds £7.25, OAPs £6.25, children £4.50, freedom ticket £10, OAPs £8, children £5.50 • Other information: Art gallery. Regular garden tours and talks programme ◑ 🍵 ✕ 🐌 **WC** 🐕 🌿 ⛱ ♨ ⚘

Originally laid out in the 1770s by 'Capability' Brown, the gardens and park retain many of his characteristic features, most notably a majestic lake and a well-wooded horizon. Sir Charles Barry's 1840s' terrace contains formal parterres and fountains, herbaceous borders and bedding. The terrace has been restored, the intricate patterns of the parterre have been re-created – with a European Union grant – to Barry's original designs after decades under grass, and the West Garden on the upper terrace was given an elegant new design by the late David Hicks. Nineteenth-century rhododendrons enrich the edge of the lake; other features in this woodland setting are a vaguely Japanese bog garden housing a good collection of hostas below the lake's cascade. Parkland, excellently maintained with trees and shrubs, is being further replanted. Children will enjoy the bird garden and the adventure playgrounds.

Hillsborough Walled Garden

Middlewood Road, Sheffield S6 4HD. Tel: (0114) 281 2167

Hillsborough Community Development Trust • Adjacent to Hillsborough Library • Open all year, Mon – Fri, 9am – 5pm (closes 4.30pm Fri), Sat, Sun (during summer months only) 2 – 5pm and Bank Holidays (check before travelling) • Entrance: free but donations welcome • Other information: Parking for disabled only ○ 🅿 🏠 WC ♿ 💷 🍴 ⚲

The site embraces four different gardens: a wildlife area, a lawn with herbaceous borders, a woodland glade and a formal garden with raised beds for easy use by disabled gardeners. There are many architectural features, and varied gardens including herb, a vegetable and nursery gardens, a Victorian heated garden and a garden for the visually handicapped. Planned, created and run by the community, this is not just an area to look at and enjoy, but everyone is encouraged to help with its upkeep – tools are available on site and plants always welcomed.

The Hollies Park ★

Weetwood Lane, Leeds LS16 5NZ.
Tel: (0113) 247 8361 (Parks and Countryside)

Leeds City Council • In NW Leeds, off A660 Leeds – Otley road • Open all year, daily, during daylight hours • Entrance: free ○ 🏠 WC ⚐

The original layout is Victorian, and the gardens were given to Leeds Corporation in 1921 by the Brown family in memory of a son killed during World War I. The fine informal, largely woodland garden features woody plants, especially rhododendrons. Ferns flourish throughout the gardens and a varied collection of hydrangeas provides late summer colour. Many slightly tender subjects thrive in the pleasant microclimate. Several National Collections are held here, including those of hemerocallis, hostas and deutzias, and probably the most comprehensive philadelphus collection in Europe.

Land Farm

Colden, Hebden Bridge, Calderdale HA7 7PJ. Tel: (01422) 842260

Mr and Mrs J. Williams • 3½ m NE of Todmorden, off A646 between Sowerby Bridge and Todmorden. Call at visitor centre in Hebden Bridge for map • Open

May to Aug, Sat, Sun and Bank Holiday Mons, 10am – 5pm. Parties welcome
• *Entrance: £3, Parties £5 per person incl. supper (2003 prices)* ◑ ✘ WC ⬳
🌶 ♨ ⚲

A four-acre garden created by the owners on a north-facing site 300 metres up in the Pennines. Designed as a low-maintenance garden, it nevertheless contains a wide diversity of shrubs, herbaceous plants and alpines. A woodland garden has rhododendrons and cornus underplanted with herbaceous plants. *Tropaeolum speciosum* runs in glorious riot through parts of the garden. There is also an art gallery in the former barn.

30 Latchmere Road

Leeds LS16 5DF. Tel: (0113) 275 1261

Frieda Brown • NW of Leeds off A6120 (ring road to Bradford). Turn up Fillingfir Drive, right at postbox, then left into Latchmere Road • Open for horticultural societies, garden clubs and tourist parties by appt only • Entrance: £2, children 50p • Other information: No parking in Latchmere Road ◑ ☕ WC 🌶

A well-known garden of exceptional merit created from scratch over the last forty years, and a good example of inspired design on a small scale. Herbaceous plants, ferns, climbers and shrubs all contribute to a series of mini-features through which the visitor passes in a controlled circuit of the garden. These include a clematis collection, sink gardens, pools, a patio and an alpine garden. The different levels and all the paving, retaining walls and steps have been built by the owners from local stone.

Lister Park [Historic Public Park Grade II]

Keighley Road, Bradford. Tel: (01274) 431535

City of Bradford Metropolitan Council • $1\frac{1}{2}$ m N of Bradford centre (Forster Square) on A650 Bradford – Keighley road • Open all year, daily, during daylight hours • Entrance: free • Other information: Cartwright Hall, City Art Gallery and Museum open all year, daily except Mon ○ ☕ ✘ WC ♿ ⬳ ⚲ ☕

The 55-acre park was given to the city by a local mill owner, Sir Samuel Cunliffe-Lister, in 1870, and has been restored through a Heritage Lottery Fund grant. Six of its buildings are listed. There is an attractive formal bedding display in front of the Cartwright Hall and gallery and an interesting floral clock – a rare example of Victorian ingenuity. The tranquil Mughal garden adjoining illustrates the simplicity and symmetry of the fusion of Islamic and Hindu styles. The old botanical garden behind the hall includes a geological trail, and boating, games and summer entertainments are on offer for both children and adults.

Nostell Priory [Historic Park Grade II*]

Doncaster Road, Nostell, Wakefield WF4 1QE. Tel: (01924) 863892

The National Trust • 6m SE of Wakefield on A638 • House open 27th March to Oct, Wed – Sun, plus 9th April and Bank Holiday Mons, 1 – 5pm • Garden open 6th to 21st March, 6th Nov to 19th Dec, Sat and Sun; 11am – 4.30pm; 27th March to Oct, Wed – Sun, 11am – 5.30pm. Also open Good Fri and Bank Holiday Mons • Entrance: £2.50, children £1.20 (house and garden £5, children £2.50, family £12.50) • Other information: Batricar available. Special events and fairs (separate charge) ◑ 🍲 🍴 WC ⅍ 🎗 💡 ⚲

The dark, brooding eighteenth-century mansion by Robert Adam sits in open parkland with an attractive lake and a variety of well-established trees. A fine rose garden is the main gardening feature, together with extensive lakeside gardens planted with magnolias and rhododendrons, a summerhouse, a Gothick archway and a cock-fighting pit. One of the most attractive Gothick buildings, with later additions by Robert Adam, has been restored.

People's Park [Historic Public Park Grade II*]

Hopwood Lane, Halifax. Tel: (01422) 359454

Metropolitan Borough of Calderdale • Open all year, daily, 8am – dusk • Entrance: free ○ 🍴 ⅍ ⟁ 💡

A gift by Francis Crossley to the town, this is a good example of a Victorian park. Designed by Joseph Paxton, it was opened in 1857, and in 1874 a bandstand was added. Queen Victoria presented two swans to the park in 1861. The pavilion was designed by Stokes and has a statue of Crossley by Joseph Durham; the statues on the terrace are by Francesco Bienaime. Restoration of the park, including the water features and the pavilion, and new landscaping, is now complete, and the atmosphere is being rejuvenated with a varied events programme and community involvement.

Sheffield Botanical Gardens [Historic Public Park Grade II]

Sheffield S10 2LN. Tel: (0114) 267 6496

Sheffield Council • ½ m from A625, 1½ m SW of city centre • Open all year, daily except 25th Dec, 10am – dusk • Entrance: free ○ 🍲 ✕ 🍴 WC ⅍ ⟁ 🎗 💡 ⚲

These historic gardens (opened in 1836) are popular with visitors for the peace and seclusion of 19 sheltered acres so close to the city centre. Facilities have been improved with the conversion of the curator's house into a tearoom/restaurant. This is just one of the improvements made possible by a Heritage Lottery Fund award of £5m, with a further £1.25m matched funding being raised by the Friends of the Botanical Gardens and the Sheffield Botanical Gardens Trust. The jewels in the crown – the impressive glass pavilions with their linking glass corridors – have been beautifully restored and planted. The 90-metre linear glasshouse displays plant collections from around the warm temperate world. The next phase includes work on the bear pit and the Pan statue, and concentrates on restoration of the landscape and plantings, retaining the nineteenth-century character of the gardens.

Temple Newsam Park [Historic Garden Grade II]

Leeds LS15 0AD. Tel: (0113) 264 5535

Leeds City Council • 3m E of Leeds, signed off A63/A6120 ring road junction and junction 46 on M1 • House open all year, except Jan, Tues – Sun, 10.30am – 5pm (closes 4pm in winter) • Park open all year, daily, dawn – dusk; National Collections open Mon – Fri, 11am – 3pm, Sat and Sun, 11am – 2pm • Entrance: free ○ 🍵 🧺 WC ⅊ ⇘ ♿ ☂ ⚲

Most people visit the house to see its remarkable collection of furniture, but set in the remnants of a 'Capability' Brown landscape of the 1760s (much reduced by a golf course and open-cast mining) is a wide diversity of gardens. A rhododendron and azalea walk leads to small ponds with a bog garden and arboretum, beyond which is a large walled rose garden and greenhouses containing collections of ivies, cacti and some rather dashing wall-trained pelargoniums. Several National Collections, including delphiniums, phlox, asters, charm and cascade chrysanthemums, are held here. Also within the large walled garden are traditional borders considered to be amongst the best in England.

Tropical World ★ [within Roundhay Park – Historic Park Grade II]

Roundhay Park, Roundhay, Leeds LS8 2ER. Tel: (0113) 266 1850

Leeds City Council • S of A6120 northern ring, off A58 Roundhay Road from city centre • Open all year, daily, except 25th Dec, 10am – 6pm • Entrance: £3, children (8–15) £2, under-8s and Leeds card holders free • Other information: Dogs in park only, on lead ○ 🍵 🧺 WC ⅊ ⇘ ☂ ⚲

The extensive parkland with its fine trees is an extravagant setting for the pure horticultural extravaganza of the canal gardens with their formal bedding and generous collections. These were once the kitchen and ornamental gardens of the Nicholson family, who sold the site to the Leeds Corporation in 1871. The exotic houses have the largest collection outside Kew, with exotic butterflies and birds. Waterfalls and pools are surrounded by tropical plants, and the arid house holds a large collection of cacti and succulents. There is an underwater world of plants and fish, an insect house and a nocturnal house where bush babies, monkeys and other animals can be seen.

Wentworth Castle Gardens ★ [Historic Park Grade I]

Lowe Lane, Stainborough, Barnsley S75 3ET. Tel: (01226) 731269

Barnsley Metropolitan Borough Council • 3m SW of Barnsley off M1 junction 37, 2m along minor roads signed to Oxspring, Gilroyd and Northern College • Open, mainly for guided tours, mid-April to June, Tues – Thurs and selected Suns; July and Aug, Tues, Thurs; selected dates in Oct – telephone for details ● ⅊

One of the most exciting gardens in Yorkshire, laid out mainly under the direction of William Wentworth between 1739 and 1791. The award of a second-stage Heritage Lottery Fund grant of £10.3m for the restoration of the pleasure gardens, parkland and walled garden has been made. Barnsley Council's development package is in conjunction with the Northern College (which owns and occupies the house). Among the many features are a three-quarter-mile-long serpentine lake, monuments to Queen Anne and Lady Mary Wortley Montagu, and the stunning Gothick folly of Stainborough Castle, constructed on the highest point of the estate, which forms a fitting dramatic climax to the gardens. The garden holds National Collections of species magnolias and species rhododendrons; there are also extensive new plantings of camellias, especially the *C.* x *williamsii* hybrids, which also have National Collection status.

York Gate ★

Back Church Lane, Adel, Leeds LS16 8DW. Tel: (0113) 267 8240

Perennial (formerly The Gardeners' Royal Benevolent Society) • *2¼ m SE of Bramhope, off A660* • *Open April to Sept, Thurs, Sun and Bank Holiday Mons, 2 – 5pm, plus Thurs evenings in July, 6.30 – 9pm, and for parties by appt* • *Entrance: £3, children free* ● **WC**

A garden created by the Spencer family and bequeathed by the late Sybil Spencer to the Gardeners' Royal Benevolent Society. Bought by the Spencers in 1951, this was a bleak farmhouse and unpromising area of land. When her husband died, her son took over the design and in a tragically short life he achieved a garden of rare delight, using local stone, cobble stones and gravel to create a structure of impeccable taste and style and great horticultural interest. As to the design, the late Arthur Hellyer remarked on its debt to Hidcote, but noted that many of the ideas used there in 10 acres are here confined to barely one. He also commented on the clever use of architectural features and topiary. 'This is a garden made for discovery,' he said, as 'from no vantage point is it possible to see the whole.' It is also a plantsman's garden, maintaining a quality collection arranged in clearly defined model features. These include an extraordinary miniature pinetum, fern and peony borders, a herb garden with summerhouse, a kitchen garden and white borders.

Yorkshire Sculpture Park [within Bretton Park Historic Park Grade II]

Bretton Hall, West Bretton, Wakefield WF4 4LG. Tel: (01924) 830302

Yorkshire Sculpture Park, Independent Charitable Trust • *6m NW of Barnsley, 6m SW of Wakefield at West Bretton. Leave M1 at junction 38* • *Open all year, daily, except 24th, 25th, 31st Dec, 10am – 6pm (closes 4pm in winter)* • *Entrance: free but donation welcomed. Parking £1.50 per car* • *Other information: Coaches by prior arrangement. Access Sculpture Trail suitable for wheelchairs. Visitor centre and indoor galleries* ○ ● ✕ ▦ WC ও ⬙ ⊞ ♦ ⚲

This, Britain's first permanent sculpture park was established in 1977, and is now considered to be one of Europe's leading open-air galleries. The Palladian-style house and its 500 acres of formal gardens, woods, lakes and parkland provide a fine setting for temporary and permanent exhibitions. The layout makes it possible to view sculpture in garden as well as 'public' settings that demand a more monumental approach by the sculptor. The park hosts temporary exhibitions by international sculptors, as well as rotating its own permanent collection.

THE REPUBLIC OF IRELAND & NORTHERN IRELAND

Two-starred gardens are marked on the map with a black square.

NORTHERN IRELAND

The National Trust Ulster Gardens Scheme runs private garden openings on special days and by appointment. For a list of gardens opening in 2004 telephone (028) 9751 0721.

Antrim Castle Gardens [Historic Garden]

Randalstown Road, Co. Antrim BT41 4LH. Tel: (028) 9442 8000

Antrim Borough Council Arts and Heritage Service • Access from A6 Randalstown Road • Open all year, daily, 9.30am – dusk. Guided tours for parties at any time by arrangement • Entrance: Individuals free. Small parties £2, concessions £1; parties of 40 or more £1 per person; school parties 50p per child • Other information: Refreshments by arrangement for groups. Interpretative display in Clotworthy Arts Centre ○ 🏫 **WC** ⛐ ⚔️ 🌡️ ⚘

A rare example of a demesne where the main elements survive as laid out for a late-seventeenth-century castle (now demolished). The canals, connected by a cascade, are lined with clipped lime and hornbeam hedges. Paths criss-cross through the wooded wilderness, the main avenue of which leads to an airy clearing with a round pond reflecting sky and trees. Following a restoration project, a large parterre has been planted with varieties known in the seventeenth century and is set off by a quincunx grove of standard hornbeam (new) and an immense yew hedge (old). The adjacent Anglo-Norman motte retains its spiral path; access can be gained by collecting a key from the arts centre (£5 refundable deposit), and it is worth a climb to the top to see the lower course of the Sixmilewater river, the centre of the town of Antrim, and the 37-acre ornamental site below – a fraction of a once-vast estate stretching as far as the eye could see.

The Argory [Historic Demesne]

Moy, Dungannon, Co. Tyrone BT71 6NA. Tel: (028) 8778 4753

The National Trust • 4m NE of Moy, 3m from M1 junction 14 • House open • Grounds and garden open all year, daily, 10am – 8pm (closes 4pm Oct to April) • Entrance: £4.10, children £2.10. Parking charge £2.10 (2003 prices) • Other information: Coaches must use M1 junction 13 because of weight restrictions. Parking 100 metres from house ◐ 🍽️ 🏫 **WC** ⛐ ⚔️ 🛍️ 🌡️ ⚘

The lawns of the pleasure ground slope down past yew arbours to two pavilions, one a pump house, the other a garden house. Beyond, the visitor can walk under pollarded limes along the banks of the Blackwater River, and there are other woodland walks in this tranquil landscape. A splash of summer colour near the house attracts the eye to an enclosed early-nineteenth-century sundial garden of box-edged rose beds. There is a riverside walk of 1 ½ miles.

Ballywalter Park [Historic Garden]

Ballywalter, Nr Newtownards, Co. Down BT22 2PAN. Tel: (028) 4275 8264

Dunleath Estates • 20m E of Belfast, 10m SE of Newtownards off B5 between Greyabbey and Ballywalter. Turn right at T-junction facing gates and follow wall to entrance on left opposite farm • Open by appt only (please telephone Mon – Fri between 9am and 1pm) • Entrance: house or garden £4 each (house and garden £7) • Other information: PYO in season ☽

The fine mid-nineteenth-century Italianate house by the architect Lanyon, with an elegant conservatory wing, was praised by Sir John Betjeman. The surrounding grounds are an amalgam of two earlier 'landscaped' demesnes, embellished for the present house with a rock garden around a stream with bridges, also by Lanyon. The notable rhododendron collection is sheltered by mature trees throughout the park. A rose pergola and restored glasshouse decorate the walled garden.

Belfast Botanic Gardens Park [Historic Park]

Stranmillis Road, Belfast City BT7 ILP. Tel: (028) 9032 4902

Belfast City Council Parks Department • Between Queen's University and Ulster Museum, Stranmillis. Buses 69, 84 and 85 • Open all year, daily, 7.30am – dusk. Palm House and Tropical Ravine, summer, weekdays, 10am – 5pm, weekends and public holidays, 2 – 5pm (closes 4pm in winter). Guided tours and parties at any time by arrangement • Entrance: free. Guided tours £10 • Other information: Refreshments in Ulster Museum ○ ▨ ᵫ 🜨 ♟

Established in 1828, this became a public park in 1895. As well as two magnificent double herbaceous borders and a rose garden with 8000 roses, there are two other reasons to visit this park – the curvilinear iron and glass conservatory (1839–52) and the Palm House one of the finest Victorian glasshouses (Richard Turner built only the wings; the dome is by Young of Edinburgh, restored in the 1970s). It contains a finely displayed collection of tropical plants, while massed pot plants are changed throughout the seasons in a cooler wing. The restored Tropical Ravine House is the greater delight, a perfect piece of 'High Victoriana' with ferns, bananas, lush tropical vines and tree ferns, goldfish in the Amazon lily pond, and a waterfall worked with a chain-pull. Marvellous, evocative of crinoline days.

Benvarden House [Historic Garden]

Ballybogey, Ballymoney, Co. Antrim BT53 6NN. Tel: (028) 2074 1331

Mr and Mrs Hugh Montgomery • 4m E of Coleraine off B67. Signposted • Open June to Aug, Tues – Sun and Bank Holiday Mons, 12 noon – 5.30pm, and at other times by appt • Entrance: £3 ◑ ▱ ▨ WC ᵫ ✿

The eighteenth-century house is set in lawns where the visitor can wander along the banks of the Bush River, which is spanned at this point by an elegant Victorian iron bridge, 36 metres long, leading to a pond surrounded by yews, rhododendrons and azaleas. The walled garden has a curved and brick-faced three-metre high wall, lined with old espalier-trained apple and pear trees and focused on a round goldfish pond and fountain. Vertical interest is achieved by climbers scrambling over former glasshouse frames, beneath which seats are provided. The adjoining one-acre traditional kitchen garden is in full production and contains melon and tomato houses, potting sheds and a gardener's bothy, fruit trees and box hedges.

Castle Ward [Historic Demesne]

Strangford, Downpatrick, Co. Down BT30 7LS. Tel: (028) 4488 1204

The National Trust • 7m NE of Downpatrick, 1½ m W of Strangford on A25, on S shore of Strangford Lough. Entrance by Ballyculter Lodge • House open – telephone for details • Estate, gardens and grounds open Oct to April, daily, 11am – 4pm, May to Sept, 10am – 8pm • Entrance: Estate and grounds £3. Estate, grounds and house £4.70. Parking charge £1 when house and other facilities closed ○ 🍵 ✕ WC ⎃ ⋈ 🏛 🖈 ⚲

Beautifully situated on a peninsula near the mouth of Strangford Lough, the landscape park enhances the 1760s' house with its classical west front and Gothick east front. Both house and decorative Lady Anne's Temple command the heights; below lie an impressive canal and yew walks, features retained from the gardens of a previous early-eighteenth-century house. The sunken Windsor Garden has lost much of its intricate bedding but there are colourful borders containing an interesting range of plants, some quite rare, leading to the rockery and a sentinel row of cordylines and Florence Court yews.

Castlewellan National Arboretum ★★ [Historic Demesne]

Castlewellan, Co. Down BT31 9BU. Tel: (028) 4477 8664

Forest Service, Dept of Agriculture (Northern Ireland) • 25m S of Belfast, 4m NW of Newcastle, in Castlewellan • Open all year, daily • Entrance: cars £4, minibuses £10, coaches £25 • Other information: Disabled parking. Refreshments in summer only. Caravan and camping ground in park ○ 🍵 WC ⎃ ⋈

The walled garden, now called the Annesley Garden, contains an outstanding collection of mature trees and shrubs, many planted before the late nineteenth century by the Earl Annesley. Original specimens of some of Castlewellan's cultivars thrive here, in fine condition. In the spring and summer there are many rhododendrons in bloom and scarlet Chilean fire bushes (*Embothrium coccineum*). In midsummer, a snow-carpet consists of the fallen petals of an unequalled collection of eucryphias. In all, there are 34 champion specimen trees in one area of just nine acres: *Cupressus macrocarpa* 'Lutea', *Dacrycarpus dacrydioides* (syn. *Podocarpus dacrydioides*), *Dacrydium colensoi*, *Juniperus recurva* and *Picea breweriana*. The garden has 15 southern-hemisphere broad-leaved champions, including *Pittosporum tenuifolium*, *Crinodendron hookerianum*, *Eucryphia cordi-*

folia. Half of these specimens are also thought to be the oldest examples in cultivation. Apart from the trees there are bulbs, herbaceous borders, two restored fountain pools, topiary of Irish yew and, in summer, an impressive show of tropaeolum. Beyond the walls the arboretum extends for a further 85 acres in the Forest Park. Signposted walks lead round the magnificent lake. A major new piece of landscaping, the largest and longest yew-hedge maze in the world, represents the path to peace in Northern Ireland.

Crom Estate [Historic Demesne]

Newtownbutler, Fermanagh BT92 8AP.
Tel: (028) 6773 8174; (028) 6773 8118 (Visitor Centre)

The National Trust • 3m W of Newtownbutler on Crom road, signed from Lisnaskea and Newtownbutler • Open April to Sept, daily, 10am – 6pm (opens 12 noon Sun, closes 8pm July and Aug) • Entrance: £4 parking charge for cars and boats • Other information: Batricar available. Visitor Centre with jetty for cruiser access, play area and wildlife exhibition. Fishing and boat hire available in summer. Castle not owned by Trust – please respect areas marked 'Private'. Tea room open July and Aug, daily; otherwise weekends and Bank Holidays only. Holiday cottages available ◑ 🍷 🍴 WC ♿ ⚐ ♨ 🍷 ✎

Although no formal gardens remain, many lovely walks can be enjoyed at this heavily wooded lough shore and island demesne, including a beautiful rhododendron walk in the American Garden, which also has fine specimens of azaleas and magnolias, at their peak in April and May. The autumn colours are spectacular, and a pair of ancient and venerable yew trees must be visited. The aim is to keep up the estate as a nature conservation site. Cross the White Bridge to Inisherk Island and survey the naturally picturesque landscape enhanced by W.S. Gilpin in the 1830s for the present house. The many interesting estate buildings, such as the boat house, the tea house and the island folly, Crichton Tower, are used as eye-catchers and surprises, and the local church and ruins of the seventeenth-century Old Castle are incorporated into the vistas.

Florence Court [Historic Demesne]

Florencecourt, Enniskillen, Co. Fermanagh BT92 1DB. Tel: (028) 6634 8249

The National Trust • 8m SW of Enniskillen, via A4 Sligo road and A32 Swanlinbar road, 4m from Marble Arch Caves • House open April, May and Sept, Sat, Sun and Bank Holiday Mons, 12 noon – 6pm; June to Aug, daily, 12 noon – 6pm (June weekdays opens 1pm) • Estate open all year, daily, Oct to March, 10am – 4pm, April to Sept, 10am – 8pm. Closed 25th Dec • Entrance: Forest Park and Pleasure Gardens £2.50 per car (house £4, children £2, family £10, parties £3 per person) (2003 prices) • Other information: Batricar available ○ 🍷 ✕ 🍴 WC ♿ ⚐ ♨ 🍷 ✎

The original, the mother of all Irish yews (*Taxus baccata* 'Fastigiata'), still grows in the original garden site – accessible by well-marked woodland paths and about a quarter of a mile from the splendid mansion at Florence Court, although strong shoes are essential, especially in the rainy season, if you wish to pay your respects to the venerable 250-year-old tree. Well worth the walk, the gravel path allows glimpses of the mountains and the handsome 'Brownian' park in front of the house. Some fine weeping beeches, Japanese maples and old rhododendrons grow in the pleasure grounds. Other features include an ice-house, a water-driven saw mill and a restored summerhouse, an eel bridge and a hydraulic ram. The three-acre walled garden, including the listed Rose Cottage and Gate Lodges, has recently been acquired by the Trust. The nearby caves are worth visiting too, making a rewarding day out.

28 Killyfaddy Road

Magherafelt, Co. Londonderry BT45 6EX. Tel: (028) 7963 2180

Ann Buchanan • 10m NE of Cookstown off A31. From Magherafelt, take Moneymore road. After ¼ m Killyfaddy Road is 2nd on left opposite filling station. Gardens 1m further along, both sides of road • Open April to Sept, Wed – Sat, 1 – 5pm, and by appt • Entrance: donation to charity ◐ 🌺 WC ♿ ☙ ❧

An acre of informal country garden created over three decades, densely planted with an extensive range of herbaceous perennials plus trees, shrubs, alpines, fruit, vegetables and a small orchard. The 'wild' garden in a separate site across the road has woodland and shade areas and a wildlife pond with associated bog plants.

Mount Stewart ★★ [Historic Garden]

Greyabbey, Newtownards, Co. Down BT22 2AD. Tel: (028) 4278 8387

The National Trust • 15m E of Belfast, 5m SE of Newtownards on A20 Portaferry road • House open different times – telephone for details • Lakeside gardens and walk open March to Nov from 10am, closing times vary depending on season. Formal garden open March, Sat, Sun and 17th March, 10am – 4pm; April to Oct, daily, 10am – 8pm (closes 6pm April and Oct) • Entrance: £3.90, children £2.10, family £8.85, parties £3.65 per person (2003 prices) • Other information: Parking 300 metres away. Two pre-bookable battery wheelchairs available ◐ 🍽 ✕ 🌺 WC ♿ ⬑ ☙ 🛍 🔔 ❧

Of all Ireland's gardens this is the one not to miss. Any adjective that evokes beauty can be applied to it, and it's fun too. In the gardens fronting of the eighteenth- and nineteenth-century house is a collection of statuary depicting British political and public figures as animals. The planting here is formal, with rectangular beds of hot and cool colours. Beyond in the informal gardens are mature trees and shrubs – a botanical collection with few equals, planted with great panache and maintained with outstanding attention to detail. Spires of giant lilies (cardiocrinums), aspiring eucalyptus, banks of rhododendrons, ferns and blue poppies, rivers of candelabra primulas, and much more. Walk along the lakeside path to the hill that affords a view over the lake to the house. Rare tender shrubs such as *Metrosideros umbellatus* from Australasia flourish here outside the walled family cemetery. Leading from it is the Jubilee Avenue and its statue of a white stag. Mount Stewart should be seen several times during the year truly to savour its rich tapestry of plants and water, buildings and trees. The Temple of the Winds, James 'Athenian' Stuart's banqueting hall of 1782–5, is memorable.

Rowallane Garden ★★ [Historic Garden]

Saintfield, Ballynahinch, Co. Down BT24 7LH. Tel: (028) 9751 0131

The National Trust • ½ m S of Saintfield on A7 Belfast – Downpatrick road • Open May to Sept, daily, 10am – 8pm; Oct to April, daily, 10am – 4pm. Closed 24th Dec to 1st Jan • Entrance: £3.10, children £1.30, family £7.30, parties £2.10 per person ○ ☕ 🏛 WC & ⟐ ⌀ 🔦

While famous as a 52-acre rhododendron garden and certainly excellent in this regard, Rowallane has much more to interest keen gardeners. In summer, the walled garden blossoms in lemon and blue, while hoherias scatter their white petals in the wind and in secluded places a pocket-handkerchief tree blows. There is a restored Victorian bandstand (music-filled on some summer weekends) and a rock garden with primulas, meconopsis, heathers, etc. Any season will be interesting, and for the real enthusiast there are rhododendron species and cultivars in bloom from October to August. A National Collection of large-flowered penstemons is here. A feature is made of *Hypericum* 'Rowallane' at the entrance to the walled garden; within are the original plant of *Viburnum plicatum* 'Rowallane' and the original *Chaenomeles* x *superba* 'Rowallane'. The wildflower meadows are becoming famed for such comparative rarities as wild orchids, and as the garden is almost organic in cultivation, wildlife abounds.

Seaforde House [Historic Garden]

Downpatrick, Co. Down BT30 8PG. Tel: (028) 4481 1225

Mr Patrick and Lady Anthea Forde • 22m S of Belfast on A24 Belfast – Newcastle road • Open all year, daily except 25th Dec to 1st Jan, Mon – Sat, 10am – 5pm, Sun, 1 – 6pm (Nov to Feb, Mon – Fri only) • Entrance: £2.80, children £1.70 ○ ☕ ✕ 🏛 WC & ⌀ 🏠 🔦 ⚲

The fine landscaped park can be glimpsed on the way to the vast walled garden, half of which is a commercial nursery with the attraction of a butterfly house which also displays a collection of tropical plants. The other half is an ornamental garden bedecked in late summer with blooms of eucryphia that make up a National Collection. The hornbeam maze has a rose-clad arbour at the centre, the vantage point for which is a 1992 Mogul tower. Beyond the walled garden is the Pheasantry, a verdant valley enclosed by mature trees, full of noteworthy plants collected over many years and still expanding.

Sir Thomas and Lady Dixon Park [Historic Park]

Upper Malone Road, Belfast. Tel: (028) 906 11506 / 903 20802

Belfast Park Department • S of Belfast city centre, on Upper Malone Road • Open all year, daily, 8am – sunset • Entrance: free ○ ☕ WC & ⟐ ⚲

This 128-acre park, presented to the City of Belfast in 1959, is part of a demesne established in the eighteenth century. The main feature today is the International Rose Trial area, where some 20,000 rose bushes can been seen in carefully labelled beds following the contours of the park. One display has old varieties demonstrating the history of the rose. Elsewhere there are riverside meadows by the River Lagan, a walled garden, international camellia trials and a Japanese garden constructed in 1990. A secluded children's playground and band performances during the summer make it enjoyable for all the family.

THE REPUBLIC OF IRELAND

No register of Historic Gardens has been published for the Republic of Ireland. The GGIRP refers to The Great Gardens of Ireland Restoration Programme, initiated in 1994, which has seen the renaissance of 26 historic parks and gardens.

Altamont

Tullow, Co. Carlow. Tel: (59) 91 59444

Deparment of Environment • 19km SE of Carlow, 8km S of Tullow, off Tullow-Bunclody road (N80/81) near Ballon • Telephone for opening times and details • Entrance: €2.75, OAPs €2, students/children €1.25, family €7, groups €2 per person • Other information: Garden centre. Coaches welcome ◐ 🛍 WC ও ৺

The lily-filled lake, surrounded by fine, mature trees, forms a backdrop for a gently sloping lawn. A central walkway formally planted with Irish yews and roses leads from the house to the lake. There is a beautiful fern-leaved beech, and other ancient beeches form the Nun's Walk. A long walk through the demesne leads to the River Slaney with diversions to a bog garden, through an Ice-Age glen of ancient oaks undercarpeted with bluebells. The late owner Mrs North's passion for trees, old-fashioned roses and unusual plants is evident, and hopefully the garden will be kept in the spirit she intended. A flower border in her memory was planted in 2000.

Amergen

Walshestown, Ovens, Co. Cork. Tel: (21) 733 1326

Mrs Christine Fehily • Take N22 Cork – Killarney road, 9km W of Cork, turn right at Dan Sheahan's pub, follow road to crossroads, turn right into cul-de-sac for about 1.5km. Garden on right • Open for parties by appt • Entrance: €4.50 ◑ WC ও

A plantsman's garden in a beautiful setting overlooking the valley of the River Lee. Behind the house is a modest arboretum that merges into mixed borders interspersed with informal lawns. The driveway divides the main garden from a slope thickly planted with shrubs and trees. Paths meander through this area, where lush *Geranium maderense* and handsome dogwoods vividly demonstrate the mildness of the Cork climate. Many tender plants can be grown outdoors, including *Melianthus major, Acacia melanoxylon* and correa, so interesting and unusual shrubs and perennials – *Viburnum harryanum, Mimulus aurantiacus* – abound.

Annes Grove

Castletownroche, Near Mallow, Co. Cork. Tel: (22) 26145

Mr and Mrs F.P. Grove Annesley • 2.5km N of Castletownroche, between Fermoy and Mallow • Open 17th March to Sept, Mon – Sat, 10am – 5pm, Sun, 1 – 6pm, and at other times by appt • Entrance: €5, OAPs and students €3, children €2. Reductions for pre-booked parties ◑ 🍴 <u>WC</u> ♿ ⬧ 🐾 ✎

This is an archetypal 'Robinsonian' (alias wild) garden. Rhododendron species and cultivars arch over and spill towards the pathways, carpeting them with fallen blossoms. Steep, sometimes slippery paths descend at various places into the valley of the Awbeg river (which inspired Edmund Spenser). The statuesque conifers planted in the valley make a colourful tapestry behind the river garden, with mimulus, daylilies and candelabra primroses in profusion. The glory of the garden is, however, the collection of rhododendron species, many of them introduced through subscription to Kingdon Ward expeditions. Visitors may spot hidden surprises – a superb *Juniperus recurva* 'Castlewellan', a mature pocket-handkerchief tree (*Davidia involucrata*) and other exotic flowering trees.

Ardcarraig ★

Oranswell, Bushypark, Co. Galway. Tel: (91) 524336

Mrs Lorna MacMahon • From Galway – Oughterard road, take second left past Glenlo Abbey Hotel; garden is on left • Open 19th May, 10am – 9pm, and by appt • Entrance: €4, parties of 15 or more €3.50 per person • Other information: Refreshments and plants for sale on open day only ◐ WC

In front of the house is a collage of heathers and conifers, with spring and autumn-flowering bulbs; ordinary but attractive. Beside it is a formal, sunken garden, with a pergola covered by clematis and a terracotta *pithoi* as the focal point; handsome, but not unusual. The path then enters a wild hazel wood carpeted with bluebells, ramsons and ferns; nature's garden. A clearing ablaze with scented azaleas in spring and roses and geraniums in summer is the first surprise. The path winds on to a pool surrounded by blue Himalayan poppies, hostas and candelabra primulas. And on . . . to a bubbling peat-stained stream that chatters over granite rocks to a bog garden with heathers and skunk cabbage, to a stunning tranquil Japanese hill and pool garden, while the boulder beyond suggests Mount Fuji. And on . . . to Harry's Garden, full of plants given to Lorna in memory of her late husband, and planted (with a pick!) among the natural granite boulders. The latest venture is a moss garden in the Japanese style.

Ardgillan Castle and Garden

Balbriggan, Co. Dublin. Tel: (1) 849 2212 (Castle), (1) 849 2324 (Garden)

Fingal County Council Parks • 24km N of Dublin, between Balbriggan and Skerries. Signposted off N1 • Castle open all year, daily except Mon (but open Bank Holiday Mons and Mons in July and Aug). Closed 23rd Dec to 1st Jan •

Garden open all year, daily, 10am – 6pm (closes winter 4.30pm). Park open all year, daily, 10am – 6pm (closes up to 9pm depending on season). Conducted tours June to Aug, Thurs, 3.30pm • Entrance: free but guided tours €2 (castle tours €4, concessions €2.50, family €9) ○ 🍽 🚌 WC & ◁ ℘ B&B

The approach to the castle is one of the most spectacular in Ireland, with views northwards along the coast to the Carlingford and Mourne mountains, and the castle itself nestled in a hollow. The castle, built in 1738 by the Revd Robert Taylor, now houses an eclectic assortment of eighteenth- and nineteenth-century furniture, and an important collection of seventeenth-century 'Down Survey' maps of Ireland. The demesne today covers about 194 acres, and within it are various gardens. A fine Victorian conservatory rescued from another house has been re-erected and is now the centrepiece of the formal rose garden. In the walled garden a unique, free-standing brick wall with 20 alcoves is now planted with fruit. The walled garden is divided into sections which include box-edged herb and vegetable gardens, a fruit garden and ornamental gardens displaying a good mix of shrubs, perennials and rock plants. Many of the beds were created recently and are not part of the original layout, but they contain some choice plants. The garden has been grant-aided under the GGIRP for remedial work on its woodland paths, rose garden (which now includes Edwardian and Victorian cultivars) and a small garden museum, and to provide some new plant stock to extend its collections. A National Collection of potentillas is held here. Don't miss the ice-house, a short way along the woodland walk.

Ardnamona

Lough Eske, Co. Donegal. Tel: (73) 22650

Kieran and Amabel Clarke • On NW shore of Lough Eske, approached from Donegal, following signs for Harvey's Point • Open all year daily, 10am – 5pm, and by appt • Entrance: €5 ○ ◁ ℘ B&B

William Robinson would have been proud of this garden created by the Wallaces between 1880 and 1932. Ardnamona is wild gardening at its most exuberant and refined. Imagine a Himalayan mountain slope cloaked with primeval rhododendron forest, 18 metres tall, with a carpet of fallen leaves underfoot embroidered in discarded flowers – you are close to imagining Ardnamona. The rhododendrons are mainly over 100 years old, and they proclaim their age with proud clean trunks, coloured from cinnamon to purple, and canopies well beyond reach. Opened in 1992, this garden (once neglected, now again cared for) will welcome visitors. Rhododendron enthusiasts will need little more encouragement than the prospect of being in paradise.

Ballindoolin House and Garden

Carbury, via Edenderry, Co. Kildare. Tel: (405) 31430

The Molony family • 5km N of Edenderry on R401. Also signposted from N4 between Enfield and Kinnegad • House open; guided tours only (extra charge) •

Open May to Sept, daily except Mon, 12 noon – 6pm, and by appt at other times • Entrance: €5, children over 5 €2.50 ◑ ☕ ✕ <u>WC</u> ♿ ☙ 🎁 ⚲

A medium-sized demesne surrounding an 1821 Georgian house which still retains its original interior and furnishings. Some of the farmyard buildings and outhouses still await repair, but the two-acre walled garden has been restored under the GGIRP. It has aged espaliered apple trees in various stages of decrepitude, which have been carefully kept and are charming, setting the atmosphere for the garden. A melon-pit ruin has also been conserved. The soil is rich and fertile, and the old borders have been beautifully replanted with a wide range of herbaceous perennials, roses and herbs. Every year the new plantings get better and better, and a good variety of vegetables and fruit thrive once again in the warm microclimate, providing much of the produce for the restaurant. The wonderfully preserved walls include a high, brick-lined south-facing fruit wall, which has also been replanted. Outside the walled garden a path leads past a quirky little rockery towards the trefoil-shaped dovecote, on to the lime kiln, the 'Iron Age' mound and the woodland walk, where a long beech avenue leads into the woods and back towards the house.

Ballinlough Castle Gardens

Clonmellon, Co. Westmeath. Tel: (46) 33135

Sir John and Lady Nugent • On N52 between Kells and Mullingar, 3km from Clonmellon • Open May to Sept, Sat, Sun and Bank Holiday Mons, 12 noon – 6pm, and at other times by appt. Closed 3rd to 16th Aug. Check opening times before travelling • Entrance: €6, concessions €5, party rates on application
◑ ☕ ✕ <u>WC</u> ♿ ☙

The gardens, woods and lakes were restored in 1998 under the GGIRP. The present castle dates from the seventeenth century, with eighteenth- and nine-teenth-century additions, but the history of the site goes way back to 1400. The long avenue through the demesne hints at good things to come, and as the house comes into view on its mound above the two lakes it is truly delightful. The arched gateway into the first of four walled enclosures leads to a formal pool, mature trees and flowering shrubs, and on to double herbaceous borders. Lady Nugent has filled the gardens with choice plants, fruit, herbs and vegetables, some old, many newly planted and all well cared for. Sir John and the garden staff have become proficient under-gardeners, and a real team spirit is evident. The formality of the walled gardens gives way to free-style wild plantings along the woodland paths, leading down to two rock bridges, a summerhouse, and a planted rockery and glade. A walk around the lake is rewarded by the view from the far side, where the castle seems to float above the water's edge. Swans have recolonised the lakes, and other creatures are settling in again.

Ballymaloe Cookery School Gardens

Shanagarry, Co. Cork. Tel: (21) 464 6785

Tim and Darina Allen • 36km E of Cork, between Cloyne and Ballycotton • Open April to Sept, daily, 10am – 6pm. Guided tours for parties by

arrangement • *Entrance: €5* • *Other information: Booking for groups essential*
◑ ᗕ ⫞ ⛫ ⚲

Take the bones of an old Quaker garden and begin afresh – that is what Darina Allen has done at Kinoith (and she hasn't finished yet). The antique beech hedges are being clipped again, and within their shelter are compartments, each one different and refreshing. The first is the flower garden with short herbaceous borders, and beside a small pool is a summerhouse, the floor of which is patterned with shards of Delft. Beyond is the herb garden, where dwarf box hedges delineate a formal pattern of beds planted mainly with culinary herbs. These compartments can be enjoyed from ground level and also from a viewing platform. The pool garden lies outside the old hedges, and has an incomplete folly. A double herbaceous border, planted in 1996, leads to a plain garden house with Gothic windows. 'Please do not touch my insides' is a friendly piece of advice, for the interior of this unassuming building is decorated with myriad shells. The organic vegetable garden appeals directly to the eye with its tapestry of vegetables and edible flowers.

Bantry House and Gardens ★

Bantry, Co. Cork. Tel: (27) 50047

Mr and Mrs E. Shelswell-White • *On outskirts of Bantry on Cork road* • *House open* • *Gardens open March to Oct, daily, 9am – 6pm* • *Entrance: €4, children free, (house and garden €9.50, concessions and students €8, children free)* • *Other information: Annual music festival, last week in June (house closed) – telephone for details* ◑ **WC** ᗕ ⪪ ⫞ ⛾ ⚲

Bantry House is worth a visit to see the house in its setting, quite apart from its magnificent garden. The gardens were created from 1844 to 1867 while in the ownership of the 2nd Earl of Bantry, Richard White, who also built up an impressive art collection as a result of his Grand Tour travels. His artistic ambitions drove him to develop the house and its setting, so formal parterres, terraces and beds were laid out around the house; behind is his amazing staircase of a hundred steps stretching up the steep hillside. Those who reach the top are rewarded with the most stunning view of the house and gardens below and Bantry Bay sweeping out to the broad Atlantic beyond. Statues, urns and balustrading encircle and embellish the gardens; copies of original terracotta urns which punctuate the great flight of steps are filled with *Osmanthus delavayi*. There is a definite Italian air about the place – and its warm humid climate has inevitably influenced the plants that will grow there towards Japanese and Chinese wisterias, magnolias, myrtles, *Trachelospermum asiaticum* – the lakeside gardens of Como and Maggiore spring to mind here. The results achieved under the GGIRP are impressive: the extensive drainage system has been recovered, the parterre surrounding the nineteenth-century wisteria circle and fountain completed, the round bed at the entrance to the house replanted, and the 14 round beds to the north overlooking the bay re-created. The rose garden is currently under review.

Belvedere

Mullingar, Co. Westmeath. Tel: (44) 49060

Westmeath County Council • 8km S of Mullingar on N52 Tullamore road • House and garden open all year, daily; May to Aug, Mon – Fri, 9.30am – 6pm, Sat, Sun and Bank Holiday Mons, 10.30am – 7.00pm; April, Sept, Oct, 10.30am – 6pm; Nov to March, 10.30am – 4.30pm (last admission 1 hour before closing) • Entrance: €6, children €4, family €17 ○ 🍵 ✕ 🛍 WC ♿ 🦮 ♨ 🏛 🦺 ⚲

The eighteenth-century hunting lodge, formal garden, Victorian walled garden and landscaped park, extending over 160 acres on the shores of Lough Ennell, have been restored thanks to a €4.4 million grant. There are fine views of the lough and islands from the terraces which drop in steps to the water. The Jealous Wall is one of those typically Gothick-Irish follies, built in 1750 to separate squabbling brothers. It looks antique and is impressive. There are also 6km of trails and a children's play area. An exhibition in the restored stables relates the story of the Wicked Earl and the Mary Molesworth scandal, the history of the estate and its restoration. Its real glory is the eighteenth-century parkland, follies – including Thomas Wright's Gothick arch – and woods.

Birr Castle Demesne ★

Birr, Co. Offaly. Tel: (509) 20336

The Earl and Countess of Rosse • 130km SW of Dublin, 38km S of Athlone, on N52 in Birr • Open all year, daily, March to Oct, 9am – 6pm; Nov to Feb, 10am – 4pm. Guided tours by arrangement • Entrance: €7, OAPs and students €5, children €3.50, family €20, parties of 20 or more €5.70 per person, students and OAPs €4.50 • Other information: Parking outside castle gates. Picnics in walled garden only. Castle not open. Historic Science Centre ○ 🍵 🛍 WC ♿ 🦮 ♨ 🏛 🦺 ⚲

The castle's Gothick front dominates vistas which strike through the park and at whose centre is the restored 'Leviathan', (the Great Telescope which made Birr the world's astronomical Mecca in the middle of the nineteenth century and of which demonstrations are given regularly). All around, in profusion, are rare trees and shrubs, many raised from seed received from central China from the 1930s. Over one of the rivers is a beautiful suspension bridge, while a hidden glen boasts a Victorian fernery with its own waterfall and fountain. Evergreen conifers, golden willows, carpets of daffodils, and world-record box hedges, magnolias galore, a cherry avenue and the original plant of *Paeonia* 'Anne Rosse' are mere selections of the many attractions. Recent improvements include the transformation of the old formal terraces with millennium gardens: new water features and wooden statuary complement the hornbeam cloisters. A secret winter garden with a romantic thatched winter bower dominating a glade of snowdrops has been restored. The demesne contains over fifty of the champion trees of the British Isles, as well as geographic collections from Mexico, Pakistan and Yunnan, the last in a corner of Tipperary to which it extends across a further bridge.

Bunratty Castle and Knappogue Castle

Bunratty, Co. Clare. Tel: (61) 360788

Shannon Heritage • Both castles located between Ennis and Limerick off N18. Signposted • Open: Bunratty, all year, daily, 9.30am – 5.30pm (last admission 4.15pm); Knappogue, mid-April to early-Oct, 9.30am – 5pm (last admission 4.15pm) • Entrance: charge NEW � ✕ WC ♿ ♀ ✑

The two neighbouring fifteenth-century castles, under the same ownership, have a variety of gardens offering an enjoyable family day out. The grounds of Bunratty Castle are now occupied by the vernacular buildings of the Folk Park, each complemented by an appropriate garden. At the far end of the park is the early-nineteenth-century *Bunratty House*, next to a pretty Regency-style walled flower garden with a traditional gardener's bothy. Knappogue Castle has a large walled garden in a tranquil setting close by. Planted today as a flower and herb garden, the wall borders are filled with an attractive mixture of shrubs and herbaceous plants. Spacious lawns are divided by the old path systems and amply supplied with seats.

Butterstream ★★

Trim, Co. Meath. Tel: (46) 36017

Jim Reynolds • Signposted from Trim • Open May to Sept, daily, 11am – 6pm • Entrance: €6 ◑ WC ♿

A single-handed work of art, Butterstream is considered to be one of the finest gardens in Ireland. A series of compartments, containing different arrangements of plants, varies from a formal box-hedged garden of old roses and lilies to an informal gold garden carpeted with ferns and hostas. A formal pool, replete with water lilies and carp, is flagged in Liscannor stone, and large pots of box topiary stand sentinel. A view across the rich pastures of adjoining farmland adds to the sense of a Tuscan villa garden. The large tennis lawn has a restrained gallery of clematis, deep purple hedges and a rustic summerhouse. Features include a Gothick pavilion and a maturing yew obelisk. Twin canals of immense length and elegant proportions have been added and the garden continues to be developed with great enthusiasm and style.

Coolcarrigan House and Gardens

Naas, Co. Kildare. Tel: (45) 863 512/834 1141

Mr and Mrs Wilson-Wright • 17.5km N of Naas, 14.5km W of Clane on minor road. Signposted • Open April to Sept, Mon – Fri, by appt only • Entrance: €8 ◑ ▥ WC ♿

The Victorian house (occasionally open) was built in 1838. The 10-acre gardens are mainly planted with shrubs and trees. The large and much-admired collection of rare and unusual trees and shrubs was formed with the advice of Sir Harold Hillier many years ago; they are dotted about the lawns in informal style as specimens. A large and well-maintained Victorian greenhouse dominates the main garden, and a fine herbaceous border fronted by an immaculate lawn completes the picture.

Derreen ★

Lauragh, Killarney, Co. Kerry. Tel: (64) 83588

Charles Bigham • 24km SW of Kenmare on R571 road along S of Kenmare Bay, towards Healy Pass • Open April to Oct, daily, 11am – 6pm • Entrance: €5, children €2 • Other information: Picnic area near car park only ◑ ☕ 🛍 **WC** ♿ ⬗ ९

The broad sweep of plush lawn and the bald outcroppings of rock by the house do not prepare visitors for the lushness of the walks which weave through native woodlands and palisades of jade-stemmed bamboo. The evocatively named King's Oozy – a path that has a hankering to be a river – leads to a grove of tall, archaic tree-ferns (*Dicksonia antarctica*) with socks of filmy ferns. Wellies are the plantsman's only requirement to enjoy the large collection of rhododendrons that shelter among clipped entanglements of *Gaultheria shallon*. This is probably one of the wettest places in these islands, a fact you're reminded of by the lushness.

The Dillon Garden ★★

45 Sandford Road, Ranelagh, Dublin 6

Helen and Val Dillon • 10-min. drive or ½ -hour walk from city centre in a cul-de-sac off Sandford Road just after Merton Road and church • Open March, July, Aug, daily; April to June, Sept, Sun; all 2 – 6pm. Parties of 15 or more at any time by written appt • Entrance: €5 • Other information: Possible for wheelchairs but limited access ◑ **WC** ♿ ⬯

Within a walled rectangular garden, typical of Dublin's Georgian town houses, Helen Dillon has created one of the best town gardens in Ireland. Set around a newly created canal, the mixed borders of shrubs and herbaceous perennials are changeful, each season revealing unusual plants and exciting colour combinations. Exploration reveals a necklace of secret rooms with raised beds for rarities, such as lady's slipper orchids or double-flowered *Trillium grandiflorum*. On the sunken terrace, terracotta pots sprout more rare plants. Clumps of *Dierama pulcherrimum* arch over the sphinxes, and a small alpine house and conservatory shelter the choicest species – *Lapageria rosea*, prize-winning ferns, alpines and bulbs. A new area of dramatic foliage plants is being developed.

Dunloe Castle Gardens

Hotel Dunloe Castle, Beaufort, Killarney, Co. Kerry. Tel: (64) 44111

Killarney Hotels Ltd • 6km W of Killarney, off Killorglin Road. Signposted • Open early May to Sept, but opening date varies – check with hotel. Parties by appt only • Entrance: individuals free, parties €63.40 per coach • Other information: Toilet facilities in hotel ◑ ☕ ✕ **WC** ♿ ⬗ ९ **B&B**

On a superb site facing the Gap of Dunloe lie the imposing buildings of the Hotel Dunloe Castle, opened in 1965, surrounded by acres of parkland and gardens with magnificent and unusual trees and shrubs. Visitors and hotel guests may wander freely and appreciate the well-kept lawns and colourful planting, the walled garden and the ruined fort of Dunloe Castle. The more serious garden visitor will spot such tender specimens as *Eriobotrya deflexa*, *Glyptostrobus pensilis*, *Banksia marginata* and *Telopea oreades* with the aid of the plan and catalogue compiled by Roy Lancaster. Plantings of 1920 have been continually added to and the whole is impeccably maintained. Plants, however, are becoming crowded and tough decisions will have to be made in the near future to allow the choicest to achieve their full potential.

Earlscliffe ★★

Baron's Brae, Ceanchor Road, Baily, Co. Dublin. Tel: (1) 832 2556

Dr David Robinson • *8km NE of city centre on Howth. At end of Ceanchor Road, enter through last gate on left signed to Baron's Brae* • *Open for parties by appt only* • *Entrance: prices on application* ◐ **WC**

Few gardens can match Earlscliffe for variety or advantage. It is perched on the cliffs looking south over Dublin Bay (a view to rival the Bay of Naples) on the southern side of the Hill of Howth, a peninsula almost encircled by sea. Severe frost is rare and there is an almost constant breeze – just what the most tender species need. The collection of plants in these six acres is astonishing. A memorable forest of *Echium pininana*, the spire-shaped, blue-blossomed bugloss from the Canary Isles, is naturalised here. An octopus-like weeping cedar groping a thicket of the Chatham Islands daisy-bushes (*Olearia* 'Henry Travers'), a grove of bananas that flower and fruit, and proteas and waxy yellow-blossomed heathers from South Africa greet the visitor. Many eucalyptus species thrive, not to mention the cupressus-like *Callitris rhomboidea*, *Juania australis*, *Daphniphyllum macropodum*, *Araucaria bidwillii*, *Cordyline baueri* – one could go on and on. The garden itself goes on and on: four new acres were taken in hand a few years ago, and a grove of 100 *Luma apiculata*, the cinnamon-stemmed myrtle, was planted for the millennium.

Enniscoe House Gardens

Castlehill, Crossmolina, via Ballina, Co. Mayo. Tel: (96) 31112

Mrs Susan Kellett • *After Ballina, turn sharp left in Crossmolina at statue, and drive for 4km on R315 (Pontoon and Castlebar road). Gates and signs on left* • *Open April to Sept, daily, Mon – Fri, 10am – 6pm; Sat, Sun, 2 – 6pm* • *Entrance: €6, children €2* ◐ 🍽 🏺 **WC** ♿ 🕊 ⚘ **B&B**

Set near the shores of Lough Conn, the estate dates from the seventeenth century, the picturesque house (now a country house hotel with good fishing and cuisine) from the eighteenth. The surrounding landscape is beautiful and unspoilt. The pleasure grounds were developed in the 1870s, but the woods may be a remnant of original woodland taken into ownership in the 1600s and managed ever since. The walled gardens were derelict from the 1950s until the present owner received grant aid from the GGIRP. The ornamental garden within the old walls has been faithfully restored to its Edwardian origins, and today is bright with annual bedding and borders filled with perennials and shrubs. The paths are smartly gravelled, the box hedging trim and the lawns settling down. The fruit and vegetable garden linked to it by a fern-draped rustic arch has been taken over by a small local co-operative, and sells produce to visitors.

An Féar Gorta (Tea and Garden Rooms)

Ballyvaghan, Co. Clare. Tel: (65) 707 7157

Catherine and Brendan O'Donoghue • In Ballyvaghan, on sea-front • Open June to mid-Sept, Mon – Sat, 11am – 5.30pm • Entrance: free ◑ 💺 WC ᒃ ⬧

The Burren, John Betjeman's 'Stony seaboard, far and foreign' . . . is this simple garden's dramatic backdrop. Catmint spills over the native limestone, shrubby cinquefoils sparkle in the sun, butterfly bushes burst with blossom and are a-flutter with insects. There are several compartments, in front of and behind the traditional cottages, all different but each one filled with shrubs and perennials that thrive by the edge of the sea. A conservatory contains other joys, including the red banana passion flower (*Passiflora antioquiensis*) and, appropriately, the cup-and-saucer vine (*Cobaea scandens*). You can sit under their shade, sipping tea and eating scrumptious cakes, enjoying the view.

Fernhill Gardens

Sandyford, Co. Dublin. Tel: (1) 295 6000

Mrs Sally Walker • 13km S of city centre on R117 Dublin – Enniskerry road • Open March to Sept, Tues – Sat and Bank Holiday Mons, 11am – 5pm, Sun, 2 – 6pm • Entrance: €5, OAPs €4, children €3 (under 5 free) ◑ 🍴 WC ᒃ 🌿

The garden is situated on the eastern slope of the Dublin Mountains and has a laurel lawn, some fine nineteenth-century plantings and an excellent flowering specimen of *Michelia doltsopa*. The plantings of rhododendron species and cultivars provide spectacles of colour from early spring into mid-summer; many of the more tender rhododendrons flourish here. The walkways through the wooded areas wind steeply past many other shrubs – pieris and camellias are also outstanding. There is a rock garden and a water garden near the house, and drifts of daffodils in the spring. In the summer there are the roses and a good collection of herbaceous plants, many used as underplanting through the woodland.

Fota Arboretum and Gardens ★

Fota Estate, Carrigtwohill, Co. Cork. Tel: (21) 481 2728

Department of Environment • 15.5km E of Cork, on Cobh road • Arboretum open all year, daily, 9am – 6pm (Sun opens 11am, Nov to March closes 5pm) • Entrance: free for arboretum. Automatic pay barrier to car park • Other information: Refreshments and shop in Fota House ◑ 💺 🍴 WC ᒃ ⬧ 🍷 ☕

Perhaps the wonders of Fota are best appreciated in summer when the obvious distractions like camellias, embothriums, drimys, pieris and most of the rhododendrons have finished flowering. There is no lack of colour: the walls sparkle with abutilons and cestrums, and the myrtles take on a pinkish hue. *Davidia involucrata* may be bereft of handkerchiefs, but admire instead the elaborate flowers of *Magnolia* x *wieseneri*, or the frothy white blooms of *Eucalyptus delegatensis*. Now is the time to appreciate the complicated growth of the Chilean hazel, the immense canopy of the fern-leaved beech, a perfect *Pinus montezumae* and the marvellous bark of the stone pine. Note the wickedly spiny species of colletia and the elegance of *Restio subverticillatus*, then spend a few minutes in the cool fernery and the Victorian orangery, which contains a fine collection of contemporary plants. This, and a section of the Pleasure Gardens known as the Italian Garden, have both been restored.

Garinish Island

(see ILNACULLIN)

Gash Gardens

Castletown, Mountrath, Co. Laois. Tel: (502) 32247

The Keenan family • S of Mountrath, 1km off N7 Dublin – Limerick road. Signposted • Open May to Sept – telephone for dates and times. Parties welcome by appt • Entrance: €4 • Other information: Children not admitted ◗ 🐌 WC ♿ 🌶

Developed by the late Noel Keenan and now lovingly looked after by his daughter Mary, this is a plantsman's garden full of treasures. Water features include a lily pond, a stream garden, a cascade and a bog garden. There is also an extensive rock garden, herbaceous borders, a riverside walk, a beech walk and a laburnum arch. This garden deserves to be better known.

Georgian House and Garden

2 Pery Square, Limerick, Co. Limerick. Tel: (61) 314130

Limerick Civic Trust • In Limerick • House and garden open all year, Mon – Fri, 10am – 4.30pm, Sat, Sun by appt (closed Bank Holidays) • Entrance: €5 (house and garden) • Other information: Teas by arrangement ○ WC ♿ 🚻 ♀

A handsome early-nineteenth-century town house in a terrace overlooking the public gardens of Pery Square has recently been conserved and renovated. The garden at the rear, enclosed by high brick walls and backed by the coach house, has been restored to complement the house. It comprises a central lawn, surrounded by neatly maintained wall borders planted with favourites of the era that give interest throughout the year.

Glenveagh Castle Gardens ★

Glenveagh National Park, Churchill, Co. Donegal. Tel: (74) 37088/37090/37262

Department of Environment • 24km NW of Letterkenny • Castle open, €2.50, OAPs €1.90, children/students €1.20, family €6.50, parties of 20 or more €190 • Garden open 15th March to 2nd Nov, 10am – 5pm, and at other times by appt • Entrance: €2.50, OAPs and parties per person €2, students and children €1.50 • Other information: Parking at visitor centre. Access to garden and castle by shuttle bus (€2) ◑ 🍽 ✕ 🛍 **WC** ♿ 🐕 ℗

The centrepiece of the Glenveagh National Park is the castle and surrounding gardens, set above Lough Veagh and encircled by high peat-blanketed mountains in the middle of the Donegal highlands. In the garden the surprises are countless, with each outdoor room given a different treatment. The two-acre lawn in the pleasure grounds is fringed by rhododendron shrubberies, tree ferns, eucryphias and mass plantings of hostas, rodgersias and astilbes. Beyond, pathways wind through oak woods in which grow scented rhododendrons and numerous other tender trees and shrubs. Here classical elements are added: one happens upon terraced enclosures furnished with Italian statuary and massive terracotta pots. In the *jardin potager* next to the castle each plot, bounded by herbaceous borders, is planted with heritage vegetable varieties, Irish apple cultivars, the unique single red *Dahlia* 'Matt Armour' and rank upon rank of flowering herbs. This is a paradise for plantsmen and gardeners keen on seeing fine and unusual specimens. Linger, and walk the mountain sides, then take the last bus back to the remarkable heather-roofed visitor centre with its imaginative landscaping.

Glin Castle Gardens

Glin, Co. Limerick. Tel: (68) 34173/34112

Madam Fitzgerald and the Knight of Glin • 48km W of Limerick on N69 • Open by appt only • Entrance: €5 • Other information: Accommodation available ◑ ⌂ **B&B**

The stylish and romantic castle looks over a formal setting to the north and a well-wooded demesne to the south. The formal garden could not be simpler, with its lawns and two domed bays flanking a path to a sundial and an elegant *Parrotia persica*, beyond which is a meadow with daffodils and a woodland with fine old trees. Magnolias and bluebells bring their spring flowering, and in early summer rhododendrons are still providing a splash of colour, in contrast to the cool tones of a large *Abutilon vitifolium*, while the grey walls of the castle are relieved by climbing plants. A shady walk with broad-leafed rhododendrons is being developed in a wood east of the main garden. An outstanding feature is the walled garden on a steep slope, with its mathematically neat rows of vegetables and herbs, figs, fruit, roses and clematis, a castellated henhouse, a rustic temple with marble incumbent, and a lovely view across the Shannon over the walls and undulating slate roofs of the old battlemented, cobblestoned stableyard. If you like kitchen gardens, Glin's will please you. Behind the kitchen garden, a path ascends gently to a circle of twentieth-century standing stones and, beyond, to a Gothic hermitage surrounded by ferns.

Graigueconna ★

Old Connaught, Bray, Co. Wicklow. Tel: (1) 282 2273

Mr and Mrs John Brown • 19km SE of Dublin city centre. Take N11, then slip road to Bray and turn right at traffic lights. From S take N11 towards Dublin, then slip road signed to Bray/Enniskerry/Rathmichael. Turn left for Graigueconna • Open May to July, 9am – 6pm, by appt only for parties of four or more; and for Wicklow Gardens Festival • Entrance: €5 • Other information: Coffee provided for small groups by arrangement ◑ ▣ WC ♿

This three-acre garden was created early last century by Lewis Meredith, who wrote *Rock gardens – how to make and maintain them* (1906), one of the earliest 'text books' on this topic. His rock garden lies hidden at the end of a specially laid railway track along which rocks were trundled. Today, this track is a grassy path, punctuated by Irish yews and lined with excellent mixed borders of herbaceous perennials and shrubs. The rock garden, while intact, is planted for easier maintenance with ground-cover species, bulbs and ferns, along with many interesting southern-hemisphere shrubs. There are numerous 'old' roses on the walls and in shrubberies. Near the house are tender and unusual plants, throughout the borders are uncommon herbaceous perennials, while the conservatory houses tender southern-hemisphere species and a collection of arisaema. The whole place is painstakingly cared for.

Heywood Garden

Ballinakill, Co. Laois. Tel: (502) 33563

Department of Environment • 5km SE of Abbeyleix. Turn E in Abbeyleix signed Ballinakill. Outside Ballinakill • Open all year, daily, during daylight hours • Entrance: free ○ ♿

Edwin Lutyens' walled garden with pergola and lawns is acknowledged as his finest small-scale work in Ireland. It is a gem, now restored close to its original state as far as the walls and ornaments are concerned. On the driveway leading towards the school buildings is an eighteenth-century folly. Heywood has now been recognised as a heritage garden of historic and architectural importance.

Ilnacullin (Garinish Island)

Glengarriff, Co. Cork. Tel: (27) 63040

Department of Environment • On island in Bantry Bay • Open March, Oct, Mon – Sat, 10am – 4.30pm, Sun, 1 – 5pm; April to June, Sept, Mon – Sat, 10am – 6.30pm, Sun, 1 – 6.30pm; July and Aug, Mon – Sat, 9.30am – 6.30pm, Sun, 11am – 6.30pm (last landing 1 hour before closing) • Entrance: €3.10, OAPs €2.20, students and children €1.20, family €7.60, parties of 20 or more €2.20 per person (2003 prices) ◑ ▣ WC ♿ ⬢ ♨

The boat trip across the sheltered inlets of Bantry Bay past sun-bathing seals, with views of the Caha Mountains, is doubly rewarding; landing at the slipway you gain entrance to one of Ireland's gardening jewels, begun in the early 1900s. Most visitors cluster around the Casita – an Italianate garden – and reflecting pool, designed by Harold Peto, to enjoy (on clear days) spectacular scenery, and some quite indifferent annual bedding. But walk beyond, to the Temple of the Winds, through shrubberies filled with plants usually confined indoors, tree ferns, southern-hemisphere conifers, rhodo-dendron species and cultivars. A flight of stone steps leads to the Martello tower, and thence the path returns to the walled garden with its double-sided herbaceous border.

Iveagh Gardens

Clonmel Street, Dublin 2. Tel: (1) 475 7816

Department of Environment • Access via Clonmel Street or National Concert Hall, Earlsfort Terrace • Open all year, daily, 8.30am – 6pm (opens 10am Sun and Bank Holiday Mons, closes earlier Oct to March). Closed 5th Dec, 17th March) • Entrance: free • Other information: Wheelchairs via Clonmel Street entrance only ○ &

Ranked among the finest and least known of Dublin's parks and gardens, they were designed by Ninian Niven in 1863 and include a rustic grotto, a cascade, fountains, a maze, a rosarium, archery grounds, a wilderness and woodlands. An ongoing programme of restoration is underway, and many of the highlights of the gardens – the fountains, the cascade and the rosarium – have already been tackled, but a lot remains to be done and good plantings are needed.

The Japanese Garden

Irish National Stud, Tully, Kildare, Co. Kildare. Tel: (45) 521617/522963

Irish National Stud • 40km SW of Dublin, 1.5km off M/N7 outside Kildare • Open mid-Feb to mid-Nov, daily, 9.30am – 6pm. Guided tours available • Entrance: by combined ticket for Japanese Garden, St Fiachra's Garden, Irish National Stud and Horse Museum €7.50, OAPs and students €6, children €4, family €18 (2003 prices) • Other information: Picnics in car park only. Lego area for children ○ ⛔ ✕ WC ⟨⟩ 🛗

Devised by Colonel William Hall-Walker (later Lord Wavertree), a wealthy Scotsman of a famous brewery family, and laid out 1906–10 by the Japanese Eida and his son Minoru, the garden symbolises the 'Life of Man'. This is not a plantsman's garden, and few of the plants are Japanese; to be sure there are some excellent old maples, but many of the trees and shrubs are clipped and shaped beyond reason. The overshadowing Scots pines are exquisite. A pathway meanders through artificial caves into a watery stream, past the tranquil ponds and on to the weeping trees of the grave. Beautiful stone lanterns grace the site, which is in the style of a Japanese tea garden. New in 1999 was the creation of *St Fiachra's Garden*, 'a garden in commemoration of the Patron Saint of Gardeners in his home country of Ireland', as the National Stud puts it.

John F. Kennedy Arboretum

New Ross, Co. Wexford. Tel: (51) 388171

Department of Environment • 12km S of New Ross • Open all year, daily except 25th Dec and 9th April; April, 10am – 6.30pm (closes 8pm May to Aug, 5pm Oct to March) • Entrance: €2.75, OAPs €2, students and children €1.25, family €7 • Other information: Refreshments and shop available mid-March to Oct, sometimes Suns only. Visitor centre with Kennedy memorial ○ 🍵 🛍 <u>WC</u> ♿ 🚲 ♨ ♀

A spacious modern arboretum laid out in botanical sequence with rides; from the summit of a nearby hill is a superb panorama not only of the arboretum but also of parts of six counties. Best to begin at the viewpoint – turn left just beyond the main entrance and drive to the summit car park to see the layout. At the arboretum be prepared for a long walk; fortunately those not keen on gardening tend to linger near the café so that the distant reaches are quiet and empty. Planting began in the 1960s, and now 4500 different trees and shrubs are growing, ranging from conifers to flowering shrubs. Most species are represented by several specimens, and keen plantsmen can take their time examining the groups. A colourful planting of dwarf conifers is on the western side, a small lake on the east. While primarily a scientific collection, the arboretum is now achieving an established reputation.

Kilfane Glen and Waterfall

Thomastown, Co. Kilkenny. Tel: (56) 24558

Mrs Susan Mosse • 19km SE of Kilkenny, 6.5km N of Thomastown, signed off N9 • Open July, Aug, daily, 11am – 6pm, and for parties of 10 or more at other times by appt • Entrance: €5.50, OAPs €5, children €4.50, family €15 ◑ 🛍 WC ♿ ♨

This romantic woodland garden dates from 1790, when the glen was designed to display nature in all her terrifying beauty, *à la* Wordsworth. It has the requisite romantic traits including a hermit's grotto, a *cottage orné* and a waterfall, so that present-day visitors can enjoy the beauties just as their predecessors did under the tuition of the gentry of Kilfane House. A good leaflet with a suggested walk tells the reader when to feel the *frisson*.

Killruddery House and Gardens ★

Bray, Co. Wicklow. Tel: (1) 286 3405

The Earl and Countess of Meath • 23km S of Dublin, just beyond Bray. Follow signs off roundabout on Bray/Greystones road. From N11 (1st exit for Bray travelling N; 3rd exit for Bray/Greystones travelling S) follow signs off roundabout • House open May, June and Sept, daily, 1 – 5pm with conducted tours, and at other dates and times for pre-arranged parties • Garden open April, Sat and Sun, 1 – 5pm; May to Sept, daily, 1 – 5pm. Guided tours for parties of 20 or more by appt (extra charge €30 per group) • Entrance: €5, OAPs/students €4, children €2 (house and garden €8, OAPs/students €6.50, children €3, parties of 20 or more €6.50 per person). All children must be accompanied • Other information: Teas and meals for groups by arrangement ◑ WC ♿

Killruddery is unique in having the most extensive early formal gardens, still in their original style, surviving in Ireland, dating largely from the seventeenth century with nineteenth-century embellishments. The joy of the garden is the formal hedging, known as 'The Angles', set beside the formal canals which lead to a ride into the distant hills. There is a collection of nineteenth-century French cast statuary, a sylvan theatre created in bay, and a fountain pool enclosed in a beech hedge. The fine nineteenth-century conservatory has been completely re-roofed, its original Turner dome put back and its unique collection of statues conserved; the marble statuary within has been restored. The garden deserves to be better known. Nearby is the *National Gardens Exhibition Centre* at Kilquade, a one-stop shop for gardeners and individual gardens created by different designers.

Kilmacurragh

Kilbride, Rathdrum, Co. Wicklow. Tel: (1) 647 3000

Department of Environment • 48km S of Dublin, 8km S of Wicklow off N11. Turn right at Old Tap pub. After 1m turn left at T-junction. Entrance through gateway with curved granite wall and sequoiadendrons • Opening dates and prices: for information ring National Botanic Gardens on (1) 837 4388 ◖

This garden is rated highly because of its atmosphere and magnificent ancient plants. It was created by Thomas Acton in the mid- to late-nineteenth century. Behind the derelict eyesore of a house there was an incomparable avenue composed of alternating Irish yews and crimson rhododendrons, although in recent years there has been much storm damage. Beyond, paths wind through the arboretum under mighty rhododendrons. The trees include many un-equalled specimens – rare conifers abound. If you can, visit it when crocus blossom is in the meadow, when the rhododendron flowers are tumbling down, at any time for elegant decrepitude. The garden is now managed, as Thomas Acton always wished, as an adjunct to the National Botanic Gardens, Glasnevin (see entry).

Kilmokea

Great Island, Campile, Co. Wexford. Tel: (51) 388109

Mark and Emma Hewlett • 13km S of New Ross, 0.5km off R733 New Ross – Ballyhack road towards River Barrow • Open March to Oct, daily, 10am – 6pm • Entrance: €6, accompanied children under 16 €3 ◖ 🍴 ✕ <u>WC</u> ♿ ⬥ 🐾 🛍 ⚲

The gardens of the rectory, developed over the past 60 years, have matured splendidly in the gentle microclimate of Waterford Harbour. The contrast between the formal and the informal is marvellously displayed here. It is impossible to decide which is the more inspired – a series of enclosed gardens featuring an herbaceous border, topiary and an Italian garden, etc., or the woodland garden, which was started on the site of an old mill and where the smaller and rarer rhododendrons, candelabra primulas and tender shrubs excel beneath a canopy of conifers and exotic trees, alongside a stream and its falls. The influence of Peto is discernible, the imaginative hand of the previous owners, the Prices, is paramount. Admire also the pergolas, gazebos and boardwalks. A yin and yang garden has been planted by the present owners, with white and yellows representing the cool element and reds and oranges the hot, and a large organic *potager* was added in 2003.

Knockabbey Castle

Ardee, Co. Louth. Tel: (677) 8816

Cyril O'Brien • 13m SW of Dundalk, 8M NW of Ardee. Take N2 N from Ardee to junction N020425; castle signposted from there • Open May to September, Tues – Sun and Bank Holiday Mons, 10.30am – 5.30pm • Entrance: €6, children €4, family €16 (house and gardens €10, children €8, family €28) • Other information: Refreshments by prior arrangement NEW ◗ WC &

The grounds that evolved over many generations have been skilfully revived in recent years by the present owner, with grant aid from the GGIRP. Terraces from the attractively castellated house lead, via an expertly maintained double herbaceous border, to mown paths in the parkland that meander between fine mature specimen trees. Beyond, well-constructed paths are linked by metal bridges and run through woodland beside a series of ornamental ponds, once formal fish ponds. The culmination of this walk is a restored eighteenth-century stone garden building, known as the tea house, which is encircled by majestic lime trees. There are many carefully placed seats and a wooden summerhouse from which to enjoy the view back towards the replica Victorian glasshouse and its colourful surrounding bedding.

Kylemore Abbey

Connemara, Co. Galway. Tel: (95) 41146

Benedictine Nuns • On N59 9km NE of Letterfrack • Abbey open March to Nov, daily except Christmas week and Good Friday, 9.30am – 5.30pm (Dec to Feb, 10.30am – 4.30pm) • Garden open Easter to Oct, daily, 10.30am – 4.30pm • Entrance: house and garden €7, concessions €6, parties of 10 or more €6 per person • Other information: Shop and tearoom open Mar to Nov ◗ 🍴 ✕ WC & 🐾 🏛 ☕

Set in spectacular Connemara landscape, the 1860s' Scottish Baronial house is reflected in a lake and backed by tree-covered mountains. The trees are some of the hundreds of thousands planted by the original owner, Mitchell Henry, who also established an elaborate six-acre walled garden in a clement spot a mile away from the house. Kylemore Castle became Kylemore Abbey when it was bought by Benedictine nuns in the 1920s. A portion of the walled garden was maintained for many years, but it had become overgrown and the buildings dilapidated until the nuns, aided by a GGIRP grant, decided in 1995 to restore the walled garden to its late-nineteenth-century splendour and to conserve the buildings. Half the garden has become again an ornamental flower garden, containing typical annual beds in lawns, the other half was a fruit and vegetable garden, now fully replanted. The two areas are separated by a tree-lined stream. Restoration of the 21 glasshouses in a handsome range has begun. The head gardener's house (sadly not lived in), bothy, toolshed and lime kiln (from which the heat for the glasshouses was piped) are on view, and traditional Victorian favourites and exotic plants can be enjoyed once more. Recipient of an Europa Nostra Award in 2002.

Lakemount ★

Barnavara Hill, Glanmire, Co. Cork. Tel: (86) 811 0241

Brian Cross • 8km E of Cork off R639, at top of Barnavara Hill above Glanmire • Open April to Sept, daily, 2.30 – 5pm, and by appt • Entrance: €5.50, tours €6.50 per person ◑ ☕ ✕ WC ♿ 🅿️

A skilfully designed and immaculately maintained two-acre hillside garden, with rhododendrons, azaleas and camellias in spring and a wealth of summer interest and colour, especially from hydrangeas. There are paved areas on different levels, a poolhouse and planthouse with exotics such as *Lochroma cassia* and tibouchina, while to the rear of the house a lawn slopes gently from a rock garden to beds with a mixed planting of trees, shrubs and herbaceous plants. This is an evolving garden with many unusual plantings, most recently in the old orchard and in meadows now filled with wild flowers fringed with rare trees and shrubs. A large pond has also been added.

Lakeview

Mullagh, Co. Cavan. Tel: (46) 42480

Daphne and Jonathan Shackleton • 2km W of Mullagh on Virginia road • Open May to Sept, Fri – Sun and Bank Holiday Mons, 2 – 6pm, and at other times by appt • Entrance: €6 ◐ 🍽 WC ♿ 🅿️ 🌱 ♻

This charming old walled garden, organically managed throughout, slopes downhill beside the house which overlooks natural wildflower meadows and Mullagh Lake. Rescued in the last few years, the traditional path layout and old apples trees form a framework to different areas, each crammed with a superb collection of thriving plants. An ornamental vegetable garden and cottage garden beds end the long double herbaceous border, and a yellow and lemon herbaceous border is a feature of the summer months. Seasonal interest evolves in luxuriant wall borders and in a small woodland. Many of the plants growing in the garden are for sale in the nursery.

Larchill Arcadian Gardens

Kilcock, Co. Kildare. Tel: (1) 628 7354

Michael and Louisa de las Casas • 5km from Kilcock on Dunslaughlin Road • Open June to Aug, daily, except Mons; May, Sept, Sat, Sun and Bank Holiday Mons; all 12 noon – 6pm • Entrance: €7, children €5, family €25, parties by arrangement ● ☕ 🍽 WC ♿ ⬳ 🌱 🏬 🅿️ ♻

The modest mid-eighteenth-century house overlooks a tree-lined parkland landscape. A circulatory walk through the trees leads to several unique rustic follies, including the Fox's Earth and a sham fort on an island in the lake (no longer used for mock sea battles but by resting wild fowl). Rare breeds of cattle graze in the park, and other rare domestic breeds live in the attractive farmyard. Contemporary design and colourful planting in the walled garden near the house provide a bright area of contrast to the calming greens of the parkland. The follies have been conserved, the lake flooded and the entire site restored with the aid of a grant from the GGIRP.

Lismore Castle Gardens

Lismore, Co. Waterford. Tel: (58) 54424

The Marquess of Hartington • 57.5km SW of Waterford in Lismore • Open April to Sept, daily, 1.45 – 4.45pm (opens 11am July, Aug) • Entrance: €5, children under 16 €2.50. Parties of 20 or more during working hours €4.50 per person, children €2.25 • Other information: Toilet facilities, inc. disabled, nearby ◑ 🍴 <u>WC</u> & ⬥ ♀

The situation of the castle overlooking the River Blackwater is stunning. There are two gardens linked by the gatehouse entrance: the upper, reached by a stairway in the gatehouse, leads to a terrace with vegetables and flowers, a reduced glasshouse by Joseph Paxton (with an interesting ridge-and-furrow roof) and a fine view from the main axis to the church spire emphasised by a new herbaceous border. In the lower garden, several steps down from the gatehouse, are a few meritricious plants, but the principal feature, an ancient yew walk, is wonderful. Remarkable too are the contemporary sculptures so skilfully inserted into the landscape by Lord Hartington. Edmund Spenser is said to have written *The Fairie Queene* here.

Lisnavagh

Rathvilly, Co. Carlow. Tel: (59 91) 61104

Lord and Lady Rathdonnell • 2.5km SE of Rathvilly off N81. Signposted • Open by appt only • Entrance: €5, children €2 ◑ <u>WC</u> &

Originally designed by Daniel Robertson in the 1850s with panoramic views of the Wicklow hills and Mount Leinster, the 10-acre gardens have a wonderful array of majestic trees and shrubs, including magnificent rhododendrons, azaleas, camellias, embothriums and many unusual plants, as well as some spectacular Irish yews. They also boast a large walled garden with peacocks strutting amongst the old fruit trees, mixed borders and a small rock garden. There are endless woodland walks with all sorts of wildlife.

Lodge Park Walled Garden

Straffan, Co. Kildare. Tel: (1) 628 8412

Mr and Mrs Robert Guinness • 20km N of Dublin. Take N4 to Maynooth or Lucan or N7 to Kill. Follow signs to Straffan and steam museum, 1.5km from village • Open June, July, daily, except Mons; Aug, Tues – Fri, all 2.30 – 5.30pm, and at other times by appt • Entrance: €4 ◑ 🍴 ✕ 🍴 <u>WC</u> & ℘ 🏛 ⏻

The two-acre walled garden dates from the late eighteenth century and provided produce and flowers for the house. The present owners have been restoring it over a number of years, adding their own personal touches to the layout. It is filled with a great assortment of rare flowering plants, herbs, salad crops and fruit and is beautifully kept – the potting shed must be the most perfect example of its kind of cleanliness and order. The lack of commerciality is refreshing, and despite being relatively unknown its high standards mark it out as a gardener's garden.

Loughcrew Historic Gardens

Oldcastle, Co. Meath. Tel: (49) 854 1922

Mr and Mrs Charles Naper • 85km NW of Dublin off N3, 5km from Oldcastle off Mullingar road • Open all year, daily: 17th March to Sept, 12.30 – 5pm; Oct to 16th March, 1 – 4pm • Entrance: €5, OAPs €4.50, children €3, family €15, parties €4.50 per person ○ 🍵 🖼 WC ⟁ ⬦ 🌿 ♨ ☕ ◕

An extraordinary survival of a seventeenth-century demesne, retaining many of its features through the waxing and waning of the family fortunes. The remarkable yew walk dates from the mid-1660s and has few rivals for the beauty and girth of its individual trees. The lime avenue runs down in a straight and elegant sweep to an ancient burial ground. The tower house alone is worth a visit. A massive centre motte is the focal point of the garden; behind it a huge cedar spews a water cascade from its base into a dark pool. This 'devil's cauldron' has been planted in fiery colours and terminates the main herbaceous border. A yew parterre fronts the site of the ruined seventeenth-century longhouse, where a carved wooden doorframe echoes the original. A slender and elegant canal flows parallel to the replanted herbaceous border, which itself skirts the outside of the old walled garden. Many of the original features of the garden and pleasure ground have been repaired, restored or unashamedly reinvented. The atmosphere of the whole place is one of considerable antiquity blended with an artistic approach.

Marlay Park

Grange Road, Rathfarnham, Dublin 18. Tel: (1) 493 4059

Dun Laoghaire-Rathdown County Council • In Rathfarnham, signposted on Brehon Road/Grange Road • House open by appt • Park open, all year, dawn – dusk. Walled garden, May to Sept, Tues – Sun, 12 noon – 5pm • Entrance: park free, walled garden €3, children €2 (2003 prices) ○ 🍵 🖼 WC ⟁ ⬦ 🌿 ♨ ☕ ◕

The extensive 200-acre public park under the Dublin mountains, with the Little Dargle River running through, contains a lake, lawns and fine old trees. Once the demesne of the La Touche banking family, the late-eighteenth-century house has recently been sensitively restored for public use. The adjacent large walled garden has also been restored with the aid of a grant from the GGIRP. The garden was traditionally divided into three parts, two of which are on view. On entering through the head gardener's house, the central position is taken by an attractive Regency-style ornamental flower garden, containing colourful flowerbeds of mixed bedding fashionable in that era. Features of interest, such as a shrubbery, an orangery, a rustic summerhouse and a fountain embellish the site. Another section of the walled garden contains a large kitchen garden, set out in a traditional early-nineteenth-century manner, containing vegetables and fruit known to have been grown at that time, many now rare.

Mount Congreve ★★

Kilmeaden, Co. Waterford. Tel: (51) 384115 (Office)

Mr Ambrose Congreve • Open April to Oct, Tues, Fri, 9am – 5pm, strictly by appt for conducted tours and coach parties • Entrance: individuals free, coaches €300 – €400 per coach • Other information: No children under 12 ● **WC**

In emulation of Exbury, the owner has amassed an unequalled collection of rhododendron, camellia and magnolia species and cultivars, with many other trees as icing on the cake. It is a staggering collection which cannot be described adequately in a single entry: 100 acres of shrubs, mass upon mass, since every cultivar is planted in groups. In addition to the flowering shrub collections, which include Mount Congreve hybrids, there are many other splendours, including a whole series of surprises, one of the most spectacular being a pagoda at the base of 25-metre cliffs. Highlights are memorable. In early March a forest of *Magnolia campbellii* offers pink to white goblets to the rooks. A languid walled garden has a fine eighteenth-century vinery and range of glasshouses. In the borders is an extensive collection of herbaceous plants arranged in order of monthly flowering – May to July, a large arrangement for August, plus a border for September and October – an unusual idea. There is far too much here to appreciate in one visit and it is satisfying to know the garden has been left to the nation.

Mount Usher ★★

Ashford, Co. Wicklow. Tel: (404) 40116

Mrs Madelaine Jay • 50km S of Dublin, 6.5km NW of Wicklow, on N11 at Ashford • Open 5th March to Oct, daily, 10.30am – 6pm • Entrance: €6, OAPs, students and children €5. Special rates for parties of 20 or more. Guided tours (€30) must be pre-booked ◗ 🍽 **WC** ♿ 🏪

The Vartry River flows through this exquisite garden over weirs and under bridges which allow visitors to meander through the collections. It is a plant-lovers' paradise. *Pinus montezumae* is always first port of call, a shimmering tree, magnificent when the bluebells are in flower. Throughout are drifts of rhododendrons, fine trees and shrubs, including many that are difficult to cultivate outdoors in other parts of Britain and Ireland. The grove of eucalyptus at the lower end of the valley is memorable; a kiwi-fruit vine (*Actinidia chinensis*) cloaks the piers of a bridge, and beside the tennis court is the gigantic original *Eucryphia* x *nymansensis* 'Mount Usher'. In spring, bulbs, magnolias, a procession of rhododendrons and camellias, in summer eucryphias and leptospermums, in autumn russet and crimson leaves falling from maples – a garden for all seasons.

Muckross House and Gardens ★

Killarney National Park, Killarney, Co. Kerry. Tel: (64) 31947/31440

National Parks and Wildlife Service • 6.5km S of Killarney on N71 Kenmare road • House open (admission charge) • Gardens open all year, daily • Entrance: free ○ 🍽 ✕ 🖐 <u>WC</u> ⅙ ⬀ 🛍 ⚲

The garden around the house is almost incidental to the spectacle of the lakes and mountains of Killarney; indeed, it is principally renowned as a viewing area for the wild grandeur of the mountains. The lawns sweep to clumps of old rhododendrons and Scots pines, and there is a huge natural rock garden. Quiet corners abound along the lough-shore walks, and anyone interested in trees and shrubs is strongly recommended to head for the recently developed arboretum area (it can be reached by car easily – follow the signpost) and is a short walk from the house). There, good specimen trees surround a wooden pergola of imaginative design, and there are plantings of tender shrubs in the wild, shaded woods beyond, which, with their unique flora and ancient yews and the almost immortal strawberry trees (*Arbutus unedo*), are enticing.

National Botanic Gardens, Glasnevin ★

Glasnevin, Dublin 9. Tel: (1) 837 4388

Department of Environment • 1.5km N of city centre on Botanic Road close to cemetery • Open all year, daily except 25th Dec, summer, 9am – 6pm, winter, 10am – 4.30pm (opens 11am Sun). Opening times for glasshouses posted at entrance • Entrance: free ○ 🍽 ✕ <u>WC</u> ⅙ 🛍 ⚑

This historic garden is changing yearly but retains much of its Victorian atmosphere. The plant collections and glasshouses are undergoing restoration and renewal. There are interesting new planting schemes near the entrance and around the Curvilinear Range, and the Great Palm House of 1884 will reopen in Spring 2004. The Turner Conservatory (1843–69), the finest in Ireland, has been restored and planted with cycads and related plants, with south-east Asian rhododendrons (sect. Vireya) and plants from the South African fynbos and dry temperate areas of Australia and South America. Recent developments include a sensory garden and a greatly expanded display of Chinese plants. Glasnevin is undoubtedly worth visiting and highlights are hard to enumerate, but a few outstanding plants may be mentioned: *Zelkova carpinifolia* (especially in winter a marvellously architectural tree); the ancient wisteria on the Chain Tent (*c.* 1836); the weeping Atlas cedar (*Cedrus atlantica* 'Pendula'); Chusan palms planted in 1870; *Parrotia persica* (near entrance, wonderful in February and October); and of course 'The Last Rose of Summer'. The gardens hold a National Collection of garryas.

The Phoenix Park

Dublin 8. Tel: (1) 821 3021

Department of Environment • N of River Liffey. From city centre follow signs to 'The West', or take No. 10 bus to Phoenix Park • Open all year, daily, 7am –

11pm • Entrance: free • Other information: Guided tours of aras an Uachtarin (residence of President of Ireland), Sat from 9.45am from visitor centre ○ 💭 ✕ 🍵 WC 👤 🐾 🏺

This is one of the largest enclosed parks in any European city, replete with a herd of fallow deer, some splendid monuments and great houses, most of which are accessible to the public by request. The Phoenix monument has been relocated to its original position on the main avenue. The planting is large-scale – the avenues of horse chestnuts, limes and beeches are spectacular in blossom and in autumn, and gas lights twinkle at night the whole way along the ceremonial avenue. The People's Garden, near the main city entrance, is the only part where there is intensive gardening, but the park is a place to be lost in among the hawthorns and the wild flowers. There is an information centre near the Phoenix monument.

Powerscourt ★

Enniskerry, Co. Wicklow. Tel: (1) 204 6000

Slazenger family • 19km S of Dublin, just outside Enniskerry • House open, with exhibition on history of estate and gardens • Gardens open all year, daily except 25th, 26th Dec, 9.30am – 5.30pm (closes dusk Nov to Feb) • Entrance: €6, OAPs and students €5, children (5–16) €3, under 5 free. Waterfall (not part of garden) €4, (house and garden €8, OAPs/students €6.50, children €4) • Other information: Apartment available ○ 💭 ✕ 🍵 WC 👤 🐾 🌿 🏺 🍵 🐾

This is a 'grand garden', a massive statement of the triumph of art over the natural landscape. In its present form, with an amphitheatre of terraces and great central axis (mid-nineteenth century), it is largely the design of the inimitable Daniel Robertson. In some ways it is beyond compare – the axis formed by the ceremonial stairway leading down to the Triton Pond and jet, and stretching beyond to the Great Sugarloaf Mountain, is justly famous. We recommend that you walk along the terrace towards the Pepperpot, and on through the mature conifers which Lord Powerscourt collected. The Pepperpot tower has been restored and visitors can climb it to view 'the killing hollow' and the North American specimen trees in the tower valley. Wander on to the edge of the pond and look up along the stairway past the monumental terraces to the façade of the house. That's the view of Powerscourt that is breathtaking – a man-made amphitheatre guarded by winged horses. Statuary and the famous perspective gate, an avenue of monkey puzzles and a beech wood along the avenue add to the glory.

Primrose Hill ★

Lucan, Co. Dublin. Tel: (1) 628 0373

Mrs Cicely and Mr Robin Hall • 13km W of city centre off N4. Turn right signed to Lucan, drive through village and, after Garda (police) station, take steep, narrow Primrose Lane on left. Continue to top and through black gateway • House open • Garden open Feb, daily, 2pm – dusk, June to July, daily, 2 – 6pm, and at other times by appt • Entrance: €5 ◐ WC 🌿

The garden is approached up a beech avenue, flanked by a developing three-acre arboretum. The garden itself is not much bigger than one acre, yet it succeeds in housing a fine collection of snowdrops – the biggest and certainly the most named collection, including some of their own 'Primrose Hill' seedlings, glorious in flower. It is unusual for a garden to boast that February is its best month – but undoubtedly it is here, starting the visiting season; to return in late spring and summer when the borders are in full colour is an added joy. The herbaceous plants are lovingly cared for and planted in humus-rich compost in large clumps, giving a generous effect to the borders. Irises are high on the priority list, and so are lobelias (two named ones originated here), lilies, kniphofias and, of course, *Primula auricula* 'Old Irish Blue', plus many others.

45 Sandford Road

(see THE DILLON GARDEN)

St Anne's Park

Raheny, Dublin 3. Tel: (1) 833 8898/1859

Dublin City Council, Mount Prospect Avenue • Open all year daily • Entrance: free ○ 🏠 WC ♿ ⟷ 🚰 ⚲

The park was once the grounds to a grand Victorian mansion, long since demolished but retaining many features of the gardens and fine mature trees. The establishment of the rose garden was inspired by the memory of the vigorous pinky-white Bourbon rose, 'Souvenir de St Anne's', which was discovered in the gardens. The main reason for visiting the large public park today is to see the outstanding display of roses in the 14-acre rose garden where thousands of blooms flourish. The height of the season, June and July, peaks with the Rose Festival held each July. It is one of the few rose gardens which holds trials for the newest unnamed varieties of roses judged by a jury of local and world experts each year. There is also a garden dedicated to patio and miniature roses.

Strokestown Park ★

Strokestown, Co. Roscommon. Tel: (071 96) 33013

The Westward Group • 23km W of Longford on N5 • House open • Park open mid-March to Oct, daily, 11am – 5.30pm. Parties by arrangement • Entrance: park free; garden €5, concessions €3.80; house, museum and garden €12, concessions €10 • Other information: Restaurant, garden shop and toilet facilities at Famine Museum ◑ ☕ ✕ 🏠 WC ♿ ⟷ 🌿 🏪 🚰 ⚲

The neo-Palladian house, entered from one of the broadest streets in Ireland, was purchased in 1979 by a local company, who put in motion a restoration plan involving the refurbishment of the house, the replanting of the remaining parkland and the creation of new gardens within the old walls. In the five-acre garden is one of the largest double herbaceous borders in these islands, resplendent from the top – silver, blue and white – to the bottom – purple, red and yellow – and repeated for much of its 146 metres. Handsome gates (from Rockingham near Boyle) have been restored and re-erected, the pool and the pergola completed, a yew and beech hedge planted. The old summer-house is close by the new maze and croquet lawn. A rose garden, a wildflower meadow and a fern walk are the latest achievements. The two-acre Georgian walled fruit and vegetable garden, the 1780 vinery, the 1740 banqueting folly and the Regency gazebo tower have all been restored.

Talbot Botanic Gardens ★

Malahide Castle, Malahide, Co. Dublin.
Tel: (1) 846 2456; (1) 890 5629 (Parks Department, Dublin)

Fingal County Council • 16km N of Dublin in Malahide • Castle open • Gardens open May to Sept, daily, 2 – 5pm, and to parties by appt. Conducted tour of walled garden and glasshouses, May to Sept, Wed, 2pm, or at any time by appt • Entrance: €3.50, parties €3 per person ◑ ☕ ✕ WC <u>WC</u> ♿ ⏛ ☙ 🍴 ☙ ⚲

A 22-acre botanic garden within the 290-acre estate of Malahide with the castle centre stage. The castle was home to the Talbot family for 800 years until the death of Lord Milo Talbot in 1973; in 1976 the estate was acquired by the local authority. The garden is in two sections – the 18-acre West Lawn area of non-ericaceous plants, and a four-acre walled garden of more tender plants. Seven glasshouses – ranging from a large Victorian conservatory to a small pit house – are devoted to different groups of plants. Non-horticultural entertainments include a model railway, dolls museum and a children's playground.

Tullynally Castle

Castlepollard, Co. Westmeath. Tel: (44) 61159

Thomas Pakenham • 1.5km NW of Castlepollard on R395 Granard road • Castle open • Grounds open May to Aug, daily, 2 – 6pm, and at other times by appt • Entrance: €5, children €2 ◑ ☕ ✕ 🖼 WC ♿ ⏛ ☙ 🍴 ☙

The elaborate early-eighteenth-century formal garden of canals and basins was succeeded by romantic parkland and pleasure grounds in the best Reptonian manner. They encompass two artificial lakes and a grotto of fantastic eroded limestone from nearby Lough Derravaragh. The present owner has added new features: a Gothick summerhouse, a Chinese garden complete with pagoda and a Tibetan garden of waterfalls and ponds. Walled gardens beyond have extensive flower borders and an avenue of memorable 200-year-old yews. The energetic can undertake a mile-long walk through woodland encircling the park, which offers splendid views of the castle.

SCOTLAND

Two-starred gardens are marked on the maps with a black square.

Abbotsford [Historic Scotland Inventory]

Melrose, Scottish Borders TD6 9BQ. Tel: (01896) 752043

Dame Jean Maxwell-Scott • 1m S of Galashiels, 3m W of Melrose on A6091, turn SW onto B6360. Just S of A72 • House open as garden • Garden open 15th March to Oct, daily, 9.30am – 5pm (but Sunday opening times vary seasonally) • Entrance: £4.20, children £2.10, parties £3.40 per person, children £1.70 (2003 prices) ◐ 🍵 🖼 WC ⚲ ⟁ ⛲

Sir Walter Scott's magnificent house astride a river valley was built between 1817 and 1821 to satisfy his yearning to become a laird, and its garden is rich in Scottish allusions. A yew hedge to the south of the house has medallions inset from an old cross, which was also used to make a fountain in the same formal garden. The River Tweed flows past the house, and there are fine views across a stretch of garden. Herbaceous beds lead to a Gothic-type fern house filled with other plants beside ferns. However, dedicated Scott scholars will find most interest in the house, amongst historical relics collected by the laird himself.

Abriachan Garden and Nursery

Loch Ness Side, Inverness, Highland IV3 8LA. Tel: (01463) 861232

Mr and Mrs Davidson • 9m S of Inverness off B862 on main Loch Ness road; ignore side roads signed to Abriachan • Open Feb to Nov, daily, 9am – dusk • Entrance: £2 (collecting box) ○ 🍵 🖼 ⟁ 🌿

Although this is officially a retail nursery, it is also a fascinating hillside garden of over four acres – a plantsman's joy with paved viewing areas and secluded seats from which to contemplate the ever-mysterious Loch Ness. The clever terracing of the beds ensures that plants are seen from every angle and level, and one cannot resist climbing onwards and upwards along the network of paths meandering into the woodland. The owners have obviously worked very hard, and the planting content is comprehensive and professional, ranging from bog plants to gravel lovers and alpines, especially primulas, meconopsis, gentians and campanulas. Enticingly, most of the plants on view are also for sale.

Achamore Gardens ★ [Historic Scotland Inventory]

Isle of Gigha, Argyll and Bute PA41 7AD. Tel: (01583) 505267

Isle of Gigha Heritage Trust • Take A83 to Tayinloan then ferry to Gigha • Open all year, daily • Entrance: £2, children £1, collecting box (2003 prices) • Other information: Refreshments at hotel ○ 🍵 ✕ WC ⚲ ⟁ 🌿 ⛲ 🍴 🐾

An amazing idea to create such a superb garden on the Isle of Gigha. The journey there is via most beautiful countryside finishing up with the ferry trip, surrounded by squawking sea birds. In 1944 Sir James Horlick purchased the whole island with the sole purpose of creating a garden in which to grow the rare and the unusual. This was accomplished with the advice of James Russell, and the overall effect is tropical. A delightful woodland landscape was planted with a vast collection from around the world. Few gardens outside the national botanic collections can claim such diversity and rarity. The rhododendrons are unsurpassed in variety, quality and sheer visual magnitude, with fine specimens of tender species such as *R. lindleyi, R. fragrantissimum*, and *R. macabeanum*, and there are many varieties of camellias, cordylines, primulas and Asiatic exotica. Many genera are represented by very good specimens, thriving in Gigha's mildness. There is a fine *Pinus montezumae* in the walled garden; drifts of Asiatic primulas feature around the especially pretty woodland pond. A visit to Gigha is a must for the keen plantsman and avid gardener; now that it has been put in trust for the local community, its future seems secure.

Achnacloich [Historic Scotland Inventory]

Connel, Oban, Argyll and Bute PA37 1PR. Tel: (01631) 710221

Mrs T.E. Nelson • 3m E of Connel off A85 • Open April to Oct, daily, 10am – 6pm • Entrance: £1.50, OAPs £1, children free • Other information: Dogs on lead please ◑ ⅊

A small castellated Scottish baronial house beautifully situated above the loch on a rocky cliff, with fine views to Loch Etive and the surrounding countryside. A curved drive sweeps past massed bulbs in spring, and later there are azaleas and fine Japanese maples; autumn colour is good throughout the garden. The natural woodland with its interlinked glades is beautiful in spring with bluebells, primroses and wood anemones, while other gaps are planted with primulas, magnolias, rare shrubs and rhododendrons. There are two water gardens, and the garden walks have been extended, taking in an oak wood planted with large-leaved rhododendrons.

Allangrange

Munlochy, Black Isle, Ross and Cromarty, Highland IV8 8NZ.
Tel: (01463) 811249

Major and Mrs A. Cameron • 5m N of Inverness, signed from A9 • Open several days during summer for charity, 2 – 5.30pm, and at other times by appt • Entrance: £2, children 20p ● ⬤ ▦ WC ⅊ ⬧ ⌀

A most attractive garden which spills down the hillside in a series of descending terraces merging naturally with the rolling agricultural landscape of the Black Isle. The formal part incorporates white and mauve gardens, many old and shrub roses, tree peonies and a small corner for plants of variegated foliage. In July climbing Himalayan roses, including *Rosa filipes* 'Kiftsgate', make a spectacular display. There is also a small pool garden, and to the rear of the house a woodland garden with unusual rhododendrons, primulas, meconopsis and *Cardiocrinum giganteum*. The hand of an accomplished flower painter, Elizabeth Cameron, shows itself everywhere.

An Cala [Historic Scotland Inventory]

Easdale, Isle of Seil, Argyll PA34 4RF. Tel: (01852) 300237

Mrs Sheila Downie • 16m SW of Oban. Signed to Easdale on B844 off A816 Oban – Campbelltown road • Open April to Oct, daily, 10am – 6pm • Entrance: £2 ◑ 🦶 **WC** ♿ ⬨ ℺

A little jewel of under five acres designed in the 1930s in front of a row of old distillery cottages, nestling into the surrounding cliffs. The stream, with its ponds and little waterfall, is an essential element in a series of different spaces filled with sophisticated colour. This is how azaleas and rhododendrons should be planted on the small scale – enhancing rather than dominating the picture. Local slate paths invite the visitor into each well-planned corner. Just over the gate, in a different world, are ocean and islands.

Arbuthnott House [Historic Scotland Inventory]

Laurencekirk, Kincardineshire AB30 1PA. Tel: (01561) 361226

The Viscount of Arbuthnott • 22m S of Aberdeen, 3m from Inverbervie on B967 between A90 (A94) and A92 • Open all year, daily, 9am – 5pm • Entrance: £2, children £1 • Other information: Refreshments available at Grassic Gibbon Centre in village ○ **WC**

The enclosed garden dates from the late seventeenth century and with the policies is contained within the valley of the Bervie Water. The entrance drive is flanked by rhododendrons and in spring the verges are full of primroses and celandines. The drive crosses a fine bridge topped by imposing urns before reaching the house set high on a promontory, with most of the garden sloping steeply to the river. The design is unusual in that it has always been treated as an extension of the house, rather than being laid out at some distance. The sloping part has four grassed terraces and this pattern is dissected by diagonal grassed walks radiating out in a manner reminiscent of the Union Jack. This fixed structure creates long garden rooms and vistas as the garden is explored. Although the garden plan is very old, much of today's mature planting was done by Lady Arbuthnott in the 1920s, and this is continued by the present Lady Arbuthnott. Herbaceous borders, old roses, shrub roses and ramblers, shrubs underplanted with hostas, primulas, meconopsis and lilies, lilacs and viburnums provide colour throughout the summer. A metal stag for target practice stands at the bottom of the slope by the lade (millstream).

Ardanaiseig Garden and Hotel [Historic Scotland Inventory]

Kilchrenan, Argyll and Bute PA35 1HE. Tel: (01866) 833333

4m E of Kilchrenan on B845 • Open April to Oct, 9am – 8pm • Entrance: by collection box at car park, £2, OAPs and children free • Other information: Refreshments at hotel. No children under 8 ◑ 🍽 ✕ **WC** ⬨ ℺

A picturesque 10-mile drive from Taynuilt down the peninsular makes a fitting introduction to this traditional Argyll garden. Attractive slate paths guide the visitor round 20 acres of well-planted woodland set behind an 1834 baronial house, now a comfortable hotel, with lovely views across Loch Awe. The species and hybrid rhododendrons are particularly fine. Note the unusual curved walls of the walled garden.

Ardchattan Priory [Historic Scotland Inventory]

Oban, Argyll and Bute PA37 1RQ. Tel: (01796) 481355

10m NE of Oban. Cross Connel Bridge on A828 N and turn first right to Ardchattan • Open April to Oct, daily, 9am – 6pm • Entrance: £2 ◑ **WC** ⟐ ⟐

A charming garden with spectacular views over Loch Etive. The extensive lawn to the front of the house is encircled by herbaceous, rose and shrub borders and a rockery. Either side of the drive, the wild garden is full of roses, shrubs and ornamental trees. The garden surrounds a priory (now a private house) founded by the Valescaullian Order in 1230. The ruined chapel and its early graveyard are open with the garden.

Ardkinglas Woodland Garden [Historic Scotland Inventory]

Cairndow, Argyll and Bute PA26 8BH. Tel: (01499) 600261

Mr David Sumsion • On A83 Loch Lomond – Inveraray road. Signposted • Open all year, daily, during daylight hours • Entrance: £3, children under 16 free ○ ▆ ▆ **WC** ⟐ ⟐ ⟐ ⟐ ⟐

Following a large-scale, long-term programme aimed at conserving and rejuvenating the historic plant collection, a sense of balance and atmosphere is being restored to this dramatic landscape setting above the shores of Loch Fyne. There are panoramic views from the gazebo (linger to read the literary quotations inscribed within). The next generation of plants is well and truly established amongst bluebells and ferns. A further area has new footpaths and a bridge over the River Kinglas giving access to a seventeenth-century mill. The garden contains five champion trees including the 'mightiest conifer in Europe', a silver fir (*Abies alba*) with a girth in excess of 10 metres, and one of the tallest trees in Britain, a grand fir (*Abies grandis*) at just over 67 metres.

Ardmaddy Castle

By Oban, Argyll PA34 4QY. Tel: (01852) 300353

Mr and Mrs Charles Struthers • 13m SW of Oban. Signed from B844 to Easdale along narrow road • Open all year, daily, 9am – dusk • Entrance: £2.50 ○ ▆ **WC** ⟐ ⟐ ⟐ ⟐

The handsome but modest fifteenth-century castle, with steps up to its *piano nobile*, faces both ways – outwards with wide views to the islands and the sea, inwards on the garden side towards steep surrounding woods and a formal walled garden. In the eighteenth century Ardmaddy marked the western extent of the Earl of Breadalbane's estate, enabling him to ride from one side of

Scotland to the other on his own land – until all was gambled away in the early twentieth century. The walled garden set below the castle has traditional box hedge compartments, large numbers of species and hybrid rhododendrons and an increasing collection of herbaceous plants and flowering shrubs and trees as well as an immaculate vegetable section. A water garden with two ponds, and a woodland garden with walks add further interest. There is always a good selection of home-grown plants and vegetables (in season) on sale.

Ardtornish [Historic Scotland Inventory]

Lochaline, Morvern, Highland PA34 5UZ. Tel: (01967) 421288 (Estate Office)

Ardtornish Estate Company • 30m SW of Corran. From Corran ferry, 9m SW of Fort William, cross to Morvern and take route left on A861 towards Lochaline, then left on A884. Gardens are 2m before Lochaline on left • Open April to Oct, daily, 10am – 4.30pm • Entrance: £3, children free (collecting box) • Other information: 14 self-catering units available, 5 in house ◑ ⑆ ⬧ ⅋ ℺

A plantsman's garden with a particularly fine and extensive collection of unusual shrubs, deciduous trees and rhododendrons set against a background of conifers, a loch and outstanding Highland scenery. The gardens have developed over the past hundred years or more following the first house on the site, established by a distiller from London in the 1860s. They are on a steeply sloping site and rainfall is heavy. Mrs Raven's late husband wrote a book, *The Botanist's Garden* (now republished), about their other garden, Docwra's Manor (see entry in Cambridgeshire), and he assisted his wife to follow in her parents' footsteps in trying to establish a plantsman's paradise here. Apart from the area around the house, there is a pleasing air of informality about the gardens, which include Bob's Glen with *Rhododendron thomsonii* and *R. prattii*, a larger glen with still more species and hybrid rhododendrons, and a kitchen garden under separate management nearby, where good-quality plants are for sale.

Arduaine Garden ★★ [Historic Scotland Inventory]

Oban, Argyll and Bute PA34 4XQ. Tel: (01852) 200366

*The National Trust for Scotland • On A816, 20m S of Oban, 18m N of Lochgilphead. Joint entrance with Loch Melfort Hotel • Open all year, daily, 9.30am – sunset • Entrance: £3.50, concessions and children £2.60, family £9.50 • Other information: Refreshments at hotel adjacent ○ ▥ **WC** ⑆*

Arduaine was conceived and begun in 1898 by James Arthur Campbell, possibly with advice from Osgood Mackenzie, creator of Inverewe Garden (see entry). The Essex nurserymen Edmund and Harry Wright restored the garden after they acquired it in 1971 and gave it to the Trust in 1992. This plantsman's garden consists of an outstanding 20 acres on a promontory bounded by Loch Melfort and the Sound of Jura, climatically favoured by the North Atlantic Drift – make the effort to climb to the high viewing point to enjoy the panorama of ocean, coasts and islands. Although its fame rests largely on its outstanding rhododendrons, azaleas, magnolias and other rare and tender trees and shrubs (the rhododendron collection around 400 species and ranks high in importance in Scotland), the garden has far more than botanical interest to offer. Trees and shrubs, some over a hundred years old and thickly underplanted, tower overhead as they, and visitors, climb the glen, while at the lower level hostas, ferns, candelabra primulas, meconopsis and numerous other flower and foliage perennials cluster around lawns and along the sides of the watercourses.

Armadale Castle Gardens [Historic Scotland Inventory]

Armadale, Sleat, Isle of Skye IV45 8RS. Tel: (01471) 844305

Clan Donald Lands Trust • 14m S of Broadford at S end of Skye, close to Mallaig ferry • Open all year, daily, 9.30am – 5.30pm • Entrance: £4.60, concessions £3.20, family £14, parties of 8 or more £2.90 per person • Other information: Guided tours with head gardener available. Visitor centre open April to Oct. Two electric wheelchairs available ○ ☕ ✕ 🍴 WC ⅙ ⬦ 🌿 👜 🐾 ⚲

This fine garden is so well groomed that it has almost the atmosphere of a city park. The cultivated areas have been sympathetically developed to include pond gardens with scree planting, a long herbaceous border with raised walk behind the ruined castle, lawns with ornamental trees and a romantic garden planted within one of the ruined sections of the castle. Surrounding the cultivated area are four miles of nature trails set within 50 acres of woodland and wildflower meadows. Although Armadale is further north than Moscow, the climate is warm and everywhere there are inspiring views up Loch Nevis to Mallaig and Knoydart. Allow plenty of time to get here: the 14-mile approach road is single-track in places and every oncoming driver must be acknowledged and thanked. The new *Museum of the Isles*, located within the garden, is included in the admission charge and worth visiting.

Attadale

Strathcarron, Wester Ross, Ross-shire IV54 8YX. Tel: (01520) 722217

Mr and Mrs Ewen Macpherson • 15m NE of Kyle of Lochalsh, on A890 between Strathcarron and Strome • Open April to Oct, daily except Sun, 10am – 5.30pm • Entrance: £3, children £1 • Other information: Honesty box, maps and leaflets inside gate. Car park 50 yards from garden; disabled parking by Attadale House. Light refreshments and meals available at Carron Restaurant 1½ m away ◑ ☕ ✕ 🍴 WC ⅙ ⬦ 🌿 ⚲

Inside the gate a stream and ponds all along one side of the drive are beautifully planted with candelabra primulas, irises, giant gunneras and bamboos. A bridge over a waterfall links the water garden with the upper rhododendron walk, commanding views of the sea and hills. Sculpture from Zimbabwe and a bronze by Bridget McCrum are reflected in the ponds, and a bronze crested eagle perches on a cliff. The formal kitchen garden has a slate urn by Joe Smith; beyond a recently built geodesic dome houses a collection of exotic ferns, and is surrounded by hardy ferns, including tree ferns, backed by dripping cliffs. A path leads down to a dell of rhododendrons planted by the Schroder family nearly a century ago, then on along a woodland path to the new Japanese garden, where lichened rocks and gravel imitate the River of Life and the Mystic Isles of the West. The symmetrical sunken garden in front of the 1755 house (not open) provides a complete contrast. Visitors are advised to wear waterproof shoes.

Ballindalloch Castle

Grantown–on–Spey, Banffshire, Highland AB37 9AX. Tel: (01807) 500205

Mrs Oliver MacPherson-Grant Russell • Halfway between Grantown-on-Spey and Keith on A95. Signposted • Castle open • Garden open 9th April to Sept, daily except Sat, 10.30am – 5pm, and at other times by appt • Entrance: grounds £2 (castle and gardens £6) • Other information: Dog-walking area ◐ ● ✕ ▥ WC � ⬥ ℘ ⬛ ♟ ℺

What a pleasure to find a garden of this scale and calibre set in the magnificent Spey valley. One of the most attractive feature is the 1937 rock garden, which comes tumbling down the hillside onto the most impressive lawn in the land. It takes three men two days to mow and edge it. The owners have completely renovated all the borders over the years and transformed the old walled garden into a rose and fountain parterre garden which has matured most attractively. The daffodil season and the river/woodland walks are particularly lovely. A small parterre at the side of the house shows how stunning humble nepeta and *Alchemilla mollis* can be when all else is eaten by the deer.

Balmoral Castle [Historic Scotland Inventory]

Ballater, Aberdeenshire AB35 5TB. Tel: (013397) 42534 (Estates Office)

H.M. The Queen • 6m W of Ballater on A93 at Crathie • Castle ballroom and carriage exhibitions open • Gardens and grounds open April to July, daily, 10am – 5pm • Entrance: £4.50, OAPs £3.50, children (5–16) £1, under 5 free ◐ ● ✕ ▥ WC ⅃ ⬥ ℘ ⬛

Balmoral, the personal home of Her Majesty the Queen in Scotland, is Gaelic for 'majestic dwelling'. There had been earlier castles on the same site before the estate was purchased in 1852 by Prince Albert, consort to Queen Victoria. She called Balmoral 'this dear paradise', and she and the Prince immediately began making a three-acre garden about the castle and planting the grounds with rare coniferous and broad-leaved forest trees. Queen Mary added the sunken rose garden in 1932, and since 1953 the Queen and Prince Philip have made other improvements and extensions, the latest being the water garden, created in 1979 close to Queen Victoria's garden cottage. There are herbaceous borders, but generally the gardens are natural in style. Throughout the grounds statues and cairns have been erected in memory of Queen Victoria's family and their descendants, and specimen trees labelled with the names of the visiting dignitaries who planted them.

The Bank House

Glenfarg, Perth PH2 9NZ. Tel: (01577) 830275

Mr and Mrs C.B. Lascelles • 10m SW of Perth off B996 between M90 junctions 8 and 9. In Glenfarg, 50 metres along Ladeside, by Glenfarg Hotel • Open by appt • Entrance: £5, children free ● ⅃ ⬥ ℺

The main garden is approached through a paved area with additional planting above low retaining walls. An apple and clematis tunnel leads the visitor onwards to large curved beds set into lawns on a gently sloping site. A horseshoe-shaped yew hedge underplanted with yellow archangel and star of Bethlehem is a fine spring feature; bulbs and early-flowering herbaceous plants carry the display through to summer. The owners have built up an eclectic collection of rare and unusual plants of much merit, and these are grown to perfection using organic gardening techniques. The careful planting, with great regard to colour and form, makes for an instructive visit. A smaller garden across the street, with a 'flowform cascade' water feature and a yin and yang circular bed, may be visited at any time. Ornamental trees have been planted in a field, where a pond has been created and a wildflower meadow sown.

Bargany [Historic Scotland Inventory]

Girvan, South Ayrshire KA26 9QL. Tel: (01465) 871249

John Dalrymple-Hamilton • 18m SW of Ayr off B734 Girvan – Dailly road • Open May, Sat – Mon, 12 noon – 5pm • Entrance: £2, children under 12 free

This is a woodland garden, densely planted with splendid ancient rhododendrons, azaleas, fine trees and conifers. Wonderfully diverse paths make for a relaxed stroll round a charming lily pond, rock garden and walled garden.

Barguillean's 'Angus Garden'

Taynuilt, Argyll and Bute PA35 1JS. Tel: (01866) 822048

Mr Sam S. MacDonald • 5m SE of Oban, 3m SW of Taynuilt. Take minor road to Kilmore off A85 at Taynuilt Hotel • Open all year, daily, dawn – dusk. Parties welcome by prior appt in writing • Entrance: £2, children free

Set on a Highland hillside overlooking a lochan with views to Ben Cruachan, this is a nine-acre woodland garden with no formal paths or borders, but with areas of established rhododendrons, azaleas and conifers and some rare trees and shrubs. It is interesting to compare the new planting, combining modern rhododendron hybrids from the north-west of the United States within native birch and oak woodland, with established rhododendron gardens of the west coast. Described by its owner as a place of tranquillity and love, it was created by Betty Macdonald in memory of her writer/journalist son, killed in Cyprus during the 1956 troubles.

Beatrix Potter Garden

Birnam, Perth and Kinross PH8 0DS. Tel: (01350) 727674 (Birnam Institute)

Perthshire and Kinross Council • 13m NW of Perth in Birnam, at centre of short loop diversion from A9 • Open all year, daily except 25th, 26th Dec, 1st, 2nd Jan • Entrance: free • Other information: Refreshments and shop at new B.I. Arts Community and Conference Centre nearby, plus Beatrix Potter exhibition (£1 charge, children 50p)

The garden displays bronze sculptures of animals in their natural surroundings, as they were first observed by Beatrix Potter before she humanised them into her enduringly famous characters. Only on an ornamental roadside gate donated by Frederick Warne do we find Peter Rabbit in the blue jacket so familiar to his fans. In her diaries Potter reveals that some of her characters were based upon people she met in the Birnam area during her many visits.

Bell's Cherrybank Gardens and Scottish National Heather Collection ★

Bell's Cherrybank Centre, Cherrybank, Perth PH2 0PF. Tel: (01738) 627330

Diageo • Off A93 in southern outskirts of Perth, approx 1m from Broxden roundabout • Open under Scotland's Garden Trust – telephone (01738) 472800 for details • Entrance: charge • Other information: Guide dogs only
🕐 🖵 wc ᴑ ⚘ ♨ ☕ ✄

This modern garden surrounding commercial offices is in fact two gardens, the first laid out in the early 1970s, plus the Scottish National Collection of heathers, begun in 1983. There are now over 900 varieties, all in superb condition. Other plant collections are well maintained and beautifully designed. Interest is sustained throughout by water features, modern sculptures, pleasant vistas, a tiny putting green, tubular bells and an aviary. The play area includes a roundabout for wheelchair-bound children. The Bell's Pride of Perth Exhibition is also on the site. Ownership having passed to Scotland's Garden Trust, these 8 acres are being subsumed into Scotland's first national garden – 62 acres in extent, described as a 'garden for the 21st century', with a variety of features including a rocky gorge, an arboretum, water gardens, grass terraces and a wildflower meadow. It is due to be completed in 2007.

Benmore Botanic Garden ★★ [Historic Scotland Inventory]

Dunoon, Argyll, Argyll and Bute PA23 8QU. Tel: (01369) 706261

Royal Botanic Garden Edinburgh • 7m N of Dunoon, W of A815 at Benmore. Signposted • Open March to Oct, daily, 10am – 6pm (closes 5pm March, Oct), and at other times by appt • Entrance: £3.50, concessions £3, children £1, family £8. Membership inc. Dawyck and Logan Botanic Gardens (see entries) available 🌓 🖵 ✕ wc ᴑ ⚘ ♨ ☕ ✄

This regional garden of the Royal Botanic Garden Edinburgh is a magnificent mountainside garden set in the dramatic location of the Cowal Peninsula. It is world-famous for its collections of flowering trees and shrubs. From Britain's finest avenue of giant redwoods (*Sequoiadendron giganteum*) planted in 1863, a variety of trails spreads out. More than 250 species of rhododendron and an extensive magnolia collection provide a positive array of colour on the hillside beside the River Eachaig. Other features include a formal garden with memorials and stately conifers, an informal pond, the Glen Massan arboretum with some of the tallest trees in Scotland, a Chilean rainforest and a Bhutanese glade. A short climb leads to a stunning viewpoint looking out across the garden, Strath Eck and the Holy Loch to the Firth of Clyde and beyond.

Biggar Park ★

Biggar, South Lanarkshire ML12 6JS. Tel: (01899) 220185

Capt. and Mrs David Barnes • 30m SW of Edinburgh at S end of Biggar on A702 • Open May to July to individuals and especially to parties by appt • Entrance: £2 • Other information: Teas by arrangement ● 🏵

A Japanese garden of tranquillity welcomes the visitor to this well-planned 10-acre plantsman's garden. The efficient labelling adds greatly to the enjoyment when walking through the woodland and the small arboretum and admiring the well-planted ornamental pond, all carefully designed to give year-round interest. This starts with a stunning display of daffodils, followed by glades of meconopsis, rhododendrons and azaleas in early summer before the huge herbaceous borders burst into colour. The centrepiece, however, must be the outstanding walled garden, reached through a fine rockery bank beside the eighteenth-century mansion house. The view through the wrought-iron gate stretches the length of a 45-metre double herbaceous border, attractively backed by swags of thick ornamental rope hanging from rose 'pillars', whilst either side is divided into intensively planted sections intersected by pleasing grass paths and plots of fruit and vegetables.

Blackhills House

Lhanbryde, Elgin, Moray IV30 8QU. Tel: (01343) 842223

Mr and Mrs John Christie • 4m E of Elgin off A96. Take B9103 southwards, then minor road • Open 16th, 23rd May, and by appt at other times • Entrance: £2, children free • Other information: Teas on open days only. Self-catering accommodation ● 🖰 🏵 WC & ⟨Þ 🌿 🍴 ⚲

The east coast of Scotland is not, with a few exceptions, noted for its rhododendron gardens, but this garden in the Laich of Moray should be visited for its collection of species rhododendrons in early May and hybrids in late May. Both sorts are spread under tree cover in a steep-sided valley with many fine specimen trees. These include a davidia, a Japanese red cedar (*Cryptomeria japonica*), Brewer's weeping spruce and a golden chestnut (*Chrysolepis chrysophylla*) – a rare chestnut relative from North America. The finest rhododendrons are those in the subsections Falconera, Grandia and Taliensia, but the genus is well represented as a whole. The wooded valley opens to reveal two lakes with plantings of maples and other Asiatic plants. Thomas North Christie, who was responsible for the early planting in the 1920s, corresponded at length and exchanged the latest introductions with his neighbour the Brodie of Brodie.

Blair Castle ★ [Historic Scotland Inventory]

Blair Atholl, Pitlochry, Perthshire PH18 5TL. Tel: (01796) 481207

The Manager, The Blair Charitable Trust • 35m N of Perth on A9 2m N at Blair Atholl. Signposted • House open as garden • Garden open April to Oct, daily, 10am – 5.30pm (last entry 4.30pm), Nov to March by appt • Entrance: £2, children £1, OAPs/students £1, family £5 (house and grounds £6.70, children £4, OAPs £5.70, students £5.40, family £17) ○ 🍵 ✕ 🏛 **WC** ♿ 🚲 👜 ♿ 🐾

Magical and blazing white, the castle remains one of Scotland's most important, most visited and best presented historic houses in private hands. The magnificent 2500-acre managed park and landscape were begun in 1730 by the 2nd Duke of Atholl in the French manner, with geometrically patterned avenues and walks radiating out from the castle. His most important legacy was the nine-acre walled Hercules Garden of 1758, named after the life-size lead statue by John Cheere which overlooks it. It is unique, not only for its scale, but also for the fact that it contains extensive water features. A series of delightful ponds, planted islands and peninsulars form a central axis from which fruit tree orchards – faithfully reproduced, but without the original underplanting of fruit and vegetables – slope gently upwards to herbaceous borders, yew buttresses and elegant gravel walks backed by the original eighteenth-century walls. A charming apple-store museum, a nineteenth-century folly, statuary, an ogee-roofed pavilion and a Chinoiserie bridge all add to the beauty of this unusual garden in its splendid Highland setting.

Blairquhan [Historic Scotland Inventory]

Maybole, South Ayrshire KA19 7LZ. Tel: (01655) 770239

James Hunter Blair • 12m S of Ayr, 7m SE of Maybole on B7045. Signposted • House open • Garden open 24th July to 22nd Aug, Tues – Sun, 1.30 – 4.15pm; grounds open 1.30 – 6pm • Entrance: £5, OAPs £4, children £3 (house and garden) ◑ 🍵 🏛 **WC** ♿ 🚲 🌿 👜 ♿ 🐾

The castle is approached by a three-mile drive along the River Girvan, giving good opportunities to admire the extensive wood and parkland. The three-acre walled garden has been redesigned with ornamental planting, and there is an 1860 pinetum.

Bolfracks [Historic Scotland Inventory]

Aberfeldy, Perth and Kinross PH15 2EX. Tel: (01887) 820344

Mr R.A. Price • 2m W of Aberfeldy on A827 towards Loch Tay • Open April to Oct, daily, 10am – 6pm • Entrance: £3, children free (honesty box at gate) ◑ **WC** 🌿 🐾

There has been a garden on this site for two centuries, but the present garden was started by the owner's grandparents in the 1920s and reshaped by his uncle over the last thirty years. Three acres of plantsman's garden are well laid out within a walled enclosure and demonstrate the potential of an exposed hillside site with a northerly aspect. Astounding views over the Tay Valley are matched by the garden's own interesting features, including peat walls and a stream garden. There are masses of fine bulbs in spring and good autumn colour. An excellent collection of mainly dwarf rhododendrons has been established over the years and gives a wonderful display in May and June. Gentians, meconopsis, ericaceous plants and celmisias do well on this soil. The walled garden contains a collection of old and modern shrub roses and rambling roses and a great variety of herbaceous perennials.

Branklyn Garden ★ [Historic Scotland Inventory]

116 Dundee Road, Perth, Perth and Kinross PH2 7BB. Tel: (01738) 625535

The National Trust for Scotland • ½ m from Friarton Bridge on A90, then A859 to Perth • Open April to Sept, daily, 9.30am – 5pm • Entrance: £5, OAPs and children £3.75, family £13.50. Pre-booked parties of 20 or more £2 per person • Other information: Steep lane to garden. Parking, including coaches and disabled, 500 yards from main gate. Possible for wheelchairs but some paths too narrow ◐ 🍽 WC 🌿 ♿ 🚻

John and Dorothy Renton created this garden nearly within sight and certainly within sound of the centre of Perth. Work commenced in 1922, and in 1955 Dorothy was awarded the Veitch Memorial Medal by the Royal Horticultural Society. The National Trust for Scotland took over the garden in 1968, after the death of Dorothy in 1966 and of her husband the following year. It extends to nearly two acres, the main interest being its Sino-Himalayan alpine and ericaceous plants and magnificent scree/rock gardens. There is also a splendid collection of dwarf rhododendrons. Essential work continues to maintain Branklyn's rightful reputation as an outstanding plantsman's garden. It is impossible to describe all the fascinating things to be found here, from the fine trees to the comprehensive collection of dwarf and smaller rhododendrons, the meconopsis to the notholirions. This is a garden that repays many visits.

Brodick Castle ★ [Historic Scotland Inventory]

Isle of Arran, North Ayrshire KA27 8HY. Tel: (01770) 302202

The National Trust for Scotland • On Isle of Arran, 2m N of Brodick. Ferry from Ardrossan or Kintyre • Gardens and country park usually open all year, daily, 9.30am – sunset, but advisable to check. • Entrance: £3.50, concessions £2.60, parties of 20 or more £2 per person (castle and gardens £7, concessions £5.30, pre-booked parties of 20 or more £5.60 per person) (2003 prices) • Other information: Wheelchair available ○ ☕ ✕ 🍽 WC ♿ 🎧 🌿 🚻 🦮

High above the shores of the Firth of Clyde and guarding the approaches to Western Scotland is a castle of locally quarried sandstone. The garden was an overgrown jungle of rhododendrons until it was restored by the Duchess of Montrose after World War I. She was much helped after 1930 when her daughter married John Boscawen of Tresco Abbey (see entry in Cornwall). Many trees and plants arrived at that time by boat from Tresco in the Scillies; others came from subscriptions to the second generation of great plant-hunters like Kingdon-Ward and, in particular, George Forrest, one of the greatest of all collectors. Plants from the Himalayas, Burma, China and South America, normally considered tender, flourish in the mild climate. There is a good display of primulas in the bog garden. The walled formal garden to the east of the castle is over 250 years old and has recently been restored as an

Edwardian garden with herbaceous plants, annuals and roses. It is impossible to list all the treasures of the woodland garden, but perhaps the most surprising is the huge size of the specimens in the lower rhododendron walk, where *R. sinogrande* are found with leaves up to 60 centimetres long. Opposite Brodick on the W side of the island, 5 miles north of Blackwaterfoot, is *Dougarie Lodge*, an impressive castellated terrace garden created in 1905 to celebrate the marriage of Mary Louise, daughter of the 12th Duke of Hamilton to the 6th Duke of Montrose. A fine plantsman's garden with a good range of semi-hardy trees and plants, and lovely views towards the Mull of Kintyre. [Open one day in summer for SGS and by appt; telephone Mr and Mrs Gibbs on (01475) 337355 for details.]

Broughton House ★ [Historic Scotland Inventory]

**12 High Street, Kirkcudbright, Dumfries and Galloway DG6 4JX.
Tel: (01557) 330437**

The National Trust for Scotland • 28m SW of Dumfries. Take A75 from Dumfries past Castle Douglas, then 1m past Bridge of Dee take A711 to Kirkcudbright. Signposted • House closed during 2004 for restoration work • Garden open Feb, March, Oct, Mon – Fri, 11am – 4pm, April to Sept, Mon – Sat, 11am – 5pm (opens 1pm Suns). Advisable to telephone or email (broughtonhouse@nts.org.uk) before travelling • Entrance: £2, OAPs £1 (honesty box) ◑ WC ▯ ⚭

Created by an artist, E.A. Hornel, who lived here from 1901 to 1933, this fascinating garden reflects an interest in oriental art following his visit to Japan, and incorporates both Japanese and Scottish features. After his death the house became a museum and its surroundings were gradually restored. The garden starts with a sunken courtyard, beyond which is a pleasant hybrid, a cross between 'fantasy Japan and fantasy old-world cottage garden'. Japanese cherries blossom over skilful low-level planting in the sunken courtyard, and further down are all the elements of a much larger garden: rose parterre, pergola, glasshouse, box hedges and herbaceous borders, all looking remarkably uncrowded. Charming lily pools have flat stepping stones and dramatic boulders, and are fed by an immense rainwater tank. At the end of the long central walk, beyond a hedge, is the River Dee with its mudflats and saltings.

Broughton Place

Broughton, Biggar, Scottish Borders ML12 6HJ. Tel: (01899) 830234

Jane and Graham Buchanan-Dunlop, Mr and Mrs R.C. Carr, H. Graham and G. Reilly • 29m SW of Edinburgh, just N of Broughton on A701 Edinburgh – Moffat road. Follow signs for Broughton Gallery • Open April to Sept, daily except Wed, 10.30am – 6pm • Entrance: by donation to collection box • Other information: Alternative entrance for wheelchairs ◑ WC ♿ ▱ ⚮

Winding up the towering eighteenth-century beech avenue, you come to the magnificent turreted modern mansion designed by Sir Basil Spence, cushioned into the surrounding Tweeddale hills. Although nearly 300 metres above sea level, the effects of frosts are limited by the hillside location. The owners have a thriving art gallery, and it is through this that the visitor gains entry into the charming three-acre garden. Meandering paths lead up and down well-kept borders full of rare and interesting plants, mainly herbaceous perennials.

Bughtrig

**Leitholm, Coldstream, Berwickshire, Scottish Borders TD12 4JP.
Tel: (01890) 840678**

Major General and The Hon. Mrs Charles Ramsay • 5m N of Coldstream, $\frac{1}{4}$ m E of Leitholm on B6461 • Open 15th June to 15th Sept, daily, 11am – 5pm • Entrance: £2, children under 18 £1, inc. donation to SGS • Other information: Special arrangements for bona fide parties to garden, and occasionally to house. Sometimes possible for parties of up to 6 persons to stay in house ◑ 🏠 ♿

Bughtrig has been owned by just three families since the fourteenth century. The traditional Scottish family garden was designed for amenity; unusually it is hedged rather than walled, and sited close to the house. Its two-and-a-half acres contain an interesting combination of herbaceous perennials, shrubs, annuals and fruit, surrounded by fine specimen trees which provide remarkable shelter.

Cally Gardens and Nursery [Historic Scotland Inventory]

**Gatehouse of Fleet, Castle Douglas, Dumfries and Galloway DG7 2DJ.
Tel: (01557) 815029 (Infoline)**

Mr Michael Wickenden • 30m SW of Dumfries via A75. Take Gatehouse turning and turn left through Cally Palace Hotel gateway. Signposted • Open 10th April to 26th Sept, Tues – Fri, 2 – 5.30pm, Sat and Sun, 10am – 5.30pm • Entrance: £2.50, children under 13 free ◑ WC ♿ ⬧ ♨

Three hundred Glasgow children 'dug for Victory' here in World War II and the gardens have flourished since the present owner arrived. A specialist nursery in the two-and-three-quarter-acre, eighteenth-century walled garden has large beds of herbaceous plants and many unusual varieties, well worth a visit by plant lovers. There is a impressive collection of perennial geraniums, kniphofias, crocosmias and others – 3500 varieties in all. Ninety-five per cent of the plants in the sales area are propagated on the premises, some from seed collected abroad or sent in botanic garden exchanges, and a changing selection of several hundred is available pot-grown. A favourite with visitors is the spread of meconopsis (Himalayan blue poppies) when in season in early June. The Cally Oak Woods which surround the nursery have nature trails. Catalogue available (3 x 1st-class stamps).

Cambo Gardens

Kingsbarns, St Andrews, Fife KY16 8QD. Tel: (01333) 450313

Mr and Mrs P. Erskine • 6m SE of St Andrews on A917 between Kingsbarns and Crail • Open all year, daily, 10am – dusk • Entrance: £3, children free • Other information: Self-catering accommodation available ◯ 🏠 WC ♿ ⬧ ♨ ♨ B&B

This romantic Victorian walled garden is designed around the Cambo burn with weeping willows, a waterfall and rose-clad wrought-iron bridges. Naturalistic plantings of rare and interesting herbaceous perennials add to the informal atmosphere of the garden. There are masses of spring bulbs, a lilac walk with 26 cultivars, over 250 old-fashioned and rambling roses, and glowing September borders. Beyond the walled garden a woodland garden includes a September meadow of colchicums, and 70 acres of woodland walks leading to the sea are carpeted in early spring with snowflakes, aconites and a spectacular display of snowdrops (over 160 specialist varieties).

Carnell ★ [Historic Scotland Inventory]

Hurlford, Kilmarnock, South Ayrshire KA1 5JS. Tel: (01563) 884236

Mr and Mrs J.R. Findlay and Mr and Mrs Michael Findlay • 4m SE of Kilmarnock, NW of Mauchline on A76, 1½ m off A719 • Open probably 27th July, 2 – 5.30pm, and to private parties by appt • Entrance: £3, children under 12 free • Other information: Sixteenth-century pele tower ● 🍽 WC ♿ ⟁ ⌘

Eighty years ago this was a limestone quarry – now it is an exquisite example of 90 metres of linear herbaceous borders facing a rectangular pool, with informal planting as a contrast on the opposite bank. There is a phlox and shrub border, an interesting rock garden and a walled garden. Oriental features include a Chinese gazebo and Burmese dragons, all mementos of Commander Findlay's travels. Climbing the slope behind the pavilion in the south-east corner is the rock garden. The garden adjacent to the house has long herbaceous borders and a shrub and lily collection. The entrance is through an archway bedecked with a 'Kiftsgate' rose.

Castle Fraser [Historic Scotland Inventory]

Sauchen, Inverurie, Aberdeenshire AB51 7LD. Tel: (01330) 833463

The National Trust for Scotland • 15m NW of Aberdeen, off B993 near Kemnay • Castle open Easter, then May to Sept, daily, Oct, weekends • Garden open all year, daily, 9am – 6pm • Entrance: free. Castle and garden £7, concessions £5.25, family £19, parties £4 per person, school parties £1 per child (2003 prices) • Other information: Dogs on dog trail only ○ 🍽 🏠 WC ♿ ⟁ ⌘ 🛍 ☕

The grounds – the setting for one of the most spectacular of the castles of Mar – consist of a designed landscape of the last seventeenth and early eighteenth centuries with eighteenth-century agricultural developments; the work of Thomas White (1794) was followed by 'natural-style' improvements of c. 1800. The deep, south-facing herbaceous border designed in 1959 by James Russell, and the planting carried out in the walled garden by Eric Robson along traditional lines in the 1970s, are being substantially reworked. A woodland garden is being developed around the walled garden, together with a woodland play area with an amphitheatre. There are excellent views from the castle, and extensive walks in the grounds include superb views of the castle in its parkland setting and outwards to nearby hills, notably Bennachie.

Castle Kennedy ★★ [Historic Scotland Inventory]

Stranraer, Wigtownshire, Dumfries and Galloway DG9 8BX. Tel: (01776) 702024

The Earl of Stair • 5m E of Stranraer on A75 • Open April to Sept, daily, 10am – 5pm • Entrance: £3, OAPs £2, children £1. Discount for parties of 20 or more (2003 prices) ◐ 🍺 🖼 WC ♿ ✿ 🛍 ♋

One of Scotland's most famous gardens, set on a peninsula between two lochs and well worth a visit for its sheer 75-acre magnificence and spectacular spring colour. The gardens were originally laid out in 1730 around the ruins of his castle home by Field Marshal the 2nd Earl of Stair, who used his unoccupied dragoons to effect a major remoulding of the landscape, combining large formal swathes of mown grassland with massive formal gardens, criss-crossed by avenues and *allées* of large specimen trees. The garden is internationally famous for its pinetum, for its good variety of tender trees and for its species rhododendrons, including many of Sir Joseph Hooker's original introductions from his Himalayan expeditions. The monkey-puzzle avenue, now sadly a little tattered, was once the finest in the world; there is also an avenue of noble firs underplanted with embothriums and eucryphias. An impressive two-acre circular lily pond puts everyone else's in their proper place, and a good walk from this brings the visitor back to the ruined castle and its walled garden, well planted with themed borders.

Castle of Mey ★★ [Historic Scotland Inventory]

Thurso, Caithness, Highland KW14 8XH.

The Queen Elizabeth Castle of Mey Trust • 1½ m from Mey on A836 • Open 24th May to 30th July, 12th Aug to 30th Sept, daily except Mon, 11am – 5pm (opens 2pm Sun) • Entrance: £6, £5 parties and OAPs ◐ WC ♿ 🛶 ✿ 🛍

The castle dates from the late sixteenth century and was renovated by H.M. The Queen Mother between 1952 and 1955. Gardening would not be possible in such an exposed position without the protection of the 'Great Wall of Mey'. Within the walled garden, she collected her favourite flowers; many were gifts and have special meaning. The personal private feeling pervades the whole garden, which is especially well planted and well maintained. The colour schemes are very good, blending the garden with the vast natural panorama within which it is situated.

Cawdor Castle ★ [Historic Scotland Inventory]

Cawdor, Nairn, Highland IV12 5RD. Tel: (01667) 404401

The Dowager Countess Cawdor • Between Inverness and Nairn on B9090 off A96 • Castle open • Garden open May to 10th Oct, daily, 10am – 5.30pm • Entrance: £3.50 (castle and garden £6.30, OAPs £5.30, children £3.50. Family £18.60. Parties of 20 or more £5.50 per person) (2003 prices) ◐ 🍺 ✕ 🖼 WC ♿ 🛍

Frequently referred to as one of the Highland's most romantic castles and steeped in history, Cawdor Castle is a fourteenth-century keep with seventeenth- and nineteenth-century additions. The surrounding parkland is handsome and well kept, though not in the grand tradition of classic landscapes. To the side of the castle is the formal garden, where recently added wrought-iron arches frame extensive herbaceous borders, a peony border, a very old hedge of mixed varieties of *Rosa pimpinellifolia* (the Scots or Burnet rose), a rose tunnel, old apple trees with climbing roses, interesting shrubs and lilies. An abundance of lavender and pinks completes a rather Edwardian atmosphere. The castle wall shelters exochordas, *Abutilon vitifolium*, *Carpenteria californica* and *Rosa banksiae*. Pillar-box red seats create an unusual note in this splendidly flowery place, but the owner likes them. The walled garden below the castle has been restored with a holly maze, a thistle garden, a laburnum walk and a white garden. The latter is a 'Paradise garden', preceded by Earth represented as a knot garden, and between the two lies Purgatory. There are fine views everywhere of the castle, the park and the surrounding countryside, which one can enjoy more actively by walking one of the five nature trails, varying in length from half a mile to five miles. Further developments include the Auchindoune gardens, where Arabella Lennox-Boyd helped with the planting.

Clan Donald Visitor Centre

(see ARMADALE CASTLE GARDENS)

Cluny House ★ [Historic Scotland Inventory]

Aberfeldy, Perth and Kinross PH15 2JT. Tel: (01887) 820795

Mr J. and Mrs W. Mattingley • 32m NW of Perth. N of Aberfeldy, over Wade's Bridge, take A827 Weem – Strathtay road. House signed after 3m • Open March to Oct, daily, 10am – 6pm • Entrance: £3, children free ◑ 🍽 ⚘

Unlike most other gardens, this is as truly wild as one can find – friendly weeds grow unchecked for fear of disturbing an extensive collection of Asiatic primulas. Sheltered slopes create a moist microclimate where all the plants flourish abundantly, including a Wellingtonia with the British near-record girth of over 11 metres. In the superb woodland garden many of the plants were propagated from seed acquired by Mrs Mattingley's father on the Ludlow/Sherriff expedition to Bhutan in 1948. Special treats are the carpets of bulbs, trilliums and meconopsis, a fine selection of Japanese acers, *Prunus serrula*, hundreds of different rhododendrons, *Cardiocrinum giganteum*, massive lysichitons and many fine specimen trees. The garden is managed on strictly organic principles, and it is delightful to see native wild flowers and garden plants growing together in harmony and profusion.

Colzium Lennox Estate

Kilsyth, Glasgow G65 0PY. Tel: (01236) 828150

North Lanarkshire Council • 14m NE of Glasgow, ½ m E of Kilsyth on A803 • House and museum open by appt • Estate open all year, daily. Walled garden open April to Sept, daily, 12 noon – 7pm; Oct to March, Sat and Sun only, 12 noon – 4pm • Entrance: free ○ **WC** ও ⟨⟩

An outstanding collection of conifers, including dwarf cultivars, and rare trees in a beautifully designed large walled garden. Everything is well labelled and immaculately maintained; even gravel paths are raked. There are also 100 varieties each of snowdrops and crocuses. Other attractions include a seventeenth-century ice-house, a glen walk, a fifteenth-century tower house, an arboretum, a curling pond and a clock theatre.

Corsock House

Corsock, Castle Douglas, Dumfries and Galloway DG7 3NJ. Tel: (01644) 440250

Mr and Mrs M.L. Ingall • 10m N of Castle Douglas on A712. Signed from A75 onto B794 • Probably open 23rd May for SGS, and by appt • Entrance: £2, children 50p (2003 prices) • Other information: Refreshments on open day ◐

A most attractive 20-acre woodland garden with exceptionally fine plantings both of trees (*Fagus sylvatica*, Wellingtonia, oak, Douglas fir, cercidiphyllum, acer) and of rhododendrons (*R. thomsonii, lacteum, loderi, prattii, sutchuenense*). The knowledgeable owner has contributed most imaginatively to the layout of the gardens over the last forty years, creating glades, planting vistas of azaleas and personally building a temple and *trompe-l'œil* bridge which give the gardens a classical atmosphere. An impressive highlight is the large water garden, again cleverly laid out and with water-edge plantings set off by a background of mature trees with good autumn colour.

Crarae Garden ★★ [Historic Scotland Inventory]

Minard, Inveraray, Argyll and Bute PA32 8YA. Tel: (01546) 886614

National Trust for Scotland • 11m SW of Inveraray on A83 • Open all year, daily, 9.30am – sunset • Entrance: £3.50, concessions and children £2.60, family £9.50 • Other information: Visitor centre open April to Sept, daily, 10am – 5pm ○ 🍽 🏪 **WC** ♿ ⬗ 🛒

Crarae, previously owned by the Crarae Charitable Trust, and one of the most important of Scottish woodland gardens, was forced to close in June 2001 due to lack of resources. A successful £1.5 million fund-raising campaign by the National Trust for Scotland raised an endowment sufficient to take on the property and to guarantee the continuity of the garden. The property was reopened in April 2002, and a phased programme of restoration is underway. The gardens were originally planned by Grace, Lady Campbell in the early part of last century, possibly inspired by her nephew Reginald Farrer, the famous traveller and plant collector. Subsequently her son, Sir George Campbell (1894–1967), spent many years creating this superb Himalayan ravine set in a Highland glen. Using surplus seed from the great plant expeditions, numerous gifts from knowledgeable friends and the shared expertise of a network of famous horticulturists, he planted a variety of rare trees (his first love), together with exotic shrubs and species rhododendrons, which now form great canopies above the winding paths. These, together with many other plants from the temperate world, make a magnificent spectacle of colour and differing perspectives, the whole enlivened by splendid torrents and waterfalls. The autumn colouring of sorbus, acers, prunus, cotoneasters and berberis is one of the great features of the garden, which contains a National Collection of nothofagus.

Crathes Castle Garden ★★ [Historic Scotland Inventory]

Crathes Castle, Banchory, Aberdeenshire AB31 5QJ. Tel: (01330) 844525

The National Trust for Scotland • 3m E of Banchory, 15m SW of Aberdeen on A93 • Castle open April to Sept, daily, 10.30am – 5.30pm (timed entry system; last admission 4.45pm), Oct, daily, 10.30am – 4.30pm (last admission 3.45pm), and at other times by appt • Garden and grounds open all year, daily, 9am – dusk • Entrance: castle, garden and grounds £9, concessions and children £6.50. Pre-booked parties of 20 or more £7 per person, concessions £5.25 (2003 prices) • Other information: Parking 400 metres from gardens (charge for non-Trust members). Dogs on nature trail in grounds only ○ 💮 ✕ 🍴 WC ⅄ ⟁ 🌿 ⊞ 💡 ⚲

The romantic castle, set in flowing lawns, dates from 1596, and looks much as it did in the mid-eighteenth century. There is no record of how the garden looked then, although the splendid yew topiary of 1702 survives. Sir James Burnett, who inherited the estate in the 1920s, was a keen collector, his wife an inspired herbaceous garden designer, and the garden today reflects their achievements. In all there are eight gardens, each with a different character and varied planting schemes, often compared to Hidcote but with evident inspiration from Jekyll, who visited Crathes and was most impressed. The terraces and sloping terrain increase the dramatic effect. Rare shrubs reflect Burnett's interest in the Far East, while the splendid wide herbaceous borders with clever plant associations were Lady Burnett's creation, the most famous being the white border. There are many specialist areas, such as the trough garden; the large greenhouses contain a National Collection of Malmaison carnations. Extensive wild gardens and grounds with picnic areas and marked trails.

Cruickshank Botanic Garden

St Machar Drive, Aberdeen AB24 3UU. Tel: (01224) 272704

The Cruickshank Trust and University of Aberdeen • 1½ m N of city centre in Old Aberdeen. Entrance in Chanonry. Signposted • Open all year, Mon – Fri, 9am – 4.30pm; May to Sept, Sat, Sun, 2 – 5pm • Entrance: free. Children must be accompanied by adult ○ 💮 ⅄

Endowed by Miss Anne H. Cruickshank in 1898 to cater for teaching and research in botany at the University of Aberdeen and for the public good, the original six acres were designed by George Nicholson of Kew. That layout disappeared with World War I. The long wall, herbaceous border and sunken garden date from 1920 but much reverted to vegetable cultivation during World War II. In 1970 the garden was extended and a new rock garden made. A terrace garden was added by the long wall in 1980, a new rose garden completed in 1986 and the peat walls restored in 1988. The rock garden, with a series of connecting pools, has interesting alpines, bulbs and dwarf shrubs. A small woodland area is rich in meconopsis, primulas, rhododendrons and hellebores. Proximity to the North Sea does not permit good growth of large conifers, with the exception of dawn redwood and *Pinus radiata*, but there are fine species lilacs, witch hazels, and the long wall shelters more tender exotics. The total area of the present garden is 11 acres, of which four are planted as an arboretum – this is reached by a path from the summit of the rock gardens.

Culross Palace [Historic Scotland Inventory]

Culross, Dunfermline, Fife KY12 8JH. Tel: (01383) 880359

The National Trust for Scotland • 12m W of Forth Bridge off A985 • Open 19th April to May, Sept, daily, 12 noon – 5pm • Entrance: palace and garden £5, OAPs £4, family £13.50 (2003 prices) ◑ ☕ WC ⚘ 🏛 ❂ ☙

A small area packed full of fascinating plants and features, including the old poultry breed, the Scots Dumpy. The atmosphere of the seventeenth-century garden is evoked by the crushed-shell paths, and great attention paid to detail – clay watering cans, plants in baskets and hurdles, bee skeps in wall niches. On the walled terrace a kitchen and ornamental garden of the period is planted with an abundance of fruit, vegetables and herbs. Head gardener Mark Jeffery describes this as a historical showpiece which runs on organic principles; the walled area contains truly old-fashioned vegetables which flourish in a relatively frost-free environment.

Culzean Castle ★★ [Historic Scotland Inventory]

Maybole, South Ayrshire KA19 8LE. Tel: (01655) 884400

The National Trust for Scotland • 12m S of Ayr on A719 coast road • Castle open • Gardens and country park open April to Oct, daily, 10am – 5pm • Entrance: £5, concessions and children £3.75, parties £4 per person (castle, grounds and country park £9, concessions £6.50, family £23, parties £7 per person) ◑ ☕ ✕ 🗎 WC ♿ ⟲ ⚘ 🏛 ❂

Over 200,000 people a year visit Culzean, regarded by many as the flagship of The National Trust for Scotland. The castle was originally a medieval fortified house atop the Ayrshire cliffs, but was extensively restructured by Robert Adam from 1777 in what has become known as his 'Culzean' style. This is reflected in the many fine architectural features scattered throughout the grounds, and in particular the handsome home farm courtyard, now a visitor centre. Restoration work continues. A major undertaking was the consolidation and partial rebuilding of Robert Adam's unique viaduct. The camellia house, a picturesque 1818 glasshouse, has been beautifully restored to its original use as an orangery, and the fountain in the garden below the castle has been repaired and replumbed. The southern walled garden has been completely redesigned and the vinery rebuilt on the original site based on its Victorian plan. The Swan Pond buildings have been conserved and repaired along with the beautiful bridge to the north. The restored pagoda is now spectacular, and the Dolphin House turned into an environmental education centre for school visits. The country-park landscape covers 600 acres with a network of woodland and cliff-top paths; the gardens themselves occupy a spacious 30 acres and include all the traditional elements of a grand garden at the turn of the century, the main ones being a fine pleasure garden with a fountain and a vast walled garden with herbaceous and vegetable plantings.

Dalmeny: The House [Historic Scotland Inventory]

South Queensferry, Edinburgh EH30 9TQ. Tel: (0131) 331 1888

Grounds around house open July and Aug, Sun – Tues, 2 – 5.30pm. Parties by arrangement at other times • Entrance: free (house and collection £4, OAPs £3.50, students £3, children (10–16) £2, under 10 free. Parties of 20 or more £3 per person during opening hours) (2003 prices) ● ◗ WC ໒

Some one and a half miles from Mons Hill (see below) is the Garden Valley and other ornamental areas close to the house. They feature rhododendrons, azaleas and specimen trees, and are worth seeing if the house itself is to be visited.

Dalmeny: The Park [Historic Scotland Park]

Mons Hill, Dalmeny Estate, South Queensferry, Edinburgh. Tel: (0131) 331 1888

The Earl of Rosebery • 7m W of Edinburgh city centre off A90 • Mons Hill open for charity one Sun late Feb/early March, depending on snowdrops • Entrance: £2, children free (2003 prices) ● ◗ WC ໒

Mons Hill is a partially wooded hill of semi-natural hardwoods with several acres of wild snowdrops and outstanding views (weather permitting) towards the Pentland Hills, Edinburgh and the Firth of Forth. The snowdrops are over a quarter of a mile uphill from the car park and must be seen to be believed, although Wellington boots are recommended. There is no possibility of taking wheelchairs or vehicles up the hill.

Dawyck Botanic Garden ★ [Historic Scotland Inventory]

Stobo, Peeblesshire, Scottish Borders EH45 9JU. Tel: (01721) 760254

Royal Botanic Garden Edinburgh • 20m SW of Edinburgh, 8m SW of Peebles on B712 • Open 14th Feb to 15th Nov, daily, 10am (closing times vary), and at other times by appt • Entrance: £3.50, concessions £3, children £1, family £8. Season tickets inc. Logan and Younger Botanic Gardens (see entries) available • Other information: Guide dogs only ◖ ◗ ▒ WC ໒ ✿ ⚒

This is a specialist garden of the Royal Botanic Garden Edinburgh (see entry). With over 300 years of tree planting, Dawyck is one of the world's finest arboretums; its collections include rare Chinese conifers and the unique Dawyck beech. At the entrance is the formal azalea terrace which leads the visitor into Scrape Glen, and from here paths cross the slopes of Scrape Hill, with the burn tumbling down under the Swiss bridge in the middle of the glen. The mature specimen trees tower majestically above a variety of flowering trees and shrubs. From further up the hill there are magnificent views of the garden, including the beech walk with its tree-top outlook. In the Heron Wood is the first cryptogamic sanctuary and reserve for non-flowering plants;

illustrated panels provide details of the essential role played by these plants. The fine stonework and terracing on bridges, balustrades and urns was produced by Italian craftsmen in the 1820s.

Druimavuic House Gardens

Appin, Argyll and Bute PA38 4BQ. Tel: (01631) 730242

Mr and Mrs Newman Burberry • 4m S of Appin on A828 Oban – Fort William road, turn left at new road bridge. Signposted • Open April to June, daily, 10am – 6pm • Entrance: £1.50, children free ◑ 🍴 ♿ ⬦ 🐾 ♿

A romantic site which was begun after World War 1 but has now been replanted and cultivated by its dedicated owners. The humorous and descriptive guide states that 'the real architect of Druimavuic Gardens is Nature', but they have certainly embellished her work most successfully. The stream garden makes an immediate impact with colourful clumps of many varieties of primulas (*florindae*, *vialii* and 'Inverewe') and meconopsis mixed in with other varied spring plantings. The well-planted woodland garden has lovely open oil-painting views of cattle watering in the loch below. There is an excellent working kitchen garden with strawberries grown at eye level.

Drum Castle [Historic Scotland Inventory]

Drumoak, by Banchory, Aberdeenshire AB31 5EY. Tel: (01330) 811204

The National Trust for Scotland • 10m W of Aberdeen, 3m W of Peterculter, off A93 • Garden open April to Sept, daily, 10am – 6pm. Grounds open all year, daily, 9.30am – sunset • Entrance: grounds free, garden only £2.50, concessions £1.90 (castle, garden and grounds £7, children and concessions £5.25; parties of 20 or more £5.60 per person (2003 prices) • Garden: ◑ 💺 🍴 **WC** ♿ 🐾 👜 🌡 *Grounds:* ○ ⬦ ♿

Within the old walled garden of the castle, the Trust has established a 'garden of historic roses' which was officially opened in June 1991 as part of its Diamond Jubilee celebrations. The four quadrants of the garden are designed and planted with roses and herbaceous or other plants appropriate to the seventeenth, eighteenth, nineteenth and twentieth centuries. The central feature is a copy of the gazebo at Tyninghame, East Lothian (see entry), and a small garden house in one corner, now restored, acts as an interpretative centre. The grounds around the castle also contain a pond garden, interesting conifers, spacious lawns and walks in the Old Wood of Drum, a SSSI.

Drumlanrig Castle [Historic Scotland Inventory]

Thornhill, Dumfries and Galloway DG3 4AQ. Tel: (01848) 330248/600283

The Duke of Buccleuch • 16m SW of M74 Junction 14, 18m NW of Dumfries, 3m N of Thornhill on A76, between A77 and A75. Signposted • Castle open 9th to 12th April; May to 22nd Aug • Garden and country park open 9th April to Sept, daily, 11am – 5pm • Entrance: £3 (extra charge for house) ◑ 💺 ✕ 🍴 **WC** ♿ 👜 ♿

Built in the late seventeenth century by William Douglas, 1st Duke of Queensberry, Drumlanrig is one of Scotland's finest and most palatial residences. The formal terraces and parterres around and below the house reflect this contemporary 'grand manner', in a magnificent setting. The parterres were first restored to their former glory in the Victorian era by two of the foremost designers of their day, Charles M'Intosh and David Thomson who, in the fashion of the time, introduced a variety of foreign plants and shrubs as well as many of the exotic conifers still thriving in the woodland walk today. These include one of the oldest Douglas firs in the UK, the tallest weeping beech (*Fagus sylvatica* 'Pendula') and an early fan-trained *Ginkgo biloba*. A charming heather-root pavilion in the woodland walk overlooks the tumbling Marr burn. The gardens were simplified during the two world wars and are now being beautifully restored again. The four parterres, all with different plants and colour themes, are a stunning sight from the 220-yard-long terrace above; the Shawl Parterre in particular has a pretty design using circles, ovals and hearts. Annuals are used on an impressive scale: 2000 pink and white begonias, 2000 *Cineraria (Senecio)* 'Silver Dust' and 1000 antirrhinums.

Drummond Castle Gardens ★★ [Historic Scotland Inventory]

Muthill, Crieff, Perth and Kinross PH5 2AA.
Tel: (01764) 681257 (681433 weekends)

Grimsthorpe and Drummond Castle Trust Ltd • 2m S of Crieff on A822 • Open 9th to 12th April, then May to Oct, daily, all 1 – 6pm (last admission 5pm) • Entrance: £3.50, OAPs £2.50, children £1.50 ◖ **WC** ♿ ⬥ ⬛

These magnificent parterre gardens were first laid out in 1630 by the 2nd Earl of Perth; at their centre was a multi-faced obelisk sundial which still indicates the time all over the world. The gardens were greatly enhanced during the seventeenth century and reached their zenith during the 1830s when a descendant created one of the most significant revival gardens of the Victorian period, much admired by Queen Victoria. Parterres were traditionally designed as architectural extensions of the mansion or castle. The parterre here takes the form of a long St Andrew's Cross and is one of the finest in Scotland, particularly when viewed from the 120-metre-long terrace 20 metres above. The whole garden is ornamented by 36 statues and numerous fountains and urns, all strategically placed as focal points or at the end of long vistas. Numerous box-edged compartments of intricate design are infilled, mostly with roses, antirrhinums, dahlias and lavenders, in the Drummond heraldic colours. The visual impact of the 207 clipped evergreens, intricate box compartments and stonemasonry is unforgettable.

Dun Ard ★

Main Street, Fintry, Stirlingshire G63 0XE. Tel: (01360) 860369.

Mr Alastair Morton and Mr Niall Manning • 17m SW of Stirling. 17m N of Glasgow on B822 • Open by appt only • Entrance: free ●

An exceptionally well-planned organic garden incorporating many of the most stimulating elements of contemporary horticultural design, all carved out of a sloping three-acre field. Areas of exuberant planting are interspersed with minimalist, restful or wild areas, so that visitors are always ready for the next surprise as they climb ever onwards and upwards, culminating at a sandstone pyramid with a bird's-eye view over the whole garden, the valley and the mountains beyond. All the features sought after by today's gardeners are here – a *potager*, an early garden, a rose parterre, a bulb meadow, a still pool enclosed by a beech hedge, a bog garden, a formal pleached hornbeam avenue and, best of all, a late garden planted in hot colours in the increasingly popular continental matrix style, combining wild and herbaceous patchwork planting, viewed in all its deliciousness from a smart decking platform.

Dunbeath Castle ★

Dunbeath, Caithness KW6 6EY. Tel: (01593) 731308

Mr and Mrs S.W. Murray Threipland • 6m NE of Berriedale off A9. Turn right at Dunbeath village post office, then right again • Open for SGS and for parties by appt • Entrance: £4, OAPs and children £2 NEW ● 💺 🏺 WC

The immaculately harled clifftop castle, dating from the fourteenth century, is dramatically outlined against the sea as one approaches down a tunnel of trees giving way to steep, deep-cut grass banks crowned on each side by two large walled gardens. The right-hand one has now been beautifully re-created with the help of the designer Xa Tollemache with a turret viewpoint over the garden as a whole and behind to the castle and the glinting sea. Although the layout is traditional, with three mown grass axes and a central path creating eight compartments, these are broad and generously scaled, with the outer paths unusually wide and the whole threaded together with decorative metalwork. A water feature with cupola, a laburnum pergola across the width of the garden, a gazebo, plant supports and border backdrops are all designed using the same metalwork, giving the garden structure, height and unity. Two well-clipped fuschia hedges run the length of the garden, providing the outer shelter walls of the compartments and small parterres. These are paired so as to make a colourful and attractive pattern of vegetables, fruit and flowers. The outer walls themselves have herbaceous planting at their feet and are clad alternatively with *Cytisus battandieri*, *Hydrangea petiolaris*, actinidia, lonicera, escallonia, *Humulus lupulus* 'Aureus' and a variety of roses. Dunbeath's outstanding position and the quality and design of its garden makes this an exceptional visit, combined perhaps with Langwell, Dunrobin and West Drummie (see entries).

Dunrobin Castle Gardens ★ [Historic Scotland Inventory]

Golspie, Sutherland, Highland KW10 6SF. Tel: (01408) 633177/633268

The Sutherland Trust • 1m NE of Golspie on A9 • Castle open • Garden open April to 15th Oct, daily, 10.30am – 4.30pm (opens 12 noon Suns April to June, Sept and Oct, closes 5.30pm June to Sept) • Entrance: £6.50, concessions £5.70, family £18, parties £5.50 per person, OAPs, £5.70, children £4.50 • Other information: Falconry displays ◐ 💺 🏺 WC 🦽 ♿ ⚘

These Victorian formal gardens were designed in the grand French style to echo the architecture of the castle, which rises high above them and looks out over the Moray Firth. They were created by the architect Sir Charles Barry in 1850. Descending the stone terraces, one can see the round garden (evocative of the Scottish shield, perhaps), grove, parterre and herbaceous borders laid out beneath. The round ponds, all furnished with fountains, are a particular feature, together with the wrought-iron Westminster gates. Roses have been replaced with hardy geraniums, antirrhinums and *Potentilla fruticosa* 'Abbots-wood'; the interest continues from tulips in spring through to the autumn-flowering lilies. An eighteenth-century summerhouse, converted into a museum in the nineteenth century, is now also open to the public and well worth seeing. Other developments include the removal of the shrubbery and its replacement by 20 wooden pyramids covered in roses, clematis and sweet peas and interplanted with small ornamental trees to continue the French style visible elsewhere. In the policies there are many woodland walks.

Dunvegan Castle [Historic Scotland Inventory]

Isle of Skye IV55 8WF. Tel: (01470) 521206

MacLeod Estate • 14m NW of Portree, beyond A850/A863 junction • Castle open • Garden open all year, daily, 10am – 5.30pm (closes 4pm Nov to mid-March) • Entrance: £4, children £2.50 (castle and gardens £6, concessions £5.50, children £3.50) (2003 prices) ○ ▨ ✕ ▩ **WC** ♿ ⬤ ▨ ⬛ ♨ ⚲

A superb backcloth for the castle which stands on the shores of Loch Dunvegan, the gardens have three areas of interest. First, a round garden with a boxwood parterre of 16 triangular beds, three mixed borders for summer show and a fern house. Second, an expanding woodland waterfall dell, which carries the season on past rhododendron time. The meconopsis and giant cardiocrinums are breathtaking in this setting, but note also tiny maidenhair ferns, native woodsage and other treasures. Third, an exciting two-acre walled garden, created by head gardener Thomas Shephard on a long-derelict site and open to the public since 1998. Laid out on a formal plan, the four quarters each have a focus of interest: a lawn with a sorbus avenue; a raised pool with gravel surround pierced by plants; a triangle with an internal yew triangle; and an unusual stepped 'temple' evocative of Mayan architecture. The surrounding paths spill over with helianthemums, cistus and other Mediterranean plants. Non-gardeners can take an exciting boat trip to the nearby seal colony – on a calm day.

Edzell Castle ★ [Historic Scotland Inventory]

Edzell, Brechin, Angus DD9 7UE. Tel: (01356) 648631

Historic Scotland • 6m N of Brechin. Take A90 (A94) and after 2m fork left on B966 • Ruins open (closed Thurs pm and Fri in winter) • Garden open April to Sept, daily, 9.30am – 6pm (opens 2pm Sun, closes 4pm Oct to March) • Entrance: £3, OAPs £2.30, children (5–16) £1, under 5 free) ○ ▩ **WC** ♿ ⬤ ▨ ⬛ ⬤ ⚲

In 1604 Sir David Lindsay made a remarkable small pleasance walled garden at his fortress at Edzell; as reconstructed, it gives us a clear idea of how his garden might have looked in its heyday. By the time they came under the care of H.M. Office of Works in 1932, the garden and castle had lain in ruins for over 150 years. Although the plantings date from the 1930s, they are elaborate examples in the manner of the period of the early seventeenth century. Meticulously kept parterres of box, lawn, and bedding are contained within the original walls of unique and curious design. There are 43 panels of alternating chequered niches and 21 sculptured symbolic figures with large recesses below for flowers. The whole is laid out to be viewed from a corner summerhouse and the windows of the now-ruined castle. Edzell itself is a good example of an ordered Victorian Scottish Highland village, with shops, a tea room and two hotels.

Falkland Palace Garden [Historic Scotland Inventory]

Falkland, Fife KY7 7BU. Tel: (01337) 857397

The National Trust for Scotland • 11m N of Kirkcaldy via A92 and A912. M90 junction 8 from Forth Road Bridge • Palace open as garden (last tour of palace 5pm) • Garden open March to 26th Oct, Mon – Sat, 10am – 6pm, Sun, 1 – 4.30pm • Entrance: £3, OAPs £2, children £1 (palace and garden £7, OAPs £5.25, children £3, family £19) • Other information: Parking 100 metres from palace. Toilet facilities in town car park and next to NTS shop ◑ 🍴 WC ♿

This was originally the garden at the sixteenth-century palace, which was the hunting lodge for the Stuart monarchs. Kings and queens from James II to Charles II enjoyed the Fife landscape and the grounds of the Renaissance palace. During World War II the garden was a 'Dig for Victory' effort and was thereafter remodelled by the landscape designer Percy Cane. The palace itself lends a gracious and dignified atmosphere to this three-acre garden. The shrub island borders are now fully mature and provide a good illustration of how to break up large areas of lawn. The main herbaceous border, recently replanted, runs the full depth of the garden and is maturing well, and there is a memorable narrow border filled with delphiniums. In addition, visitors can see the royal tennis court (i.e. real tennis) where occasional competitions of this old game are still staged, and an outdoor chequers game near the herb garden. There is also an orchard. Note the interesting village houses nearby.

Finlaystone [Historic Scotland Inventory]

Langbank, Renfrewshire PA14 6TJ. Tel: (01475) 540285

Mr George Gordon MacMillan of MacMillan • 8m W of Glasgow Airport, on A8 W of Langbank • Open all year, daily, 10.30am – 5pm • Entrance: £3, OAPs and children £2 • Other information: Doll museum and Celtic exhibition in visitor centre. Play area ◯ 🍴 🍴 WC ♿ ⟁ ♿ ♀

Designed in 1900 and enhanced and tended over the last fifty years by the late Lady MacMillan, much respected *doyenne* of Scottish gardens, and her family, this spacious garden is imaginatively laid out over 10 acres, with a further 70 acres of mature woodland walks. There are large, elegant lawns framed by long herbaceous borders, interesting shrubberies and mature copper beeches looking down over the River Clyde. John Knox's tree, a Celtic paving 'maze', a paved fragrant garden and a bog garden are added attractions, and for children there are unusual woodland play areas. A walled garden is planted in the shape of a Celtic ring cross.

Floors Castle [Historic Scotland Inventory]

Roxburghe Estates Office, Kelso, Roxburghshire TD5 7SF. Tel: (01573) 223333

The Duke of Roxburghe • Well signposted on outskirts of Kelso • Open 9th April to Oct, 11am – 4.30pm • Entrance: (house and garden) £5.75, OAPs/students £4.75, children £3.25, family £15; grounds only £3 (2003 prices) ○ 🍵 ✕ 🎒 WC ♿ ⟁ 🌿 🛒 🔦 ⚲

Floors is, architecturally, one of Scotland's grandest country houses – a real swagger castle – magnificently situated with glorious views across a huge sweep of open parkland. The 1857 walled kitchen garden is of equally stately proportions and contains the classic mix of glasshouses, herbaceous borders, fruit, vegetables and annuals. The borders – long, broad and packed with colour – have a backing of chain swags covered with the bright pink rose 'American Pillar'. The large children's playground is conveniently, but not aesthetically, sited within the walled garden. Recent additions are a woodland garden and a two-acre parterre, designed in the French style and featuring the intertwined initials of the present Duke and Duchess. Much use has been made of traditional box, with contrast and highlighting provided by *Euonymus fortunei* 'Emerald 'n' Gold'.

Glamis Castle [Historic Scotland Inventory]

Glamis, Forfar, Angus DD8 1RJ. Tel: (01307) 840393

The Earl of Strathmore and Kinghorne • 5m W of Forfar on A94 • Castle open, guided tours • Garden open late March to Oct, daily, 10.30am – 5.30pm (last admission 4.45pm) (opens 10am July, Aug) • Entrance: £3.50, OAPs, students and children (5–16) £2.50, disabled persons free (castle and grounds £6.70, OAPs and students £5, children (5–16) £3.50, family £18). Reductions for parties of 20 or more ◑ 🍵 ✕ 🎒 WC ♿ ⟁ 🛒 🔦 ⚲

At the end of a long, tree-lined avenue and against the backdrop of mountain and moorland, the turrets and spires of Glamis Castle beckon the visitor. Although much older, the park was landscaped in the 1790s by a garden designer working under the influence of 'Capability' Brown, and the avenue was replanted about 1820. On the lawn near the castle is an intriguing Baroque sundial, six and a half metres tall and with a face for every week of the year. On the east side of the castle a two-acre Italian garden consists of high yew hedges, herbaceous borders, a fountain and seventeenth-century-style gazebos. The pinetum, planted c.1870, is now open to visitors. Glamis was the childhood home of H.M. Queen Elizabeth The Queen Mother.

Glasgow Botanic Gardens [Historic Scotland Inventory]

730 Great Western Road, Glasgow G12 0UE. Tel: (0141) 334 2422

Glasgow City Council • Near city centre on corner of Great Western Road and Queen Margaret Drive • Open all year, daily, 7am – dusk. Kibble Palace

Glasshouse closed in 2004. Main range open 10am – 4.45pm • Entrance: free
○ 🐌 <u>WC</u> ⅋ ⬦ 🌱 ⚲

A pleasant afternoon's walk with well-maintained herbaceous, shrub and annual borders. A greatly extended herb garden has recently been completed and includes a unique Scottish garden containing plants native to Scotland with explanatory labels on how they have been utilised over centuries. In the nearby tropical glasshouses are displays of orchids and the National Collection of species begonias, also cacti and economic plants – all meticulously maintained. The Arid Adaptations house has on display some of the most bizarre plants in the world; the unique development of island plants is also demonstrated here. Although the Victorian Kibble Palace – the chief attraction here – will not reopen until 2005, there is a new rose garden of mainly scented shrub roses.

14 Glebe Crescent

Tillicoultry, Clackmananshire FK13 6PB. Tel: (01259) 750484

Mrs Joy McCorgray • 8m W of Stirling on A91 at east end of village; signed by yellow arrow at Glebe Crescent • Open for SGS, and by appt • Entrance: £2, children free 🐛 🕐 ⅋ 🌱 ⚲

This delightful half-acre plantsman's garden is designed to fill every corner with a different plant setting and thus a different 'feel'. Clever terracing of the natural slope ensures that the garden does not seem unduly overcrowded and yet, believe it or not, there is a Japanese koi carp pool, a collection of bonsai, a perfumed garden, a formal courtyard area, a conifer lawn, over 40 ornamental grasses and a woodland area with a large collection of rare ferns, arisaemas, hellebores and trilliums. Notable are the unusual *Cercidiphyllum japonicum* 'Ruby', and the variegated angelica tree (*Aralia elata* 'Aureovariegata') and many people covet the beautiful Japanese umbrella pine (*Sciadopitys verticillata*). The owner says: 'There's a lot squashed into this garden.' Indeed there is.

Glen Grant Garden

Rothes, Aberlour, Moray AB38 7BS. Tel: (01340) 832118

Glen Grant Distillery • 10m SE of Elgin on A941, on main roundabout in Rothes • Open April to Oct, daily, 10am – 4pm (opens 12.30 – 4pm on Sun) • Entrance: free • Other information: Distillery tours ◑ WC ⅋ 🏛

The garden was originally developed in 1866 up the distillery's glen by 'The Major' James Grant, son of the founder, and a legendary innovator, socialiser and traveller. Using exotic plants collected on his travels, he enhanced the natural setting with paths that meandered through orchards, lawns and wooded glades up to the gorge and a rustic bridge over the tumbling burn which flows through on its way to the River Spey. Thanks to the firm of Chivas Brothers, the garden is currently being restored with exact replicas, including the heather-thatched dram hut.

Glenarn ★ [Historic Scotland Inventory]

Rhu, Helensburgh, Dunbartonshire G84 8LL. Tel: (01436) 820493

Michael and Sue Thornley • On A814 between Helensburgh and Garelochhead. Go up Pier Road to Glenarn Road • Open 21st March to 21st Sept, daily, dawn – dusk • Entrance: £3, OAPs/children £1.50 • Other information: Refreshments on certain open days only ◑ 🍴 ⟨⟩ ⌗ ⚲

Established in the 1920s by the Gibson family, this is a very special woodland garden. An earlier Victorian garden had been fed by the famous plant expeditions. Well-kept paths meander round a 10-acre sheltered bowl, sometimes tunnelling under superb giant species rhododendrons (including a *R. falconeri* grown from seed supplied by Hooker in 1849), sometimes allowing a glorious vista across the garden to the Clyde estuary, and sometimes stopping the visitor short to gaze with unstinted admiration at 12-metre magnolias, pieris, olearias, eucryphias and hoherias. The owners, both professional architects, acquired Glenarn some years ago and with almost no help are successfully replanting and restoring where necessary, whilst retaining the special atmosphere created by such magnificent growth. The rock garden falls steeply down past the daffodil lawn to the house with its tall, twisting chimney pots; work is continuing to expose the quarry face and restore the scree bed.

Glenbervie House [Historic Scotland Inventory]

Drumlithie, Stonehaven, Kincardineshire AB39 3YA. Tel: (01569) 740226

Mrs C.S. MacPhie • 8m NE of Laurencekirk, 6m from Stonehaven off A90 Laurencekirk – Stonehaven road. On minor road 3m W of Drumlithie • Open one day for charity, and by appt • Entrance: £2.50, children 80p ◑ 🍴 🍽 WC ⟨⟩

Two very different gardens may be enjoyed here – a traditional Scottish walled garden on a slope, and a woodland garden by a stream. Occupying one wall of an enclosed garden is a fine example of a Victorian conservatory, with a great diversity of pot plants and climbers on the walls. Elsewhere in the walled area is a typical mix of herbaceous plants, fruit, vegetables and summer bedding. There are many shrub and old roses, and on walls and pillars a variety of climbing and rambler roses. Spring brings good displays of bulbs, and the woodland garden with its drifts of primulas, ferns and interesting shrubs is beautiful in early summer. There are fine trees near the house.

Glendoick Gardens ★ [Historic Scotland Inventory]

Glendoick, Glencarse, Perth and Kinross PH2 7NS. Tel: (01738) 860205 (Nursery); (01738) 860260 (Garden Centre)

Mr and Mrs Peter Cox and Kenneth Cox • 8m E of Perth, 14m SW of Dundee on A90 • Open mid-April to mid-June, Mon – Fri, 10am – 4pm, 2nd, 16th May for SGS; and for parties by appt in May • Entrance: £4 (£2.50 on SGS days), children under 5 free ◑ 🍴 ✕ WC ♿ ⌗ 🏠

One of the most comprehensive collections of rhododendrons in the world, started by Euan H.M. Cox in the 1920s and considerably augmented since then by his son, daughter-in-law and grandson; many specimens were collected by them in south-east Asia. The rhododendrons are enhanced by an understorey of perennials, including meconopsis, primulas, trilliums, lilies and nomocharis, swelled by naturalised and native plants. Near the fine Georgian mansion are dwarf rhododendrons and azaleas, and a small arboretum and a collection of conifers complement the many mature trees. Trial beds of new hybrid rhododendrons have been planted in the walled garden.

Glenwhan Garden

Dunragit, Stranraer, Wigtownshire, Dumfries and Galloway DG9 8PH. Tel: (01581) 400222

Mr and Mrs Knott • 7m E of Stranraer, 1m off A75 at Dunragit. Signposted • Open April to Sept, daily, 10am – 5pm, and by appt. Evening visits by arrangement • Entrance: £3.50, OAPs £3, children £1, toddlers free, family £8.50, season ticket £10, conducted tours for parties of 20 or more £15 • Other information: Picnics permitted on request. Dogs strictly on leads (dog-walking area). Plants for sale in nursery ◑ ♨ ✕ ▧ **WC** ᕕ ⟳ ℘ 🏛 ⚐ ℺

This exciting 12-acre garden has commanding views over Luce Bay and the Mull of Galloway, and is set in an area of natural beauty with many rocky outcrops. Because of the Gulf Stream and consequent mild climate, exotic plants thrive amongst the huge collections of trees, shrubs and plants. Seats and walkways abound in the maze of hilly plantings, mostly overlooking the central lakes and bog gardens, and sculptures are placed in carefully selected locations. Collections, whether of genera, reminders of friends or particular themes of interest, are to be seen everywhere. The garden continues to expand and mature. There are enchanting woodland walks where species rhododendrons flourish amongst many different kinds of primulas.

Greenbank Garden ★ [Historic Scotland Inventory]

Flenders Road, Clarkston, Glasgow G76 8RB. Tel: (0141) 616 5125/5126

The National Trust for Scotland • From Clarkston Toll in S Glasgow take Mearns Road for 1m. Signposted • Open all year, daily except 25th, 26th Dec and 1st, 2nd Jan, 9.30am – sunset • Entrance: £3.50, concessions and children £2.60 • Other information: Conducted tours and demonstrations on second Sat of each month. Refreshments in summer only. Catering for parties and guided tours by arrangement. Dogs in woodland only, on lead ◯ ♨ **WC** ᕕ ⟳ ℘ 🏛 ⚐

The large old walled garden of an eighteenth-century house has been divided into many sections, offering imaginative practical demonstrations to illustrate the design and planting of small gardens. The colour combinations are especially good. All the plants are in good condition and admirably labelled. An old hard tennis court in the corner has been converted into a spacious and pleasant area full of ideas for disabled and infirm gardeners, with raised beds and a waist-high running-water pond. Wheelchair access to the glasshouse and potting shed allows disabled people to attend classes and work here. Woodland walks are filled with spring bulbs and shrubs and there are usually Highland cattle in the paddock. A National Collection of bergenias is held here.

Hill of Tarvit [Historic Scotland Inventory]

Cupar, Fife KY15 5PB. Tel: (01334) 653127

The National Trust for Scotland • 2½ m S of Cupar off A916 • House open April to Sept, daily, 1 – 5pm; Oct, Sat, Sun, 1 – 5pm • Grounds open all year, daily, 9.30am – sunset • Entrance: House and grounds £5, children and concessions £3.75 family £13.50, parties of 20 or more £4 per person. Car parking charge extra • Other information: Shop and tea room open from 12 noon daily ○ 🍽 🏺 WC 👤 🐕 🌿 🏛 🕯 ⚲

The garden surrounds the charming Edwardian mansion designed in 1906 for a Dundee financier by Sir Robert Lorimer, who also laid out the grounds to the south of the house: the views over Fife are particularly fine. Good-size borders are filled with an attractive variety of perennials, annuals and heaths, and the grounds as a whole contain many unusual ornamental trees and shrubs now reaching maturity. The plantings are regularly upgraded to include newer and more unusual specimens. There is a lovely rose garden. This is a good garden for amateurs and keen plantspersons alike. A massive two-day plant sale is held the first weekend in October – there is no entry charge, and the public queue at the gate well before the opening.

The Hirsel [Historic Scotland Inventory]

Coldstream, Berwickshire TD12 4LP. Tel: (01890) 882834

The Earl of Home • 9m NE of Kelso, 15m SW of Berwick-on-Tweed, W of Coldstream on A697 • Open all year, daily during daylight hours • Entrance: parking charge £2 per car • Other information: Craft workshops ○ 🍽 🏺 WC 👤 🐕 ⚲

The house is not open, but at all seasons of the year the grounds have much of interest and enjoyment for the visitor who values the peace and ever-changing beauty of the countryside. There is something here for the ornithologist, botanist, geologist, forester, zoologist, historian and archaeologist. In spring, snowdrops and aconites and then acres of daffodils herald the coming summer as the birds, resident and migrant, of which 169 have been definitely identified within the estate boundaries, start busying themselves around their nesting sites. In May and June the rhododendron wood, Dundock, is justly famous for its kaleidoscopic colouring and breathtaking scents. Rose beds, herbaceous and shrub borders follow through the summer. In October and November, the leaves turning on trees and shrubs provide attractive autumn colouring, and hundreds of duck, geese and gulls make the lake their nightly home. In winter the same trees are stark but magnificent in their skeletal forms against storm clouds and sunsets.

House of Pitmuies ★★ [Historic Scotland Inventory]

Guthrie, By Forfar, Angus DD8 2SN. Tel: (01241) 828245

Mrs Farquhar Ogilvie • 1½ m W of Friockheim, on A932 • House open for parties by appt • Garden open April to Oct, daily, 10am – 5pm, and at other times by appt • Entrance: £2.50 by collection box • Other information: Teas by arrangement for parties visiting house ◑ 🍴 WC ♿ ⟁ ⚘

In the grounds of an attractive eighteenth-century house and courtyard, these beautiful walled gardens lead down towards a small river with an informal riverside walk and two unusual buildings – a turreted dovecot and a Gothick wash-house. There are rhododendron glades with unusual trees and shrubs, but pride of place must go to the spectacular semi-formal gardens behind the house, where exquisite old-fashioned roses and a series of long borders containing a dramatic and superbly composed palette of massed delphiniums and other herbaceous perennials in June and July constitute one of the most memorable displays of its type to be found in Scotland.

Latterly the gardens have evolved with new plantings, vistas and focal points, and the conversion of a former tennis court has allowed for new habitats and a greater diversity of plants. The supremely knowledgeable owner has lived in the house since 1966 and known the place for half a century.

House of Tongue ★ [Historic Scotland Inventory]

Tongue, Lairg, Sutherland, Highland IV27 4XH. Tel: (01847) 611209

The Countess of Sutherland • 1m N of Tongue off A838 • Open 31st July, 2 – 6pm for charity, and at other times by appt • Entrance: £2.50, children (under 12) 50p ● ♿ ⟁ ⚘

Sheltered from wind and salt by tall trees, this walled garden is a haven in an otherwise-exposed environment. Adjoining the seventeenth-century house, it is laid out after the traditional Scottish acre, with gravel and grass walks between herbaceous beds, hedged vegetable plots and orchard. A stepped beech-hedged walk leads up to a high terrace which commands a fine view over the Kyle of Tongue. The centrepiece of the garden is Lord Reay's sundial (1714), a sculpted obelisk of unusual design.

Innes House Garden [Historic Scotland Inventory]

Elgin, Moray IV30 8NG. Tel: (01343) 842410

Mr and Mrs Mark Tennant • 5m E of Elgin, off A96 on B9103 Lossiemouth road • Open to parties by appt only • Entrance: charge • Further information: Teas by prior arrangement ●

An extensive ornamental garden divided into compartments, the whole framed by a wide variety of mature and interesting trees. The garden was replanned and reorientated by the present owner's great-grandmother in 1912, when yew hedges were planted, providing a central walk. The large trees in the park are a major feature of the property – 47 varieties are represented, many estimated to be over 200 years old, including rare oaks, unusual maples, beeches and specimen trees such as *Arbutus menziesii, Davida involucrata* and *Cercidiphyllum japonicum*. There are beautiful mature rhododendrons, different varieties flowering over a long period, and an azalea walk.

Inveresk Lodge Gardens [Historic Scotland Inventory]

Musselburgh, East Lothian EH21 6BQ. Tel: (0131) 665 1855

The National Trust for Scotland • 6m E of Edinburgh, S of Musselburgh via A6124 • Open all year, daily, 10am – 6pm (Nov to March closes 4.30pm) • Entrance: £2 (honesty box) ○ 🐾 WC ஃ ♀ ९

The large garden of the seventeenth-century house (not open) is surrounded by high and ancient stone walls; the south-facing aspect provides a warm microclimate for tender plants and a wide range of climbers. A small courtyard opens out unexpectedly onto a croquet lawn dominated at one end by an old yew. The large Edwardian glasshouse contains the National Collection of tropaeolums, plus exotic climbers, tree ferns, a grapevine and an aviary. Semi-formal in character, the three acres of garden were redesigned in the 1960s, with a shrub rose border originally designed by Graham Stuart Thomas, an azalea border, a white border flanked by a *Prunus nigra* hedge, a spring border with a circular lawn, and a newly laid juniper terrace. The garden slopes gently downwards, giving fine views of the Pentland Hills. The village itself, a unique, unspoilt example of eighteenth-century villa development, open under the Scotland Garden Scheme on alternate years, is open this year.

Inverewe Garden ★★ [Historic Scotland Inventory]

Poolewe, Ross–shire, Highland IV22 2LG. Tel: (01445) 781200

The National Trust for Scotland • 6m NE of Gairloch on A832 • Open all year, daily, 9.30am – 9pm (closes 5pm Oct to March) • Entrance: £7, concessions £5.25, family £19, parties £5.25 per person • Other information: Restaurant and shop open April to Oct only ○ 🍽 ✕ 🐾 WC ஃ ❧ 🎂 ♀

This garden is spectacular. Created from 1865 on the shores of the sea loch, Loch Ewe, it covers the entire Am Ploc Ard peninsula. Planned as a wild garden around two dwarf willows on peat and sandstone, it has been developed as a series of walks through herbaceous and rock gardens, a wet valley, a rhododendron walk and an orchard. A traditional sloping walled garden with glorious sea views and colourful terraces is filled with a mixture of herbaceous plants, roses and vegetables. It is a plantsman's garden (labelling is discreet), containing many tender species from Australia, New Zealand, China and the Americas, sheltered by mature beech and pine trees. Plants include National Collections of olearias and rhododendrons. The garden is well tended and way-marked. Note: midge-repellent is advisable and on sale at the main desk.

Inwood

Carberry, Musselburgh EH21 8PZ. Tel: (0131) 665 4550

Irvine and Lindsay Morrison • 6m E of Edinburgh. From A1 Edinburgh – Berwick Road take A6124 signed to Dalkeith. Follow signs for Carberry Candles;

garden is opposite shop • Open April to Sept, Tues, Thurs, 2 – 5pm, and by appt • Entrance: £2, children free ◑ 💻 <u>WC</u> ⅋ ℐ 🏠 **B&B**

A delightful plantsman's garden of just over an acre created since 1984. Full use is made of a small front garden designed for late summer colour containing an exciting variety of tender and lush-foliage plants. Through the garden gate boundary fences blaze with prolific rambling roses ('Blush Rambler', 'Paul's Himalayan Musk' and 'Sander's White Rambler'), and carefully chosen plants complement each other in colour-themed island beds, where roses and unpruned clematis scramble over shrubs to reach up into the central heights of *Viburnum plicatum* 'Pink Beauty', *Pyrus salicifolia* 'Pendula', and a beautiful *Cornus controversa* 'Variegata'. Neat mown lawn extends into the woodland area with appropriate shrubs and ornamental trees; rare plants are constantly being added to the shade beds and pond. The owner has also cleverly created a large polythene-lined 'bog-bed' – an excellent idea that really works and adds glamorous foliage to a dry shady area. If you are lucky, the permanent plant stall will have some of the owner's prize-winning begonias for sale.

Johnston Gardens

Viewfield Road, Aberdeen. Tel: (01224) 522734

Aberdeen City Council • In Aberdeen, ½ m S of Queens Road (A944 to Alford), ¼ m W of junction with ring road • Open all year, daily, 8am – 1 hour before dusk • Entrance: free ○ <u>WC</u> ⅋ ◁▷

When Johnston House was demolished and the grounds sold for redevelopment, it was impossible to utilise the deepest area of the ravine. This was converted into a water and rock garden by the City of Aberdeen Parks and Recreation Department. The result is a congenial oasis of trees, shrubs and mature rhododendrons surrounding a small lake complete with an island, bridges and resident waterfowl. The rock and scree gardens contain some interesting alpine plants.

Jura House

Ardfin, Isle of Jura, Argyll and Bute PA60 7XX. Tel: Peter Cool (01496) 820315

Riley-Smith family • On Jura, 5m SE of ferry terminal off A846. Vehicle ferries from Kennacraig by Tarbert to Port Askaig, Islay, and from Islay to Feolin, Jura • Open all year, daily, 9am – 5pm • Entrance: £2.50, children (5-16) £1 (collecting box) • Other information: Teas available June to Aug, Mon – Fri only. Possible for wheelchairs but sloping gravel paths ○ 💻 🍽 <u>WC</u> ⅋ ◁▷ ℐ 🏠 ᛩ

A circular walk around the Jura House estate illustrates the rich natural history and geology of the island. Starting from the car park, the visitor walks through native woodland and follows the fuchsia-clad banks of the burn to where it plunges into a ravine, filled with ferns and lichens, over the raised beach to the sea. Spectacular views of the Islay coast accompany the steep path down to the shore. Dykes and rock formations are home to wild scree plants and scrubby trees, and here is an example of machair – dune grassland. After the climb back up the cliff, signs guide the visitor to the garden proper. This organic walled garden is a sheltered haven with many unusual plants, including a collection of Australasian origin. Linger awhile before continuing on the woodland path back to the lodge.

Kailzie Gardens ★ [Historic Scotland Inventory]

Peebles, Peebleshire, Scottish Borders EH45 9HT. Tel: (01721) 720007

Lady Angela Buchan-Hepburn • 2½ m SE of Peebles on B7062 • Garden and trout pond open all year, daily, 11am – 5.30pm (in winter, during daylight hours) • Entrance: mid-March to May; £2.50, children (5–14) 75p; June to Oct, £3, children (5–14) £1; Nov to mid-March, £2, children 50p (honesty box); snowdrop days, as advertised. Telephone for party rates • Other information: Holiday cottage available ○ 🍽 ✕ 🏕 WC ⬦ & ℘ 🏛 🔦 ✆

'A Pleasure Garden' is the description in one of the advertisements for Kailzie (pronounced Kailie), and very apt it is too. The gardens of 17 acres are situated in a particularly attractive area of the beautiful Tweed Valley and are surrounded by breathtaking views. The old mansion was pulled down in 1962 and the vast walled garden, which still houses the magnificent greenhouse, has been transformed by the present owner from vegetables to a garden of meandering lawns and island beds full of interesting shrubs and plants, notably fuchsias and geraniums. There are many surprises, including snowdrops in drifts in February and March, a choice flower area, secret gardens, loving seats invitingly placed under garlanded arbours and several thoughtfully sited pieces of statuary. A magnificent fountain at the end of the herbaceous borders leads on to woods and stately trees, and from here you may stroll down the Major's Walk, lined with laburnum and underplanted with rhododendrons, azaleas, blue poppies and primulas. An 18-hole putting green and an osprey watch viewing centre opened in 2003.

Kellie Castle [Historic Scotland Inventory]

Pittenweem, Fife KY10 2RF. Tel: (01333) 720271

The National Trust for Scotland • 3m NW of Pittenweem on B9171 towards Arncroach • Castle open (telephone for details) • Garden and grounds open all year, daily, 9.30am – sunset • Entrance: £2, children £1 (castle and garden extra charge) • Other information: Parking 100 metres, closer for disabled. Refreshments and shop only when castle open ○ 🍽 🏕 WC & ⬦ ℘ 🏛 🔦 ✆

The garden appears to be seventeenth-century in plan, embellished by Professor James Lorimer and his family in late Victorian times. Entered by a door in a high wall, the one-and-a-half acres inspire dreams within every gardener's reach. Simple borders, such as one of nepeta, capture the imagination as hundreds of bees and butterflies work the flowers. Areas of lawn are contained within box hedges, and roses on arches and trellises abound. In one corner, behind a trellis, is a small romantic garden-within-a-garden. A large, green-painted commemorative seat – designed by the architect Hew Lorimer provides a focus at the end of one of the main walks. There is an orchard, with wall-trained fruit, and a collection of old and unusual varieties of vegetables produced by organic gardening methods. Outside the walled garden, mown walks wind through the meadow and woodland, which is a haze of wild garlic in late spring.

Kilbryde Castle

Dunblane, Perthshire FK15 9NF. Tel: (01786) 824897

Sir James Campbell • 9m NW of Stirling, off A820 Dunblane – Doune road • Open 16th May, 20th June, 2 – 5pm, for charity, and by appt • Entrance: £2, OAPs and children £1.50; non-open day charge £3 ● ● WC ఆ

The 20-acre garden was created by the present owner's parents, whose passions were rhododendrons, azaleas, clematis and bulbs. The garden is in two parts – a partly walled upper garden with island beds full of colour on a south-facing slope, and a lovely woodland garden on either bank of a stream well planted with rhododendrons and azaleas under a canopy of mature trees. The best time to visit is spring, particularly the end of May.

Kildrummy Castle Gardens ★ [Historic Scotland Inventory]

Alford, Aberdeenshire AB33 8RA. Tel: (01975) 571203/571277

Kildrummy Castle Garden Trust • 2m SW of Mossat, 10m W of Alford, 17m SW of Huntly. Take A944 from Alford, following signs to Kildrummy, and turn left onto A97. From Huntly turn right onto A97 • Open April to Oct, daily, 10am – 5pm • Entrance: £2, children (5–16) free (2003 price) • Other information: Cars park inside hotel main entrance, coaches in delivery entrance. Woodland walks and children's play area ◑ ● ▦ WC ఆ ⬠ ⌀ ⛏ ∾

The gardens are set in a deep ravine between the ruins of a thirteenth-century castle and a Tudor-style house, now a hotel. The rock garden, by Backhouse of York (1904), occupies the site of the quarry which provided the stone for the castle. The narrowest part of the ravine is crossed by a copy of the towering fourteenth-century Auld Brig O'Balgownie (Old Aberdeen Bridge) built by Colonel Ogston in 1900. This affords a spectacular bird's-eye view of both sides of the water garden commissioned from a firm of Japanese landscape gardeners in the same period; Backhouse continued the planting. In April the reflections in the still water of pools increase the impact of the luxuriant *Lysichiton americanus*, and later come primulas, Nepalese poppies and a notable *Schizophragma hydrangeoides*. There are also fine maples, rhododendron species and hybrids, oaks and conifers. Although a severe frost pocket, the garden can grow embothriums, dieramas and other choice plants. The garden is especially beautiful in autumn with colchicums in flower and acers in brilliant leaf.

Kinross House Gardens [Historic Scotland Inventory]

Kinross, Kinross–shire KY13 8ET. Tel: (01577) 862900

Mr James Montgomery • 13m N of Dunfermline, E of M90, in Kinross • Open May to Sept, daily, 10am – 7pm • Entrance: £2, children 50p ◑ ఆ

Four acres of walled garden, all beautifully maintained, surround the mansion designed in the 1680s and restored early this century. The walls, surmounted by fine statuary, have decorative gates. This is a formal garden of spacious lawn, clipped hedging, herbaceous borders, some with colour themes, and rose borders round the fountain. There are yew hedges in interesting shapes, with well-placed seating for those in a contemplative mood or wishing to view Loch Leven Castle on the nearby island. It was here that Mary Queen of Scots was imprisoned in 1567; though it has no garden, it would be churlish not to walk to the pier to make the short boat trip to its sombre walls.

Kittoch Mill

Busby Road, Carmunnock, Glasgow G76 9BJ. Tel: (0141) 6444712

Margaret and Les Watson • 4m NW of East Kilbride, on B759 Busby – Carmunnock road • Open for parties by appt • Entrance: £50 per group (max. 20 people) ◐

A small organic country garden on the site of an ancient water mill. It includes a 25-foot waterfall and a small Japanese-style garden adjacent to a SSSI and home to 300 hostas.

Landform Ueda at the Gallery of Modern Art

75 Belford Road, Edinburgh EH4 3DR. Tel: (0131) 624 6200

National Galleries of Scotland • Between Scottish National Gallery of Modern Art and Dean Gallery • Open all year, daily, 10am – 5pm (closes 7pm Thurs) • Entrance: free NEW 🍴 🏛

Designed in 2002 by American architectural historian Charles Jencks for the Scottish National Gallery of Modern Art, the Landform Ueda (named for a Japanese scientist) is a serpentine stepped mound of mown grass with three crescent-shaped pools from which rise gentle spiral paths. The design, which is both innovative and strangely pleasing to the eye, is based on the rhythmic patterns that occur in nature, such as weather systems. These create a series of curves which overlap but never repeat and are attracted to a point or basin. Jencks 'looked at the inherent principles of natural movement and designed the Ueda to reflect and heighten these natural forces'. Once you actually see it, the above description becomes quite understandable. The Landform is seven metres high and occupies 300 square metres; from the paths there is also a good elevated view over the two galleries' grounds and their fine collection of sculptures, and towards the handsome Edinburgh skyline. Jencks' own garden, *Portrack* in Dumfriesshire, is open on one day in 2004 for SGS.

Langwell [Historic Scotland Inventory]

Berriedale, Caithness, Highland KW7 6HE.
Tel: (01593) 751237 or (01593) 751278 (Head Gardener)

The Lady Anne Bentinck • 2m W of Berriedale off A9 • Open two days in Aug for SGS, and by appt • Entrance: £2 ◐ 🍴 WC ♿ ⚲

A lovely traditional two-acre walled garden. It has a sadly short season, due to the fact that it is almost as far to the north-east as it is possible to go, but inspires commensurate interest and admiration as a result. The cruciform layout lends itself to dramatic 64-metre-long herbaceous borders specialising in plants that are not only colourful but also manage to thrive in these conditions. They are framed by yew hedges, behind which lie vegetable and fruit sections – all immaculately maintained.

Lawhead Croft

Tarbrax, West Calder, West Lothian EH55 8LW.

Sue and Hector Riddell • 12m SW of Balerno, 6m NE of Carnwath on A70 towards Tarbrax • Open for charity June to Sept, daily, at any reasonable time, and for parties by written appt only • Entrance: £2, children 20p • Other information: No coaches down farm road (no turning room) ◗ 🏵

Nearly 300 metres up in the midst of the bleak Lanarkshire moors, the present owners have planted hedges and laboriously carved out a luxuriant garden. Grass walks lead from one interesting border to another, full of unusual plants. Colour associations and leaf contrasts are carefully thought out. There is an enchanting series of garden rooms, all with a different theme. Great ideas include an excellent bonsai collection. Recently most of the vegetable garden has been swept away and replanted in a great sweep of curved, tiered and circular beds of spectacular and original design.

Leckmelm Shrubbery and Arboretum [Historic Scotland Inventory]

Little Leckmelm House, Lochbroom, Ullapool, Ross-shire IV23 2RH.

Mr and Mrs Peter Troughton • 4m S of Ullapool on A835 • Open April to Sept, daily, 10am – 6pm • Entrance: £1.50 ◗ 🍽

Situated on the shore of Loch Broom and warmed by the Gulf Stream, the 10-acre arboretum is full of fine species rhododendrons and mature trees, various shrubs and bamboos. Originally planted in 1870, it was abandoned for fifty years in the 1930s until reclamation started in 1984, and is now restored to its former Victorian glory. Note particularly the venerable old weeping beech whose spread covers at least a third of an acre, and the largest *Chamaecyparis lawsoniana* 'Wisselii' in Europe. A map and planting plan are available in the car park.

Leith Hall and Gardens ★ [Historic Scotland Inventory]

Huntly, Aberdeenshire AB54 4NQ. Tel: (01464) 831216

The National Trust for Scotland • 34m NW of Aberdeen, 1m W of Kennethmont on B9002 • Hall open (inc. exhibition) 9th to 12th April, May to Sept, Fri – Tues, 12 noon – 5pm (last admission 4.15pm) • Garden and grounds open all year, daily, 9.30am – dusk • Entrance: £2.50, OAPs and children £1.90, pre-booked parties of 20 or more £2 per person (hall and gardens £7, OAPs and children £5.25, pre-booked parties of 20 or more £5.60 per person) • Other information: Dogs outside walled garden only ○ 🍽 🏵 WC 🍴

The gardens are being restored and it is the old garden, remote from the house, that offers the greatest pleasure to the enthusiast. This comprises a series of small spaces, sheltered by walls and hedges, rising on a gentle slope from the west drive. It includes long borders and a large, well-stocked rock garden with a stream and gravel paths. The simple, romantic design allows a tremendous display of flowers during the whole of summer and early autumn; especially fine are magenta *Geranium psilostemon* and an entire border of solid catmint. There are no courtyards and no dominating architecture, just massive plantings of perennials and the odd rarity amongst the rocks. The circular moon gate at the top of the garden leads to the old turnpike road. Woodland walks throughout the designed landscape take in ponds and views down the garden.

Linn Botanic Gardens

Cove, Helensburgh, Dunbartonshire, Argyll and Bute G84 0NR.
Tel: (01436) 842242

Mr J.H.K. Taggart • 6m S of Garelochhead, ¾ m N of Cove on shore of Loch Long • Open March to Oct, daily, dawn – dusk • Entrance: £3.50, OAPs £3, students and teenagers £2, accompanied children 12 and under free • Other information: Entirely unsuitable for wheelchairs and prams. Light refreshments for organised tours. Plants for sale in adjacent nursery, open daily, 11am – 5pm
○ 🏠 WC ♿ ✿

The garden has been developed in its present form since 1971 (the villa dates from the 1860s), with thousands of unusual, exotic and rare plants. Water is a constant presence: in the extensive water garden, in formal ponds and fountains, in the glen with its tumbling waterfall, and, beyond the garden, in the views down to the Firth of Clyde from the terrace. There are also herbaceous borders, a rockery and a cliff garden. A one-kilometre signed route takes visitors through all parts of the garden; a useful leaflet is available.

Little Sparta ★★ [Historic Scotland Inventory]

Dunsyre, Lanark, South Lanarkshire ML11 8NG.

Dr Ian Hamilton Finlay • Turn off A721 at Newbiggin for Dunsyre. 1m W of Dunsyre turn up unmarked farm track signed to Stonypath and Little Sparta. Alternatively take A702 from Edinburgh, turning off at Dolphinton; road signed to Dunsyre • Open probably mid-June to Sept, Fri and Sun, 2 – 5pm • Entrance: free, but donation to Little Sparta Trust welcome ●

Described by Sir Roy Strong as the most original contemporary garden in the country, the garden is now mercifully open to the public once more. On arrival at the gate to the property a beautifully carved wooden sign greets the visitor, giving a hint of the fine craft that combines with the art of this admired sculptor. Hamilton Finlay believes that a garden should both appeal to all the senses and provoke thought, both serious and trivial, and he has therefore revived the art of emblematic gardening which died out in Britain in the seventeenth century, although his personal philosophy is inspired more closely by the eighteenth-century poet-gardeners Alexander Pope and William Shenstone. He has achieved an international reputation in the process. It is impossible to describe Little Sparta briefly, except to say that he has transformed a sizeable hill farmstead 1000 feet above sea level in the Pentland Hills (starting in 1996 with the idea of establishing a testing-ground for his sculptures) into a garden full of classical inscriptions and images, allusions and symbols. Not all are easily understood or interpreted – *n'importe*, as this is a garden, not a crossword puzzle.

Lochalsh Woodland Garden (Balmacara Estate)

Lochalsh House, Balmacara, Kyle, Ross–shire, Highland IV40 8DN. Tel: (01599) 566325

The National Trust for Scotland • 3m E of Kyle of Lochalsh off A87 • Open all year, daily, 9am – dusk • Entrance: £2, children £1 • Other information: Parking off A87 with ½ m walk to garden, closer parking by prior arrangement ○ 🍴 WC ♿ ♋

The garden is approached down the wooded road through the village of Glaick on the lochside. From there, across the water, rise the magnificent mountains of Skye and Knoydart. Woodland planting on this steep-sided, 11-acre site began in 1887 around Lochalsh House, and the canopy of beeches, larches, oaks and pines is now outstanding. Ornamental plantings began in the late 1950s with large-leaved rhododendrons, followed from the 1980s to the present day by shrubs from China, Japan, the Himalayas and Australasia. Paths created through the woods give a choice of walks. Alongside these and in glades, logs have been used to build curved, raised beds for plantings which include hydrangeas, fuchsias, bamboos and ferns.

Logan Botanic Garden ★★ [Historic Scotland Inventory]

Port Logan, Stranraer, Wigtownshire, Dumfries and Galloway DG9 9ND. Tel: (01776) 860231

Royal Botanic Garden Edinburgh • 14m S of Stranraer, off B7065. Signposted • Open March to Oct, daily, 10am – 6pm (closes 5pm March, Oct) and at other times by arrangement • Entrance: £3.50, concessions £3, children £1, family ticket £8. Local membership scheme, inc. Dawyck and Benmore Botanic Gardens (see entries), available • Other information: Discovery Centre and Sound Alive guided tours. Guide dogs only ◑ 🍽 ✕ WC ♿ 🌿 ♨

This is a regional garden of the Royal Botanic Garden Edinburgh (see entry). In the far south-west of Scotland on a peninsula washed by the Gulf Stream, Logan's mild climate allows a fine collection of exotic plants to be grown in the open. Flourishing here are beautiful specimens from South and Central America, Southern Africa, Australasia and the Mediterranean which survive outside in few other British gardens. Throughout the summer it is ablaze with colour. One of the best Scottish collections of tender perennials includes diascias, fuchsias and salvias. As the season progresses rhododendrons, primulas, meconopsis and other acid-loving plants come into bloom on the peat walls, a feature first developed here. The walled garden was established over a century ago and contains many smaller gardens. Major features are the water garden with the original cabbage palms and tree ferns, and the terrace garden framed by an avenue of Chusan palms. The woodland garden is wild by contrast, with glades of eucalyptus and magnolias surrounded by many unusual flowering trees and shrubs. All in all, a fascinating tour of exotic plant collections native mainly to the southern hemisphere.

Malleny Garden [Historic Scotland Inventory]

Balerno, Edinburgh EH14 7AF. Tel: (0131) 449 2283

The National Trust for Scotland • In Balerno, off A70 Edinburgh – Lanark road • Open all year, daily, 10am – 6pm (or dusk if earlier) • Entrance: £2, OAPs/children £1 (2003 prices) ○ 🍴 **WC** ♿ 🌱

Aptly described as The National Trust for Scotland's secret garden, Malleny seems an old and valued friend soon after meeting and reflects the thoughtful planning by the head gardener and his talented wife. An impressive deodar cedar reigns over this three-acre walled garden, assisted by a square of early-seventeenth-century clipped yews and by yew hedges. As well as holding a National Collection of nineteenth-century shrub roses, Malleny's four-metre-wide herbaceous borders are superb, as is the large glasshouse containing a summer display of flowering plants. Don't forget to admire the attractive herb and ornamental vegetable garden, laid out in traditional manner.

Manderston ★★ [Historic Scotland Inventory]

Duns, Scottish Borders TD11 3PP. Tel: (01361) 883450

Lord Palmer • 2m E of Duns on A6105 • House open • Gardens open mid-May to Sept, Sun, Thurs and Bank Holiday Mons, 2pm – dusk. Also for parties at any time of year by appt • Entrance: £6.50, children £3 (house and garden), gardens only £3.50, children £1.50. Reduced rate for parties of 20 or more (2003 prices) ● ☕ 🍴 **WC** ♿ 🍽️ 🎁

One of the last great classic houses to be built in Britain, designed by John Kinross and modelled on Robert Adam's Kedleston Hall. It was described in 1905 as a 'charming mansion inexhaustible in its attractions', and this might equally well apply to the gardens, which remain an impressive example of gardening on the grand scale. Four magnificent formal terraces planted in Edwardian style overlook a narrow serpentine lake, and a Chinoiserie bridging dam tempts one over to the woodland garden on the far side, thus elegantly effecting the transition from formal to informal. The woodland garden has an outstanding collection of azaleas and rhododendrons, and is at its best in May. The formal walled gardens to the north of the house are a lasting tribute to the very best of the Edwardian era, when 24 gardeners were employed to do what two now accomplish to the same immaculately high standard. Gilded gates open on to a panorama of colourful planting on different levels, with fountains, statuary and a charming rose pergola all complementing each other. Even the greenhouses were given lavish treatment, with the walls created from lumps of limestone to resemble an exotic planted grotto. Fifty-six acres of formal and informal beauty.

Megginch Castle [Historic Scotland Inventory]

Errol, Perthshire PH2 7SW. Tel: (01821) 642222

Lady Strange • 8m E of Perth off A85 Perth – Dundee road • Open April to Oct, daily, 2 – 5.30pm • Entrance: £3, children (over 5) £1 (2003 prices) ◑ &.
⟁ ℺

Originally a fifteenth-century tower house (not open), Megginch, meaning Beautiful Island, was considerably restructured by Robert Adam in 1790 and by successive generations, and this gives the gardens and the Gothick courtyard of 1806 a timeless atmosphere. A fountain parterre to the west of the house is of particular interest for its yew and variegated holly topiary, including an unusual yew crown planted to commemorate Queen Victoria's Jubilee. There are four clumps of thousand-year-old yews, at 22 metres the highest in Scotland. Try and visit Megginch during August when a stunning 110-metre double border – the length of the eighteenth-century walled garden – is a glorious blaze of annual plantings. So many dahlias can rarely have been displayed. An adjacent sixteenth-century walled area contains an interesting astrological garden with plants relevant to each sign. Peacocks abound.

Mellerstain ★ [Historic Scotland Inventory]

Gordon, Berwickshire TD3 6LG. Tel: (01573) 410225

The Earl of Haddington • 6m NW of Kelso off A6089 • House open as garden, 12.30 – 5pm • Garden open 9th to 12th April; May to Sept, daily except Tues, Sat; Oct, Sun; all 11.30 – 5.30pm (last admission 4.30pm), and to parties of 20 or more at other times by appt • Entrance: £3, children free (house and garden £5.50, parties of 20 or more £5 per person) • Other information: Craft gallery ◑ ▆ WC &. ⟁ ℘ ⊪ ℺

The house is a rare example of the work of the Adam family; both William and his son Robert worked on the building. The garden is formal, composed of dignified terraces, balustraded and 'lightly' planted with climbers and simple topiary, because even when labour was plentiful a mere six gardeners were employed. The great glory of the garden is the landscape, complete with lake and woodlands in the style of Brown and Repton, but redesigned early this century by Sir Reginald Blomfield. The view of the Cheviot Hills from the terraces is one of the finest to be found in this lovely area of the Scottish Borders. Mellerstain is a must for lovers of the formal landscape.

Mertoun [Historic Scotland Inventory]

St Boswells, Melrose, Roxburghshire TD6 0EA. Tel: (01835) 823236

The Duke of Sutherland • 8m SE of Galashiels, 2m NE of St Boswells on B6404 • Open April to Sept, Sat, Sun and Bank Holiday Mons, 2 – 6pm • Entrance: £2, OAPs £1.50, children (under 14) 50p ◐ WC &.

Overlooking the Tweed and with Mertoun House in the background, this is a lovely garden in which to wander and admire the mature specimen trees, azaleas and daffodils, and the most attractive ornamental pond flanked by a good herbaceous border. The focal point is the immaculate three-acre walled garden, which is everything a proper kitchen garden should be. Walking up from a 1567 dovecot, thought to be the oldest in the country, through a healthy orchard, the visitor reaches the box hedges, raised beds and glass-houses of the main area. Vegetables, herbs and bright flowers for the house vie for attention with figs and peaches in the well-stocked glasshouses.

Monteviot [Historic Scotland Inventory]

Jedburgh, Scottish Borders TD8 6TJ. Tel: (01835) 830380 (mornings)

5m NE of Jedburgh. Turn off A68 onto B6400 to Nisbet. Entrance second turn on right • Open April to Oct, daily, 12 noon – 5pm. Parties must book with Administrator • Entrance: £2, children under 16 free (2003 prices) • Other information: Refreshments at Harestanes Countryside Visitor Centre, ½ m ◑ **WC** & ⟨⊅⟩ ⋒

The river garden running down to the River Teviot has been extensively replanted with herbaceous perennials and shrubs to a more informal design. Beside it, the semi-enclosed terraced rose gardens overlooking the river have a large collection of hybrid teas, floribundas and shrub roses. The pinetum is full of unusual trees, and nearby a water garden has been created, planted with hybrid rhododendrons and azaleas. A new feature incorporates cascading water flowing through bridges into a pool. A circular route has been laid out around the gardens, and there are fine views.

Mount Stuart ★★ [Historic Scotland Inventory]

Rothesay, Isle of Bute. Argyll and Bute PA20 9LR. Tel: (01700) 503877

Mount Stuart Trust • Take ferry from Wemyss Bay. Garden is 5½ m S of Rothesay ferry terminal on A844 • House open as garden, 11am – 5pm (last admission 3.45pm) • Garden open May to Sept, daily except Tues and Thurs, 10am – 6pm. Guided tours available • Entrance: £3.50, OAPs £3, children £2 (house and garden £7, OAPs £5.50, children £2). Party discounts available (2003 prices) ◑ ⬛ ✕ ▦ **WC** & ⋒ ⛪ ⚑

Incorporated in the 300 acres of designed landscape and waymarked woodland walks, there is a wealth of horticultural interest here, and one of the most elegant drives in the country. The gardens contain a considerable mature pinetum of 1860 and a magnificent old lime tree avenue leading to the shore, but they have been restored and augmented over the last decade by the 6th Marquess and his wife. In conjunction with the Royal Botanic Garden Edin-burgh, 100 acres have also been set aside to grow endangered conifer species from all over the world. Rock gardens provide decorative features near the house, but the two most important elements are the kitchen garden and the 'Wee' garden. The latter is actually eight acres of mixed and exotic plantings with emphasis on species from the southern hemisphere. It is set in the mildest part of the grounds and grows some of the most tender plants to be found outside the glasshouse, some flourishing to unusual size. The kitchen garden, originally designed as an ornamental *potager* by the late Rosemary Verey, has been redesigned for the 7th Marquess by James Alexander-Sinclair in the form of six large beds, planted with bold imagination in a scheme based on the colour wheel. Set in the middle is the Pavilion Glasshouse planted with rare flora from SE Asia. One of Scotland's finest gardens. Then visit the magnificent Victorian fern house and attractive garden at *Ascog Hall*, just south of Rothesay. [Open Easter to October, Wed – Sun, 10am – 5pm.]

Netherbyres [Historic Scotland Inventory]

Eyemouth, Berwickshire, Scottish Borders TD14 5SE. Tel: (01890) 750337

Colonel S.J. Furness • 8m NW of Berwick-upon-Tweed, $\frac{1}{4}$ m from Eyemouth on A1107 • Open twice yearly in April and July for charity, and April to Sept for small parties by appt • Entrance: £2.50, children £1.50 ● & ⬦

Although the Victorian conservatory and vineries were demolished to make way for a modern house and conservatory, the garden is worth seeing for the unique elliptical walls, built before 1750. The present layout dates from the 1860s, and constitutes one of the few Scottish walled gardens with a traditional mix of fruit, flowers and vegetables still fully cultivated on traditional lines. A central gazebo and a shrub border have been added.

Novar

Evanton, Ross-shire IV16 9XL. Tel: (01349) 830126

Mr and Mrs Ronald Munro Ferguson • 7m NE of Dingwall off A9, and B817 between Evanton and junction with A836 • Open for SGS, and for parties of 8 or more by appt • Entrance: £4.50 NEW ● ● WC &

A charming series of mature planted natural ponds forms part of the mansion house gardens, fed by streams gushing over stone steps and monumental waterfalls. A formal semi-circular parterre was built to celebrate the millennium, the back edge of which drops down as a five-foot wall to form a handsome ha-ha overlooking the park. There is also a five-acre traditional walled garden with charming arched entrances. Peaceful lawns and mature trees offset a large eighteenth-century oval pond embellished with a contemporary bronze figure.

Pitmedden Garden ★ [Historic Scotland Inventory]

Pitmedden Village, Ellon, Aberdeenshire AB41 7PD. Tel: (01651) 842352

The National Trust for Scotland • 14m N of Aberdeen. 1m W of Pitmedden, 1m N of Udny on A920 • Open May to Sept, daily, 10am – 5.30pm • Entrance: £5, concessions £3.75, parties £4, children £3.75, family £13.50 • Other information: Coaches please book if tea is required. Wheelchairs supplied. Museum of farming life ● ● ● WC & ⬦ ✿ ⊞ ♀ ♀

The Great Garden at Pitmedden exhibits the taste of seventeenth-century garden-makers and their love of patterns made to be viewed from above. This rectangular parterre garden is enclosed by high terraces on three sides and by a wall on the fourth. Simple topiary and box hedging abound. The south- and west-facing walls, lined by fine herbaceous borders, are covered by a great variety of old apple trees in both fan and espalier styles, producing nearly one ton of fruit at the end of the season. Ornamental patterns are cut in box on a grand scale, infilled with 40,000 annuals. The overall impact is striking when viewed from the original ogivally roofed stone pavilion at the north of the garden or when walking along the terraces. When the Trust acquired Pitmedden in 1952 all that survived was the masonry, and since nothing remained of the original design, contemporary seventeenth-century plans for the garden at the Palace of Holyrood in Edinburgh were used in re-creating what is seen today.

Pollok House [Historic Scotland Inventory]

Pollokshaws Road, Glasgow G43 1AT. Tel: (0141) 616 6410

The National Trust for Scotland • 3½ m S of city centre. In Pollokshaws take A736. Signposted • House open • Garden open all year, daily, 10am – 5pm (closed 25th, 26th Dec, 1st, 2nd Jan) • Entrance: free (house £5) ○ 🍴 🍴 **WC** ♿ 🐕 🎫 🌂 ♒

A visit to Pollok House offers a full day's entertainment. Next to the house is a lovely formal terrace of box parterres. There are borders near the water and a nineteenth-century woodland garden on the ridge nearby. The stone gazebos have ogee roofs. The house holds the Stirling Maxwell collection of European paintings, and in the grounds, famous for their bluebells in spring, is The Burrell Collection, one of the world's finest modern galleries, housing decorative and fine arts. The building was designed to complement the woodland, and the parkland around is beautifully planted and maintained.

Portmore ★

Eddleston, Peebleshire, Scottish Borders EH45 8QU. Tel: (01721) 730296

Mr and Mrs D.L. Reid • ½ m N of Eddleston, on A703 Peebles – Edinburgh road • Open for SGS in mid-July, and for parties by appt • Entrance: £2.50 ◑ **WC** 🐕

It is a joy to see an old neglected estate brought lovingly back to life. The long drive winds up through woods, fields and little lochs to the Edwardian mansion which proudly overlooks the rolling acres. Parterres have recently been planted at the far side of the house, and shrub-filled woodland walks are being planned. The wonder of the place is the large walled garden designed and replanted by Chrissy Reid with great taste and flair – she cares particularly about colours and the effect at the entrance is magical. The soft mixture of pale greens, blues, mauves and white delights the eye in the herbaceous borders and leads the gaze to the greenhouses stuffed full of geraniums, pelargoniums, streptocarpus, fuchsias, etc. Leading off these there is an enchanting cool, dripping Victorian Italianate grotto, fern-filled. The remainder of the garden is divided into squares of *potagers*, herb gardens, cherry walks, rose gardens, all surmounted with wonderful wrought-iron arches. Even the luxurious-looking fruit is protected by wire held up by three elegant arches.

Priorwood Garden [Historic Scotland Inventory]

Melrose, Ettrick and Lauderdale, Scottish Borders TD6 9PX. Tel: (01896) 822493

The National Trust for Scotland • On A6091 in Melrose • Open 9th – 12th April then May to 24th Dec, Mon – Sat, 12 noon – 5pm, Sun, 1 – 5pm (opens 10am Mon – Sat, July and Aug) • Entrance: £2.50, OAPs £1.90, children £1
🕐 🖼 & ⬧ 🌿 🛒 🚻 ⚓

Purchased by the Trust in 1974, this was originally the walled garden belonging to Priorwood House, now Melrose Youth Hostel. The garden has been developed for the production of dried flowers, and by drying them in dessicants – as the ancient Egyptians did – the range of plants has been greatly increased to include some 700 varieties of annual and herbaceous plants. The ↘ is also an orchard, which has been designed to show the development of the apple tree in Britain, and a woodland area. The eighteenth-century garden walls are complemented by ornamental ironwork thought to be the work of Lutyens.

Royal Botanic Garden Edinburgh ★★ [Historic Scotland Inventory]

Inverleith Row, Edinburgh EH3 5LR. Tel: (0131) 552 7171

1m N of city centre at Inverleith. Signposted • Open all year, daily, 10am (closes between 4pm and 7pm depending on season). Closed 25th Dec, 1st Jan. Garden tours operate April to Sept, daily, 11am and 2pm from West Gate • Entrance: free • Other information: Exhibition hall and Inverleith House gallery open. Guide dogs only ○ 🍽 ✕ wc & 🌿 🛒 🚻 ⚓

Set on a hillside with magnificent panoramic views of the city, this is one of the finest botanic gardens in the world; arguably the finest garden, physically, of its type in Britain. Established in the seventeenth century on an area the size of a tennis court, it now extends to 75 acres. Rhododendrons and azaleas abound, and in spring their stunning flowers provide a blaze of colour and intriguing scents. The world-renowned rock garden is spanned by a long bridge over the stream. In summer, marsh orchids, lilies, saxifrages and bell-shaped campanulas give brilliant colour. There are also peat and woodland gardens and a stunning herbaceous border. The arboretum sweeps along the garden's southern boundary. A relatively recent addition is the Chinese hillside on the south-facing slope of Inverleith Hill, which includes a spectacular wild-water ravine crossed by bridges, tumbling down into a tranquil pond at the bottom of the hillside. A *Ting* (pavilion) provides an ideal place to relax. The glasshouses, featuring Britain's tallest palm house, leads the visitor on a trail of discovery through the temperate and tropical regions of the world, featuring passion flowers, cycads (some over 200 years old) and species that provide everyday necessities such as food, clothes and medicine.

Scone Palace Gardens [Historic Scotland Inventory]

Perth, Perth and Kinross PH2 6BD. Tel: (01738) 552300

The Earl and Countess of Mansfield • Just outside Perth on A93 Perth – Braemar road • Palace and grounds open April to Oct, daily, 9.30am – 5.15pm • Entrance: £3.25, OAPs/students £2.65, children £1.80 (palace and gardens £6.35, OAPs/students £5.50, children £3.75, family £18) ◑ ☕ ✕ WC ♿

The 100 acres of gardens, surrounding the site of Macbeth's ancient city of Scone, include the famous nineteenth-century pinetum with magnificent towering trees and *Sequoia giganteum* over 48 metres tall; a second pinetum with over 60 specimens was planted in 1977. There is also an acer collection, a butterfly garden, a 30-metre-long laburnum pergola and a beech maze designed by Adrian Fisher, opened in 1998, which comprises 2000 beech trees in the shape of the Murray Star. Taking their turn in season are spectacularly massed daffodils, a primrose drive, rhododendrons and azaleas. The renowned explorer/plant collector, David Douglas, born at Scone, supplied the garden with many of his discoveries, and one of his firs survives. His life is marked by an exhibition in the palace, where there are always orchids in flower, the owners having the largest collection in the country.

Shepherd House ★

Inveresk, East Lothian EH21 7TH. Tel: (0131) 665 2570

Sir Charles and Lady Fraser • 7m E of Edinburgh. From A1 take A6094 exit, signed to Wallyford and Dalkeith, and follow brown tourist-signs to Inveresk Lodge Gardens. House is opposite lodge at junction of main road and Crookston Road • Open four times a year for SGS, and by appt • Entrance: £2.50 • Other information: Teas and plant stall on charity open days only ◕ ♿

The most arresting feature of this one-acre plantsman's garden is a timelessly elegant stone water rill, which flows for 37 metres from a raised pond with a four-jet fountain at the end of the garden to a central bronze fountain with a girl washing her hair, set just above the alpine wall of a prettily planted terrace and parterre in front of the seventeenth-century house. Over and beside the rill are alternate arches and blue trellises, pillars clothed with *Vitis coignetiae* and 'Bobbie James', 'Wedding Day', 'Seagull' and bronze 'Ghislaine de Féligonde' roses, underplanted with allium and nepeta. A decorative arbour sets off more old-fashioned and Scottish roses in a special bed protected by the old stone walls of the garden, and the lawn path meanders on past 'cool' and 'hot' borders through shady trees, a meadow garden, a shrub border, finally curving round to two immaculate *potager* areas with twin arbours of trained pear trees. The garden is also full of sculptural surprises. Some – bird baths, sundials and tulip-filled urns – are elegant, while others – lead pigeons in the undergrowth, a large copper rose stuck in a bush and eye-stopping giant topiary creatures – are delightfully quirky. Lady Fraser is an accomplished botanical artist and with her trained eye for beauty and detail has created with her equally knowledgeable husband one of the best smaller gardens in Scotland.

St Andrew's Botanic Garden

Canongate, St Andrews KY16 8RT. Tel: (01334) 476452/477178

Fife Council • ½ m from town centre, signed in Canongate • Open all year, daily, 10am – 7pm (closes 4pm Oct to April). Glasshouse open daily, 10am – 4pm • Entrance: £2, concessions and children (5–16) £1 (2003 prices) • Other information: Private tours by prior arrangement. Winter lectures and courses held ○ 🍽 🗑 WC ♿ 🌿 ♺

On its present site the garden dates from 1960, covering 18 acres along the Kinness Burn; in 1987 it was leased by the university to the local council. Although the botanical collections are now increasingly adapted for low maintenance, the areas of specialised planting remain excellent. Visitors will find something of interest all year; even in winter a pleasant afternoon may be spent in the greenhouses among the arid, alpine and temperate-zone plants. The pond and rock garden are particularly attractive, and the order beds are a valuable educational aid, rarely seen elsewhere. There are good collections of cotoneasters, sorbus and berberis, and stunning clumps of *Lathraea clandestina*.

Stobo Castle Water Gardens [Historic Scotland Inventory]

Peebles, Scottish Borders EH45 8NY. Tel: (01721) 760245

Hugh and Charles Seymour • 6m SW of Peebles on B712, 12m E of Biggar • Open for SGS, and by appt, but advisable to confirm in writing in addition to telephoning • Entrance: £2, children free ● 🍽 ⬥ 🌿 ♺

The enduring appeal of water is exemplified here; the planting, although most attractive, takes second place to the visual impact of clear water flowing down a series of cascades and waterfalls. Japanese bridges and stepping stones invite frequent crossings from side to side, and peaceful rills stray from the main torrent to create one huge water garden. In fine landscape-garden tradition, man has contrived to manipulate nature – in this case a large earth dam across a steep valley – into something of classical delight. The dam was faced with stone to create a magnificent waterfall and the resulting flow is impressive even in dry summers. Many mature trees.

Teviot Water Garden

Kirkbank House, Eckford, Kelso, Scottish Borders TD5 8LE. Tel: (01835) 850734/253

Mr and Mrs Hamish Wilson • Between Kelso and Jedburgh on A698 • Open all year, daily, 10am – 5pm • Entrance: free ◑ 🍽 ✕ WC 🌿 🛍 ♺

Created over the years from a stony riverside field, these gardens occupy a spectacular position on a steep north-west-facing bank of the River Teviot. A series of terraces linked by waterfalls displays a wide range of plants, giving a varied show throughout the summer months. Aquatic plants are a speciality, but this intimate and tranquil garden also contains a selection of choice perennials, grasses, ferns and bamboos. The shop stocks plants and other items needed by the water garden enthusiast, from fish to pumps and liners.

Threave Garden and Estate ★ [Historic Scotland Inventory]

**Stewartry, Castle Douglas, Dumfries and Galloway DG7 1RX.
Tel: (01556) 502575**

*The National Trust for Scotland • 1m W of Castle Douglas off A75 • House
open March to Oct, Wed, Thurs, Fri, Sun, 11am – 4pm • Garden open all year,
daily, 9.30am – dusk (walled garden and glasshouses close 5pm). • Entrance:
Garden £5, OAPs and children £3.75, family £13.50, parties £4 per person,
school parties £1 per child (house and garden £9, OAPs £6.50, parties £7 per
person, family £23) • Other information: Exhibition in visitor and countryside
centre, March to Dec, daily* ○ 🍵 ✗ 🛍 WC ⓖ ⬦ ☙ 🏮 🍴 ⚲

The Threave estate, which extends to 1500 acres, includes the famous 65-acre
garden which has been used as a school of horticulture since 1960 and caters for
trainee gardeners. Numerous perennials, annuals, trees and shrubs are used in
imaginative ways and maintained by the resident horticultural students. For
the visitor the principal interest is the working walled garden with its range of
glasshouses, vegetables, orchard and wall-trained fruit. This may be contrasted
with the less formal woodland and rock gardens, heath garden and arboretum.
The garden is famous for its collection of daffodils, complemented in spring by
rhododendrons and flowering trees and shrubs.

Tillypronie [Historic Scotland Inventory]

Tarland, Aboyne, Aberdeenshire AB34 4XX. Tel: (013398) 81238

*The Hon. Philip Astor • 4½ m W of Tarland via A97 Dinnet – Huntly road •
Open 6th June, 29th Aug for charity, 2 – 5pm • Entrance: £2, children £1*
● 🍵 WC ⓖ ⬦ ☙ ⚲

Set on the south-facing slope of a hill at over 300 metres above sea level, this is
a cold garden, but shelter belts dating from the mid-1800s ensure that a wide
range of plants can be grown; more shelter planting was added from 1925 to
1951. The overall layout was completed in the 1920s, the work of George
Dillistone of Tunbridge Wells. The terraces below the house date from the
same period and support narrow herbaceous borders. The house walls provide
shelter for less hardy climbers, and trained *Buddleia davidii* cultivars make a good
display in August. Curved stone steps lead between extensive heather gardens
to lawns sweeping down to the ponds with their colourful plantings of astilbes,
filipendulas, lysichitons, primulas and ferns. Azaleas and rhododendrons
feature strongly in June, and there are fine specimens of *Picea breweriana* and
many other conifers and an area devoted to dwarf varieties. A rock garden and
a Golden Jubilee garden are recent arrivals. Spectacular views end with the
Grampians on the horizon.

Torosay Castle and Gardens [Historic Scotland Inventory]

Craignure, Isle of Mull, Argyll and Bute PA65 6AY. Tel: (01680) 812421

*Mr Christopher James • 1½ m S from Craignure. Steamer 6 times daily April to
Oct (2 to 4 times daily Nov to March) from Oban to Craignure. Narrow-gauge*

railway from Craignure ferry. Or take Lochaline to Fishnish ferry, then travel 7m S on A849 • Castle open, Easter to Oct, 10.30am – 5pm • Garden open all year, April to Oct, 9am – 7pm (or dusk in winter) • Entrance: £5, OAPs and students £4, children £1.75 (castle and gardens) (2003 prices) ○ ☕ 🍽 WC ♿ ⟨⟩ 🌿 🏪 🔦

The house in baronial castle style by Bryce (1858) is complemented by a formal Italianate main garden based on a series of descending terraces with an unusual statue walk. This features one of the richest collections of Italian Rococo statuary in Britain and alone justifies the crossing from Oban to Mull. Vaguely reminiscent of Powis Castle (see entry in Wales), it makes a dramatic contrast with the rugged island scenery. The peripheral gardens around the formal terraces are also a contrast – a newly restored informal water garden and an Oriental garden looking out over Duart Bay, and a small rock garden. Rhododendrons and azaleas are a feature but less important than in other west-coast gardens, and there is a collection of Australian and New Zealand trees and shrubs. A major 15-year restoration is under way, and 2000 species and cultivars have been planted over the past five years. Outside the main garden, the owners, in conjunction with the Royal Botanic Garden Edinburgh, have created a five-acre Chilean wood and underplanted another two-acre wood with plants from the collection of the late Jim Russell.

Tyninghame House ★ [Historic Scotland Inventory]

Tyninghame, East Linton, East Lothian EH42 1XW.

Tyninghame Gardens Ltd • 25m E of Edinburgh between Haddington and Dunbar. N of A1, 2m E of A198 • Open 9th May, 27th June for charity, 1 – 5pm • Entrance: £2 ◐ ☕ 🍽 WC ♿ ⟨⟩ 🌿 ⚲

Tyninghame is renowned for the gardens created by the Dowager Lady Haddington from 1947 onwards, which have been described as of 'ravishing beauty'. They consist of a formal rose garden, terraces, a secret garden, an Italian garden and an area of woodland. When her husband died in 1986, her son reluctantly sold the house, but those who worried about the garden's future need not have feared, as the conversion and addition of two houses was handled by Kit Martin with great sensitivity. The garden is close to the sea, with fine views in all directions.

Tyninghame Walled Garden [Historic Scotland Inventory]

Dunbar, East Lothian EH42 1XW. Tel: (01620) 860559

Mrs Charles Gwyn • 25m E of Edinburgh N of A1. Take turning to North Berwick and Tyninghame on A198; after 1m turn right through archway • Open two day for SGS, and by appt, 1 – 5pm • Entrance: £2, children free ◐ 🍽 WC ♿ ⟨⟩ 🌿

The heated brick walls and gateways here date from 1760, making it one of the earliest walled gardens in Scotland. The name, however, does not perhaps do justice to the treasury of specialist trees and plants contained within its immaculate four and a half acres. The clean-cut layout (redesigned in the 1960s by James Russell) is best viewed from the delightful 1832 camellia house attached to the main house beside a magnificent *Magnolia grandiflora*. Straight ahead stretches a grass *allée* of clipped yew walls, niched to offset eight classical statues and centred on a Florentine fountain. This *allée* divides the entire garden lengthways; the transverse paths consist of a rose pergola and a well-planted rose walk. As well as extensive borders of mixed planting, there is also a spacious lawned *potager* and an eye-catching collection of bearded irises. The two outstanding areas are the almost monastic espaliered apple-tree walk, 90 metres long, with Bacchus and Diana as the focal points at either end, and the comprehensive collection of mature exotic and unusual trees, too numerous to mention. On the whole of the right-hand side of the garden they have been cleverly under-planted with huge sweeping beds.

University of Dundee Botanic Garden

Riverside Drive, Dundee DD2 1QH. Tel: (01382) 647190

University of Dundee • 2½ m from city centre on A90 Perth road. Signposted • Open all year, daily, 10am – 4.30pm (closes 3.30pm Nov to Feb) • Entrance: £2, OAPs £1, children £1, family £5 ⏰ 🍴 🥾 **WC** ♿ 🛍 🔍 ⚓

Founded in 1971 as a source of plant material for teaching and research purposes, the garden has always been open to the public for their pleasure. The planting around the glasshouse and large pond near the entrance is extremely attractive and reminiscent of a private rather than a botanic garden. The large area beyond has plants grouped according to region or habitat, including many Scottish natives; though mainly composed of trees and shrubs, the artistic layout ensures plenty to see of interest as well as beauty. The glasshouse is brimful of fine specimens, from tropical to temperate zones, from rainforest to desert – a pleasure whatever the weather is like outside. In all, a very varied 23 acres.

West Drummuie Garden

West Drummuie, Golspie, Sutherland, Highland KW10 6TA. Tel: (01408) 633493

Mrs Elizabeth Woollcombe • 1m S of Golspie off A9. At white milestone, turn up hill and bear right at fork to last house • Open mid-April to early Oct by appt only • Entrance: donations welcome • Other information: No coaches please ● ⬧ 🔍 ⚓

A small private garden imbued with the spirit of the owner (a gardener of forty years' experience), set on a steep slope at the foot of Ben Bhraggie overlooking the Dornoch Firth. Protected from the salty east winds by hedges of *Griselinia littoralis*, hebe and escallonia, it is a garden of woodland and water. Pieris, *Crinodendron hookerianum*, *Azara microphylla*, hoheria and *Corokia cotoneaster* flower well, and *Mysotidium hortensia* overwinters thanks to a covering of seaweed. Dogs are much in evidence, and bantams act as slug controllers. All the owner's favourite treasures are propagated and for sale.

WALES

Two-starred gardens are marked on the map with a black square.

Aberglasney Gardens ★ [Welsh Historic Garden Grade II*]

Llangathen, Llandeilo, Carmarthenshire SA32 8QH. Tel: (01558) 668998

Aberglasney Restoration Trust • 3m W of Llandeilo on A40. Turn S at Broak Oak junction • Open April to Oct, daily, 10am – 6pm (last entry 5pm); in winter telephone for opening details • Entrance: £5.50, OAPs £4.50, disabled £3, children £2.50, family ticket £14 ◑ ⛾ ✕ 🧺 WC ⅼ ♨ 🏛

Here are gardens lost in time. Records for Aberglasney go back to the mid-fifteenth century, when mention was made of nine gardens, orchards and vineyards. Around 1600 the Bishop of St David's bought the estate to turn it into a private palace, and it is probably he who built the gatehouse and the marvellous cloister garden. To the side of the house is a yew tunnel unique in Britain. After many years of neglect the gardens are being restored with great care and attention to detail. The large upper walled garden was designed by Penelope Hobhouse to complement the historic site, and the lower walled garden is home to vegetables, herbs and plants grown for cutting. The wooded area known as Bishop Rudd's Walk has fine collections of rare and unusual woodland plants. Pigeon House Wood is a natural, unspoilt area where you may sit in the shade of splendid beech trees and other woodland planting. The restoration of the formal cloister garden, devoted to plants typically grown in an early-seventeenth-century garden, was completed two years ago.

Bodnant Garden ★★ [Welsh Historic Garden Grade I]

Tal-y-Cafn, Colwyn Bay, Conwy LL28 5RE. Tel: (01492) 650460

The National Trust • 8m S of Llandudno, just off A470 • Garden open mid-March to Oct, daily, 10am – 5pm • Entrance: £5.50, children £2.75 • Other information: Parking 50 metres from garden. Plant centre (not NT) adjacent ◑ ⛾ ✕ WC ⅼ ♨ 🏛

One of the finest gardens in the country, not only for the magnificent collections of rhododendrons, camellias and magnolias but also for its beautiful setting above the River Conwy and extensive views of the Snowdon range. The garden, which covers 80 acres, has many interesting features, the best-known being the laburnum arch, which in late May and early June is an overwhelming mass of bloom. Others include the lily terrace, the curved and stepped pergola, the canal terrace, Pin Mill and the dell garden. In the dell is the tallest redwood in the country, the 45-metre *Sequoia sempervirens*. These, together with the outstanding autumn colours, make it a garden for all seasons. The whole effect was created by four generations of the Aberconway family (who bought Bodnant in 1874), aided by three generations of the Puddle family as head gardeners.

Bodrhyddan [Welsh Historic Garden Grade II*]

Rhuddlan, Denbighshire LL18 5SB. Tel: (01745) 590414

Lord Langford • 4m SE of Rhyl. Take A5151 Rhuddlan – Dyserth road and turn left. Signposted • House open • Garden open June to Sept, Tues, Thurs, 2 – 5.30pm • Entrance: £2 (house and garden £4, children under 16 £2) ◑ 🍵 🏠 WC ♿ ⬇ ♋

The box-edged parterre was laid out by William Andrews Nesfield – the father of the equally renowned William Eden Nesfield – who designed the 1875 alterations to the house. The paths are bordered by clipped yew and, to the north-west, the Pleasance, part of a larger area known on very old maps as the Grove. This is probably because it embraces St Mary's Well, revered since pagan times and covered now by a 1612 Inigo Jones pavilion, said to have been used for clandestine marriages. The two-acre Pleasance, originally a Victorian shrubbery, has been restored; it has four ponds, fine mature trees and many new plantings, and an additional area has been developed as a wild garden, picnic spot and new woodland walk.

Bodysgallen Hall ★ [Welsh Historic Garden Grade I]

Llandudno, Gwynedd LL30 1RS. Tel: (01492) 584466

Historic House Hotels • 2m S of Llandudno. At A55/A470 junction turn onto A470 towards Llandudno. Hall is 1m on right • Open all year, daily • Entrance: free to guests using hotel facilities • Other information: Refreshments in hotel ○ 🍵 ✕ WC B&B

The Garden has written that 'there can be few better living examples of early seventeenth-century gardens anywhere in England and Wales'. Both house and gardens have been restored to a high standard. The limestone outcrops provide an interesting array of rockeries and terraces; major features include a parterre sympathetically planted with herbs, and a formal walled rose garden. The fine trees and shrubs include a medlar and a mulberry, and woodland walks add a further dimension to a magnificent award-winning garden.

Cae Hir ★

Cribyn, Lampeter, Ceredigion SA48 7NG. Tel: (01570) 470839

Mr Will Akkermans • 5m NW of Lampeter off A482. Turn left onto B4337 at Temple Bar; garden is 2m on left • Open daily except Mon (but open Bank Holiday Mons), 1 – 6pm • Entrance: £2.50, OAPs £2, children 50p ◑ 🍵 🏠 WC ♿ ⬇ 🌣 💡 ♋

Begun nearly twenty years ago, the garden has been made and is managed by just one man. Its six acres – four on one side of the road where the house is situated and two on the other – slope, very gently at first, then more steeply from a natural stream and a series of informal wildlife pools at the bottom to a summerhouse at the top with fine views of the surrounding countryside. Near the top, an 18-metre-long laburnum crescent is underplanted with *Rosa rugosa* and edged with *Geranium macrorrhizum*; immediately below, a neatly clipped yew hedge echoes the crescent shape. This formality of design occurs throughout the garden, and yet there is no formal feel to it. The discreet rooms, several themed by colour, are separated by large swathes of grass punctuated by standard trees. The owner's necessary choice of tough plants that don't need a lot of looking after has been turned to good effect: he uses them dramatically and often in masses. Trees are his passion, and he clearly enjoys trimming them into unusual shapes – he has a separate bonsai area. Most intriguing. Nearby on the B4342, near Talsarn, is the *Winllan Wildlife Garden*, not so much a garden as several acres bordering the River Aeron devoted to encouraging wildflowers and wildlife. [Open for NGS, June, daily, 2 – 5pm and in July, Aug by appt only – telephone (01570) 470612.]

Cefn Bere

Cae Deintur, Dolgellau, Gwynedd LL40 2YS. Tel: (01341) 422768

Mr and Mrs Maldwyn Thomas • Leave Dolgellau on A496 signed to Barmouth. Crossing River Wnion, turn left at top of bridge. After 50 metres turn right, then second right behind school; continue up hill to left-hand bend, and house is fourth on right • Open spring, summer and autumn by appt only • Entrance: by donation to collecting box ◐

This relatively small garden has a diverse collection of plants, amassed over the last 45 years. There are good trees, a wide variety of shrubs, climbers, perennials and bulbs – all planted informally within a formal framework, and designed to be in sympathy with the magnificent view of the Cadair Idris escarpment. There are also peat and bulb frames, stone troughs and an alpine house to bring the visitor back to earth.

Centre for Alternative Technology

Machynlleth, Powys SY20 9AZ. Tel: (01654) 705950

C.A.T. • 3m N of Machynlleth on A487. Also access by water-balanced cliff railway, Easter to Oct • Open all year, daily except 25th Dec and mid-Jan, 10am – 5pm (4pm in winter) • Entrance: £7, OAPs, claimants and students £5, children £3.60, family £26 (2003 prices). Discounts for arrival by public transport or bicycle • Other information: Parking inc. coaches at base of site, but for elderly and disabled at top of steep drive. Guide dogs only ○ ♥ ✕ ▓ ⓷ ♨ ⊞ ⓠ ℺

High in a former slate quarry, and at the heart of the environmentally friendly community here, is the most exciting garden. Compactly laid out, using natural and recycled materials to form harmoniously shaped raised beds, ponds and walks, the garden is vibrant (in June) with colour and insect life drawn to the organically grown flowers and companion-planted vegetables. There are suggestions, too, for urban gardeners and displays of land reclamation, wildlife gardening, composting, weed and pest control. Wind turbines and solar fountains in different sizes and designs could be considered unusual, if highly functional, garden sculptures. Whether you want to experience the

world of the worm in the underground mole hole, or wander gently by one of
the lakes, be sure not to miss the view from the balcony of the water-balanced
railway. A new information centre has been built from rammed earth and
insulated with sheep's wool.

Chirk Castle ★ [Welsh Historic Garden Grade I]

Chirk, Wrexham, Clwyd LL14 5AF. Tel: (01691) 777701

*The National Trust • 10m SW of Wrexham, 2m W of Chirk off A5, 1½ m up
private drive • Castle open as gardens but 12 noon – 5pm • Gardens open Feb,
Sat and Sun (telephone to check times), 12 noon – 4pm; then 2nd April to 2nd
Nov, daily except Mon and Tues (but open Bank Holiday Mons, 11am – 6pm
(last admission 4.30pm); Oct, Nov, Wed – Sun, 11am – 5pm (last admission
3.30pm) • Entrance: £3.60, children £1.80 (less in Feb) (castle and garden
£5.80, children £2.90, family £14.50) • Other information: Parking 350 metres
from garden; courtesy coach offers transport* ☀ 🍽 ✕ 🛍 WC ♿ 🏛 ☕ ♀

The castle, its walls now covered with climbing plants, dates from 1300 and is
set in an eighteenth-century landscaped park. Six acres of trees and flowering
shrubs, including rhododendrons and azaleas, were mostly planted by Lady
Margaret Myddleton; they contrast with the yews in the formal garden, which
were planted in the 1870s by Richard Biddulph. The rose garden contains
mainly old cluster-flowered (floribunda) roses. From the terrace, with its fine
views over Shropshire and Cheshire, the visitor passes to the classical pavilion,
then along a lime tree avenue to a statue of Hercules. There is interesting
nineteenth-century topiary, a rockery and an old hawk house, and a pleasure-
ground wood to stroll in. Chirk is described by the Trust as a 'family' garden.

Clyne Gardens ★ [Welsh Historic Garden Grade I]

Blackpill, Swansea, West Glamorgan SA3 5AR. Tel: (01792) 401737

*Swansea City Council • From Swansea take A4067 Mumbles road and turn
right into car park of Woodmans Inn • Open all year, daily, 8am – dusk.
Telephone for details of garden tours • Entrance: free • Other information: 'Clyne
in Bloom' and rare plants sale in May* ○ 🛍 WC ♿ 🏕 ☕ ♀

Fifty acres of well-kept nineteenth-century woodland garden and open parkland with considerable botanical interest. Three National Collections are held
here – pieris, enkianthus and rhododendron (Trifolia and Falconera subsections) – although they are not easy to find. Tree lovers will be well rewarded.
There are many fine specimens, including the tallest recorded magnolia in
Britain, *M. campbellii* Alba group. The most interesting time to visit is undoubtedly the spring, when the enormous collection of rhododendrons (the
largest in Wales with over 800 varieties, some of them are very rare) are at
their best. These are mostly found on the banks of the stream that runs
through the garden and make for a glorious walk ending up at the Japanese
bridge. The bog garden is also situated in this area with extensive plantings of
Gunnera manicata, candelabra primulas and other moisture-lovers. Pick your
time right and there will also be lovely swathes of bluebells and wood garlic.

Colby Woodland Garden [Welsh Historic Garden Grade II]

Stepaside, Amroth, Narberth, Pembrokeshire SA67 8PP. Tel: (01834) 811885

The National Trust • 10m SW of St Clear, near Amroth on Carmarthen Bay off A477 • Open April to Oct, daily, 10am – 5pm; walled garden 11am – 5pm. Guided walks available with head gardener • Entrance: £3, children £1.50, family £7.50, pre-booked parties of 15 or more £2.50 per person, children £1.25 (2003 prices) • Other information: Plant fair – telephone for details. Parking 50 metres from garden, disabled may park closer. Coaches welcome. Gallery ○ ☕ ▧ WC ⟁ ⟿ ▨ ⊞ ▮ ⟋

This early-nineteenth-century estate garden round a Nash-style house is now mainly woodland with some formal gardens. The walled garden is planted informally for ornamental effect. The woodland garden has many rhododendrons and some interesting trees. A new hydrangea bed gives further summer interest. Delightful autumn colour.

Cwm-Pibau

New Moat, Clarbeston Road, Haverfordwest, Pembrokeshire SA63 4RE. Tel: (01437) 532454

Mrs Drew • 10m NE of Haverfordwest. Take A40 through Robeston Wathen, turn left on B4313, follow signs to New Moat. 3m from Clarbeston Road on outskirts of New Moat, take concealed drive on left and continue for $\frac{1}{2}$ m, keeping left • Open by appt for charity • Entrance: £2 ◕ ▧ WC ⟿

Created by the owner since 1978, the garden has as a background mature woodland, and the long driveway is a difficult uphill walk (although on charity days it is possible to get a lift down and back to the car). Rhododendrons have been planted along the side of the drive, which leads to lawns and herbaceous plantings near the house. Paths are then signposted down through five acres of shrub plantings and along a stream fringed with moisture-lovers. This area is still young, but leads on to five more acres of woodland planted with embothriums, rhododendrons and rare shrubs.

The Dingle ★

Welshpool, Powys SY21 9JD. Tel: (01938) 555145

Mr and Mrs Roy Joseph • 3m NW of Welshpool. Take A490 for 1m to Llanfyllin then turn left signed to Dingle Nursery or Frochas. After $1\frac{1}{2}$ m fork left • Open all year, daily, except Tues and 25th Dec to 2nd Jan, 9am – 5pm • Entrance: £2 for charity, children free • Other information: Possible for wheelchairs but steep in places ○ ☕ ▧ WC ⟁ ⟿ ▨

Set on the steep slopes of a verdant Welsh valley, this garden is partly a woodland creation of over 4000 carefully chosen trees and shrubs and partly colour-coordinated beds planned to look good all year. The owners began by damming the stream (the dingle) that flows through the site, and have created a large pool which now sets off the garden superbly. There is a grove of acers, with many other interesting specimens such as *Davidia involucrata* and many different pittosporums. The real treat has to remain the nursery, which is worth driving many, many miles to reach.

Dolwen ★

Cefn Coch, Llanrhaeadr-ym-Mochnant, Powys SY10 0BU. Tel: (01691) 780411

J. Marriott and B. Yarwood • 14m W of Oswestry, on B4580 Oswestry – Llanrhaeadr road. Turn sharp right in Llanrhaeadr at Three Tuns Inn • Open May to Aug, Fri, first and last Sun in month, 2 – 4.30pm (please telephone to check). Parties welcome by appt • Entrance: £2 ◑ 🍵 🏫 WC ⬥ ℘ 🎋 ♀

A dramatic woodland and water garden situated high in the Berwyn hills with splendid views. What started as a small cottage garden was extended by the previous owner, Frances Denby, to two-and-a-half acres, with the extra land used to great advantage. Striking plants in the water areas include *Salix fargesii* and *S. udensis* 'Sekka', but she was careful not to overplant the margins of the three ponds, which she referred to as 'The Lake District'. Large boulders are sited imaginatively, and contemporary sculpture adds charm in unexpected places; so do the bridges, some of which have unusual origins. As well as shrubs and climbing roses, there are wonderful trees. Many of the uncommon plants here were supplied by the *Crug Farm Nursery* near Caernarfon.

Donadea Lodge

Babell, Flintshire CH8 8QD. Tel: (01352) 720204

Mr and Mrs Patrick Beaumont • 8m E of St Asaph. Turn off A541 Mold – Denbigh road at Afonwen, signed to Babell, and at T-junction turn left; or take A55 then B5122 to Caerwys and third turn on left • Open May to July by appt • Entrance: £2, children 20p ◑ WC ♿ ⬥ ℘

The garden demonstrates what creative design can achieve on a very long site. On one side an avenue of mature lime trees is a fine feature in its own right. The other side is a mixed border of bays and small islands, each with its own restrained and carefully thought-out colour scheme, often achieved using unusual plants in unexpected but entirely effective combinations. A particular feature is the use of roses and clematis.

Dyffryn Gardens ★ [Welsh Historic Garden Grade I]

St Nicholas, Cardiff, Vale of Glamorgan CF5 6SU. Tel: (029) 2059 3328

Vale of Glamorgan Council • 4m SW of Cardiff on A4232 turn S on A4050 and W to A48 • Open all year, daily, 10am – dusk • Entrance: £3, OAPs and children £2, family £6.50 ○ 🍵 🏫 WC ♿ ⬥ ℘ 🎋 ♀

What is happening at Dyffryn, one of Wales's largest landscape gardens and also one of its best-kept secrets, is one of the Heritage Lottery Fund's most intelligent acts of garden funding. With the help of a huge grant – some £6.15 million – Thomas Mawson's 1904 plans for the distinguished horticulturist Reginald Cory are to be used as the basis for a full-scale restoration over the first three years of the new century. Major projects are the reinstatement of the lake and the restoration of the walled kitchen garden and its magnificent glasshouse. Arguably one of the most important gardens of the Edwardian era, here are herbaceous borders on an heroic scale, croquet and archery lawns, panel gardens featuring box-hedged flower beds, rose gardens, a heather bank, a rockery, an arboretum and a series of themed garden rooms, including the Pompeian Garden with a Grade-II-listed garden building open.

Erddig ★ [Welsh Historic Garden Grade I]

Wrexham, Clwyd LL13 0YT. Tel: (01978) 355314

The National Trust • 2m S of Wrexham off A525 or A483 • House open 12 noon – 5pm (closes 4pm from 1st Oct) • Garden open April to Oct, daily except Thurs and Fri, 11am – 6pm (closes 5pm from 1st Oct). Conducted tours for parties by prior arrangement • Entrance: £3.40, children £1.70, pre-booked parties of 15 or more £2.70 per person, family £8.50 (house and garden £6.60, children £3.30, family £16.50, pre-booked parties £5.30 per person) (2003 prices) • Other information: Parking 100 metres from garden. Wheelchairs provided. Dogs in parkland only, on lead ◑ ⬛ ✕ 🖼 WC ♿ ✿ 🏵 ♨

The gardens, a rare example of early-eighteenth-century formal design, were almost lost along with the house, but have now been carefully restored. The large walled garden contains varieties of fruit trees known to have been grown there during that period, and there is a canal garden and fish pool. South of the canal walk is a Victorian flower garden, and other Victorian additions include the parterre and yew walk. A National Collection of ivies is here, also a narcissus collection. Apple Day is celebrated in October.

Farchynys Cottage

Bontddu, Gwynedd LL42 1TN. Tel: (01341) 430245

Mrs G. Townshend • 4m W of Dolgellau on A496 Dolgellau – Barmouth road. After Bontddu on right. Signposted • Open April to June, daily except Sat, Wed, 2.30pm – 6pm • Entrance: £1.50 ◑ WC

This woodland garden overlooking the Mawddach estuary is set in natural oak and conifer woodland. There is much new planting, but azaleas, rhododendrons and magnolias are well established and repay a spring visit. A small sculpture garden has been established.

Foxbrush

Aber Pwll, Port Dinorwic, Gwynedd LL56 4JZ. Tel: (01248) 670463

Mr and Mrs B.S. Osborne • 3m SW of Bangor on B4507 (old Caernarfon road) N of A487. Avoiding new bypass, enter village. House on left after high estate wall, opposite layby. Signed to Felinheli • Open by appt only • Entrance: £1.50, children free ● ⬛ 🖼 WC ⤵ 🏵 ✎

A private three-acre plantswoman's garden, created single-handedly from a wilderness on the site of a sixteenth-century mill. Narrow paths meander through romantic plantings of rare treasures and sudden surprises, over bridges and under tunnels of laburnum and a 14-metre rose and clematis pergola, past herbaceous borders, a croquet lawn, a river and ponds. Although essentially a spring garden (despite ferocious flooding), it is much admired throughout the summer, too.

Glansevern Hall Gardens [Welsh Historic Garden Grade II*]

Berriew, Welshpool, Powys SY21 8AH. Tel: (01686) 640200

G.E and M.B Thomas • From Welshpool take A483 S. After 5m entrance on left by bridge over River Rhiew • Open May to Sept, Fri, Sat and Bank Holiday Mons, 12 noon – 6pm • Entrance: £3, OAPs £2, children free ◐ ⬤ ✕ WC &. ⬱ ⌆ ⛫

The mature 18-acre garden is set in a wider parkland on the banks of the River Severn, and is noted for its range of unusual trees. A four-acre lake has islands where swans, ducks and other waterfowl breed. The streams, which form a water garden and feed the lake, are planted along the banks with moisture-loving plants and shrubs. A large area of lawn contains mature trees and herbaceous borders. Notable too are the fountain with its surround and walk festooned with wisteria, the restored rockery and grotto, the walled garden (completely replanted in 2002), and the rose gardens.

Hilton Court ★

Roch, Haverfordwest, Pembrokeshire SA62 6AE. Tel: (01437) 710262

Mr and Mrs Peter Lynch • 6m NW of Haverfordwest off A487 St Davids road. About ³/₄ m beyond Simpson Cross signed on left • Open all year, daily: Feb, 10.30am – 4pm; March to Aug, 10am – 5.30pm; Sept, 10.30am – 5pm; Oct to Dec, 10.30am – 4pm. Closed Jan • Entrance: £1 ◔ ⬤ ✕ WC ⌆ ⛫

The garden has been developed by the present owners within the framework of the 12-acre grounds of an old estate, the house dating from 1735. Several lakes have been formed and the main water areas can be viewed from the decking area next to the teashop and from the platform surrouned by two ornamental ponds. The woodland walk is 200 years old. The garden is associated with a delightful garden centre arranged in a novel way so that plants are located near others that require similar conditions. Stone out-buildings house craft workshops. The drive to the gardens has views over the cliffs and shoreline of St Bride's Bay. The coast is subject to the gales off the Irish Sea and so a feature of the nursery is a selection of plants that can withstand both wind and salt spray. Aquatic plants are also a speciality.

Maenan Hall

Llanrwst, Conwy LL26 0UL. Tel: (01492) 640441

The Hon. Mr and Mrs Christopher McLaren • 2m N of Llanrwst on E side of A470, ¹/₄ m S of Maenan Abbey Hotel • Open 25th April, 23rd May, 22nd Aug for charity, 10.30am – 5.30pm (last admission 4.30pm) • Entrance: £2.50, children £1.50 ◐ ⬤ WC &. ⬱ ⌆ ⚲

Created in 1956 by the late Christabel, Lady Aberconway are formal gardens surrounding the Elizabethan and Queen Anne house, with less formal gardens in the mature woodland beyond. Her son and daughter-in-law, the present owners, have extended the planting of ornamental trees and shrubs in both settings. Azaleas, rhododendrons and camellias, the latter situated in a dell at the base of a cliff, make a spring visit rewarding, while a large number of eucryphias are spectacular in late summer.

Museum of Welsh Life and
St Fagans Castle ★ [Welsh Historic Garden Grade I]

St Fagans, Cardiff, South Glamorgan CF5 6XB. Tel: (029) 2057 3500

National Museum of Wales • Near M4 junction 33. Signposted • Open all year, daily, 10am – 5pm or 6pm. Closed 24th to 26th Dec • Entrance: free ○ ☕ ✕ 🍴 <u>WC</u> & ◁ 🚽 💡 ♋

An historic garden with terraces, herb and knot gardens, a hornbeam tunnel, an old grove of mulberry trees and a vinery. The Rosery of 1900 has been restored with the original varieties. Mature trees, both coniferous and broad-leaved, are an impresssive feature, as are the broad high terraces with massive stone walls hosting many climbing plants. Beneath are large fish ponds containing carp, bream and tench, traditionally farmed over the years to feed the household. In the grounds rhododendrons are underplanted with spring bulbs. The range of glasshouses is in poor condition, but plans for a complete restoration are in hand. Elsewhere the restoration and replanting of the formal gardens continue to reflect the Edwardian spirit. The restored Arts and Crafts Italian garden was opened in 2003. Gardens attached to re-erected buildings from all over Wales are also being developed to re-create the differences in social status and period, using traditional horticultural techniques, tools and vegetable varieties.

National Botanic Garden of Wales ★ [Welsh Historic Garden Grade II]

Middleton Hall, Llanarthne, Carmarthenshire SA32 8HG.
Tel: (01558) 667132/667134

Trustees, NBGW • 8m E of Carmarthen, 7m W of Llandeilo off A48(M) • Open all year, daily, 10am – 6pm (last admission 1 hour before closing) • Entrance: £6.95, concessions £5, children £3.50, family £17.50 • Other information: Free buggy hire for disabled. Coaches must pre-book ● ☕ ✕ <u>WC</u> & 🚽 💡

The vast new £43-million garden, supported by £22 million from the Millennium Commission, is located at the Regency estate of Middleton Hall, deep in the beautiful Towy valley. Its scale and purpose is summed up in its centre-piece, the Great Glasshouse, a stunning 91-metre-long 'teardrop' structure designed by architects Foster and Partners. Within the world's largest single-span glasshouse, visitors can walk through and wonder at plants, landscapes and waterfalls normally found in threatened Mediterranean environments. A 300-metre-long broadwalk of herbaceous plants and flowers leads through the middle of the garden, passing the unique double-walled garden and towards the Wallace Garden, which demonstrates the history of plant genetics. Visitors can also explore a necklace of three lakes, features of the late-eighteenth-century water park, where plants cultivated in slate beds adjoin the natural setting of gentle Welsh countryside, parkland and grassland; Paxton's View, site of the former mansion, offers a panorama down the valley.

Pant-yr-Holiad ★

Rhydlewis, Llandysul, Ceredigion SA44 5ST. Tel: (01239) 851493

Mr and Mrs G. Taylor • 12m NE of Cardigan. Take A487 coast road to Brynhoffnant, then B4334 towards Rhydlewis for 1m, turn left and garden is second left • Open two Suns in spring for NGS, and at other times for pre-booked parties by appt • Entrance: £2.50, children £1 (2003 prices) ● 🍵 WC ✿

This five-acre woodland garden, created by the owners since 1971, was started in an area of natural woodland backing onto the farmhouse. Since then hundreds of rhododendrons (species and hybrids) have been planted along the banks. Acers, eucalyptus, eucryphias and many other rare and unusual trees have now reached maturity, and the paths wander in and around to give something to please the eye wherever the visitor may care to look. A stream runs through the middle of the garden, creating a boggy area which is home to iris and primulas, numerous species of ferns and a *Rhododendron macabeanum*. A fairly recent addition is a summer walk, along which slate-edged beds are filled with herbaceous plants, including a collection of penstemons. A small pergola has a rose-embowered seat from which the fine view over the valley may be enjoyed, and the remainder of the walk is beneath arches of climbing roses. Nearer the house is a walled garden, alpine beds, a series of pools for ornamental waterfowl and a *potager*-style kitchen garden.

Pencarreg ★

Glyn Garth, Menai Bridge, Gwynedd LL59 5NS. Tel: (01248) 713545

Miss G. Jones • 1½ m NE of A545 Menai Bridge towards Beaumaris. Glan y Menai drive is turning on right, Pencarreg 100 metres on right • Open all year by appt • Entrance: charity box • Other information: Parking in lay-by on main road, limited parking in courtyard for small cars and disabled ● WC ♿

This beautiful garden, with a wealth of species planted for all-year interest, has colour achieved by the use of common and unusual shrubs. A small stream creates another sympathetically exploited feature. The garden ends at the cliff edge and this, too, has been skilfully planted. The views are remarkable.

Penlan-Uchaf Farm Gardens

Gwaun Valley, Fishguard, Pembrokeshire SA65 9UA. Tel: (01348) 881388

Mr and Mrs Vaughan • 7m SE of Fishguard, 4m S of Newport. From Fishguard take B4313 Narberth road and after 4m turn left signed to Cwm Gwaun/Gwaun Valley (Pontvane). From Newport take Gwaun Valley road. Next to Sychpant Forest car park • Open 7th March to Nov (weather permitting), daily, 9am – dusk •

Entrance: £2.50, children 50p, disabled persons and children under 3 free • Other information: Cars carrying wheelchairs may set down at main garden. Up to 22-seater coaches and minibuses permitted ❶ 🍵 🏞 WC ⏀ ⌀ ℺

A medium-sized garden on a hillside near the top of the Gwaun Valley. The drive is very steep, but the view from the tea room is worth the effort. This is a young garden but the owners, realising that its position will make many trees and shrubs an impossibility, have chosen alpines and herbaceous borders and planted a 27-metre pergola with sweet peas. There are some 30,000 spring bulbs, and fuchsias, geraniums and annuals give plenty of colour later. A raised herb garden, suitable for wheelchair visitors and the blind, contains more than 100 different herbs and wild flowers.

Penpergwm Lodge

Abergavenny, Monmouthshire NP7 9AS. Tel: (01873) 840208

Mrs C. Boyle • 2½ m SE of Abergavenny off B4598 Usk road. Turn left opposite King of Prussia Inn. Entrance 300 metres on left • Open April to Sept, Thurs – Sun, 2 – 6pm • Entrance: £2.50 • Other information: Teas on Sat and Sun only ❶ 🍵 WC ⏀ ⌀ ℺ B&B

This spacious three-acre garden forms the centrepiece for an established and successful school of gardening, which offers day-long workshops. Broad south-facing terraces command views over wide expanses of lawn well screened by mature trees and shrubs. A vine pergola makes a bold statement and provides a visual link with the house, while a formal garden of yew and box creates a delightful and effective enclosure. Old-fashioned roses, herbaceous perennials and an imaginative vegetable garden contribute interest throughout the season. The nursery sells unusual plants. A folly tower adds a new dimension to the garden.

Penrhyn Castle ★ [Welsh Historic Garden Grade II*]

Bangor, Gwynedd LL57 4HN. Tel: (01248) 353084

The National Trust • 1m E of Bangor on A5122 • Castle open 12 noon – 5pm (opens 11am July, Aug) • Garden open 27th March to Oct, daily except Tues, 11am – 5pm (opens 10am July, Aug) • Entrance: £5, children £2.50 (castle and garden £7, children £3.50, family £17.50, parties £5.50 per person) • Other information: Golf buggy available if pre-booked ❶ 🍵 ✕ 🏞 WC ♿ ⏀ 🍴 ℺

The large garden covers 48 acres with some fine specimen trees, shrubs and a Victorian walled garden in terraces with pools, lawns and a wild garden. Although the original house dated from the eighteenth century, the gardens are very much early-Victorian, contemporary with the present castle designed by Thomas Hopper. A giant tree fern, which will dwarf any children who visit, has been sent from Tasmania to take its place in a specialist collection that also includes another giant, gunnera, and the Australian bottle brush plant. These can be found in the spectacular bog garden beyond the walled garden.

Picton Castle ★ [Welsh Historic Garden Grade II*]

Haverfordwest, Pembrokeshire SA62 4AS. Tel: (01437) 751326

Picton Castle Trust • 4m SE of Haverfordwest off A40. Signposted • Castle open for conducted tours April to Sept. Telephone for details • Garden open April to Oct, daily except Mon (but open Bank Holiday Mons), 10.30am – 5pm • Entrance: gardens and gallery £3.95, OAPs £3.75, children £1.95 (castle, gardens and gallery £4.95, OAPs £4.75, children £1.95) ◑ ⬛ ✕ 🍽 <u>WC</u> ♿ ⬦ ⌁ 🏛 🔦 🜊

The grounds extend over nearly 40 acres, with woodland walks among massive oaks and giant redwoods. Rarities include the biggest *Rhododendron* 'Old Port' in existence and a metasequoia, a deciduous conifer presumed extinct but rediscovered in China in 1941. In June all these exotic shrubs reach their full splendour. In the walled garden are herb borders and summer-flowering plants, with a pond and fountain creating a cool and calming atmosphere.

Plas Brondanw ★ [Welsh Historic Garden Grade I]

Llanfrothen, Penrhyndeudraeth, Gwynedd LL48 6SW. Tel: (07880) 766741

5m NE of Porthmadog between Llanfrothen and Croesor • Open all year, daily, 10am – 5pm • Entrance: £1.50, children 25p ○ **WC**

This garden, in the grounds of the house given to Sir Clough Williams-Ellis by his father, is quite separate from the village of Portmeirion (see entry), and was created by the architect over a period of seventy years. His main objective was to provide a series of dramatic and romantic prospects inspired by the great gardens of Italy; it includes architectural features, such as the orangery. Visitors should walk up the avenue that leads past a dramatic chasm to the folly, from which there is a fine view of Snowdon – indeed mountains are visible from the end of every vista. Williams-Ellis made a prodigious investment in hedging and topiary (mostly yew) and the present head gardener has calculated that the former, if laid flat, would cover four acres. Hydrangeas and ferns flourish in the damp climate.

Plas Newydd ★ [Welsh Historic Garden Grade I]

Llanfairpwll, Anglesey LL61 6DQ. Tel: (01248) 714795

The National Trust • 4m SW of Menai Bridge, 2m S of Llanfairpwll via A5 • House with military museum open as gardens, 12 noon – 5pm • Garden open 27th March to 3rd Nov, Sat – Wed and Good Friday, 11am – 5.30pm (last admission 4.30pm). Rhododendron garden open April to early June only. Guided tours by arrangement • Entrance: £3, children £1.50 (house and gardens £5, children £2.50, family £12, pre-booked parties of 15 or more £4.50 per person) • Other information: Parking ¼ m from house. Complimentary minibus service between car park and house, and shuttle service available in garden ◑ ⬛ ✕ 🍽 <u>WC</u> ♿ ⬦ 🏛 🔦 🜊

The eighteenth-century house by James Wyatt is worth visiting, mainly to see Rex Whistler's largest painting. Humphry Repton's suggestion of 'plantations . . . to soften a bleak country and shelter the ground from violent winds' has resulted in an informal open-plan garden, with shrub plantings in the lawns and parkland, which slopes down to the Menai Strait and frames the view of the Snowdonia peaks. There is a formal Italian-style garden to the front of the house. A new arbour has replaced a conservatory on the top terrace with a tufa mound, from which water falls to a pool on the bottom terrace. The pool has a new Italianate fountain to add to the overall Mediterranean effect of this formal area within the parkland. The influence of the Gulf Stream enables the successful cultivation of many frost-tender shrubs, and a special rhododendron garden is open in the spring when the gardens are at their best, although they are expertly tended throughout the year. Major restoration of the Italianate terrace garden continues and includes the building of a deep grotto and the replanting of the mixed borders. The marine and woodland paths along the Menai Straits have also been restored. Summer brings displays of hydrangeas, while autumn colour appears in the ever-changing arboretum of southern-hemisphere trees and shrubs, and wild flowers appear in their seasons. There is an adventure trail for children.

Plas-yn-Rhiw [Welsh Historic Garden Grade II]

Pwllheli, Gwynedd LL53 8AB. Tel: (01758) 780219

The National Trust • Near tip of Lleyn Peninsular. 16m SW of Pwllheli, take A499 and B4413. Signposted at Botwnnog • House open (numbers limited) • Garden and snowdrop wood open some weekends Jan and Feb (telephone to check); also open 27th March to May, daily except Tues and Wed; 2nd June to 1st Oct, daily except Tues; 2nd to 24th Oct, Sat and Sun only; 25th to 31st Oct, Mon – Fri; all 12 noon – 5pm • Entrance: £2, children £1; garden and snowdrop wood £2.50 (house and garden £3.40, children £1.70, family ticket £8. Pre-booked evening parties £1.40 extra per person) • Other information: Parking 80 metres from garden. No coaches ◑ 🛍 **WC** 🌿 ♿ 🔦

This is essentially a cottage garden, laid out around a partly medieval manor house on the west shore of Hell's Mouth Bay. Flowering trees and shrubs, rhododendrons, camellias and magnolias are divided by formal box hedges and grass paths extending to three quarters of an acre. A snowdrop wood stands on high ground above the garden.

Portmeirion ★ [Welsh Historic Garden Grade II*]

Penrhyndeudraeth, Gwynedd LL48 6ET. Tel: (01766) 770228 (Hotel Reception)

2m SE of Porthmadog near A487 • Open all year, daily except 25th Dec, 9.30am – 5.30pm • Entrance: £5.50, OAPs £4.20, children £2.60, under 5 free, family £12.60, season ticket £35 (2003 prices) • Other information: Parking at top of village. Difficult for wheelchairs as steep in places ○ 🍽 ✕ 🛍 **WC** 🌿 ♿ ⚲

Architect Sir Clough Williams-Ellis's wild essay into the picturesque is a triumph of eclecticism, with Gothick, Renaissance and Victorian buildings arranged as an Italianate village around a harbour and set in 70 acres of sub-tropical woodlands criss-crossed by paths. This light opera is played out against the backdrop of the Cambrian mountains and the vast empty sweep of estuary sands. The gentle humour of the architecture extends to the plantings in both horizontal and vertical planes – in the formal gardens and in the wild luxuriance which clings to the rocky crags. Portmeirion provides one of Britain's most stimulating objects for an excursion, and during the period of the June festival in nearby Criccieth there are other good gardens open in the district. Write for details (with s.a.e.) to Criccieth Festival Office, PO Box 3, 52 High Street, Criccieth LL52 0BW.

Powis Castle and Garden ★★ [Welsh Historic Garden Grade I]

Welshpool, Powys SY21 8RF. Tel: (01938) 551929

The National Trust • ¾ m S of Welshpool on A483. Signposted • Castle open, 1 – 5pm • Garden open 31st March to June, Wed – Sun and Bank Holiday Mons; July, Aug, Tues – Sun and Bank Holiday Mon; Sept to Oct, Wed – Sun; all 11am – 6pm • Entrance: £5.75, children (5–16) £2.75, under 5 free, family £14, parties £4.75 per person (castle, garden and museum £8.25, children (5–16) £4, under 5 free, family £20.50, parties £7.25 per person) • Other information: Events programme and guided tours of garden – telephone for details. Picnics in park outside garden only. Problematic for wheelchairs and pushchairs as very steep with steps ◑ ☕ ✗ <u>WC</u> ♿ ⌖ 🛒 ⚲

The garden was originally laid out in the 1680s, based on formal designs by William Winde, who had just finished at Cliveden (see entry in Buckinghamshire) – another cliff-hanger. The most notable features are the broad hanging terraces, interestingly planted and with huge clipped yews. The terraces are inspired by those of the Palace of St Germain-en-Laye near Paris, where the 1st Marquis of Powis joined James II in exile in 1689. On the second terrace, above the orangery, are fine urns. Statuary by van Nost's workshop stands in front of the deeply recessed brick alcoves of the aviary. The late-eighteenth-century changes to the garden as a result of the English landscape style are attributed to William Emes. Advantage was taken of the many microclimates to develop the ornamental plantings during the nineteenth century, and the kitchen garden of the lower garden was transformed into a formal flower garden in 1911 by Lady Violet, wife of the 4th Earl. Unusual and tender plants and climbers now prosper in the shelter of the walls and hedges. The planting schemes are superb. The box-edged terraces have notable displays of clematis and pittosporums; in season *Abutilon vitifolium* 'Tennant's White' matched with *Rosa banksiae* 'Lutea' and *R.* 'Gloire de Dijon' are inspiring, the collection of ceanothus cloaking the terraces magnificent; in late summer the eucryphias repeat the performance. The basket-weave terracotta pots continue to be planted with a masterly touch. The more recent gardens below, lying towards the Severn valley, are planted with old-fashioned roses and cottage-garden plants, with arches of vines continuing the formality in enclosed hedged rooms. This garden is not for the faint-hearted because it is very steep, but it is well worth the effort to enjoy the views which are as fine as any, anywhere.

Ridler's Garden ★

St Peter's, Terrace, Swansea SA2 0FW. Tel: (01792) 588217

Mr and Mrs Tony Ridler • At M4 Junction 47 turn S on A483. After 3m turn right at traffic lights opposite carpet warehouse; at next traffic lights turn left. Entrance to garden is off footpath for Cockett Pond play area • Open for NGS 2nd May, 6th June, 4th July, 2 – 5pm, and by appt • Entrance: £2 NEW ● ▣ WC

Behind his modest terraced house in the suburbs of Swansea, graphic designer Tony Ridler has created within half an acre one of the most exciting gardens you are likely to see. The drama of the place engages you from the moment you enter, when you are faced with a formal avenue of yew containing a sea of box balls and standard Portuguese laurels clipped neatly into lollipops. In an enclosed compartment off this avenue are exquisitely crafted topiary spirals mulched with white cockleshells. Further paths create new vistas, mostly with focal points of sculpture. Plants, although chosen with care and forethought, play a supporting role – they are there to emphasise and complement the atmosphere, mostly used in blocks and with repetition. The black-painted walls used to define some of the spaces and boundaries make a strikingly successful backdrop to the planting. Beyond a quiet courtyard of grass squares and sculpture, the formal kitchen garden is the most intensively planted area. Topiary pyramids and standard gooseberries add height, and the alternating purple and green foliage of the vegetables reinforces the overall impression of symmetry and order.

Singleton Botanic Gardens ★

Singleton Park, Swansea, West Glamorgan SA2 9DU. Tel: (01792) 298637

Swansea City Council • In Swansea. Entrance in Gower Road • Open all year, daily, 9am – 6pm (4.30pm in winter) • Entrance: free • Other information: Refreshments during Aug only ○ WC &

A four-and-a-half-acre garden with herbaceous borders, rockeries, rose beds and an interesting collection of trees and shrubs, including tapestry hedges using a variety of different shrubs. Newly erected temperate and tropical glasshouses contain an extensive range of rare and unusual plants, including orchids, bromeliads and epiphytes. While in Swansea, visit the 1600-square-metre hothouse *Plantasia*. Divided into arid, tropical and humid zones, it contains over 5000 plants and much wildlife. [Signed from city centre and open all year, daily except Mondays.]

Tredegar House [Welsh Historic Park Grade II*]

Newport, Gwent NP10 8YW. Tel: (01633) 815880

Newport City Council • 3m S of Newport. Signed from A48 and M4 junction 28 • House open April to Sept, Wed – Sun, 11.30am – 4pm • Park open daily, dawn – dusk • Entrance: free; house £5.25, OAPs £3.85, children free (2003 prices) • Other information: Dogs in park only, on lead ◑ ▣ ▧ WC & ⬥ ⬛ ♙ ⚲

Behind the impressive Restoration house and its adjacent orangery and stables are three large walled enclosures. This is the main gardened area. The middle one is dominated by an ancient cedar of Lebanon and several mature magnolias; at the base of the walls a herbaceous border is designed to have colour throughout the summer and autumn months. On one side of this enclosure is the orchard and the head gardener's cottage. But the most interesting area is the Orangery Garden on the other side. Here, recent archaeological excavations revealed the remnant of a massive late seventeenth-century mineral parterre. This unique find has been reconstructed using coal, sand, gravels and sea shells and is punctuated by carefully clipped standards of box. Two large *Magnolia grandiflora* stand at the entrance to the orangery.

Upton Castle [Welsh Historic Garden Grade II]

Cosheston, Pembroke Dock, Pembrokeshire SA72 4SE. Tel: (01646) 651782

Canon and Mrs H.J.N. Skelton • 2m NE of Pembroke off A477. In Cosheston turn right. Castle signed on left • Open April to Oct, daily except Sat, 10am – 5pm, but check before travelling • Entrance: £2, children £1, family £5. Season tickets available • Other information: Approach roads very narrow. No coaches ◑ ▓ WC ⑇ ⇦

The grounds of the part-thirteenth-century castle were planted as a garden in the 1930s with a large collection of rhododendrons and camellia species and hybrids of the period. These have grown into large mature specimens to which the Pembrokeshire Coast National Park, which has a management agreement with the owners, has added new cultivars. Large specimens of redwood, drimys and chestnut-leaved oak, embothriums and a particularly magnificent *Magnolia campbellii*, planted in 1936, and *Davidia involucrata*, planted in 1968, are among the 250 or more kinds of trees and shrubs growing in the grounds. A walk through the woods leads down to the Carew River. The old walled garden is now mostly grass, with fruit and vegetables and two greenhouses. There are also formal terraces with herbaceous borders and rose beds, and a medieval chapel.

Veddw House ★

Devauden, Monmouthshire NP16 6PH. Tel: (01291) 650836

Anne Wareham and Charles Hawes • 5m NW of Chepstow off B4293. In Devauden, signed from pub on green • Open June to Aug, Sun and Bank Holiday Mons, 2 – 5pm, and for parties of 10 or more afternoons or evenings by appt April to Sept • Entrance: £3.50, children £1 (2003 prices) ◑ ▓ WC ⑇ ⑨

Situated on a sheltered slope near the Wye Valley, framed by old beech woods and with views in all directions, this garden is the product of enthusiastic labour by the owners since 1987. There are two acres of flower garden and meadow and two acres of woodland where the trees are embellished by decorative plaques and quotations. The generously planted borders include repeat plantings of many unusual varieties, and around every corner is something of interest – a magnolia walk, a cotoneaster walk with rampant rambler roses growing through it, a philadelphus border. In front of the house four rectangular beds are punctuated by balls of clipped evergreens; nearby is a grey border. The formal vegetable garden is enclosed by borders of old scented roses and 40 varieties of clematis on trellis and arches. From here an arch leads into the orchard and the meadow, full of bulbs in spring and grasses and wild flowers in summer. Behind the house the ground slopes steeply upwards, with paths and steps leading to viewpoints. Yew hedges enclose a formal garden planted with cornfield annuals, and a new garden has been created with a black reflecting pool and a seat with an arching back that echoes curves found elsewhere in the garden – in long low paths and a sinuous beech hedge. Overlooking these gardens is another fascinating parterre, where box hedges form compartments replicating the 1824 tithe map of the area. The spaces between are filled with a variety of grasses. Further up still is a hazel coppice and the wood with its superb old beech trees, sorbus and hornbeam.

Whimble Garden and Nursery

Kinnerton, Presteigne, Powys LD8 2PD. Tel: (01547) 560413

E.M. Taylor and R.T. Lancett • 6m W of Presteigne; signposted from A44 at Walton (going from Kington towards Rhayader) • Open April to mid-October, Wed – Sun and Bank Holiday Mons, 10.30am – 5.30pm • Entrance: free
◑ ☕ WC ♿

Tucked away on a south-facing slope of the Radnor Valley, this small but richly planted garden is not only a most effective shop window for the adjoining nursery but a joy in its own right. Specialising in unusual herbaceous plants and climbers, everything is carefully chosen for beauty of colour and form. An airy 'church' made from wire mesh creates an eccentric and attractive framework for many varieties of climbing rose and rare clematis – the latter one of the nursery's specialities. The views of the surrounding hills are spectacular, and the adjoining meadow not only boasts a newly created nuttery but a 'pre-historic' earthwork. A subtle tapestry of colour throughout the season (appropriate as the owner's winter job is restoring old carpets), this is an inspiring and satisfying garden to visit – you will not go home empty-handed!

Wyndcliffe Court [Welsh Historic Garden Grade II*]

St Arvans, Chepstow, Monmouthshire NP16 6EY. Tel: (01291) 622352

Mr and Mrs H.A.P. Clay • Off Wye Valley road from Chepstow • Open 1st June for NGS, 8th July, 5th Aug, various days for charity, and by appt for private parties • Entrance: £2.50 • Other information: Garden only accessible for wheelchairs on terrace ◕ ☕ WC ♿

An Arts and Crafts house designed by Eric Francis, with a landscape garden to match created by Avray Tipping. The house and its garden date from 1922, and although maintenance is not up to the high standards of that period it is worth visiting as a period piece that has remained largely unchanged. From a broad paved terrace, two flights of steps descend to the topiary terrace with its semi-circular pool; the topiary yew drums are matched by ten rectangular beds of annuals. The next level is a bowling green. Beyond the charming summerhouse is a sunken garden with a long rectangular pool. Long herbaceous borders lead to the large walled vegetable garden, much of it devoted to flowers and shrubs. Fine views.

CHANNEL ISLANDS

GUERNSEY AND SARK

Candie Gardens

Candie Road, St Peter Port GY1 1UG. Tel: (01481) 720904

States of Guernsey • In St Peter Port, off Candie Road • Open all year, daily, 8am – sunset (5pm in winter) • Entrance: free • Other information: Teas, toilet facilities, (inc. disabled), shop and events in Guernsey Museum and Art Gallery ○ ☕ 🏬 WC & 🐟 🏧 🎪 ⚲

Situated on a slope overlooking the harbour at St Peter Port, there are wonderful views over the islands of Herm and Sark from the gardens. Created over 100 years ago, they contain statues of Queen Victoria and Victor Hugo, who lived on Guernsey in exile from 1855 to 1871. The Lower Gardens used to be the walled fruit and vegetable garden of Candie House (now the Priaulx Library) but were remodelled as a public garden in 1887. A rare surviving example of a Victorian public flower garden, they have been sympathetically restored. Guernsey's mild climate and the shelter afforded by the garden walls has enabled many varieties of exotic plants from all over the world to be grown, including a magnificent Canary palm considered to be the largest in the British Isles, a huge *Gingko biloba*, camellias, rhododendrons, ferns, aquatics and a South African bulb collection which originated in the late nineteenth century. The gardens also contain herbaceous borders and two 1792 show glasshouses in an excellent state of preservation. The Guernsey Museum and Art Gallery, built around an original Victorian bandstand, and the Priaulx Reference and Genealogical Library are here.

The Hermitage

Les Maindonnaux, St Martin GY4 6AJ.
Tel: (01481) 237035 or Guernsey Tourist Information (01481) 723552

Anne and Tony Curr • 1½ m S of St Peter Port • Open one or two days a year, and for private parties by appt • Entrance: £3 ● WC &

Dating from the 1750s, the house is surrounded by about three acres of landscaped gardens, dominated by a very tall Monterey cypress some 200 years old. From this vantage point visitors can view a small lake surrounded by giant gunneras, ligularias and other moisture-loving plants, fed by freshwater springs to the obvious enjoyment of the resident ducks and moorhens. Nearby azaleas, rhododendrons, camellias and fuchsias grow in abundance in a woodland setting. A walled garden offers shelter to fine specimens of *Cestrum elegans*, *Clethra arborea*, *Clianthus puniceus*, *Crinodendron hookerianum*, giant echiums and many other unusual shrubs and perennials.

Mille Fleurs

Rue du Bordage, St Pierre du Bois GY7 9DW. Tel: (01481) 263911

Mr and Mrs D. Russell • 6m SW of St Peter Port. 100 metres down lane from Rue de Quanteraine/Rue du Bordage junction • Open one or two days a year, and for parties by appt • Entrance: £3.50 • Other information: Self-catering cottages available ◑

Natural country gardens of some three acres set in a peaceful, wooded conservation valley. The areas around the house and holiday cottages are a profusion of roses, clematis, penstemons and other herbaceous perennials, with sweetly scented honeysuckle and jasmine framing arches and doorways. Paths flanked by lilies, lavender and other fragrant plants meander down to the bottom of the valley, where more tender, sub-tropical plants flourish in the sheltered microclimate. A natural spring feeds into two ponds surrounded by mature tree ferns and giant gunneras amid huge stands of arum lilies. A large mature fig tree and a host of terracotta pots brimming with red pelargoniums and cordylines, together with banks of crocosmias, phormiums and euphorbias, lend a Mediterranean feel to the swimming-pool area.

La Petite Vallée

Rue de Putron, St Peter Port GY1 2TE. Tel: (01481) 238866

Mrs Jennifer Monachan • 2m S of central St Peter Port • Open occasionally for charity – check with local paper or tourist information office (Tel: (01481) 726611) ◑ WC ♿

This is a garden full of surprises and excitement, since it reflects the enthusiasm and passions that the owner has lavished on this three-acre valley going down towards the sea. Wildflower meadows, shrubberies, rose gardens, a folly, a stream, along with herb, water and terrace gardens all flow into each other with effortless ease. One of the best in the Channel Islands.

Les Prés de Jerbourg

St Martin GY4 6BN. Tel: (01481) 236158

Paul Chilcott • Drive to Jerbourg Point car park; garden is at end of little cliff road • Open April to Sept, daily, 2 – 5pm, and by appt • Entrance: £2, children free (all donations to local charities) ◑ WC ♿ ✿ ☕

A series of gardens has remarkably been created since 1988 from a couple of clifftop fields on one of the most exposed positions in the islands, using sycamore, Scots pine (which figures in a painting by Renoir) and blackthorn as windbreaks. It is well worth the 400-metre walk just for the views over virtually all the other islands and France. The garden has now expanded to include a Japanese garden, a meadow area, rock, gravel and rose gardens. There are also shrubberies and a conservatory, and the owner continues to take in more land as further windbreaks come into effect. The plants and shrubs native to warmer parts of the world, new to many British gardeners, are particularly interesting, not only from a colour combination and aesthetic point of view, but because of their resistance to high winds off the sea.

Sausmarez Manor Exotic Woodland Garden

St Martins, Guernsey GY4 6SG. Tel: (01481) 235571

Mr Peter de Sausmarez • $1\frac{1}{2}$ m S of St Peter Port, off Fort Road • Manor open mid-week in summer • Garden open all year, daily, 10.30am – 5.30pm (or dusk if earlier). Guided tours for parties by appt • Entrance: £3, OAPs/children £2.50, disabled persons and babies free • Other information: Rare plant sale 31st May. Doll's house collection. Pitch and putt course. Sculpture park, ride-on trains. Available for holiday let ○ 🍽 ✕ WC ♿ 🏛 ♨ ⚲

Set around two small lakes in an ancient wood is a garden which has been crammed with the unusual and rare to give an exotic feel. It is strewn with plants from many parts of the world, particularly the sub-tropics and the Mediterranean, which survive in Guernsey's mellow maritime climate. Collections of yuccas, ferns, camellias (over 300), bamboos, hebes, bananas, echiums, lilies, palm trees, fuchsias, as well as hydrangeas, hostas, azaleas, pittosporums, clematis, rhododendrons, cyclamens, impatiens, giant grasses etc., all jostle with indigenous wild flowers. No pesticides are used so wildlife flourishes. A new poetry trail winds through the wood. Also here is the Art Park, showing around 200 pieces of sculpture by about 90 British, European, African, American and local artists, all for sale.

La Seigneurie

Sark GY9 OSF. Tel: (01481) 832345 (Sark Tourism)

Seigneur Mr J.M. Beaumont • $\frac{1}{2}$ m NW of Creux Harbour, Sark • Open 14th April to 24th Oct, Mon – Fri, 10am – 5pm, and Sat, July to Sept for charity • Entrance: £1.20, children 60p ◑ WC ♿ ⚲

The grounds and walled garden of La Seigneurie, the residence of the Seigneurs of Sark, are beautifully maintained. Visit in spring and early summer for the camellias, azaleas and rhododendrons, later for roses, old-fashioned annuals, and in autumn for the glowing colours of dahlias and fuchsias. The walled garden contains clematis, geraniums, lapagerias, abutilons, osteospermums and many sub-tropical and tender plants. There is a *potager*, a wild pond area, a restored Victorian greenhouse with vines and bougainvilleas, a hedge maze for children, and a small outdoor museum with antique cannons. The Gothick *colombier* may still be seen behind the house.

JERSEY

Creux Baillot Cottage

Le Chemin des Garennes, St Ouen JE3 2FE. Tel: (01534) 482191

Judith Quérée • $\frac{1}{4}$ m N of St Ouen. Location map provided or directions given when booking made • Open May to Sept, Tues, Wed, Thurs, 11am and 2pm (or by arrangement), by appt only for conducted tours • Entrance £4 ◑ ⚲

This garden, largely laid out as a cottage garden, belongs to a dedicated plantsperson. With 1700 different species and cultivars, it is a living encyclopaedia of the rare and unusual packed into a ¼ –acre site in a secluded valley. To name but a few, there are 170 different clematis, 25 species of corydalis, 50 types of iris. An unusual feature with a charming sculpture, a curtain of chains for climbers, a raised walkway through a bog garden with a small wooden boat and a collection of anchors lend nautical and humorous touches to a serious garden.

Domaine Des Vaux

La Rue de Bas, St Lawrence JE3 1JG.

Mr and Mrs Marcus Binney • 2m N of St Helier • Open one Sun, 2 – 5pm, for charity (check with Jersey Tourist Board (01534) 500700). Private parties by prior arrangement with owners in writing • Entrance: £4 (2003 price) ● ☕ ▨ **WC** ⬥ ☂

Marcus Binney, architectural correspondent of *The Times*, has a passion for the preservation of architecture and landscape, and these tastes are very much reflected in his and his wife Anne's delightful garden. It is in two completely contrasting parts. The top is a formal Italianate garden, set around and above a sunken rectangular lawn, and the borders here are a riot of unusual and familiar perennials and shrubs. This perfect formal garden was created by the previous generation, Sir George and Lady Binney, and designed by Walter Ison. Lady Binney planted with an eye for colour in foliage as much as in flowers, as is evidenced by the grey and silver borders facing the yellow, gold and bronze ones. The Binneys have planted a small formal herb garden on a triangular theme and have created a *jardinière* and a pair of long flower borders. The lower garden is a semi-wild and quite steep valley with a string of ponds connected by a stream. In spring the valley and wood are at their best, with a carpet of wild Jersey narcissi under camellias, azaleas and rhododendrons. A magnificent *Magnolia campbellii* has reached maturity and flowers abundantly in March. Of particular note are the camellias in both gardens and an interesting collection of conifers, and other trees planted to give year-round foliage colour in a small arboretum. A newly created Mediterranean Garden stands at the top of the valley with a collection of planted pots which reflect the colours of the south of France and Italy.

Eric Young Orchid Foundation

Victoria Village, Trinity JE3 5HH. Tel: (01534) 861963

The Eric Young Charitable Trust • 1½ m N of St Helier • Open all year except 1st Jan, 25th, 26th Dec, Wed – Sat, 10am – 4pm • Entrance: £2.50, OAPs £1.50, students £1.50, children £1 • Other information: Plants for sale when available ○ ☕ ▨ **WC** ♿ ⬥ ♨ ⬛

This exquisite collection, described as 'the finest private collection of orchids in Europe, possibly the world', was built up by the late Eric Young, who came to Jersey after World War II. In 1958 he merged his own collection with that of a Sanders nursery which was closing down, and continued to acquire new plants. The purpose-built centre, which has won many awards, consists of eight growing houses and a landscaped display area where visitors may view these exotic flowers in close detail. From November to April there are cymbidiums, paphiopedilums, odontoglossums and calanthes, from May to June cattleyas, miltonias and odontoglossums and from June to October, phalaenopsis, miltonias and odontoglossums. (The beauty of these flowers is inversely proportional to the difficulty of their names.)

Howard Davis Park

St Saviour.

In St Helier, between St Clement's Road and Don Road • Open all year, daily: Oct to March, 8.30am – 4.30pm; April to May, 8am – 8pm; June to Sept, 8am – 10pm • Entrance: free (charge for bandstand seats) ○ 🍽 ✕ 🥪 WC ♿ 🚻 ☕

Given by T.B. Davis, a great benefactor of the island, in memory of his son who was killed in World War I, this is the most famous of Jersey's public gardens. Colourful sub-tropical trees and plants flourish here, and the bandstand is the venue for an excellent variety of live entertainment from May to September. Other public parks in St Helier are Parade Gardens, off Parade Place, and Victoria Park, off St Aubins Road/Cheapside. Both contain interesting statues.

Jersey Lavender

Rue du Pont Marquet, St Brelade JE3 8DS. Tel: (01534) 742933

Alastair and Eleanor Christie • 3m W of St Helier near Pont Marquet Country Park • Open 10th May to 18th Sept, Mon – Sat, 10am – 5pm • Entrance: £3, children free ◐ 🍽 ✕ WC ♿ 🛍 🏵 ⛪ ☕

This lavender farm was started in 1983 and now covers nine acres. Visitors are invited to walk around the main fields, planted with six varieties of lavender, to enjoy their different colours and scents. Harvesting starts in late June, and the distillation and perfume-bottling processes may be seen. There is an extensive garden of herbs, including a National Collection of lavenders and a collection of 75 different species of bamboos.

Jersey Zoological Park

Les Augres Manor, Trinity JE3 5BP. Tel: (01534) 860000

Durrell Wildlife Conservation Trust • 2½ m NW of St Helier on B361 • Open daily except 25th Dec, 9.30am – 6pm or dusk if earlier • Entrance: £9, OAPs £7.50, children £6.50. Parties of 10 or more £2 less per person ○ 🍽 ✕ 🥪 WC ♿ ⛪ 🚻 ☕

Over 100 rare and endangered species of animals reside within the 31 acres of parkland and water gardens. The late author and naturalist Gerald Durrell founded the Zoo as a sanctuary forty years ago. Today Sumatran orang-utans, Andean bears and Montserrat orioles, rescued from beneath the smouldering volcano, live in lush, spacious environments, which closely replicate their native habitats. Madagascar lemurs and tiny lion tamarins from Brazil live free in the Zoo's woodland, leaping through the trees.

Samarès Manor

St Clement JE2 6QW. Tel: (01534) 870551

Vincent Obbard • 2m E of St Helier • Manor (guided tours mornings daily except Sun, £1.95 extra) open • Garden open 12th April to 11th Oct, daily, 10am – 5pm • Entrance: £4.95, OAPs £4.50, children £1.95, under 5 free • Other information: Craft centre ◑ 💟 ✕ 🍱 <u>WC</u> ⬤ 🌿 🏬 🎪 ℃

The name Samares is derived from the French for salt marsh, and indeed sea salt was once extracted from marshy land nearby. It is not known who built the existing manor house, which has passed through many owners, but the grounds have developed gradually. By 1680 they were famed for their trees. The present garden was the work of Sir James Knott, who bought the property in 1924 and had it developed, employing 40 gardeners, at a cost of £100,000. Two quite different gardens here: a herb garden specialising in culinary and medicinal herbs in a partially walled garden leading to a lakeside area, and a Japanese garden. Of particular note are the camellias, the *Taxodium distichum* in the lake and the rocks imported from Cumberland.

Les Vaux

Rozel Valley, St Martins JE3 6AJ. Tel: (01534) 861102

Rhona, Lady Guthrie • 6m NE of St Helier • Open March to Sept for parties by appt • Entrance: £3 • Other information: Garden steep in parts, so not ideal for unfit or disabled visitors ⬤ 🍱 WC ⬤ ⬦ ℃

Sheltered within a steep-sided valley, the garden encompasses a variety of styles and an eclectic range of trees, shrubs, herbaceous plants and sculptures. The owner's artistry and love of unusual plants is lavished around lawns and bare rocks, on serene slopes and in richly filled shrubberies and borders. Now the garden has been increased in size with a new area which includes a couple of small lakes linked by a stream and bordered by saplings to form a nature reserve garden. Red squirrels are already regular visitors.

SYMBOLS
NEW entries new for 2004; ○ open all year; ◐ open most of year; ◑ open during main season; ⬤ open rarely and/or by appt; 💟 teas/light refreshments; ✕ meals; 🍱 picnics permitted; WC toilet facilities; <u>WC</u> toilet facilities, inc. disabled; ⬤ partly wheelchair-accessible; ⬦ dogs on lead; 🌿 plants for sale; 🏬 shop; 🎪 events held; ℃ children-friendly; B&B bed and breakfast available.

EUROPE

Throughout the *Guide* two-starred gardens are marked on the maps with a bold square.

For some years the *Guide* has included a selection of gardens in Europe, concentrating on those which are a reasonable distance from the Channel ports or some other points of entry such as a Eurostar station.

FRANCE

Paris Gardens

Central Paris: *The Tuileries Garden* near the Louvre (being restored, including *Le Jardin du Carrousel*. Christopher Bradley-Hole in his description has written that the Wirtz family 'have used yew hedges, planted in an extensive *patte d'oie* converging on the Arc de Triomphe, to make sense of some of the disparate geometry of the site'); *Parc Monçeau* on boulevard. de Courcelles (nineteenth-century nannyland); *The Luxembourg Gardens* on the Left Bank (*grandeur ancienne*); *The Fondation Cartier* has a gallery and garden for *'l'art contemporain'* at 261 boulevard Raspail (Tel: 42.18.56.51). Here Patrick Blanc has created a spectacular jungle-like hanging garden above the entrance which links the boulevard trees to the Fondation's rear garden; *Jardin des Plantes* also on the Left Bank, Pont d'Austerlitz; *Place des Vosges*, which landscape architect Gordon Haynes calls 'a masterpiece' of design and an excellent venue for picnics purchased in rue St Antoine and rue Birague to the south. An exhibition was held in 2000 at *Bagatelle* near the Trianon and this may be a regular event; there is also an elegant rose garden there.

Inner suburbs: *Parc André Citroën* (the most exciting modern park in Paris); *Jardin Albert Kahn* at Boulogne Billancourt (several gardens including an authentic Japanese garden); *Fondation Cartier Sculpture Garden* in Jovy-en-Jonas (20 minutes by train or RER line B. Good café). In the Marais is a new garden, simple and elegant, dedicated to the late Diana, Princess of Wales.

Outer suburbs: *Parc Caillebotte*, Yerres, near Orly (garden of the painter who launched Monet); *Roseraie de L'Hay les Roses* (famous rose garden in the corner of a large municipal park near Orly); *La Bagatelle* on the edge of the Bois de Boulogne in Neuilly (perhaps the most elegant display of roses in the world).

Ile de France: *Château de St Jean de Beauregard*, 28km S of Paris at Les Ulis (one of the best *potagers*), which hosts an annual plant fair (telephone 1.60.12.00.01 for details).

Shows

Two other major garden events are held every year within reasonable distance of Paris. Les Journées de Plantes de Courson is held every May and October (now in its eighteenth year) in the seventeenth-century Château de Courson, 35km south of Paris. Dubbed the 'French Chelsea', this is an international plant sale with exhibitors and nurserymen from all over Europe, organised by the château owners, Patrice and Hélène Fustier, who were awarded the RHS Gold

Veitch medal in 1993. To reach Courson from Paris, take the train (line C RER) from Alma, Les Invalides or Austerlitz stations to Breuillet or Bruyères-Le-Châtel on Dourden route (first four carriages of train only), then shuttle bus or taxi from Breuillet to Courson (6km). For 2003 dates and prices, telephone 1.64.58.90. Further south, 185km from Paris, the Festival des Jardins, now in its eleventh year, takes place at the Château de Chaumont. Dozens of miniature gardens are on show, created by designers from all over the world. The festival runs from mid-June to mid-October. There is a regular train service from Austerliz to Chaumont-sur-Loire, sometimes having to change at Blois. For further information and prices, telephone 1.48.04.84.59.

Arboretum d'Harcourt

27800 Harcourt, Normandie. Tel: 2.32.46.29.70; Fax: 2.32.46.53.38

Open daily except Tues: March to 14th June, 2pm – 6pm, 15th June to 14th Sept, 10.30am – 6.30pm, 15th Sept to 14th Nov, 2pm – 6pm

A nine-hectare arboretum set in a 94-hectare forest, started in 1802 and including many fine trees from North America.

Botanica

79 rue de Fruges, 62130 Hernicourt–Sauricourt. Tel: 3.21.04.04.03

Open March to Oct, Thurs – Sun, 10am – 5pm

A beautifully landscaped garden with fine trees and good collections of herbaceous perennials. Landscaped lake with rustic bridge.

Chantilly ★

60500 Chantilly. Tel: 3.44.62.62.62; Fax: 3.44.62.62.61

Open all year, daily, 10am – 6pm. 45-minute train around the park available, with commentary in French and English.

Acknowledged as one of André Le Nôtre's greatest creations, notable for its magnificent scale and water features.

Château d'Ambleville

95710 Bray–et–Lû. Tel: 1.34.67.71.34

Open April to 15th Oct, Sat, Sun and public holidays, 10.30 – 6.30pm

Italian gardens created between the two world wars, expressed as terraces, topiary and water.

Château de Bagatelle

133 route de Paris, 80100 Abbeville. Tel: 3.22.24.02/69

Open July and Aug, daily except Tues, 2 – 6pm, and for parties by appt

Complementing the picturesque eighteenth-century castle, a box-edged parterre, sculptures and pleached limes. Fine trees in the park.

Château de la Ballue

35560 Bazouges-la-Pérouse, Brittany. Tel: 2.99.97.47.86; Fax: 2.99.97.47.70

Open 15th April to 15th Oct, daily, 1 – 5.30pm, and in winter by appt

A series of theatrical gardens in the Baroque or Mannerist style of the sixteenth and seventeenth centuries, created in 1973 and now restored.

Château de Beaumesnil ★

27410 Beaumesnil. Tel/Fax: 2.32.44.40.09

Open April to Oct, daily, except Mon, 10am – 12 noon, 2 – 6pm

Designed by La Quintinye in 1640 and extensively remodelled in the eighteenth century. Features include a formal garden, an unusual labyrinth and lakeside walks.

Château de Bizy

27200 Vernon. Tel: 2.32.51.00.82; Fax: 2.32.21.66.54

Open April to Oct, daily, except Mon, 10am – 12 noon, 2 – 6pm

Surrounding the nineteenth-century château, a series of elaborate cascades, fountains and statuary, lime and yew walks and an attractive park.

Château de Bosmelet

76720 Auffay. Tel: 2.35.32.81.07; Fax: 2.35.32.84.62

Garden open for groups all year, 1 – 7pm. Potager open May to Oct, daily except Tues and Thurs

A re-creation of the classical French design laid out in 1715 by Le Colinet, first gardener to André Le Nôtre at Versailles, and including an ancient lime avenue and a fine ornamental kitchen garden.

Château de Brécy ★★

14480 St Gabriel-Brécy. Tel/Fax: 2.31.80.11.48

Open April to 2nd Nov, Tues, Thurs and Sun, 2.30 – 6.30pm, and for groups at other times by appt

A seventeenth-century garden laid out on five terraces in the Italian style in the 1650s – sophisticated, architectural and compact.

Château de Canon ★★

14270 Mézidon. Tel: 2.31.20.05.07/2.31.28.77.04; Fax: 2.31.20.65.17

Open July to Oct, daily, 2 – 7pm

Unchanged since the mid-eighteenth century, a combination of French and English picturesque styles, including an Anglo-Chinese garden.

Château de Caradeuc

35190 Bécherel, Brittany. Tel: 2.99.66.77.76

Open April to June, Sept and Oct, weekends; July to Aug, daily, 2.30pm – 6pm

A garden restored in the traditional French manner in the late nineteenth century, distinguished by *allées*, vistas, statues and monuments.

Château de Compiègne ★

60200 Compiègne. Tel: 3.44.38.47.00

Open all year, daily except Tues and public holidays, 10am – 6pm

An important restoration project, noted especially for the magnificent vista and trellis-covered walk commissioned by Napoleon to complement a garden dating originally from the reign of Louis XV.

Château de Corbeil-Cerf

60110 Corbeil-Cerf. Tel: 3.44.52.02.43

Open by appt to groups only

A series of rides cut through the forest surrounding the château, with a formal area to the north and four other modern gardens.

Château de Galleville ★

76560 Douderville, Normandie. Tel: 2.35.96.52.40

Open May to Oct for groups by appt. Guided visits mid-July to Aug

An elegant contemporary design uniting the seventeenth-century château with its garden and magnificent park.

Château de Martinvast

50690 Martinvast. Tel: 2.33.52.02.23

Open all year, Sat, Sun and public holidays, 2 – 7pm, by written appt only

A wooded park created in the English manner in 1820, with extensive water features, complementing the Gothick château.

Château de Miromesnil

Tourville sur Arques, 76550 Offranville. Tel/Fax: 2.35.85.02.80

Open May to mid-Oct, daily, except Tues, 2 – 6pm

A garden notable for its connection with Guy de Maupassant, magnificent beech wood and charming traditional *potager*.

Château de Nacqueville

50460 Urville-Nacqueville, Nr Cherbourg, Manche. Tel: 2.33.03.01.02

Open all year, Tues and Fri. Guided visits only, hourly from 2pm to 5pm

A park in the English style, created in the 1830s, damaged in World War II and now restored, set in a green valley sheltered by wooded escarpments.

Château de Vauville

50440 Beaumont-Hague, E. Cherbourg. Tel: 2.33.52.71.41; Fax: 2.33.52.72.31

Open July and Aug, daily. Guided visits only hourly from 2.30pm to 5.30pm

A post-war garden, informal in its style and Mediterranean in its planting, specialising in exotic and succulent plants arranged in a series of 'green rooms'.

Château de Vendeuvre

14170 Saint-Pierre-sur-Dives.

Open May to Sept, daily; March, April, Nov, Dec, weekends and public holidays; all 10am – 6pm

A classical château and lake and many contemporary ideas, including new plantings and intriguing architectural and water features.

Clos du Coudray

76850 Etaimpuis, Normandie. Tel: 2.35.34.96.85

Open Easter to 2nd Nov, Thurs – Sun, 10am – 7pm

Thousands of different plant species grouped into 22 distinctive areas within clipped hedges or meandering paths – a succession of delightful surprises.

Ermenonville (Parc Jean–Jacques Rousseau) ★

1 rue Ren de Girardin, 60950 Ermenonville. Tel: 3.44.54.01.58; Fax: 3.44.54.04.96

Open Easter to Oct, Sat and Sun; June to Sept, daily except Tues, all 1.30 – 7pm

A natural landscape of grass, trees and water embellished with statues and follies in the Stowe/Painshill tradition and indelibly associated with the great philosopher.

Herbarium des Remparts

80230 St Valéry-sur-Somme. Tel: 3.22.26.90.72

Open May to 15th Nov, daily, 10am – 12 noon, 3 – 6pm

A well-laid-out collection of medicinal, aromatic and culinary herbs and other plants useful to man, within the walls of an old convent garden.

Les Hortillonages

54 Boulevard Beauville, 80000 Amiens. Tel: 3.22.92.12.18

Open April to Oct, daily, 2 – between 5 and 8pm, depending on season

Unique. Small electric boats take visitors around these former vegetable gardens (filled now with flowers), intersected by numerous small canals. Striking views of Amiens Cathedral.

Jardin d'Angélique

Hameau du Pigrard, Route de Lyons, 76520 Montmain, Normandie. Tel: 2.35.79.08.12

Open 15th April to Oct, daily, 10am – 7pm

A small garden dedicated to the beauty of life in memory of a lost daughter, filled with roses and perennials in a subtle combination of scents and colours, plus a newer, more formal garden.

Jardins de Maizicourt

80370 Maizicourt. Tel: 3.22.32.69.64

Open May to Oct, June and Sept, daily, 2 – 6pm

Clipped box hedges, herbaceous borders and old roses, all planted with impeccable taste. The small church over the garden wall is worth visiting, (key with garden owner).

Jardin de Plantbessin

14490 Castillon, Calvados, Nr Bayeux. Tel: 2.31.92.56.03; Fax: 2.31.22.70.09

Open 15th May to 1st June, Mon – Sat; 2nd June to 14th July, daily; 15th July to 15th Oct, Mon – Sat, all 2.30 – 6pm

A delightful setting for a fine nursery, laid out in garden 'rooms', including herbaceous borders and water, Japanese and herb gardens – a plantsman's delight.

Jardin des Plantes, Caen

Rue Desmoneux, 14000 Caen. Tel: 2.31.30.432.63

Open all year, daily, 8am – between 5.30 and 7.30pm, (Suns and public holidays open 2pm). Tropical greenhouses, 2 – 5pm • Entrance: free

A pleasant public garden founded in 1736, with a park added in 1805 – fine trees, rare shrubs, plant order beds, a rock garden and a pond.

Jardin des Plantes, Rouen

**114 ter avenue des Martyrs de la Résistance, 76100 Rouen.
Tel: 2.35.72.36.36/2.32.18.21.30**

*Open all year, daily, 8am – between 5.15 and 7.45pm. Greenhouses 8 – 11am,
1.30 – 4.30pm • Entrance: free*

A well-maintained eight-hectare park with interesting plants, attractive
greenhouses and order beds.

Jardins de Valloires

80120 Argoules. Tel: 3.22.23.53.55

Open mid-March to Oct, daily, 10am – 5pm (closes 6.30pm, May to Sept)

Designed by one of France's foremost garden designers, Gilles Clément.
Evoking the peace and contemplation of its monastic past, spacious
lawns, subdued flower combinations, a rosery and a cloister furnished
with yew columns and a parterre, a water garden and a garden of the
five senses.

Jardin de Yves Gosse de Gorre

2 rue du bois, 62270 Séricourt. Tel: 3.21.03.64.42

Open April to Oct, Tues – Sat, 9am – 12 noon, 2 – 6pm

Good collection of species roses, chosen especially for their colourful heps,
together with amusing topiary, and colour-themed rooms.

Jardin Exotique

Roscoff, 29680 Brittany. Tel: 2.98.61.29.19 (summer); Fax: 2.98.61.12.34

*Open all year, daily: Feb, Dec, times vary but always open 2 – 5.30pm; May to
Oct, mornings and 2 – 5.30pm; Feb, Mar, Nov, Dec, closed Tues*

The giant echiums are spectacular. Over 2000 species of exotic plants grown in
an informal seaside setting, fringing paths, pools, waterfalls and rocky outcrops.

Jardin Georges Delaselle

29253 Ile de Batz, Finistère, Brittany. Tel: 2.98.61.75.65

Open April to Sept, daily

A late-nineteenth-century plantsman's garden sheltered, nurtured and
now restored, with many palms and exotics from the southern hemisphere complementing the Bronze Age tombs and excellent modern
sculptures.

Jardins et Pépinières de Cotelle

76370 Derchigny–Graincourt. Tel: 2.35.83.61.38

Open late April to mid-Nov, Mon – Sat, 10am – 12 noon and 2 – 5pm;
occasionally open Suns, May, June, Oct

A garden created by a nurseryman and his painter wife around their nursery of unusual plants.

Manoir du Fay

Rue du Grand Fay, 76190 Yvetot, Normandie. Tel: 2.35.56.24.73

Open May to Oct, one Sun per month, 2 – 6pm, and by appt

Behind a seventeenth-century manor house, a *potager* re-created in the traditional manner using entirely organic principles.

Parc et Jardins du Château d'Harcourt

14220 Thury-Harcourt. Tel: 2.31.79.65.41 or 2.31.79.72.05

Open April and Oct, Sun and public holidays, May to Sept, daily, all 2.30 – 6.30pm

A dazzling spring and summer garden with a profusion of flowers laid out with consummate artistry on a sloping site: a world away from the dramatic ruins of the château destroyed in World War II and its 70 hectares of park and gardens.

Parc Floral de Haute-Bretagne

353133 Le Châtellier. Tel: 2.99.95.48.32

Open mid-March to mid-Nov

A late-eighteenth-century garden in the English style with a series of gardens on an international theme: Persian, Greek, Himalayan etc.

Parc Floral des Moutiers ★★

76119 Varengeville-sur-Mer. Tel: 2.35.85.10.02

Open mid-March to mid-Nov, and for groups by appt

A Lutyens garden with Jekyll undertones surrounding a characterful house, combining formality, exuberant planting and archetypal architectural features in a satisfying Anglo-French alliance.

Shamrock

Route du Manoir d'Ango, 76119 Varengeville-sur-Mer. Tel: 2.35.04.02.33;

Open July to Oct, Fri, Sat, Sun and public holidays, 10am – 12 noon, 2.30pm – 6pm

Possibly the largest collection of hydrangeas in the world, with over 6000 different species and varieties brought together by Corinne Malet.

Le Vasterival ★★

76119 Ste-Marguerite-sur-Mer. Tel: 2.35.85.12.05

Open by appt only

A garden created since 1957 by an outstanding plantswoman, the Princess Sturdza, informal in layout, immaculately cultivated, fascinating at any season.

BELGIUM

Brussels Gardens

Brussels itself has a number of gardens open at all times, including *Abbaye de la Cambre*, *Bois de la Cambre*, the *Jean Massart Experimental Garden*, *Parc Léopold* on rue Belliard and the park in the City Centre. Other gardens include *Parc Tenbosch* (with outstanding trees) on chaussée de Vleurgat, and *Maison d'Erasme*, 31 rue du Chapitre Anderlecht. *Parc Solvay* on chaussée de la Hulpe and *Jardins du Museé van Buuren*, 41 rue Leo Errera are in the south of the city. Ten kilometres north of Brussels is the *National Botanic Garden*, open daily 9am – sunset. Once a year, usually in April/May, the King of Belgium opens the conservatories in the *Laeken Royal Palace* on the northern outskirts of the city.

Annevoie ★★

5537 Annevoie-Rouillon, Anhee.

Open April to Oct, daily, 9.30am – 6.30pm

An historically important garden, created in the mid-eighteenth century with elements borrowed from the Italian, French and English styles, linked by a network of water features, including some spectacular fountains, fine urns and statues and superb trees.

Arboretum Kalmthout

Heuvel 2, B–2920 Kalmthout. Tel: 3.666.6741

Open 15th March to 15th Nov, daily, 10am – 5pm

The largest dendrological collection in Belgium, a 10-acre arboretum of outstanding quality with many collections of rare and unusual trees and shrubs.

Château d'Attre ★

Avenue du Château, 7941 Attre, Brugelette. Tel: 32.68.45.44.60

Open by appt only: April to Oct, Sat, Sun; July, Aug, daily, except Wed; all 10am – 12 noon, 2 – 6pm

A picturesque 28-hectare park with magnificent old trees and interesting follies and garden building.

Château de Belœil

rue du Château, Belóil, pres Mons. Tel: 32.69.68.96.55

Open April to Oct, Sat, Sun; July, Aug, daily except Wed; all 10am – 6pm

An exceptional garden with a great six-hectare lake flanked by garden characterful 'rooms', plus 10km of spectacular hedges and other foliage features.

Château de Hex

B–3870 Heers. Tel: 12.74.73.41

Open 11th to 13th June and 10th to 12th Sept, all 10am – 5pm

Five hectares of formal garden set in 60 hectares of English-style park, all in a beautiful natural site, with a huge collection of old roses and a traditional *potager*.

Château de Leeuwergem ★

B–9620 Zottegem. Tel: 93.60.08.73

Open May to 1st Oct by appt only

A park with a rare eighteenth-century *théâtre de verdure* (still in regular use), and formal gardens laid out in 1702 in the French classical style – a splendid counterpoint to the spare simplicity of the château.

Château Fort d'Ecaussinnes (Le Potager)

Rue de Seneffe, 7191 Ecaussinnes–Lalaing. Tel: 67.44.24.90

Open all year, daily except Mon; Easter to 1st Nov, 10am – 8pm, 2nd Nov to Easter, 8am – 4pm

A seventeenth-century walled ornamental *potager* across a private road from the medieval castle, reputedly the first garden in Belgium to be listed.

Château s'Gravenwezel

2970 s'Gravenwezel, Schilde. Tel: 36.58.14.70

A 40-hectare formal park surrounding an ancient castle, reinvigorated by leading designer Jacques Wirtz with wide walks, extensive tree planting and the restoration of the eighteenth-century garden plan in the English landscape style, plus an attractive botanical garden and a redesigned walled garden.

Hof ter Weyden

Greefstraat 1, 2910 Essen. Tel: 36.77.22.74

Open 2 days in June, 10am – 6pm, and by appt

Three distinctive planting areas surrounding an old farmhouse and its historic barn: a formal rose garden, an architectural garden divided by hedges, and an orchard, with a double row of poplars and a lake linking the garden with the countryside.

Park van Beervelde

Beervelde-Dorp 75, B-9080 Lochristi. Tel: 93.55.55.40

Open by appt

A 20-hectare arboretum and garden in the English landscape style, with a spectacular flowering of Ghent azaleas in May.

Rekem Garden ★

Achter St Pieter 24, 3621 Rekem-Lanaken. Tel: 89.71.46.92

A small, immaculately maintained garden sheltered by fine hedges, with an unusual central pavilion of *Cornus mas* and distinctive areas planted with an artist's eye for design and colour.

Vlaamse Toontuinen (Flemish Show Gardens)

1 Houtmarkt, Hoegaarden 3320. Tel: 16.76.78.43/16.76.56.39;

Within a walled park, a permanent exhibition of 22 different types of gardens, all designed by landscape architects and professional gardeners, plus nature trails, a sculpture exhibition and horticultural displays.

NETHERLANDS

Amsterdam Canal Gardens

During the 'Amsterdam Canal Garden in Bloom' weekend of 18th – 20th June some 20 individual, institutional and museum gardens (both classical and contemporary) will open to the public. The entry through the fine seventeenth- and eighteen-century houses is worth the visit by itself. Several houses offer sandwiches and drinks. Opening hours are 10am – 5pm, and a day ticket costs E10. Telephone 203.20.36.60, email info@museumvanloon.nl or visit the website on www.museumvanloon.nl.

Broekstraat 17 ★

6999 De Hummelo. Tel: 314.38.1120

The highly original creation of one of the gurus of the contemporary Dutch style of naturalistic gardening, Piet Oudolf, and his wife Anja, displaying the masterly orchestration of nature that won him the top prize at Chelsea 2000.

Huys de Dohm

De Doom 48–50, 6419 CX Heerlen. Tel: 45.571.0470

Open several days 31st May to 15th June, 10am – 5pm or 8.30 – 9.30pm

Restored since 1980 as a series of outdoor rooms, including double herbaceous borders, a delightful *potager* and topiary, white, water and wild gardens, reflecting the character of the small, ancient castle and its hunting lodge.

De Kempenhof

Zuiverseweg 4, 4357 NM Domburg. Tel: 118.58.16.47

Open by appt

A two-hectare garden focused on a splendid all-season double herbaceous border, with island beds, roses, hellebores and an avenue planted with ornamental grasses for additional seasonal interest.

Leiden Botanic Garden ★

Hortus Botanicus, Rapenburg 73, Leiden. Tel: 71.527.7249

Open April to Sept, Mon – Sat, Oct to March 2003, Mon – Fri, all 9am – 5pm

Clusius's late-sixteenth-century garden reconstructed as the original, with 60 beds and ancient trees, plus a general garden with other features of interest.

Paleis Het Loo, National Museum ★★

Koninklijk Park 1, 7315 JA Apeldoorn. Tel: 55.577.2400

Open all year, daily except Mon (but open Bank Holiday Mons), 10am – 5pm

William Prince of Orange's magnificent formal garden of 1684, transformed into a landscape park, then destroyed and now triumphantly restored to its original design, including a sunken garden, parterres, elaborate water conceits, an upper garden with a curved colonnade, and delightful gardens near the palace.

Priona Gardens

Schnineslootweg 13, Schninesloot. Tel: 523.68.17.34

Open May to Sept, Thurs to Sat, 10am – 5pm, Sun, 2 – 6pm

The naturalistic garden of Henk Gerritsen, combining artistry and a profound knowledge of wild flowers and their habitats.

Slot der Nisse

Dorpsplein 4443 AE, Nisse. Tel: 113.64.94.69

Open by appt

A modern garden for the coachhouse of a demolished castle – delightful ingredients include a lovely herb garden, a natural pond, double white borders, an orchard, a spring avenue with medlars, and fine views.

J.P. Thijsse–Park

Prins Bernhardlaan 8, Amstelveen, Amsterdam. Tel: 205.40.42.65

A public 'new-wave' park created post-war and devoted to plants that grow in the wild, with large and varied groups of plants creating an entirely natural feeling, all connected by a long and narrow meandering pond.

De Tintelhof

Golsteinseweg 24, 4351 SC Veere. Tel: 118.61.45.20

Open by appt

A garden of well-balanced herbaceous borders, many old and modern roses in a frame of trimmed hedges and clipped evergreens, and a contrasting area of woodland, all sensitively integrated into its surroundings.

In de Tuinen van Ruinen

Achterma 20, 7963 PM Ruinen. Tel: 522.47.26.55

Open 30th April to Oct, Wed – Sun, 10am – 5pm

A magical meadow-like garden in the new Dutch style contrived by former owner Ton ter Linden, one of the acknowledged masters of the art.

KEY TO MAPS

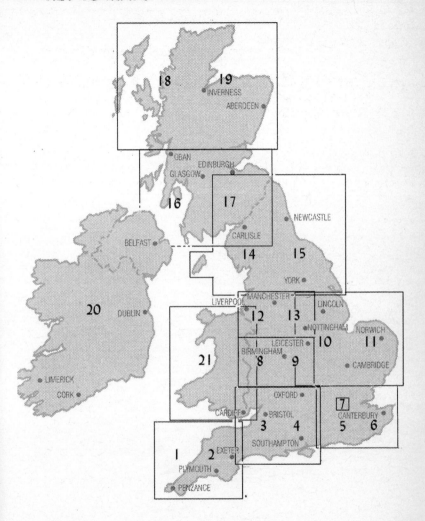

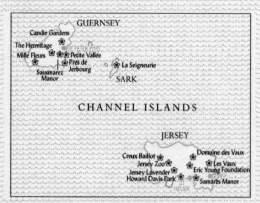

GUERNSEY

Candie Gardens

The Hermitage
Mille Fleurs   Petite Vallée
     Près de
     Jerbourg   La Seigneurie
Sausmarez
Manor   SARK

CHANNEL ISLANDS

JERSEY

              Domaine des Vaux
Creux Baillot
Jersey Zoo   Les Vaux
Jersey Lavender   Eric Young Foundation
Howard Davis Park
             Samarès Manor

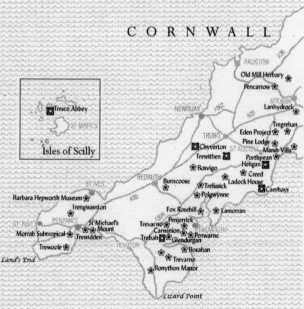

C O R N W A L L

PADSTOW

Old Mill Herbary
Pencarrow

Lanhydrock
NEWQUAY
Tregrehan
Eden Project
Pine Lodge
TRURO
Chyverton   ST AUSTELL   Marsh Villa
Trewithen   Porthpean
      Heligan
Bosvigo   Creed
REDRUTH
Burncoose   Ladock House
     Trelissick
     Polgwynne   Caerhays
ST IVES

Barbara Hepworth Museum

Trengwainton   Fox Rosehill   Lamorran
          Penjerrick
PENZANCE   Trevarno   FALMOUTH
   St Michael's   Carwinion
   Mount   Trebah   Penwarne
Morrab Subtropical   Trewidden   Glendurgan
           Bosahan
Trewoofe
Land's End   Trevarno
      HELSTON
      Bonython Manor

Lizard Point

Tresco Abbey
ST MARY'S
Isles of Scilly

2

Lundy

Woodborough

Greencombe

Arlington Court

Dunster Castle

Marwood Hill

SOMERSET

Tapeley Park

Castle Hill

Hartland Abbey

Docton Mill

RHS Garden Rosemoor

Knightshayes

DEVON

Killerton

University of Exeter

Cleave House

Andrew's Corner

Castle Drogo

Gidleigh Park

Bickham House

Bicton College

Bicton Park

Lee Ford

Endsleigh House

Dartmoor

Ken Caro

Cotehele

The Garden House

Buckland Abbey

Hill House

Dartington

Boconnoc

St Martin's Manor

Ince Castle

Tudor Rose

Lukesland

Paignton Zoo

Headland

Antony

Saltram House

Greenway

Mount Edgcumbe

Coleton Fishacre

Blackpool Garden

Overbecks

Start Point

ENGLISH CHANNEL

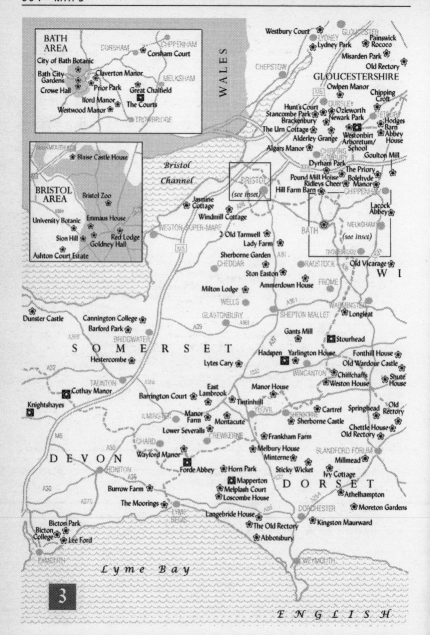

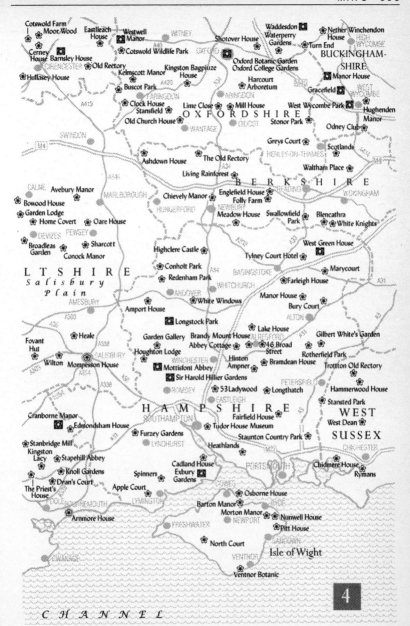

5

H E R T S

Knebworth
Seal Point
Hanbury Manor Hotel
Mackerye End House
Gibberd Garden

Ascott
Waddesdon
Ashridge Management College
Jenningsbury
Hatfield House

Nether Winchenden
Turn End

Campden Cottage
The Abbot's House
Capel Manor
7A Ellesmere Gardens
Myddelton House

Manor House
Blossoms
Chenies Manor
Beale Arboretum

Gracefield
Spindrift
Hughenden Manor
Cheslyn House

West Wycombe Park

B U C K S

Odney Club
Cliveden

Waltham Place
Scotlands

B E R K S

Frogmore Gardens

LONDON AREA

Map 7

Valley Gardens
Savill Garden
Great Fosters

The Walled Garden
Little Lodge

Englefield House
Swallowfield Park
Blencathra
White Knights

The Green House
Claremont
Painshill

Folly Farm
Old Rectory

RHS Wisley
Beverstone

Down House

West Green House

Knightsmeed

Tylney Hall

Sutton Place

S U R R E Y

Tilsey
Place
Squerryes
Court
Emmetts
Chartwell

Marycourt
Heathersett
Guildford Castle
Clandon Park
Poelsden Lacey

Chart's Edge
Edenbridge Ho.

Manor House
Bury Court

Chilworth Manor
Loseley Park
Busbridge Lakes
Vale End
Albury Pk
Brook Lodge
Goddards
Bates Green
Winkworth Arbor.
Red Oaks
Langshott Manor
Hever Castle
Old Budehurst
Wayshode Manor

Munstead Wood
Leith Hill
Hannah Peschar
Coverwood Lakes

Barnett Hill

Gilbert White's Garden
Crosswater Farm
Rotherfield Pk

Street House
Feathercombe
Ramster
Vann

Yew Tree Cottage
Orchards

H A N T S

Standen
Gravelye Manor

Duckyls

Shulbrede Priory
Frith Hill

High Beeches
Selehurst
Leonardslee
Nymans

Wakehurst
Place
Borde Hill

Sheffield
Park
Clinton
Lodge

Petworth House
Hammerwood House

Trotton
Old Rectory

Coates Manor
Somerset Lodge
Parham House

Town Place

Stansted Park

W E S T   S U S S E X

Champs
Hill
Little
Wantley
Chantry Green House

E A S T

West Dean
Staunton Country Park
Weald & Downland Sculpture at Goodwood
St Mary's House

Monk's House
Charleston

Denmans
Burpham Place

Chidmere House
Rymans
Berri Court
Highdown
Royal Pavilion

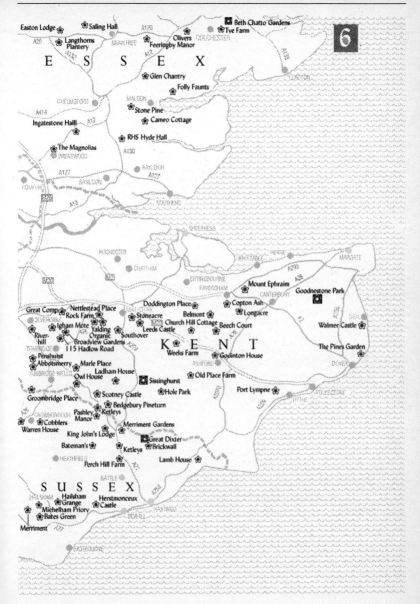

6

Easton Lodge
Saling Hall
A120
Beth Chatto Gardens
Tye Farm
Langthorns
Plantery
Olivers
Feeringby Manor
COLCHESTER
A120
A20
A12
A130

E   S   S   E   X

Glen Chantry

Folly Faunts

CHELMSFORD
A414
MALDON
Stone Pine
Ingatestone Hall
A12
Cameo Cottage

The Magnolias
BRENTWOOD
A130
RHS Hyde Hall

A127
RAYLEIGH
A127
BASILDON
A13
SOUTHEND

SHEERNESS

ROCHESTER
WHITSTABLE
HERNE
MARGATE
A299
CHATHAM
SITTINGBOURNE
FAVERSHAM
Mount Ephraim
CANTERBURY
Goodnestone Park
Copton Ash
Longacre
A2
DEAL
Doddington Place
Belmont
Walmer Castle
Great Comp
Nettlestead Place
Rock Farm
Stoneacre
Church Hill Cottage
Beech Court
SEVENOAKS
Igham Mote
Yalding
Organic
Leeds Castle
The Pines Garden
River-
hill
Southover
Broadview Gardens
K • E • N • T
DOVER
TONBRIDGE
115 Hadlow Road
Weeks Farm
Godinton House
Penshurst
ASHFORD
Abbotsmerry
Marle Place
Ladham House
Old Place Farm
TUNBRIDGE WELLS
Owl House
Sissinghurst
Groombridge Place
Scotney Castle
Hole Park
Port Lympne
Bedgebury Pineturn
FOLKESTONE
Pashley
Manor
Ketleys
HYTHE
Cobblers
Warren House
Merriment Gardens
King John's Lodge
Great Dixter
Bateman's
Ketleys
Brickwall
Lamb House
Perch Hill Farm

BATTLE
S   U   S   S   E   X
HAILSHAM
Hailsham
Grange
Herstmonceux
Castle
HASTINGS
Michelham Priory
Bates Green
BEXHILL
Merriment
A27
EASTBOURNE

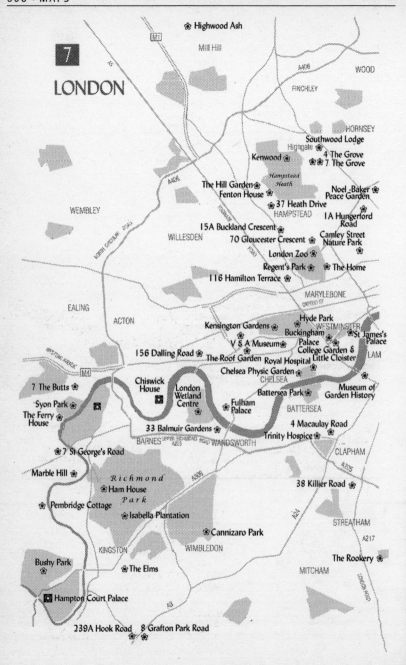

7

LONDON

Highwood Ash

MILL HILL

WOOD

A406

FINCHLEY

HORNSEY

Southwood Lodge

Highgate

4 The Grove

Kenwood

7 The Grove

Hampstead
Heath

The Hill Garden
Fenton House

Noel Baker
Peace Garden

37 Heath Drive

HAMPSTEAD

1A Hungerford
Road

WEMBLEY

15A Buckland Crescent

Camley Street
Nature Park

WILLESDEN

70 Gloucester Crescent

London Zoo

The Home

Regent's Park

116 Hamilton Terrace

EALING

MARYLEBONE

OXFORD ST

Hyde Park

ACTON

Kensington Gardens

Buckingham
Palace

WESTMINSTER

St James's
Palace

V & A Museum

156 Dalling Road

The Roof Garden

College Garden &
Little Cloister

Royal Hospital

LAM

Chelsea Physic Garden

CHELSEA

Chiswick
House

7 The Butts

Battersea Park

Museum of
Garden History

London
Wetland
Centre

Fulham
Palace

Syon Park

The Ferry
House

BATTERSEA

33 Balmuir Gardens

4 Macaulay Road

BARNES UPPER RICHMOND ROAD
A205

WANDSWORTH

Trinity Hospice

CLAPHAM

7 St George's Road

A205

Marble Hill

Richmond

A306

38 Killier Road

Ham House

Park

A24

Pembridge Cottage

Isabella Plantation

STREATHAM

A217

Cannizaro Park

KINGSTON

WIMBLEDON

The Rookery

Bushy Park

The Elms

MITCHAM

LONDON ROAD

Hampton Court Palace

A3

239A Hook Road   8 Grafton Park Road

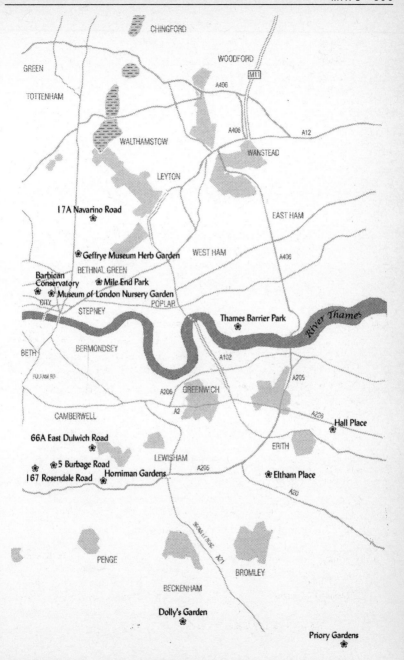

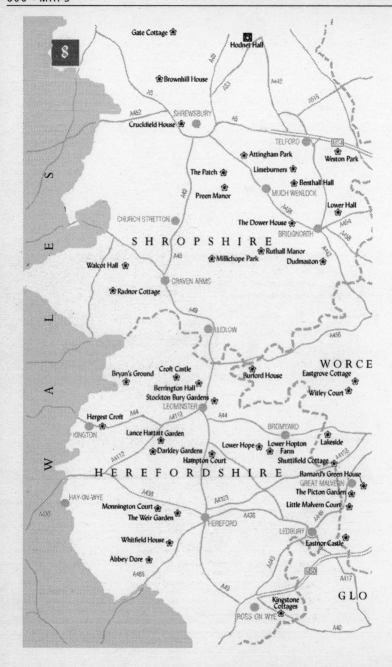

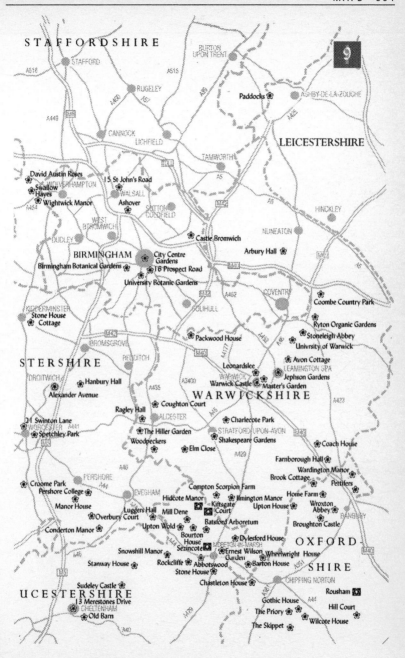

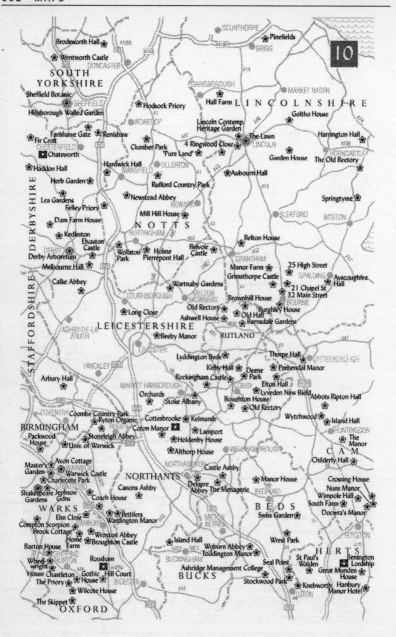

10

Brodsworth Hall
Pinefields
Wentworth Castle
SCUNTHORPE
DONCASTER
BRIGG
SOUTH
YORKSHIRE
GAINSBOROUGH
MARKET RASEN
Sheffield Botanic
SHEFFIELD
Hall Farm
LINCOLNSHIRE
Hodsock Priory
Hillsborough Walled Garden
Goltho House
WORKSOP
Lincoln Contemp.
Heritage Garden
Harrington Hall
Fanshawe Gate
Renishaw
Fir Croft
The Lawn
CHESTERFIELD
Clumber Park
4 Ringwood Close
LINCOLN
Chatsworth
'Pure Land'
Garden House
The Old Rectory
Haddon Hall
Hardwick Hall
HORNCASTLE
OLLERTON
MANSFIELD
Aubourn Hall
Herb Garden
Lea Gardens
Rufford Country Park
DERBYSHIRE
Felley Priory
Newstead Abbey
NEWARK
Springtyme
Dam Farm House
NOTTS
Mill Hill House
SLEAFORD
BOSTON
Kedleston
NOTTINGHAM
Belton House
Elvaston
Castle
Wollaton
Holme
Belvoir
GRANTHAM
Derby Arboretum
Park
Pierrepont Hall
Castle
Manor Farm
25 High Street
Melbourne Hall
Grimsthorpe Castle
SPALDING
Ayscoughfee
STAFFORDSHIRE
Wartnaby Gardens
21 Chapel St
Hall
Calke Abbey
Brownhill House
32 Main Street
MELTON
LOUGHBOROUGH
MOWBRAY
BOURNE
Long Close
Old Rectory
Burghley House
Ashwell House
Old Hall
Barnsdale Gardens
LEICESTERSHIRE
Beeby Manor
RUTLAND
ASHBY-DE-LA-
ZOUCH
LEICESTER
Lyddington Bede
Thorpe Hall
PETERBOROUGH
Kirby Hall
Deene
Prebendal Manor
HINCKLEY
Rockingham Castle
Park
Arbury Hall
Elton Hall
MARKET HARBOROUGH
Lyveden New Bield
Abbots Ripton Hall
Orchards
Stoke Albany
Boughton House
Cottesbrooke
Kelmarsh
Old Rectory
Wytchwood
Island Hall
Coombe Country Park
Coton Manor
HUNTINGDON
BIRMINGHAM
Ryton Organic
Lamport
The
Packwood
Stoneleigh Abbey
Holdenby House
CAM.
Manor
House
Univ. of Warwick
Althorp House
WELLINGBOROUGH
Childerly Hall
Master's
Avon Cottage
WARWICK
Garden
Warwick Castle
NORTHAMPTON
Castle Ashby
Crossing House
Charlecote Park
NORTHANTS
Manor House
Nuns Manor
Shakespeare Jephson
Canons Ashby
Delapre
BEDFORD
Wimpole Hall
Gardens Gdns
Coach House
Abbey The Menagerie
BEDS
South Farm
Docwra's Manor
WARKS
Elm Close
Pettifers
Swiss Garden
Compton Scorpion
Wardington Manor
MILTON
Brook Cottage
Home
KEYNES
Barton House
Wroxton Abbey
Farm
Island Hall
Wrest Park
BANBURY
Broughton Castle
Woburn Abbey
HERTS
Wheel
BICESTER
Rousham
Toddington Manor
Benington
wright
Seal Point
St Paul's
Lordship
House Chastleton
Gothic
Hill Court
Ashridge Management College
Walden
Great Munden
The Priory
House
BUCKS
Stockwood Park
House
Wilcote House
Knebworth
Hanbury
LUTON
Manor Hotel
The Skippet
OXFORD

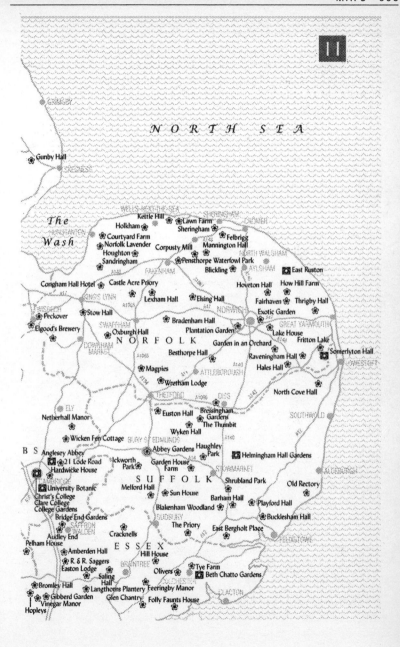

11

NORTH SEA

The Wash

Gunby Hall

Kettle Hill
Holkham
Lawn Farm
Sheringham
Courtyard Farm
Felbrigg
Norfolk Lavender
Corpusty Mill
Mannington Hall
Houghton
Sandringham
Penthorpe Waterfowl Park
Blickling
East Ruston
Congham Hall Hotel
Castle Acre Priory
Hoveton Hall
How Hill Farm
Lexham Hall
Elsing Hall
Fairhaven
Thrigby Hall
Peckover
Stow Hall
Exotic Garden
Elgood's Brewery
Oxburgh Hall
Bradenham Hall
Plantation Garden
Lake House
Fritton Lake
NORFOLK
Garden in an Orchard
Somerlyton Hall
Besthorpe Hall
Raveningham Hall
Magpies
Hales Hall
Wretham Lodge
Euston Hall
Bressingham
Gardens
The Thumbit
North Cove Hall
Netherhall Manor
Wyken Hall
Wicken Fen Cottage
Abbey Gardens
Haughley
Park
Helmingham Hall Gardens
B S
Anglesey Abbey
21 Lode Road
Ickworth
Park
Garden House
Farm
Hardwicke House
University Botanic
SUFFOLK
Shrubland Park
Old Rectory
Christ's College
Melford Hall
Clare College
Sun House
Barham Hall
College Gardens
Playford Hall
Bridge End Gardens
Blakenham Woodland
Bucklesham Hall
Audley End
Cracknells
The Priory
East Bergholt Place
Pelham House
Amberden Hall
ESSEX
Hill House
R. & R. Saggers
Easton Lodge
Saling
Hall
Olivers
Tye Farm
Bromley Hall
Langthorns Plantery
Feeringbuy Manor
Beth Chatto Gardens
Gibberd Garden
Glen Chantry
Folly Faunts House
Vinegar Manor
Hopleys

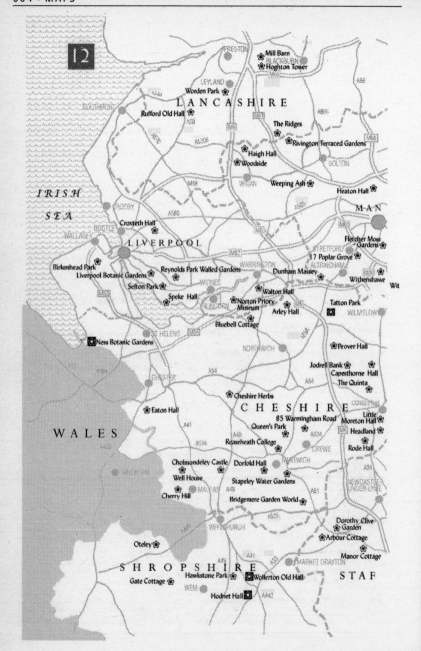

12

Mill Barn 🌢
BLACKBURN
Hoghton Tower 🌢

PRESTON

LEYLAND

Worden Park 🌢

LANCASHIRE

Rufford Old Hall 🌢

The Ridges 🌢

Rivington Terraced Gardens 🌢

Haigh Hall 🌢
Woodside 🌢

WIGAN

BOLTON

Weeping Ash 🌢

Heaton Hall 🌢

IRISH

SEA

CROSBY

MAN

BOOTLE

Croxteth Hall 🌢

Fletcher Moss
Gardens 🌢

LIVERPOOL

STRETFORD

17 Poplar Grove 🌢

ALTRINCHAM

WARRINGTON

Birkenhead Park 🌢

Reynolds Park Walled Gardens 🌢

Dunham Massey 🌢

Liverpool Botanic Gardens 🌢

Sefton Park 🌢

Withenshawe 🌢

Wit

Speke Hall 🌢

Walton Hall 🌢

RUNCORN

Norton Priory
Museum 🌢

Tatton Park 🏛

Arley Hall 🌢

WILMSLOW

Bluebell Cottage 🌢

ST HELENS

Ness Botanic Gardens 🏛

NORTHWICH

Peover Hall 🌢

CHESTER

Jodrell Bank 🌢

Capesthorne Hall 🌢

CONGLETON

The Quinta 🌢

Cheshire Herbs 🌢

CHESHIRE

Little
Moreton Hall 🌢

Eaton Hall 🌢

85 Warmingham Road 🌢

Queen's Park 🌢

Headland 🌢

Reaseheath College 🌢

CREWE

Rode Hall 🌢

Cholmondeley Castle 🌢

Dorfold Hall 🌢

Well House 🌢

NEWCASTLE-
UNDER-LYNE

Stapeley Water Gardens 🌢

Cherry Hill 🌢

MALPAS

WALES

Bridgemere Garden World 🌢

WREXHAM

Dorothy Clive
Garden 🌢

WHITCHURCH

Arbour Cottage 🌢

Oteley 🌢

Manor Cottage 🌢

MARKET DRAYTON

SHROPSHIRE

STAF

Hawkstone Park 🌢

Wollerton Old Hall 🌢

Gate Cottage 🌢

WEM

Hodnet Hall 🏛

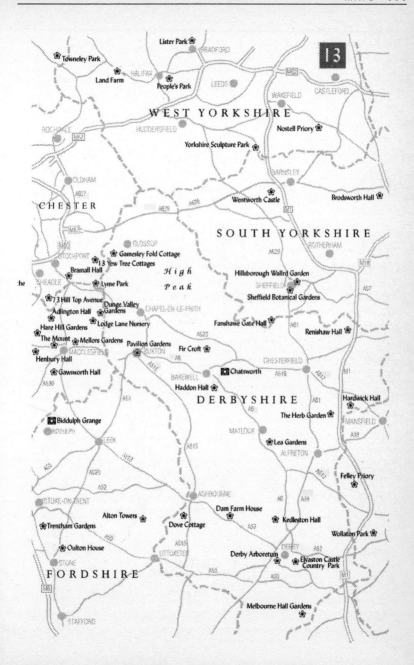

13

Lister Park 🏵 BRADFORD
Towneley Park 🏵
Land Farm 🏵 HALIFAX
People's Park 🏵 LEEDS
WAKEFIELD CASTLEFORD

WEST YORKSHIRE

ROCHDALE HUDDERSFIELD
Nostell Priory 🏵
Yorkshire Sculpture Park 🏵
BARNSLEY
OLDHAM
CHESTER Wentworth Castle 🏵 Brodsworth Hall 🏵

SOUTH YORKSHIRE
GLOSSOP ROTHERHAM
Gamesley Fold Cottage 🏵
13 Yew Tree Cottages 🏵
Bramall Hall 🏵 High Hillsborough Wall'rd Garden 🏵
STOCKPORT Peak SHEFFIELD
Lyme Park 🏵 Sheffield Botanical Gardens 🏵
73 Hill Top Avenue 🏵 Dunge Valley CHAPEL-EN-LE-FRITH
Adlington Hall 🏵 Gardens 🏵 Fanshawe Gate Hall 🏵
Hare Hill Gardens 🏵 Lodge Lane Nursery 🏵 Renishaw Hall 🏵
The Mount 🏵 Mellors Gardens 🏵 Pavilion Gardens 🏵
Henbury Hall 🏵 MACCLESFIELD BUXTON Fir Croft 🏵 CHESTERFIELD
Gawsworth Hall 🏵 BAKEWELL Chatsworth 🏵
Haddon Hall 🏵
DERBYSHIRE Hardwick Hall 🏵
Biddulph Grange 🏵 The Herb Garden 🏵 MANSFIELD
BIDDULPH MATLOCK
LEEK Lea Gardens 🏵
ALFRETON
Felley Priory 🏵
STOKE-ON-TRENT ASHBOURNE
Alton Towers 🏵 Dam Farm House 🏵
Trentham Gardens 🏵 Dove Cottage 🏵 Kedleston Hall 🏵
Wollaton Park 🏵
Oulton House 🏵 UTTOXETER Derby Arboretum 🏵 DERBY
STONE Elvaston Castle
FORDSHIRE Country Park 🏵
STAFFORD Melbourne Hall Gardens 🏵

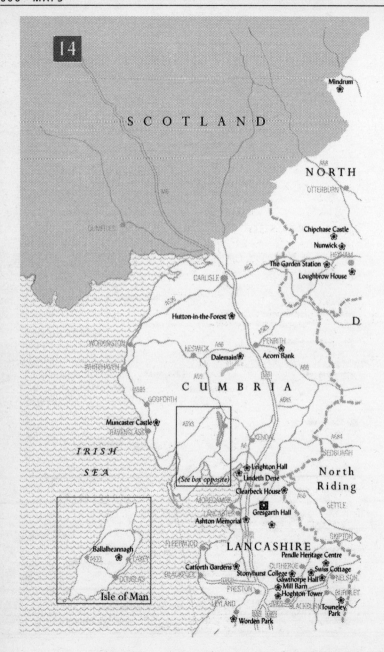

14

S C O T L A N D

Mindrum ✿

N O R T H

A68

OTTERBURN

Chipchase Castle ✿

Nunwick ✿

HEXHAM

The Garden Station ✿

Loughbrow House ✿

D

CARLISLE

Hutton-in-the-Forest ✿

PENRITH

KESWICK

Dalemain ✿

Acorn Bank ✿

C U M B R I A

GOSFORTH

Muncaster Castle ✿

KENDAL

SEDBURGH

I R I S H
S E A

North
Riding

(See box opposite)

Leighton Hall ✿

Lindeth Dene ✿

Clearbeck House ✿

SETTLE

MORECAMBE

Gresgarth Hall ✿

SKIPTON

Ashton Memorial ✿

Ballalheannagh ✿

PEEL

LANCASHIRE

Pendle Heritage Centre ✿

Catforth Gardens ✿

Stonyhurst College ✿

Swiss Cottage ✿

CLITHEROE

NELSON

Gawthorpe Hall ✿

DOUGLAS

Mill Barn ✿

Hoghton Tower ✿

BURNLEY

Isle of Man

PRESTON

BLACKBURN

Towneley
Park

LEYLAND

Worden Park ✿

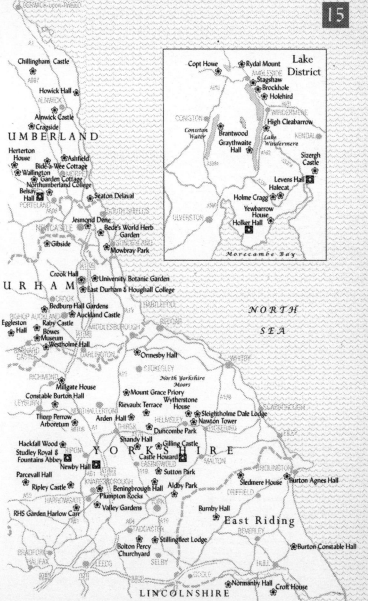

15

Chillingham Castle

Howick Hall

ALNWICK

Alnwick Castle
Cragside

UMBERLAND

Herterton
House
Ashfield
Bide-a-Wee Cottage
Wallington
Garden Cottage
Northumberland College
Belsay
Hall
PORTLAND

Seaton Delaval

SOUTH SHIELDS

Jesmond Dene

NEWCASTLE
Bede's World Herb
Garden
SUNDERLAND
Gibside
Mowbray Park

Copt Howe   Rydal Mount   Lake
                                        District
                    AMBLESIDE
                    Stagshaw
                    Brockhole
                    Holehird
                    WINDERMERE
CONISTON
                                        High Cleabarrow
Coniston
Water   Brantwood   Lake   KENDAL
            Graythwaite   Windermere
            Hall
                                        Sizergh
                                        Castle
A590
                                        Levens Hall
                                        Halecat
                    Holme Cragg
ULVERSTON   Yewbarrow
                    House
                    Holker Hall

                    Morecambe Bay

Crook Hall
                University Botanic Garden
URHAM   East Durham & Houghall College
CROOK
                                                HARTLEPOOL
BISHOP AUCKLAND   Bedburn Hall Gardens
                   Auckland Castle
Eggleston   Raby Castle   MIDDLESBROUGH
Hall   Bowes
                   Museum
                   Westholme Hall   NORTH
DARLINGTON
                                                         SEA
RICHMOND   Ormesby Hall
                            STOKESLEY
                                                         WHITBY
                            North Yorkshire
                            Moors
            Millgate House   Mount Grace Priory
Constable Burton Hall   Wytherstone
LEYBURN   Rievaulx Terrace   House
                                                         A169
Thorp Perrow   Arden Hall   Sleightholme Dale Lodge
Arboretum   Nawton Tower
                THIRSK   HELMSLEY
                    Duncombe Park
        Shandy Hall
Hackfall Wood   Gilling Castle
RIPON   E
Studley Royal &   Castle Howard
Fountains Abbey   MALTON
        Newby Hall   YORKSHIRE
Parcevall Hall
                            Sutton Park
Ripley Castle
                   Beningbrough Hall   Aldby Park   Sledmere House   Burton Agnes Hall
HARROGATE   Plumpton Rocks   DRIFFIELD
RHS Garden Harlow Carr   Valley Gardens
                                        Burnby Hall
        A64   TADCASTER   BEVERLEY
                                        East Riding
        Bolton Percy   Stillingfleet Lodge
        Churchyard
BRADFORD   Burton Constable Hall
HALIFAX   LEEDS
                   SELBY
                                        Normanby Hall   Croft House

        LINCOLNSHIRE

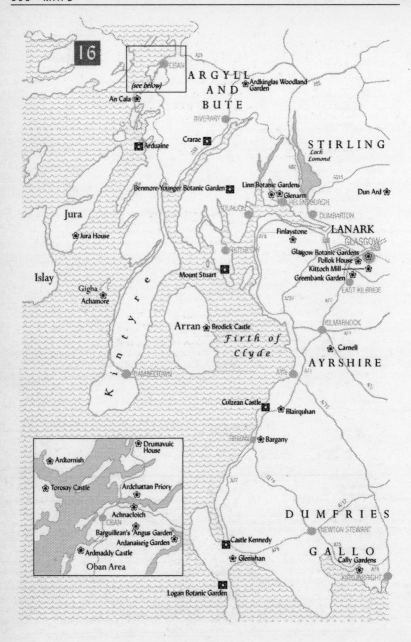

16

(see below)

OBAN

ARGYLL
AND
BUTE

☀ Ardkinglas Woodland
Garden

An Cala ☀

INVERARY

STIRLING

☀ Arduaine   Crarae ☀

*Loch
Lomond*

Benmore-Younger Botanic Garden ☀

Linn Botanic Gardens

☀ Glenarn

Dun Ard ☀

DUNOON

Jura

HELENSBURGH

DUMBARTON

☀ Jura House

Finlaystone

LANARK

GLASGOW

Islay

Glasgow Botanic Gardens ☀
Pollok House ☀
Kittoch Mill
Greenbank Garden ☀

Gigha
☀ Achamore

EAST KILBRIDE

KILMARNOCK

Arran ☀ Brodick Castle

*Firth of
Clyde*

☀ Carnell

AYRSHIRE

CAMPBELTOWN

AYR

Culzean Castle ☀

☀ Blairquhan

GIRVAN

☀ Bargany

DUMFRIES

NEWTON STEWART

Castle Kennedy ☀

GALLO

☀ Glenwhan

Cally Gardens ☀

KIRKCUDBRIGHT

Logan Botanic Garden ☀

☀ Drumavuic
House

☀ Ardtornish

☀ Torosay Castle   Ardchattan Priory

Achnacloich
OBAN
Barguillean's 'Angus Garden'
Ardanaiseig Garden ☀
☀ Ardmaddy Castle

Oban Area

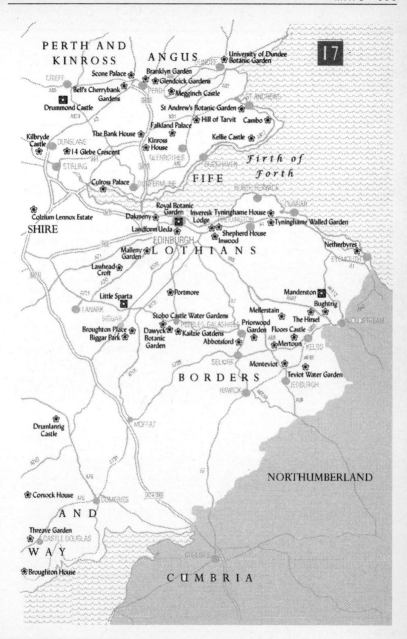

17

PERTH AND
KINROSS

Scone Palace

Bell's Cherrybank
Gardens

Drummond Castle

Kilbryde
Castle

The Bank House

14 Glebe Crescent

Culross Palace

Colzium Lennox Estate

SHIRE

Lawhead
Croft

Little Sparta

Broughton Place
Biggar Park

Drumlanrig
Castle

Corsock House

AND

Threave Garden

WAY

Broughton House

ANGUS

Branklyn Garden
Glendoick Gardens

Megginch Castle

St Andrew's Botanic Garden
Hill of Tarvit   Cambo
Falkland Palace
Kinross
House

Kellie Castle

FIFE

University of Dundee
Botanic Garden

Firth of
Forth

Royal Botanic
Garden   Inveresk Tyninghame House
Dalmeny   Lodge
Landform Ueda   Tyninghame Walled Garden
Shepherd House
Inwood
Malleny   LOTHIANS
Garden

Netherbyres

Portmore

Stobo Castle Water Gardens
Dawyck   Kailzie Gardens
Botanic   Abbotsford
Garden

Manderston
Bughtrig
Mellerstain
Priorwood   The Hirsel
Garden   Floors Castle

Mertoun

Monteviot

BORDERS

Teviot Water Garden

NORTHUMBERLAND

CUMBRIA

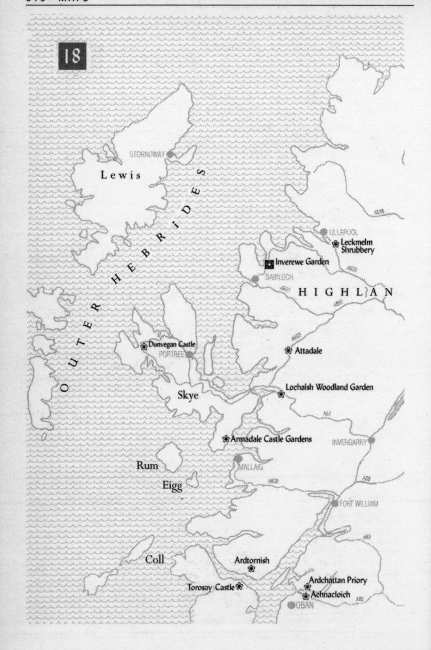

18

STORNOWAY

Lewis

O U T E R   H E B R I D E S

ULLAPOOL

🏵 Leckmelm
Shrubbery

🏵 Inverewe Garden

GAIRLOCH

H I G H L A N

Dunvegan Castle 🏵

PORTREE

🏵 Attadale

Skye

🏵 Lochalsh Woodland Garden

🏵 Armadale Castle Gardens

INVERGARRY

Rum

MALLAIG

Eigg

FORT WILLIAM

Coll

🏵 Ardtornish

Ardchattan Priory 🏵

Torosay Castle 🏵

🏵 Achnacloich

OBAN

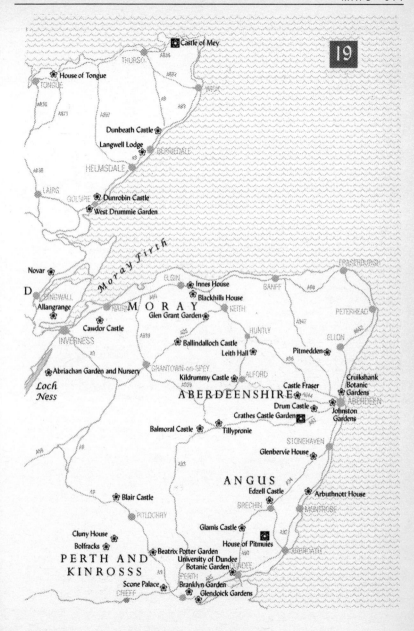

19

Castle of Mey

THURSO

House of Tongue

TONGUE

Dunbeath Castle

Langwell Lodge

HELMSDALE

LAIRG

GOLSPIE

Dunrobin Castle

West Drummie Garden

Moray Firth

Novar

DINGWALL

Allangrange

ELGIN

Innes House

Blackhills House

MORAY

Glen Grant Garden

NAIRN

KEITH

Cawdor Castle

INVERNESS

Ballindalloch Castle

Leith Hall

HUNTLY

Pitmedden

Abriachan Garden and Nursery

GRANTOWN-on-SPEY

*Loch
Ness*

Kildrummy Castle

ALFORD

Castle Fraser

Cruikshank
Botanic
Gardens

ABERDEENSHIRE

ABERDEEN

Drum Castle

Johnston
Gardens

Crathes Castle Garden

Balmoral Castle

Tillypronie

STONEHAVEN

Glenbervie House

ANGUS

Edzell Castle

Arbuthnott House

Blair Castle

BRECHIN

MONTROSE

PITLOCHRY

Glamis Castle

Cluny House

House of Pitmuies

Bolfracks

Beatrix Potter Garden

University of Dundee
Botanic Garden

ARBROATH

PERTH AND
KINROSSS

DUNDEE

Scone Palace

Branklyn Garden

PERTH

CRIEFF

Glendoick Gardens

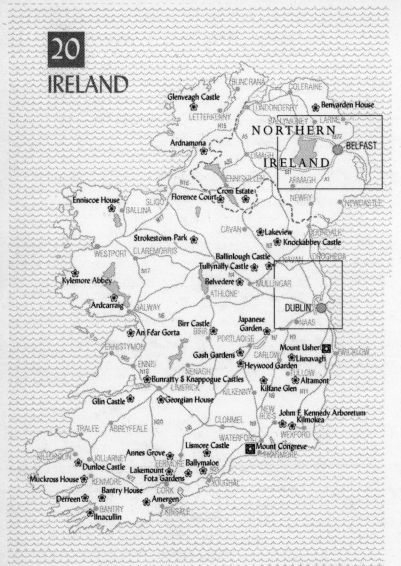

20

IRELAND

Glenveagh Castle

Benvarden House

BUNCRANA

COLERAINE

LONDONDERRY

BALLYMONEY

LARNE

LETTERKENNY

N15

A5

NORTHERN

Ardnamona

OMAGH

IRELAND

BELFAST

N3

ENNISKILLEN

ARMAGH

A1

NEWCASTLE

Enniscoe House

Florence Court

Crom Estate

NEWRY

SLIGO

BALLINA

N17

CAVAN

Lakeview

DUNDALK

Strokestown Park

Knockabbey Castle

DROGHEDA

CLAREMORRIS

NAVAN

WESTPORT

Ballinlough Castle

Tullynally Castle

Kylemore Abbey

N17

Belvedere

MULLINGAR

Ardcarraig

GALWAY

ATHLONE

DUBLIN

N6

Birr Castle

Japanese Garden

NAAS

An Féar Gorta

BIRR

N3

ENNISTYMON

PORTLAOISE

Mount Usher

WICKLOW

ENNIS

Gash Gardens

CARLOW

Lisnavagh

N18

NENAGH

Heywood Garden

TULLOW

Bunratty & Knappogue Castles

Altamont

LIMERICK

KILKENNY

Kilfane Glen

N11

Glin Castle

Georgian House

NEW ROSS

John F. Kennedy Arboretum

TRALEE

ABBEYFEALE

N20

CLONMEL

Kilmokea

WEXFORD

KILLORGLIN

Lismore Castle

WATERFORD

Mount Congreve

KILLARNEY

Annes Grove

KENMARE

Ballymaloe

Dunloe Castle

Lakemount

Muckross House

KENMARE

Fota Gardens

YOUGHAL

Derreen

Bantry House

CORK

Amergen

BANTRY

KINSALE

Ilnacullin

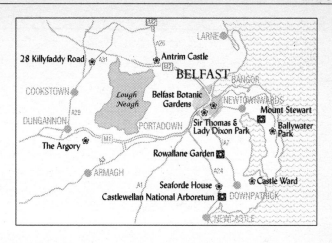

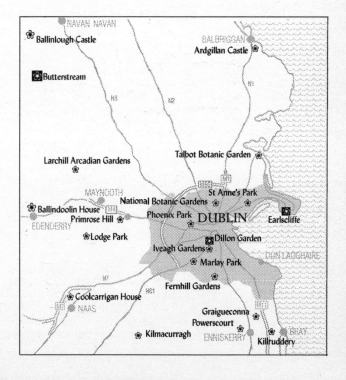

21
WALES

LIVERPOOL

CHESHIRE

SHROPSHIRE

HEREFORDSHIRE

Cardigan

Bay

Bristol Channel

SOMERSET

HOLYHEAD

Anglesey

LLANDUDNO

PRESTATYN

Bodrhyddan Hall

Pencarreg

MENAI BRIDGE

Bodysgallen Hall

Donadea lodge

Plas Newydd

Penrhyn
Castle

Bodnant Garden

Foxbrush

Maenan Hall

MOLD

BETWYS-Y-COED

WREXHAM

LLANGOLLEN

Plas Brondanw

FFESTINIOG

Chirk Castle

Erddig

OSWESTRY

Portmeirion

BALA

PWLLHELI

Plas-yn-Rhiw

Dolwen

SHREWSBURY

Farchynys Cottage

BARMOUTH

Cefn Bere

The Dingle

DOLGELLAU

Centre for
Alternative
Technology

Powis Castle

ABERDYFI

Glansevern Hall

NEWTOWN

MACHYNLLETH

Whimble Garden

LEOMINSTER

ABERYSTWYTH

ABERAERON

TREGARON

LAMPETER

BUILTH WELLS

HAY-ON-WYE

Pant-yr-Holiad

Caer Hir

CARDIGAN

LLANDOVERY

Penlan-Uchaf Farm

FISHGUARD

BRECON

Donadea Lodge

Hilton Court

Cwm Pibau

CARMARTHEN

National Botanic
Garden of Wales

MONMOUTH

HAVERFORDWEST

Picton Castle

Aberglasney

ST CLEARS

Colby Woodland Garden

Upton Castle

Penpergwm Lodge

TENBY

Clyne Gardens

Veddw House

Ridler's Garden

Wyndcliffe Court

Singleton Botanic Gardens

SWANSEA

Tredegar

NEWPORT

Museum of Welsh Life

CARDIFF

Dyffryn Gardens

BRISTOL

EUROPE

On the map which follows we include a selection of fine gardens in France, Belgium and Holland, concentrating on those which are a reasonable distance from the Channel ports or some other points of entry such as a Eurostar station. Regional leaflets are available at many tourist offices and other outlets in those countries. French speakers should pay a visit to the French bookshop (Librairie La Page) at 7 Harrington Road, London SW7 (Tel: (020) 7589 2849), where they may buy or order such useful guides as Michel Racine's *Jardins en France* (published by Acres Sud and revised in 2003) or the Guide Charme *Parcs et Jardins en France*. Alas, Mitchell Beazley's *Gardens of France* by Patrick Taylor and *Gardens of The Netherlands and Belgium* by Barbara Abbs are out of print.

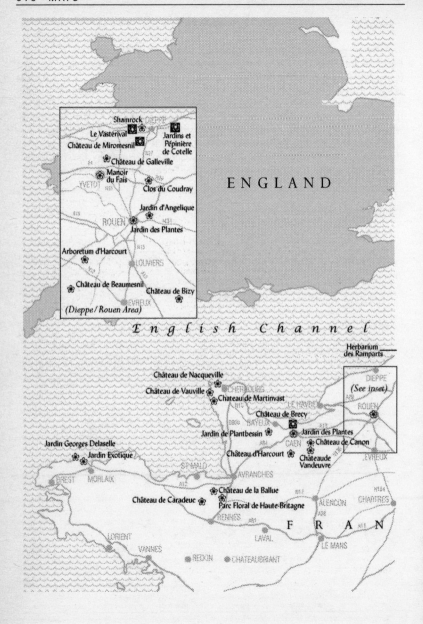

Shamrock
Le Vasterival
Château de Miromesnil
Jardins et Pépinière de Cotelle
Château de Galleville
Manoir du Fais
Clos du Coudray
Jardin d'Angelique
ROUEN
Jardin des Plantes
Arboretum d'Harcourt
LOUVIERS
Château de Beaumesnil
Château de Bizy
EVREUX
(Dieppe/Rouen Area)

YVETOT

ENGLAND

English Channel

Herbarium des Ramparts

DIEPPE
(See inset)
ROUEN
EVREUX

Château de Nacqueville
Château de Vauville
CHERBOURG
Château de Martinvast
LE HAVRE
Château de Brecy
BAYEUX
Jardin de Plantbessin
Jardin des Plantes
Jardin Georges Delaselle
CAEN
Château de Canon
Jardin Exotique
Château d'Harcourt
Château de Vandeuvre
BREST
MORLAIX
ST-MALO
AVRANCHES
Château de la Ballue
Château de Caradeuc
Parc Floral de Haute-Britagne
ALENCON
CHARTRES
RENNES
LORIENT
LAVAL
FRAN
VANNES
LE MANS
REDON
CHATEAUBRIANT

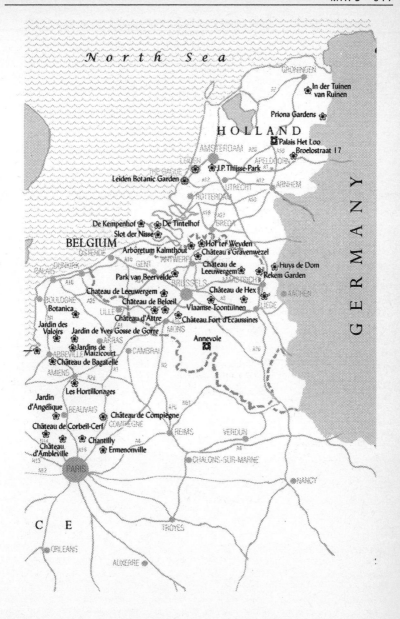

North Sea

GRONINGEN

In der Tuinen
van Ruinen

Priona Gardens

HOLLAND

AMSTERDAM

APELDOORN

Palais Het Loo
Broelostraat 17

LEIDEN

THE HAGUE

J.P. Thijsse-Park

Leiden Botanic Garden

UTRECHT

ARNHEM

ROTTERDAM

De Kempenhof — De Tintelhof

BREDA

Slot der Nisse

BELGIUM

OOSTENDE

Arboretum Kalmthout

Hof ter Weyden
Château s'Gravenwezel

ANTWERP

DUNKERK

GENT

Park van Beervelde

Château de
Leeuwergem

Huys de Dom

Rekem Garden

CALAIS

BRUSSELS

HASSELT

AACHEN

Château de Leeuwergem

Château de Hex

BOULOGNE

LILLE

Château de Belœil

Vlaamse Toontuinen

LIEGE

Botanica

Château d'Attre

Château Fort d'Ecaussines

Jardin des
Valoirs

Jardin de Yves Gosse de Gorre

MONS

ARRAS

Annevoie

Jardins de
Maizicourt

CAMBRAI

Château de Bagatelle

AMIENS

Les Hortillonages

BEAUVAIS

Jardin
d'Angélique

Château de Corbeil-Cerf

Château de Compiègne

COMPIEGNE

REIMS

VERDUN

Château
d'Ambleville

Chantilly

Ermenonville

CHALONS-SUR-MARNE

PARIS

NANCY

C E

TROYES

ORLEANS

AUXERRE

GERMANY

Websites for Gardens in the *Guide*

Many private and publicly owned gardens now have their own websites, and these are listed below. We have not listed individually the websites for gardens owned by the National Trust. The easiest way to access a National Trust garden is to type in their website followed by the house name in full, e.g. nationaltrust.org.uk/mottisfontabbey. For the National Trust for Scotland (nts.org.uk), English Heritage (english-heritage.org.uk) and the Department of Environment in the Republic of Ireland (heritageireland.ie or environ.ie) you should access the main website and follow the instructions. **Note: All website addresses must have www. as a prefix**.

Other useful websites for garden visitors are: CADW (Welsh Historic Monuments) (www.cadw.wales.gov.uk); Historic Houses Association (www.hha.org.uk); Historic Royal Palaces (www.hrp.org.uk); Historic Scotland (www.historic-scotland.gov.uk); Landmark Trust (www.landmarktrust. co.uk); The National Gardens Scheme (www.ngs.org.uk). The website for all the Royal Horticultural Society's gardens isrhs.org.uk.

Bedfordshire
kathybrownsgarden.
  homestead.com
toddingtonmanor.co.uk
woburnabbey.co.uk

Berkshire
englefield.co.uk
royal.gov.uk
livingrainforest.org
waltham-place.org.uk

Birmingham Area
birminghambotanicgardens.
  org.uk
cbhgt.swinternet.co.uk
birmingham.gov.uk
botanic.bham.ac.uk

Bristol Area
bristol-city.gov.uk
bristolzoo.org.uk
emmaus-house.co.uk
goldneyhall.com
bristol-city.gov.uk

Buckinghamshire
ascottestate.co.uk
waddesdon.org.uk

Cambridgeshire
christs.cam.ac.uk
clare.cam.ac.uk
elgoods-brewery.co.uk
greenknowe.co.uk
botanic.cam.ac.uk
wicken.org.uk
wimpole.org

Cheshire
adlingtonhall.com
arleyestate.zuunet.co.uk
bluebellcottagegardens.co.uk
bridgemere.co.uk
capesthorne.com
cheshireherbs.com
dungevalley.co.uk
gawsworthhall.com
jb.man.ac.uk/scicen
merseyworld.com/nessgardens
nortonpriory.org
crewe-nantwich.gov.uk
tattongardensociety.co.uk
stapeleywatergardens.com
tattongardensociety.co.uk
warrington.gov.uk

Cornwall
tate.org.uk
bosvigo.com
burncoose.co.uk
caerhays.co.uk
carwinion.com
edenproject.com
headlandgarden.co.uk
heligan.com
marshvillagardens.com
penwith.gov.uk
cornwalltouristboard.co.uk
oldmillherbary.co.uk
pencarrow.co.uk
pine-lodge.co.uk
trebah-garden.co.uk
tresco.co.uk
trewithengardens.co.uk

Cumbria
brantwood.org.uk
dalemain.com
cragview.demon.co.uk

holker-hall.co.uk
levenshall.co.uk
muncaster.co.uk
rydalmount.co.uk

Derbyshire
chatsworth.org
fanshawegate.org.uk
gamesleyfold.fsnet.co.uk
haddonhall.co.uk
melbournehall.com
highpeak.gov.uk
sitwell.co.uk

Devon
bictongardens.co.uk
burrowfarmgardens.co.uk
castlehilldevon.co.uk
hostas-uk.com
dartington.u-net.com
doctonmill.co.uk
thegardenhouse.org.uk
gidleigh.com
hartlandabbey.com
hillhousenursery.co.uk
tapestry.org.uk
paigntonzoo.org.uk
ex.ac.uk

Dorset
abbotsbury-tourism.co.uk
mdmusic.com/arnmore
athelhampton.co.uk
cranborne.co.uk
fordeabbey.co.uk
kmc.ac.uk
knollgardens.co.uk
mapperton.com
sherbornecastle.com
springheadtrust.co.uk
stickywicket.co.uk

Durham
auckland-castle.co.uk
bowesmuseum.org.uk
crookhallgardens.co.uk
rabycastle.com
durham.ac.uk

Essex
bethchatto.co.uk
uttlesford.gov.uk
eastonlodge.co.uk
thegibberdgarden.co.uk
themagnolias.co.uk
rhs.org.uk

Gloucestershire
batsford-arboretum.co.uk
bourtonhouse.com
framptoncourtestate.uk.com
specialplants.net
kiftsgate.co.uk
gardenvisit-cotswolds.co.uk
westonbirtarboretum.com
owlpen.com
rococogarden.co.uk
rodmarton-manor.co.uk
sudeleycastle.co.uk
lesleyrossergardens.co.uk
westonbirt.gloucs.sch.uk

Hampshire & Isle of Wight
applecourt.com
brandymount.co.uk
exbury.co.uk
gardengallery.uk.com
highclearcastle.co.uk
houghtonlodge.co.uk
longstockpark.co.uk
gertrudejekyllgarden.co.uk
hilliergardens.org.uk
spinnersgarden.com
hants.gov.uk/leisure/coparks/
    Staunton
southampton.gov.uk/leisure/
    heritage
tylneyhall.com
brading.co.uk
wightfarmholidays.co.uk/
    northcourt
botanic.co.uk

Herefordshire
hortus.co.uk
darkleyhouse.co.uk
hamptoncourt.org.uk
hergest.co.uk

Hertfordshire
ashridge.org
bealeshotels.co.uk
beningtonlordship.co.uk
hatfield-house.co.uk
hopleys.co.uk
knebworthhouse.com

Kent
abbotsmerry.co.uk
bedgeburypinetum.org.uk
beechcourtgardens.co.uk
belmont-house.org
hadlow.ac.uk
goodnestoneparkgardens.co.uk
greatcomp.co.uk
groombridge.co.uk
hevercastle.co.uk
leeds-castle.co.uk
marleplace.co.uk
mountephraimgardens.co.uk
nettlesteadplace.co.uk
owlhouse.com
penshurstplace.com
pinesgardenandmuseum.co.uk
howletts.net
rockfarmhousebandb.co.uk
squerryes.co.uk
hdra.org.uk

Lancashire
williamsonpark.com
arabellalennoxboyd.com
hoghtontower.co.uk
leightonhall.co.uk
htnw.co.uk
bents.co.uk
woodsidegarden.net
southribble.gov.uk

Leicestershire
belvoircastle.com
longclose.org.uk
5e.biglobe.ne.jp/~orchards
wartnabyplantlabels.co.uk

Lincolnshire
burghley.co.uk
doddingtonhall.com
grimsthorpe.co.uk
gunbyhall.ic24.net
hall-farm.co.uk
northlincs.gov.uk/normanby

Liverpool & Wirral
croxteth.co.uk

London
wandsworth.gov.uk
the-royal-collection.org.uk
royalparks.org.uk
wildlondon.org.uk
merton.gov.uk
capel.ac.uk
cpgarden.demon.co.uk
CIP.com
westminster-abbey.org
geffrye-museum.org.uk
hrp.org.uk
gardenphotolibrary.com
horniman.ac.uk
royalparks.gov.uk
royalparks.gov.uk
zsl.org
museumgardenhistory.org.uk
museumoflondon.org.uk
leevalleypark.com
kew.org
chelsea-pensioners.org.uk
royalparks.gov.uk
syonpark.co.uk
thamesbarrierpark.org.uk

Newcastle upon Tyne
bedesworld.co.uk
newcastle.gov.uk
twmuseums.org.uk

Norfolk
bradenhamhall.co.uk
bressingham.co.uk
e-ruston-
    oldvicaragegardens.co.uk
exoticgarden.com
norfolkbroads.com/Fairhaven
blooms-online.com
frittonlake.co.uk
haleshall.com
holkham.co.uk
hovetonhallgardens.co.uk
manningtongardens.co.uk
norfolk-lavender.co.uk
pensthorpe.com
plantationgarden.co.uk
raveningham.com
sandringhamestate.co.uk

Northamptonshire
althorp.com
boughtonhouse.org.uk
cotonmanor.co.uk
cottesbrooke.hall.co.uk
deenepark.com
holdenby.com
kelmarsh.com
lamporthall.co.uk
oldrectorygardens.co.uk
prebendal-mnor.co.uk
rockinghamcastle.com

Northumberland
alnwickgarden.com
bide-a-wee.co.uk
chillingham-castle.com
thegardenstation.co.uk
northland.ac.uk

Nottinghamshire
snowdrops.co.uk
holmepierreponthall.com
pgmail.clara.net/mhpg
newsteadabbey.org.uk
ruffordcraftcentre.org.uk
wollatonhall.org.uk

Oxfordshire
blenheimpalace.com
broughtoncastle.demon.co.uk
buscot-park.com
cotswoldwildlifepark.co.uk
andrewlawson.com
botanic-garden.ox.ac.uk
kelmscottmanor.co.uk
kingstonbagpuizehouse.org.uk
botanic-garden.ox.ac.uk
rousham.org
stonor.com
wardingtonmanor.co.uk
waterperrygardens.co.uk

Rutland
barnsdalegardens.co.uk

Shropshire
eleventowns.co.uk
greatbritishgardens.co.uk
hawkstone.co.uk
walcothall.com
weston-park.com
wollertonoldhallgarden.com

Somerset
americanmuseum.org
eastlambrook.com
gantsmill.co.uk
hadspengarden.co.uk
hestercombegardens.com
bologrew.pwp.blueyonder.co.uk
lowerseveralls.co.uk
stoneaston.co.uk

Staffordshire
altontowers.com
dorothyclivegardens.co.uk
trenthamgardens.co.uk

Suffolk
edmundsbury.gov.uk
suffolktopattractions.com
helmingham.com
shrublandpark.co.uk
somerleyton.co.uk

Surrey
cha.org.uk
sundialgroup.com
busbridgelakes.co.uk
coverwoodlakes.co.uk
rhododendrons.com
dunsboroughpark.com
gatton-park.org.uk
landmarktrust.co.uk
greatfosters.co.uk
guildford.gov.uk
hannahpescharsculpture.com
langshottmanor.com
loseley-park.com
painshill.co.uk
savillgarden.co.uk
titsey.com
cornusweb.co.uk

Sussex, East
batesgreen.co.uk
frewcoll.demon.co.uk
charleston.org.uk
greatdixter.co.uk
herstmonceux-castle.com
merriments.co.uk
sussexpast.co.uk
pashleymanorgardens.com
thecuttinggarden.com
royalpavilion.brighton.co.uk

Sussex, West
bordehill.co.uk
chidmere.com
denmans-garden.co.uk
highbeeches.com
leonardslee.com
hellyers.co.uk
parhaminsussex.co.uk
sculpture.org.uk

kew.org
wealddown.co.uk
westdean.org.uk

Warwickshire
coughtoncourt.co.uk
ragleyhall.com
hdra.org.uk
shakespeare.org.uk
stoneleighabbey.org
warwick-castle.co.uk

Wiltshire
abbeyhousegardens.co.uk
bowood.org
corsham-court.com
secretgardendesigns.co.uk
ifordmanor.co.uk
rushmore-estate.co.uk
longleat.co.uk
poundhillplants.co.uk
wiltonhouse.com
Worcestershire
burford.co.uk
eastgrove.co.uk
eastnorcastle.com
luggershall.com
overbury.org.uk
pershore.ac.uk
autumnnasters.co.uk
spetchleygardens.co.uk
shcn.co.uk

Yorkshire (N. & E. Riding)
burnbyhallgardens.co.uk
burton-agnes.com
castlehoward.co.uk
constableburtongardens.co.uk
duncombepark.com
milllgatehouse.com
newbyhall.com
parcevallhallgardens.co.uk
rhs.org.uk
ripleycastle.co.uk
shandy-hall.org.uk
stillingfleetlodgenurseries.co.uk
fountainsabbey.org.uk
thorpperrow.com
harrogate.gov.uk

Yorkshire (S. & W. Area)
bramhampark.co.uk
harewood.org
hcdt.4t.com
calderdale.gov.uk
sbg.org.uk
leeds.gov.uk
leeds.gov.uk
perennial.org.uk
ysp.co.uk

Ireland
antrim.gov.uk
belfastcity.gov.uk
benvarden.com
forestserviceni.gov.uk/
    arboretum.htm
seafordegardens.com
annesgrovegardens.com
ardnamona.com

cookingisfun.ie
bantryhouse.ie
belvedere-house.ie
birrcastle.com
dillongarden.com
killarneyhotels.ie
earlscliffe.com
enniscoe.com
zenith.ie/fota
limerickcivictrust.ie
glincastle.com
irish-national-stud.ie
NicholasMosse.com
killruddery.com
kilmokea.com
kylemoreabbey.com
lakemount.yahoo
lakeviewgardens.net
larchill.com
lismorecastle.com
lisnavagh.com
steam-museum.ie
loughcrew.com
irishtabletop.com
mount-usher-gardens.com
powerscourt.ie
dublincorp.ie
strokestownpark.ie
fingalcoco.ie

Scotland
melrose.bordernet.co.uk/
    abbotsford
lochnessgardens.com
isle-of-gigha.co.uk
allangrange.co.uk
ardanaiseig-hotel.com
gardens-of-argyll.co.uk
ardkinglas.com
ardtornish.co.uk
clandonald.com
attadale.com
ballindallochcastle.co.uk
balmoralcastle.com
birnaminstitute.com
rbge.org.uk
blackhills.org.uk
blair-castle.co.uk
blairquhan.co.uk
bolfracks.com
camboestate.com
castlekennedygarden.co.uk
castleofmey.org.uk
cawdorcastle.com
northian.gov.uk
dalmany.co.uk
rbge.org.uk
drum-castle.org.uk
buccleuch.com
drummondcastlegardens.co.uk
highlandescape.com
dunvegancastle.com
finlaystone.co.uk
floorscastle.com
glamis-castle.co.uk
gardens-of-argyll.co.uk
glendoick.com
glenwhan.co.uk
pitmuies.com
inwoodgarden.com

aberdeen.gov.uk
jurahouseandgardens.co.uk
kildrummy-castle-gardens.co.uk
kinrosshouse.com
rbge.org.uk
manderston.co.uk
rbge.org.uk
scone-palace.co.uk
st-andrews-botanic.org
teviotwatergardens.co.uk
torosay.co.uk

Wales
aberglasney.org.uk
bodysgallen.com
cardiganshirecoastandcountry.
    com
cat.org.uk
dinglenurseries.co.uk
dyffryngardens.org.uk
hiltongardensandcrafts.co.uk
gardenofwales.org.uk
penplants.com
pictoncastle.co.uk

portmeirion-village.com
newport.gov.uk
pembrokeshirecoast.org.uk

Channel Islands
gov.gg/boa
millefleurs.co.uk
artparks.co.uk
sark-tourism.com
judith.queree.freewebspace.com
ericyoungorchidfoundation.co.uk
jerseylavender.co.uk

Index

An * indicates that the garden or nursery is mentioned in the text of another garden entry; # means that only garden names, addresses and contact details, with perhaps a very brief description, are given.